REINFORCED CONCRETE DESIGN

FOURTH EDITION

About the Authors

Dr. S Unnikrishna Pillai pursued his engineering education at the University of Kerala and Queen's University, Canada. He has taught at College of Engineering, Thiruvananthapuram; Queen's University, Canada; University of Sulaimaniya, Iraq; Royal Military College of Canada and Regional Engineering College (presently NIT), Calicut. As the Founder-Director of the Co-operative Academy of Professional Education (CAPE), he has built up five Engineering Colleges and a Medical College in Kerala. His major research interests have been in the areas of Limit States Design of concrete structures, Strength and Stability of Beam-Columns in metal structures and Rehabilitation of structures. He also has wide experience in design and construction of various RC structures.

Dr. Pillai has published several technical papers, authored the book *Reinforced Concrete Design* (McGraw-Hill Ryerson, Canada) and co-authored '*Ch. 8 – Beam-Columns*' of *SSRC Guide to Stability Design Criteria for Metal Structures, 3rd Ed.* (Edited by Bruce G. Johnston; John Wiley & Sons, New York, 1976). He has received several awards, including Kerala University Scholarships for First Rank, Canadian Commonwealth Scholarship, UP Government National Award, and Fellowship of NRC, Canada.

Prof. Devdas Menon pursued his civil engineering education at IIT Madras and IIT Delhi. Soon after graduation, he worked as a structural engineer at New Delhi, and later took to academics, teaching initially at REC Calicut and later at IIT Madras (since 1998). He is presently Professor & PC Varghese Institute Chair at the Department of Civil Engineering at IIT Madras. He is a structural consultant involved in various infrastructure projects.

Prof. Menon's primary research interests are in the area of structural concrete design. He has also carried out innovative research and development in affordable and sustainable building systems and in biomechanical orthopaedic devices. He has published numerous technical papers and has been conferred several awards for his contributions to teaching and research. He has a special interest in developing codes of practice and has served as Chairman of the Bureau of Indian Standards CED38 Committee on *Special Structures* since 2006. He is the author of textbooks titled *Structural Analysis* and *Advanced Structural Analysis*, and the editor of *Trends in Prestressed Concrete* and *Handbook on Seismic Retrofit of Buildings*.

Prof. Menon promotes a holistic approach to education and on finding meaning and fulfilment in life through self-awareness and inner transformation. He has given numerous invited talks on this theme and is the author of popular books titled *Stop sleepwalking through life!* and *Spirituality at work*.

Cover Feature:

THE WORLD TOWERS, Mumbai, composed of three residential towers of uniquely curvilinear shape forming a stunning sculpture of reinforced concrete and glass. WORLD ONE, with 80 storeys is the tallest of the three, at 273m (895 ft) and has 257 apartments. Developers: The Lodha Group. Architect: Pei Cobb Freed & Partners, New York. Structural Engineers: Leslie E. Robertson Associates, New York. Courtesy: Dr. Prasad Marepalli, The Lodha Group.

REINFORCED CONCRETE DESIGN

FOURTH EDITION

S Unnikrishna Pillai
Fellow, American Society of Civil Engineers
Formerly Principal, Regional Engineering College (now NIT), Calicut

Devdas Menon
Professor & PC Varghese Institute Chair
Department of Civil Engineering
Indian Institute of Technology, Madras

McGraw Hill Education (India) Private Limited

Published by McGraw Hill Education (India) Private Limited,
Registered Office: Anjana Complex No: 5/90 A, Butt Road, St. Thomas Mount, Chennai – 600016, Tamil Nadu, India.

Reinforced Concrete Design, 4e

Fourth reprint 2026

Print Edition
ISBN -13: 978-93-5460-102-6
ISBN -10: 93-5460-102-2

E-book Edition
ISBN -13: 978-93-5460-103-3
ISBN -10: 93-5460-103-0

05 06 07 08 09 MAG 30 29 28 27 26

Typeset at The Composers, 260, C.A. Apt., Paschim Vihar, New Delhi 110 063 and printed and bound in India at Magic International Pvt. Ltd., Plot No. 26E, Sector-31, (Industrial), Site IV, Greater Noida 201306

Cover Designer: Kapil Gupta
Cover Image Source: Shutterstock

Visit us at: www.mheducation.co.in
Toll free in India: 1800 103 5875
Write to us at: support.india@mheducation.com
CIN: U80302TN2010PTC111532

Preface

This book on *Reinforced Concrete Design* has undergone regular revisions following its first publication in 1998 – in order to keep pace with developments in theory and practice, and corresponding periodic revisions and updates in the provisions of IS 456 and related codes. We are grateful to students, teachers and design engineers, who have been using this book during the past two decades, for their feedback and suggestions, which have also contributed to the evolution of the book. Additional topics have been introduced in every new edition of the book.

This fourth edition of *Reinforced Concrete Design* has many new features, including a new book size (with a larger page layout). The contents of the 17 chapters of the third edition have been thoroughly reviewed and updated, and two additional chapters have now been introduced: Chapter 18 titled *Design of liquid storage tanks* and Chapter 19 titled *Estimation of wind and seismic forces on buildings*. In all chapters, the primary *Learning Objectives* have been introduced at the beginning. It is hoped that the new chapters will be useful not only to students and teachers, but also practising engineers who seek clarity in understanding of the recent code revisions in IS 3370 (Part 2), IS 875 (Part 3) and IS 1893 (Part 1).

Several new sections have been introduced in the earlier chapters. The additional topics include *yield line analysis of rectangular beam-supported slabs, shear walls, footings subjected to bi-axial bending and uplift, modelling of diaphragms, chords and collectors*. The topic of *strut-and-tie method* has been significantly expanded, with additional design examples (pile cap, corbel and deep beam). The chapter on earthquake-resistant design has also been modified as per the latest code provisions. All example problems have been reworked using M 25 grade concrete and Fe 500 grade steel, which are being increasingly used in current practice. Several figures are revised and a few new figures have been introduced for improved clarity. Review questions and references have been expanded and updated. A graded series of laboratory assignments of the *design-build-test-analyse-report* type have been added as Appendix C. Another addition, very helpful to the user, is a comprehensive *List of Symbols* used.

However, the unique features of the earlier editions relating to coverage and planning of contents, description and illustration, presentation and overall organisation of the text have been retained. Also, the chapters on structural systems, good detailing and construction practices, earthquake-resistant design, and selected special topics as well as the design aids, which made the book stand apart, have all been expanded and retained. Yet another unique feature introduced in this edition is *Margin Notes*: callouts giving key insights relevant to the topic under discussion. With these and the additions and revisions mentioned earlier (all of practical relevance), this book presents a state-of-the-art coverage of all the topics in reinforced concrete design generally required for a civil engineering degree programme in Indian universities. Several advanced topics in the book are also relevant at the post-graduate level and will be of use to post-graduate students, teachers and practising engineers.

Chapter 1 introduces the concepts of reinforced concrete structures and structural systems. Chapters 2 and 3 discuss the basic material properties and basic design safety concepts respectively. Chapter 4 deals with the elastic and inelastic behaviour of reinforced concrete beams under flexure. Chapter 5 discusses the design of beams and one-way slabs for flexure. Chapters 6, 7 and 8 explain design for shear, bond and torsion respectively. Chapter 9 deals with analysis for design moments in continuous systems, while Chapter 10 discusses serviceability limit states: deflection and cracking. Chapter 11 explains in detail the design of two-way slab systems whereas Chapters 12, 13 and 14 discuss the design concepts of staircases, compression members, footings and retaining walls. The short-length Chapters 15 and 16 provide useful information on good detailing, construction practices and special provisions for earthquake-resistant design. Chapter 17 explains some selected special topics such as design for shear by compression field theory, design by strut-and-tie method, and fire resistance. The new Chapter 18 covers the design of liquid storage tanks, with a focus on limit states design, while the new Chapter 19 explains the estimation of forces due to wind and earthquake on buildings using the latest code provisions.

This book lays great emphasis on conceptual clarity and strength in fundamentals. The student is encouraged to raise questions, to relate to field experience, to develop a 'structural sense', to appreciate proper 'documentation' and 'detailing', to analyse results and to synthesize knowledge; and the 'design-build-test-analyse-report' type laboratory projects now introduced will help practice such capabilities. A set of stimulating 'review questions' and 'multiple choice questions' have been included at the end of each chapter, in addition to a large number of illustrative worked examples. An exhaustive set of problems (with answers for 'analysis' type problems) is also included at the end of each chapter. Typical questions used in GATE examination have also been incorporated. Extensive chapter-wise references are also listed to enable the research-minded to pursue further study.

We would like to place on record our gratitude to the excellent support given by our former doctoral students in preparing this edition – in particular, Dr. Najeeb Shariff for his contribution to the new Chapters 18 and 19, Dr. Bijily Balakrishnan for her contribution in improving Chapters 11 and 14, Dr. Indu Geevar for her contribution in improving Chapters 14 and 17, and Dr. P Harikrishna (Chief Scientist and Head, Wind Engineering Lab, CSIR-SERC) for reviewing Chapter 19. We also wish to acknowledge gratefully the many valuable suggestions made for the improvement of this edition and the excellent support rendered by the team at McGraw Hill Education, the publishers of this book. Finally, we express our gratitude to our colleagues, students, friends and family members, who contributed in their own ways in making this book possible.

Feedback and suggestions from readers for improving this book in any manner would be very much appreciated.

We dedicate this book to students of civil/structural engineering, with a hope that they will find the learning of reinforced concrete design a rewarding experience.

S Unnikrishna Pillai
Devdas Menon

Contents

CHAPTER 1

Reinforced Concrete Structures

LEARNING OBJECTIVES

After studying this chapter, you will be able to:

- *Explain the why, where, when and how about uses of reinforced concrete*
- *Describe the objectives of structural design*
- *Discuss the different structural systems used in reinforced concrete structures and their roles in resisting load effects*
- *Apply the National Codes of Practice*

1.1 Introduction

Traditionally, the study of **reinforced concrete design** begins directly with a chapter on materials, followed by chapters dealing with design. In this book, a departure is made from that convention. It is desirable for the student to first have an overview of the world of reinforced concrete structures, before plunging into the finer details of the subject. Accordingly, this chapter gives a general introduction to reinforced concrete and its applications. It also explains the role of structural design in reinforced concrete construction and outlines the various structural systems that are commonly adopted in these buildings.

It is well known that concrete is a common structural material. But how common it is and how much a part it plays in our daily lives is perhaps not well known – or rather, not often realised. Structural concrete is used extensively in the construction of various kinds of buildings, stadia, auditoria, pavements, bridges, piers, breakwaters, berthing structures, dams, waterways, pipes, water tanks, swimming pools, cooling towers, bunkers and silos, chimneys, communication towers, tunnels, and the like. It is the most commonly used construction material, consumed at a rate of approximately one ton for every living human being. 'Man consumes no material except water in such tremendous quantities' [Ref. 1.1].

Pictures of some typical examples of reinforced concrete structures are shown in Figures 1.1–1.5. Perhaps, some day in the future, you may be called upon to design similar (if not, more exciting) structures! The student will do well to bear this goal in mind.

Fig. 1.1 Ferrocement Boat – The first known example of reinforced concrete is a boat, patented in 1848 by Joseph-Louis Lambot.

Fig. 1.2 A modern reinforced concrete multi-storeyed building – one of the tallest in New Delhi (102 m): Jawahar Vyapar Bhavan [*Architects: Raj Rewal and Kuldip Singh, Project Consultants: Engineers India Limited*].
Structural concept: joist floor supported on Vierendeel girders (arranged in a 'plug on' fashion), cantilevered from core walls. *Source: Shutterstock.*

Fig. 1.3 The Bahá'i House of Worship, New Delhi – a unique lotus-shaped reinforced concrete structure, with a complex shell geometry involving spheres, cylinders, toroids and cones *[Architect: Faríburz Sahbá, Structural Consultants: Flint & Neill, Contractor: Larsen & Toubro Ltd.] Source: Shutterstock.*

Fig. 1.4 C N Tower – a communications tower at Toronto, Canada, rising to a height of 550 m, making it, when completed, the tallest reinforced concrete tower in the world. (The picture also shows an elevator car which travels vertically along the shaft of the tower). *Photo by S. Unnikrishna Pillai.*

Fig. 1.5 A reinforced concrete bow-string girder bridge spanning across the Bharathapuzha River at Kuttippuram, Kerala. *Photo by S. Unnikrishna Pillai.*

1.2 Plain and Reinforced Concrete

1.2.1 Plain Concrete

Concrete is any solid mass made with a cementing medium; the ingredients usually comprise sand, gravel, cement and water.

Concrete is defined [Ref. 1.2] as any solid mass made with the use of a cementing medium; the ingredients generally comprise sand, gravel, cement and water. That the mixing together of such disparate and discrete materials can result in a *solid mass* (of any desired shape), with well-defined properties, is a wonder in itself. Concrete has been in use as a building material for more than a hundred and fifty years. Its success and popularity may be largely attributed to (1) durability under hostile environments (including resistance to water), (2) ease with which it can be cast into a variety of shapes and sizes, and (3) its relative economy and easy availability. The main strength of concrete lies in its compression-bearing ability, which surpasses that of traditional materials like brick and stone masonry. Advances in *concrete technology*, during the past four decades in particular, have now made it possible to produce a wide range of concrete grades, varying in mass density (1200–2500 kg/m^3) and compressive strength (10–100 MPa).

Concrete is remarkably strong in compression, but is equally remarkably weak in tension! [Figure 1.6(a)]. Its tensile 'strength' is approximately one-tenth of its compressive 'strength'. Hence, the use of **plain concrete** as a structural material is limited to situations where significant tensile stresses and strains do not develop, as in hollow (or solid) block wall construction, small pedestals and 'mass concrete' applications (in dams, etc.).

Concrete cast with embedded steel bars is reinforced concrete; the steel reinforcement serves to resist tensile stresses and provides ductility.

1.2.2 Reinforced Concrete

Concrete would not have gained its present status as a principal building material, but for the invention of **reinforced concrete,** which is concrete

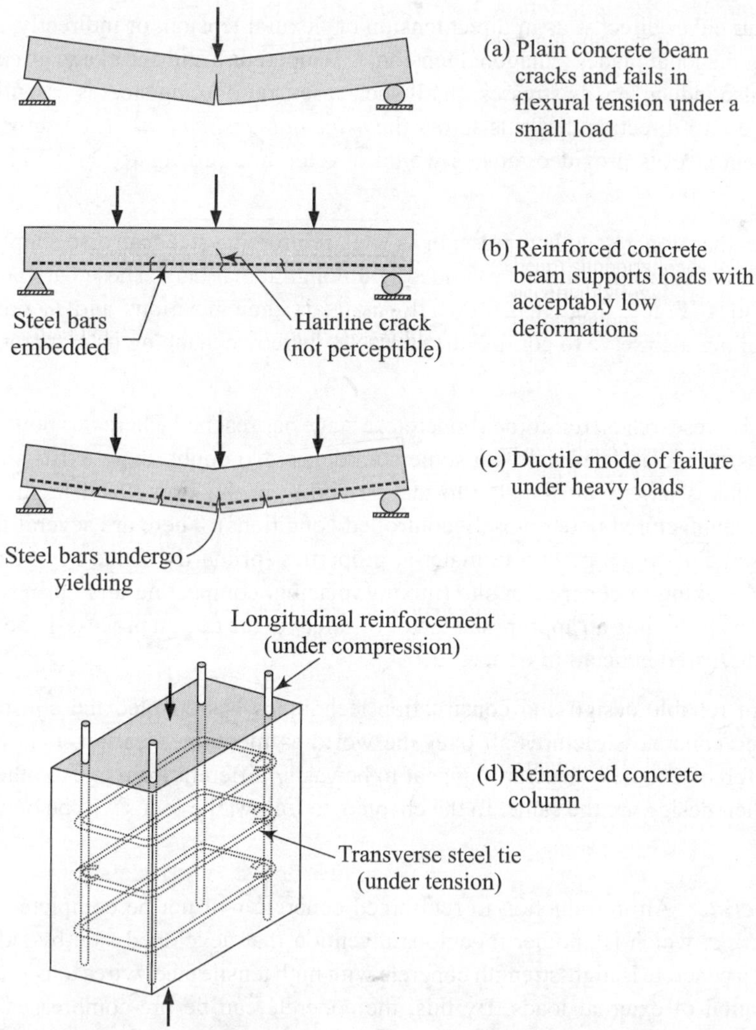

Fig. 1.6 Contribution of steel bars in reinforced concrete.

with steel bars embedded in it. The idea of reinforcing concrete with steel has resulted in a new *composite* material, having the ability to resist significant tensile stresses as well, which was otherwise impossible. Thus, the construction of flexural members, such as beams and slabs, became viable with this new material. The steel bars (embedded in the tension zone of the concrete) compensate for the concrete's inability to resist tension, effectively carrying all the tension, without separating from the concrete [Figure 1.6(b)]. The *bond* between steel and the surrounding concrete ensures *strain compatibility*, i.e., the strain at any point in the steel is equal to that in the adjoining concrete. Moreover, the reinforcing steel imparts *ductility* to a material that is otherwise brittle. This implies that if a properly reinforced beam were to fail, then such a failure would be preceded by large deflections caused by the yielding of steel, thereby giving ample warning of the impending collapse [Figure 1.6(c)].

Tensile stresses occur either directly, as in direct tension or flexural tension, or indirectly, as in shear, which causes tension along diagonal planes ('diagonal tension'). Temperature and shrinkage effects and restraint to deformations may also induce tensile stresses. In all such cases, reinforcing steel is essential, and should be appropriately located, in a direction that cuts across the *principal tensile planes* (i.e., across potential tensile cracks). If insufficient steel is provided, cracks would develop and propagate, and could possibly lead to failure.

Being much stronger than concrete in compression as well, reinforcing steel can also supplement concrete in bearing compressive forces, as in columns provided with longitudinal bars. These bars need to be confined by transverse steel ties [Figure 1.6(d)], in order to maintain their positions and to prevent their lateral buckling. The lateral ties also serve to confine the concrete, thereby enhancing its compression load-bearing capacity.

As a result of extensive research on reinforced concrete, a stage has reached where it is now possible to predict the behaviour of this composite material with some confidence. No doubt, there exists some uncertainty in the prediction, but this is largely attributable to the variability in the strength of in-situ concrete (which, unlike steel, is not manufactured under closely controlled conditions). There are several factors which lead to this variability, some of which pertain to material properties (primarily of the aggregates), while others pertain to the actual making of concrete at site (mixing, placing, compacting and curing). This uncertainty can be taken care of by providing an appropriate factor of safety in the design process. [The topic of structural safety in design is discussed in detail in Chapter 3.]

The development of reliable design and construction techniques has enabled the construction of a wide variety of reinforced concrete structures all over the world as mentioned earlier. It is worth noting that, although these reinforced concrete structures appear to be vastly different from one another, the actual principles underlying their design are the same. In the chapters to follow, the focus will be on these fundamental principles.

Prestressed Concrete An introduction to reinforced concrete will not be complete without a mention of *prestressed concrete*, which is another ingenious invention that developed side-by-side with reinforced concrete. Prestressed concrete is high-strength concrete with high tensile steel wires tensioned and embedded, prior to the application of external loads. By this, the concrete can be pre-compressed to such a degree that, after the structure is loaded, there is practically no net tension developed in the beam. Prestressed concrete finds application in situations where long spans are encountered (as in bridges), or where cracks (even hairline) in concrete are not permitted (as in pressure vessels, pipes and water tanks), or where fatigue loading is encountered (as in rail track sleepers), etc.

Fibre-Reinforced Concrete and Ferrocement Recent developments in *concrete composites* have resulted in several new products that aim to improve the tensile strength of concrete, and to impart ductility. Among these, *fibre-reinforced concrete* and *ferrocement* constitute important developments. In the former, steel or glass fibres are incorporated in concrete at the time of mixing; in the latter, thin sections are formed by embedding multiple layers of steel wire mesh in cement mortar. Although ferrocement has gained popularity only in recent years, it represents one of the earliest applications of reinforced concrete to be experimented with [Figure 1.1].

This book is concerned with reinforced concrete; hence, no further discussion on other concrete composites will be made.

1.3 Objectives of Structural Design

The design of a structure must satisfy three basic requirements:

1. *Stability* to prevent overturning, sliding or buckling of the structure, or parts of it, under the action of loads;
2. *Strength* to resist safely the stresses induced by the loads, including environmental loads, in the various structural members and their connections; and
3. *Serviceability* to ensure satisfactory performance under *service load* conditions – which implies providing adequate ***stiffness*** and reinforcements to contain deflections, crack-widths and vibrations within acceptable limits, and also providing ***impermeability*** and ***durability*** (including corrosion-resistance), etc.

The **strength** aspect includes ***fire resistance*** and ***structural integrity*** requirements. There are three other considerations that a sensible designer ought to bear in mind, viz., **economy, aesthetics** and **sustainability**. One can always design a massive structure, which has more-than-adequate stability, strength and serviceability, but the ensuing cost of the structure may be exorbitant, and the end product, far from aesthetic. At times, there may be conflicts between engineering and architectural requirements. In the words of Felix Candela [Ref. 1.3], the designer of a remarkably wide range of reinforced concrete shell structures,

> '... the architect has no weapons to fight against the scientific arguments of the engineer. A dialogue is impossible between two people who speak different languages. The result of the struggle is generally the same: science prevails, and the final design has generally lost the eventual charm and fitness of detail dreamed by the architect.'

It is indeed a challenge, and a responsibility, for the structural designer to design a structure that is not only appropriate for the architecture, but also strikes the right balance between safety and economy [Ref. 1.4]. The design should also be environmentally sustainable in terms of the use of limited natural resources.

1.4 Reinforced Concrete Construction

Reinforced concrete construction is not the outcome of structural design alone. It is a collaborative venture involving the client, the architect, the structural engineer, the construction engineer/project manager and the contractor. Other specialists may also have to be consulted, with regard to soil investigation, water supply, sanitation, fire protection, transportation, heating, ventilation, air-conditioning, acoustics, electrical services, etc. Typically, a construction project involves three phases viz., *planning, design* (including *analysis*) and *construction* (including *contracting*).

> **Cooperation and collaboration amongst the major stakeholders (client, architect, structural engineer, construction engineer and contractor) is the key to success in the construction project.**

1. Planning Phase It is the job of the architect/planner to conceive and plan the architectural layout of the building, to suit the functional requirements of the client, with due regard to aesthetic, environmental and economic considerations. Structural feasibility is also an important consideration, and for this the structural designer has to be consulted.

2. Design Phase Once the preliminary plans have been approved, the actual details of the project have to be worked out (on paper) by the various consultants. In the case of the structural engineer/consultant, the tasks involved are (i) selection of the most appropriate structural system and initial proportioning of members, (ii) estimation of loads on the structure, (iii) **structural analysis** for the determination of the stress resultants (member forces) and displacements induced by various load combinations, (iv) **structural design** of the actual proportions (member sizes, reinforcement details) and grades of materials required for *safety* and *serviceability* under the calculated member forces, and (v) submission of *working drawings* that are detailed enough to be stamped 'good for construction'.

3. Construction Phase The plans and designs conceived on paper get translated into concrete (!) reality. A structure may be well-planned and well-designed, but it also has to be well-built. And for this, the responsibility lies not only with the contractor who is entrusted with the execution, but also with the construction engineers who undertake supervision on behalf of the consultants/owners. The work calls for proper management of various resources, viz., manpower, materials, machinery, money and time. It also requires familiarity with various construction techniques and specifications. In particular, expertise in concrete technology is essential, to ensure the proper mixing, handling, placing, compaction and curing of concrete. Management of contracts and following proper procedures, systems and documentation are also important aspects of the construction phase, especially in public works. However, these are beyond the scope of this book.

During the construction phase, some redesign may also be required – in the event of unforeseen contingencies, such as complications in foundations, non-availability of specified materials, etc.

1.5 Structural Systems

A structural system is an assemblage of load-carrying elements such as slabs, beams, walls, columns and foundations acting integrally to carry and transmit to the supporting ground, the loads acting on it.

Any structure is made up of *structural elements* (load-carrying, such as beams and columns) and *non-structural elements* (such as partitions, false ceilings, doors). The structural elements, put together, constitute the 'structural system'. Its function is to resist effectively the action of gravitational and environmental loads, and to transmit the resulting forces to the supporting ground, without significantly disturbing the geometry, integrity and serviceability of the structure.

Most of the structural elements may be considered, from the viewpoint of simplified analysis, as *one-dimensional* (skeletal) elements (such as beams, columns, arches, truss elements) or *two-dimensional* elements (such as slabs, plates and shells). A few structural elements (such as shell-edge beam junctions, perforated shear walls) may require more rigorous analysis.

Consider, for example, a reinforced concrete overhead water tank structure [Figure 1.7]. The structural system essentially comprises three subsystems, viz., the tank, the staging and the foundation, which are distinct from one another in the sense that they are generally designed, as well as constructed, in separate stages. The tank, in this example, is made up of a dome-shaped shell roof, a cylindrical side-wall (with stiffening ring beams at top and bottom), a conical portion below the lower ring beam, a flat circular base slab, and a main ring beam, which is supported by the columns of the staging. The staging comprises a three-dimensional framework of beams and columns, which are 'fixed' to the foundation. The foundation is a 'raft', comprising a slab in the shape of an annular ring, stiffened by a ring beam on top, and resting on firm soil below. The loads acting on the structure are due to *dead loads* (due to self-weight), *live loads* (due to water in the tank, maintenance on the roof), *wind loads* (acting on the exposed surface areas of the tank and staging), and *seismic loads* (due to earthquake induced ground excitation). The effect of the loads acting on the tank are transmitted to the staging through the main ring beam; the effect of the loads on the staging are, in turn, transmitted to the foundation, and ultimately to the ground below.

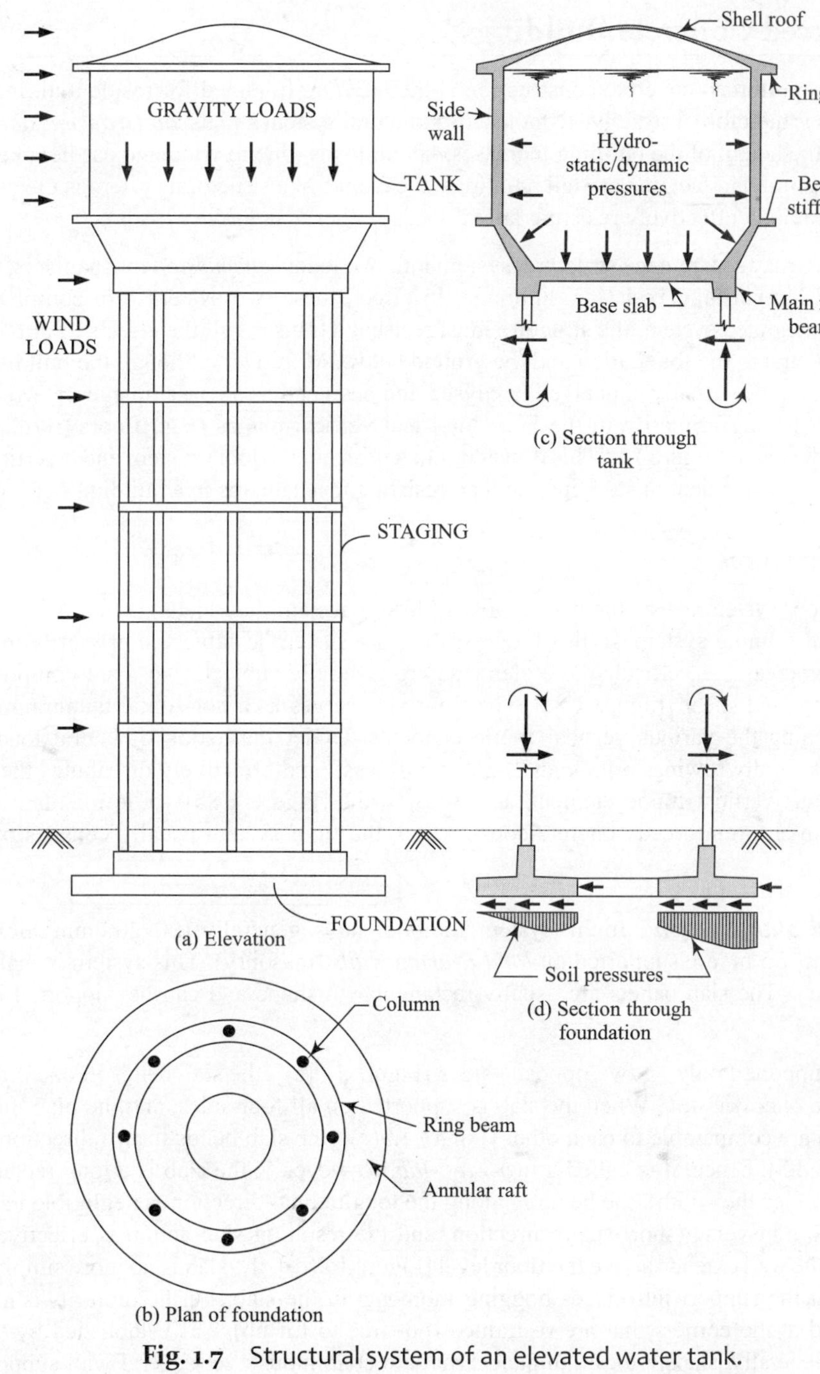

Fig. 1.7 Structural system of an elevated water tank.

1.6 Reinforced Concrete Buildings

The most common reinforced concrete construction is the *building* (planned for residential, institutional or commercial use). It is therefore instructive to look at its structural system and its *load transmission* mechanism in some detail. As the height of the building increases, lateral loads (due to wind and earthquake) make their presence felt increasingly; in fact, in very tall buildings, the choice of a structural system is dictated primarily by its relative economy in effectively resisting lateral loads (rather than gravity loads).

For convenience, we may separate the structural system into two load *transmission* mechanisms, viz., **gravity load resisting** and **lateral load resisting**, although, in effect, these two systems are complementary and interactive. As an integrated system, the structure must resist and transmit all the effects of gravity loads and lateral loads acting on it to the foundation and the ground below. Moreover, although the building is a three-dimensional structure, it is usually conceived, analysed and designed as an assemblage of two-dimensional (planar) sub-systems lying primarily in the horizontal and vertical planes (e.g., floors, roof, walls, plane frames, etc.), as indicated in Figure 1.8. This division into a horizontal (floor) system and a vertical (framing) system is particularly convenient in studying the load resisting mechanisms in a building.

1.6.1 Floor Systems

The (horizontal) floor system resists the gravity loads (dead loads and live loads) acting on it and transmits these to the vertical framing system. In this process, the floor system is subjected primarily to flexure and transverse shear, whereas the vertical frame elements are generally subjected to axial compression, often coupled with flexure and shear [Figure 1.8a]. The floor also serves as a horizontal diaphragm connecting together and stiffening the various vertical frame elements. Under the action of lateral loads, the floor diaphragm behaves rigidly (owing to its high in-plane stiffness), and effectively distributes the lateral load effects to the various vertical frame elements and shear walls [Figure 1.8b] while maintaining the floor geometry. In cast-in-situ reinforced concrete construction, the floor system usually consists of one of the following.

Wall-Supported Slab System In this system, the floor slabs, generally 100–200 mm thick with spans ranging from 3 m to 7.5 m, are supported on *load-bearing walls* (masonry). This system is mainly adopted in low-rise buildings. The slab panels are usually rectangular in shape and can be supported in a number of ways.

When the slab is supported only on two opposite sides [Figure 1.9(a)], the slab bends in one direction only; hence, it is called a *one-way slab*. When the slab is supported on all four sides, and the plan dimensions of length and breadth are comparable to each other [Figure 1.9(c)], the slab bends in two directions (along the length and the breadth); hence, it is called a *two-way slab*. However, if the slab is a long rectangle (length greater than about twice the width), the bending along the longitudinal direction is negligible in comparison with that along the transverse (short-span) direction, and the resulting slab action is effectively one-way [Figure 1.9(b)]. If the wall extends above the floor level [Figure 1.9(d)], the slab is no more simply supported; the partial fixity at the support introduces hogging moments in the slab. Furthermore, twisting moments are also introduced at the corners that are restrained (not free to lift up) – as established by the classical theory of plates. Generally, slabs are cast in panels that are continuous over several wall supports, and are called *one-way continuous* [Figure 1.9(e)] or *two-way continuous* slabs, depending on whether the bending is predominantly along one direction or two directions. Hogging moments are induced in the slab in the regions near the intermediate support.

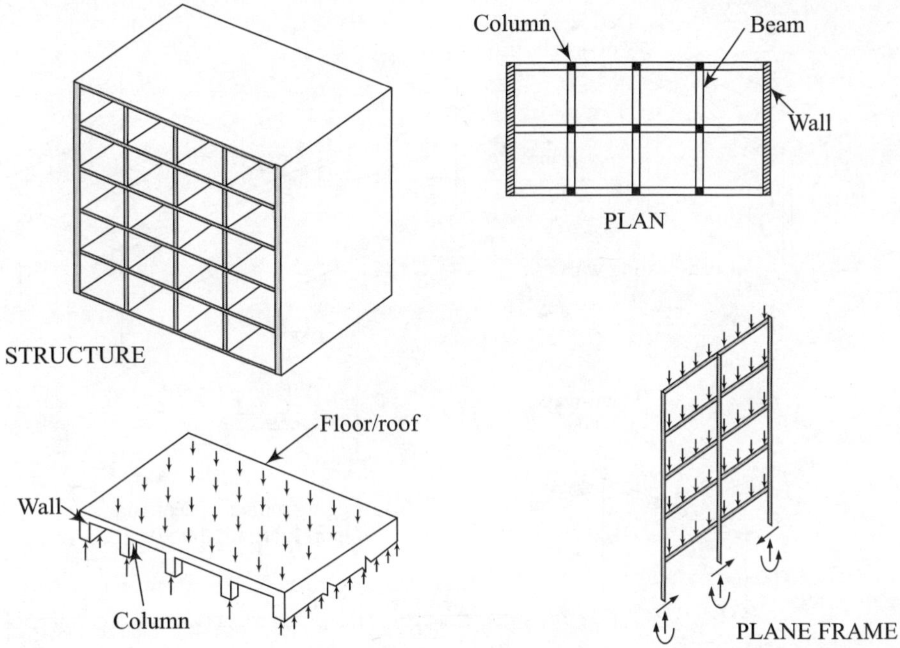

(a) Vertical load transmission

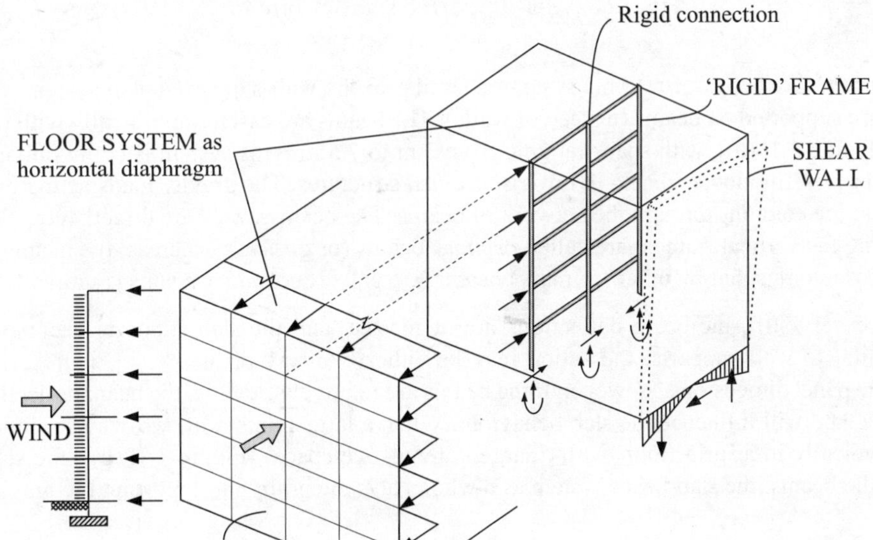

(b) Lateral load transmission

Fig. 1.8 Load transmission mechanisms.

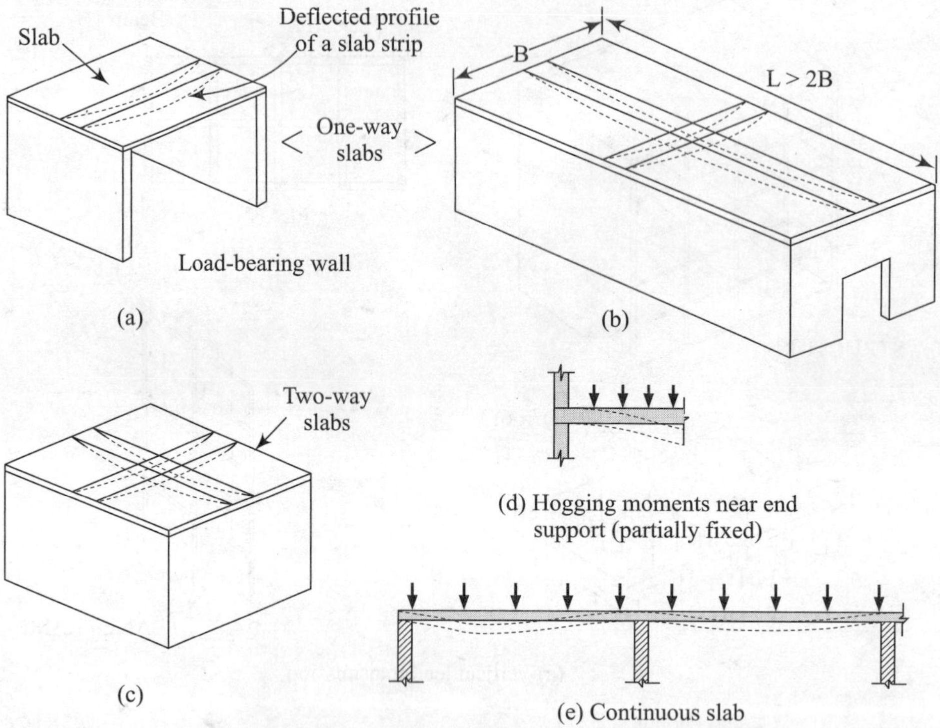

Fig. 1.9 Wall-supported slab systems.

Beam-Supported Slab System This system is similar to the wall-supported slab system, except that the floor slabs are supported on beams (instead of walls). The beams are cast monolithically with the slabs in a grid pattern [Figure 1.10(a)], with spans ranging from 3 m to 7.5 m. This system is commonly adopted in high-rise building construction, and also in low-rise *framed* structures. The gravity loads acting on the slabs are transmitted to the columns through the network of beams. The beams which are directly connected to the columns (forming the vertical frames) are called *primary* beams (or *girders*); whereas, the beams which are supported, not by columns, but by other (primary) beams, are called *secondary* beams [Figures 1.10(b),(c)].

If the beams are very stiff, the beam deflections are negligible, and the slab supports become relatively unyielding, similar to wall supports; the action may be either two-way or one-way [Figures 1.10(b),(c)], depending on the panel dimensions. However, if the beams are relatively flexible, the beam deflections are no longer negligible and will influence the slab behaviour. When a large number of two-way secondary beams are involved (typically in a 'grid floor' with a large column-free space) [Figure 1.10(d)], the slabs do not really 'rest' on the beams; the slab-beam system as a whole, acts integrally in supporting the gravity loads.

Ribbed Slab System This is a special type of 'grid floor' slab-beam system (also known as *joist floor*), in which the 'slab', called *topping*, is very thin (50–100 mm) and the 'beams', called *ribs*, are very slender and closely spaced (less than 1.5 m apart). The ribs have a thickness of not less than 65 mm and a depth that is three-to-four times the thickness.

The ribs may be designed in one-way or two-way patterns [Figures 1.11(a),(b)], and are generally cast-in-situ, although precast construction is also possible.

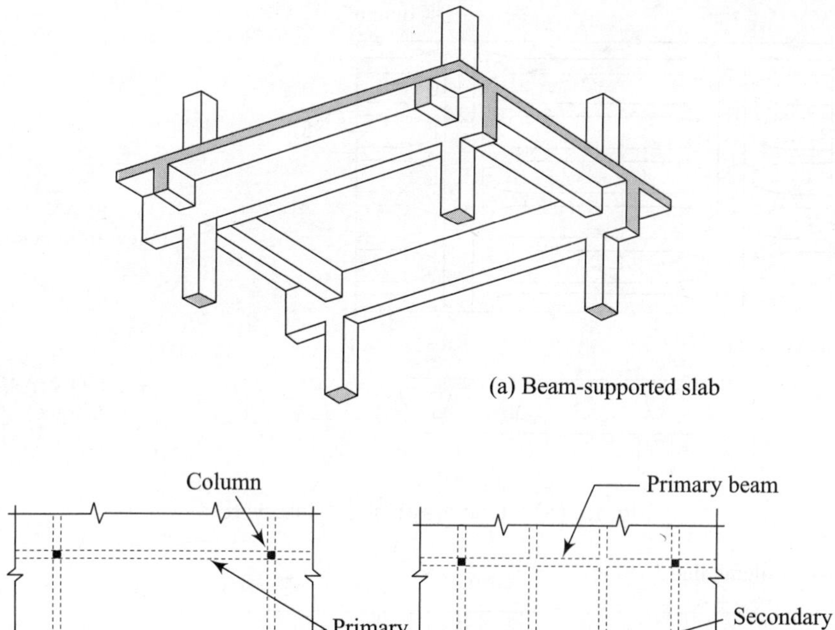

(a) Beam-supported slab

(b) Two-way system

(c) One-way system

(d) Grid beam-supported slab

Fig. 1.10 Beam-supported slab systems.

Two-way ribbed slabs are sometimes called *waffle slabs*. Along the outer edges, the ribbed-slab system is generally supported on stiff edge beams or walls. In wall-supported systems, the thickness of the rib resting on the wall is usually increased to match the wall thickness for improved bearing. Waffle slabs, used in large-span construction, may rest directly on columns; in this case, the slab is made solid in the neighbourhood of the column [Figure 1.11(b)].

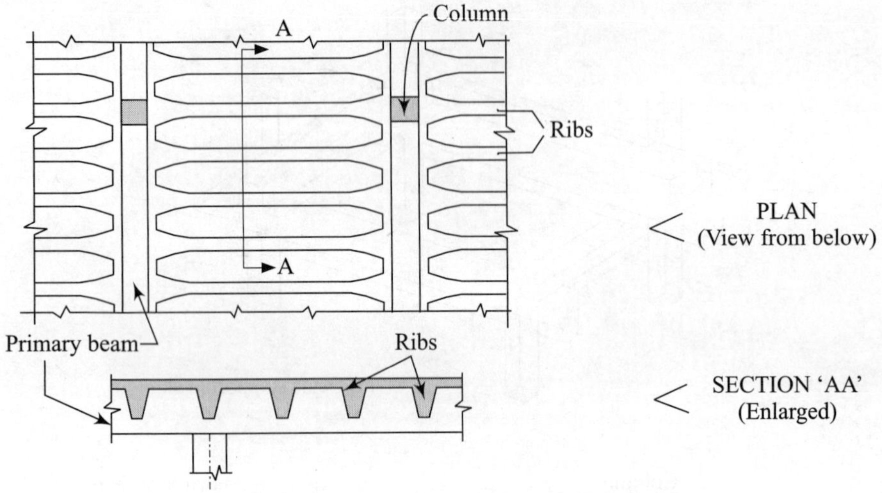

Fig. 1.11(a) One-way ribbed slab system.

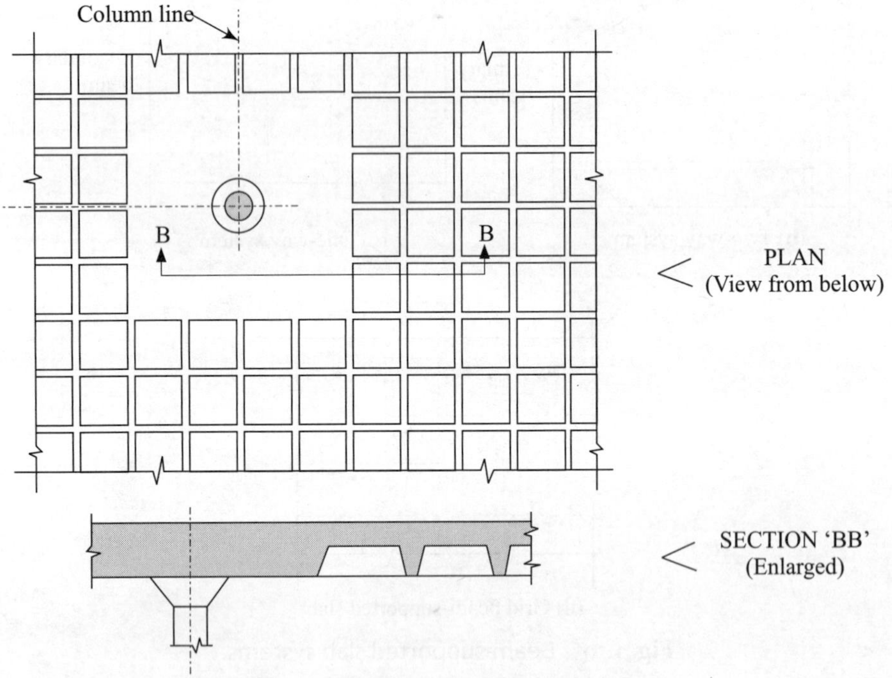

Fig. 1.11(b) Two-way ribbed (waffle) slab system.

Flat Plate System Here, the floor slab is supported directly on the columns, without the presence of stiffening beams, except at the periphery [Figure 1.12]. It has a uniform thickness of about 125–250 mm for spans of 4.5–6 m. Its load-carrying capacity is restricted by the limited shear strength and hogging moment capacity at the column supports. Because it is relatively thin and has a flat under-surface, it is called a *flat plate*, and certainly has much architectural appeal. It is used at locations (such as in apartments and hotels) where floor loads are low, spans are not large, and plane soffits serve as ceilings. Reinforced concrete flat-plate systems are relatively rare in India, but prestressed concrete (post-tensioned) flat plate systems are now gaining popularity.

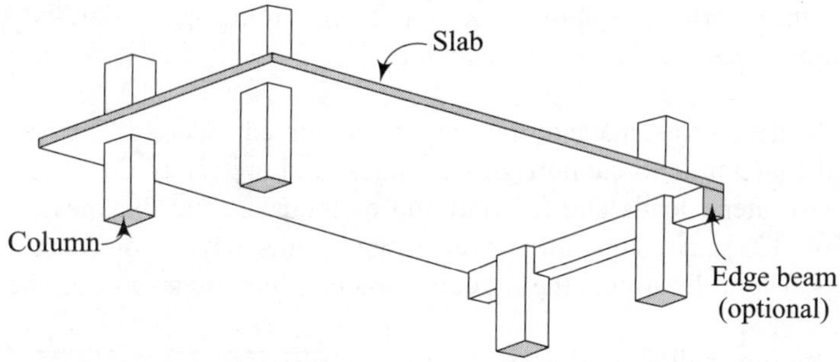

Fig. 1.12 Flat plate system.

Flat Slab System This is a more acceptable concept to many designers [Figure 1.13]. The flat slabs are plates that are stiffened near the column supports by means of 'drop panels' and/or 'column capitals' (which are generally concealed under 'drop ceilings'). Compared to the flat plate system, the flat slab system is suitable for higher loads and larger spans, because of its enhanced capacity in resisting shear and hogging moments near the supports. The slab thickness varies from 125 mm to 300 mm for spans of 4–9 m. Among the various floor systems, the flat slab system is the one with the highest dead load per unit area.

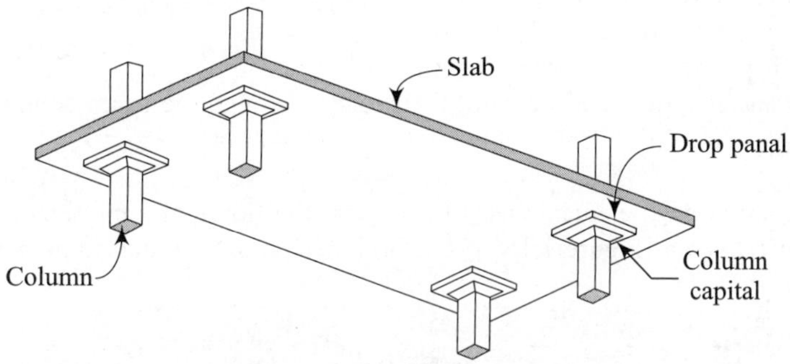

Fig. 1.13 Flat slab system.

1.6.2 Vertical Framing System

The vertical framing system resists the gravity loads and lateral loads from the floor system and transmits these effects to the foundation and ground below. The framing system is made up of a three-dimensional framework of beams and columns. For convenience, we may divide the framework into separate *plane frames* in the transverse and longitudinal directions of the building.

In cast-in-situ reinforced concrete construction, the vertical framing system usually comprises the following.

Columns These are skeletal structural elements, whose cross-sectional shapes may be rectangular, square, circular, L-shaped, etc. – often as specified by the architect. The size of the column section is dictated, from a structural viewpoint, by its height and the loads acting on it – which, in turn, depend on the type of floor system, spacing of columns, number of storeys, etc. The column is generally designed to resist axial compression combined with (biaxial) bending moments that are induced by 'frame action' under gravity and lateral loads. These load effects are more pronounced in the lower storeys of tall buildings; hence, high strength concrete (up to 50 MPa) with high reinforcement area (up to 6 per cent of the concrete area) is frequently adopted in such cases, to minimise the column size. In some locations such as atriums, the column height between floor slabs may be excessive (more than one storey height); in such cases, it is structurally desirable to reduce the unsupported length of the column by providing appropriate *tie beams*; otherwise, the columns should be properly designed as *slender columns*.

Walls These are vertical elements, made of masonry or reinforced concrete. They are called *bearing walls* if their main structural function is to support gravity loads, and are referred to as *shear walls* if they are mainly required to resist lateral loads due to wind and earthquake. The thickness of reinforced concrete bearing walls varies from 125 mm to 200 mm; however, shear walls may be considerably thicker in the lower storeys of tall buildings. The walls around the lift cores of a building often serve as shear walls.

Transfer Girders In some buildings, the architectural planning is such that large column-free spaces are required in the lower floors – for banquet/convention halls (in hotels), lobbies, parking areas, etc.

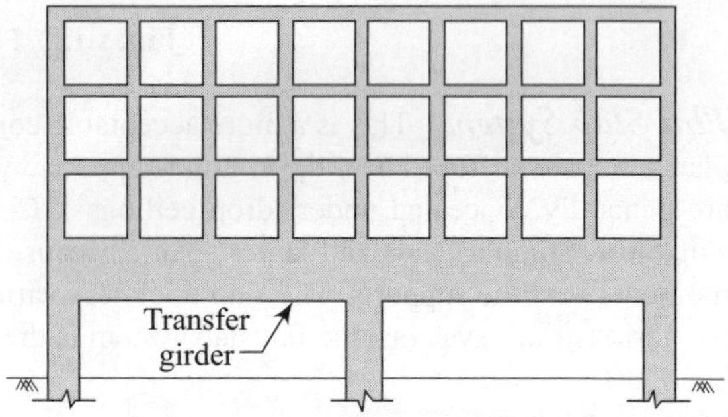

Fig. 1.14 Use of transfer girder.

In such cases, the vertical load-bearing elements (columns, bearing walls) of the upper floors are not allowed to continue downwards, through the lower floors, to the foundations below. This problem can be resolved by providing a very heavy beam, called *transfer girder*, whose depth may extend over one full storey [Figure 1.14]. The upper-storey columns terminate above the transfer girder, and transmit their loads, through the beam action of the girder, to the main columns that support the girder from below.

Suspenders These are vertical elements used to suspend the floors of a multi-storeyed building from a central reinforced concrete core [Figure 1.15]. Structural steel is often found to be better suited for use as

Fig. 1.15 The 'Hanging' building – Yayasan Sabah Headquarters, Kota Kinabalu, Sabah, Malaysian Borneo. The 30 floors (33 m dia) of the building are suspended along their periphery with 96 high tensile steel rods, 38 mm thick, hung from radial steel brackets attached to the top of a 14.3 m dia reinforced concrete core. At their inside edges, the floors are supported by brackets on the core. The core, which rises 122 m from the ground to the helipad at top, houses the elevators and services. *Photo by S. Unnikrishna Pillai.*

suspenders (also called *hangers*), because the force to be resisted is direct tension; moreover, steel hangers take up very little of the floor space. These suspenders may be hung from large cantilevered beams, cross-braced trusses, Vierendeel girders or brackets attached to the reinforced concrete core at the roof or at intermediate levels.

It may be noted that the vertical elements in the bow-string girder of Figure 1.5 also act as suspenders, transmitting the loads of the bridge deck to the arches spanning between the piers.

1.6.3 Lateral Load Resisting Systems

The horizontal and vertical sub-systems of a structural system interact and jointly resist both gravity loads and lateral loads. Lateral load effects (due to wind and earthquake) predominate in tall buildings, and govern the selection of the structural system.

Lateral load resisting systems of reinforced concrete buildings generally consist of one of the following.

Frames These are generally composed of columns and beams [Figures 1.8(b) and 1.16(a)]. Their ability to resist lateral loads is entirely due to the rigidities of the beam-column connections and the moment-resisting

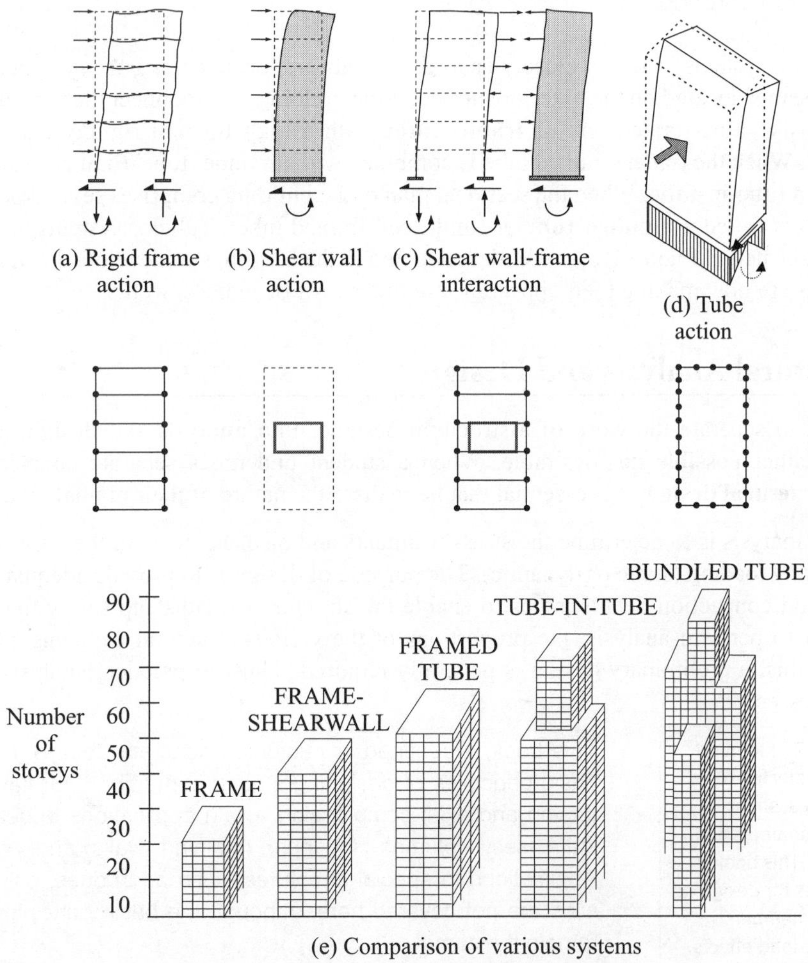

Fig. 1.16 Lateral load-resisting systems.

capacities of the individual members. They are often (albeit mistakenly) called 'rigid frames', because the ends of the various members framing into a joint are 'rigidly' connected in such a way as to ensure that they all undergo the same rotation under the action of loads. In 'flat plate' or 'flat slab' system, a certain width of the slab, along the column line, takes the place of the beam in 'frame action'. Frames are used as the sole lateral load-resisting system in buildings with up to 15 to 20 storeys [Figure 1.16(e)].

Shear Walls These are solid walls, which usually extend over the full height of the building. They are commonly located at the lift/staircase core regions. Shear walls are also frequently placed along the transverse direction of a building, either as exterior (facade) walls or as interior walls. The walls are very stiff, having considerable depth in the direction of lateral loads [Figure 1.16(b)]; they resist loads by bending like vertical cantilevers, fixed at the base.

The various walls and co-existing frames in a building are linked at the different floor levels by means of the floor system, which distributes the lateral loads to these different systems appropriately. The interaction between the shear walls and the frames is structurally advantageous in that the walls restrain the frame deformations in the lower storeys, while the frames restrain the wall deformations in the upper storeys [Figure 1.16(c)]. Frame-shear wall systems are generally considered in buildings up to about 40 storeys, as indicated in Figure 1.16(e) [Ref. 1.5].

Tubes These are systems in which closely-spaced columns are located along the periphery of a building. Deep spandrel beams, located on the exterior surface of the building, interconnect these columns. The entire system behaves like a perforated box or **framed tube** with a high flexural rigidity against lateral loads [Figure 1.16(d)]. When the (outer) framed tube is combined with an 'inner tube' (or a central shear core), the system is called a **tube-in-tube**. When the sectional plan of the building comprises several perforated tubular *cells*, the system is called a **bundled tube** or 'multi-cell framed tube'. Tubular systems are effective up to 80 storeys, as indicated in Figure 1.16(e). Widely adopted in the big cities of developed countries, these sky-scraping systems are now making their appearance in the metros of India as well.

1.7 Structural Analysis and Design

It is convenient to separate the work of a structural designer into **analysis** and **design,** although a rigid separation is neither possible nor desirable. When a student undergoes separate courses on **structural analysis** and **structural design**, it is essential that he realises the nature of their mutual relationship.

The purpose of analysis is to determine the stress resultants and displacements in the various members of a structure under any loading (static or dynamic). The purpose of design is to provide adequate member sizes, reinforcement and connection details, so as to enable the structure to withstand safely the calculated load effects. In order to perform analysis, the proportions of the various structural elements should be known in advance; for this, a preliminary design is generally required. Thus, in practice, analysis and design are interactive processes.

The forces that a RC member/section can be subjected to include axial forces, shear forces, bending moments and twisting moment. This book details procedures for designing and detailing RC members/sections for these load effects.

This book is confined to reinforced concrete **design**. It covers the basic principles of designing structural members for flexure, shear, torsion and axial compression – with applications to beams, slabs, staircases, columns, footings, retaining walls and water tanks. Applications to special structures, such as bridges, chimneys, and silos are not covered here, although the basic principles of design remain the same.

Furthermore, the various methods of analysis of structures [Ref. 1.6-1.9] clearly lie outside the scope of this book. However, some approximations in analysis, as permitted by design codes, are discussed in some of the chapters to follow.

1.7.1 Exposure to Construction Practices

In reinforced concrete structures, **construction practices** are as important as the **design**. Indeed, for a correct understanding of design as well as the Code provisions, some exposure to concrete laboratory work (see Appendix C) and to actual reinforced concrete construction work in the field is required.

> Frequently, major concrete structures are constructed right in the college campus (or nearby). Students (and teachers!) should take full advantage of these opportunities to visit the sites and supplement and reinforce the theory they learn in the class room. Learning can emerge from both good practice and bad practice!
>
> **Supplement theoretical study with real-life practical learning.**

1.8 Design Codes and Handbooks

1.8.1 Purpose of Codes

National building codes have been formulated in different countries to lay down guidelines for the design and construction of structures. The codes have evolved from the collective wisdom of expert structural engineers, gained over the years. These codes are periodically revised to bring them in line with current research, and often, current trends.

The codes serve at least four distinct functions. Firstly, they ensure adequate structural safety, by specifying certain essential minimum requirements for design. Secondly, they render the task of the designer relatively simple; often, the results of sophisticated analyses are made available in the form of a simple formula or chart. Thirdly, the codes ensure a measure of consistency among different designers. Finally, they have some legal validity, in that they protect the structural designer from any liability due to structural failures that are caused by inadequate supervision and/or faulty material and construction.

> The codes are not meant to serve as a substitute for basic understanding and engineering judgement. The student is, therefore, forewarned that he will make a poor designer if he succumbs to the unfortunate (and all-too-common) habit of blindly following the codes. On the contrary, in order to improve his understanding, he must learn to question the code provisions – as, indeed, he must, nearly everything in life!
>
> **While codes attempt to ensure minimum requirements, try to think beyond the codes.**

1.8.2 Basic Code for Design

The design procedures described in this book conform to the following Indian code, published by the Bureau of Indian Standards, New Delhi:

IS 456: 2000 – Plain and reinforced concrete – Code of practice (fourth revision)

This code shall henceforth be referred to as 'the Code' in the chapters to follow. References have also been made to other national codes, such as ACI 318, BS 8110, CSA CAN3-A23.3 and Eurocode, wherever relevant.

1.8.3 Loading Standards

The loads to be considered for structural design are specified in the following loading standards:

IS 875 (Parts 1-5): 1987 – Code of practice for design loads (other than earthquake) for buildings and structures (second revision)

Part 1: Dead loads
Part 2: Imposed (live) loads
Part 3: Wind loads (third revision - 2015)
Part 4: Snow loads
Part 5: Special loads and load combinations

IS 1893: 2016 – Criteria for earthquake resistant design of structures – Part 1: General Provisions and Buildings (fourth revision).

1.8.4 Design Handbooks

The Bureau of Indian Standards has also published the following handbooks, which serve as useful supplements to the 1978 version of the Code. Although the handbooks need to be updated to bring them in line with the revised (2000 version) of the Code, many of the provisions continue to be valid (especially with regard to structural design provisions).

SP 16: 1980 – Design Aids for Reinforced Concrete to IS 456: 1978
SP 23: 1982 – Handbook on Concrete Mixes
SP 24: 1983 – Explanatory Handbook on IS 456: 1978
SP 34: 1987 – Handbook on Concrete Reinforcement and Detailing

1.8.5 Other Related Codes

There are several other codes that the designer may need to refer to. The codes dealing with material specifications and testing are listed at the end of Chapter 2. Chapter 16 of this book deals with special design provisions related to earthquake-resistant design of reinforced concrete structures. The codes related to this topic are:

IS 13920: 2016 – Ductile detailing of reinforced concrete structures subjected to seismic forces.
IS 3370: 2021 – Code of practice for concrete structures for retaining aqueous liquids.

Other codes dealing with the design of special structures, such as bridges, folded plates and shells, chimneys, bunkers and silos, are not covered in this book, the scope of which is limited to basic reinforced concrete design.

REVIEW QUESTIONS

1.1 Ascribe reasons to why concrete is gaining the status of the most widely used construction material?

1.2 The occurrence of *flexural tension* in reinforced concrete is well known. Cite practical examples where tension occurs in other forms in reinforced concrete.

1.3 Explain the role of *transverse steel ties* [Figure 1.6(d)] in reinforced concrete columns?

1.4 A reinforced concrete canopy slab, designed as a cantilever, is under construction. Prior to the removal of the formwork, doubts are expressed about the safety of the structure. It is proposed to prop up the free edge of the cantilever with a beam supported on pillars. Comment on this proposal.

1.5 Describe the main objectives of structural design.

1.6 List the steps involved in the process of structural design.

1.7 Distinguish between structural *analysis* and structural *design*.

1.8 Consider a typical reinforced concrete building in your institution. Identify the various structural elements in the structural system of the building, and briefly explain how the loads are transmitted to the supporting ground.

1.9 Consider a symmetrical portal frame ABCD with the columns (AB and CD) 4 m high, fixed at the base points A and D. The beam BC has a span of 6 m and supports a uniformly distributed load of 100 kN. From structural analysis, it is found that at each fixed base support, the reactions developed are 50 kN (vertical), 30 kN (horizontal) and 40 kN m (moment). With the help of free body, bending moment, shear force and axial force diagrams, determine the stress resultants in the design of the beam BC and the column AB (or CD).

1.10 Enumerate the various types of gravity load bearing systems and lateral load resisting systems used in reinforced concrete buildings.

REFERENCES

1.1 Mehta, P K and Monteiro, P J M, *Concrete: Microstructure, Properties and Materials*, Indian edition, Indian Concrete Institute, Chennai, 1997

1.2 Neville, A M and Brooks, J J , *Concrete Technology*, ELBS edition, Longman, London, 1990

1.3 Faber, C, *Candela, The Shell Builder*, Architectural Press, London, 1960

1.4 Salvadori, M and Heller, M, *Structure in Architecture*, Prentice-Hall International, 1986

1.5 Fintel, M, *Handbook of Concrete Engineering*, Second edition, (Van Nostrand Co., New York), C.B.S. Publishers and Distributors, Delhi, 1986

1.6 Menon, D, *Structural Analysis*, Second Edition, Narosa Publishing House, Delhi, 2017

1.7 Menon, D, *Advanced Structural Analysis*, Second Edition, Narosa Publishing House, 2017

1.8 Clough, R W and Penzien, J, *Dynamics of Structures*, Second edition, McGraw-Hill International edition, 1993

1.9 Taranath, B S, *Structural Analysis and Design of Tall Buildings*, McGraw-Hill International edition, 1988

CHAPTER 2

Basic Material Properties

LEARNING OBJECTIVES

After studying this chapter, you will be able to:

- *Define/discuss the different constituents of concrete, their properties and standard tests, and about various admixtures*
- *Identify the factors influencing strength and properties of hardened concrete, their standard tests, stress-strain relations, behaviour under combined stresses, and long-term effects*
- *Define/explain/discuss the aspects related to durability of concrete*
- *Specify the various types, sizes and grades of reinforcing steel, their behaviour and stress-strain characteristics; and Code specifications related to concrete materials*

2.1 Introduction

In order to learn to design reinforced concrete structures, it is essential to begin with an understanding of the basic materials, viz., **concrete** (including its ingredients) and **reinforcing steel**. Accordingly, this chapter describes briefly some of the important properties of these basic materials.

Much of this chapter is devoted to concrete rather than steel, because the designer (as well as the builder) needs to know more about concrete, which, unlike steel, is not usually manufactured in factories under controlled conditions. Concrete is generally prepared at the site itself, although *ready-mixed* concrete and *precast* concrete are also used in some cases.

2.1.1 Concrete Technology

> With exactly the same constituents, one can make concrete of very high quality or very poor quality. To learn how to do the former (and not the latter), apply the principles of concrete technology.

The making of 'good' concrete is decidedly not an easy job. This is clear from the all-too-common 'bad' concrete. Both good and bad concrete can be prepared from exactly the same constituents: cement, aggregate, water (and, sometimes, admixtures). It is the mix proportions, the 'know-how' and the 'do-how' that makes the difference.

Good concrete is one that has the desired qualities of strength, impermeability, durability, etc., in the *hardened state*. To achieve this, the concrete has to be 'satisfactory' in the *fresh state* (which includes the stages of mixing, handling, placing, compacting and curing). Broadly, this means that the *mix* must be of the right proportions, and must be *cohesive* enough to be *transported* and *placed* without *segregation* by the means available, and its *consistency* must be such that it is *workable* and can be *compacted* by the means that are actually available for the job.

A competent concrete technologist will be able to get a fair idea of the nature and properties of hardened concrete by observation and a few simple tests on the fresh concrete. If found unsatisfactory, suitable remedial measures can and should be adopted without having to wait until the concrete hardens, by which time it will be too late to effect corrections.

> **Concrete technology deals with the properties of concrete for various applications: appropriate choice and mixing of the ingredients of concrete, as well as compaction and curing, govern the properties of hardened concrete.**

'Concrete technology' is a complete subject in itself, and the reader is advised to consult standard textbooks on the subject [Ref. 2.1, 2.2, 2.3] for a detailed study. In the following sections, some salient features of making concrete (covering both ingredients and process) are discussed, followed by a detailed description of the properties of hardened concrete and reinforcing steel.

2.2 Cement

Cement may be described as a material with adhesive and cohesive properties that make it capable of bonding mineral fragments ('aggregates') into a compact whole [Ref. 2.1]. In this process, it imparts *strength* and *durability* to the hardened mass called concrete. The cements used in the making of concrete are called *hydraulic cements* – so named, because they have the property of reacting chemically with water in an exothermic (heat-generating) process called *hydration* that results in water-resistant products†. The products of hydration form a viscous *cement paste*, which coats the aggregate surfaces and fills some of the void spaces between the aggregate pieces. The cement paste loses consistency ('stiffens') on account of gradual loss of 'free water', through adsorption and evaporation, and subsequently 'sets', transforming the mixture into a solid mass. If the *consistency* of the cement paste is either excessively 'harsh' or excessively 'wet', there is a danger of *segregation*, i.e., the aggregate tends to separate out of the mix; this will adversely affect the quality of the hardened concrete and may also result in a 'honeycomb' appearance. The freshly set cement paste gains strength with time ('hardens'), on account of progressive filling of the void spaces in the paste with the reaction products, also resulting in a decrease in porosity and permeability.

> **Does increasing cement content enhance concrete quality?**

> There is a common misconception regarding the role of cement in concrete. Many people (including some civil engineers) assume that it is desirable to put in as much cement as possible in a concrete mix – provided, of course, cost is not a constraint. This is simply not true. The use of excessive cement results in cracking of concrete (due to the *heat of hydration* generated and due to *plastic shrinkage* of the cement paste), and leads to increased long-term effects of *creep* and *drying shrinkage* of hardened concrete, resulting in undesirable large deflections and cracking.

† Cements derived from calcination of gypsum or limestone are 'non-hydraulic' because their products of hydration are not resistant to water; however, the addition of pozzolanic materials can render gypsum and lime cements 'hydraulic' [Ref. 2.2].

2.2.1 Portland Cements

The most common type of hydraulic cement used in the manufacture of concrete is known as *Portland cement*, which is available in various forms.

Portland cement was first patented in England in 1824, and was so named because its grey colour resembled a limestone (quarried in Dorset) called 'Portland stone'. Portland cement is made by burning together, to about 1400°C, an intimate mixture (in the form of a slurry) of limestone (or chalk) with alumina-, silica- and iron oxide-bearing materials (such as clay or shale), and grinding the resulting 'clinker' into a fine powder, after cooling and adding a little gypsum. The cement contains four major compounds, viz., tricalcium silicate (C_3S), dicalcium silicate (C_2S), tricalcium aluminate (C_3A) and tetracalcium aluminoferrite (C_4AF). By altering the relative proportions of these major compounds, and including appropriate *additives*, different types of Portland cement, with different properties, can be made. For instance, increased proportions of C_3S and C_3A contribute to high early strength; on the contrary, an increased proportion of C_2S retards the early development of strength (and generates less heat of hydration), but enhances ultimate strength [Ref. 2.2]. Adjusting the fineness of cement can also control these properties.

The use of any one of the following types of Portland cement is permitted by the Code (IS 456: 2000):

Ordinary Portland Cement (OPC) presently available in three different 'grades' (denoting compressive strength), viz., C33, C43 and C53, conforming to IS 269: 2015. The numbers 33, 43 and 53 correspond to the 28-day (characteristic[†]) compressive strengths of cement, as obtained from standard tests on cement-sand mortar specimens. These are most commonly used in general concrete construction, where there is no special durability requirement (such as exposure to 'sulphate attack').

Rapid Hardening Portland Cement (RHPC) conforming to IS 8041: 1990, is similar to OPC, except that it has more C_3S and less C_2S, and it is ground more finely. It is used in situations where a rapid development of strength is desired (e.g., when formwork is to be removed early for reuse).

Portland Slag Cement (PSC) conforming to IS 455: 2015, is made by inter-grinding Portland cement clinker and granulated *blast furnace slag* (which is a waste product in the manufacture of pig iron). It has fairly high sulphate resistance, rendering it suitable for use in environments exposed to sulphates (in the soil or in ground water).

Portland Pozzolana Cements (PPC) *flyash based* or *calcined clay based,* conforming respectively to Parts 1 and 2 of IS 1489: 2015, involves the addition of 'pozzolana' (flyash or calcined clay) – a mineral additive containing silica; the pozzolana is generally cheaper than the cement it replaces. These cements hydrate and gain strength relatively slowly, and therefore require *curing* over a comparatively longer period. They are suitable in situations (such as mass concreting) where a low rate of heat of hydration is desired.

Hydrophobic Portland Cement (HPC) conforming to IS 8043: 1991, is obtained by inter-grinding Portland cement with 0.1–0.4 per cent of oleic acid or stearic acid. The 'hydrophobic' (water-resistant) property is due to the formation of a water-repellent film around each particle of cement. During the mixing

[†] The term 'characteristic strength' is defined in Section 2.6.1. Higher grade OPC is now widely available in India, and is achieved in cement manufacture by increased proportion of lime (which enhances C_3S) and increased fineness (up to 325 kg/m^2). The higher the grade of cement, the quicker will be the strength gain of the concrete mixture. However, in the long run, the strength development curves more or less converge for the various grades of cement.

of concrete, this film is broken, thereby making it possible for normal hydration to take place. Although its early strength is low, this cement is suitable in situations where cement bags are required to be stored for a prolonged period under unfavourable conditions, because it deteriorates very little.

Low Heat Portland Cement (LHPC) conforming to IS 12600: 1989, is Portland cement with relatively lower contents of the more rapidly hydrating compounds, C_3S and C_3A. The process of hydration is slow (as with PPC), and the consequent rate of heat generation is also low. This is desirable in mass concreting of gravity dams; as otherwise, the excessive heat of hydration can result in serious cracking. However, because of the slower rate of strength gain, adequate precaution should be taken in their use such as with regard to removal of formwork, etc.

Sulphate Resisting Portland Cement (SRPC) conforming to IS 12330: 1988, is Portland cement with a very low C_3A content and ground finer than OPC. This cement is 'sulphate-resistant' because the disintegration of concrete, caused by the reaction of C_3A in hardened cement with a sulphate salt from outside is inhibited. SRPC is therefore ideally suited for use in concrete structures located in soils where sulphates are present. However, recent research indicates that the use of SRPC is not beneficial in environments where chlorides are present.

Portland White Cement (PWC) conforming to IS 8042: 2015, is Portland cement made from raw materials of low iron content, the clinker for which is fired by a reducing flame. Special precautions are required during the grinding of the clinker to avoid contamination. The addition of pigments to a white cement concrete mix makes it possible to produce concrete with pastel colours. White cement is far more expensive, compared to OPC, and is used mainly for architectural purposes – in floor and wall finishes, swimming pool surfaces, etc.

The Code permits the use of combinations of Portland cements with mineral admixtures, provided they meet the desired performance standards. The term 'blended cements' is now gaining popularity; it refers to cements obtained by combination with various pozzolanic admixtures such as *flyash* (of proper quality) and *ground granulated blast furnace slag*.

2.2.2 Other Cements

The Code also permits the use of the following special cements 'under special circumstances' – mainly prevention of chemical attack. However, the use of these cements should be done judiciously and with special care.

High Alumina Cement (HAC) or Aluminous Cement conforming to IS 6452: 1989, is very different in its composition from Portland cements. The raw materials used for its manufacture consist of 'bauxite' (which is a clay with high alumina content) and limestone (or chalk). It has good resistance against attack by sulphates and some dilute acids, and is particularly recommended in marine environments; it also shows a very high rate of strength development.

Supersulphated Cement (SC) conforming to IS 6909: 1990, is made by inter-grinding a mixture of 80–85 per cent of granulated blast furnace slag with 10–15 per cent of dead-burnt gypsum and about 5 per cent Portland cement clinker. It is highly resistant to sea water, and can withstand high concentrations of sulphates found in soil or ground water; it is also resistant to peaty acids and oils.

2.2.3 Tests on Cements

Testing of cement quality is very important in the production of quality concrete. The quality of cement is determined on the basis of its conformity to the performance characteristics given in the respective IS specification for the cement. Any special features or such other performance characteristics claimed/indicated by manufacturers alongside the 'Statutory Quality Marking' or otherwise have no relation with characteristics guaranteed by the Quality Marking as relevant to that cement. Consumers should go by the characteristics given in the corresponding IS specification or seek expert advice (Cl. 5.1.3 of the Code).

Tests are performed in accordance with IS 4032: 1985 and IS 4031 (Parts 1-15) : 1988 - 1999 to assess the following:

- ***Chemical composition*** Analysis to determine the composition of various oxides (of calcium, silica, aluminium, iron, magnesium and sulphur) present in the cement and to ensure that impurities are within the prescribed limits;
- ***Fineness*** A measure of the size of the cement particles, in terms of specific surface (i.e., surface area per unit mass); increased fineness enhances the rate of hydration, and hence, also strength development[†];
- ***Normal consistency*** Determination of the quantity of water to be mixed to produce 'standard paste';
- ***Initial and final setting times*** Measures of the rate of solidification of standard cement paste (using a 'Vicat needle'); the 'initial setting time' indicates the time when the paste becomes unworkable (to be not less than 30–45 min usually for OPC), whereas the 'final setting time' refers to the time to reach a state of complete solidification (to be not greater than 375–600 min for OPC);
- ***Soundness*** A quality which indicates that the cement paste, once it has set, does not undergo appreciable change in volume (causing concrete to crack); and
- ***Strength*** Measured in terms of the stress at failure of hardened cement-sand mortar specimens, subject to compression and tension tests.

2.3 Aggregate

Since aggregate occupies about three-quarters of the volume of concrete, it contributes significantly to the structural performance of concrete, especially *strength*, *durability* and *volume stability*.

Aggregate is formed from natural sources by the process of weathering and abrasion, or by artificially crushing a larger parent (rock) mass. Other types of aggregates may be used for *plain concrete members* (Code Cl. 5.3.1), however, as far as possible, preference shall be given to natural aggregates. Aggregate is generally categorised into **fine aggregate** (particle size between 0.075 mm and 4.75 mm) and **coarse aggregate** (particle size larger than 4.75 mm), as described in IS 383: 2016.

Sand, taken from river beds and pits, is normally used as fine aggregate, after it is cleaned and rendered free from silt, clay and other impurities; stone (quarry) dust is sometimes used as a partial replacement for sand.

Gravel and crushed rock are normally used as coarse aggregate. The maximum size of coarse aggregate to be used in reinforced concrete work depends on the thickness of the structural member and the space available around the reinforcing bars. Generally, a maximum *nominal*[‡] size of 20 mm is found to be satisfactory in

---

[†] Modern cements are considerably finer than their predecessors, on account of improved grinding technology; accordingly, these cements also turn out to be stronger in the early stages. However, the heat of hydration released is also higher.

[‡] The term 'nominal' (commonly used in reinforced concrete design practice) refers to the *expected* value of any parameter, such as dimension and material strength. The *actual* value may be somewhat different, depending on admissible tolerances.

RC structural elements. However, in cases where the member happens to be very thin, the Code (Cl. 5.3.3) specifies that the size should be restricted to one-fourth of the minimum thickness of the member. In the case of heavily reinforced members, it should be restricted to 5 mm less than the minimum clear spacing between bars or minimum *cover* to reinforcement, whichever is smaller. In such situations, the maximum nominal size is frequently taken as 10 mm. In situations where there is no restriction to the flow of concrete, as in most plain concrete work, there is no such restriction on the maximum aggregate size. It is common to use aggregate up to 40 mm nominal size in the *base concrete* underneath foundations. The Code (Cl. 5.3.3) even permits the use of 'plums' above 160 mm in certain cases of mass concreting up to a maximum limit of 20 per cent by volume of concrete. *Plums* are large random-shaped stones dropped into freshly-placed mass concrete to economise on the concrete; such mass concrete is sometimes called 'Cyclopean concrete' [Ref. 2.8].

Mention may also be made of a special type of aggregate, known as lightweight aggregate, which (although not used for reinforced concrete work) is sometimes used to manufacture 'lightweight concrete' masonry blocks, which have low unit weight and good thermal insulation and fire resistance properties. Lightweight aggregate may be obtained from natural sources (such as diatomite, pumice, etc.) or artificially, in the form of 'sintered fly ash' or 'bloated clay' (conforming to IS 9142: 1979).

2.3.1 Aggregate Properties and Tests

A number of tests have been described in IS 2386 (Parts 1-8): 1963 to assess the quality of the aggregate, in terms of the following physical and mechanical properties:

- ***Particle size, shape and surface texture*** 'Size' and 'shape' influence *strength*; 'shape' and 'texture' influence *bond* (between the aggregate and the cement paste) – for instance, it is found that *angular* and somewhat *porous* aggregates are conducive to good bond;
- ***Geological classification*** Based on the mineral type of the parent rock;
- ***Specific gravity and bulk density*** Of aggregate particle and aggregate whole respectively;
- ***Moisture content, water absorption and bulking of sand*** The moisture present in aggregate or the moisture that may be absorbed by the aggregate, as the case may be, must be accounted for in the determination of the quantity of water to be added to the concrete mix; moreover, the presence of water films in between sand particles results in an increase in volume (bulking of sand) that must be accounted for in case *volume batching* is employed in mix preparation;
- ***Strength*** Resistance to compression, measured in terms of the *aggregate crushing value*;
- ***Toughness*** Resistance to impact, measured in terms of the *aggregate impact value*;
- ***Hardness*** Resistance to wear, measured in terms of the *aggregate abrasion value*;
- ***Soundness*** Which indicates whether or not the aggregate undergoes appreciable volume changes due to alternate thermal changes, wetting and drying, freezing and thawing; and
- ***Deleterious constituents*** These may be iron pyrites, coal, mica, clay, silt, salt and organic impurities, which can adversely affect the hydration of cement, the bond with cement paste, the strength and the durability of hardened concrete.

2.3.2 Grading Requirements of Aggregate

'Grading' is the particle size distribution of aggregate; it is measured by *sieve analysis* [IS 2386 (Part 1): 1963], and is generally described by means of a *grading curve*, which depicts the 'cumulative percentage passing' against the standard IS sieve sizes.

The grading (as well as the type and size) of aggregate is a major factor which influences the *workability* of fresh concrete, and its consequent degree of *compaction*. This is of extreme importance with regard to the quality of hardened concrete, because incomplete compaction results in *voids*, thereby lowering the *density* of the concrete and preventing it from attaining its full compressive strength capability [Figure 2.1]; furthermore, the impermeability and durability characteristics get adversely affected. It is seen from Figure 2.1 that as little as 5 per cent of voids can lower the strength by as much as 32 per cent.

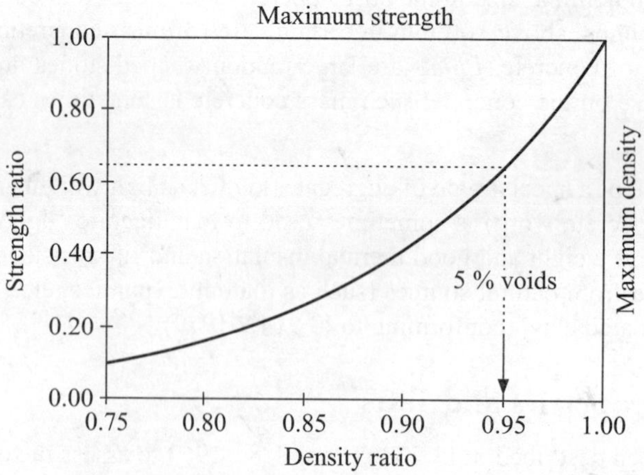

Fig. 2.1 Relation between density ratio and strength ratio [Ref. 2.1].

From an economic viewpoint, it may appear desirable to aim for maximum density by a proper grading of aggregate alone – with the smaller particles fitting, as much as possible, into the voids of the larger particles in the dry state, thereby limiting the use of the (more expensive) cement paste to filling in the voids in the fine aggregate. Unfortunately, such a concrete mix is prone to be 'harsh' and unworkable. Moreover, it is very likely to *segregate*, with the coarser particles separating out or settling more than the finer particles.

The cement paste must be in sufficient quantity to be able to coat properly all the aggregate surfaces, to achieve the required workability, and to ensure that the particle sizes are distributed as homogeneously as possible without segregation. The presence of more 'fines' (sand and cement) in a mix is found to improve both workability and resistance to segregation, because the fines tend to 'lubricate' the larger particles, and also fill into their voids as *mortar*. However, too much of fine aggregate in a mix is considered to be undesirable, because the durability and impermeability of the hardened concrete may be adversely affected.

Concrete mix design involves the determination of the optimal proportions of the ingredients (typically, cement, water, fine and coarse aggregate) to produce concrete with the desired workability, strength and durability. This is covered in IS 10262.

On account of these and other interacting factors, it is difficult to arrive at a unique 'ideal' grading in *mix design*. In practice, grading limits are recommended in codes and specifications, which are found *to produce a strong and workable concrete* [Ref. 2.3].

2.4 Water

Water has a significant role to play in the making of concrete – in *mixing* of fresh concrete and in *curing* of concrete while hardening. In order to ensure proper strength development and durability of concrete, it is necessary that the water used for mixing and curing is free from impurities such as oils, acids, alkalis, salts, sugar and organic materials.

Water that is fit for human consumption (i.e., *potable water*) is generally considered to be suitable for concreting. However, when the potability of the water is suspect, it is advisable to perform a chemical analysis of the water, in accordance with IS 3025 (Parts 17-32). The pH value of the water should not be less than 6. The concentrations of solids in water should be within certain 'permissible limits' that are specified in the Code (Cl. 5.4). In particular, the content of sulphates (as SO_3) is limited to 400 mg/l, while that of chlorides is restricted to 500 mg/l in reinforced concrete (and 2000 mg/l in plain concrete)[†]. Sea water is particularly unsuitable for mixing or curing of concrete. The Code also recommends testing for initial setting time of cement paste (as per IS 4031 (Part 5): 1988) and compressive strength of concrete cubes (as per IS 516: 1959), when there is doubt regarding the suitability of the water for proper strength development of concrete.

2.4.1 Water Content and Workability of Concrete

The water in a concrete mix is required not only for hydration with cement, but also for *workability. 'Workability' may be defined as 'that property of the freshly mixed concrete (or mortar) which determines the ease and homogeneity with which it can be mixed, placed, compacted and finished'* [Ref. 2.8]. The main factor that influences workability is the water content (in the absence of admixtures), as the 'inter-particle lubrication' is enhanced by the mere addition of water. The amount of water required for lubrication depends on the aggregate type, texture and grading: finer particles require more water to wet their larger specific surface; angular aggregates require more water than rounded ones of the same size; aggregates with greater porosity consume more water from the mix.

Water content in a mix is also related to the fineness of cement – the finer the cement, the greater the need for water – for hydration as well as for workability.

It may be recalled that workability is required to facilitate *full placement* in the formwork (even in areas of restricted access) and *full compaction*, minimising the voids in concrete. If a mix is too dry, bubbles of entrapped air create voids, and there is also danger of *segregation* [refer Section 2.3.2]. The addition of water provides for better cohesion of the mix and better compaction, and causes the air bubbles to get expelled. However, there is a danger in adding too much water, because it would be water, rather than cement paste, that takes the place of the air bubbles. This water evaporates subsequently, leaving behind voids. Hence, even if the fresh concrete were to be 'fully compacted', voids may still be present in the hardened concrete, adversely affecting its strength, impermeability, etc. Moreover, there is the danger of segregation of 'grout' (cement plus water) in a very wet mix. The excess water tends to rise to the surface of such a mix, as the solid constituents settle downwards; this is called *bleeding*.

> The 'optimum' water content in a mix is that at which the *sum of volumes* of entrapped air and of entrapped water is a minimum, and for which the density achievable (by the method of compaction employed) is a maximum [Ref. 2.1].

The Code recommends that the workability of concrete should be controlled by the direct measurement of water content in the mix. For this, workability should be checked at frequent intervals, by one of the standard tests (*slump, compacting factor*, or *vee-bee*), described in IS 1199: 1959. The Code (Cl. 7.1) also

[†] Steel reinforcing bars embedded in concrete are highly prone to corrosion in the presence of chlorides (as explained in Section 2.13.3); hence, the Code imposes a stricter control on the chloride content in reinforced concrete, compared to plain concrete.

recommends certain ranges of slump, compacting factor and vee-bee time that are considered desirable for various 'degrees of workability' (very low, low, medium, high) and placing conditions.

For the purpose of *mix design* [refer Section 2.7], the water content is usually taken in the range 180–200 lit/m^3 (unless admixtures are used). If the aggregate is wet, then this should be appropriately accounted for, by measuring the moisture content in the aggregate [refer Cl. 10.2 of the Code].

2.4.2 Water-Cement Ratio and Strength

The addition of water in a concrete mix improves workability. However, the water should not be much in excess of that required for hydration. The **water-cement ratio,** defined as the ratio of the *mass* of 'free water' (i.e., excluding that absorbed by the aggregate) to that of cement in a mix, is the major factor that controls the strength and many other properties of concrete. In practice, this ratio lies generally in the range of 0.35 to 0.65, although the purely chemical requirement (for the purpose of complete hydration of cement) is only about 0.25.

> *Abrams' law:* For any given set of concreting materials, the strength of concrete is inversely related to the mass ratio of water to cement.

It is seen that the compressive strength of hardened concrete is inversely proportional to the water-cement ratio, provided the mix is of workable consistency; this is the so-called **Abrams' law**. A reduction in the water-cement ratio generally results in an increased quality of concrete, in terms of density, strength, impermeability, reduced shrinkage and creep, etc.

In *mix design* (refer Section 2.7.2), the water-cement ratio is selected on the basis of the desired 28-day compressive strength of concrete *and* the 28-day[†] compressive strength of the cement to be used. For this purpose, appropriate design charts may be made use of [Ref. 2.4 and IS 10262: 2019]. A simple chart (in which 'strength' is non-dimensionalised) developed for this purpose [Ref. 2.5] is shown in Figure 2.2.

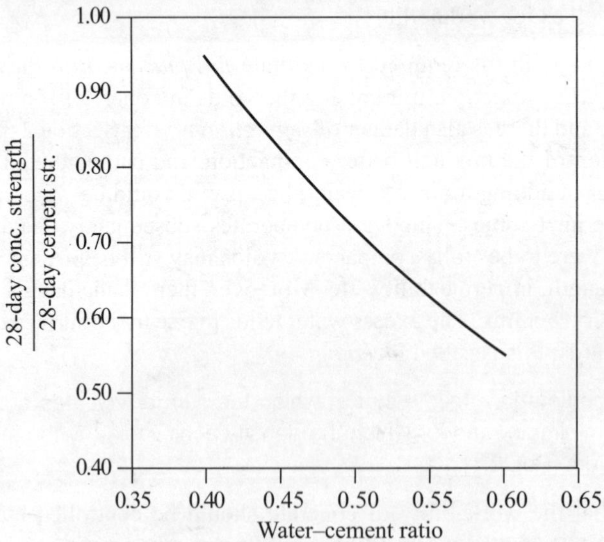

Fig. 2.2 Relation between water-cement ratio and compressive strength [Ref. 2.5].

[†] The earlier practice of specifying 7-day strength is discarded, as it is found that some types of cement (such as RHPC) gain early high strength, but the strength at 28-days is no different from that of other cements (such as PPC) which gain strength relatively slowly. Most cements and concretes attain a major part of their long-term strength in about 28 days.

It is found that water-cement ratios of 0.4, 0.5 and 0.6 are expected to produce respectively 28-day concrete strengths that are about 0.95, 0.72 and 0.55 times the 28-day strength of the cement used.

2.4.3 Water for Curing

The water in a concrete mix takes one of the following three forms, as a consequence of hydration [Ref. 2.3]:

1. ***Combined water*** Which is chemically combined with the products of hydration; it is non-evaporable;
2. ***Gel water*** Which is held physically or adsorbed on the surface area of the 'cement gel' (solid hydrates located in tiny, impermeable 'gel pores'); and
3. ***Capillary water*** Which partially occupies the 'capillary pores' that constitute the space in the cement paste remaining after accounting for the volumes of cement gel and unhydrated cement; this water is easily evaporated.

If the hardened cement paste is only partly hydrated (as is usually the case, soon after casting), the capillary pores tend to become interconnected; this results in low strength, increased permeability and increased vulnerability of the concrete to chemical attack. All these problems can be overcome, to a large extent, if the degree of hydration is sufficiently high for the capillary pore system to become 'segmented' through partial blocking by the newly developed cement gel.

Curing is the name given to procedures that are employed for actively promoting the hydration of cement in a suitable environment during the early stages of hardening of concrete. The Code (Cl. 13.5) defines it as 'the process of preventing the loss of moisture from the concrete while maintaining a satisfactory temperature regime'. Curing is essential for producing 'good' concrete that has the desired strength, impermeability and durability, and is of particular importance in situations where the water-cement ratio is low, or the cement has a high rate of strength development or if the pozzolanic content is high.

Moist curing aims to keep the concrete as nearly saturated as possible at normal temperature – by continually spraying water, or by 'ponding', or by covering the concrete with a layer of any kind of 'sacking' which is kept wet. The ingress of curing water into the capillary pores stimulates hydration. This process, in fact, goes on, even after active curing has stopped, by absorption of the moisture in the atmosphere. The period of curing should be as long as conveniently possible in practice. The Code specifies the duration as 'at least seven days from the date of placing of concrete in case of OPC' under normal weather conditions, and at least 10 days when dry and hot weather conditions are encountered. When mineral admixtures or blended cements are used, the recommended minimum period is 10 days, which should preferably be extended to 14 days or more.

Moist curing improves the concrete strength very rapidly in the first few days; subsequently, the gain in strength becomes less and less, as shown in Figure 2.3. The figure also shows the drastic loss in strength if moist curing is avoided altogether.

Increase in temperature is found to enhance the rate of hydration and the consequent rate of gain of strength. However, the early application of high temperature is found to reduce the long-term strength of concrete [Ref. 2.3]. Hence, it is desirable to take appropriate steps to reduce the temperature of fresh concrete when concreting is done in hot weather.

In some cases, as in the manufacture of prefabricated components, a high early strength is desired, to facilitate handling and transfer of the concrete products soon after casting. In such cases, methods of *accelerated curing* such as 'steam curing' or the more advanced 'autoclave curing' are resorted to. In *steam curing*, steam at atmospheric pressure takes the place of water for curing.

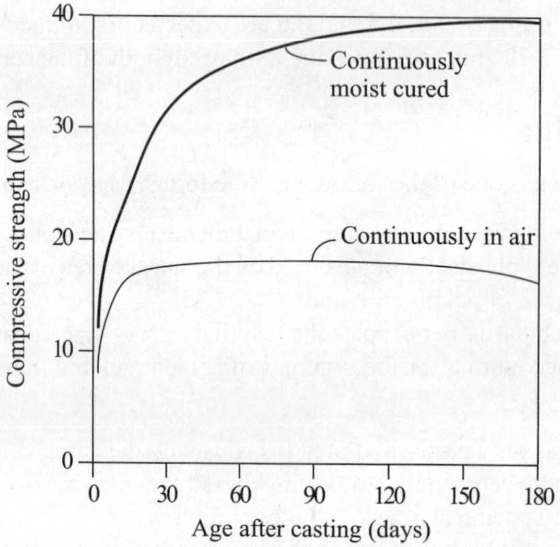

Fig. 2.3 Influence of moist curing on concrete strength [Ref. 2.6].

In special cases, *membrane curing* may be resorted to, in lieu of moist curing, by applying either special compounds (usually sprayed on the surface) or impermeable membranes (such as polyethylene sheeting) to all exposed concrete surfaces immediately after the setting of concrete, to prevent the evaporation of water.

2.5 Admixtures

Admixtures are additives that are introduced in a concrete mix to modify the properties of concrete in its fresh and hardened states. Some guidelines for admixtures are given in IS 9103: 1999. A large number of proprietary products are currently available; their desirable effects are advertised in the market. These, as well as possible undesirable effects, need to be examined scientifically, before they are advocated [Ref. 2.7]. The Code (Cl. 5.5.3) recommends, 'the workability, compressive strength and the slump loss of concrete with and without the use of admixtures shall be established during the trial mixes before the use of admixtures'. Also, the use of admixtures should not impair durability and increase the risk of corrosion to reinforcement.

Admixtures are either 'chemical' (liquid) or 'mineral' (fine granular) in form. They are now being increasingly used in concrete production, particularly when there is an emphasis on either 'high strength' or 'high performance' (durability). The use of chemical admixtures is inevitable in the production of *ready-mixed concrete*, which involves transportation over large distances of fresh concrete that is manufactured under controlled conditions at a batching plant.

2.5.1 Types of Chemical Admixtures

Some of the more important chemical admixtures are briefly described here:

Accelerators

Chemicals (notably, calcium chloride) to accelerate the hardening or the development of early strength of concrete; these are generally used when urgent repairs are undertaken, or while concreting in cold weather;

Retarders

Chemicals (including sugar) to retard the setting of concrete, and thereby also to reduce the generation of heat; these are generally used in hot weather concreting and in *ready-mixed concrete*;

Water-reducers (or *Plasticizers*)

Chemicals to improve plasticity in the fresh concrete; these are mainly used for achieving higher strength by reducing the water-cement ratio; or for improving workability (for a given water-cement ratio) to facilitate placement of concrete in locations that are not easily accessible;

Superplasticizers (or *High-range Water-reducers*)

Chemicals that have higher dosage levels and are supposedly superior to conventional water-reducers; they are used for the same purposes as water-reducers, viz., to produce high-strength concrete or to produce 'flowing' concrete;

Air-entraining Agents

Organic compounds (such as animal/vegetable fats and oils, wood resins) which introduce discrete and microscopic air bubble cavities that occupy up to 5 per cent of the volume of concrete; these are mainly used for protecting concrete from damage due to alternate freezing and thawing;

Bonding Admixtures

Polymer emulsions (latexes) to improve the adherence of fresh concrete to (old) hardened concrete; they are ideally suited for repair work.

2.5.2 Types of Mineral Admixtures

Mineral Admixtures

These are used either as partial replacement of cement or in combination with cement, at the time of mixing, in order to modify the properties of concrete or achieve economy. Some of the more important mineral admixtures are described briefly here.

Pozzolanas

These are materials containing amorphous silica, which, in finely divided form and in the presence of water, chemically react with calcium hydroxide at ordinary temperatures to form compounds possessing cementitious properties; the Code (Cl. 5.2) permits their use, provided uniform blending with cement is ensured. Many of the pozzolanas (especially fly ash) are industrial 'waste products' whose disposal raise environmental concerns; their use in concrete making, hence, is commendable. These include the following:

- *fly ash* Ash precipitated electrostatically or mechanically from exhaust gases in coal-fired power plants, conforming to Grade 1 of IS 3812;
- *ground granulated blast-furnace slag* Conforming to IS 12089, has good pozzolanic properties, and produces concrete with improved resistance to chemical attack;
- *silica fume* (or *micro silica*) Obtained as a by-product of the silicon industry, is found to be not only pozzolanic in character but also capable of producing very dense concrete, and is finding increasing use in the production of high-strength and high-performance concrete;
- *rice husk ash* Produced by burning rice husk at controlled temperatures;
- *metakaoline* Obtained by calcination of kaolinitic clay (a natural pozzolana), followed by grinding;

Gas-forming Admixtures

Powdered zinc, powdered aluminium and *hydrogen peroxide*, which generate gas bubbles in a sand-cement matrix; they are used in the manufacture of lightweight *aerated concrete* – which, although not suitable for heavy load-bearing purposes, can be used for its high thermal insulation properties.

2.6 Grade of Concrete

The desired properties of concrete are its compressive strength, tensile strength, shear strength, bond strength, density, impermeability, durability, etc. Among these, the property that can be easily tested, and is perhaps the most valuable (from the viewpoint of structural design) is the *compressive strength*. This is measured by standard tests on concrete cube (or cylinder) specimens. Many of the other important properties of concrete can be inferred from the compressive strength, using correlations that have been experimentally established.

The quality or *grade* of concrete is designated in terms of a number, which denotes its *characteristic* compressive strength (of 150 mm cubes at 28-days), expressed in MPa (or, equivalently, N/mm^2). The number is usually preceded by the letter 'M', which refers to 'mix'. Thus, for example, M 20 grade concrete denotes a concrete whose mix is so designed as to generate a **characteristic strength** of 20 MPa; the meaning of this term is explained in the next section.

In the 2000 revision of the Code, the selection of the minimum grade of concrete is dictated by considerations of durability, and is related to the kind of environment that the structure is exposed to [refer Table 5 of the Code]. The minimum grade of concrete in reinforced concrete work has been upgraded from M 15 to M 20 in the 2000 code revision†. However, this is applicable only under 'mild' exposure conditions. An exposure condition is considered 'mild' when the concrete surface is protected against weather or aggressive conditions and is not situated in a coastal area. Under more adverse environmental exposure‡ conditions, higher grades of concrete are called for. For 'moderate', 'severe', 'very severe' and 'extreme' exposure conditions, the minimum grades prescribed are M 25, M 30, M 35 and M 40 respectively, for reinforced concrete work [Cl. 6.1.2 of the Code]. It should be noted that the higher grades specified here are dictated, not by the need for higher compressive strength, but by the need for improved durability [refer Section 2.13]. The need is for 'high performance' concrete, and it is only incidental that this high performance (obtained, for example, by reducing the water-cement ratio and adding mineral admixtures such as silica fume) is correlated with high strength. In practice, although M20 is the minimum grade specified for reinforced concrete, it is prudent to adopt a higher grade.

There are specific applications that may call for the grade of concrete to be decided on the basis of considerations of strength, rather than durability. For example, the use of high strength is desirable in the columns of very tall buildings, in order to reduce their cross-sectional dimensions; this is desirable even under 'mild' environmental exposure. Similarly, high strength concrete is required in prestressed concrete construction [refer IS 1343: 2012]. The definition of the term 'high strength' has been changing over the years, with technological advancements resulting in the development of higher strengths. The present Code (in its recent revision) describes grades of concrete above M 60 as 'high strength concrete'. Concrete grades in the range M 25 to M 55 are described as 'standard strength concrete', and grades in the range M 10 to M 20 are termed 'ordinary concrete' [refer Table 2 of the Code].

† It may be noted that the traditional 'nominal mix' of 1:2:4 (cement: sand: coarse aggregate, by weight), which used to conform approximately to M 15 grade of concrete (using OPC of C 33 grade), is presently found to yield higher grades (M 20 and higher), with the use of C 43 and C 53 grades of cement, which are now commonly available in the market

‡ The different types of exposure are described in detail in Section 2.13.1.

2.6.1 Characteristic Strength

Concrete is a material whose strength is subject to considerable *variability*. Cube specimens that are taken from the same mix give different values of compressive strength in laboratory tests. This may be attributed largely to the non-homogeneous nature of concrete. The variability in the strength evidently depends on the degree of quality control [Figure 2.4]. Statistically, it is measured in terms of either the 'standard deviation' (σ) or the coefficient of variation (*cov*), which is the ratio of the standard deviation to the mean strength (f_{cm}).

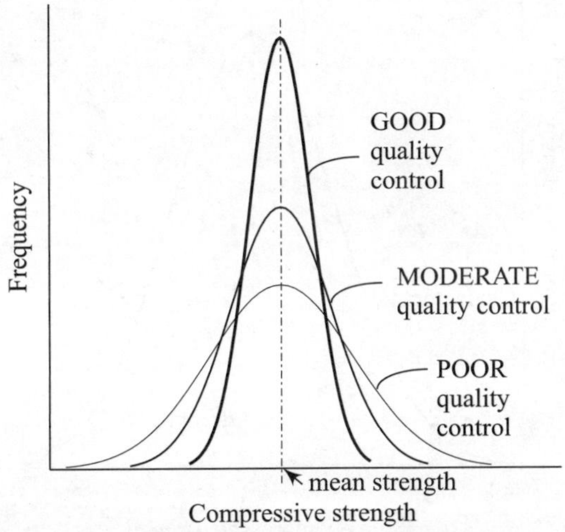

Fig. 2.4 Influence of quality control on the frequency distribution of concrete strength.

Experimental studies have revealed that the probability distribution of concrete strength (for a given mix, as determined by compression tests on a large number of specimens) is approximately 'normal' (Gaussian) [Ref. 2.9]. The coefficient of variation is generally in the range of 0.01 to 0.02; it is expected to reduce with increasing grade of concrete, in view of the need for increased quality control.

In view of the significant variability in the compressive strength, it is necessary to ensure that the designer has a reasonable assurance of a certain minimum strength of concrete. This is provided by the Code by defining a *characteristic strength*, which is applicable to any material (concrete or steel):

> '**Characteristic strength** is defined as the strength of material below which not more than 5 per cent of the test results are expected to fall.'

Accordingly, the mean strength of the concrete f_{cm} (as obtained from 28-day compression tests) has to be significantly greater than the 5-percentile characteristic strength f_{ck} that is specified by the designer [Figure 2.5].

2.7 Concrete Mix Design

The design of a concrete mix for a specified *grade* involves the economical selection of the relative proportions (and types) of cement, fine aggregate, coarse aggregate and water (and admixtures, if any). Although compliance with respect to 'characteristic strength' is the main criterion for acceptance, it is implicit that the concrete must also have the desired *workability* in the fresh state, and *impermeability* and *durability* in the hardened state.

2.7.1 Nominal Mix Concrete

Concrete mix design is an involved process that calls for some expertise from the mix designer/construction engineer/contractor. This is not often available. Traditionally, mixes were specified in terms of fixed proportions of cement : sand : coarse aggregate (by mass preferably, or by volume) such as 1 : 2 : 4, 1 : 1.5 : 3, etc., – which were rather crude and incorrect translations of concrete grades M 15, M 20, etc.

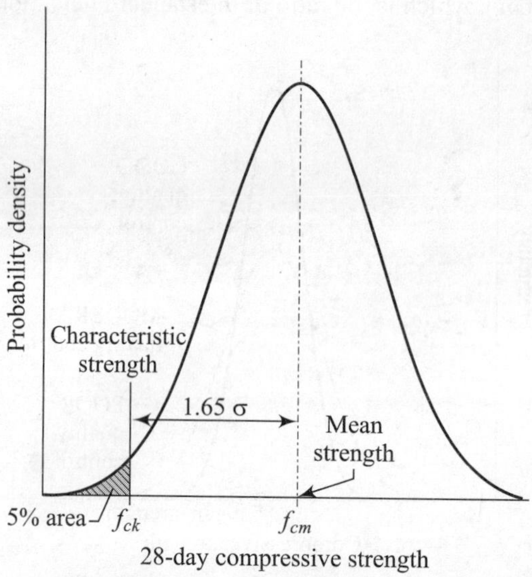

Fig. 2.5 Idealised normal distribution of concrete strength.

The Code (Table 9) attempts to provide more realistic 'nominal mix' proportions for M 5, M 7.5, M 10, M 15 and M 20 grades of concrete, in terms of the total mass of aggregate, proportion of fine aggregate to coarse aggregate and volume of water to be used per 50 kg mass of cement (i.e., one bag of cement). Such *nominal mix concrete* is permitted in 'ordinary concrete construction', which does not call for concrete grades higher than M 20.

However, the Code clearly highlights (Cl. 9.1.1) that *design mix concrete*, based on the principles of 'mix design', is definitely preferred to 'nominal mix concrete'. In practice, it is found that design mix concrete not only yields concrete of the desired quality, but also often works out to be more economical than nominal mix concrete.

2.7.2 Design Mix Concrete

Several methods of mix design have been evolved over the years in different countries, and have become codified – such as the ACI practice [Ref. 2.10–2.12], the British practice [Ref. 2.13], etc. In India, recommendations for mix design are given in IS 10262: 2019 and SP 23: 1982 [Ref. 2.4]. These are merely 'recommendations'; in practice, any proven method of design may be adopted. All that matters finally is that the designed mix must meet the desired requirements in the fresh and hardened states. The steps involved in the Indian Standard recommendations for mix design are summarised as follows:

1. Determine the *mean target strength* f_{cm} from the desired 'characteristic strength' f_{ck} [Figure 2.5]:

$$f_{cm} = f_{ck} + 1.65\sigma \tag{2.1}$$

where the standard deviation σ depends on the quality control, which may be assumed for design in the first instance, and are listed in Table 8 of the Code. As test results of samples are available, actual calculated value is to be used.

2. Determine the *water-cement ratio*, based on the 28-day strength of cement and the mean target strength of concrete, using appropriate charts (such as Figure 2.2); this ratio should not exceed the limits specified in Table 5 of the Code (for durability considerations).
3. Determine the *water content* V_w based on workability requirements, and select the ratio of fine aggregate to coarse aggregate (by mass), based on the type and grading of the aggregate; the former is generally in the range of 180–200 lit/m^3 (unless admixtures are employed), and the latter is generally 1:2 or in the range of 1:1½ to 1:2½.
4. Calculate the *cement content* M_c (in kg/m^3) by dividing the water content by the water-cement ratio, and ensure that the cement content is not less than that specified in the Code [Tables 4 and 5] for durability considerations. [Note that the Code (Cl.8.2.4.2) cautions against the use of cement content (not including fly ash and ground granulated blast furnace slag) in excess of 450 kg/m^3 in order to control shrinkage and thermal cracks]. Also, calculate the masses of fine aggregate M_{fa} and coarse aggregate M_{ca} based on the 'absolute volume principle':

$$\frac{M_c}{\rho_c} + \frac{M_{fa}}{\rho_{fa}} + \frac{M_{ca}}{\rho_{ca}} + V_w + V_v = 1.0 \tag{2.2}$$

where ρ_c, ρ_{fa}, ρ_{ca} denote the mass densities of cement, fine aggregate and coarse aggregate respectively, and V_v and V_w denote respectively the volumes of voids (approx. 2 per cent) and water per cubic metre of concrete.

5. Determine the weight of ingredients per batch, based on the capacity of the concrete mixer.

2.8 Behaviour of Concrete under Uniaxial Compression

The strength of concrete under *uniaxial compression* is determined by loading 'standard test cubes' (150 mm size) to failure in a compression testing machine, as per IS 516: 1959. The test specimens are generally tested 28 days after casting (and continuous curing). The loading is *strain-controlled* and generally applied at a uniform strain rate of 0.001 mm/mm per minute in a standard test. The maximum stress attained during the loading process is referred to as the *cube strength* of concrete. As discussed in Section 2.6.1, the cube strength is subject to variability; its characteristic (5-percentile) and mean values are denoted by f_{ck} and f_{cm} respectively.

Uniaxial compression occurs in a member (such as a strut) subject to a purely axial compressive force acting along its centroidal axis – without any eccentricity causing bending.

In some countries (such as USA), 'standard test *cylinders*' (150 mm diameter and 300 mm high) are used instead of *cubes*. The *cylinder strength* is found to be invariably lower than the 'cube strength' for the same quality (mix) of concrete; its nominal value, termed as 'specified cylinder strength' by the ACI code [Ref. 2.21], is denoted by f_c'.

It should be noted that among the various properties of concrete, the one that is actually measured in practice most often is the compressive strength. The measured value of compressive strength can be correlated to many other important properties such as tensile strength, shear strength, modulus of elasticity, etc. (as discussed in the sections to follow).

The characteristic compressive strength of concrete, f_{ck}, is a very important property. The modulus of elasticity, modulus of rupture and shear strength of concrete can be related to $\sqrt{f_{ck}}$, vide Eqs. 2.4, 2.6 and 6.10.

2.8.1 Influence of Size of Test Specimen

It has been observed that the *height/width ratio* and the *cross-sectional dimensions* of the test specimen have a pronounced effect on the compressive strength (maximum stress level) obtained from the uniaxial compression test. These effects are illustrated in Figure 2.6 for cylinder specimens.

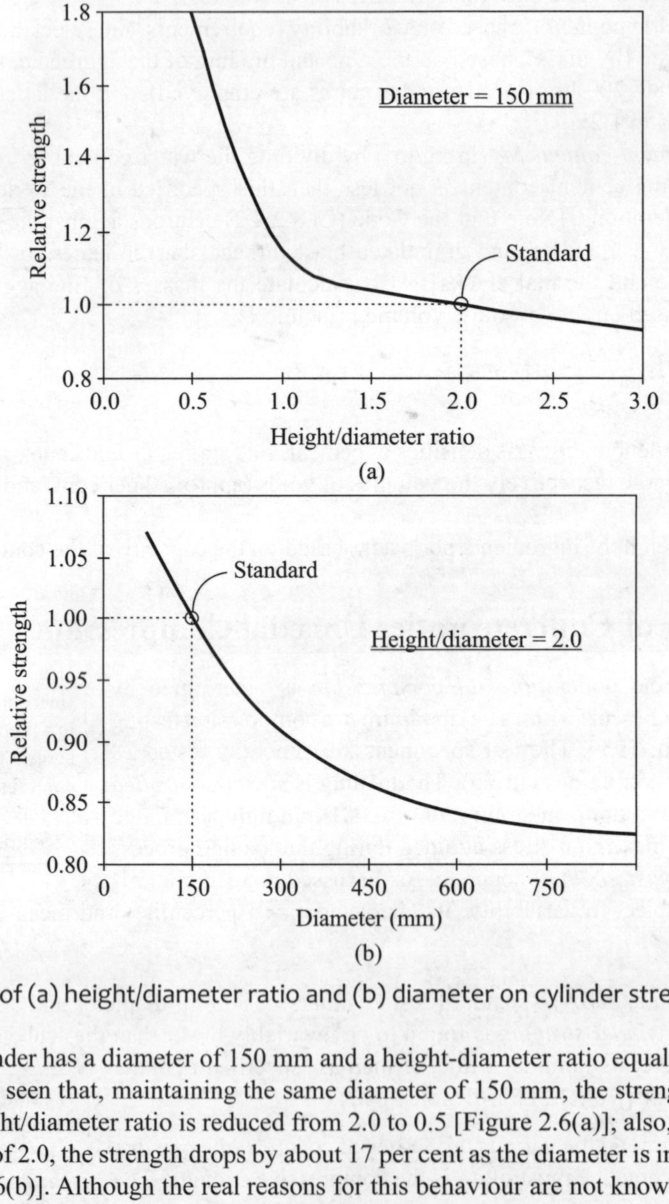

Fig. 2.6 Influence of (a) height/diameter ratio and (b) diameter on cylinder strength [Ref. 2.3, 2.14].

The standard test cylinder has a diameter of 150 mm and a height-diameter ratio equal to 2.0. With reference to this 'standard', it is seen that, maintaining the same diameter of 150 mm, the strength increases by about 80 per cent as the height/diameter ratio is reduced from 2.0 to 0.5 [Figure 2.6(a)]; also, maintaining the same height/diameter ratio of 2.0, the strength drops by about 17 per cent as the diameter is increased from 150 mm to 900 mm [Figure 2.6(b)]. Although the real reasons for this behaviour are not known with certainty, some plausible explanations that have been proposed are discussed below.

Firstly, a proper measure of uniaxial compressive stress can be obtained (in terms of load divided by cross-sectional area) only if the stress is *uniformly distributed* across the cross-section of the longitudinally loaded test specimen. Such a state of stress can be expected only at some distance away from the top and bottom surfaces where the loading is applied (*St. Venant's principle*) – which is possible only if the height/width ratio of the specimen is sufficiently large.

Secondly, *uniaxial* compression implies that the specimen is not subject to lateral loading or lateral restraint. However, in practice, lateral restraint, known as *platen restraint*, is bound to manifest owing to the friction between the end surfaces of the concrete specimen and the adjacent steel platens of the testing machine. This introduces radial (inward) shear forces at the top and bottom surfaces, resulting in restraint against free lateral displacements.

The effect of this lateral restraint is to enhance the *compressive strength* (maximum stress prior to failure) in the longitudinal direction; this effect dies down with increasing distance from the platen restraint. Thus, the value of the compressive strength depends on the *height/width ratio* of the specimen; the greater this ratio, the lesser the strength, because the less is the beneficial influence of the lateral restraint at the (weakest) section, located near the mid-height of the specimen.

The reduction in compressive strength with increasing size, while maintaining the same height/width ratio [Figure 2.6(b)], is attributed to *size effect* – a phenomenon which requires a *fracture mechanics* background for understanding.

From the above, it also follows that the 'standard test *cube*' (which has a height/width ratio of 1.0) would register a compressive strength that is higher than that of the 'standard test *cylinder*' (with a height/diameter ratio of 2.0), made of the same concrete, and that the cylinder strength is closer to the true uniaxial compressive strength of concrete. The cube strength is found to be approximately 1.25 times the cylinder strength [Ref. 2.3], whereby $f_c' \approx 0.8 f_{cm}$. For design purposes, the cube strength that is relied upon by the Code is the 'characteristic strength' f_{ck}.

Accordingly, the relation between the cube strength and the cylinder strength takes the following form:

$$f_c' \approx 0.8 f_{ck} \tag{2.3}$$

2.8.2 Stress-Strain Curves

Typical stress-strain curves of concrete (of various grades), obtained from standard uniaxial compression tests, are shown in Figure 2.7. The curves are somewhat linear in the very early phase of loading; the non-linearity begins to gain significance when the stress level exceeds about one-third to one-half of the maximum. The maximum stress is reached at a strain approximately equal to 0.002; beyond this point, an increase in strain is accompanied by a decrease in stress. For the usual range of concrete strengths, the strain at failure is in the range of 0.003 to 0.005.

> The higher the concrete grade, the steeper is the initial portion of the stress-strain curve, the sharper the peak of the curve, and the lesser the failure strain. For low-strength concrete, the curve has a relatively flat top and a high failure strain.

> **As concrete compressive strength increases, the ultimate failure strain decreases: concrete becomes more brittle.**

When the stress level reaches 70–90 per cent of the maximum, internal micro-cracks are initiated in the mortar throughout the concrete mass, roughly parallel to the direction of the applied loading [Ref. 2.15]. The concrete tends to expand laterally, and longitudinal cracks become visible when the lateral strain (due to the *Poisson effect*) exceeds the limiting tensile strain of concrete (0.0001–0.0002). The cracks generally occur at the aggregate-mortar interface. As a result of the associated larger lateral extensions, the apparent Poisson's ratio increases sharply [Ref. 2.16].

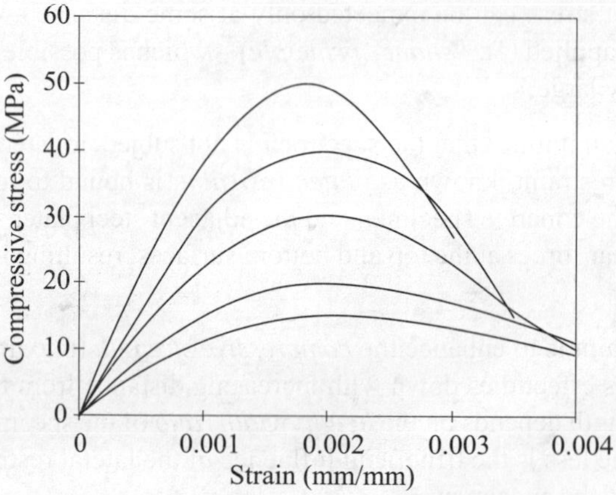

Fig. 2.7 Typical stress-strain curves of concrete in compression.

The descending branch of the stress-strain curve can be fully traced only if the strain-controlled application of the load is properly achieved. For this, the testing machine must be sufficiently rigid† (i.e., it must have a very high value of load per unit deformation); otherwise, the concrete is likely to fail abruptly (sometimes, explosively) almost immediately after the maximum stress is reached. The fall in stress with increasing strain is a phenomenon which is not clearly understood; it is associated with extensive *micro-cracking* in the mortar, and is sometimes called *strain-softening* of concrete [Ref. 2.17]. Stress-strain relationship of cracked concrete in compression is discussed in Section 17.1.3.

Stress-strain relation in flexural compression is nearly identical to that observed in a compression test.

Experimental studies [Ref. 2.17, 2.18] have also confirmed that the stress-strain relation for the compression zone of a reinforced concrete *flexural member* is nearly identical to that obtained for uniaxial compression. For the purpose of design of reinforced concrete flexural members, various simplified stress-strain curves have been adopted by different codes.

2.8.3 Modulus of Elasticity and Poisson's Ratio

Concrete is not really an *elastic* material, i.e., it does not fully recover its original dimensions upon unloading. It is not only *non-elastic*; it is also *non-linear* (i.e., the stress-strain curve is nonlinear). Hence, the conventional 'elastic *constants*' (*modulus of elasticity* and *Poisson's ratio*) are not strictly applicable to a material like concrete. Nevertheless, these find place in design practice, because, despite their obvious limitations when related to concrete, they are material properties that have to be necessarily considered in the conventional *linear elastic analysis/design* of reinforced concrete structures.

Modulus of Elasticity

The *Young's modulus of elasticity* is a constant, defined as the ratio, within the *linear elastic* range, of axial stress to axial strain, under uniaxial loading. In the case of concrete under uniaxial compression, it has some validity in the very initial portion of the stress-strain curve, which is practically linear [Figure 2.8]; that is, when the loading is of low intensity, and of very short duration. If the loading is sustained for a relatively long duration, inelastic *creep* effects come into play, even at relatively low stress levels [refer Section 2.11]. Besides, non-linearities are also likely to be introduced on account of shrinkage.

† Alternatively, a *screw-type* loading mechanism may be used.

The *initial tangent modulus* [Figure 2.8] is, therefore, sometimes considered to be a measure of the **dynamic modulus** of elasticity of concrete [Ref. 2.3]; it finds application in some cases of cyclic loading (wind- or earthquake-induced), where long-term effects are negligible. However, even in such cases, the non-elastic behaviour of concrete manifests, particularly if high intensity cyclic loads are involved; in such cases, a pronounced *hysterisis effect* is observed, with each cycle of loading producing incremental permanent deformation [Ref. 2.18].

In the usual problems of structural analysis, based on *linear static analysis*, it is the **static modulus** of elasticity that needs to be considered. It may be noted that when the loads on a structure (such as dead loads) are of long duration, the long-term effects of creep reduce the effective modulus of elasticity significantly. Although it is difficult to separate the *long-term strains* induced by creep (and shrinkage) from the *short-term 'elastic' strains*, this is usually done at a conceptual level, for convenience. Accordingly, while estimating the deflection of a reinforced concrete beam, the total deflection is assumed to be a sum of an 'instantaneous' elastic deflection (caused by the loads) and the 'long-term' deflections induced by creep and shrinkage [refer Chapter 10]. The *short-term static modulus of elasticity (E_c)* is used in computing the 'instantaneous' elastic deflection.

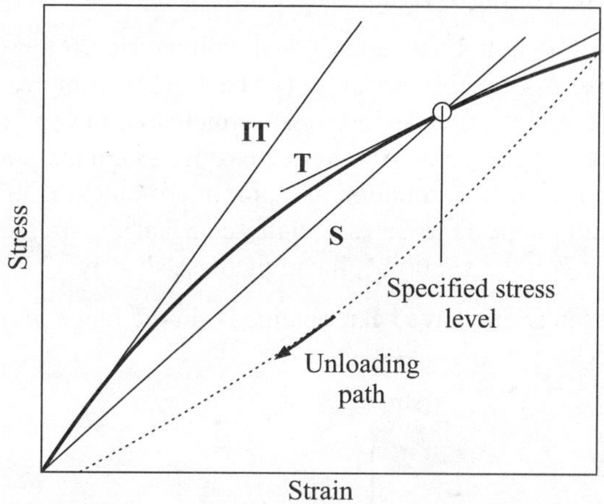

Fig. 2.8 Various descriptions of modulus of elasticity of concrete: (IT ≡ initial tangent, T ≡ tangent, S ≡ secant)

Various descriptions of E_c are possible, such as *initial tangent modulus*, *tangent modulus* (at a specified stress level), *secant modulus* (at a specified stress level), etc., – as shown in Figure 2.8. Among these, the **secant modulus** at a stress of about one-third the cube strength of concrete is generally found acceptable in representing an average value of E_c under service load conditions (static loading) [Ref. 2.3].

The Code (Cl. 6.2.3.1) gives the following empirical expression for the static modulus E_c (in *MPa* units) in terms of the characteristic cube strength (in MPa units):

$$E_c = 5000\sqrt{f_{ck}} \tag{2.4}$$

It may be noted that the earlier version of IS 456 had recommended $E_c = 5700\sqrt{f_{ck}}$, which was found to overestimate the elastic modulus.

Note that in Eq. 2.4, the constant 5000 has the unit of $(\text{MPa})^{1/2}$ and the equation is 'unit-sensitive'. For use in units other than MPa, the constant 5000 has to be suitably modified. This is the case with several other empirical equations related to concrete (e.g., Eq. 2.6 in Section 2.9.1).

The ACI code [Ref. 2.21] gives an alternative formula† for E_c in terms of the specified cylinder strength f_c' and the mass density of concrete ρ_c (in kg/m^3):

$$E_c = 0.0427\sqrt{\rho_c^{\,3} f_c'} \tag{2.4a}$$

Considering $\rho_c = 2400$ kg/m^3 for normal-weight concrete and applying Eq. 2.3, the above expression reduces to $E_c \approx 4500\sqrt{f_{ck}}$, which gives values of E_c that are about 10 per cent less than those given by the present IS Code formula [Eq. 2.4].

From a design viewpoint, the use of a lower value of E_c will result in a more conservative (larger) estimate of the short-term elastic deflection of a flexural member.

Poisson's Ratio

This is another elastic constant, defined as *the ratio of the lateral strain to the longitudinal strain*, under uniform axial stress. When a concrete prism is subjected to a uniaxial compression test, the longitudinal compressive strains are accompanied by lateral tensile strains. The prism as a whole also undergoes a volume change, which can be measured in terms of *volumetric strain*.

Typical observed variations of longitudinal, lateral and volumetric strains are depicted in Figure 2.9 [Ref. 2.16]. It is seen that at a stress equal to about 80 per cent of the compressive strength, there is a point of inflection on the volumetric strain curve. As the stress is increased beyond this point, the rate of volume reduction decreases; soon thereafter, the volume stops decreasing, and in fact, *starts increasing*. It is believed that this inflection point coincides with the initiation of major micro-cracking in the concrete, leading to large lateral extensions. Poisson's ratio appears to be essentially constant for stresses below the inflection point. At higher stresses, the apparent Poisson's ratio begins to increase sharply.

Widely varying values of Poisson's ratio have been obtained – in the range of 0.10 to 0.30. A value of about 0.2 is usually considered for design.

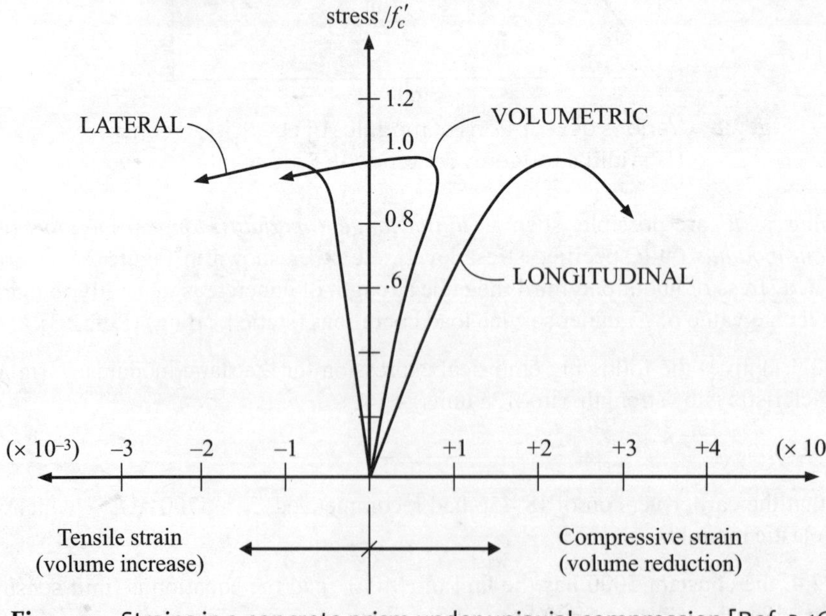

Fig. 2.9 Strains in a concrete prism under uniaxial compression [Ref. 2.16].

† The original formula in the ACI code, expressed in FPS units, is converted to SI units.

2.8.4 Influence of Duration of Loading on Stress-Strain Curve

The standard compression test is usually completed in less than 10 minutes, the loading being gradually applied at a uniform strain rate of 0.001 mm/mm per minute. When the load is applied at a faster strain rate (which occurs, for instance, when an impact load is suddenly applied), it is found that both the modulus of elasticity and the strength of concrete increase, although the failure strain decreases [Ref. 2.19, 2.20].

On the other hand, when the load is applied at a slow strain rate, such that the duration of loading is increased from 10 minutes to as much as *one year* or more, there is a slight reduction in compressive strength, accompanied by a decrease in the modulus of elasticity and a significant increase in the failure strain, as depicted in Figure 2.10; the stress-strain curve also becomes relatively flat after the maximum stress is reached.

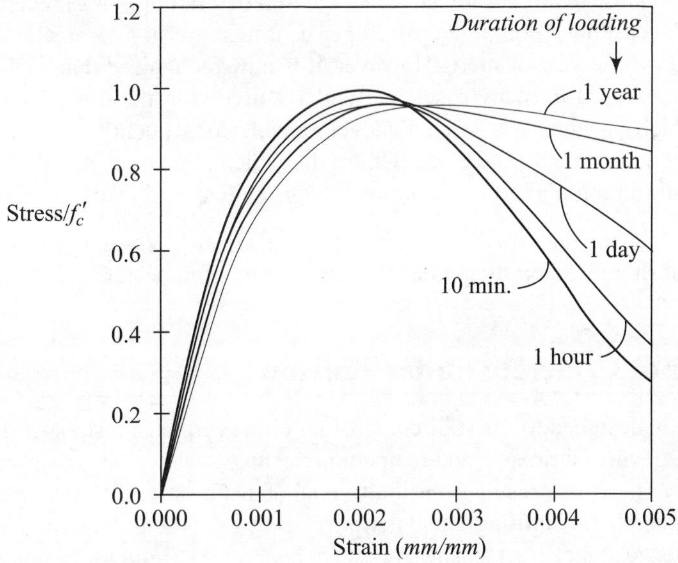

Fig. 2.10 Influence of duration of loading (strain-controlled) on the stress-strain curve of concrete [Ref. 2.20].

It has also been reported [Ref. 2.20] that long-term *sustained loading* at a constant stress level results not only in *creep strains* [refer Section 2.11], but also in a reduced compressive strength of concrete.

2.8.5 Maximum Compressive Stress of Concrete in Design Practice

The compressive strength of concrete in an actual concrete structure cannot be expected to be exactly the same as that obtained from a standard uniaxial compression test for the same quality of concrete. There are many factors responsible for this difference in strength, mainly, the effects of duration of loading, size of the member (*size effect*), the strain gradient and the multi-axial state of stress.

The value of the maximum compressive stress (strength) of concrete is generally taken as 0.85 times the 'specified cylinder strength' (f_c'), for the design of reinforced concrete structural members (compression members as well as flexural members) [Ref. 2.17, 2.20]. This works out approximately [Eq. 2.3] to 0.67 times the 'characteristic cube strength' (f_{ck}) – as adopted by the Code. The Code also limits the failure strain of concrete to 0.002 under direct compression and 0.0035 under flexure.

When the predominant loading that governs the design of a structure is *short-term* rather than *sustained* (as in tall reinforced concrete chimneys subject to wind loading), it may be too conservative to limit the compressive strength to 0.85 (or 0.67); in such cases, it appears reasonable to adopt a suitably higher compressive strength [Ref. 2.22, 2.9].

When the occurrence of permanent sustained loads on a structure is delayed, then, instead of a reduction in compressive strength, some increase in strength (and in the quality of concrete, in general) can be expected due to the tendency of freshly hardened concrete to gain in strength with age, beyond 28 days. This occurs due to the process of continued hydration of cement in hardened concrete, by absorption of moisture from the atmosphere; this is particularly effective in a humid environment.

The earlier version of the Code allowed an increase in the estimation of the *characteristic strength* of concrete when a member (such as a foundation or lower-storey column of a tall building) receives its full design load more than a month after casting. A maximum of 20 per cent increase in f_{ck} was allowed if the operation of the full load is delayed by one year or more. However, it is now recognised that such a significant increase in strength may not be realised in many cases, particularly involving the use of high-grade cement (with increased fineness), which has high early strength development. Consequently, the values of age factors have been deleted in the present version of the Code (Cl. 6.2.1), which stipulates, 'the design should be based on the 28 days characteristic strength of concrete unless there is evidence to justify a higher strength'.

The use of age factors (based on actual investigations) can assist in assessing the actual behaviour of a distressed structure, but should generally not be taken advantage of in design.

2.9 Behaviour of Concrete under Tension

Concrete is not normally designed to resist direct tension. However, tensile stresses do develop in concrete members as a result of flexure, shrinkage and temperature changes, as well as in structures like water tanks. Principal tensile stresses may also result from multi-axial states of stress. Often cracking in concrete is a result of the tensile strength (or limiting tensile strain) being exceeded. As pure shear causes tension on diagonal planes, knowledge of the direct tensile strength of concrete is useful for estimating the shear/torsional strength of beams with unreinforced webs, etc. Also, a knowledge of the flexural tensile strength of concrete is necessary for estimation of the 'moment at first crack'†, required for the computation of deflections and crack widths in flexural members.

As pointed out earlier, concrete is very weak in tension, the direct tensile strength being only about 7 to 15 per cent of the compressive strength [Ref. 2.6]. It is difficult to perform a *direct* tension test on a concrete specimen, as it requires a purely axial tensile force to be applied, free of any misalignment and secondary stress in the specimen at the grips of the testing machine. Hence, *indirect* tension tests are resorted to, usually the *flexure test* or the *cylinder splitting test.*

2.9.1 Modulus of Rupture

In the *flexure test* most commonly employed [refer IS 516: 1959], a 'standard' plain concrete beam of a square or rectangular cross-section is simply supported and subjected to third-points loading until failure. Assuming a linear stress distribution across the cross-section, the theoretical maximum tensile stress reached in the extreme fibre is termed the *modulus of rupture* (f_{cr}).

† Refer Chapter 4 for computation of *cracking moment* M_{cr}

It is obtained by applying the flexure formula:

$$f_{cr} = \frac{M}{Z} \tag{2.5}$$

where M is the bending moment causing failure, and Z is the section modulus.

However, the actual stress distribution is not really linear, and the modulus of rupture so computed is found to be greater than the direct tensile strength by as much as 60–100 per cent [Ref. 2.6]. Nevertheless, f_{cr} is the appropriate tensile strength to be considered in the evaluation of the *cracking moment* (M_{cr}) of a beam by the flexure formula, as the same assumptions are involved in its calculation.

The Code (Cl. 6.2.2) suggests the following empirical formula for estimating f_{cr}:

$$f_{cr} = 0.7\sqrt{f_{ck}} \tag{2.6}$$

where f_{cr} and f_{ck} are in MPa units.

The corresponding formula suggested by the ACI Code [Ref. 2.21] is:

$$f_{cr} = 0.623\sqrt{f_c'} \tag{2.6a}$$

From a design viewpoint, the use of a lower value of f_{cr} results in a more conservative (lower) estimate of the 'cracking moment'.

2.9.2 Splitting Tensile Strength

The *cylinder splitting test* is the easiest to perform and gives more uniform results compared to other tension tests. In this test [refer IS 5816: 1999], a 'standard' plain concrete cylinder (of the same type as used for the compression test) is loaded in compression *on its side* along a diametral plane. Failure occurs by the splitting of the cylinder along the loaded plane [Figure 2.11]. In an elastic homogeneous cylinder, this loading produces a nearly uniform tensile stress across the loaded plane as shown in Figure 2.11(b).

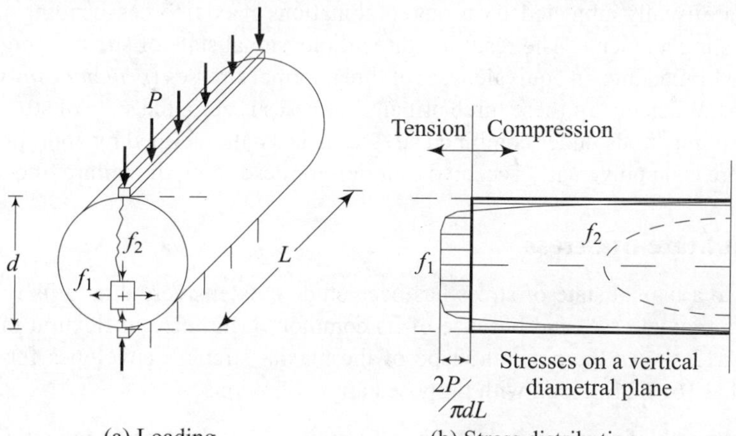

Fig. 2.11 Cylinder splitting test for tensile strength.

From theory of elasticity, the following formula for the evaluation of the *splitting tensile strength* f_{ct} is obtained:

$$f_{ct} = \frac{2P}{\pi d L} \tag{2.7}$$

where P is the maximum applied load, d is the diameter and L is the length of the cylinder.

It has been found that for normal density concrete the splitting strength is about two-thirds of the modulus of rupture [Ref. 2.23]. (The Code does not provide an empirical formula for estimating f_{ct} as it does for f_{cr}).

2.9.3 Stress-Strain Curve of Concrete in Tension

Concrete has a low failure strain in uniaxial tension. It is found to be in the range of 0.0001 to 0.0002. The stress-strain curve in tension is generally approximated as a straight line from the origin to the failure point. The modulus of elasticity in tension is taken to be the same as that in compression. As the tensile strength of concrete is very low, and often ignored in design, the tensile stress-strain relation is of little practical value.

2.9.4 Shear Strength and Tensile Strength

Concrete is rarely subjected to conditions of pure shear; hence, the strength of concrete in *pure shear* is of little practical relevance in design. Moreover, a state of pure shear is accompanied by principal tensile stresses of equal magnitude on a diagonal plane, and since the tensile strength of concrete is less than its shear strength, failure invariably occurs in tension. This, incidentally, makes it difficult to experimentally determine the resistance of concrete to pure shearing stresses. A reliable assessment of the shear strength can be obtained only from tests under combined stresses. On the basis of such studies, the strength of concrete in pure shear has been reported to be in the range of 10–20 per cent of its compressive strength [Ref. 2.14]. In normal design practice, the shear strength of concrete is governed by its tensile strength, because of the associated principal tensile (diagonal tension) stresses and the need to control cracking of concrete.

2.10 Behaviour of Concrete under Combined Stresses

Structural members are usually subjected to various combinations of axial forces, bending moments, transverse shear forces and twisting moments. The resulting three-dimensional state of stress acting at any point on an element may be transformed into an equivalent set of three normal stresses (*principal stresses*) acting in three orthogonal directions. When one of these three principal stresses is zero, the state of stress is termed *biaxial*. The failure strength of materials under combined stresses is normally defined by appropriate failure criteria. However, as yet, there is no universally accepted criterion for describing the failure of concrete.

2.10.1 Biaxial State of Stress

Concrete subjected to a biaxial state of stress has been studied extensively due to its relative simplicity in comparison with the triaxial case, and because of its common occurrence in flexural members, plates and thin shells. Figure 2.12 shows the general shape of the biaxial strength envelopes for concrete, obtained experimentally [Ref. 2.16, 2.24], along with proposed approximations.

It is found that the strength of concrete in *biaxial compression* is greater than in *uniaxial compression* by up to 27 per cent. The *biaxial tensile strength* is nearly equal to its *uniaxial tensile strength*. However, in the region of combined compression and tension, the compressive strength decreases nearly linearly with an increase in the accompanying tensile stress. Observed failure modes suggest that tensile strains are of vital importance in the failure criteria and failure mechanism of concrete for both uniaxial and biaxial states of stress [Ref. 2.24].

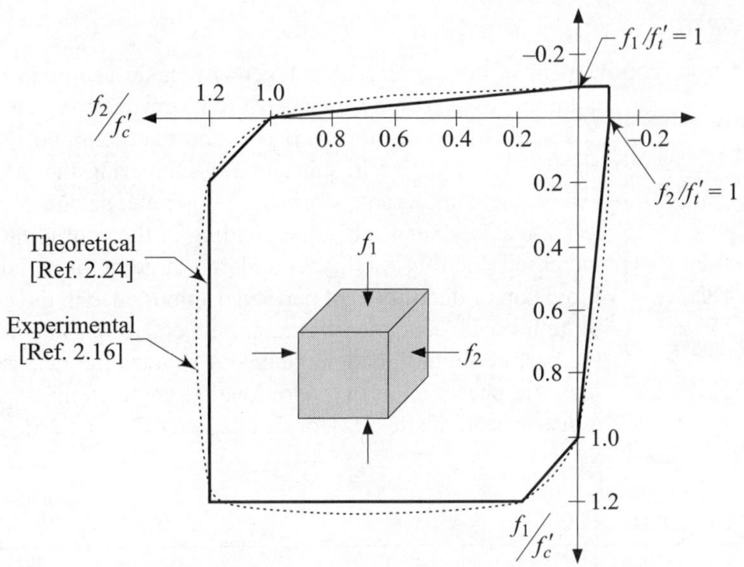

Fig. 2.12 Failure stress envelope – biaxial stress [Ref. 2.16, 2.24].

2.10.2 Influence of Shear Stress

Normal stresses are accompanied by shear stresses on planes other than the *principal planes*. For a prediction of the strength of concrete in a general biaxial state of stress, *Mohr's theory of failure* is sometimes used. A more accurate (experiment based) failure envelope for the case of direct stress (compression or tension) in one direction, combined with shear stress, is shown in Figure 2.13 [Ref. 2.25].

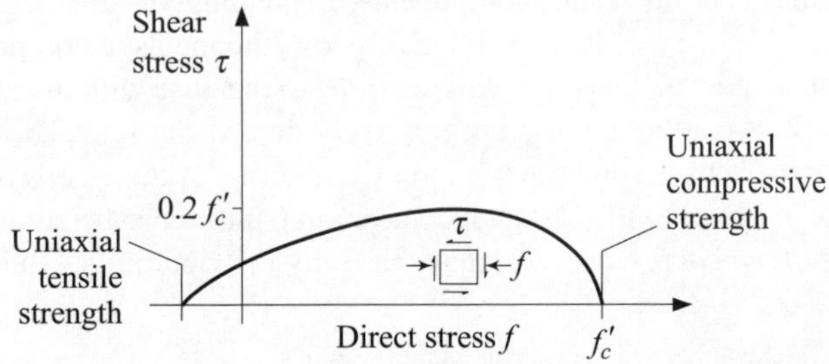

Fig. 2.13 Failure stress envelope – direct stress combined with shear stress [Ref. 2.25].

It is seen that the compressive strength (as well as the tensile strength) of concrete is reduced by the presence of shear stress. Also, the shear strength of concrete is enhanced by the application of direct compression (except in the extreme case of very high compression), whereas it is (expectedly) reduced by the application of direct tension.

2.10.3 Behaviour under Triaxial Compression

When concrete is subject to compression in three orthogonal directions, its *strength* and *ductility* are greatly enhanced [Ref. 2.26, 2.27]. This effect is attributed to the all-round *confinement* of concrete, which reduces significantly the tendency for internal cracking and volume increase just prior to failure.

Effect of Confinement

The benefit derived from confinement of concrete is advantageously made use of in reinforced concrete columns, by providing transverse reinforcement in the form of steel hoops and spirals [Figure 1.6(c)]. It is found that continuous circular spirals are particularly effective in substantially increasing the ductility, and to some extent, the compressive strength of concrete; square or rectangular ties are less effective [Ref. 2.28]. The yielding of the confining steel contributes to increased ductility (ability to undergo large deformations prior to failure). Provision of ductility is of particular importance in the design and *detailing* of reinforced concrete structures subject to *seismic loads* (especially at the beam-column junctions), since it enables the material to enter into the inelastic phase, imparting additional strength to the structure by means of redistribution of stresses [for details, refer Chapter 16].

> Effective confinement of concrete enhances its strength and ductility while reducing internal cracking. It is resorted to in columns, hinging regions, joints subject to reversed/cyclical loading, detailing for earthquake resistance, anchorages, bearing regions, etc.

2.11 Creep of Concrete

2.11.1 Time-Dependent Behaviour under Sustained Loading

When concrete is subject to sustained compressive loading, its deformation keeps increasing with time, even though the stress level is not altered. The time-dependent component† of the total strain is termed **creep**. The time-dependent behaviour of the total strain in concrete (considering both 'instantaneous' strain and creep strain) is depicted in Figure 2.14.

The *instantaneous strain* is that which is assumed to occur 'instantaneously' on application of the loading. This may have both 'elastic' and 'inelastic' components, depending on the stress level [Figure 2.6]. In practice, as the stress level under service loads is relatively low, the inelastic component is negligible. If the stress is maintained at a constant level, the strain will continue to increase with time (as indicated by the solid line in the curve in Figure 2.14), although at a progressively decreasing rate. The increase in strain at any time is termed the *creep strain*. This is sometimes expressed in terms of the *creep coefficient* (C_t), defined as the ratio of the creep strain at time t to the instantaneous strain ('initial elastic strain'). The maximum value of C_t is called the *ultimate creep coefficient* (designated as θ by the Code); its value is found to vary widely in the range 1.3 to 4.2 [Ref. 2.29].

If the sustained load is removed at any time, the strain follows the curve shown by the dashed line in Figure 2.14. There is an instantaneous recovery of strain by an amount equal to the elastic strain (to the extent permitted by the prevailing modulus of elasticity) due to the load removed at this age. This is followed by a gradual decrease in strain, which is termed as *creep recovery*.

Based on the mechanism involved, creep is classified as basic creep and drying creep. Basic creep occurs when the concrete member exhibits time-dependent deformation under sustained load without the influence of drying, for example under 100% relative humidity conditions or when the member is sealed, and thereby drying is prevented. Drying creep occurs when the time-dependent deformation under sustained load is influenced by drying, as in the case of all exposed members.

† Excluding strains introduced by shrinkage and temperature variations.

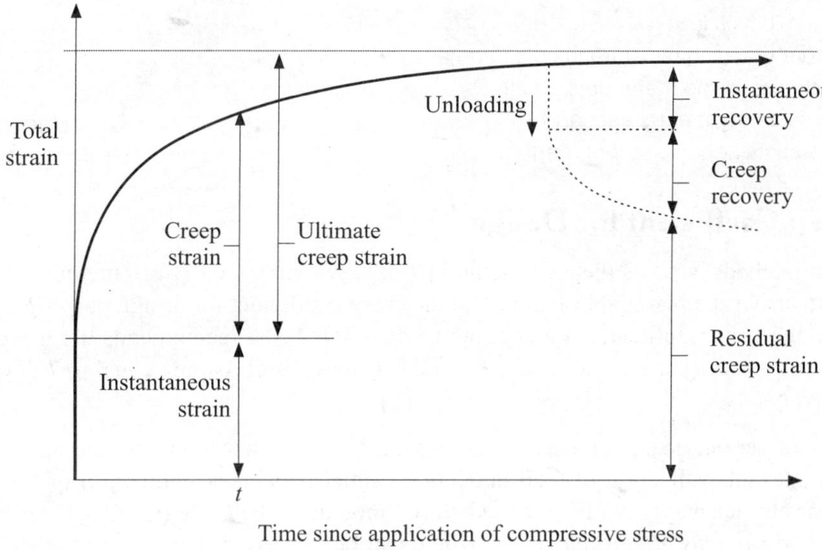

Fig. 2.14 Typical strain-time curve for concrete in uniaxial compression.

2.11.2 Effects of Creep

The exact mechanism of creep in concrete is still not fully understood. It is generally attributed to internal movement of adsorbed water, viscous flow or sliding between the gel particles, moisture loss and the growth in micro-cracks.

Creep of concrete results in the following detrimental effects in reinforced concrete structures:

- increased deflection of beams and slabs;
- increased deflection of slender columns (possibly leading to buckling);
- gradual transfer of load from concrete to reinforcing steel in compression members (possibly leading to yielding of steel);
- loss of prestress in prestressed concrete;

> **Long-term deflection due to creep (plus shrinkage and temperature effects) may be as large as 2–3 times the short-term deflection and hence these effects need due consideration.**

However, some effects of creep may even be beneficial – such as reduction of stresses induced by non-uniform or restrained shrinkage, resulting in a reduction of cracking [Ref. 2.3]. Also, in cases of stresses induced by imposed deformations (as with settlement of supports), creep effects tend to reduce the stresses.

2.11.3 Factors Influencing Creep

There are a number of independent and interacting factors related to the material properties and composition, curing and environmental conditions, and loading conditions that influence the magnitude of creep [Ref. 2.29]. In general, creep *increases* when:

- cement content is high;
- water-cement ratio is high;
- aggregate content is low;
- air entrainment is high;

- relative humidity is low;
- temperature (causing moisture loss) is high;
- size / thickness of the member is small;
- loading occurs at an early age; and
- loading is sustained over a long period.

2.11.4 Creep Coefficient for Design

Several empirical methods, such as the ACI method [Ref. 2.29] and the CEB-FIP method [Ref. 2.30], have been developed to arrive at a reasonable estimate of the creep coefficient for design purposes. In the absence of data related to the factors influencing creep, the Code (Cl. 6.2.5.1) recommends the use of the *ultimate creep coefficient* (θ) – with values equal to 2.2, 1.6 and 1.1, for ages of loading equal to 7 days, 28 days and one year respectively.

Within the range of service loads, creep may be assumed to be proportional to the applied stress. This assumption facilitates the estimation of total deflection (initial plus creep deflection) of flexural members by the usual linear elastic analysis with a reduced elastic modulus. The Code (Cl. C 4.1) terms this reduced modulus as *effective modulus of elasticity* (E_{ce}), which can be expressed[†] in terms of the short-term elastic modulus (E_c) and the ultimate creep coefficient (θ) as follows:

$$E_{ce} = \frac{E_c}{1+\theta} \tag{2.8}$$

Details of computation of long-term deflections of reinforced concrete beams due to creep are covered in Chapter 10.

2.12 Shrinkage and Temperature Effects in Concrete

2.12.1 Shrinkage

Concrete shrinks in the hardened state due to loss of moisture by evaporation; the consequent reduction in volume is termed *drying shrinkage* (often, simply *shrinkage*). Like creep, shrinkage introduces time-dependent strains in concrete [Figure 2.15].

Shrinkage and creep are not independent phenomena. However, for convenience, it is normal practice to treat their effects as separate, independent and additive. All the factors related to constituent material properties, composition of mix, curing and environmental conditions, member size and age that affect creep also affect shrinkage.

However, unlike creep, shrinkage strains are independent of the stress conditions in the concrete. Also, shrinkage is reversible to a great extent, i.e., alternating dry and wet conditions will cause alternating volume changes in concrete.

Shrinkage can be classified as autogenous shrinkage and drying shrinkage. Autogenous shrinkage occurs as a result of the self-desiccation property of concrete, when the loss of moisture is prevented, as in the case of a sealed specimen. Drying shrinkage occurs when the moisture loss is allowed from inside the specimen.

[†] For a more detailed explanation, refer Chapter 10 (Figure 10.12).

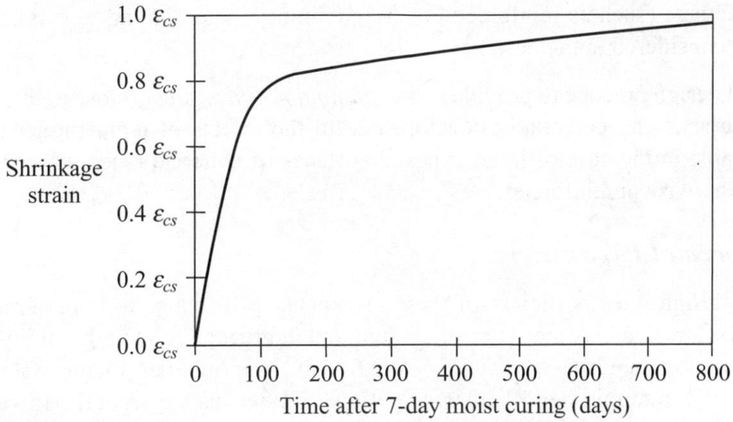

Fig. 2.15 Typical variation of shrinkage with time.

When shrinkage is restrained, as it often is in concrete structures, tensile stresses develop, and, if excessive, may lead to cracking. Similarly, a differential shrinkage, due to a moisture or thermal gradient, or due to a differential restraint to shrinkage (caused, for example, by unsymmetrically placed reinforcement in a beam) will result in internal stresses, curvature and deflections. Shrinkage, like creep, also leads to a loss of prestress in prestressed concrete structures.

Since the primary cause of shrinkage is moisture loss from the cement paste phase of the concrete, it can be minimised by keeping the unit water content in the mix as low as possible and the total aggregate content as high as possible.

Shrinkage Strain for Design

Shrinkage is usually expressed as a linear strain (mm/mm). Empirical methods [Ref. 2.29, 2.30] are available for the estimation of the shrinkage strains for the purpose of design. Wide variations in the value of the *ultimate shrinkage strain* (ε_{cs}) – up to 0.001 mm/mm – have been reported. In the absence of reliable data, the Code (Cl. 6.2.4.1) recommends the use of an ultimate shrinkage strain value of 0.0003 mm/mm; this appears to be rather low, in comparison with ACI recommendation [Ref. 2.29] of an average value of 0.0008 mm/mm for moist-cured concrete.

Details of computation of long-term deflections of reinforced concrete beams due to shrinkage are covered in Chapter 10.

2.12.2 Temperature Effects

Concrete expands with a temperature rise and contracts as the temperature drops; thermal contraction, in fact, produces effects similar to shrinkage.

As a consequence of seasonal variations in temperature, internal stresses are induced in structures (which are statically indeterminate), owing to restrictions in free movements. In order to limit the development of temperature stresses in reinforced concrete buildings with large plan dimensions, it is desirable to provide suitable *expansion joints* at appropriate locations – particularly where there are marked changes in plan dimensions [refer Cl. 27 of the Code].

Temperature stresses also develop on account of differential temperature (thermal gradient), as in roof slabs (particularly of air-conditioned rooms) exposed to the sun, or in chimneys which release hot gases. In the design of many structures (such as reinforced concrete chimneys and cooling towers), 'temperature loads' need to be specially considered in the design.

In general, it is good design practice to provide some *nominal reinforcement* (close to the surface) in concrete at locations where cracks can potentially develop, due to the effects of temperature and shrinkage. This is particularly desirable in the case of large exposed surfaces of concrete (such as web faces of large-size beams) which are otherwise unreinforced.

Coefficient of Thermal Expansion

For the purpose of design, the coefficient of thermal expansion of concrete is required. This is found to depend on various factors, such as the types of cement and aggregate, relative humidity, member size, etc. The Code (Cl. 6.2.6) recommends values ranging from 6×10^{-6} mm/mm per °C (for concrete with calcareous aggregate) to 12×10^{-6} mm/mm per °C (for concrete with siliceous aggregate). However, for the design of special structures such as water tanks, chimneys, bins and silos, a value of 11×10^{-6} mm/mm per °C is recommended [Ref. 2.33]. This is very close to the coefficient of thermal expansion of steel (which is about 12×10^{-6} mm/mm per °C), so that there is little likelihood of any differential thermal expansion and associated relative movements between the steel and surrounding concrete.

2.13 Durability of Concrete

If concrete is to serve the purpose for which it is designed during its intended lifetime, it has to be *durable*. Unfortunately, many reinforced concrete structures built in the past (particularly, the not-too-distant past) in adverse environments have shown signs of increased structural distress, mainly† due to **chemical attack**, causing deterioration of concrete and corrosion of reinforcing steel. Loss of durability results in a reduced life of the structure. In an attempt to give increased importance to durability considerations, the recent revision of the Code has strengthened the provisions pertaining to durability, by shifting the guidelines from the Appendix (of the earlier Code) to the main body of the Code (Cl. 8), and by enhancing their scope and impact. These changes are in line with other national codes, such as BS 8100 and ACI 318.

Loss of durability in concrete structures is essentially attributable to two classes of factors, viz., external factors and internal factors. The external factors pertain to the type of environment to which the concrete is exposed, whereas the internal factors pertain to characteristics inherent to the built concrete. Primary among the internal factors is the relative **permeability** of the concrete, as chemical attack can occur only if harmful chemicals can ingress into the concrete. Chemical attack is caused by the ingress of water, oxygen, carbon dioxide, chlorides, sulphates, and other harmful chemicals (borne by surrounding ground or sea water, soil or humid atmosphere). It can also occur due to the presence of deleterious constituents (such as chlorides, sulphates and alkali-reactive aggregate) in the original concrete mix. Concrete members that are relatively thin or have inadequate cover to reinforcement are particularly vulnerable. Lack of good drainage of water to avoid standing pools and rundown of water along exposed surfaces, and cracks in concrete also lead to ingress of water and deterioration of concrete. Impermeability is governed by the constituents and workmanship used in making concrete. Despite the remarkable advances in concrete technology, regrettably, workmanship remains very poor in many construction sites in India, especially of smaller size projects.

Durability in concrete can be realised if the various internal factors are suitably accounted for (or modified), during the design and construction stages, to ensure that the concrete has the desired resistance to the

† Other factors include 'abrasive' actions on concrete surfaces (caused, for example, by machinery and metal tyres) and 'freezing and thawing' actions.

anticipated external factors. Otherwise, the task of repairing and rehabilitating concrete that has been damaged (for want of proper design and quality of construction) can prove to be difficult and expensive.

The most effective ways of providing for increased durability of concrete against chemical attack in a known adverse environment are by the following:

Effective ways of providing for increased durability.

- reducing permeability by
  - providing high grade of concrete
  - using adequate cement content
  - using well-graded, dense aggregate
  - using low water-cement ratio
  - using appropriate admixtures (including silica fume)
  - achieving maximum compaction
  - achieving effective curing
  - using appropriate surface coatings and impermeable membranes
  - avoiding sharp corners and locations where compaction is difficult
  - taking care while designing to minimise possible cracks
- providing direct protection to embedded steel against corrosion by
  - providing adequate clear cover
  - using appropriate corrosion-resistant or coated steel
  - using sophisticated techniques such as cathodic protection
- providing appropriate type of cement having the desired chemical resistance to sulphates and/or chlorides
- controlling the chloride and sulphate contents in the concrete mix constituents (within the limits specified in Cl. 8.2.5 of the Code)
- avoiding the use of alkali-reactive aggregate
- providing air-entraining admixtures when resistance against freezing and thawing is required
- providing adequate thickness of members
- providing adequate reinforcement designed to contain crack widths within acceptable limits
- providing adequate drainage on concrete surfaces to avoid water retention (e.g., 'ponding' in roof slabs)

2.13.1 Environmental Exposure Conditions and Code Requirements

The Code (Cl. 8.2.2.1) identifies five categories of 'environmental exposure conditions', viz., **'mild'**, **'moderate'**, **'severe'**, **'very severe'** and **'extreme'**, in increasing degree of severity. The purpose of this categorisation is mainly to provide a basis for enforcing certain minimum requirements aimed at providing the desired performance related to the severity of exposure. These requirements, having implications in both design and construction of reinforced concrete work, pertain to the following:

- minimum grade of concrete (varying from M 20 to M 40)
- minimum clear cover to reinforcement (20 mm to 75 mm)
- minimum cement content (300 to 360 kg/m^3 for 20 mm size aggregates)
- maximum water-cement ratio (0.55 to 0.40)
- acceptable limits of surface width of cracks (0.1 mm to 0.3 mm)

Code requirements related to exposure conditions to be considered at design and construction stage.

The descriptions of the five categories of environmental exposure, as well as the corresponding specifications for the minimum grade of concrete, 'nominal cover'† (minimum clear cover to reinforcement), minimum

† Additional cover requirements pertaining to fire resistance are given in Table 16A of the Code.

cement content and maximum free water-cement ratio, for reinforced concrete work, are summarised in Table 2.1†. These specifications incorporated in the revised Code constitute perhaps the most significant changes in the Code, having tremendous practical (and economic) implications. These recommendations have been long overdue, and are in line with international practice.

It may be noted that in the same structure, different members may be subject to different categories of exposure. For example, a reinforced concrete building located in a port city (such as Chennai or Mumbai) would be exposed to a coastal environment, which qualifies to be categorised as 'severe' (or 'very severe', in case it is very near the beach, exposed to sea water spray). However, for concrete members located well inside the building (excepting foundations), sheltered from direct rain and aggressive atmospheric environment, the exposure category may be lowered by one level of severity; i.e., from 'severe' to 'moderate' (or 'very severe' to 'severe').

Table 2.1 *Exposure conditions and requirements for RC work with normal aggregate (20 mm nominal size)*

Exposure Category	Description	Min. Grade	Min. Cover (mm)	Min. Cement (kg/m^3)	Max. Free w/c ratio
Mild	Protected against weather or aggressive conditions, except if located in coastal area	M 20	20*	300	0.55
Moderate	Sheltered from severe rain or freezing whilst wet, or Exposed to condensation and rain, or Continuously under water, or In contact with or buried under non-aggressive soil or ground water, or Sheltered from saturated 'salt air' in coastal area	M 25	30	300	0.50
Severe	Exposed to severe rain, alternate wetting and drying or occasional freezing whilst wet or severe condensation, or Completely immersed in sea water, or Exposed to coastal environment	M 30	45**	320	0.45
Very severe	Exposed to sea water spray, corrosive fumes or severe freezing whilst wet, or In contact with or buried under aggressive sub-soil or ground water	M 35	50	340	0.45
Extreme	Members in tidal zone, or Members in direct contact with liquid/ solid aggressive chemicals	M 40	75	360	0.40

* can be reduced to 15 mm, if the bar diameter is less than 12 mm.

** can be reduced by 5 mm, if M 35 or higher grade is used.

† The requirements for plain concrete (given in Table 5 of the Code) are not shown here.

Accordingly, corresponding to the 'severe' category, the roof† slab must be (at least) of M 30 grade concrete and its reinforcement should have a minimum clear cover of 45 mm. These values may be compared to M 15 grade and 15 mm cover hitherto adopted in design practice, as per IS 456: 1978. The increase in capital investment on account of the substantial increase in slab thickness and enhanced grade of concrete may appear to be drastic, but should be weighed against the significant gain in terms of prolonged maintenance-free life of the structure.

2.13.2 Permeability of Concrete

As mentioned earlier, reducing the permeability of concrete is perhaps the most effective way of enhancing durability. *Impermeability* is also a major *serviceability* requirement – particularly in water tanks, sewage tanks, gas purifiers, pipes and pressure vessels. In ordinary construction, roof slabs need to be impermeable against the ingress of rain water.

Permeability of concrete is directly related to the *porosity* of the cement paste, the distribution of *capillary pores* and the presence of *micro-cracks* (induced by shrinkage effects, tensile stresses, etc.). The main factors influencing capillary porosity are the *water-cement ratio* and the *degree of hydration*. The use of a **low water-cement ratio, adequate cement** and **effective curing** contribute significantly to reduced permeability. The steps to be taken to reduce permeability were listed in the previous Section. In addition, it is essential for the concrete to be dense; this requires the use of **well-graded, dense aggregate** and **good compaction**. For given aggregates, the cement content should be sufficient to provide adequate workability with a low water-cement ratio so that concrete can be completely compacted with the means available. The use of appropriate chemical admixtures (such as superplasticisers) can facilitate working with a reduced water-cement ratio, and the use of mineral admixtures such as silica fume can contribute to making a dense concrete with reduced porosity.

Provision of appropriate tested surface coatings and impermeable membranes also provide additional protection in extreme situations.

2.13.3 Chemical Attack on Concrete

The main sources of chemical attack, causing deterioration of concrete are sulphates, sea water (containing chlorides, sulphates, etc.), acids and alkali-aggregate reaction.

Sulphate Attack

Sulphates present in the soil or in ground (or sea) water attack hardened concrete that is relatively permeable. Sulphates of sodium and potassium, and magnesium in particular, react with calcium hydroxide and C_3A to form calcium sulphate ('gypsum') and calcium sulphoaluminate ('ettringite') – which occupy a greater volume than the compounds they replace [Ref. 2.3]. This leads to expansion and disruption (cracking or disintegration) of hardened concrete. Sulphate-attacked concrete has a characteristic whitish appearance ('efflorescence' – due to leaching of calcium hydroxide), and is prone to cracking and spalling of concrete.

Resistance to sulphate attack can be improved by the use of special cements such as PSC, SRPC, HAC and SC [refer Section 2.2.1], and by reducing the permeability of concrete. Recommendations regarding the choice of type of cement, minimum cement content and maximum water-cement ratio, for exposure to different concentrations of sulphates (expressed as SO_3) in soil and ground water are given in Table 4 of the Code. The Code recommends the use of Portland slag cement (PSC) with slag content more than 50 per cent, and in cases of extreme sulphate concentration, recommends the use of supersulphated cement (SC)‡ and sulphate resistant

† In the case of intermediate floor slabs, the grade of concrete can be reduced to M 25 and the clear cover to 30 mm, corresponding to 'moderate' exposure.

‡ However, use of supersulphated cement in situations where the ambient temperature exceeds 40°C is discouraged.

cement (SRC). The specified minimum cement content is in the range 280 to 400 kg/m^3 and the maximum free water-cement ratio is in the range 0.55 to 0.40 respectively for increasing concentrations of sulphates.

Sea Water Attack

Sea water contains chlorides in addition to sulphates – the combination of which results in a gradual increase in porosity and a consequent decrease in strength. The same measures used to prevent sulphate attack are applicable here. However, the use of sulphate resistant cement (SRC) is not recommended. The Code recommends the use of OPC with C_3A content in the range 5–8 per cent and the use of blast furnace slag cement (PSC). In particular, *low permeability* is highly desirable. The inclusion of silica fume admixture can contribute to the making of the densest possible concrete. The use of soft or porous aggregate should be avoided. Concrete shall be at least M 30 Grade in case of reinforced concrete. The use of a higher cement content (of at least 350 kg/m^3) above the low-tide water level, along with a lower water-cement ratio (of about 0.40) is recommended, owing to the extreme severity of exposure in this region, where construction joints should also be avoided [Ref. 2.30]. Adequate *cover to reinforcement* and other measures to prevent corrosion are of special importance to prevent chloride attack on reinforcement.

Alkali-Aggregate Reaction

Some aggregates containing reactive silica are prone to reaction with alkalis (Na_2O and K_2O) in the cement paste. The reaction, however, is possible only in the presence of a high moisture content within the concrete. The reaction eventually leads to expansion, cracking and disruption of concrete, although the occurrence of damage may be delayed, sometimes by five years or so [Ref. 2.3]. Care must be taken to avoid the use of such aggregates for concreting. Also, the use of low alkali OPC and inclusion of pozzolana are recommended by the Code (Cl. 8.2.5.4). The Code also recommends measures to reduce the degree of saturation of concrete during service by the use of impermeable membranes in situations where the possibility of alkali-aggregate reaction is suspected.

2.13.4 Corrosion of Reinforcing Steel

The mechanism of corrosion of reinforcing steel, embedded in concrete, is attributed to electrochemical action. Differences in the electrochemical potential on the steel surface results in the formation of anodic and cathodic regions, which are connected by some salt solution acting as an electrolyte.

Steel in freshly cast concrete is generally free from corrosion because of the formation of a thin protective film of iron oxide due to the strongly alkaline environment produced by the hydration of cement. This passive protection is broken when the pH value of the regions adjoining the steel falls below about 9. This can occur either by *carbonation* (reaction of carbon dioxide in the atmosphere with the alkalis in the cement paste) or by the ingress of *soluble chlorides*. The extent of carbonation penetration or chloride penetration depends, to a great extent, on the *permeability* of concrete in the *cover* region. The increased cover stipulated in the recent code revision will contribute to increased protection against corrosion, provided, of course, the cover concrete is of good quality (low permeability). However, it may be noted that increased cover also contributes to increased flexural crack-widths [Ref. 2.31], and it is necessary to contain the cracking by suitable reinforcement design and detailing [refer Chapter 10].

The electrochemical process of corrosion takes place in the presence of the electrolytic solution and water and oxygen. The consequent formation and accumulation of rust can result in a significant increase in the volume of steel and a loss of strength; the swelling pressures cause cracking and spalling of concrete, thereby allowing further ingress of carbonation or chloride penetration. Unless remedial measures are quickly adopted, corrosion is likely to propagate and lead eventually to structural failure. *Cathodic protection* is the most effective (although expensive) way of arresting corrosion [Ref. 2.32].

Prevention is easier (and less costly) than cure. If it is known in advance that the structure is to be located in an adverse environment, the designer should aim for structural durability at the design stage itself, by adopting suitable measures such as

- *control crack widths* in reinforced concrete by suitable design [refer Chapter 10], or by resorting to partial or full *prestressing*;
- provide *increased cover* to reinforcement [refer Cl. 26.4.2 of the Code];
- ensure *low permeability* by specifying optimum cement content, minimum water-cement ratio, proper compaction and curing;
- specify the use of special *corrosion-resistant steel or fusion bonded epoxy steel*;
- use of special cements;
- use of cathodic protection.

Corrosion of reinforcement is a common problem. Prevention is better than cure! The preventive measures at design and construction stages are easier, more effective and cheaper than repair measures undertaken after damage.

2.14 Reinforcing Steel

As explained earlier (Section 1.2), concrete is reinforced with steel primarily to make up for concrete's incapacity for tensile resistance. Steel embedded in concrete, called reinforcing steel, can effectively take up the tension that is induced due to flexural tension, direct tension, 'diagonal tension' or environmental effects. Reinforcing steel also imparts ductility to a material that is otherwise brittle. Furthermore, steel is stronger than concrete in compression also; hence, concrete can be advantageously reinforced with steel for bearing compressive stresses as well, as is commonly done in columns.

2.14.1 Types, Sizes and Grades

Reinforcing steel is generally provided in the form of bars, wires or welded wire fabric.

Reinforcing bars (referred to as *rebars*) are available in *nominal* diameters[†] ranging from 5 mm to 50 mm, and may be *plain* or *deformed*. In the case of the latter, 'deformations', in the form of lugs or protrusions, are provided on the surface to enhance the *bond* between steel and concrete, and to mechanically inhibit the longitudinal movement of the bar relative to the concrete around it. The bars that are most commonly used are **high strength deformed bars** (generally *cold-twisted*), conforming to IS 1786: 2008, and having a 'specified yield strength' of 415 MPa. Deformed bars of a higher specified strength of 500, 550 and 600 MPa may also be used in special cases. Plain **mild steel** bars are less commonly used in reinforced concrete, because they possess less strength (250 MPa yield strength) and cost approximately the same as high-strength deformed bars; however, they are used in practice in situations where nominal reinforcement is called for. Low strength steel is also preferred in special situations where deflections and crack widths need to be controlled [refer Chapter 10], or where high ductility is required, as in earthquake-resistant design [refer Chapter 16]. The Code also permits the use of *medium tensile steel* (which has a higher strength than mild steel); but this is rarely used in practice. The requirements of both mild steel and medium tensile steel are covered in IS 432 (Part 1): 1982.

For the purpose of reinforced concrete design, the Code grades reinforcing steel in terms of the 'specified yield strength'. In IS 456: 2000, only three grades have been specified, viz., Fe 250, Fe 415, and Fe 500,

[†] The bar sizes (nominal diameters in mm) presently available in India are – 5, 6, 8, 10, 12, 16, 18, 20, 22, 25, 28, 32, 36, 40, 45 and 50.

conforming to specified yield strengths of 250 MPa, 415 MPa and 500 MPa respectively. However, additional grades, Fe 415D, Fe 500D, Fe 550 D and Fe 600 have been recently introduced in the code, IS 1786: 2008, to include higher strength of 550 MPa and 600 MPa and higher ductility (denoted by letter 'D'). The specified yield strength normally refers to a guaranteed minimum. The actual yield strength of the steel is usually somewhat **higher** than the specified value. The Code (Cl. 36.1) specifies that the 'specified yield strength' may be treated as the *characteristic strength* of reinforcing steel. In some cases (e.g., in ductile, earthquake resistant design – see Chapter 16) it is **undesirable** to have a yield strength much higher than that considered in design.

Hard-drawn steel wire fabrics, conforming to IS 1566: 1982, are sometimes used in thin slabs and in some precast products (such as pipes). Their sizes are specified in terms of mesh size and wire diameter.

Rolled steel sections, conforming to Grade A of IS 2062: 2011, are also permitted by the Code in *composite construction*; however, this is strictly not in the purview of reinforced concrete design, and hence is not discussed in this book.

Rust on Reinforcement

Rust on reinforcing steel (prior to concreting) is not an uncommon sight at construction sites. Loose mill scale, loose rust, oil, mud, etc., are considered harmful for the bond with concrete, and should be removed before fixing of reinforcement [Cl. 5.6.1 of the Code]. However, research has shown that a normal amount of rust on deformed bars and wire fabric is perhaps not undesirable, because it increases the bond with concrete [Ref. 2.33]; however, the rust should not be excessive as to violate the specified tolerances on the size of the reinforcement.

2.14.2 Stress-Strain Curves

The stress-strain curve of reinforcing steel is obtained by performing a standard *tension test* [refer IS 1608: 2018]. Typical stress-strain curves for the three grades of steel are depicted in Figure 2.16.

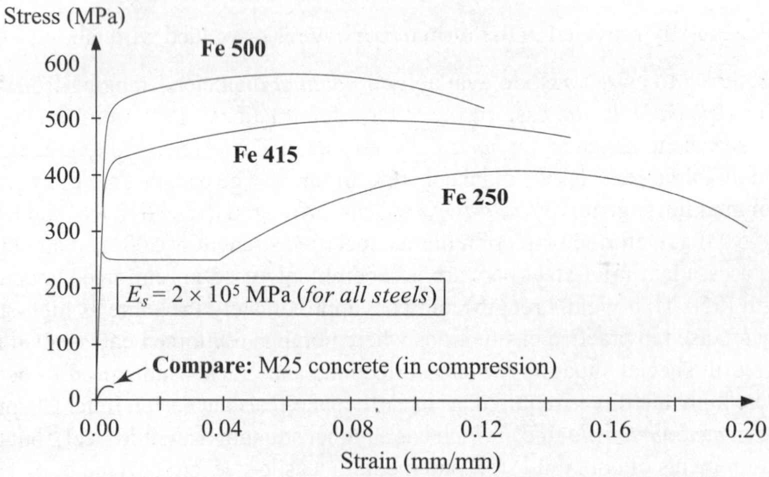

Fig. 2.16 Typical stress-strain curves for reinforcing steels.†

† For comparison, the stress-strain curve for M25 concrete is also plotted to the same scale. Note the enormous difference in ultimate strength and strain and elastic modulus between concrete and steel. For steel, the stress-strain curve in compression is identical to the one in tension (provided buckling is restrained). In contrast, for concrete, the tensile strength and strain are only a small fraction of the corresponding values in compression.

For all grades, there is an initial linear elastic portion with constant slope, which gives a *modulus of elasticity* (E_s) that is practically the same for all grades. The Code (Cl. 5.6.3) specifies that the value of E_s to be considered in design is 2×10^5 MPa (N/mm^2).

The stress-strain curve of mild steel (*hot rolled*) is characterised by an initial linearly elastic part that is followed by an *yield plateau* (where the strain increases at almost constant stress), followed in turn by a *strain hardening range* in which the stress once again increases with increasing strain (although at a decreasing rate) until the peak stress (*tensile strength*) is reached. Finally, there is a descending branch wherein the *nominal stress* (load divided by original area) decreases until *fracture* occurs. (The *actual* stress, in terms of load divided by the current reduced area, will, however, show an increasing trend). For Fe 250 grade steel, the ultimate tensile strength is specified as 412 MPa, and the minimum percentage elongation (on a specified gauge length) is 20–22 per cent. [refer IS 432 (Part 1): 1982].

The process of *cold-working* involves stretching and twisting of mild steel, beyond the yield plateau, and subsequently releasing the load, as indicated by the line *BCD* in Figure 2.17. This steel on reloading will follow the path *DEF*. It can be seen that by unloading after the yield stress has been exceeded and reloading, a hysteresis loop is formed. The unloading and reloading curves *BCD* and *DEF* are initially very nearly parallel to the original elastic loading line *OA*. The hysteresis loop shown in Figure 2.17 is greatly exaggerated and, except under continuous reversed cyclic loading, the unloading and reloading paths in this region may be assumed to be overlapping, elastic and parallel to line *OA*. Thus, upon reloading, the steel follows a linear elastic path (with the same modulus of elasticity E_s as the original mild steel) up to the point where the unloading started – the new raised 'yield point'. (The point of yielding is **not likely to be well-defined** if the point of unloading lies beyond the yield plateau.) Thereafter, the material enters into the *strain hardening* range, following the path indicated by the curve *FGH*, which is virtually a continuation of the curve *OAB* [Figure 2.17]. It can also be seen that cold-working results in a residual strain in the steel, represented by *OD* in Figure 2.17.

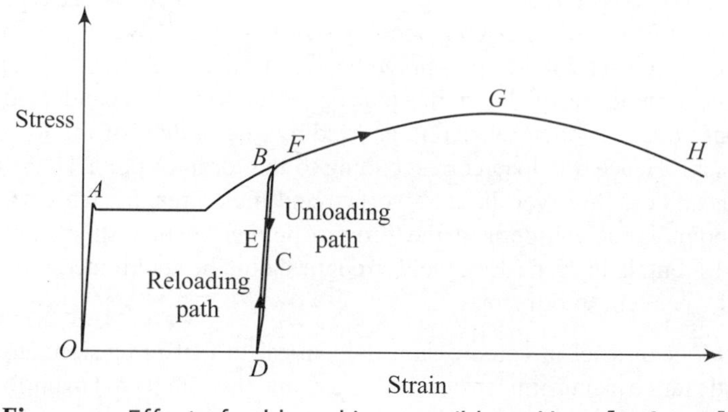

Fig. 2.17 Effect of cold-working on mild steel bars [Ref. 2.34].

It should be noted that although the process of cold-working effectively increases the 'yield strength' of the steel, it also reduces the ductility in the material. Higher yield strengths can be achieved by suitably selecting the point of unloading in the strain hardening range, and by using higher grades of mild steel. It also follows that increasing yield strength through cold-working results in a decreased margin between yield strength and ultimate strength.

For Fe 415, Fe 500, Fe 550 and Fe 600 grades steel, the ultimate tensile strength is expected to be at least 485, 545, 585 and 600 MPa respectively with percentage elongations of 14.5, 12.0, 10.0 and 10.0 per cent respectively, as per recent revised IS 1786: 2008. This code for deformed bars also permits the use of bars of higher ductility (especially suited for earthquake-resistant design), with grades Fe 415D, Fe 500D and Fe 550D with percentage elongations of 18.0, 16.0 and 14.50, and with minimum ultimate tensile strengths of 500, 565 and 600 MPa respectively. For design purposes, the increase in strength beyond the 'yield point' (due to strain-hardening) is generally ignored. Most design codes recommend the use of an ideal *elasto-plastic* stress-strain curve (with an initial linear elastic line up to yield, followed by a line at constant stress, denoting the post-yielding behaviour).

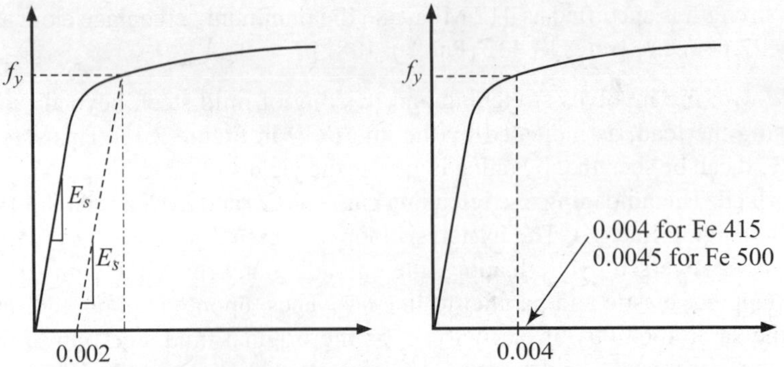

(a) 0.2 per cent proof stress (b) Stress at specified (yield) strain

Fig. 2.18 Definition of yield strength – high strength steel.

In the absence of a definite yield point, the 0.2 per cent 'proof stress'† is generally taken as the yield strength [Figure 2.18(a)]. It is also admissible to take the yield strength as the stress corresponding to a specified strain (0.004 and 0.0045 for Fe 415 and Fe 500 grades respectively; see Cl. 8.2 of IS 1786: 2008) as shown in Figure 2.18(b)‡. **A note of caution** will be appropriate here. For mild steel such as grade Fe 250 [see Figure 2.16], there is a sharp and pronounced yielding. In a tension test on such steel conducted on a relatively 'stiff' testing machine, because of the sudden relaxation at yielding, the pointer of the load dial of the machine 'hesitates' or 'drops back'. Hence, the load corresponding to the 'drop of pointer' can be taken as the yield load with reasonable accuracy. However, in cold-worked and high strength steels whose yielding is more gradual and the 'yield point' is not well-defined, the 'drop-of-pointer' method should not be used to determine the yield load and yield strength. In such cases, yield strength should be determined from the measured stress-strain diagram as the 0.2 per cent 'proof stress'§.

The stress-strain behaviour of steel in compression is identical to that in tension. However, if the steel is stressed into the inelastic range in uniform tension, unloaded, and then subjected to uniform compression (i.e., reversed loading), it is found that the stress-strain curve in compression becomes non-linear at a stress much

† The stress at which a non-proportional elongation equal to 0.2 per cent of the original gauge length takes place [IS 1786: 2008 & 1608: 2005]; stress level, which on unloading, results in a residual strain of 0.002.

‡ These strains are indeed the sum of 0.002 and f_y/E_s for the respective grades [see Figure 2.18(b)].

§ It has come to the notice of the authors that some educational institutions conducting commercial tests have been adopting the 'drop-of-pointer' method even for high strength reinforcing steel specimens. As a result, yield strengths far greater than the real values have been erroneously reported. Hence, this note of caution.

lower than the initial yield strength [Figure 2.19]. This is referred to as the '*Bauschinger effect*' [Ref. 2.28]. In this case, the hysteresis loop is also more pronounced. In inelastic deformation processes involving continual reversal of stress (such as metal working, high intensity reversed seismic loading, etc.), the Bauschinger effect is very important and cannot be ignored. In other cases, where the loading is within the elastic range or where there is in general no more than one stress reversal, the Bauschinger effect can safely be neglected.

The stress-strain curve for steel under compression is generally taken to be the same as under tension.

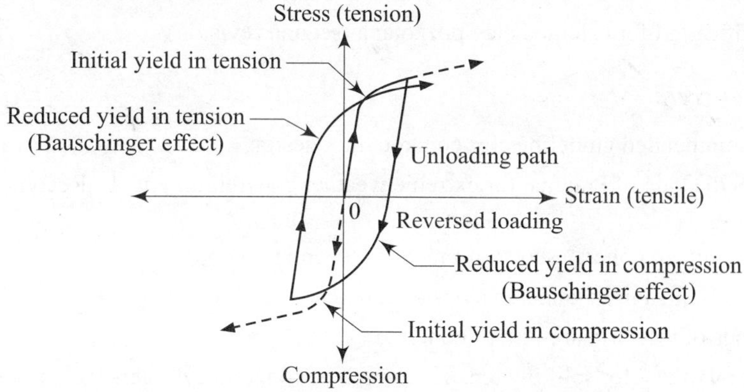

Fig. 2.19 Bauschinger effect and hysteresis.

2.15 List of Relevant Indian Standards

All the codes on *material specifications* that have been referred to in this chapter are listed as follows:

Standards on Cement

IS 269:2015 Specification for Ordinary Portland cement (sixth revision)

IS 8041:1990 Specification for rapid hardening Portland cement (second revision)

IS 455:2015 Specification for Portland slag cement (fifth revision)

IS 1489:2015 Specification for Portland pozzolana cement

Part I: Flyash based (fourth revision)

Part II: Calcined clay based (fourth revision)

IS 12600:1989 Specification for low heat Portland cement

IS 12330:1988 Specification for sulphate resisting Portland cement

IS 8042:2015 Specification for white Portland cement (third revision)

IS 8043:1991 Specification for hydrophobic Portland cement (second revision)

IS 6452:1989 Specification for high alumina cement for structural use (first revision)

IS 6909:1990 Specification for supersulphated cement (first revision)

IS 4031:1988 Methods of physical tests for hydraulic cement

Standards on Aggregate, Water and Admixtures

IS 383:2016 Specification for coarse and fine aggregates from natural sources for concrete (third revision)

IS 9142:2018 Specification for artificial lightweight aggregates for concrete masonry units

IS 2386 (Parts 1–8) Methods of tests for aggregate for concrete

IS 3025 (Parts 17–32) Methods of sampling and test (physical and chemical) for water and waste water

IS 9103:1999 Specification for admixtures for concrete (first revision)

IS 3812:2013 Specification for flyash for use as pozzolana and admixture (second revision)

IS 1344:1981 Specification for calcined clay pozzolana (second revision)

Standards on Concrete

IS 10262:2019 Recommended guidelines for concrete mix design

IS 7861 (Part 1):1975 Code of Practice for extreme weather concreting: Part 1 Recommended practice for hot weather concreting

IS 4926:2003 Ready-mixed concrete-code of practice (second revision)

IS 1199:1959 Methods of sampling and analysis of concrete

IS 516:1959 Methods of tests for strength of concrete

IS 5816:1999 Method of test for splitting tensile strength of concrete cylinders (first revision)

IS 3370 (Part 1):2009 Code of Practice for the storage of liquids: Part 1General

IS 1343:2012 Code of Practice for Prestressed Concrete (second revision)

Standards on Reinforcing Steel

IS 432 (Part 1):1982 Specification for mild steel and medium tensile steel bars for concrete reinforcement (third revision)

IS 1786:2008 High strength deformed steel bars and wires for concrete reinforcement-specification

IS 1566:1982 Specification for hard-drawn steel wire fabric for concrete reinforcement (second revision)

IS 2062:2006 Steel for general structural purposes-Specification (sixth revision)

IS 1608:2018 Metallic materials - Tensile testing at ambient temperature (fourth revision)

REVIEW QUESTIONS

2.1 Discuss the types of cement that are suitable for (a) *mass concreting*, (b) resistance to *sulphate attack*.

2.2 Explain how development of strength and heat of hydration be controlled in cement manufacture.

2.3 Can the use of excessive cement in concrete be harmful?

2.4 Discuss the meaning of the terms *stiffening*, *setting* and *hardening* with reference to cement paste?

2.5 What is the basis for deciding the maximum size of coarse aggregate in concrete work?

2.6 Discuss what is meant by *segregation* of concrete. Under what circumstances does it take place?

2.7 What is meant by *workability* of concrete, and how is it measured?

2.8 Discuss the role of water in producing 'good' concrete.

2.9 Mention the different types of 'admixtures' and their applications.

2.10 (a) Define *characteristic strength*. (b) Determine the 'mean target strength' required for the mix design of M25 concrete, assuming moderate quality control.

2.11 Enumerate the steps involved in the Indian Standard method of *mix design*.

2.12 Why is the *cube strength* different from the *cylinder strength* for the same grade of concrete?

2.13 Can concrete be assumed to be a *linear elastic* material? Discuss.

2.14 Distinguish between *static modulus* and *dynamic modulus* of elasticity of concrete.

2.15 Discuss the variations of longitudinal, lateral and volumetric strains that are observable in a typical uniaxial compression test on a concrete prism.

2.16 Why does the Code limit the compressive strength of concrete in structural design to 0.67 f_{ck}, and not f_{ck}?

2.17 Is the *modulus of rupture* of concrete equal to its *direct tensile strength*? Discuss.

2.18 The standard flexure test makes use of a 'third-point loading'. Is this necessary? Can a single point load at midspan be used as an alternative?

2.19 Why is it not possible to determine the *shear strength* of concrete by subjecting it to a state of pure shear?

2.20 What is the advantage of confinement of concrete? Give suitable examples to illustrate your point.

2.21 What does 'creep of concrete' mean? Is creep harmful or beneficial?

2.22 How is it that the deflection of a simply supported reinforced concrete beam increases due to shrinkage of concrete?

2.23 Consider a simple portal frame (with fixed base) made of reinforced concrete. Sketch the approximate shape of the deflection curve caused by (a) a uniform shrinkage strain, (b) a uniform temperature rise.

2.24 Consider the temperature gradient across the shell thickness of a reinforced concrete chimney (with tubular cross-section). Where would you provide reinforcing steel to resist tensile stresses due to the effect of temperature alone (caused by the emission of hot gases): close to the outer circumference or close to the inner circumference? Justify your answer.

2.25 Define 'durable concrete'? Discuss the ways of ensuring durability.

2.26 Cite two examples each for the five categories of 'environmental exposure' described in the Code.

2.27 Describe the main factors that affect the *permeability* of concrete.

2.28 Discuss briefly the factors that lead to corrosion of reinforcing steel.

2.29 Explain the steps a designer can adopt at the design stage to ensure the *durability* of a reinforced concrete *offshore structure*?

2.30 Discuss *strain hardening* of steel? How is it related to the *grade* of reinforcing steel?

2.31 What is meant by cold-working of mild steel? How does it affect the structural properties of the steel?

2.32 Explain *Bauschinger effect*? Where is it relevant?

2.33 For M25 concrete with creep coefficient of 1.5, the long-term static modulus of elasticity (expressed in MPa) as per the provisions of IS:456-2000 is ________ [GATE 2016]

2.34 When a specimen of M25 concrete is loaded to a stress level of 12.5 MPa, a strain of 500×10^{-6} is recorded. If this load is allowed to stand for a long time, the strain increases to 1000×10^{-6}. In accordance with the provisions of IS:456-2000, considering the long-term effects, the effective modulus of elasticity of the concrete (in MPa) is ___________ [GATE 2019]

REFERENCES

2.1 Neville, A M, *Properties of Concrete*, Second edition, Pitman Publishing Co., London, 1973

2.2 Mehta, P K and Monteiro, P J M, *Concrete: Microstructure, Properties and Materials*, Indian edition, Indian Concrete Institute, Chennai, 1997

2.3 Neville, A M and Brooks, J J, *Concrete Technology*, ELBS edition, Longman, London, 1990

2.4 *Design of Concrete Mixes*, Special Publication SP:23, Bureau of Indian Standards, New Delhi, 1982

2.5 Rao, P S and Aravindan, P K, *Concrete Mix Design Practice – Need for a Fresh Approach*, Indian Concrete Journal, May 1990, pp 234–237

2.6 Price, W H, *Factors Influencing Concrete Strength*, Journal ACI, Vol. 47, Feb. 1951, pp 417–432

2.7 *Guide for Use of Admixtures in Concrete*, ACI Committee Report 212.2 R-81, Am. Conc. Inst., Detroit, Michigan, USA, 1981

2.8 *Cement and Concrete Terminology*, ACI (Committee 116) Special Publication SP-19, Am. Conc. Inst., Detroit, Michigan, USA, 1967

2.9 Ellingwood, B, Galambos, T V, MacGregor, J G and Cornell, C A, *Development of a Probability Based Load Criterion for American National Standard A58*, Special Publication No.577, National Bureau of Standards, Washington DC, 1980

2.10 *Standard Practice for Selecting Proportions for Normal, Heavyweight and Mass Concrete*, ACI Standard 211.1–81, Am. Conc. Inst., Detroit, Michigan, USA, 1981

2.11 *Standard Practice for Selecting Proportions for Structural Lightweight Concrete*, ACI Standard 211.2–81, Am. Conc. Inst., Detroit, Michigan, USA, 1981

2.12 *Standard Practice for Selecting Proportions for No-Slump Concrete*, ACI Standard 211.3–75 (revised), Am. Conc. Inst., Detroit, Michigan, USA, 1980

2.13 Teychenne, D C, Franklin, R E, Erntroy, H C, *Design of Normal Concrete Mixes*, Dept. of Environment, Her Majesty's Stationary Office, London, 1975

2.14 Kesler, C E, *Hardened Concrete Strength*, 'Tests and Properties of Concrete', ASTM Special Testing Publication No. 169–A, Am. Soc. for Testing and Materials, 1966, pp 144–159

2.15 Hsu, T T C et al, *Microcracking of Plain Concrete and the Shape of the Stress-Strain Curve*, Journal ACI, Vol. 60, Feb. 1963, pp 209–223

2.16 Kupfer, H, Hilsdorf, H K and Rüsch, H, *Behaviour of Concrete Under Biaxial Stresses*, Journal ACI, Vol. 66, Aug. 1969, pp 655–666

2.17 Hognestad, E, Hanson, N W and McHenry, D, *Concrete Stress Distribution in Ultimate Strength Design*, Journal ACI, Vol. 52, Dec. 1955, pp 455–479

2.18 Sinha, B P, Gerstle, K H and Tulin, LG, *Stress-Strain Relationships for Concrete Under Cyclic Loading*, Journal ACI, Vol. 61, Feb. 1964, pp 195–211

2.19 ACI Committee 439, *Effect of Steel Strength and Reinforcement Ratio on the Mode of Failure and Strain Energy Capacity of R.C. Beams*, Journal ACI, Vol. 66, March 1969, pp 165–173

2.20 Rüsch, H, *Researches Towards a General Flexural Theory for Structural Concrete*, Journal ACI, Vol. 57, July 1960, pp 1–28

2.21 *Building Code Requirements for Reinforced Concrete*, ACI Standard 318–89, Am. Conc. Inst., Detroit, Michigan, USA, 1989

2.22 Rao, P S and Menon, D, *Ultimate Strength of Tubular R C Tower Sections Under Wind Loading*, Indian Concrete Journal, Feb. 1995, pp 117–123

2.23 Wright, P J F, *Comments on an Indirect Tensile Test on Concrete Cylinders*, Magazine of Concrete Research, No. 20, 1955, p. 87

2.24 Tasuji, M E, Slate, F O and Nilson, A H, *Stress-Strain Response and Fracture of Concrete in Biaxial Loading*, Journal ACI, Vol. 75, July 1978, pp 306–312

2.25 Bresler, B and Pister, K S, *Strength of Concrete Under Combined Stresses*, Journal ACI, Vol. 55, Sept. 1958, pp 321–345

2.26 Richart, F E, Brandtzaeg, A and Brown, R L, *A Study of the Failure of Concrete Under Combined Stresses*, Univ. of Illinois Engineering Experimental Station, Bulletin No. 185, 1928

2.27 Gerstle, K H et al, *Strength of Concrete Under Multi-axial Stress States*, ACI Publication SP–55, Am. Conc. Inst., Detroit, Michigan, USA, 1978, pp 103–131

2.28 Park, R and Paulay, T, *Reinforced Concrete Structures*, John Wiley & Sons, Inc., New York, 1975

2.29 ACI Committee 209, *Prediction of Creep, Shrinkage and Temperature Effects in Concrete Structures*, SP–27, Am. Conc. Inst., Detroit, Michigan, USA, 1971, pp 51–93

2.30 CEB-FIP, *International Recommendations for the Design and Construction of Concrete Structures*, Comité Européen du Béton-Fédération Internationale de la Précontrainte, Paris, 1970

2.31 Gouthaman, A and Menon, D, *Increased Cover Specifications in IS 456 (2000) – Crack-width Implications in RC Slabs*, Indian Concrete Journal, Sept. 2001, pp 581–586

2.32 ACI Committee 201, *Guide to Durable Concrete*, Journal ACI, Vol. 74, 1977, pp 573–609

2.33 *Explanatory Handbook on Indian Standard Code of Practice for Plain and Reinforced Concrete* (*IS 456:1978*), Special Publication SP:24, Bureau of Indian Standards, New Delhi, 1983

2.34 Purushothaman, P, *Reinforced Concrete Structural Elements — Behaviour, Analysis and Design,* Tata McGraw Hill Publication Co. Ltd., New Delhi, 1984

2.35 Sengupta, A K, *Constitutive Models for Plain and Reinforced Concrete – An Overview*, Indian Concrete Journal, Aug. 2003, pp 1244-1250

CHAPTER 3

Basic Design Concepts

LEARNING OBJECTIVES

After studying this chapter, you will be able to:

- *Explain the methods for providing safety factors in structural design*
- *Discuss the different methods for design of reinforced concrete structures*
- *Explain Limit States Design and related Code requirements*

3.1 Introduction

Having gained a general overview of reinforced concrete structures (Chapter 1) and an understanding of the basic material properties (Chapter 2), it is time to get into the actual details of the design process. This chapter introduces the basic concepts relating to performance criteria in reinforced concrete design.

3.1.1 Design Considerations

The aim of structural design is to design a structure so that it fulfils its intended purpose during its intended lifetime with adequate *safety* (in terms of strength, stability and structural integrity), adequate *serviceability* (in terms of stiffness, durability, etc.) and *economy*.

Safety, serviceability, economy and sustainability are the primary design considerations.

Collapse of a structure or a part of it would include rupture, fracture, buckling, overturning, sliding, etc.

Serviceability relates to deflections, cracking, vibrations, etc., which affect the appearance and durability of the structure and the comforts of the occupants.

Safety implies that the likelihood of (partial or total) collapse of the structure is acceptably low not only under the normal expected loads (*service loads*), but also under abnormal but probable *overloads* (such as due to live loads, earthquake and/or extreme wind). Collapse may occur due to various possibilities such as exceeding the load-bearing capacity, overturning, sliding, buckling, fatigue, fracture, etc. Another related aspect of safety is *structural integrity* (see Introduction to Chapter 15). The objective here is to minimise the likelihood of *progressive collapse* triggered by a local failure.

Serviceability implies satisfactory performance of the structure under *service loads*, without discomfort to the user due to excessive *deflection, cracking, vibration*, etc. Other considerations that come under the purview of serviceability are *durability, impermeability*, *acoustic* and *thermal* *insulation*, etc. A design that adequately satisfies the 'safety' requirement need not necessarily satisfy the 'serviceability' requirement. For example, a thin reinforced concrete slab can be made safe against collapse (by suitable reinforcement); but if it is too thin, it is likely to result in excessive deflections, crack-widths and permeability (leakage), and the exposed steel becomes vulnerable to corrosion (thereby affecting durability).

Increasing the design *margins of safety* can enhance safety and serviceability; but this increases the cost of the structure. In considering overall **economy**, the increased cost associated with increased safety margins should be weighed against the potential losses that could result from any damage.

Two other terms, repeatedly being used here, need to be defined. The term **service load** (or **working load**) refers to the expected load to which the structure is subjected to in its normal use/service. It *does not include* any possible overloading or any *safety factors*. The term **ultimate load** refers to the maximum load the member or structure, as the case may be, can carry before failure.

3.1.2 Design Philosophies

Over the years, various design philosophies have evolved in different parts of the world, with regard to reinforced concrete design. A 'design philosophy' is built up on a few fundamental premises (assumptions), and is reflective of a way of thinking.

The earliest codified design philosophy is the **working stress method** of design (WSM). Close to a hundred years old, this traditional method of design, based on *linear elastic theory*, is still surviving in some countries (including India), although it is now side lined by the modern *limit states design* philosophy. In the recent (2000) revision of the Code (IS 456), the provisions relating to the WSM design procedure have been relegated from the main text of the Code to an Annexure (Annex. B) 'so as to give greater emphasis to limit state design' (as stated in the 'Foreword').

Design philosophies have evolved over time from elastic theory and working stress method, through ultimate load design and reliability-based methods, to limit states design and inelastic analysis (including moment redistribution and yield line theory).

Historically, the design procedure to follow the WSM was the **ultimate load method** of design (ULM), which was developed in the 1950s. Based on the (ultimate) strength of reinforced concrete at *ultimate loads*, it evolved and gradually gained acceptance. This method was introduced as an alternative to WSM in the ACI code in 1956 and the British Code in 1957, and subsequently in the Indian Code (IS 456) in 1964.

Probabilistic concepts of design developed over the years† and received a major impetus from the mid-1960s onwards. The philosophy was based on the theory that the various uncertainties in design could be handled more rationally in the mathematical framework of probability theory. The risk involved in the design was quantified in terms of a *probability of failure*. Such probabilistic methods came to be known as **reliability-based methods**. However, there was little acceptance for this theory in professional practice, mainly because the theory appeared to be complicated and intractable (mathematically and numerically).

In order to gain code acceptance, the probabilistic 'reliability-based' approach had to be simplified and reduced to a deterministic format involving *multiple (partial) safety factors* (rather than *probability of failure*). The European Committee for Concrete (CEB) and the International Federation for Prestressing (FIP) were among the earliest to introduce the philosophy of ***limit states method*** (LSM) of design, which is reliability-based in concept [Ref. 3.2]. Based on the CEB-FIP recommendations, LSM was introduced in the British Code CP 110 (1973) [now BS 8110 (1997)], and the Indian Code IS 456 (1978). In the United States, LSM was introduced in a slightly different format (*strength design* and *serviceability design*) in the ACI 318–71 (now ACI 318–19).

† For a detailed history, consult Ref. 3.1.

Thus, the past several decades witnessed an evolution in design philosophy – from the traditional 'working stress method', through the 'ultimate load method', to the modern 'limit states method' of design.

3.2 Working Stress Method (WSM)

This was the traditional method of design not only for reinforced concrete, but also for structural steel and timber design. The conceptual basis of WSM is simple. The method basically assumes that the structural material behaves in a *linear elastic* manner, and that adequate safety can be ensured by suitably restricting the stresses in the material induced by the expected 'working loads' (service loads) on the structure. As the specified *permissible* ('allowable') stresses are kept well below the material strength (i.e., in the initial phase of the stress-strain curve), the assumption of linear elastic behaviour is considered justifiable. The ratio of the strength of the material to the permissible stress is often referred to as the *factor of safety* and this provides for possible overloads.

The stresses under the applied loads are analysed by applying methods of 'strength of materials' such as the simple bending theory. In order to apply such methods to a composite material like reinforced concrete, *strain compatibility* (due to bond) is assumed, whereby the strain in the reinforcing steel is assumed to be equal to that in the adjoining concrete to which it is bonded. Furthermore, as the stresses in concrete and steel are assumed to be linearly related to their respective strains, it follows that the stress in steel is linearly related to that in the adjoining concrete by a constant factor (called the *modular ratio*), defined as the ratio of the modulus of elasticity of steel to that of concrete.

However, the main assumption of linear elastic behaviour and the tacit assumption that the stresses under working loads can be kept within the 'permissible stresses' are not found to be realistic. Many factors are responsible for this – such as the long-term effects of creep and shrinkage, the effects of stress concentrations, and other secondary effects. All such effects result in significant local increases in stresses into the inelastic range and *redistribution* of the calculated stresses[†]. Moreover, WSM does not provide a realistic measure of the actual factor of safety underlying a design. WSM also fails to discriminate between different types of loads that act simultaneously, but have different degrees of uncertainty. This can, at times, result in very unconservative designs, particularly when two different loads (say, dead loads and wind loads) have counteracting effects [Ref. 3.4].

Nevertheless, in defence against these and other shortcomings levelled against WSM, it may be stated that most structures designed in accordance with WSM have been generally performing satisfactorily for many years and generally have larger real safety factors than in LSM. The design usually results in relatively large sections of structural members (compared to ULM and LSM), thereby resulting in better serviceability performance (less deflections, crack-widths, etc.) under the usual working loads. The method is also notable for its essential simplicity – in concept, as well as application.

Although WSM has been superseded by LSM in the design code for general RC structures (IS 456) several decades ago, it continued to be the accepted method of design in India for certain special structures such as RC bridges (IRC 21), liquid storage tanks (IS 3370) and chimneys (IS 4998); however, LSM has now been incorporated in all these codes (IRC 112, IS 3370, IS 4998) in the past decade, in line with international practice.

[†] For example, in the case of reinforced concrete columns subjected to sustained service loads, it is found that redistribution of stresses takes place with time to such an extent that the 'permissible' stress in reinforcing steel will not only be exceeded, but the stress is even likely to reach yield stress – thereby upsetting the assumptions and calculations of WSM based on a constant modular ratio [Ref. 3.3].

Furthermore, serviceability (deflection, crack width, etc.) checks are carried out under *service loads* and at these load levels, the elastic theory is more appropriate.

3.3 Ultimate Load Method

With the growing realisation of the shortcomings of WSM in reinforced concrete design, and with increased understanding of the behaviour of reinforced concrete at *ultimate loads*, the ultimate load method of design (ULM) evolved in the 1950s and became an alternative to WSM. This method is sometimes also referred to as the *load factor method* or the *ultimate strength method.*

In this method, the stress condition at the state of impending *failure* of the section (i.e., at the *ultimate strength*) is analysed, and the non-linear stress-strain curves of concrete and steel are made use of. The concept of 'modular ratio' and its associated problems are avoided entirely in this method. The safety measure in the design is introduced by an appropriate choice of the *load factor*, defined as the ratio of the ultimate load (design load) to the working load. The ultimate load method makes it possible for different types of loads to be assigned different *load factors* under combined loading conditions, thereby overcoming the related shortcoming of WSM.

This method generally results in more slender sections, and often more economical designs of beams and columns (compared to WSM), particularly when high strength reinforcing steel and concrete are used.

However, the satisfactory 'strength' performance at *ultimate loads* does not guarantee satisfactory 'serviceability' performance at the normal *service loads*. The designs sometimes result in excessive deflections and crack-widths under service loads, owing to the slender sections resulting from the use of high strength reinforcing steel and concrete.

Moreover, the use of the non-linear stress-strain behaviour for the design of sections becomes truly meaningful only if appropriate *non-linear analysis* is performed on the structure for determining the load effects as well. Unfortunately, such a structural analysis is generally not performed on reinforced concrete structures (except in the *yield line theory* for slabs), owing to the difficulties in predicting the behaviour of 'plastic hinges' in reinforced concrete. Commonly, the distribution of stress resultants at ultimate load is taken as the distribution at service loads, magnified by the load factor(s); in other words, analysis is still based on linear elastic theory. This is illogical and clearly in error, because significant inelastic behaviour and *redistribution* of stress resultants takes place, as the loading is increased from service loads to ultimate loads.

> Yield line theory provides an economical and rational analysis of slabs and beam-slab systems at the limit state of collapse; this is discussed in detail in Chapter 11.

3.4 Probabilistic Analysis and Design

3.4.1 Uncertainties in Design

Safety margins are provided in design to safeguard against the risk of failure (*collapse* or *unserviceability*). In the traditional methods of design, these safety margins were assigned (in terms of 'permissible stresses' in WSM and 'load factors' in ULM) primarily on the basis of engineering judgement. Structures designed according to these traditional methods were found, in general, to be free from failure. However, the scientific basis underlying the provision of safety margins in design has been questioned time and again. As a result of persistent efforts over the past several decades in various fields of engineering, the science of reliability-based design evolved with the objective of providing a rational solution to the problem of 'adequate safety'.

The main variables in design calculations that are subject to varying degrees of uncertainty and randomness are the *loads* [Figure 3.1, for example], *material properties* [Figure 3.2, for example] and *dimensions*. Further, there are idealisations and simplifying assumptions used in the theories of structural analysis and design. There are also several other variable and often unforeseen factors that influence the prediction of strength and serviceability – such as construction methods, workmanship and quality control, intended service life of the structure, possible future change of use, frequency of loading, etc.

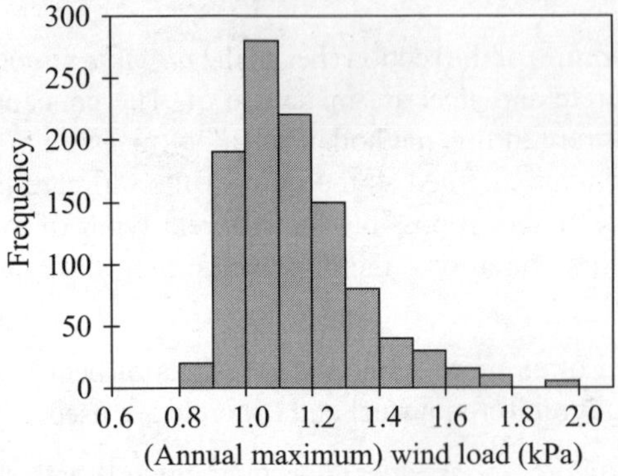

Fig. 3.1 Typical example of frequency distribution of wind loads on a structure.

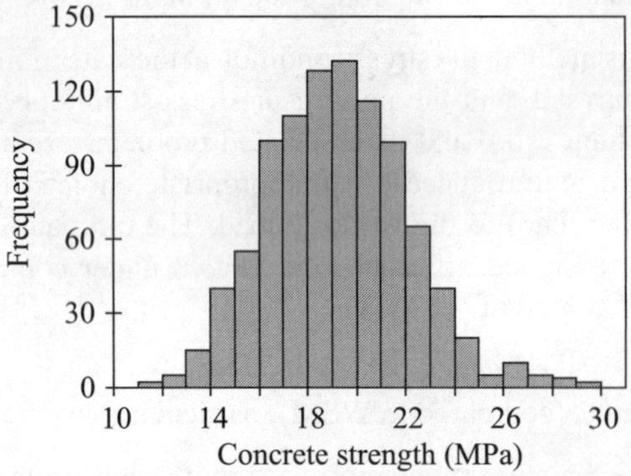

Fig. 3.2 Typical example of frequency distribution of concrete strength.

Thus, the problem facing the designer is to design economically on the basis of

> '...prediction through imperfect mathematical theories of the performance of structural systems constructed by fallible humans from material with variable properties, when these systems are subjected to an unpredictable natural environment' [Ref. 3.5]

It should be evident that any realistic, rational and quantitative representation of safety must be based on *statistical* and *probabilistic* analysis. [Recent attempts include the application of *fuzzy logic* also.]

> All variables in structural design – related to loads, material properties, design theories, environmental effects, as well as factors related to construction, such as workmanship, quality control, etc., – are subject to uncertainties and randomness.

3.4.2 Classical Reliability Models

In this section, a simple introduction to reliability-based design is given. Two simple 'classical' models are considered here – one for 'strength design' and the other for 'serviceability design'.

Strength Design Model

The (lifetime maximum) *load effect* ***S*** on a structure and the ultimate *resistance* ***R*** of the structure (both expressed in terms of a stress resultant such as bending moment at a critical section) are treated as *random variables* whose respective probability density functions $f_S(S)$ and $f_R(R)$ are known [Figure 3.3]. It is also assumed that ***S*** and ***R*** are statistically independent, which is approximately true for cases of normal static loading.

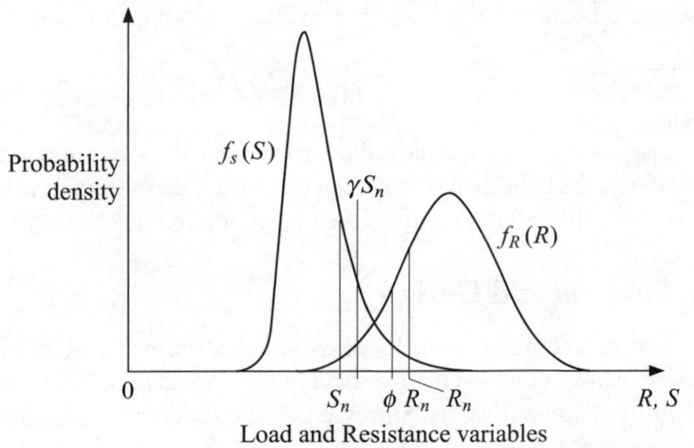

Fig. 3.3 Classical reliability model for strength design.

If $\boldsymbol{S} < \boldsymbol{R}$, the structure is expected to be safe, and if $\boldsymbol{S} > \boldsymbol{R}$, the structure is expected to fail. It is evident from Figure 3.3 that there is always a probability, however small, that failure may occur due to the exceeding of the load-bearing capacity of the structure (or structural element under consideration).

The *probability of failure* P_f may be calculated as follows:

$$P_f = \text{Prob}\left[\{R < S\} \cap \{0 < S < \infty\}\right]$$

$$P_f = \int_0^{\infty} f_S(S)\left[\int_0^{S} f_R(R)\,dR\right]dS \tag{3.1}$$

The desired margin(s) of safety (expressed in terms of one or more *factors of safety*) can thus be related to the desired ('target') probability of failure P_f.

Serviceability Design Model

Here, the variable to be considered is a *serviceability* parameter Δ (representing deflection, crack-width, etc.). Failure is considered to occur when the specified limit (maximum allowable limit of serviceability) Δ_{all} is exceeded [Figure 3.4]. It may be noted that unlike the previous model, here the limit defining failure is deterministic, and not probabilistic.

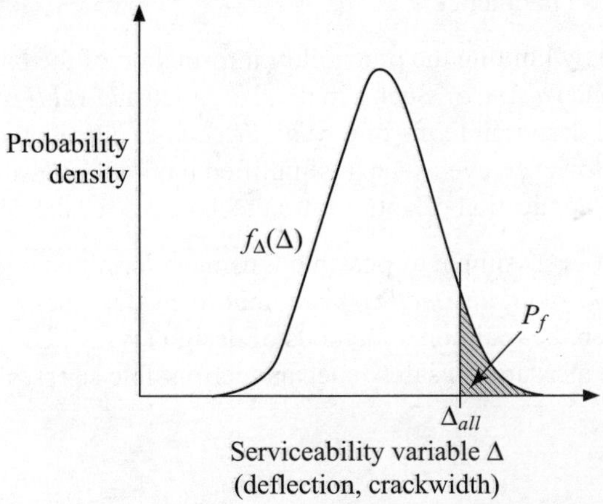

Fig. 3.4 Classical reliability model for serviceability design.

Accordingly, in this case, the probability of failure P_f may be obtained as follows:

Probability of failure can be brought down to an acceptable level, consistent with economy, but cannot be brought to zero.

$$P_f = \int_{\Delta_{all}}^{\infty} f_\Delta(\Delta)\, d\Delta \tag{3.2}$$

where f_Δ denotes the probability density function of Δ. Here also, the probability of failure can be restricted to a 'target' value, by suitably selecting the safety margin in the design.

3.4.3 Reliability Analysis and Design

From the discussions in the preceding section, it follows that a rational and quantitative solution to the problem of 'adequate safety' can be obtained by quantifying the acceptable risk in terms of target probability of failure or *target reliability*. ['Reliability' is expressed as the complement of the probability of failure, i.e., equal to $(1 - P_f)$.]

Evaluating the probability of failure P_f (or the reliability) underlying a given structure is termed *reliability analysis*, whereas designing a structure to meet the target reliability is termed *reliability design* [Ref. 3.6].

However, in practice, there are considerable difficulties involved in reliability analysis and design. Firstly, the problem becomes complicated when a large number of load and resistance 'basic variables' are involved, as is usually the case. The integral [Eq. 3.1] becomes multi-dimensional and quite formidable to solve (even with sophisticated techniques such as *simulation* with 'variance reduction'). Secondly, it is difficult to obtain statistical data regarding the joint probability distribution of the multiple variables. Thirdly, 'target reliabilities' are hard to define, since losses associated with failures are influenced by economic, social and moral considerations, which are difficult to quantify. Fourthly, it is now recognized that 'human error' is a major factor causing failure, and this is difficult to express probabilistically [Ref. 3.1].

3.4.4 Levels of Reliability Methods

There exist a number of *levels* of reliability analysis. These are differentiated by the extent of probabilistic information that is used [Ref. 3.1].

A full-scale probabilistic analysis (of the type discussed in Section 3.4.3) is generally described as a *Level III reliability method*. It is highly advanced, mathematically difficult, and generally used at a research level. It is clearly unsuitable for general use in practice.

The problem can be simplified by limiting the probability information of the basic variables to their 'second moment statistics' (i.e., *mean* and *variance*). Such a method is called a *Level II reliability method*. It evaluates the risk underlying a structural design in terms of a *reliability index* β (in lieu of the 'probability of failure' P_f used in Level III method). However, even such a 'simplified method' is unsuitable for day-to-day use in a design office, as it requires the application of optimisation techniques for the determination of β.

For code use, the method must be as simple as possible – using deterministic rather than probabilistic data. Such a method is called a *Level I reliability method*. The 'multiple safety factor' format of *limit states design* comes under this category. Even the traditional methods of design (WSM, ULM) belong to this category as they make use of deterministic measures of safety such as 'permissible stresses' and 'load factors'.

3.5 Limit States Method

The philosophy of the limit states method of design (LSM) represents a definite advancement over the traditional design philosophies. Unlike WSM, which based calculations on service load conditions alone, and unlike ULM, which based calculations on ultimate load conditions alone, LSM aims for a comprehensive and rational solution to the design problem, by considering *safety* at ultimate loads and *serviceability* at working loads.

> Limit states design attempts to design the structure so that the probability of reaching *Safety limit states* under likely overloads and *Serviceability limit states* under normal service loads is acceptably low.

The LSM philosophy uses a multiple safety factor format which attempts to provide *adequate safety* at ultimate loads as well as *adequate serviceability* at service loads, by considering all possible 'limit states' (defined in the next section). The selection of the various multiple safety factors is supposed to have a sound probabilistic basis, involving the separate consideration of different kinds of failure, types of materials and types of loads. In this sense, LSM is more than a mere extension of WSM and ULM. It represents a new 'paradigm' – a modern philosophy.

3.5.1 Limit States

A ***limit state*** is a state of impending *failure*, beyond which a structure ceases to perform its intended function satisfactorily, in terms of either *safety* or *serviceability*; i.e., it either *collapses* or becomes *unserviceable*.

There are two types of limit states:

1. *Ultimate limit states* (or 'limit states of collapse'), which deal with strength, overturning, sliding, buckling, fatigue fracture, etc.
2. *Serviceability limit states* which deal with discomfort to occupancy and/or malfunction, caused by excessive deflection, crack-width, vibration, leakage, etc., and also loss of durability, etc.

3.5.2 Multiple Safety Factor Formats

The objective of limit states design is to ensure that the probability of any limit state being reached is acceptably low. This is made possible by specifying appropriate *multiple safety factors* for each limit state (Level I reliability). Of course, in order to be meaningful, the specified values of the safety factors should result (more-or-less) in a 'target reliability'. Evidently, this requires a proper reliability study to be done by the code-making authorities.

Most national codes introduced multiple safety factors in limit states design in the 1970s – primarily based on experience, tradition and engineering judgement [Ref. 3.7]. Subsequently, codes have been engaged in the process of *code calibration* – to determine the range of the reliability index β (or its equivalent probability of failure P_f) underlying the specified safety factors for different practical situations [Ref. 3.1, 3.6, 3.8]. With every code revision, conscious attempts are made to specify more rational reliability-based safety factors, in order to achieve practical designs that are *satisfactory* and *consistent* in terms of the degree of safety, reliability and economy.

3.5.3 Load and Resistance Factor Design Format

> Conceptually, the attempt is to ensure safety by over-estimating the load effects and under-estimating the member/structure strength by applying load and resistance factors respectively to their nominal values.

Of the many multiple safety factor formats in vogue, perhaps the simplest to understand is the Load and Resistance Factor Design (LRFD) format, which is adopted by the ACI Code [Ref. 3.5, 3.8, 3.9]. Applying the LRFD concept to the classical reliability model [Figure 3.3], adequate safety requires the following condition to be satisfied:

$$\textit{Design Resistance } (\phi R_n) \geq \textit{Design Load effect } (\gamma S_n) \qquad (3.3)$$

where R_n and S_n denote the nominal or characteristic values of *resistance* ***R*** and *load effect* ***S***, respectively; ϕ and γ denote the ***strength reduction factor*** and ***load factor***, respectively. The strength reduction factor ϕ accounts for 'under-strength', i.e., possible shortfall in the computed 'nominal' resistance, owing to uncertainties related to material strengths, dimensions, theoretical assumptions, etc., and accordingly, it is less than unity. On the contrary, the load factor γ, which accounts for 'overloading' and the uncertainties associated with S_n, is generally greater than unity.

Eq. 3.3 may be rearranged as

$$S_n < \frac{R_n}{\gamma/\varphi} \qquad (3.3\text{ a})$$

which is representative of the safety concept underlying WSM, γ/ϕ here denoting the 'factor of safety' applied to the material strength, in order to arrive at the *permissible stress* for design.

Alternatively, Eq. 3.3 may be rearranged as

$$R_n \geq (\gamma/\varphi)\, S_n \qquad (3.3\text{ b})$$

which is representative of the safety concept underlying ULM, γ/ϕ here denoting the so-called 'load factor' (ULM terminology) applied to the load in order to arrive at the *ultimate load* for design.

3.5.4 Partial Safety Factor Format

The multiple safety factor format recommended by CEB–FIP [Ref. 3.2], and adopted by the Code, is the so-called *partial safety factor* format, which may be expressed as follows:

$$R_d \geq S_d \qquad (3.4)$$

where R_d is the *design resistance* computed using the reduced material strengths $0.67f_{ck}/\gamma_c$ and f_y/γ_s, involving two separate *partial (material) safety factors* γ_c (for concrete) and γ_s (for steel), in lieu of a single overall strength reduction factor ϕ, and S_d is the *design load effect* computed for the enhanced loads ($\gamma_D.DL$, $\gamma_L.LL$, $\gamma_Q.QL$,) involving separate *partial load factors* γ_D (for dead load), γ_L (for live load), γ_Q (for wind *or*† earthquake load). The other terms involved are the *nominal* compressive strength of concrete $0.67f_{ck}$ (refer Section 2.8.5) and the *nominal* yield strength of steel f_y on the side of the resistance, and the *nominal* load effects DL, LL and QL representing dead loads, live loads and wind/earthquake loads, respectively.

It may be noted that, whereas the multiplication factor ϕ is generally less than unity, the dividing factors γ_c and γ_s are greater than unity – giving the same effect. All the *load factors* are generally greater than unity, because over-estimation usually results in improved safety. However, one notable exception to this rule is the dead load factor γ_D which is taken as 0.8 or 0.9 while considering stability against overturning or sliding, or while considering reversal of stresses when dead loads are combined with wind/earthquake loads; in such cases, under-estimating the counteracting effects of dead load results in greater safety.

† Either wind *or* earthquake loads is considered at a time. The probability of the joint occurrence of an earthquake as well as an extreme wind is considered to be negligible.

One other effect to be considered in the selection of load factors is the reduced probability of different types of loads (DL, LL, QL) acting simultaneously at their peak values. Thus, it is usual to reduce the load factors when three or more types of loads are considered acting concurrently; this is referred to sometimes as the 'load combination effect'.

3.6 Code Recommendations for Limit States Design

The salient features of LSM, as prescribed by the Code, are covered here. Details of the design procedure for various limit states of collapse and serviceability are covered in subsequent chapters.

3.6.1 Characteristic Strengths and Loads

The general definition of the **characteristic strength** of a material (concrete or steel) was given in Section 2.6.1. It corresponds to the 5-percentile strength value. In the case of reinforcing steel, it refers to the 'specified yield stress' as mentioned in Section 2.14.1.

The **characteristic load** is defined as the load that *'has a 95 per cent probability of not being exceeded during the life of the structure'* (Cl. 36.2 of the Code). However, in the absence of statistical data regarding loads, the *nominal* values specified for dead, live and wind loads are to be taken from IS 875 (Parts 1 & 2 : 1987 and Part 3 : 2015) and the values for 'seismic loads' (earthquake loads) from IS 1893 (Part 1) : 2016.

3.6.2 Partial Safety Factors for Materials

The ***design strength*** (i.e., the ***factored strength***) of concrete or reinforcing steel is obtained by dividing the **characteristic strength** by the appropriate **partial safety factor**. In the case of concrete, while f_{ck} is the characteristic *cube* strength, the strength of concrete in the *actual structure* is taken as 0.67 f_{ck} [refer Section 2.8.5], and hence the *design strength* of concrete is $0.67 f_{ck}/\gamma_c$.

For *ultimate limit states*, the Code specifies $\gamma_c = 1.5$ and $\gamma_s = 1.15$. A higher partial safety factor has been assigned to concrete, compared to reinforcing steel, evidently because of the higher variability associated with it.

For *serviceability limit states*, $\gamma_c = \gamma_s = 1.0$. A safety factor of unity is appropriate here, because the interest is in estimating the *actual* deflections and crack-widths under the service loads, and not 'safe' (conservative) values.

3.6.3 Partial Safety Factors for Loads

Three different load combinations have been specified (Cl. 36.4.1 of Code) involving the combined effects of dead loads (DL), 'imposed' or live loads (LL) and wind/earthquake loads (QL).

The code recommends the following weighted combinations for estimating the *ultimate load effect* (UL) and the *serviceability load effect* (SL):

Ultimate limit states

- UL = 1.5 (DL + LL)
- UL = 1.5 (DL + QL) or (0.9 DL + 1.5 QL)
- UL = 1.2 (DL + LL + QL)

The reduced load factor of 1.2 in the third combination above recognises the reduced probability of all the three loads acting together at their possible peak values.

For the purpose of structural design, the design resistance (using the material partial safety factors) should be greater than or equal to the maximum load effect that arises from the above load combinations [Eq. 3.4].

The Code makes a departure from the usual convention (adopted by other codes) of assigning a *lower* load factor for DL in comparison with the more variable LL – apparently on the grounds that it is more convenient in practice to deal with all *gravity* loads (dead plus live) together [Ref. 3.10]. Besides, applying an average load factor of 1.5 to the combined gravity loads is, in general, likely to have about the same effect as, say, (1.4 DL + 1.6 LL) – which is adopted by BS 8110.

Serviceability limit states

- SL = 1.0 (DL + LL)
- SL = 1.0 (DL + QL)
- SL = (1.0 DL) + (0.8 LL) + (0.8 QL)

The use of a partial load factor of unity, in general, is appropriate, because it implies *service load* conditions – which is required for 'serviceability design'. However, when live loads and wind loads are combined, it is improbable that both will reach their characteristic values simultaneously; hence a lower load factor is assigned to LL and QL in the third combination, to account for the reduced probability of concurrent occurrence at peak values.

Other Load Combinations

Other loads to be considered, but not listed in the Code (Table 18) include the effects of creep, shrinkage, temperature variation and support settlement. Although a load factor of unity may be appropriate while considering these load effects (in addition to gravity loads) for 'serviceability limit states', the following combinations are recommended [Ref. 3.10] for 'ultimate limit states':

- UL = 0.75 (1.4 DL + 1.4 TL + 1.7 LL)
- UL = 1.4 (DL + TL)

where TL represents the structural effects due to temperature variation, creep, shrinkage or support settlement.

> *Flexural compression* refers to compression caused by bending moment (in flexural members such as beams and slabs), whereas *direct compression* refers to axial compression (as in struts and columns subject to pure axial loading) and *eccentric compression* refers to compression caused by a combination of bending moment and axial compression (as in beam-columns in framed buildings).

3.6.4 Design Stress-Strain Curve for Concrete

The *characteristic* and *design* stress-strain curves specified by the Code for concrete in ***flexural compression*** are depicted in Figure 3.5. The maximum stress in the concrete in the structure is restricted to 0.67 f_{ck} for reasons explained in Section 2.8.5. The curves consist of a parabola in the initial region up to a strain of 0.002 (where the slope becomes zero), and a straight line thereafter, at a constant stress level up to an *ultimate strain* of 0.0035.

For the purpose of *limit states design*, the appropriate partial safety factor γ_c has to be applied, and γ_c is equal to 1.5 for the consideration of ultimate limit states [refer Section 3.6.2]. Thus, the factored or 'design strength curve' is obtained by simply scaling down the ordinates of the strength curve for concrete in the structure – dividing by γ_c [Figure 3.5]. Accordingly, the maximum *design stress* becomes equal to $0.447f_{ck}$, and the formula for the design compressive stress f_c corresponding to any strain $\varepsilon \leq 0.0035$ is given by

$$f_c = \begin{cases} 0.447\, f_{ck} \left[2\left(\dfrac{\varepsilon}{0.002}\right) - \left(\dfrac{\varepsilon}{0.002}\right)^2 \right] & \text{for } \varepsilon < 0.002 \\ 0.447\, f_{ck} & \text{for } 0.002 \leq \varepsilon \leq 0.0035 \end{cases} \tag{3.5}$$

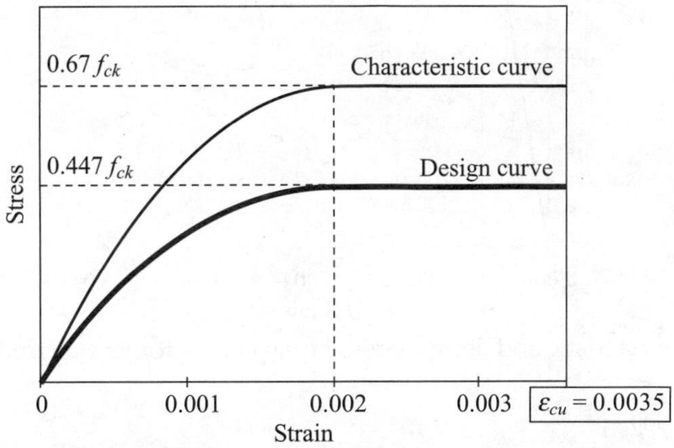

Fig. 3.5 Characteristic and design stress-strain curves for concrete in flexural compression.

When concrete is subjected to ***uniform compression***, as in the case of a concentrically loaded short column, the *ultimate strain* is limited to 0.002, and the corresponding *maximum design stress* is $0.447f_{ck}$. The stress-strain curve has no relevance in the limit state of collapse under (pure) compression of concrete, and hence is not given by the Code.

When concrete is subject to ***axial compression combined with flexure***, the ultimate strain is limited to a value between 0.002 and 0.0035, depending on the location of the neutral axis [refer Chapter 13]. The maximum design stress level remains unchanged at $0.447f_{ck}$.

3.6.5 Design Stress-Strain Curve for Reinforcing Steel

The *characteristic* and *design* stress-strain curves specified by the Code for various grades of reinforcing steel (in tension or compression) are shown in Figures 3.6 and 3.7. The design yield strength f_{yd} is obtained by dividing the specified yield strength f_y by the partial safety factor $\gamma_s = 1.15$ (for ultimate limit states); accordingly, $f_{yd} = 0.87 f_y$. In the case of mild steel (Fe 250), which has a well-defined yield point, the behaviour is assumed to be perfectly linear-elastic up to a design stress level of $0.87 f_y$ and a corresponding design yield strain $\varepsilon_y = 0.87 f_y / E_s$; for larger strains, the design stress level remains constant at $0.87 f_y$ [Figure 3.6].

In the case of cold-worked bars (Fe 415 and Fe 500), which have no specific yield point, the transition from linear elastic behaviour to nonlinear behaviour is assumed to occur at a stress level equal to 0.8 times f_y in the *characteristic* curve and 0.8 times f_{yd} in the *design* curve. The full design yield strength $0.87 f_y$ is assumed to correspond to a 'proof strain' of 0.002; i.e., the design yield strain ε_y is to be taken as $0.87 f_y / E_s + 0.002$, as shown in Figure 3.7. The non-linear region is approximated as piecewise linear segments. The coordinates of the salient points of the design stress-strain curve for Fe 415 and Fe 500 are listed in Tables 3.1 and 3.2. The design stress, corresponding to any given strain, can be obtained by linear interpolation from Table 3.2.

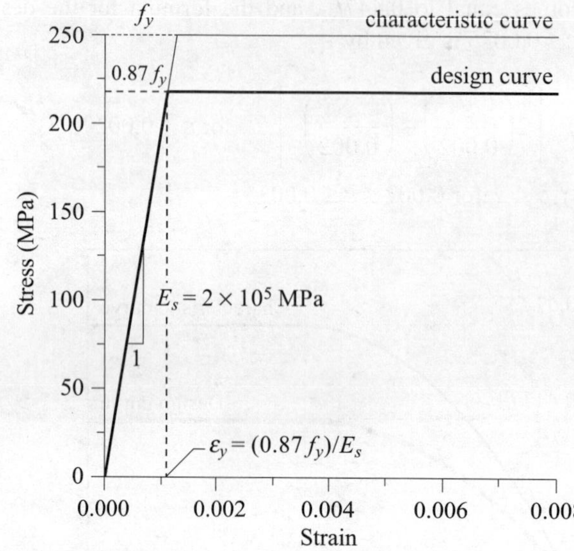

Fig. 3.6 Characteristic and design stress-strain curves for **Fe 250** grade mild steel.

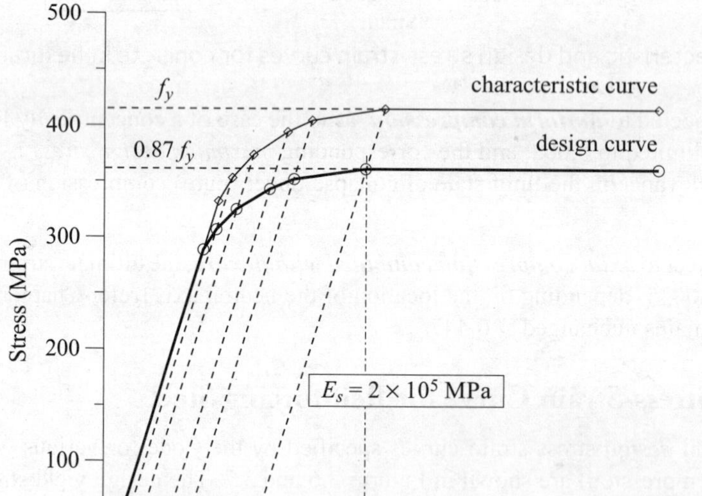

Fig. 3.7 Characteristic and design stress-strain curves for **Fe 415** grade cold-worked steel[†].

† The characteristic and design stress-strain curves for Fe 500 grade cold-worked steel is similar; in this case, f_y shall be taken as 500 MPa (instead of 415 MPa).

It may be noted that whereas in the case of concrete [Figure 3.5], the partial safety factor γ_c is applicable at *all* stress levels, in the case of reinforcing steel, the partial safety factor γ_s is applicable only for the inelastic region [Figures 3.6, 3.7]. This may be ascribed to the fact that in the case of concrete, the stress-strain curve (including the short-term modulus of elasticity) is directly affected by changes in the compressive strength of concrete [refer Figure 2.7]; however, this is not the case for steel whose modulus of elasticity is independent of the variations in the yield strength.

Table 3.1 *Salient points on the stress-strain curve for cold-worked steels*

Design Stress/(f_{yd})	.80	.85	.90	.95	.975	1.0
Inelastic Strain	0.0000	0.0001	0.0003	0.0007	0.0010	0.0020

Table 3.2 *Design stresses at specified strains for (a)* **Fe 415** *and (b)* **Fe 500**

Fe 415		**Fe 500**	
Strain	**Stress (*MPa*)**	**Strain**	**Stress (*MPa*)**
0.000 00	0.0	0.000 00	0.0
0.001 44	288.7	0.001 74	347.8
0.001 63	306.7	0.001 95	369.6
0.001 92	324.8	0.002 26	391.3
0.002 41	342.8	0.002 77	413.0
0.002 76	351.8	0.003 12	423.9
0.003 80	360.9	0.004 17	434.8

REVIEW QUESTIONS

3.1 Discuss the merits and demerits of the traditional methods of design (working stress method, ultimate load method).

3.2 Explain how *creep* of concrete affects *modular ratio*.

3.3 Demonstrate the difference between *deterministic* design and *probabilistic* design.

3.4 Show that an alternative expression for the *probability of failure* for the classical reliability problem of safety [refer Eq. 3.1] can be obtained as

$$P_f = 1 - \int_0^{\infty} f_R(R)\left[\int_0^{S} f_S(S)\,dS\right]dR$$

3.5 Why is it difficult to undertake a fully probabilistic design of a structure in practice?

3.6 Explain *limit state*. Discuss the different 'limit states' to be considered in reinforced concrete design.

3.7 The maximum moments at a section in a reinforced concrete beam (end section) are obtained (for different independent service load conditions) from structural analysis, as −50 kNm, −80 kNm, ±120 kNm and ±180 kNm under dead loads, live loads, wind loads and earthquake loads respectively. Determine the *ultimate design* moments ('negative' as well as 'positive') to be considered (as per the Code) for the limit state of collapse (flexure).

3.8 Explain the basis for the selection of partial safety factors (for loads and materials) by the Code for 'serviceability limit states'.

3.9 Discuss why is the partial safety factor for concrete (γ_c) greater than that for reinforcing steel (γ_s) in the consideration of ultimate limit states?

3.10 Why is it that γ_c is applicable at all stress levels whereas γ_s is applicable only near the 'yield stress' level?

3.11 Is the use of a single (overall) *strength reduction factor* ϕ more suitable than two separate *partial safety factors* γ_c and γ_s? Give your views.

3.12 Describe *calibration* of codes and why is it required.

3.13 Determine the *design stress* levels (at ultimate limit states) in (a) Fe 250, (b) Fe 415 and (c) Fe 500 grades of steel, corresponding to tensile strains of (i) 0.001, (ii) 0.002, (iii) 0.003 and (iv) 0.004.

REFERENCES

3.1 Madsen, H O, Krenk, S and Lind, N C, *Methods of Structural Safety*, Prentice-Hall Inc., Englewood Cliffs, N J, 1986

3.2 CEB-FIP, *International Recommendations for the Design and Construction of Concrete Structures*, Comité Européen du Béton-Fédération Internationale de la Précontrainte, Paris, 1970

3.3 Park, R and Paulay, T, *Reinforced Concrete Structures*, John Wiley & Sons, Inc., New York, 1975

3.4 Rao, P S and Menon, D, *Safety Considerations in Wind-Resistant Design of R C Chimneys*, Journal of Instn. of Engineers (India) — Civil Engg Div., Vol. 76, Part 4, pp 242–248

3.5 Cornell, C A, *A Probability-Based Structural Code*, Journal ACI, Vol. 66, Dec. 1969, pp 974–985

3.6 Ranganathan, R, *Reliability Analysis and Design of Structures*, Tata McGraw-Hill Publication Co. Ltd., New Delhi, 1990

3.7 Ellingwood, B, *Reliability Basis for Load and Resistance Factors for R C Design*, NBS Building Science Series 110, National Bureau of Standards, Washington DC, 1978

3.8 Ellingwood, B, Galambos, T V, MacGregor, J G and Cornell, C A, *Development of a Probability Based Load Criterion for American National Standard A58*, Special Publication No.577, National Bureau of Standards, Washington D.C., 1980

3.9 Ravindra, M K and Galambos, T V, *Load and Resistance Factor Design for Steel*, ASCE Journal of Struct. Div., Vol. 104, Sept. 1978, pp 1337–1353

3.10 *Explanatory Handbook on Indian Standard Code of Practice for Plain and Reinforced Concrete (IS 456:1978)*, Special Publication SP:24, Bureau of Indian Standards, New Delhi, 1983

CHAPTER 4

Behaviour in Flexure

LEARNING OBJECTIVES

After studying this chapter, you will be able to:

- *Discuss flexural behaviour of RC members under loading up to collapse*
- *Derive formulae for stresses, strains and moments of resistance of RC flexural members at service and ultimate loads*
- *Apply Code provisions and prepare helpful analysis/design aids*
- *Do analysis for stresses and flexural strengths of beams of various types*

4.1 Introduction

Flexure or *bending* is commonly encountered in structural elements such as *beams* and *slabs* (as well as *plates* and *shells*) which are transversely loaded. Flexure also occurs in *columns* and *walls* that are subjected to eccentric loading, lateral pressures and/or lateral displacements.

'Flexure' usually occurs in combination with *transverse shear*, and sometimes in combination with other structural actions, such as *axial compression* (or *tension*) and *torsion*. For convenience, the behaviour of reinforced concrete in flexure alone is considered in this chapter. The effects of shear, torsion and axial force are considered separately in subsequent chapters, as also their combined effects.

Furthermore, the actual *design* of reinforced concrete elements (in flexure) is deferred to the next chapter (Chapter 5). The scope of this chapter is limited to discussing the overall behaviour of reinforced concrete in flexure, and includes the *analysis* of beam sections.

4.1.1 Two Kinds of Problems: Analysis and Design

There are two kinds of problems commonly encountered in structural design practice. In the first kind, termed *analysis* (or 'review') problems, the complete cross-sectional dimensions (including details of reinforcing steel), as well as the material properties of the member are known. It is desired to compute (1) the stresses in the materials (or deflections, crack-widths, etc.) under given loads or (2) the allowable or ultimate bending moments (loads) that the member can resist. The 'analysis' referred to here (with regard to *stresses* in a given beam *section*) should not be confused with 'structural analysis', which refers to the determination of *stress resultants* (i.e., bending moments, shear forces, etc.) in an entire *structure* (such as a frame) or a structural element (such as a beam).

The second type of problem involves *design.* In this case, the load effects (stress resultants) are known from structural analysis, and it is required to select appropriate grades of materials and to arrive at the member dimensions and reinforcement details required to resist the load effects. It is evident that there are many possible solutions to a design problem, whereas the solution to an analysis problem is unique. As mentioned earlier, the topic of 'design for flexure' is dealt with in the next chapter.

4.1.2 Bending Moments in Beams from Structural Analysis

The beam is a very commonly used structural element. It may exist independently, or may form a component of a structural framework (as in 'grids' and 'rigid frames'). In all such cases, the beam is treated as a *one-dimensional* (line) element (with known material and geometric properties) for the purpose of structural analysis.

Commonly, at any point in the beam line element, the stress resultants to be determined from structural analysis are the *bending moment* (M) and the transverse *shear force* (V). A *twisting moment* (T) may also exist in some situations (e.g., when the loading is eccentric to the 'shear centre' axis). Frequently, an *axial force* (N) – tensile or compressive – exists in combination with M and V, as shown in Figure 4.1. The effect of the axial force may be neglected if the normal stresses induced by it are relatively low (as is often the case in *beams*, unlike *columns*), and especially so when it is compressive. Occasionally, a beam may be subject to *biaxial bending*, involving bending moments and transverse shear forces in two orthogonal planes (as when a beam is laterally loaded, both vertically and horizontally).

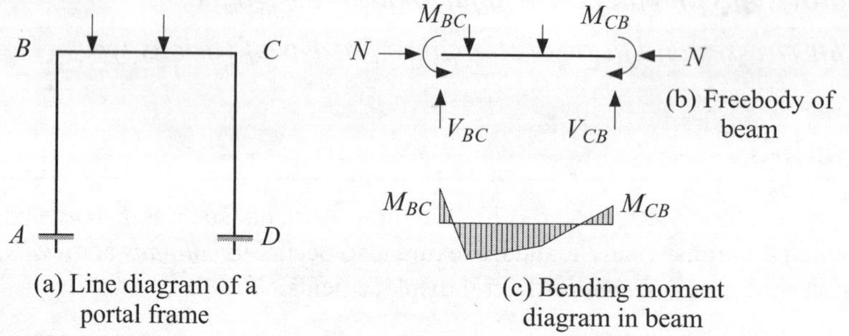

Fig. 4.1 Structural analysis to determine bending moments in a beam.

In the present context, it is assumed that the distribution of bending moments along the length of the beam is known from structural analysis [Figure 4.1(c)]. The effect of uniaxial bending moment (M) alone at a given beam section is investigated in this chapter.

4.1.3 From Bending Moment to Flexural Stresses

Although in structural analysis, it suffices to treat the beam as a one-dimensional element, the fact is that the beam is actually three-dimensional. Each point on the one-dimensional beam element is representative of a cross-section (usually rectangular) of the actual three-dimensional beam. The 'bending moment' at any section of the beam due to the action of external load gives rise to *normal stresses* in the beam cross section (compressive and tensile) in concrete and reinforcing steel. The resultant of these stresses is the resisting moment (*cf.* theory of simple bending), which equilibrates with the applied moment at the section under consideration.

In the sections to follow in this chapter, the relationship between the bending moment (M) and the flexural (normal) stresses in concrete and steel (at various stages of loading) is described.

4.2 Theory of Flexure for Homogeneous Materials

Reinforced concrete is a *composite* material. Before developing a theory of flexure for such a material, it is instructive to review the conventional 'theory of flexure' which was originally developed for a *homogeneous* material (such as structural steel). [It is presumed that the reader is familiar with the *simple theory of bending/ flexure* and only a brief recapitulation is presented here].

4.2.1 Fundamental Assumption

> **Regions of members where the assumption of plane section remaining plane is valid are known as 'flexural regions' where theory of flexure is applicable. Regions where the assumption is not valid are designated 'disturbed or discontinuous' regions.**

The fundamental assumption in flexural theory is that plane cross-sections (taken normal to the longitudinal axis of the beam) remain *plane* even after the beam bends. This assumption is generally found to be valid for beams of usual proportions† [Ref. 4.1, 4.2]. For initially straight members, the assumption implies that the distribution of *normal strains* across the beam cross-section is *linear* [Figure 4.2(a), (b)]. That is, the normal strain at any points in the beam section is proportional to its distance from the *neutral* axis. For the case of a 'sagging' (designated 'positive' in this book) moment, as indicated in Figure 4.2, the top 'fibres' (above the neutral axis) are subjected to compression and the bottom 'fibres' (below the neutral axis) to tension, with the maximum strains occurring at the most extreme (top/bottom) surfaces. Of course, if

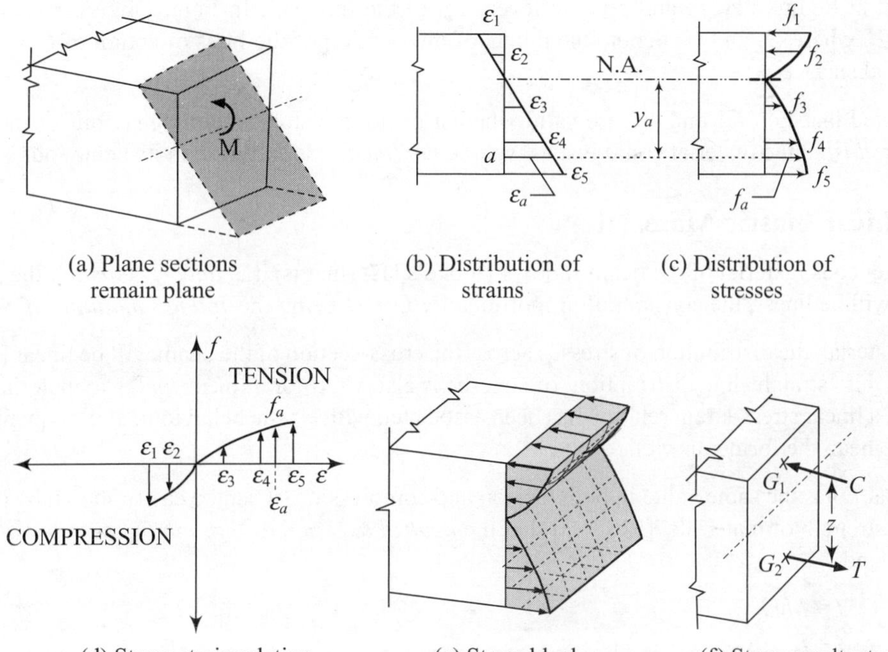

Fig. 4.2 Homogeneous section under flexure.

† In 'deep beams' (i.e., beams whose depths are comparable to their spans), this assumption is not valid as significant *warping* of the cross-section occurs, on account of shear deformations.

the moment is 'hogging' ('negative'), as in the case of a cantilever, the top fibres will be in tension and the bottom fibres in compression.

4.2.2 Distribution of Stresses

The normal stress induced by flexure (*flexural stress*) at any point such as *a* in Figure 4.2(b) depends on the normal strain ε_a at that level. This stress f_a corresponding to strain ε_a is determined from the stress-strain relation for the material [Figure 4.2(d)]. Thus, corresponding to each strain level (such as ε_1, ε_2, ε_3, ...) in Figure 4.2(b), the corresponding stress level (f_1, f_2, f_3), indicated in Figure 4.2(c) is obtainable from the stress-strain curve [Figure 4.2(d)]. As the distribution of strains is *linear* (with strains increasing in the *y*-direction from a zero value at the neutral axis) and as the stress-strain curve is plotted on a linear scale (with strains increasing along the *x*-axis), it follows that the distribution of stresses in the beam section will be identical to that in the stress-strain curve, but turned through 90 degrees.

The location of the *neutral axis* (NA) and the magnitude of the *flexural stresses* are obtained by solving two simple equations of static equilibrium:

$$C = T \tag{4.1}$$

$$M = Cz \tag{4.2a}$$

or

$$M = Tz \tag{4.2b}$$

where *C* and *T* denote the resultant compression and tension acting on the cross section respectively [refer 'stress block' in Figure 4.2(e)], and *z* is the lever arm of the 'couple'. In Figure 4.2(f), *z* is shown as the distance G_1G_2, where G_1 and G_2 denote the points of intersection of the lines of action of *C* and *T* with the cross-sectional surface.

It may be noted that Eqs 4.1 and 4.2 are valid whether or not the stress-strain behaviour of the material is *linear* and/or *elastic*; the material could just as well be *nonlinear* and *inelastic* in its behaviour.

4.2.3 Linear Elastic Material

If the homogeneous material of the beam follows Hooke's law (that is, it is *linearly elastic*), the stress-strain distribution will be linear, the constant of proportionality $E = f/\varepsilon$ being the *Young's modulus of elasticity*.

For such a material, the distribution of stresses across the cross-section of the beam will be linear [Figure 4.3]. Incidentally, this 'straight-line distribution' of stresses is also valid for a linear *inelastic* material. However, traditionally, a linear stress-strain relation has been associated with elastic behaviour, and frequently the latter is implied to mean the former as well.

Assuming that *E* has the same value in both tension and compression, it can be easily shown by applying the methods of 'strength of materials' [Ref. 4.3] that the *neutral axis passes through the centroid of the section* [Figure 4.3], and

$$f = My/I \tag{4.3}$$

$$M = f_{max} I / y_{max} \tag{4.4}$$

where

$f \equiv$ flexural stress at any point at a distance *y* from the neutral axis,
$f_{max} \equiv$ flexural stress in the extreme fibre ($y = y_{max}$),
$I \equiv$ second moment of area about the neutral axis, and
$M \equiv$ bending moment at the section.

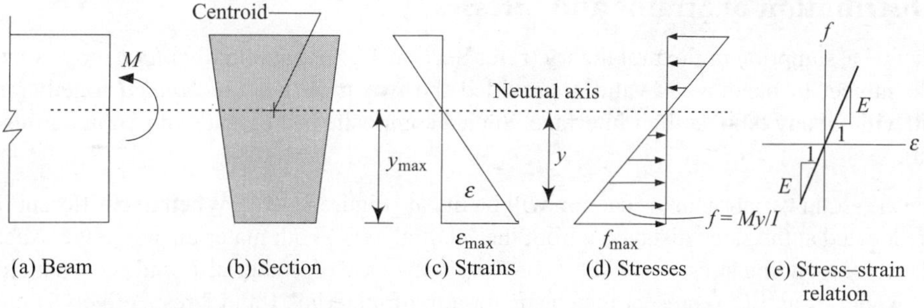

Fig. 4.3 Linear elastic stress distribution in flexure.

4.3 Linear Elastic Analysis of Composite Sections

The analysis described in Section 4.2.3 [including Eqs 4.3, 4.4] is not directly applicable to *non-homogeneous* materials like reinforced concrete. For 'composite' materials, made of two (or more) different (linear elastic) materials [Figure 4.4(a)], the theory has to be suitably modified.

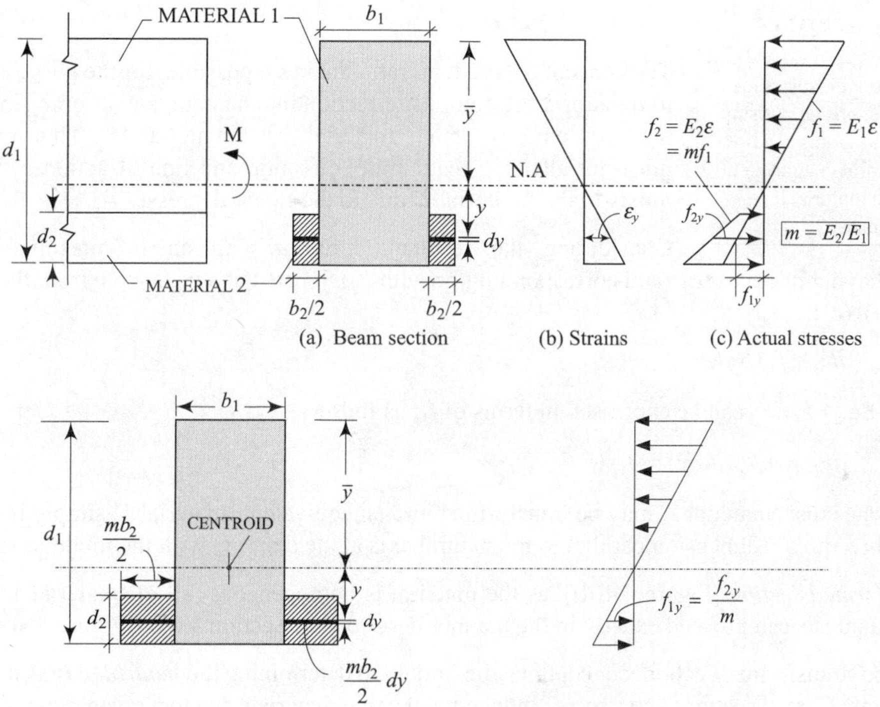

Fig. 4.4 Concept of 'transformed section'.

4.3.1 Distribution of Strains and Stresses

The fundamental assumption in flexural theory (refer Section 4.2.1) that initially *plane cross-sections remain plane*, while subject to bending, is valid – provided the two materials are *bonded* together to act as an integral unit, without any 'slip' at their interface. Such a composite beam, made of two materials is shown in Figure 4.4(a).

Accordingly, the strain variation in the section will be linear [Figure 4.4(b)]. When two different (but bonded) materials are located at the same distance y from the 'neutral axis', both materials will have exactly the same strain ε_y. The corresponding stresses will be $f_{1y} = E_1\varepsilon_y$ in the case of 'material 1' and $f_{2y} = E_2\varepsilon_y$ in the case of 'material 2', where E_1 and E_2 represent the elastic moduli of materials 1 and 2 respectively [Figure 4.4(c)].

The stress f_{2y} in the 'material 2' can be expressed in terms of the corresponding stress f_{1y} in the 'material 1' (at points located at the same distance y from the neutral axis) as follows:

$$f_{2y} = mf_{1y} \tag{4.5}$$

$$m = E_2/E_1 \tag{4.6}$$

The ratio of the two moduli of elasticity, m, is called the *modular ratio*.

4.3.2 Concept of 'Transformed Section'

> Within the linear elastic range, composite sections comprising two or more materials can be transformed into an equivalent section of one material for analysis purposes.

The concept of 'modular ratio' makes it possible, for the purpose of analysis, to transform the composite section into an equivalent homogeneous section made up entirely of one material (say, 'material 1'). This transformation must not alter the magnitude, direction and line of action of the resultant *forces* in the 'material 2' due to the flexural stresses f_{2y}.

Considering the resultant force dF_2 in an infinitesimal element of 'material 2' having thickness dy (and corresponding breadth b_2), located at a distance y from the neutral axis [Figure 4.4(a), (c)],

$$dF_2 = f_{2y}(b_2dy)$$

Substituting Eq. 4.5, dF_2 can be expressed in terms of f_{1y} as follows:

$$dF_2 = mf_{1y}(b_2dy) = f_{1y}(mb_2)dy \tag{4.7}$$

Eq. 4.7 indicates that 'material 2' may be transformed into an equivalent 'material 1' simply by multiplying the original breadth b_2 (dimension parallel to the neutral axis at the depth y) with the modular ratio m.

In the *transformed section* [Figure 4.4(d)], as the material is homogeneous (all of 'material 1') and 'linear elastic', the analysis can proceed exactly in the manner described in Section 4.2.3; [Figure 4.4(e)].

The use of the 'transformed section' concept may be limited to determining the *neutral axis* as the 'centroidal axis' of the transformed section. The stresses induced in the two materials due to a given moment can then be determined by applying the basic equations of static equilibrium [Eqs 4.1, 4.2].

Alternatively, the stresses can be computed with the 'transformed section' itself, by applying the flexure formula [Eq. 4.3]; in this case the second moment of area I_g of the 'transformed section' has to be considered. The stresses thus computed with reference to 'material 1' can be converted to the equivalent stresses in 'material 2' by involving the 'modular ratio' concept [Eq. 4.5].

4.4 Modular Ratio and Cracking Moment

4.4.1 Modular Ratio in Reinforced Concrete

In the case of the *working stress* analysis of reinforced concrete sections, it is usual to transform the composite section into an equivalent *concrete* section. Accordingly, for reinforced concrete, the 'modular ratio' m [Eq. 4.6] is defined as the ratio of the elastic modulus of steel to that of concrete.

As discussed earlier (Sections 2.8.3, 2.11.1), the modulus of elasticity of concrete is *not a constant* (unlike that of steel). The 'short-term static modulus' E_c, given by Eq. 2.4, is not considered appropriate for determining the modular ratio m because it ignores the long-term effects of *creep* under sustained loading. Partly taking this into account, the Code [(Cl. B-1.3(d)] suggests the following approximate formula for determining the modular ratio:

$$m = 280/(3\sigma_{cbc}) \tag{4.8}$$

implying that $m\sigma_{cbc}$ is a constant† [Ref. 4.9]:

$$m\sigma_{cbc} = 280/3 \tag{4.9}$$

where σ_{cbc} is the *permissible* compressive stress of concrete in bending (refer Table 21 of the Code). Values of σ_{cbc} (in MPa units) and m for different grades of concrete are listed in Table 4.1.

Table 4.1 *Values of σ_{cbc} and m for different concrete grades*

Concrete Grade	σ_{cbc} (MPa)	Modular ratio 'm'
M 15	5.0	18.67
M 20	7.0	13.33
M 25	8.5	10.98
M 30	10.0	9.33
M 35	11.5	8.11
M 40	13.0	7.18
M 45	14.5	6.44
M 50	16.0	5.83

4.4.2 Transformed Area of Reinforcing Steel

Tension Steel

Applying the concept of 'transformed section', the area of tension reinforcement steel A_{st} is transformed into equivalent concrete area as mA_{st}. This transformation is valid in reinforced concrete not only for flexural members but also for members subjected to *direct tension* [refer Cl. B-2.1.1 of the Code].

The stress in the tension steel, f_{st}, is obtained from the corresponding stress f_{cs} in the equivalent 'transformed' concrete (at the level of the steel) as $f_{st} = mf_{cs}$.

† This concept is used subsequently in some derivations. Hence, for consistency in calculations, the value of m (given by Eq. 4.8) should *not* be rounded off to an integer (as done in the traditional WSM).

Compression Steel

When reinforcing steel is provided in compression in reinforced concrete beams or columns, the modular ratio to be considered for transformation is generally greater than that used for tension steel [Eq. 4.9]. This is because the long-term effects of creep and shrinkage of concrete, as well as the nonlinearity at higher strains in concrete, result in much larger compressive stresses in the compression steel than those indicated by the linear elastic theory using the normally specified value of m. Accordingly, the Code recommends that the transformed area of compression steel A_{sc} be taken as $1.5mA_{sc}$, rather than mA_{sc} [refer Cl. B-4.1 of the Code].

The stress in the compression steel, f_{sc}, is obtained from the corresponding stress f_{csc} in the equivalent 'transformed' concrete (at the level of the compression steel) as $f_{sc} = 1.5mf_{csc}$

It may be noted that, while considering the area of *concrete* (under compression) in the transformed section, the *net* area A_c, i.e., gross area A_g minus A_{sc} (making allowance for the concrete area displaced by the steel area) should be considered.

4.4.3 Cracking Moment

'Cracking moment' or 'moment at first crack' is a property of a RC beam section; it is the moment at which the maximum flexural tensile stress reaches the modulus of rupture of concrete.

Concrete in the extreme tension fibre of a beam section is expected to crack (for the first time) when the stress reaches the value of the *modulus of rupture* f_{cr} [refer Section 2.9.1]. At this stage, the maximum strains in compression and tension are of a low order. Hence, assuming a linear stress-strain relation for concrete in both tension and compression, with same elastic modulus, the following formula is obtained [applying Eq. 4.4] for the 'moment at first crack' or *cracking moment* M_{cr}:

$$M_{cr} = f_{cr}\frac{I_T}{y_t} \tag{4.10}$$

where y_t is the distance between the neutral axis and the extreme tension fibre, and I_T is the second moment of area of the transformed reinforced concrete section with reference to the NA.

If the contribution of the transformed area of reinforcing steel is not significant, an approximate value M_{cr} is obtainable by considering the 'gross (concrete) section', i.e., treating the beam section as a *plain concrete* section.

If the beam is very lightly loaded (or designed to be crack-free), the maximum applied bending moment may be less than M_{cr}. In such a case of 'uncracked section', the concrete and steel both participate in resisting tension. The computation of stresses for such a situation is described in Example 4.1.

Example 4.1

A reinforced concrete beam of rectangular section has the cross-sectional dimensions shown in Figure 4.5(a). Assuming M 25 grade concrete and Fe 500 grade steel, compute (i) the cracking moment and (ii) the stresses due to an applied moment of 50 kNm.

Solution

Material Properties: For M 25 concrete,

- modular ratio, $m = 10.98$ [Eq. 4.8 or Table 4.1]
- modulus of rupture $f_{cr} = 0.7\sqrt{25} = 3.5$ MPa [Eq. 2.6]

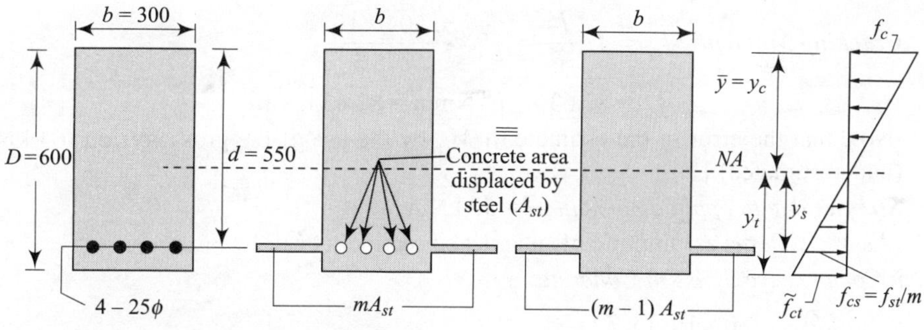

(a) Beam section (b) Transformed section (c) Stresses

Fig. 4.5 Example 4.1 – 'Uncracked section.'

Approximate *Cracking Moment* (assuming *gross* section):

- Section modulus $Z = \dfrac{bD^2}{6} = \dfrac{300 \times 600^2}{6} = 18 \times 10^6 \text{ mm}^3$

$\Rightarrow$ Cracking moment

$M_{cr} \approx f_{cr} Z = 3.5 \text{ N/mm}^2 \times 18 \times 10^6 \text{ mm}^3 = 63 \times 10^6 \text{ Nmm}$ †

$= \mathbf{63 \text{ kNm}}$

Transformed Section Properties:

- *Area of tension steel* $A_{st} = 4 \times \pi(25)^2/4 = 1963 \text{ mm}^2$
The transformed area A_T comprises the concrete area $A_g - A_{st}$ plus the transformed steel area mA_{st}. It is convenient to take this as the sum of the gross concrete area A_g and the additional contribution due to steel as $(m - 1)A_{st}$ [Figure 4.5(b)]:
$$A_t = bD + (m - 1)A_{st}$$
- *Depth of neutral axis* $\bar{y}$:
Equating moments of areas of the transformed section about the top edge,
$$A_T \bar{y} = (bD)(D/2) + (m - 1)A_{st}(d)$$
$$\bar{y} = \frac{(300 \times 600)(300) + (10.98 - 1)(1963)(550)}{(300 \times 600) + (9.98 \times 1963)} = 324.5 \text{ mm}$$
$\Rightarrow$ distance from NA to extreme compression fibre $y_c = 324.5$ mm,
distance from NA to extreme tension fibre $y_t = 600 - 324.5 = 275.5$ mm
distance from NA to reinforcing steel $y_s = 550 - 324.5 = 225.5$ mm
- *Transformed second moment of area:*
$$I_T = by_c^3/3 + by_t^3/3 + (m-1)A_{st}(y_s)^2$$
$$= 300 \times (324.5^3 + 275.5^3)/3 + (9.98 \times 1963)(225.5)^2 = 6.504 \times 10^9 \text{ mm}^4$$

† It is reasonable and adequate to include only three significant figures for *final* results in calculations. This practice is followed in this book.

(i) ***Cracking Moment*** $M_{cr} = f_{cr}\dfrac{I_T}{y_t} = 3.5 \times \dfrac{6.504 \times 10^9}{275.5}$

$= 82.63 \times 10^6$ Nmm = **82.63 kNm**

[Note that the error in the estimate of M_{cr} by the use of the gross section (63 kNm) is 31% (underestimated).]

(ii) ***Stresses*** *due to applied moment* $M = 50$ kNm:

(As $M < M_{cr}$, the assumption of 'uncracked section' is valid.)

- *Maximum Compressive Stress in Concrete:*

$$f_c = \frac{My_c}{I_T} = \frac{(50 \times 10^6) \times 324.5}{6.504 \times 10^9} = \mathbf{2.49\ MPa}$$

- *Maximum Tensile Stress in Concrete:*

$$\tilde{f}_{ct} = \frac{My_t}{I_T} = f_c\left(\frac{y_t}{y_c}\right) \Rightarrow \tilde{f}_{ct} = 2.49 \times \left(\frac{275.5}{324.5}\right) = \mathbf{2.11\ MPa}\ (< f_{cr} = 3.5\ \text{MPa})$$

- *Tensile Stress in Steel:*

From the stress distribution diagram [Figure 4.5(c)],

$$f_{st} = mf_{cs}$$

where $f_{cs} = f_c\left(\dfrac{y_s}{y_c}\right) = \tilde{f}_{ct}\left(\dfrac{y_s}{y_t}\right)$

$$\Rightarrow \quad f_{st} = 10.98 \times 2.49 \times \left(\frac{225.5}{324.5}\right) = \mathbf{18.99\ MPa}$$

4.5 Flexural Behaviour of Reinforced Concrete

The general behaviour of reinforced concrete beam sections under flexure is discussed in detail here. The behaviour of the section at various stages of loading is described – from the initial *uncracked phase* to the final (ultimate) condition at *collapse* (due to the flexural resistance capacity of the section being exceeded). For convenience, it is assumed that the beam section is rectangular and that only tension reinforcing steel is provided [Figure 4.6].

4.5.1 Uncracked Phase

Consider a simply supported beam subjected to gradually increasing load [Figure 4.6(a)]. The central segment of the beam is subjected to pure flexure. In the early stages of loading, the applied moment (at any section) is less than the cracking moment M_{cr} and the maximum tensile stress $\tilde{f}_{ct}$ in the concrete is less than its flexural tensile strength f_{cr}. This phase is the *uncracked* phase, wherein the *entire* section is effective in resisting the moment and is under stress. The distribution of strains and stresses are as indicated in Figure 4.6(c). The calculation of stresses for a given moment is as shown in Example 4.1; similarly, the 'allowable moment' for given 'permissible stresses' can be computed.

The uncracked phase reaches its limit when the applied moment M becomes equal to the cracking moment M_{cr}. In the concrete stress-strain curve shown in Figure 4.6(b), the uncracked phase falls within the initial linear portion OA.

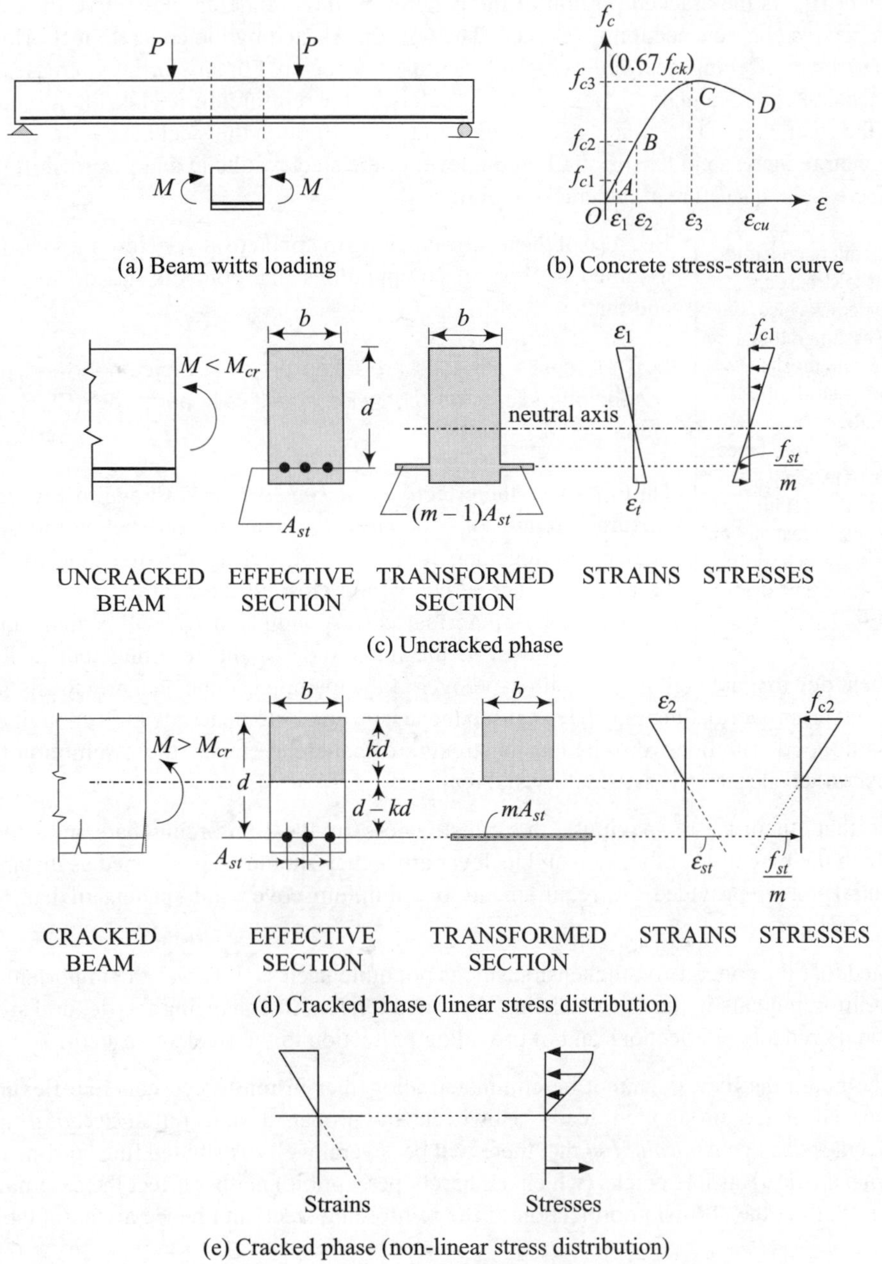

Fig. 4.6 Behaviour of reinforced concrete beam under increasing moment.

4.5.2 Linear Elastic Cracked Phase

As the applied moment exceeds M_{cr}, the maximum tensile stress in concrete exceeds the *flexural tensile strength* of concrete and the section begins to *crack* on the tension side. The cracks are initiated in the bottom (tensile) fibres of the beam, and with increasing loading, widen and propagate gradually towards the neutral axis [Figure 4.6(d)]. As the cracked portion of the concrete is now rendered ineffective in resisting tensile stresses, the *effective* concrete section is reduced. The tension resisted by the concrete just prior to cracking is transferred to the reinforcing steel at the cracked section of the beam. For any further increase in the applied moment, the tension component has to be contributed solely by the reinforcing steel. With the sudden increase in tension in the steel, there is the associated increase in tensile strain in the steel bars at the cracked section. This relatively large increase in tensile strain at the level of the steel results in an upward shift of the neutral axis and an increase in curvature at the cracked section.

At the crack location, concrete carries no tensile stresses. In between the cracks also, it is generally assumed that concrete carries no tensile stresses – for the strength assessment in RC design. However, the tensile resistance of concrete (in between cracks) is accounted for in serviceability design (estimation of deflections and crack-width) and in compression field theory (refer Section 17.2).

Because of the tensile cracking of concrete at very low stresses, it is generally assumed in flexural computations that concrete has no tensile resistance, and that:

> '...all tensile stresses are taken up by reinforcement and none by concrete, except as otherwise specifically permitted' [Cl. B-1.3(b) of the Code].

On this basis, the effective *cracked section* is shown in Figure 4.6(d). The flexural strength of concrete in the tension zone below the neutral axis is neglected altogether. It is true that, during the first-time loading, a small part of the concrete below and close to the neutral axis (where the tensile strains are less than that corresponding to f_{cr}) will remain uncracked and effective. However, the magnitude of the resulting tensile force and the internal moment due to it are negligibly small. Moreover, if the loading is done on a previously loaded beam, it is possible that prior overloading may have caused the tensile cracks to penetrate high enough to effectively eliminate this little contribution from the tensile strength of concrete. Hence, the assumption that concrete resists no flexural tensile stress is satisfactory and realistic.

It is obvious that, in order to maximise the effectiveness of the reinforcing bars in resisting flexure (in terms of both the magnitude of tension and its lever arm), they should be positioned as distant as possible from the neutral axis – provided the requirements of minimum cover and spacing of bars are satisfied [refer Section 5.2].

It may be noted that the concrete on the tension side is not quite useless. It serves the important functions of holding the reinforcing bars in place, of resisting shear and torsion, of enhancing the flexural stiffness of the beam and thereby reducing deflections and of providing protection to the steel against corrosion and fire.

It may also be noted that cracks cannot be eliminated altogether in reinforced concrete flexural members under the normal range of applied loads. However, by proper design for *serviceability limit state* [Chapter 10], cracks can be *controlled* so that there will be several well-distributed fine hairline cracks rather than a few wide cracks. Hairline cracks (which are barely perceptible) neither affect the external appearance of the beam nor affect the corrosion protection of the reinforcing steel, and hence are acceptable in normal situations.

Finally, it may be noted that the stresses under service loads are usually in the 'cracked section' phase and within the *linear elastic* range. Hence, such an analysis (refer Section 4.3), involving the use of the 'modular ratio' concept, is called for in investigating the *limit states of serviceability* (calculation of deflections and crack-widths) as well as in the traditional *working stress method* of design (refer Section 3.2). The assumption of linear elastic behaviour is acceptable for beams with tension reinforcement, as long as the calculated maximum stress in concrete (under flexural compression) is less than about one-third of the cube strength [see the nearly linear part OAB of the stress-strain curve in Figure 4.6(b)] and the steel stress is within the elastic limit (which is usually the case). However, when compression reinforcement is introduced, the modular ratio for the compression steel has to be suitably modified, as explained in Section 4.4.2.

Expressions for the stresses and the moment of resistance (based on 'permissible stresses') of reinforced concrete sections, using the linear elastic stress distribution and the concept of cracked-transformed sections, are derived in Section 4.6.

4.5.3 Stages Leading to Limit State of Collapse

As the applied moment on the beam section is increased beyond the 'linear elastic cracked phase', the concrete strains and stresses enter the nonlinear range BCD in Figure 4.6(b). For example, if the strain in the extreme compression fibre reaches a value of ε_3 (equal to 0.002, according to the Code), corresponding to the maximum stress level $0.67f_{ck}$, the compressive stress distribution in the cracked section (above the neutral axis) will take the shape of the curve OBC in Figure 4.6(b), as shown in Figure 4.6(e). This occurs because the 'fundamental assumption' of a linear strain distribution holds good at all stages of loading, as validated experimentally [Ref. 4.2, 4.4].

The behaviour of the beam in the nonlinear phase depends on the amount of reinforcing steel provided.

The reinforcing steel can sustain very high tensile strains, due to the ductile behaviour of steel, following 'yielding'; the ultimate strain can be in the range of 0.12 to 0.20. However, the concrete can accommodate compressive strains which are much lower in comparison; the 'ultimate compressive strain' ε_{cu} is in the range of 0.003 to 0.0045. As will be seen later, the final collapse of a normal beam at the ultimate limit state is caused inevitably by the crushing of concrete in compression, regardless of whether the tension steel has yielded or not. If the tension steel yields at the ultimate limit state, the beam is said to be *under-reinforced*; otherwise, if the steel does not yield, the beam is said to be *over-reinforced.* The terms 'under-' and 'over-' are used with reference to a benchmark condition called the 'balanced' section. If the area of tension steel provided at a beam section is less than that required for the *balanced* section condition, the beam is *under-reinforced*; otherwise, if the steel area is in excess, the beam is *over-reinforced.*

Balanced Section

A 'balanced section' is one in which the area of tension steel is such that at the *ultimate limit state*, the two limiting conditions are reached *simultaneously*; viz., the compressive strain in the extreme fibre of the concrete reaches the ultimate strain ε_{cu}, and the tensile strain at the level of the centroid of the steel reaches the 'yield strain' ε_y. The failure of such a section, termed '*balanced failure*', is expected to occur by the simultaneous initiation of crushing of concrete and yielding of steel.

Under-Reinforced Section

An 'under-reinforced section' is one in which the area of tension steel is such that as the ultimate limit state is approached, the yield strain ε_y is reached in the steel before the ultimate compressive strain is reached in the extreme fibre of the concrete. When the reinforcement strain reaches ε_y (and the stress reaches the yield strength f_y), the corresponding maximum concrete strain is less than ε_{cu} – as depicted in 'stage 1' of Figure 4.7. The equilibrium conditions are given by $C = T = A_{st}f_y$ and $M = Tz_1$.

A slight increase in the load (moment) at this stage causes the steel to *yield* and elongate significantly, without any significant increase in stress. The marked increase in tensile strain causes the neutral axis to shift upwards, thus tending to reduce the area of the concrete under compression. As the total tension T remains essentially constant at $A_{st}f_y$, the compressive stresses (and hence, the strains) have to increase in order to maintain equilibrium ($C = T$). This situation is represented by 'stage 2' in Figure 4.7. The corresponding moment of resistance is given by $M = Tz_2$, and represents a marginal increase over the moment at 'stage 1' owing to the slight increase in the lever arm – from z_1 to z_2. [Conversely, one can also see that any increase in load (and moment) beyond the first yield of steel requires (with T constant) an increase in lever arm and hence a rise in the neutral axis level].

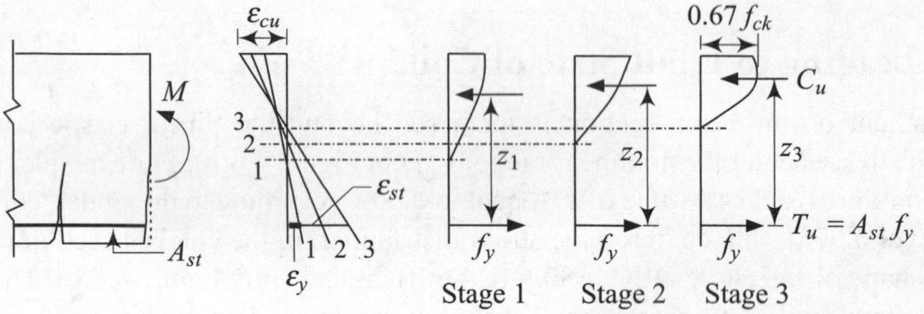

Fig. 4.7 Behaviour of under-reinforced section (tension failure).

This process is accompanied by wider and deeper tensile cracks and increased beam curvatures and deflections, due to the relatively rapid increase in the tensile strain. The process continues until the maximum strain in concrete reaches the ultimate compressive strain of concrete ε_{cu} ('stage 3'), resulting in the crushing of concrete in the limited compression zone.

It is to be noted that the increase in the moment of resistance between 'stage 1' and 'stage 3' is marginal, being attributable solely to the slight increase in the lever arm z. However, there is a substantial increase in curvature, deflection, and width as well as spread of cracking during this process.

As indicated in Figure 4.8, the curvature φ (rotation per unit length) can be conveniently measured from the linear strain distribution as:

$$\varphi = \frac{\varepsilon_c + \varepsilon_{st}}{d} \tag{4.11}$$

where ε_c is the compressive strain in the extreme concrete fibre, ε_{st} is the strain at the centroid of the tension steel, and d is the *effective depth* of the beam section.

Effective depth of a beam is defined as 'the distance between the *centroid* of the area of tension reinforcement and the maximum compression fibre' (Cl. 23.0 of the Code). Reinforcing bars are usually provided in multiple numbers, and sometimes in multiple layers, due to size and spacing constraints. In flexural computations, it is generally assumed that the entire steel area resisting tension is located at the centroid of the bar group, and that all the bars carry the same stress – corresponding to the centroid level (i.e., at the effective depth).

> Behaviour where the section/member undergoes large curvatures and deflections maintaining near constant strength before failure, giving ample warning of impending failure, is termed 'ductile' and is a desired quality.

The failure of an under-reinforced beam is termed as *tension failure* – so called because the primary cause of failure is the yielding in tension of the steel. The onset of failure is gradual, giving ample prior *warning* of the impending collapse by way of increased curvatures, deflections and cracking. Hence, such a mode of failure is highly preferred in design practice. The actual collapse, although triggered by the yielding of steel, occurs by means of the eventual crushing of concrete in compression ('secondary compression failure'). A sketch of the moment-curvature relation for an under-reinforced beam is shown in Figure 4.8(a). The large increase in curvature (rotation per unit length), prior to collapse, is indicative of a typical *ductile* mode of failure.

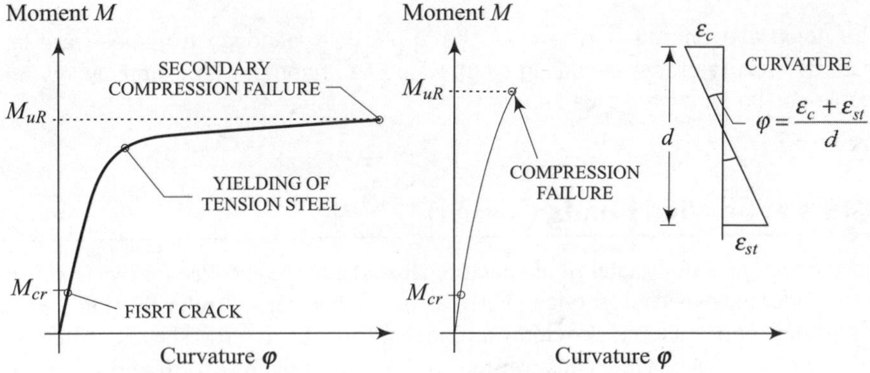

(a) Under-reinforced beam (b) Over-reinforced beam

Fig. 4.8 Moment-curvature relations.

Over-Reinforced Section

An 'over-reinforced' section is one in which the area of tension steel is such that at the ultimate limit state, the ultimate compressive strain in concrete is reached, however the tensile strain in the reinforcing steel is less than the yield strain ε_y [Figure 4.9].

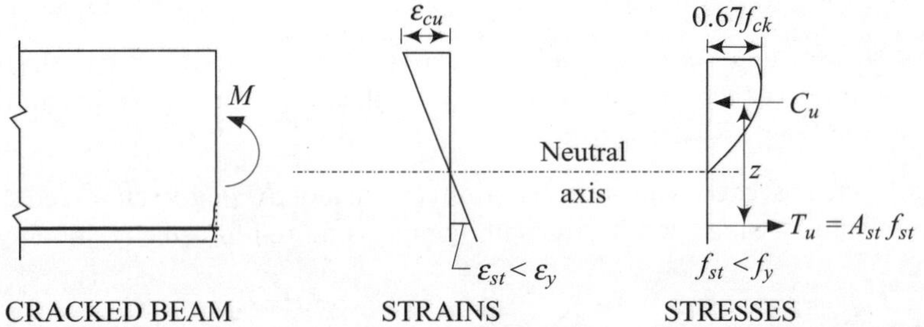

Fig. 4.9 Behaviour of over-reinforced section (compression failure).

The concrete fails in compression before the steel reaches its yield point. Hence, this type of failure is termed *compression failure*. The failure occurs (often, explosively) without warning.

> A primary 'compression failure' of a beam section/member, without prior yielding of steel in tension, is a brittle failure (occurring without any warning). and hence is considered undesirable.

In this case, the tension steel remains in the elastic range up to collapse. As the limit state of collapse is approached, the tensile stress in steel increases proportionately with the tensile strain, whereas the compressive stress in concrete does not increase proportionately with the compressive strain, because it is in the nonlinear range. Hence, in order to maintain equilibrium ($C = T$), the area of concrete under compression has to increase; this is enabled by a lowering of the neutral axis. The strains across the section remain relatively low. Consequently, the curvatures [Figure 4.8(b)], deflections and crack-widths – all the 'distress' signals – also remain relatively low in sharp contrast with the behaviour of the under-reinforced section at failure. Because the failure is sudden (without any signs of warning) and the deflections and curvatures remain low right up to failure, this type of failure is termed a *brittle* failure. For this reason, over-reinforced flexural members are not permitted by the Code.

> It should be noted that one other type of failure is possible, although extremely rare in practice. This is failure by *fracture* of the reinforcing steel, which can happen with extremely low amounts of reinforcements and under dynamic loading.

4.6 Analysis at Service Loads (WSM)

Sections designed for *ultimate* limit states (under factored loads) must be checked for *serviceability* (deflection, crack-width, etc.) under the expected 'service loads', as mentioned earlier [refer Section 3.5]. The details of the calculations of deflections and crack-widths are covered in Chapter 10. These calculations require the computation of stresses under service loads. Moreover, these calculations form part of the working stress method of design (WSM). The **basic assumptions** involved in the analysis at the service load stage (Cl. B-1.3 of the Code) are summarised here. (These assumptions have already been explained earlier.)

(a) Plane sections normal to the beam axis remain plane after bending, i.e., in an initially straight beam, strain varies linearly over the depth of the section.
(b) All tensile stresses are resisted by the reinforcement, and none by concrete (except in the uncracked phase).
(c) Stresses are linearly proportional to strains – for both concrete and steel.
(d) The modular ratio, $m = E_s/E_c$, has the value, $280/(3\sigma_{cbc})$ [Eq. 4.8]

The expressions for stresses under service loads are derived here, using the linear elastic theory and the cracked-transformed section concept [refer Section 4.3]. Further, the expressions for 'allowable moment of resistance', based on WSM, are also derived.

The simple rectangular cross-section with tension reinforcement alone ('singly reinforced section') is studied first. Subsequently, 'flanged beams' and beams with compression reinforcement ('doubly reinforced') are dealt with.

4.6.1 Stresses in Singly Reinforced Rectangular Sections

Figure 4.10(a) shows a 'singly reinforced' rectangular section of a beam, subjected to a specified (load) moment M (assumed sagging). For this beam section, the corresponding 'cracked-transformed section' is shown in Figure 4.10(c). The concrete on the tension side of the neutral axis is neglected. The neutral axis (NA) is located by the line passing through the 'centroid' of transformed section, and perpendicular to the plane of bending.

Expressing the depth of the neutral axis (from the extreme compression fibres) as a fraction k of the *effective depth d*, and equating the moments of the compression and tension areas about the NA,

$$\frac{b(kd)^2}{2} = mA_{st}(d - kd) \tag{4.12}$$

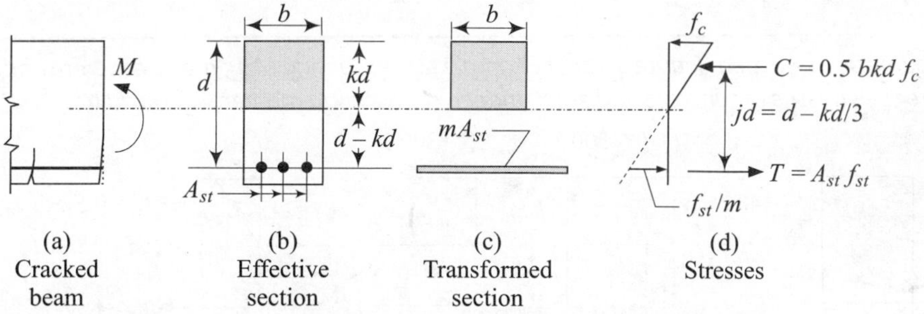

Fig. 4.10 Concept of 'cracked-transformed section.'

This quadratic equation can be easily solved to determine *kd*. Of the two roots, only one is acceptable, namely $0 < k < 1$. The resulting expression for *k* can be obtained as

$$k = \sqrt{2\rho m + (\rho m)^2} - \rho m \tag{4.13}$$

where ρ is termed the *reinforcement ratio*, given by:

$$\rho \equiv \frac{A_{st}}{bd} \tag{4.14}$$

The *second moment of area* of the cracked–transformed section, I_{cr}, is given by:

$$I_{cr} = \frac{b(kd)^3}{3} + mA_{st}(d - kd)^2 \tag{4.15}$$

Knowing the neutral axis location and the second moment of area, the stresses in the concrete (and steel) in the composite section [Figure 4.10(d)] due to the applied moment *M* may be computed from the flexure formula $f = My/I$, as explained in Section 4.3 (and Example 4.1). The same results could be obtained more simply and directly, by considering the static equilibrium of resultant forces and moments [Eqs 4.1 and 4.2]. Referring to Figure 4.10,

$$C = \frac{bkd}{2} f_c \tag{4.16}$$

$$T = A_{st} f_{st} \tag{4.17}$$

$$j = (1 - k/3) \tag{4.18}$$

$$M = Cjd = Tjd$$

from which $$f_c = \frac{M}{0.5b(kd)(jd)} \tag{4.19}$$

and $$f_{st} = \frac{M}{A_{st}\, jd} \tag{4.20}$$

It is to be noted that if two points in the stress distribution diagram are known (such as k and f_c), then the stress at any level can be computed using similar triangles. Thus, f_{st} may be alternatively obtained as:

$$f_{st} = mf_c \frac{d - kd}{kd} = mf_c \left(\frac{1-k}{k}\right) \tag{4.21}$$

Example 4.2

Consider the same beam section [Figure 4.11] of Example 4.1. Assuming M 25 grade concrete and Fe 500 grade steel, compute the stresses in concrete and steel under a service load moment of 140 kNm.

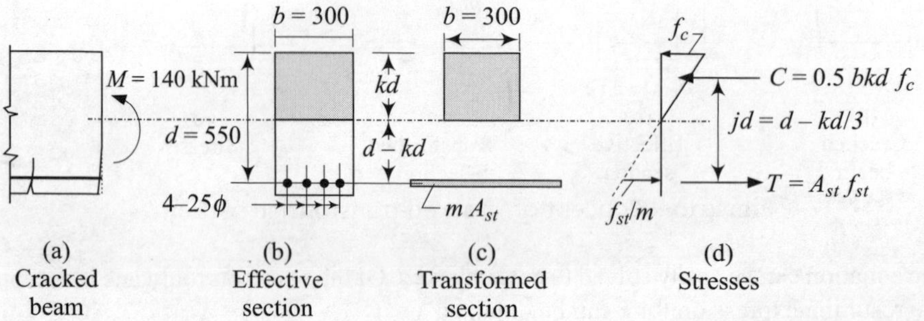

Fig. 4.11 Example 4.2 – 'cracked section'.

Solution

From Example 4.1, it is seen that M_{cr} = 82.63 kNm. For the present problem M = 140 kNm > M_{cr}. Hence, the section would have 'cracked'. The cracked-transformed section is shown in Figure 4.11.

Transformed Section Properties:

- Modular ratio m = 10.98 (for M 25 concrete)
- Transformed steel area = mAst

  = 10.98 × 1963 = **21554 mm²**
- Equating moments of areas about the neutral (centroidal) axis,

$$\frac{300(kd)^2}{2} = 21554(550 - kd)$$

Solving, $kd = 218.31$ mm

⇒ neutral axis depth factor $k = 218.31/550 = 0.397$

⇒ lever arm $jd = d - kd/3 = 477.2$ mm

Stresses:

- *Maximum Concrete Stress:*

  Taking moments about the tension steel centroid,

$$M = 0.5\, f_c b(kd)(jd)$$

$$\Rightarrow \quad f_c = \frac{140 \times 10^6}{0.5 \times 300 \times 218.31 \times 477.2} = \mathbf{8.96\ MPa}$$

- *Tensile Stress in Steel:*

  Taking moments about the line of action of C,

$$M = f_{st} A_{st}(jd)$$

$$\Rightarrow \quad f_{st} = \frac{140 \times 10^6}{1963 \times 477.2} = \mathbf{149.4\ MPa}$$

Alternatively, considering the linear stress distribution [Figure 4.10]:

$$f_{st} = 10.98 \times 8.96 \times \frac{1 - 0.397}{0.397} = \mathbf{149.4\ MPa}$$

[*Note:* The maximum concrete stress f_c exceeds the permissible stress $\sigma_{cbc} = 8.5$ MPa for M 25 concrete [refer Section 4.6.2]; hence the beam is not 'safe' according to WSM provision of the Code although the steel stress is within allowable limit.]

- Note that the same results can be obtained by the 'flexure formula' $f = My/I_{cr}$, where

$$I_{cr} = \frac{300 \times (218.31)^3}{3} + 21554(550 - 218.31)^2 = 3.412 \times 10^9 \text{ mm}^4$$

Accordingly, $f_c = \dfrac{My_c}{I_{cr}} = \dfrac{(140 \times 10^6) \times 218.31}{3.412 \times 10^9} = \mathbf{8.96\ MPa}$

$$f_{st} = m\frac{M(d - kd)}{I_{cr}} = \frac{10.98 \times (140 \times 10^6) \times (550 - 218.31)}{3.412 \times 10^9} = \mathbf{149.4\ MPa} \text{ (as before)}$$

4.6.2 Permissible Stresses

In the traditional working stress method, analysis requires the designer to verify that the calculated stresses [Eqs 4.19 and 4.20] under service loads are within '*permissible limits*'. The 'permissible stress' in concrete under flexural compression (denoted as σ_{cbc} by the Code) is as given in Table 4.1.

The 'permissible stress' in tension steel σ_{st} (specified in Table 22 of the Code) takes values of 140 MPa, 230 MPa and 275 MPa for Fe 250, Fe 415 and Fe 500 grades respectively. However, for Fe 250 grade, the permissible stress is *reduced* to 130 MPa if the bar diameter exceeds 20 mm.

In the case of reinforcing steel under compression in flexural members, the permissible stress σ_{sc} is limited to *the calculated compressive stress in the surrounding concrete multiplied by* 1.5 *times the modular ratio or* $\tilde{\sigma}_{sc}$ (maximum permissible compressive stress in steel given in Table 22 of the Code), *whichever is lower*†. The specified values of $\tilde{\sigma}_{sc}$ are 130 MPa, 190 MPa and 190 MPa for Fe 250, Fe 415 and Fe 500 grades respectively.

4.6.3 Allowable Bending Moment

When it is desired to compute the 'allowable bending moment' capacity of a beam of known cross-section, in accordance with WSM, the procedure to be adopted is very similar to that given in Section 4.6.1 and Example 4.2. Here, the stresses in concrete and steel (f_c and f_{st}) are taken as their respective 'permissible stresses' (σ_{cbc} and σ_{st}) as specified in Section 4.6.2.

Considering the moment with reference to the tension steel [Figure 4.10],

$$M_{all} = A_{st}\sigma_{st} jd \tag{4.22a}$$

Considering the moment with reference to the compression in concrete [Figure 4.10],

$$M_{all} = 0.5\ \sigma_{cbc}\ b(kb)(jd) \tag{4.22b}$$

In a given beam section, the permissible stresses in both steel and concrete may not be reached simultaneously. Hence, the lower of the two moments computed by Eqs 4.22a and 4.22b will give the correct permissible moment, and the corresponding stress (either f_{st} or f_c) will be the one to reach the permissible limit.

† Generally, the value of 1.5m times the calculated compressive stress is lower than $\tilde{\sigma}_{sc}$, and hence controls.

Alternatively, with the knowledge of certain constants (discussed in the subsection to follow), it is possible to predict whether it is the steel or the concrete that controls M_{all}.

'Balanced (WSM)' Section Constants

A balanced (WSM) section is one in which the maximum concrete compressive stress and the maximum steel tensile stress reach their allowable values simultaneously.

In *the working stress method*, the 'balanced' section is one in which both tensile steel stress f_{st} and maximum compressive stress f_c simultaneously reach their allowable limits σ_{st} and σ_{cbc} respectively [Figure 4.12] under *service loads*. The corresponding area of steel A_{st} is denoted as $A_{st,b}$; the percentage reinforcement $p_t \equiv 100A_{st,b}/bd$ is denoted as $p_{t,b}$; the neutral axis depth factor is denoted as k_b; the lever arm depth factor is denoted as j_b; and the allowable moment of the section is denoted as M_{wb}.

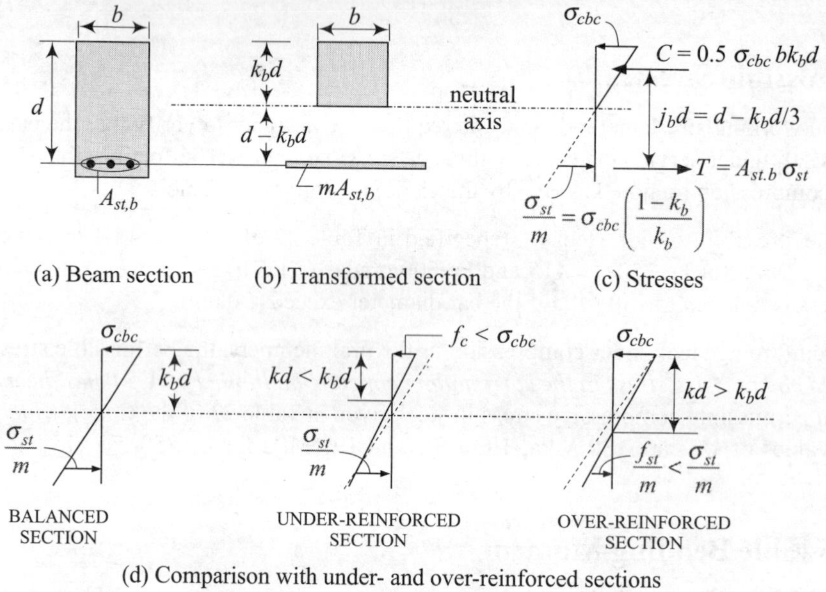

Fig. 4.12 'Balanced (WSM)' section.

For such a case, from the linear distribution of stresses [Figure 4.12(c)] in the transformed-cracked section [Eq. 4.21], it follows that:

$$\sigma_{st} = m\sigma_{cbc} \times \frac{1-k_b}{k_b}$$

The product $m\sigma_{cbc}$ is a constant, equal to 280/ 3, according to the Code [Eq. 4.9], whereby the above equation can be solved to give:

$$k_b = \frac{280}{280 + 3\sigma_{st}} \tag{4.23}$$

where σ_{st} is in MPa units.

Thus, it is seen that the neutral axis depth factor (k_b) of a 'balanced (WSM)' section depends only on the permissible tensile stress in steel.

Further, considering the equilibrium of forces $C=T$, it follows that

$$0.5\sigma_{cbc}\,b(k_b d) = A_{st,b}\sigma_{st}$$

$$\Rightarrow \qquad \frac{100A_{st,b}}{bd} \equiv p_{t,b} = 50k_b \times \frac{\sigma_{cbc}}{\sigma_{st}} \tag{4.24}$$

Finally, considering moment equilibrium,

$$M_{wb} = C(j_b d) = 0.5\sigma_{cbc} b\,(k_b d)\left(1-\frac{k_b}{3}\right)d$$

$$\Rightarrow \qquad \frac{M_{wb}}{\sigma_{cbc}bd^2} \equiv Q_b = 0.5k_b\left(1-\frac{k_b}{3}\right) \tag{4.25}$$

It may be noted that Eqs 4.23 to 4.25 are expressed in non-dimensional form. The quantities on the right-hand sides of the equations reduce to constants (for given material grades). Some typical values of the constants k_b, $p_{t,b}$ and Q_b are listed in Table 4.2.

Table 4.2 *Constants for the balanced 'WSM' section*

Steel Grade		Fe 250 ($\phi > 20$ mm)	Fe 250 ($\phi \le 20$ mm)	Fe 415	Fe 500
k_b		0.4179	0.4000	0.2887	0.2534
$p_{t,b}$	M 20	1.1251	1.0000	0.4394	0.3225
	M 25	1.3662	1.2143	0.5334	0.3916
	M 30	1.6073	1.4286	0.6276	0.4607
	M 35	1.8484	1.6429	0.7218	0.5298
	M 40	2.0895	1.8571	0.8159	0.5989
	M 45	2.3306	2.0714	0.9100	0.6681
	M 50	2.5717	2.2857	1.0042	0.7372
$Q_b \equiv M_{wb}/\sigma_{cbc}\,bd^2$		0.1798	0.1733	0.1304	0.1160

'Under-Reinforced (WSM)' Sections

According to the traditional WSM terminology, a given section is said to be 'under-reinforced (WSM)' if its area of tension steel is less than that corresponding to balanced conditions (i.e., $A_{st,b}$); so that the tensile stress in steel reaches the allowable limit before the maximum compressive stress in concrete reaches its allowable limit, and the allowable moment capacity is limited by the stress in steel, and not by the stress in concrete [i.e., $f_{st} = \sigma_{st}$ and $f_c < \sigma_{cbc}$].

With the help of the 'balanced (WSM)' section constants, it is possible to predict whether a given section is 'under-reinforced (WSM)' or not. If the section is 'under-reinforced (WSM)', $k < k_b$ [Figure 4.12(d)] and $p_t < p_{t,b}$; both conditions are equivalent, and either one may be checked.

Accordingly, the allowable moment is given by:

$$M_{all} = (A_{st}\,\sigma_{st}) \times (d - kd/3) \qquad \text{for} \quad k < k_b \tag{4.26}$$

The corresponding maximum compressive stress in concrete is obtained by applying the condition of force equilibrium ($C = T$), (or from the stress distribution diagram knowing σ_{st} and k).

$$0.5 f_c bkd = A_{st}\sigma_{st}$$

$$\Rightarrow \quad f_c = \frac{2A_{st}\sigma_{st}}{bkd} = \frac{p_t\sigma_{st}}{50k} \tag{4.27}$$

'Over-Reinforced (WSM)' Sections

According to the traditional WSM terminology, a given section is said to be 'over-reinforced (WSM)' if its area of tension steel is more than $A_{st,b}$, so that allowable limiting stress is reached in the concrete before the steel stress reaches the limiting value, and the allowable moment capacity is limited by the stress in concrete, and not by the stress in steel [i.e., $f_c = \sigma_{cbc}$ and $f_{st} < \sigma_{st}$]

Evidently, for such a section, $k > k_b$ [Figure 4.12(d)] and $p_t > p_{t,b}$. The allowable moment is given by

$$M_{all} = (0.5\sigma_{cbc}\, bkd)(d - kd/3) \quad \text{for} \quad k > k_b \tag{4.28}$$

The corresponding stress in the tension steel is obtained (by applying the condition T=C) as:

$$f_{st} = \frac{0.5\sigma_{cbc} bkd}{A_{st}} = \frac{50\sigma_{cbc}k}{p_t} \tag{4.29}$$

'Balanced condition' for service load state (WSM) and ultimate load state (LSM) are different. To avoid confusion, when the reference is to WSM, the term WSM is inserted in parenthesis in this book.

These definitions of 'balanced (WSM)', 'under-reinforced (WSM)' and 'over-reinforced (WSM)', with reference to **service load** conditions, should not be confused with the definitions for balanced/under-reinforced/over-reinforced given earlier (in Section 4.5.3) with reference to the **ultimate limit state**. In order to distinguish the WSM descriptions, the term 'WSM' should be preferably attached (in parenthesis) – as done consistently in this chapter.

Variation of M_{all} with p_t

On the basis of Eq. 4.13, Eq. 4.26 and Eq. 4.28, the values of $M_{all}/(bd^2)$, in MPa units, corresponding to increasing values of p_t have been computed and plotted in Figure 4.13 – for two commonly used concrete grades (M 20, M 30), each combined with two steel grades (Fe 250[†], Fe 500).

Each curve in Figure 4.13 is characterised by two distinctive portions: the initial segment (thick line), which is practically linear, conforms to *under-reinforced* (*WSM*) sections; this is followed by a non-linear segment (thin line), which conforms to *over-reinforced* (*WSM*) sections. The kink in each curve, marking the transition from 'under-reinforced (WSM)' to 'over-reinforced (WSM)', evidently corresponds to the *balanced* (*WSM*) section.

From the trends depicted in Figure 4.13, it follows that (expectedly), the allowable moment capacity increases with increase in tensile reinforcement area. In fact, for 'under-reinforced (WSM)' sections, M_{all} increases rapidly and nearly proportionately with p_t for $p_t < p_{t,b}$. Further, although the rate of gain in M_{all} increases with the use of higher strength steel, the 'balanced' section limit is reached at a lower percentage of steel.

[†] Assuming bar diameter $\phi \leq 20$ mm.

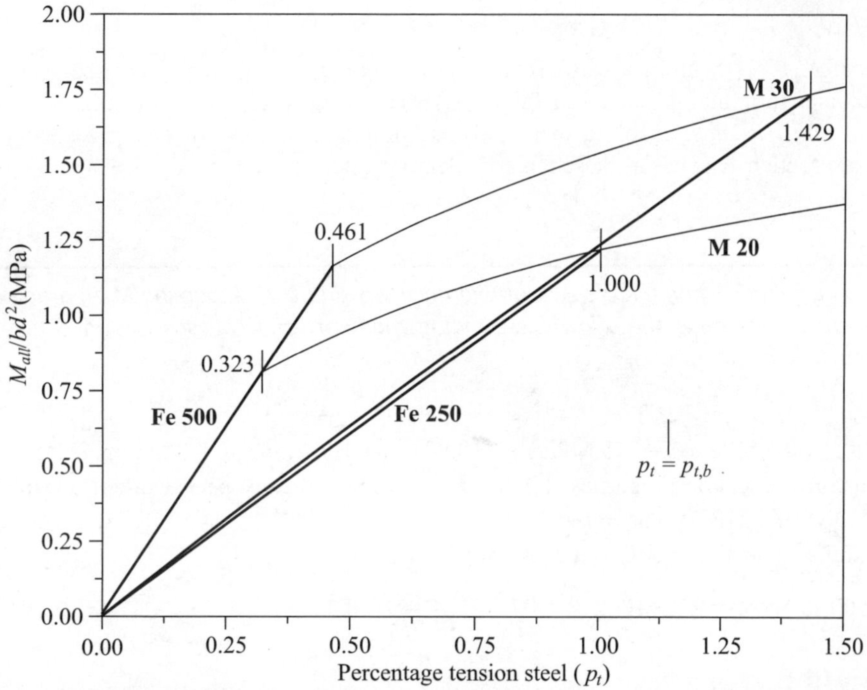

Fig. 4.13 Variation of M_{all}/bd^2 with p_t for different grades of concrete and steel.

> Improving the grade of concrete has practically no effect on M_{all} (for a given p_t) for under-reinforced (WSM) sections, except that the 'balanced section' limit is raised.

For $p_t > p_{t,b}$ (i.e., for 'over-reinforced (WSM)' sections), the rate of gain in allowable moment capacity with increase in tensile reinforcement area drops off rapidly. Also, improving the grade of steel has no effect on M_{all} (for a given p_t and grade of concrete) for over-reinforced sections, except that the value of $p_{t,b}$ is lowered. This is so, because the allowable limit of stress is reached in concrete in *compression,* and, unless the compression capacity is suitably enhanced†, there is not much to gain in boosting the flexural tensile capacity of the beam section – either by adding more tension steel area or by improving the grade of steel.

> For this reason, 'over-reinforced (WSM)' beams are considered to be highly uneconomical in the traditional WSM method of design.

Finally, it may be noted that 'over-reinforced (WSM)' sections often may turn out to be *under-reinforced* with reference to the *ultimate limit state* (leading to *ductile* failure), except when the percentage of tension steel is very high. For example, when M 20 concrete and Fe 500 steel are used in a beam section, if the tension steel area exceeds 0.323 per cent, by the working stress method the section is 'over-reinforced (WSM)', – but it is *under-reinforced* in the ultimate limit state (up to tension steel area of 0.759 per cent) [refer Section 4.7].

† By improving the grade of concrete and/or providing compression reinforcement ('doubly reinforced' section).

Analysis Aids

The variation of M_{all}/bd^2 with p_t for different grades of concrete and steel (depicted in Figure 4.13) is expressed in tabular form and presented in Tables A.1(a) and (b) in Appendix A of this book. These tables serve as useful *analysis aids*, enabling the rapid determination of M_{all} for any given singly reinforced rectangular beam section. The use of these tables is demonstrated in Example 4.3.

Example 4.3

Consider the same beam section [Figure 4.11 of Examples 4.1 and 4.2]. Assuming M 25 grade concrete and Fe 500 grade steel, determine the allowable bending moment, and the stresses in concrete and steel corresponding to this moment.

Solution

- Given: $\sigma_{cbc} = 8.5$ MPa, $\sigma_{st} = 275$ MPa, $m = 10.98$, $A_{st} = 1963$ mm^2, $b = 300$ mm, $d = 550$ mm.
- The transformed section properties [Figure 4.11(b)] have already been worked out in Example 4.2. Accordingly, $kd = 218.31$ mm $\Rightarrow k = 0.397$.
  The neutral axis depth factor k_b is a constant [Eq. 4.23].
  For Fe 500 steel ($\sigma_{st} = 275$ MPa), $k_b = \dfrac{280}{280 + 3(275)} = 0.2534$

Stresses:

As $k > k_b$, the section is 'over-reinforced (WSM)'. [Alternatively, $p_t = \dfrac{100 \times 1963}{300 \times 550} = 1.190$. $p_{t,b} =$ 0.3916 for M 25 concrete with Fe 500 steel. As $p_t > p_{t,b}$, the section is 'over-reinforced (WSM)']. Accordingly, the concrete stress controls, and $f_c = \sigma_{cbc} =$ **8.5 MPa** (for M 25 concrete).

- Applying $T = C$,

$$f_{st} = \frac{0.5\sigma_{cbc}\, b(kd)}{A_{st}} = \frac{0.5 \times 8.5 \times 300 \times 218.31}{1963} = \mathbf{141.8\ MPa} \qquad (< \sigma_{st} = 275\ \text{MPa})$$

  Alternatively, considering the linear stress distribution,

$$f_{st} = mf_c \frac{(1-k)}{k} = 10.98 \times 8.5 \left(\frac{1 - 0.397}{0.397}\right) = \mathbf{141.8\ MPa}\ \text{(as before)}$$

Allowable bending moment:

- Taking moments of forces about the tension steel centroid,

$$M_{all} = (0.5\sigma_{cbc} bkd)(d - kd/3) = (0.5 \times 8.5 \times 300 \times 218.31)(550 - 218.31/3)$$
$$= 132.8 \times 10^6\ \text{Nmm} = \mathbf{133\ kNm}$$

- [Alternatively, using the analysis aids given in Table A.1(a), for $p_t = 1.190$ and M 25 concrete with Fe500 steel, $\dfrac{M_{all}}{bd^2} = 1.46$ MPa

$$\Rightarrow \quad M_{all} = 1.46 \times 300 \times 550^2 = 132.8 \times 10^6\ \text{Nmm} = \mathbf{133\ kNm}\ \text{(as before)]}$$

4.6.4 Analysis of Singly Reinforced Flanged Sections

In the previous discussions, beams of *rectangular section* (which are most common) and with tensile steel alone ('singly reinforced') were considered, for the sake of simplicity. The procedure of analysis is similar for other cross-sectional shapes.

Frequently, beams of rectangular section are built with flanges (slab cast integrally) – at top or bottom. If the flanges are located in the compression zone, they become effective (partly or wholly) in adding significantly to the area of the concrete in compression. However, if the flanges are located in the tension zone, the concrete in the flanges becomes ineffective in cracked section analysis.

T-beams and L-beams

Beams having effectively T-*sections* and L-*sections* (called T-beams and L-beams) are commonly encountered in beam-supported slab floor systems [refer Figures 1.10, 4.14]. In such situations, a portion of the slab acts integrally with the beam and bends in the longitudinal direction of the beam. This slab portion is called the *flange* of the T- or L-beam. The beam portion below the flange is often termed the *web*, although, technically, the web is the full rectangular portion of the beam other than the overhanging parts of the flange. Indeed, in shear calculations, the web is interpreted in this manner.

When the flange is relatively wide, the flexural compressive stress is not uniform over its width. The stress varies from a maximum in the web region to progressively lower values at points farther away from the web[†]. In order to operate within the framework of the theory of flexure, which assumes a *uniform* stress distribution across the *width* of the section, it is necessary to define a *reduced effective flange width.*

The 'effective width of flange' may be defined as the width of a hypothetical flange that resists in-plane compressive stresses of uniform magnitude equal to the peak stress in the original wide flange, such that the value of the resultant longitudinal compressive force is the same (Figure 4.14).

The effective flange width is found to increase with increased span, increased web width and increased flange thickness. It also depends on the type of loading[‡] (concentrated, distributed, etc.) and the support conditions (simply supported, continuous, etc.). Approximate formulae for estimating the 'effective width of flange' b_f (Cl. 23.1.2 of Code) are given as follows:

$$b_f = \begin{cases} l_0/6 + b_w + 6D_f & \text{for T-beams} \\ l_0/12 + b_w + 3D_f & \text{for L-beams} \end{cases} \tag{4.30a}$$

where b_w is the breadth of the web, D_f is the thickness of the flange [Figure 4.14], and l_0 is the 'distance between points of zero moments in the beam' (which may be assumed as 0.7 times the effective span in continuous beams and frames). Obviously, b_f cannot extend beyond the slab portion tributary to a beam, i.e., the actual width of slab available. Hence, the calculated b_f should be restricted to a value that does not exceed $(s_1 + s_2)/2$ in the case of T-beams, and $s_1/2 + b_w/2$ in the case of L-beams, where the spacings s_1 and s_2 of the beams are as marked in Figure 4.14.

† The term 'shear lag' is sometimes used to explain this behaviour. The longitudinal stresses at the junction of the web and flange are transmitted through in-plane shear to the flange regions. The resulting shear deformations in the flange are maximum at the junction and reduce progressively at regions farther away from the web. Such 'shear lag' behaviour can be easily visualised in the case of a rectangular piece of sponge that is compressed in the middle.

‡ For example, it is seen that the equivalent flange width is less when a concentrated load is applied at the midspan of a simply supported beam, compared to the case when the same load is applied as a uniformly distributed load.

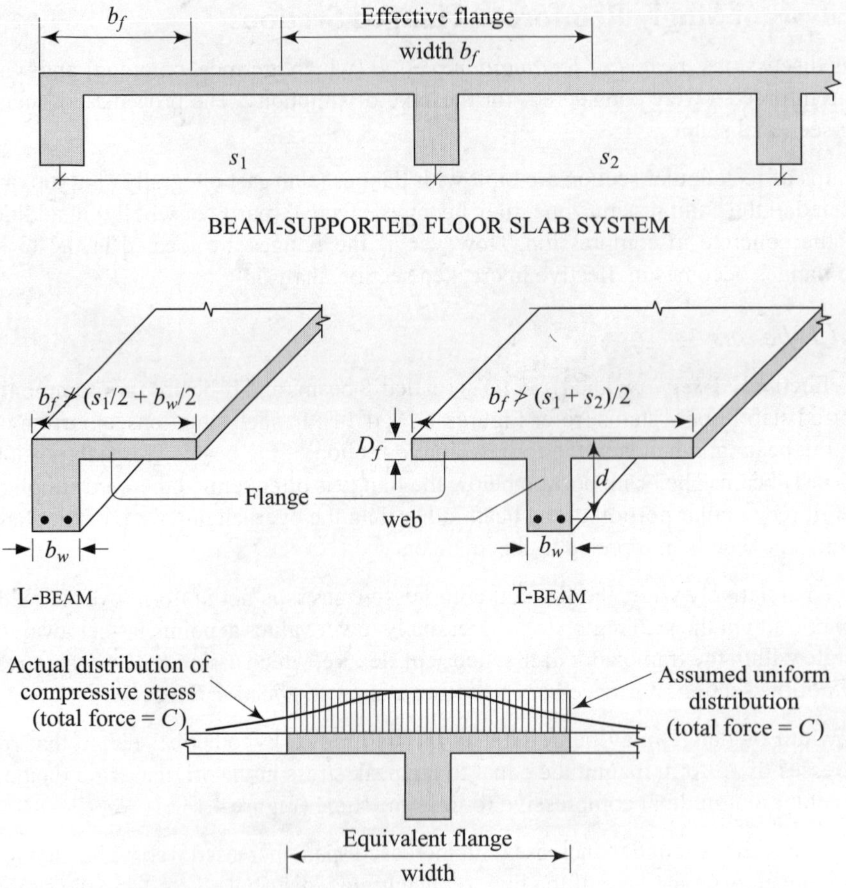

Fig. 4.14 T-beams and L-beams in beam-supported floor slab systems.

In some situations, *isolated* T-beams and L-beams are encountered, i.e., the slab is discontinuous at the sides, as in a footbridge or a 'stringer beam' of a staircase. In such cases, the Code [Cl. 23.1.2(c)] recommends the use of the following formula to estimate the 'effective width of flange' b_f:

$$b_f = \begin{cases} \dfrac{l_0}{l_0/b + 4} + b_w \le b & \text{for isolated T-beams} \\ \dfrac{0.5l_0}{l_0/b + 4} + b_w \le b & \text{for isolated L-beams} \end{cases} \tag{4.30b}$$

where b denotes the *actual* width of flange; evidently, the calculated value of b_f should not exceed b.

Analysis of T-beams and L-beams

The neutral axis may lie either within the flange [Figure 4.15(b)] or in the web of the flanged beam [Figure 4.15(c)]. In the former case $(kd \le D_f)$, as all the concrete on the tension side of the neutral axis is assumed ineffective in flexural computations, the flanged beam may just as well be treated as a *rectangular* beam having a width b_f and an *effective depth d.* The analytical procedures described in Sections 4.6.1 and 4.6.3, therefore, are identically applicable here, the only difference being that b_f is to be used in lieu of b.

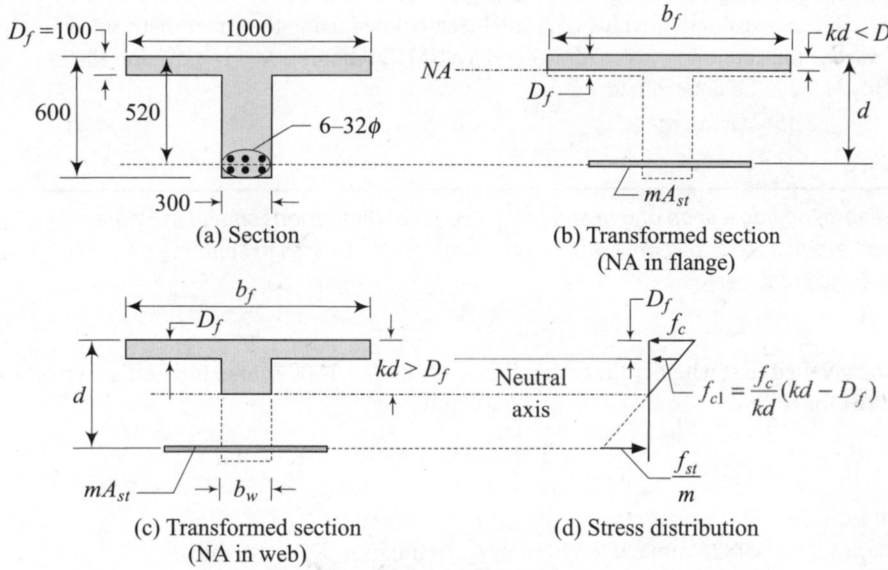

Fig. 4.15 Example 4.4 – Cracked section analysis (WSM) of a T-beam.

In the case $kd > D_f$, the area of concrete in compression spreads into the web region of the beam [Figure 4.15(c)]. The exact location of the neutral axis (i.e., kd) is determined by equating moments of areas of the cracked-transformed section in tension and compression [Eq. 4.31] and solving for kd:

$$(b_f - b_w)D_f(kd - D_f/2) + b_w(kd)^2/2 = mA_{st}(d - kd) \tag{4.31}$$

This is valid only if the resulting kd exceeds D_f.

With reference to the stress distribution shown in Figure 4.15(d), the area of the concrete in compression can be conveniently obtained by considering the difference between the two rectangles $b_f \times kd$ and $(b_f - b_w) \times (kd - D_f)$. Accordingly, considering equilibrium of forces ($C = T$),

$$\frac{1}{2}f_c\, b_f\,(kd) - \frac{1}{2}f_{c1}\,(b_f - b_w)(kd - D_f) = A_{st}f_{st} \tag{4.32}$$

where $$f_{c1} = f_c\left(\frac{kd - D_f}{kd}\right) \tag{4.33}$$

Also, taking moments of forces about the centroid of tension steel,

$$M = \frac{1}{2}f_c\, b_f\,(kd)(d - kd/3) - \frac{1}{2}f_{c1}(b_f - b_w)(kd - D_f)\{d - D_f - (kd - D_f)/3\} \tag{4.34}$$

If the problem is one of determining the stresses f_c and f_{st} for a given moment M, then f_c may be determined first by solving Eq. 4.34 (after substituting Eq. 4.33) and f_{st} can then be determined either by solving Eq. 4.32, or by considering similar triangles in the stress distribution diagram (Eq. 4.21). On the other hand, if the problem is one of determining the allowable moment capacity (M_{all}) of the section, then it should first be verified whether the section is 'under–reinforced (WSM)' or 'over-reinforced (WSM)' – by comparing the neutral axis depth factor k with k_b (given by Eq. 4.23). If $k < k_b$, the section is 'under–reinforced (WSM),' whereby $f_{st} = \sigma_{st}$. The corresponding value of f_c can be calculated using the stress distribution diagram. On the other hand, if $k > k_b$, the section is 'over-reinforced (WSM)', whereby $f_c = \sigma_{cbc}$. Using the appropriate value of f_c in Eq. 4.34, M_{all} can be determined.

Example 4.4

An isolated T-beam, having a span of 6 m and cross-sectional dimensions shown in Figure 4.15(a), is subjected to a service load moment of 250 kNm. Compute the maximum stresses in concrete and steel, assuming M 25 concrete and Fe 250 steel.

Solution

- It must be verified first whether the actual flange width b = 1000 mm is fully effective or not. Applying Eq. 4.30(b) for isolated T-beams with l_0 = 6000 mm

$$b_f = \frac{l_0}{l_0/b+4} + b_w = \frac{6000}{6+4} + 300 = \mathbf{900\ mm} < (b = 1000\ \text{mm})$$

- Modular ratio (for M 25 concrete) m =10.98
- $A_{st} = 6 \times \pi(32^2)/4 = 4826\ \text{mm}^2$, d = 520 mm, b_w = 300 mm, D_f = 100 mm

Neutral axis depth:

- First assuming $kd \le D_f$ [Figure 4.15(b)], and equating moments of compression and (transformed) tension areas about the neutral axis,

$$b_f \times (kd)^2/2 = mA_{st}(d - kd) \Rightarrow 900 \times (kd)^2/2 = 10.98 \times 4826 \times (520 - kd)$$

  Solving, kd = 195.5 mm.
  As this is greater than D_f = 100 mm, the assumption $kd \le D_f$ is incorrect.
- For $kd > D_f$, the neutral axis is located in the web [Figure 4.15(c)],

$$(900 - 300)(100)(kd - 50) + 300(kd)^2/2 = 10.98 \times 4826 \times (520 - kd)$$

  Solving, kd = **211.2 mm**

Stresses:

- Relating the compressive stress f_{c1} at the flange bottom to f_c,

$$f_{c1} = f_c\left(\frac{211.2 - 100}{211.2}\right) = 0.527 f_c$$

- Compressive force $C = 0.5 f_c b_f (kd) - 0.5 f_{c1}(b_f - b_w)(kd - D_f)$

$$= 0.5f_c[(900 \times 211.2) - 0.527 \times (900 - 300)(211.2 - 100)]$$
$$= 0.5f_c[(190080) - (35161)]\ \text{N}$$

- Taking moments of forces about the tension steel centroid,

$$250 \times 10^6 = 0.5 f_c\left[(190080)(520 - 211.2/3) - (35161)\left(520 - 100 - \frac{211.2 - 100}{3}\right)\right]$$

  Solving, f_c = **6.94 MPa**
  (which, incidentally, is less than the permissible stress σ_{cbc} = 8.5 MPa for M 25 concrete).

- Now applying $C = T$,

  $0.5 \times 6.94 \times [190080 - 35161] = 4826 f_{st}$

  $\Rightarrow \quad f_{st} = \mathbf{111\ MPa}$

- Alternatively, from the stress distribution diagram [Figure 4.15(d)]

  $$f_{st} = m f_c \left(\frac{d - kd}{kd} \right) \Rightarrow f_{st} = \frac{10.98 \times 6.94(520 - 211.2)}{211.2} = \mathbf{111\ MPa} \text{ (as before)}$$

  (which, incidentally, is less than the permissible stress $\sigma_{st} = 130$ MPa)

Example 4.5

For the T-beam problem in Example 4.4, determine the allowable moment capacity.

Solution

- From the previous Example, the neutral axis depth factor

  $k = 211.2/520 = 0.4062$

- For a 'balanced section', as per Eq. 4.23,

  $$k_b = \frac{280}{280 + (3 \times 130)} = 0.4179$$

- As $k < k_b$, the section is 'under-reinforced (WSM)'.

  Accordingly, $f_{st} = \sigma_{st} = 130$ MPa (for Fe 250 steel, $\phi > 20$ mm);

  $$f_c = \left(\frac{kd}{d - kd} \right) \left(\frac{f_{st}}{m} \right) = \left(\frac{211.2}{520 - 211.2} \right) \left(\frac{130}{10.98} \right) = \mathbf{8.09\ MPa}$$

  $f_{c1} = 0.527 f_c = \mathbf{4.3\ MPa}$

  Substituting in Eq. 4.34,

- $$M_{all} = \frac{1}{2} \times 8.09 \times 900 \times 211.2 \times (520 - 211.2/3)$$
  $$- \frac{1}{2} \times 4.3 \times (900 - 300) \times (211.2 - 100) \times \left[520 - 100 - \left(\frac{211.2 - 100}{3} \right) \right]$$

  $= 291.4 \times 10^6$ Nmm $=$ **291.4 kNm**

- *Note:*

  The answer could have been easily obtained using the result of Example 4.4, and making use of the *linear elastic* assumption underlying WSM. A compressive stress $f_c = 6.94$ MPa results from a moment $M = 250$ kNm. Hence, the allowable stress $f_c = 8.09$ MPa corresponds to a moment $M_{all} = 250 \times \left(\frac{8.09}{6.94} \right)$ = 291.4 kNm (as before).

4.6.5 Analysis of Doubly Reinforced Sections

When *compression reinforcement* is provided in addition to *tension* reinforcement in beams, such beams are termed *doubly reinforced* beams. *Hanger bars* of nominal diameter, used for the purpose of holding stirrups, do not normally qualify as compression reinforcement – unless the area of such bars is significant (greater than 0.2 per cent).

In the discussions related to Figure 4.13, it was shown that merely providing tension steel in excess of that required for the 'balanced section' ($p_{t,b}$) is not an effective way of improving the allowable moment capacity of the section, because the increase in the beam's capacity to carry flexural tension (with $f_{st} = \sigma_{st}$) is not matched by a corresponding increase in its capacity to carry flexural compression. One of the ways of solving this problem is by providing compression steel.

It may further be recalled (refer Section 4.6.2) that the *permissible stress* in compression steel (σ_{sc}) is generally restricted to 1.5 m times the stress in the adjoining concrete (f_{csc}). Accordingly, the 'transformed section' takes the configuration shown in Figure 4.16(b) for rectangular sections. For convenience, the concrete area under compression (i.e., above the NA) is treated as the 'gross' concrete area, i.e., disregarding the area displaced by the steel embedded therein. The concrete area displaced by the embedded compression bars (area A_{sc}) is accounted for by taking the 'effective' transformed area of steel as $(1.5m - 1)A_{sc}$. The compression steel is generally kept as close to the face of the extreme compression concrete fibre as permitted by considerations of minimum cover, in order to maximise its effectiveness. The distance between the centroid of the compression steel and the extreme compression fibre in concrete is usually denoted by d'.

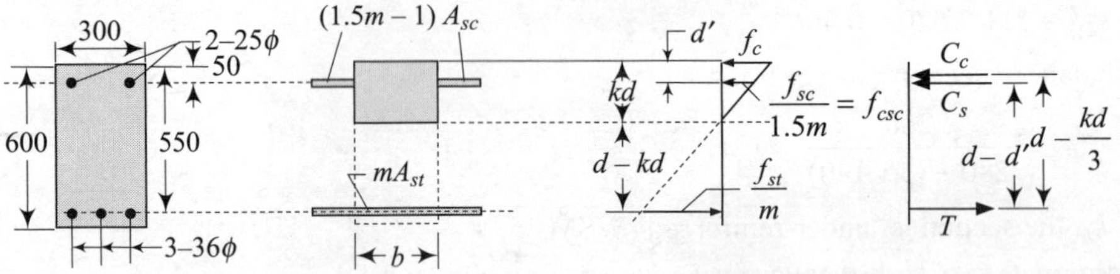

(a) Beam section (b) Transformed section (c) Stresses (d) Resultant forces

Fig. 4.16 Cracked section analysis of a doubly-reinforced beam.

Rectangular Sections

Referring to the transformed section shown in Figure 4.16(b), the neutral axis is determined by solving the following equation (considering moments of areas about the NA),

$$\frac{b(kd)^2}{2} + (1.5m - 1)A_{sc}(kd - d') = mA_{st}(d - kd) \tag{4.35}$$

The force equilibrium equation is given by:

$$C_c + C_s = T \tag{4.36}$$

where C_c and C_s denote the net compressive forces in concrete and steel respectively:

$$C_c = 0.5 f_c b(kd) \tag{4.37a}$$

$$C_s = (1.5mf_{csc})A_{sc} - f_{csc}A_{sc}$$

$$\Rightarrow \quad C_s = (1.5m - 1)A_{sc}f_{csc} \tag{4.37b}$$

Where $$f_{csc} = f_c\left(\frac{kd - d'}{kd}\right) \tag{4.38}$$

And $T = A_{st}f_{st}$ (as before)

Further, taking moments of forces about the centroid of the tension steel,

$$M = C_c(d - kd/3) + C_s(d - d') \tag{4.39}$$

Flanged Sections

If the neutral axis falls inside the flange ($kd \leq D_f$), then the section can be effectively treated as a rectangular section, $b_f \times d$, as discussed earlier.

However, if $kd > D_f$, the equation to determine the neutral axis (in lieu of Eq. 4.35) is as follows:

$$(b_f - b_w)D_f(kd - D_f/2) + b_w(kd)^2/2 + (1.5m - 1)A_{sc}(kd - d') = mA_{st}(d - kd) \tag{4.40}$$

In the force equilibrium equation [Eq. 4.36], the net compressive force in concrete is determined (as before) by considering the difference between the two rectangles $b_f \times kd$ and $(b_f - b_w) \times (kd - D_f)$ – whereby,

$$C_c = 0.5f_c\left[b_f(kd) - (b_f - b_w)\frac{(kd - D_f)^2}{kd}\right] \tag{4.41}$$

Finally, the moment equilibrium equation [Eq. 4.39] takes the following form:

$$M = 0.5f_c\left[b_f(kd)(d - kd/3) - (b_f - b_w)\frac{(kd - D_f)^2}{kd}\left(d - D_f - \frac{kd - D_f}{3}\right)\right] + (1.5m - 1)A_{sc}f_c\frac{(kd - d')}{kd}(d - d') \tag{4.42}$$

It may be noted that although Eq. 4.42 appears rather lengthy, it can be derived easily from first principles.

Example 4.6

The cross-sectional dimensions of a doubly reinforced beam are shown in Figure 4.16(a). Determine the stresses in concrete and steel corresponding to a service load moment of 191 kNm. Further, determine the allowable moment on the beam section. Assume M 25 concrete and Fe 250 steel

Solution

- Given: $b = 300$ mm, $d = 550$ mm, $d' = 50$ mm, $\sigma_{cbc} = 8.5$ MPa, $\sigma_{st} = 130$ MPa ($\phi > 20$ mm)

Transformed section properties [Figure 4.16(b)]:

- modular ratio $m = 10.98$ (for M 25 concrete)

$$A_{st} = 3 \times \frac{\pi \times (36)^2}{4} = 3054 \text{ mm}^2; \; A_{sc} = 2 \times \frac{\pi \times (25)^2}{4} = 982 \text{ mm}^2$$

- Transformed tension steel area = $mA_{st} = 33533$ mm^2
- Transformed compression steel area = $(1.5m - 1)A_{sc} = 15192$ mm^2

Neutral axis depth:

- Considering moments of areas about the neutral axis,

$$\frac{300(kd)^2}{2} + 15192\,(kd - 50) = 33533(550 - kd)$$

Solving, $kd = 230.5$ mm.

Stresses due to M = 191 kNm:

- Considering the linear stress distribution [Figure 4.16(c)],

$$f_{csc} = f_c\left(\frac{230.5-50}{230.5}\right) = 0.7831 f_c$$

$$C_c = 0.5 \times f_c \times 300 \times 230.5 = 34578 f_c$$

$$C_s = 15192 \times 0.7831 \times f_c = 11896 f_c$$

- Taking moments about the tension steel centroid,

$$M = C_c(d - kd/3) + C_s(d - d')$$

$$\Rightarrow \quad 191 \times 10^6 = f_c\left[34578 \times (550 - 230.5/3) + 11896 \times (550 - 50)\right]$$

$$\Rightarrow \quad f_c = \mathbf{8.561\ MPa}$$

(which, incidentally, exceeds $\sigma_{cbc} = 8.5$ MPa)

- *Compressive stress in steel:*

$$f_{sc} = 1.5 m f_{csc} = 1.5 \times 10.98 \times (0.7831 \times 8.561) = \mathbf{110\ MPa}$$

- *Tensile stress in steel:*

$$f_{st} = mf_c\left(\frac{d-kd}{kd}\right) = 10.98 \times 8.561 \times \left(\frac{550-230.5}{230.5}\right) = \mathbf{130\ MPa}$$

[Alternatively, $C_c + C_s = T \Rightarrow f_{st} = \dfrac{8.561(34578 + 11896)}{3054}$
$= 130$ MPa (as before).

Allowable bending moment:

- For a 'balanced (WSM) section', $k_b = \dfrac{280}{280 + 3(130)} = 0.4179$

For the given section, $k = 230.5/550 = 0.4190 > k_b = 0.4179$
Hence the section is 'over-reinforced (WSM)',
whereby $f_c = \sigma_{cbc} = 8.5$ MPa.

$$M_{all} = 8.5\left[34578 \times (550 - 230.5/3) + 11896 \times (500)\right]$$

$$= 189.6 \times 10^6 \text{ Nmm} = \mathbf{189.6\ kNm}$$

[Alternatively, $M_{all} = 191 \times \left(\dfrac{8.5}{8.561}\right) = 189.6$ kNm]

Example 4.7

In the previous Example, it is seen that the service load moment of 191 kNm exceeds the allowable moment (equal to 189.6 MPa). If the problem were a design problem (instead of an analysis problem), how is it possible to arrive at the appropriate values of A_{st} and A_{sc} (without changing the size of the section and the grades of concrete and steel) so that the allowable moment is raised to 191 kNm?

Solution

- As explained earlier (with reference to Figure 4.13), 'over–reinforced (WSM)' sections are uneconomical. This is true not only for 'singly reinforced' sections, but also 'doubly reinforced' sections. The neutral axis depth kd should be ideally restricted to that corresponding to the balanced section ($k_b d = 0.4179 \times 550 = 229.8$ mm). Accordingly, applying Eq. 4.35,

$$300 \times (229.8)^2/2 + (1.5 \times 10.98 - 1)\,A_{sc}\,(229.8 - 50) = 10.98A_{st}\,(550 - 229.8)$$

$$\Rightarrow \quad A_{st} = (0.8A_{sc} + 2253)\ \text{mm}^2$$

A_{sc} is to be determined from Eq. 4.39 for $M = 191$ kNm and $f_c = \sigma_{cbc} = 8.5$ MPa,

$$191 \times 10^6 = (0.5 \times 8.5 \times 300 \times 229.8) \times (550 - 229.8/3) + (1.5 \times 10.98 - 1)A_{sc} \times 8.5 \times \frac{(229.8 - 50) \times (550 - 50)}{229.8}$$

$$\Rightarrow \quad A_{sc} = \mathbf{1017\ mm^2}$$

whereby $A_{st} = 0.8 \times 1017 + 2253 =$ **3058 mm²**

- **Alternative Solution:**

Let

$$A_{st} = A_{st1} + A_{st2} \tag{4.43}$$

where, A_{st1} corresponds to the area required for a *singly reinforced* 'balanced (WSM)' section[†], and A_{st2} corresponds to the additional tension steel (with $f_{st} = \sigma_{st}$) required to resist the moment $M - M_{wb}$, in combination with the compression steel A_{SC} whose stress is given by 1.5m times f_{csc}, where

$$f_{csc} = \sigma_{cbc}\left(1 - \frac{d'}{k_b d}\right) \tag{4.44}$$

[In doubly reinforced sections, the stress 1.5 mf_{csc} is generally less than the maximum limit $\tilde{\sigma}_{sc}$ given in Section 4.6.2.]

Accordingly,

$$A_{st1} = \frac{M_{wb}}{\sigma_{st} d(1 - k_b/3)} \tag{4.45}$$

$$A_{st2} = \frac{M - M_{wb}}{\sigma_{st}(d - d')} \tag{4.46}$$

$$A_{sc} = \frac{M - M_{wb}}{(1.5m - 1)\,f_{csc}\,(d - d')} \tag{4.47}$$

The formula for M_{wb} is obtainable by Eq. 4.25. For the present problem, applying the various formulae with $k_b = 0.418$, $b = 300$ mm, $d = 550$ mm, $m = 10.98$, $\sigma_{st} = 130$ MPa, $\sigma_{cbc} = 8.5$ MPa, and $M = 191 \times 10^6$ Nmm,

$$M_{wb} = 0.5 \times 8.5 \times 300 \times (0.4179 \times 550) \times (1 - 0.4179/3)550 \qquad \text{[Eq. 4.25]}$$

$$= 138.72 \times 10^6\ \text{Nmm}$$

$$A_{st1} = \frac{138.72 \times 10^6}{130 \times 550(1 - 0.4179/3)} = 2254\ \text{mm}^2 \qquad \text{[Eq. 4.45]}$$

$$A_{st2} = \frac{(191.0 - 138.72) \times 10^6}{130(550 - 50)} = 804\ \text{mm}^2 \qquad \text{[Eq. 4.46]}$$

---

† Note that allowance has to be made for the area A_{sc} displaced by the concrete; this is done in the calculation for the required area of the compression steel [Eq. 4.47].

$\therefore \quad A_{st} = 2254 + 804 = \mathbf{3058\ mm^2}$ [Eq. 4.43]

$$f_{csc} = 8.5 \times \left(1 - \frac{50}{0.4179 \times 550}\right) = 6.651 \text{ MPa} \quad \text{[Eq. 4.44]}$$

$$\Rightarrow \quad A_{sc} = \frac{(191.0 - 138.72) \times 10^6}{(1.5 \times 10.98 - 1)(6.651)(550 - 50)} = \mathbf{1016\ mm^2} \quad \text{[Eq. 4.47]}$$

Example 4.8

Consider the T-beam section of Example 4.4 with additional compression reinforcement of 3–32ϕ bars of Fe 250 grade and d′ = 50 mm. Determine the allowable moment capacity.

Solution

- Given: $b_f = 850$ mm, $D_f = 100$ mm, $b_w = 250$ mm, $d = 520$ mm, $A_{st} = 3695$ mm^2, $m = 10.98$ (for M 25 concrete), $d' = 50$ mm,

$$A_{sc} = \frac{3 \times \pi \times (32)^2}{4} = 2413 \text{ mm}^2$$

Transformed tension steel area $= mA_{st} = 52979$ mm^2

Transformed compression steel area $= (1.5m - 1)A_{sc} = 37329$ mm^2

- Assuming first $kd \le D_f$, and $kd > d'$, and solving Eq. 4.35 with $b = b_f$,

$kd = 174.3$ mm

As $\quad kd > D_f$, the assumption $kd \le D_f$, is incorrect.

- Now solving Eq. 4.40 for $kd \ge D_f$, $kd = 182.5$ mm $\Rightarrow k = 182.5/520 = 0.3509$

For a 'balanced (WSM)' section with $\sigma_{st} = 130$ MPa [Eq. 4.23], $k_b = 0.4179$

- As $k = 0.3509 < k_b$, the section is 'under-reinforced (WSM)' whereby $f_{st} = \sigma_{st} = 130$ MPa. Considering the linear stress distribution [Eq. 4.32(b)],

$$f_c = \frac{130}{10.98} \times \frac{182.5}{520 - 182.5} = 6.4 \text{ MPa } (< \sigma_{cbc} = 8.5 \text{ MPa})$$

- Substituting in Eq. 4.42,

$M_{all} = \mathbf{295\ kNm}$

Two points may be noted with regard to *working stress design* of doubly-reinforced sections:

1. There is no advantage in using high strength steel as compression reinforcement as the permissible stress* is relatively low and unrelated to the grade of steel.
2. In order to resist a very high moment, a large area of compression steel is called for; the A_{sc} required may even exceed A_{st}

These are serious shortcomings of WSM, which result in uneconomical designs. Owing to these and other reasons explained in Chapter 3, WSM is no longer employed in practical designs – being replaced by the more rational *limit states design*.

* Refer Section 4.6.2

4.7 Analysis at Ultimate Limit State

Whereas the previous section (Section 4.6) dealt with the 'analysis at *service loads*', the present section deals with the 'analysis at *ultimate loads*'. The former is based on the *working stress method* (WSM) and is also applicable to the analysis of 'serviceability limit states', whereas the latter is based on the 'ultimate limit state' of the *limit states method* (LSM).

Having studied analysis at '*service loads*' in some detail (including the solution to a number of Example problems), it is likely that the student may get somewhat confused while undertaking the task of analysing the same problems at '*ultimate loads*'. The important question that is likely to disturb the student is –why go through this process of analysing at service loads as well as ultimate loads? The answer to this question was given in Chapter 3, where it was explained that a structure has to be both **safe** (at various *ultimate* limit states) and **serviceable** (at various *serviceability* limit states). At ultimate limit states, the load levels are those corresponding to impending failure of structure, whereas at serviceability limit states, the load levels and stresses are those applicable in the day-to-day service of the structure. This section investigates the 'safety' of flexural members (of given design) at the *ultimate limit state in flexure*. The previous section discussed the calculation of flexural stresses under service loads required for serviceability analysis (described in Chapter 10), and also the calculation of 'allowable bending moment' based on the WSM concept of *permissible stresses*. The latter was included to enable the student to gain a first-hand understanding of the traditional (and, earlier much-used) working stress method – which retains a place in the Code, albeit as an Appendix, and is sometimes used in the design of special structures such as water tanks and road bridges.

Therefore, the student will do well to keep in perspective the background of the present section, dealing with the *analysis* at the 'ultimate limit state in flexure'. The expressions derived here will find use again in the next chapter (Chapter 5), which deals with the *design* of reinforced concrete beams at the ultimate limit state in flexure.

In this section, the Code procedure for analysis is discussed. The calculations are based on the idealised stress-strain curves for concrete and steel, as specified by the Code. Moreover, the *design* stress-strain curves (involving partial safety factors γ_c, γ_s) are used, as explained in Section 3.6.

4.7.1 Assumptions in Analysis

The behaviour of reinforced concrete beam sections at ultimate loads has been explained in detail in Section 4.5.3. The basic assumptions involved in the analysis at the ultimate limit state of flexure (Cl. 38.1 of the Code) are listed here [see also Figure 4.17]. (Most of these assumptions have already been explained earlier.)

(a) Plane sections normal to the beam axis remain plane after bending, i.e., in an initially straight beam, strain varies linearly over the depth of the section.

(b) The maximum compressive strain in concrete (at the outermost fibre) ε_{cu} shall be taken as 0.0035 [Figure 4.17(b)]. This is so, because regardless of whether the beam is *under-reinforced* or *over-reinforced*, collapse invariably occurs by the crushing of concrete (as explained in Section 4.5.3).

(c) The *design stress-strain curve* of concrete in flexural compression (recommended by the Code) is as depicted in Figure 3.5. [The Code also permits the use of any other shape of the stress-strain curve *which results in substantial agreement with the results of tests.*] The partial safety factor $\gamma_c = 1.5$ is to be applied.

(d) The tensile strength of the concrete is ignored.

(e) The *design stress-strain curves* for mild steel and cold-worked bars are as depicted in Figures 3.6 and 3.7 respectively. Here too, the partial safety factor $\gamma_s = 1.15$ is to be applied.

(f) The strain ε_{st} in the tension reinforcement (at its centroid) at the ultimate limit state shall not be less than ε^*_{st} [Figure 4.17], defined as:

$$\varepsilon^*_{st} \equiv (0.87 f_y / E_s) + 0.002 \tag{4.48}$$

This is equivalent to defining the yield stress f_y of steel as the stress corresponding to 0.002 strain offset (0.2% proof stress) – regardless of whether the steel has a well-defined yield point or not. The yield strain corresponding to f_y is then given by $0.002 + f_y/E_s$. Introducing the partial safety factor $\gamma_s = 1.15$ to allow for the variability in the steel strength, the *design*† *yield strength*, $f_{yd} = f_y/1.15 = \phi_s f_y = 0.87 f_y$ and using this in lieu of f_y, the yield strain ε_y [refer Figure 3.7] is given by:

$$\varepsilon_y = 0.002 + (0.87 f_y/E_s) \equiv \varepsilon^*_{st}$$

In the case of mild steel, which has a well-defined yield point ($\varepsilon_y = 0.87 f_y/E_s$, as shown in Figure 3.6), the requirement (f) cited above may appear to be conservative. However, the Code specifies a uniform criterion [Eq. 4.48] for *all* grades of steel. The intention here is to ensure that 'yielding' of the tension steel takes place at the ultimate limit state, so that the consequent failure is *ductile* in nature, providing ample warning of the impending collapse.

4.7.2 Limiting Depth of Neutral Axis

Based on the assumption given above, an expression for the depth of the neutral axis at the ultimate limit state, x_u, can be easily obtained from the strain diagram in Figure 4.17(b). Considering similar triangles,

$$\frac{x_u}{d} = \frac{0.0035}{0.0035 + \varepsilon_{st}} \tag{4.49}$$

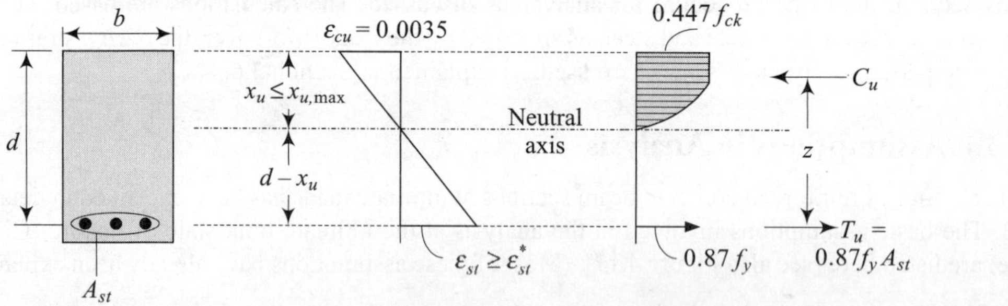

(a) Beam section (b) Strains (c) Stresses

Fig. 4.17 Behaviour of singly reinforced rectangular section at ultimate limit state in flexure.

According to the Code [requirement (f) in Section 4.7.1], $\varepsilon_{st} \geq \varepsilon^*_{st}$, implying that there is a limiting (maximum) value of the neutral axis depth $x_{u,\max}$ corresponding to $\varepsilon_{st} = \varepsilon^*_{st}$. This is obtained by substituting the expression for ε^*_{st} [Eq. 4.48] in Eq. 4.49:

† It is interesting to note that the use of the *design* yield stress $f_{yd} = 0.87 f_y$, instead of the characteristic yield stress f_y, results in a slightly *lesser* (and hence, less conservative!) value of the yield strain ε_y [refer Figures 3.6, 3.7]. The addition of 0.002 [Eq. 4.48] will offset this. The factor $0.87 = 1/\gamma_s$, denoted by ϕ_s, is also known as the 'material resistance factor' for steel.

$$\frac{x_{u,\max}}{d} = \frac{0.0035}{0.0055 + 0.87 f_y / E_s} \tag{4.50}$$

The values of $x_{u,\max}/d$ for different grades of steel, obtained by applying Eq. 4.50, are listed in Table 4.3. Being dependant only on the limiting strains in concrete and steel, it may be noted that the constants given in Table 4.3 are applicable to all cross-sectional shapes, and remain valid for doubly reinforced sections as well.

Table 4.3 *Limiting depth of neutral axis for different grades of steel*

Steel Grade	Fe 250	Fe 415	Fe 500
$x_{u,\max}/d$	0.5313	0.4791	0.4560

The limiting depth of neutral axis $x_{u,\max}$ corresponds to the so-called *balanced* section, i.e., a section that is expected to result in a 'balanced' failure (i.e., simultaneous attainment of limiting compressive strain of 0.0035 in concrete and the minimum specified tensile strain to ensure yielding in steel, given by Eq. 4.48) at the ultimate limit state in flexure [refer Section 4.5.3]. If the neutral axis depth x_u is less than $x_{u,\max}$, then the section is *under-reinforced* (resulting in a 'tension' failure); whereas if x_u exceeds $x_{u,\max}$, it is *over-reinforced* (resulting in a 'compression' failure).

4.7.3 Analysis of Singly Reinforced Rectangular Sections

Analysis of a given reinforced concrete section at the ultimate limit state of flexure implies the determination of the *ultimate moment of resistance* M_{uR} of the section. This is easily obtained from the couple resulting from the flexural stresses [Figure 4.17(c)]:

$$M_{uR} = C_u \cdot z = T_u \cdot z \tag{4.51}$$

where C_u and T_u are the resultant (ultimate) forces in compression and tension respectively, and z is the lever arm.

$$T_u = f_{st} A_{st} \tag{4.52}$$

where

$$f_{st} = 0.87 f_y \quad \text{for} \quad x_u \le x_{u,\max}$$

and the line of action of T_u corresponds to the level of the centroid of the tension steel.

Concrete Stress Block in Compression

In order to determine the magnitude of C_u and its line of action, it is necessary to analyse the *concrete stress block* in compression. As ultimate failure of a reinforced concrete beam in flexure occurs by the crushing of concrete, for both under- and over-reinforced beams, the shape of the compressive stress distribution ('stress block') at failure will be, in both cases, as shown in Figure 4.18[also refer assumptions (b) and (c) in Section 4.7.1]. The value of C_u can be computed knowing that the compressive stress in concrete is uniform at $0.447 f_{ck}$ for a depth of $3x_u/7$, and below this it varies parabolically over a depth of $4x_u/7$ to zero at the neutral axis [Figure 4.18].

> Over time and across National Codes, rectangular, trapezoidal, parabolic and other shapes have been used for concrete stress-strain relationship. IS 456 (2000) Cl. 38.1.c permits the use of such relationships.

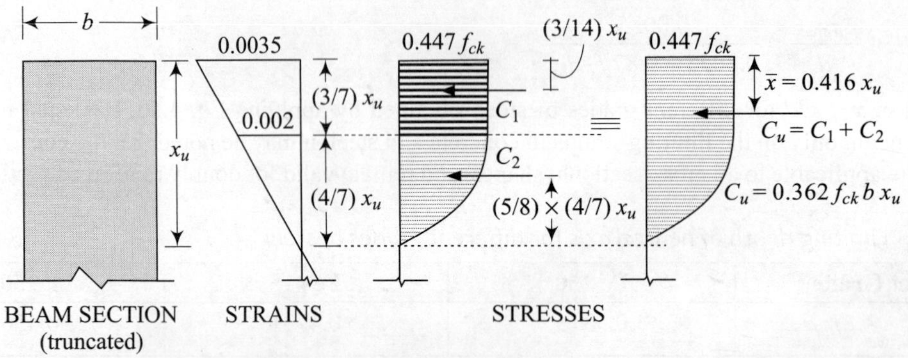

Fig. 4.18 Concrete stress-block parameters in compression.

For a rectangular section of width b,

$$C_u = 0.447 f_{ck}\, b\left[\frac{3x_u}{7} + \left(\frac{2}{3}\times\frac{4x_u}{7}\right)\right]$$

$$\Rightarrow \qquad C_u = 0.362 f_{ck} b x_u \tag{4.53}$$

Also, the line of action of C_u is determined by the centroid of the stress block, located at a distance $\bar{x}$ from the concrete fibres subjected to the maximum compressive strain. Accordingly, considering moments of compressive forces C_u, C_1 and C_2 [Figure 4.18] about the maximum compressive strain location,

$$(0.362 f_{ck} b x_u)\times\bar{x} = (0.447 f_{ck} b x_u)\left[\left(\frac{3}{7}\right)\left(\frac{1.5x_u}{7}\right) + \left(\frac{2}{3}\times\frac{4}{7}\right)\left(x_u - \frac{5}{8}\times\frac{4x_u}{7}\right)\right]$$

Solving,

$$\bar{x} = 0.416\, x_u \tag{4.54}$$

Depth of Neutral Axis

> The definition of neutral axis depth, x_u, of a RC beam section in LSM is distinctly different from that defined earlier in WSM (which is identical with the depth, x, of the centroidal axis)

For any given section, the depth of the neutral axis should be such that $C_u = T_u$, satisfying equilibrium of forces. Equating $C_u = T_u$, with expressions for C_u and T_u, given by Eq. 4.53 and Eq. 4.52 respectively:

$$x_u = \frac{0.87 f_y A_{st}}{0.362 f_{ck} b}, \quad \text{valid only if resulting } x_u \le x_{u,\max} \tag{4.55}$$

For the condition $x_u > x_{u,\max}$, $\varepsilon_{st} < \varepsilon^*_{st}$ [Figure 4.17], implying that, at the ultimate limit state, the steel would not have 'yielded' (as per the proof stress definition† for f_y) and the steel stress cannot be taken as $f_y/\gamma_s = 0.87 f_y$. Hence Eq. 4.52 and therefore Eq. 4.55 are not applicable. When the steel has not yielded, the true location of the neutral axis is obtained by a trial-and-error method, called *strain compatibility method*, involving the following steps:

† In the case of low-grade mild steel (Fe 250), which has a sharply defined yield point, the steel would have yielded and reached f_y even at a strain slightly lower than ε^*_{st}. In such cases, one may find that $f_{st} = 0.87 f_y$ even for values of x_u slightly in excess of $x_{u,\max}$.

1. Assume a suitable initial (trial) value of x_u.
2. Determine ε_{st} by considering *strain compatibility* [Eq. 4.49]:

$$\varepsilon_{st} = 0.0035(d/x_u - 1) \tag{4.56}$$

3. Determine the *design stress* f_{st} corresponding to ε_{st} using the design stress-strain curve [Figure 3.7, Table 3.2].
4. Derive the value of x_u corresponding to f_{st} by considering $T_u = f_{st} A_{st}$ and applying the force equilibrium condition $C_u = T_u$, whereby

$$x_u = \frac{f_{st} A_{st}}{0.362 f_{ck} b} \tag{4.57}$$

5. Compare this value of x_u with the value used in step (1). If the difference between the two values is acceptably small, accept the value given by step (4); otherwise, repeat steps (2) to (5) with an improved (say, average) value of x_u, until convergence.

Ultimate Moment of Resistance

The *ultimate moment of resistance* M_{uR} of a given beam section is obtainable from Eq. 4.51. The lever arm z, for the case of the singly reinforced rectangular section [Figure 4.17(d), Figure 4.18] is given by

$$z = d - 0.416x_u \tag{4.58}$$

Accordingly, in terms of the concrete compressive strength,

$$M_{uR} = 0.362 f_{ck} b x_u (d - 0.416x_u) \quad \text{for all } x_u \tag{4.59}$$

Alternatively, in terms of the steel tensile stress,

$$M_{uR} = f_{st} A_{st} (d - 0.416 x_u) \quad \text{for all } x_u \tag{4.60}$$

with $\quad f_{st} = 0.87 f_y \quad \text{for} \quad x_u \le x_{u,\max}$

Limiting Moment of Resistance

The *limiting moment of resistance* $M_{u,\lim}$ of a given (singly reinforced, rectangular) section, according to the Code (Cl. G–1.1), corresponds to the condition $x_u = x_{u,\max}$, defined by Eq. 4.50. From Eq. 4.59, it follows that:

$$M_{u,\lim} = 0.362 f_{ck} b x_{u,\max} (d - 0.416 x_{u,\max}) \tag{4.61}$$

$$\Rightarrow \quad \frac{M_{u,\lim}}{f_{ck} b d^2} \equiv K = 0.362\left(\frac{x_{u,\max}}{d}\right)\left(1 - 0.416\frac{x_{u,\max}}{d}\right) \tag{4.61a}$$

The values of the non-dimensional parameter K for different grades of steel [refer Table 4.3] are obtained as 0.1498, 0.1389 and 0.1338 for Fe 250, Fe 415 and Fe 500 respectively.

Limiting Percentage Tensile Steel

Corresponding to the limiting moment of resistance $M_{u,\lim}$, there is a limiting percentage tensile steel $p_{t,\lim} = 100 \times A_{st,\lim}/bd$. An expression for $p_{t,\lim}$ is obtainable from Eq. 4.55 with $x_u = x_{u,\max}$:

$$\frac{x_{u,\max}}{d} = \frac{0.87 f_y}{0.362 f_{ck}} \times \frac{p_{t,\lim}}{100}$$

$$\Rightarrow \qquad p_{t,\text{lim}} = 41.61\left(\frac{f_{ck}}{f_y}\right)\left(\frac{x_{u,\max}}{d}\right) \tag{4.62}$$

The values of $p_{t,\text{lim}}$ and $M_{u,\text{lim}}/bd^2$ (in MPa units) for, different combinations of steel and concrete grades are listed in Table 4.4. These values correspond to the so-called 'balanced' section [refer Section 4.5.3] for a singly reinforced rectangular section.

Table 4.4 *Limiting values of $p_{t,lim}$ and $M_{u,lim}/bd^2$ for singly reinforced rectangular beam sections for various grades of steel and concrete.*

(a) $p_{t,\text{lim}}$ values

	M 20	M 25	M 30	M 35	M 40	M 45	M 50
Fe 250	1.769	2.211	2.653	3.095	3.537	3.979	4.421
Fe 415	0.961	1.201	1.441	1.681	1.921	2.162	2.402
Fe 500	0.759	0.949	1.138	1.328	1.518	1.708	1.897

(b) $M_{u,\text{lim}}/bd^2$ values (MPa)

	M 20	M 25	M 30	M 35	M 40	M 45	M 50
Fe 250	2.996	3.746	4.495	5.244	5.993	6.742	7.491
Fe 415	2.777	3.472	4.166	4.860	5.555	6.249	6.943
Fe 500	2.675	3.444	4.013	4.682	5.350	6.019	6.688

Safety at Ultimate Limit State in Flexure

The bending moment expected at a beam section at the *ultimate limit state* due to the *factored loads* is called the *factored moment* M_u. For the consideration of various combinations of loads (dead loads, live loads, wind loads, etc.), appropriate load factors should be applied to the specified 'characteristic' loads (as explained in Chapter 3), and the factored moment M_u is determined by structural analysis.

The beam section will be considered to be 'safe', according to the Code, if its ultimate moment of resistance M_{uR} is greater than or equal to the factored moment M_u. In other words, for such a design, the *probability of failure* is acceptably low. It is also the intention of the Code to ensure that at ultimate failure in flexure, the type of failure should be a *tension (ductile) failure* – as explained earlier. For this reason, the Code requires the designer to ensure that $x_u \le x_{u,\max}$ [Table 4.3], whereby it follows that, *for a singly reinforced rectangular section*, the tensile reinforcement percentage p_t should not exceed $p_{t,\text{lim}}$ and the ultimate moment of resistance M_{uR} should not exceed $M_{u,\text{lim}}$ [Table 4.4]. The Code (Cl. G–1.1d) clearly states:

> 'If x_u/d is greater than the limiting value, the section shall be redesigned.'

The topic of *design* is covered in detail in Chapter 5. The present chapter deals with analysis – and, in *analysis*, it is not unlikely to encounter beam sections (already constructed) in which $p_t > p_{t,\text{lim}}$, whereby $x_u > x_{u,\max}$ and $M_{uR} > M_{u,\text{lim}}$. In such 'over-reinforced' sections, the *strength* requirement may be satisfied, but not the *ductility*† requirement. The question arises: are such sections acceptable? The answer, in general, would be in

† The ductility requirement may be partly satisfied in the case of mild steel (Fe 250), even if x_u slightly exceeds $x_{u,\max}$; this is explained later with reference to Figure 4.19.

the negative, except in certain special situations where the section itself is not 'critical' in terms of ductility, and will not lead to a *brittle failure* of the structure under the given *factored loads*. In such exceptional cases, where $M_{uR} > M_u$, and inelastic flexural response[†] is never expected to occur under the given *factored loads*, over-reinforced sections cannot be strictly objected to.

It may be noted that the exact determination of M_{uR} of an over-reinforced section generally involves considerable computational effort, as explained in the next section. An approximate (but conservative) estimate of the ultimate moment capacity of such a section is given by the limiting moment of resistance, $M_{u,\text{lim}}$, which can be easily computed.

Variation of M_{uR} with p_t (for singly reinforced rectangular sections)

$p_t \le p_{t,\text{lim}}$

For $x_u \le x_{u,\max}$, it is possible to arrive at a simple closed–form expression for the ultimate moment of resistance of a given section with a $p_t \le p_{t,\text{lim}}$. First, expressing A_{st} in terms of *pt*:

$$A_{st} = \frac{p_t bd}{100} \tag{4.63}$$

and then substituting in Eq. 4.55,

$$x_u = \frac{0.87}{0.362}\frac{f_y}{f_{ck}}\frac{p_t d}{100} \tag{4.64}$$

Further substituting Eq. 4.63 and Eq. 4.64 in Eq. 4.60,

$$M_{uR} = 0.87 f_y \frac{p_t}{100} bd^2 \left(1 - \frac{0.416 \times 0.87}{0.362}\frac{f_y}{f_{ck}}\frac{p_t}{100}\right)$$

$$\Rightarrow \quad \frac{M_{uR}}{bd^2} = 0.87 f_y \frac{p_t}{100}\left(1 - 1.000\frac{f_y}{f_{ck}}\frac{p_t}{100}\right) \quad \text{for} \quad p_t \le p_{t,\text{lim}} \tag{4.65}$$

$p_t > p_{t,\text{lim}}$

For $p_t > p_{t,\text{lim}}$[‡], $x_u > x_{u,\max}$, whereby the stress in the tension steel at ultimate moment takes a value f_{st} which, in general, is less than the *design yield stress* and not known in advance, and depends on the value of x_u [Eq. 4.56].

To determine f_{st}, the (trial-and-error) *strain compatibility method* (described earlier) has to be employed. The final expression, comparable to Eq. 4.65, takes the following form:

$$\frac{M_{uR}}{bd^2} = f_{st}\frac{p_t}{100}\left(1 - \frac{0.416}{0.362}\frac{f_{st}}{f_{ck}}\frac{p_t}{100}\right) \tag{4.66}$$

[†] for details on 'plastic hinge' formation at the ultimate limit state, refer Chapter 9.

[‡] This condition $p_t > p_{t,\text{lim}}$ is not permitted in *design*. Its only relevance is in *analysis*.

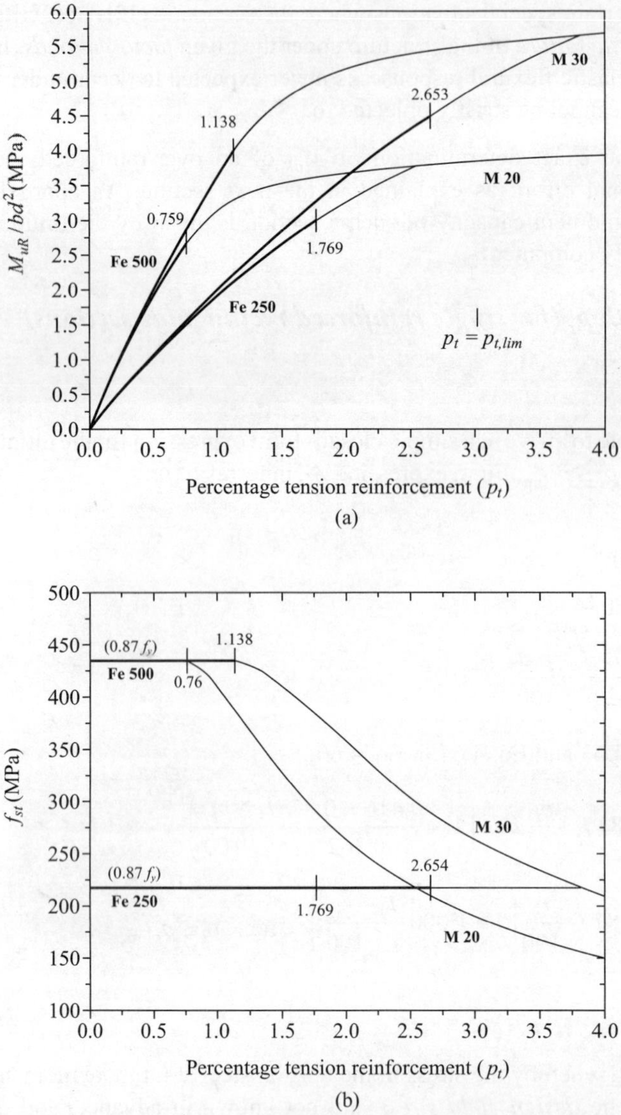

Fig. 4.19 Variation of (a) M_{uR}/bd^2 and (b) f_{st} with p_t.

where $f_{st} \leq 0.87 f_y$ has to satisfy the force equilibrium condition [Eq. 4.57], and the strain ε_{st} corresponding to f_{st} [Figures 3.6, 3.7] must satisfy the strain compatibility condition [Eq. 4.56]. For convenience, Eq. 4.57 is re-arranged as follows:

$$\frac{x_u}{d} = \frac{f_{st}}{0.362 f_{ck}} \frac{p_t}{100} \tag{4.67}$$

The steps involved in the 'strain-compatibility method for determining M_{uR}/bd^2 for a given p_t, are as follows:

1. Assume an initial (trial) value of x_u/d, in excess of $x_{u,max}/d$; an upper limit for trial x_u/d is obtained from Eq. 4.67 with f_{st} assumed $= 0.87f_y$;
2. Determine ε_{st} using Eq. 4.56;
3. Determine f_{st} from ε_{st} using the *design* stress-strain curves [Figures 3.6, 3.7];
4. Calculate the new value of x_u/d using Eq. 4.67;
5. Compare the new value of x_u/d with the old value. If the difference is within acceptable tolerance, proceed to step (6); otherwise, repeat steps (2) to (5) until convergence is attained.
6. Apply Eq. 4.66 and determine M_{uR}/bd^2.

A quick solution can be obtained by means of a computer program. The relationship between M_{uR}/bd^2 (expressed in MPa units) and p_t is plotted in Figure 4.19(a) for two typical grades of steel (Fe 250 and Fe 500) combined with the commonly used grades of concrete (M 20 and M 30). The corresponding relationship between stress f_{st} (at the ultimate limit state) and p_t is depicted in Figure 4.19(b). The relatively thick lines represent the under-reinforced condition $p_t \leq p_{t,\lim}$ (i.e., $M_{uR} \leq M_{uR,\lim}$), whereas the thin lines denote the over-reinforced condition $p_t > p_{t,\lim}$ (i.e., $M_{uR} > M_{uR,\lim}$), and the transition points are marked by thin vertical lines.

It can be seen that these curves in Figure 4.19(a) (for the ultimate limit state) bear resemblance with the corresponding curves in Figure 4.13 (for the service load state).

> The gain in M_{uR} with increase in p_t follows a nearly linear relationship almost up to the 'balanced' point. Also the gain in M_{uR} with higher grades of concrete is marginal for low values of p_t and becomes pronounced only when p_t exceeds $p_{t,\lim}$.

It may be noted from Figure 4.19(b) that with the steel percentage limited to $p_{t,\lim}$, as ultimate moment of resistance M_{uR} is reached, the steel would have already 'yielded' ($f_{st} = 0.87f_y$) and gone into the domain of large inelastic strains, thus ensuring a ductile response. For $p_t > p_{t,\lim}$, the tension steel would not have 'yielded' at the ultimate limit state, with the definition of steel strain at balanced condition as $\varepsilon_{st}^* = 0.002 + (0.87f_y)/E_s$ [refer Section 4.7.1]. However, in the case of Fe 250 steel [Figure 3.6], it can be seen that 'yielding' will actually take place even with a p_t slightly in excess of $p_{t,\lim}$ (or with a steel strain less than ε_{st}^*).

> Hence, in the case of Fe 250 steel, the actual 'under-reinforced' (ductile failure) behaviour extends to some p_t values greater than $p_{t,\lim}$ [Figure 4.19]. However, as explained earlier, the use of p_t values in this range is not permitted by the Code for *design* purpose.

It can also be seen that the gain in M_{uR} with p_t falls off significantly, and somewhat exponentially, beyond the point where f_{st} drops below $0.87f_y$. Beyond the 'balanced' point, there is a stage when the ultimate moment capacity is dictated entirely by the compressive strength of concrete, and hence does not depend on the grade of steel; in this range, $\varepsilon_{st} << \varepsilon_y$, whereby the steel stress is given by $f_{st} = E_s\varepsilon_{st}$, regardless of the grade of steel, and the same $T_u = A_{st}f_{st}$ is obtained whether Fe 250 or Fe 500 steel is used. This is indicated by the merging together of the thin lines (for a given concrete grade, and for Fe 250 and Fe 500 steel grades) in Figure 4.19(a).

> It is thus evident that over-reinforced sections are undesirable not only from the perspective of the loss in ductility, but also from the practical viewpoint of economy.

Analysis Aids

The variation of M_u/bd^2 with p_t for different grades of concrete and steel (depicted in Figure 4.19) is expressed in tabular form and presented in Tables A.2(a), (b) in Appendix A of this book. As with analysis by WSM [Tables A.1(a), (b)], these tables serve as useful *analysis aids*. They enable rapid determination of the ultimate moment capacity of any given singly reinforced rectangular beam section. The use of these tables is demonstrated in Example 4.11.

Example 4.9

Determine the neutral axis depth x_u (at the ultimate limit state) for the beam section in Example 4.2.

Solution

- Given: $b = 300$ mm, $d = 550$ mm, $A_{st} = 1963$ mm^2, $f_y = 500$ MPa, $f_{ck} = 25$ MPa
- For Fe 500 steel, $x_{u,\max}/d = 0.456$ [Table 4.3 or Eq. 4.50]
  $\Rightarrow \quad x_{u,\max} = 0.456 \times 550 = 250.8$ mm
- Assuming $x_u \leq x_{u,\max}$ and applying the force equilibrium condition $C_u = T_u$

$$x_u = \frac{0.87 \times 500 \times 1963}{0.362 \times 25 \times 300} = 314.5 \text{ mm } (> x_{u,\max} = 250.8 \text{ mm})$$

- As $x_u > x_{u,\max}$, steel would not have 'yielded'; accordingly, the 'strain compatibility method' is adopted to obtain the correct value of x_u.

  First Cycle :
  1. assume $x_u \approx (251 + 315)/2 = 283$ mm
  2. strain compatibility $\Rightarrow \varepsilon_{st} = 0.0035\left(\dfrac{550}{283} - 1\right) = 0.00330$
  3. $\Rightarrow f_{st} = 423.9 + (434.8 - 423.9)\left(\dfrac{330 - 312}{417 - 312}\right) = 425.8$ MPa [refer Table 3.2, for Fe 500]
  4. $C_u = T_u \Rightarrow x_u = f_{st} \times \left(\dfrac{1963}{0.362 \times 25 \times 300}\right) = 425.8 \times (0.7230) = 307.8$ mm

  Second Cycle :
  1. assume $x_u \approx (308 + 283)/2 = 295.5$ mm
  2. $\Rightarrow \varepsilon_{st} = 0.0035\left(\dfrac{550}{295.5} - 1\right) = 0.00301$
  3. $\Rightarrow$ [Table 3.2] $f_{st} = 420.5$ MPa
  4. $x_u = 420.5 \times (0.7230) = 304$ mm

  Third Cycle :
  1. assume $x_u \approx (304 + 296)/2 = 300$ mm
  2. $\Rightarrow \varepsilon_{st} = 0.0035\left(\dfrac{550}{300} - 1\right) = 0.00292$
  3. $\Rightarrow f_{st} = 413 + (423.9 - 413) \times \left(\dfrac{292 - 277}{312 - 277}\right) = 417.7$ MPa
  4. $x_u = 417.7 \times (0.7230) = 301.9$ mm

     The final value of x_u may be taken as: $x_u =$ **302 mm**

Example 4.10

Repeat the problem in Example 4.9, considering Fe 250 grade steel in lieu of Fe 500.

Solution

- Given: $b = 300$ mm, $d = 550$ mm, $A_{st} = 1963$ mm^2, $f_y = 250$ MPa, $f_{ck} = 25$ MPa
- For Fe 250 steel, $x_{u,max}/d = 0.5313$ [Table 4.3, Eq. 4.50]

$\Rightarrow \quad x_{u,max} = 0.5313 \times 550 = 292.2$ mm

- Assuming $x_u \leq x_{u,max}$, and applying the force equilibrium condition

$$x_u = \frac{0.87 \times 250 \times 1963}{0.362 \times 25 \times 300} = 157.3 \text{ mm} < x_{u,max} = 292.2 \text{ mm}$$

Therefore, x_u =**157.3 mm**

Example 4.11

Determine the ultimate moments of resistance for the beam sections in (a) Example 4.9 and (b) Example 4.10.

Solution

(a)

- Given: $b = 300$ mm, $d = 550$ mm, $A_{st} = 1963$ mm^2, $f_y = 500$ MPa, $f_{ck} = 25$ MPa
- $x_u = 302$ mm $> x_{u,max} = 250.8$ mm (from Example 4.9).
- Taking moments about the tension steel centroid,

$$M_{uR} = 0.362 f_{ck} b x_u (d - 0.416 x_u) = 0.362 \times 25 \times 300 \times 302 \times (550 - 0.416 \times 302)$$
$$= 347.9 \times 10^6 \text{ Nmm} = \mathbf{348 \text{ kNm}}$$

- Note that M_{uR} can also be calculated in terms of the steel tensile stress f_{st}, which is less than $0.87 f_y$, as $x_u > x_{u,max}$. From the last cycle of iteration in Example 4.9, the value of f_{st} is obtained as 417.7 MPa.

$\Rightarrow \quad M_{uR} = f_{st} A_{st} (d - 0.416 x_u) =$ **348 kNm** (as before)

Note that it is easier to evaluate M_{uR} in terms of the concrete strength.

Alternative (using analysis aids)

$$p_t = \frac{100 \times 1963}{300 \times 550} = 1.190$$

Referring to Table A.2(a) – for M 25 concrete and Fe 500 steel, for $p_t = 1.190$,

$$\frac{M_{uR}}{bd^2} = (3.814 + 3.845)/2 = 3.830 \text{ MPa}$$

$\Rightarrow \quad M_{uR} = 3.830 \times 300 \times 550^2 = 347.6 \times 10^6$ Nmm

= **348 kNm** (exactly as obtained earlier)

(b)

- Given: $b = 300$ mm, $d = 550$ mm, $A_{st} = 1963$ mm^2, $f_y = 250$ MPa, $f_{ck} = 25$ MPa
- $x_u = 157.3$ mm $< x_{u,max} = 292.2$ mm (from Example 4.10)

- Taking moments about the tension steel centroid,

$$M_{uR} = 0.362 \times 25 \times 300 \times 157.3 \times (550 - 0.416 \times 157.3)$$
$$= 206.9 \times 10^6 \text{ Nmm} = \mathbf{207\ kNm}$$

- Alternatively, as $x_u < x_{u,\max}$, it follows that $f_{st} = 0.87f_y$, and

$$M_{uR} = 0.87 f_y A_{st} (d - 0.416 x_u)$$
$$= 0.87 \times 250 \times 1963 \times (550 - 0.416 \times 157.3)$$
$$= 206.8 \times 10^6 \text{ Nmm} = \mathbf{207\ kNm}$$

Alternative (using analysis aids)

$p_t = 1.190$ (as in the previous case).

Referring to Table A.2(a) – for M 25 concrete and Fe 250 steel,

$$\frac{M_{uR}}{bd^2} = (2.264 + 2.297)/2 = 2.281 \text{ MPa}$$

$$\Rightarrow \quad M_{uR} = 2.281 \times 300 \times 550^2 = 207.0 \times 10^6 \text{ Nmm}$$
$$= \mathbf{207\ kNm} \text{ (exactly as obtained earlier)}$$

4.7.4 Analysis of Singly Reinforced Flanged Sections

Flanged beams (T-beams and L-beams) were introduced in Section 4.6.4, where the analysis at *service loads* was discussed. The present section deals with the analysis of these beam sections at the *ultimate limit state.*

The procedure for analysing flanged beams at ultimate loads depends on whether the neutral axis is located in the flange region [Figure 4.20(a)] or in the web region [Figure 4.20(b)].

If the neutral axis lies within the flange (i.e., $x_u \leq D_f$), then – as in the analysis at service loads [refer Section 4.6.4] – all the concrete on the tension side of the neutral axis is assumed ineffective, and the T-section may be analysed as a rectangular section of width b_f and effective depth d [Figure 4.20(a)]. Accordingly, Eq. 4.55 and Eq. 4.59 are applicable with b replaced by b_f.

If the neutral axis lies in the web region (i.e., $x_u > D_f$), then the compressive stress is carried by the concrete in the flange and a portion of the web, as shown in Figure 4.20(b). It is convenient to consider the contributions to the resultant compressive force C_u, from the *web*† portion ($b_w \times x_u$) and the *overhanging flange* portion (width $b_f - b_w$) separately, and to sum up these effects. Estimating the compressive force C_{uw} in the 'web' and its moment contribution M_{uw} is easy, as the full stress block is operative:

$$C_{uw} = 0.362 f_{ck} b_w x_u \tag{4.68a}$$
$$M_{uw} = C_{uw} (d - 0.416\, x_u) \tag{4.68b}$$

However, estimating the compressive force C_{uf} in the flange is rendered difficult by the fact that the stress block for the flange portions may comprise a rectangular area plus a truncated parabolic area [Figure 4.20(c)]. A general expression for the total area of the stress block operative in the flange, as well as an expression for the centroidal location of the stress block, is not convenient to derive for such a case. However, when the portion of the stress block over the flange depth contains only the rectangular part (having a uniform stress $0.447f_{ck}$), which occurs when $3x_u/7 \geq D_f$, (i.e., $D_f/x_u \leq 3/7 = 0.43$), as shown in Figure 4.20(b), an expression for C_{uf} and its moment contribution M_{uf} can easily be formulated (see Code Cl. G-2.3 and G-2.2).

† The 'web' comprises the portion of the beam excluding the overhanging parts of the flange.

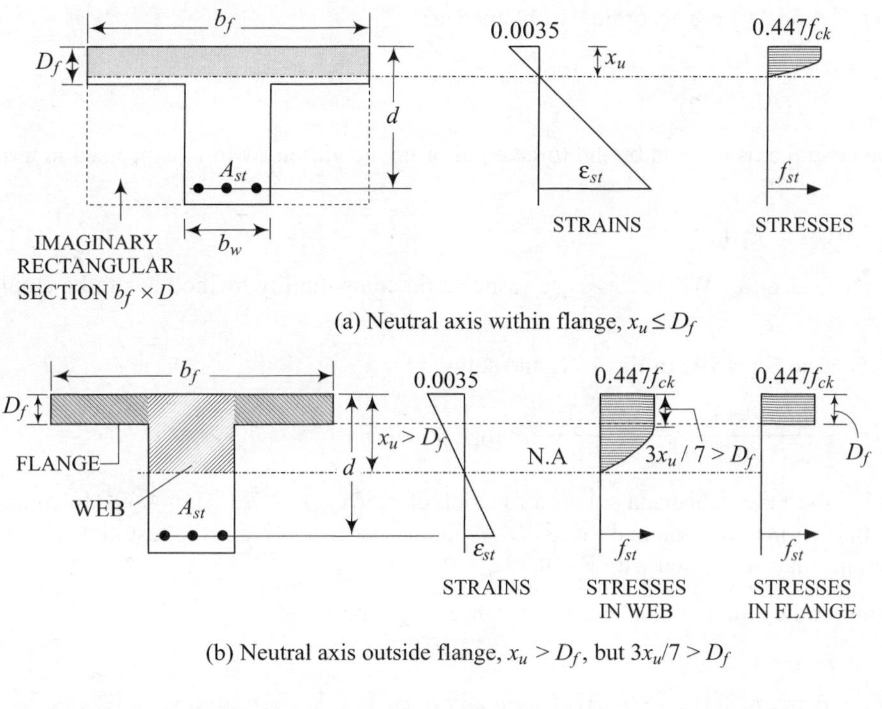

Fig. 4.20 Behaviour of flanged beam section at ultimate limit state.

For the case, $1 < x_u / D_f < 7/3$, (i.e., $D_f/x_u > 0.43$) an *equivalent* rectangular stress block with uniform stress $0.447f_{ck}$ and a reduced depth $y_f \leq D_f$ (having area $0.447f_{ck}\, y_f$) can be conceived, for convenience, as shown in Figure 4.20(c). The expression for y_f given in the Code (Cl. G-2.3 and G-2.2.1) is necessarily an approximation, because it cannot satisfy the *two* conditions of 'equivalence', in terms of area† of stress block as well as centroidal location. A general expression for y_f may be specified for any $x_u > D_f$; (Code Cl. G-2.3):

$$y_f = \begin{cases} 0.15x_u + 0.65D_f & \text{for } 1 < x_u/D_f < 7/3 \\ D_f & \text{for } x_u/D_f \geq 7/3 \end{cases} \tag{4.69}$$

† It may be noted that the equivalence in terms of area is approximately satisfied at the limiting conditions $x_u/D_f = 1$, and exactly satisfied for $x_u/D_f \geq 7/3$.

The expressions for C_{uf} and M_{uf} are accordingly obtained as:

$$C_{uf} = 0.447 f_{ck} (b_f - b_w) y_f \quad \text{for} \quad x_u > D_f \tag{4.70a}$$

$$M_{uf} = C_{uf} (d - y_f/2) \tag{4.70b}$$

The location of the neutral axis is fixed by the force equilibrium condition (with y_f expressed in terms of x_u [Eq. 4.69]).

$$C_{uw} + C_{uf} = f_{st} A_{st} \tag{4.71}$$

where $f_{st} = 0.87 f_y$ for $x_u \le x_{u,\max}$. Where $x_u > x_{u,\max}$, the strain compatibility method has to be employed to determine x_u.

Substituting Eq. 4.68a and Eq. 4.70a in Eq. 4.71, and solving for x_u,

$$x_u = \frac{f_{st} A_{st} - 0.447 f_{ck} (b_f - b_w) y_f}{0.362 f_{ck} b_w} \quad \text{for} \quad x_u > D_f \tag{4.72}$$

Note that in Eq. 4.72, y_f on the right-hand side is a function of x_u if $x_u/D_f < 7/3$; [Eq. 4.69]. In computing x_u using Eq. 4.72, initially it may be assumed that $x_u/D_f \ge 7/3$ and hence $y_f = D_f$; if the resulting x_u is less than 7/3 D_f, the calculations may be revised with $y_f = 0.15 x_u + 0.65 D_f$.

The final expression for the ultimate moment of resistance M_{uR} is obtained as:

$$M_{uR} = M_{uw} + M_{uf} \tag{4.73}$$

$$\Rightarrow \quad M_{uR} = 0.362 f_{ck} b_w x_u (d - 0.416 x_u) + 0.447 f_{ck} (b_f - b_w) y_f (d - y_f/2) \tag{4.74}$$

The Code (Cl. G-2.3) recommends Eqs 4.74 and 4.69 for computation of M_{uR}.

Limiting Moment of Resistance

The limiting moment of resistance $M_{u,\lim}$ is obtained for the condition $x_u = x_{u,\max}$, where $x_{u,\max}$ takes the values of $0.531d$, $0.479d$ and $0.456d$ for Fe 250, Fe 415 and Fe 500 grades of tensile steel reinforcement [refer Table 4.3]. The condition $x_u/D_f \ge 7/3$ in Eq. 4.69, for the typical case of Fe 415, works out, for $x_u = x_{u,\max}$, as $0.479d/D_f \ge 7/3$, i.e., $D_f/d \le 0.205$. For the limiting moment calculations, the Code (Cl. G–2.2) suggests a simplified condition of $D_f/d \le 0.2$ for *all* grades of steel – to represent the condition $x_u/D_f \ge 7/3$ when $y_f = D_f$.

Accordingly, Eq. 4.74 and Eq. 4.69 take the following forms:

$$M_{u,\lim} = 0.362 f_{ck} b_w x_{u,\max} (d - 0.416 x_{u,\max}) + 0.447 f_{ck} (b_f - b_w) y_f (d - y_f/2) \quad \text{for} \quad x_{u,\max} > D_f \tag{4.75}$$

where

$$y_f = \begin{cases} 0.15 x_{u,\max} + 0.65 D_f & \text{for } D_f/d > 0.2 \\ D_f & \text{for } D_f/d \le 0.2 \end{cases} \tag{4.76}$$

The advantage of using Eq. 4.76 in lieu of the more exact Eq. 4.69 (with $x_u = x_{u,\max}$) is that the estimation of y_f is made somewhat simpler. Of course, for $x_{u,\max} \le D_f$ (i.e., neutral axis within the flange), as for a rectangular section of width b_f:

$$M_{u,\lim} = 0.362 f_{ck} b_f x_{u,\max} (d - 0.416 x_{u,\max}) \quad \text{for} \quad x_{u,\max} \le D_f \tag{4.77}$$

When it is found by *analysis* of a given T-section that $x_u > x_{u,max}$, then the strain compatibility method has to be applied. As an approximate and conservative estimate, M_{uR} may be taken as $M_{u,lim}$, given by Eq. 4.76/4.77. From the point of view of *design* (to be discussed in Chapter 5), $M_{u,lim}$ provides a measure of the ultimate moment capacity that can be expected from a T-section of given proportions with tension reinforcements only. If the section has to be designed for a *factored moment* $M_u > M_{u,lim}$, then this calls for the provision of compression reinforcement and corresponding additional tension reinforcement.

Example 4.12

Determine the ultimate moment of resistance for the T-section in Example 4.4

Solution

- Given: $b_f = 900$ mm, $D_f = 100$ mm, $b_w = 300$ mm, $d = 520$ mm, $A_{st} = 4825$ mm^2, $f_y = 250$ MPa and $f_{ck} = 25$ MPa
- $x_{u,max}/d = 0.531$ for Fe 250 $\Rightarrow x_{u,max} = 0.531 \times 520 = 276.1$ mm
- First assuming $x_u \le D_f$ and $x_u \le x_{u,max}$, and considering force equilibrium

$$C_u = T_u \Rightarrow 0.362 f_{ck} b_f x_u = 0.87 f_y A_{st}$$

$$\Rightarrow \quad x_u = \frac{0.87 \times 250 \times 4825}{0.362 \times 25 \times 900} = 128.8 \text{ mm} > D_f = 100 \text{ mm}$$

Hence, this calculated value of x_u is not correct, as $x_u > D_f$.

- As $x_u > D_f$, the compression in the 'web' is given by

$$C_{uw} = 0.362 f_{ck} b_w x_u$$
$$= 0.362 \times 25 \times 300 \times x_u = (2715 x_u) \text{ N}$$

- Assuming $x_u \ge 7/3\, D_f = 233.3$ mm, the compression in the 'flange' is given by

$$C_{uf} = 0.447 f_{ck} (b_f - b_w) D_f$$
$$= 0.447 \times 25 \times (900 - 300) \times 100 = 670500 \text{ N}$$

- Also assuming $x_u \le x_{u,max} = 276.1$ mm, $f_{st} = 0.87 f_y$, and

$$T_u = 0.87 \times 250 \times 4825 = 1049438 \text{ N}$$

Applying the force equilibrium condition ($C_{uw} + C_{uf} = T_u$),

$$2715 x_u + 670500 = 1049438 \Rightarrow x_u = 139.6 \text{ mm} < 7/3\, D_f = 233.3 \text{ mm}$$

Hence, this calculated value of x_u is also not correct.

- As $D_f < x_u < 7/3\, D_f$, the depth $y_f (\le D_f)$ of the equivalent concrete stress block is obtained as:

$$y_f = 0.15 x_u + 0.65 D_f = (0.15 x_u + 65) \text{ mm}$$

$$\Rightarrow \quad C_{uf} = 670500 \times \left(y_f / D_f \right) = (1005.7 x_u + 435825) \text{ N}$$

- $C_{uw} + C_{uf} = T_u$

$$\Rightarrow \quad 2715 x_u + (1005.7 x_u + 435825) = 1049437$$

$\Rightarrow$ $x_u =$ **164.9 mm** $< x_{u,max}$; hence, the assumption $f_{st} = 0.87 f_y$ is OK.

$\Rightarrow$ $y_f = (0.15 \times 164.9) + 65.0 = 89.7$ mm

- Taking moments of C_{uw} and C_{uf} about the centroid of tension steel,

$$M_{uR} = C_{uw} (d - 0.416 x_u) + C_{uf} (d - y_f/2)$$
$$= (2715 \times 164.9) \times (520 - 0.416 \times 164.9) + (1005.7 \times 164.9 + 435825) \times (520 - 89.7/2)$$
$$= 488 \times 10^6 \text{ Nmm} = \mathbf{488 \text{ kNm}}$$

Example 4.13

Repeat the T-section problem in Example 4.12, considering 9–32ϕ bars instead of 6–32ϕ bars.

Solution

- Given: $b_f = 900$ mm, $D_f = 100$ mm, $b_w = 300$ mm, $d = 520$ mm, $f_y = 250$ MPa and $f_{ck} = 25$ MPa,

$$A_{st} = 9 \times \frac{\pi}{4} \times (32)^2 = 7238 \text{ mm}^2$$

- $x_{u,\max} = 276.1$ mm (as in Example 4.12)
- First assuming $x_u \leq D_f$ and $x_u \leq x_{u,\max}$,

$$x_u = \frac{0.87 \times 250 \times 7238}{0.362 \times 25 \times 900} = 193.3 \text{ mm} > D_f = 100 \text{ mm}$$

Hence this calculated value of x_u is not correct.

- As $x_u > D_f$,

$$C_{uw} = 0.362 \times 25 \times 300 x_u$$
$$= (2715 x_u) \text{ N}$$

- Assuming $x_u \geq 7/3 D_f = 233.3$ mm, $y_f = D_f = 100$ mm and

$$C_{uf} = 0.447 \times 25 \times (900 - 300) \times 100$$
$$= 670500 \text{ N}$$

- Further assuming $x_u \leq x_{u,\max} = 276.1$ mm, $f_{st} = 0.87 f_y$, and

$$T_u = 0.87 \times 250 \times 7238 = 1574265 \text{ N}$$

- Applying the force equilibrium condition ($C_{uw} + C_{uf} = T_u$),

$$x_u = \frac{1574265 - 670500}{2715} = \mathbf{332.9} \text{ mm},$$

which implies $x_u > 7/3 D_f = 233.3$ mm, but not $x_u \leq x_{u,\max} = 276.1$ mm

The section is over-reinforced as per the Code provisions.

Exact Solution (considering *strain compatibility*)

- Corresponding to $x_u = 332.9$ mm, $\varepsilon_{st} = 0.0035(520/332.9 - 1) = 0.00197$ [Eq. 4.56] which is clearly greater than the strain at yield for Fe 250, i.e., $0.87 \times 250/(2.0 \times 10^5) = 0.00109$

  Hence, the design steel stress is indeed $f_{st} = 0.87 f_y$, and the so calculated $x_u = 332.9$ mm is the correct depth of the neutral axis†.

  Accordingly,

$$M_{uR} = C_{uw}(d - 0.416 x_u) + C_{uf}(d - D_f/2)$$
$$= (2715 \times 332.9) \times (520 - 0.416 \times 332.9) + 670500 \times (520 - 50)$$
$$= 659.9 \times 10^6 \text{ Nmm} = \mathbf{660\ kNm} > M_{u,\lim}$$

  This is the correct estimate of the ultimate moment capacity of the section; as the steel strain is beyond the yield strain a limited amount of ductile behaviour can also be expected. However, as per the

† This is a case where, being Fe 250 grade steel with a sharp yield point, the strain at first yield, $\varepsilon_y = f_y/E_s$, is lower than the strain for the 'balanced' condition ε_{st}^* specified by the Code. Hence, even though $x_u > x_{u,\max}$, the steel has yielded. See also Figure 4.19(b).

Code, this will not qualify as an admissible under-reinforced section since $x_u > x_{u,\max}$. [Note that if the ε_{st} computed had turned out to be less than ε_y, $f_{st} < 0.87f_y$ and a trial-and-error procedure has to be resorted to.]

Approximate Solution

- An approximate and conservative solution for M_{uR} can be obtained by limiting x_u to $x_{u,\max} = 276.1$ mm, and taking moments of C_{uw} and C_{uf} about the centroid of the tension steel (Note that, following the Code procedure, $D_f/d = 100/520 = 0.192 < 0.2 \Rightarrow y_f = D_f = 100$ mm [Eq. 4.76]). Accordingly,

$$M_{uR} \approx M_{u,\lim} = C_{uw}(d - 0.416x_{u,\max}) + C_{uf}(d - D_f/2)$$

$$= (2715 \times 276.1) \times (520 - 0.416 \times 276.1) + 670500 \times (520 - 50)$$

$$= \mathbf{619\ kNm}$$

4.7.5 Analysis of Doubly Reinforced Sections

Doubly reinforced beam sections (i.e., sections with compression steel as well as tension steel) were introduced in Section 4.6.5, where the analysis at *service loads* was discussed. The present section deals with the analysis of these beam sections (rectangular) at the *ultimate limit state.*

The distributions of stresses and strains in a 'doubly reinforced' rectangular section [Figure 4.21] are similar to those obtained in a 'singly reinforced' section [Figure 4.17], except that there is a stress f_{sc} in the compression steel (area A_{sc}) which also needs to be accounted for. This stress f_{sc} may or may not reach the design yield stress $0.87f_y$, depending on the strain ε_{sc} in the compression steel. An expression for ε_{sc} can be easily obtained from strain compatibility [Figure 4.21(b)]:

$$\varepsilon_{sc} = 0.0035 \times \left(1 - {d'}/{x_u}\right) \tag{4.78}$$

where d' is the distance between the centroid of the compression steel and the extreme compression fibre in the concrete. In practice, the ratio d'/d is found to vary in the range 0.05 to 0.20. It can be shown that the compression steel will, in most cases, attain the design yield stress ($f_{sc} = 0.87f_y$) in the case of Fe 250 grade steel, but is generally unlikely to do so in the case of Fe 415 and Fe 500 (because of their higher strains at yield). Values of the stress f_{sc} (corresponding to $x_u = x_{u.\max}$) for various grades of steel and ratios of d'/d are listed in Table 4.5.

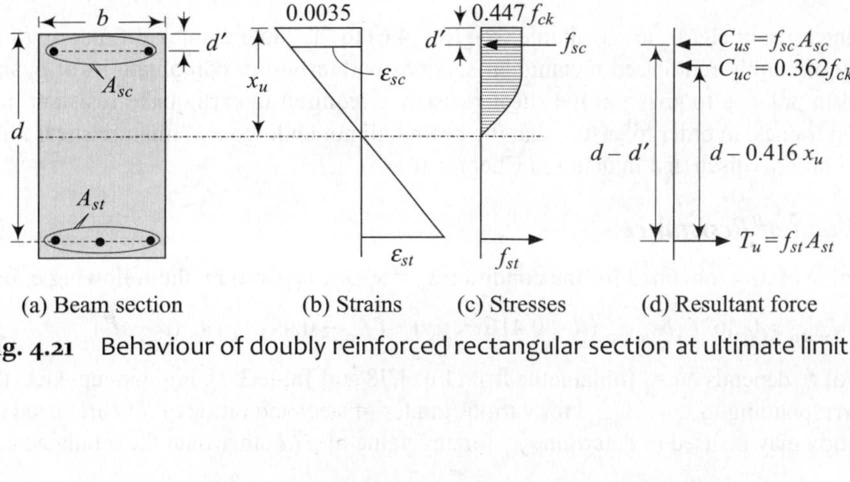

Fig. 4.21 Behaviour of doubly reinforced rectangular section at ultimate limit state.

Table 4.5 *Value of f_{sc} (in MPa units) at $x_u = x_{u,max}$ – for various d′/d ratios and different grades of compression steel*

Grade of steel	d′/d			
	0.05	**0.10**	**0.15**	**0.20**
Fe 250	217.5	217.5	217.5	217.5
Fe 415	355.1	351.9	342.4	329.2
Fe 500	423.9	411.3	395.1	370.3

Applying the condition of force equilibrium [Figure 4.21(d)]

$$C_{uc} + C_{us} = T_u \tag{4.79}$$

where C_{uc} and C_{us} denote, respectively, the resultant compressive forces in the concrete and the compression steel. For convenience, the full area of the concrete under compression ($b \times x_u$) is assumed to be effective in estimating C_{uc}. The force in concrete area displaced by steel (equal to A_{sc}, stressed to a level that is exactly or nearly equal to $0.447f_{ck}$, the stress in concrete) already included in C_{uc}, is accounted for in the estimation of C_{us} as follows:

$$C_{uc} = 0.362f_{ck}bx_u \tag{4.80a}$$

$$C_{us} = (f_{sc} - 0.447f_{ck})A_{sc} \tag{4.80b}$$

$T_u = f_{st}A_{st}$, where $f_{st} = 0.87f_y$ if $x_u \le x_{u,\max}$. Accordingly, the depth of the neutral axis x_u is obtainable from Eq. 4.79 as:

$$x_u = \frac{f_{st}A_{st} - (f_{sc} - 0.447\,f_{ck})\,A_{sc}}{0.362\,f_{ck}b} \tag{4.81}$$

This equation provides a closed-form solution to x_u only if $f_{st} = 0.87f_y$ and $f_{sc} = 0.87f_y$; otherwise, f_{st} and f_{sc} will depend on x_u. Initially the values of f_{sc} and f_{st} may be taken as $0.87f_y$, and then revised, if necessary, employing the *strain compatibility* method. This is demonstrated in Example 4.15.

Having determined f_{sc} and x_u, the ultimate moment of resistance can be calculated by considering moments of C_{uc} and C_{us} about the centroid of the tension steel [Figure 4.21(d)] as follows:

$$M_{uR} = C_{uc}(d - 0.416x_u) + C_{us}(d - d') \tag{4.82}$$

Design aids, in the form of charts, are available (see Ref. 4.6) to facilitate a quick estimation of the ultimate moment capacity of doubly reinforced rectangular sections with arbitrary combinations of p_t and p_c. These charts are useful in practice to arrive at the shear resistance required in earthquake-resistant design of RC beams in building frames, in order to ensure that the beam will not undergo a premature shear failure prior to a ductile flexural failure (discussed in detail in Chapter 16).

Limiting Moment of Resistance

The 'limiting' value of M_{uR}, obtained for the condition $x_u = x_{u,\max}$, is given by the following expression:

$$M_{u,\lim} = 0.362f_{ck}bx_{u,\max}(d - 0.416x_{u,\max}) + (f_{sc} - 0.447f_{ck})A_{sc}(d - d') \tag{4.83}$$

where the value of f_{sc} depends on ε_{sc} (obtainable from Eq. 4.78 and Table 3.2). For convenience, the values of the stress f_{sc} (corresponding to $x_u = x_{u,\max}$) for various grades of steel and ratios of d'/d are listed in Table 4.5. Linear interpolation may be used to determine f_{sc} for any value of d'/d other than the tabulated constants.

Example 4.14

Determine the ultimate moment of resistance of the doubly reinforced beam section of Example 4.6.

Solution

- Given: $b = 300$ mm, $d = 550$ mm, $A_{st} = 3054$ mm^2, $f_y = 250$ MPa and $f_{ck} = 25$ MPa, $d' = 50$ mm, $A_{sc} = 982$ mm^2
- $x_{u,\max}/d = 0.531$ for Fe 250 $\Rightarrow x_{u,\max} = 0.531 \times 550 = 292.1$ mm
- Assuming $f_{sc} = f_{st} = 0.87f_y$, and considering force equilibrium:

$$C_{uc} + C_{us} = T_u, \text{ with}$$
$$C_{uc} = 0.362 \times 25 \times 300 \times x_u = (2715x_u) \text{ N}$$
$$C_{us} = (0.87 \times 250 - 0.447 \times 25) \times 982 = 202611 \text{ N}$$
$$T_u = 0.87 \times 250 \times 3054 = 664245 \text{ N}$$
$$\Rightarrow \quad 2715x_u + 202611 = 664245$$
$$\Rightarrow \quad x_u = \mathbf{170\ mm} < x_{u,\max} = 292.1 \text{ mm}$$

Hence, the assumption $f_{st} = 0.87f_y$ is justified.

- Also, $\varepsilon_{sc} = 0.0035(1 - 50/170) = 0.00247 > \varepsilon_y = \dfrac{0.87 \times 250}{2 \times 10^5} = 0.00109$

$\Rightarrow \quad f_{sc} = 0.87 f_y$ is also justified.

- *Ultimate moment of resistance*

$$M_{uR} = C_{uc}(d - 0.416x_u) + C_{us} \times (d - d')$$
$$= (2715 \times 170) \times (550 - 0.416 \times 170) + 202611 \times (550 - 50)$$
$$= 322.5 \times 10^6 \text{ Nmm} = \mathbf{323\ kNm}$$

Example 4.15

Repeat the problem in Example 4.14, considering Fe 500 instead of Fe 250.

Solution

- Given: $b = 300$ mm, $d = 550$ mm, $A_{st} = 3054$ mm^2, $f_y = 500$ MPa and $f_{ck} = 25$ MPa, $d' = 50$ mm, $A_{sc} = 982$ mm^2
- $x_{u,\max}/d = 0.456$ for Fe 500 $\Rightarrow$ $x_{u,\max} = 0.456 \times 550 = 250.8$ mm
- Assuming $f_{sc} = f_{st} = 0.87 \times f_y$, and considering force equilibrium [Eq. 4.81],

$$x_u = \frac{(0.87 \times 500 \times 3054) - (0.87 \times 500 - 0.447 \times 25) \times 982}{0.362 \times 25 \times 300}$$
$$= 336 \text{ mm} > x_{u,\max} = 250.8 \text{ mm}$$

The section is over-reinforced.

Exact Solution (considering *strain compatibility*):

- Applying [Eq. 4.81] : $x_u = \dfrac{f_{st} \times 3054 - (f_{sc} - 0.447 \times 25) \times 982}{0.362 \times 25 \times 300}$

$$\Rightarrow \quad x_u = (3054 f_{st} - 982 f_{sc} + 10974)/2715$$

First Cycle:

1. x_u lies within the two limits above; 250.8 mm $< x_u <$ 336 mm

2. Assume $x_u \approx \frac{1}{2}(250.8 + 336) = 293$ mm
3. [Eq. 4.78] $\Rightarrow \varepsilon_{sc} = 0.0035(1 - 50/293) = 0.0029$
4. [Eq. 4.56] $\Rightarrow \varepsilon_{st} = 0.0035(550/293 - 1) = 0.00307$
5. [Table 3.2] $\Rightarrow f_{sc} = 413 + (423.9 - 413) \times (290 - 277)/(312 - 277)$
   $= 417.05$ MPa
   and $f_{st} = 413 + (423.9 - 413) \times (307 - 277)/(312 - 277)$
   $= 422.3$ MPa
6. $\Rightarrow x_u = (3054 \times 422.3 - 982 \times 417.1 + 10974)/2715 = 328.3$ mm

Second Cycle :

1. Assume $x_u \approx \frac{1}{2}(293 + 328) = 311$ mm
2. [Eq. 4.78] $\Rightarrow \varepsilon_{sc} = 0.00294$
3. [Eq. 4.56] $\Rightarrow \varepsilon_{st} = 0.00269$
4. [Table 3.2] $\Rightarrow f_{sc} = 418.3$ MPa and $f_{st} = 409.6$ MPa
5. $\Rightarrow x_u = (3054 \times 409.6 - 982 \times 418.3 + 10974)/2715 = 314$ mm

Third Cycle:

1. $x_u \approx \frac{1}{2}(311 + 314) = 312.5$ mm
2. [Eq. 4.78] $\Rightarrow \varepsilon_{sc} = 0.00294; \Rightarrow f_{sc} = 418.3$ MPa
3. [Eq. 4.56] $\Rightarrow \varepsilon_{st} = 0.00266$
4. [Table 3.2] $\Rightarrow f_{st} = 408.3$ MPa
5. $\Rightarrow x_u = (3054 \times 408.3 - 982 \times 418.3 + 10974)/2715 = 312$ mm (converged)

- Taking $x_u = 312$ mm, and applying Eq. 4.82,
  $M_{uR} = (0.362 \times 25 \times 300 \times 312) \times (550 - 0.416 \times 312) + (418.3 - 0.447 \times 25) \times 982 \times (550 - 50)$
  $= 555.9 \times 10^6$ Nmm = **556 kNm**
  (*Note:* $\varepsilon_{st} < \varepsilon^*_{st}, f_{st} < 0.87 f_y$, and this moment is associated with *brittle* failure)

Approximate Solution

- As an approximate and conservative estimate, limiting x_u to $x_{u,max} = 250.8$ mm,
  $\varepsilon_{sc} = 0.0035(1 - 50/250.8) = 0.00280$
  $\Rightarrow \quad f_{sc} = 413.9$ MPa [Table 3.2]
  [This value is alternatively obtainable from Table 4.5 for $d'/d = 0.09$ and Fe 500]
  Accordingly, limiting the ultimate moment of resistance M_{uR} to the 'limiting moment' $M_{u,lim}$ [Eq. 4.83],
  $M_{u,lim} = 0.362 \times 25 \times 300 \times 250.8 \times (550 - 0.416 \times 250.8)$
  $+ (413.9 - 0.447 \times 25) \times 982 \times (550 - 50) = 501 \times 10^6$ Nmm = **501 kNm**

Example 4.16

Determine the ultimate moment of resistance of the doubly reinforced section shown in Figure 4.22. Assume M 25 concrete and Fe 500 steel.

Solution

- Given: $b = 300$ mm, $d = 655$ mm, $d' = 45$ mm, $f_y = 500$ MPa and $f_{ck} = 25$ MPa $A_{sc} = \pi(25)^2/4 \times 2 = 491 \times 2 = 982 \text{ mm}^2$, $A_{st} = 491 \times 4 = 1964 \text{ mm}^2$
- $x_{u,\max}/d = 0.456$ for Fe 500 $\Rightarrow x_{u,\max} = 0.456 \times 655 = 298.7$ mm
- Assuming (for a first approximation) $f_{sc} = f_{st} = 0.87f_y$,

$$C_{uc} = 0.362 \times 25 \times 300 \times x_u = (2715x_u)\text{ N}$$
$$C_{us} = (0.87 \times 500 - 0.447 \times 25) \times 982 = 416196 \text{ N}$$
$$T_u = 0.87 \times 500 \times 1964 = 854340 \text{ N}$$

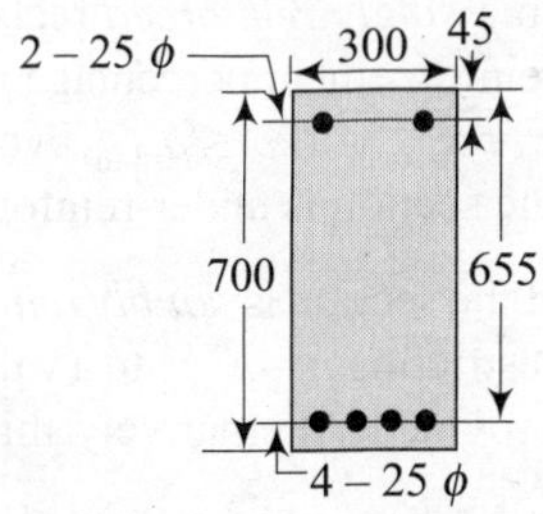

Fig. 4.22 Example 4.16.

- Considering force equilibrium : $C_{uc} + C_{us} = T_u$,

$$2715x_u + 416196 = 854340$$
$$\Rightarrow \quad x_u = 161.4 \text{ mm} < x_{u,\max} = 298.7 \text{ mm}$$

- The assumption $f_{st} = 0.87f_y$ is justified

Further, $\varepsilon_{sc} = 0.0035(1 - 45/161.4) = 0.00252$

For Fe 415, $\varepsilon_y = \dfrac{0.87 \times 500}{2 \times 10^5} + 0.002 = 0.0042$

As $\varepsilon_{sc} < \varepsilon_y$, the assumption $f_{sc} = 0.87f_y$ is not justified, whereby the calculated value of C_{us} (and hence of $x_u = 161.4$ mm) is also not correct. The correct value has to be obtained iteratively using *strain compatibility*.

First cycle :

- Assuming $\varepsilon_{sc} = 0.00252$,

$$f_{sc} = 391.3 + (413 - 391.3) \times \frac{252 - 226}{277 - 226} = 402.4 \text{ MPa}$$
$$\Rightarrow \quad C_{us} = (402.4 - 0.447 \times 25) \times 982 = 384183 \text{ N}$$
$$C_{uc} + C_{us} = T_u \Rightarrow x_u = \frac{854340 - 384183}{2715} = 173.2 \text{ mm}$$
$$\Rightarrow \quad \varepsilon_{sc} = 0.0035(1 - 45/173.2) = 0.00259 \approx 0.00252 \text{ (calculated earlier)}$$

Second cycle :

- Assuming $\varepsilon_{sc} = 0.00259$,

$$f_{sc} = 391.3 + (413 - 391.3) \times \frac{259 - 226}{277 - 226} = 405.3 \text{ MPa}$$
$$\Rightarrow \quad C_{us} = (405.3 - 0.447 \times 25) \times 982 = 387031 \text{ N}$$
$$\Rightarrow \quad x_u = \frac{854340 - 387031}{2715} = 172.1 \text{ mm (converged)}$$

- Taking $x_u = 172.1$ mm,

$$M_{uR} = C_{uc}(d - 0.416x_u) + C_{us}(d - d')$$
$$= (2715 \times 172.1)(655 - 0.416 \times 172.1) + 387031(655 - 45)$$
$$= 508.7 \times 10^6 \text{ Nmm} = \textbf{509 kNm}$$

4.7.6 Balanced Doubly Reinforced Sections

'Over-reinforced' sections are undesirable, both from the Code viewpoint of lack of ductile failure, as well as the practical viewpoint of loss of economy. Hence, from a *design* viewpoint it is necessary to restrict the depth of the neutral axis to the limit prescribed by the Code [Eq. 4.50].

In a *singly reinforced* rectangular beam, the requirement $x_u \le x_{u,\max}$ can be ensured by limiting the tension reinforcement percentage $p_t \le p_{t,\lim}$ where $p_{t,\lim}$ (given by Eq. 4.62) corresponds to the 'balanced' condition $x_u = x_{u,\max}$. If $p_t \le p_{t,\lim}$, even if compression reinforcement is provided (i.e., the beam is 'doubly reinforced'), the section is under-reinforced and the condition $x_u < x_{u,\max}$ is satisfied.

If the section is *doubly reinforced* with $p_t > p_{t,\lim}$ and $p_c > 0$, then the requirement $x_u \le x_{u,\max}$, can be ensured by restricting $p_t - p_{t,\lim}$ to a value commensurate with the percentage compression reinforcement ($p_c = 100A_{sc}/bd$) provided. Alternatively, this can be ensured by providing adequate compression steel (p_c) for a given $p_t > p_{t,\lim}$.

It is convenient to visualise p_t as comprising a component $p_{t,\lim}$ [Eq. 4.62] and another component ($p_t - p_{t,\lim}$); the tensile force in the former is visualised as being balanced by the compressive force in the concrete $C_{uc} = 0.362 f_{ck} b x_{u,\max}$, and in the latter by the compressive force in the compression steel C_{us} alone. Accordingly, considering force equilibrium in the latter parts, and denoting the value of p_c for 'balanced' section a p_c^*:

$$0.87 f_y \frac{(p_t - p_{t,\lim})bd}{100} = (f_{sc} - 0.447 f_{ck}) \frac{p_c^*}{100} bd$$

$$\Rightarrow \quad p_c^* = \frac{0.870 f_y}{f_{sc} - 0.447 f_{ck}} (p_t - p_{t,\lim}) \quad \text{for} \quad x_u = x_{u,\max} \tag{4.84}$$

where f_{sc} is obtainable from Table 4.5, or using Eq. 4.78 and Tables 3.1 and 3.2.

It also follows that if the actual p_c provided in a beam section exceeds p_c^* (given by Eq. 4.84), then $x_u < x_{u,\max}$, and hence the beam is 'under-reinforced'. On the other hand, if $p_c < p_c^*$, then the beam is 'over-reinforced'.

In the case of a 'balanced' section an expression for $M_{uR} = M_{u,\lim-DR}$ can be derived in terms of the percentage tensile steel (p_t) as follows:

$$M_{u,\lim-DR} = (0.87 f_y) \left[\frac{p_{t,\lim} bd}{100} (d - 0.416 x_{u,\max}) + \frac{(p_t - p_{t,\lim})bd}{100} (d - d') \right]$$

$$\Rightarrow \quad \frac{M_{u,\lim-DR}}{bd^2} = (0.87 f_y) \left[\frac{p_{t,\lim}}{100} \left(1 - 0.416 \frac{x_{u,\max}}{d} \right) + \frac{(p_t - p_{t,\lim})}{100} \left(1 - d'/d \right) \right] \tag{4.85}$$

where the additional subscript 'DR' (for *doubly reinforced* section) is inserted – to avoid confusion with the $M_{u,\lim}$ defined earlier for the *singly reinforced* section. The corresponding percentage compression steel $p_c = p_c^*$ is as given by Eq. 4.84.

4.8 Analysis of Slabs as Rectangular Beams

Slabs under flexure behave in much the same way as beams. A slab of uniform thickness subject to a bending moment uniformly distributed over its width [Figure 4.23] may be treated as a wide shallow beam for the purpose of analysis and design.

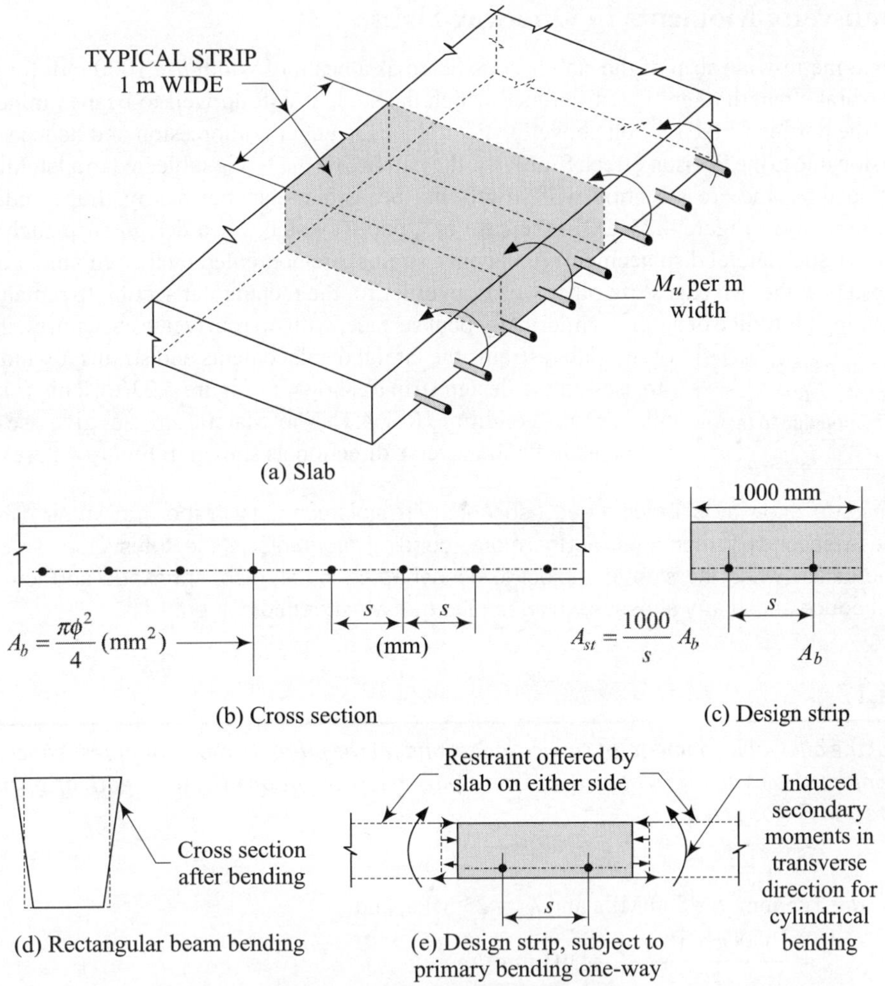

Fig. 4.23 Analysis of slabs.

In such slabs, the reinforcing bars are usually spaced uniformly over the width of the slab. For convenience, computations are generally based on a typical one-metre-wide strip of the slab considered as a beam [Figure 4.23(c)], i.e., with $b = 1000$ mm. The loads are generally uniformly distributed† and expressed in units of kN/m^2.

If s is the centre-to-centre spacing of bars in mm, then the number of bars in the 1-metre-wide strip is given by $1000/s$. Accordingly, denoting A_b as the cross-sectional area of one bar (equal to $\pi \phi^2/4$), the area of tensile steel (A_{st}), expressed in units of mm^2/m, is given by

$$A_{st} = 1000\, A_b/s \tag{4.86}$$

In practice, reinforced concrete slabs are generally under-reinforced and singly reinforced. In the example to follow, the analysis of a typical slab is undertaken to determine the moment resisting capacity at *working* loads as well as at the *ultimate limit state*.

† When concentrated loads act on a one-way slab, the simplified procedure given in Cl. 24.3.2 of the Code may be adopted.

4.8.1 Transverse Moments in One-way Slabs

Although a one-metre-wide strip of the slab is considered as a beam of width b = 1000 mm for the analysis/design for flexural strength, there is a difference which the student will do well to bear in mind. As a beam bends (sags), the portion of the section above the neutral axis is under compression and hence subjected to a lateral expansion due to the Poisson effect. Similarly, the part below the NA is subjected to a lateral contraction. Hence, after bending, the cross section will strictly not be rectangular, but nearly[†] trapezoidal, as shown (greatly exaggerated) in Figure 4.23(d). In the case of a one-way slab, for a design strip such as shown in Figure 4.23(c, e), such lateral displacements (and hence strains) are prevented by the remainder of the slab on either side (except at the two edges). In other words, in order for the rectangular section to remain rectangular even after bending (as a slice of a long cylindrically bent surface, with no transverse curvature), the remainder of the slab restrains the lateral displacements and strains, by inducing lateral stresses on the design strip as shown in Figure 4.23(e). This is known as the 'plain strain' condition [Ref. 4.1]. These lateral stresses give rise to secondary moments in the transverse direction as shown in Figure 4.23(e).

One-way slabs do develop bending moments in the transverse direction due to the 'Poisson effect'.

Hence, even a one-way slab will need ('secondary') reinforcements in the transverse direction to resist these secondary moments. Furthermore, bending moments in the transverse direction are generated locally when the slab is subject to concentrated loads. Also, shrinkage and temperature effects introduce secondary stresses which require transverse reinforcement.

Example 4.17

Determine (a) the allowable moment (at service loads) and (b) the ultimate moment of resistance of a 150 mm thick slab, reinforced with 10 mm ϕ bars at 200 mm spacing located at an effective depth of 125 mm. Assume M 25 concrete and Fe 500 steel.

Solution

- Given : d = 125 mm, f_y =500 MPa and f_{ck} = 25 MPa, and

$$A_{st} = \frac{1000(\pi \times 10^2/4)}{200} = 393 \text{ mm}^2/\text{m}$$

(a) Analysis at working loads :

For M 25 concrete, σ_{cbc} = 8.5 MPa and m = 10.98

For Fe 500 steel, σ_{st} = 275 MPa and $k_b = \dfrac{280}{280 + 3\sigma_{st}} = 0.253$

The neutral axis depth kd is obtained by considering moments of areas in the transformed–cracked section [Eq. 4.12], and considering b = 1000 mm

$$1000 \times (kd)^2/2 = 10.98 \times 393 \times (125 - kd)$$

Solving, kd = 28.81 mm < $k_b d$ = 0.253 × 125 = 31.6 mm

Hence, the section is 'under–reinforced (WSM)'.

$\Rightarrow \quad f_{st} = \sigma_{st}$ = 275 MPa

$M_{all} = \sigma_{st} A_{st} (d - kd/3)$

[†] To be exact, just as the beam undergoes a 'sagging' curvature along the span, there will be a 'hogging' ('anticlastic') curvature in the transverse direction. Thus the top surface will be curved rather than straight [see Ref. 4.1].

$= 275 \times 393 \times (125 - 28.81/3)$
$= 12.47 \times 10^6$ N mm/m = **12.5 kNm/m**

(b) Analysis at ultimate limit state

For Fe 500 steel, $x_{u,\max} = 0.456 \times 125 = 57$ mm

- Assuming $x_u \le x_{u,\max}$, and considering $C_u = T_u$,

$$x_u = \frac{0.87 f_y A_{st}}{0.362 f_{ck} b} = \frac{0.87 \times 500 \times 393}{0.362 \times 25 \times 1000} = 18.89 \text{ mm} < x_{u,\max}$$

Accordingly,

$$M_{uR} = 0.362 f_{ck}\, b x_u (d - 0.416 x_u)$$
$$= 0.362 \times 25 \times 1000 \times 18.89 \times (125 - 0.416 \times 18.89)$$
$$= 20 \times 10^6 \text{ N mm/m} = \mathbf{20\ kNm/m}$$

- Alternatively,

$$p_t = \frac{100 \times 393}{1000 \times 125} = 0.314 < p_{t,\lim} = 0.949 \text{ [Table 4.4]}$$

Applying Eq. 4.65, or using analysis aids [Table A.2(a)],

$$\frac{M_{uR}}{bd^2} = 0.87 \times 500 \times \frac{0.314}{100} \times \left(1 - \frac{500}{25} \times \frac{0.314}{100}\right) = 1.28 \text{ MPa}$$

$$\Rightarrow \quad M_{uR} = 1.28 \times 1000 \times 125^2 = 20 \times 10^6 \text{ Nmm/m} = \mathbf{20\ kNm/m}$$

REVIEW QUESTIONS

4.1 Describe the fundamental assumption in flexural theory. Is it valid at the ultimate state?

4.2 Explain the concept of 'transformed section', as applied to the analysis of reinforced concrete beams under service loads.

4.3 Discuss why does the Code specify an effectively higher modular ratio for compression reinforcement, as compared to tension reinforcement.

4.4 Justify the assumption that concrete resists no flexural tensile stress in reinforced concrete beams.

4.5 Describe the moment-curvature relationship for reinforced concrete beams. What are the possible modes of failure?

4.6 The term 'balanced section' is used in both *working stress method* (WSM) and *limit state method* (LSM). Discuss the difference in meaning.

4.7 State why is it undesirable to design over-reinforced sections in (a) WSM, (b) LSM.

4.8 The concept of locating the *neutral axis* as a *centroidal axis* (in a reinforced concrete beam section under flexure) is applied in WSM, but not in LSM. Why?

4.9 Is it uneconomical to use high strength steel as compression reinforcement in design by WSM. Give your views with reasons.

4.10 Justify the Code specification for the limiting neutral axis depth in LSM.

4.11 'The ultimate moment of resistance of a singly reinforced beam section can be calculated either in terms of the concrete compressive strength or the steel tensile strength'. Is this statement justified in all cases?

4.12 Compute and plot the ratio M_{uR}/M_{all} for a given singly reinforced beam section for values of p_t in the range 0.0 to 2.0, considering combinations of (i) M 25 and Fe 250, and (ii) M 25 and Fe 500. (Refer Figures 4.13 and 4.19). Comment on the graphs generated, in terms of the safety underlying beam sections that are designed in accordance with WSM.

4.13 Define 'effective flange width'.

4.14 What are the various factors that influence the effective flange width in a T-beam? To what extent are these factors accommodated in the empirical formula given in the Code?

4.15 Is it correct to model the interior beams in a continuous beam-supported slab system as T-beams for determining their flexural strength at *all* sections?

4.16 Discuss the variation of the ultimate moment of resistance of a singly reinforced beam of given rectangular cross-section and material properties with the area of tension steel.

4.17 Explain how the neutral axis is located in T-beam sections (at the ultimate limit state), given that it lies outside the flange.

4.18 Given percentages of tension steel (p_t) and compression steel (p_c) of a doubly reinforced section, how is it possible to decide whether the beam is under-reinforced or over-reinforced (at the ultimate limit state)?

4.19 Show that the procedure for analysing the flexural strength of reinforced concrete slabs is similar to that of beams.

4.20 Demonstrate the significant differences in behaviour in bending of a beam of rectangular section and a strip of a very wide one-way slab.

4.21 Is it necessary to provide transverse reinforcement in a one-way slab. Discuss why.

4.22 'A reinforced concrete beam can be considered to be *safe* in flexure if its ultimate moment of resistance (as per Code) at any section exceeds the factored moment due to the loads at that section'. Explain the meaning of *safety* as implied in this statement. Does the Code call for any additional requirement to be satisfied for 'safety'?

4.23 If a balanced singly reinforced beam section is experimentally tested to failure, what is the ratio of actual moment capacity to predicted capacity (as per Code) likely to be? (*Hint:* to estimate actual strength, no safety factors should be applied; also, there is no effect of sustained loading).

4.24 According to IS 456-2000, which one of the following statements about the depth of neutral axis $x_{u,\text{bal}}$ for a balanced reinforced concrete section is correct?

(a) $x_{u,\text{bal}}$ depends on the grade of concrete only; (b) $x_{u,\text{bal}}$ depends on the grade of steel only; (c) $x_{u,\text{bal}}$ depends on both the grade of concrete and grade of steel; (d) $x_{u,\text{bal}}$ does not depend on the grade of concrete and grade of steel. [GATE 2017]

4.25 A singly-reinforced rectangular concrete beam of width 300 mm and effective depth 400 mm is to be designed using M25 grade concrete and Fe500 grade reinforcing steel. For the beam to be under-reinforced, the maximum number of 16 mm diameter reinforcing bars that can be provided is:

(a) 3 (b) 4 (c) 5 (d) 6 [GATE 2018]

4.26 Consider the singly reinforced beam section given in Figure 4.24(a). The stress block parameters for the cross-section from IS;456-2000 are given in Figure 4.24(b). The moment of resistance for the given section by the limit state method is ______________ kN-m. [GATE 2015]

4.27 In the reinforced beam section shown in Figure 4.25, the nominal cover provided at the bottom of the beam as per IS 456-2000 is:

(a) 30 mm (b) 36 mm (c) 42 mm (d) 50 mm [GATE 2019]

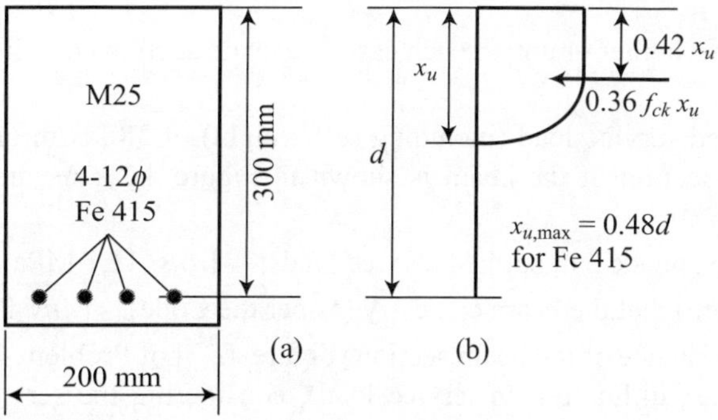

Fig. 4.24

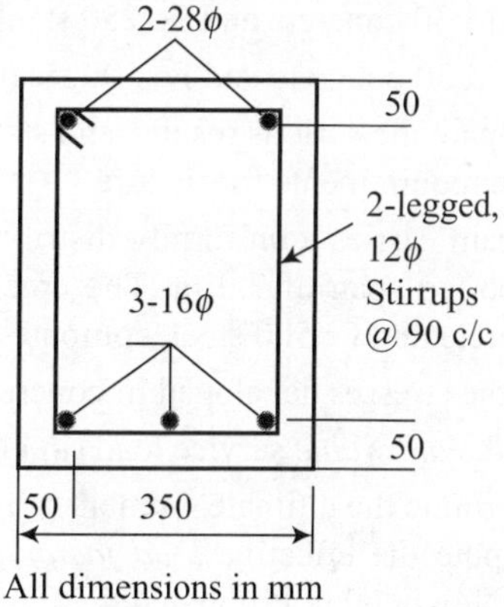

Fig. 4.25

PROBLEMS

4.1 A beam has a rectangular section as shown in Figure 4.26. Assuming M 25 concrete and Fe 250 steel,

(a) compute the stresses in concrete and steel under a service load moment of 125 kNm. Check the calculations using the flexure formula. [*Ans.* 4.93 MPa; 85 MPa]

(b) determine the *allowable moment* capacity of the section under service loads. Also determine the corresponding stresses induced in concrete and steel. [*Ans.* 192 kNm; 7.55 MPa; 130 MPa]

4.2 Determine the *allowable moment* capacity of the beam section [Figure 4.26] of Problem 4.1, as well as the corresponding stresses in concrete and steel (under service loads), considering

(i) M 25 concrete and Fe 500 steel; [*Ans.* 216 kNm; 8.5 MPa; 146 MPa]

(ii) M 30 concrete and Fe 250 steel. [*Ans.* 193 kNm; 8.04 MPa; 130 MPa]

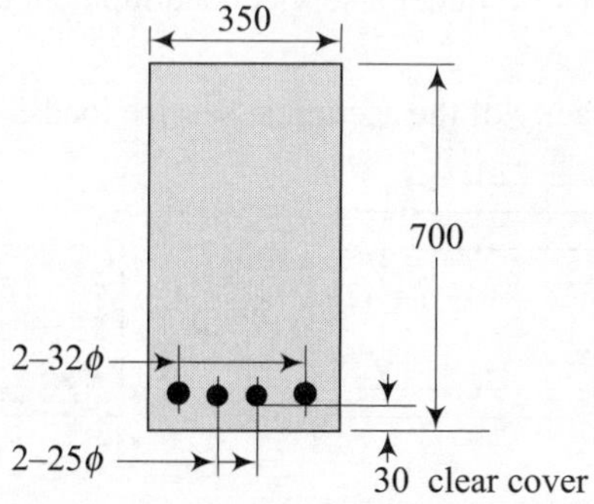

Fig. 4.26 Problems 4.1–4.3.

4.3 Determine the *ultimate* moment of resistance of the beam section [Figure 4.26] of Problem 4.1, considering

(i) M 25 concrete and Fe 250 steel; [*Ans.* 327 kNm]

(ii) M 25 concrete and Fe 500 steel; [*Ans.* 560 kNm]

(iii) M 30 concrete and Fe 250 steel; [*Ans.* 334 kNm]

(iv) M 30 concrete and Fe 500 steel. [*Ans.* 598 kNm]

Compare the various results, and state whether or not, in each case, the beam section complies with the Code requirements for flexure.

4.4 A beam carries a uniformly distributed service load (including self-weight) of 38 kN/m on a simply supported span of 7.0 m. The cross-section of the beam is shown in Figure 4.27. Assuming M 25 concrete and Fe 500 steel, compute

(a) the stresses developed in concrete and steel at applied service loads; [*Ans.* 11.1 MPa; 207 MPa]

(b) the *allowable* service load (in kN/m) that the beam can carry (as per the Code). [*Ans.* 29.1 kN/m]

4.5 Determine the ultimate moment of resistance of the beam section [Figure 4.27] of Problem 4.4. Hence, compute the effective *load factor* (i.e., ultimate load/service load), considering the service load of 38 kN/m cited in Problem 4.4. [*Ans.* 445 kNm; 1.91]

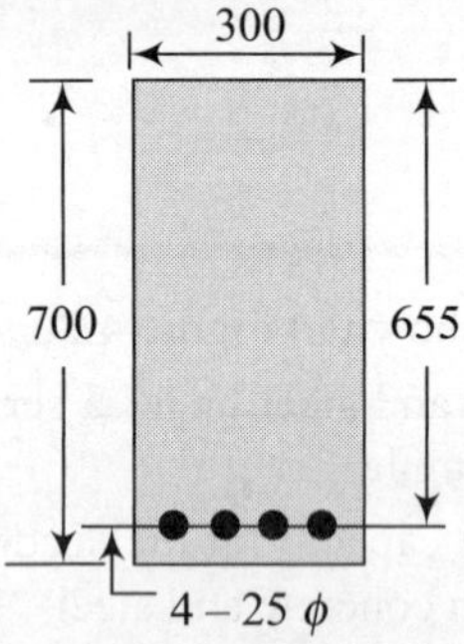

Fig. 4.27 Problems 4.4–4.5.

4.6 The cross-sectional dimensions of a T-beam are given in Figure 4.28. Assuming M 25 concrete and Fe 500 steel, compute:

(a) the stresses in concrete and steel under a service load moment of 150 kNm;

[*Ans.* 4.82 MPa; 115.2 MPa]

(b) the *allowable* moment capacity of the section at service loads. [*Ans.* 265 kNm]

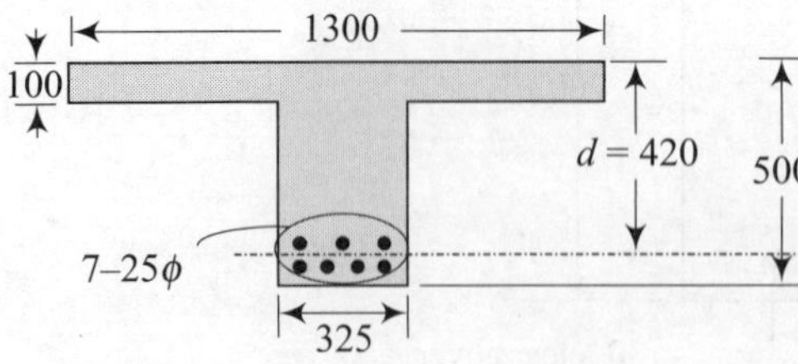

Fig. 4.28 Problems 4.6 – 4.7.

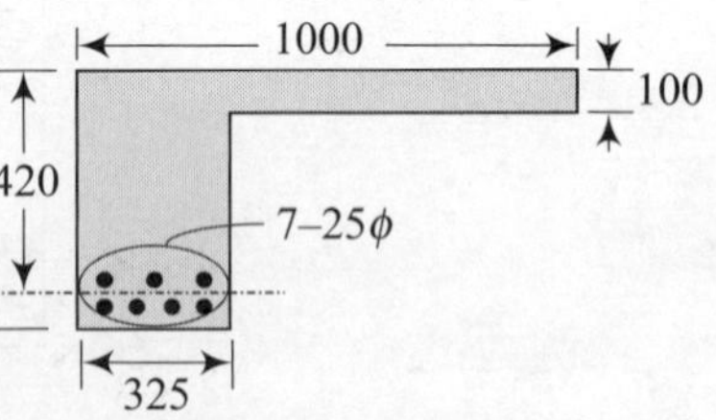

Fig. 4.29 Problems 4.8 – 4.9.

4.7 Determine the ultimate moment of resistance of the T-beam section [Figure 4.28] of Problem 4.6. [*Ans.* 547 kNm]

4.8 Assuming M 25 concrete and Fe500 steel, compute the ultimate moment of resistance of the L-beam section shown in Figure 4.29. [*Ans.* 512 kNm]

4.9 Determine the ultimate moment of resistance of the L-section [Figure 4.29] of Problem 4.8, considering Fe 250 grade steel (in lieu of Fe500). [*Ans.* 288 kNm]

4.10 A doubly reinforced beam section is shown in Figure 4.30. Assuming M 25 concrete and Fe 500 steel, compute

(a) the stresses in concrete and steel under a service load moment of 125 kNm;

[*Ans.* 11.5 MPa; 136 MPa; 169 MPa]

(b) the allowable service load moment capacity of section. [*Ans.* 92 kNm]

4.11 Determine the ultimate moment of resistance of the beam section [Figure 4.30] of Problem 4.10.

[*Ans.* 301 kNm]

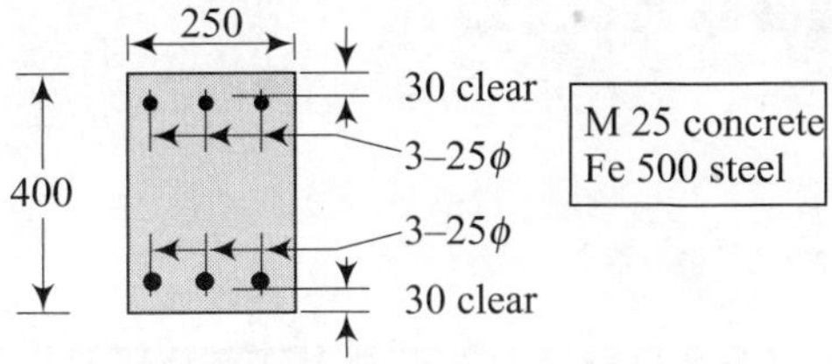

Fig. 4.30 Problems 4.10–4.12.

4.12 Repeat Problem 4.11, considering the compression bars to comprise 3–20ϕ (instead of 3–25ϕ, as shown in Figure 4.30). [*Ans.* 252 kNm]

4.13 Determine (a) the allowable moment (at service loads) and (b) the ultimate moment of resistance of a 100 mm thick slab, reinforced with 8 mm ϕ bars at 200 mm spacing located at an effective depth of 75 mm. Assume M 25 concrete and Fe 500 steel. [*Ans.* (a) 4.77 kNm/m;

(b) 7.64 kNm/m]

4.14 A simply supported *one–way* slab has an effective span of 3.5 metres. It is 150 mm thick, and is reinforced with 10 mm ϕ bars @ 200 mm spacing located at an effective depth of 125 mm. Assuming M 25 concrete and Fe 500 steel, determine the superimposed service load (in kN/m^2) that the slab can safely carry (i) according to WSM, and (ii) according to LSM (assuming a load factor of 1.5).

[*Ans.* (i) 4.4 kN/m^2;

(ii) 4.95 kN/m^2]

REFERENCES

4.1 Timoshenko, S P and Goodier, J N, *Theory of Elasticity*, Second edition, McGraw-Hill, 1951

4.2 Hognestad, E, Hanson, N W and McHenry, D, *Concrete Stress Distribution in Ultimate Strength Design*, Journal ACI, Vol. 52, Dec. 1955, pp 455–479

4.3 Popov, E P, *Mechanics of Solids*, Prentice-Hall Inc., Englewood Cliffs, New Jersey, 1976

4.4 Rüsch, H, *Researches Towards a General Flexural Theory for Structural Concrete*, Journal ACI, Vol. 57, July 1960, pp 1–28

4.5 — *Explanatory Handbook on Indian Standard Code of Practice for Plain and Reinforced Concrete (IS 456:1978)*, Special Publication SP:24, Bureau of Indian Standards, New Delhi, 1983

4.6 Chugh, R and Menon, D, *Design aids for estimation of shear in seismic design of RC beams*, Indian Concrete Journal, Vol. 79, No. 3, March 2005, pp 22–28

Design of Beams and One-Way Slabs for Flexure

CHAPTER 5

LEARNING OBJECTIVES

After studying this chapter, you will be able to:

- *Comply with general guidelines and Code requirements while designing and detailing flexural members*
- *Design singly and doubly reinforced flexural members of various cross-sectional shapes*
- *Curtail flexural reinforcement and provide adequate development lengths at critical sections as per Code*

5.1 Introduction

In the previous chapter, the behaviour of reinforced concrete beams (and one-way slabs) was explained, and procedures given for the **analysis** of sections. Analysis of beam sections may involve calculations of (1) stresses under known service load moments, (2) allowable service load moments M_{all} (working stress method) and (3) ultimate moment of resistance M_{uR} (limit states method). It may be noted that the results of the analysis of a *given* beam section are unique, being dictated solely by the conditions of equilibrium of forces and compatibility of strains. On the basis of these computations, it is possible to decide whether or not the beam is 'safe' under known moments.

In design, there is no unique solution; several alternative designs are possible.

The **design** problem is somewhat the reverse of the *analysis* problem. The external loads (or load effects), material properties and the skeletal dimensions of the beam are given, and it is required to arrive at suitable cross-sectional dimensions and details of the reinforcing steel, which would give adequate *safety* and *serviceability*. In designing for flexure, the distribution of bending moments along the length of the beam must be known from structural analysis. For this, the initial cross-sectional dimensions have to be assumed in order to estimate dead loads; this is also required for the analysis of indeterminate structures (such as continuous beams). The adequacy of the assumed dimensions should be verified and suitable changes made, if required.

Unlike the *analysis* problem, the *design* problem does not have a unique solution because the flexural strength of a section is dependent on its width and effective depth, and on the area of reinforcement; and there are several combinations of these which would give the required strength. Different designers may come up with different solutions, all of which may meet the desired requirements.

Of course, it is possible to conceive an 'optimal' solution – by formulating the problem as an *optimisation* problem[†] [Ref. 5.1]. However, such a mathematically intensive procedure is not commonly adopted, nor warranted in standard design practice.

A complete design of a beam involves considerations of safety under the *ultimate limit states* in flexure, shear, torsion and bond, as well as considerations of the *serviceability limit states* of deflection, crack-width, durability, etc.

The present chapter focuses on the considerations of safety under the ultimate limit state of flexure alone. Considerations of other limit states are covered in detail in subsequent chapters. However, some acceptance criteria under serviceability limit states are introduced indirectly, such as by specifying limiting span/depth ratios (for deflection control) and clear cover to reinforcement (for durability).

> The traditional *working stress method* (WSM) of design is not considered here, as it is no longer used in practice, being superseded by the *limit states method* (LSM) of design. WSM is no longer recommended by most international Codes on reinforced concrete design. In the last (2000) revision of the Code (IS 456), the provisions relating to the WSM design procedure, as an alternative to LSM, have been relegated from the main text of the Code to an Annexure (Annexure B). It is generally not used in practice – except in the design of liquid retaining structures and bridges. However, most modern codes insist on LSM even for such structures, where the serviceability limit state of cracking is a major criterion; crack-widths are best *directly* controlled (as in LSM), rather than *indirectly* by permissible stresses in steel and concrete (as in WSM).

Prior to taking up problems related to design in flexure, it is necessary to have first an understanding of the requirements related to the placing of flexural reinforcement, control of deflection, as well as other guidelines for the selection of member sizes. These are discussed in the following sections.

5.2 Requirements of Flexural Reinforcement

5.2.1 Concrete Cover

> **Failure to provide adequate concrete cover for the reinforcement is a common mistake; it can severely damage the performance and durability of the structure.**

Clear cover is the distance measured from the exposed concrete surface (without plaster and other finishes) to the nearest surface of the reinforcing bar. The Code (Cl. 26.4.1) defines the term *nominal cover* as 'the design depth of concrete cover to all steel reinforcements, including links'. This cover is required to protect the reinforcing bars from corrosion and fire, and also to give the reinforcing bars sufficient embedment to enable them to be stressed without 'slipping' (losing bond with the concrete). The 2000 revision in the Code, with its emphasis on increased durability, has incorporated increased cover requirements, based on the severity of the environmental exposure conditions (refer Table 2.1). The minimum values for the 'nominal cover' to meet *durability* requirements, depending on exposure condition, are summarised in Table 5.1.

As corrosion of reinforcing bars is a common and serious occurrence, it is advisable to specify liberal clear cover in general (particularly in excessively wet and humid environments, and in coastal areas). It may be

† That is, suitably defining an 'objective function' and various 'constraints', involving economy, deflection control, crack control, ductility requirements, headroom limitations, reinforcement percentage limits, etc., and a set of variables such as width, depth, material properties, area of reinforcement, etc.

noted that in actual construction, the clear cover obtained may be (and often is) less than the specified clear cover; however, this should be within the tolerance allowed and appropriate allowance should be made for such errors in construction. In this context, it is important to note the revised tolerance specified in IS 456: 2000, according to which the maximum deviation in clear cover from the value specified by the designer are '+10 mm and –0 mm†'.

Table 5.1 *Nominal cover requirements based on exposure conditions*

Exposure Condition	Minimum Grade	Nominal Cover (mm) (not less than)	Allowance Permitted
Mild	M 20	20	Can be reduced by 5 mm for main rebars less than 12 mm dia
Moderate	M 25	30	
Severe	M 30	45	Can be reduced by 5 mm if concrete grade is M35 and higher
Very severe	M 35	50	
Extreme	M 40	75	

The clause in the earlier version of the Code, limiting the *maximum* clear cover in any construction to 75 mm has, for some reason, been eliminated in the revised code. The general message underlying the revised recommendations in the code pertaining to clear cover seems to be: 'the more the cover, the more durable the concrete'. Unfortunately, the code does not also convey the message that the provision of very large covers (100 mm or more) is undesirable, and can be counter-productive, causing increased crack-widths, particularly in flexural members (such as slabs and beams). Large crack-widths (greater than 0.3 mm) permit the ingress of moisture and chemical attack to the concrete, resulting in possible corrosion to reinforcement and deterioration of concrete. There is little use in providing increased cover to reinforcement, if that cover is cracked, and the likelihood of cracking increases with increased cover. It is, therefore, necessary to impose an upper limit to clear cover (usually 75 mm), and to enforce the checking for the limit state of cracking when large covers are provided (Ref. 5.2).

It may be noted that in the earlier version of the Code, the clear cover requirements were based on the type of structural element (for example, 15 mm in slabs, 25 mm in beams, 40 mm in columns, etc.). The clear cover specifications are now made applicable for *all reinforcements* (including stirrups and ties) and in all types of structural elements. However, certain minimum clear cover requirements have been specified in Cl. 26.4.2.1 of the Code for columns (for longitudinal bars, in any case not less than 40 mm except for bars under 12 mm dia.) and in Cl. 26.4.2.2 for footings (50 mm in general). These are discussed in Chapters 13 and 14.

In addition, the Code has introduced nominal cover requirements, based on *fire resistance* (in terms of hours) required. These provisions have been apparently borrowed from BS 8110. They are described in Cl. 26.4.3 of the Code. In general, for a nominal 1-hour fire resistance, the nominal cover specified is 20 mm for beams and slabs, and 40 mm for columns. Larger cover is required only if the structural element under consideration has to be specially designed for fire resistance.

† That is, no reduction in clear cover is permitted; an increase in clear cover up to 10 mm above the specified nominal cover is allowed.

5.2.2 Spacing of Reinforcing Bars

The Code specifies minimum and maximum limits for the spacing between parallel reinforcing bars in a layer. The *minimum* limits are necessary to ensure that the concrete can be placed easily in between and around the bars during the placement of fresh concrete. The *maximum* limits are specified for bars in tension for the purpose of controlling crack-widths and improving bond.

The minimum spacing limits can be met without difficulty in slabs in general, because of the large widths available and the relatively low percentage of flexural reinforcement required. However, in the case of beams, which have limited widths and are required to accommodate relatively large areas of flexural reinforcement, the minimum spacing requirements can sometimes govern the selection of the widths of the beams. If all the reinforcing bars cannot be accommodated in a single layer with the necessary clearance between the bars and the clear cover on the two sides [Figure 5.1], the options are:

It is a common sight at construction sites to see reinforcing bars so crowded together, especially at junctions of members, that it is nearly impossible for the coarse aggregate in the concrete mix to pass through; the designer has to avoid this situation by proper detailing.

- to increase the beam width;
- to place the bars in two or more layers, properly separated [Figure 5.1(a)]; and
- to bundle groups of parallel bars (two, three or four bars in each bundle) [Figure 5.1(c)].

When placed in two or more layers, the bars in the upper layers must come directly above those in the bottom layer, with the required clearance. While fixing the overall size of the beam or the thickness of the slab, it is desirable to use multiples of 5 mm for slabs and 50 mm (or 25 mm) for beams. This will be convenient in the construction of the formwork. The requirements for placement of flexural reinforcement are described in Cl. 26.3 of the Code. The salient features of these specifications are summarised in Figure 5.1. The student is advised to read the relevant clauses in the Code, while studying Figure 5.1. The requirements for singly reinforced beams, slabs and doubly reinforced beams are depicted in parts (a), (b) and (c) respectively of Figure 5.1.

Stirrups provided in beams serve as transverse shear reinforcement [refer Chapter 6]. In singly reinforced beams, they may be provided as U-shaped stirrups, with two hanger bars at top [Figure 5.1(a)]. However, it is more common to provide fully closed rectangular stirrups [Figure 5.1(c)], for both singly and doubly reinforced sections; this is mandatory in the latter case for the effective functioning of the compression steel. Stirrups required for resisting torsion must also be of the closed form [refer Chapter 7].

In addition to the requirements indicated in Figure 5.1, the Code specifies limits to the maximum spacing of tension reinforcing bars in beams for crack control [refer Table 15 of the Code]. It may be noted that, for a given area of tension reinforcement, providing several small-diameter bars (that are well distributed in one or more layers in the extreme tension zone) is more effective in controlling cracks and improving bond than providing fewer bars of larger diameter. For this reason, the Code (Cl. 26.5.2.2 & 26.3.3b) limits the maximum diameter of reinforcing bars in slabs to one-eighth of the total thickness of the slab, and the maximum spacing of such main bars to $3d$ or 300 mm (whichever is less) [Figure 5.1(b)]. However, it may be noted that when large cover is provided, more stringent bar spacing may be required to achieve the desired crack control [Ref. 5.2].

Furthermore, in relatively deep flexural members, since tension reinforcements are generally provided close to the tension face in order to get the maximum effective depth, a substantial portion of the web below the neutral axis will be in tension but without reinforcements. Tension reinforcement properly distributed

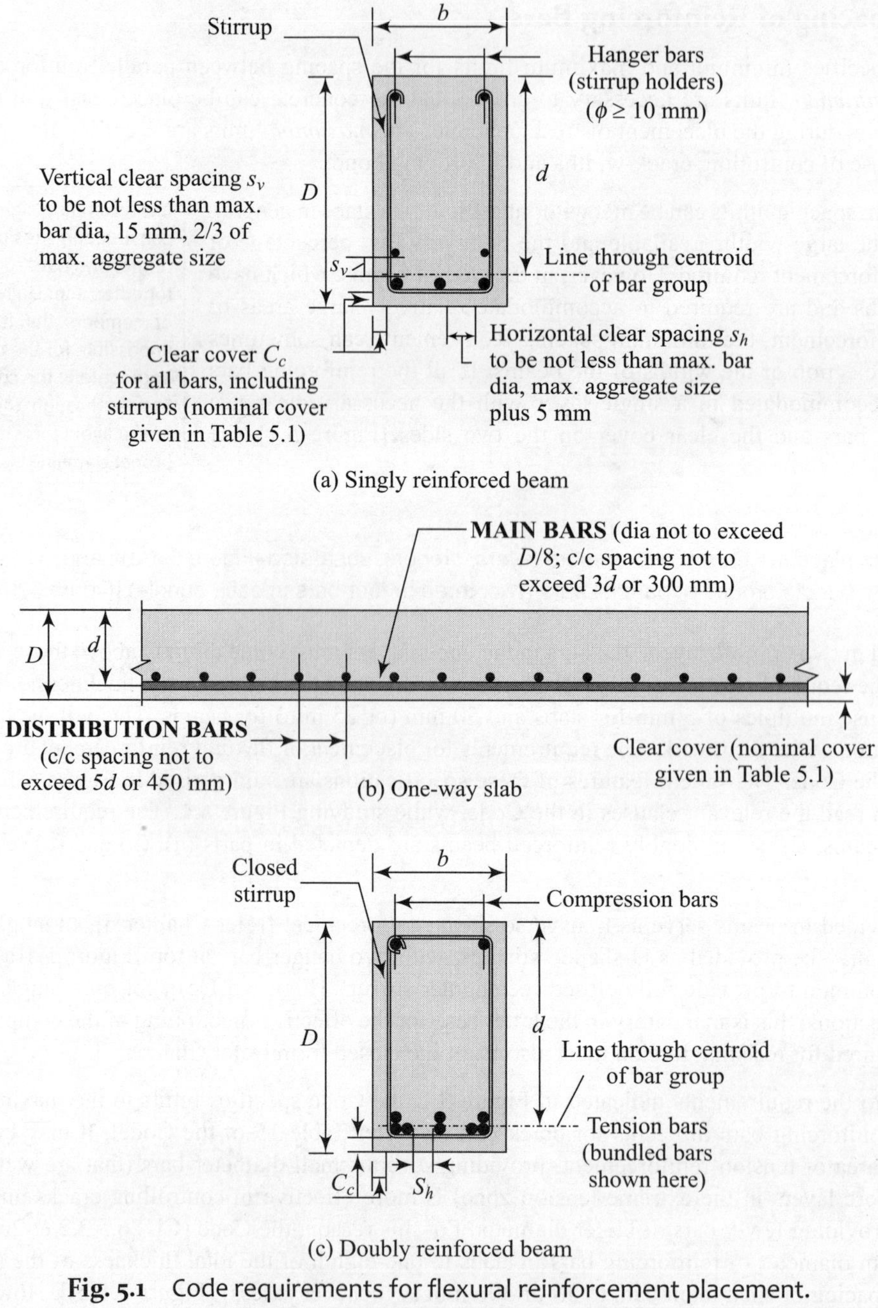

Fig. 5.1 Code requirements for flexural reinforcement placement.

will, no doubt, control the crack width at its level; however, wider cracks may develop higher up in the web. Moreover, as explained in Section 2.12, cracking can occur in large unreinforced exposed faces of concrete on account of shrinkage and temperature variations. In order to control such cracks, as well as to improve resistance against lateral buckling of the *web* [Ref. 5.3], the Code (Cl. 26.5.1.3) requires *side face reinforcement* to be provided along the two faces of beams with overall depth exceeding 750 mm:

'the total area of such reinforcement shall be not less than 0.1 percent of the web area and shall be distributed *equally* on two faces at a spacing not exceeding 300 mm or *web* thickness whichever is less'

5.2.3 Minimum and Maximum Areas† of Flexural Reinforcement

A minimum area of tension reinforcing steel is required in flexural members not only to resist possible load effects, but also to control cracking in concrete due to shrinkage and temperature variations. It was shown in Section 4.4.3 that a *plain* concrete beam will fail at a moment equal to the cracking moment M_{cr}. Naturally, the minimum reinforcement in a *reinforced* concrete beam must be such as to develop an ultimate moment of resistance at least equal to M_{cr}.

Minimum Tension Reinforcement in Beams

In the case of beams, the Code (Cl. 26.5.1.1) prescribes the following:

$$\frac{(A_{st})_{\min}}{bd} = \frac{0.85}{f_y} \tag{5.1}$$

which gives $(p_t)_{\min} \equiv \dfrac{100(A_{st})_{\min}}{bd}$ values equal to 0.340, 0.205 and 0.170 for Fe 250, Fe 415 and Fe 500 grades of steel respectively. In the case of flanged beams, the width of the web b_w should be considered in lieu of b.

It can be shown that the $(A_{st})_{\min}$ given by Eq. 5.1 results in an ultimate moment of resistance that is approximately equal to the 'cracking moment' of an identical plain concrete section. Thus, the minimum reinforcement requirement ensures that a sudden failure is avoided at $M = M_{cr}$.

Minimum Flexural Reinforcement in Slabs

As specified in Cl. 26.5.2, the minimum reinforcement $(A_{st})_{\min}$ in either direction in slabs is given by

$$(A_{st})_{\min} = \begin{cases} 0.0015A_g & \text{for Fe 250} \\ 0.0012A_g & \text{for Fe 415 and Fe 500} \end{cases} \tag{5.2}$$

where A_g denotes the *gross* area of the section ($b \times D$).

In the design of one-way slabs, this minimum reinforcement is also to be provided for the *secondary* (or *distributor*) *reinforcement* (refer Section 4.8.1) along the direction perpendicular to the main reinforcement‡, with the spacing of such bars not exceeding $5d$ or 450 mm (whichever is less) [Figure 5.1(b)]. It may be noted that in the case of slabs, sudden failure due to an overload is less likely owing to better lateral distribution of the load effects. Hence, the minimum steel requirements of slabs are based on considerations of shrinkage and temperature effects alone, and not on strength. Accordingly, the specified value of $(p_t)_{\min}$ is somewhat smaller in the case of slabs, compared to beams. However, for exposure conditions where crack control is of special importance, reinforcement in excess of that given by Eq. 5.2 should be provided.

† The limits specified here (as per IS 456) are applicable to reinforced concrete flexural members in general. However, for earthquake-resistant design ('ductile detailing'), different limits are applicable; this is described in Chapter 16.

‡ Note that the direction of the secondary reinforcement need not be the same as that of the long span. This case is encountered, for example, in a slab supported on opposite edges, with the actual span dimension being larger than the transverse dimension.

Maximum Flexural Reinforcement in Beams

Providing excessive reinforcement[†] in beams can result in congestion (particularly at beam-column junctions), thereby adversely affecting the proper placement and compaction of concrete. For this reason, the Code (Cl. 26.5.1) restricts the area of tension reinforcement (A_{st}) as well as compression reinforcement (A_{sc}) in beams to a maximum value of 0.04 *bD*. If both A_{sc} and A_{st} are provided at their maximum limits, the total area ($A_{sc} + A_{st}$) of steel would be equal to 8 per cent of the gross area of the beam section; this is rather excessive. It is recommended that such high reinforcement areas should be generally avoided by suitable design measures. These include:

- increasing the beam size (especially depth);
- improving the grades of concrete and steel.

5.3 Requirements for Deflection Control

> By providing initial upward camber in slabs and beams, where possible, deflection can be offset to the desired degree.

Excessive deflections in slabs and beams are generally undesirable as they adversely affect the appearance and efficiency of the structure and of the other elements (such as partitions, equipment) they support, cause psychological discomfort to the occupants of the building, grossly alter the slopes/levels of floor surfaces, and also lead to excessive crack-widths and subsequent loss of durability and ponding in roof slabs.

> *Flexural rigidity* of a beam section is given by *EI*, the product of elastic modulus, *E*, and second moment of area, *I*; flexural cracking reduces flexural rigidity, and this effect has to be taken into account in deflection calculations.

The selection of cross-sectional sizes of flexural members (thicknesses of slabs, in particular) is often governed by the need to control deflections under service loads. For a given loading and span, the deflection in a reinforced concrete beam or slab is inversely proportional to its *flexural rigidity*. It is also dependent on factors related to long-term effects of creep and shrinkage [refer Sections 2.11, 2.12]. From the point of view of design, it is the ratio of the maximum deflection to the span that is of concern, and that needs to be limited. The Code (Cl. 23.2a) specifies a limit of span/250 to the final deflection due to *all* loads (including long-term effects of temperature, creep and shrinkage). Additional limits are also specified in Cl. 23.2(b) of the Code – to prevent damage to partitions and finishes [refer Chapter 10 for details].

The explicit computation of maximum deflection can be rather laborious and made difficult by the need to specify a number of parameters (such as creep coefficient and shrinkage strain as well as actual service loads), which are not known with precision at the design stage. For convenience in design, and as an alternative to the actual calculation of deflection, the Code recommends certain maximum admissible span/effective depth (l/d) ratios (i.e., minimum depths) which are expected to satisfy the requirements of deflection control ($\Delta/l < 1/250$). It should be noted however, that meeting the (l/d) limits is no guarantee that the deflections are under control, especially in members with large spans and heavy loading and where creep and shrinkage effects can be substantial. Thus, explicit calculations of deflections (refer Chapter 10) become necessary under the following situations [Ref. 5.3]:

- when the specified l/d limits are exceeded;
- when the loading on the structure is abnormal; and
- when stringent deflection control is required.

[†] Heavy reinforcement may be designed in doubly reinforced beam sections and in flanged beam sections, without resulting in *over-reinforced* sections.

5.3.1 Deflection Control by Limiting Span/Depth Ratios

For a rectangular beam, made of a linearly elastic material, the ratio of the maximum elastic deflection to the span (Δ/l) will be a constant if the span/overall depth ratio (l/D) is kept constant. This can be proved as follows for the case of a simply supported rectangular beam, subjected to a uniformly distributed load w per unit length:

$$\Delta = \frac{5}{384}\frac{wl^4}{EI} \tag{5.3a}$$

$$M_{max} = \frac{wl^2}{8}$$

$$\Rightarrow \quad w = (M_{max})\frac{8}{l^2} = (\sigma Z)\frac{8}{l^2} = \left(\sigma \frac{bD^2}{6}\right)\frac{8}{l^2} \tag{5.3b}$$

where σ is the bending stress at service loads and $z = bD^2/6$ is the section modulus.

Substituting Eq. 5.3(b) and $I = bD^3/12$ in Eq. 5.3(a), it can be shown that

$$\left(\frac{\Delta}{l}\right) = \text{constant} \times \left(\frac{l}{D}\right) \tag{5.4}$$

where, in the present case of a simply supported beam with uniformly distributed loading, the 'constant' works out to $5\sigma/(24E)$.

Eq. 5.4 is generalised, and holds good for all types of loading and boundary conditions (with appropriately different constants). It is thus seen that, by limiting the l/D ratio, deflection (in terms of Δ/l) can be controlled.

Eq. 5.4 is not directly applicable in the case of reinforced concrete, because it is not a linearly elastic material and the parameters σ, Z and E are not constants, being dependent on such factors as the state of cracking, the percentage of reinforcement, as well as the long-term effects of creep and shrinkage. The Code however adopts this concept, with suitable approximations, and prescribes limiting l/d ratios for the purpose of deflection control.

5.3.2 Code Recommendations for Span/Effective Depth Ratios

For prismatic beams of rectangular sections and slabs of uniform thicknesses and *spans*[†] *up to* 10 m, the limiting l/d ratios are specified by the Code (Cl. 23.2.1) as:

$$(l/d)_{max} = (l/d)_{basic} \times k_t \times k_c \tag{5.5}$$

where $$(l/d)_{basic} = \begin{cases} 7 \text{ for cantilever spans} \\ 20 \text{ for simply supported spans} \\ 26 \text{ for continuous spans} \end{cases}$$

and the *modification factors* k_t (which varies with p_t and f_{st}) and k_c (which varies with p_c) are as given in Figures 4 and 5 of the Code (based on Ref. 5.4). Alternatively, the values of these 'modification factors' can be obtained from Tables 5.2 and 5.3 which are based on the figures given in the Code [Ref. 5.4]. For spans above 10 m, the limiting l/d ratios may be multiplied by 10/span in meters, except for cantilevers.

[†] The Code (Cl. 22.2) uses the term *effective span*, defined as the clear span plus effective depth, or centre-to-centre support distance, whichever is smaller.

It can be seen from Table 5.2 that the values of k_t increase with the use of lower percentages and lower service load stress levels[†] of tension reinforcement. This is attributable to the fact that, under given service loads, lower values of p_t and f_{st} are indicative of larger beam (or slab) cross-sections, resulting in higher flexural rigidity, and hence lesser deflections. Alternatively, for given cross-sections, lower values of p_t and f_{st} are indicative of lower design loads and lower strains distributed across the cross-section, and hence lower curvatures and lesser deflections. The use of *mild steel* bars (Fe 250), with relatively low allowable stress levels, is particularly effective in reducing deflections; the values of k_t are invariably greater than unity – even at high p_t values. The calculation of the stress in the tension steel f_{st} should ideally be worked out considering the transformed cracked section properties. However, for convenience, the Code permits an approximate calculation of f_{st}, given as follows:

$$f_{st} = 0.58 f_y \frac{\text{Area of steel required}}{\text{Area of steel provided}}$$

> It should be noted that, in the estimation of k_t for the control of deflections in continuous beams and slabs, the value of p_t and f_{st} should be calculated at the *midspan region*; however, in the case of cantilevers, p_t and f_{st} should be calculated at the support [Ref. 5.3].

Table 5.2 *Modification factor k_t for different values of p_t and f_{st} [Ref. Figure 4 of IS 456: 2000]*

$p_t \equiv \dfrac{100 A_{st}}{bd}$	f_{st} (MPa)				
	120	145	190	240	290
0.2	–	–	–	1.68	1.40
0.3	–	–	1.89	1.47	1.23
0.4	–	–	1.68	1.34	1.13
0.5	–	1.95	1.53	1.23	1.04
0.6	–	1.79	1.43	1.17	0.98
0.8	1.78	1.57	1.29	1.06	0.90
1.0	1.60	1.42	1.20	0.99	0.85
1.2	1.50	1.33	1.12	0.95	0.81
1.4	1.41	1.26	1.08	0.92	0.78
1.6	1.34	1.21	1.03	0.88	0.75
1.8	1.30	1.17	0.99	0.85	0.72
2.0	1.23	1.12	0.97	0.83	0.71
2.2	1.20	1.10	0.94	0.82	0.70
2.4	1.18	1.06	0.91	0.81	0.69
2.6	1.15	1.04	0.90	0.80	0.68
2.8	1.13	1.02	0.89	0.79	0.67
3.0	1.11	1.00	0.88	0.78	0.67

Table 5.3 *Modification factor k_c for different values of p_c [Ref. Figure 5 of IS 456: 2000]*

$p_c \equiv \dfrac{100 A_{sc}}{bd}$	k_c
0.00	1.00
0.25	1.08
0.50	1.14
0.75	1.20
1.00	1.25
1.25	1.29
1.50	1.33
1.75	1.36
2.00	1.39
2.25	1.42
2.50	1.45
2.75	1.48
3.00	1.50

From Table 5.3, it can be seen that the provision of compression steel can significantly contribute towards reducing deflections. For example, the modification factor k_c takes values of 1.25 and 1.50 for values of p_c equal to 1 per cent and 3 per cent respectively – for all grades of compression steel. This beneficial effect of compression reinforcement is attributable to its contributions in reducing differential *shrinkage* strains across the reinforced concrete section and in reducing the maximum creep strain in concrete [refer Section 2.12 and Chapter 10], thereby reducing long-term deflections due to shrinkage and creep.

In the case of *flanged beams*, the Code (Cl. 23.2.1e) recommends that the values of p_t and p_c considered in estimating the modification factors k_t and k_c should be

[†] In the earlier version of the Code, the modification factor k_t was a function of the characteristic (yield) strength, f_y; this has been corrected in the 2000 revision of the Code.

based on an area of section equal to $b_f d$, and that the calculated $(l/d)_{max}$ [Eq. 5.5] should be further modified by a 'reduction factor' which depends on b_w/b_f (as given in Figure 6 of the Code). However, this code procedure has been found to give anomalous results – as reported in the Explanatory Handbook to the Code [Ref. 5.3]. Hence, it is recommended that, for the purpose of using Eq. 5.5, the overhanging portions of the flanges be ignored, and that the beam be treated as a rectangular beam with width b_w and effective depth d; this will give conservative results.

5.4 Guidelines for Selection of Member Sizes

As explained in Sections 5.2 and 5.3, the selection of flexural member sizes (from a structural viewpoint) is often dictated by serviceability criteria (need to control deflections and crack-widths) as well as requirements related to the placement of reinforcement. However, there are other structural, economic and architectural considerations that come into play in the design of reinforced concrete beams.

The cost of concrete, steel and formwork in RC members typically forms only a small fraction of the overall cost of a building project. Attempts to minimise their quantities must be weighed against desired long-term performance. It is imperative to ensure that the Code-specified limit states of collapse and serviceability are not violated.

5.4.1 General Guidelines for Beam Sizes

The design problem does not have a unique solution (Section 5.1). Many choices of beam sizes are feasible in any given design situation. In general, for the purpose of designing for flexure, it is economical to opt for singly reinforced sections with moderate percentage tension reinforcement ($p_t \approx 0.5$ to 0.8 times $p_{t,lim}$).

Given a choice between increasing either the width of a beam or its depth, it is always advantageous to resort to the latter. This results not only in improved moment resisting capacity, but also in improved flexural stiffness, and hence, less deflections, curvatures and crack-widths. However, very deep beams are generally not desirable, as they result in a loss of headroom or an overall increase in the building height. In general, the recommended ratio of overall depth (D) to width (b) in rectangular beam sections is in the range of 1.5 to 2. It may be higher (up to 3 or even more) for beams carrying very heavy loads, such as bridge girders. The width and depth of beams are also governed by the shear force on the section [refer Chapter 6]. Often, architectural considerations dictate the sizes of beams. If these are too restrictive, then the desired strength of the beam in flexure can be provided by making it 'doubly reinforced' and/or by providing high strength concrete and steel. In the case of beam-supported slab systems which are cast integrally, the beams can be advantageously modelled as 'flanged beams', as explained earlier.

In the case of building frames, the width of beams should, in general, be less than or equal to the lateral dimension of the columns into which they frame. Beam widths of 200 mm, 250 mm and 300 mm are common in practice world-wide. Where the beam is required to support a masonry wall, the width of the beam is often made such that its sides are flush with the finished surfaces of the wall; thus, beam widths of 230 mm are also encountered in practice in India. In design practice, the overall depths of beams are often fixed in relation to their spans. Span to *overall depth* ratios of 10 to 16 are generally found to be economical in the case of simply supported and continuous beams. However, in the case of cantilevers, lower ratios are adopted, and the beams are generally tapered in depth along their lengths, for economy. Such traditional heuristic methods of fixing the depth of beams are generally satisfactory from the viewpoint of deflection control – for the normal range of loads.

From practical considerations, it is desirable to limit the number of different beam sizes in the same structure to a few standard modular sizes, as this will greatly convenience the construction of formwork, and permit reusability of forms.

5.4.2 General Guidelines for Slab Thicknesses

In the case of *slabs*, whose thicknesses are very small in comparison with the depths of beams, the limiting span/depth ratios of Eq. 5.5 will generally govern the proportioning. In practice, Fe 415 grade steel is most commonly used, and for such steel, a p_t value of about 0.4–0.5 per cent may be assumed for preliminary proportioning. This gives a k_t value of about 1.25 [Table 5.2]; accordingly, the required *effective depth* (for preliminary design) works out to about span/25 for simply supported slabs and about span/32 for continuous slabs.

In order to determine the thickness of the slab, the clear cover (based on exposure, refer Table 5.1) plus half the bar diameter of the main reinforcement (usually along the shorter span) have to be added to the effective depth, as indicated in Figure 5.1(b). The calculated value of the thickness should be rounded off to the nearest multiple of 5 mm or 10 mm.

5.4.3 Deep Beams and Slender Beams

In certain extreme situations, the designer may be called upon to deal with very low span/depth ratios. In such cases, where the depth of the beam becomes comparable to its span, the beam is referred to as a *deep beam*†. It calls for special design requirements, which are covered in Cl. 29 of the Code.

In other situations, *slender beams* may be encountered. When the length of a beam is excessive in comparison with its cross-sectional dimensions (particularly its width *b*), there is a possibility of *instability* due to slenderness – in particular, lateral buckling in the compression zone. The Code (Cl. 23.3) specifies certain 'slenderness limits' to ensure *lateral stability*. The clear distance between lateral restraints should not exceed $60b$ or $250\, b^2/d$, whichever is less, in the case of simply supported and continuous beams. For a cantilever, the distance from the free end to the edge of the support should not exceed $25b$ or $100\, b^2/d$, whichever is less.

Recent research [Ref. 5.8 and 5.9], based on experimental studies, indicate that, in addition to geometrical parameters, other parameters contributing to the lateral flexural stiffness and torsional stiffness of the beam (such as percentage of longitudinal and transverse reinforcement and grade of concrete), influence the limiting slenderness ratio. Moreover, these studies show that there is a reduction in the ultimate moment capacity of beams whose slenderness approach the limiting slenderness causing lateral flexural-torsional instability.

5.5 Design of Singly Reinforced Rectangular Sections

The design problem is generally one of determining the cross-sectional dimensions of a beam, viz., *b* and *D* (including *d*), and the area of tension steel A_{st} required to resist a known factored moment M_u. The material properties f_{ck} and f_y are generally prescribed/selected on the basis of exposure conditions, availability and economy. For normal applications, Fe 415 grade steel is used, and either M 20 or M 25 grade concrete is used (for exposures rated 'severe', 'very severe' and 'extreme', the minimum concrete grades specified are M 30, M 35 and M 40 respectively, as shown in Table 5.1). As explained earlier in Section 4.7.3, for under-reinforced sections, the influence of f_{ck} on the ultimate moment of resistance M_{uR} is relatively small; hence, the use of high strength concrete is not beneficial from the point of economy, although it is desirable from the point of durability.

† By definition, a 'deep beam' is one whose *l/D* ratio is less than 2.0 for a simply supported beam, and 2.5 for a continuous beam [refer Cl. 29.1 of the Code].

The basic requirement for *safety* at the 'ultimate limit state of flexure' is that the factored moment M_u should not exceed the ultimate moment of resistance M_{uR}, and that the failure at the limit state should be *ductile*. Accordingly, the *design equation* for flexure is given by:

$$M_u \leq M_{uR} \quad \text{with } x_u \leq x_{u,\max}$$

This implies that, for singly reinforced beam sections, Eq. 4.65 is applicable, with $M_u = M_{uR}$:

$$\frac{M_u}{bd^2} \equiv R = 0.87 f_y \left(\frac{p_t}{100}\right)\left[1 - \frac{f_y}{f_{ck}}\left(\frac{p_t}{100}\right)\right] \quad \text{for } p_t \leq p_{t,\lim} \tag{5.6}$$

For any chosen value of p_t, the constant $R \equiv \dfrac{M_u}{bd^2}$ (in MPa units) is determined from Eq. 5.6 (or, alternatively from the *analysis aids* given in Table A.2). The limiting percentage tension reinforcement $p_{t,\lim}$ and the corresponding $R_{\lim} \equiv M_{u,\lim}/(bd^2)$ are constants given by Eq. 4.62 and 4.61(a):

$$p_{t,\lim} = \begin{cases} 0.0884\ f_{ck} & \text{for Fe 250} \\ 0.0480\ f_{ck} & \text{for Fe 415} \\ 0.0379\ f_{ck} & \text{for Fe 500} \end{cases} \tag{5.7}$$

$$R_{\lim} = \frac{M_{u,\lim}}{bd^2} = \begin{cases} 0.1498\ f_{ck} & \text{for Fe 250} \\ 0.1389\ f_{ck} & \text{for Fe 415} \\ 0.1338\ f_{ck} & \text{for Fe 500} \end{cases} \tag{5.8}$$

5.5.1 Fixing Dimensions of Rectangular Section

Obviously, there are several combinations of p_t, b and d (or D) which can satisfy Eq. 5.6. If two of the three quantities are suitably assumed, the required value of the third can be computed. Thus, the problem is simplified if the values of b and D are either given (by architectural considerations) or arrived at on some logical basis. Another common approach is to select a value for p_t in the admissible range, using which the required value of bd^2 and hence an acceptable combination of b and d can be computed.

In the case of slabs, b is taken as 1000 mm (as explained in Section 4.8) and d is governed by the limiting l/d ratios for deflection control (refer Section 5.3.2). As suggested in Section 5.4.2, a trial value of d may be assumed as approximately $l/25$ for simply supported spans, $l/32$ for continuous spans and $l/8$ for cantilevers. The overall depth D may be taken as d plus effective cover. The effective cover will be the sum of the clear cover, the diameter of the stirrup and half the bar diameter (in the case of a single layer of tension reinforcement). Assuming a stirrup diameter of 10 mm and a bar diameter of 20 mm, the effective cover will be in the range of 40–95 mm, depending on the exposure condition†.

In the case of beams, it is generally found economical to adopt under-reinforced sections with $p_t < p_{t,\lim}$. For a chosen p_t, the value of R can be computed using the expression on the right-hand side of Eq. 5.6, and with this, the required $bd^2 = M_u/R$. Several combinations of b and d are possible. The value of b may be suitably fixed as 200 mm, 250 mm, 300 mm, etc., and the value of d is given by:

$$d = \sqrt{\frac{M_u}{Rb}} \tag{5.9}$$

† Effective cover (in mm) may be taken as 40, 50, 65, 70 and 95 respectively for mild, moderate, severe, very severe and extreme conditions of exposure.

where M_u is the factored moment† (in N mm). The minimum value of d corresponding to the limiting case $p_t = p_{t,\text{lim}}$ is obtained by substituting $R = R_{\text{lim}}$ (given by Eq. 5.8). It is desirable to adopt a value of d which is larger than d_{min} in order to obtain an under-reinforced section. The overall depth of the beam may be taken as $D > d_{\text{min}}$ + effective cover, and should be expressed in rounded figures (for ease in formwork construction). Multiples of 50 mm (or 25 mm) are generally adopted in practice. However, as explained earlier, the resulting D/b ratio should neither be excessive nor too small; ideally, it should be in the range 1.5 to 2.0. If the resulting D/b ratio is unacceptable and needs to be modified, this can be achieved by suitably modifying b, recalculating d (using Eq. 5.9) and fixing D.

Having fixed the rounded-off value of D, the correct value of the effective depth d can be obtained (assuming that the reinforcing bars can be accommodated in one layer) as follows:

$$d = D - (\text{clear cover}) - \phi_{\text{tie}} - \frac{\phi}{2}$$

If the bars need to be accommodated in two or more layers, the values of D and d should be fixed accordingly [refer Figure 5.1].

5.5.2 Determining Area of Tension Steel

At this stage of the design process, b and d are known, and it is desired to determine the required A_{st} so that the section has an ultimate moment of resistance M_{uR} equal to the factored moment M_u.

From Eq. 4.60, considering $M_u = M_{uR}$ and $x_u < x_{u,\text{max}}$, it follows that:

$$(A_{st})_{\text{reqd}} = \frac{M_u}{0.87 f_y d (1 - 0.416 x_u/d)} \tag{5.10}$$

where x_u/d is obtained by solving Eq. 4.59:

$$M_u = 0.362 f_{ck} bd^2 \left(\frac{x_u}{d}\right)\left[1 - 0.416\left(\frac{x_u}{d}\right)\right]$$

$$\Rightarrow \qquad 0.416\left(\frac{x_u}{d}\right)^2 - \left(\frac{x_u}{d}\right) + \frac{M_u}{0.362 f_{ck} bd^2} = 0$$

which is a quadratic equation, whose solution gives:

$$\frac{x_u}{d} = 1.202\left[1 - \sqrt{1 - 4.597 R/f_{ck}}\right] \tag{5.11}$$

where, as mentioned earlier, $R \equiv M_u/bd^2$.

It is also possible to calculate $(A_{st})_{\text{reqd}}$ directly from Eq. 5.6, without having to determine x_u/d. By re-arranging Eq 5.6,

$$\frac{f_y}{f_{ck}}\left(\frac{p_t}{100}\right)^2 - \left(\frac{p_t}{100}\right) + \frac{R}{0.87 f_y} = 0$$

which is a quadratic equation, whose solution gives:

† This will include the contribution of the self-weight of the flexural member. A conservative estimate of the size of the member may be made at the initial stage, for calculating self-weight. The unit weight of concrete should be taken as 25 kN/m^3 [Cl. 19.2.1 of Code; see also Appendix B.1 of this book].

$$\frac{p_t}{100} \equiv \frac{(A_{st})_{\text{reqd}}}{bd} = \frac{f_{ck}}{2f_y}\left[1-\sqrt{1-4.598R/f_{ck}}\,\right] \tag{5.12}$$

The above formula provides a convenient and direct estimate of the area of tension reinforcement in singly reinforced rectangular sections.

Alternative: Use of Design Aids

In practice, this is the most widely used method. Expressing the relationship between $R \equiv M_u/(bd^2)$ and p_t [Eq. 5.12] in the form of charts or tables for various combinations of f_y and f_{ck} is relatively simple. These are available in design handbooks such as SP : 16 [Ref. 5.5]. The tabular format is generally more convenient to deal with than the Chart.

Accordingly, Tables A.3(a) and A.3(b) have been developed (based on Eq. 5.12) for M 20, M 25, M 30 and M 35 grades of concrete, each table covering the three grades of steel [Fe 250, Fe 415 and Fe 500]; these tables are placed in Appendix A of this book. For a given value of R, and specified values of f_y and f_{ck}, the desired value of p_t can be read off (using linear interpolation for intermediate values).

Converting Area of Steel to Bars

The calculated area of steel $(A_{st})_{\text{reqd}}$ has to be expressed in terms of bars of specified nominal diameter ϕ and number (or spacing). Familiarity with the standard bar areas ($A_b = \pi\phi^2/4$) [Table 5.4] renders this task easy.

Table 5.4 *Standard bar areas ($A_b = \pi\phi^2/4$) and mass per metre (kg/m)*

ϕ (mm)	6	8	10	12	14	16	18	20	22	25	28	32	36
A_b (mm^2)	28.3	50.3	78.5	113	154	201	254	314	380	491	616	804	1018
Mass kg/m	.222	.395	.616	.887	1.21	1.58	1.99	2.46	2.98	3.85	4.84	6.31	7.99

For a chosen bar diameter ϕ, the number of bars required to provide the area of tension steel A_{st} is given by A_{st}/A_b, taken as a whole number. Alternatively, for a chosen number of bars, the appropriate bar diameter can be worked out. In some cases, it may be economical to select a combination of two different bar diameters (close to each other) in order to arrive at an area of steel as close as possible to the A_{st} calculated. As explained earlier, in the case of slab, the area of steel is expressed in terms of centre-to-centre spacing of bars, given by

$$s_{\text{reqd}} = 1000A_b/(A_{st})_{\text{reqd}}$$

The actual spacing provided should be rounded off to the nearest *lower* multiple of 5 mm or 10 mm.

For convenience, Tables A.5 and A.6 (provided in Appendix A) may be referred to – for a quick selection of bar diameter and number/spacing of bars. The values of bar areas given in Table 5.4 are also obtainable from Table A.5. Table 5.4 also gives the mass per metre length of the bars which may be useful in cost estimation.

The arrangement of bars finally proposed must comply with the Code requirements for placement of flexural reinforcement described in Section 5.2.

5.5.3 Design Check for Strength and Deflection Control

The actual A_{st} and d provided should be worked out, and it should be ensured that the consequent p_t is less than $p_{t,\text{lim}}$ (for ductile failure at the ultimate limit state). It is good practice to calculate the actual M_{uR} of the section designed (using Eq. 4.65 or 4.66), and thereby ensure that the actual $M_{uR} \geq M_u$.

A check on the adequacy of the depth provided for deflection control is also called for in flexural members. In the case of beams, the limiting (l/d) ratio given by Eq. 5.5 is generally more-than-adequately satisfied by singly reinforced sections. However, in the case of slabs, the criteria for deflection control are generally critical. In anticipation of this, it is necessary to adopt a suitable value of d at the initial stage of the design itself, as explained in Section 5.5.1.

The section should be suitably redesigned if it is found to be inadequate.

Example 5.1

A rectangular reinforced concrete beam, located inside a building in a coastal town, is simply supported on two masonry walls 230 mm thick and 6 m apart (centre-to-centre). The beam has to carry, in addition to its own weight, a distributed live load of 10 kN/m and a dead load of 5 kN/m. Design the beam section for maximum moment at midspan. Assume Fe 500 steel.

Solution

The beam is located inside the building, although in a coastal area, and thereby protected against weather, and not directly exposed to 'coastal environment'†. Hence, according to the Code (Table 3), the exposure condition may be taken as 'moderate'. The corresponding grade of concrete may be taken as M 25 and the clear cover as 30 mm. This cover will be adequate for normal fire resistance requirement also.

Determining M_u for design

- Assume a trial cross-section $b = 250$ mm, and $D = 600$ mm (span/10).

  Let $d = D - 50 = 550$ mm.

  ∴ Effective span (Cl. 22.2 of Code)

$$l = \begin{cases} 6.0 \text{ m} & \text{(distance between supports)} \\ (6.0 - 0.23) + 0.55 = 6.32 & \text{(clear span} + d) \end{cases}$$

  Taking the lesser value (as per Code), $l = 6.0$ m
- Distributed load due to self-weight

$$\Delta w_{DL} = 25 \text{ kN/m}^3 \times 0.25 \text{ m} \times 0.6 \text{ m} = 3.75 \text{ kN/m}$$

  ∴ Total $w_{DL} = 5.0 + 3.75 = 8.75$ kN/m, $w_{LL} = 10.0$ kN/m (given)
- ∴ Factored load (as per Code):

$$w_u = 1.5(w_{DL} + w_{LL}) = 1.5(8.75 + 10.0) = 28.1 \text{ kN/m}$$

- ⇒ Factored Moment (maximum at midspan)

$$M_u = w_u l^2/8 = 28.1 \times 6.0^2/8 = 126 \text{ kN/m}$$

Fixing up b, d and D

- For Fe 500 steel, $M_{u,\lim} = 0.1338 f_{ck} bd^2$ [Eq. 5.8]
- For M 25 concrete,

$$f_{ck} = 25 \text{ MPa} \Rightarrow R_{\lim} \equiv \frac{M_{u,\lim}}{bd^2} = 0.1338 \times 25 = 3.345 \text{ MPa}$$

- Assuming b = 250 mm, for a singly reinforced section, the minimum value of d, corresponding to $x_u = x_{u,\max}$ is given by

† Had the beam been located in the roof, the exposure condition would be 'severe'. Further, if the structure is located at the seafront (subject to sea water spray), the exposure condition would be 'very severe', according to the Code.

$$d_{min} = \sqrt{\frac{M_u}{R_{lim} b}} = \sqrt{\frac{126 \times 10^6}{3.345 \times 250}} = 388 \text{ mm}$$

- Adopt D = 450 mm[†]. Assuming 20ϕ bars, 8ϕ stirrups and clear cover of 30 mm, (note that specified cover is required for the stirrups as well),
  $d = 450 - 30 - 8 - 20/2 = 402$ mm

Determining $(A_{st})_{reqd}$

- $R \equiv \frac{M_u}{bd^2} = \frac{126 \times 10^6}{250 \times 402^2} = 3.119$ MPa

  $$R = 0.87 f_y \left(\frac{p_t}{100}\right)\left[1 - \frac{f_y}{f_{ck}} \times \frac{p_t}{100}\right]$$

  Solving this quadratic equation in terms of p_t [Eq. 5.12],

- $$\frac{p_t}{100} \equiv \frac{A_{st}}{bd} = \frac{25}{2(500)}\left[1 - \sqrt{1 - \frac{4.598 \times 3.119}{25}}\right] = 8.676 \times 10^{-3}$$

  $$\Rightarrow \qquad (A_{st})_{reqd} = (8.676 \times 10^{-3}) \times 250 \times 402 = 872 \text{ mm}^2$$

- [Alternatively, using 'design aids' [Table A.3(a)], for M_u/bd^2 = 3.119 MPa, M 25 concrete and Fe 500 steel, p_t = 0.867 – which gives the same result].

Detailing

- Using 3 bars in one layer, $3 \times (\pi\phi^2/4) = 872$ mm² $\Rightarrow \phi_{reqd} = 19.2$ mm.
  Provide **3–20ϕ** bars, for which $A_{st} = 3 \times (314) = 942$ mm² > 872 mm². The placement of bars [Figure 5.2] complies with the clearances specified by the Code.

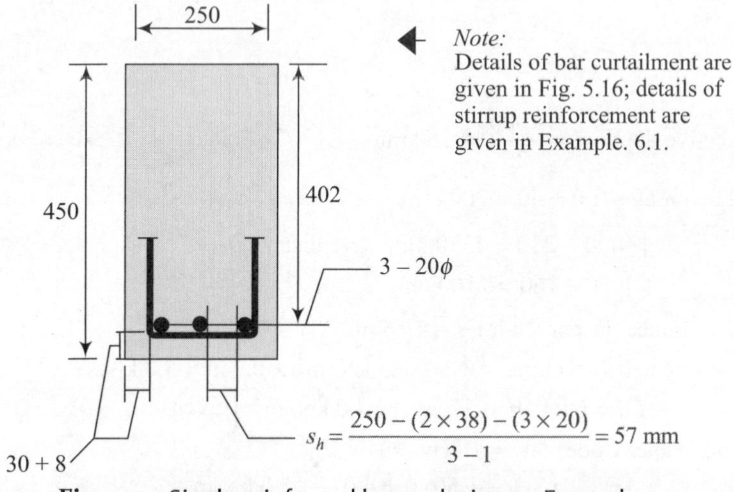

Fig. 5.2 Singly reinforced beam design — Example 5.1,

[†] The resulting D/b ratio is 1.8, which is satisfactory.

Design Checks

- (a) *For strength in flexure*

Actual $d = 450 - 30 - 8 - 20/2 = 402$ mm.

$$\Rightarrow \quad p_t = \frac{100 \times 942}{250 \times 402} = 0.937 < p_{t,\mathrm{lim}} = 0.947$$

$$\Rightarrow \quad M_{uR} = 0.87 \times 500 \times \left(\frac{0.937}{100}\right)\left[1 - \frac{500}{25}\left(\frac{0.937}{100}\right)\right] \times 250 \times 402^2$$

$$= 133.8 \times 10^6 \text{ Nmm} > M_u = 126 \text{ kNm — Hence, safe.}$$

[*Note*: As the actual depth provided (402 mm) is greater than the calculation value ($d = 388$ mm), and as the A_{st} provided (942 mm^2) is also greater than the A_{st} required (872 mm^2), it is evident (without the need for further proof) that the section is safe in flexure.]

- (b) *For deflection control*:

For $p_t = 0.937$, and

$$f_s = 0.58 f_y \left(\frac{A_{st(\mathrm{req})}}{A_{st(\mathrm{provided})}}\right) = 0.58 \times 500 \times \left(\frac{872}{942}\right) = 268.4 \text{ MPa}$$

$k_t = 0.918$ (from Figure 4 of Code or Table 5.2),

and, as $p_c = 0$ (singly reinforced beam), $k_c = 1$

$$\Rightarrow \quad \text{[Eq 5.5]: } (l/d)_{\max} = 20 \times 0.918 \times 1 = 18.36$$

$$(l/d)_{\text{provided}} = 6000/402 = 14.93 < (l/d)_{\max} \text{ — Hence, OK.}$$

Example 5.2

Design a one-way slab, with a clear span of 4.0 m, simply supported on 230 mm thick masonry walls, and subjected to a live load of 4 kN/m^2 and a surface finish of 1 kN/m^2. Assume Fe 500 steel. Assume that the slab is subjected to moderate exposure conditions.

Solution

Determining M_u

- Assume an effective depth $d \approx \dfrac{4000}{25} = 160$ mm

and an overall depth $D = 160 + 40 = 200$ mm

$$\therefore \text{ Effective span } l = \begin{cases} 4000 + 230 = 4230 \text{ mm} & \text{(c/c distance)} \\ 4000 + 160 = 4160 \text{ mm} \end{cases}$$

Taking the lesser values (as per Code), $l = 4.16$ m.

- Distributed load due to self-weight, $\Delta w_{DL} = 25 \text{ kN/m}^3 \times 0.2 \text{ m} = 5.0 \text{ kN/m}^2$

$$\therefore \quad w_{DL} = 5.0 + 1.0 = 6.0 \text{ kN/m}^2 \; ; \; w_{LL} = 4.0 \text{ kN/m}^2 \text{ (given)}$$

- $\therefore$ Factored load (as per Code) : $w_u = 1.5(w_{DL} + w_{LL})$

$$= 1.5(6.0 + 4.0) = 15.0 \text{ kN/m}^2$$

- $\Rightarrow$ Factored Moment (maximum at midspan)

$$M_u = w_u l^2/8 = 15.0 \times 4.16^2/8 = \mathbf{32.4\ kNm/m}$$

Determining A_{st} (main bars)

- $R \equiv \frac{M_u}{bd^2} = \frac{32.4 \times 10^6}{10^3 \times 160^2} = 1.267$ MPa
- For moderate exposure conditions, considering M25 grade concrete, $f_{ck} = 25$ MPa and applying Eq. 5.12,

$$\Rightarrow \qquad \frac{p_t}{100} \equiv \frac{A_{st}}{bd} = \frac{25}{2(500)}\left[1 - \sqrt{1 - \frac{4.598 \times 1.267}{25}}\right] = 0.310 \times 10^{-2}$$

- $\Rightarrow (A_{st})_{\text{reqd}} = (0.310 \times 10^{-2}) \times 1000 \times 160 = 497$ mm^2/m. [Alternatively, using 'design aids' [Table A.3(a)], the same result is obtained].
- Spacing of bars $s = 1000 A_b / A_{st}$
  Assuming 10ϕ bars ($A_b = \pi \times 10^2/4 = 78.5$ mm^2),
  spacing $s_{\text{reqd}} = 1000 \times 78.5/497 = 158$ mm
  [Alternatively, this can be obtained from Table A.6].
- Maximum spacing limits: $3d = 3 \times 160 = 480$ mm or 300 mm (whichever less)
  ∴ Provide 10ϕ @ 150 mm c/c for main reinforcement.

Distribution bars

(to be provided at right angles, in plan, to the main reinforcement – refer Section 5.2.3)

- $(A_{st})_{\text{dist}} = 0.0012 \times 1000 \times 200 = 240$ mm^2/m.
  Assuming 8ϕ bars ($A_b = \pi \times 8^2/4 = 50.3$ mm^2),
  Spacing $s_{\text{reqd}} = 1000 \times 50.3 / 240 = 208$ mm.
  Maximum spacing limit: $5d = 5 \times 160 = 800$ mm or 450 mm (whichever is less)
  ∴ Provide 8ϕ @ 200 mm c/c for distribution bars.

Strength check

- Providing a clear cover of 30 mm, $d = 200 - 30 - 10/2 = 165$ mm.

$$A_{st} = \frac{1000 \times 78.5}{150} = 523 \text{ mm}^2/\text{m}$$

$$\Rightarrow \qquad p_t = \frac{100 \times 523}{1000 \times 165} = 0.316; < p_{t,\lim} = 0.94$$

  As the actual depth provided (165 mm) is greater than the calculation value (160 mm), and the steel area provided is also greater than the calculation value, it is evident that the section is safe in flexure.

Deflection control check

- For $p_t = 0.316$ and $f_s = 0.58 \times 500 \times \frac{507}{523} = 281$ N/mm^2,

  $k_t = 1.26$ [Figure 4 of Code or Table 5.2]

$$\Rightarrow \qquad (l/d)_{\max} = 20 \times 1.26 = 25.2$$

  $(l/d)_{\text{provided}} = 4160/165 = 25.2$, which is just equal to the limiting value

— Hence, OK.

Detailing

> ***Detailing*** **is much more than the detailing of reinforcements for the member designed. Proper placement of reinforcement at joints, junctions, connections, etc., is critical for the safety of the structure (refer Ch. 15).**

The complete detailing of the slab† is indicated in Figure 5.3; this meets the Code requirements [refer Section 5.5]. Alternate bars of the main reinforcement are bent up (cranked) near the supports at a distance of 0.1 l from the support (Cl. D-1.6 of Code) – in order to resist any flexural tension that may possibly arise on account of partial fixity at the support [refer Figure 1.9(d)].

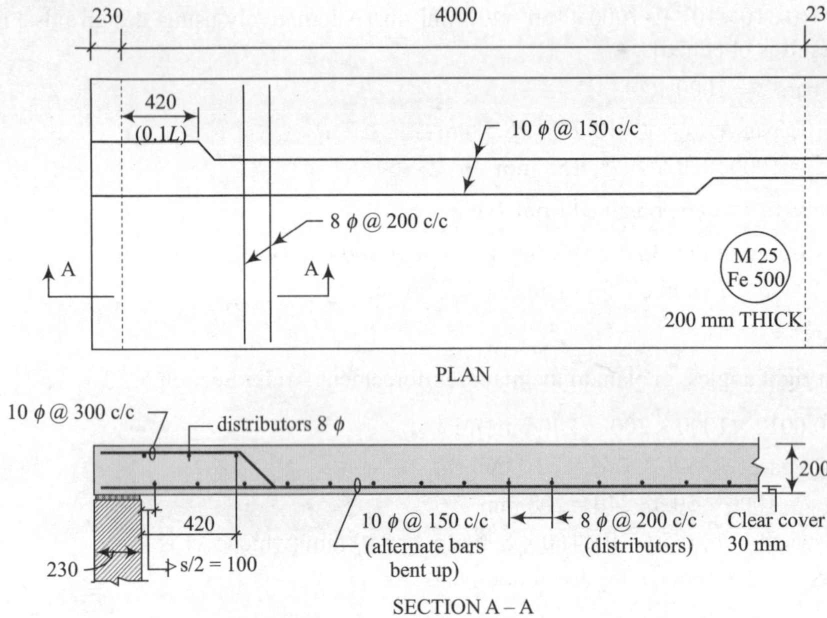

Fig. 5.3 Details of a one-way slab – Example 5.2.

5.6 Design of Continuous One-Way Slabs

In wall-supported and beam-supported slab floor systems (with stiff beams‡) [refer Section 1.6.1], the slab panels are generally continuous over several supporting walls/beams. When the bending is predominantly in one direction [Figure 1.9(b), (e)], the slab is called a *one-way continuous* slab system.

5.6.1 Simplified Structural Analysis – Use of Moment Coefficients

In order to determine the distribution of bending moments under the design loads (dead loads plus live loads), *structural analysis* has to be performed. For convenience, a strip of 1 *metre* width [Figure 5.4(a)] is considered (i.e., b = 1000 mm) for analysis and design. As the live loads (unlike the dead loads) are not

† Plans are generally drawn to a scale of 1:50 or 1:100, and section details to a scale of 1:10 or 1:20.

‡ Literature has established that the 'stiff' beams supporting the slab (unless extremely stiff), may not provide non-yielding supports. This has been discussed in detail in Chapter 11. Even though, the current design methodology can be followed which will give an over-conservative design.

expected to act all the time, various arrangements of live load have to be considered [refer Cl. 22.4.1 of the Code] in order to determine the maximum load effects; this is discussed in detail in Chapter 9. The (linear elastic) analysis may be done by methods such as the 'moment distribution method' or more appropriately using a commercially-available structural analysis software.

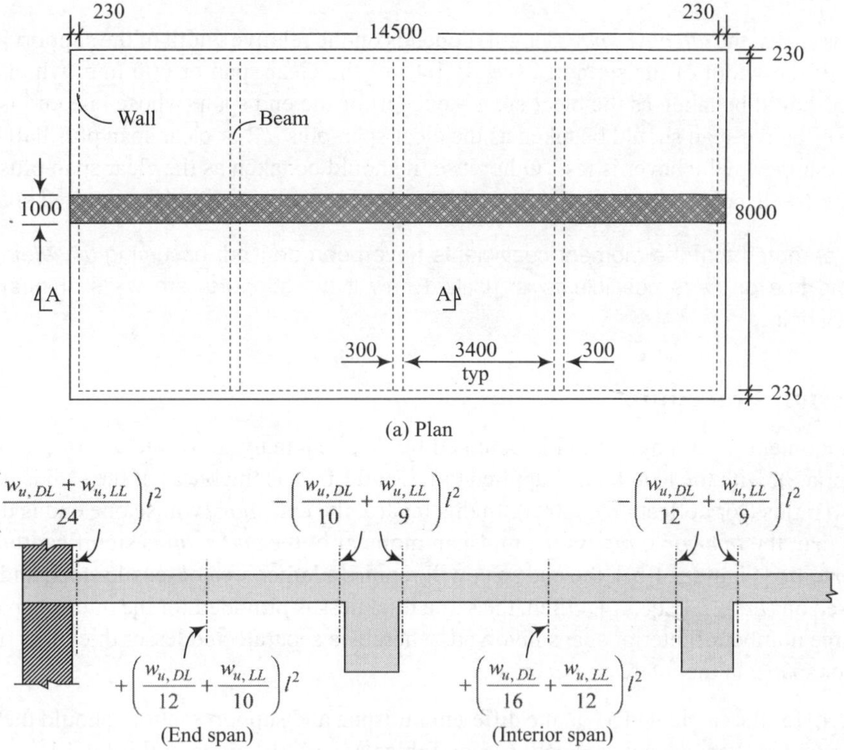

(b) Section A – A; Design Moments at Critical Sections
(not to scale)

Fig. 5.4 A continuous one-way slab floor system – Example 5.3.

For convenience, the Code (Cl. 22.5) lists *moment coefficients* (as well as *shear coefficients*[†]) that are close to the 'exact' values of the maximum load effects obtainable from rigorous analyses on an infinite number of equal spans on point supports [refer Ref. 5.3]. The moment coefficients [Table 12 of the Code] are depicted in Figure 5.4(b). These are applicable to cases of (uniformly loaded) one-way continuous slabs and (secondary) continuous beams with at least three spans '*which do not differ by more than 15 per cent of the longest*'. In the case of two adjacent spans which are either unequal or unequally loaded, for the negative moment at the support, the average of the two values may be taken. The 'shear coefficients' given by the Code are not shown here, as slabs do not generally have to be checked for shear, the shear stresses being kept in check by the adequate depths provided for deflection control [refer Chapter 6].

In any span, the maximum sagging ('positive') moment is assumed to be located at the midspan location, and the maximum hogging ('negative') moment at the face of the support (wall/beam). The magnitude of

[†] The 'shear coefficients' [Table 13 of the Code] are required in the design of continuous secondary beams.

the moment due to the factored dead load $w_{u,DL}$ (per unit length) is obtained by multiplying $w_{u,DL}$ with the relevant moment coefficient and the square of the *effective span l.* Similarly, the moment due to the factored live load $w_{u,LL}$ is obtained.

Effective Span

For continuous spans, the *effective span* (length) depends on the relative width of the support [vide Cl. 22.2(b) of the Code]. If the width of the support exceeds 1/12 of the clear span or 600 mm, whichever is less, the effective span should be taken as the clear span – except for the end span (whose one end is discontinuous) for which the effective span should be taken as the clear span plus $d/2$ or clear span plus half the width of the discontinuous support, whichever is less. Otherwise, it should be taken as the clear span plus effective depth or centre-to-centre distance between supports, whichever is less (as for simply supported spans).

> It should be noted that the moment coefficients have been derived, assuming *unyielding* supports. Hence, the use of these coefficients is justified only if the supports are walls or beams that are adequately rigid.

5.6.2 Design Procedure

The factored moment M_u at any section is obtained by detailed analysis (or the use of moment coefficients where appropriate), with the load factors applied to DL and LL. The thickness of the slab is usually governed by limiting l/d ratios (for deflection control). In this regard, the *end span* (whose one end is discontinuous) is more critical than the *interior span*. As the midspan moment in the *end span* is significantly larger than that in the *interior span* [Figure 5.4(b)], the end span will require a larger area of tensile steel, and will govern the thickness based on $(l/d)_{max}$ [Eq. 5.5]. Often, the same thickness is provided for the interior spans also – unless there are a large number of interior spans involved, whereby a separate and lesser thickness may be specified for the interior spans, in the interest of economy.

The required A_{st} for the calculated M_u at the different midspan and support sections should then be determined – by applying Eq. 5.12 or 'design aids' [SP : 16 or Tables A.3(a), (b) given in this book].

The 'positive' and 'negative' moment reinforcement required in the midspan and support regions may be provided in one of two alternative ways, as shown in Figures 5.5(a) and (b). In the first method, separate reinforcement is detailed for the positive moments and the negative moments [Figure 5.5(a)]. Alternatively, in the second method, the top ('negative moment') reinforcement over a support region may be provided by bending up alternate bars of the bottom ('positive moment') reinforcement from either side of the support, with additional bars provided (at top), if required.

The calculated spacings (required theoretically) in different spans/support regions are *not* directly provided as such (including rounding off to the nearest lower multiple of 5 mm or 10 mm). In practice, it is found desirable to correlate the spacings requirements at the different locations of the continuous slab, and to provide either the same spacing s or a fraction/multiple of it ($s/4$, $s/2$, $2s$ etc.) in all spans/supports, so that placement (including bending up over support) becomes convenient. *Detailing* of *bar cut-off* (curtailment), bending and extensions are discussed in Section 5.9. This involves detailed calculations (involving the bending moment envelope) which are not necessary in the present case, as a simplified analysis (using moment coefficients) is adopted. Accordingly, the details shown in Figure 5.5, based on the recommendations of SP : 34 [Ref. 5.5], may be adopted for such continuous slabs.

The proposed design should be checked for adequacy in terms of deflection control. Appropriate distribution bars should also be provided, as required by the Code.

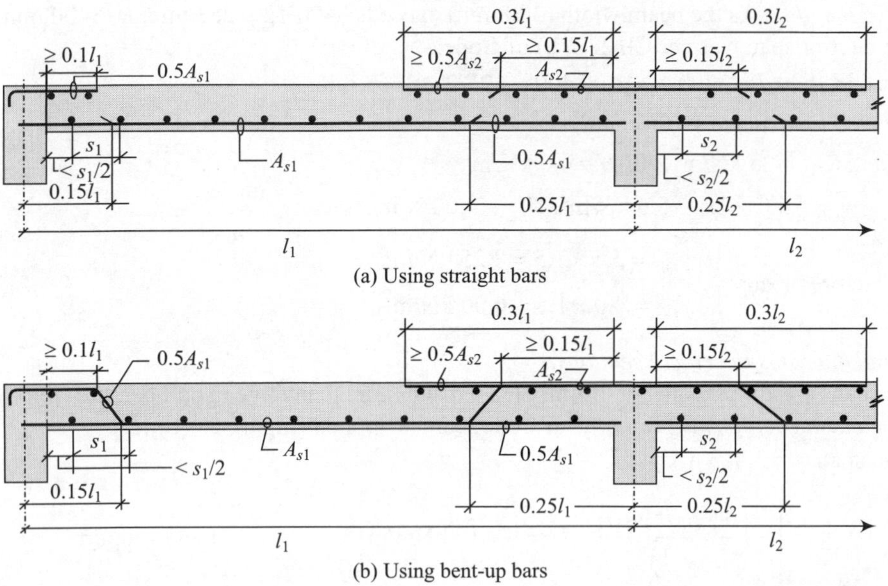

Fig. 5.5 Arrangement of main reinforcement in one-way continuous slabs [Ref. 5.6].

Example 5.3

The plan of a floor slab system, covering an area 8.0 m × 14.5 m (clear spans) is shown in Figure 5.4(a). The slab rests on a 230 mm thick masonry wall all around. For economy, the span of the slab is reduced by providing three (equally spaced) intermediate beams along the 8.0 m direction, as shown. The specified floor loading consists of a live load of 4 kN/m², and a dead load (due to floor finish, partitions etc.) of 1.5 kN/m² in addition to the self-weight. Assuming Fe 500 steel, design and detail the floor slab. Assume the beam is subjected to moderate exposure conditions.

Solution

- Assuming each beam to be 300 mm wide, the clear spacing between beams is equal to (14.5 – 0.3 × 3)/4 = 3.4 m. Each slab panel (with clear spans 3.4 m × 8.0 m) has an *L/B* ratio greater than 2.0, and hence may be treated as *one-way* (*continuous*) [refer Section 1.6.1]. The grade of concrete may be taken as M 25.

Determining Values of M_u at Critical Sections

Consider a 1-m wide design strip [Figure 5.4(a)].

- *Thickness of slab*:
  Assume a uniform thickness for both *end span* and *interior span*. The 'end span', which is critical, is discontinuous on one edge and continuous at the other.
  Accordingly, assuming $(l/d)_{max} \approx 1.23 \times (20+26)/2^{\dagger} = 28$,
  $d_{min} \approx 3500/28 = 125$ mm (for an assumed effective span of $l = 3.5$ m)
  Assume overall depth $D \approx 125 + 35 = 160$ mm for all spans and $d = 125$ mm.

† Modification factor k_t corresponding to $p_t \approx 0.3$ and $f_s = 290$ N/mm² [refer Section 5.3.2].

- *Effective length, l*: As the beam width (300 mm) exceeds 3400/12 = 283 mm, l =3400 mm (clear span) for the interior span – as per Cl. 22.2(b) of Code.
  For the *end span*, $l = 3400 + d/2 = 3400 + 125/2 = 3463$ mm.
- *Distributed load due to self-weight*:

$$\Delta w_{DL} = 25 \text{ kN/m}^3 \times 0.16 = 4.0 \text{ kN/m}^2$$

$$\therefore \quad w_{DL} = 4.0 + 1.5 = 5.5 \text{ kN/m}^2;\ w_{LL} = 4.0 \text{ kN/m}^2 \text{ (given)}$$

- $\therefore$ Factored loads $\begin{cases} w_{u,DL} = 5.5 \times 1.5 = 8.25 \text{ kN/m}^2 \\ w_{u,LL} = 4.0 \times 1.5 = 6.00 \text{ kN/m}^2 \end{cases}$
- *Factored moments at critical sections*:
  As the spans are almost equal, uniformly loaded and more than three in number, the simplified analysis using *moment coefficients* [Table 12 of Code] can be applied [Figure 5.4(b)].
  For end span ($l = 3.463$ m),

$$M_u = \begin{cases} -\left(\dfrac{w_{u,DL} + w_{u,LL}}{24}\right) l^2 = -7.12 \text{ kNm/m} & \text{at end support} \\ +\left(\dfrac{w_{u,DL}}{12} + \dfrac{w_{u,LL}}{10}\right) l^2 = +15.44 \text{ kNm/m} & \text{at midspan} \\ -\left(\dfrac{w_{u,DL}}{10} + \dfrac{w_{u,LL}}{9}\right) l^2 = -17.89 \text{ kNm/m} & \text{at interior support} \end{cases}$$

For interior span ($l = 3.400$ m),

$$M_u = \begin{cases} -\left(\dfrac{w_{u,DL}}{10} + \dfrac{w_{u,LL}}{9}\right) l^2 = -17.24 \text{ kNm/m} & \text{at first interior support} \\ +\left(\dfrac{w_{u,DL}}{16} + \dfrac{w_{u,LL}}{12}\right) l^2 = +11.74 \text{ kNm/m} & \text{at midspan} \\ -\left(\dfrac{w_{u,DL}}{12} + \dfrac{w_{u,LL}}{9}\right) l^2 = -15.65 \text{ kNm/m} & \text{at interior support} \end{cases}$$

At the first interior support, an average value of M_u should be considered:

$$M_u = -(17.89 + 17.24)/2 = -17.6 \text{ kNm/m}$$

Determining A_{st}

- For the maximum moment, $M_u = -17.6$ kNm/m at the first interior support,

$$R \equiv \frac{M_u}{bd^2} = \frac{17.6 \times 10^6}{1000 \times 125^2} = 1.126 \text{ MPa}$$

Applying Eq. 5.12, or using design aids (Table A.3(a)), for M 25 concrete (since the slab is subjected to moderate exposure conditions) and Fe 500 steel,

$$\frac{p_t}{100} = \frac{25}{2(500)}\left[1 - \sqrt{1 - (4.598 \times 1.126/25)}\right] = 0.274 \times 10^{-2}$$

$$(p_t)_{reqd} = 0.274 \Rightarrow (A_{st})_{reqd} = \frac{0.274}{100} \times 1000 \times 125 = 342 \text{ mm}^2/\text{m}$$

Assuming 10ϕ bars (A_b = 78.5 mm²), spacing reqd. = 1000 × 78.5/342 = 229 mm

Alternatively, for 8ϕ bars (A_b = 50.3 mm²), spacing reqd. = $\frac{1000 \times 50.3}{342}$ = 147 mm

[*Note*: maximum spacing allowed = 3 × 125 = 375 mm (> 300 mm)]

- For convenience, the results for all $(A_{st})_{reqd}$ at the various sections are tabulated in Table 5.5, after performing appropriate calculations (as shown for M_u = 17.6 kNm/m). The Table also shows the details of the actual steel provided (assuming the arrangement of bars shown in Figure 5.5(a)).
- Distribution bars: $(A_{st})_{min}$ = 0.0012bD = 192 mm²/m. Provide 8 mmϕ @ 250c/c

Deflection control check

- Maximum midspan steel in the end span:

  $(A_{st})_{provided}$: 8ϕ @ 140 c/c = 1000 × 50.3/140 = 359 mm²/m

  Providing a clear cover of 30 mm, d = 160 – 30 – 8/2 = 126 mm

  $\Rightarrow$ p_t = 100 × 359/(1000 × 126) = 0.285, f_s = 0.58 × 500 × 342/359 = 276.3 N/mm²

  $\Rightarrow$ k_t = 1.3 [Table 5.2]

  $\Rightarrow$ $(l/d)_{max}$ = 1.3 × (20 + 26) /2 = 29.9

  $(l/d)_{provided}$ = 3463/126 = 27.5 < 29.9 $\Rightarrow$ OK

  Evidently, the limiting (l/d) ratio will be satisfied by the interior span as well.

Table 5.5 *Calculation of A_{st} at critical locations of a one-way continuous slab system – Example 5.3*

Location	End Span		Interior Span		
	End support	Midspan	First int. support	Midspan	Int. support
M_u (kNm/m)	–7.1	+15.4	–17.6	+11.7	–15.6
M_u/bd^2 (MPa)	0.456	0.988	1.126	0.751	1.002
$(p_t)_{reqd}$	0.107	0.239	0.274	0.179	0.242
$(A_{st})_{reqd}$ (mm²/m)	134	298	342	224	303
$(A_{st})_{min}$ (mm²/m)	0.0012bD = 0.0012 × 10³ × 160 = 192				
Reqd. Spacing (mm) using (a) 10ϕ (b) 8ϕ	 409 262	 263 169	 230 147	 351 224	 259 166
Max. spacing (mm)	3 × d = 3 × 126 = 378 (> 300)				
Spacing of bars provided 10ϕ 8ϕ	(top) — 250	(bottom) — 140	(top) — 140	(bottom) — 150	(top) — 140

Detailing : The sectional details of the design are shown in Figure 5.6.

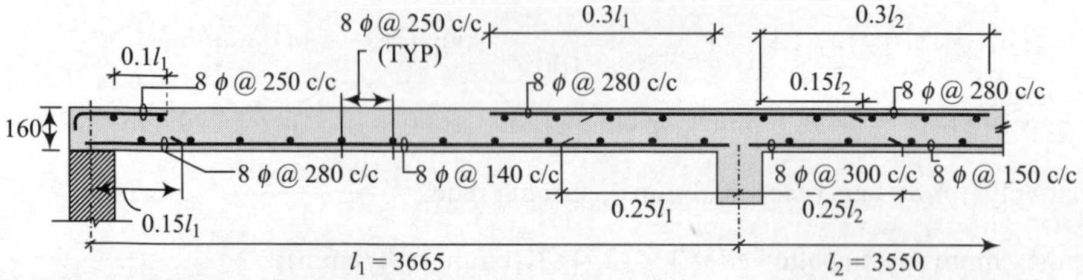

Fig. 5.6 Details of one-way continuous slab – Example 5.3.

5.7 Design of Doubly Reinforced Rectangular Sections

As explained earlier, doubly reinforced sections are generally resorted to in situations where the cross-sectional dimensions of the beam are restricted (by architectural or other considerations) and where singly reinforced sections (with $p_t = p_{t,\lim}$) are not adequate in terms of moment-resisting capacity. Doubly reinforced beams are also used in situations where reversal of moments is likely (as in multi-storeyed frames subjected to lateral loads). The presence of compression reinforcement reduces long-term deflections due to shrinkage and creep (refer Sections 5.3.2 and 10.4). All compression reinforcement must be enclosed by *closed* stirrups [Figure 5.1(c)], in order to prevent their possible buckling and to provide some ductility by confinement of concrete.

5.7.1 Design Formulas

As the dimensions of the beam section already are fixed, the design problem is one of determining the areas of reinforcement required in tension (A_{st}) and compression (A_{sc}).

As explained in Section 4.7.5, from the design point of view, it is necessary to limit the neutral axis depth x_u to $x_{u,max}$. This can be done conveniently by considering $x_u = x_{u,\max}$ and resolving the factored moment $M_u = M_{uR}$ into two components [Figure 5.7]:

$$M_u = M_{uR} = M_{u,\lim} + \Delta M_u \tag{5.13}$$

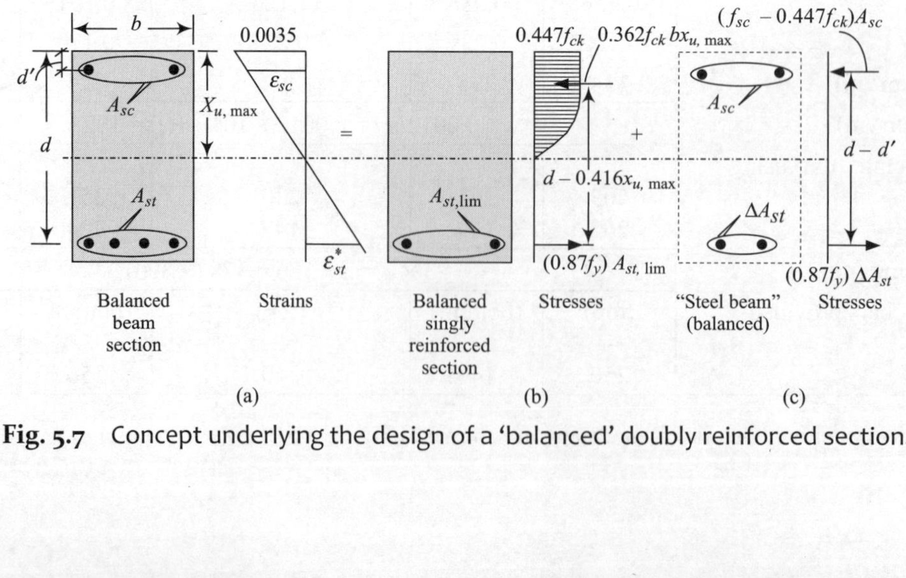

Fig. 5.7 Concept underlying the design of a 'balanced' doubly reinforced section.

where $M_{u,\lim}$ is the limiting moment capacity of a singly reinforced 'balanced' section (without compression steel) [Figure 5.7(b)] given by Eq. 5.8, and ΔM_u is the additional moment capacity desired from the compression steel A_{sc} and the corresponding additional tension steel ΔA_{st} – which may be visualised as the flanges of an equivalent 'steel beam' [Figure 5.7(c)]. As the contribution of concrete in compression is entirely accounted for in $M_{u,\lim}$, it does not contribute to ΔM_u. The distribution of strains, given by the condition, [Figure 5.7(a)] is identical for both the components, and the corresponding distributions of stresses are as shown in Figures 5.7(b) and (c).

If p_t denotes the total percentage of tension steel required for a 'balanced' doubly reinforced section, then corresponding to Eq. 5.13, it can also be resolved into two components.

$$p_t = p_{t,\lim} + \Delta p_t \tag{5.14a}$$

or

$$A_{st} = A_{st,\lim} + \Delta A_{st} \tag{5.14b}$$

where $A_{st,\lim} = p_{t,\lim}\, bd/100$ (or given by Eq. 5.7) is the tension steel corresponding to $M_{u,\lim}$ and $\Delta p_t = 100(\Delta A_{st})/bd$ is that corresponding to ΔM_u. Evidently, the moment ΔM_u is obtained from a couple comprising a (compressive) force $(f_{sc} - 0.447 f_{ck})A_{sc}$ and an equal and opposite (tensile) force $(0.87 f_y\, \Delta A_{st})$, with a lever arm $(d - d')$. The stress f_{sc} in the compression steel (at the ultimate limit state) depends on the strain ε_{sc} (given by Eq. 4.78) which is controlled by the linear strain distribution with the neutral axis located at $x = x_{u,\max}$ [Figure 5.7(a)]. Values of f_{sc} for different grades of steel and typical d'/d ratios are listed in Table 4.5. (It may be noted from Table 4.5 that the full design yield stress is attained only in the case of mild steel.) Based on the above, following formulas are obtainable:

$$\Delta A_{st} = \frac{M_u - M_{u,\lim}}{0.87 f_y (d - d')} \tag{5.15a}$$

$$\frac{\Delta p_t}{100} = \frac{R - R_{\lim}}{0.87 f_y (1 - d'/d)} \tag{5.15b}$$

$$p_t = p_{t,\lim} + \frac{100(R - R_{\lim})}{0.87 f_y (1 - d'/d)} \tag{5.16}$$

where $R \equiv M_u/bd^2$ and $R_{\lim} \equiv M_{u,\lim}/bd^2$.

$$A_{sc} = \frac{(0.87 f_y)(\Delta A_{st})}{f_{sc} - 0.447 f_{ck}} \tag{5.17a}$$

or

$$p_c = \frac{0.87 f_y (p_t - p_{t,\lim})}{f_{sc} - 0.447 f_{ck}} \tag{5.17b}$$

Applying Eq. 5.16 and Eq. 5.17b, design aids can be generated to give values of p_t and p_c for a given $M_u/(bd^2)$ – for various combinations of concrete and steel grades and different d'/d ratios. These have been developed in Table A.4 (placed in Appendix A of this book) for the commonly used combination of M 20 and M 25 grades of concrete with Fe 500 steel. Four typical ratios of d'/d (viz., 0.05, 0.10, 0.15, and 0.20) are covered in Table A.4. The Design Handbook, SP 16 [Ref. 5.5], gives such tables for other combinations of concrete and steel grades.

5.7.2 Design Procedure for Given M_u

Determining A_{st}

For a given rectangular section (with given b, d, and given f_{ck}, f_y), the limiting moment capacity for a singly reinforced section ($M_{u,\text{lim}}$) should be first determined, using Eq. 5.8. If $M_{u,\text{lim}}$ is greater than or equal to the factored moment M_u, the section should be designed as a singly reinforced section – as described in Section 5.5.2. Otherwise (for $M_u > M_{u,\text{lim}}$), the section should be designed as a doubly reinforced section.

The value of $p_{t,\text{lim}}$ is determined from Eq. 5.7, and the values of ΔA_{st} from Eq. 5.15(a) assuming a suitable value for d'. The total $(A_{st})_{\text{reqd}}$ is then obtained from Eq. 5.14(b). The bars should be suitably selected such that the A_{st} actually provided is as close as possible in magnitude to, but not less than $(A_{st})_{\text{reqd}}$. Tables A.5 and A.6 may be used for this purpose.

If the placement of bars results in a new value of the effective depth d which is significantly different from the original value assumed, $M_{u,\text{lim}}$, $A_{st,\text{lim}}$ and $(A_{st})_{\text{reqd}}$ should be recalculated at this stage itself.

Determining A_{sc}

Using the value of ΔA_{st} *actually provided*, the value of $(A_{sc})_{\text{reqd}}$ may be calculated from Eq. 5.17a. The value of f_{sc} can be obtained from the value of ε_{sc} [Figure 5.7(a) or Eq. 4.78] and the stress-strain relation [Table 3.2], or alternatively from Table 4.5 by interpolating for the calculated value of d'/d. The compression bars should be suitably selected such that the A_{sc} provided is as close as possible (but not less than $(A_{sc})_{\text{reqd}}$). Such a design procedure will result invariably in an adequately 'safe' design with $M_{uR} \geq M_u$ and $x_u \leq x_{u,\max}$; however, a design check for strength is always desirable.

Note that in the above calculations, the $(A_{sc})_{\text{reqd}}$ is computed corresponding to the 'ΔA_{st} *actually provided*' and *not* the 'ΔA_{st} *required*' (as computed from Eq. 5.15a). This is because the ΔA_{st} *actually provided* may be slightly in excess of ΔA_{st} *required*, and basing the latter (the lower value) for computing $(A_{sc})_{\text{reqd}}$ may result in the section being slightly *over-reinforced*. In other words, ΔA_{st} and A_{sc} actually provided must be in conformity with the strain distribution in Figure 5.7a.

Alternative: Using Design Aids

Design aids (Table A.4, SP:16) may be used to determine the $(p_t)_{\text{reqd}}$ and $(p_c)_{\text{reqd}}$ for the calculated value of M_u/bd^2; accordingly, A_{st} and A_{sc} are suitably provided. This is the most commonly adopted method in practice. However, it should be noted that if the A_{st} actually provided is well in excess of the $(A_{st})_{\text{reqd}}$, there is a possibility of ending up with an *over-reinforced section*, with $x_u > x_{u,\max}$ (see *Note* above). In order to avoid such a situation, (which is undesirable, and also not permitted by the Code), a correspondingly higher value of A_{sc} should be provided [Eq. 5.17a] such that the resulting $p_c > p_c^*$ (given by Eq. 4.84).

> A design check for safety in flexural strength is desirable – by properly analysing the designed section. It may be noted, however, that designers in practice, who are habituated with the use of design aids, often neglect to do this. It is often assumed that the strength design requirements are automatically satisfied if the values of p_t and p_c provided are in excess of that given in the tables. This is not always true – as demonstrated in Example 5.4.

Check for Deflection Control

The limiting (l/d) ratio for deflection control [Eq. 5.5] is generally satisfied by doubly reinforced beams, on account of the modification factor (k_c) for the compression steel [Table 5.3]. However, in the case of relatively shallow beams, a check for deflection control becomes necessary.

Example 5.4

Design the flexural reinforcement for the beam in Example 5.1, given that its size is limited to 250 mm × 400 mm, and that it has to carry, in addition to the loads already mentioned, a concentrated dead load of 30 kN placed at the midspan point. Assume that the beam is subjected to moderate exposure conditions.

Solution

Determining Mu for design

Given $b = 250$ mm, $D = 400$ mm, $f_{ck} = 25$ MPa , $f_y = 500$ MPa

Let $d = D - 50 = 350$ mm.

⇒ Effective span $l = 6.0$ m (as in Example 5.1).

- Loads: $w_{DL} = 5.0$ kN/m + Δw_{DL} (self-weight), $W_{DL} = 30$ kN at midspan
  Due to self-weight, $\Delta w_{DL} = 25 \times 0.25 \times 0.4 = 2.5$ kN/m, $w_{LL} = 10.0$ kN/m
  Factored Load: $w_u = (5.0 + 2.5 + 10.0) \times 1.5 = 26.25$ kN/m
  and $W_u = 30 \times 1.5 = 45$ kN (at midspan)
- ∴ Factored Moment (maximum at midspan):
  $M_u = 26.25 \times 6.0^2/8 + 45{\times}6.0/4 = 185.6$ kNm = **186 kNm**.

Singly reinforced or doubly reinforced section?

- For $M_{u,\lim} = 0.1338 f_{ck} bd^2 = 0.1338 \times 25 \times 250 \times 350^2$ (for Fe 500 with M 25)
  $= 102.4 \times 10^6$ Nmm = 102 kNm

  As $M_u > M_{u,\lim}$, the section has to be doubly reinforced, with $p_t > p_{t,\lim}$, where $p_{t,\lim} = 41.61\left(\dfrac{f_{ck}}{f_y}\right)\left(\dfrac{x_{u,\max}}{d}\right)$ = 0.947 for Fe 500 with M 25.

Determining A_{st}

- Considering a 'balanced section' ($x_u = x_{u,\max}$),

$$A_{st} = A_{st,\lim} + \Delta A_{st}$$

Where $A_{st,\lim} = \dfrac{0.947}{100} \times 250 \times 350 = 829 \text{ mm}^2$

- Assuming 20 mm ϕ bars for compression steel,

  $d' \approx 48$ mm (30 mm clear cover + 8 mm stirrup $+\phi/2$)

$$(\Delta A_{st})_{\text{reqd}} = \frac{(186 - 102) \times 10^6}{0.87 \times 500 \times (350 - 48)} = 639 \text{ mm}^2$$

$$\therefore \quad (A_{st})_{\text{reqd}} = 829 + 639 = 1467 \text{ mm}^2$$

Using 3 bars, $\phi_{\text{reqd}} = \sqrt{\dfrac{1467/3}{\pi/4}} = 24.9$ mm

Provide 3 nos 25 mm ϕ [$A_{st} = 3 \times 491 = 1473$ mm^2]

- Actual d (assuming 30 mm clear cover and 8 mm stirrups):

$$d = 400 - (30 + 8 + 25/2) = 349.5 \text{ mm} < 350 \text{ mm assumed earlier}$$

Revising the above calculations with $d = 349.5$ mm,

$$M_{u,\lim} = 102.1 \text{ kNm}, A_{st,\lim} = 0.947 \times 250 \times 349.5/100 = 827.4 \text{ mm}^2,$$

$$(\Delta A_{st})_{\text{reqd}} = 639 \text{ mm}^2, (A_{st})_{\text{reqd}} = 827 + 639 = 1467 \text{ mm}^2,$$

$$\therefore \quad \text{Actual } (\Delta A_{st})_{\text{provided}} = 1473 - 827 = 646 \text{ mm}^2$$

Determining A_{sc}

- Assuming $x_u = x_{u,\max}$, for $d'/d = 48/349.5 = 0.137$, from Table 4.5,

$$f_{sc} = 411.3 - (411.3 - 395.1) \times \frac{0.137 - 0.100}{0.15 - 0.10} = 399.3 \text{ MPa}$$

[Alternatively, applying $x_{u,\max}/d = 0.456$ in Eq. 4.78,

$$\varepsilon_{sc} = 0.0035(1 - 0.137/0.456) = 0.00244$$

$$\Rightarrow \quad f_{sc} = 399.3 \text{ MPa (from Table 3.2 or design stress-strain curve)]}$$

$$(A_{sc})_{\text{reqd}} = \frac{0.87 f_y (\Delta A_{st})}{f_{sc} - 0.447 f_{ck}} = \frac{(0.87 \times 500) \times 646}{399.3 - (0.447 \times 25)} = 724 \text{ mm}^2$$

$$\text{Using 2 bars, } \phi_{\text{reqd}} = \sqrt{\frac{724/2}{\pi/4}} = 21.5 \text{ mm}$$

$$\text{Using 3 bars, } \phi_{\text{reqd}} = \sqrt{\frac{724/3}{\pi/4}} = 17.53 \text{ mm}$$

Provide 3 nos 20 mm ϕ [$A_{sc} = 3 \times 314 = 942 \text{ mm}^2 > 725 \text{ mm}^2$].
The proposed section is shown in Figure 5.8.
[As an exercise in analysis, the student may verify that this section satisfies the design conditions: $M_{uR} \geq M_u$ and $x_u \leq x_{u,\max}$.]

Alternative method: using design aids

Assuming $d = 350$ mm, $d' = 50$ mm,

$$\frac{M_u}{bd^2} = \frac{186 \times 10^6}{250 \times 350^2} = 6.073 \text{ MPa}$$

Referring to Table A.4d (M 25 concrete and Fe 500 steel), for $d'/d = 50/350 = 0.143$ and $M_u/bd^2 = 6.073$ MPa, by linear interpolation,

$$p_t \approx 1.64 \Rightarrow (A_{st})_{\text{reqd}} = \frac{1.64}{100} \times 250 \times 350 = 1435 \text{ mm}^2$$

$$p_c \approx 0.76 \Rightarrow (A_{sc})_{\text{reqd}} = \frac{0.76}{100} \times 250 \times 350 = 665 \text{ mm}^2$$

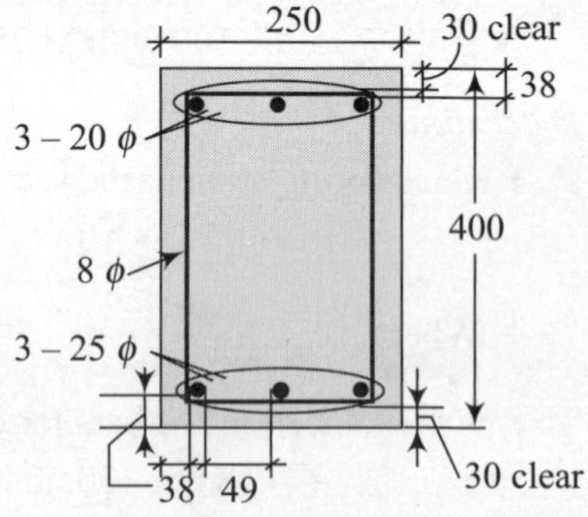

Fig. 5.8 Doubly reinforced section design – Example 5.4.

Provide 3–25ϕ for tension steel [$A_{st} = 3 \times 490 = 1470 \text{ mm}^2 > 1435$]
and 4–16ϕ for compression steel [$A_{sc} = 4 \times 201 = 804 \text{ mm}^2 > 665$]

Design check

- To ensure $x_u \le x_{u,\max}$, it suffices to establish $p_c \ge p_c^*$ [Eq. 4.84]

  Actual d provided: $d = 400 - 30 - 8 - 25/2 = 349.5$ mm;

  $d' = 30 + 16/2 + 8 = 46$ mm

  For $d'/d = 46/349.5 = 0.132, f_{sc} = 401$ MPa [Table 4.5].

  [Alternatively, $\varepsilon_{sc} = 0.0035(1 - 0.132/0.456) = 0.00249$

  $\Rightarrow \quad f_{sc} = 401$ MPa (Table 3.2).]

  Actual p_t provided: $p_t = 100 \times 1470/(250 \times 349.5) = 1.68$

  Actual p_c provided: $p_c = 100 \times 804/(250 \times 349.5) = 0.92$

$$p_c^* = \frac{0.87 f_y (p_t - p_{t,\lim})}{f_{sc} - 0.447 f_{ck}} = \frac{0.87 \times 500 \times (1.68 - 0.947)}{401 - (0.447 \times 25)} = 0.82$$

- As p_c is greater than p_c^*, the section is under-reinforced [This can also be verified by applying Eq. 4.81, which gives $x_u/d = 0.414 < x_{u,\max}/d = 0.456$.]

  Check for deflection control

  $p_t = 1.68$ and $f_{st} = 0.58 \times 500 \times 1435/1470 = 283.1$ MPa

  $\Rightarrow \quad k_t = 0.752$ [Table 5.2 or Figure 4 of Code]

  $p_c = 0.92 \Rightarrow k_c = 1.234$ [Table 5.3 or Figure 5 of Code]

- Applying Eq. 5.5,

  $(l/d)_{\max} = 20 \times 0.752 \times 1.234 = 18.56$

  $(l/d)_{\text{provided}} = 6000/349.5 = 17.16 < 18.56$ — Hence OK

5.8 Design of Flanged Beam Sections

T-beams and L-beams were introduced in Section 4.6.4. The integral† connection between the slab and the beam in cast in-situ construction makes the two act integrally, so that some portion of the slab functions as a flange of the beam. It should be noted that the flange is effective only when it is on the compression side, i.e., when the beam is in a 'sagging' mode of flexure (not 'hogging') with the slab on top. Alternatively, if the beam is 'upturned' (inverted T-beam) and it is subjected to 'hogging' moments (as in a cantilever), the T-beam action is effective, as the flange is under compression.

Ideal flanged beam action occurs when the flange dimensions are relatively small while the beam is deep – as in the case of closely spaced long-span bridge girders in a T-beam bridge. The beam is invariably heavily reinforced in such cases.

5.8.1 Transverse Reinforcement in Flange

The integral action between the flange and the web is usually ensured by the transverse bars in the slab and the stirrups in the beam. In the case of isolated flanged beams (as in spandrel beams of staircases), the detailing of reinforcement depicted in Figure 5.9(a) may be adopted. The overhanging portions of the slab should be designed as cantilevers and the reinforcement provided accordingly.

† Where the slab and beam are not cast monolithically, flanged beam action cannot be assumed, unless special shear connectors are provided at the interface between beam and the slab.

Adequate transverse reinforcement must be provided near the top of the flange. Such reinforcement is usually present in the form of negative moment reinforcement in the continuous slabs which span across and form the flanges of the T-beams. When this is not the case (as in slabs where the main bars run *parallel* to the beam), the Code (Cl. 23.1.1b) specifies that transverse reinforcement should be provided in the flange of the T-beam (or L-beam) as shown in Figure 5.9(b). The area of such steel should be not less than 60 per cent of the main area of steel provided at the midspan of the slab, and should extend on either side of the beam to a distance not less than one-fourth of the span of the beam.

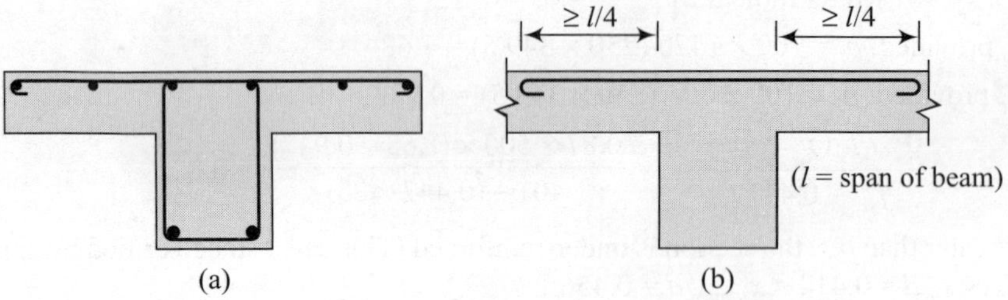

Fig. 5.9 Detailing of flanged beams to ensure integral action of slab and beam.

5.8.2 Design Procedure

In the case of a *continuous* flanged beam, the negative moment at the face of the support generally exceeds the maximum positive moment (at or near the midspan), and hence governs the proportioning of the beam cross-section. In such cases of negative moment, if the slab is located on top of the beam (as is usually the case), the flange is under flexural tension and hence the concrete in the flange is rendered ineffective. The beam section at the support is therefore to be designed as a rectangular section for the factored negative moment†. Towards the midspan of the beam, however, the beam behaves as a proper flanged beam (with the flange under flexural compression). As the width of the web b_w and the overall depth D are already fixed from design considerations at the support, all that remains to be determined is the area of reinforcing steel; the *effective width of flange* is determined as suggested by the Code [Eq. 4.30].

In simply supported flanged beams, however, the web dimensions must also be designed (if not otherwise specified). The width of the web is generally fixed as 250 mm, 300 mm, 350 mm (as for a rectangular section), and the overall depth assumed to be approximately span/13 to span/16. An approximate estimate of the area of tension steel A_{st} can be obtained as follows:

$$(A_{st})_{\text{reqd}} = \frac{M_u}{0.87 f_y z} \tag{5.18}$$

where the lever arm z may be taken approximately as $0.9d$ or $(d - D_f/2)$, whichever is larger. If convenient, the reinforcement should be accommodated in one layer – although, often this may not be possible. When the tension steel is provided in more than one layer, the effective depth gets reduced.

The determination of the actual reinforcement in a flanged beam depends on the location of the neutral axis x_u, which, of course, should be limited to $x_{u,\max}$. If M_u exceeds $M_{u,\lim}$ for a singly reinforced flanged section, the depth of the section should be suitably increased; otherwise, a doubly reinforced section is to be designed.

† In such cases it is desirable to distribute the tension steel at the top of the web across the effective width of the flange, to protect the integral flange from cracking – as recommended by the ACI Code. Alternatively, additional reinforcement may be provided in the flange region for this purpose.

Neutral Axis within Flange ($x_u \le D_f$):

This is, by far, the most common situation encountered in building design. Because of the very large compressive concrete area contributed by the flange in T-beams and L-beams of usual proportions, the neutral axis lies within the flange ($x_u \le D_f$), whereby the section behaves like a rectangular section having width b_f and effective depth d.

A simple way of first checking $x_u \le D_f$ is by verifying $M_u \le (M_{uR})_{x_u = D_f}$ where $(M_{uR})_{x_u = D_f}$ is the limiting ultimate moment of resistance for the condition $x_u = D_f$ and is given by

$$(M_{uR})_{x_u = D_f} = 0.362 f_{ck} b_f D_f (d - 0.416 D_f) \tag{5.19}$$

It may be noted that the above equation is meaningful only if $x_{u,\max} > D_f$. In rare situations involving very thick flanges and relatively shallow beams, $x_{u,\max}$ may be less than D_f. In such cases, $M_{u,\lim}$ is obtained by substituting $x_{u,\max}$ in place of D_f in Eq. 5.19.

Neutral Axis within Web ($x_u > D_f$):

When $M_u > (M_{uR})_{x_u = D_f}$, it follows that $x_u > D_f$. The accurate determination of x_u can be somewhat laborious†. As explained in Chapter 4, the contributions of the compressive forces C_{uw} and C_{uf} in the 'web' and 'flange' may be accounted for separately as follows:

$$M_u = C_{uw}(d - 0.416 x_u) + C_{uf}(d - y_f/2) \tag{5.20}$$

where,

$$C_{uw} = 0.362 f_{ck} b_w x_u \tag{5.21}$$

$$C_{uf} = 0.447 f_{ck} (b_f - b_w) y_f \tag{5.22}$$

and the equivalent flange thickness y_f is equal to or less than D_f depending on whether x_u exceeds $7D_f/3$ or not.

For $x_{u,\max} \ge 7D_f/3$, the value of the ultimate moment of resistance $(M_{uR})_{x_u = 7D_f/3}$ corresponding to $x_u = 7D_f/3$ and $y_f = D_f$ may be first computed. If the factored moment $M_u \ge (M_{uR})_{x_u = 7D_f/3}$, it follows that $x_u > 7D_f/3$ and $y_f = D_f$. Otherwise, $D_f < x_u < 7D_f/3$ for $(M_{uR})_{x_u = D_f} < M_u < (M_{uR})_{x_u = 7D_f/3}$ and

$$y_f = 0.15 x_u + 0.65 D_f \tag{5.23}$$

Inserting the appropriate value – D_f or the expression for y_f (given by Eq. 5.23) — in Eq. 5.20, the resulting quadratic equation (in terms of the unknown x_u) can be solved to yield the correct value of x_u. Corresponding to this value of x_u, the values of C_{uw} and C_{uf} can be computed [Eq. 5.21, 5.22] and the required A_{st} obtained by solving the force equilibrium equation.

$$T_u = 0.87 f_y A_{st} = C_{uw} + C_{uf}$$

$$\Rightarrow \qquad (A_{st})_{\text{reqd}} = \frac{C_{uw} + C_{uf}}{0.87 f_y} \tag{5.24}$$

† As an alternative to this procedure, a design based on the approximate estimate of A_{st} [Eq. 5.18] may be assumed, and the resulting section *analysed* to determine M_{uR}. The design becomes acceptable if $M_{uR} \ge M_u$ and $x_u \le x_{u,\max}$.

Example 5.5

Design the interior beam in the floor system in Example 5.3 [Figure 5.4(a)]. Assume that the beam is subjected to moderate exposure conditions. Use Fe 500 steel.

Solution

- The slab is one-way, spanning between the beams, which are simply supported and hence behave as T-beams [$l_0 = 8230$ mm, $D_f = 160$ mm, $b_w = 300$ mm].
  Effective flange width (Cl 23.1.2 Code):
  $$b_f = l_0/6 + b_w + 6D_f \text{ [Eq. 4.30]}$$
  $$= 8230/6 + 300 + (6 \times 160) = 2632 \text{ mm},$$
  which is acceptable as it is less than b_w + clear span of slab (300 + 3400 = 3700).
- Assume overall depth $D \approx l/15 = 550$ mm.
  $\Rightarrow$ effective depth $d \approx 500$ mm.
  $\Rightarrow$ effective span $l = 8.0 + 0.23$ m = 8.23 m (less than 8.0 + 0.5 = 8.5 m).

Determining M_u for design

- Distributed loads from slab (refer Example 5.3):
  $$w_{DL} = 5.5 \text{ kN/m}^2 \times 3.7 \text{ m} = 20.35 \text{ kN/m}$$
  $$w_{LL} = 4.0 \text{ kN/m}^2 \times 3.7 \text{ m} = 14.8 \text{ kN/m}$$
  Additional dead load due to self-weight of *web:*
  $$\Delta w_{DL} = 25 \times 0.3 \times (0.55 - 0.16) = 2.93 \text{ kN/m}$$
- $\therefore$ Factored load $w_u = 1.5 \times (20.35 + 14.8 + 2.93) = 57.12$ kN/m
- $\Rightarrow$ Factored moment (maximum at midspan)
  $$M_u = w_u l^2/8 = 57.12 \times 8.23^2/8 = 484 \text{ kNm}$$

Determining approximate A_{st}

- Assuming a lever arm z equal to the larger of $0.9d = 450$ mm and $d - D_f/2 = 420$ mm, i.e., $z \approx 450$ mm,
  $$(A_{st})_{reqd} = \frac{M_u}{0.87 f_y z} \approx \frac{484 \times 10^6}{0.87 \times 500 \times 450} = 2472.54 \text{ mm}^2$$
- Providing 3 bars, $\phi_{reqd} = \sqrt{\frac{2472/3}{\pi/4}} = 32.4$ mm

  or, providing 4 bars, $\phi_{reqd} = \sqrt{\frac{2472/4}{\pi/4}} = 28.1$ mm
- [Alternatively, this is obtainable from Table A.4.]
  It may be observed that the bars (either 3–36ϕ or 4–32ϕ) can be accommodated in one layer, given $b_w = 300$ mm. Assuming 32 mm ϕ bars and 8 mm ϕ stirrups,
  $\Rightarrow$ Actual $d = 550 - 32 - 8 - 32/2 = 494$ mm
  (clear cover shall not be less than the diameter of the bar)

Determining actual A_{st}

$x_{u,\max} = 0.456 \times 494 = 225 \text{ mm} > D_f = 160$ mm

- Assuming the neutral axis to be located at $x_u = D_f$

$$(M_{uR})_{x_u=D_f} = 0.362 \times 25 \times 2632 \times 160 \times (494 - 0.416 \times 160) \text{ [for M 25 concrete]}$$
$$= 1629 \times 10^6 \text{ Nmm} > M_u = 484 \text{ kNm}$$

Hence, the neutral axis is located definitely within the flange ($x_u < D_f$).

- Accordingly, designing the T-section as a singly reinforced rectangular section with $b = b_f = 2632$ mm and $d = 494$ mm,

$$R \equiv \frac{M_u}{bd^2} = \frac{484 \times 10^6}{2632 \times 494^2} = 0.753 \text{ MPa}$$

$$\frac{(p_t)_{\text{reqd}}}{100} = \frac{25}{2 \times 500}\left[1 - \sqrt{1 - \frac{4.598 \times 0.753}{25}}\right] = 0.18 \times 10^{-2}$$

$$\Rightarrow \quad (A_{st})_{\text{reqd}} = \frac{0.18}{100} \times 2632 \times 494 = 2334 \text{ mm}^2$$

(which incidentally is about 6 per cent less than the approximate value calculated earlier).

- Provide 2–32ϕ plus 2–25ϕ bars

[$A_{st} = (2 \times 804) + (2 \times 490) = 2590 \text{ mm}^2 > 2334 \text{ mm}^2$]

The cross-section of the beam, showing the location of bars, is depicted in Figure 5.10.

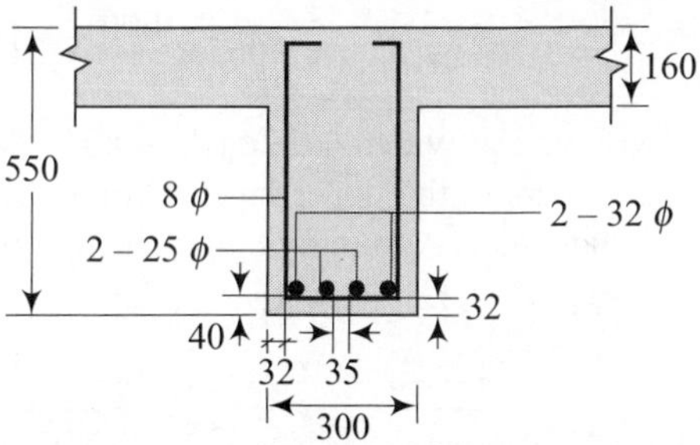

Fig. 5.10 T-beam of Example 5.5.

Check for Deflection Control

- Ignoring the contribution of flanges (conservative) [refer Section 5.3.2],

$$p_t = \frac{100 \times 2590}{300 \times 494} = 1.75; \; f_s = 0.58 \times 500 \times \frac{2334}{2590} = 261.33 \text{ MPa}$$

$$\Rightarrow \quad k_t = 0.72 \text{ [Table 5.2]}$$

$$\Rightarrow \quad (l/d)_{\max} = 20 \times 0.72 \times 1 = 14.4 \text{ [Eq. 5.5]}$$

$$(l/d)_{\text{provided}} = 8230/494 = 16.66 > 14.4$$

– Hence, not OK. Hence, either do detailed calculation of deflections and check (refer Ch. 10), or revise the design with an overall depth of beam of 600 mm.

Example 5.6

A continuous T-beam has the cross-sectional dimensions shown in Figure 5.11(a). The web dimensions have been determined from the consideration of negative moment at support and shear strength requirements. The span is 10 m and the design moment at midspan under factored loads is 800 kNm. Determine the flexural reinforcement requirement at midspan. Consider Fe 500 steel. Assume that the beam is subjected to moderate exposure conditions.

Solution

Determining approximate A_{st}

- *Effective flange width b_f*

Actual flange width provided = 1500 mm; D_f = 100 mm, b_w = 300 mm.

Maximum width permitted = (0.7 × 10000)/6 + 300 + (6 × 100) = 2067 mm > 1500 mm

$\therefore \quad b_f = 1500$ mm

- Assuming $d \approx 650$ mm and a lever arm z equal to the larger of $0.9d = 585$ mm and $d - D_f/2 = 600$ mm, i.e., $z \approx 600$ mm,

$$(A_{st})_{\text{reqd}} \approx \frac{800 \times 10^6}{0.87 \times 500 \times 600} = 3065 \text{ mm}^2$$

- Providing 4 bars, $\phi_{\text{reqd}} = \sqrt{\dfrac{3065/4}{\pi/4}} = 31.2$ mm, i.e., 32 mm.

  As 4–32ϕ bars cannot be accommodated in one layer within the width $b_w = 300$ mm, two layers are required.

  Assuming a reduced $d \approx 625$ mm, $z \approx 625 - 100/2 = 575$ mm.

$$\Rightarrow \quad (A_{st})_{\text{reqd}} \approx 3065 \times \frac{600}{575} = 3198 \text{ mm}^2$$

- ∴ the provided 4–32ϕ [$A_{st} = 804 \times 4 = 3216$ mm^2] reinforcement, with 2 bars in the lower layer plus 2 bars in the upper layer, with a clear vertical separation of 32 mm – as shown in Figure 5.11(b), is adequate. Assuming 8 mm stirrups and a clear 32 mm cover to *stirrups*,

$$\Rightarrow \quad d = 700 - 32 - 8 - 32 - 16 = 612 \text{ mm}$$

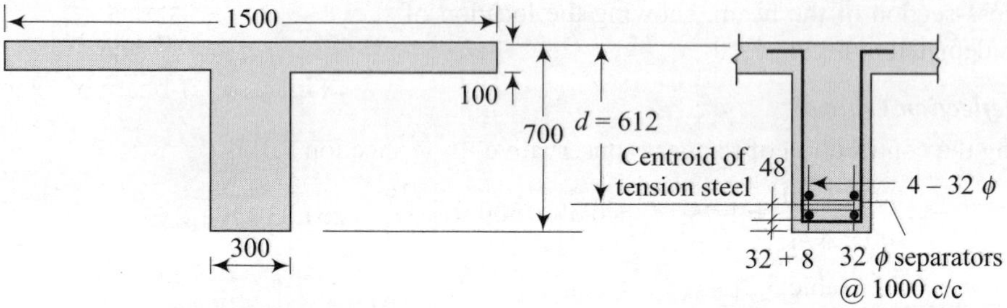

(a) Given section (b) Proposed reinforcement

Fig. 5.11 T-beam of Example 5.6.

Determining actual A_{st}

$$x_{u,\max} = 0.456 \times 612 = 279 \text{ mm}$$

- As $x_{u,\max} > D_f = 100$ mm, the condition $x_u = D_f$ satisfies $x_u \le x_{u,\max}$:
- Assuming M 25 concrete, $f_{ck} = 25$ MPa

$$(M_{uR})_{x_u = D_f} = 0.362 \times 25 \times 1500 \times 100 \times (612 - 0.416 \times 100)$$
$$= 774.3 \times 10^6 \text{ Nmm} < M_u = 800 \text{ kNm}$$

$$\Rightarrow \quad x_u > D_f \text{ and } M_u = C_{uw}(d - 0.416\, x_u) + C_{uf}(d - y_f/2),$$

where $C_{uw} = 0.362 f_{ck}\, b_w\, x_u = 0.362 \times 25 \times 300 x_u = (2715 x_u)$ N

and $\quad C_{uf} = 0.447 f_{ck}\,(b_f - b_w) y_f = 0.447 \times 25 \times (1500 - 300) y_f = (13410 y_f)$ N

- Considering $x_u = 7D_f/3 = 233$ mm ($< x_{u,max} = 279$ mm), $y_f = D_f = 100$ mm

$$\Rightarrow \quad (M_{uR})_{x_u = 7D_f/3} = (2715 \times 233)(612 - 0.416 \times 233) + (13410 \times 100) \times (612 - 100/2)$$
$$= 1079.5 \times 10^6 \text{ Nmm} > M_u = 800 \text{ kNm}$$

- Evidently, $D_f < x_u < \frac{7}{3}D_f$, for which $y_f = 0.15x_u + 0.65D_f$

$$\Rightarrow \quad C_{uf} = 13410(0.15x_u + 0.65 \times 100) = (2011.5x_u + 871650)\text{ N}$$

$$M_u = 800 \times 10^6 = (2715x_u)(612 - 0.416x_u) + (2011.5x_u + 871650) \times [612 - (0.15x_u + 65)/2]$$

$$= -1280.3x_u^2 + 2827244.3x_u + 505.12 \times 10^6$$

Solving this quadratic equation,

$$x_u = 109.7\text{ mm} < x_{u,\max} = 279\text{ mm}$$

$$\Rightarrow \quad y_f = 0.15x_u + 65 = 81.5\text{ mm}$$

- Applying $T_u = 0.87f_yA_{st} = C_{uw} + C_{uf}$,

$$(A_{st})_{\text{reqd}} = \frac{(2715 \times 109.7) + (13410 \times 81.5)}{0.87 \times 500} = \mathbf{3197\ mm^2}$$

The reinforcement (4–32ϕ; A_{st} = 3216 mm^2, based on the approximate estimate of A_{st} [Figure 5.11(b)] is evidently adequate and appropriate.

5.9 Curtailment of Flexural Tension Reinforcement

In simply supported beams, the maximum (positive) bending moment occurs at or near the midspan, and the beam section is accordingly designed. Similarly, in continuous spans, the cross-section at the face of the support is designed for the maximum negative moment, and the cross-section at the midspan region is designed for the maximum positive moment. Although the bending moment progressively decreases away from these critical sections, the same overall dimensions of the beam are usually maintained throughout the length of the beam – mainly for convenience in formwork construction.

In order to achieve economy in the design, it is desirable to progressively curtail ('cut-off') the flexural tension reinforcement, commensurate with the decrease in bending moment. However, there are several other factors to be considered in arriving at the actual bar cut-off points – such as unexpected shifts in maximum moments, development length requirements, influence on shear strength (more exactly, the additional tensile stresses due to shear – see Section 6.7.5) and development of diagonal tension cracks due to the effects of discontinuity. Accordingly, the Code (Cl. 26.2.3) has listed out a number of requirements that need to be considered for the curtailment of flexural reinforcement.

5.9.1 Theoretical Bar Cut-off Points

> The 'theoretical cut-off point' for a bar in a flexural member is that point beyond which it is (theoretically) no longer needed to resist the design moment.

In a prismatic beam (with constant *b*, *d*) the required area of tension reinforcement varies nearly linearly with the bending moment. This was indicated in Figure 4.19, and can further be demonstrated for a uniformly loaded and simply supported beam [Figure 5.12a] as follows.

Let A_{st} be the tension steel area required at the section of maximum factored moment $M_{u,max}$ [Figures 5.12(b), (c)], and let A_{st1} be the tension steel area required at a section where the factored moment decreases to M_{u1}. Evidently,

$$A_{st} = \frac{M_{u,\max}}{0.87 f_y z} \text{ and } A_{st1} = \frac{M_{u1}}{0.87 f_y z_1}$$

$$\Rightarrow \quad \frac{A_{st1}}{A_{st}} = \frac{M_{u1}}{M_{u,\max}} \times \frac{z}{z_1} \approx \frac{M_{u1}}{M_{u,\max}}, \text{ as } \frac{z}{z_1} \approx 1$$

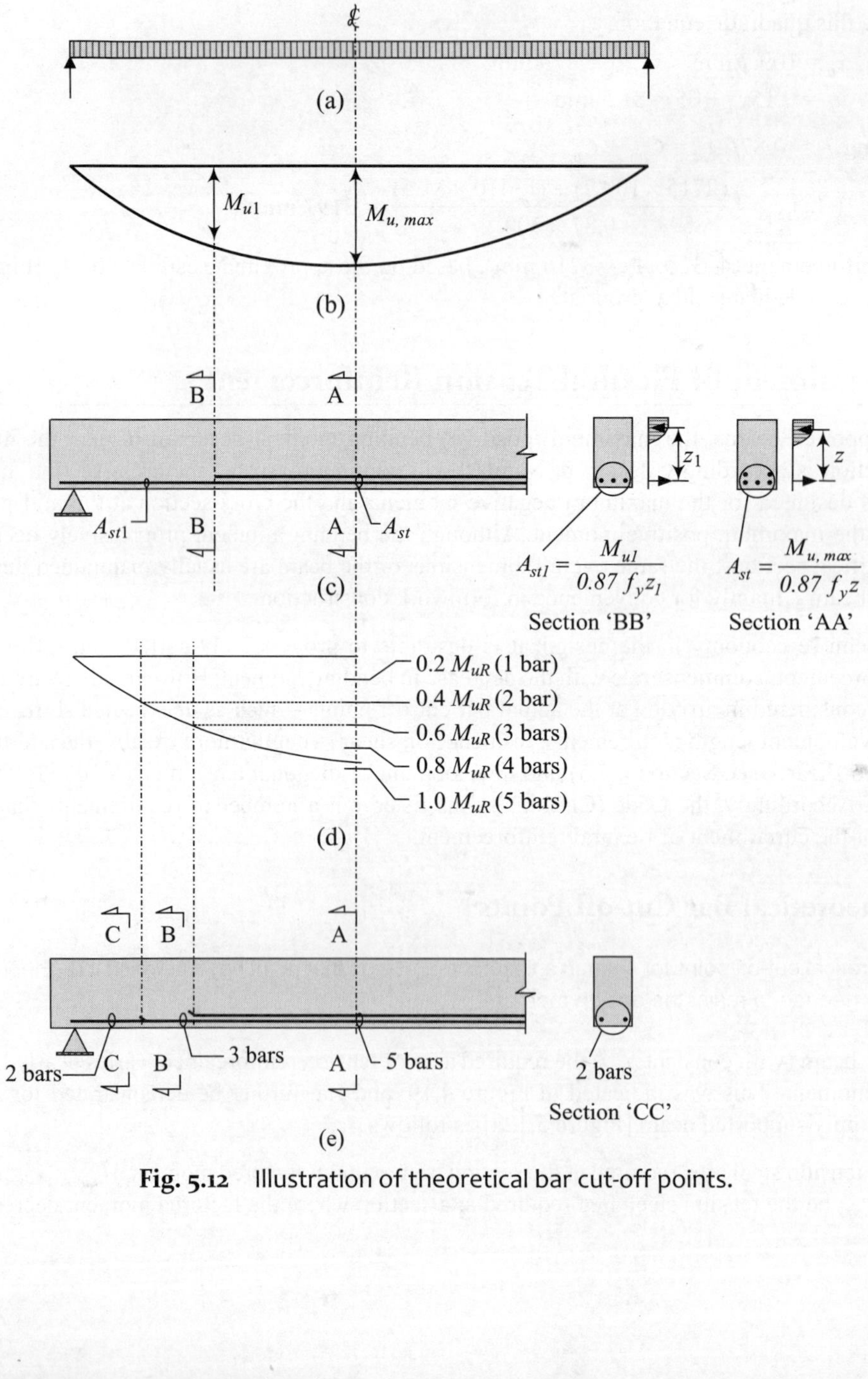

Fig. 5.12 Illustration of theoretical bar cut-off points.

Actually, the lever arm ratio z/z_1 decreases slightly below unity at sections further removed from the critical section, as the area of steel is reduced [Figure 5.12(c)]. Accordingly, the approximation $A_{st1} \approx (M_{u1}/M_{u,\max})A_{st}$ is acceptable as it results in slightly conservative estimates of A_{st1}. Based on this, it can be seen that at a section where the moment is, say, 60 per cent of $M_{u,\max}$, the reinforcement area required is only 60 per cent of the designed area A_{st}, and the remaining 40 per cent may be 'cut off' – as far as the flexural requirement is concerned.

As bars are available only in discrete sizes and can be provided only in full numbers, the actual reinforcement provided in practice at the critical section is often slightly greater than the calculated area A_{st}. Also, bars to be cut off are selected in terms of numbers rather than percentage of areas. Hence, for detailing of bar cut-off, it is appropriate to consider the strength contributed by each bar in terms of the critical section's ultimate moment resisting capacity. If there are n bars provided at the critical section, and if the bars are all of the same diameter, then the strength per bar is M_{uR}/n, where M_{uR} is the *actual* ultimate moment of resistance at the critical section.

Thus, for example, as shown in Figures 5.12(d),(e), the 'theoretical cut-off point' for the first two bars (of the group of 5 bars) occurs at a section where the factored moment is equal to $(n–2)M_{uR}/n$. Similarly, the theoretical cut-off point for the third bar occurs at the section where the factored moment is equal to $(n–3) M_{uR}/n$, and so on. Note that bars to be cut-off are selected such that the remaining bars yield a symmetrical placement within the cross section.

In determining the theoretical bar cut-off points in this manner, the factored bending moment diagram must represent the possible maximum at each section, i.e., the *moment envelope* must be considered [Figure 5.13].

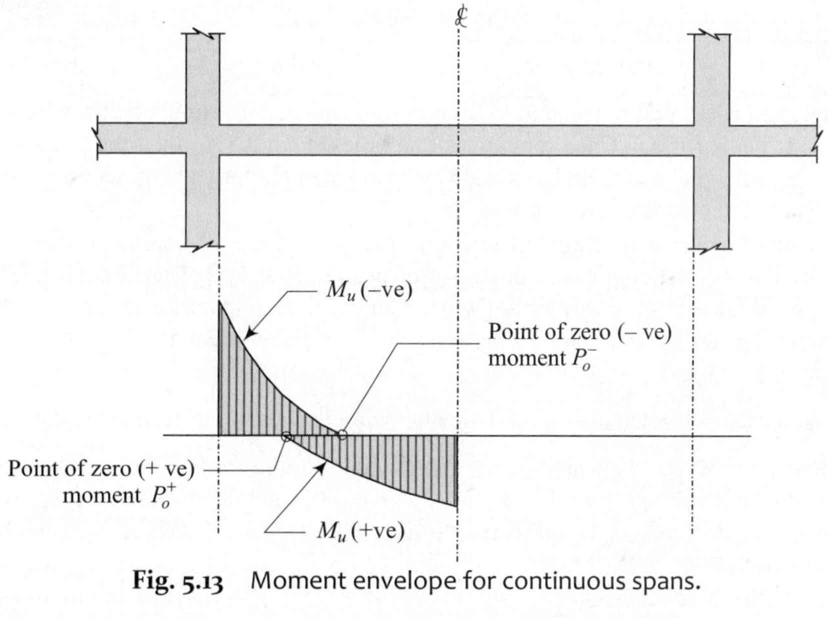

Fig. 5.13 Moment envelope for continuous spans.

This is of particular significance where moving loads are involved and in continuous spans where the loading patterns (of live loads) for the maximum negative moment at supports and for the maximum positive moment in the span are different [refer Chapter 9]. In a continuous span, the *point of zero moment*† for the negative

† It is not appropriate to use the term *point of inflection* here, as the reference is to a bending moment *envelope*. A point of inflection occurs where there is a change in sign of curvature (and hence, of bending moment) under a given loading.

moment envelope (marked P_0^- in Figure 5.13) is often different from that of the positive moment envelope, (marked P_0^+ in Figure 5.13).

5.9.2 Restrictions on Theoretical Bar Cut-off Points

As mentioned earlier, the *actual* bar cut-off points differ from the 'theoretical' ones for a number of reasons, some of which are described below:

- **Unexpected shifts in design moments:** The theoretical bending moment diagrams represent idealisations or 'best estimates'; these are subject to some variability on account of the assumptions and approximations involved in the calculation of load and load effects, yielding of supports, etc.
- **Development length requirements:** The stress at the end of a bar is zero; it builds up gradually along its length through bond with the surrounding concrete [refer Chapter 8]. In order to develop the full design stress ($0.87f_y$) in the bar at a section, a minimum *development length* L_d is required on either side of the section. Some typical values of L_d/ϕ (in accordance with the Code – Cl. 26.2.1) are listed in Table 5.6.

  Table 5.6 *L_d/ϕ values for fully stressed bars in tension**

Grade of Steel	Grade of concrete				
	M 20	M 25	M 30	M 35	M 40 and above
Fe 250	45	39	36	32	29
Fe 415	47	40	38	33	30
Fe 500	57	49	45	40	36

  *for bars in *compression*, multiply these values of L_d/ϕ by 0.8.

  For example, if Fe 415 grade steel and M 20 concrete are used, L_d should be taken as 47 times the bar diameter ϕ. If the bar is subjected to a stress that is less than $0.87f_y$, then the required 'development length' is proportionately less. No bar should be terminated abruptly at any section, without extending it by the required development length.
- **Development of premature diagonal tension cracks:** Cutting off bars in the tension zone lowers substantially the shear strength (and ductility) of beams [Ref. 5.7]. The discontinuity at the cut end of the bar introduces stress concentration which can cause premature flexural cracks that may further develop into diagonal tension cracks – particularly if the shear stress at this section is relatively high [refer Chapter 6].

  Such a diagonal tension crack in a flexural member without shear reinforcement is shown in Figure 5.14.

  The equilibrium of forces† indicated on the free body in Figure 5.14(c) shows that the tensile force in the reinforcement at section '*b-b*' (located at $d.\cot\theta \approx d$ beyond the theoretical cut-off point at section '*a-a*') depends on the moment M_{u1} at section '*a-a*'. Thus, the area of steel required at section '*a-a*' must extend up to section '*b-b*'. The effect of shear on longitudinal steel requirement can also be considered more directly. Sections 6.7.5 and 17.1 show that shear force also causes a longitudinal tension in the section. Thus, the total tensile reinforcement required at a section such as '*a-a*' is the sum of that required for the bending moment at the section, M_{u1}, and that required for the associated shear force V_u.

† The forces due to 'aggregate interlock' and 'dowel action' in the reinforcing bars [refer Chapter 6] are neglected here.

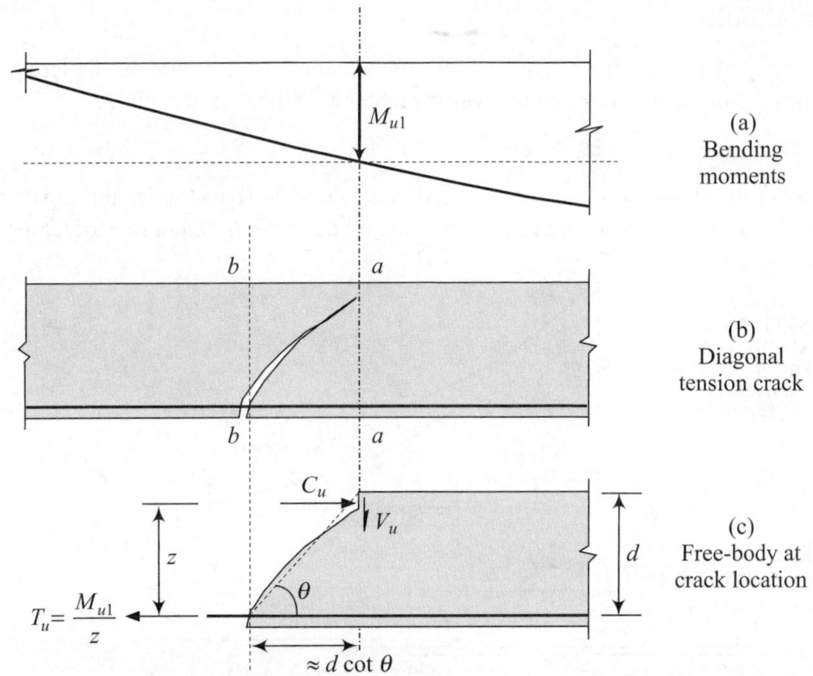

Fig. 5.14 Influence of diagonal tension crack on tension steel stress.

5.9.3 Code Requirements

In view of the various considerations involved in the curtailment of flexural reinforcement, the Code (Cl. 26.2.3) has specified certain requirements.

Shear Strength Requirements for Curtailment

To safeguard against the development of diagonal tension cracks, the tension steel should not be terminated unless *any one* of the following three requirements is satisfied:

1. The shear at the cut-off point does not exceed two-thirds of the shear resisting capacity of the section.
2. Excess stirrups are provided over a distance of $0.75d$ from the cut-off point having an area A_{sv} and a spacing s_v such that:

$$A_{sv} \geq \frac{0.4 b_w s_v}{f_y} \quad ; \quad s_v \leq \frac{d}{8\beta_b}$$

   where β_b is the ratio of the area of bars cut off to the total area of the bars at the section.
3. For 36 mm ϕ and smaller bars, the continuing bars provide at least twice the area required for flexure at the cut-off point *and* the shear does not exceed three-fourth of the shear resisting capacity of the section.

   The additional longitudinal tension due to shear is taken care of by extension of bars beyond the theoretical point of cut-off as given below.

End Extension of Bars

The extension of bars beyond the theoretical cut-off points, denoted L_a, should not be less than the effective depth *d,* or 12 times the bar diameter ϕ, whichever is greater as indicated in Figure 5.15.

$$L_a \geq d \quad \text{and} \quad L_a \geq 12\phi$$

This requirement of 'end extension' should be satisfied by the *curtailed* bars (i.e., assuming there are additional continuing bars) of both positive moment reinforcement and negative moment reinforcement [Figure 5.15].

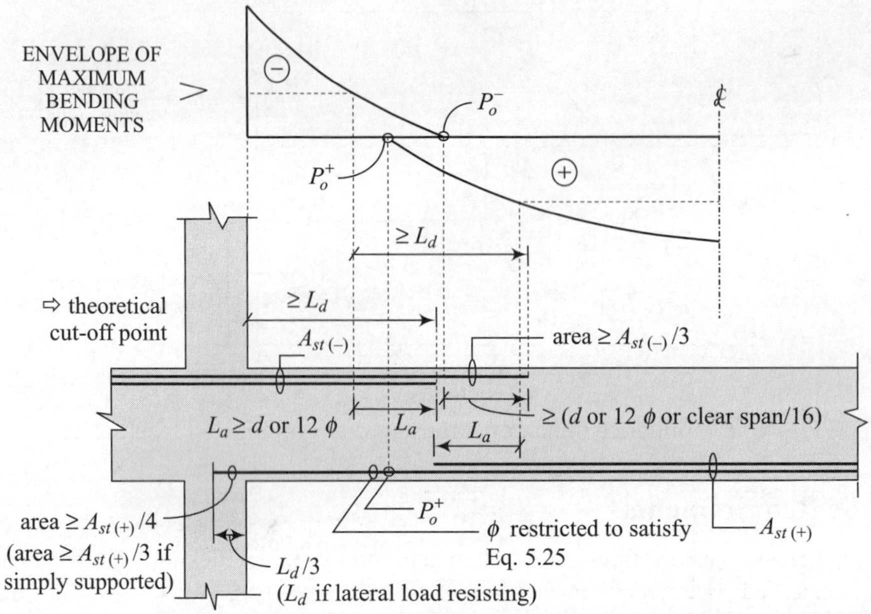

Fig. 5.15 Code requirements (Cl. 25.2.3) for curtailment of tension reinforcement.

For the continuing bars which are to be *finally terminated,* different requirements are applicable, regarding continuation beyond the point of zero moment (where they are no longer required theoretically). In the case of negative moment reinforcement, at least one-third of the total steel provided at the face of the support must extend beyond the *point of zero moment* (P_o^-) for a distance not less than *d*, 12ϕ or 1/16 times the clear span. In the case of positive moment reinforcement, at least one-third of the total steel in simply supported members and one-fourth the total steel in continuous members should be extended straight into the support by a distance not less than $L_d/3$ [Figure 5.15]. If the support width is inadequate to provide this embedment, the bars should be suitably anchored by bending/hooks.

Development Length Requirements

As mentioned earlier, no bar should be terminated without providing the required development length L_d [Table 5.6] on either side of the point of maximum design stress ($0.87f_y$). At the supports at exterior columns, the bars may be bent (standard 90-degree bend) to anchor them suitably and thus provide the required L_d – for the negative moment reinforcement.

In the case of positive moment reinforcement of beams (in frames) that constitute part of a lateral load resisting system, the Code requires that such steel should also be anchored into the support by a length L_d beyond the face of the support.

Every point of stress in a bar requires a corresponding 'development length' that is directly proportional to the bar diameter ϕ as well as the stress level at the point. The values of L_d generally specified [Table 5.6] correspond to the 'fully stressed' condition ($f_{st} = 0.87f_y$) which occurs at a 'critical section'. However, providing a length L_d on either side of the critical section does not necessarily ensure that adequate embedment (or development length) is available at *all* stressed points along the length of the bar to develop the actual flexural stress (f_{st}) generated in the bar – except when the variation of f_{st} in the bar is linear (which occurs only when the bending moment falls off linearly). In particular, the 'positive' moment regions of beams with distributed loading require special consideration, as in such regions the moment diagram, and hence the variation of f_{st} in the bar is nonlinear (and convex), whereas the bar stress development over the length L_d is assumed to be linear.

This is illustrated with the aid of Figure 5.16, which shows a typical nonlinear variation of bending moment near a simple support of a beam. For the purposes of illustration, it is assumed that the theoretical cut-off point of a group of bars (marked 'a') is at point A, located at a distance equal to L_d of the continuing group of bars (marked 'b') from the point of zero moment (support C). At A, bars 'b' are fully stressed ($f_{st} = 0.87f_y$) and possess an ultimate moment of resistance M_{uR} equal to the factored moment M_A. As these bars are terminated at C, it follows that the bar stress will decrease linearly (assuming uniform bond stress distribution) from $0.87f_y$ at A to zero at C, and hence the moment resisting capacity will also drop linearly from M_A to zero, as depicted by the dotted line A″C′ in Figure 5.16. Evidently, this means that the ultimate moment capacity at any intermediate point (such as B at, say, $0.4L_d$ from C) in the region AC will generally fall short of the factored moment M_B, as shown in Figure 5.16.

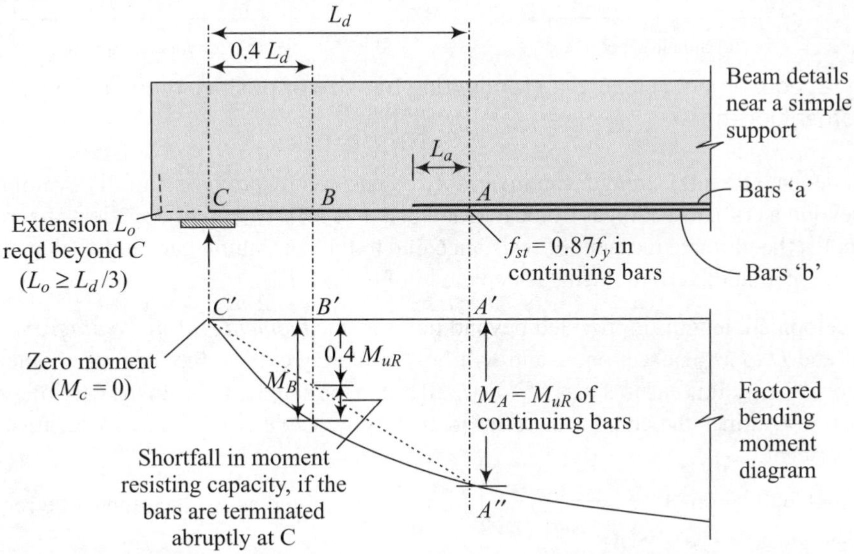

Fig. 5.16 Need for extending bars beyond point of zero moment.

Clearly, this indicates the need for an adequate extension (L_o) of the tension bars beyond the point of zero moment (either at a simple support or at a point of inflection). How much to extend, of course, depends on how nonlinear the variation of the factored moment (M_u) is, in the region CA near the point of zero moment.

A measure of this rate of change of the factored moment is given by the factored shear force V_u (= dM_u/dx) at the point of zero moment, C [Figure 5.17].

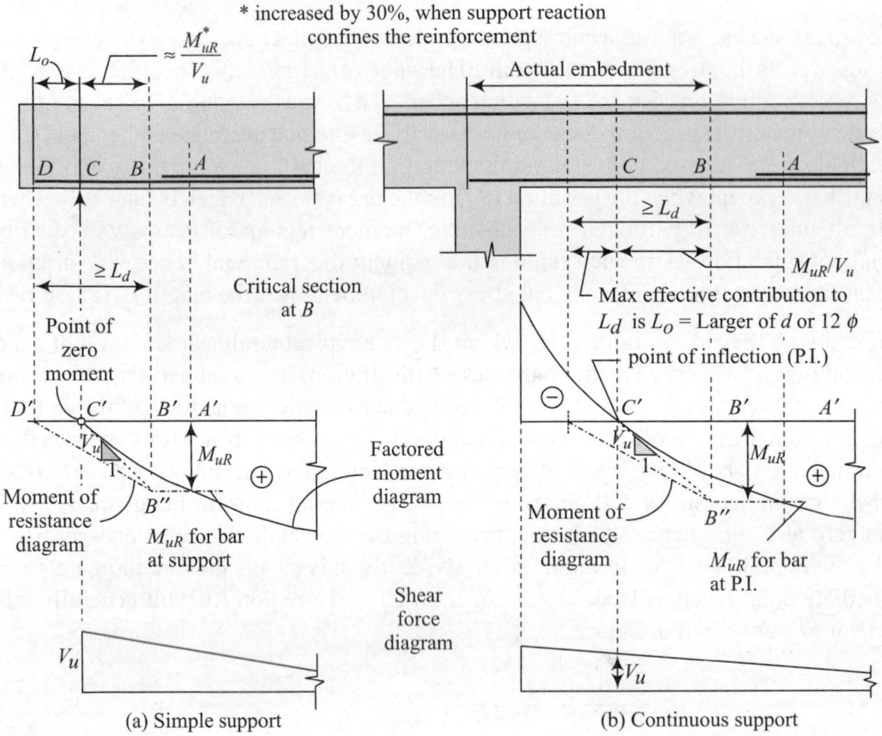

Fig. 5.17 Code requirement (Cl. 26.2.3c) for limiting bar size of positive moment requirement at zero moment location.

It is seen that adequate flexural strength can invariably be ensured by providing a full development length L_d to a point D beyond a critical section at B, located at a distance M_{uR}/V_u from the section of zero moment (C). Here, M_{uR} denotes the ultimate moment of resistance due to the continuing bars and V_u denotes the factored shear force at the section of zero moment, as depicted in Figure 5.17.

With a full development length L_d provided beyond point B, the *moment resistance diagram* will vary from zero at the bar end *D* to M_{uR} at section B, and will lie completely outside the factored moment diagram [as shown in Figure 5.17(a)]; this ensures that $M_{uR} > M_u$ all along the segment CA. In the case of a simple support where the reaction confines the ends of the reinforcement, the Code (Cl. 26.2.3.3c) permits an increase in M_{uR}/V_u by 30 per cent.

If the anchorage length beyond the zero-moment location is denoted as L_o, then the Code requirement may be expressed as:

$$(M_{uR}/V_u)^* + L_o \geq L_d \tag{5.25}$$

or,

$$L_o \geq L_d - (M_{uR}/V_u)^* \tag{5.25a}$$

where $(M_{uR}/V_u)^* = 1.3M_{uR}/V_u$ at a simple support with a confining reaction, and M_{uR}/V_u otherwise.

At a point of inflection, the anchorage length L_o is limited to the effective depth d or 12ϕ, whichever is greater. At a simple support although the entire embedment length beyond the centre of support (including the equivalent anchorage value of any hook† or mechanical anchorage) qualifies as a proper measure of L_o, there may be practical limitations. The most effective way of satisfying Eq. 5.25 is by controlling the bar diameter ϕ, thereby reducing L_d.

> The Code (Cl. 26.2.3.3c) explicitly states that the purpose of the requirement given by Eq. 5.25 is to limit the bar diameter of positive tension reinforcement at a zero-moment location. It is apparent that the objective is to ensure adequate development length and moment resisting capacity at locations such as depicted in Figure 5.17.

Curtailment of Bundled Bars

Where *bundled bars* (provided as tension reinforcement) are to be curtailed, the individual bars in a bundle must be terminated at different points that are at least 40 bar diameters apart. This, however, is not applicable for bundles terminating at a support.

It is desirable to curtail first the bars in a bundle that are closer to the neutral axis; this is also desirable when bars (not bundled) are provided in multiple layers.

The 'development length' for each bar in a bundle should be taken as $1.1L_d$, $1.2L_d$, and $1.33L_d$ for 2-bar bundles, 3-bar bundles and 4-bar bundles respectively, where L_d is the development length for an individual bar.

5.9.4 Bending of Bars

As an alternative to curtailment, *bending* ('cranking') of bars may be resorted to. In continuous beams, some of the bars (usually, not more than two at a time) may be bent over (at intervals, if large numbers are involved) from the bottom side of the beam to the top side, and continued over the support to form part of the negative moment reinforcement. Such a system is shown in Figure 5.5(b) for one-way continuous slabs. The bars are usually bent at an angle of 45°, although angles up to 60° are also resorted to in practice for relatively deep beams. The bent portion of the bar contributes to increased shear strength of the beam section by resisting diagonal tensile stresses and restraining the spread of diagonal tension cracks [refer Chapter 6]. This contrasts with the adverse effect of bar curtailment on shear strength.

The discontinuity effects discussed in Section 5.9.2 are, therefore, less severe for bars which are bent, in comparison with bars which are cut off. Hence a requirement that the *bend points* be extended beyond the 'theoretical bar cut-off points' by the end extension distance ($L_a \geq d$ or 12ϕ) may be too conservative. It has been suggested [Ref. 5.6] that for bar extension purpose, a bent bar may be considered effective up to a section where the bar crosses the mid-depth of the beam; this would reduce the extension required by $d/2$. However, for bar extension, the Code does not distinguish between cut-off bars and bent bars.

Example 5.7

Design a suitable longitudinal arrangement of the tension reinforcement (including bar cut-off) for the simply supported beam of Example 5.1.

† The anchorage value of a standard U-type hook should be taken as 16ϕ. If bends are provided, an anchorage value of 4ϕ should be taken for each 45° bend, subject to a maximum of 16ϕ [Cl. 26.2.2.1b of the Code].

Solution

- Given: From Example 5.1, $A_{st} = 942\ \text{mm}^2$ (3–20ϕ), $b = 250$ mm, $d = 402$ mm, $f_y = 500$ MPa, $f_{ck} = 25$ MPa, factored load $w_u = 28.1$ kN/m, span = 6.0 m [Figure 5.18(a)], $M_{u,\max} = 126$ kNm, $(M_{uR})_{3\text{bars}} = 133.8$ kNm.
- The middle bar (of 20ϕ) may be curtailed. Let the theoretical cut-off point be at a distance x from the support. The value of x can be obtained by solving the moment equilibrium equation:

$$M_x = V_u x - w_u x^2/2$$

where M_x is the ultimate moment of resistance of the two-continuing 20ϕ bars:

$$M_x \approx (2 \times 314/942) \times 133.8\ \text{kNm} = 89.2\ \text{kNm [Figure 5.18(b)]}$$

$$V_u = w_u l/2 = 28.1 \times 3.0 = 84.3\ \text{kN}$$

$$\Rightarrow \quad 84.3x - 28.1\,x^2/2 = 89.2$$

$$\Rightarrow \quad x^2 - 6x + 6.349 = 0$$

Solving, $x = 1.372$ m = 1372 mm

- ***End extension for curtailed bar***

Bar extension beyond theoretical cut-off point is given by $d = 402$ mm, which is greater than 12ϕ = 240 mm.

∴ Actual point of termination = 1372 – 402 = 970 mm from the centre of support [Figure 5.18(c)].

- ***Check bar size limitation at support***

$$\left(1.3\frac{M_{uR}}{V_u} + L_o\right) \text{ must exceed } L_d \text{ [Eq. 5.25].}$$

For Fe 500 steel and M 25 concrete, $L_d = 49 \times 20 = 980$ mm [Table 5.6].

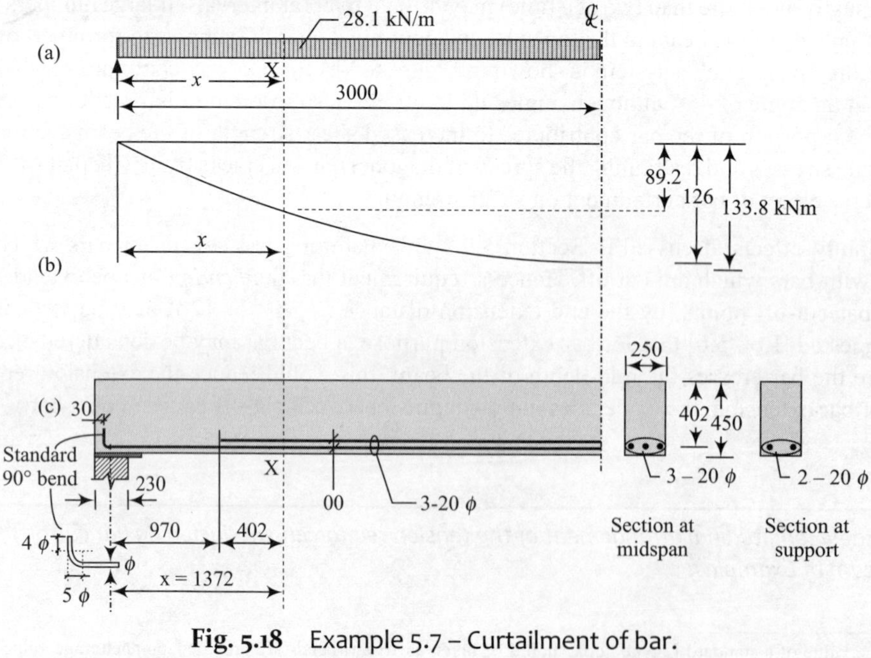

Fig. 5.18 Example 5.7 – Curtailment of bar.

For the continuing two bars, M_{uR} = 89.2 kNm

$$\Rightarrow \quad \left(1.3\frac{M_{uR}}{V_u} + L_o\right) = 1.3 \times \frac{89.2 \times 10^3}{84.3} + L_o = (1376 \text{ mm} + L_o)$$

which exceeds L_d = 980 mm, regardless of L_o. Hence, the bar diameter ϕ = 20 mm is acceptable.

- ***Extension over support for continuing bars***

  At the simple support the two bars must extend beyond the face of the support by a distance not less than: $L_d/3$ = 980/3 = 327 mm

  which is not possible over a support width of 230 mm (with end cover of 30 mm minimum) – unless the bar is bent upwards. Accordingly, provide standard 90° bend with 4ϕ extension, having a total anchorage value of 12ϕ = 240 mm, as shown in Figure 5.18(c).

  ∴ Embedment length with 90° bend = (230 – 30 – 5 × 20) + 240 = 340 mm >$L_d/3$ –Hence, OK

- ***Development length requirements***
  1. For the curtailed bar, the critical section is at midspan; the length provided (3000 – 970 = 2030 mm) is well in excess of L_d = 980 mm.
  2. For the continuing bars, the requirement $M_u^*/V_u + L_o \geq L_d$ has been satisfied.

  –Hence, OK

- ***Shear strength requirements for curtailment***

  This is covered in Example 6.1 of Chapter 6.

REVIEW QUESTIONS

5.1 Discuss why does the Code imposes minimum and maximum limits with regard to (a) spacing, (b) percentage area of flexural reinforcement?

5.2 Compare the advantages and disadvantages of providing large clear cover to reinforcement in flexural members.

5.3 Show that deflection control in normal flexural members can be achieved by limiting span/effective depth ratios.

5.4 Explain the dependence of span/effective depth ratios (for deflection control, as per Code) on the percentage tension and compression reinforcement, as well as the grade of tension steel.

5.5 Under what circumstances are doubly reinforced beams resorted to?

5.6 Reinforced concrete slabs are generally singly reinforced. Why not doubly reinforced?

5.7 A designer provides areas of tension and compression reinforcement (in a doubly reinforced beam) that result in percentage p_t and p_c in *excess* of the values obtained from *design tables* (corresponding to a given M_u/bd^2). Is it guaranteed that the design will meet all the Code requirements?

5.8 Discuss the proportioning of sections in T-beam design.

5.9 What is a 'theoretical bar cut-off point'? Why does the Code disallow curtailment of flexural tension reinforcement at this point?

5.10 Discuss the influence of diagonal tension cracks on the tension steel stress in a flexural member.

5.11 Discuss the Code requirement related to ensuring adequate development length in the bars near the zero moment location.

5.12 A reinforced concrete beam has a width of 250 mm and effective depth of 400 mm, and is reinforced with Fe415 steel. As per IS: 456: 2000 provisions, the minimum and maximum amount of tensile reinforcement (in mm^2) for the section are, respectively:

(A) 205 and 4000 (B) 270 and 2000 (C) 300 and 2500 (D) 250 and 3500

5.13 With Fe500 grade steel, the minimum percentage of tension reinforcement required in reinforced concrete beams of rectangular cross-section (considering effective depth in the calculation of area), as per IS: 456-2000, is ______

5.14 A reinforced concrete slab is simply supported at two opposite ends on 230 mm thick masonry walls spaced at 3.3 m centre-to-centre, and has an effective depth of 80 mm. As per IS: 456: 2000, the effective span of the slab is ______

PROBLEMS

5.1 A rectangular beam of span 7 m (centre-to-centre of supports), resting on 300 mm wide simple supports, is to carry a uniformly distributed dead load (excluding self-weight) of 15 kN/m and a live load of 20 kN/m. Using Fe 500 steel, design the beam section at midspan, based on first principles. Check the adequacy of the section for strength, using design aids. Also perform a check for deflection control. Assume that the beam is subjected to moderate exposure conditions.

5.2 Design a suitable arrangement of the tension reinforcement (including bar cut-off) for the beam in Problem 5.1

5.3 Design the beam section in Problem 5.1, given that the overall beam depth is restricted to 550 mm.

5.4 Design a one-way slab, with a clear span of 5.0 m, simply supported on 230 mm thick masonry walls, and subjected to a live load of 3 kN/m^2 and a surface finish load of 1 kN/m^2, using Fe 500 steel. Assume that the beam is subjected to (a) mild exposure and (b) very severe exposure, and compare the results.

5.5 Repeat Problem 5.4, considering Fe 250 steel in lieu of Fe 500 steel.

5.6 The floor plan of a building is shown in Figure 5.19. The specified floor loading consists of a live load of 5.0 kN/m^2 and a dead load of 2.5 kN/m^2 (excluding self-weight). Design the slab thickness and reinforcement area required at the various critical sections, using Fe 500 steel. Assume that the beam is subjected to moderate exposure conditions.

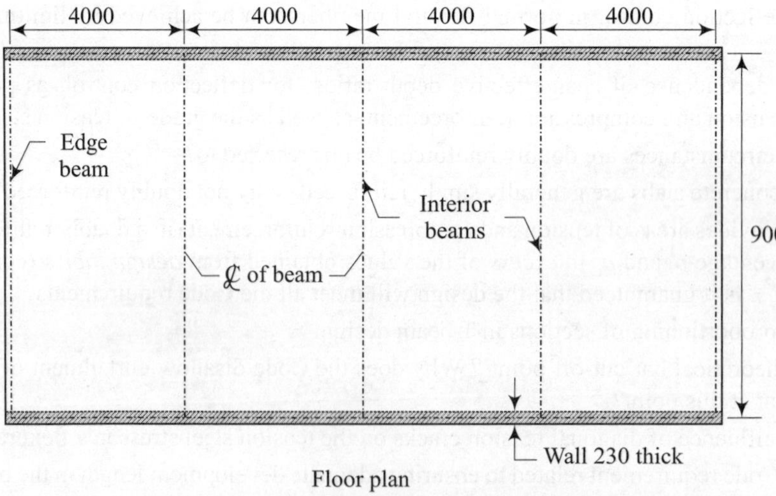

Fig. 5.19 Floor system – Problems 5.6 – 5.8.

5.7 Design the interior beam of the floor system in Figure 5.19, considering the beam to be simply supported.

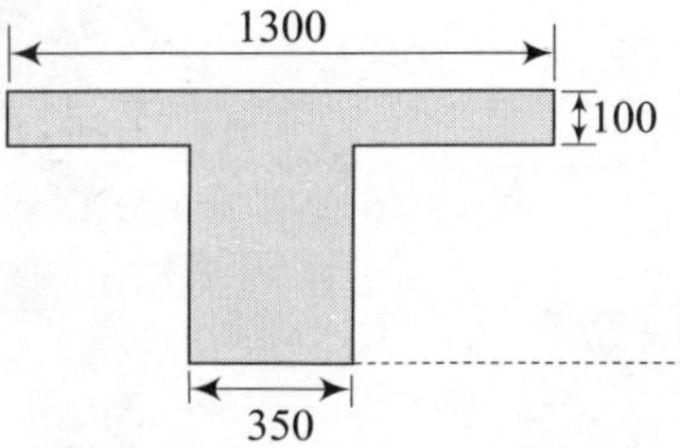

Fig. 5.20 Problem 5.9

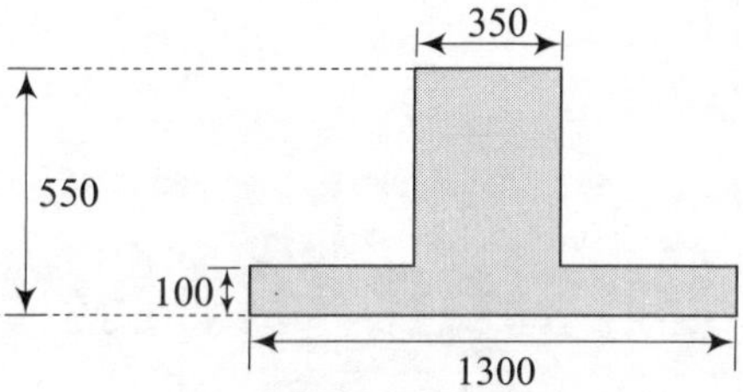

Fig. 5.21 Problem 5.10

5.8 Design the edge beam (L-beam) of the floor system in Figure 5.19, with the width of the web equal to 250 mm. Assume the beam to be simply supported and neglect the effect of torsion.

5.9 A T-beam of 8 m clear span, simply supported on wall supports 230 mm wide, is subjected to a dead load of 20 kN/m (including self-weight) and a live load of 25 kN/m. The overall size of the beam is given in Figure 5.20. Design the beam for tension reinforcement and detail the bar cut-off. Assume that 50 per cent of bars are to be cut off. Use Fe 500 steel. Assume moderate exposure conditions.

5.10 The section of a cantilever (inverted T-beam) is shown in Figure 5.21. The cantilever has a clear span of 4 m and carries a total distributed load of 25 kN/m (including self-weight) and a concentrated load of 50 kN at the free end. Design and detail the tension reinforcement, considering the cantilever to be supported from a 600 mm wide column. Assume that the beam is subjected to severe exposure conditions.

5.11 Work out the bar cut-off details for the beam designed in Example 5.5.

REFERENCES

5.1 Arora, J S, *Introduction to Optimum Design*, McGraw-Hill International edition, 1989

5.2 Gouthaman, A and Menon, D, *Increased Cover Specifications in IS 456 (2000) – Crack-width Implications in RC Slabs*, Indian Concrete Journal, Sept. 2001, pp 581–586

5.3 — *Explanatory Handbook on Indian Standard Code of Practice for Plain and Reinforced Concrete (IS 456:1978)*, Special Publication SP:24, Bureau of Indian Standards, New Delhi, 1983

5.4 Beeby, A W, *Modified Proposals for Controlling Deflection by Means of Ratios of Span to Effective Depth*, Cement and Concrete Association, Publ. No. 42.456, London, April 1971

5.5 — *Design Aids (for Reinforced Concrete) to IS 456 : 1978*, Special Publication SP:16, Bureau of Indian Standards, New Delhi, 1980

5.6 — *Handbook on Concrete Reinforcement and Detailing,* Special Publication SP 34, Bureau of Indian Standards, New Delhi, 1987

5.7 ASCE-ACI Committee 426, *The Shear Strength of Reinforced Concrete Members*, ASCE Journal, Struct. Div., Vol. 99, June 1973, pp 1091–1187

5.8 P Revathi and D Menon, *Estimation of Critical Buckling Moments in Slender Reinforced Concrete Beams*, ACI Structural Journal, American Concrete Institute, Vol. 103, No. 2, pp 296-303, March/April 2006

5.9 P Revathi and D Menon, *Slenderness Effects in Reinforced Concrete Beams*, ACI Structural Journal, American Concrete Institute, Vol. 104, No. 4, pp 412-419, July/August 2007

CHAPTER 6

Design for Shear

LEARNING OBJECTIVES

After studying this chapter, you will be able to:

- *Explain the behaviour of Reinforced Concrete members under shear force*
- *Identify critical sections for shear design and compute design shear forces*
- *Design and detail shear reinforcement of different types, conforming with specifications*
- *Describe shear-friction theory and demonstrate where it is applicable*

6.1 Introduction

Bending moments are generally accompanied by transverse shear forces, and sometimes by axial forces and torsion as well. The ultimate limit state considered in Chapters 4 and 5 dealt with flexure (bending) alone. This chapter deals with the ultimate limit state in *flexural shear*, i.e., shear associated with a varying bending moment. Commonly, flexural shear is simply referred to as 'shear'. The method described in this chapter (for convenience, referred to as the *Conventional Method* or the '*Simplified Method*') is intended to be used for the design of '*flexural regions*' of members; i.e., beams, columns, or walls (or portions of the member as are) designed by the conventional theory of flexure, in which the assumption that '*plane sections remain plane*' is reasonably valid. In this method, the transverse reinforcement is designed for the shear, while the longitudinal reinforcement is designed for the combined effects of flexure and axial (compressive only) load. The effects of shear on the longitudinal reinforcement (Section 5.9.2) are taken care of by bar detailing requirements.

> The conventional method is applicable to *flexural regions*. For *disturbed regions*, resort to strut-and-tie method (refer Ch. 17).

In the case of slabs, this type of shear is sometimes referred to as *one-way shear* – as distinct from *two-way shear* ('punching shear'), which is associated with the possibility of punching through a relatively thin slab by a concentrated column load (refer Chapter 11). Another type of shear that needs consideration is *torsional shear* (due to torsion), which, when it occurs, generally does so in combination with flexural shear; this is covered in Chapter 7.

> Shear in slabs (*one-way* as well as *two-way*) is discussed in Ch. 11.
>
> Torsional shear (alone and in combination with *flexural shear*) is discussed in Ch. 7.

A more general method for shear and torsion design, based on the so-called *Compression Field Theory*, is presented in Chapter 17. In this method, the member is designed for the combined effects of flexure, shear, axial (compressive or tensile) load and torsion.

A method based on the 'Strut-and-Tie Model' is also presented in Chapter 17. This method is particularly suitable for the design of regions where the assumption that 'plane sections remain plane' is not applicable. Such regions include deep beams, parts of members with a deep shear span, brackets and corbels, pile caps, regions with abrupt changes in cross-section (web openings in beams and articulations in girders), disturbed regions (such as intersection of two beams and beam-column joints) and regions near discontinuities.

Interface shear transfer and the shear-friction procedure are also described in this chapter (Section 6.9). This is applicable for situations involving the possibility of shear failure in the form of sliding along a plane of weakness.

Failure of a reinforced concrete beam in flexural shear often may not lead to an immediate *collapse* by itself. However, it can significantly reduce flexural strength (moment-bearing capacity) as well as ductility. Hence, the state of (impending) shear failure is treated by the Code as an *ultimate limit state* (i.e., limit state of collapse) for design purposes.

The behaviour of reinforced concrete under shear (flexural shear alone or in combination with torsion and axial forces) is very complex – mainly because of its non-homogeneity, presence of cracks and reinforcement, and the nonlinearity in its material response. The current understanding of and design procedures for shear effects are, to a large measure, based on the results of extensive tests and simplifying assumptions, rather than on an exact and universally accepted theory.

6.2 Shear Stresses in Homogeneous Rectangular Beams

In order to gain an insight into the causes of flexural shear failure in reinforced concrete, the stress distribution in a homogeneous elastic beam of rectangular section is reviewed here. In such a beam, loaded as shown in Figure 6.1(a), any transverse section (marked 'XX'), in general, is subjected to a bending moment M and a transverse shear force V.

From basic mechanics of materials [Ref. 6.1], it is known that the *flexural* (*normal*) *stress* f_x and the *shear stress* τ at any point in the section, located at a distance y from the neutral axis, are given by:

$$f_x = \frac{My}{I}$$

$$\tau = \frac{VQ}{Ib} \tag{6.1}$$

where I is the second moment of area of the section about the neutral axis, Q the first moment of area about the neutral axis of the portion of the section above the layer at distance y from the NA, and b is the width of the beam at the layer at which τ is calculated. The distributions of f_x and τ are depicted in Figure 6.1(b). It may be noted that the variation of shear stress is parabolic, with a maximum value at the neutral axis and zero values at the top and bottom of the section.

Considering an element at a distance y from the NA [Figure 6.1(c)], and neglecting any possible vertical normal stress f_y caused by the surface loads, the combined flexural and shear stresses can be resolved into

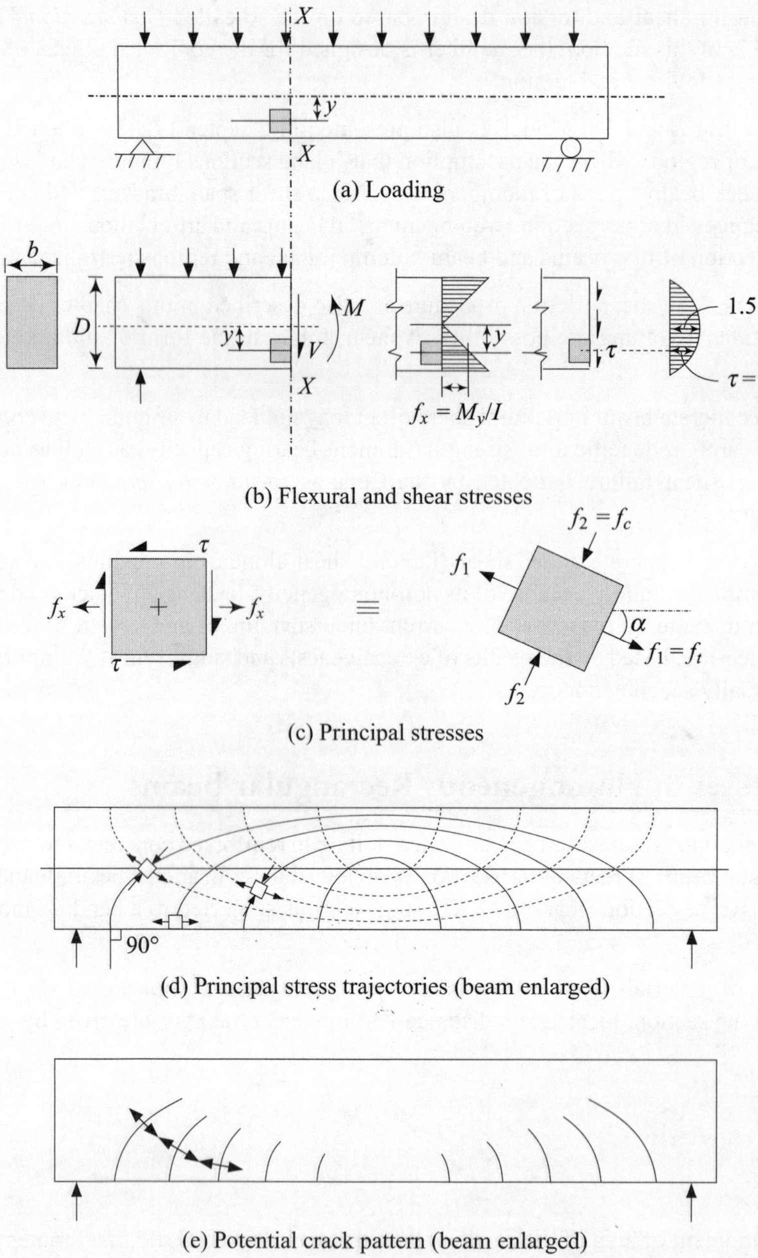

Fig. 6.1 Stress distribution in homogeneous beams of rectangular section.

equivalent *principal stresses* f_1 and f_2 acting on orthogonal planes, inclined at an angle α to the beam axis (as shown):

$$f_{1,2} = \frac{1}{2} f_x \pm \sqrt{\left(\frac{1}{2} f_x\right)^2 + \tau^2} \tag{6.2}$$

$$\tan 2\alpha = \frac{2\tau}{f_x} \tag{6.3}$$

In general, the stress f_1 is tensile (say $= f_t$) and f_2 is compressive (say $= f_c$). The relative magnitudes of f_t and f_c and their directions depend on the relative values of f_x and τ [Eq. 6.2, 6.3]. In particular, at the top and bottom fibres where shear stress τ is zero, it follows from Eq. 6.3 that $\alpha = 0$, indicating that one of the principal stresses is in a direction parallel to the surface, and the other perpendicular to it, the latter being zero in the present case†. Thus, along the top face, the nonzero stress parallel to the beam axis is f_c, and along the bottom face, it is f_t. On the other hand, a condition of 'pure shear' occurs for elements located at the neutral axis (where τ is maximum and $f_x = 0$), whereby $f_t = f_c = \tau_{max}$ and $\alpha = 45°$. The stress pattern is indicated in Figure 6.1(d), which depicts the *principal stress trajectories*‡ in the beam.

In a material like concrete which is weak in tension, tensile cracks would develop in a direction that is perpendicular to that of the principal tensile stress. Thus the compressive stress trajectories [firm lines in Figure 6.1(d)] indicate *potential* crack patterns (depending on the magnitude of the tensile stress), as shown in Figure 6.1(e). It should be noted, however, that once a crack develops, the stress distributions depicted here are no longer valid in that region, as the effective section gets altered and the above equations are no longer valid.

6.3 Behaviour of Reinforced Concrete Under Shear

6.3.1 Modes of Cracking

In reinforced concrete beams of usual proportions, subjected to relatively high flexural stresses f_x and low shear stresses τ, the maximum principal tensile stress is invariably given by the flexural stress $f_{x,max}$ in the outer fibre (bottom face of the beam in Figure 6.1) at the peak moment locations; the resulting cracks are termed *flexural cracks* [Figure 6.2(a)]. These are controlled and the tensile stresses are carried by the tension bars. On the other hand, in short-span beams which are relatively deep and have thin webs (as in *I*-sections) and are subjected to high shear stresses τ (due to heavy concentrated loads) and relatively low flexural stresses f_x, it is likely that the maximum principal tensile stress is located at the neutral axis level at an inclination $\alpha = 45°$ (to the longitudinal axis of the beam); the resulting cracks (which generally occur near the supports, where shear force is maximum) are termed *web shear cracks* or *diagonal tension cracks* [Figure 6.2(b)].

In general, in a beam under flexure and shear, a biaxial state of combined tension and compression exists at various points, as shown in Figure 6.1. As explained in Section 2.10.2, the presence of shear stress reduces the *strength* of concrete in compression as well as tension. Accordingly, the tensile strength of the concrete in a reinforced concrete beam subjected to flexural shear will be less than the uniaxial tensile strength of concrete. The so-called 'diagonal tension cracks' can be expected to occur in reinforced concrete beams in general, and appropriate *shear reinforcement* is required to prevent the propagation of these cracks. When a 'flexural crack' occurs in combination with a 'diagonal tension crack' (as is usually the case), the crack is sometimes referred to as a *flexure-shear crack* [Figure 6.2(c)]. In such a case, it is the flexural crack that usually forms first, and due to the increased shear stresses at the tip of the crack, this flexural crack extends into a diagonal tension crack.

†This assumes that stress f_y at the top surface due to any load applied on the surface can be neglected

‡'Principal stress trajectories' are a set of orthogonal curves whose tangent/normal at any regular point indicate the directions of the principal stresses at that point. In Figure 6.1(d), the firm lines indicate directions of compressive stress, and the broken lines indicate directions of tensile stress.

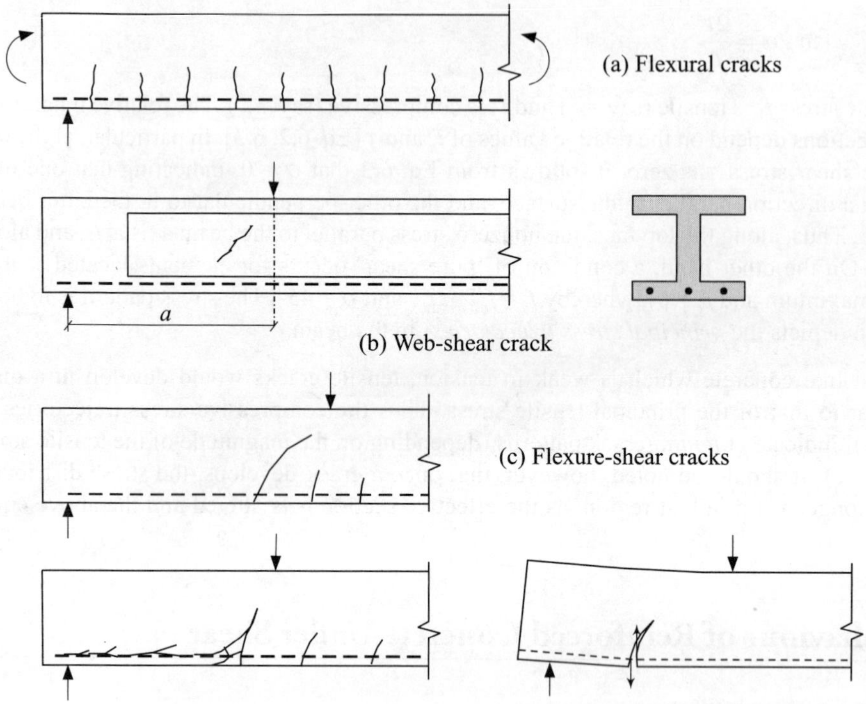

Fig. 6.2 Modes of cracking

> *Dowel action* in general refers to the restraining effect of reinforcement running across a crack (or separation), restricting relative transverse movement of the separated concrete at the crack interface. In the case of an inclined shear crack, it refers to the restraining effect of longitudinal tension bars, which tend to 'kink' at the crack location, generating a transverse 'dowel force' that resists shear force.

Sometimes, the inclined crack propagates along the tension reinforcement towards the support [Figure 6.2(d)]. Such cracks are referred to as *secondary cracks* or *splitting cracks*. These are attributed to the wedging action of the tension bar deformations and to the transverse 'dowel forces' introduced by the tension bars functioning as *dowels* across the crack, resisting relative transverse displacements between the two segments of the beam (*dowel action*) [Figure 6.2(e)].

6.3.2 Shear Transfer Mechanisms

There are several mechanisms by which shear is transmitted between two adjacent planes in a reinforced concrete beam. The prominent among these are identified in Figure 6.3, which shows the freebody of one segment of a reinforced concrete beam separated by a flexure-shear crack.

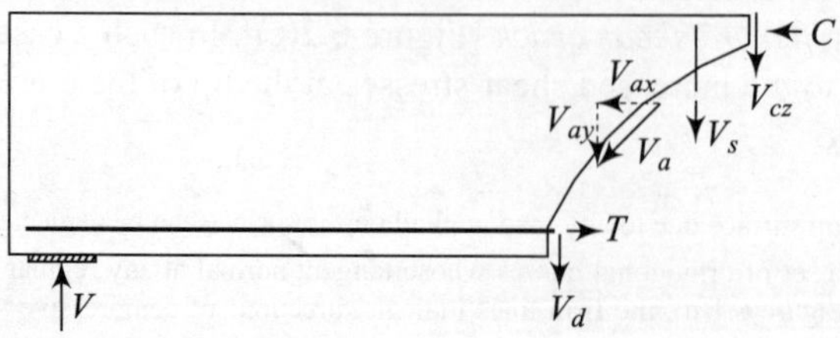

Fig. 6.3 Internal forces acting at a flexural-shear crack.

The transverse (external) shear force is denoted as V (and has a maximum value near the support, equal to the support reaction). It is resisted by various mechanisms, the major ones [Figure 6.3] being:

1. shear resistance V_{cz} of the uncracked portion of concrete;
2. vertical component V_{ay} of the 'interface shear' (*aggregate interlock*) force V_a;
3. dowel force V_d in the tension reinforcement (due to dowel action); and
4. shear resistance V_s carried by the shear (transverse) reinforcement, if any.

The interface shear V_a is a tangential force transmitted along the inclined plane of the crack, resulting from the friction against relative slip between the interlocking surfaces of the crack. Its contribution can be significant, if the crack-width is limited. The dowel force V_d comes from 'dowel action' [Figure 6.2(e)], as explained earlier.

The equilibrium of vertical forces in Figure 6.3 results in the relation:

$$V = V_{cz} + V_{ay} + V_d + V_s \tag{6.4}$$

The relative contribution of the various mechanisms depends on the loading stage, the extent of cracking and the material and geometric properties of the beam. Prior to flexural cracking, the applied shear is resisted almost entirely by the uncracked concrete ($V \approx V_{cz}$). At the commencement of flexural cracking, there is a redistribution of stresses, and some interface shear V_a and dowel action V_d develop. At the stage of diagonal tension cracking, the shear reinforcement (hitherto practically unstressed) that intercepts the crack undergoes a sudden increase in tensile strain and stress. All the four major mechanisms are effective at this stage. The subsequent behaviour, including the failure mode and the ultimate strength in shear, depends on how the mechanisms of shear transfer break down and how successfully the shear resisting forces are redistributed.

The presence of increased longitudinal reinforcement in the flexural tension zone not only contributes to enhanced dowel action (V_d), but also serves to control the propagation of flexural cracks and contributes to increasing the depth of the neutral axis, and thereby the depth of the uncracked concrete in compression; this enhances the contributions of V_a and V_{cz}. Thus, the higher the percentage tension reinforcement, the greater the shear resistance in the concrete – up to a limit.

Beams without Shear Reinforcement

In beams without shear reinforcement, the component V_s is absent altogether. Moreover, in the absence of *stirrups* enclosing the longitudinal bars, there is little restraint against splitting failure, and the dowel force V_d is small. Furthermore, the crack propagation is unrestrained, and hence, fairly rapid, resulting in a fall in the aggregate interface force V_a and also a reduction in the area of the uncracked concrete (in the limited compression zone) which contributes to V_{cz}. However, in relatively deep beams, *tied-arch action* [Figure 6.4(b)] may develop following inclined cracking, thereby transferring part of the load to the support, and so reducing the effective shear force at the section. Indeed, the 'sectional model' is not valid in this case and the strut-and-tie model is more appropriate.

Thus, in beams without shear reinforcement, the breakdown of any of the shear transfer mechanisms may cause immediate failure, as there is little scope for redistribution. Further, owing to the uncertainties associated with all the above effects, it is difficult to predict precisely the behaviour and the strength *beyond the stage of diagonal cracking* in beams without shear reinforcement.

As seen in Chapter 5, design for flexure is done so as to ensure a ductile flexural failure. The objective of shear design is to avoid premature brittle shear failures, such as those displayed by beams without web

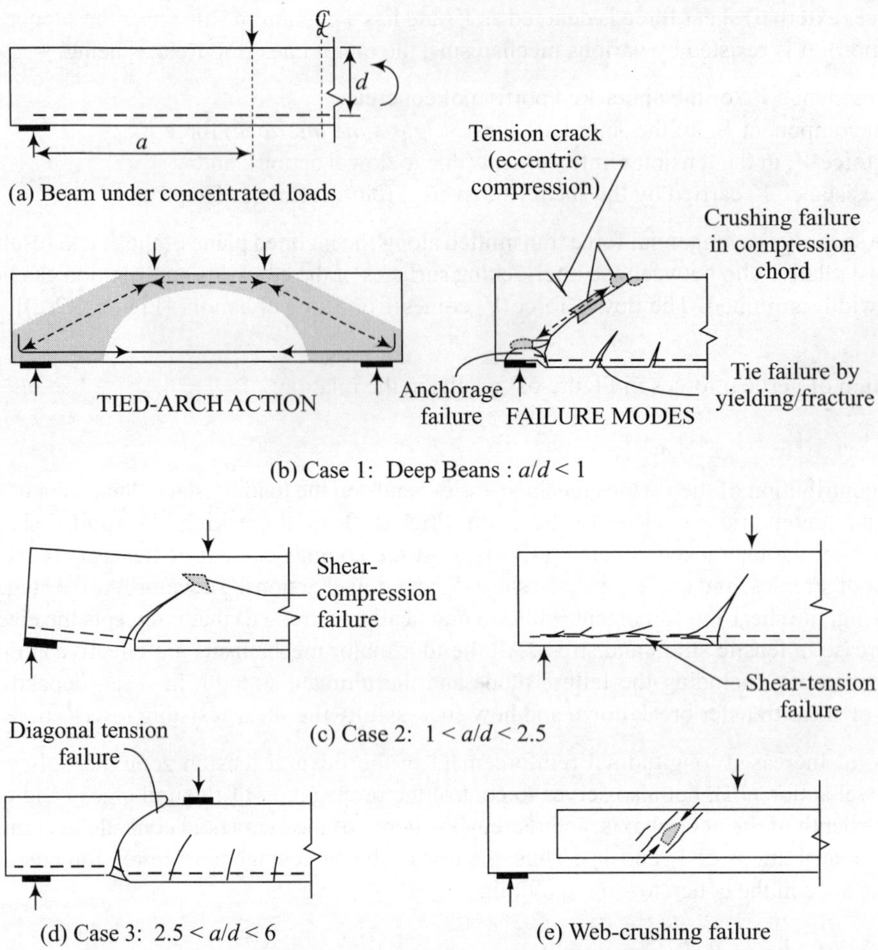

Fig. 6.4 Typical shear failure modes.

reinforcement, before the attainment of the full flexural strength. Members should be designed so that the shear capacity is high enough to ensure a ductile flexural failure.

Beams with Shear Reinforcement

In beams with moderate amounts of shear reinforcement, shear resistance continues to increase even after inclined cracking, until the shear reinforcement yields in tension, and the force V_s cannot exceed its ultimate value V_{us}. Any additional shear V has to be resisted by increments in V_{cz}, V_d and/or V_{ay}. With progressively widening crack-width (now accelerated by the yielding of shear reinforcement), V_{ay} decreases (instead of increasing), thereby forcing V_{cz} and V_d to increase at a faster rate until either a splitting (dowel) failure occurs or the concrete in the compression zone gets crushed under the combined effects of flexural compressive stress and shear stress.

Owing to the pronounced yielding of the shear reinforcement, the failure of shear reinforced beams is gradual and ductile in nature – unlike beams without shear reinforcement, whose failure in shear is sudden and brittle in nature. However, if excessive shear reinforcement is provided, it is likely that the 'shear-compression' mode of failure [see next section] will occur first, and this is undesirable, as such a failure will occur suddenly, without warning.

6.3.3 Shear Failure Modes

As explained earlier (with reference to Eq. 6.2), the magnitude and direction of the maximum principal tensile stress, and hence the development and growth of inclined cracks are influenced by the relative magnitudes of the flexural stress f_x and the shear stress τ. As an approximation, stresses f_x and τ can be considered proportional to $M/(bd^2)$ and $V/(bd)$ respectively, where M and V are the applied bending moment and shear force respectively at the beam section under consideration, b is the width and d the effective depth.

Accordingly,

$$\frac{f_x}{\tau} = \frac{F_1 M/(bd^2)}{F_2 V/(bd)} = F_3 \frac{M}{Vd} \tag{6.5}$$

where F_1, F_2, F_3 are constants of proportionality. For beams subjected to concentrated loads [Figure 6.4(a)], the ratio M/V at the critical section subjected to the *maximum* V works out exactly to the distance a, called *shear span*, between the support and the load. In such a case, the ratio $M/(Vd)$ becomes equal to a/d, the shear span-depth ratio, whereby Eq. 6.5 reduces to

$$\frac{f_x}{\tau} \propto \frac{a}{d} \tag{6.6}$$

It can be seen that the dimensionless ratio a/d (or $M/(Vd)$) provides a measure of the relative magnitudes of the flexural stress and the shear stress, and hence enables the prediction of the mode of failure of the beam under combined flexure and shear [Ref. 6.2, 6.3]. The prediction is based on considerable experimental evidence involving simply supported beams of rectangular cross-section subjected to symmetrical two-point loading.

Case 1: $a/d < 1$

In very deep beams ($a/d < 1$) without web reinforcement, inclined cracking transforms the beam into a *tied-arch* [Figure 6.4(b)]. The tied-arch may fail either by a breakdown of its tension element (the tie), viz., the longitudinal reinforcement (by yielding, fracture or failure of anchorage) or a breakdown of its compression chord – the strut (crushing of concrete), as shown in Figure 6.4(b).

Case 2: $1 < a/d < 2.5$

In relatively short beams with a/d in the range of 1 to 2.5, the failure is initiated by an inclined crack – usually a *flexure-shear crack*. The actual failure may take place either by (1) crushing of the reduced concrete section above the tip of the crack under combined shear and compression, termed *shear-compression* failure or (2) secondary cracking along the tension reinforcement, termed *shear-tension* failure. Both these types of failure usually occur before the flexural strength (full moment-resisting capacity) of the beam is attained.

However, when the loads and reactions applied on the top and bottom surfaces of the beam are so located as to induce a vertical compressive stress in concrete between the load and the reaction, the shear strength may be increased significantly – requiring very heavy loads to cause inclined cracking.

Case 3: 2.5 < a/d < 6

Normal beams have *a/d* ratios in excess of 2.5. Such beams may fail either in shear or in flexure. The limiting *a/d* ratio above which flexural failure is certain depends on the tension steel area as well as strength of concrete and steel; generally, it is in the neighbourhood of 6.

For beams with *a/d* ratios in the range 2.5 to 6, flexural tension cracks develop early. Failure in shear occurs by the propagation of inclined flexural-shear cracks. As mentioned earlier, if shear (web) reinforcement is not provided, the cracks extend rapidly to the top of the beam; the failure occurs suddenly and is termed *diagonal tension* failure [Figure 6.4(d)]. Addition of web reinforcement enhances the shear strength considerably. Loads can be carried until failure occurs in a *shear-tension* mode (yielding of the shear reinforcement) or in a *shear-compression* mode†, or in a *flexural* mode.

Web-Crushing Failure

In addition to the modes described above, thin-webbed members (such as *I*-beams with web reinforcement) may fail by the crushing of concrete in the web portion between the inclined cracks under diagonal compression forces [Figure 6.4(e)].

6.4 Nominal Shear Stress

The concept of *average shear stress* τ_{av} in a beam section is used in mechanics of materials, with reference to a homogeneous elastic material [Figure 6.1]. It is defined as

$$\tau_{av} = \frac{\text{shear force}}{\text{area of cross section}}$$

For simplicity, this parameter is used as a *measure* of the shear stresses in a reinforced concrete beam section as well.

6.4.1 Members with Uniform Depth

For *prismatic* members of rectangular (or flanged) sections, the Code (Cl. 40.1) uses the term *nominal shear stress* τ_v, defined at the ultimate limit state, as follows:

$$\tau_v = \frac{V_u}{bd} \tag{6.7}$$

where V_u is the *factored* shear force at the section under consideration, b is the width of the beam (taken as the web width b_w in flanged beams), and d the effective depth of the section.

It should be noted that τ_v is merely a parameter intended to aid design and to control shear stresses in reinforced concrete; it does not actually represent the true average shear stress (whose distribution is quite complex in reinforced concrete).

† If web steel is excessive, it may not yield; instead, concrete in diagonal compression gets crushed.

6.4.2 Members with Varying Depth

In the case of members with varying depth [Figure 6.5], the nominal shear stress, defined by Eq. 6.7, needs to be modified, to account for the contribution of the vertical component of the flexural tensile force T_u which is inclined at an angle β to the longitudinal direction.

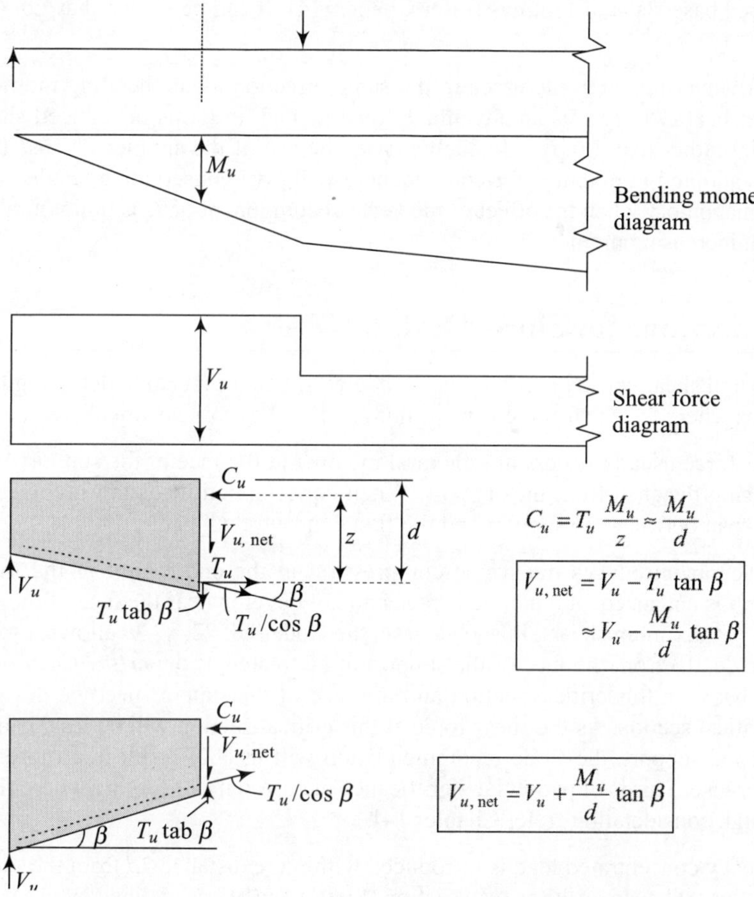

Fig. 6.5 Design shear force in beams of variable depth.

Assuming the horizontal component of T_u as $M_u/z \approx M_u/d$, it can be seen from Figure 6.5 that the *net shear force* $V_{u,\text{net}}$ for which the section should be designed is:

$$V_{u,\text{net}} = V_u \pm \frac{M_u}{d} \tan\beta \tag{6.8}$$

Accordingly, the *nominal shear stress* (Cl. 40.1.1 of the Code), defined with respect to $V_{u,\text{net}}$, is obtained as

$$\tau_v = \frac{V_u \pm \dfrac{M_u}{d}\tan\beta}{bd} \tag{6.9}$$

where V_u and M_u are the applied factored shear force and bending moment at the section under consideration. The negative sign in Eqs 6.8, 6.9 applies where M_u *increases* in the same direction as the depth increases and the positive sign applies where M_u decreases in this direction, as shown clearly in Figure 6.5.

A similar adjustment to the shear V_u and the nominal shear stress τ_v is called for when the flexural compression C_u is inclined to the longitudinal axis of the beam, i.e., the compression face is sloping. Such a situation is encountered in tapered base slabs of footings [refer Chapter 14]. It can be shown that Eq. 6.9 holds good in this case also.

It may be noted that when the depth increases in the same direction as the bending moment (as is usually the case in cantilever beams†), there is an advantage to be gained, in terms of reduced shear stress, by the application of Eq. 6.9 rather than Eq. 6.7. In such a case, the use of the simpler Eq. 6.7 for nominal shear stress τ_v (sometimes adopted in practice, for convenience) will give conservative results. However, the use of Eq. 6.9 becomes mandatory when the effect of the vertical component of T_u is unfavourable, i.e., when the depth decreases with increasing moment.

6.5 Critical Sections for Shear Design

In designing for flexural shear, the *critical sections* to be investigated first (for calculating the nominal shear stress τ_v) are the ones where the shear force is maximum and/or the cross-sectional area is minimal.

The maximum shear force usually occurs in a flexural member at the face of the support, and progressively reduces with increasing distance from the support. When concentrated loads are involved, the shear force remains high in the span between the support and the first concentrated load.

When a support reaction introduces transverse compression in the end region of the member, the shear strength of this region is enhanced, and inclined cracks do not develop near the face of the support (which is usually the location of maximum shear). In such a case, the Code (Cl. 22.6.2.1) allows a section located at a distance d (effective depth) from the face of the support to be treated as the *critical section* [Figure 6.6(a)]. The beam segment between this critical section and the face of the support need be designed only for the shear force at the critical section. As the shear force at this critical section will be less than (or equal to) the value at the face of the support, the Code recommendation will usually result in a more favourable (less) value of τ_v than otherwise. This is of particular significance in base slabs of footing where flexural (one-way) shear is a major design consideration [refer Chapter 14].

However, when a heavy concentrated load is introduced within the distance $2d$ from the face of the support, then the face of the support becomes the critical section [Figure 6.6(b)], as inclined cracks can develop within this region if the shear strength is exceeded. In such cases, closely spaced stirrups should be designed and provided in the region between the concentrated load and the support face.

Also, when the favourable effect of transverse compression from the reaction is absent – as in a suspended beam [Figure 6.6(c)], or a beam (or bracket) connected to the side of another supporting beam [Figure 6.6(d)] – the critical section for shear should be taken at the face of the support.

In the latter case [Figure 6.6(d)], special shear reinforcement detailing is called for – to ensure that effective shear transfer takes place between the *supported* beam (or bracket in some situation) and the *supporting* beam and to eliminate a push-out failure of the supporting beam. It is recommended [Ref. 6.8] that full depth stirrups (also referred to as hanger reinforcements) should be designed in both the supported member and the supporting member in the vicinity of the interface for 'hanging up' a portion of the interface shear, equal to $V_u(1 - h_b/D)$, the dimensions h_b and D being as shown in Figure 6.7. The shear reinforcement (stirrups) so

† For example, in balanced cantilever bridge girders with parabolically varying soffits.

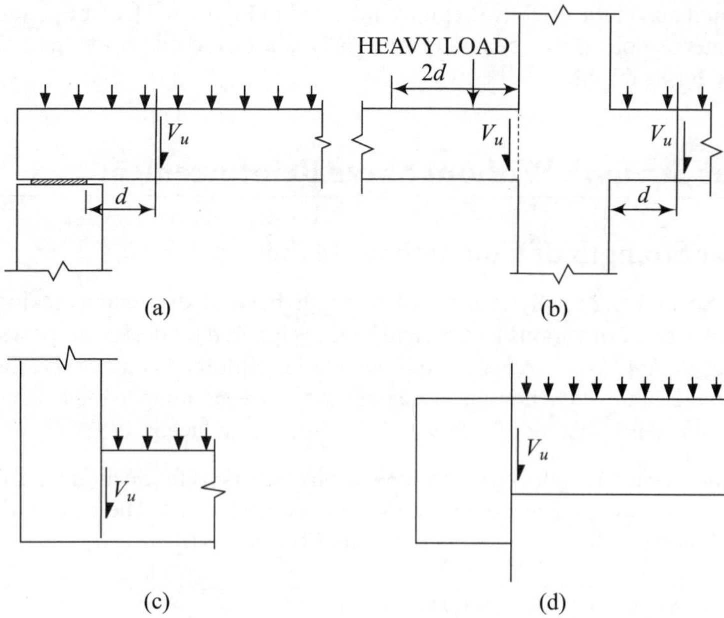

Fig. 6.6 Critical sections for shear at support.

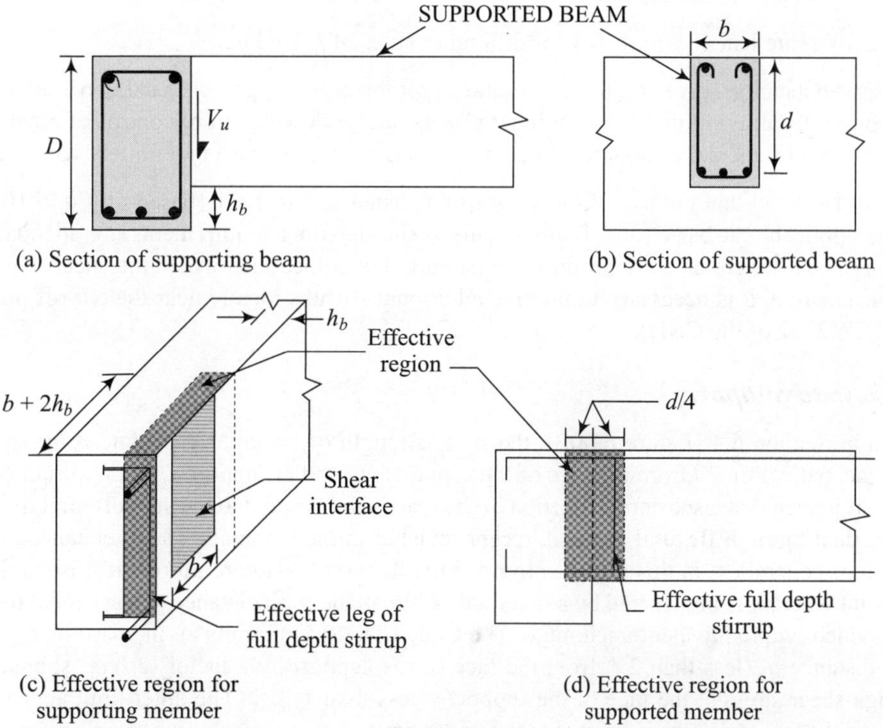

Fig. 6.7 Detailing of stirrups for interface shear at indirect support.

designed must be accommodated in the effective regions indicated in Figure 6.7 [refer Section 6.8 for design procedure]. Indeed, the intersection of two beams (Figure 6.7) is a disturbed region, and the strut-and-tie model is more appropriate for its design.

6.6 Design Shear Strength Without Shear Reinforcement

6.6.1 Design Shear Strength of Concrete in Beams

As explained earlier in Section 6.2.2, the margin of strength beyond diagonal cracking is subject to considerable fluctuation on account of various factors, and hence is ignored for design purposes [Ref. 6.4, 6.5]. Accordingly, the (average) *design shear strength* τ_c of concrete in reinforced concrete beams without shear reinforcement is limited to the value of the nominal shear stress τ_v corresponding to the load at which the first inclined crack develops; some partial factor of safety ($\approx$ 1.2) is also introduced.

The magnitude of the design shear strength τ_c depends on various factors (refer Section 6.3.2) that are related to the grade of concrete (f_{ck}) and the percentage tension steel $p_t = 100A_{st}/(bd)$. The values of τ_c given in the Code (Table 19) are based on the following empirical formula [Ref. 6.5, 6.6]:

$$\tau_c = 0.85\sqrt{(0.8f_{ck})}(\sqrt{1+5\beta} - 1)/(6\beta) \tag{6.10}$$

where $$\beta \equiv \begin{cases}(0.8\, f_{ck})/(6.89\, p_t) \\ 1\end{cases} \text{ whichever is greater} \tag{6.10a}$$

Typical values of τ_c are listed in Table 6.1 for different values of f_{ck} and p_t.

It may be observed that, for a given f_{ck}, there is a value of p_t (corresponding to $\beta = 1$ in Eq. 6.10a), beyond which τ_c remains constant, implying that the beneficial effects due to dowel action, control of crack propagation and increased depth of uncracked concrete in compression, cannot increase indefinitely with increasing p_t.

Further, it may be noted that the use of the values of τ_c listed in Table 6.1 (based on Eq. 6.10) for a given value of p_t is applicable at bar cut-off regions, only if the detailing requirements are adequately satisfied (refer Section 5.9.3). Where bars are proposed to be curtailed at locations where the shear requirements are not otherwise satisfied, it is necessary to provide additional stirrups locally near the cut-off points (thereby satisfying Cl. 26.2.3.2 of the Code).

Sections Close to Supports

As explained in Section 6.4 [Figure 6.6(a)], the shear strength of concrete is enhanced in regions close to the support (located within $2d$ from the face of the support), when the support reaction introduces transverse compression. It is seen that a substantial portion of the load is transmitted to the support directly through strut action, rather than through flexural shear. A recent revision in the Code allows for enhancement of design shear strength of concrete τ_c in this region, provided the flexural tension reinforcement is extended on each side of the point where it is intersected by a potential failure plane for a distance at least equal to the effective depth, or provided with equivalent anchorage. The Code (Cl. 40.5) permits an increase in τ_c at any section located at a distance a_v (less than $2d$) from the face of the support by a factor $(2d)/a_v$, subject to the limit that the design shear stress at the face of the support is less than $\tau_{c,\max}$. [The latter limit appears redundant, since the nominal shear stress, τ_v, is limited to the upper limit of $\tau_{c,\max}$ in any case (see Section 6.6.3 below)]. However, this increase should be used with caution, as it is implied that as the critical section approaches

Table 6.1 *Design Shear Strength of Concrete τ_c (MPa)*

$p_t = \dfrac{100A_{st}}{bd}$	Concrete grade				
	M 20	M 25	M 30	M 35	M 40 and above
0.2	0.326	0.331	0.334	0.337	0.339
0.3	0.388	0.395	0.400	0.403	0.407
0.4	0.437	0.446	0.452	0.457	0.461
0.5	0.478	0.489	0.497	0.503	0.508
0.6	0.514	0.526	0.536	0.543	0.549
0.7	0.546	0.559	0.570	0.578	0.585
0.8	0.574	0.589	0.601	0.611	0.618
0.9	0.599	0.616	0.630	0.640	0.649
1.0	0.623	0.641	0.656	0.667	0.677
1.1	0.644	0.664	0.680	0.692	0.703
1.2	0.664	0.686	0.703	0.716	0.727
1.3	0.682	0.706	0.724	0.738	0.750
1.4	0.700	0.725	0.744	0.759	0.771
1.5	0.716	0.742	0.762	0.779	0.792
1.6	0.731	0.759	0.780	0.797	0.811
1.7	0.746	0.775	0.797	0.815	0.830
1.8	0.760	0.790	0.813	0.832	0.847
1.9	0.773	0.804	0.828	0.848	0.864
2.0	0.785	0.818	0.843	0.864	0.880
2.1	0.797	0.831	0.857	0.878	0.896
2.2	0.808	0.843	0.871	0.893	0.911
2.3	0.819	0.855	0.883	0.906	0.925
2.4	0.821	0.867	0.896	0.919	0.939
2.5	0.821	0.878	0.908	0.932	0.952
2.6	0.821	0.888	0.919	0.944	0.965
2.7	0.821	0.899	0.930	0.956	0.978
2.8	0.821	0.909	0.941	0.968	0.990
2.9	0.821	0.918	0.952	0.979	1.001
3.0	0.821	0.918	0.962	0.989	1.013
3.1	0.821	0.918	0.971	1.000	1.024
3.2	0.821	0.918	0.981	1.010	1.034
3.3	0.821	0.918	0.990	1.020	1.045
3.4	0.821	0.918	0.999	1.029	1.055
3.5	0.821	0.918	1.006	1.039	1.065
3.6	0.821	0.918	1.006	1.048	1.074

(Contd.)

$p_t = \frac{100A_{st}}{bd}$	Concrete grade				
	M 20	M 25	M 30	M 35	M 40 and above
3.7	0.821	0.918	1.006	1.056	1.084
3.8	0.821	0.918	1.006	1.065	1.093
3.9	0.821	0.918	1.006	1.073	1.102
4.0	0.821	0.918	1.006	1.081	1.110
4.1	0.821	0.918	1.006	1.087	1.119
4.2	0.821	0.918	1.006	1.087	1.127
4.3	0.821	0.918	1.006	1.087	1.135
4.4	0.821	0.918	1.006	1.087	1.143
4.5	0.821	0.918	1.006	1.087	1.151
4.6	0.821	0.918	1.006	1.087	1.158
4.7	0.821	0.918	1.006	1.087	1.162

the face of the support, the shear strength will increase asymptotically, which is not realistic. The authors suggest that the shear strength in concrete for sections within a distance d from the face of the support should be limited to $2\tau_c$.

For beams carrying generally uniform load, or where the principal load is located farther than $2d$ from face of support, the increase in τ_c may be ignored. In such cases, the shear design calculations may be based on the critical section given in Section 6.5 and the same shear reinforcement provided within the distance d also.

6.6.2 Design Shear Strength of Concrete in Slabs

Experimental studies [Ref. 6.2-6.4] have shown that slabs and shallow beams fail at loads corresponding to a nominal stress that is higher than that applicable for beams of usual proportion. Moreover, the thinner the slab, the greater is the increase in shear strength. In recognition of this, the Code (Cl. 40.2.1.1) suggests an increased shear strength, equal to $k\tau_c$ for 'solid slabs' (i.e., not including *ribbed slabs*), the multiplication factor k having a value in the range 1.0 to 1.3, expressed as follows:

$$k = \begin{cases} 1.3 & \text{for } D \leq 150 \text{ mm} \\ 1.6 - 0.002D & \text{for } 150 < D < 300 \text{ mm} \\ 1.0 & \text{for } D \geq 300 \text{ mm} \end{cases} \tag{6.11}$$

where D is the overall depth of the slab in mm.

It should be noted that these provisions for design shear strength are applicable only for considerations of *flexural shear* (or 'one-way shear'). For *flat slabs* and column footings, *punching shear* ('two-way shear') has to be considered, which involve different considerations of shear strength [refer Chapter 11].

Slabs under distributed loadings generally do not need reinforcement for flexural (one-way) shear.

In general, slabs subjected to normal distributed loads satisfy the requirement $\tau_v < k\tau_c$, and hence do not need shear reinforcement. This is mainly attributable to the fact that the thickness of the slab (controlled by limiting deflection criteria) is usually adequate in terms of shear capacity. This is demonstrated in Example 6.1.

6.6.3 Influence of Axial Force on Design Shear Strength

In Section 2.10.2, it was indicated that the actual shear strength of concrete is generally improved in the presence of uniaxial compression and weakened in the presence of uniaxial tension.

As explained earlier (in Section 6.6.1), the design shear strength is based on a safe estimate of the limiting nominal stress at which the first inclined crack develops. The effect of an axial *compressive* force is to delay the formation of both flexural and inclined cracks, and also to decrease the angle of inclination α of the inclined cracks to the longitudinal axis [Ref. 6.5]. Likewise, an axial *tensile* force is expected to do exactly the reverse, i.e., it will decrease the shear strength, accelerate the process of cracking and increase the angle α of the inclined cracks.

Accordingly, the Code (Cl. 40.2.2) specifies that the design shear strength in the presence of *axial compression* should be taken as $\delta\tau_c$, the multiplying factor δ being defined as:

$$\delta = \begin{cases} 1 + \dfrac{3P_u}{A_g f_{ck}} \\ 1.5 \end{cases} \text{whichever is less} \tag{6.12}$$

where P_u is the factored compressive force (in *N*), A_g is the gross area of the section (in mm^2) and f_{ck} is the characteristic strength of concrete (in MPa).

Although the Code does not explicitly mention the case of *axial tension*, it is evident that some reduction in design shear strength is called for in such a case. The following simplified expression for δ, based on the ACI Code [Ref. 6.7], may be used:

$$\delta = 1 + \frac{P_u}{3.45\ A_g} \quad \text{for } P_u < 0 \tag{6.13}$$

where P_u is the factored axial tension (in N), with a negative sign.

Alternatively, when axial tension is also present, design for shear may be done based on the Compression Field Theory or the Strut-and-Tie Model, described in Chapter 17.

6.7 Design Shear Strength With Shear Reinforcement

6.7.1 Types of Shear Reinforcement

Shear reinforcement, also known as *web reinforcement* and *transverse reinforcement*, may consist of any one of the following systems (Cl. 40.4 of the Code)

- stirrups perpendicular to the beam axis;
- stirrups inclined (at 45° or more) to the beam axis; and
- longitudinal bars bent-up (usually, not more than two at a time) at 45° to 60° to the beam axis, combined with stirrups.

By far, the most common type of shear reinforcement is the *two-legged stirrup*, comprising a closed or open loop, with its ends anchored properly around longitudinal bars/stirrup-holders (to develop the yield strength in

> ***Two-legged*** **refers to the two legs of the stirrup that are effective in intercepting the shear crack; in design of stirrups in relatively wide beams subject to heavy shear force (as in bridge girders), it is common to use four-legged or six-legged stirrups.**

In beams subject to reversal of shear force, closed stirrups placed perpendicular to the beam axis are required.

tension). It is placed perpendicular to the member axis ('vertical† stirrup'), and may or may not be combined with bent-up bars, as shown in Figure 6.8.

The direction of bending up of the tension bar (or the direction of the inclined stirrup) should be such that it intercepts the potential inclined (diagonal tension) crack, nearly at right angles, thereby most effectively restraining the opening up and propagation of crack. The bent-up bar must be properly anchored; in order to be effective, a full 'development length' L_d is required beyond the midpoint of the inclined portion of the bar.

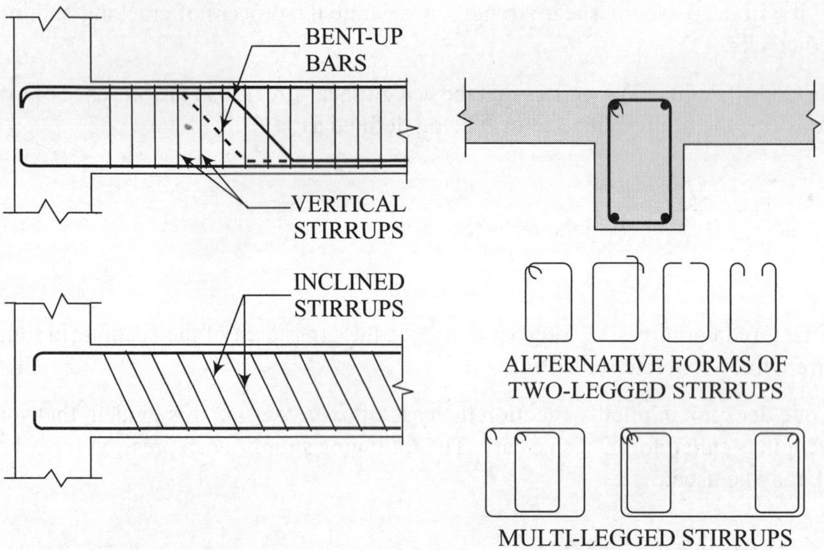

Fig. 6.8 Types of shear reinforcement.

The stirrup (particularly, the inclined stirrup) is considered to be most effective in enhancing the overall shear resistance of the beam, because in addition to contributing in much the same way as the bent-up bar, it contributes significantly towards improved *dowel action* of the longitudinal tension bars, by restraining the latter from undergoing transverse (dowel) displacements. There is concern that stirrups inclined at less than 45° to the longitudinal reinforcement will slip along the longitudinal bars and hence are not recommended. Strictly, simple U-shaped ('open') stirrups with the free ends anchored properly around stirrup-holders in the compression zone by hooks suffice as shear reinforcement. However, 'closed' loops are called for in resisting torsion and confining the compression reinforcement (when provided, in doubly reinforced beams). It is desirable to locate the hook in the closed stirrup in the compression zone, rather than the tension zone, for improved anchorage and to avoid crack initiation.

The shear resistance of bent-up bars cannot be fully relied upon, unless stirrups are also provided, to ensure adequate development of dowel action of the longitudinal bars. The Code (Cl. 40.4) specifies that

> 'Where bent-up bars are provided, their contribution towards shear resistance shall not be more than half that of the total shear reinforcement'

† The term vertical is commonly used (as in the Code), with the assumption that the beam axis is horizontal (as is commonly the case); the term is also (although inappropriate) used in the case of beams inclined to the horizontal. The term 'transverse' is more appropriate.

6.7.2 Factors Contributing to Ultimate Shear Resistance

If V_{uc} and V_{us} denote respectively the ultimate shear resistance of the concrete and the shear reinforcement, then the total *ultimate shear resistance* V_{uR} at any section of the beam is given by

$$V_{uR} = V_{uc} + V_{us} \tag{6.14}$$

In Eq. 6.14, the shear resistance V_{uc} of concrete is made up of all the components V_{cz}, V_{ay} and V_d of Eq. 6.4. Although the relative magnitudes of these components of V_{uc} vary with the stage of loading and the state of cracking (refer Section 6.3.2), their aggregate value V_{uc} is assumed to be constant, and obtainable from the design strength of concrete τ_c as

$$V_{uc} = \tau_c bd \tag{6.15}$$

This follows from the concept of τ_c as the 'safe' limiting value of the nominal shear stress τ_v (given by Eq. 6.7) of concrete *without* shear reinforcement. In beams *with* shear reinforcement, it is found from actual measurements of strain (in the shear reinforcement) that, prior to the formation of diagonal tension cracks, there is practically no tensile stress developed in the shear reinforcement [Ref. 6.2]. Accordingly, V_{uc} denotes the shear resistance at the stage of initiation of diagonal cracking in flexural members, regardless of whether or not shear reinforcement is provided.

As explained earlier in Section 6.3.2, all the four shear transfer mechanisms (V_{cz}, V_{ay}, V_d, V_s) become operational, following the development of inclined cracks. The shear reinforcement contributes significantly to the overall shear resistance by increasing or maintaining the individual components V_{cz}, V_{ay} and V_d of Eq. 6.4, in addition to directly contributing by means of the tension V_s in the legs of the stirrup and the bent-up portions of the bent-up bars (where provided).

For simplicity, it is assumed that the contribution $V_{cz} + V_{ay} + V_d$ remains practically unchanged following the stage of inclined cracking. Hence, V_{uc} (calculated using Eq. 6.15) is assumed to represent the shear resistance of the concrete at the ultimate limit state in beams with shear reinforcement as well. Further, as explained in Section 6.3.2, once the shear reinforcement starts yielding in tension, its shear resisting capacity remains practically constant as V_{us}. Expressions for V_{us} are derived in Section 6.7.4.

From a design viewpoint, suitable shear reinforcement has to be designed if the factored shear V_u exceeds V_{uc} (i.e., τ_v exceeds τ_c), and the shear resistance[†] required from the web reinforcement is given by

$$V_{us} \geq V_u - V_{uc} = (\tau_v - \tau_c)bd \tag{6.16}$$

6.7.3 Limiting Ultimate Shear Resistance

As explained earlier, the yielding of the shear reinforcement at the ultimate limit state is essential to ensure a *ductile* failure (with ample warning). However, such a failure will not occur if the shear reinforcement provided is excessive. If the total cross-sectional area A_{sv} of the stirrup legs and the bent-up bars exceeds a certain limit, it is likely that the section becomes stronger in diagonal tension compared to diagonal compression. Hence, a *shear-compression* failure [Figure 6.4(c)] may occur even before the shear reinforcement has yielded (and thus realised its full potential). Such a situation is undesirable due to the *brittle* nature of the failure; moreover, it turns out to be uneconomical, in much the same way as over-reinforced beams.

† It may be noted that the stirrups will be in tension, and have to be designed for the numerical value of $V_u - V_{uc}$, regardless of whether V_u acts upward or downward.

In order to prevent such shear-compression failures and to ensure yielding of the shear reinforcement at the ultimate limit state, the Code (Cl. 40.2.3) has indirectly imposed a limit on the resistance V_{us}, by limiting the ultimate shear resistance V_{uR}:

$$V_{uR,\,\lim} = \tau_{c,\,\max}\, bd \tag{6.17}$$

where $\tau_{c,\,\max}$ ($\approx 0.62\sqrt{f_{ck}}$) is given values (in MPa) of 2.4, 2.8, 3.1, 3.4, 3.7 and 3.9 for concrete grades M 15, M 20, M 25, M 30, M 35 and M 40 respectively (vide Table 20 of the Code).

Thus, if the calculated nominal shear stress τ_v ($=V_u/bd$) at a beam section exceeds the limit $\tau_{c,\max}$ (or the factored shear force V_u exceeds $V_{uR,\lim}$), the design should be suitably revised, either by improving the grade of concrete (thereby, raising $\tau_{c,\max}$) or increasing the dimensions of the beam (thereby, lowering τ_v). The increase in $\tau_{c,\max}$ with the compressive strength of concrete follows logically from the fact that the shear strength in diagonal compression gets enhanced.

In the case of solid slabs, the Code (Cl. 40.2.3.1) specifies that τ_v should not exceed $0.5\tau_{c,\max}$ (i.e., 1.2 MPa for M 15, 1.4 MPa for M 20, 1.55 MPa for M 25, 1.7 MPa for M 30, 1.85 MPa for M 35 and 1.95 MPa for M 40 concrete).

6.7.4 Shear Resistance of Web Reinforcement

> Shear reinforcements in beams are also referred to as web reinforcement and transverse reinforcement

Traditionally, the action of web reinforcement in reinforced concrete beams has been explained with the aid of the *truss analogy*, the simplest form of which is shown in Figure 6.9. This design model was first enunciated by Ritter in 1899 and explained in more detail by Mörsch in 1902. In this model, a reinforced concrete beam with inclined cracks is idealised as a pin-jointed truss The flexural compression zone of concrete at the top of the beam acts as the top chord of the truss, the longitudinal tension reinforcement forms the bottom chord, the stirrups act as the vertical tension members and the concrete in compression in-between the inclined cracks act as the diagonal members of the truss. (The truss model is akin to the Strut-and-Tie model).

In this model, the compression diagonals do not have to go from top of one stirrup to the bottom of the next. In reality, rather than having discrete diagonal compressive struts, there is a continuous field of diagonal compression contributing to shear resistance.

The truss model is a helpful tool in visualising the forces in the stirrups (under tension) and the concrete (under diagonal compression), and in providing a basis for simplified design concepts and methods. However, this model does not recognise fully the actual action of the web reinforcement and its effect on the various types of shear transfer mechanisms identified in Figure 6.3.

Figure 6.9(b) shows one segment of the beam separated by a diagonal tension crack. This is an idealisation of Figure 6.9(a), wherein the diagonal crack is assumed to be straight, inclined at an angle θ to the beam axis and extends over the full depth of the beam. The general case of inclined stirrups is considered in the freebody in Figure 6.9(b); only the forces in the web reinforcement that contribute to the resistance V_{us} are shown.

The inclined stirrups are assumed to be placed at an angle α (not less than 45° in design practice) with the beam axis, and spaced s_v apart measured along the beam axis. If A_{sv} is the total cross-sectional area of one stirrup (considering all the legs intercepting the inclined crack) and $0.87f_y$ is the design yield stress in it

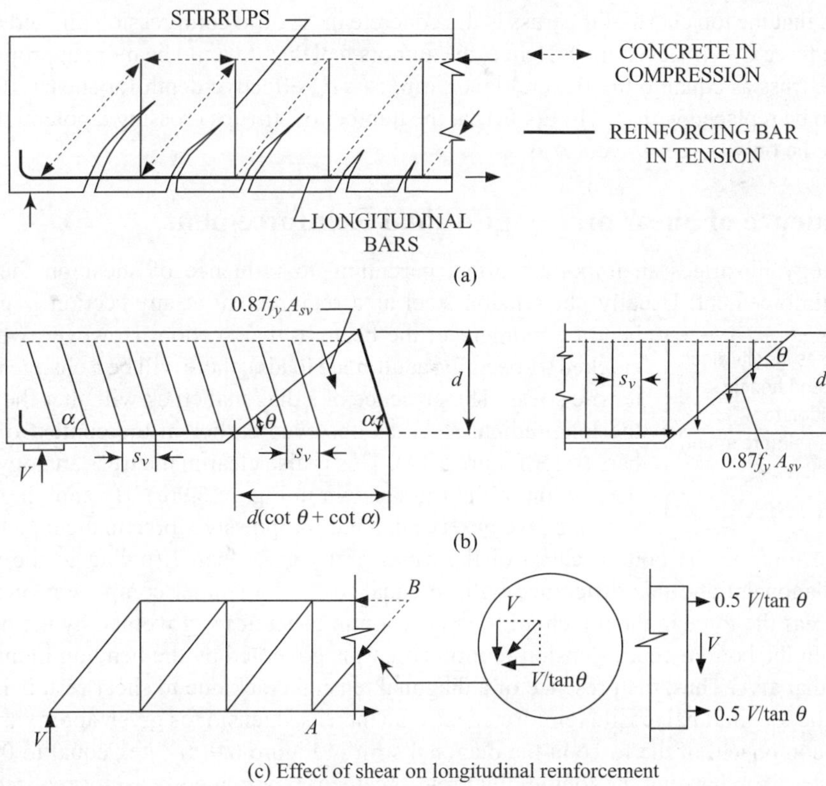

Fig. 6.9 Classical truss analogy for action of web reinforcement.

(assuming yielding at the ultimate limit state), then the total shear resistance of all the stirrups intercepting the crack is given by:

$$V_{us} = \text{(vertical component of tension per stirrup)} \times \text{(number of stirrups)}$$

$$\Rightarrow \quad V_{us} = (0.87\, f_y A_{sv} \sin \alpha) \times d(\cot \theta + \cot \alpha)/s_v \tag{6.18a}$$

Assuming, for convenience, that the crack is inclined at $\theta = 45^\circ$, the above relation simplifies to

$$V_{us} = 0.87\, f_y A_{sv}(d/s_v)(\sin \alpha + \cos \alpha) \tag{6.18b}$$

The case of 'vertical stirrups' may be considered as a special case with $\alpha = 90^\circ$. Hence, for vertical stirrups, the shear resistance V_{us} is obtained from Eq. 6.18b as

$$V_{us} = 0.87\, f_y A_{sv}\, d/s_v \tag{6.19}$$

The shear resistance of *bent-up bars* may also be obtained from Eq. 6.18 – when a series of single or parallel bent-up bars are provided at regular intervals in the manner of inclined stirrups. However, when a *single* bar or a single group of parallel bars are bent-up at the same location at an angle α, the vertical component of the total tension in these bars is given† by

$$V_{us} = 0.87\, f_y A_{sv} \sin \alpha \tag{6.20}$$

† It may be noted that Eq. 6.20 is applicable only in the limited region where the bar is bent up.

It may be noted that the top chord of the truss is the concrete in flexural compression aligned along the centre of compressive force $C = M/(\text{lever arm})$. Hence, the authors feel that it would be more appropriate to consider the depth of the truss as equal to the flexural lever arm, z (= d_v, effective depth for shear). If so, in Eqs 6.18 to 6.20, d has to be replaced with d_v. [In Eq. 6.18a, the number of stirrups crossing a potential diagonal crack will in any case be only $d_v (\cot\theta + \cot\alpha)/s_v$.]

6.7.5 Influence of Shear on Longitudinal Reinforcement

> **Shear force causes longitudinal tension as well, and hence requires, in addition to transverse shear reinforcement, longitudinal tension reinforcement.**

The truss analogy illustrates an important effect pertaining to influence of shear on the tension in the longitudinal reinforcement. Usually, the tension steel area requirement at any section is governed by the bending moment in the beam at that section. However, when the beam is cracked (especially, at ultimate loads), there will be a change in the calculated tensile stress. The presence of a diagonal crack will alter the tensile stress in the longitudinal steel, as observed earlier in the context of curtailment of bars (refer Figure 5.14). This is also clear in the truss analogy, as revealed by the section of the truss shown in Figure 6.9(c). By applying the 'method of sections', we observe that the compressive force in the top chord will be less than the tensile force in the bottom chord of the truss in any given panel (owing to the presence of the compression diagonals) and this difference will be equal to the horizontal component of the force in the diagonal. Whereas the force in the top chord (compression in concrete) is governed by the bending moment at A, the force in the bottom chord (tension reinforcement) is governed by the bending moment at B, which is higher than that at A. Thus, the presence of a diagonal tension crack due to shear results in an increase in the tension in the longitudinal tensile reinforcement. The increased tension is given approximately by half of the horizontal component of the force in the diagonal strut in Figure 6.9(c)†; i.e., equal to $0.5\ V/\tan\theta$. This influence of shear in enhancing the longitudinal reinforcement requirement was not realised till the 1950s. Even now, this is not directly reflected in the I.S. Code provisions as a specified additional amount of longitudinal reinforcement required for shear. (However, the compression field theory for shear design, discussed in Chapter 17, does account for this effect directly). Instead, it is accounted for indirectly by provisions for extension of flexural reinforcements (Cl. 26.2.3 – see also Sections 5.9.2 and 5.9.3). The Code (Cl. 26.2.3.1) requires that the flexural tension reinforcement be extended for a distance of d or 12ϕ, whichever is greater, beyond the location required for flexure alone. Here ϕ is the nominal diameter of the longitudinal bar concerned, and the provision is applicable for locations other than at the supports of simple spans and at the free ends of cantilevers with concentrated loads. This provision is equivalent to the outward shifting of the design moment diagram by a distance of d or 12ϕ (Figure 6.10a). At simple supports and at free ends of cantilevers, similar effect of shear on longitudinal reinforcement has to be accounted for somewhat differently, as explained below.

Anchorage of Longitudinal Reinforcements at End Supports

At simple supports and near free ends of cantilevers, the flexural tension reinforcement should be capable of resisting a tensile force of $V_f - 0.5\ V_s$ at the inside edge of the bearing area, where V_s is the factored shear resistance provided by the shear reinforcement in this location. This expression can be derived from

† The horizontal component of the force in the diagonal strut, equal to $V/\tan\theta$ is assumed to be balanced equally by forces in the top and bottom chords. This, incidentally, also implies that there will be a reduction in the longitudinal compression in the top chord, equal to $0.5\ V/\tan\theta$.

equilibrium considerations of the forces in the free body diagram of the support region, separated by a diagonal crack [Figure 6.10b]. Taking moments about A and neglecting small quantities of second order,

$$V_f z \approx Tz + V_s z/2$$

$$\Rightarrow \quad T = V_f - 0.5V_s \tag{6.21}$$

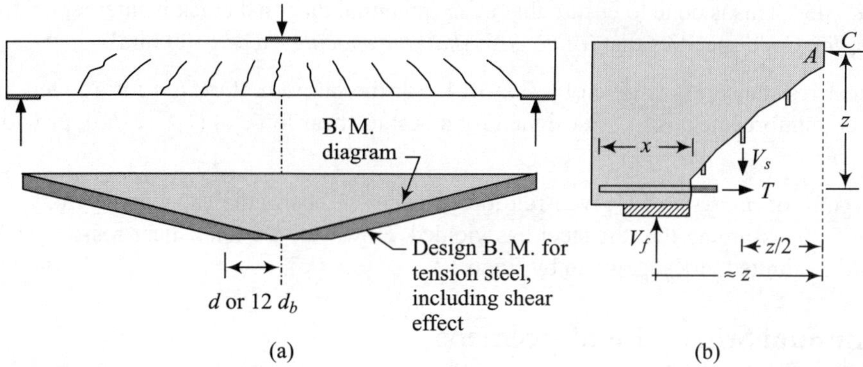

Fig. 6.10 Design bending moment for tension steel, including shear effect.

Thus, the embedment length available at the interior edge of the support should be adequate to develop a force of $T = V_f - 0.5V_s$ in the longitudinal reinforcements. If the actual straight embedment length available at the support, x, is less than the development length, L_d, the stress that can be developed in the bar at the critical section at the inside edge of the bearing area (Figure 6.10b) may be taken as:

$$f_s = 0.87 f_y (x/L_d)$$

and the bar force developed is

$$A_s f_s = A_s\, 0.87\, f_y (x/L_d) \geq T$$

Alternatively, the embedment length required to develop the required stress f_s in the bar (or the required force T in the bars) can be computed as:

$$x = \frac{f_s}{0.87\, f_y} L_d \geq \frac{T L_d}{A_s\, 0.87\, f_y}$$

If the straight length available is inadequate, sufficient anchorage should be provided with bends, hooks or mechanical devices.

The Code does not have any requirements to provide for the above, except Cl. 40.5.1 which requires that the bars be extended on either side of where it intersects the crack by a distance at least equal to the effective depth. However, this is coupled with the use of enhanced shear strength of sections close to supports. Where the enhanced strength is not taken advantage of, there is no requirement to check the anchorage requirement at support. The authors suggest that the anchorage requirement at simple end supports should be met, and furthermore, that providing an extension by an effective depth may not be adequate in all cases (see also Example 17.1 in Chapter 17).

Code Recommendations

Equations 6.18-6.20 are given in the Code under Cl. 40.4. Further, the Code limits the maximum value of f_y to 415 MPa, as higher strength reinforcement may be rendered brittle at the sharp bends of the web reinforcement; also, a shear compression failure could precede the yielding of the high strength steel.

The Code (Cl. 26.5.1.5) also limits the value of the spacing s_v to 0.75 d for 'vertical' stirrups and d for inclined stirrups with $\alpha = 45°$. This is done to ensure that every potential diagonal crack is intercepted by at least one stirrup. Further, the Code specifies that '*in no case shall the spacing exceed* 300 mm'.

The overall shear resistance V_{uR} is given by Eq. 6.14. For the purpose of *design* for a given factored shear force V_u, the web reinforcement is to be designed for a design shear force of ($V_u - \tau_c bd$), provided $\tau_v \leq \tau_{c,\max}$ (i.e., $V_u < V_{uR,\lim}$).

From the viewpoint of *analysis* of a given reinforced concrete beam, the capacity V_{us} may be determined from Eqs 6.18–6.20, assuming that the steel has yielded. However, the total shear resistance V_{uR}, given by Eq. 6.14, should be limited to $V_{uR,\lim}$ given by Eq. 6.17.

6.7.6 Minimum Stirrup Reinforcement

The Code (Cl. 26.5.1.6) specifies a minimum shear reinforcement to be provided in the form of stirrups in all beams where the calculated nominal shear stress $\tau_v \geq 0.5\tau_c$:

$$\frac{A_{sv}}{bs_v} \geq \frac{0.4}{0.87 f_y} \quad \text{when } \tau_v \geq 0.5\tau_c \tag{6.22}$$

$$\Rightarrow \qquad s_v < \frac{2.175 f_y A_{sv}}{b} \tag{6.23}$$

The minimum reinforcement controls the propagation of a diagonal crack and also alters the pattern of cracking before failure. If overloaded in shear, while regions without shear reinforcement can fail in shear upon the formation of the first diagonal crack, regions with minimum shear reinforcement will develop several wide diagonal cracks prior to failure.

The maximum spacing of stirrups should also comply with the requirements described earlier. For normal 'vertical' stirrups, the requirement is

$$s_v \leq \begin{cases} 0.75d \\ 300 \text{ mm} \end{cases} \quad \text{whichever is less} \tag{6.24}$$

The Code objective in recommending such minimum shear reinforcement is to prevent the sudden formation of an inclined crack in an unreinforced (or very lightly reinforced) web, possibly leading to an abrupt failure. Further, the provision of nominal web reinforcement restrains the growth of inclined shear cracks, improves the dowel action of the longitudinal tension bars, introduces ductility in shear and provides a warning of the impending failure.

6.8 Shear Design for Circular Sections

Beam-columns of circular section are commonly encountered in practice in the form of bridge piers, columns in buildings and foundation piles. Although IS 456: 2000 code is silent on the shear design of circular sections, a few international standards discuss them. Shear tests of members with circular sections have indicated that in the estimation of shear capacity, the effective area can be taken as the gross area of an equivalent rectangular section [Ref. 6.10]. The ACI 318-19 code [Ref. 6.7] recommends that the effective depth d of the equivalent rectangular section may be approximated as $0.8D$ and the width b as D (where D is the diameter of the solid circular section), in the estimation of shear strength of circular sections (see Figure 6.11). Accordingly, the following approximation may be adopted to evaluate V_{uc}.

$$V_{uc} = 0.8\ \tau_c D^2 \tag{6.25}$$

Studies have also indicated that circular ties/stirrups do not have the same effectiveness as that of a rectangular ties/stirrups and hence some modification in the shear contribution of the circular ties or spirals has been proposed [Ref. 6.11–6.12].

Applied Technology Council (ATC 32) [Ref. 6.13] recommends the following formula for the shear strength of circular ties, V_{us}:

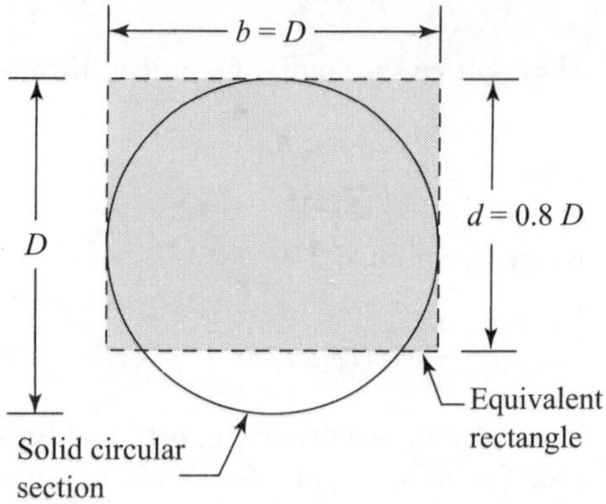

Fig. 6.11 Equivalent rectangular cross-sectional area for shear design.

$$V_{us} = \frac{\pi}{2}\frac{A_{sv1} f_{yd} D'}{s_v} \tag{6.26}$$

where A_{sv1} is the area of the tie, f_{yd} is the design yield stress of the reinforcing bar including the material safety factor, D' is the diameter of the tie and s_v is the spacing of the ties.

6.9 Additional Comments on Shear Reinforcement Design

- Consistent with the truss model, to be effective, transverse shear reinforcement must tie together the longitudinal tension reinforcement and the flexural compression zone of the member.
- *Bent-up bars* generally give lower shear strength and often result in wider cracks than stirrups. Major inclined cracks tend to occur at bend points. Their effectiveness is also sensitive to misplacement. Hence, unless there is a series of such bars bent up at relatively close spacings (as is possible in long-span bridge girders), there is not much economy resulting from considering their shear strength contribution. In normal situations, where there are only a few isolated bent-up bars scattered widely along the span, their shear strength contribution (not available at all sections) is ignored. Accordingly, the stirrups are designed to carry the full excess shear, given by:

$$V_{us} = (\tau_v - \tau_c)bd \tag{6.27}$$

- *Inclined stirrups* are most effective in reducing the width of the inclined cracks, and are desirable when full depth transverse cracks are likely (as in beams with high axial tension). However, such reinforcement may be rendered entirely ineffective if the direction of the shear force is reversed (as under seismic loads†).
- '*Vertical*' *stirrups* are the ones most commonly employed in practice. It should be noted that the use of closely spaced stirrups of smaller diameter gives better crack control than stirrups of larger

† Special provisions for shear reinforcement design, under earthquake loading, are covered in Chapter 16.

diameter placed relatively far apart. The diameter is usually 8 mm, 10 mm or 12 mm. Where heavy shear reinforcement is called for, multiple-legged stirrups should be employed (as often required in the beams of slab-beam footings).

- For *n*-legged stirrups of diameter ϕ_s

$$A_{sv} = n\pi\phi_s^2/4 \tag{6.28}$$

The required spacing s_v of 'vertical stirrups' for a selected diameter ϕ_s is given by applying Eq. 6.19, as:

$$s_v \leq \frac{0.87 f_y A_{sv}}{V_{us}/d} \tag{6.29}$$

where (from Eq. 6.27),

$$\frac{V_{us}}{d} = (\tau_v - \tau_c)b \tag{6.30}$$

It can also be seen from Eq. 6.19 and Eq. 6.28, that for a given arrangement of vertical stirrups (with specified n, ϕ_s, s_v), the shear resistance in terms of V_{us}/d is a constant (in N/mm units) given by

$$\frac{V_{us}}{d} = \frac{0.87 f_y A_{sv}}{s_v} \tag{6.31}$$

Accordingly, suitable design aids can be prepared expressing the above equation, as done in Table 62 of SP : 16 [Ref. 6.9] – to enable a quick design of vertical stirrups, for a specified V_{us}/d.

The stirrup bar diameter is usually kept the same for the entire span of the beam. Theoretically, the required spacing of stirrups will vary continuously along the length of the beam owing to the variation in the shear force V_u. However, stirrups are usually arranged with the spacing kept uniform over portions of the span – satisfying the requirements of shear strength [Eq. 6.29] and maximum spacing [Eqs 6.23, 6.24]. The first stirrup should be placed at not more than one-half spacing ($s_v/2$) from the face of the support†.

- A longitudinal bar (at least a 'hanger bar' of nominal diameter) must be located at every bend‡ in a stirrup. Stirrups must be anchored so as to develop its yield strength without any slip. The ends of the stirrup enclosing the longitudinal bars should satisfy *anchorage* requirements (discussed in Chapter 8).
- Although the Code does not call for shear reinforcement in portions of beams where $\tau_v < \tau_c/2$, it is good design practice to provide minimum (nominal) stirrups [Eq. 6.23] in this region – to improve ductility, give adequate warning of distress and to restrain inclined cracks in the event of accidental overloading.
- The factored shear force V_u to be considered for design at any section must take into account possible variations in the arrangement of live loads. The construction of *shear envelope* for this purpose is demonstrated in Examples 6.1 and 6.3.
- Termination of flexural reinforcement in the tension zone can lower the shear strength of beams (refer Section 5.9). Hence, such sections may also be critical and have to be checked for shear; if necessary, additional stirrups should be provided over a distance of 0.75*d* from the cut-off point to satisfy the Code requirement (Cl. 26.2.3.2). This is demonstrated in Examples 6.1 and 6.3.
- When reversal of stresses occurs, as in the case of earthquake loading or reversed wind direction, the shear strength of the (previously cracked) concrete cannot be relied upon. In such cases, the stirrups

† See Section 6.5 and Figure 6.7 regarding special case involving shear transfer.

‡ The stirrup is tied to this longitudinal bar using 'binding wire'.

should be designed to take the *entire shear*. Moreover, the stirrups should necessarily be in the form of closed loops placed perpendicular to the member axis. [The details of earthquake-resistant design for shear are described in Chapter 14.]

6.10 Interface Shear and Shear Friction

6.10.1 Shear-Friction

There are situations where shear has to be transferred across a defined plane of weakness, nearly parallel to the shear force and along which slip could occur (Figure 6.12). Examples are planes of existing or potential cracks, interface between dissimilar materials, interfaces between elements such as webs and flanges, and interface between concrete placed at different times. In such cases, possible failure involves sliding along the plane of weakness rather than diagonal tension. Therefore, it would be appropriate to consider shear resistance developed along such planes in the form of resistance to the tendency to slip. The *shear-friction* concept is a method to do this.

When two bodies are in contact with a normal reaction, R, across the surface of contact, the frictional resistance, F, acting tangential to this surface and resisting relative slip is known to be $F = \mu R$, where μ is the coefficient of friction (Figure 6.13a). Figure 6.13(b) shows an idealised cracked concrete specimen loaded in shear. In such a specimen, a clamping force between the two faces of the crack can be induced by providing reinforcement (shear-friction reinforcement, A_{vf}) perpendicular to the crack surface. Any slip between the two faces of the rough irregular crack causes the faces to ride upon each other, which opens up the crack (Figure 6.13c). This in turn induces tensile forces in the reinforcement, which ultimately yields (Figure 6.13d). The tension in the reinforcement is balanced by compressive force, R, in the concrete across the crack. If the area of reinforcement is A_{vf} and yield stress f_y, at ultimate, the clamping force between the two faces is $R = A_{vf}f_y$, and the frictional resistance is $\Sigma F = A_{vf}f_y\,\mu$.

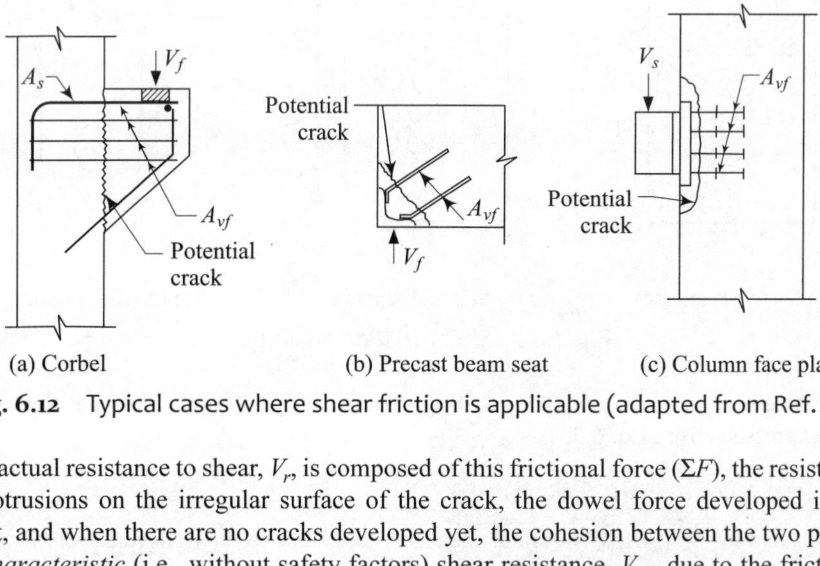

Fig. 6.12 Typical cases where shear friction is applicable (adapted from Ref. 6.10).

In reality, the actual resistance to shear, V_r, is composed of this frictional force (ΣF), the resistance to shearing off of the protrusions on the irregular surface of the crack, the dowel force developed in the transverse reinforcement, and when there are no cracks developed yet, the cohesion between the two parts as well. The *nominal* or *characteristic* (i.e., without safety factors) shear resistance, V_{sn}, due to the friction between the crack faces, is given by Eq. 6.32. Other less simple methods of calculation have been proposed (Ref. 6.11,

6.12) which result in predictions of shear transfer resistance in substantial agreement with comprehensive test results.

For shear-friction reinforcement placed perpendicular to the shear plane,

$$V_{sn} = A_{vf} f_y \mu \tag{6.32}$$

where, V_{sn} = nominal shear resistance due to the assumed friction part alone contributed by reinforcement stress

A_{vf} = area of shear-friction reinforcement, placed normal to the plane of possible slip

μ = coefficient of friction.

Shear-friction reinforcement may also be placed at an angle α_f to the shear plane, such that the shear force produces tension in the shear-friction reinforcement, as shown in Figures 6.14(a), (b) (i.e., $\alpha_f \leq 90°$). As the shear-friction reinforcement yields, the tensile force in the reinforcement is $A_{vf}f_y$, which has a component parallel to the shear plane of $A_{vf}f_y \cos\alpha_f$, and a component normal to the plane equal to $A_{vf}f_y \sin \alpha_f$. The latter produces the clamping force. The total force resisting shear is then obtained as $A_{vf}f_y \cos \alpha_f + \mu.A_{vf}f_y \sin \alpha_f$, and the nominal shear resistance is given by:

$$V_{sn} = A_{vf}f_y (\cos \alpha_f + \mu \sin \alpha_f) \tag{6.33}$$

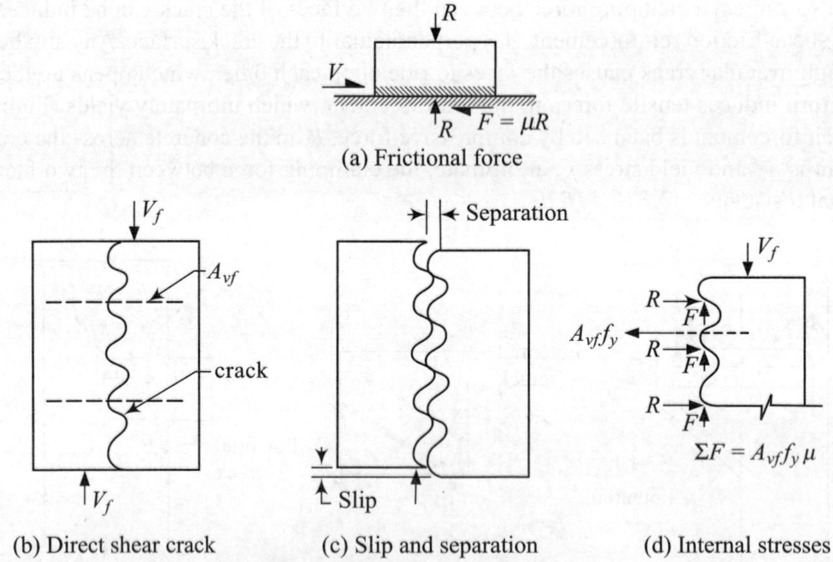

Fig. 6.13 Shear-friction analogy.

If the area of concrete section at the interface resisting shear transfer is A_{cv}, the nominal shear resistance per unit area can be expressed (from Eq. 6.33) as:

$$v_{sn} = \rho_v f_y \cos \alpha_f + \mu(\rho_v f_y \sin \alpha_f) \tag{6.33a}$$

where $\rho_v = A_{vf}/A_{cv}$, and $v_{sn} = V_{sn}/A_{cv}$ = nominal shear resistance due to the transverse reinforcement.

If there is a load, N, normal to the interface, this will either increase or decrease the effective normal pressure across the interface, and correspondingly affect the shear resistance associated with shear-friction, depending on whether it is compressive or tensile (Figure 6.14d). Taking N positive if compressive, the effective normal pressure R across the interface will then be:

$$R = A_{vf} f_y \sin \alpha_f + N$$

Reinforcement inclined at an angle $\alpha_f > 90°$ is ineffective in resisting interface shear, because, as relative slip between the two parts occurs and the reinforcement deforms, the effect is to separate the two parts farther rather than to introduce any clamping forces (Figure 6.14c). Hence reinforcement with $\alpha_f \leq 90°$ (i.e., placed such that shear force produces tension in the bar) only is effective as shear-friction reinforcement. [Indeed, this type of inclined bars will be more effective than bars perpendicular to the interface as tensile strains are initiated in the former sooner and more effectively than in the latter].

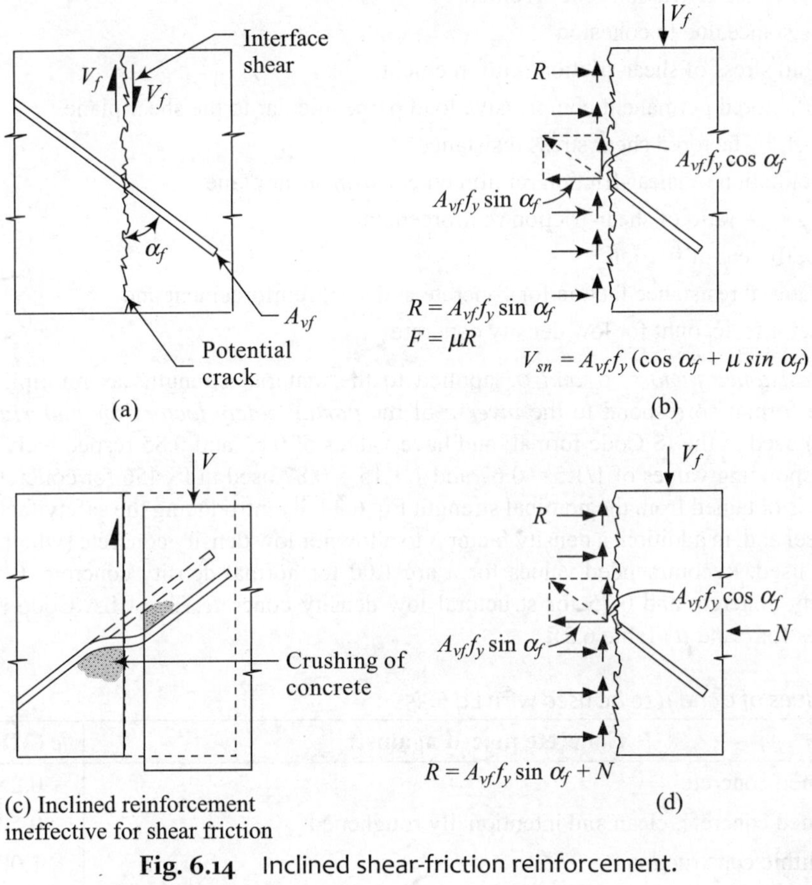

Fig. 6.14 Inclined shear-friction reinforcement.

If allowance is made for the shear strength contribution due to the cohesion between the two parts across the interface, the nominal shear resistance (for the general case of inclined shear-friction reinforcement and normal force N) can be obtained as:

$$v_{rn} = c + \mu(\rho_v f_y \sin \alpha_f + N/A_g) + \rho_v f_y \cos \alpha_f \tag{6.34}$$

where c = stress due to cohesion

N = load across shear plane (positive if compressive and negative if tensile)

6.10.2 Recommendation for Interface Shear Transfer

The Code IS 456: 2000 does not give any guidance related to shear friction concepts. The Canadian standard CSA A23.3 recommends the following formula for determining the factored interface shear resistance, v_r, based on the shear-friction concept:

$$v_r = \lambda\phi_c(c + \mu\sigma) + \phi_s\rho_v f_y \cos\alpha_f \quad (6.35)$$

where, $\sigma = \rho_v f_y \sin\alpha_f + N/A_g$ (6.36)

A_{cv} ≡ area of concrete section resisting shear

A_g ≡ gross area of section transferring N

A_{vf} ≡ area of shear-friction reinforcement

c ≡ resistance due to cohesion

f_y ≡ yield stress of shear-friction reinforcement

N ≡ unfactored permanent compressive load perpendicular to the shear plane

$v_r \equiv V_r/A_{cv}$ = factored shear stress resistance

α_f ≡ inclination of shear-friction reinforcement with shear plane

$\rho_v \equiv A_{vf}/A_{cv}$ = ratio of shear-friction reinforcement

μ ≡ coefficient of friction

ϕ_c, ϕ_s ≡ material resistance factors for concrete and steel reinforcement and

λ ≡ factor to account for low density concrete

The *material resistance factors*, ϕ_c *and* ϕ_s, applied to the material strengths as multipliers, used in the Canadian Code format correspond to the *inverse* of the *partial safety factors for materials* (see Sections 3.5.4 and 3.6.2) used in the IS Code format; and have values of 0.65 and 0.85 respectively. These compare well with corresponding values of 1/1.5 = 0.67 and 1/1.15 = 0.87 used in IS 456 for concrete and steel. The design Eq. 6.35 is obtained from the nominal strength Eq. 6.34, by introducing the safety factors ϕ_c and ϕ_s for concrete and steel and, in addition, a density factor λ to allow for low density concrete (which has lower shear strength) when used. Recommended values for λ are 1.00 for normal density concrete, 0.85 for structural semi-low density concrete and 0.75 for structural low-density concrete. The CSA Code recommends the following values for c and μ (Table 6.2):

Table 6.2 *Values of c and μ to be used with Eq 6.35*

Case	Concrete placed against:	c (MPa)	μ
1	Hardened concrete	0.25	0.60
2	Hardened concrete, clean and intentionally roughened	0.50	1.00
3	Monolithic construction	1.00	1.40
4	As-rolled structural steel and anchored by headed studs or reinforcing bars	0.00	0.60

An upper limit on the first term of Eq. 6.35, $\lambda\phi_c(c + \mu\sigma)$, is specified, equal to $0.25\phi_c f_c'$, to avoid failure of concrete by crushing (here f_c' is the cylinder strength of concrete).

Any direct tension, N_f, across the shear plane must be provided for by additional reinforcement having an area equal to $N_f/(\phi_s f_y)$. Such tensile forces may be caused by restraint of deformations due to temperature change, creep and shrinkage, etc. Although there is a beneficial effect of a permanently occurring net compressive force across the shear plane that reduces the amount of shear-friction reinforcement required, it is prudent to ignore this effect. When there is a bending moment acting on the shear plane, the flexural tensile and compressive forces balance each other, and the ultimate compressive force across the plane (which induces the frictional resistance) is equal to $A_s f_y$. Hence, the flexural reinforcement area, A_s, can be included in the area A_{vf} for computing V_r. When there is no bending moment acting on the shear plane, the shear-friction reinforcement is best distributed uniformly along the shear plane in order to minimise crack widths. When a bending moment also exists, most of the shear-friction reinforcement is placed closer to the tension face to provide the required effective depth. Since it is assumed that the shear-friction reinforcement yields at the ultimate strength, it must be anchored on both sides of the shear plane so as to develop the specified yield strength in tension.

Equation 6.35 can be adapted to the IS code format by introducing the corresponding partial safety factors. Thus introducing the factors given in Section 3.6.2, the interface shear resistance may be taken as:

$$v_r = 0.447(c + \mu\sigma) + 0.87\rho_v f_y \cos \alpha_f \tag{6.37}$$

where, $\sigma = \rho_v f_y \sin \alpha_f + N/A_g$

Values for c and μ given in Table 6.2 may be adopted. The corresponding upper limit on the first term of Eq. 6.37 will be $0.13 f_{ck}$.

6.11 Shear Connectors in Flexural Members

6.11.1 Shear along Horizontal Planes

The shear stress distribution in a homogeneous elastic beam was discussed in Section 6.2 and presented in Figure 6.1. Just as a vertical section is subjected to shear stresses as shown in Figure 6.1(b), every horizontal plane in the beam is also subjected to shear stresses, as shown in the top and bottom faces of the element depicted in Figure 6.1(c). At times, a beam is made up of two dissimilar materials, such as a rolled steel joist with a concrete compression flange as shown in Figure 6.15(a). Similarly, under special circumstances, a concrete beam may be cast in two steps (such as a precast part and a cast-in-situ part, or a slab cast over a prestressed concrete beam) with a horizontal layer forming the interface between the concrete cast at different times (Figure 6.15(b)). In such a situation, if the beam is to act as a single composite integral flexural member with the entire cross section acting integrally (rather than as two separate beams, one sitting on top of the other with a discontinuity along the plane of contact), provision has to be made to transmit the horizontal shear across the interface and prevent relative slippage between the parts above and below. In a composite beam such as shown in Figure 6.15(a), this is achieved by providing *shear connectors* in the form of studs, channel shapes, etc., welded on top of the steel beam as shown in Figure 6.15(c). In the case of beams with concrete-to-concrete interface, as in Figure 6.15(b), providing full depth stirrups together with the bond and friction along the interface can provide shear connection [Figure 6.15(d)].

Sometimes, attempts are made to strengthen a flexural member in distress by increasing the depth by casting another layer on top. Such a layer will not be effective unless positive and effective steps are taken to have shear transfer across the interface. Cleaning and chipping the surface of the older member, application of bonding materials, etc., will not be effective except for very small localised areas. The engineer should be wary of such dubious steps for the rehabilitation of distressed members.

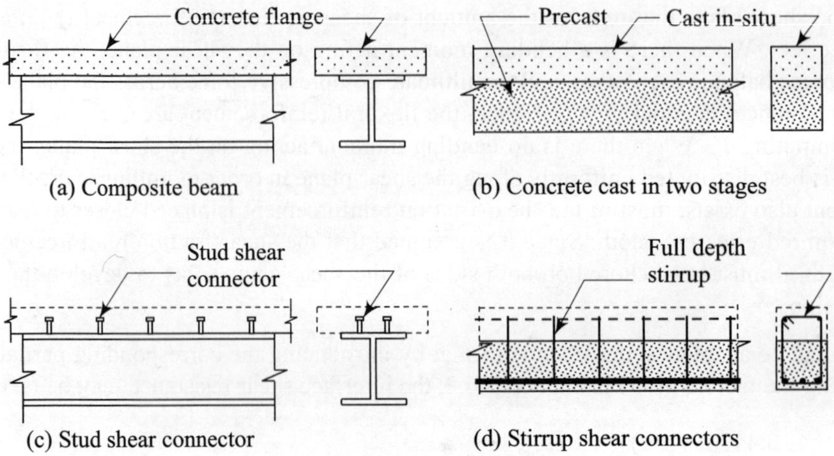

Fig. 6.15 Shear connectors.

6.12 Shear Design Examples – Conventional Method

Example 6.1

The simply supported beam in Example 5.1 (and Example 5.7) is provided with web reinforcement of 8 mm plain (Fe 250) bar U-stirrups at a uniform spacing of 200 mm, as shown in Figure 6.16(a). Check the adequacy of the shear design. If necessary, revise the design.

Solution

- ***Factored loads*** *[refer Example 5.1]*:
  Dead Load $w_{u,DL} = 1.5 \times 8.75 = 13.1$ kN/m
  Live Load $w_{u,LL} = 1.5 \times 10.0 = 15.0$ kN/m

- ***Factored shear force envelope***
  The placement of live load† giving the maximum shear force (V_u) at any section X on the left-half of the span is shown in Figure 6.16(b). (The dead load acts on the entire span). Although the resulting shape of the shear envelope is curvilinear, it is adequate and conservative to consider the shear force envelope to vary as a straight line between the maximum values computed for the support and for the midspan.

  At support, $V_u = (13.1 + 15.0) \times 6.0/2 = 84.3$ kN

  At midspan‡, $V_u = 0 + (15.0 \times 3.0)/4 = 11.25$ kN

  The factored shear force diagram is shown in Figure 6.16(c).

- ***Factored shear force at critical section near support***
  The critical section for shear is at a distance $d = 399$ mm from the face of support, i.e., $230/2 + 399 = 514$ mm from the centre of support [Figure 6.16(a)].

† This follows from the influence line diagram for shear force at the section X [refer any basic text on structural analysis].

‡ The live load is placed only on one-half of the span for maximum shear force at the midspan section [refer Figure 6.16(b)].

The factored shear force at this section is obtainable from the shear force envelope [Figure 6.16(c)]:

$$V_u = 11.25 + (84.3 - 11.25) \times \frac{3000 - 514}{3000} = 71.8 \text{ kN}$$

- ***Check adequacy of section***

Nominal shear stress $\tau_v = \dfrac{V_u}{bd} = \dfrac{71.8 \times 10^3}{250 \times 399} = 0.72$ MPa $< \tau_{c,max} = 3.1$ MPa (for M 25 concrete). Hence the size of the section is adequate.

- ***Design shear resistance at critical section***

At the critical section, A_{st} (due to 2 – 20 ϕ) = 314 × 2 = 628 mm^2

$$p_t = \frac{100 \times 628}{250 \times 399} = 0.63$$

⇒ Design shear strength of concrete (from Eq. 6.10 or Table 6.1, for M 25 grade):

$$\tau_c = 0.536 \text{ MPa} < \tau_v = 0.72 \text{ MPa}$$

⇒ $$V_{uc} = 0.536 \times 250 \times 399 = 53466 \text{ N} = 53.47 \text{ kN}$$

Shear resistance of 'vertical' stirrups (8ϕ @ 200 c/c, Fe 250 grade):

$$A_{sv} = 2 \times 50.3 = 100.6 \text{ mm}^2,\ s_v = 200 \text{ mm}$$

$$V_{us} = 0.87 f_y A_{sv}\, d/s_v$$

$$= 0.87 \times 250 \times 100.6 \times 399/200 = 43651 \text{ N}$$

$$= 43.65 \text{ kN}$$

∴ Total shear resistance at critical section:

$$V_{uR} = V_{uc} + V_{us} = 53.47 + 43.65 = 97.12 \text{ kN} > V_u = 71.8 \text{ kN}$$

Hence, the section is safe in shear.

- ***Check minimum stirrup requirements (maximum spacing)***

Eq. 6.22: $$(s_v)_{max} = 2.175 f_y A_{sv}/b$$

$$= 2.175 \times 250 \times 100.6/250$$

$$= 219 \text{ mm}$$

$$(s_v)_{provided} = 200 \text{ mm} < (s_v)_{max} \quad \Rightarrow \quad \text{OK}$$

Further, applying Eq. 6.24,

$$s_v \le \begin{cases} 0.75d = 0.75 \times 399 = 299 \text{ mm} \\ 300 \text{ mm} \end{cases}$$

which are evidently satisfied by s_v = 200 mm.

- ***Check shear strength at bar cut-off point***
  The cut-off point is located at 973 mm from centre of support [Figure 6.16(a)].

  Factored shear at cut-off point [from Figure 6.16(c)]:

$$V_u = 11.25 + (84.3 - 11.25) \times \frac{3000 - 973}{3000} = 60.61 \text{ kN}$$

  Shear resistance of the section $V_{uR} = 97.12$ kN

$$\frac{2}{3} \text{ shear resistance} = \frac{2}{3} \times 97.12 = 64.75 \text{ kN} > V_u = 60.61 \text{ kN}$$

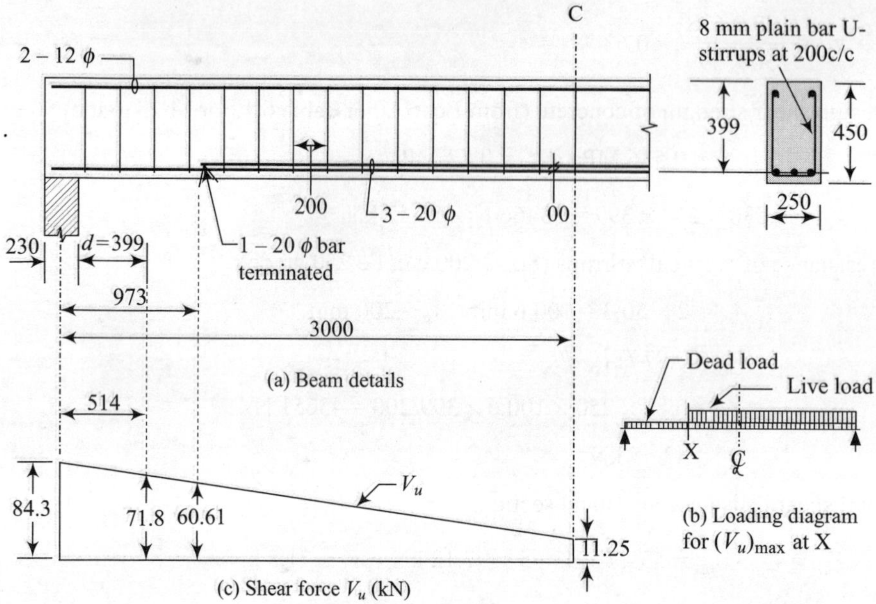

Fig. 6.16 Example 6.1.

As shear strength requirements (Cl. 26.2.3.2(a) of the Code, Section 5.9.3) are satisfied, no additional checks are required.

Example 6.2

Slabs, in general, do not require shear reinforcement, as the depth provided (based on deflection criteria) is usually adequate to meet shear strength requirements. Verify this in the case of the one-way slab of Example 5.2.

Solution

- *Given*: Slab thickness = 200 mm, Effective depth = 165 mm, f_{ck} = 25 MPa (from Example 5.2)
  A_{st} provided at support (10ϕ @ 300 c/c) = 262 mm^2/m

$$\Rightarrow \qquad p_t = \frac{100 \times 262}{1000 \times 165} = 0.16$$

Factored load (DL + LL) $w_u = 15$ kN/m^2

simply supported span $l = 4.165$ m

- It is convenient to prove that the section has adequate shear strength at the support itself, which has the maximum factored shear, rather than at d from the face of support:

  $V_u = 15 \times 4.165/2 = 31.24$ kN/m

  Nominal shear stress $\tau_v = \dfrac{V_u}{bd} = \dfrac{31.24 \times 10^3}{10^3 \times 165} = 0.189$ MPa

  Design shear strength (from Eq. 6.10): for M 25 concrete and $p_t = 0.16$,

  $\tau_c = 0.3$ MPa

  This value may further be enhanced by a multiplying factor

  $k = 1.6 - 0.002 \times 200 = 1.2$ [Eq. 6.11]

  $\Rightarrow \qquad k\tau_c = 1.2 \times 0.3 = 0.36$ MPa

  $>> \tau_v = 0.189$ MPa

- As the section is safe at the support section itself (where shear is maximum), there is no need to confirm this at the 'critical' section located d away from the face of support.

Example 6.3

Design the shear reinforcement for the beam in Example 5.4. Assume the curtailment of longitudinal bars as shown in Figure 6.17(a). Assume Fe 415 grade steel for the shear reinforcement.

Solution

- ***Factored loads*** [refer Example 5.4]:

  Dead Load $w_{u,DL} = 7.5$ kN/m $\times$ 1.5 = 11.25 kN/m

  Additional DL $W_{u,DL}$: 30 × 1.5 = 45.0 kN concentrated at midspan

  Live Load $w_{u,LL} = 10$ kN/m $\times$ 1.5 = 15.0 kN/m

- ***Factored shear force envelope***

  As explained in the Example 6.1 it is adequate and conservative to consider the shear force envelope to vary as a straight line between the maximum values computed at the support and at the midspan.

  At support, $V_u = (11.25 + 15.0) \times 6.0/2 + 45.0/2 = 101.25$ kN

  At midspan, $V_u = 45.0/2 + (15.0 \times 3.0)/4 = 33.75$ kN

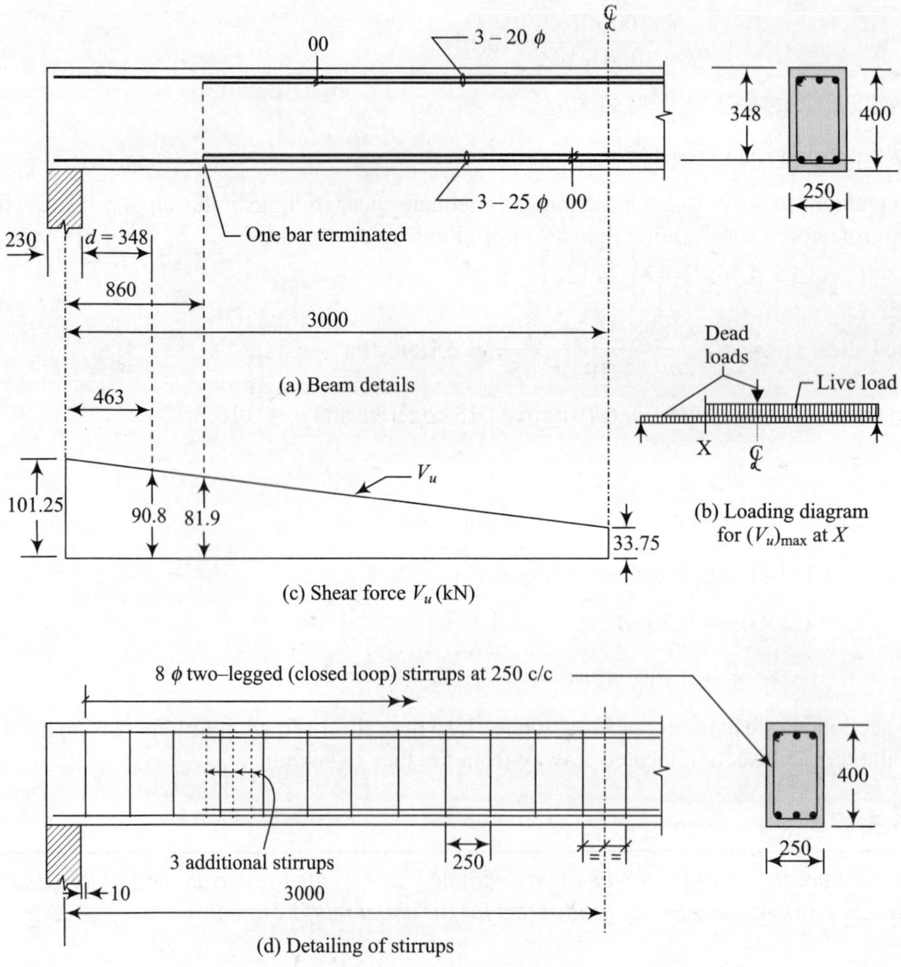

Fig. 6.17 Example 6.3.

- ***Factored shear force at critical section***

The critical section is $d = 348$ mm from the face of support, i.e.,

230/2+348 = 463 mm from the centre of support [Figure 6.17(a)].

$$V_u = 33.75 + (101.25 - 33.75) \times \frac{3000 - 463}{3000} = 90.8 \text{ kN}$$

- ***Check adequacy of section size***

Nominal shear stress $\dfrac{90.8 \times 10^3}{250 \times 348} = 1.044$ MPa

which is less than $\tau_{c,max} = 3.1$ MPa (for M 25 concrete)

Hence, the size of the section is adequate.

- ***Design shear strength of concrete***
  At the critical section, A_{st} (due to 2–25 ϕ) = 491 × 2 = 982 mm^2

$$\Rightarrow \qquad p_t = \frac{100 \times 982}{250 \times 348} = 1.129$$

$\Rightarrow$ Design shear strength of concrete (from Eq. 6.10 or Table 6.1, for M 25 concrete).
$\tau_c = 0.670$ MPa $< \tau_v = 1.044$ MPa

- ***Design of 'vertical' stirrups***
  Shear to be resisted by stirrups $V_{us} = (\tau_v - \tau_c)bd$

$$\Rightarrow \qquad \frac{V_{us}}{d} = (1.044 - 0.670) \times 250 = 93.50 \text{ N/mm}$$

Assuming 2-legged closed stirrups of 8 mm dia,

$$A_{sv} = 2 \times 50.3 = 100.6 \text{ mm}^2$$

$$\Rightarrow \qquad \text{required spacing } s_v \le \frac{0.87 f_y A_{sv}}{V_{us}/d} = \frac{0.87 \times 415 \times 100.6}{93.5} = 388 \text{ mm}$$

Code requirements for maximum spacing:

$$s_v = \begin{cases} 2.175 f_y A_{sv}/b = 2.175 \times 415 \times 100.6/250 = 363 \text{ mm} \\ 0.75d = 0.75 \times 348 = 261 \text{ mm} \\ 300 \text{ mm} \end{cases}$$

Provide 8ϕ two-legged closed stirrups at 250 mm c/c spacing.

[*Note*: The stirrups should be *closed* as the section is doubly reinforced].

- *Check shear strength at bar cut-off point*
  The cut-off point is located at 860 mm from the centre of support [Figure 6.17(a)]. The factored shear force at this section [Figure 6.17(b)] is given by:

$$V_u = 33.75 + (101.25 - 33.75) \times \frac{(3000 - 860)}{3000} = 81.9 \text{ kN}$$

$$\text{Shear resistance } \; V_{uR} = \tau_c bd + \frac{0.87 f_y A_{sv} d}{s_v}$$

$$= (0.670 \times 250 \times 348) + (0.87 \times 415 \times 100.6 \times 348)/250$$

$$= 108850 \text{ N} = 109 \text{ kN}$$

$$\frac{2}{3} \text{ shear resistance} = \frac{2}{3} \times 109 = 72.7 \text{ kN} < 81.9 \text{ kN}$$

Hence, additional stirrups must be provided over a distance of $0.75d = 261$ mm ('along the terminated bar') with a spacing $< d/8\beta_b = 348 / (8 \times 1/3) = 130$ mm [Cl. 26.2.3.2(b) of the Code].

This is achieved by adding three additional stirrups along the last portion of the cut-off bar, as shown in Figure 6.17(d).

⇒ spacing = 250/3 = 83.3 mm which is less than 130 mm

$$\text{Excess stirrup area required} = \frac{0.4bs_v}{f_y} = \frac{0.4 \times 250 \times 83.3}{415} = 20.1 \text{ mm}^2.$$

Although it suffices to provide 6 mm ϕ additional 2-legged stirrups (A_{sv} = 56.6 mm^2), from a practical viewpoint, it is convenient to use the same 8 mm ϕ (A_{sv} = 100.6 mm^2) for the additional stirrups.

REVIEW QUESTIONS

6.1 Under what conditions is the traditional method of shear design inappropriate?

6.2 Under what situations do the following modes of cracking occur in reinforced concrete beams: (a) *flexural* cracks, (b) *diagonal tension* cracks, (c) *flexural-shear* cracks and (d) *splitting* cracks?

6.3 Describe the force components that participate in the shear transfer mechanism at a flexural-shear crack location in a reinforced concrete beam.

6.4 Illustrate how the *shear span* influences the mode of shear failure.

6.5 Describe how the computation of *nominal shear stress* for beams with variable depth different from that for prismatic beams.

6.6 Generally, the *critical section* for shear in a reinforced concrete beam is located at a distance d (effective depth) away from the face of the support. Why? Under what circumstances is this not permitted?

6.7 Describe why is the design shear strength of concrete (τ_c) related to the percentage tension steel p_t?

6.8 Reinforced concrete slabs are generally safe in shear and do not require shear reinforcement. Why?

6.9 Explain how does the presence of an axial force (tension or compression) influences the shear strength of concrete.

6.10 Stirrups may be *open* or *closed*. When does it become mandatory to use *closed* stirrups?

6.11 Stirrups may be 'vertical' or inclined. When does it become mandatory to use vertical stirrups?

6.12 The shear resistance of bent-up bars cannot be counted upon, unless stirrups are also provided. Why?

6.13 Why is an upper limit $\tau_{c,\,max}$ imposed on the shear strength of a reinforced concrete beam with shear reinforcement?

6.14 Explain the action of a reinforced concrete beam (with shear reinforcement) with the aid of the *truss analogy* model.

6.15 The provision of a *minimum* stirrup reinforcement is mandatory in all reinforced concrete beams. Why?

6.16 The site of curtailment of tension reinforcement in a reinforced concrete beam is considered a critical section for shear. Why?

6.17 In the traditional method of design for shear, how is the influence of shear on longitudinal reinforcement requirement taken care of?

6.18 What are shear connectors? Where are they needed? What are the different types used?

6.19 Explain the concept of interface shear and shear friction theory? Where are these relevant?

6.20 Relate interface shear and shear connectors.

6.21 In the design for shear of RC beams, the Code suggests checks for the allowable shear strength of concrete (τ_c) as well as the maximum permissible shear stress ($\tau_{c\,max}$). The check for $\tau_{c\,max}$ is to take care of: (A) Additional shear stress due to accidental loading; (B) Possibility of failure of concrete by diagonal tension; (C) Possibility of failure of concrete by diagonal compression; (D) Ensuring the yielding of shear reinforcement.

6.22 As per IS: 456- 2000, the maximum allowable shear stress ($\tau_{c\,max}$) in a reinforced concrete beam depends on: (A) grade of concrete only; (B) grade of steel only; (C) grade of concrete and grade of steel; (D) grade of concrete and percentage of steel.

6.23 An RC beam of rectangular section has a width of 250 mm and effective depth of 350 mm, and is subjected to a factored shear force of 200 kN. Assume that τ_c = 0.62 N/mm^2, $\tau_{c,max}$ =2.8 N/mm^2 and two-legged stirrups with 10ϕ bars of Fe250 grade steel are to be used. The required stirrup spacing is ______.

PROBLEMS

6.1 A simply supported beam of 6-m span (c/c), (shown in Figure 6.18), is to carry a uniform dead load of 20 kN/m (including beam weight) and a uniform live load of 30 kNm. The width of the supporting wall is 230 mm. Assume M 25 concrete and Fe 415 steel for shear reinforcement.

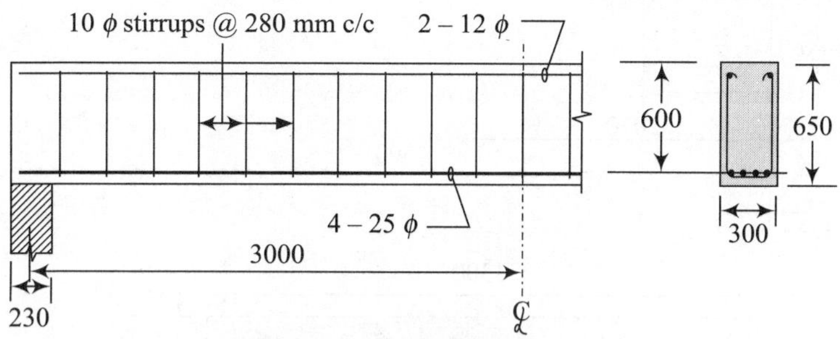

Fig. 6.18 Problem 6.1.

(a) Determine the adequacy of the 10 mm ϕ U-stirrups as shear reinforcement.

[*Ans.* adequate]

(b) If the shear reinforcement is to be provided in the form of 10ϕ stirrups inclined at 60° to the beam axis, determine the required spacing.

[*Ans.* 450 mm]

(c) If two of the tension reinforcement bars are terminated at 300 mm from the centre of the support, check the adequacy of shear strength at the bar cut-off point.

[*Ans.* inadequate]

6.2 A simply supported T-beam of 9 m span (c/c) is subjected to a dead load (including self-weight) of 20 kN/m and a live load of 25 kN/m. Details of the section and bar cut-offs are shown in Figure 6.19. Design and detail the shear reinforcement using 'vertical' stirrups. Assume M 25 concrete and Fe 415 steel for shear reinforcement.

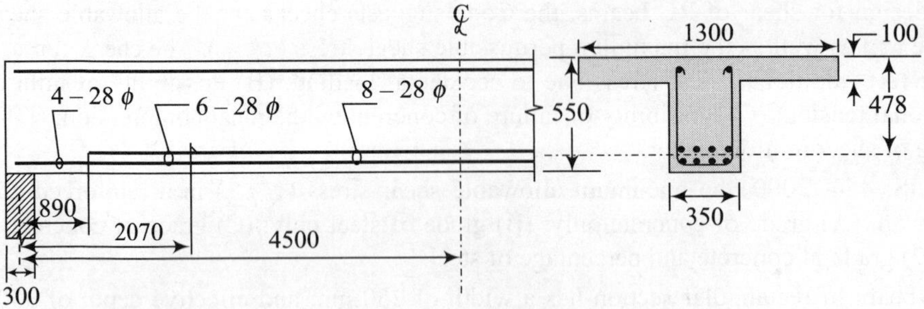

Fig. 6.19 Problem 6.2.

6.3 A simply supported beam (shown in Figure 6.20) is subjected to a dead load (including self-weight) of 20 kN/m and a live load of 20 kN/m. Design and detail the shear reinforcement using vertical stirrups. Use M 25 concrete and Fe 415 steel for shear reinforcement.

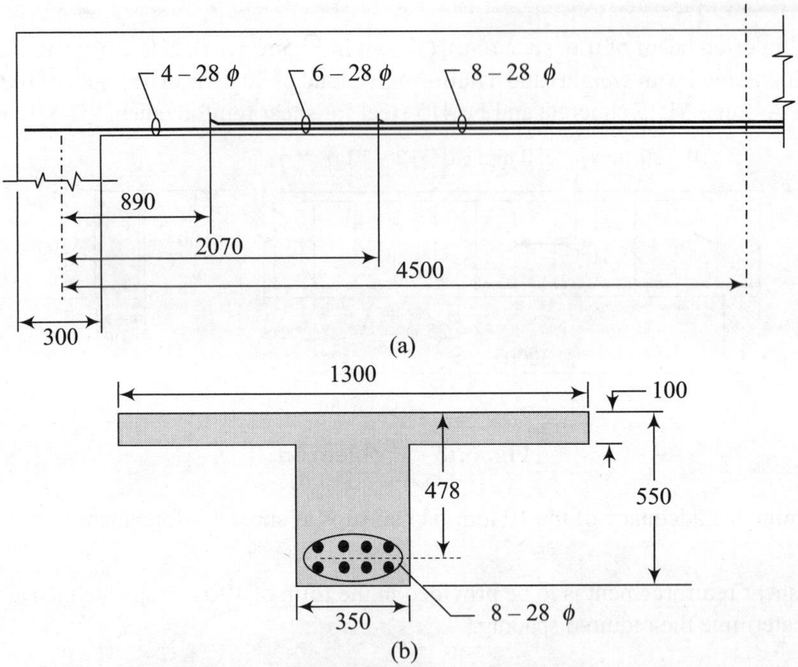

Fig. 6.20 Problem 6.3.

6.4 Figure 6.21 shows a uniformly loaded cantilever beam with the depth linearly tapered along the span. The dead load, including self-weight of the beam is 20 kN/m and the live load is 50 kN/m. Design the shear reinforcement using vertical stirrups. The bar cut-off details are as shown. Assume M 25 concrete and Fe 415 steel for shear reinforcement.

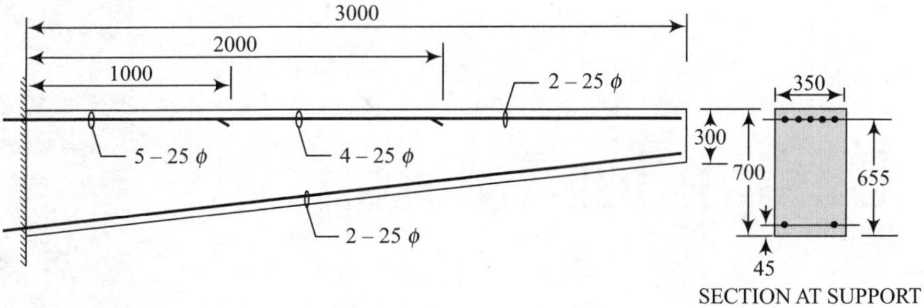

Fig. 6.21 Problem 6.4.

REFERENCES

6.1 Popov, E P, *Mechanics of Materials*, Second edition, Prentice Hall Inc., Englewood Cliffs, New Jersey, 1978

6.2 ASCE–ACI Committee 426, *The Shear Strength of Reinforced Concrete Members*, ASCE Journal, Struct. Div., Vol. 99, June 1973, pp 1091–1187

6.3 Bresler, B and MacGregor, J G, *Review of Concrete Beams Failing in Shear*, ASCE Journal, Struct. Div., Vol. 93, Feb. 1967, pp 343–372

6.4 ACI–ASCE Committee 326 Report, *Shear and Diagonal Tension*, Journal ACI, Vol. 59, Jan., Feb., and Mar., 1962, pp 1–30, 277–334 and 352–396

6.5 — *Explanatory Handbook on Indian Standard Code of Practice for Plain and Reinforced Concrete (IS 456:1978)*, Special Publication SP:24, Bureau of Indian Standards, New Delhi, 1983

6.6 Rangan, B V, *Diagonal Cracking Strengths in Shear of Reinforced Concrete Beams*, Civil Engg. Transactions, Instn of Engineers, Australia, Vol CE 14, No. 1, 1972

6.7 — *Building Code Requirements for Reinforced Concrete*, ACI Standard 318–19, Am. Conc. Inst., Detroit, Michigan, USA, 2019.

6.8 CSA Standard A23.3 – 94 — *Design of Concrete Structures*, Canadian Standards Association, Rexdale, Ontario, Canada, 1994

6.9 — *Design Aids (for Reinforced Concrete) to IS 456 : 1978*, Special Publication SP:16, Bureau of Indian Standards, New Delhi, 1980

6.10 Khalifa, J U, and Collins, M P, *Circular Reinforced Concrete Members subjected to Shear*, Publications No. 81-08, Dept of Civil Engineering, University of Toronto, Dec. 1981

6.11 Ghee, A B, *Seismic shear strength of circular bridge piers*, PhD Thesis, University of Canterbury, 1985

6.12 Balakrishnan, B, Hussain, S, Menon, D, *Assessment of shear strength of circular reinforced concrete beams*, ACI Structural Journal, 2016 Nov 1; 113(6)

6.13 Applied Technology Council. "ATC-32, improved seismic design criteria for California bridges, provisional recommendations." (1996)

6.14 *Commentary on Building Code Requirements for Structural Concrete* (ACI 318R-95), American Concrete Institute, Detroit, Michigan, 1995

6.15 Mattock, A H, *Shear Transfer in Concrete Having Reinforcement at an Angle to the Shear Plane, Shear in Reinforced Concrete*, SP-42, American Concrete Institute, Detroit, 1974, pp. 17–42

6.16 Mattock, A H, Li, W K, Wang, T C, *Shear Transfer in Lightweight Reinforced Concrete*, J. PCI, Vol. 21, No. 1, Jan.-Feb. 1976, pp. 20–39

CHAPTER

7

Design for Torsion

LEARNING OBJECTIVES

After studying this chapter, you will be able to:

- *Describe the behaviour of plain and reinforced concrete members subjected to torsion*
- *Discuss the theories and models for computing torsional strength of reinforced concrete members*
- *Design torsion reinforcement*

7.1 Introduction

Torsion when encountered in reinforced concrete members, usually occurs in combination† with flexure and transverse shear. Torsion in its 'pure' form (generally associated with metal shafts) is rarely encountered in reinforced concrete.

The interactive behaviour of torsion with bending moment and flexural shear in reinforced concrete beams is fairly complex, owing to the non-homogeneous, nonlinear and composite nature of the material and the presence of cracks. For convenience in design, codes prescribe highly simplified design procedures, which reflect a judicious blend of theoretical considerations and experimental results.

These design procedures and their bases are described in this chapter, following a brief review of the general behaviour of reinforced concrete beams under torsion.

7.2 Primary Torsion and Secondary Torsion

Torsion may be induced in a reinforced concrete member in various ways during the process of load transfer in a structural system. In reinforced concrete design, the terms 'primary torsion' and 'secondary torsion' are commonly used to refer to two different torsion-inducing situations.

† In some (relatively rare) situations, axial force (tension or compression) may also be involved.

In 'primary torsion' (also known as 'equilibrium torsion'), the torsion is induced by an eccentric loading (with respect to the shear centre at any cross-section), and equilibrium conditions† alone suffice in determining the twisting moments. In 'secondary torsion' (also known as 'compatibility torsion'), the torsion is induced by the need for the member to undergo an angle of twist to maintain deformation compatibility, and the resulting twisting moment depends on the torsional stiffness of the member.

There are some situations (such as circular beams supported on multiple columns) where both *primary torsion* and *secondary torsion* coexist.

7.2.1 Primary (or Equilibrium) Torsion

This is associated with twisting moments that are developed in a structural member to maintain static equilibrium with the external loads directly applied on the member, and are independent of the torsional stiffness of the member. In general, primary torsion is statically determinate. Such torsion must be necessarily considered in design (Code Cl. 41.1). The magnitude of the twisting moment does not depend on the torsional stiffness of the member, and is entirely determinable from statics alone. The member has to be designed for the full torsion, which is transmitted by the member to the supports. Moreover, the end(s) of the member should be suitably restrained to enable the member to resist effectively the torsion induced. Typically, *primary torsion* is induced in beams supporting lateral overhanging projections, and is caused by the eccentricity in the loading [Figure 7.1]. Such torsion is also induced in beams curved in plan and subjected to gravity loads, and in beams where the transverse loads are eccentric with respect to the *shear centre* of the cross-section.

'Primary torsion' is the torsion developed in a member due to transverse loading applied eccentric with respect to the shear centre of the cross section, and which can be calculated by applying equations of static equilibrium. The magnitude of primary torsion is independent of the torsional stiffness of the member.

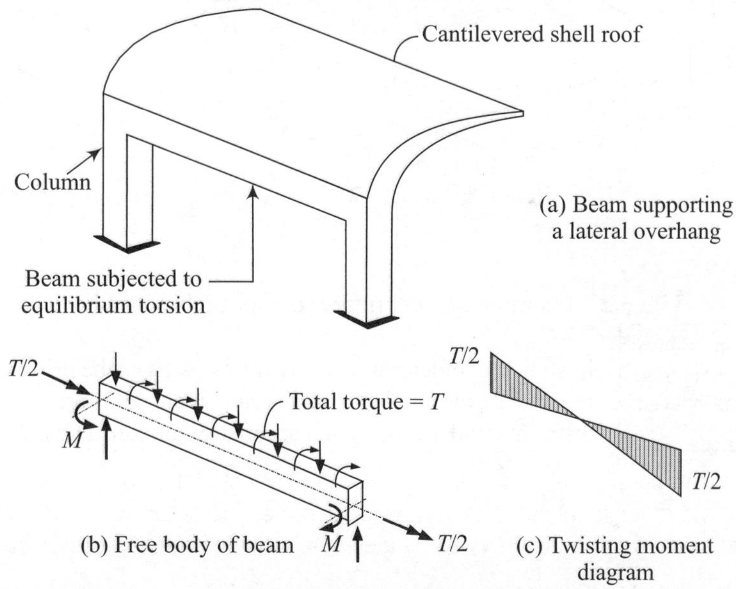

Fig. 7.1 Example of 'primary (equilibrium) torsion'.

† It must be clearly understood that this is merely a matter of terminology, and that it does not imply, for instance, equilibrium conditions need not be satisfied in cases of 'secondary (compatibility) torsion' or vice-versa!

7.2.2 Secondary (or Compatibility) Torsion

'Secondary torsion' is the torsion induced in a member subjected to a twist (angular), as a result of having to maintain deformation compatibility at junctions with connected members. The magnitude of induced secondary torsion is dependent on the torsional stiffness of the member.

This is the name given to the type of torsion induced in a structural member, as a secondary effect, by rotations (twists) applied at one or more points along the length of the member through interconnected members, rather than by directly applied loads on it. The twisting moments induced are directly dependent on the torsional stiffness of the member. These moments are generally statically indeterminate and their analysis necessarily involves (rotational) compatibility conditions; hence the term 'compatibility torsion' is also used. For example, in the floor beam system shown in Figure 7.2, the flexure of the secondary beam *BD* results in a *rotation* θ_B at the end *B*. As the primary (spandrel) beam *ABC* is monolithically connected with the secondary beam *BD* at the joint *B*, deformation *compatibility* at *B* implies an *angle of twist*, equal to θ_B, in the spandrel beam *ABC* at *B*. Corresponding to the angle θ_B, a twisting moment will develop at *B* in beam *ABC*, and a bending moment will develop at the end *B* of beam *BD*. The bending moment will be equal to, and will act in a direction opposite to the twisting moment, in order to satisfy static equilibrium. The magnitude of θ_B and the twisting/bending moment at *B* depends on the torsional stiffness of beam *ABC* and the flexural stiffness of beam *BD*. Secondary torsion is, in general, statically indeterminate.

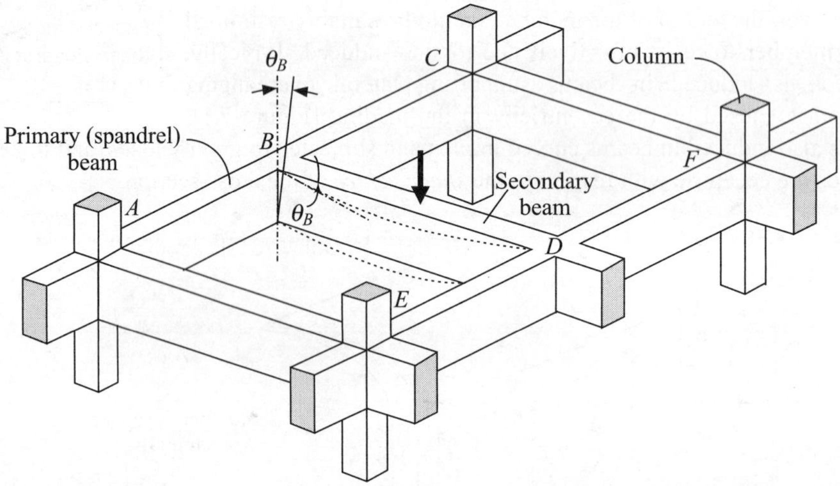

Fig. 7.2 Example of 'secondary (compatibility) torsion'.

With secondary torsion, release of the torsional restraint of the member eliminates the induced torsion.

In statically indeterminate structures (such as the grid floor system shown in Figure 7.2), the torsional restraints are 'redundant', and releasing such redundant restraints will eliminate the secondary torsion. Thus, the Code states:

'...where torsion can be eliminated by releasing redundant restraints, no specific design for torsion is necessary, provided torsional stiffness is neglected in the calculation of internal forces. Adequate control of any torsional cracking is provided by the shear reinforcement as per Cl. 40' [Cl. 41.1 of the Code].

Torsion results in diagonal tensile stresses in concrete and hence cracking. The torsional stiffness of a reinforced concrete member is drastically reduced by torsional cracking. This results in a very large increase in the angle of twist (formation of a 'torsional hinge'), and, in the case of 'secondary torsion', a significant reduction in the induced twisting moment.

With reference to Figure 7.2, application of Code Cl. 41.1 implies, in theory (although this is seldom done), providing a hinge-like connection (i.e., with no rotational restraint) at the end *B* (and *D*) of the beam *BD*; i.e., making *BD* a simply supported beam, and analysing it independent of *ABC*. In practice, Cl. 41.1 is applied by making the assumption that the torsional stiffness of beam *ABC* can be neglected (giving due recognition to the drastically reduced torsional stiffness after torsional cracking), with the result that beam *BD* becomes flexurally unrestrained at both ends. In this case, the grid system is analysed as a whole, but the value of the torsional stiffness of the member *ABC* (and *EDF*) is taken as zero† in the structural analysis for calculation of internal forces. Incidentally, this assumption helps in reducing the degree of static indeterminacy of the structure (typically, a grid floor), thereby simplifying the problem of structural analysis.

Of course, this simplification implies the acceptance of cracking and increased deformations (twist) in the torsional member. It also means that, despite the assumption of zero torsional stiffness, during the first time loading, a twisting moment up to the *cracking torque* of the plain concrete section can develop in the member, prior to torsional cracking. Hence, even with zero stiffness assumption, in order to control the cracking and to impart ductility to the member, it is necessary to provide a minimum torsional reinforcement, equal to that required to resist the 'cracking torque'. In fact, one of the intentions of the minimum stirrup reinforcement specified by the Code (Cl. 26.5.1.6) is to ensure some degree of control of torsional cracking of beams due to secondary torsion.

> The cracking torque of a RC member is the torque at which diagonal tensile cracks develop; it is very nearly equal (and taken as equal) to the ultimate torsional strength of a plain concrete member of the same cross section.

If, however, the designer chooses to consider 'secondary torsion' in analysis and design, then it is important that a realistic estimate of torsional stiffness is made for the purpose of structural analysis, and the required torsional reinforcement should be provided for the calculated twisting moment.

7.2.3 Estimation of Torsional Stiffness

Observed behaviour of reinforced concrete members under torsion [see also Section 7.3] shows that the torsional stiffness is little influenced by the amount of torsional reinforcement in the (nearly) linear elastic phase, and may be taken as that of the plain concrete section. However, once torsional cracking occurs, there is a drastic reduction in the torsional stiffness. The post-cracking torsional stiffness is only a small fraction (less than 10 per cent) of the pre-cracking stiffness, and depends on the amount of torsional reinforcement, provided in the form of closed stirrups and longitudinal bars. Heavy torsional reinforcement can, no doubt, increase the torsional resistance (strength) to a large extent, but this can be realised only at very large angles of twist (accompanied by heavy cracking).

> Hence, even with torsional reinforcement provided, in most practical situations, the maximum twisting moment developed in a reinforced concrete member under secondary torsion is the value corresponding to the torsional cracking of the member. This 'cracking torque' is very nearly the same as the failure strength obtained for an identical *plain concrete* section.

In the usual linear elastic analysis of framed structures, the *torsional stiffness* K_t (torque per unit twist T/θ) of a beam of length l is expressed as

† For greater accuracy, this value may be treated as 10 per cent of the uncracked torsional stiffness. The analysis of this indeterminate system will result in some flexural moment at end *B* in beam *BD* and twisting moments in beam *ABC*, which should be designed for.

$$K_t = \frac{GC}{l} \tag{7.1}$$

where *GC* is the *torsional rigidity*, obtained as the product of the *shear modulus G* and the geometrical parameter† *C* of the section [Ref. 7.1]. It is recommended in the Explanatory Handbook to the Code [Ref. 7.2] that *G* may be taken as 0.4 times the modulus of elasticity of concrete E_c (given by Eq. 2.4) and *C* may be taken as 0.5*K*, where *K* is the appropriate 'St. Venant torsional constant' calculated for the plain concrete section. For a rectangular section of size $b \times D$, with $b < D$,

$$K = \beta b^3 D \tag{7.2}$$

where β is a constant which depends on the *D*/*b* ratio, having values varying from 0.141 to 0.333 [Ref. 7.1]. Alternatively, the following formula [Ref. 7.1] may be used:

$$\beta = \left(1 - 0.63\frac{b}{D}\right)\Big/3 \tag{7.3}$$

For sections composed of rectangular elements (T-, L-, channel sections), the value of *K* (and hence, *C* and K_t) may be computed by summing up the individual values for each of the component rectangles, the splitting into component rectangles being so done as to maximise *K*.

7.3 General Behaviour in Torsion

7.3.1 Behaviour of Plain Concrete

The theory of torsion (St. Venant torsion) of prismatic, homogeneous members with linear elastic material having circular, non-circular and thin-walled cross-sections is described in detail in books on mechanics of materials [Ref. 7.1, 7.3]. It is seen that torsion induces shear stresses and causes warping of non-circular sections. For rectangular sections under elastic behaviour, the distribution of torsional shear stress over the cross-section is as shown in Figure 7.3.

The maximum torsional shear stress occurs at the middle of the wider face, and has a value given by

$$\tau_{t,\max} = \frac{T}{\alpha b^2 D} \tag{7.4}$$

where *T* is the twisting moment (torque), *b* and *D* are the cross-sectional dimensions (*b* being smaller), and α is a constant whose value depends on the *D*/*b* ratio; α varies from 0.208 to 1/3 for *D*/*b* varying from 1.0 to ∞. In concrete beams, it is more convenient to express the shear stresses in terms of the section width *b* and effective depth *d*. Considering the range of values for α and assuming $d \approx 0.8D$, the maximum shear stress by elastic theory will be in the range

$$\text{from} \quad \tau_{t,\max} = 3.84\frac{T}{b^2 d} \quad \text{to} \quad \tau_{t,\max} = 2.4\frac{T}{b^2 d} \tag{7.4a}$$

† *C* is a property of the section having the same relationship to the torsional stiffness of a rectangular section as the polar moment of inertia has for a circular section.

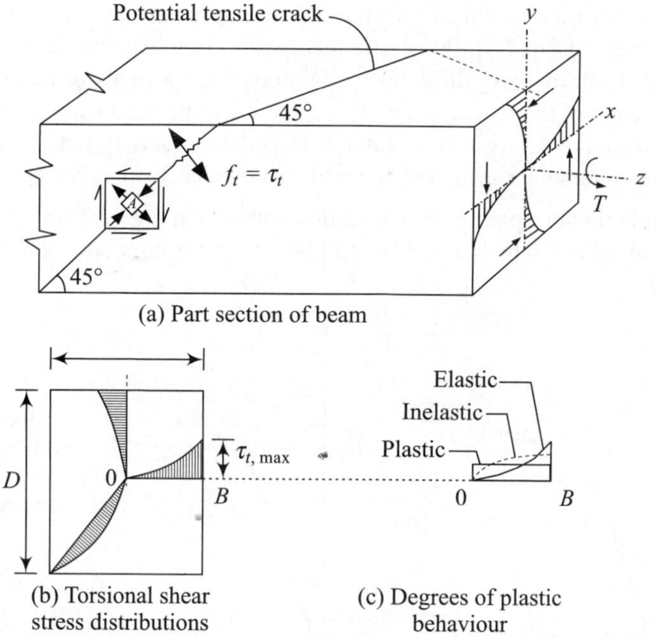

Fig. 7.3 Torsional shear stresses in a beam of rectangular section.

By elastic theory, the shear stresses are zero at the four corners of the cross section [Figure 7.3(b)]. In reality, there will be considerable redistribution of the shear stresses along the outer fibres before cracks are developed all around and the section fails, particularly so if the cracks are intercepted by at least minimal reinforcements. If such inelastic behaviour is considered, the maximum shear stress will be much lower than indicated by Eq. 7.4(a).

> In RC members, torsional shear stresses result in diagonal tension and lead to diagonal cracking.

The state of *pure shear* develops direct tensile and compressive stresses along the diagonal directions, as shown in the element at A in Figure 7.3(a). The principal tensile and compressive stress trajectories spiral around the beam in orthogonal directions at 45° to the beam axis. One such line (across which the principal tensile stress f_t acts) is marked in Figure 7.3(a); it is evidently a potential line of crack in the case of concrete. Such a crack would develop in a concrete beam when the maximum diagonal tensile stress f_t reaches the tensile strength of concrete. Owing to the brittle nature of concrete under tension, the crack will rapidly penetrate inwards from the outer surface of the cross-section. This effectively destroys the torsional resistance, which is primarily contributed by the stresses in the outer fibres (that are the largest in magnitude and also have the greatest lever arm). Hence, in a plain concrete member, the diagonal torsional cracking in the outer fibres would lead, almost immediately, to a sudden failure of the entire section. Of course, as the point of failure is approached, some degree of plasticity is developed, resulting in somewhat larger stresses in the interior fibres than what the elastic theory would indicate. Sometimes, for simplicity, the material is assumed to be rigid plastic with a uniform stress distribution over the entire cross-section [Figure 7.3(c)].

> The cracking torque, T_{cr}, of a RC member/section, taken equal to the ultimate torsional strength of an identical plain concrete section, may be obtained by equating the theoretical nominal maximum torsional shear stress in the latter to the tensile strength of concrete.

The *cracking torque* T_{cr} provides a measure of the ultimate torsional resistance (strength) of a plain concrete section. It is generally computed by equating the theoretical nominal maximum torsional shear stress $\tau_{t,\max}$ (which is a measure of the resulting diagonal tension) to the tensile strength of concrete. Various expressions for T_{cr} have been derived based on (a) elastic theory [given by Eq. 7.4], (b) plastic theory, (c) skew bending theory and (d) equivalent tube analogy [Ref. 7.4, 7.5]. Each of these different expressions for T_{cr} needs to be correlated experimentally with an appropriate measure of the tensile strength of concrete to be used with it. The Code has adopted the *design shear strength of concrete* τ_c [given by Table 6.1] as the measure of tensile strength, for convenience in combining the effects of torsional shear and flexural shear [refer Section 7.4.1].

A typical torque-twist relation for a plain concrete section is shown in Figure 7.4(a) [Ref. 7.6]. The relationship is somewhat linear up to failure, which is sudden and brittle, and occurs immediately after the formation of the first torsional crack.

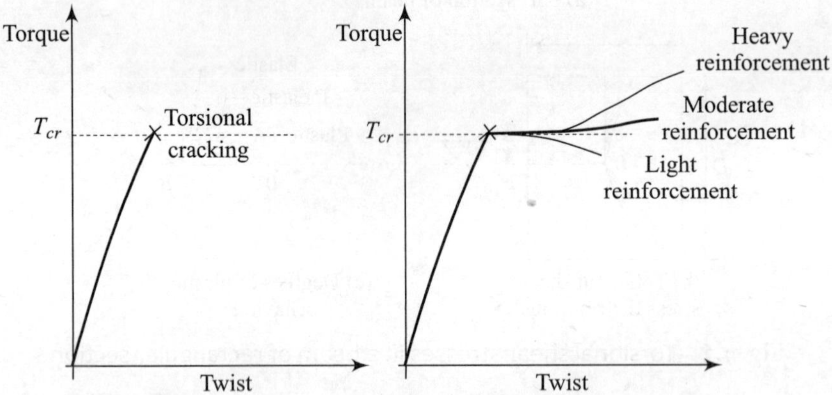

(a) Plain concrete (b) Torsionally reinforced concrete

Fig. 7.4 Typical torque-twist curves for concrete members in pure torsion.

7.3.2 Behaviour of Concrete with Torsional Reinforcement

As mentioned earlier, the failure of a plain concrete member in torsion is caused by torsional cracking due to the diagonal tensile stresses. Hence, the ideal way of reinforcing the beam against torsion is by providing the steel in the form of a spiral along the direction of the principal tensile stresses. However, this is often impractical, and the usual form of torsional reinforcement consists of a combination of longitudinal and transverse reinforcement – the former in the form of bars distributed around the cross-section, close to the periphery, and the latter in the form of closed rectangular stirrups, placed perpendicular to the beam axis. It may be noted here that the longitudinal reinforcement (on the tension side) is also needed for flexure and the transverse reinforcement is needed for shear.

> **In RC members subjected to torsion, a minimum amount of torsional reinforcement is necessary for crack control and for ductility in torsional response.**

The torque-twist behaviour of (torsionally) reinforced concrete member is similar to that of plain concrete until the formation of the first torsional crack (corresponding to the cracking torque T_{cr}), as shown in Figure 7.4(b) [Ref. 7.7]. The value of T_{cr} is insensitive to the presence of torsional reinforcement, and is practically the same as for an identical plain concrete section. When cracking occurs, there is a large increase in twist under nearly constant torque, due to a drastic loss of torsional stiffness [Figure 7.5]. Beyond this, however, the strength and behaviour depend on the amount of torsional reinforcement present in the beam.

For very small amounts of torsional reinforcement, no increase in torsional strength beyond T_{cr} is possible, and failure occurs soon after the first crack, in a brittle manner. Increasing the torsional reinforcement will no doubt increase the ultimate torsional strength and the (ductile) failure is preceded by yielding of steel, but this can be realized only at very large angles of twist. However, the strength cannot be raised indefinitely with increasing torsional reinforcement as crushing of concrete in diagonal compression may precede, and thereby prevent, the yielding of the reinforcement in tension.

The torsional stiffness after cracking is primarily dependent on the amount of torsional reinforcement, and is usually in the range of 0–10 per cent of the value prior to cracking.

7.4 Design Strength in Torsion

7.4.1 Design Torsional Strength without Torsional Reinforcement

As already indicated, the strength of a torsionally reinforced member at torsional cracking T_{cr} is practically the same as the failure strength of a plain concrete member under pure torsion. Although several methods have been developed to compute T_{cr}, the *plastic theory* approach is described here, as the Code recommendation can be explained on its basis.

> With plastic theory, the shear stress distribution will be uniform over the section, as shown in Figure 7.3(c).

Cracking Torque

The idealised assumption that the unreinforced section is fully plasticised at the point of failure implies that the shear stress is constant throughout the section, having a magnitude $\tau_{t,\max}$ [Figure 7.3(c)]. The resultant shears are obtainable from the shear flow diagram, as shown in Figure 7.5.

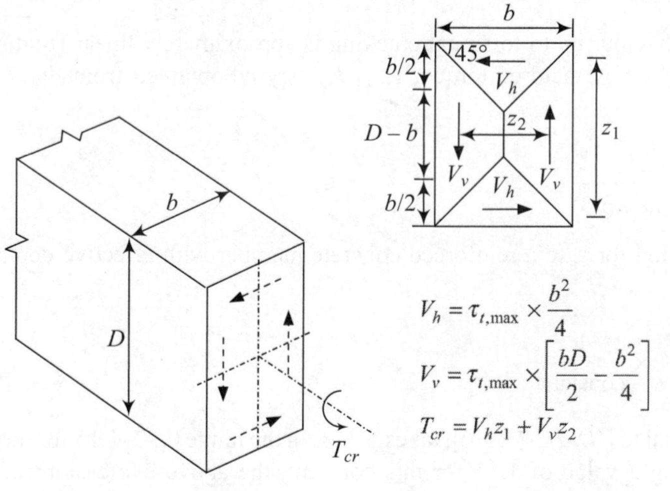

(a) (b)

Fig. 7.5 Plastic theory to determine T_{cr}

The resultant horizontal shear V_h is simply obtained by multiplying the tributary area, triangular-shaped, (equal to $b^2/4$) by $\tau_{t,\max}$. Similarly, the resultant vertical shear V_v is obtained by multiplying the trapezoidal tributary area ($bD/2 - b^2/4$) by $\tau_{t,\max}$. The two equal and opposite V_h forces form a couple which has a lever arm $z_1 = D - b/3$. Similarly, the two equal and opposite V_v forces form another couple, with a lever arm z_2, which can be shown to be:

$$z_2 = 2 \times \frac{3D - b}{3(2D - b)} \times \frac{b}{2}$$

The summation of the two couple-moments gives the desired value of T_{cr}:

$$T_{cr} = V_h z_1 + V_v z_2$$

$$= \tau_{t,\max}\left[\left(\frac{b^2}{4}\right)\left(D - \frac{b}{3}\right) + \left(\frac{bD}{2} - \frac{b^2}{4}\right)\left(\frac{b}{3} \times \frac{3D - b}{2D - b}\right)\right]$$

$$\Rightarrow \quad T_{cr} = \tau_{t,\max}\frac{b^2}{2}\left(D - \frac{b}{3}\right) \tag{7.5}$$

The above relation can also be derived using the so-called 'sand heap' analogy. Evidently, the assumption of full plasticisation of the section is not justified for a material like concrete and Eq. 7.5 will over-estimate T_{cr}. Hence, a correction factor has to be applied, by either modifying the expression in Eq. 7.5, or by using a reduced value of $\tau_{t,\max}$ (which is otherwise equal to the tensile strength of concrete) – to conform with experimental results. Test results indicate an ultimate strength value of $\tau_{t,\max}$ (MPa units) of about $0.2\sqrt{f_{ck}}$, to be used with Eq. 7.5.

Torsional Shear Stress

As the torque-twist behaviour up to torsional cracking is approximately linear [Figure 7.4], torsional shear stress τ_t corresponding to any factored torque, $T_u \le T_{cr}$ may be obtained from Eq. 7.5 for a plain concrete rectangular section as

$$\tau_t = \frac{2T_u}{b^2(D - b/3)} \tag{7.6}$$

Extending this expression for τ_t to a reinforced concrete member with effective depth d, Eq. 7.6 reduces to the following form:

$$\tau_t \approx \frac{2T_u}{b^2 d} \times \frac{1}{\text{constant}}$$

where the constant, equal to $[(D/d) - (b/3d)]$, takes values in the range 0.92–1.15 for most rectangular sections in practice. Considering a value of 1.15 for this constant, the above expression reduces to the following simplified form:

$$\tau_t = \frac{1.73(T_u/b)}{bd}$$

Note that the above expression is similar to the elastic theory solutions [Eq. 7.4(a)] although the constant is different. The Code gives an expression for torsional shear stress as:

$$\tau_t = \frac{1.6(T_u/b)}{bd} \tag{7.7}$$

where T_u is the twisting moment acting on the section, b is the width of the rectangular beam (or the width of the web of the flanged beam) and d the effective depth.

It may be noted here that this expression [Eq. 7.7] for torsional stress τ_t has a form similar to that of the 'nominal' (flexural) shear stress $\tau_v = V_u/bd$ (given by Eq. 6.7). By comparison, it follows that $(1.6T_u/b)$ provides a measure of the 'equivalent torsional shear'.

Need for Torsional Reinforcement

Stresses due to flexural shear and torsional shear are additive only on one side of a beam, they act in opposite directions on the other side.

Torsional reinforcement has to be suitably designed when the torsional shear stress τ_t exceeds the shear strength τ_c of the plain concrete section. Where flexural shear V_u occurs in combination with torsional shear (as is commonly the case), the combined shear stress (flexural plus torsional) has to be considered. For the purpose of evaluating the combined shear stress, the term *equivalent shear* V_e is used by the Code (Cl. 41.3.1) to express the combined shear effects on a reinforced concrete beam, subject to flexural shear and torsional shear:

$$V_e = V_u + 1.6\frac{T_u}{b} \tag{7.8}$$

It may be noted that the shear† due to V_u and T_u are additive only on one side of the beam; they act in opposite directions on the other side.

The equivalent nominal shear stress, τ_{ve}, is given by

$$\tau_{ve} = \frac{V_u + 1.6T_u/b}{bd} \tag{7.9}$$

If τ_{ve} exceeds $\tau_{c,\max}$ [refer Section 6.6], the section has to be suitably redesigned – by increasing the cross-sectional area (especially width) and/or improving the grade of concrete. If τ_{ve} is less than the design shear strength of concrete τ_c [refer Section 6.6], only the minimum stirrup reinforcement need be provided, as explained in Section 6.7.6. If the value of τ_{ve} lies between τ_c and $\tau_{c,\max}$, suitable torsional reinforcement (both transverse and longitudinal) has to be designed for the combined effects of shear and torsion.

7.4.2 Torsional Strength with Torsional Reinforcement

The space truss model assumes a three-dimensional (four-sided) tubular truss comprising a continuous series of diagonal concrete struts connected to longitudinal and transverse steel ties. These reinforcements and surrounding layer of concrete effectively function as a thin-walled tube.

Several theories have been proposed for the computation of the torsional strength of reinforced concrete members with torsional reinforcement – notably the *space-truss analogy* and the *skew bending* theory [Ref. 7.9–7.12].

Space Truss Analogy

The space truss analogy – a strut-and-tie model – is essentially an extension of the *plane truss analogy* [Figure 6.9] used to explain flexural shear

† Care must be taken to express V_u and T_u in consistent units, i.e., V_u in N and T_u in Nmm, b in mm and d in mm.

resistance. The 'space-truss model' (illustrated in Figure 7.6) is an idealisation of the effective portion of the beam, comprising the longitudinal and transverse torsional reinforcement and the surrounding layer of concrete. It is this 'thin-walled tube' which becomes fully effective at the post-torsional cracking phase. The truss is made up of the corner longitudinal bars as stringers (ties), the closed stirrup legs as transverse ties, and the concrete between diagonal cracks as compression diagonals (struts).

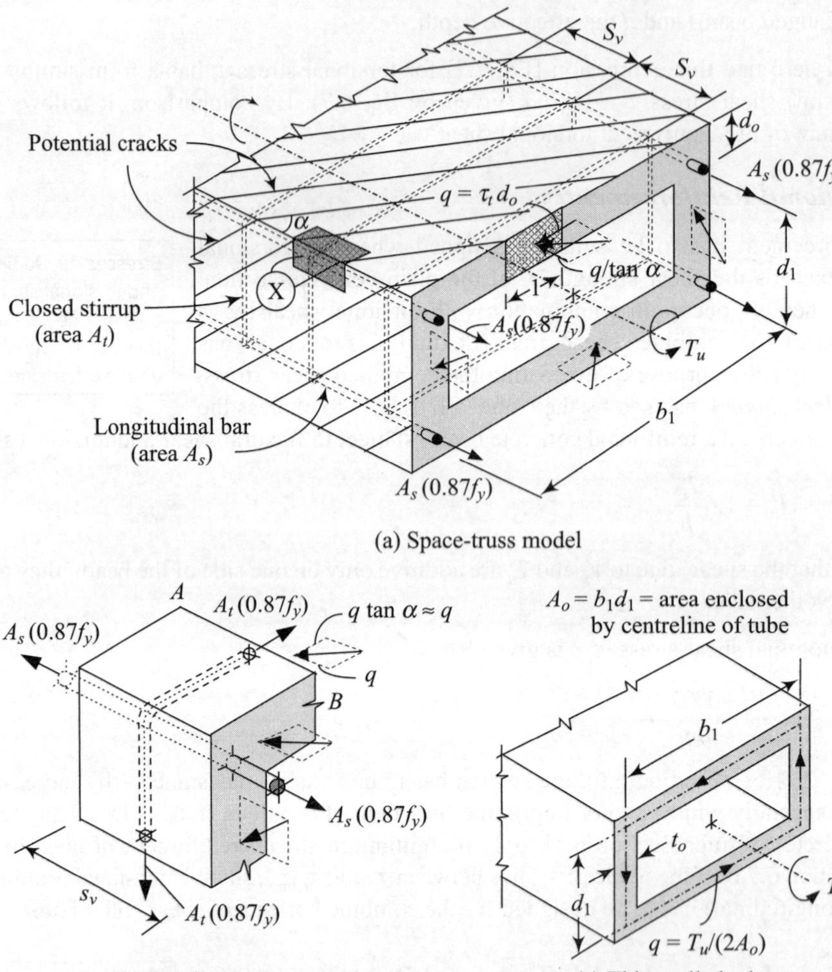

(a) Space-truss model

(b) Detail 'X'

(c) Thin-walled tube (box section)

Fig. 7.6 The idealised space-truss model.

For a closed thin-walled tube, the shear flow q (force per unit length) across the thickness of the tube [Ref. 7.1] is uniform and is given by:

$$q = \frac{T_u}{2A_o} = \frac{T_u}{2b_1 d_1} \tag{7.10}$$

where A_o is the area enclosed by the centreline of the thickness and b_1 and d_1 denote the width and depth of A_o, taken as the centre-to-centre distances between the corner bars in the directions of the width and the depth respectively. Eq. 7.10 can be derived from Figure 7.6(c). The forces in the two vertical sides (= qd_1) form a couple with lever arm b_1 giving torque = qd_1b_1. Similarly, the forces in the two horizontal sides contribute torque = qb_1d_1. The total torque T_u is given by $2qb_1d_1 = 2qA_o$.

The shear stress, τ, can be obtained from the shear flow per unit length of the tube thickness, q, as:

$$\tau = \frac{q}{1 \times t_o} = \frac{T_u}{2A_o t_o} = \frac{T_u}{2b_1 d_1 t_o} \tag{7.11}$$

where t_o is the wall thickness of the equivalent tube [Figure 7.6].

In one approach using equivalent tube concept to rectangular concrete sections of usual proportions (Ref. 7.5, 7.10), the actual cross section is replaced by an equivalent thin-walled tube having the same external dimension as the actual section, but with wall thickness $t_o = 0.75\, A_c/p_c$ and area enclosed by centreline of the wall thickness, A_o, ≈ (2/3) A_c; where p_c is the external perimeter of the actual section and A_c = area enclosed within perimeter p_c. With these assumptions, Eq. 7.11 reduces to Eq. 7.11a. With the torsional shear stress τ taken as the diagonal cracking stress of concrete, Eq. 7.11a may be used to compute the cracking torque T_{cr}.

$$\tau = \frac{T_u p_c}{A_c^2} \tag{7.11a}$$

Considering equilibrium of forces normal to section AB [Figure 7.6(b)], the total force in each transverse reinforcement (stirrup) is given by $qs_v \tan\alpha$ where s_v is the spacing of the stirrups and α is the inclination of the diagonal crack. Further, assuming that the stirrup has yielded in tension at the ultimate limit state (with a design stress of $0.87f_y$), it follows from force equilibrium that

$$A_t(0.87f_y) = qs_v \tan\alpha \tag{7.12}$$

where A_t is the cross-sectional area of the stirrup bar (equal to $A_{sv}/2$ for two legged stirrups). Assuming torsional cracks (under pure torsion) occur at 45° to the longitudinal axis of the beam, Eq. 7.12 reduces to:

$$A_t(0.87f_y) = qs_v \tag{7.13}$$

Substituting Eq. 7.10 in the above equation, the following expression is obtained for the ultimate strength $T_u = T_{uR}$ in torsion:

$$T_{uR} = 2A_t b_1 d_1 (0.87 f_y)/s_v \tag{7.14}$$

For the general case with crack inclination at angle α [Eq. 7.12] and *without* the partial safety factor for steel (0.87), the nominal ultimate strength, T_{un}, is obtained as:

$$T_{un} = 2A_o A_t f_y/(s_v \tan\alpha) \tag{7.14a}$$

Further, assuming that the longitudinal steel (symmetrically placed with respect to the beam axis) has also yielded at the ultimate limit state, it follows from longitudinal force equilibrium [Figure 7.6(a)] that:

$$A_l(0.87 f_{yl}) = \frac{q}{\tan\alpha} \times 2(b_1 + d_1) \tag{7.15}$$

where $A_l \equiv \Sigma A_s$ is the total area of the longitudinal steel and f_{yl} its yield strength.

Substituting Eq. 7.10 in the above equation and for $\alpha = 45°$, the following expression is obtained for the ultimate strength $T_u = T_{uR}$ in torsion:

$$T_{uR} = A_l b_1 d_1 (0.87 f_{yl})/(b_1 + d_1) \tag{7.16}$$

Again, for the general case with crack inclination at angle α and *without* partial safety factor for steel (= 0.87), the nominal strength is obtained as:

$$T_{un} = A_o A_l f_{yl} \tan \alpha/(b_1 + d_1) \tag{7.16a}$$

The two alternative expressions for T_{uR}, viz., Eq. 7.14 and Eq. 7.16, (or Eqs 7.14a and 7.16a for the general case) will give identical results only if the following relation between the areas of longitudinal steel and transverse steel (as torsional reinforcement) is satisfied:

for $\alpha = 45°$,
$$\frac{A_l f_{yl}}{2(b_1 + d_1)} = \frac{A_t f_y}{s_v} \tag{7.17}$$

or for general case with crack inclination at α,
$$\frac{A_l f_{yl} \tan \alpha}{2(b_1 + d_1)} = \frac{A_t f_y}{s_v \tan \alpha} \tag{7.17a}$$

If both transverse and longitudinal steel have the same yield strength, Eq. 7.17 can be simplified as Eq. 7.17b. The left-hand side of this equation gives the thickness of a thin steel tube of dimensions $b_1 \times d_1$ having same cross-sectional area as the longitudinal reinforcement. Similarly, the right-hand side gives the thickness of a similar tube having transverse cross-sectional area equal to the transverse reinforcement.

$$\frac{A_l}{2(b_1 + d_1)} = \frac{A_t}{s_v} \tag{7.17b}$$

If the relation given by the Eq. 7.17 (or 7.17a) is not satisfied, then T_{uR} may be computed by combining Eq. 7.14 and Eq. 7.16 [Ref. 7.10], taking into account the areas of both transverse and longitudinal reinforcements, as given in Eq. 7.18. This equation is analogous to considering a steel tube with thickness equal to the square root of the product of the two equivalent thicknesses mentioned in the above paragraph. Eq. 7.18 can be derived by substituting the value of tan α obtained from Eq. 7.17a into Eq. 7.14a or 7.16a and then applying the partial safety factor.

$$T_{uR} = 2b_1 d_1 \sqrt{\left(\frac{A_t f_y}{s_v}\right)\left(\frac{A_l \times f_{yl}}{2(b_1 + d_1)}\right)} \times 0.87 \tag{7.18}$$

To ensure that the member does not fail suddenly in a brittle manner after the development of torsional cracks, the torsional strength of the cracked reinforced section must be at least equal to the cracking torque T_{cr} (computed without considering any safety factor).

For any design torsional moment, T_u (= T_{uR}), Eq. 7.14 and Eq. 7.17 give the required areas for transverse and longitudinal reinforcements respectively. These areas A_t and A_l calculated for the effect of torsion alone, should then be added to the corresponding reinforcement required to resist shear and flexure respectively. This procedure is adopted by many codes – *but not the IS Code*. The provisions in the IS Code are based on the *skew bending theory* for rectangular beams and not on the space truss analogy [Ref. 7.2].

Skew Bending Theory

The post-cracking behaviour of reinforced concrete members may be alternatively studied on the basis of the *mechanism of failure*, rather than on the basis of stresses [Ref. 7.10, 7.13]. In the consideration of the failure mechanism, the *combined* action of torsion with flexure and shear has to be taken into account.

Addition of torsion to flexure skews the failure surface in the direction of the resultant moment-torsion vector and analysis is based on this mode of failure.

Three modes of failure have been identified for beams subjected to combined flexure and torsion [Figure 7.7]. The action of torsion is to *skew* the failure surface (which is otherwise vertical under the action of flexure alone); the skewing is in the direction of the resultant moment-torsion vector. The most common type of failure is as shown in Mode 1 [Figure 7.7(b)] – with bending predominating over torsion and the compression zone (shown shaded) remaining on top, albeit skewed ($\theta < 45°$). This type of failure (sometimes called 'modified bending failure') will occur in wide beams, even if torsion is relatively high. However, if a beam with a *narrow* section ($D >> b$) is subject to predominant torsion, a Mode 2 type of failure [Figure 7.7(c)] is likely, with the compression zone skewed to a side of the section; this type of failure is sometimes called a *lateral bending* failure. A third mode of failure – Mode 3 [Figure 7.7(d)] – is possible when the compression zone occurs at the bottom and the area of the longitudinal top steel is much less than that of the bottom steel; this type of failure is sometimes called a *negative bending* failure.

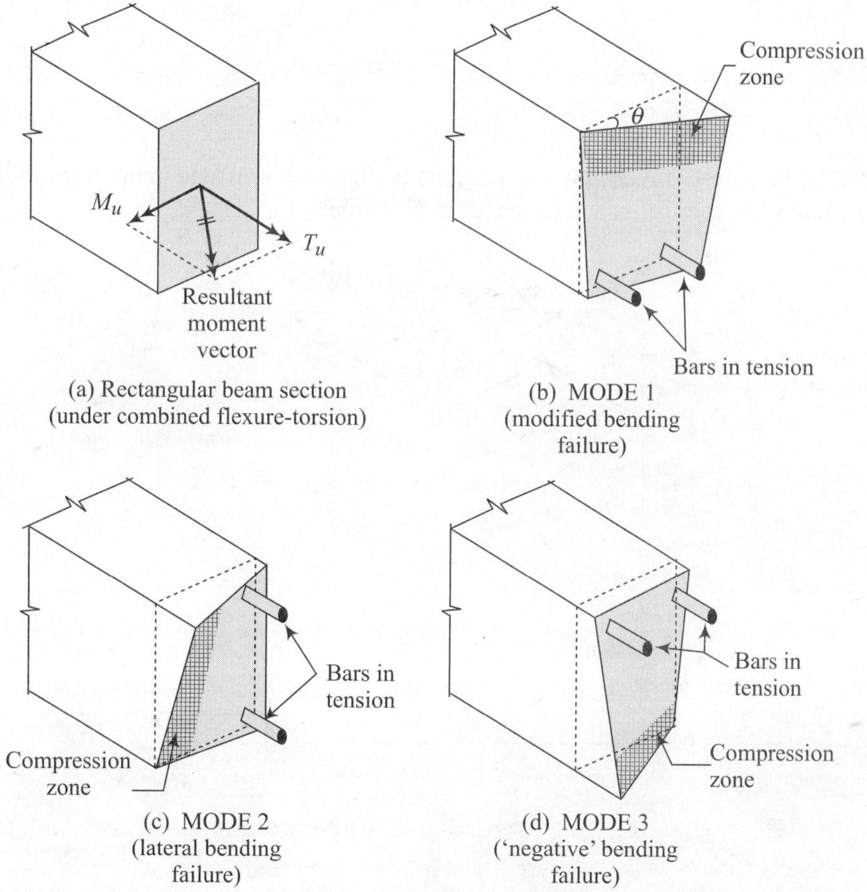

Fig. 7.7 Failure modes for combined flexure and torsion.

In a beam with a square cross-section, with symmetrical longitudinal reinforcement, subjected to pure torsion, the three modes become identical.

Expressions for the ultimate strength in torsion have been derived for each of the three possible modes of failure. The interested reader is advised to refer to Ref. 7.13 (or Ref. 7.14) for the derivation of these expressions. It is customary to check for all the three modes and to choose the lowest value of the torsional strength.

It may be noted that the presence of shear may cause a beam to fail at a lower strength. The Code attempts to prevent the possibility of such shear type of failure by the concept of designing for *equivalent shear* [refer Section 7.4.4].

7.4.3 Design Strength in Torsion Combined with Flexure

The strength of a member subjected to combined torsion (T_u) and flexure (M_u) is best described in terms of the interaction of T_u/T_{uR} with M_u/M_{uR}, where T_{uR} and M_{uR} denote respectively the strengths of the member under *pure torsion* and *pure flexure* respectively. The following parabolic interaction formulas [Ref. 7.15] have been proposed, based on experimental studies on rectangular reinforced beams:

Mode 1 failure: $$\left(\frac{A'_s}{A_s}\right)\left(\frac{T_u}{T_{uR}}\right)^2 + \left(\frac{M_u}{M_{uR}}\right) \leq 1 \qquad (7.19a)$$

Mode 3 failure : $$\left(\frac{T_u}{T_{uR}}\right)^2 - \left(\frac{A_s}{A'_s}\right)\left(\frac{M_u}{M_{uR}}\right) \leq 1 \qquad (7.19b)$$

Where A_s and A'_s denote, respectively, the areas of longitudinal steel provided in the 'flexural tension zone' and 'flexural compression zone' of the rectangular beam section.

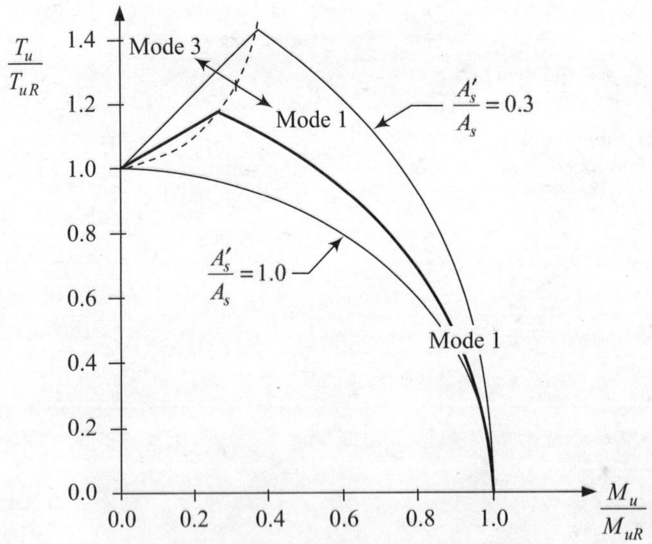

Fig. 7.8 Torsion-flexure interaction.

The torsion-flexure *interaction curves*, based on Eq. 7.19, are depicted in Figure 7.8 for A_s'/A_s in the range 0.3 to 1.0. Each curve represents a 'failure envelope', in the sense that any combination of T_u/T_{uR} and M_u/M_{uR} that falls outside the area bounded by the curve and the coordinate axes is 'unsafe'. In general, it is seen that the torsional strength (T_u) increases beyond the 'pure torsion' strength (T_{uR}) in the presence of bending moment (M_u) – provided M_u/M_{uR} is low and A_s'/A_s is also low. In such cases, failure may occur in Mode 3 (i.e., initiated by the yielding of the compression steel) at very low values of M_u/M_{uR} [Figure 7.8]. In general, however, a Mode 1 failure is likely to occur (i.e., initiated by the yielding of the 'tension' steel); this becomes inevitable when A_s' is equal to A_s.

It may also be noted from Figure 7.8 that the presence of torsion invariably brings down the flexural strength of the reinforced concrete member.

IS Code Provisions for Design of Longitudinal Reinforcement

The Code (Cl. 41.4.2) recommends a simplified skew-bending based formulation [Ref. 7.15] for the design of longitudinal reinforcement to resist torsion combined with flexure in beams with rectangular sections. The torsional moment T_u is converted into an effective bending moment M_t defined† as follows:

$$M_t = T_u(1 + D/b)/1.7 \tag{7.20}$$

where D is the overall depth and b the width of the beam.

M_t, so calculated, is combined with the actual bending moment M_u at the section, to give 'equivalent bending moments', M_{e1} and M_{e2}:

$$M_{e1} = M_t + M_u \tag{7.21a}$$

$$M_{e2} = M_t - M_u \tag{7.21b}$$

The longitudinal reinforcement area A_{st} is designed to resist the equivalent moment M_{e1}, and this steel is to be located in the 'flexural tension zone'. In addition, if $M_{e2} > 0$ (i.e., $M_t > M_u$), then a reinforcement area A_{st}' is to be designed to resist this equivalent moment, and this steel is to be located in the 'flexural compression zone'.

It follows from the above that in the limiting case of 'pure torsion' (i.e., with $M_u = 0$), *equal* longitudinal reinforcement is required at the top and bottom of the rectangular beam, each capable of resisting an equivalent bending moment equal to M_t.

7.4.4 Design Strength in Torsion Combined with Shear

Torsion-shear interaction curves have been proposed [Ref. 7.16], similar to torsion-flexure interaction curves. In general, the interaction between T_u/T_{uR} and V_u/V_{uR} takes the following form:

$$\left(\frac{T_u}{T_{uR}}\right)^{\alpha} + \left(\frac{V_u}{V_{uR}}\right)^{\alpha} \le 1 \tag{7.22}$$

T_u and V_u are the given factored twisting moment and factored shear force respectively; T_{uR} and V_{uR} are the ultimate strengths in 'pure torsion' and 'flexural shear' (without torsion) respectively; α is a constant, for

† This formula can alternatively be generated from the space-truss analogy [Figure 7.6(a) and Eq. 7.16], by visualising the longitudinal tensile forces in the bars (located either at top or at bottom) as those required to resist an effective bending moment $M_t \approx A_l(0.87f_{yl})d_1$ which can be shown to be equal to $T_u(1 + d_1/b_1)$; the Code has simplified this formula to the form given in Eq. 7.20.

which values in the range 1 to 2 have been proposed [Figure 7.9]. A value of α equal to unity results in a linear interaction and generally provides a conservative estimate.

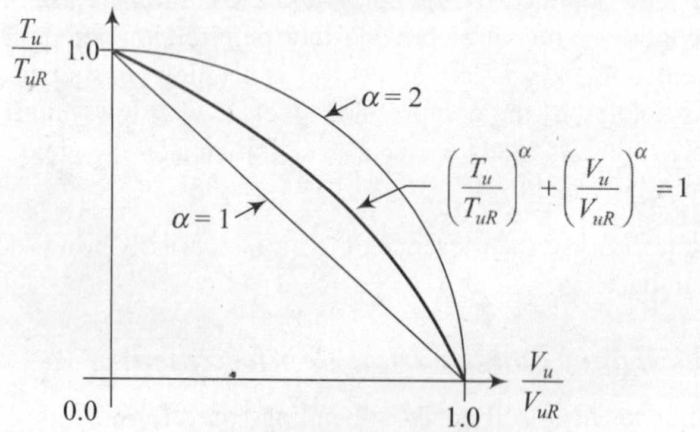

Fig. 7.9 Torsion-shear interaction.

IS Code Provisions for Design of Transverse Reinforcement

The Code provisions (Cl. 41.4.3) for the design of transverse stirrup reinforcement (2-legged, closed) are based on the skew-bending theory and are aimed at resisting a Mode 2 failure [Figure 7.7(b)], caused by a large torsion combined with a small flexural shear:

$$A_{sv} = \frac{T_u s_v}{b_1 d_1 (0.87 f_y)} + \frac{V_u s_v}{2.5 d_1 (0.87 f_y)} \tag{7.23}$$

where $A_{sv} = 2A_t$ is the total area of two legs of the stirrup; s_v is the centre-to-centre spacing of the stirrups; b_1 and d_1 are the centre-to-centre distances between the corner bars along the width and depth respectively; and T_u and V_u are the factored twisting moment and factored shear force acting at the section under consideration.

It may be observed that for the extreme case of strength in 'pure torsion' (i.e., with $V_u = 0$ and $T_u = T_{uR}$), Eq. 7.23 becomes exactly equivalent to Eq. 7.14, which was derived using the space-truss analogy.

In addition to Eq. 7.23, the Code (Cl. 41.4.3) specifies a minimum limit to the *total* area of transverse reinforcement:

$$A_{sv} \geq \frac{(\tau_{ve} - \tau_c)\, b s_v}{0.87 f_y} \tag{7.24}$$

where τ_{ve} is the 'equivalent nominal shear stress' given by Eq. 7.9. Note that when T_u approaches zero, Eq. 7.23 does not converge to the shear only case [Eqs 6.28 and 6.29]. The purpose of Eq. 7.24 is to cover this and provide adequate resistance against flexural shear failure, which is indicated in situations where T_u is negligible in comparison with V_u. Indeed, for the extreme case of $T_u = 0$, Eq. 7.24 becomes exactly equivalent to Eq. 6.29, which was derived for flexural shear. It may be noted that the contribution of inclined stirrups and bent up bars can be included in the calculation of A_{sv} in Eq. 7.24, but not Eq. 7.23.

Distribution of Torsional Reinforcement

The Code (Cl. 26.5.1.7a) specifies maximum limits to the spacing s_v of the stirrups provided as torsional reinforcement – to ensure the development of post-cracking torsional resistance, to control crack-widths and to control the fall in torsional stiffness on account of torsional cracks:

$$s_v \le \begin{cases} x_1 \\ (x_1 + y_1)/4 \\ 300 \text{ mm} \end{cases} \tag{7.25}$$

where x_1 and y_1 are, respectively, the short and long centre-to-centre dimensions of the rectangular closed stirrups. The spacing s_v should satisfy *all* the limits given in Eq. 7.25.

The Code (Cl. 26.5.1.7b) also recommends that the '*longitudinal reinforcement shall be placed as close as is practicable to the corners of the cross-section, and in all cases, there shall be at least one longitudinal bar in each corner of the ties*'.

Further, if the torsional member has a cross-sectional dimension (usually, overall depth rather than width) that exceeds 450 mm, additional longitudinal bars are required to be provided as side face reinforcement, with an area not less than 0.1 per cent of the web area. These bars are to be distributed equally on the two faces at a spacing not exceeding 300 mm or web thickness, whichever is less.

7.5 Analysis and Design Examples

Example 7.1

A plain concrete beam (M 25 grade concrete) has a rectangular section, 300 mm wide and 500 mm deep (overall). Estimate the 'cracking torque'. Also determine the limiting torque beyond which torsional reinforcement is required (as per the Code), assuming τ_c = 0.3 MPa.

Solution

- ***Using the plastic theory formula*** [Eq. 7.5]:

$$T_{cr} = \frac{1}{2}\tau_{t,\max} b^2 (D - b/3)$$

where b = 300 mm, D = 500 mm.

Assuming $\tau_{t,\max} \approx 0.2\sqrt{f_{ck}} = 0.2\sqrt{25} = 1$ MPa

$$\Rightarrow \qquad T_{cr} = \frac{1}{2}(1) \times 300^2 \times (500 - 300/3)$$

$$= 18 \times 10^6 \text{ Nmm} = \mathbf{18\ kNm}$$

- As per IS Code formulation, torsion has to be combined with shear for deciding whether or not torsional reinforcement is required.

Torsional reinforcement is required if $\tau_v > \tau_c$, i.e., $\dfrac{V_u + 1.6T_u/b}{bd} > \tau_c$

Assuming $V_u = 0$, $d \approx 0.9D = 450$ mm and $\tau_c = 0.3$ MPa,

$$\Rightarrow \qquad \frac{0 + 1.6(T_u \times 10^6/300)}{300 \times 450} > 0.30$$

$$\Rightarrow \qquad T_u > 7.59 \times 10^6 \text{ Nmm} = \mathbf{7.6\ kNm}$$

Example 7.2

The beam of Example 7.1 is reinforced (using Fe 500 grade steel) as shown in Figure 7.10(a). Determine the design torsional resistance of the beam under pure torsion. Assume moderate exposure condition.

Solution

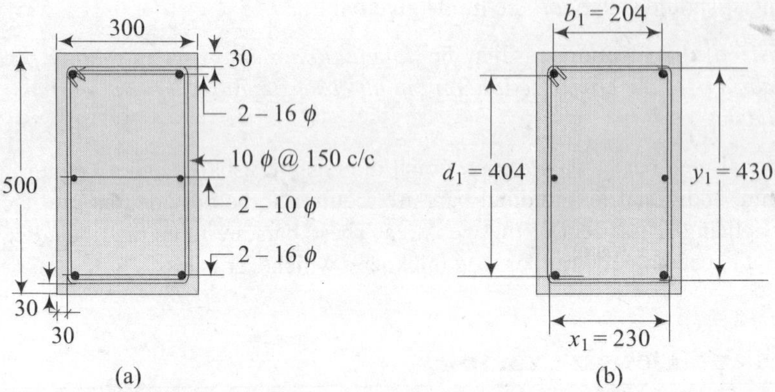

Fig. 7.10 Example 7.2.

- Given $b = 300$ mm, $D = 500$ mm, $f_{ck} = 25$ MPa, $f_{yl} = 500$ MPa, $f_{yt} = 415$ MPa (due to the limitation in the yield strength of transverse reinforcement),
  A_l (due to 4–16 ϕ plus 2–10ϕ) = (201 × 4) + (78.5 × 2) = 961 mm^2.

  A_t(10ϕ stirrup) = 78.5 mm^2, $A_{sv} = 2A_t = 157$ mm^2

  $s_v = 150$ mm

  $b_1 = 300 - 30 \times 2 - 10 \times 2 - 16 = 204$ mm

  $d_1 = 500 - 30 \times 2 - 10 \times 2 - 16 = 404$ mm [Figure 7.10(b)]

- Applying the general space truss formulation, considering the contribution of both transverse and longitudinal reinforcements [Eq. 7.18]:

$$T_{uR} = 2b_1d_1\sqrt{\left(\frac{0.87f_yA_t}{s_v}\right)\left(\frac{0.87f_{yl}A_l}{2(b_1+d_1)}\right)}$$

$$= 2 \times 204 \times 404 \times \sqrt{\left(\frac{0.87 \times 415 \times 78.5}{150}\right)\left(\frac{0.87 \times 500 \times 961}{2(204+404)}\right)}$$

$$= 42.01 \times 10^6 \text{ Nmm} = \mathbf{42\ kNm}$$

  which is greater than $T_{cr} = 18$ kNm (refer Example 7.1).

- Alternatively, using the IS Code formula, considering shear-torsion interaction [Eq. 7.23] with $V_u = 0$, which corresponds to the space truss formulation considering the contribution of the transverse reinforcement alone [Eq. 7.14]:

$$T_{uR} = A_{sv}b_1d_1(0.87f_y)/s_v$$

$$= 157 \times 204 \times 404 \times (0.87 \times 415)/150$$

$$= 31.1 \times 10^6 \text{ Nmm} = \mathbf{31.1\ kNm}$$

- In the above formulation, we had tacitly assumed that the torsional strength is governed by shear considerations and not 'equivalent moment'. The reader may verify this assumption by checking the equivalent moment capacity due to the longitudinal reinforcement[†] using Eq. 7.20.

Example 7.3

A beam, framing between columns, has an effective span of 5.0 m and supports a cantilevered projection, 1 m wide [Figure 7.11(a)] throughout its length. Assume that the cross-sectional details of the beam are exactly the same as in Example 7.2 [Figure 7.10]. Determine the adequacy of the section (as per IS Code), assuming a total uniformly distributed load (DL + LL) of 5 kN/m² on the cantilever projection as shown. Assume fixity at the ends of the beam against torsion as well as flexure.

Solution

Structural Analysis

This is a problem involving primary torsion, combined with flexure and shear.

- *Loads on beam* [Figure 7.11(b)]:

  from projection: $5.0 \text{ kN/m}^2 \times 1m = 5.0$ kN/m
  from self-weight: $25.0 \times 0.3 \times 0.5 = 3.75$ "
  8.75 kN/m

  Assuming a load factor of 1.5,
  Factored distributed load $w_u = 8.75 \times 1.5 = 13.13$ kN/m

  Eccentricity of cantilever load from beam centreline $= 1.0/2 + 0.3/2 = 0.65$ m

  $\therefore$ Factored distributed torque $t_u = (5.0 \times 0.65) \times 1.5 = 4.88$ kNm/m

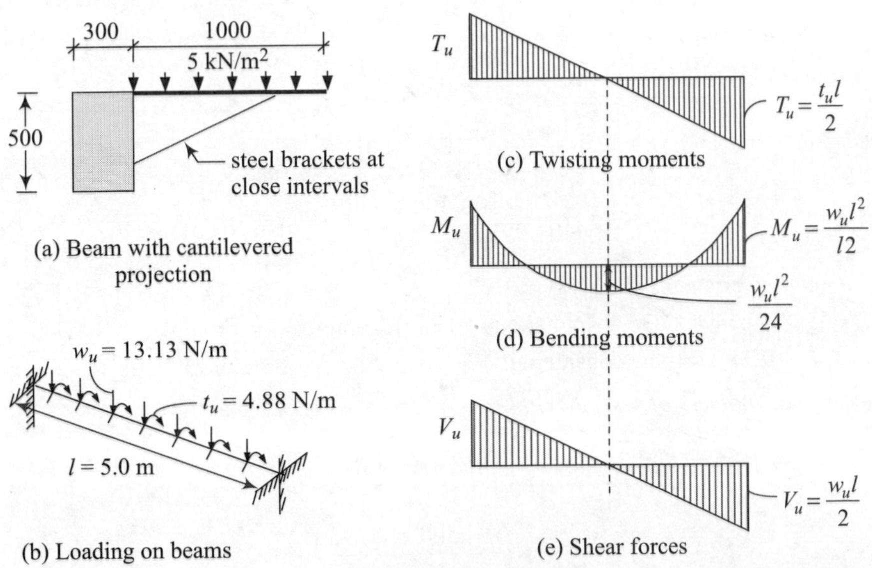

Fig. 7.11 Example 7.3.

† The corresponding value of M_{uR} is 73.3 kNm, whereby $T_u = 46.7$ kNm [Eq. 7.20].

- *Stress resultants*:

Max. twisting moment (at support) $T_u = \frac{t_u l}{2} = 4.88\left(\frac{5.0}{2}\right) = 12.20$ kNm.

Max. bending moment (at support) $M_u = \frac{w_u l^2}{12} = 27.35$ kNm (hogging).

Max. shear force (at support) $V_u = \frac{w_u l}{2} = 32.82$ kN.

The distributions of twisting moment, bending moment and shear force are shown in Figures 7.11(c), (d), and (e). Evidently, the critical section for checking the adequacy of the beam under the combined effects of T_u, M_u and V_u is at the support [at midspan, $T_u = 0$, $V_u = 0$].

Need for torsional reinforcement

- *Equivalent nominal shear stress* [Eq. 7.9]:

$$\tau_{ve} = \frac{V_u + 1.6T_u/b}{bd} \qquad (d = 500 - 30 - 10 - 8 = 452 \text{ mm})$$

$$= \frac{(32.82\times10^3) + 1.6(12.20\times10^6)/300}{300\times452} = 0.722 \text{ MPa}$$

$< \tau_{c\,\max} = 3.1$ MPa (for M25 concrete), hence section size is adequate.

- *Shear strength of concrete* [Eq. 6.10]:

$$A_{st} = 402 \text{ mm}^2 \;\Rightarrow\; p_t = \frac{402\times100}{300\times452} = 0.296 \;\Rightarrow\; \beta = 0.8\times25/(6.89\times0.296) = 9.81 > 1.0$$

$$\Rightarrow \quad \tau_c = 0.85\sqrt{(0.8\times25)}\left(\sqrt{(1+5\times9.81)}-1\right)\Big/(6\times9.81) = 0.392 \text{ MPa}$$

- *As* $\tau_{ve} > \tau_c$, *torsional reinforcement is required.*

Adequacy of longitudinal reinforcement

- *Effective bending moment* $M_t = T_u\left(\frac{1+D/b}{1.7}\right)$ [Eq. 7.20]

$$= 12.20\left(\frac{1+500/300}{1.7}\right) = 19.14 \text{ kNm}$$

- *Equivalent bending moments* [Eq. 7.21]:
  $M_{e1} = M_t + M_u = 19.14 + 27.35 = 46.49$ kNm (with flexural tension on top)
  $M_{e2} = M_t - M_u < 0 \Rightarrow$ not to be considered.
- *Ultimate resisting moment of section with* $A_{st} = 402$ mm² ($p_t = 0.296$ at top)

$$M_{uR} = 0.87f_y\frac{p_t}{100}\left(1-\frac{f_y}{f_{ck}}\frac{p_t}{100}\right)bd^2 \quad \text{[Eq. 4.65]}$$

$$= 0.870\times500\times\frac{0.296}{100}\times\left(1-\frac{500}{25}\times\frac{0.296}{100}\right)\times300\times452^2$$

$$= 74.25\times10^6 \text{ Nmm} = 74.3 \text{ kNm}$$

- $M_{uR} > M_e = 46.4n9$ kNm $\Rightarrow$ safe.

Adequacy of side face reinforcement

- As the depth (500 mm) exceeds 450 mm, additional $A_{st} = 0.001\ bD = 150\ \text{mm}^2$ is required at a spacing less than 300 mm, distributed equally on the two side faces. This has been provided in the form of 2–10ϕ bars (157 mm^2) [Figure 7.10(a)].

— Hence, OK.

Adequacy of transverse reinforcement

- Area of 2-legged 10ϕ stirrups provided, $A_{sv} = 157\ \text{mm}^2$
  This should exceed the requirements given by Eq. 7.23 and Eq. 7.24

  $s_v = 150$ mm, $b_1 = 204$ mm, $d_1 = 404$ mm [Figures 7.10(a), (b)]

- [Eq. 7.23]: $(A_{sv})_{\text{reqd}} = (T_u/b_1 + V_u/2.5)(s_v/(d_1 0.87 f_y))$

$$= (12.20 \times 10^6/204 + 32.82 \times 10^3/2.5) \times \frac{150}{404(0.87 \times 415)}$$

$$= 75\ \text{mm}^2 < 157\ \text{mm}^2 \text{ provided} \quad \Rightarrow \quad \text{OK.}$$

- Minimum limit of area of transverse reinforcement [Eq. 7.24]:

$$(A_{sv})_{\text{reqd}} = \frac{(\tau_{ve} - \tau_c) b s_v}{0.87 f_y}$$

$$= \frac{(0.722 - 0.386) \times 300 \times 150}{0.87 \times 415}$$

$$= 41.1\ \text{mm}^2 < 157\ \text{mm}^2 \text{ provided} \quad \Rightarrow \quad \text{OK.}$$

- Further, the spacing of stirrups provided ($s_v = 150$ mm) should satisfy the requirements of Eq. 7.25:

$$(s_v)_{\text{reqd}} \le \begin{cases} x_1 = 204 + 16 + 10 = 230 \text{ mm} \\ (x_1 + y_1)/4 = (230 + 430)/4 = 165 \text{ mm} \\ 0.75d = 0.75 \times 452 = 339 \text{ mm} \end{cases}$$

$$(s_v)_{\text{provided}} = 150 \text{ mm} < (s_v)_{\text{reqd}} \quad \Rightarrow \quad \text{OK.}$$

- Hence, the section provided is adequate in all respects.

Example 7.4

Design the torsional reinforcement in a rectangular beam section, 350 mm wide and 750 mm deep, subjected to an ultimate twisting moment of 140 kNm, combined with an ultimate (hogging) bending moment of 200 kNm and an ultimate-shear force of 110 kN. Assume M 25 concrete, Fe 500 steel and mild exposure conditions.

Solution

- Given: $b = 350$ mm, $D = 750$ mm, $f_{ck} = 25$ MPa, $f_y = 500$ MPa, $T_u = 140$ kNm, $M_u = 200$ kNm, $V_u = 110$ kN
  Minimum required cover to the stirrups is 20 mm. Assuming 50 mm effective cover all around, $d = 700$ mm.

Design of longitudinal reinforcement

- *Effective bending moment due to torsion*:

$$M_t = T_u(1 + D/b)/1.7$$
$$= 140 \times (1 + 750/350)/1.7 = 259 \text{ kNm}$$

- *Equivalent bending moments for design*:

$$M_e = M_t \pm M_u$$
$$= 259 \pm 200 = \begin{cases} 459 \text{ kNm} & \text{(flexural tension at top)} \\ 59 \text{ kNm} & \text{(flexural tension at bottom)} \end{cases}$$

- *Design of top steel*:

$$R_1 \equiv \frac{M_{e1}}{bd^2} = \frac{459 \times 10^6}{350 \times (700)^2} = 2.676 \text{ MPa}$$
$$< \frac{M_{u,\lim}}{bd^2} = 0.1338 \times 25 = 3.345 \text{ MPa}$$

$\Rightarrow$ [Eq. 5.12]: $$\frac{p_t}{100} \equiv \frac{A_{st}}{bd} = \frac{f_{ck}}{2f_y}\left[1 - \sqrt{1 - 4.598\, R_1/f_{ck}}\right]$$
$$= \frac{25}{2(500)}\left[1 - \sqrt{1 - 4.598 \times 2.676/25}\right]$$
$$= 0.718 \times 10^{-2}$$

[Note: The same result is obtainable directly using Design Aids – Table A.3(a) or SP : 16].

$\Rightarrow$ $(A_{st})_{\text{reqd}} = 0.718 \times 10^{-2} \times 350 \times 700 = 1760 \text{ mm}^2$

Provide 2–28ϕ + 2–20ϕ at top [$A_{st} = (616 \times 2) + (314 \times 2) = 1860 \text{ mm}^2$]

- *Design of bottom steel*:

$$R_2 \equiv \frac{M_{e2}}{bd^2} = \frac{59 \times 10^6}{350 \times (700)^2} = 0.344 \text{ MPa}$$

$$\therefore \quad \frac{(p_t)_{\text{reqd}}}{100} = \frac{25}{2(500)}\left[1 - \sqrt{1 - \frac{4.598 \times 0.344}{25}}\right] = 0.0803 \times 10^{-2} \text{ (very low)}$$

Provide minimum reinforcement: $\dfrac{A_{st}}{bd} = \dfrac{0.85}{500} = 0.17 \times 10^{-2}$

$\Rightarrow$ $(A_{st})_{\text{reqd}} = 0.17 \times 10^{-2} \times 350 \times 700 = 417 \text{ mm}^2$

Provide 3–16ϕ ($A_{st} = 201 \times 3 = 603 \text{ mm}^2$) at bottom.

- *Side face reinforcement*:
  As $D > 450$ mm, side face reinforcement for torsion is required.

  $(A_{st})_{\text{reqd}} = 0.001bD = 0.001 \times 350 \times 750 = 263 \text{ mm}^2$

  Provide 4–10ϕ ($A_{st} = 78.5 \times 4 = 314 \text{ mm}^2$), two bars on each side face. The (vertical) spacing between longitudinal bars will be less than 300 mm, as required by the Code. The designed cross-section is shown in Figure 7.12.

Design of transverse reinforcement

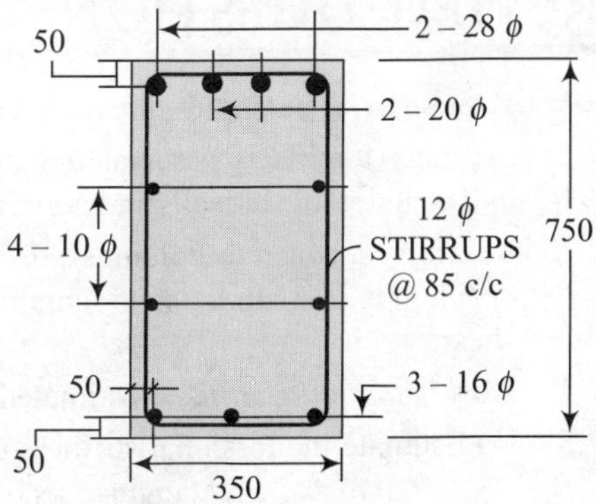

Fig. 7.12 Example 7.4.

- Equivalent nominal shear stress:

$$\tau_{ve} = \frac{V_u + 1.6T_u/b}{bd}$$

$$= \frac{(110 \times 10^3) + 1.6 \times (140 \times 10^6)/350}{350 \times 700}$$

$$= 3.06 \text{ MPa}$$

$$< \tau_{c,\max} = 3.1 \text{ MPa (for M 25 concrete)}$$

- Shear strength of concrete [Eq. 6.10]:

For $p_t = \dfrac{1860 \times 100}{350 \times 700} = 0.76, \beta = 3.82$

$\Rightarrow \quad \tau_c = 0.58$ MPa (for M 25 concrete)

- As torsional shear is relatively high, Eq. 7.23 is likely to govern the design of stirrups (rather than Eq. 7.24). Assuming 10 ϕ 2-legged stirrups, $A_{sv} = 78.5 \times 2 = 157 \text{ mm}^2$.

$$\Rightarrow \qquad (s_v)_{\text{reqd}} = \frac{A_{sv} d_1 (0.87 f_y)}{T_u/b_1 + V_u/2.5}$$

With 50 mm effective cover assumed all around, [Figure 7.12].

$$d_1 = 750 - 50 \times 2 = 650 \text{ mm}$$

$$b_1 = 350 - 50 \times 2 = 250 \text{ mm}$$

$$\Rightarrow \qquad (s_v)_{\text{reqd}} = \frac{157 \times 650 \times (0.87 \times 415)}{(140 \times 10^6/250) + (110 \times 10^3/2.5)} = 61.0 \text{ mm (low)}$$

Alternatively, providing 12ϕ 2-legged stirrups, $A_{sv} = 113 \times 2 = 226 \text{ mm}^2$

$$\Rightarrow \qquad (s_v)_{\text{reqd}} = 61.0 \times \frac{226}{157} = 87.8 \text{ mm}$$

Further, applying Eq. 7.24,

$$(s_v)_{\text{reqd}} = \frac{0.87 f_y A_{sv}}{(\tau_{ve} - \tau_e)b} = \frac{0.87 \times 415 \times 226}{(3.06 - 0.618) \times 350} = 94 \text{ mm}$$

- Maximum spacing requirements [Eq. 7.25]:

$$(s_v) \le \begin{cases} x_1 = 250 + 28 + 12 = 290 \text{ mm} \\ (x_1 + y_1)/4 = (290 + 650 + 34)/4 = 243 \text{ mm} \\ 300 \text{ mm} \end{cases}$$

Provide 12ϕ 2-legged stirrups at 85 mm c/c [Figure 7.12]

- Check cover:
With 50 mm effective cover, 12ϕ stirrups and 28ϕ longitudinal bars, clear cover to stirrups is: $50 - 12 - 28/2 = 24$ mm, > 20 mm $\Rightarrow$ OK.

REVIEW QUESTIONS

7.1 Explain, with examples, the difference between *primary torsion* and *secondary torsion.*

7.2 'Primary torsion is associated with statically determinate structures, whereas secondary torsion is associated with statically indeterminate structures'. Is this statement true? Comment.

7.3 Reinforced concrete columns are rarely subjected to torsion. Cite an example where this situation occurs, i.e., torsion exists in combination with axial compression, and perhaps also with flexure and shear.

7.4 How is *torsional stiffness* estimated for 'secondary torsion'?

7.5 (a) Estimate the torsional stiffness of a reinforced concrete beam element (of a frame), having a span $l = 6.0$ m and a rectangular section with width $b = 200$ mm and overall depth $D = 500$ mm. Assume M 25 concrete.

(b) Compare the torsional stiffness with the flexural stiffness, $4EI/l$, for the same beam element.

7.6 In the case of a *circular* shaft subject to pure torsion, it is well known that the maximum torsional shear stress occurs at locations of maximum radius. If the member has a *rectangular* (instead of circular) cross-section, the corner points are the ones located furthest from the shaft axis. However, the torsional shear stress at these points is not the maximum; the stress, in fact, is zero! [refer Figure 7.3(b)]. Why?

7.7 Discuss the torque-twist relationship for (a) *plain concrete* and (b) *reinforced concrete* members subjected to pure torsion.

7.8 Inclined stirrups and bent-up bars are considered suitable for shear reinforcement, but not torsional reinforcement. Why?

7.9 For a thin-walled tubular section of arbitrary shape (but uniform thickness) subjected to pure torsion T_u, the *shear flow q* can be assumed to be constant (in the plasticised state) at all points on the centreline of the thickness. Using this concept, derive the relationship [Eq. 7.9] between q and T_u in terms of A_o, the area enclosed by the centreline of the thickness.

7.10 Briefly explain the concept underlying the space truss analogy for estimating torsional strength of a reinforced concrete beam.

7.11 Briefly discuss the different modes of failure under combined flexure and torsion.

7.12 Briefly discuss torsion-shear interaction of reinforced concrete beams.

PROBLEMS

7.1 Determine the design torsional resistance of the beam shown in Figure 7.13 under pure torsion by (i) IS Code procedure, (ii) general space truss formulation. Assume M 25 concrete and Fe 500 steel.

Ans. (i) 48.6 kNm (ii) 62.2 kNm

7.2 For the beam section shown in Figure 7.13, derive and hence plot suitable interaction relationships (satisfying IS Code requirements) between:

(a) torsion and bending ($T_u - M_u$)

(b) torsion and shear ($T_u - V_u$)

Plot T_u on the y-axis in both cases.

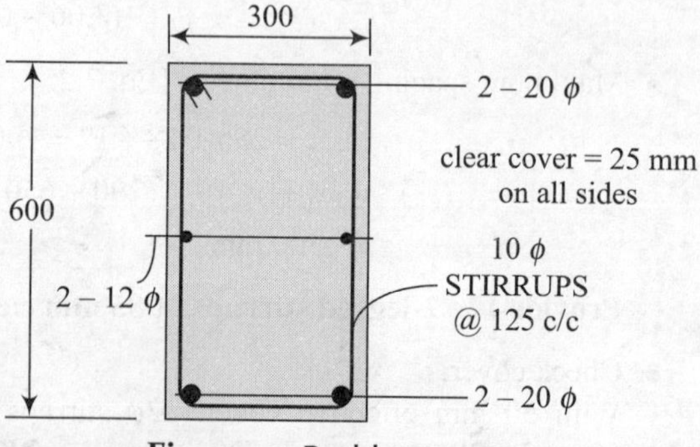

Fig. 7.13 Problems 7.1, 7.2.

7.3 Consider the problem described in Example 7.3 as a *design* problem instead of an *analysis* problem. Consider a total distributed service load of 10 kN/m^2 (instead of 5 kN/m^2) on the 1 m wide cantilever projection [Figure 7.11]. Design the reinforcement in the beam section (300 mm × 500 mm), assuming M 25 concrete, moderate exposure conditions and Fe 415 steel.

7.4 Design a rectangular beam section, 300 mm wide and 550 mm deep (overall), subjected to an ultimate twisting moment of 25 kNm, combined with an ultimate bending moment of 60 kNm and an ultimate-shear force of 50 kN. Assume M 20 concrete, moderate exposure conditions and Fe 415 steel.

7.5 Repeat the Problem 7.4, considering an ultimate twisting moment of 50 kNm (instead of 25 kNm).

7.6 Consider a circular girder of radius $R = 5$ m with rectangular cross-section, 350 mm wide and 750 mm deep (overall), supported symmetrically on 8 pillars [Figure 7.14(a)]. Design and detail one typical span (AB) of the girder, assuming M 20 concrete and Fe 415 steel. The total ultimate (uniformly distributed) load on span AB may be taken as $W_u = 1400$ kN, inclusive of self-weight of the girder. Expressions for the bending moment (M_u), twisting moment (T_u) and shear force (V_u) at any location θ (in radians) [Figure 7.14(b)] can be derived from first principles. For convenience, these expressions are summarised below:

$$M_u = (W_u R)[0.5 \sin\theta + 1.20711 \cos\theta - 1.27324]$$

$$T_u = (W_u R)[1.20711 \sin\theta - 0.5 \cos\theta - 4\theta/\pi + 0.5]$$

$$V_u = 0.5\, W_u\, (1 - 8\theta/\pi)$$

Assume moderate exposure conditions.

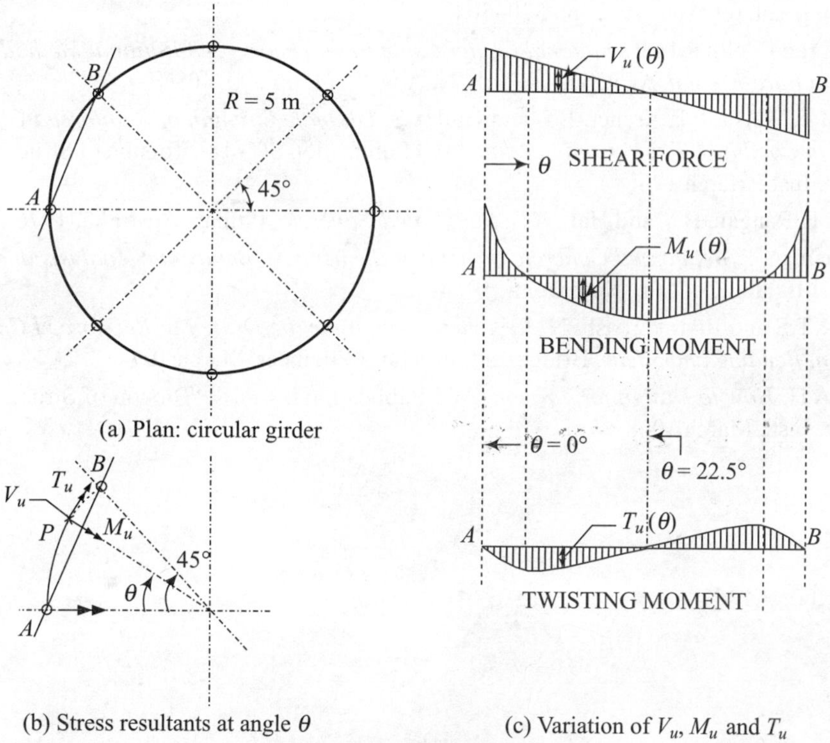

(b) Stress resultants at angle θ (c) Variation of V_u, M_u and T_u

Fig. 7.14 Problem 7.6.

REFERENCES

7.1 Timoshenko, S, and Goodier, J N, *Theory of Elasticity*, Third edition, McGraw-Hill, New York, 1970

7.2 — *Explanatory Handbook on Indian Standard Code of Practice for Plain and Reinforced Concrete (IS 456:1978)*, Special Publication SP:24, Bureau of Indian Standards, New Delhi, 1983

7.3 Popov, E P, *Mechanics of Materials*, Second edition, Prentice-Hall, Englewood Cliffs, New Jersey, 1978

7.4 Hsu, T T C, *Plain Concrete Rectangular Sections*, Torsion of Structural Concrete, ACI Publication SP – 18, Am. Conc. Inst., Detroit, 1968, pp 207–238

7.5 Collins, M P, *The Torque-Twist Characteristics of Reinforced Concrete Beams*, Inelasticity and Nonlinearity in Structural Concrete, SM Study No. 8, University of Waterloo Press, Waterloo, 1972, pp 211–232

7.6 Cowan, H J, *Reinforced and Prestressed Concrete in Torsion*, Edward Arnold Ltd., London, 1965

7.7 Hsu, T T C, *Behaviour of Reinforced Concrete Rectangular Members*, ACI Publication SP – 18, 'Torsion of Structural Concrete' Am. Conc. Inst., Detroit, 1968, pp 261–306

7.8 —*Structural Use of Concrete : Part 2 : Code of Practice for Special Circumstances*, BS 8110 : Part 2 : 1985, British Standards Institution, 1985

7.9 Hsu, T T C, *Ultimate Torque of Reinforced Rectangular Beams*, ASCE Journal, Struct. Div., Vol. 94, Feb. 1968, pp 485–510

7.10 Lampert, P and Collins, M P, *Torsion, Bending and Confusion — An Attempt to Establish the Facts*, ACI Journal, Vol. 69, Aug. 1972, pp 500–504

7.11 Mitchell, D and Collins, M P, *Diagonal Compression Field Theory — A Rational Method for Structural Concrete in Pure Torsion*, ACI Journal, Vol. 71, Aug. 1974, pp 396–408

7.12 Collins, M P, Walsh, P F, Archer, F E and Hall A S, *Ultimate Strength of Reinforced Concrete Beams Subjected to Combined Torsion and Bending*, ACI Publication SP – 18, 'Torsion of Structural Concrete', Am. Conc. Inst., March 1966

7.13 Warner, R F, Rangan, B V and Hall, A S, *Reinforced Concrete,* Pitman, Australia, 1976

7.14 Purushothaman, P, *Reinforced Concrete Structural Elements — Behaviour, Analysis and Design,* Tata McGraw-Hill Publ. Co. Ltd., New Delhi, 1984

7.15 Iyengar, K T S and Ram Parkash, N, *Recommendation for the Design of Reinforced Concrete Beams for Torsion, Bending and Shear*, Bridge and Structural Engineer, March 1974

7.16 Mattock, A H, *How to Design for Torsion*, ACI Publication SP – 18, 'Torsion of Structural Concrete', Am. Conc. Inst., March 1968

CHAPTER

8

Design for Bond

LEARNING OBJECTIVES

After studying this chapter, you will be able to:

- *Interpret the mechanisms of bond resistance and bond failure in reinforced concrete*
- *Describe reinforcement splicing procedures and related Code specifications*
- *Check for adequacy of anchorage/development length and to redesign if necessary, and to design splices for reinforcement*

8.1 Introduction

'Bond' in reinforced concrete refers to the adhesion between the reinforcing steel and the surrounding concrete. It is this *bond* which is responsible for the transfer of axial force from a reinforcing bar to the surrounding concrete, thereby providing *strain compatibility* and 'composite action' of concrete and steel [refer Section 1.2.2]. If this bond is inadequate, 'slipping' of the reinforcing bar will occur, destroying full 'composite action'. Hence, the fundamental assumption of the theory of flexure, viz., plane sections remain plane even after bending, becomes valid in reinforced concrete only if the mechanism of bond is fully effective.

> Bond is the mechanism through which the axial force in the reinforcing steel is transferred to the surrounding concrete, ensuring strain compatibility, stress variations (as required) and composite action.

It is through the action of *bond resistance* that the axial stress (tensile or compressive) in a reinforcing bar can undergo variation from point to point along its length. This is required to accommodate the variation in bending moment along the length of the flexural member. Had the bond been absent, the stress at all points on a straight bar would be constant†, as in a string or a straight cable.

8.1.1 Mechanisms of Bond Resistance

Bond resistance in reinforced concrete is achieved through the following mechanisms:

1. Chemical adhesion – due to a gum-like property in the products of hydration (formed during the making of concrete).

† Such a situation is encountered in prestressed concrete – in *unbonded post-tensioned* members.

2. Frictional resistance – due to the surface roughness of the reinforcement and the grip exerted by the concrete shrinkage.
3. Mechanical interlock – due to the surface protrusions or 'ribs' (oriented transversely to the bar axis) provided in deformed bars.

Evidently, the resistance due to 'mechanical interlock' (which is considerable) is not available when *plain* bars are used. For this reason, many foreign codes prohibit the use of plain bars in reinforced concrete – except for lateral spirals, and for stirrups and ties smaller than 10 mm in diameter. However, there is no such restriction, as yet, in the IS Code.

8.1.2 Bond Stress

> Bond stress is the tangential component of the resistance to slip developed along the contact surface between the reinforcing bar and the surrounding concrete.

Bond resistance is achieved by the development of tangential (shear) stress components along the interface (contact surface) between the reinforcing bar and the surrounding concrete. The stress so developed at the interface is called *bond stress*, and is expressed in terms of the tangential force per unit nominal surface area of the reinforcing bar.

8.1.3 Two Types of Bond

There are two types of loading situations which induce bond stresses, and accordingly 'bond' is characterised as:

1. *Flexural bond*
2. *Anchorage bond* or *development bond*

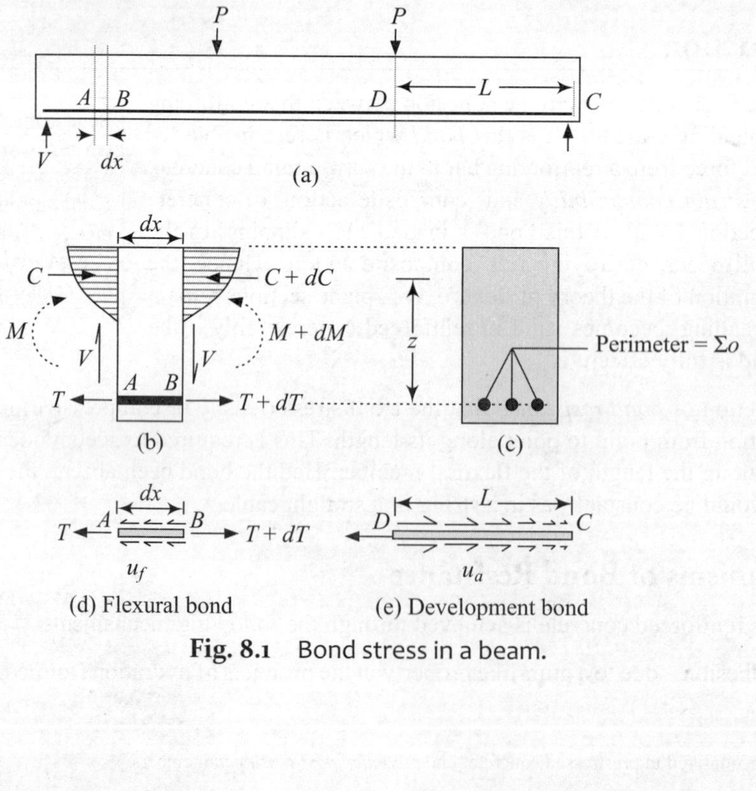

Fig. 8.1 Bond stress in a beam.

'Flexural bond' is that which arises in flexural members on account of shear or a variation in bending moment, which in turn causes a variation in axial tension along the length of a reinforcing bar [Figure 8.1(d)]. Evidently, flexural bond is critical at points where the shear ($V = dM/dx$) is significant.

'Flexural bond' is associated with variation in bending moment and hence in axial force in the reinforcing bar along the span.

'Anchorage bond' (or 'development bond') is that which arises over the length of anchorage provided for a bar or near the end (or cut-off point) of a reinforcing bar; this bond resists the 'pulling out' of the bar if it is in tension [Figure 8.1(e)†], or conversely, the 'pushing in' of the bar if it is in compression.

'Anchorage bond' refers to the bond formed over the length of anchorage (or the development length) provided, in order to develop the desired stress in the reinforcing bar at the critical section.

These two types of bonds are discussed in detail in the sections to follow.

8.2 Flexural Bond

As mentioned earlier, variation in tension along the length of a reinforcing bar, owing to varying bending moment, is made possible through *flexural bond.* The flexural stresses at two adjacent sections of a beam, dx apart, subjected to a differential moment dM, is depicted in Figure 8.1(b). With the usual assumptions made in flexural design, the differential tension dT in the tension steel over the length dx is given by

$$dT = \frac{dM}{z} \tag{8.1}$$

where z is the *lever arm*.

This unbalanced bar force is transferred to the surrounding concrete by means of 'flexural bond' developed along the interface. Assuming the flexural (local) bond stress u_f to be uniformly distributed over the interface in the elemental length dx, equilibrium of forces gives:

$$u_f(\Sigma o)dx = dT \tag{8.2}$$

where Σo is the total perimeter of the bars at the beam section under consideration [Figure 8.1(c)].

From Eq. 8.2, it is evident that the bond stress is directly proportional to the change in the bar force. Combining Eq. 8.2 with Eq. 8.1, the following expression for the local bond stress u_f is obtained:

$$u_f = \frac{dM/dx}{(\Sigma o)z} \tag{8.3a}$$

Alternatively, in terms of the transverse shear force at the section $V = dM/dx$,

$$u_f = \frac{V}{(\Sigma o)z} \tag{8.3b}$$

It follows that flexural bond stress is high at locations of high shear, and that this bond stress can be effectively reduced by increasing Σo, by providing an increased number of bars of smaller diameter (to give the same required A_{st}).

† Segments of the reinforcing bar along *CD* in Figure 8.1(a) have both flexural bond and anchorage bond. An example of anchorage bond alone is the portion *CD* of the bar in Figure 8.3(a).

It may be noted that the actual bond stress will be influenced by *flexural cracking*, *local slip*, *splitting* and other secondary effects – which are not accounted for in Eq. 8.3. In particular, flexural cracking has a major influence in governing the magnitude and distribution of local bond stresses.

8.2.1 Effect of Flexural Cracking on Flexural Bond Stress

From Eq. 8.3(b), it appears that the flexural (local) bond stress u_f has a variation that is similar to and governed by the variation of the transverse shear force V. In fact, it would appear that in regions of constant moment, where shear is zero, there would be no bond stress developed at all. However, this is not true. The tensile force T in the reinforcement varies between flexural crack locations, even in regions of constant moment, as indicated in Figure 8.2.

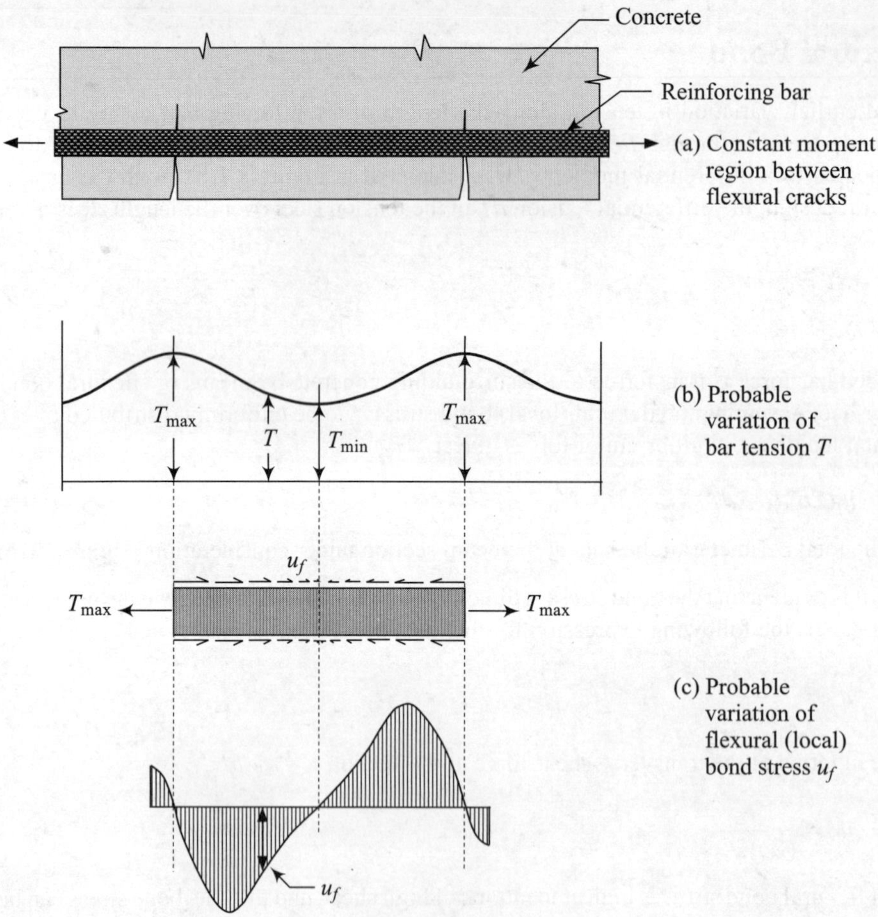

Fig. 8.2 Effect of flexural cracks on flexural bond stress in constant moment region.

At the flexural crack location, the tension is carried by the reinforcement alone, whereas in between the cracks, concrete carries some tension and thereby partially relieves the tension in the steel bars. As local bond stress is proportional to the rate of change of bar force [Eq. 8.2], local bond stresses do develop in such situations.

The bond stresses follow a distribution somewhat like that shown in Figure 8.2(c), with the direction of the bond stress reversing between the cracks [Ref. 8.1]. The net bond force between the cracks will, of course, be zero in a region of constant moment. When the moment varies between the flexural cracks, the bond stress distribution will differ from that shown in Figure 8.2(c), such that the net bond force is equal to the unbalanced tension in the bars between the cracks [Eq. 8.2].

Beam tests show that longitudinal splitting cracks tend to get initiated near the flexural crack locations where the local peak bond stresses can be high. The use of large diameter bars particularly renders the beam vulnerable to splitting and/or local slip.

Finally, it may be noted that flexural cracks are generally not present in the compression zone. For this reason, flexural bond is less critical in a compression bar, compared to a tension bar with an identical axial force.

8.3 Anchorage (Development) Bond

As mentioned earlier, *anchorage bond* or *development bond* is the bond developed near the extreme end (or cut-off point) of a bar subjected to tension (or compression). This situation is depicted in the cantilever beam of Figure 8.3, where it is seen that the tensile stress in the bar segment varies from a maximum (f_s) at the continuous end D to practically zero at the discontinuous end C.

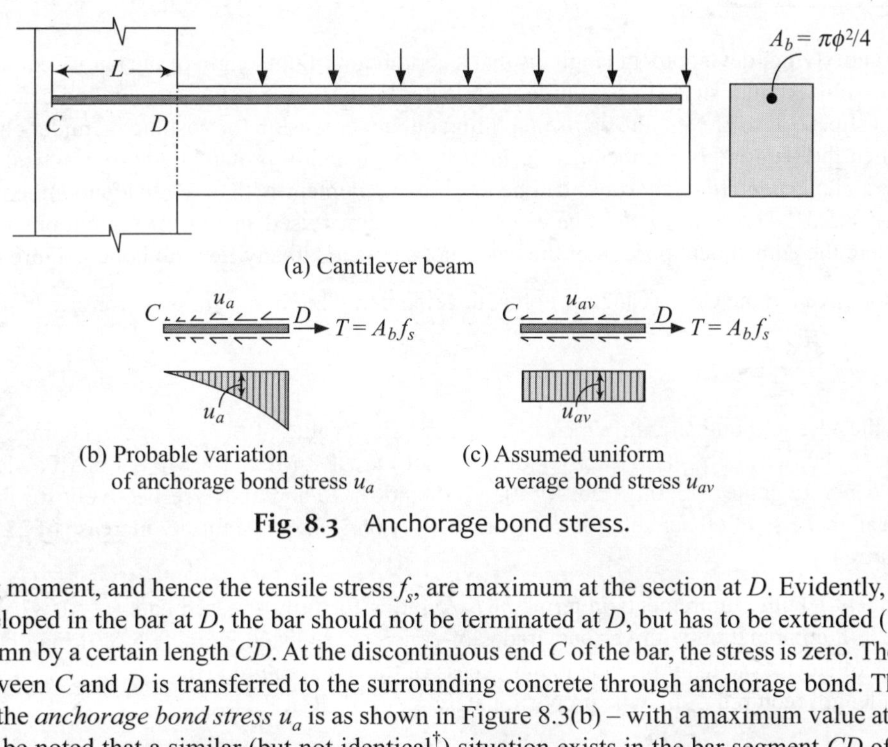

Fig. 8.3 Anchorage bond stress.

The bending moment, and hence the tensile stress f_s, are maximum at the section at D. Evidently, if a stress f_s is to be developed in the bar at D, the bar should not be terminated at D, but has to be extended ('anchored') into the column by a certain length CD. At the discontinuous end C of the bar, the stress is zero. The difference in force between C and D is transferred to the surrounding concrete through anchorage bond. The probable variation of the *anchorage bond stress* u_a is as shown in Figure 8.3(b) – with a maximum value at D and zero at C. It may be noted that a similar (but not identical†) situation exists in the bar segment CD of the simply supported beam in Figure 8.1(a).

† It can be seen that in the case shown in Figure 8.1(a), flexural bond coexists with anchorage bond, owing to variation of bending moment in the segment CD.

An expression for an *average* bond stress u_{av} can be derived by assuming a uniform bond stress distribution over the length L of the bar of diameter ϕ [Figure 8.3(c)], and considering equilibrium of forces as given below:

$$(\pi\phi L)u_{av} = (\pi\phi^2/4)f_s \quad \Rightarrow \quad u_{av} = \frac{\phi f_s}{4L} \tag{8.4}$$

This bond stress may be viewed as the average bond stress generated over a length L in order to *develop* a maximum tensile (or compressive) stress f_s at a critical section; hence, this type of bond is referred to as 'development bond'. Alternatively, this bond may be viewed as that required to provide *anchorage* for a critically stressed bar; hence, it is also referred to as 'anchorage bond'.

8.3.1 Development Length

At every section, the reinforcing bar must have developed in it the required axial force. This is achieved by ensuring that the bar has adequate development length in *both* directions (i.e., on either sides).

The term *development length* has already been introduced in Section 5.9.2, in relation to restrictions on theoretical bar cut-off points. The concept of 'development length' is explained in the Code as follows:

> 'The calculated tension or compression in any bar at any section shall be developed on each side of the section by an appropriate development length or end anchorage or by a combination thereof' [Cl. 26.2].

The concept underlying 'development length' is that a certain minimum length of the bar is required on either side of a point of maximum steel stress in order to transfer the bar force to the surrounding concrete through bond, without slip, so as to prevent the bar from pulling out under tension (or pushing in, under compression). However, when the required bar embedment cannot be conveniently provided due to practical difficulties, *bends*, *hooks* and *mechanical anchorages* can be used to supplement with an equivalent embedment length [refer Section 8.5.3]. The term *anchorage length* is sometimes used in lieu of 'development length' in situations where the embedment portion of the bar is not subjected to any flexural bond [Figure 8.3].

The expression given in the Code (Cl. 26.2.1) for 'development length' $\tilde{L}_d$† follows from Eq. 8.4:

$$\tilde{L}_d = \frac{\phi f_s}{4\tau_{bd}} \tag{8.5}$$

where τ_{bd} is the 'design bond stress', which is the permissible value of the average anchorage bond stress u_a. The values specified for τ_{bd} (Cl. 26.2.1.1 of the Code) are 1.2 MPa, 1.4 MPa, 1.5 MPa, 1.7 MPa and 1.9 MPa for concrete grades M 20, M 25, M 30, M 35 and M 40 and above respectively for *plain bars in tension*, with an increase of 60 per cent for *deformed bars in tension*, and a further increase of 25 per cent for *bars in compression*.

The development length requirements in terms of L_d/ϕ ratios for fully stressed bars ($f_s = 0.87f_y$) of various grades of steel in combination with various grades of concrete are listed in Table 5.6. It may be noted that when the area of steel A_s actually provided is in excess of the area required (for $f_s = 0.87f_y$), then the actual development length required $\tilde{L}_d$ may be proportionately reduced [Ref. 8.5]:

$$\tilde{L}_d = L_d \times \frac{(A_s)_{\text{reqd}}}{(A_s)_{\text{provided}}} \tag{8.6}$$

† In this book, the notation L_d is reserved for development length of fully stressed bars ($f_s = 0.87f_y$). For $f_s < 0.87f_y$, evidently $\tilde{L}_d = L_d(f_s/0.87f_y)$.

In the case of bundled bars, the Code specifies that the '*development length of each bar of bundled bars shall be that for the individual bar, increased by* 10 *percent for two bars in contact,* 20 *percent for three bars in contact and* 33 *percent for four bars in contact.*' Such an increase in development length is warranted because of the reduction in anchorage bond caused by the reduced interface surface between the steel and the surrounding concrete.

8.4 Bond Failure and Bond Strength

8.4.1 Bond Failure Mechanisms

The mechanisms that initiate bond failure may be any one or combination of the following:

- break-up of adhesion between the bar and the concrete;
- longitudinal splitting of the concrete around the bar;
- crushing of the concrete in front of the bar ribs (in deformed bars); and
- shearing of the concrete keyed between the ribs along a cylindrical surface surrounding the ribs (in deformed bars).

> **Axial forces in deformed bars cause wedging action at the lugs, resulting in radial outward forces tending to split the concrete - refer Figures 8.4 (c),(d).**

The most common type of bond failure mechanism is the pulling loose of the reinforcement bar, following the *longitudinal splitting* of the concrete along the bar embedment [Figure 8.4]. Occasionally, failure occurs with the bar pulling out of the concrete, leaving a circular hole without causing extensive splitting of the concrete. Such a failure may occur with plain smooth bars placed with large cover, and with very small diameter deformed bars (wires) having large concrete cover [Ref. 8.1]. However, with deformed bars and with the normal cover provided in ordinary beams, bond failure is usually a result of longitudinal splitting.

In the case of ribbed bars, the bearing pressure between the rib and the concrete is inclined to the bar axis [Figure 8.4(b)]. This introduces radial forces in the concrete ('wedging action'), causing circumferential tensile stresses in the concrete surrounding the bar (similar to the stresses in a pipe subjected to internal pressure [Figures 8.4(c),(d)]) and tending to split the concrete along the weakest plane [Ref. 8.2–8.4]. Splitting occurs along the thinnest surrounding concrete section, and the direction of the splitting crack ('bottom splitting' or 'side splitting') depends on the relative values of the bottom cover, side cover and bar spacing as shown in Figure 8.4(b).

Splitting cracks usually appear on the surface as extensions of flexural or diagonal tension cracks in flexural members, beginning in regions of high local bond stress [Figure 8.2]. With increased loads, these cracks propagate gradually along the length of embedment ('longitudinal splitting') with local splitting at regions of high local bond stress and associated redistribution of bond stresses. It is found that in a normal beam, local splitting can develop over 60–75 per cent of the bar length without loss of average bond strength and without adversely affecting the load-carrying capacity of the beam [Ref. 8.1]. The presence of stirrups offers resistance to the propagation of continuous longitudinal splitting cracks [Figure 8.5]. However, in beams without stirrups, the failure due to bond can occur early and suddenly, as the longitudinal split runs through to the end of the bar without the resistance offered by the stirrups.

> **Stirrups help resist splitting forces, in addition to confining concrete, and in general, improve bond strength.**

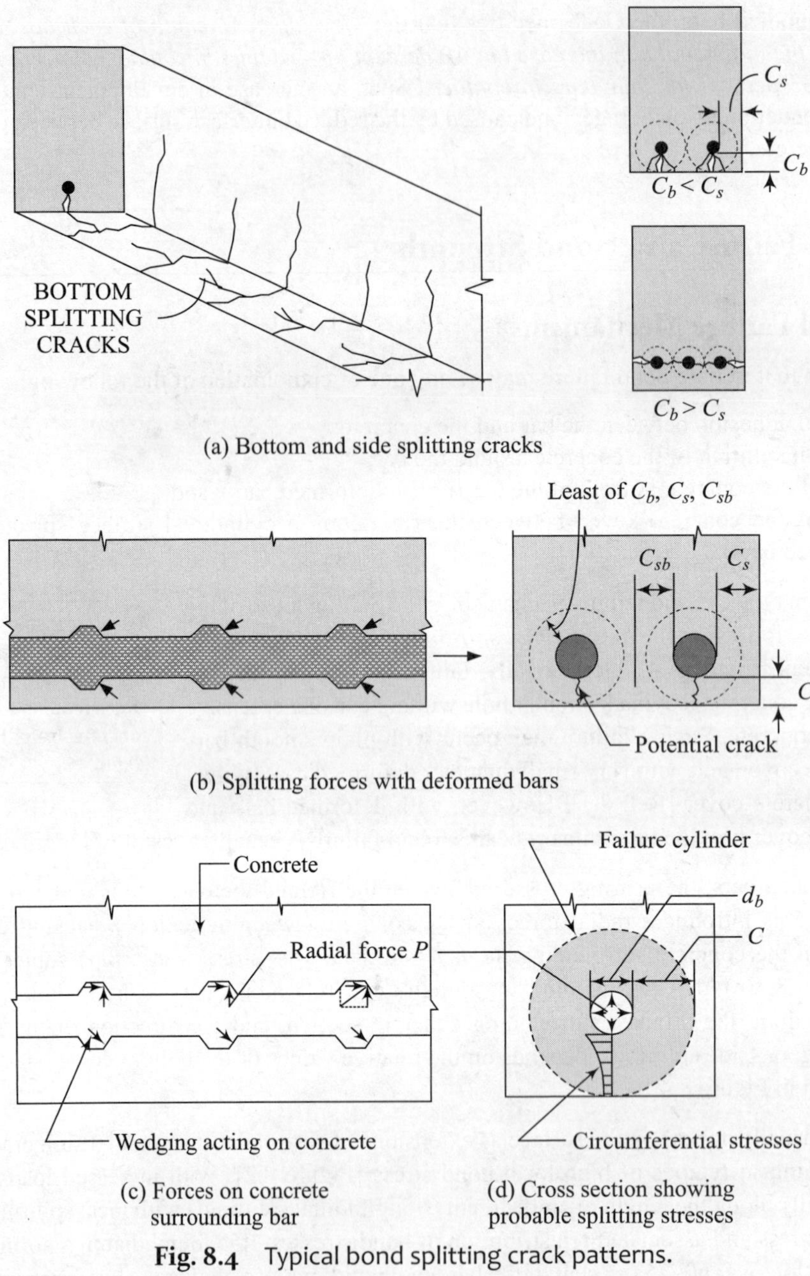

Fig. 8.4 Typical bond splitting crack patterns.

A simply supported beam can act as a two-hinged arch, and so carry substantial loads, even if the bond is destroyed over the length of the bar, provided the tension bars are suitably anchored at their ends [Figure 8.6]. (See the strut-and-tie concept in Section 17.3). However, the deflections and crack-widths of such a beam may be excessive. The anchorage may be realised over an adequate length of embedment beyond the face of the support, and/or by bends and hooks or mechanical anchorages (welded plates, nuts and bolts, etc.).

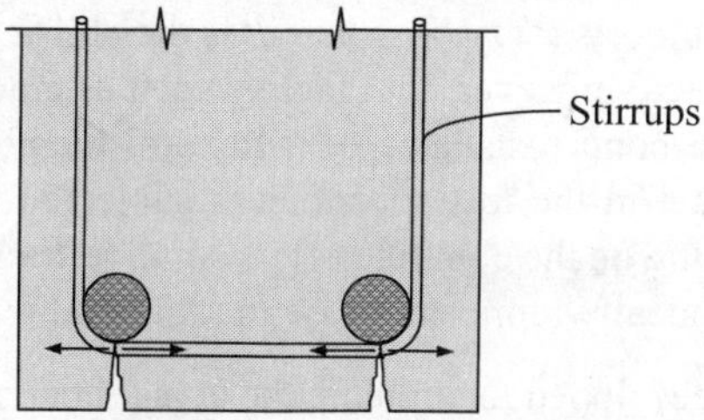

Fig. 8.5 Stirrups resisting tensile forces due to bond.

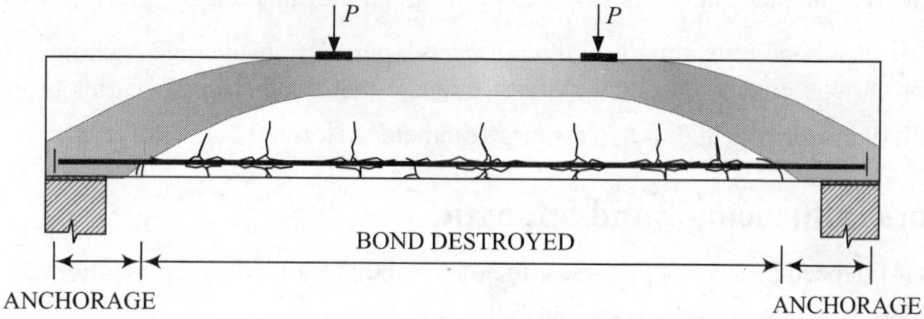

Fig. 8.6 Tied-arch action with bar anchorage alone.

8.4.2 Bond Tests

Bond strength is usually ascertained by means of *pull out* tests or some sort of beam tests. The typical 'pull out' test is shown schematically in Figure 8.7(a). A bar embedded in a concrete cylinder or prism is pulled until failure occurs by splitting, excessive slip or pull-out.

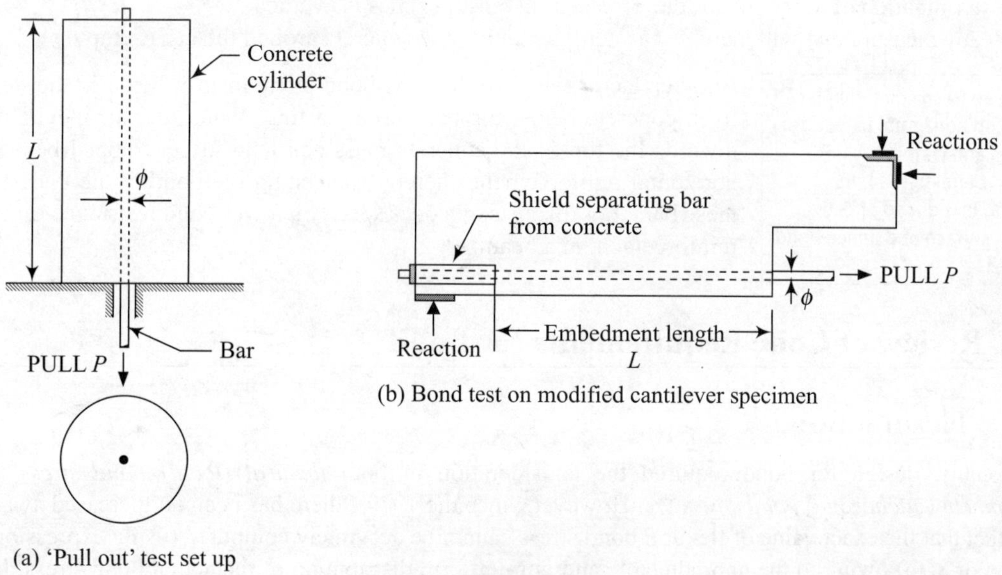

Fig. 8.7 Bond tests.

The *nominal bond strength* is computed as $P/(\pi\phi L)$, where P is the pull at failure, ϕ the bar diameter and L the length of embedment. It may be noted, however, that factors such as cracking (flexural or diagonal tension) and dowel forces, which lower the bond resistance of a flexural member, are not present in a concentric pull-out test. Moreover, the concrete in the test specimen is subjected to a state of compression (and not tension), and the friction at the bearing on the concrete offers some restraint against splitting. Hence, the bond conditions in a pull-out test do not ideally represent those in a flexural member.

Of the several types of beam tests developed to simulate the actual bond conditions, one test set-up is shown in Figure 8.7(b) [Ref. 8.3]. The bond strength measured from such a test, using the same expression $[P/(\pi\phi L)]$ as for a pull-out test, is bound to give a lesser (and more accurate) measure of the bond strength than the pull-out strength. However, the pull-out test is easier to perform, and for this reason, more commonly performed.

From the results of such bond tests, the 'design bond stress' (permissible average anchorage bond stress), τ_{bd}, is arrived at – for various grades of concrete. Tests indicate that bond strength varies proportionately with $\sqrt{f_{ck}}/\phi$ for small diameter bars and $\sqrt{f_{ck}}$ for large diameter deformed bars [Ref. 8.1].

8.4.3 Factors Influencing Bond Strength

Bond strength is influenced by several factors, some of which have already been mentioned. In general, bond strength is enhanced when the following measures are adopted:

- deformed (ribbed) bars are used instead of *plain* bars;
- smaller bar diameters are used;
- higher grade of concrete (improved tensile strength) is used;
- increased cover is provided around each bar;
- increased length of embedment, bends and/or hooks are provided;
- mechanical anchorages are employed;
- stirrups with increased area, reduced spacing and/or higher grade of steel are used;
- termination of longitudinal reinforcement in tension zones is avoided;
- any measure that will increase the confinement of the concrete around the bar is employed.

With deep fresh concrete placed below top horizontal bars, air bubbles and water may get trapped beneath the bars, resulting in reduced effective contact surface and hence bond strength.

Another factor which influences bond strength in a beam is the depth of fresh concrete below the bar during casting. Water and air inevitably rise towards the top of the concrete mass and tend to get trapped beneath the horizontal reinforcement, thereby weakening the bond at the underside of these bars. For this reason, codes specify a lower bond resistance for the top reinforcement in a beam.

8.5 Review of Code Requirements for Bond

8.5.1 Flexural Bond

Traditionally, design for bond required the consideration of both *flexural (local) bond stress* u_f and *development (anchorage) bond stress* u_{av}. However, since the 1970s, there has been an increased awareness of the fact that the exact value of flexural bond stress cannot be accurately computed (using expressions like Eq. 8.3a or 8.3b) owing to the unpredictable and non-uniform distribution of the actual bond stress. In fact, it is found that localised bond failures can and do occur, despite the checks provided by Eq. 8.3. However, as explained earlier, these local failures do not impair the strength of the beam (in terms of ultimate load-carrying capacity) provided the bars are adequately anchored at their ends [Figure 8.6]. Thus, the concept underlying limit state design for flexural bond has shifted from the control of local bond stresses (whose predicted values are unrealistic) to the development of required bar stresses through provision of adequate *anchorage* – at simple supports and at bar cut-off points.

The Code requirement for such a check on anchorage, in terms of *development length* plus *end anchorage* and the variation of tensile stress in the bar [Eq. 5.25], has already been discussed at length in Section 5.9.3, and illustrated with several examples.

8.5.2 Development (Anchorage) Bond

The computed stress at *every section* of a reinforcing bar (whether in tension or compression) must be developed on *both* sides of the section – by providing adequate 'development length', $\tilde{L}_d$. Such development length is usually available near the midspan locations of normal beams (where sagging moments are generally maximum) and support locations of continuous beams (where hogging moments are generally maximum). Special checking is generally called for in the following instances only:

- in flexural members that have relatively short spans;
- at simple supports and points of inflection [refer Section 5.9.3];
- at points of bar cut-off [refer Section 5.9.3];
- at cantilever supports;
- at beam-column joints in lateral load resisting frames;
- for stirrups and transverse ties; and
- at *lap splices* [refer Section 8.6].

8.5.3 Bends, Hooks and Mechanical Anchorages

Bends, conforming to standards, are frequently resorted to in order to provide *anchorage*, contributing to the requirements of development length of bars in tension. The Code (Cl. 26.2.2.1) specifies that '*the anchorage value of a bend shall be taken as* 4 *times the diameter of the bar for each* 45° *bend, subject to a maximum of* 16 *times the diameter of the bar*'.

Commonly a 'standard 90° bend' (anchorage value = 8ϕ) is adopted [Figure 8.8(a)], including a minimum extension of 4ϕ. Any additional extension beyond the bend also qualifies to be included in development length calculations. The exact calculation for additional length required, if any, beyond the standard 90° bend is shown in Figure 8.8(c). However, it is sufficiently accurate and conservative to take this as $= L_d - L_{straight}$. More conveniently, the total length of the leg CB beyond the straight bar, including the bend, may be taken as $= L_d - L_{straight} + 5.5\phi$, as shown in Figure 8.8(c). When the bend is turned around 180° and extended beyond by 4ϕ (anchorage value = 16ϕ), it is called a *standard U-type hook* [Figure 8.8(b)]. The minimum (internal) turning radius (r in Figure 8.8) specified for a hook is 2ϕ for plain mild steel bars and 4ϕ for cold-worked deformed bars [Ref. 8.5]. Hooks are generally considered mandatory for *plain* bars in tension [refer Cl. 26.2.2.1a of the Code]. Note that in Fig. 8.8(c), the radius r is taken as 4ϕ.

Bends and hooks are ineffective in anchoring bars in compression. Hence, Code (Cl. 26.2.2.2) specifies that for bars in compression, only the projected length of hooks, bends and straight lengths beyond bends shall be considered for development length. However, for bars in compression, it is doubtful whether extensions beyond bends can meaningfully provide anchorage.

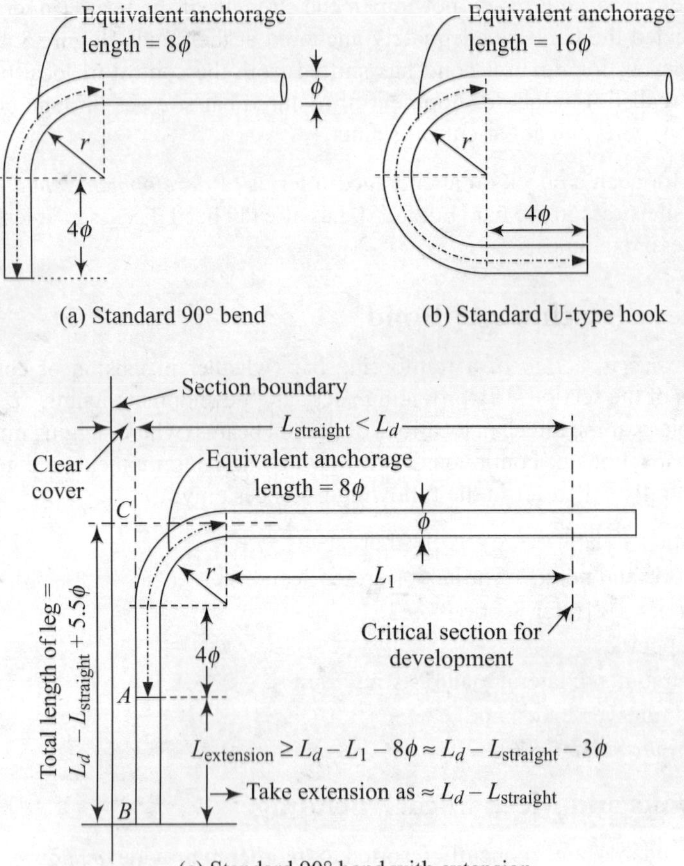

Fig. 8.8 Anchorage lengths of standard bends and hooks.

In the case of stirrup (and transverse tie) reinforcement, the Code (Cl. 26.2.2.4b) specifies that *complete anchorage shall be deemed to have been provided* if any of the following specifications is satisfied:

- 90° bend around a bar of diameter not less than the stirrup diameter ϕ, with an extension of at least 8ϕ;
- 135° bend with an extension of at least 6ϕ;
- 180° bend with an extension of at least 4ϕ.

A word of caution is appropriate here. In situations were closed ties are required (as in columns and for torsion), the effectiveness of the 90° bend with a straight bar extension is doubtful unless the concrete cover around the hook is restrained against spalling.

It may be noted that bends and hooks introduce bearing stresses in the concrete that they bear against. To ensure that these bearing stresses are not excessive, the turning radius r (in Figure 8.8) should be sufficiently large. The Code (Cl. 26.2.2.5) recommends a check on the bearing stress f_b inside any bend, calculated as follows:

$$f_b = \frac{F_{bt}}{r\phi} \tag{8.7}$$

where F_{bt} is the design tensile force in the bar (or group of bars), r the internal radius of the bend, and ϕ the bar diameter (or size of bar of equivalent area in case of a bundle). The calculated bearing stress should not exceed a limiting bearing stress, given by $1.5f_{ck}/(1 + 2\phi/a)$, where a is the centre-to-centre spacing between bars perpendicular to the bend, or, in the case of bars adjacent to the face of the member, the clear cover plus the bar diameter ϕ. For fully stressed bars,

$$F_{bt} = 0.87 f_y \left(\frac{\pi\phi^2}{4}\right)$$

Accordingly, it can be shown that the limiting radius is given by

$$r \geq 0.456\phi\left(\frac{f_y}{f_{ck}}\right)\left(1+\frac{2\phi}{a}\right) \tag{8.8}$$

Mechanical anchorages in the form of welded plates, nuts and bolts, etc., can be used, provided they are *capable of developing the strength of the bar without damage to concrete* (Cl. 26.2.2.3 of the Code). In general, the effectiveness of such devices must be ascertained through tests.

8.6 Splicing of Reinforcement

Splices are regions of stress concentrations, and thereby, potential zones of weakness; they are to be avoided at locations of high moments/shears; they are ideally staggered.

Splices are required when bars placed short of their required length (due to non-availability of longer bars) need to be extended. Splices are also required when the bar diameter has to be changed along the length (as is sometimes done in columns). The purpose of 'splicing' is to transfer effectively the axial force from the terminating bar to the connecting (continuing) bar with the same line of action at the junction. This invariably introduces stress concentrations in the surrounding concrete. These effects should be minimised by:

- using proper splicing techniques;
- keeping the splice locations away from sections with high flexural/shear stresses; and
- staggering the locations of splicing in the individual bars of a group (as, typically in a column).

The Code recommends that

> "splices in flexural members should not be at sections where the bending moment is more than 50 percent of the moment of resistance; and not more than half the bars shall be spliced at a section" (Cl. 26.2.5).

When splicing in such situations becomes unavoidable, special precautions need to be employed, such as

- increasing the length of lap (in *lap splices* and *lap welding*);
- using spirals or closely-spaced stirrups around the length of the splice.

Splicing is generally done in one of the following three ways:

1. Lapping of bars (*lap splice*)
2. Welding of bars (*welded splice*)
3. Mechanical connection.

8.6.1 Lap Splices

Lap splices are achieved by overlapping the bars over a certain length, thereby enabling the transfer of axial force from the terminating bar to the connecting bar through the mechanism of anchorage (development) bond with the surrounding concrete – [Figure 8.9(a)]. The cracking and splitting behaviour observed in *lap splice tests* are found to be similar to those in *anchorage bond tests* [Ref. 8.2].

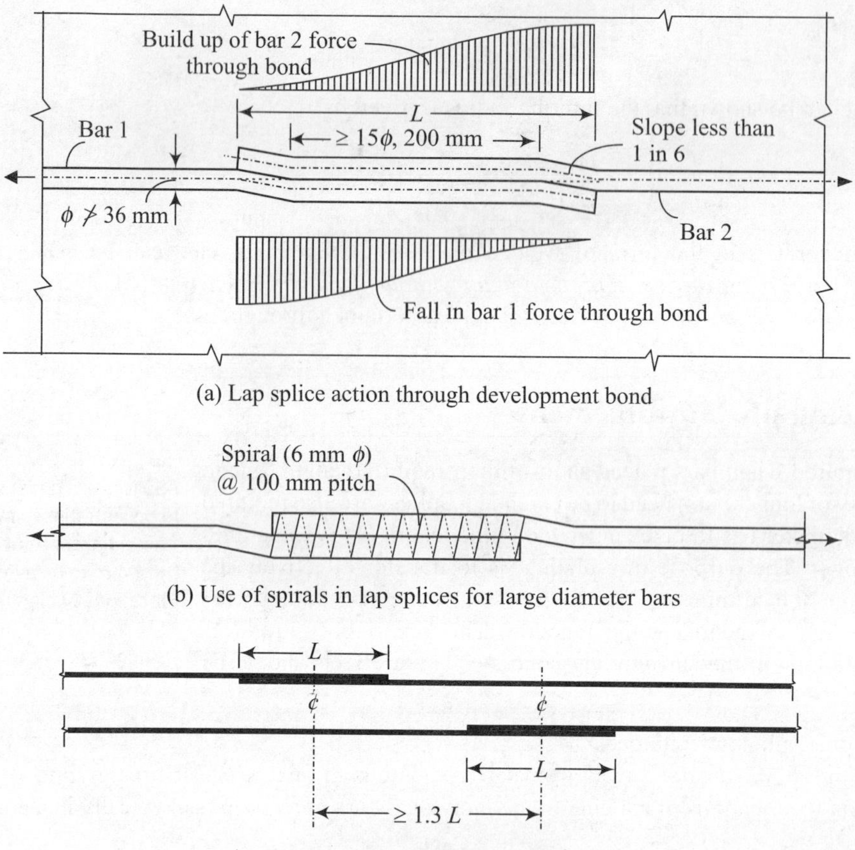

(a) Lap splice action through development bond

(b) Use of spirals in lap splices for large diameter bars

(c) Staggered splicing of bars

Fig. 8.9 Lap splices.

Lap splices are usually not permitted for very large diameter bars ($\phi > 36$ mm), for which *welded splices* are recommended. However, where welding is not practicable, the Code (Cl. 26.2.5.1a) permits lap splices with additional *spirals* around the lapped bars [Figure 8.9(b)].

It is desirable to bend the bars slightly (particularly large diameter bars) near the splice location in order to ensure a collinear transfer of force (without eccentricity), as shown in Figure 8.9(a). The Code specifies that the straight length of the lap should not be less than 15ϕ or 200 mm. As the force transfer is through development bond, the lap length should at least be equal to the *development length* $\tilde{L}_d$. The Code (Cl. 26.2.5.1c,d) specifies a lap length of $\tilde{L}_d$ for bars in flexural tension, 2 $\tilde{L}_d$ for bars in direct tension and

$\tilde{L}_d$ (computed for compression) for bars in compression. Furthermore, in no case should the lap length be less than 30ϕ under flexural or direct tension and 24ϕ under compression†. When bars of two different diameters are to be spliced, the lap length should be calculated on the basis of the smaller diameter. Splices in tension members shall be enclosed in spirals made of bars not less than 6 mm diameter with pitch not more than 100 mm.

In the revised Code, some additional clauses have been incorporated (Cl. 26.2.5.1c) to account for the reduction in bond strength with regard to rebars located near the top region [refer Section 8.4.3‡]. When lapping of tension reinforcement is required at the top of a beam (usually near a continuous support location or a beam-column junction) and the clear cover is less than twice the diameter of the lapped bar, the lapped length should be increased by a factor of 1.4. If the rebar is required to turn around a corner (as in an exterior beam-column junction), the lapped length should be increased by a factor of 2.0. This factor may be limited to 1.4 in the case of corner bars when the clear cover on top is adequate but the side cover (to the vertical face) is less than twice the diameter of the lapped bar.

When more than one bar requires splicing, care must be taken to ensure that the splicing is staggered, with a minimum (centre-to-centre) separation of 1.3 times the lap length, as indicated in Figure 8.9(c). It is also desirable to provide (extra) transverse ties (especially in columns), connecting the various longitudinal bars in the spliced region. In the case of *bundled bars*, the lap length should be calculated considering the increased $\tilde{L}_d$ [refer Section 8.3.1], and the individual splices within a bundle should be staggered.

8.6.2 Welded Splices and Mechanical Connections

Welded splices and *mechanical connections* are particularly suitable for large diameter bars. This results in reduced consumption of reinforcing steel. It is desirable to subject such splices to *tension tests* in order to ensure adequacy of strength [refer Cl. 12.4 of the Code]. Welding of cold-worked bars needs special precautions owing to the possibility of a loss in strength on account of welding heat [Ref. 8.6]. The Code (Cl. 26.2.5.2) recommends that the design strength of a welded splice should in general be limited to 80 per cent of the design strength of the bar for tension splices.

Butt welding of bars is generally adopted in welded splices. The bars to be spliced should be of the same diameter. Additional two or three symmetrically positioned small diameter lap bars may also be provided (especially when the bars are subjected to tension) and fillet welded to the main bars. Even in the case of 'lap splices', *lap welding* (at intervals of 5ϕ) may be resorted to in order to reduce the lap length.

End-bearing splices are permitted by the Code (Cl. 26.2.5.3) for bars subject to compression. This involves *square cutting* the ends of the bars and welding the bar ends to suitable bearing plates that are embedded within the concrete cover.

† Columns are frequently subjected to compression combined with bending. Hence, it may be prudent to calculate the lap length, assuming *flexural tension*, and *not* compression.

‡ As explained in Section 8.4.3, this reduction in bond strength is strictly applicable for all situations, not only lapping. It may also be noted that the reduction in bond strength of top reinforcement may not be significant in shallow members.

8.7 Design Examples

Example 8.1

Check the adequacy of the anchorage provided for the longitudinal bars in the cantilever beam shown in Figure 8.10 and suggest appropriate modifications, if required. The beam is subjected to a uniformly distributed factored load of 100 kN (total, including self-weight). Assume M 25 concrete and Fe 500 steel, deformed bars.

Solution

Preliminary check on anchorage length

- Assuming the bars are fully stressed at the location of maximum moment (i.e., face of column support), full development length L_d is required for anchorage of the bars inside the column, beyond this section.

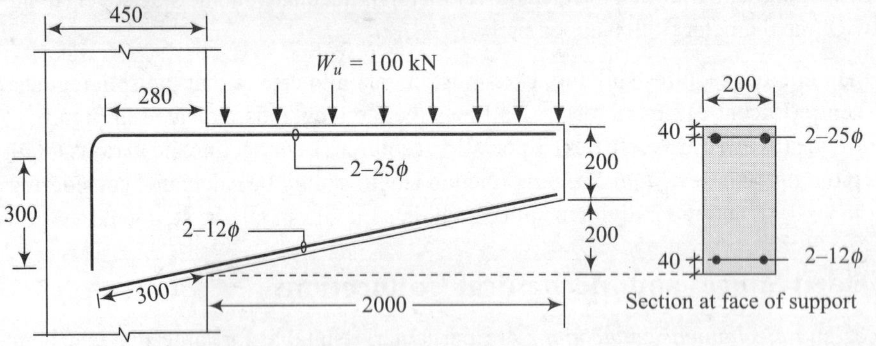

Fig. 8.10 Example 8.1.

- *For the tension bars* (2–25ϕ at top), $L_d = \left(\dfrac{0.87 f_y}{4\tau_{bd}}\right)\phi = 49\phi$

  [This follows from f_y = 500 MPa and τ_{bd} = 1.4 MPa × 1.6 for M 25 concrete with Fe 500 steel deformed bars; L_d/ϕ ratios are also listed in Table 5.6]

  ⇒ $L_d = 49 \times 25 = 1225$ mm

  Actual anchorage length provided (including effect of the 90° bend and extension of bar beyond bend and minimum extension 4ϕ) = 280 + (8 × 25) + 200 = 680 mm

  $< L_d = 1225$ ⇒ Not OK.

- *For the compression bars* (2–12ϕ at bottom),
  τ_{bd} can be increased by 25 per cent, whereby $L_d = (49\phi) \times 0.8$

  ⇒ $L_d = 49 \times 12 \times 0.8 = 470$ mm

  Actual anchorage length provided = 300 mm.

  $< L_d = 470$ mm ⇒ Not OK.

- Before providing increased anchorage length, it is desirable to verify whether the bars are fully stressed under the given loading, and to make more precise development length ($\tilde{L}_d$) calculations [refer Eq. 8.6].

Actual anchorage length required

- *Maximum factored moment at the critical section:*

$$M_u = W_u \times L/2 = 100 \text{ kN} \times (2.0 \text{ m})/2 = 100 \text{ kNm}$$

$$b = 200 \text{ mm}, d = 400 - 40 = 360 \text{ mm}$$

$$\Rightarrow \quad \frac{M_u}{bd^2} = \frac{100 \times 10^6}{200 \times 360^2} = 3.858 \text{ MPa} > \frac{M_{u,\text{limit}}}{bd^2} = 0.1338 \times 25$$

$$= 3.345 \text{ MPa (for M 25)}$$

Hence, the section has to be doubly-reinforced.

- Using Design Aids [Table A.5 or SP : 16], with $d'/d = 40/360 = 0.11$

$$(p_t)_{\text{reqd}} = 1.08 \quad \Rightarrow \quad (A_{st})_{\text{reqd}} = (1.08/100) \times (200 \times 360) = 778 \text{ mm}^2$$

$$(p_c)_{\text{reqd}} = 0.15 \quad \Rightarrow \quad (A_{sc})_{\text{reqd}} = (0.15/100) \times (200 \times 360) = 108 \text{ mm}^2$$

$$(A_{st})_{\text{provided}} = 2 \times 491 = 982 \text{ mm}^2 > 778 \text{ mm}^2$$

$$(A_{sc})_{\text{provided}} = 2 \times 113 = 226 \text{ mm}^2 > 108 \text{ mm}^2$$

- Anchorage length provided, including the 90° bend value = 280 + 8 × 25 + (300 – 4 × 25) = 680 mm
- Actual anchorage length required $= \tilde{L}_d = \dfrac{(A_s)_{\text{reqd}}}{(A_s)_{\text{provided}}} \times L_d$

$\Rightarrow$ For the *tension* bars, $\tilde{L}_d = \dfrac{778}{982} \times 1225 = 971 \text{ mm} > 680 \text{ mm provided.}$

For the *compression* bars, $\tilde{L}_d = \dfrac{108}{226} \times 470 = 225 \text{ mm} < 300 \text{ mm provided.}$

$\Rightarrow$ Not OK for the tension bars.

Modifications proposed

- It is desirable to reduce the anchorage length requirements by providing smaller diameter bars:
- For *tension* bars (at top), *provide* 3–20 mm ϕ or 4–16 mm ϕ (instead of 2–25ϕ):

$\Rightarrow$ $A_{st} = 3 \times 314 = 942 \text{ mm}^2$ or $A_{st} = 4 \times 201 = 804 \text{ mm}^2 > 778 \text{ mm}^2$ required.

$\tilde{L} \approx L_d = 49 \times 20 = 980$ mm or $49 \times 16 = 784$ mm > 680 mm provided

$\Rightarrow$ Extend the bars further by 980 – 680 = 300 mm for 20 mm ϕ or 784 – 680 = 104 mm for 16 mm ϕ.

— Hence OK.

Example 8.2

The plan of a ground floor column in a building is shown in Figure 8.11(a). It is desired to reduce the longitudinal bar diameter from 28 mm to 20 mm above the second-floor level. Design and detail a suitable lap splice. Assume M 25 concrete and Fe 500 steel.

Solution

- As the column is subjected to compression combined with flexure, some of the bars may be under tension. Hence, the lap length should be calculated, assuming flexural tension, i.e., $L = L_d$ or 30ϕ, whichever is greater. Moreover, at the splice location, as the smaller diameter (20 mm ϕ) bars are adequate in providing the desired strength, the lap length calculation should be based on the smaller diameter:

$$L = \begin{cases} L_d = \dfrac{0.87 \times 500\phi}{4 \times (1.4 \times 1.60)} = 49\phi \quad \text{(greater)} \\ 30\phi \end{cases} \Rightarrow \quad L = 49\phi$$

$$\Rightarrow \qquad L = 49 \times 20 = 980 \text{ mm}$$

- *Staggered splicing:*
  As required by the Code (Cl. 25.2.5.1), the splicing of the bars should be ideally staggered with a minimum (centre-to-centre) separation of

$$1.3L = 1.3 \times 980 = 1275 \text{ mm}$$

The splice detail is shown in Figure 8.11(b).

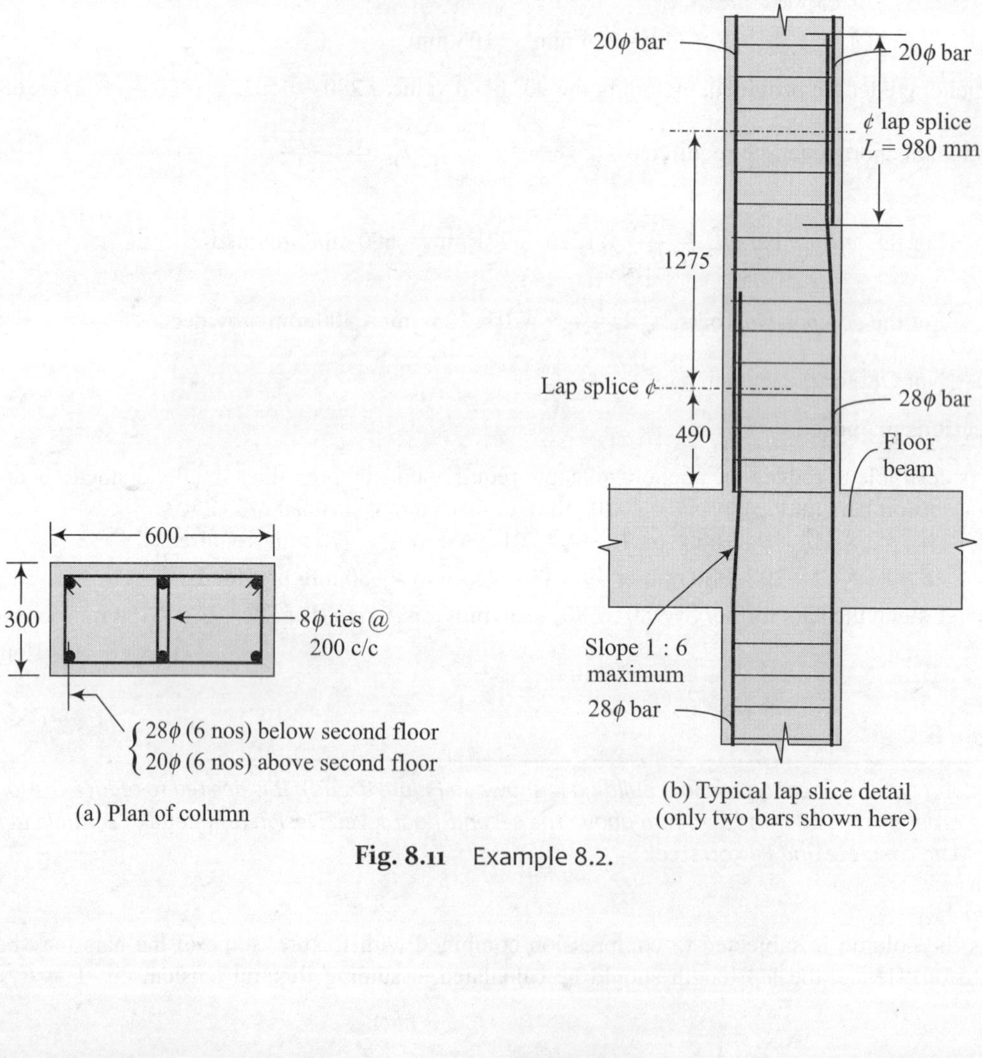

Fig. 8.11 Example 8.2.

REVIEW QUESTIONS

8.1 How is the assumption that *plane sections remain plane even after bending* related to 'bond' in reinforced concrete?

8.2 What are the mechanisms by which bond resistance is mobilised in reinforced concrete?

8.3 Explain clearly the difference between *flexural bond* and *development bond.*

8.4 There is no direct check on *flexural bond stress* in the present Code. Comment on this.

8.5 Define 'development length'. What is its significance?

8.6 Briefly describe the various bond failure mechanisms.

8.7 How is *bond strength* of concrete measured in the laboratory?

8.8 Enumerate the main factors that influence *bond strength*.

8.9 Can there be a difference in the bond resistance of identical bars placed at the *top* and *bottom* of a beam? If so, why? Does the current Code IS 456 recognise this in (i) development length, (ii) lap splice?

8.10 Briefly describe the situations where a check on *development bond* is called for.

8.11 What is the most effective way of reducing the development length requirement of bars in tension?

8.12 Discuss the criterion for deciding the minimum turning radius in a bend in a reinforcing bar

8.13 Determine the minimum internal radius at a bend in a 20 mm ϕ bar of Fe 415 grade in concrete of grade M 20. Assume that the centre-to-centre spacing of bars normal to the bend is 100 mm.

8.14 Explain the purpose of *splicing* of reinforcement. What are the different ways by which this can be achieved?

8.15 Describe why is a *welded splice* generally preferred to a *lap splice*.

8.16 How would you decide on the location of a splice in the tension reinforcement in a flexural member?

8.17 When there is a marked change in the direction of a bar, care must be taken to ensure that the resultant force in the bar at the bend point does not have a component that tends to break the concrete cover. Cite a suitable example and suggest detailing measures to solve such a problem.

8.18 The development length of a deformed reinforcement bar can be expressed as $\phi f_s/(k\ \tau_{bd})$. From IS: 456-2000, the value of k can be calculated as ________.

8.19 As per IS: 456-2000, the lap length of a reinforcement bar of diameter ϕ under compression shall be:
(A) $\geq 15\phi$ (B) $\geq 24\phi$ (C) $\geq 30\phi$ (D) 40ϕ

PROBLEMS

8.1 The outline of a typical (exterior) beam-column joint is shown in Figure 8.12. The maximum factored moment in the beam at the face of the column is found to be 350 kNm (hogging) under gravity loads. Design the flexural reinforcement in the beam at this critical section, and determine the desired anchorage for the reinforcement. Mark the reinforcement and anchorage details in Figure 8.12. Assume M 25 concrete and Fe 500 steel.

8.2 In the case of the beam of Problem 8.1 [Figure 8.12], it is seen that under lateral (wind) loads combined with gravity loads, the maximum factored design moments are obtained as 350 kNm (hogging) or 150 kNm (sagging). Does the earlier design (solution to Problem 8.1) need any modification? Detail the modification, if any.

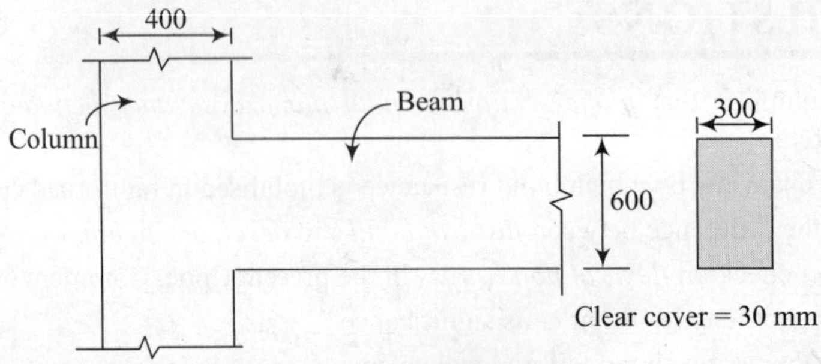

Fig. 8.12 Problem 8.1.

8.3 In a reinforced concrete tension member, a 16 mm ϕ bar has to be lap spliced with a 20 mm ϕ bar. Assuming M 25 concrete and Fe 500 steel, design a suitable lap splice.

8.4 The plan of a column (with 4–25ϕ bars plus 4–20ϕ bars) at a certain level in a multi-storeyed building is shown in Figure 8.13. It is desired to reduce the longitudinal bar sizes from 25 mm to 20 mm, and from 20 mm to 16 mm, above the next floor level. Design and detail suitable lap splices. Assume M 25 concrete and Fe 500 steel.

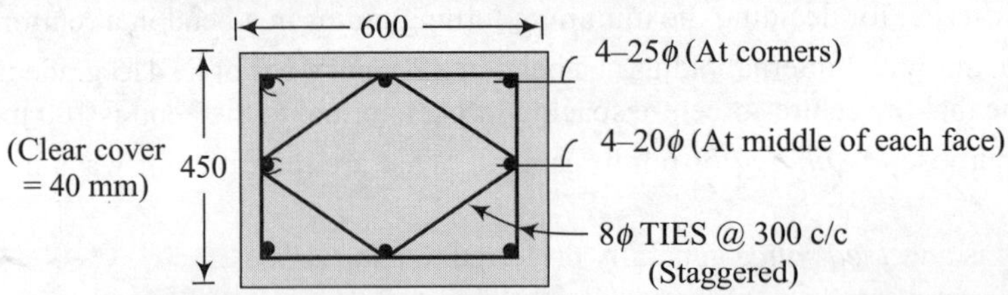

Fig. 8.13 Problem 8.4.

REFERENCES

8.1 ACI Committee 408, *Bond Stress — The State of the Art*, Journal ACI, Vol. 63, Oct. 1966, pp 1161–1190.

8.2 Orangun, C O, Jirsa, J O and Breen, J E, *A Re-evaluation of Test Data on Development Length and Splices*, Journal ACI, Vol. 74, March 1977, pp 114–122.

8.3 Kemp, E L and Wilhelm, W J, *Investigation of the Parameters Influencing Bond Cracking*, Journal ACI, Vol. 76, Jan. 1979, pp 47–71.

8.4 Jimenez, R, White, R N and Gergely, P, *Bond and Dowel Capacities of Reinforced Concrete*, Journal ACI, Vol. 76, Jan. 1979, pp 73–92.

8.5 — *Handbook on Concrete Reinforcement and Detailing*, Special Publication SP 34, Bureau of Indian Standards, New Delhi, 1987.

8.6 — *Recommendations for Welding Cold Worked Bars for Reinforced Concrete Construction* (first revision), IS 9417 : 1989, Bureau of Indian Standards, New Delhi, 1989.

CHAPTER 9

Analysis for Design Moments in Continuous Systems

LEARNING OBJECTIVES

After studying this chapter, you will be able to:

- *Undertake analysis of continuous systems and adopt simplified and approximate methods for analysis.*
- *Implement inelastic analysis, moment redistribution and related Code provisions*

9.1 Introduction

The behaviour and design of flexural members subjected to given bending moments were covered in Chapters 4 and 5. In the design procedure, it was assumed implicitly that *the distribution of bending moments along the length of the beam is known from structural analysis* (as stated in Section 4.1.2). It is not within the scope of this book to describe detailed and exact methods of analysis of indeterminate structures. However, there are many approximations, assumptions and simplified procedures permitted by codes, which assist in the analysis of indeterminate structures and these are discussed here. In particular, this chapter deals with the following aspects:

- Gravity load patterns for maximum moments
- Simplified (approximate) methods of analysis
- Proportioning of member sizes for preliminary design
- Estimation of stiffnesses of frame elements
- Adjustments in calculated moments at beam-column junctions
- Inelastic analysis and moment redistribution

9.1.1 Approximations in Structural Analysis

In a typical reinforced concrete building [refer Section 1.6], the structural system is quite complex. The structure is three-dimensional, comprising floor slabs, beams, columns and footings, which are monolithically connected and act integrally to resist gravity loads (dead loads, live loads) and lateral loads (wind loads, seismic loads). The nature of the load transfer mechanisms [Figure 1.8] and the various load combinations (as well as the associated load factors) have already been discussed in Sections 1.6 and 3.6 respectively.

Gravity Load Patterns

From the viewpoint of designing for the limit state in flexure, what is essentially required is the distribution of the maximum ('positive' as well as 'negative') bending moments (*moment envelope*) under the 'worst' combination of *factored loads*. This is a problem of structural analysis, and for this purpose, the Code (Cl. 22.1) recommends that *all structures may be analysed by the linear elastic theory to calculate internal actions produced by design loads*. In order to simplify the analysis, the effects of *gravity loads* and *lateral loads* may be considered separately and their results superimposed†, after applying appropriate weighting factors (load factors), to give the design *factored moments* (as well as shear forces, axial forces and twisting moments). In the case of *live loads*, special loading patterns have to be considered so that the loads are so placed as to produce the worst effects at the design section considered. These loading patterns, as well as the related Code simplifications, are discussed in Section 9.2.

Simplified Methods of Frame Analysis

While using computer software for analysis, the designer should be fully aware of the modelling and assumptions used in the software and make sure they are consistent with those of the problem at hand. Inappropriate modelling can give unrealistic or erroneous outputs.

The analysis of a complete three-dimensional space frame subjected to various combinations and patterns of loading is complex. Computer programs are widely used for detailed analysis of structures based on matrix methods and finite element methods. Several computer software packages are commercially available for analysis with complex models using one-, two- and three-dimensional elements and both linear and non-linear behaviour (such as ETABS, RFEM, SAP, STAAD). These are essential tools for a large design office and major projects, however, that level of complexity may not be required to analyse typical reinforced concrete structures, for which recourse may be made to simpler and simplified methods of analysis.

In order to simplify the analysis, the three-dimensional framed structure is generally divided into a series of independent parallel *plane frames* along the column lines in the longitudinal and transverse directions of the building, as shown in Figure 9.1. To analyse the gravity load effects, these plane frames may further be simplified into continuous beams or partial frames. The Code also permits the use of certain moment and shear coefficients for continuous beams, which directly give the design moments and shear forces. Simplified methods are also suggested in the Code for analysing plane frames subjected to gravity loads as well as lateral‡ loads. These methods are described in Section 9.3.

Unless the structure is very unsymmetrical or very tall or of major importance, the simplified methods of analysis are usually adequate. In such cases, rigorous analyses can be avoided. From a practical design viewpoint, it should be appreciated that when considerable uncertainties exist with regard to the loads and material properties (inputs of structural analysis), the very concept of an nth order accuracy in the computation of design moments is questionable. A good designer is, therefore, one who makes sensible decisions regarding the modelling and analysis of the structural system, depending on its behaviour and complexity. With the increased availability of software packages, the modern trend is to let the computer do all the analyses as a 'black box', with as much rigour as is available with the software. However, the results of such analyses are highly dependent on the input data fed into the computer, and errors in the input – conceptual or numerical

† The *principle of superposition* is strictly applicable only in a 'first order' analysis, where the structure is assumed to behave in a linear elastic manner. In cases where deflections are significant, a 'second order' analysis (involving the so-called *P–Δ effect*) may be called for; in such cases, superposition is not valid.

‡ Wind load or earthquake loads are dynamic loads, which require *dynamic analysis*. However, the Code permits the use of conventional static analysis in many cases, wherein the loads are treated as equivalent static loads.

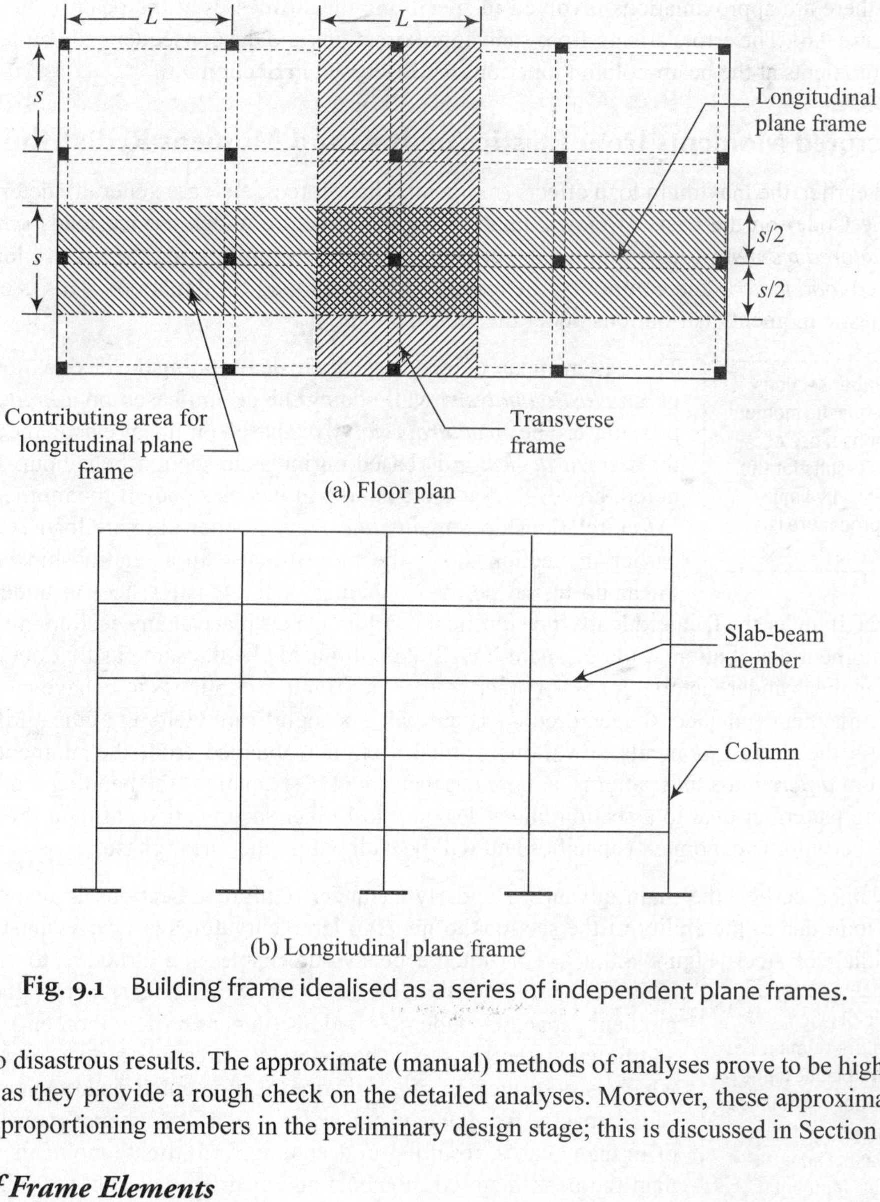

Fig. 9.1 Building frame idealised as a series of independent plane frames.

– may lead to disastrous results. The approximate (manual) methods of analyses prove to be highly useful in this context, as they provide a rough check on the detailed analyses. Moreover, these approximate methods are useful in proportioning members in the preliminary design stage; this is discussed in Section 9.4.

Stiffness of Frame Elements

The sizes of the various members must be known prior to structural analysis, not only to enable the calculation of dead loads, but also to fix the *relative stiffnesses* of the various members of the indeterminate structure. As mentioned earlier, *cracking* is unavoidable in reinforced concrete structures, and the presence of cracks complicates the determination of the stiffness (flexural, torsional or axial) of a reinforced concrete member. Accordingly, certain simplified assumptions are called for in the estimation of stiffnesses – even for the 'rigorous' methods of analysis; these are discussed in Section 9.5.

Furthermore, there are approximations involved in specifying the stiffnesses at the beam-column junctions of frames [Figure 9.6]. The errors arising from such approximations and the consequent adjustments required in the design moments at the beam-column junctions are discussed in Section 9.6.

9.1.2 Factored Moments from Elastic Analysis and Moment Redistribution

As mentioned earlier, the maximum load effects (moments, shear forces, etc.) are generally determined (vide Cl. 22.1 of the Code) on the basis of *elastic* analyses of the structure under service loads (*characteristic loads*). The *factored moments* (design moments) are then obtained by multiplying the service load moments by the specified *load factors* and combining the results of different load combinations. This is equivalent to considering elastic moment distributions under the *factored loads*.

> **Where the member sections have an elastic-plastic moment-curvature response, use of elastic analysis results for the design of sections by limit states design procedure is justified.**

There is an apparent inconsistency in determining the design moments based on an *elastic analysis*, while doing the design based on a *limit state design* procedure. The *structural analysis* is based on linear elastic theory, whereas the *structural design* is based on inelastic section behaviour. It should be noted, however, that there is no real inconsistency if the moment-curvature (M-φ) relationship remains *linear* even under ultimate loads. As explained earlier in Section 4.5.3, the moment-curvature relationship is practically linear up to the point of yielding of the tension steel in under-reinforced sections†. Thus, if under the factored loads, no significant yielding takes place at any section in the structure, the bending moment distribution at the ultimate limit state will indeed be the same as that obtained from a linear elastic analysis under factored loads. In other words, the structure continues to behave more-or-less in a linear elastic manner even under the factored loads, provided no significant yielding of the reinforcing steel takes place. As the design moments at various critical sections (obtained from the moment envelope), determined from *different* loading patterns, are greater than (or at best equal to) the bending moments due to the *one* loading pattern critical to a section under design, most other sections (excepting a few) would not have reached their ultimate moment capacities and will be well within the linear phase.

Also, as explained earlier, the main advantage underlying under-reinforced sections is that they exhibit *ductile* behaviour, due to the ability of the sections to undergo large curvatures at nearly constant moment after the yielding of steel [Figure 4.8(a)]. This ductile behaviour enables the structure to enter into an inelastic phase, wherein the sections which have reached their ultimate moment capacities undergo rotations (under constant moment). This causes additional load effects to be borne by less stressed sections – a phenomenon which is described as *redistribution* of moments (or, in general, stresses). This capacity for *moment redistribution* can be advantageously made use of in many cases, resulting in designing for ultimate moments that are less than the peak factored moments obtained from elastic analysis. The Code (Cl. 37.1.1) permits a limited redistribution of moments, provided adequate ductility is ensured at the critical sections. This is discussed in the concluding section (Section 9.7) of this chapter.

> **Bi-linear elastic-plastic moment-curvature relation and consequent plastic hinge formation in under-reinforced sections/members are the key to limit (plastic) analysis of RC structures. Moment redistribution permitted by the Code is a limited adoption of limit analysis concepts.**

† Actually, the linear M–φ relationship is valid only up to the point of yielding of the tension steel in under-reinforced sections [Figure 4.8(a)]. However, the moment of resistance at this point is practically equal to M_{uR}, which is finally attained only after a significant increase in curvature. Note that the 'idealised' M–φ relationship used even in inelastic analysis [Figure 9.8] assumes linear relationship up to a moment equal to M_{uR}.

9.2 Gravity Load Patterns for Maximum Design Moments

Gravity loads comprise *dead loads* and *live loads* – to be estimated in accordance with Parts 1 and 2 respectively of IS 875: 1987 [also refer Appendix B]. Whereas dead loads, by their inherent nature, act at all times, live loads occur randomly – both temporally and spatially. Thus, live loads need not necessarily act on the entire structure. In order to determine the maximum ('positive' as well as 'negative') moments that can occur at any section in a continuous beam or frame, it is first necessary to identify the spans (or portions of spans) to be loaded (or left unloaded) with live loads so as to create the 'worst' (most extreme) effects.

Live loads, by their nature, need not necessarily act over the whole area; they are applied only over such areas as to produce the worst effect at the section under consideration.

This can be conveniently done by sketching, qualitatively, the shape of the *influence line* for the bending moment at the section under consideration, using the *Müller-Breslau Principle* [Ref. 9.1]. A fictitious hinge is first inserted at the section under consideration, and a rotation introduced therein in a direction corresponding to the moment desired. The resulting deflected shape, corresponding to a unit value of the imposed rotation, gives the desired influence line. The influence lines for the bending moments at two sections (one in the midspan region and another near the support) in a continuous beam, and at two similar sections in a plane frame, are shown in Figures 9.2 and 9.3, respectively.

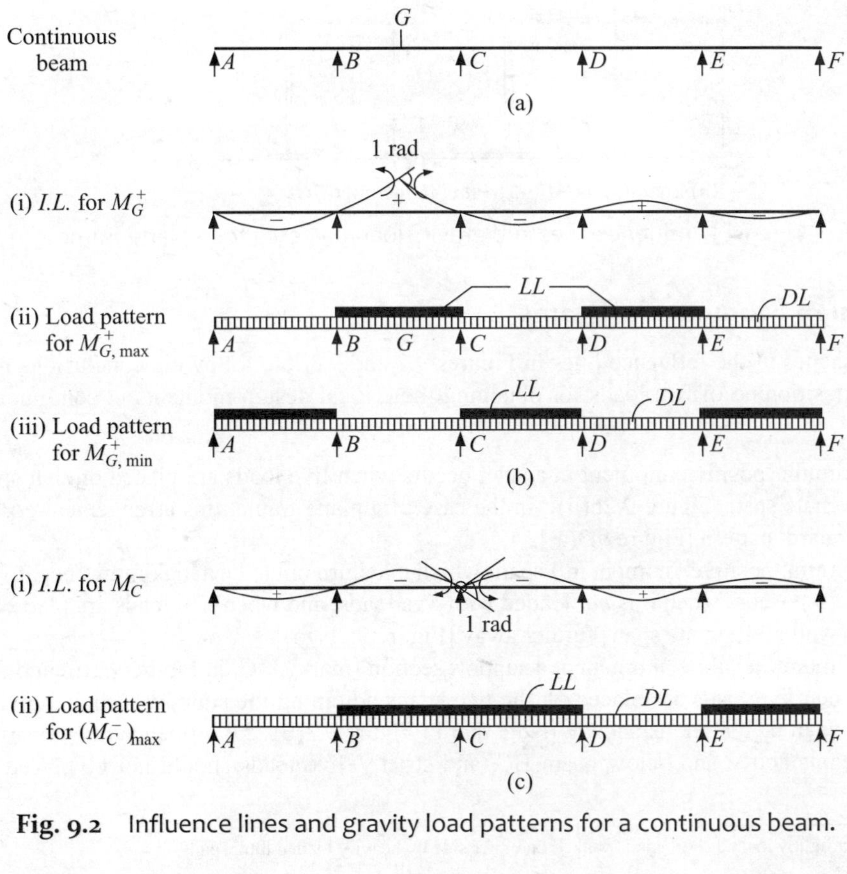

Fig. 9.2 Influence lines and gravity load patterns for a continuous beam.

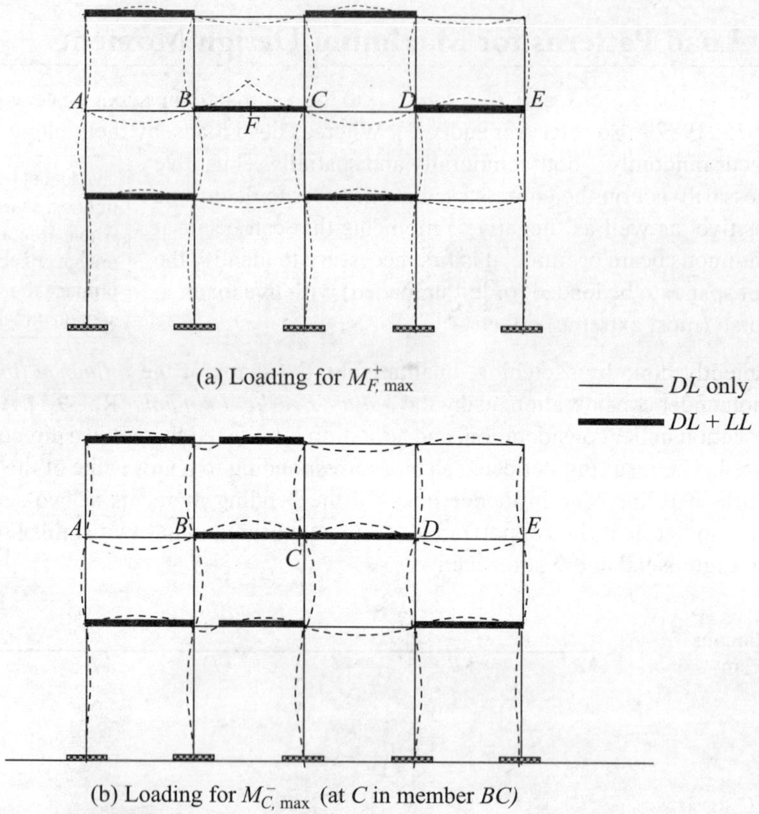

Fig. 9.3 Influence lines and gravity load patterns for a plane frame.

9.2.1 Design Moments in Beams

Based on the shapes of the influence lines in Figures 9.2 and 9.3, the following conclusions may be drawn regarding the positioning of live loads for obtaining the critical design moments in continuous beams and plane frames:

1. The maximum 'positive' moment in a span occurs when live loads are placed on that span and every other alternate span [Figure 9.2b(ii)]; in the case of a plane frame, this arrangement corresponds to a 'checkerboard' pattern [Figure 9.3(a)].
2. The minimum 'positive' moment in a span (which may turn out to be a maximum 'negative' moment in some cases†) occurs when it is *not* loaded with live loads, and when live loads are placed on adjoining spans, as well as alternate spans further away [Figure 9.2b(iii)].
3. The maximum 'negative' moment at a support section [marked 'C' in Figure 9.2(c) and Figure 9.3(b)] occurs when live loads are placed on the two spans adjoining the support section, and also on every alternate span thereafter, as shown. [Note that in Figure 9.3(b), the influence line is partially positive in the beams above and below beam BC, and strictly, live loads should not be placed on the small

† For example, in a lightly loaded short span, flanked on either side by heavily loaded long spans.

'positive' portions in these spans. However, this is ignored generally and the full live load is placed on these spans, as the error involved is small.]

4. The influence of loads on spans far removed from the sections under consideration is relatively small. Thus, there is little error in ignoring loadings on spans two panels distant from the section where moments are being determined. (This forms the basis of the substitute frame method, to be discussed in Section 9.3).

Code Recommendations

The Code recommendations for 'arrangement of imposed load' (Cl. 22.4.1) in continuous beams (and one-way slabs) and frames are in conformity with the conclusions (1) – (4) cited above. It may be noted that, with respect to the live load pattern required to estimate the maximum moment at a support section, the Code does not call for live loads to be placed on alternate spans two panels away from the support [refer span EF in Figure 9.2(c)] in addition to the placement on the two spans adjacent to the support [this is justified by conclusion (4) above].

Furthermore, in the case of frames in which the *design live load does not exceed three-fourths of the design dead load*, the Code (Cl. 22.4.1b) permits the designer to ignore altogether the problem of analysing different live load patterns. In such cases, it suffices to perform a single frame analysis for gravity loading – with full design dead load plus live load on *all* the spans. It may be noted that this major approximation is permitted only for frames, and *not* for continuous beam and one-way slabs. Also, it should be noted that *redistribution of moments* (refer Section 9.8) cannot be applied in this case [Ref. 9.2].

9.2.2 Design Moments in Columns

Bending moments in columns, unlike beams, need to be studied in association with co-existing axial compressive forces. The interaction between axial compressive strength and flexural strength of a given column section is such that its ultimate moment resisting capacity M_{uR} is nonlinearly dependent on the factored axial load P_u [refer Chapter 13]. Strictly, this calls for an investigation of all gravity load patterns that result in all possible combinations of P_u and M_u. Furthermore, the combinations should include P_u, M_{ux} and M_{uy} – considering the biaxial bending moments that occur simultaneously from the longitudinal and transverse frames connected to the same column [Figure 9.1].

However, it is generally accepted [Ref. 9.3] that considerations may be limited to gravity load patterns that result in (a) maximum eccentricity $e = M_u/P_u$ and (b) maximum P_u. The former is generally obtainable from the checkerboard patterns of loading (which are, at any rate, required to determine the maximum span moments in beams). The latter is obtained by loading *all* the panels on *all* the floors above the storey under consideration. It may be noted here that the Loading Code [IS 875 : 1987 (Part 2)] permits some reduction in live load values to account for the low probability of simultaneous occurrence of full live loads on all the floor slab areas in all the floors above. Incidentally, the live load arrangement on the floor below has some influence on the bending moment to be considered in combination with the maximum P_u. For this purpose, it is recommended [Ref. 9.3] that it is sufficient to consider live loads on a single span (the one that is longer and more heavily loaded) adjoining the lower end of the column member under consideration.

9.3 Simplified (Approximate) Methods of Analysis

9.3.1 Moment Coefficients for Continuous Beams under Gravity Loads

For typical continuous beams under gravity loading, the code recommends moment coefficients for computation of design moments, in lieu of detailed anaysis, subject to limitations.

The use of *moment coefficients* (in lieu of rigorous analyses of various gravity load patterns) was introduced in Section 5.6.1, with reference to continuous one-way slabs. These 'moment coefficients' as well as related 'shear coefficients' (Cl. 22.5.1 of the Code) are listed in Table 9.1. The use of the moment coefficients has already been demonstrated in Example 5.3.

Table 9.1 *Factored moments and shears in continuous beams using Code coefficients (Cl. 22.5 of the Code)*

(a) 'POSITIVE' MOMENTS:	
1. End spans	$+\left(\frac{w_{u,DL}}{12}+\frac{w_{u,LL}}{10}\right)l^2$
2. Interior spans	$+\left(\frac{w_{u,DL}}{16}+\frac{w_{u,LL}}{12}\right)l^2$
(b) 'NEGATIVE' MOMENTS:	
1. End support (if partially restrained)	$-\left(\frac{w_{u,DL}}{24}+\frac{w_{u,LL}}{24}\right)l^2$
2. First interior support	$-\left(\frac{w_{u,DL}}{10}+\frac{w_{u,LL}}{9}\right)l^2$
3. Other interior supports	$-\left(\frac{w_{u,DL}}{12}+\frac{w_{u,LL}}{9}\right)l^2$
(c) SHEAR FORCES:	
1. End support	
• *unrestrained*	$(0.5w_{u,DL}+0.5w_{u,LL})l$
• *partially restrained*	$(0.4w_{u,DL}+0.45w_{u,LL})l$
2. First interior support	
• *exterior face*	$(0.6w_{u,DL}+0.6w_{u,LL})l$
• *interior face*	$(0.55w_{u,DL}+0.6w_{u,LL})l$
3. Other interior supports	$(0.5w_{u,DL}+0.6w_{u,LL})l$

It may be noted that the use of the 'moment coefficients, as well as the related 'shear coefficients', for continuous beams and one-way slabs is subject to the following conditions (Cl. 22.5.1 of the Code):

- the continuous spans should be at least three in number;
- the supports should be fairly rigid and should not themselves deflect;
- beams are of uniform cross-section;

- the effective length of each span should be more-or-less the same, and at any rate should not differ by more than 15 per cent of the largest effective span;
- the loading on all spans should be 'substantially uniformly distributed'; and
- no redistribution of moments is permitted.

9.3.2 Substitute Frame Method of Frame Analysis for Gravity Loads

As explained earlier, the skeleton of a typical framed building is a three-dimensional 'rigid frame', which may be resolved, for the purpose of analysis, into a series of independent parallel 'plane frames' along the column lines in the longitudinal and transverse directions of the building. Each of these plane frames [Figure 9.4(a)] in turn, has to be analysed separately for a number of gravity load patterns as well as lateral loads.

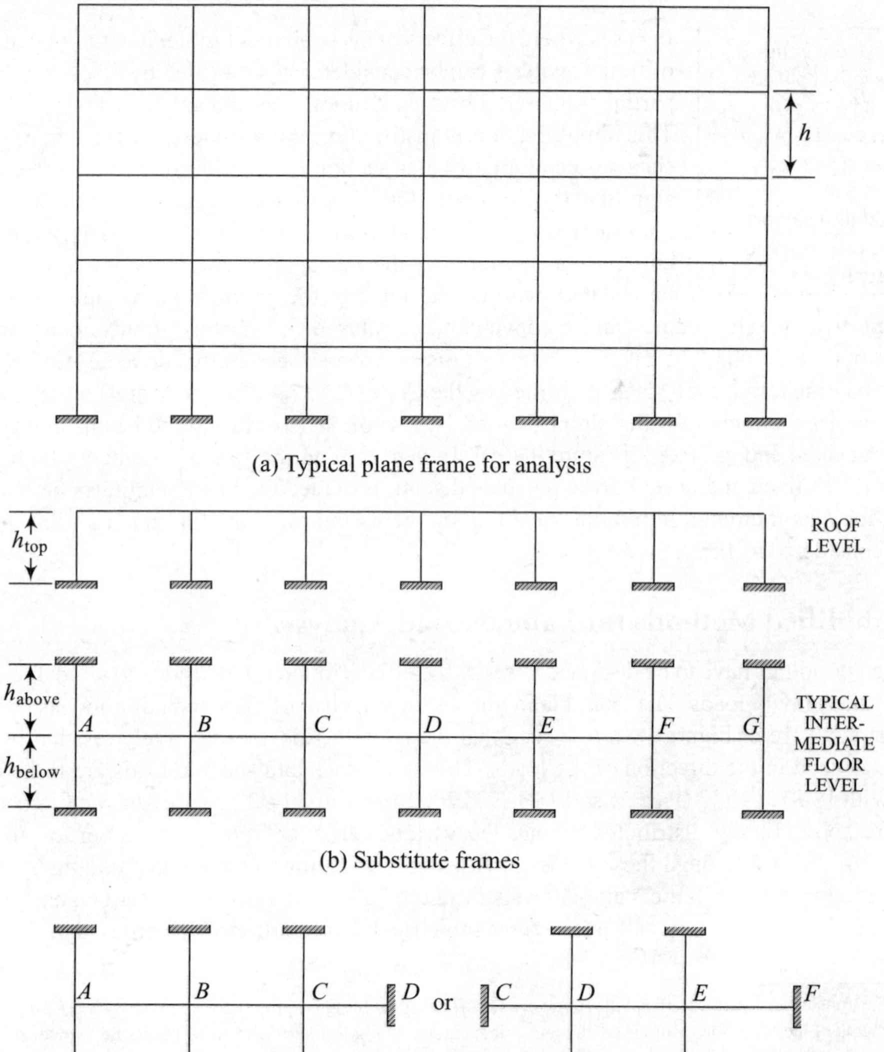

(a) Typical plane frame for analysis

(b) Substitute frames

(c) Substitute frames — truncated

Fig. 9.4 'Substitute frames' for gravity load analysis.

This is essentially a problem of structural analysis of indeterminate structures, and various techniques are available for this purpose [Ref. 9.4, 9.5]. As noted earlier, for the detailed analysis of large frames, with high indeterminacy, computer-based matrix methods are ideally suitable [Ref. 9.5]. However, the good old manual methods such as the *Moment Distribution Method* are still in vogue, and are ideally suited for analysing small *non-sway* frames under gravity loading. Convenient tabular arrangements for performing moment distribution (up to four cycles) are given in Ref. 9.6 and 9.7.

In the cases of frames that are substantially unsymmetrical or unsymmetrically loaded, and are otherwise not braced against *sway*, the effects of sway also have to be considered. For such analyses, the use of the *Moment Distribution Method* can be cumbersome, as it requires more than one distribution table to be constructed (and later combined); *Kani's Method* is better suited for such analyses, as it manages with a single distribution table.

> In brief, a 'substitute frame' is a much smaller/simplified frame consisting only of the member under consideration and neighbouring members connected to it, with members distantly located not considered, as their influence can be neglected.

In cases where the effects of sway are negligible, it is found that the problem of frame analysis can be considerably simplified by resolving the frame into partial frames ('substitute frames'), as indicated in Figure 9.4 [Ref. 9.2]. This simplification is justified on the grounds that the bending moment or shear force at a particular section (of a beam or column) is not influenced significantly by gravity loads on spans far removed from the section under consideration [refer conclusion (4) in Section 9.2.1]. Accordingly, an entire floor, comprising the beams and columns (above and below) may be isolated, with the far ends of the columns above and below considered 'fixed' [Figure 9.4(b)]. This frame can be conveniently analysed for various gravity load patterns by the moment distribution method; two cycles of moment distribution are generally adequate [Ref. 9.8, 9.2]. This method of 'substitute frame analysis' is permitted by the Code (Cl. 22.4.2). If there are a large number of bays in the substitute frame, then a further simplification is possible by truncating the beams appropriately, and treating the truncated end as 'fixed' [Figure 9.4(c)]. In determining the support moment, the beam member may be assumed as fixed at any support two panels distant, provided the beam continues beyond that point. In analysing for maximum and minimum 'positive' moments in spans, the far ends of adjacent spans may similarly be considered as fixed.

9.3.3 Simplified Methods for Lateral Load Analysis

Multi-storeyed buildings have to be designed to resist the effects of lateral loads due to wind or earthquake, in combination with gravity loads. The lateral load transfer mechanism of a framed building has been explained briefly in Chapter 1 (refer Figure 1.8). It is seen that the lateral loads are effectively resisted by the various plane frames aligned in the direction of the loads. The wind loads and seismic loads are to be estimated in accordance with IS 875: 1987 (Part 3) and IS 1893: 2002 respectively. They are assumed to act at the floor levels and are appropriately distributed among the various resisting frames (in proportion to the relative translational stiffness†). Although these loads are essentially dynamic in nature, the loading Codes prescribe equivalent static loads to facilitate static analysis in lieu of the more rigorous dynamic analysis [Ref. 9.9]. However, if the building is very tall and/or unsymmetrically proportioned, rigorous dynamic analysis is

† A measure of the translational stiffness of a plane frame in a multi-storey building is approximately given by $E(\Sigma I_c)/h$ where ΣI_c denotes the sum of moments of inertia of the columns (with appropriate axis of bending) that form part of the frame. However, the presence of an infill masonry wall can substantially increase the stiffness (up to two times or more), and this should also be accounted for. Also, if the lowermost storey of the building is free of infill walls (on account of ground floor parking), the adverse effects of reduction in mass and stiffness in this critical storey should be specially accounted for in seismic-resistant design, as advocated in IS 1893: 2002.

called for. Otherwise, in most ordinary situations, simplified static analysis is permitted by the Code (Cl. 22.4.3). In fact, the Explanatory Handbook to the Code [Ref. 9.2] states:

> 'Considerable uncertainty prevails regarding the magnitude as well as the distribution of wind and earthquake forces. Therefore, it will be sufficient, in most cases, to use an approximate method which gives an accuracy which is greater than that of the load data and other assumptions.'

The simple methods of lateral load analysis in vogue are the *Portal Method* and the *Cantilever Method* [Ref. 9.10], wherein the static indeterminacy in the frame is eliminated by making reasonable assumptions. The Portal Method, in particular, is very simple and easy to apply. It is based on the following assumptions:

> Three approximate methods for lateral load analysis of frames are *Cantilever method, Portal method* and *Factor method.*

- The inflection points of all columns and beams are located at their respective middle points.
- For any given storey, the 'storey shear' (which is equal and opposite to the sum of all lateral loads acting above the storey) is apportioned among the various columns in such a way that each interior column carries twice the shear that is carried by each exterior column.

The limitation of the Portal Method (as well as the Cantilever Method) is that it does not account for the relative stiffnesses of the various beams and columns. An improved method of analysis, which takes into account these relative stiffnesses (in locating the points of inflection and apportioning the storey shear to the various columns) is the so-called *Factor Method*, developed by Wilbur [Ref. 9.10]. This method works out to be fairly accurate, although it requires more computational effort.

9.4 Proportioning of Member Sizes for Preliminary Design

As mentioned earlier, it is necessary to estimate the cross-sectional dimensions of beams and columns prior to frame analysis and subsequent design – in order to

- assess the dead loads due to self-weight
- determine the various member stiffnesses for analysis

This requires a preliminary design, whereby the design values of bending moments, shear forces and axial forces in the various members may be approximately computed.

Gravity Load Effects

The apportioning of gravity loads to the various secondary/primary beams and columns may be done by considering the *tributary areas* shown in Figure 9.5. These areas are based on the assumption that the (uniformly distributed) gravity loads in any panel are divided among the supporting beams by lines midway between the lines of support, the load in each area is transferred to the adjacent support. In the general case of a 'two-way' rectangular slab panel, this implies a triangular shaped tributary area on each of the two short span beams and a trapezoidal area on each of the two long span beams, as shown in Figures 9.5(a), (b) [refer Cl. 24.5 of the Code]†. When the slab is 'one-way', the trapezoidal tributary area on each long span beam may be approximated (conservatively) as a simple rectangle, as indicated.

> The tributary area concept is used for computing the share of loads on beams, girders and columns. It also helps to roughly check on computer analysis outputs.

† The lines forming the two sides of the triangle may be assumed to be at 45° to the base.

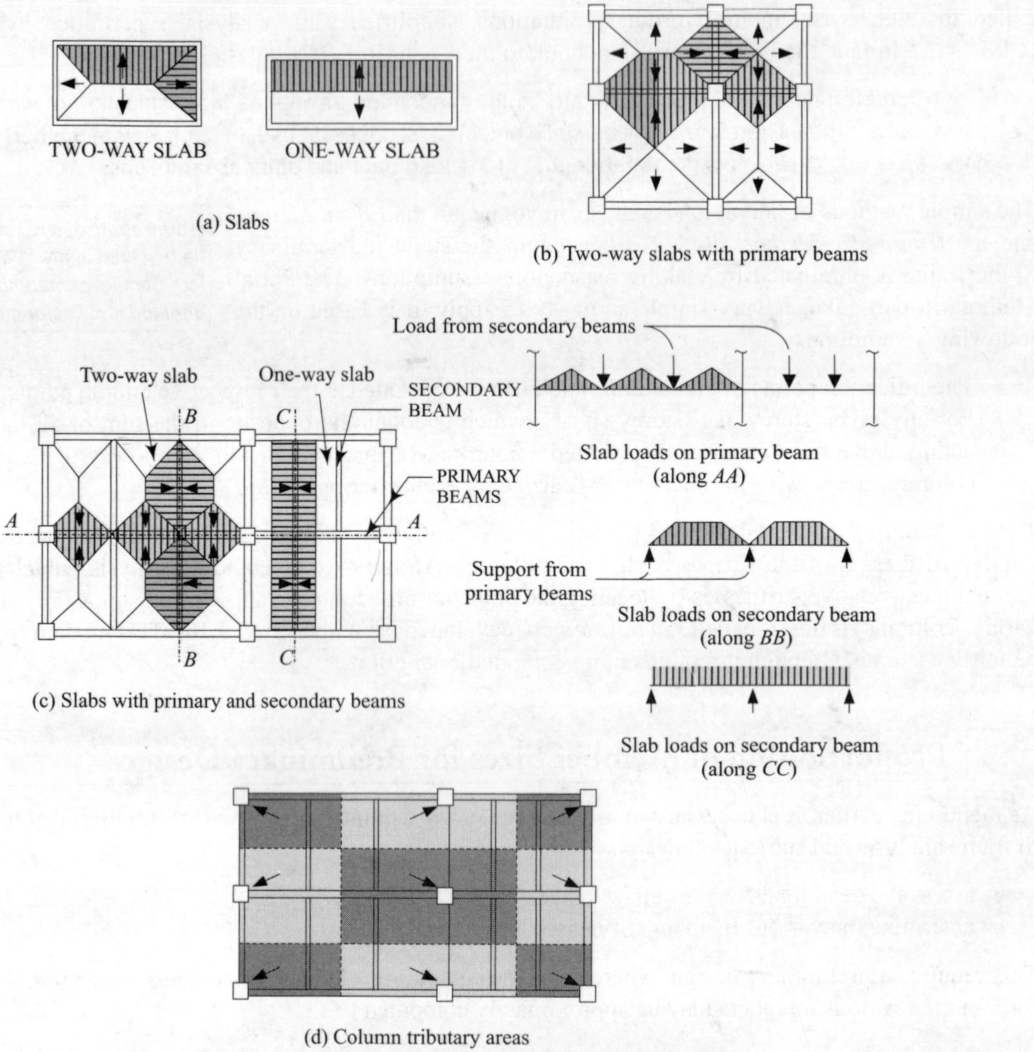

Fig. 9.5 Tributary areas for beams and columns.

When the floor system is made up of a combination of primary beams and secondary† beams, the tributary areas may be formed in a similar fashion [Figure 9.5(c)]. One-way slabs are assumed to transfer the loads only on to the longer supporting sides [Figures 9.5(a), (c)]. The loads from the 'secondary beams' are transferred as concentrated loads to the supporting 'primary beams' [Figure 9.5(c)]. However, for preliminary calculations, a uniformly distributed load may be assumed on each primary beam, with the tributary areas appropriately taken.

The axial loads on the columns at each floor level are obtained from the tributary areas of the primary beams, the load on each primary beam being shared equally by the two supporting columns. The tributary areas for

---

† 'Primary' beams (or *girders*) are those which frame into the columns, whereas 'secondary' beams are those which are supported by the primary beams – as explained in Section 1.6.1 [refer Figure 1.10]. In the load transfer scheme shown in Figure 9.5(c), it is assumed that the primary beams offer 'rigid' supports to the secondary beams.

the columns are indicated in Figure 9.5(d). In addition to the gravity loads transferred from the floor slabs, loads from masonry walls (wherever applicable) as well as self-weight of the beams/columns should be considered.

For a preliminary design, the influence of different possible live load patterns may be ignored, and all panels may be assumed to be fully loaded with dead loads plus live loads. Substitute frame analysis may be done to determine the bending moments and shear forces in the primary beams and columns; the secondary beams may be analysed as continuous beams using moment coefficients. A crude estimate of the maximum design moment in a beam may be taken as $\pm W_u l/10$, where W_u is the total factored load on the beam and l its span; similarly, the design shear force may be approximately taken as $W_u/2$.

Sizes of interior columns are primarily determined by the axial loads coming from the tributary areas of all the floors above the floor under consideration. However, exterior columns are subjected to significant bending moments (on account of unbalanced beam end moments) in addition to axial forces. Accordingly, these columns must be designed for the combined effect of axial compression and bending moment; this can be conveniently done using appropriate interaction curves (design aids), as explained in Chapter 13.

Finally, it should be noted that if the frames are unsymmetrical, the additional moments induced by sway should also be accounted for.

Lateral Load Effects

In the case of tall buildings, the effects of wind or earthquake moments are likely to influence the design bending moments in primary beams and column, especially in the lower floors. These load effects may, for the purpose of preliminary design, be determined approximately using the Portal Method described in Section 9.3.3. The design (factored) moments are obtained by combining the effects of gravity loads with lateral loads, using the specified partial load factors. Earthquake-resistant design calls for special design and detailing, as discussed in detail in Chapter 16.

9.5 Estimation of Stiffnesses of Frame Elements

A typical building frame – even a 'substitute frame' – is a statically indeterminate structure. To enable its analysis, whether by approximate methods or rigorous methods, it is necessary to know the stiffnesses (flexural, torsional, axial) of the various members that constitute the frame. Frequently, it is only the *flexural stiffness* that needs to be known. Axial stiffness is generally high, resulting in negligible axial deformations. Furthermore, as explained in Chapter 7, the torsional stiffness of a reinforced concrete member is drastically reduced following torsional cracking and hence can be ignored altogether. Recommendations for computing torsional stiffness, wherever required, are given in Section 7.2.3.

The 'flexural stiffness' of a beam element (with the far end 'fixed') is given by $4EI/l$, where EI is the 'flexural rigidity', obtained as a product of the modulus of elasticity E and the second moment of area I, and l is the length of the member. As the analysis is generally a 'linear static' analysis, the appropriate value of E is given by the static modulus of elasticity E_c, defined in Section 2.8.3. The problem lies with specifying the value of I, which must ideally reflect the degree of cracking, the amount of reinforcement and the participation of flanges (in beam-slab members).

The Code (Cl. 22.3.1) permits the calculation of flexural stiffness based on the 'gross' concrete section, the 'uncracked-transformed' section or the 'cracked-transformed' section [refer Chapter 4]; however, the *same* basis is to be applied to all the elements of the frame to be analysed. This is reasonable, because for braced frames what really matters is the *relative* stiffness, and not the absolute stiffness. The most common (and simplest) procedure is to consider the 'gross' section (i.e., ignoring both the amount of reinforcement and the degree of cracking) for calculating the second moment of area. An alternative procedure, which better reflects the higher degree of flexural cracking in beams relative to columns, is to use I_{gross} for columns and $0.5I_{gross}$ for beams [Ref. 9.11].

In slab-beam systems, the presence of the flange enhances the stiffness of the beam. However, the flanged beam action (with effective width b_f as described in Section 4.6.4) is not fully effective when the flanges are subjected to flexural tension, as in the regions of 'negative' moment. Some designers ignore the contribution of the flanges altogether (mainly for convenience) and treat the beam section as being rectangular. An improved procedure, suggested in Ref. 9.8, is to use twice the moment of inertia of the gross web section ($I = 2 \times b_w D^3/12$). This corresponds to an effective flange width $b_f \approx 6b_w$ with $D_f/D \approx 0.2$ to 0.4. The use of such a procedure eliminates the explicit consideration of the flanges; it gives reasonable results and is simple to apply, and hence is recommended by the authors of this book.

9.6 Adjustment of Design Moments at Beam-Column Junctions

While centreline dimensions of beams and columns are generally used in analysis, beams and columns need be designed only for the moments developed at their interface with the joint.

In frame analysis, *centreline* dimensions of beams and columns are generally used to define the geometry of the frame 'line diagram' [Figure 9.6(a)] (refer Cl. 22.2c of the Code). In the analysis, it is tacitly assumed that the specified flexural stiffness of any member (beam or column) is valid even at the ends of the line-member [i.e., right up to the point of intersection of the centre lines, including the zone where the column and beam merge, as shown in Figure 9.6(b)]. It is also assumed tacitly that the restraint offered by the column against vertical deflection of the beam is limited to a single point, corresponding to the centre of the beam-column junction. This results in beam deflections at points located between the centreline and the face of the column [see point 'B' in Figure 9.6(c)] – which is obviously not possible in reality.

The neglect of the increased stiffness and restraint of the beam within the column width results in a slight under-estimation of the 'negative' moment at the beam end and a corresponding over-estimation of the 'positive' moment in the span, under gravity loads. It has been shown that, in the interest of greater accuracy, the beam bending moment diagram (from frame analysis) may be adjusted† [Figure 9.6(d)] by an upward shift by $Vb/6$, where V is the shear force at the column centreline and b the width of the column support [Ref. 9.8]. This results in an adjusted 'negative' moment at the face of the column support, equal to $M_c - Vb/3$, where M_c is the theoretically computed moment at the column centreline. The slight reduction (equal to $Vb/6$) in the design 'positive' moment at midspan may be ignored; this is conservative and satisfactory.

The Code (Cl. 22.6.1) permits flexural members (in monolithic construction) to be designed for moments computed at the *faces* of the supports, as the effective depth (and hence, flexural resistance) of the flexural member (beam or column) is greatly enhanced in the region where the beam merges with the column. In the case of beams, this often results in a much lower moment than the computed 'negative' moment at the support centreline, owing to the steep variation in the bending moment diagram of the support region [Figure 9.6(d)].

† This is based on the assumption that the stiffness of the beam is infinite within the column width b, where it is monolithic with the column.

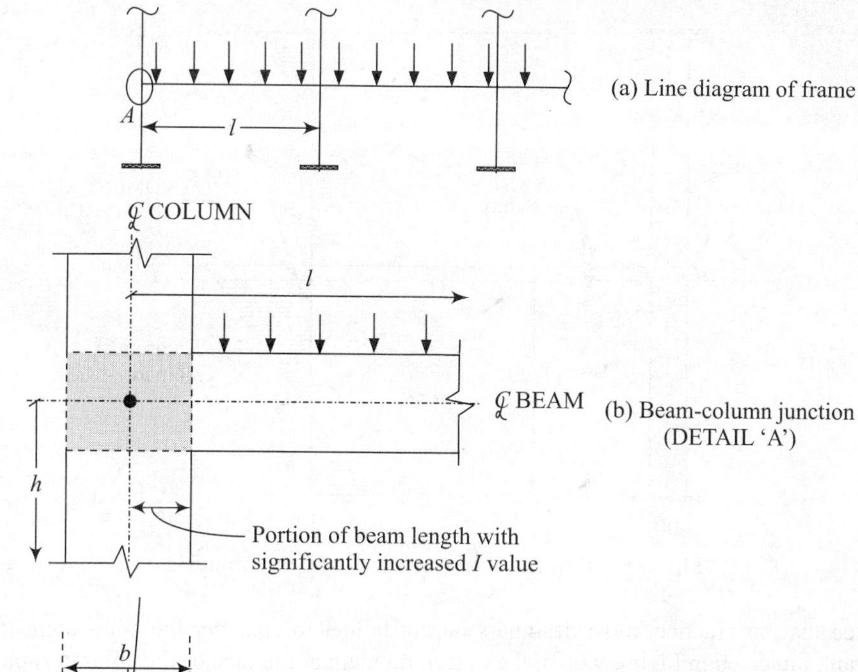

Fig. 9.6 Assumptions implicit in frame analysis at beam-column junctions.

However, in the case of columns, the moment gradient is not so significant, and so there is little to gain in taking the moment at the beam face, rather than at the beam centreline [Figure 9.7].

Also, the adjustment in the bending moment diagram due to the increased stiffness of column at the beam-column junction is generally negligible. Hence, the column moment for design may be taken as that obtained from frame analysis at the beam centreline.

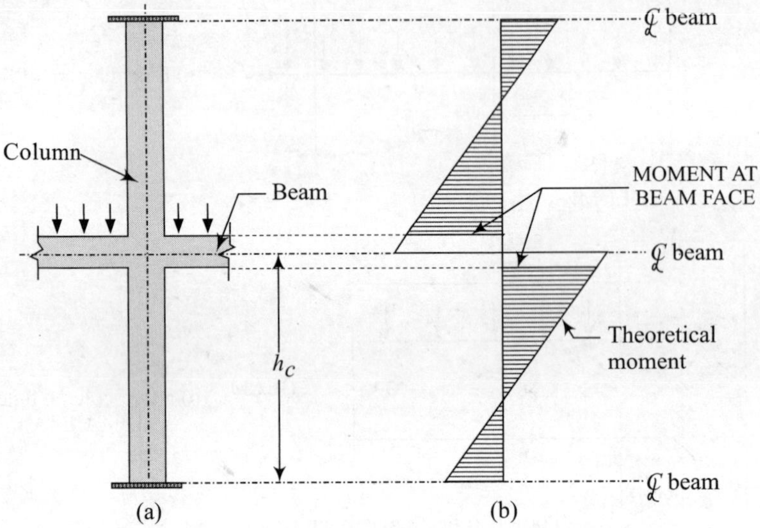

Fig. 9.7 Column moments from frame analysis.

It may be noted that, in practice, most designers do not bother to consider the adjustment in the bending moment diagram, indicated in Figure 9.6(d); the design moment at the face of the column supports is simply taken as ($M_c - Vb/2$), rather than as ($M_c - Vb/3$). This is also justifiable, if consideration is given to the possibility of *redistribution of moments*, as explained in Section 9.7.

9.7 Inelastic Analysis and Moment Redistribution

9.7.1 Limit Analysis

Reinforced concrete structures are generally analysed by the conventional *elastic theory* (refer Cl. 22.1 of the Code). In flexural members, this is tantamount to assuming a linear moment-curvature relationship, even under *factored loads*. For under-reinforced sections, this assumption is approximately true [refer Figure 4.8(a)], provided the reinforcing steel has not yielded at any section. Once yielding takes place (at any section), the behaviour of a statically indeterminate structure enters an inelastic phase, and linear elastic structural analysis is strictly no longer valid.

> The term *Limit analysis* used in RC design is analogous to *Plastic analysis* used in design of steel structures.

For a proper determination of the distribution of bending moments for loading beyond the yielding stage at any section, *inelastic* analysis is called for. This is generally referred to as *limit analysis*, when applied to reinforced concrete framed structures [Ref. 9.12–9.17], and 'plastic analysis' when applied to steel structures. In the special case of reinforced concrete slabs, the inelastic analysis usually employed is the 'yield line analysis' due to Johansen [Ref. 9.18]. The assumption generally made in limit analysis is that the moment-curvature relation is an idealised bilinear elasto-plastic relation [Figure 9.8]. This has validity only if the section is adequately under-reinforced and the reinforcing steel has a well-defined yield plateau. The ultimate moment of resistance (M_{uR}) of such sections, with specified area of steel, can be easily assessed, as described in Chapter 4.

Plastic Hinge Formation

With the idealised $M-\varphi$ relation, the ultimate moment of resistance (M_{uR}) is assumed to have been reached at a 'critical' (peak moment) section in a flexural member with the yielding of the tension steel [Figure 9.8]. On further straining (loading causing increase in curvature: $\varphi > \varphi_y$), the moment at the section cannot increase. However, the section 'yields', and the curvature continues to increase under a constant moment ($M = M_{uR}$). In general (with bending moment varying along the length of the member), the zone of 'yielding' spreads over a small region in the immediate neighbourhood of the peak moment section under consideration, permitting continued rotation, as though a 'hinge' is present at the section, but one that continues to resist a fixed moment M_{uR}. A *plastic hinge* is said to have formed at the section. If the structure is statically indeterminate, it is still stable after the formation of a plastic hinge, and for *further loading*, it behaves as a modified structure with a hinge at the plastic hinge location (and one less degree of indeterminacy). It can continue to carry additional loading (with formation of additional plastic hinges) until the limit state of collapse is reached on account of one of the following reasons:

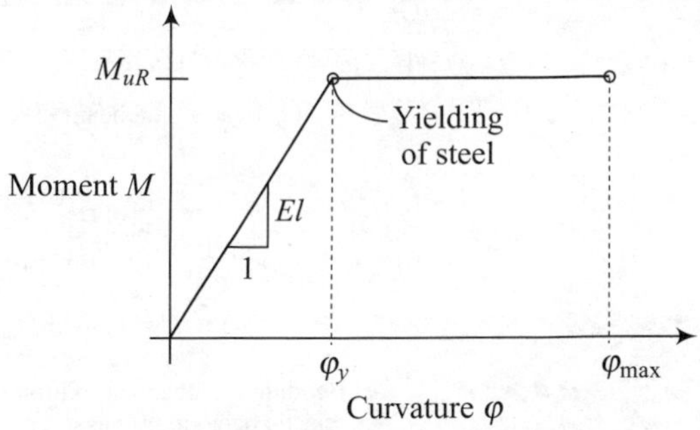

Fig. 9.8 Idealised moment-curvature relation.

> Unlike in steel structures where plastic hinges can undergo very large rotations, in RC structures, the rotation capacity of plastic hinges is limited–corresponding to limiting concrete compressive strain of 0.0035. This has limited the use of limit analysis for RC structures.

- formation of sufficient number of plastic hinges, to convert the structure (or a part of it) into a 'mechanism'
- limitation in ductile behaviour (i.e., curvature φ reaching the ultimate value φ_{max}, or, in other words a plastic hinge reaching its ultimate rotation capacity) at any one plastic hinge location, resulting in local crushing of concrete at that section

Example of Limit Analysis

A simple application of limit analysis is demonstrated here, with reference to a two-span continuous beam subjected to an increasing uniformly distributed load w per unit length [Figure 9.9(a)]. For convenience, it may be assumed that the beam has uniform flexural strength (M_{uR}) at all sections [Figure 9.9(b)]. Initially, the beam behaves elastically and the bending moment distribution by linear elastic theory is as shown in Figure 9.9(c). As the load w is increased, the limit of linear elastic behaviour of the structure is reached at a load $w = w_1$, at which the maximum moment (occurring at the continuous support, $= wl^2/8$) just reaches M_{uR} [Figure 9.9(c)], i.e.,

$$M_{uR} = \frac{w_1 l^2}{8} \quad \Rightarrow \quad w_1 = 8M_{uR}/l^2$$

At this load, a plastic hinge will form at the continuous support [Figure 9.9(d)]. However, the maximum moment in the span is only 0.5624 M_{uR}. For any additional loading, the beam behaves as a two-span beam with a hinge at support B (i.e., two simply supported spans) and the span moment alone increases [Figure 9.9(d), (f)] while the support moment remains constant at M_{uR}. How much additional load the beam can take will now depend on the plastic rotation capacity of this 'plastic hinge' or the formation of additional plastic hinges to transform the beam segments into an unstable hinged mechanism. Assuming that the support section is sufficiently under-reinforced such that it will not break down prior to the formation of the next

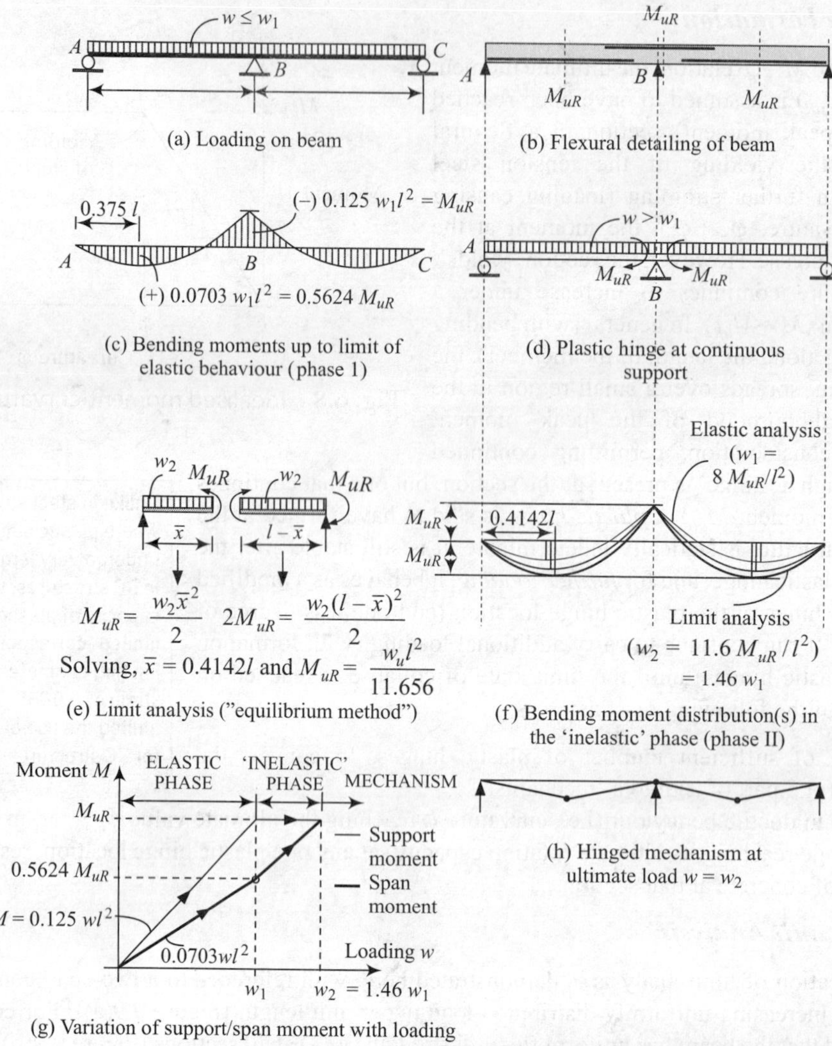

Fig. 9.9 Limit analysis of a two-span continuous beam.

plastic hinge(s), this phase of behaviour will continue until the peak moment in the span reaches M_{uR} [Figures 9.9(e),(f)]. Analysis of the structure for this condition [Figure 9.9(e)] indicates that this corresponds to a maximum span moment given by:

> A *mechanism* is said to form when the formation of a new plastic hinge renders the structure (or part of it) unstable, capable of large displacements through rotations at the hinges (plastic or real) without any (additional) resistance to applied loads.

$$M_{uR} = \frac{w_2 l^2}{11.656} \quad \Rightarrow \quad w_2 = 11.656\ M_{uR}/l^2 = 1.46\ w_1$$

As the load w_2 is reached, two additional plastic hinges† are formed in the two spans at the peak moment locations, and the structure is transformed into an unstable hinged mechanism which can deflect with no increase in load

† In this example, two plastic hinges will form simultaneously – one in each span, due to symmetry in the geometry as well as the loading.

[Figure 9.9(h)]. Obviously, w_2 is the ultimate (collapse) load of the structure, even allowing for inelastic behaviour. [Figure 9.9(h) which shows *straight* segments of the beam in-between plastic hinges should not confuse the student. The beam segments have bending moments and hence curvature along its length. However, after the formation of the last plastic hinge, there is no more increase in load and hence in moment and curvature along the beam segment, and *further* displacement will be by rigid-body rotation about the hinges, like a mechanism. It is this mechanism motion *beyond* the maximum load that is shown in Figure 9.9(h); and later in Figure 9.12(c)]

This indicates that the beam is capable of carrying additional loads up to 46 per cent beyond the limit of elastic behaviour, thanks to the ductile behaviour of the beam section at the continuous support.

The bending moment distributions in the inelastic phase are indicated in Figure 9.9(f). It is seen in this example that, after the yielding at the support section, a 'redistribution of moments' from the heavily stressed section to the lesser stressed ones takes place, with the support moment remaining constant at M_{uR} while the span moments continue to increase until they too reach M_{uR}. The variation of support moment and maximum span moment with increasing loading is shown in Figure 9.9(g). The gain in moments is linear in the 'elastic phase' ($w < w_1$), and corresponding to the formation of the first plastic hinge (at $w = w_1$), there is a discontinuity (change of slope) in each of the two *M–w* curves.

> It may be noted that the so-called 'limit analysis' is essentially a superposition of a series of 'elastic analyses', the inelasticity being confined to the plastic hinge locations. The structure gets modified – with the introduction of successive plastic hinges, and each so-called 'inelastic' phase of the analysis is in fact 'elastic' for the modified structure. This is reflected in the piece-wise linear segments of the *M–w* relationship in Figure 9.9(g).

In deriving the expression for w_2, allowing full moment redistribution on to the spans, it was assumed above that the plastic hinge at the support section will continue to yield (rotate) while resisting a moment = M_{uR}, without breakdown. If the rotation capacity† of the plastic hinge at B gets exhausted prior to the span moment reaching M_{uR}, the 'inelastic' phase will get terminated at a stage $w_1 < w < w_2$. If the plastic hinge possesses adequate ductility, then the maximum collapse load is reached at $w_u = w_2$, corresponding to the formation of a 'mechanism'.

Interestingly, it is possible to have an optimally designed structure (with variable section strengths) such that elastic analysis and limit analysis will give identical results, with no scope for any redistribution. For instance, if the beam in Figure 9.9(a) is designed such that while the support section has a strength M_{uR}, the span sections have only strengths of 0.56 M_{uR}, then just as the load w_1 is reached, hinges will form simultaneously at support as well as in the spans, resulting in the formation of a mechanism and collapse. (In reinforced concrete, even with prismatic members, it is possible to design the amount of flexural reinforcement to suit the actual moment at any section.) However, in practice, prismatic members are used and section sizes are determined by other considerations also (shear, deflection, etc.). Moreover, in general, the peak moments at different sections are under different load combinations, and there is room for moment redistribution for a given loading.

> **Ductility and the ability to yield without loss of strength and failure is a desirable characteristic/behaviour for sections of structural members.**

> In structures, as in life, some local yielding is not something to be abhorred; on the contrary it may be helpful. Such yielding and consequent redistribution of stresses takes place in most common structures and often helps in eliminating failure. For example, a steel plate under tension with a minute

† For a detailed calculation of plastic rotations, the reader is advised to consult Ref. 9.15.

(transverse) tear will have near-infinite stresses at the ends of the tear if it behaved in a *linear elastic* manner and the slightest tension would cause failure. It is the local yielding at these locations and subsequent redistribution which eliminates such a failure. Nearly all cases of stress concentrations are examples of such behaviour. One might even say – it is the localised yielding and ductility that help eliminate distress and sustain our structures!

9.7.2 Moment Redistribution

As seen in the previous section, the distribution of bending moments in a continuous beam (or frame) gets modified significantly in the inelastic phase. The term *moment redistribution* is generally used to refer to the transfer of moments to the less stressed sections as sections of peak moments yield on their ultimate capacity being reached (as witnessed in the example above). From a design viewpoint, this behaviour can be taken advantage of by attempting to effect a redistributed bending moment diagram which achieves a reduction in the maximum moment levels (and a corresponding increase in the lower moments at other locations).

Such an adjustment in the moment diagram often leads to the design of a more economical structure with better balanced proportions, and less congestion of reinforcement at the critical sections.

Considering the earlier example of the two-span continuous beam [Figure 9.10(a)], as a *design* problem (rather than an *analysis* problem), it may be seen that the designer has several alternative factored moment diagrams to choose from, depending on the amount of redistribution to be considered. If the design [Figure 9.10(b)] is to be based on a purely elastic moment distribution (without considering any redistribution) then the bending moment diagram to be considered is as shown in Figure 9.10(c), and the corresponding design support moment $M^-_{uR(E)}$ and span moment $M^+_{uR}(E)$ are obtained as:

$$M^-_{uR(E)} = M^-_{(E)} \equiv \frac{1}{8} w_u l^2$$

$$M^+_{uR(E)} = M^+_{(E)} \equiv \frac{9}{128} w_u l^2 \left(= \frac{9}{16} M^-_{(E)} \right) \tag{9.1}$$

where $M^-_{(E)}$ and $M^+_{(E)}$ denote the support and span moments in the elastic solution; the subscript (*E*) here represents *elastic* analysis†.

Reduction in Peak 'Negative' Moments

The relatively high support moment $M^-_{(E)}$ may call for a large section (if singly reinforced); alternatively, for a given limited cross-section, large amounts of reinforcement may be required. With the same gross cross section used throughout the spans, it is meaningful to even out the peak (+ve and –ve) moments. Therefore, in such situations, it is desirable to reduce the design moment at the support to a value, say $C_1 M^-_{(E)}$ (where the factor C_1 has a value less than unity), and to correspondingly increase the span (positive) moments which are otherwise relatively low. The percentage reduction in the design support moment is given by:

$$\delta M = (1 - C_1) \times 100 \tag{9.2}$$

† In this example, it is tacitly assumed that the gravity loads indicated in Figure 9.10 are entirely due to permanent loads, and that there are no variable loads.

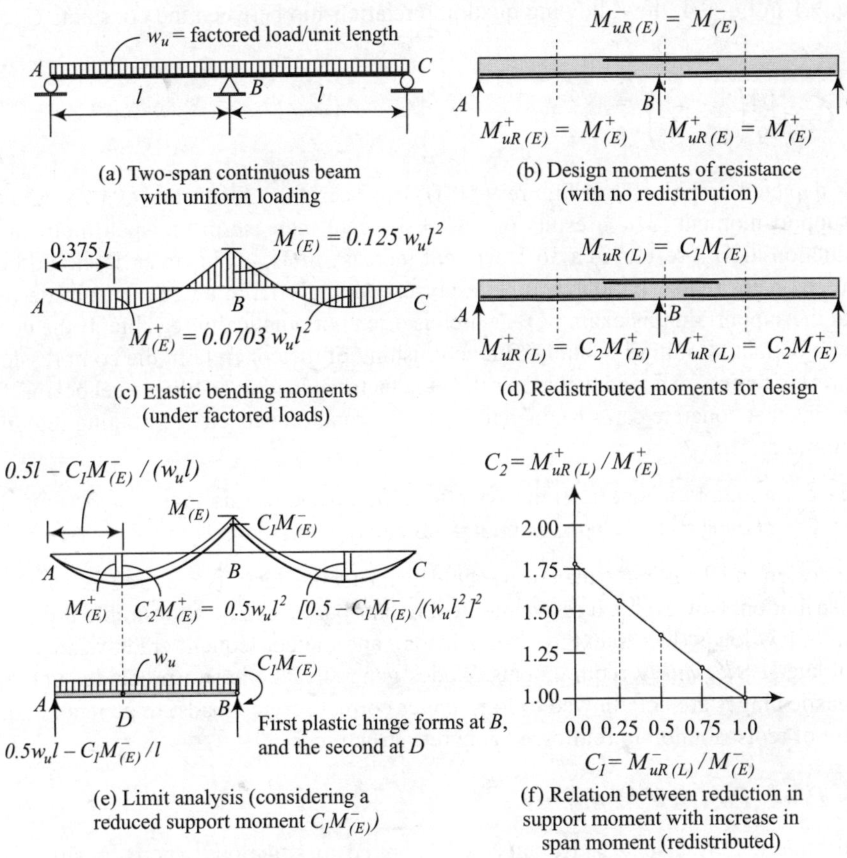

Fig. 9.10 Moment redistribution in a two-span continuous beam.

Consequent to a reduction in the support moment from $M^-_{(E)}$ to $C_1\ M^-_{(E)}$, there is an increase in the design ('positive') moment in the span region from $M^+_{(E)}$ to $C_2\ M^+_{(E)}$, where the factor C_2 obviously is greater than unity. Accordingly, as indicated in Figure 9.9(d),

$$M^-_{uR(L)} = C_1 M^-_{(E)} \tag{9.3a}$$

$$M^+_{uR(L)} = C_2 M^+_{(E)} \tag{9.3b}$$

where the subscript (L) represents *limit* analysis. The factor C_2 (indicating the increase in the elastic span moment $M^+_{(E)}$) depends on the factor C_1. The factor C_1 is fixed (based on the percentage reduction desired), and the factor C_2 has to be determined for design – by considering 'limit analysis' [Figure 9.10(e)]. It can be shown easily, by applying static equilibrium, that:

$$C_2 M^+_{(E)} = \frac{w_u l^2}{2}\left[\frac{1}{2} - \left(\frac{C_1 M^-_{(E)}}{w_u l^2}\right)\right]^2 \tag{9.4}$$

Introducing Eq. 9.1 in Eq. 9.4, the following quadratic relationship between the constants C_2 and C_1 can be established:

$$C_2 = \frac{64}{9}\left(\frac{1}{2} - \frac{C_1}{8}\right)^2 \tag{9.5}$$

This relation is depicted graphically in Figure 9.10(f). It is seen that, for instance, a 25 per cent reduction in the elastic support moment ($M^-_{(E)}$) results in a 17.3 per cent increase in the span moment ($M^+_{(E)}$) and a 50 per cent reduction in $M^-_{(E)}$ results in a 36.1 per cent increase in $M^+_{(E)}$. However, it should be noted that a large amount of moment redistribution requires a correspondingly large amount of plastic rotation of the plastic hinge (at the support, in this example) – which is often not practically feasible. If the desired ductility is not available, a premature failure is likely (due to crushing of the concrete in the compression zone at the plastic hinge forming region) at a load that is less than the factored load w_u. Unlike steel beams, the maximum compressive strains that concrete can sustain, and hence the rotation capacity of hinging regions of concrete beams, is very limited.

For the desired moment redistribution to take place, the plastic hinges that develop must have the required rotation capacities to 'hold on' without undergoing premature failure.

Through proper design and detailing, it may be possible to muster the ductility required for significant amounts of moment redistribution. However, excessive moment redistribution can be undesirable if it results in plastic hinge formation at low loads (less than the service loads), and the consequent crack-widths and deflections are likely to violate *serviceability* requirements. Codes generally attempt to preclude such a situation by ensuring that plastic hinges are not allowed to form under normal service loads. In general, codes allow only a limited amount of redistribution in reinforced concrete structures.

Reduction in Peak 'Positive' Moments

Moment redistribution† may also be advantageously applied to situations where 'positive' moments are relatively high and need to be reduced – for greater economy and less congestion of reinforcement.

For instance, with reference to the earlier example of the two-span continuous beam, if part of the total factored load w_u is due to live load $w_{u,LL}$, then the arrangement of loads for maximum span moment is as shown in Figure 9.11(a).

The maximum span moment from elastic analysis [Figure 9.11(b)] can be redistributed by allowing the first plastic hinge to form in the span region. The reduction in span moment is accompanied by a corresponding increase in the support moment [Figure 9.11(c)] – to maintain equilibrium at the limit state. Such a redistribution may be desirable if the elastic span moment is relatively high, as would be the case if the live load component in the loading is high.

9.7.3 Code Recommendations for Moment Redistribution

The Code (Cl. 37.1.1) permits the designer to select the envelope of redistributed factored moment diagrams for design, in lieu of the envelope of elastic factored moments, provided the following conditions are satisfied:

1. **Equilibrium:** The redistributed moments must be in a state of static equilibrium with the corresponding factored loads.

† It may be noted that 'redistribution' merely refers to a transfer of load effects from heavily stressed locations to less heavily (or lightly) stressed locations, regardless of whether the peak moments are 'positive' or 'negative'.

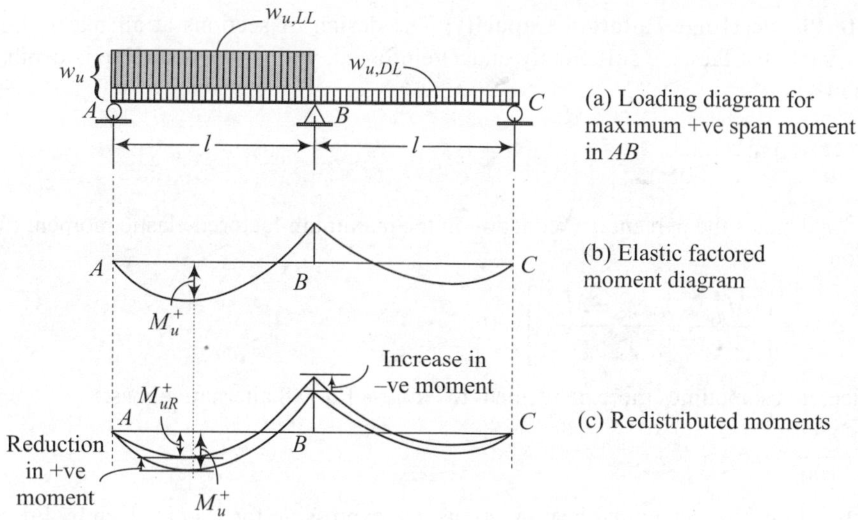

Fig. 9.11 Moment redistribution: reduction in peak positive moment.

2. **Serviceability:** The ultimate moment of resistance (M_{uR}) at any section should not be less than 70 per cent of the factored moment ($M_{u,\text{max}}$) at that section, as obtained from the elastic moment envelope (considering all loading combinations). In other words, the flexural strength at any section should not be less than that given by the elastic factored moment envelope, scaled by a factor of 0.7:

$$M_{uR} \geq 0.7(M_{u,\text{max}})_{\text{elastic}} \text{ at all sections} \tag{9.6}$$

This restriction (Cl. 37.1.1.b) is aimed at ensuring that plastic hinge formation does not take place under normal service loads, and even if it does take place, the yielding of the steel will not be so significant as to result in excessive crack-widths and deflections. It is mentioned in the Explanatory Handbook to the Code that the value of 70% is arrived at as the ratio of service loads to ultimate loads with respect to load combinations involving a uniform load factor of 1.5, as $1/1.5 = 0.67 \cong 0.7$.

3. **Low Demand for High Plastic Hinge Rotation Capacities:** The reduction in the elastic factored moment ('negative' or 'positive') at any section due to a particular combination of factored loads should not exceed 30 per cent of the absolute maximum factored moment ($M_{u\,\text{max}}$), as obtained from the envelope of factored elastic moments (considering all loading combinations). Although the basis for this clause in the Code (Cl. 37.1.1.c) is different from the previous clause (Cl. 37.1.1.b), which is based on the idea of preventing the formation of plastic hinges at service loads, for the case of gravity loading, if Cl. 37.1.1.b is satisfied, Cl. 37.1.1.c would automatically be satisfied. However, in the design of lateral load resisting frames (with number of storeys exceeding four), the Code (Cl. 37.1.1.e) imposes an additional over-riding restriction. The reduction in the elastic factored moment is restricted to 10 per cent of $M_{u,\text{max}}$. Thus,

$$(M_u)_{\text{elastic}} - M_{uR} \leq \begin{cases} 0.3(M_{u,\text{max}})_{\text{elastic}} & \text{in general} \\ 0.1(M_{u,\text{max}})_{\text{elastic}} & \text{for lateral load-resisting frames only} \end{cases} \tag{9.7}$$

This restriction is intended to ensure that the ductility requirements at the plastic hinge locations are not excessive.

4. **Adequate Plastic Hinge Rotation Capacity:** The design of sections at all plastic hinge locations should be such that they are sufficiently under-reinforced, with a *low* neutral axis depth factor (x_u/d), satisfying:

$$\frac{x_u}{d} \le 0.6 - \frac{|\delta M|}{100} \tag{9.8}$$

Where $|\delta M|$ denotes the percentage reduction in the maximum factored elastic moment $(M_{u,\max})_{\text{elastic}}$ at the section:

$$\delta M \equiv \left[\frac{(M_{u,\max})_{\text{elastic}} - M_{uR}}{(M_{u,\max})_{\text{elastic}}}\right] \times 100 \tag{9.9}$$

In practice, it is sometimes more convenient to express Eq. 9.8 alternatively as:

$$\frac{\delta M}{100} \le 0.6 - \frac{x_u}{d} \tag{9.10}$$

For singly reinforced rectangular beam sections, the expression for x_u/d is given by Eq. 5.11, which is repeated here for convenience, with $M_{uR} = M_u$,

$$\frac{x_u}{d} = 1.202\left[1 - \sqrt{1 - 4.597R/f_{ck}}\right] \tag{9.11}$$

Moment Redistribution in Beams

Low values of x_u/d (and, thus large values of δM) are generally not possible in beams without resorting to very large sections, which may be uneconomical. However, even with the extreme case of a *balanced* section (with $x_u = x_{u,\max}$), it can be shown, by applying Eq. 9.10 and Eq. 4.50 (or Table 4.3), that

$$\delta M < \begin{cases} 6.9 & \text{for Fe 250} \\ 12.1 & \text{for Fe 415} \\ 14.4 & \text{for Fe 500} \end{cases} \quad \text{with } x_u = x_{u,\max} \tag{9.12}$$

Thus, it is seen that a limited moment distribution (for example, up to 12.1 per cent for Fe 415 steel) is possible, even with the *limiting* (maximum) neutral axis depth permitted for design [refer Chapter 4], but a higher percentage is possible with lower x_u.

Inelastic Analysis of Slabs

As discussed earlier (in Chapter 5), the thicknesses of reinforced concrete slabs are generally governed by deflection control criteria, with the result that the sections are invariably under-reinforced, with low x_u/d values. Hence, significant inelastic action is possible in such cases.

It may be noted, however, that, in the case of one-way continuous slabs, (and continuous beams), no moment redistribution is permitted by the Code (Cl. 22.5.1) if the analysis is based on the use of the Code moment coefficients [Table 12 of the Code]. This is so, because such coefficients are only approximations, and minor errors are assumed to be accommodated through the inherent capacity for moment redistribution in the structure [Ref. 9.2].

In the case of *two-way* slab systems, which are statically indeterminate, detailed inelastic analysis (*yield line analysis*) is often resorted to [Figure 9.12], and, in fact, the moment coefficients given in the Code (Table 26)

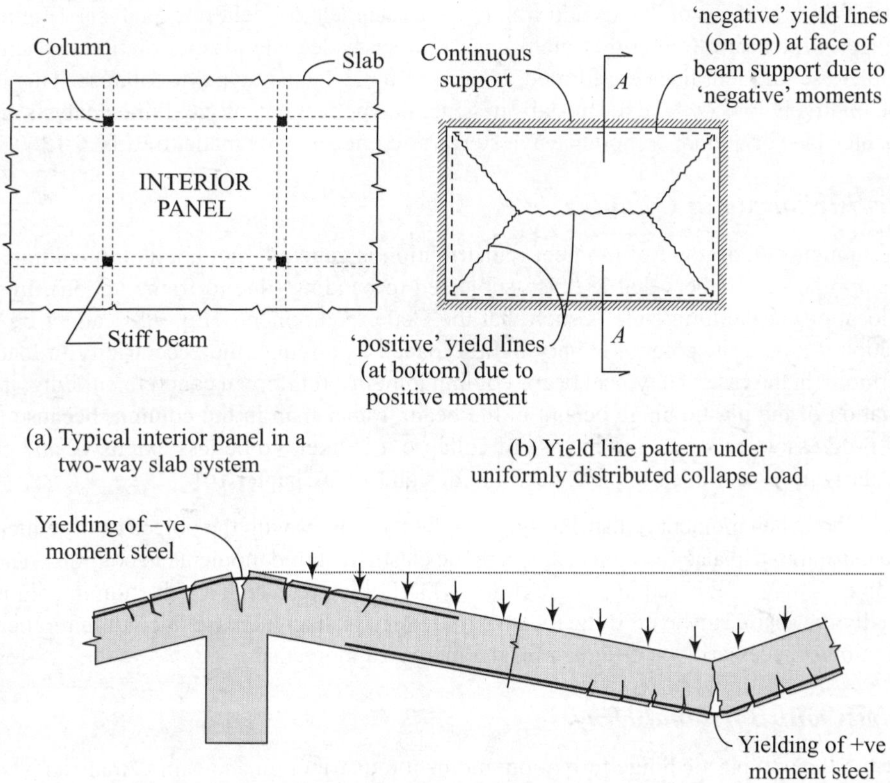

(a) Typical interior panel in a two-way slab system

(b) Yield line pattern under uniformly distributed collapse load

(c) Deflected shape at collapse (mechanism motion) (section A–A)

Fig. 9.12 Concept underlying yield line analysis of slabs.

for two-way rectangular slabs with various possible edge conditions are based on such analyses [refer Chapter 11].

> **The limit analysis concepts, applied to slabs, is known as *yield-line analysis*.**

'Yield line analysis' is the equivalent for a two-dimensional flexural member (plate or slab) of the limit analysis of a one-dimensional member (continuous beam), explained in Section 9.7.1. It is based on the elastic-plastic $M–\varphi$ relation [Figure 9.8], according to which, as the moment at a section reaches M_{uR}, a plastic hinge is formed, and therefore rotation takes place at constant moment. In slabs, peak moments occur along *lines* (such as 'negative' moments along support lines and 'positive' moments along lines near the midspan), and hence the yielding (plastic hinge formation) occurs along lines ('yield lines'), and not at sections, as in beams. In a skeletal structure (continuous beam, grid, plane frame, space frame), the ultimate (collapse) load is reached when sufficient number of plastic hinges are formed to transform the structure into a mechanism. In a similar way, the ultimate load is reached in plates when sufficient number of yield lines are formed to transform the slab into a series of plate segments† connected by 'yield lines', resulting in mechanism type behaviour [Figures 9.12(b), (c)]. Yield line theory is discussed in detail in Chapter 11.

† Such plate segment can freely rotate about the 'yield line', in much the same way as a door can rotate about a line hinge.

As in the case of limit analysis of beams and frames, it is assumed in 'yield line analysis' [Figure 9.12] that the plastic hinges which form (along the 'yield lines') possess adequate plastic rotation capacities to 'hold on' till a complete set of yield lines are formed, leading to a mechanism type of collapse. This is justifiable in view of the relatively low x_u/d values in slabs in general. Applications of yield line analysis are discussed further in Chapter 11. For a more comprehensive study, reference may be made to Refs. 9.18–9.22.

Moment Redistribution in Columns

Reduction of moments on account of moment redistribution is generally not applied to columns, which are essentially *compression* members that are also subjected to bending (due to frame action). In general, the neutral axis location† at the limit state is such that the Code requirements [Eq. 9.8] cannot be satisfied by a column section – unless the column is very lightly loaded axially and the eccentricity in loading is very large. Furthermore, in the case of a typical beam-column joint in a reinforced concrete building, it is desirable that the formation of the plastic hinge occurs in the beam, rather than in the column, because there is less likelihood of progressive collapse; and in case of collapse it is likely to be less extensive and catastrophic. This is particularly necessary in earthquake-resistant design [refer Chapter 16].

It may be noted that when moment redistribution is applied to frames with the objective of reducing the peak moments in *beams*, this will also result in changes in the elastic factored moments in columns. These changes in column moments may be ignored in design, if the redistribution results in a reduction in column moments (which is usually the case). However, if the redistribution results in an increase in column moments, then the column section must necessarily be designed for the increased moments.

Limit Analysis with Torsional Hinges

The basis for the flexural plastic hinge formation, moment redistribution and Limit Analysis is the moment-curvature relation of under-reinforced beams, which can be idealised as a bilinear elastic-plastic relation [Figure 9.8]. Interestingly, a beam with adequate torsional reinforcements has a similar bilinear elastic-plastic torque-twist relation [see Figure 7.4(b)]. With such beams, the formation of a *plastic hinge in torsion* and subsequent redistribution of torque/moments in the structure can occur [Ref. 9.23]. Limit analysis can also be extended to structures with members subjected to significant torsion, such as transversely loaded grid structures (or bridges), where the collapse mechanisms may involve torsional hinges as well [Ref. 9.24]. Recognising this, some codes [Ref. 9.3] permit the limiting of the maximum design torque, in statically indeterminate structures where reduction of torsional moment in a member can occur due to redistribution of internal forces, to $0.67T_{cr}$, provided corresponding adjustments are made to the torsions, moments and shears in the framing-in members to account for the redistribution. Here T_{cr} is the cracking torque of the spandrel beam, and $0.67T_{cr}$ represents a torque corresponding to a 'plastic torsional hinge' formation and consequent cracking and reduction in torsional stiffness.

9.8 Design Examples

Example 9.1

Analyse a three-span continuous beam (with equal spans l), subjected to a uniformly distributed load w per unit length, to determine the critical 'positive' moments M_1 (in the end span) and M_2 (in the interior span), as well as the 'negative' moment M_3 at the continuous support [Figure 9.13(a)]. Assume that the dead load (w_D)

† When the loading on the column is not very eccentric, the neutral axis will lie *outside* the cross-section.

and live load (w_L) components of the total load (w) are equal. Also assume all spans to have the same cross-section. Compare the moment coefficients obtained by

(a) elastic analysis considering total load w on all spans†;
(b) elastic analysis considering 'pattern loading';
(c) Code recommendations for moment coefficients.

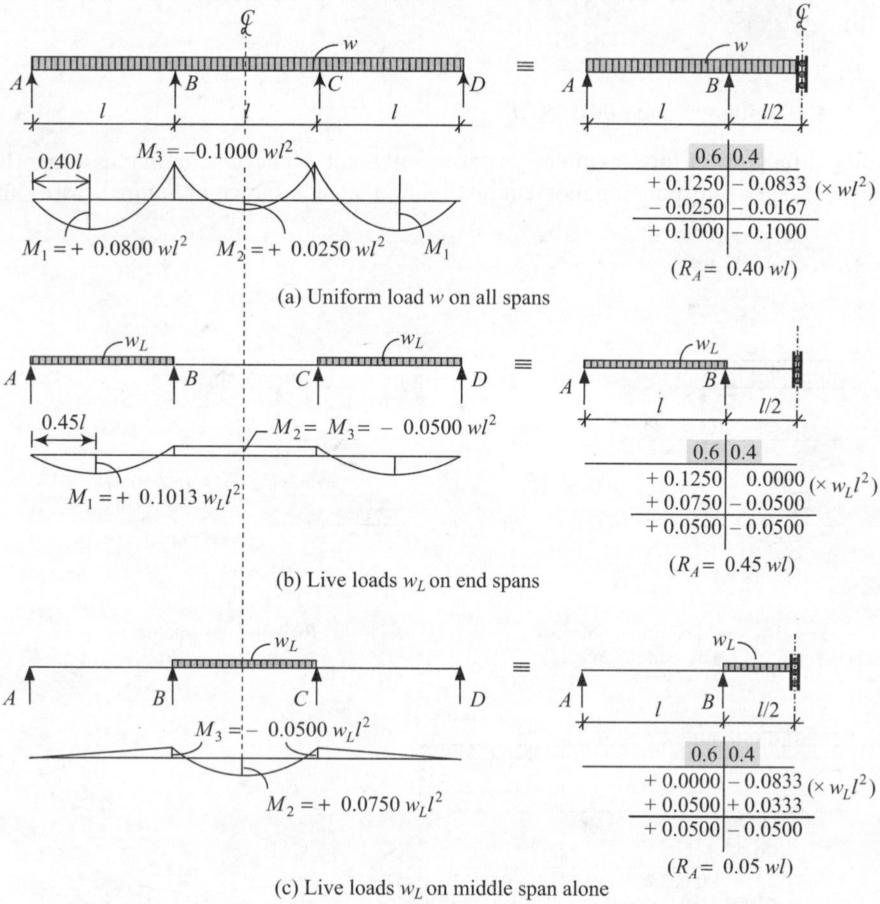

Fig. 9.13 Example 9.1 – analysis by moment distribution method.

Solution

(a) Elastic analysis considering total load (w) on all spans

By taking advantage of the symmetry in the structural geometry and loading, the analysis can be easily performed by considering a simple one-cycle moment distribution, as shown in Figure 9.13(a). The results indicate:

$$\text{span moments} \begin{cases} M_1 = +0.0800wl^2 \\ M_2 = +0.0250wl^2 \end{cases}$$

support moment $M_3 = -0.1000\ wl^2$

† Note that such an analysis is included here only for the purpose of comparison; such analysis is not permitted by the Code for design purposes.

(b) Elastic analysis considering 'pattern loading'

Here, too, the advantage of symmetry of the structure can be availed of for analysing the maximum span moments due to live loads appropriately arranged, as shown in Figures 9.13(b) and (c). The results of uniform dead loads on *all* spans is obtainable form Figure 9.13(a), by considering w_D in lieu of w. By superimposing the effects of live load and dead load contributions separately, and considering $w_L = w_D = 0.5w$, the final results (critical moments) may easily be obtained, as shown in Figures 9.14(a),(b).

$$M_1 = +0.0903\ wl^2$$

$$M_2 = +0.0500\ wl^2 \text{ and } -0.0125\ wl^2$$

The loading arrangement for maximum 'negative' moment M_3 at the continuous support is shown in Figure 9.14(c). The corresponding moment distribution table is shown in Figure 9.14(c), from which it follows that

$$M_3 = -0.1082\ wl^2$$

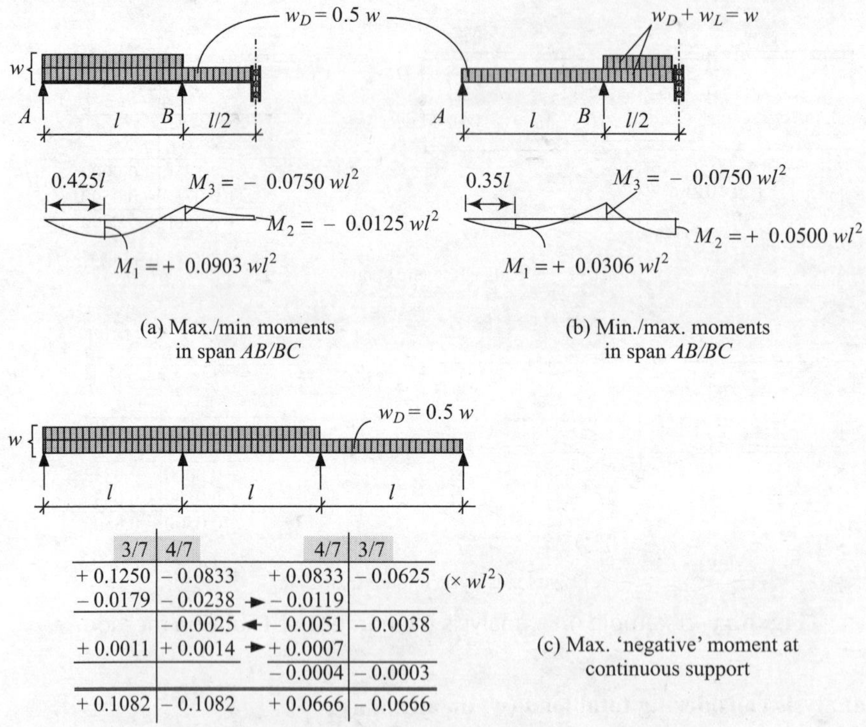

3/7	4/7		4/7	3/7
+ 0.1250	− 0.0833		+ 0.0833	− 0.0625
− 0.0179	− 0.0238	→	− 0.0119	
	− 0.0025	←	− 0.0051	− 0.0038
+ 0.0011	+ 0.0014	→	+ 0.0007	
			− 0.0004	− 0.0003
+ 0.1082	− 0.1082		+ 0.0666	− 0.0666

($\times\ wl^2$)

(c) Max. 'negative' moment at continuous support

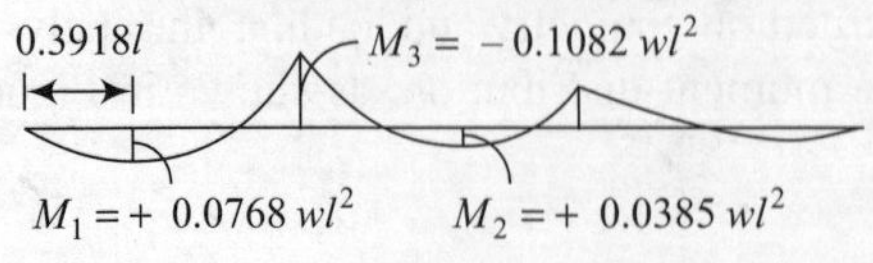

Fig. 9.14 Example 9.1 — analysis considering $w_D = w_L = 0.5\ w$.

(c) Use of Code moment coefficients

The results are easily obtainable from Table 9.1 of this chapter (Cl. 22.5):

$$\text{span moments}\begin{cases} M_1 = +(0.5w)l^2\left(\frac{1}{12}+\frac{1}{10}\right) = +0.0917wl^2 \\ M_2 = +(0.5w)l^2\left(\frac{1}{16}+\frac{1}{12}\right) = +0.0729wl^2 \end{cases}$$

$$\text{support moments } M_3 = -(0.5w)l^2\left(\frac{1}{10}+\frac{1}{9}\right) = -0.1056wl^2$$

Comparison of results

The results of moment coefficients obtained by the three methods are summarised in Table 9.2 as follows:

Table 9.2 *Example 9.1 – Moment coefficients by various methods*

Method	Span moments		Support moment
	M_1	M_2	M_3
(a) Total load on all spans	+0.0800	+0.0250	–0.1000
(b) Pattern loading	+0.0903	+0.0500 –0.0125	–0.1082
(c) Code coefficients	+0.0917	+0.0729	–0.1056

Comments

It is evident that the 'exact' analysis corresponds to case (b), viz., consideration of 'pattern loading'. With reference to these results, for the particular problem analysed, it follows that:

- the simplified consideration of total loading on all spans [case (a)] results in a 50 per cent under-estimation in the 'positive' midspan moment (M_2) in the interior span; M_1 and M_3 are also under-estimated, but marginally;
- the Code coefficient method over-estimates the midspan 'positive' moment M_2 in the interior span by as much as 45.8 per cent and the moment M_1 in the end span by 1.5 per cent;
- in general, the relatively crude method of considering total loads on all spans results in an unconservative design, whereas the use of Code moment coefficients results in a relatively conservative† design.

Example 9.2

(a) Based on the elastic factored moment envelope (i.e., considering pattern loading) obtainable from Example 9.1, design the flexural reinforcement in the three-span continuous beam of Example 9.1, given the following data:

$$w = 30 \text{ kN/m } (w_D = 15 \text{ kN/m}, w_L = 15 \text{ kN/m}); l = 8.0 \text{ m}$$

† Note that although the moment at the continuous support is slightly under-estimated (by 2.4 per cent), this difference can be easily accommodated by moment redistribution. Also, the *minimum* span moments in the *central* span are hogging in nature (requiring steel to be designed at top); however, $M_2 = -0.0125wl^2$ is relatively small and is likely to fall within the flexural strength of the nominal top steel provided.

Assume a partial load factor of 1.5 for both dead loads and live loads (as per IS Code). Use M 25 concrete and Fe 500 steel.

(b) Redesign the three-span continuous beam by applying moment redistribution (to the extent permitted by the Code).

Solution

(a)

- Factored load $w_u = 1.5 \times 30 = 45$ kN/m
  $\Rightarrow \quad w_u l^2 = 45 \times (8.0)^2 = 2880$ kNm
- The elastic factored moment envelope, based on the results of Example 9.1, is shown in Figure 9.15(a). The critical design moments are:

$$\text{span moments} \begin{cases} M_{u1} = +0.0903 w_u l^2 = +260.1 \text{ kNm (end span)} \\ M_{u2} = +0.0500 w_u l^2 = +144.0 \text{ kNm (interior span)} \end{cases}$$

[Also note that $M_{u2,\,min} = -0.0125\, w_u\, l^2$]

support moment $M_{u3} = -0.1082\, w_u\, l^2 = -311.7$ kNm

Proportioning of beam section:

- Assume a beam width $b = 300$ mm. Considering the maximum design moment of 311.7 kN/m, for an under-reinforced section,

$$\text{effective depth } d = \sqrt{\frac{M_u}{Rb}}$$

where $R_{\lim} = 0.1338 f_{ck} = 0.1338 \times 25 = 3.345$ MPa

$$\Rightarrow \quad d_{\min} = \sqrt{\frac{311.7 \times 10^6}{3.345 \times 300}} = 557.3 \text{ mm}$$

- Assume overall depth $D = 650$ mm and $d \approx 605$ mm (for an economical design)

Design of flexural reinforcement

- $$\frac{p_t}{100} \equiv \frac{A_{st}}{bd} = \frac{f_{ck}}{2 f_y}\left[1 - \sqrt{1 - 4.598 R / f_{ck}}\right]$$

  where $R \equiv \dfrac{M_u}{bd^2}$

- Considering $f_{ck} = 25$ MPa, $f_y = 500$ MPa, $b = 300$ mm, $d = 605$ mm, the following results are obtained:

1. for $M_{u1} = +260.1$ kNm, $R = 2.368$ MPa $\Rightarrow p_t = 0.623$
   $\Rightarrow (A_{st})_{reqd} = 1129 \text{ mm}^2$
   Provide 2–25ϕ + 1–16ϕ at bottom in the end span [$A_{st} = 1183 \text{ mm}^2 > 1129$]
2. for $M_{u2} = +144.0$ kNm, $R = 1.311$ MPa $\Rightarrow p_t = 0.322$
   $\Rightarrow (A_{st})_{reqd} = 585 \text{ mm}^2$
   Provide 3–16ϕ at bottom in the central span [$A_{st} = 603 \text{ mm}^2 > 585$]

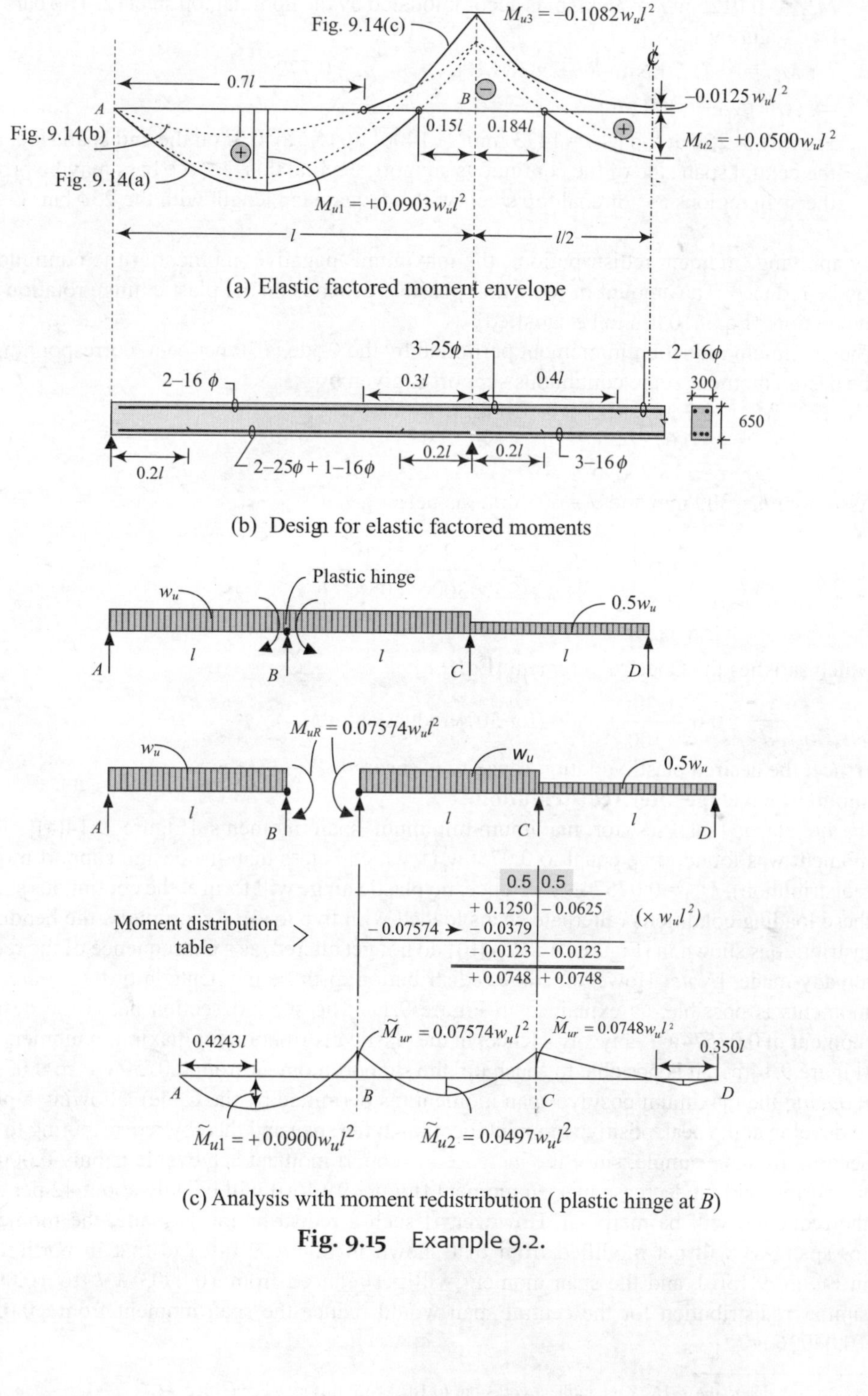

(a) Elastic factored moment envelope

(b) Design for elastic factored moments

(c) Analysis with moment redistribution (plastic hinge at B)

Fig. 9.15 Example 9.2.

$M_{u2} = -0.0125\ w_u l^2 = 36$ kNm is accommodated by the nominal top steel (2–16ϕ bars) provided† [see Figure 9.15(b)].

3. for $M_{u3} = -311.7$ kNm, $R = 2.838$ MPa $\Rightarrow$ $p_t = 0.772$

$\Rightarrow$ $(A_{st})_{reqd} = 1400\ \text{mm}^2$

Provide 3–25ϕ at top [$A_{st} = 1473\ \text{mm}^2 > 1400$] up to, say 0.3$l$ on the end span side, and 0.4l on the central span side of the continuous support; beyond this, 2–16 ϕ bars may be provided over the span regions as nominal top steel (with adequate lap length with the 25ϕ bars).

(b)

- By applying 'moment redistribution', the maximum 'negative' moment at the continuous support can be reduced. The amount of reduction possible depends on the plastic hinge rotation capacity at the section. [Eq. 9.10 has to be satisfied].
- The maximum reduction in moment permitted by the Code is 30 per cent, corresponding to which, the design moment at the continuous support is given by:

$$\tilde{M}_{u3} = 0.7\ M_{u3} = 0.7 \times (-0.1082\ w_u l^2)$$
$$= -\ 0.07574\ w_u l^2$$
$$= -\ 218.2\ \text{kNm}$$

- Assuming $b = 300$ mm and $d = 605$ mm (as before),
- [Eq. 9.11]: $$\frac{x_u}{d} = 1.202\left[1 - \sqrt{1 - \frac{4.598 \times 218.2 \times 10^6}{25 \times 300 \times 605^2}}\right]$$

$$= 0.244$$

which satisfies the Code requirement [Eq. 9.8]:

$$\frac{x_u}{d} \le 0.6 - \frac{30}{100} = 0.30 \text{ (for 30\% reduction in } M_{u3}).$$

Hence, the desired plastic rotation capacity is ensured.

Bending moment envelope after redistribution

- In the elastic analyses for maximum/minimum span moments [Figure 9.14(a)], the support moment was found to be equal to $0.0750 w_u l^2$, which is less than the design support moment (after redistribution), $\tilde{M}_{u3} = 0.07574 w_u l^2$. Hence, no plastic hinge will form at the continuous support under these loading conditions (alternate spans loaded with live load). Accordingly, the bending moment distributions shown in [Figures 9.14(a),(b)] do not get altered, as a consequence of the redistribution already made. [*Note:* However, some redistribution of these moments in order to *reduce* the span moments is possible, as explained in Figure 9.11. The support section has to be designed for a moment of $0.07574 w_u l^2$ anyway. Hence, in the elastic distribution for maximum moment in span AB [Figure 9.14(a)], it is possible to 'push up' the support moment from $0.0750 w_u l^2$ to $0.07574 w_u l^2$, by *reducing* the maximum positive span moment (as permitted by the Code), allowing a plastic hinge to develop at the peak positive moment location in the span and thereby redistributing to the support section. In this example, since the increase in support moment achievable is only $0.00074 w_u l^2$ and the corresponding decrease in span moment [Figure 9.14(a)] will be only about 42 per cent of this; the reduction will be marginal. However, if such a redistribution is made, the moment diagram for span AB will get modified from that shown in Figure 9.14(a) to that in portion AB (only) in Figure 9.15(c), and the span moment will get reduced from $+0.0903\ w_u l^2$ to $+0.0900\ w_u l^2$. A similar redistribution for the central span would reduce the span moment from $+0.0500\ w_u l^2$ to $+0.04926\ w_u l^2$.]

† The flexural strength due to the 2–16ϕ bars, in fact, works out to 101 kNm; this may be verified.

- For the loading pattern shown in Figure 9.14(c), the possibility of redistribution has been recognised by reducing the design flexural strength at the continuous support from the elastic solution value of $-0.1082\ w_u l^2$ to $\tilde{M}_{u3} = -0.07574\ w_u l^2$. What remains to be done is to calculate the revised span moments and locations of points of inflection, corresponding to the lowering of the support moment, i.e., redistribution.
- By performing an analysis of the continuous beam with a plastic hinge at the continuous support, (with $\tilde{M}_{u3} = -0.07574\ w_u l^2$) [Figure 9.15], the maximum 'positive' moments in the end span and central span are obtained as:

  end span: $\tilde{M}_{u1} = +0.0900\ w_u l^2 < (M_{u1})_{\text{elastic}} = +0.0903\ w_u l^2$

  central span: $\tilde{M}_{u2} = +0.0497\ w_u l^2 < (M_{u2})_{\text{elastic}} = +0.0500\ w_u l^2$

  In fact, the bending moment diagrams obtained, after redistribution [Figure 9.15(c)], for spans AB and BC, happens to be very much similar to those obtained earlier in Figures 9.14(a), (b).
- Thus, with redistribution effected at the support section only, it is seen that, in the case of the end span as well as the central span, the design moments remain the same as for loading conditions given in Figures 9.14(a) and (b), with $\tilde{M}_{u1} = +0.0903\ w_u l^2 = +260.1$ kNm, and $\tilde{M}_{u2} = +0.0500\ w_u l^2 = +144.0$ kNm. The corresponding 'positive' moment envelopes are shown in Figure 9.16(a). [It may be seen that if the redistributions for reducing span moments mentioned in the *note* above were also effected, the design moments in the spans would have been $+0.0900\ w_u l^2$ and $+0.0497\ w_u l^2$ respectively for end and central spans, and Figure 9.16(a) would correspondingly get modified.]
- The moment envelope is obtained by combining the bending moment diagrams of Figures 9.14(a), (b) and 9.15(c); the diagram of Figure 9.15(c) is seen to practically merge with Figures 9.14(a),(b). This is depicted in Figure 9.16(a). In combining these diagrams, the outermost lines yield the moment envelope.

Design of flexural reinforcement

- Considering $f_{ck} = 25$ MPa, $f_y = 500$ MPa, $b = 300$ mm, $d = 605$ mm (as before),
  1. For span AB, $\tilde{M}_{u1} = +260.1$ kNm, (which is identical to Part(a) of this Example).

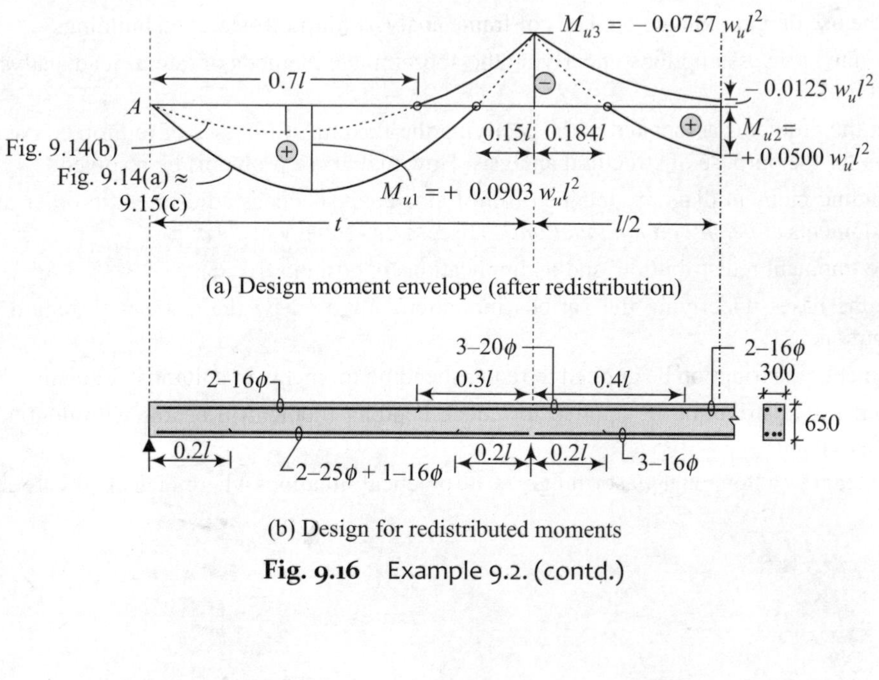

Fig. 9.16 Example 9.2. (contd.)

Provide 2–25ϕ + 1–16ϕ at bottom in the end span (A_{st} = 1183 mm^2 >1129).

Note: There is no increase in the reinforcement provided [refer Figure 9.15(b)] on account of redistribution.

2. For span BC, $\tilde{M}_{u2}$ = +144.0 kNm, (which is identical to Part(a) of this Example) *Provide* 3–16ϕ at bottom in the central span (exactly as before).

3. For the support section, $\tilde{M}_{u3}$ = –218.2 kNm, $R \equiv \dfrac{M_u}{bd^2}$ = 1.987 MPa

   $\Rightarrow\ p_t = 0.508 \Rightarrow (A_{st})_{reqd} = 923\ \text{mm}^2$

   Provide 3–20ϕ at top (A_{st} = 942 mm^2 > 923), with the bars curtailed as before and beyond this, 2–16ϕ (nominal) bars provided at top in the span region.

   Note: This results in some savings, compared to the earlier design [Figure 9.15(b)], which required 3–25ϕ

- The detailing is shown in Figure 9.16(b).

REVIEW QUESTIONS

9.1 Comment on the apparent inconsistency in combining *elastic analysis* of structures with *design* at the *ultimate limit state.*

9.2 Explain how the critical live load patterns in a plane frame can be obtained by the application of the Müller-Breslau Principle.

9.3 Under what circumstances does the Code permit the neglect of 'pattern loading' for the purpose of arriving at the critical design moments in a framed structure?

9.4 Explain why the Code disallow *moment redistribution* when bending moments in continuous beams are based on the Code moment coefficients.

9.5 Describe when is it inappropriate to apply the *substitute frame method* for multi-storeyed buildings.

9.6 Justify the use of approximate methods of frame analysis for multi-storeyed buildings.

9.7 Evaluate the basic assumptions underlying the approximate methods of lateral load analysis of multi-storeyed frames.

9.8 Interpret the problems associated with specifying the flexural stiffnesses of reinforced concrete frame members for the purpose of structural analysis. How may these problems be resolved?

9.9 'The bending moment diagram obtained from frame analysis needs adjustment in order to obtain the design moments at *beam-column junctions*'. Discuss this statement.

9.10 Describe 'moment redistribution' and its implications in design.

9.11 Explain the bases underlying the various limitations imposed by the Code with regard to moment redistribution.

9.12 Can moment redistribution be applied to reduce bending moments in columns? Explain.

9.13 Can moment redistribution be applied to reduce bending moment in beams with doubly reinforced sections? Explain.

9.14 What is meant by a 'torsional plastic hinge'? Cite practical situations where such hinges are encountered.

PROBLEMS

9.1 Repeat the problem given in Example 9.1, considering the live load component (w_L) to constitute 80 per cent of the total load (w).

Ans.: (a) $M_1 = +0.0800w_u l^2$; $M_2 = +0.0250w_u l^2$; $M_3 = -0.1000w_u l^2$

(b) $M_1 = +0.0968w_u l^2$; $M_2 = +0.0650w_u l^2$; $M_3 = -0.1143w_u l^2$

(c) $M_1 = +0.0968w_u l^2$; $M_2 = +0.0750w_u l^2$; $M_3 = -0.1089w_u l^2$

9.2 Using the results of Problem 9.1, design the three-span continuous beam, considering 25 per cent reduction in the maximum factored elastic 'negative' moment, with moment redistribution, including possible reductions in the span moments. Assume w = 30 kN/m, l = 8 m, M 25 concrete and Fe 500 steel.

9.3 Consider the symmetric portal frame in Figure 9.17. From an elastic analysis under factored loads, the hogging moment at B and C is obtained as $M_B = M_C$ = 100 kNm.

(a) Determine the ratio $M_{uR}^- : M_{uR}^+$, as required by elastic analysis, where M_{uR}^- and M_{uR}^+ denote respectively the design hogging and sagging moment capacities for the beam BC. In order to make this ratio 1:1, determine the percentage redistribution required. Draw the redistributed bending moment diagram for the portal frame, indicating the values at the critical locations.

(b) Show that the above redistribution is allowable, given that the beam is 200 mm wide, and has an effective depth of 450 mm. Assume M 25 concrete and Fe 500 steel. Also determine the area of tension steel A_{st} (mm^2) required at the support/midspan sections.

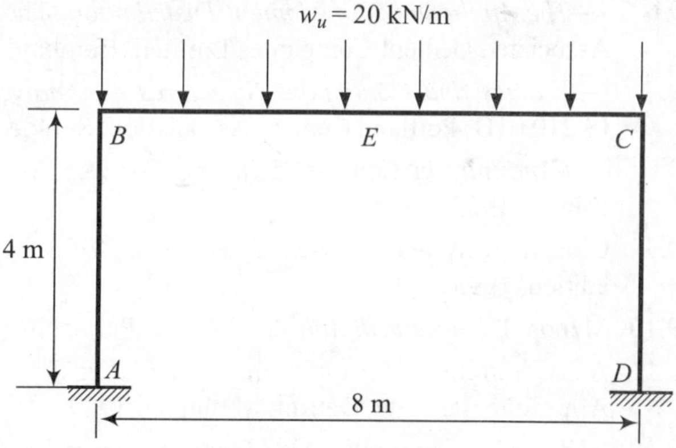

Fig. 9.17 Problem 9.3.

9.4 Analyse the design moments and sketch the moment envelope for the beam members in the *substitute frame* shown in Figure 9.18. Assume suitable dimensions for the frame members. The beams are integrally connected to a floor slab 150 mm thick.

9.5 Applying appropriate moment redistribution (to the results of Problem 9.4), design the flexural reinforcement in the beams *AB* and *BC* in Figure 9.18. Assume M 25 concrete and Fe 500 steel.

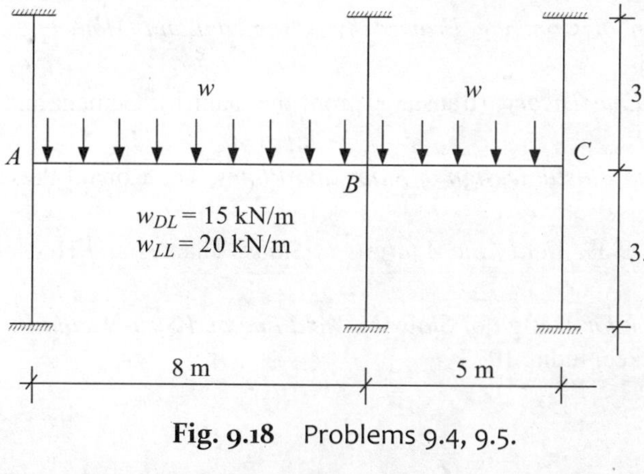

Fig. 9.18 Problems 9.4, 9.5.

REFERENCES

9.1 Hsieh, Y Y, *Elementary Theory of Structures,* Prentice-Hall, Inc., New Jersey, 1970

9.2 — *Explanatory Handbook on Indian Standard Code of Practice for Plain and Reinforced Concrete (IS 456:1978)*, Special Publication SP:24, Bureau of Indian Standards, New Delhi, 1983

9.3 CSA Standard CAN – A23.3 – 04 — *Design of Concrete Structures for Buildings*, Canadian Standards Association, Mississauga, Ontario, 2004

9.4 Wang, C K, *Intermediate Structural Analysis*, McGraw-Hill International edition, 1983

9.5 Weaver, W and Gere, J M, *Matrix Analysis of Framed Structures*, Second edition, Van Nostrand Co., New York, 1980

9.6 — *The Applications of Moment Distribution*, The Concrete Association of India, Publication of The Associated Cement Companies Limited, Bombay, 1978

9.7 — *Frames and Continuous Structures — Analysis by Moment Distribution*, Concrete Information IS 210.01D, Portland Cement Association, Skokie, Illinois, 1980

9.8 — *Continuity in Concrete Building Frames*, Fourth edition, Portland Cement Association Chicago, Illinois, 1959

9.9 Clough, R W and Penzien, J, *Dynamics of Structures*, Second edition, McGraw-Hill International edition, 1993

9.10 Menon, D, *Structural Analysis*, Narosa Publishing House, Delhi, 2008

9.11 ACI Committee 318, *Commentary on Building Code Requirements for Reinforced Concrete* (ACI 318–89), Am. Conc. Institute, Detroit, Michigan, 1989

9.12 ACI–ASCE Committee 428, *Limit Design of Reinforced Concrete Beams and Frames — Addendum*, (supplement to bibliographies published in ACI Journal in Nov. 1961 and Dec. 1962), Journal ACI, Vol. 60, Oct. 1963, pp 1471–1473

9.13 Cohn, M Z, *Limit-Design Solutions for Concrete Structures*, ASCE Journal, Struct. Div., Vol. 83, Feb. 1967, pp 37–57

9.14 Lazaro, A L and Richards, R, *Full-Range Analysis of Concrete Frames*, ASCE Journal, Struct. Div., Vol. 99, August 1973, pp 1761–1783

9.15 Baker, A L L, *Ultimate Load Theory Applied to the Design of Reinforced and Prestressed Concrete Frames*, Concrete Publications Ltd., London, 1956

9.16 Colin M A, *Limit Design of Reinforced Concrete Frames*, ASCE Journal, Struct. Div., Vol. 94, Oct. 1968, M. 2647–2483

9.17 Furlong, R W, *Design of Concrete Frames by Assigned Limit Moments*, Journal ACI, Vol. 67, Apr. 1970, pp 341–353

9.18 Johansen, K W, *Yield Line Theory*, (translated from the Danish), Cement and Concrete Association, London, 1962

9.19 Wood, R H, *Plastic and Elastic Design of Slabs and Plates*, The Ronald Press Company, New York, 1961

9.20 Jones, L L and Wood, R H, *Yield Line Analysis of Slabs*, Thames and Hudson, Chatto and Windus, London, 1967

9.21 Shukla, S N, *Handbook for Design of Slabs by Yield line and Strip Methods*, Structural Engineering Research Centre, Roorkee, India, 1973

9.22 Purushothaman, P, *Reinforced Concrete Structural Elements — Behaviour, Analysis and Design,* Tata McGraw Hill Publ. Co. Ltd., New Delhi, 1984

9.23 Pillai, S U and Bhargavan, K K, *Bending Moment-Torque Redistribution in Reinforced Concrete Frames*, Proc., Conference on Tall Buildings, Kuala Lampur, Dec. 1974, pp 4.66–4.75

9.24 Pillai, S U and Lash, S D, *Ultimate Strength of Reinforced Concrete Grid and Slab Bridges*, First International Symposium: Concrete Bridge Design, ACI Publication SP–23, Am. Conc. Institute, Detroit, 1969, pp 361–384

Serviceability Limit States: Deflection and Cracking

CHAPTER 10

LEARNING OBJECTIVES

After studying this chapter, you will be able to:

- *Explain serviceability requirements for RC members and related Code specifications*
- *Use different methods for calculations of short- and long-term deflections and check with applicable limits*
- *Evaluate probable crack-widths in different cases and implement measures for crack control*
- *Ensure serviceability conformance in RC design, in general*

10.1 Introduction

Serviceability limits related to deflection, crack width, vibration, etc., are applicable to service (working) load conditions. In modern structures, with heavier loads, longer spans and slender members, serviceability limits assume greater importance.

Limiting *l/d* ratios may not guarantee deflection control for members with large live to dead load ratios.

According to the design philosophy of the *limit states method* (refer Section 3.5), there are two distinct classes of limit states to be considered: *ultimate limit states* and *serviceability limit states*. Whereas the former deals with *safety* in terms of strength, overturning, sliding, buckling, fatigue fracture, etc., the latter deals with *serviceability* in terms of deflection, cracking, vibration, durability, etc. The aim of structural design by the LSM philosophy is to ensure both 'safety' and 'serviceability', so that the structure performs its intended function satisfactorily.

In the chapters considered hitherto, the focus has been on *ultimate* limit states (or 'limit states of collapse') dealing with *strength*[†] (flexure, shear, torsion and bond). The importance of controlling *deflection* and *cracking* has been briefly covered in Chapter 5, in terms of proper detailing of reinforcement (Section 5.2) and limiting span/effective depth ratios (Section 5.3) in beams and slabs. In fact, the Code (Cl. 42 and 43) does not require the designer to perform any explicit check on deflection or crack-width for *all normal cases*, provided the Code recommendations for limiting *l/d* ratios (for deflection control) and spacing of flexural reinforcement (for crack control) are complied with. However,

[†] The ultimate limit state of strength in *compression*, not considered so far, is discussed at length in Chapter 13. The ultimate limit states in overturning and sliding are considered in Chapter 14, in connection with the design of foundations.

the minimum depths indicated by these *l/d* ratios may not be adequate for certain sequences of shoring during construction or large live to dead load ratios. Moreover, calculation of deflection may be required for roof slabs to check for likelihood of ponding and to estimate required compensatory initial camber.

It is well recognised that, in modern practice, structural 'failures' are all-too-common in terms of serviceability, and are relatively rare in terms of safety. In particular, it is the serviceability limit state of *durability* that calls for particular attention, indeed all over the world. The problem of inadequate durability is linked not only to such factors as improper making of concrete, chemical attack from the environment and corrosion of reinforcement [refer Section 2.13], but also to inadequate cover to reinforcement [refer Section 5.2.1], improper detailing and inadequate sizes for structural members, resulting in excessive deflections and crack-widths (and consequent loss of durability). Some of these problems as well as their solutions are addressed in Chapter 15 of this book.

Adoption of limit states design and higher grades of concrete and steel in modern reinforced concrete design has led to overall thinner member sections and higher stress levels at service loads [see example in Figure 15.1]. These, in turn, have resulted in larger deflections, crack-widths, vibrations, etc., in such structures, compared to earlier ones designed by the more conservative working stress design and using mild steel and lower grades of concrete. Hence, the need for serviceability checks has assumed greater importance in present-day design.

The scope of the present chapter is limited to describing methods of explicitly calculating deflections and crack-widths in flexural members for the purpose of checking the serviceability limit states of deflections and cracking. This is required especially when the limiting *l/d* ratios of the Code are not complied with, when the specified load is abnormally high, and in special structures where limits to deflection and crack-width are of particular importance.

Deflection check is necessary where *l/d* limits are not met, specified loads are abnormally high, or the structure requires lower deflection limits.

10.2 Serviceability Limit States: Deflection

10.2.1 Deflection Limits

Various factors are involved in prescribing limits to deflection in flexural members, such as:

- aesthetic/psychological discomfort;
- crack-width limitation (limiting deflection is an indirect way of limiting crack-widths);
- effect on attached structural and non-structural elements;
- ponding in (roof) slabs.

The selection of a limit to deflection depends on the given situation, and this selection is somewhat arbitrary [Ref. 10.1].

The Code (Cl. 23.2) prescribes the following two limits for flexural members in general:

1. span/250	— the *final* deflection due to *all* loads (including long-term effects of creep and shrinkage);
2. span/350 or 20 mm (whichever is less)	— the deflection (including long-term effects of creep and shrinkage) that occur *after* the construction of partitions and finishes*.

† This involves loads applied after this stage, which in general, comprise live loads.

The first limit is based on considerations of crack control and aesthetic/psychological discomfort to occupants, and the second limit is aimed at preventing damage to partitions and finishes [Ref. 10.2]. These limits constitute broad guidelines and may be exceeded in situations where the deflections are considered to not adversely affect the appearance or efficiency of the structure.

It may be noted that the prescribed Code limits are concerned only with deflections that occur under *service loads*; hence, the partial load factor to be applied on the *characteristic* load should be taken as unity in general [refer Section 3.6.3]. Furthermore, the Code (Cl. 36.4.2.2) specifies that the modulus of elasticity and other properties to be considered in deflection calculations should be based on the characteristic strength of concrete and steel.

10.2.2 Difficulties in Accurate Prediction of Deflections

Because of the uncertainties and high variability in the factors involved in deflection calculations, such calculations yield only approximate results. Yet, they serve the purpose of deflection control.

Accurate prediction of deflections in reinforced concrete members is difficult because of the following factors:

- uncertainties in predicting the *flexural rigidity* (*EI*) of the member, which is influenced by:
  - varying degrees of tensile cracking of concrete;
  - varying amounts of flexural reinforcement;
  - variations in modulus of elasticity of concrete; and
  - variations in modulus of rupture of concrete;
- uncertainties regarding time-dependent and environmental effects which influence shrinkage and creep;
- inelastic flexural behaviour of members; and
- inherent high variability in measured deflections, even under carefully controlled laboratory conditions.

In view of the above uncertainties, approximations and simplifications are essential in deflection calculations. The calculations are considered in two parts: (i) *immediate* or short-term deflection occurring on application of the load, and (ii) additional *long-term* deflection, resulting mostly from differential shrinkage and creep under sustained loading. For calculating the 'immediate' deflection, the loading to be considered is the full load (dead plus live). However, for calculating the long-term deflection due to creep, only the 'permanent' load (dead load plus the sustained part of live load) is to be considered. Despite these simplifications and assumptions, the calculations are quite lengthy and may give the impression of being sophisticated and rigorous – which is rather illusory, in view of the random nature of deflection and its high variability. Nevertheless, in the absence of more precise information, these deflection calculations become necessary, and may be regarded as providing representative values that serve the purpose of comparison with empirically set deflection limits.

10.3 Short-term Deflection

10.3.1 Deflections by Elastic Theory

Short-term deflections, due to the applied *service* loads, are generally based on the assumption of linear elastic behaviour, and for this purpose, reinforced concrete is treated as a homogeneous material [refer Section 4.2]. Expressions for the maximum elastic deflection Δ of a homogeneous beam of effective span l and flexural rigidity EI (for any loading and support conditions) can be derived using the standard methods of structural analysis, and are available for several standard cases in handbooks [Ref. 10.3, 10.4]. Typically, they take the form:

$$\Delta = k_w \frac{Wl^3}{EI} = k_m \frac{Ml^2}{EI} \tag{10.1}$$

where W is the total load on the span, M the maximum moment, and k_w and k_m are constants which depend on the load (or moment) distribution, conditions of end restraint and variation in the flexural rigidity EI (if any). For the standard case of a simply supported beam of uniform section, subjected to a uniformly distributed load, $k_w = 5/384$ and $k_m = 5/48$, as shown in Figure 10.1(a). If the same beam is subjected instead to an end moment M alone, the midspan deflection Δ_m is given by $k_m = 1/16$ in Eq. 10.1 [Figure 10.1(b)].

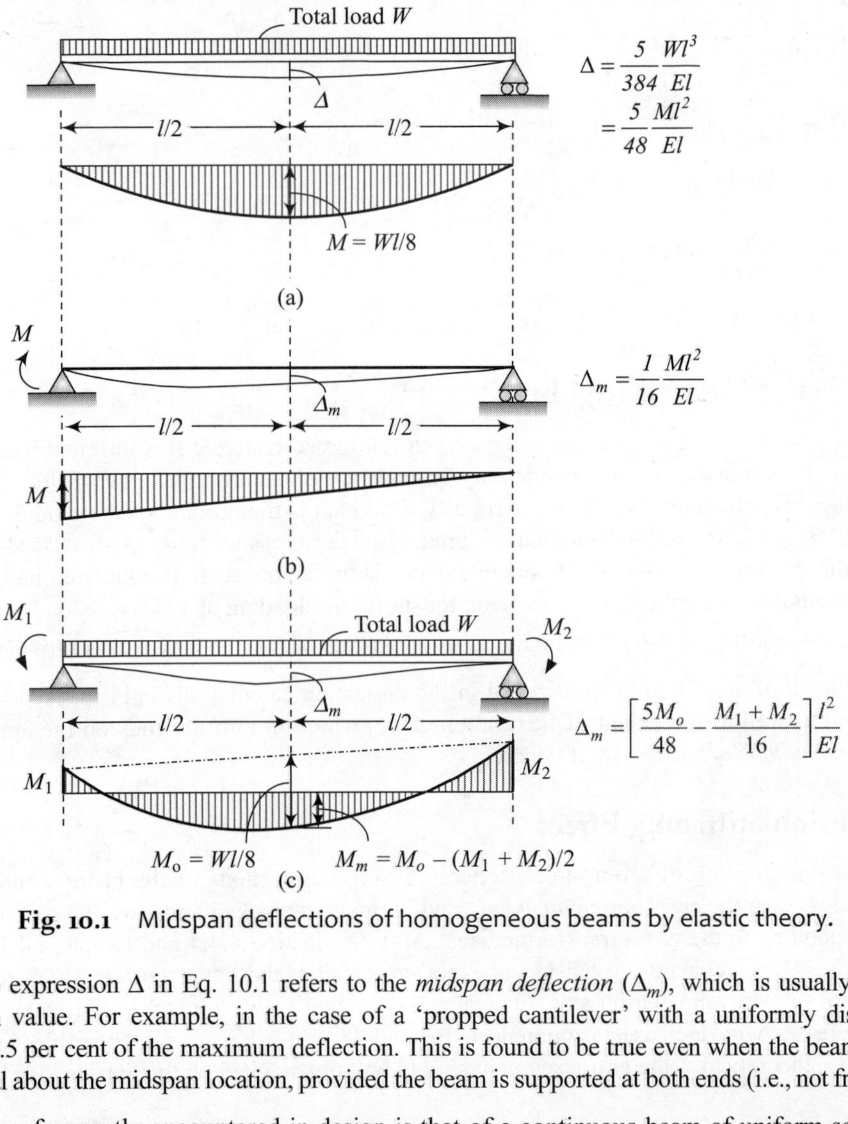

Fig. 10.1 Midspan deflections of homogeneous beams by elastic theory.

Generally, the expression Δ in Eq. 10.1 refers to the *midspan deflection* (Δ_m), which is usually very close to the maximum value. For example, in the case of a 'propped cantilever' with a uniformly distributed load, Δ_m is within 3.5 per cent of the maximum deflection. This is found to be true even when the beam or loading is unsymmetrical about the midspan location, provided the beam is supported at both ends (i.e., not free at one end).

A standard case frequently encountered in design is that of a continuous beam of uniform section, subject to a uniformly distributed load [Figure 10.1(c)]. As the support moments (M_1, M_2) are usually known from structural analysis of the statically indeterminate structure, it would be convenient to express the midspan deflection Δ_m in terms of these two moments as well as the midspan moment $M_m = M_0 - (M_1 + M_2)/2$. Applying the principle of superposition, and making use of the results of Figures 10.1(a) (b), an expression for the midspan deflection Δ_m may be derived as follows:

$$\Delta_m = \frac{5}{48}\frac{M_o l^2}{EI} - \frac{M_1 l^2}{16EI} - \frac{M_2 l^2}{16EI}$$

$$= \frac{5l^2}{48EI}\left[M_o - (3/5)(M_1 + M_2)\right]$$

where $M_o = Wl/8$

Substituting $M_m = M_o - (M_1 + M_2)/2$, and eliminating M_o,

$$\Delta_m = \frac{5l^2}{48EI}\left[M_m - (M_1 + M_2)/10\right] \tag{10.2}$$

Alternatively, eliminating $(M_1 + M_2)$,

$$\Delta_m = \frac{5l^2}{48EI}\left[1.2M_m - 0.2M_o\right] \tag{10.3}$$

Similar expressions can be worked out for concentrated loadings [Ref. 10.5].

10.3.2 Effective Flexural Rigidity

For the purpose of calculating *short-term deflections* in reinforced concrete flexural members, expressions such as Eq. 10.1–10.3, based on elastic theory, may be made use of. An important parameter that needs to be considered in these calculations is the flexural rigidity *EI*, which is the product of the modulus of elasticity of concrete[†] $E = E_c$, and the second moment of area, *I*, of the cross-section. As discussed in Chapter 2 (Section 2.8), the modulus of elasticity of concrete depends on factors such as concrete quality, age, stress level and rate or duration of applied load. However, for short-term loading up to service load levels, the Code expression [Eq. 2.4] for the short-term static modulus of elasticity $\left(E_c = 5000\sqrt{f_{ck}}\right)$ is satisfactory.

The second moment of area, *I*, to be considered in the deflection calculations is influenced by percentage of reinforcement as well as the extent of flexural cracking, which in turn depends on the applied bending moment and the *modulus of rupture* f_{cr} of concrete.

10.3.3 Tension Stiffening Effect

During the first time loading of a reinforced concrete beam, the portions of the beam where the applied moment (*M*) is less than the *cracking moment* (M_{cr}) will remain uncracked and have the second moment of area (I_T) corresponding to the gross transformed section [refer Section 4.4.3 and Example 4.1]. Where the moment exceeds M_{cr}, the concrete in tension is expected to fail at the outer tension fibres and the cracks propagate inward (towards the neutral axis). The average spacing between cracks reduces and the average crack-width increases with increase in moment *M* beyond M_{cr}. In a beam segment subject to a constant moment $M > M_{cr}$, theoretically, the entire segment should be fully cracked on the tension side of the neutral

[†] The material called 'reinforced concrete' is essentially concrete, as the embedded reinforcement comprises only a very small fraction of the volume of the reinforced concrete member.

axis. But, in practise, it is seen that this does not happen, and in fact, the flexural cracks are dispersed randomly such that there are significant portions in between the cracks, which remain uncracked, as shown in Figure 10.2(a).

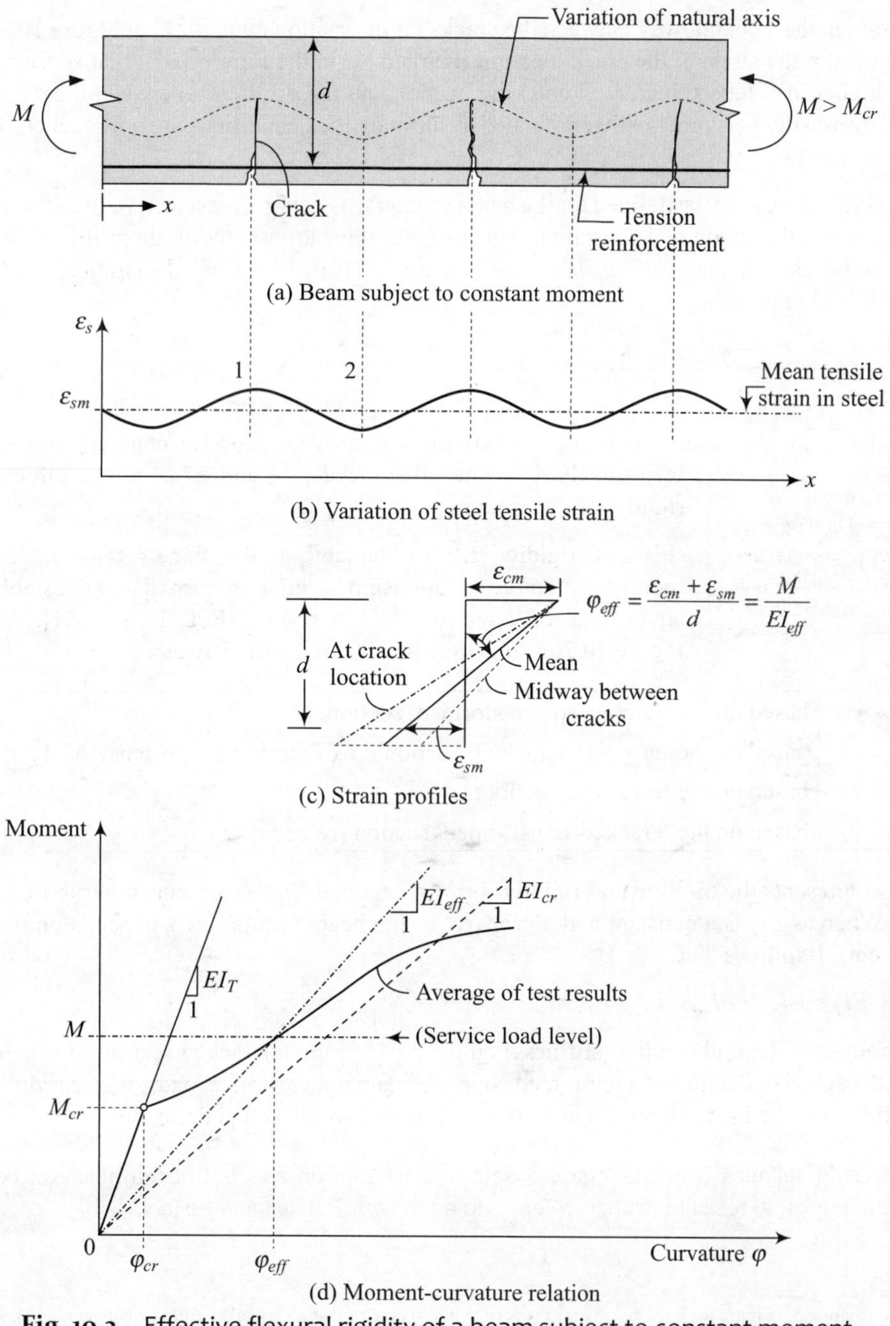

Fig. 10.2 Effective flexural rigidity of a beam subject to constant moment.

The concrete in between the cracks resists some tension, and this is reflected by a reduction in tensile strain in the reinforcement [Figure 10.2(b)], a lowering of the neutral axis [Figure 10.2(a)], a fluctuation in the bond stress† [see also Figure 8.2] as well as a reduction in curvature [Figure 10.2(c)] – with reference to these parameters calculated at the crack location.

The tensile strain in the steel midway between the cracks (at the section marked '2' in Figure 10.2) may be as low as 60 per cent of the strain at the crack location (marked '1' in the Figure 10.2) – at service load levels. Of course, at higher load levels, increased cracking occurs, and the difference between the two strains gets reduced – and eventually gets practically eliminated as ultimate load conditions are approached (in an under-reinforced beam).

An *effective curvature* φ_{eff} may be defined for the beam segment, as being representative of the mean curvature of the segment, under the action of a constant moment M. For this purpose, the strain profile to be considered may be reasonably based on the *mean strain* profile [Figure 10.2(c)], rather than the strain profile at the crack location (which is obviously higher):

$$\varphi_{eff} = \frac{\varepsilon_{cm} + \varepsilon_{sm}}{d} = \frac{M}{EI_{eff}} \tag{10.4}$$

where ε_{cm} and ε_{sm} are the mean strains in the extreme compression fibre in concrete and tension steel respectively, d is the effective depth, and EI_{eff} is the effective flexural rigidity of the section.

There are different ways for computing the flexural rigidity, *EI*, of a member – any *effective* value, EI_{eff}, used in calculations is just an approximation.

'Flexural rigidity' EI is obtainable as the slope (secant modulus) of the moment-curvature relationship, which in turn can be established from an average of a number of test results [Ref. 10.5–10.11]. As shown in Figure 10.2(d), this may be obtained variously as:

• EI_T	based on the 'uncracked-transformed' section;
• EI_{gr}	based on the 'gross' (uncracked) section, i.e., ignoring the presence of steel;
• EI_{eff}	based on the 'effective' section;
• EI_{cr}	based on the 'cracked-transformed' section [refer Eq. 4.15].

Evidently, EI_T represents the true flexural rigidity for $M < M_{cr}$, and EI_{eff} represents the true flexural rigidity for $M > M_{cr}$. Whereas EI_T is a constant and a property of the beam section, EI_{eff} depends on the load level (applied moment). It follows that:

$$EI_T > EI_{gr} > EI_{eff} > EI_{cr}$$

Thus, determining the flexural rigidity (stiffness) on the basis of the uncracked section results in an under-estimation of the actual deflection of a reinforced concrete beam under service loads; whereas doing so on the basis of the (fully) cracked section results in an over-estimation of the actual deflection.

The increase in stiffness over the 'cracked section' stiffness, on account of the ability of concrete (in between cracks) to resist tension, is referred to as the *tension stiffening* effect.

† As explained in Chapter 8, [Figure 8.2], the bond stress is zero at every crack location and also midway between cracks (in the region of constant moment); elsewhere the bond stress varies nonlinearly.

10.3.4 Effective Second Moment of Area Formulation

Various empirical expressions for the 'effective second moment of area' I_{eff} (for calculating short-term deflections in simply supported beams) have been proposed [Ref. 10.5–10.11] and incorporated in different codes. Some of these formulations are based on assumed transition moment-curvature relations [Ref. 10.5–10.8], whereas the others [Ref. 10.9–10.11] are based on assumed transition of strains/stresses in the region between cracks (and involve stress-strain relations and equilibrium of forces). The expression given in the Indian Code (IS 456: 2000, Cl. C–2.1) is based on an earlier version of the British Code, which assumes an idealised trilinear moment-curvature relation [line *OABCD* in Figure 10.3]. The initial uncracked stiffness EI_{gr} and the cracked stiffness (at ultimate load) EI_{cr} are represented by the slopes of lines *OA* and *OC* respectively. Any intermediate stiffness (EI_{eff} corresponding to line *OB*) can be interpolated by defining the slope of the intermediate line *ABC* in the region $M_{cr} < M < M_u$. The slope of this line (which commences with the cracking moment point *A*) is approximated as $0.85EI_{cr}$.

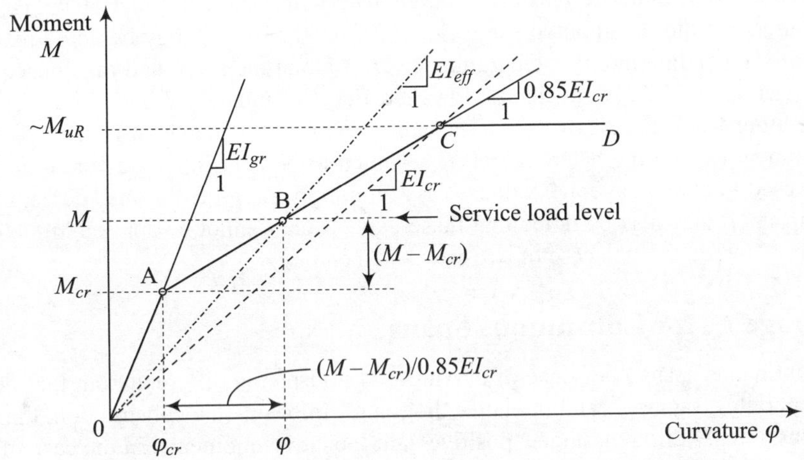

Fig. 10.3 Idealised trilinear moment-curvature relation.

It follows that:

$$EI_{eff} = \frac{M}{\varphi_{cr} + (M - M_{cr})/(0.85EI_{cr})} \quad \text{for} \quad M_{cr} \le M \le M_u$$

where $\varphi_{cr} = M_{cr}/EI_{gr}$ and $M_{cr} = f_{cr}I_{gr}/y_t$ [Note that this expression for M_{cr} is similar to Eq. 4.10, except that I_{gr}[†] is used instead of I_T]. Simplifying the above expression, it can be shown that

$$I_{eff} = \frac{I_{cr}}{1.2 - (M_{cr}/M)\eta} \quad \text{with } I_{cr} \le I_{eff} \le I_{gr} \tag{10.5a}$$

where $\eta \equiv 1.2 - I_{cr}/I_{gr}$ (10.5b)

The IS code formula for the effective moment of inertia is identical to Eq. 10.5a, except that the non-dimensional parameter η in the equation takes a more complicated form than the one given by Eq. 10.5b:

[†] The use of the *gross* section (i.e., ignoring the contribution of steel), instead of the *uncracked-transformed* section, is done for convenience.

$$\eta \equiv \frac{z}{d}\left(1-\frac{x}{d}\right)\frac{b_w}{b} \tag{10.6}$$

where $x \equiv kd$ is the depth of the neutral axis, $z \equiv jd$ the lever arm, b_w the 'breadth of the web', and b the 'breadth of the compression face'. Sometimes, the calculations will yield values of I_{eff} that may exceed I_{gr} or be less than I_{cr}. In such cases, the bounds on I_{eff}, as indicated in Eq. 10.5a, should be applied.

An alternative expression for I_{eff}, widely used in North American practice (ACI code [Ref. 10.13], Canadian code [Ref. 10.14]), is due to Branson [Ref. 10.5] and takes the form:

$$I_{eff} = I_{cr} + (I_{gr} - I_{cr})\left(\frac{M_{cr}}{M}\right)^3 \leq I_{gr} \quad \text{for } M > M_{cr} \tag{10.7}$$

Eq. 10.7 gives a value of I_{eff} which is effectively a weighted average of I_{gr} and I_{cr}.

Comparison with test results indicates reasonable agreement (within the range of ± 20 per cent !) between the deflections measured and those computed using Eq. 10.5a or Eq. 10.7. It may be noted that for the general case of a non-uniform bending moment diagram, I_{eff} varies along the span, and the consequent calculation of maximum deflection can be very difficult. However, Eqs 10.5a and 10.7 have been developed with the intention of generating a single value of I_{eff} (for the entire beam, assumed to be prismatic) in association with the *maximum* moment (M) on the beam, which is assumed to be bent in single curvature. Thus, Eq. 10.5 (or 10.7) can be used to give an average value† of I_{eff} for simply supported spans and cantilever spans, but not continuous spans. It may also be noted that these expressions cannot be applied in the case of bending combined with axial force, or in the case of two-way slab bending.

10.3.5 Average I_{eff} for Continuous Spans

In the case of continuous spans, the sense of curvature at midspan is different from that near the support; the former is (generally) 'sagging', and the latter 'hogging'. In beam-slab construction, the flanged section properties are substantially different under 'positive' and 'negative' moments; in the case of the former, the flange is effective, being under compression, but in the case of the latter, the flange is under tension [refer Sections 4.6.4, 4.7.4]. Even in the case of beams with rectangular cross-sections, there are differences in reinforcement ratios and differences in the influence of cracking in the two regions. Hence, a weighted average of the I_{eff} values at mid-span and support regions is generally recommended.

A simple expression for a weighted average $I_{eff,\,av}$, recommended in Ref. 10.5 and 10.15, is as follows:

$$I_{eff,av} = 0.7I_{eff,m} + 0.15(I_{eff,1} + I_{eff,2}) \tag{10.8a}$$

(for beams with both ends continuous)

$$I_{eff,av} = 0.85I_{eff,m} + 0.15I_{eff,cont} \tag{10.8b}$$

(for beams with one end continuous)

where the subscript m denotes the midspan location, and the subscripts *cont*, 1, 2 denote the continuous end location(s).

Typically, in a continuous span, the gravity loading pattern which produces the maximum deflection (as well as maximum 'positive' moment) is different from that which produces the maximum 'negative' moment at

† Assuming a uniform I_{eff} (calculated with respect to the *maximum* span moment) will generally result in a conservative estimate of deflection.

the supports [refer Chapter 9]. In order to account for the more widespread cracking near the support regions under these larger 'negative' moments, it becomes necessary to consider the maximum 'negative' moment at the support region for evaluating $I_{eff,1}$, $I_{eff,2}$ or $I_{eff,cont}$ using Eq. 10.5a or Eq. 10.7. Similarly, the maximum 'positive' moment should be considered for evaluating $I_{eff,m}$. Of course, once the $I_{eff,av}$ has been evaluated this way (using Eq. 10.8), the deflection calculation (using Eq. 10.3) should be based on values of M_m, M_1 and M_2, corresponding to that loading diagram which causes maximum deflection (in the span region).

It may also be noted that, generally, in continuous spans, I_{eff} values at the continuous ends have a much smaller effect† on the deflections than $I_{eff,\,m}$, and reasonable predictions of deflection can be obtained by using $I_{eff,\,m}$ alone, instead of a weighted average [Ref. 10.15]. However, when there is a significant variation in flexural rigidity (as in flanged beams), or when the negative moment at either continuous end is relatively large, the use of a weighted average such as Eq. 10.8 is recommended.

The weighted average expression given in the Code (Cl. C–2.1) for continuous beams is somewhat complicated and takes the form (similar to Eq. 10.5a):

$$I_{eff,av} = \frac{I_{cr,av}}{1.2 - (M_{cr,av}/M)\eta} \quad \text{with } I_{cr,\,av} \le I_{eff,\,av} \le I_{gr,\,av} \tag{10.9a}$$

where $I_{cr,\,av}$, $I_{gr,\,av}$ and $M_{cr,\,av}$ are to be computed as weighted averages using the following generalised expression:

$$X_{av} = k_1(X_1 + X_2)/2 + (1 - k_1)X_m \tag{10.9b}$$

where the subscripts 1 and 2 denote the two continuous support locations and m denotes the midspan location; k_1 is a weighting factor which lies between 0 and 1, and depends on the ratio of the sum of the corresponding fixed end moment $(M_{F1} + M_{F2})$ – as given in Table 21 of the Code. The expression for η in Eq. 10.9(a) is the same as that given in Eq. 10.6. It is not clear from either the Code or the Explanatory Handbook to the Code [Ref. 10.2] whether, in the case of continuous beams, the value of the applied moment M (in Eq. 10.9a) and the values of the neutral axis depth x and lever arm z (in Eq. 10.6) are to be based on the midspan location or the support location, or as a weighted average. [It appears logical that when an expression such as Eq. 10.2 is used for calculation of Δ, the M should be the moment at midspan.] In view of these uncertainties and complications, the Code procedure for evaluating $I_{eff,\,av}$ in its present form, is not generally used in design practice.

10.3.6 Effective Curvature Formulation

In the latest British code, BS: 8110 [Ref. 10.12], the use of Eq. 10.5a (involving the concept of I_{eff}) is dispensed with, and the formulation is now based on an assumed distribution of strains and stresses that attempt to account for the tension-stiffening effect more directly. From the assumed distribution of strains, the effective curvature is directly obtained [Figure 10.4], and the deflections may be computed from the effective curvatures. It may be noted that if the beam section under consideration is subject to a low bending moment, it is likely to behave as an uncracked section, and this possibility [Figure 10.4a] should also be investigated. It is stated in the British code that the curvature at any section should be taken (conservatively) as the larger of the values obtained by considering the section as (a) uncracked and (b) cracked [Figure 10.4]. This clause is intended to ensure that even if the applied bending moment is less than the cracking moment,

† This can be easily observed from the *conjugate beam method*, where the span moment in the conjugate beam (which gives Δ) is governed predominantly by the *M*/*EI* values (which is the loading on the conjugate beam) in the midspan regions than in the end regions.

it is possible that the section may behave as a cracked section due to some prior heavier loading (or cracking due to temperature and shrinkage effects)[†]. It is also mentioned that the calculation of effective curvature is to be done at the mid-span for simply supported beams and at the support section for cantilevers, and the appropriate relationship between elastic deflection and curvature used for calculating the maximum deflection [Eq. 10.1].

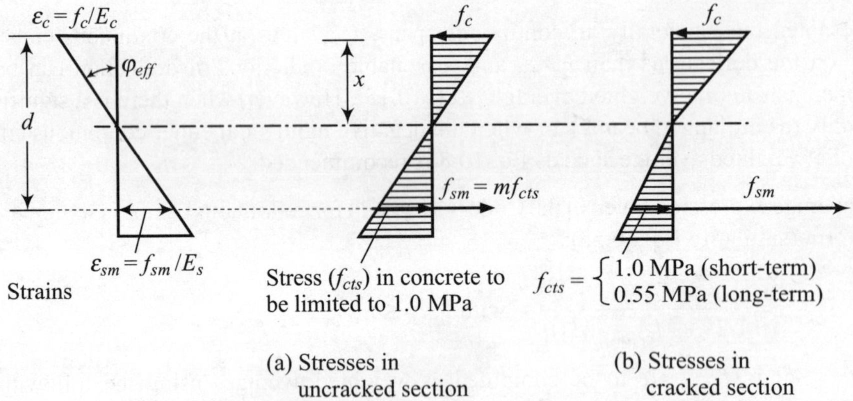

Fig. 10.4 Distribution of strains and stresses (BS 8110) for serviceability calculations, including tension stiffening effect.

It may be noted that the distribution of strains [Figure 10.4] is linear for both uncracked and cracked sections (being based on the fundamental assumption of plane sections remaining plane after bending), and the formula for effective curvature, applicable for both sections, may be easily derived using strain compatibility considerations. The formula may be expressed in terms of either the concrete compressive stress f_c:

$$\varphi_{eff} = \frac{\varepsilon_c}{x} = \frac{f_c}{xE_c} \tag{10.10a}$$

or, in terms of the mean tensile stress in steel:

$$\varphi_{eff} = \frac{\varepsilon_{sm}}{(d-x)} = \frac{f_{sm}}{(d-x)E_s} \tag{10.10b}$$

where

$f_c \equiv$ compressive stress in concrete at the extreme compression fibre

$f_{sm} \equiv$ mean tensile stress in steel

$f_{cts} \equiv$ allowable tensile stress in concrete at the level of the tension steel, to be taken appropriately.

The value of f_{cts} is to be limited to 1.0 MPa in the case of the uncracked section [Figure 10.4b], and the corresponding stress in steel is given by $f_{sm} = mf_{cts}$. It may be noted that the corresponding stress in the extreme tension fibre in concrete, given by f_{cts}. $(D - x)/(d - x)$, will be considerably less than the modulus of rupture ($0.7\sqrt{f_{ck}}$). This is done in order to ensure that when the applied moment is less than but close to

[†] Refer Example 10.1

the 'cracking moment' M_{cr}, it would be more appropriate (and conservative) to treat the section as a cracked section for the purpose of estimating deflections. The magnitude of cracking moment, by this formulation reduces to:

$$\tilde{M}_{cr} = \left(f_{cts}\frac{0.5D}{d-0.5D}\right)\left(\frac{I_{gr}}{0.5D}\right) \tag{10.11}$$

In the case of the cracked section, the maximum contribution of concrete in tension is considered by taking f_{cts} = 1.0 MPa, and considering the short-term elastic modulus E_c. However, for the purpose of calculating long-term deflections due to creep, it is recommended that a lower value, f_{cts} = 0.55 MPa, should be taken (as indicated in Figure 10.4b), and the effective modulus of elasticity (including creep coefficient) E_{ce} should be considered. It may be noted that in both the cracked and uncracked cases, the total tensile force resisted by concrete below the neutral axis may be obtained by assuming a triangular stress block.

For the uncracked section, the curvature can be obtained directly, using Eq. 10.4 with $I_{eff} = I_{gr}$ (which ignores the contribution of the steel, and effectively assumes x = 0.5D). However, for the cracked section, it is necessary to apply Eq. 10.10, which involves the neutral axis depth x and either the concrete compressive stress f_c [Eq. 10.10a] or the mean tensile stress in steel f_{sm} [Eq. 10.10b]. This cannot be directly determined by means of a closed-form solution, and an iterative (trial-and-error) procedure is required. The following force and moment equilibrium equations need to be satisfied:

$$0.5bxf_c = f_{sm}A_{st} + 0.5b(D-x)f_{ct} \tag{10.12}$$

$$M = A_{st}f_{sm}\left(d-\frac{x}{3}\right)+\frac{1}{3}bD\,f_{ct}(D-x) \tag{10.13}$$

where $$f_{ct} = \left(\frac{D-x}{d-x}\right)\times f_{cts} \tag{10.14}$$

Using strain compatibility relations [Figure 10.4],

$$f_c = \frac{x}{d-x}\frac{E_c}{E_s}f_{sm} \tag{10.15}$$

whereby $$x = \frac{d}{1+f_{sm}/(mf_c)} \tag{10.15a}$$

One may begin by assuming a trial value of the neutral axis depth x ($\approx d/3$). Next, trial values of f_{ct} and f_{sm} are calculated by solving Eq. 10.14 and 10.13 respectively. Using these values, f_c is calculated solving Eq. 10.12, and an improved value of x can now be obtained from Eq. 15a. For the next trial, an average of this value and the initial trial value of x may be considered, and the procedure repeated. Usually, convergence in the trial-and-error procedure can achieved within two or three iterations, as demonstrated in Example 10.2.

Example 10.1

For the one-way (simply supported) slab system designed in Example 5.2, compute the maximum short-term deflection due to dead loads plus live loads. Solve (a) using the concept of I_{eff} specified in IS 456: 2000, and (b) using the concept of effective curvature given in BS 8110 (1997).

Solution

- Given: $l = 4.16$ m, $D = 200$ mm, $A_{st} = 523$ mm^2/m, ($p_t = 0.316$), $d = 165$ mm,
  $f_{ck} = 25$ MPa, $f_y = 500$ MPa, $w_{DL} = 6.0$ kN/m^2 $w_{LL} = 4.0$ kN/m^2, [refer Example 5.2].
- Formula for maximum short-term deflection (at midspan):

$$\Delta = \frac{5}{384}\frac{wl^4}{EI_{eff}} = \frac{5}{48}\frac{Ml^2}{EI_{eff}}$$

- Maximum moment at midspan (under service loads – dead plus live):
  $M = (6.0 + 4.0) \times 4.16^2/8 = 21.63$ kNm per m width
- Short-term modulus of elasticity:

$$E = E_c = 5000\sqrt{f_{ck}}$$
$$= 5000\sqrt{25} = 25000 \text{ MPa}$$

(a) SOLUTION AS PER IS 456 (2000)

- $M_{cr} = f_{cr} I_{gr}/(0.5D)$

  where $f_{cr} = 0.7\sqrt{f_{ck}}$ (as per Code)

$$= 0.7\sqrt{25} = 3.5 \text{ MPa}$$

$$I_{gr} = bD^3/12 = 1000 \times (200)^3/12 = 6.667 \times 10^8 \text{ mm}^4$$

$$\Rightarrow \quad M_{cr} = 3.5 \times 6.667 \times 10^8/(0.5 \times 200)$$
$$= 23.33 \times 10^6 \text{ Nmm/m} = 23.33 \text{ kNm/m}$$
$$> M = 21.63 \text{ kNm/m (implying that the section is likely to be uncracked)}$$
$$\Rightarrow \quad I_{eff} = I_{gr} = 6.667 \times 10^8 \text{ mm}^4$$

Maximum short-term deflection (uncracked section)

$$\Delta = \frac{5}{48}\frac{Ml^2}{EI_{eff}} = \frac{5}{48} \times \frac{21.63 \times 10^6 (\text{Nmm}) \times (4160)^2 (\text{mm})^2}{25000(\text{N/mm}^2) \times (6.667 \times 10^8)(\text{mm}^4)}$$
$$= 2.34 \text{ mm } (l/1778)$$

Note: As the applied moment of 21.63 kNm/m is close to the cracking moment of 23.33 kNm/m, it may be unconservative to calculate deflections based on the uncracked section. It would be more prudent (as suggested in BS 8110) to limit the use of the uncracked section to applied moments that are less than $\tilde{M}_{cr}$ [refer Eq. 10.11 for $\tilde{M}_{cr}$]. The IS Code, however, does not give any recommendations in this regard. A recent study indicates that the use of the BS Code estimate of $\tilde{M}_{cr}$, when coupled with the IS Code procedure, results in very large deflection estimates. The authors suggest that, for the application of the IS Code procedure, the value of $\tilde{M}_{cr}$ may be taken as approximately 0.7 M_{cr}. In the present problem, the reduced cracking moment works out to:

$$\tilde{M}_{cr} = 0.7 \times 23.33 \text{ kNm/m} = 16.33 \text{ kNm/m.}$$

(The use of Eq. 10.11 results in a more conservative estimate of $\tilde{M}_{cr} = 10.26$ kNm/m).
This value (16.33 kNm/m) is considerably less than the applied moment of 21.63 kNm/m.
Hence, the section should be treated as a cracked section for calculation of short-term deflection.
For meaningful results in the estimation of I_{eff}, M_{cr} should be replaced by $\tilde{M}_{cr}$ in Eq. 10.5a.

Effective second moment of area

- $I_{eff} = \dfrac{I_{cr}}{1.2 - (\tilde{M}_{cr}/M)\eta}$

  $\eta = j(1-k)(b_w/b)$ as per IS 456 formulation

- $I_{cr} = b(kd)^3/3 + m\,A_{st}(d-kd)^2$ [see Figure 10.5]

  The neutral axis (NA) depth kd is obtainable by considering moments of areas of the cracked transformed section about the NA:

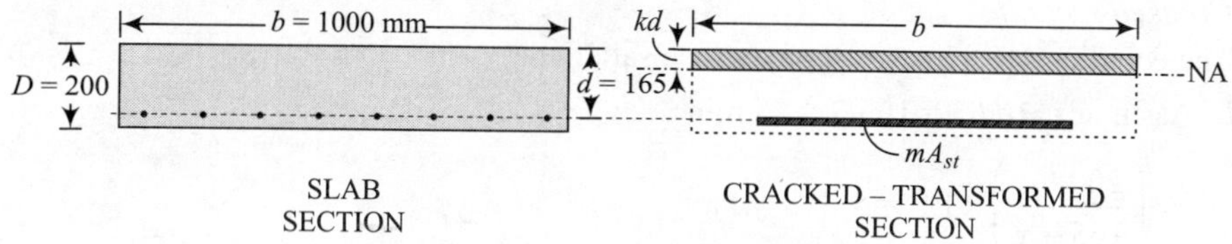

Fig. 10.5 Example 10.1.

- $b \times (kd)^2/2 = m\,A_{st}\,(d-kd)$

  where $m^{\dagger} = E_s/E_c = 2 \times 10^5/25000 = 8.0$

  $\Rightarrow \quad 1000 \times (kd)^2/2 = (8.0) \times 523\ (165 - kd)$

  Solving, $kd = 33.21$ mm $\Rightarrow k = 33.21/165 = 0.2013$

  [*Note:* k can be directly obtained from Eq. 4.13].

  $\Rightarrow \quad I_{cr} = 1000(33.21)^3/3 + (8.0 \times 523) \times (165 - 33.21)^2$

  $= 0.8488 \times 10^8\ \text{mm}^4\ (= 0.1273\, I_{gr})$

  $\eta = j(1-k)(b_w/b)$

  $= (1 - k/3)(1-k)(1) = (1 - 0.2013/3)(1 - 0.2013)$

  $= 0.7451$

$$I_{eff} = \frac{I_{cr}}{1.2 - (\tilde{M}_{cr}/M)\eta} = \frac{(0.8488 \times 10^8)}{1.2 - (16.33/21.63) \times 0.7451} = 1.3315 \times 10^8\ \text{mm}^2$$

(which lies between I_{cr} and I_{gr}) and is equal to $0.1997\, I_{gr}$).

Maximum short-term deflection (cracked section)

$$\Delta = \frac{5}{48}\frac{Ml^2}{EI_{eff}} = \frac{5}{48} \times \frac{21.63 \times 10^6 (\text{Nmm}) \times (4160)^2\ (\text{mm})^2}{25000(\text{N/mm}^2) \times (1.3315 \times 10^8)(\text{mm}^4)}$$

$= \mathbf{11.71}$ mm $(= l/355)$

[*Note:* The deflection calculated on the basis of 'cracked section' (11.71 mm) is considerably larger than the value calculated on the basis of 'uncracked section' (2.34 mm). This is because $I_{eff} = 0.1997\, I_{gr}$].

---

† *Note:* For short-term deflection calculations, E_c should be taken as the short-term modulus of elasticity. Hence, the empirical expression for *modular ratio* given by the Code for flexural design ($m = 280/3\sigma_{cbc}$) should not be used here.

(b) ALTERNATIVE SOLUTION AS PER BS 8110 (1997)

The effective curvature should be calculated assuming that the section is (i) uncracked and (ii) cracked, and the higher value is to be taken.

(i) *Uncracked section*

The curvature is given by

$$\varphi_{eff} = \frac{M}{E_c I_{gr}} = \frac{21.63 \times 10^6 \text{(Nmm)}}{25000(\text{N/mm}^2) \times (6.667 \times 10^8)(\text{mm}^4)} = \mathbf{1.298 \times 10^{-6}/mm}$$

(ii) *Cracked section*

The equations 10.11 – 10.14 have to be satisfied.

Trial 1: Assume $x \approx d/3 = 165/3 = 55$ mm

$$\Rightarrow \quad f_{ct} = \left(\frac{200 - x}{165 - x}\right) \times 1.0 = 1.318 \text{ MPa}$$

$$\Rightarrow \quad f_{sm} = \left(21.63 \times 10^6 - \frac{1000 \times 200 \times f_{ct} \times (200 - x)}{3}\right) \Big/ 523 \times \left(165 - \frac{x}{3}\right) = 116 \text{ MPa}$$

$$\Rightarrow \quad f_c = \frac{f_{sm} A_{st} + 0.5b(D - x) f_{ct}}{0.5bx} = 5.68 \text{ MPa}$$

$$\Rightarrow \quad x = \frac{165}{1 + f_{sm}/(8.0 f_c)} = 46.4 \text{ mm}$$

Trial 2: Assuming an average value $x \approx (55 + 46.4)/2 = 50.7$ mm, and repeating the procedure,

$\Rightarrow \quad f_{ct} = 1.306$ MPa

$\Rightarrow \quad f_{sm} = 111.4$ MPa

$\Rightarrow \quad f_c = 6.14$ MPa

$\Rightarrow \quad$ **x = 50.5 mm**, which indicates convergence.

The effective curvature of the cracked section may now be calculated using either Eq. 10.10a:

$$\varphi_{eff} = \frac{f_c}{xE_c} = \frac{6.14}{50.5 \times 25000} = 4.863 \times 10^{-6} \text{ per mm}$$

or Eq. 10.10b:

$$\varphi_{eff} = \frac{f_{sm}}{(d - x)E_s} = \frac{111.4}{(165 - 50.5)(2 \times 10^5)} = \mathbf{4.865 \times 10^{-6} \text{ per mm}}$$

The curvature due to the cracked section (4.865×10^{-6} per mm) is larger than the one due to uncracked section (1.298×10^{-6} per mm), and accordingly, considering this larger value, for the uniformly loaded beam,

$$\Delta = \frac{5}{48} \varphi_{eff} l^2 = \frac{5}{48} \times 4.865 \times 10^{-6} \times (4160)^2 = \mathbf{8.77 \text{ mm}}$$

which is less than **11.71 mm** predicted as per IS 456 (cracked section).

10.3.7 Additional Short-Term Deflection Due to Live Loads Alone

As mentioned in Section 10.2.1, the check on deflection involves a separate check on deflection due to live loads (including long-term effects of creep and shrinkage) that occur after the construction of partitions and finishes. This requires the calculation of the short-term deflection due to live load alone.

> The load-deflection relationship of a RC beam being non-linear, the *principle of superposition* is not applicable for deflection calculations.

Because of the variations in effective flexural rigidity with the applied moment [Figure 10.2], the load-deflection behaviour of a reinforced concrete beam is non-linear [Figure 10.6]; hence, the principle of superposition is not applicable in deflection calculations. Unlike the live loads, the dead loads act all the time. Hence, the immediate (short-term) deflection due to the live load part alone, Δ_L, has to be obtained as the difference between the short-term deflection due to dead plus live loads, Δ_{D+L}, and that due to dead load alone, Δ_D:

$$\Delta_L = \Delta_{D+L} - \Delta_D \tag{10.16}$$

This is depicted in Figure 10.6. In the calculation of Δ_D, for deciding whether to consider the section to be cracked or uncracked, it is prudent to compare the dead load moment M_D with the reduced cracking moment $\tilde{M}_{cr}$, ($\approx 0.7\ M_{cr}$), as discussed in Example 10.1(a). The section may be treated as uncracked only if M_D is less than $\tilde{M}_{cr}$.

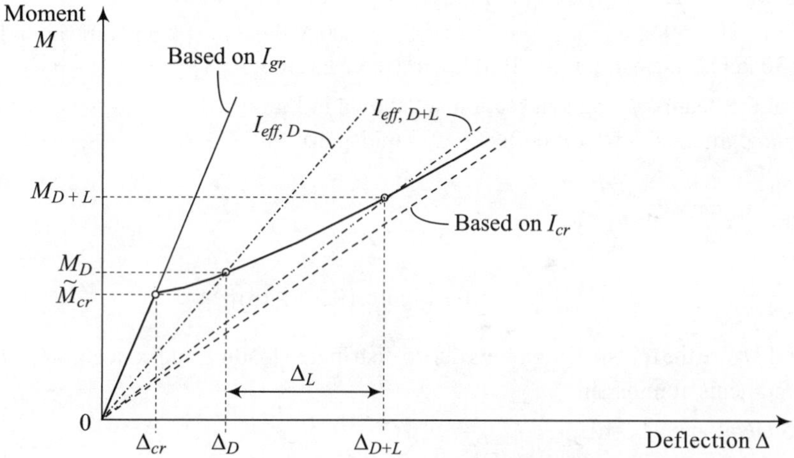

Fig. 10.6 Short-term deflections due to dead loads and live loads.

Example 10.2

For the slab of Example 10.1, determine the short-term deflection due to live loads alone.

Solution

- $\Delta_L = \Delta_{D+L} - \Delta_D$, where $\Delta_{D+L} = 11.71$ mm as per IS 456 (from Example 10.1a)

Short-term deflection due to dead loads alone: Δ_D

- $M_D = w_{DL}l^2/8 = 6.0 \times 4.162/8 = 12.98$ kNm per m width
  $< \tilde{M}_{cr} = 16.33$ kNm per m width [refer Example 10.1(a)].

Hence, the section should be treated as uncracked.

$\Rightarrow \quad I_{eff,D} = I_{gr} = 6.667 \times 10^8$ mm^4; [refer Example 10.1]

$E = E_c = 25000$ MPa

$$\Rightarrow \quad \Delta_D = \frac{5}{48}\frac{M_D l^2}{EI_{eff}} = \frac{5}{48} \times \frac{(12.98 \times 10^6) \times (4160)^2}{25000 \times (6.667 \times 10^8)}$$

$= 1.40$ mm

Short-term deflection due to live loads alone: Δ_L

$\Delta_L = \Delta_{D+L} - \Delta_D$

$= 11.71 - 1.40$

$= 10.31$ mm

Example 10.3

Determine the maximum short-term deflection under dead loads and live loads for the doubly reinforced beam of Example 5.4. Also determine the short-term deflection due to live loads only.

Solution

- Given: $l = 6.0$ m, $b = 250$ mm, $D = 400$ mm, $d = 349.5$ mm, $d' = 48$ mm, $A_{st} = 1473$ mm^2, $A_{sc} = 942.5$ mm^2, $f_{ck} = 25$ MPa, $f_y = 500$ MPa, $w_{DL} = 7.5$ kN/m (including self-weight) plus $W_{DL} = 30$ kN at midspan, $w_{LL} = 10.0$ kN/m [refer Example 5.4]
  The details of the beam loading and section are shown in Figure 10.7.
- Formula for maximum short-term deflection (at midspan):

$$\Delta = \frac{5}{384}\frac{wl^4}{EI_{eff}} + \frac{1}{48}\frac{Wl^3}{EI_{eff}}$$

$$= \frac{5}{48}\frac{l^2}{EI_{eff}}[M_1 + 0.8M_2] \qquad \text{[refer Figure 10.7(a), (b)]}$$

where M_1 and M_2 are the midspan moments due to distributed loading and concentrated load respectively.

- Maximum moments at midspan

(i) due to DL alone: $M_D = M_{1,D} + M_{2,D} = w_{DL}l^2/8 + W_{DL}l/4$

$= (7.5 \times 6.0^2/8) + (30.0 \times 6.0/4)$

$= 33.75 + 45.0 = 78.75$ kNm

(ii) due to $DL + LL$: $M_{D+L} = M_D + M_{1,L}$

$= 78.75 + (10.0 \times 6.0^2/8)$

$= 78.75 + 45.0 = 123.8$ kNm

- Short-term modulus of elasticity:

$E = E_c = 5000\sqrt{25} = 25000$ MPa

- Gross section properties:

$I_{gr} = bD^3/12 = 250 \times 400^3/12 = 13.3333 \times 10^8$ mm^4

$M_{cr} = f_{cr}I_{gr}/(0.5D)$

where $f_{cr} = 0.7\sqrt{25} = 3.50$ MPa

$\Rightarrow \quad M_{cr} = 3.50 \times (13.3333 \times 10^8)/(0.5 \times 400)$

$= 23.33 \times 10^6$ Nmm = 23.33 kNm

$\tilde{M}_{cr} = 0.7\, M_{cr} = 0.7 \times 23.33 \times 10^6 = 16.33 \times 10^6 \text{ Nmm} < M_D, M_{D+L}$

Hence, $I_{eff} < I_{gr}$

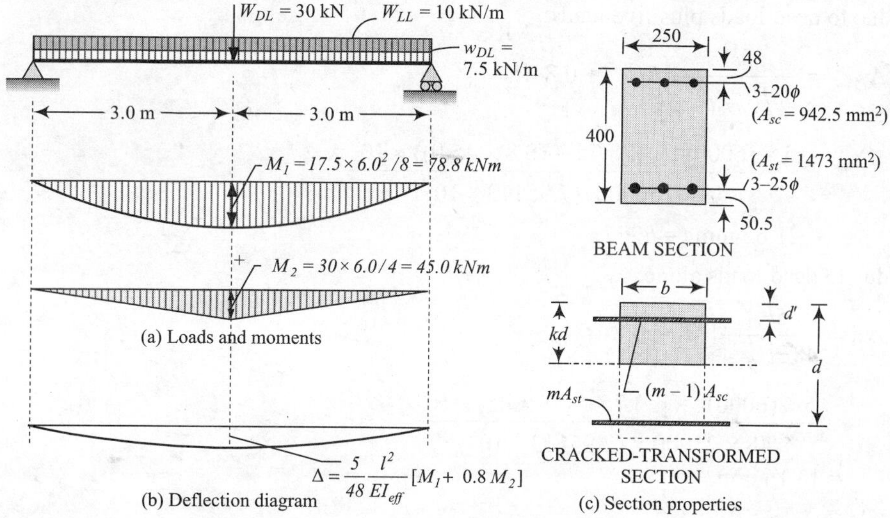

Fig. 10.7 Example 10.3.

Effective second moment of area

- $I_{eff} = \dfrac{I_{cr}}{1.2 - (\tilde{M}_{cr}/M)\eta}$;

  $\eta = j(1-k)(b_w/b)$ as per IS 456 formulation

  where $I_{cr} = b(kd)^3/3 + m\,A_{st}(d-kd)^2 + (m-1)A_{sc}(kd-d')^2$

- The NA depth, kd, is obtainable by considering moments of areas of the cracked-transformed section† about the NA (centroidal axis) [Figure 10.7(c)]

  $$b(kd)^2/2 + (m-1)A_{sc}(kd-d') = m\,A_{st}(d-kd)$$

  where $m = E_s/E_c = 2 \times 10^5/25000 = 8$

  $\Rightarrow \quad 250(kd)^2/2 + (8-1)(942.5)(kd-48) = (8 \times 1473)(349.5 - kd)$

  $\Rightarrow \quad 125(kd)^2 + 18381.5(kd) - 4435188 = 0$

  Solving, $kd = 128.7$ mm ($\Rightarrow k = 128.7/349.5 = 0.3682$)

  $\Rightarrow \quad I_{cr} = 250(128.7)^3/3 + (8 \times 1473)(349.5 - 128.7)^2 + (7 \times 942.5)(128.7 - 48)^2$

  $= 7.95113 \times 10^8 \text{ mm}^4$

  $\Rightarrow \quad \eta = j(1-k)(b_w/b) = (1 - 0.3682/3)(1 - 0.3682)1.0 = 0.5543$

† Note that the transformed area of compression steel is taken as $(m-1)A_{sc}$ and ***not*** $(1.5m-1)A_{sc}$ as considered in stress calculations [refer Section 4.6.5], because the increased modular ratio $1.5m$ (to account for creep effects) is not applicable in the context of short-term deflections.

- $M_D = 78.75$ kNm $\Rightarrow I_{eff,D}/I_{cr} = [1.2 - (16.33/78.75)(0.5543)]^{-1}$
$= 0.922 < 1.0$

As $I_{eff,\,D}$ cannot be less than I_{cr}, and $I_{eff,\,D+L} \le I_{eff,\,D}$, it follows that

$$\boldsymbol{I_{eff,\,D} = I_{eff,\,D+L} = I_{cr} = 7.95113 \times 10^8\ \text{mm}^4}$$

Maximum short-term deflection

(i) due to dead loads plus live loads:

$$\Delta_{D+L} = \frac{5l^2}{48EI_{eff,D+L}}[M_{1_{D+L}} + 0.8\,M_{2_{D+L}}]$$

$$= \frac{5 \times (6000)^2 \times \{78.75 + (0.8 \times 45.0)\} \times 10^6}{48 \times 25000 \times (7.95113 \times 10^8)}$$

$$= 21.65\ \text{mm}\ (= l/277)$$

(ii) due to dead loads alone:

$$\Delta_D = \frac{5l^2}{48EI_{eff,D}}[M_1 + 0.8\,M_2]$$

$$= \frac{5 \times (6000)^2 \times [33.75 + 0.8 \times 45] \times 10^6}{48 \times 25000 \times (7.95113 \times 10^8)}$$

$$= 13.16\ \text{mm}$$

$$\Delta_L = \Delta_{D+L} - \Delta_D$$
$$= 21.65 - 13.16$$
$$= \mathbf{8.49\ mm}$$

Note: The reader may compare the results obtained in this Example with other methods (BS 8110 and Branson's formula).

Example 10.4

For the one-way continuous slab system designed in Example 5.3, compute the maximum midspan deflection in the end span due to dead loads and live loads. Also compute the deflection due to live loads only.

Solution

- Given: $l = 3463$ m, $D = 160$ mm, $d = 126$ mm, $A_{st} = 359$ mm^2/m (at midspan), $A_{st} = 359$ mm^2/m and $A_{sc} = 179.6$ mm^2/m at first interior support (as shown in Figure 10.8), $f_{ck} = 25$ MPa, $f_y = 500$ MPa, $w_{DL} = 5.5$ kN/m^2, $w_{LL} = 4.0$ kN/m^2. [Refer Figure 10.8]

$E_c = 5000\sqrt{25} = 25000$ MPa

$m = E_s/E_c = 2 \times 10^5/25000 = 8$

$I_{gr} = 1000 \times 160^3/12 = 3.4133 \times 10^8$ mm^4

$f_{cr} = 0.7\sqrt{25} = 3.5$ MPa

$\Rightarrow \quad M_{cr} = f_{cr}I_{gr}/(0.5D) = 3.5 \times (3.4133 \times 10^8)/(0.5 \times 160)$

$= 14.93 \times 10^6$ Nmm $= 14.93$ kNm per m width

$\tilde{M}_{cr} = 0.7\,M_{cr} = 10.45$ kNm per m width

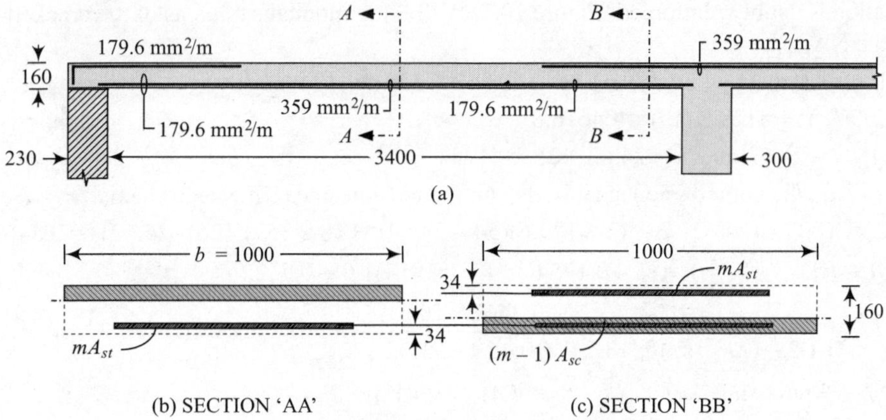

Fig. 10.8 Example 10.4.

- The moment coefficients prescribed by the Code (and used in Example 5.3) will be used here to determine the moments.

(a) *at midspan*: $M_{M,D} = w_{DL}l^2/12 = 5.5 \times 3.463^2/12$

$= 5.5$ kNm per m width $< \tilde{M}_{cr} = 10.45$ kNm

$M_{M,D+L} = M_{M,D} + w_{LL}l^2/10 = 5.5 + (4.0 \times 3.463^2/10)$

$= 10.3$ kNm per m width $< \tilde{M}_{cr}$

(b) *at end support*: $M_{1,D} = w_{DL}l^2/24 = 5.5 \times 3.463^2/24$

$= 2.75$ kNm $< \tilde{M}_{cr}$

$M_{1,D+L} = (w_{DL} + w_{LL})l^2/24 = 9.5 \times 3.463^2/24$

$= 4.75$ kNm $< \tilde{M}_{cr}$

(c) *at first interior support*:

$M_{2,D} = w_{DL}l^2/10 = 5.5 \times 3.463^2/10$

$= 6.60$ kNm per m width $< \tilde{M}_{cr}$

$M_{2,D+L} = M_{2,D} + w_{LL}l^2/9 = 6.60 + (4.0 \times 3.463^2/9)$

$= 11.93$ kNm $> \tilde{M}_{cr}$

Effective second moment of area

(a) *at midspan*:

(i) due to DL: $M_{M,D} < \tilde{M}_{cr} \Rightarrow (I_{eff,\,m})_D = I_{gr} = 3.4133 \times 10^8$ mm^4

(ii) due to $DL + LL$: $M_{M,D+L} = 10.3$ kNm $< \tilde{M}_{cr}$

$\Rightarrow (I_{eff,\,m})_{D+L} = 3.4133 \times 10^8$ mm^4

(b) *at end support*:

$M_{1,D+L} < \tilde{M}_{cr} \Rightarrow (I_{eff,\,1})_D = (I_{eff,\,1})_{D+L} = I_{gr} = 3.4133 \times 10^8$ mm^4

(c) *at first interior support*:

(i) due to DL: $M_{2,D} = 6.6$ kNm $< \tilde{M}_{cr}$

(ii) due to $DL + LL$: $M_{2,D+L} = 11.93$ kNm $> \tilde{M}_{cr}$

The section is doubly reinforced [Figure 10.8(c)]. Taking moments of areas of the cracked-transformed about the NA,

$1000 \times (kd)^2/2 + (7 \times 179.6)(kd - 34) = (8 \times 359) \times (126 - kd)$

$\Rightarrow \quad 500(kd)^2 + 4129.2\,(kd) - 404616.8 = 0$

Solving, $kd = 24.62$ mm, $k = 24.62/126 = 0.1954$

Since $kd < d'$, the compression steel is also on the tension side of the neutral axis.

$\Rightarrow \quad I_{cr} = 1000 \times (24.62)^3/3 + (8 \times 179.6)(34 - 24.62)^2 + (8 \times 359)(126 - 24.62)^2 = 0.3462 \times 10^8 \text{ mm}^4$

$\Rightarrow \quad \eta = j(1-k)(b_w/b) = (1 - 0.1954/3)(1 - 0.1954)1.0 = 0.7522$

$$\Rightarrow \quad I_{eff} = \frac{I_{cr}}{1.2 - (\tilde{M}_{cr}/M)\eta} = \frac{0.3462 \times 10^8}{1.2 - (10.45/11.93)0.7522} = 0.6398 \times 10^8$$

$M_{2,D} = 6.6 \text{ kNm} \Rightarrow (I_{eff,\,2})_D = I_{gr} = 3.4133 \times 10^8 \text{ mm}^4$

$M_{2,D+L} = 11.93 \text{ kNm} \Rightarrow (I_{eff,\,2})_{D+L} = 0.6398 \times 10^8 \text{ mm}^4 > I_{cr}$

- *Weighted average* [Equation 10.8(a)]

  $I_{eff,\,av} = 0.7 I_{eff,\,m} + 0.15(I_{eff,\,1} + I_{eff,\,2})$

  (i) under *DL*: $(I_{eff,\,av})_D = 0.7 \times (3.4133 \times 10^8) + 0.15\,(3.4133 + 3.4133) \times 10^8 = 3.4133 \times 10^8 \text{ mm}^4$
  (Under *DL*, *all* sections are uncracked and hence $I_{eff,\,av} = I_{gr} = 3.4133 \times 10^8 \text{ mm}^4$)

  (ii) under *DL* + *LL*: $(I_{eff,\,av})_{D+L} = 0.7 \times (3.4133 \times 10^8) + 0.15\,(3.4133 + 0.6398) \times 10^8 = 2.9973 \times 10^8 \text{ mm}^4$

Short-term deflection

$$\Delta \approx \Delta_m = \frac{5l^2}{48EI_{eff}}[1.2M_m - 0.2M_o] \qquad \text{(Eq. 10.3)}$$

where $M_o = wl^2/8$

(i) *due to DL*, $M_m = 5.5$ kNm, $M_o = 5.5 \times 3.463^2/8 = 8.245$ kNm

$$\Rightarrow \quad \Delta_D = \frac{5 \times (3463)^2 \times (1.2 \times 5.5 - 0.2 \times 8.245) \times 10^6}{48 \times 25000 \times (3.4133 \times 10^8)} = 0.73 \text{ mm}$$

(ii) *due to DL* + *LL*, $M_m = 10.3$ kNm , $M_o = 9.5 \times 3.463^2/8 = 14.24$ kNm

$$\Rightarrow \quad \Delta_{D+L} = \frac{5 \times (3463)^2 \times (1.2 \times 10.3 - 0.2 \times 14.24) \times 10^6}{48 \times 25000 \times (2.9973 \times 10^8)} = 1.59 \text{ mm } (= l/2178)$$

(iii) *due to LL* alone: $\Delta_L = \Delta_{D+L} - \Delta_D$
$= 1.59 - 0.73$
$= \mathbf{0.86 \text{ mm}}$

10.4 Long-term Deflection

The deflection of a reinforced concrete flexural member increases with time, mainly due to:

- differential shrinkage or temperature variation (causing differential strains across the cross-section, resulting in curvature and deflections);
- creep under sustained loading leading to increases in initial curvature; and
- temperature effects in statically indeterminate frames [Figure 10.9].

The factors affecting shrinkage and creep are related to the environment, making of concrete and loading history; these have been described in detail in Sections 2.11 and 2.12. It may be noted that, unlike creep strains, shrinkage and temperature strains are independent of the stress considerations in the concrete. Furthermore, shrinkage and temperature effects are reversible to a large extent, unlike creep effects.

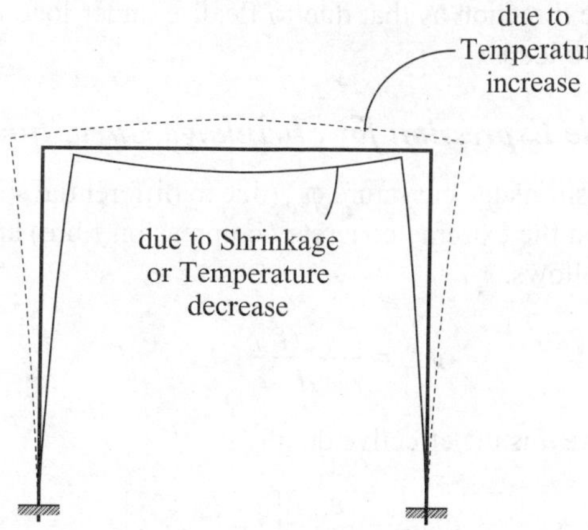

Fig. 10.9 Deflections in a statically indeterminate frame due to temperature effects or shrinkage.

The combined long-term deflection due to shrinkage, creep and temperature effects may be **as large as two to three times the short-term deflection** due to dead and live loads. It may also be noted that, whereas excessive short-term deflections can be effectively countered by *cambering*, this is not generally done in the case of long-term deflections. Providing a *camber* to a reinforced concrete flexural member implies casting the member in such a configuration that, following the removal of the formwork, the member deflects (under dead loads) into a horizontal position. This is commonly done in the case of cantilever beams and slabs.

While there may be no early indications, long-term deflections of RC flexural members could be quite large and debilitating, especially with concrete cast with poor quality control. Designers will do well to bear this in mind.

The fact that the observed deflections of a structure soon after construction are well within limits is no guarantee that this will remain so in the future. In most cases, it is the long-term deflection that gradually builds up over a period of time (2–5 years or even more), and if the total deflection exceeds the acceptable limit, a serviceability failure will occur. This aspect is often neglected and designers will do well to bear this in mind.

Additional factors which can contribute to increased long-term deflection (not considered here) include formation of new cracks, widening of earlier cracks, and effects of repeated load cycles.

10.4.1 Deflection Due to Differential Shrinkage

In an unrestrained reinforced concrete member, drying shrinkage of concrete results in shortening of the member. However, the reinforcing steel embedded in the concrete resists this shortening to some extent, with the result that compressive stress is developed in the steel, and tensile stress is developed in the concrete. When the reinforcement is placed symmetrically in the cross section, shrinkage does not result in any curvature of the member – except in statically indeterminate frame elements, where shrinkage results in an overall change in geometry of the entire frame, and has an effect similar to temperature [Figure 10.9].

When the reinforcement is unsymmetrically placed in the cross-section (as is usually the case in flexural members), differential strains are induced across the cross section – with the locations with less (or no) reinforcement shrinking more than the location with relatively high reinforcement. This is depicted in Figure 10.10(a) for a simply supported beam (where the main bars are located at the bottom), and in Figure 10.10(b) for a cantilever beam (where the main bars are on top). For convenience, it is assumed that the strain gradient is linear. The differential shrinkage causes a curvature (φ_{sh}) in the member, which is in the same direction as that due to flexure under loading. Thus, the shrinkage deflection enhances the deflection due to loads.

Code Expression for Shrinkage Curvature

The shrinkage curvature φ_{sh} (due to differential shrinkage) may be expressed in terms of the shrinkage strains ε_{sh} (at the extreme concrete compression fibre) and ε_{st} (at the level of the tension steel) [refer Figure 10.10] as follows:

$$\varphi_{sh} = \frac{\varepsilon_{sh} - \varepsilon_{st}}{d} \tag{10.17}$$

where d is the effective depth.

$$\Rightarrow \qquad \varphi_{sh} = \left(\frac{\varepsilon_{sh}}{d}\right)\left[1 - \varepsilon_{st}/\varepsilon_{sh}\right]$$

$$\Rightarrow \qquad \varphi_{sh} = \left(\frac{\varepsilon_{sh}}{D}\right)k$$

where $$k = \frac{1 - \varepsilon_{st}/\varepsilon_{sh}}{d/D}$$

The parameter, k, evidently depends, amongst other things, on the extent of asymmetry in the reinforcement provided in the cross-section. The Code (Cl. C–3.1) suggests the following expression for shrinkage curvature based on empirical fits with test data [Ref. 10.2]:

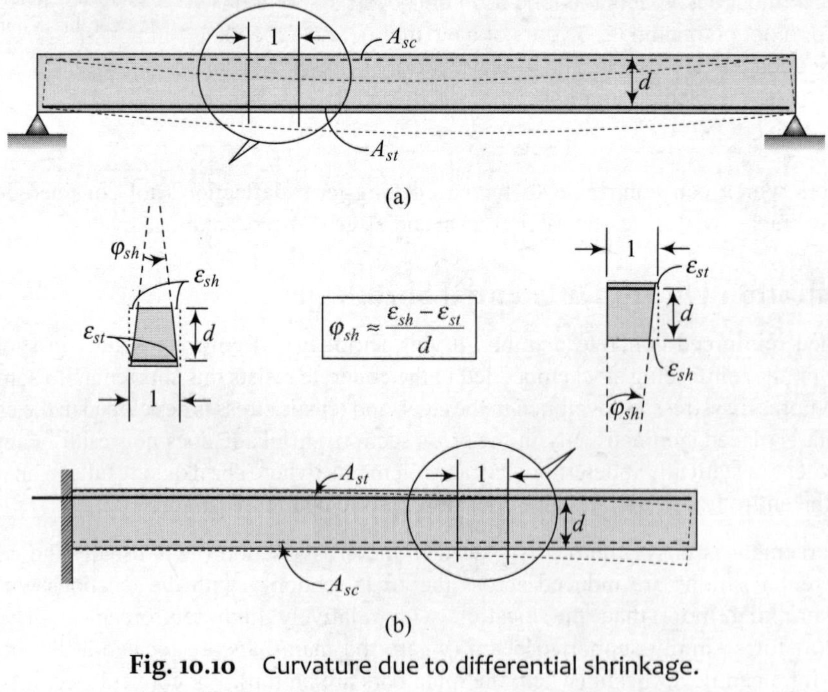

Fig. 10.10 Curvature due to differential shrinkage.

$$\varphi_{sh} = k_4 \frac{\varepsilon_{cs}}{D} \tag{10.18}$$

where, $\varepsilon_{cs} \equiv$ the ultimate shrinkage strain of concrete, and

$$k_4 = \begin{cases} 0.72(p_t - p_c)/\sqrt{p_t} \le 1.0 & \text{for } 0.25 \le (p_t - p_c) < 1.0 \\ 0.65(p_t - p_c)/\sqrt{p_t} \le 1.0 & \text{for } (p_t - p_c) \ge 1.0 \end{cases} \tag{10.19}$$

where $p_t \equiv 100A_{st}/(bd)$ and $p_c \equiv 100A_{sc}/(bd)$ denote the percentages of tension reinforcement and compression reinforcement respectively. When $p_t = p_c$ (i.e., the beam is symmetrically reinforced), $k_4 = 0$, and hence $\varphi_{sh} = 0$.

Relation Between Deflection and Shrinkage Curvature

The deflection due to shrinkage in a reinforced concrete beam depends on the variation of shrinkage curvature φ_{sh} along the span of the beam and the boundary conditions of the beam. For convenience, it may be assumed that the curvature φ_{sh} remains constant in magnitude† and merely changes sign at points of inflection, which separate the beam into *sagging* ('positive' curvature) and *hogging* ('negative' curvature) segments. This is depicted in Figure 10.11 for some typical boundary conditions.

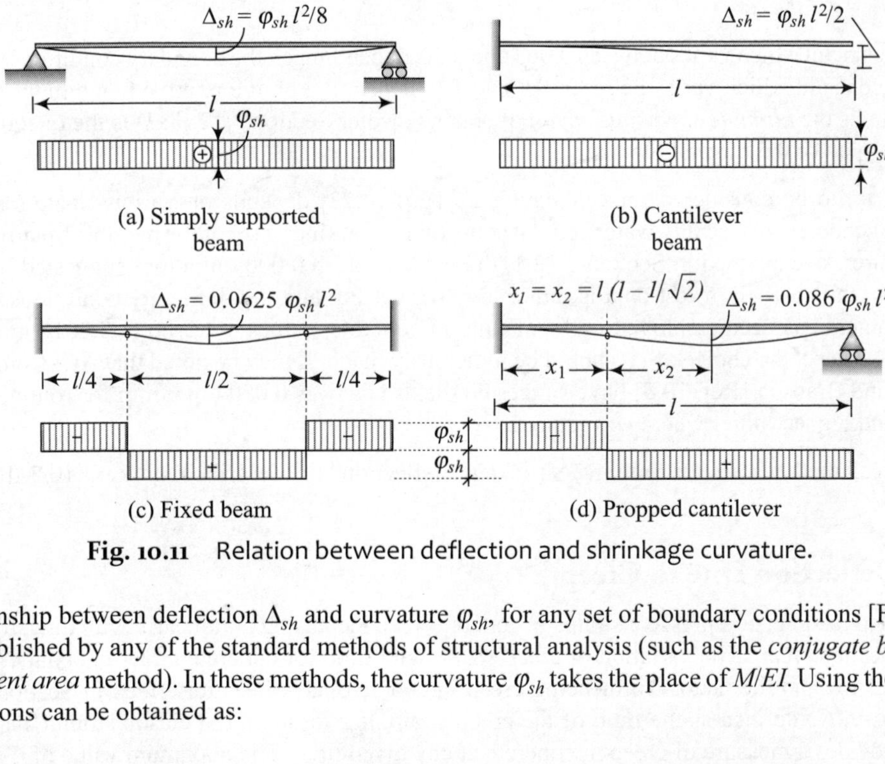

Fig. 10.11 Relation between deflection and shrinkage curvature.

The relationship between deflection Δ_{sh} and curvature φ_{sh}, for any set of boundary conditions [Figure 10.11] can be established by any of the standard methods of structural analysis (such as the *conjugate beam* method or the *moment area* method). In these methods, the curvature φ_{sh} takes the place of *M*/*EI*. Using these methods, the deflections can be obtained as:

† In actual beams, the ratio $(p_t - p_c)/\sqrt{p_t}$ in Eq . 10.19 may not be uniform along the span. It is generally satisfactory to compute this ratio (and hence, k_4) at the midspan location in simply supported and continuous beams, and at the support section in cantilever beams.

$$\Delta_{sh} = \begin{cases} 0.125\,\varphi_{sh} l^2 & \text{for simply supported beams} \\ 0.500\,\varphi_{sh} l^2 & \text{for cantilever beams} \\ 0.063\,\varphi_{sh} l^2 & \text{for fixed beams} \\ 0.086\,\varphi_{sh} l^2 & \text{for propped cantilevers} \end{cases} \tag{10.20}$$

or, in general, $\Delta_{sh} = k_3 \varphi_{sh} l^2$ (10.21)

where l is the effective span of the beam.

The ratio $(\Delta_{sh}/\varphi_{sh}\, l^2)$ is denoted by the parameter k_3 in the Code (Cl. C–3.1) and the results obtained above are summarised in the Code. For convenience, the Code permits the use of the condition of 'fixity' for continuous ends, and thus the Code recommends values of 0.086 and 0.063 for k_3 for beams continuous at one end and both ends respectively.

Expression for Maximum Shrinkage Deflection

The maximum shrinkage deflection Δ_{sh} in a reinforced concrete flexural member may be expressed (by combining Eqs 10.18 and 10.21) as follows:

$$\Delta_{sh} = k_3 k_4 \varepsilon_{cs} (l^2/D) \tag{10.22}$$

where k_3 is a constant which varies between 0.063 and 0.50, depending on the boundary conditions [Eq. 10.20]; k_4 is another constant which varies between 0.0 and 1.0, depending on the relative magnitudes of p_t and p_c [Eq. 10.19]; ε_{cs} is the *ultimate shrinkage strain* of concrete [refer Section 2.12.1]; D is the overall depth and l the effective span of the flexural member.

The value of ε_{cs} to be considered for calculating Δ_{sh} [Eq. 10.22] depends on various factors such as the constituents of concrete (especially water content at the time of mixing), size of the member, relative humidity and temperature. As explained in Section 2.12.1, the value of ε_{cs} = 0.0003 mm/mm suggested by the Code (Cl. 6.2.4.1) in the absence of test data is rather low. Under hot and low-humidity conditions, and where high water-content has been employed in the making of concrete, values of ε_{cs} up to 0.0010 mm/mm have been reported. Hence, the choice of ε_{cs} should be judiciously made. It may be noted that ACI Committee 435 [Ref. 10.17] and Branson [Ref. 10.5] have suggested the use of ε_{cs} = 0.0004 mm/mm for routine deflection calculation, and higher values wherever required.

Other empirical methods of determining shrinkage deflection are described in Ref. 10.5–10.7, 10.10, 10.16–10.18.

10.4.2 Deflection Due to Creep

Under sustained loading, compressive strains in concrete keep increasing nonlinearly with time, owing to the phenomenon called *creep*. The variation of *creep strain* with time for concrete under uniaxial compression [refer Figure 2.15] and the factors influencing creep in concrete have been described in Section 2.11. The *creep coefficient*, C_t, defined as the ratio of the creep strain, ε_{cp}, to the initial elastic strain ('instantaneous strain'), ε_i, provides a measure of creep in concrete at any given time. The maximum value of C_t, called the *ultimate creep coefficient* (designated as θ by the Code), is required for predicting the maximum deflection of a flexural member due to creep. In the absence of data related to the factors influencing creep, the Code (Cl. 6.2.5.1) recommends values of θ equal to 2.2, 1.6 and 1.1 for ages of loading equal to 7 days, 28 days and 1 year respectively.

In a flexural member, the distribution of creep strains across the depth at any cross-section is non-uniform, with a practically linear variation similar to that produced by the applied loading (i.e., bending moment). This linear variation of creep strains [Figure 10.12(b)] results in a *creep curvature,* φ_{cp}, which is additive to the *initial elastic curvature,* φ_i, and is similar in effect to the *shrinkage curvature* φ_{sh} described in Section 10.4.1. It may be noted that although the creep effect is primarily related to increased strains in *concrete* under *compression*, there is also a marginal increase in the tensile strain in the steel[†], as indicated in Figure 10.12.

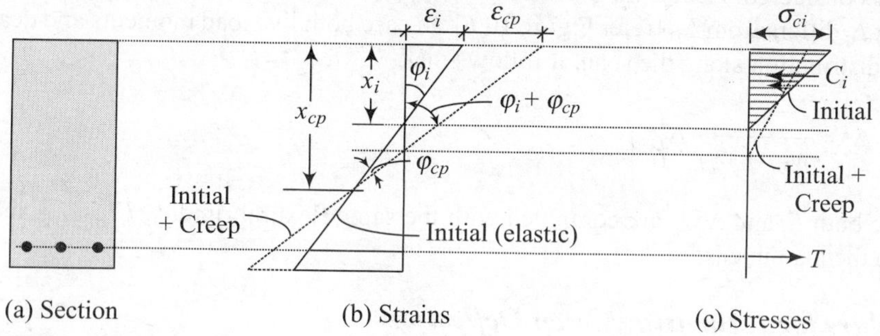

Fig. 10.12 Creep curvature in a flexural member.

Relation Between Creep Deflection and Initial Elastic Deflection

Within the range of service loads, creep curvature φ_{cp} may be assumed to be proportional to the initial elastic curvature φ_i. With reference to Figure 10.12(b),

$$\frac{\varphi_{cp}}{\varphi_i} = \frac{\varepsilon_{cp}/x_{cp}}{\varepsilon_i/x_i} = k_r C_t \tag{10.23}$$

where $C_t \equiv \varepsilon_{cp}/\varepsilon_i$ is the creep coefficient, and $k_r \equiv x_i/x_{cp}$ is the ratio of the 'initial' neutral axis depth (x_i) to the neutral axis depth due to creep (x_{cp}). As $x_i < x_{cp}$, the coefficient k_r is less than unity. For singly reinforced flexural members, $k_r \approx 0.85$ [Ref. 10.17]. The presence of compression reinforcement reduces ε_{cp} and hence φ_{cp}. To allow for this reduced curvature and deflections, the following expression is recommended by ACI [Ref. 10.17]:

$$k_r = 0.85/(1 + 0.5p_c) \tag{10.24}$$

where $p_c \equiv 100A_{sc}/bd$ is the percentage of compression reinforcement.

The variation of creep curvature φ_{cp} along the span of the flexural member may be assumed to be identical to the variation of φ_i. Hence, it follows that:

$$\frac{\Delta_{cp}}{\Delta_i} = \frac{\varphi_{cp}}{\varphi_i} = k_r C_t$$

where Δ_i and Δ_{cp} denote respectively the maximum initial elastic deflection and the additional deflection due to creep. For estimating maximum (ultimate) deflection due to creep, the 'ultimate creep coefficient' θ

[†] Steel itself is not subjected to creep. However, due to creep in concrete (see Figure 10.12), there is a slight increase in the depth of neutral axis, with a consequent reduction in the internal lever arm. Hence, to maintain static equilibrium with the applied moment at the section, there has to be a slight increase in the steel stress, and hence the steel strain.

should be used in lieu of C_t. Accordingly,

$$\Delta_{cp} = (k_r\ \theta)\Delta_i \tag{10.25}$$

where Δ_i is to be taken as the 'initial' elastic displacement due to the permanently applied loads (dead loads plus sustained part of live loads). It may be noted that although transient live loads are excluded in the computation of Δ_i, the possibility of a reduced flexural stiffness on account of prior cracking due to such live loads should be considered. Hence, the calculation of Δ_i should be based on $I_{eff,\ D+L}$, and not on $I_{eff,D}$. It is in this respect that Δ_i differs from Δ_D [refer Figure 10.6]. In case both live load moments and dead load moments have the same distribution along the span, it follows that:

$$\Delta_i = \frac{w_{DL}}{w_{DL} + w_{LL}} \Delta_{D+L} \tag{10.26}$$

This is because both Δ_i and Δ_{D+L} are computed with the same flexural rigidity, $EI_{eff,\ D+L}$ and hence they are proportional to the load intensity.

Code Procedure for Estimating Creep Deflection

The procedure given in the Code (Cl. C – 4.1) for calculating creep deflection [Eq. 10.27] is different from the ACI recommendation. Instead of determining the creep deflection Δ_{cp} directly in terms of the initial elastic deflection Δ_i (due to the permanent loads), the Code procedure involves the explicit calculation of the deflection Δ_{i+cp} due to the permanent loads (initial plus creep), using an effective modulus of elasticity $E_{ce} = E_c/(1 + \theta)$ [refer Section 2.11.4, Eq. 2.8]. The creep deflection Δ_{cp} is then obtained as the difference between Δ_{i+cp} and Δ_i:

$$\Delta_{cp} = \Delta_{i+cp} - \Delta_i \tag{10.27}$$

where Δ_{i+cp} is calculated assuming E_{ce} and the corresponding I_{eff}†, whereas Δ_i, the initial deflection due to permanent loads, is calculated assuming E_c and $I_{eff,\ D+L}$.

The Code formula for the effective modulus of elasticity is based on the reasonable assumption that the total strain in concrete ε_{i+cp} (i.e., initial elastic strain plus creep strain) is directly proportional to the stress σ_i induced by the permanent loads [Figure 10.13].

As

$$\varepsilon_{i+cp} = \varepsilon_i + \varepsilon_{cp} = \varepsilon_i(1 + \theta)$$

it follows that

$$E_{ce} \equiv \frac{\sigma_i}{\varepsilon_{i+cp}} = \frac{\sigma_i}{\varepsilon_i}\frac{1}{1+\theta} = \frac{E_c}{1+\theta} \tag{10.28}$$

where $E_c \equiv \sigma_i/\varepsilon_i$

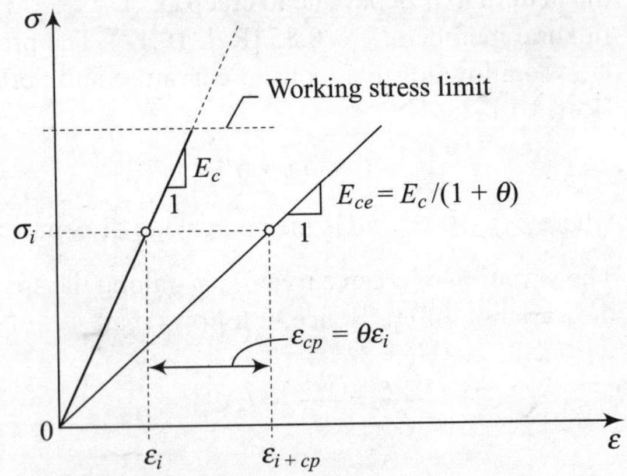

Fig. 10.13 Effective modulus of elasticity under creep.

† The increased modular ratio $m = E_s/E_{ce}$ is generally quite high, with the result that the second moment of area of the corresponding cracked-transformed section (with steel area contributions mA_{st}, mA_{sc}) will also be high – but has to be limited to I_{gr}. In case the calculated I_{cr} is less than I_{gr}, then I_{eff} has to be calculated using Eq. 10.5a and considering the moment due to dead load plus live load.

The steps involved in the Code procedure for determining Δ_{cp} may be summarised [Ref. 10.2] as follows:

1. Compute Δ_{D+L} due to the characteristic dead plus live loads (considering E_c and $I_{eff,\,D+L}$).
2. Compute Δ_i due to permanent (dead) loads alone, considering E_c and $I_{eff,\,D+L}$.
3. Compute Δ_{i+cp} due to permanent loads plus creep, considering E_{ce} and $I_{eff,\,D+L}$.
4. Calculate the creep deflection $\Delta_{cp} = \Delta_{i+cp} - \Delta_i$ [Eq. 10.27].

10.4.3 Deflection Due to Temperature Effects

As mentioned earlier with reference to Figure 10.9, seasonal changes in temperature can introduce curvatures (and stresses) in statically indeterminate frames which may be significant. The determination of bending moments due to temperature loading may be done by any of the standard methods of structural analysis of indeterminate frames. An appropriate value of the coefficient of thermal expansion should be considered – as explained in Section 2.12.2. The deflections in the various beam members may now be determined (using Eq. 10.2 or 10.3) in a manner identical to the determination of short-term deflection in continuous beams [refer Section 10.3.5]. The same procedure is applicable to deflections induced by overall shrinkage in statically indeterminate frames.

In addition to overall curvatures in an integrated structure, local deflections may be introduced in individual members (such as beams and slabs) owing to unsymmetrical reinforcement. The calculation of such deflections is similar to the calculation of deflections induced by differential shrinkage [refer Section 10.4.1]. In case of a known thermal gradient across the depth of a flexural member, a simple 'strength of materials' approach may be adopted for calculating deflections.

It may be noted, however, that in routine designs of reinforced concrete buildings, deflections due to temperature effects are rarely computed. This is largely because such deflections are not usually significant[†] and are reversible. However, the tensile stresses (and consequent cracks) induced by restraints against temperature changes can be significant, and these need to be taken care of by proper detailing of reinforcement – as explained in Section 2.12.2.

10.4.4 Checks on Total Deflection

After calculating the various components of short-term deflection (Δ_D, Δ_{D+L}) and long-term deflection (Δ_{sh}, Δ_{cp}, Δ_{temp}), the acceptability of these deflections should be verified with reference to the deflection limits specified by the Code. As explained in Section 10.2.1, two checks on total deflection are called for:

$$\Delta_{D+L} + \Delta_{\text{long-term}} \le l/250 \tag{10.29a}$$

$$\Delta_L + \Delta_{\text{long-term}} \le \begin{cases} l/350 \\ 20 \text{ mm} \end{cases} \quad \text{(whichever is less)} \tag{10.29b}$$

where

$$\Delta_{\text{long-term}} = \Delta_{sh} + \Delta_{cp} + \Delta_{\text{temp}} \tag{10.29c}$$

and l is the effective span of the flexural member under considerations.

[†] In special circumstances, these may be significant, and in such cases deflections due to temperature effects should be explicitly computed.

In case these limits are exceeded, it may be investigated if the excess can be contained by providing a *camber* (as explained earlier). Otherwise, the design of the member should be suitably revised – ideally, by enhancing the depth (and thereby the stiffness) of the member. If there are constraints on the cross-sectional dimensions, then the grade of concrete (and hence, E_c) should be increased suitably. Alternatively, measures may be taken to reduce the effective span and/or the loading on the member. Providing compression reinforcement will also reduce deflections, especially those due to shrinkage and creep.

Example 10.5

In continuation with Examples 10.1 and 10.2, determine the maximum long-term deflections due to shrinkage and creep, and hence apply the Code checks on the total deflection. Assume an ultimate shrinkage strain ε_{cs} = 0.0004 and an ultimate creep coefficient θ = 1.6.

Solution

- From Examples 10.1 and 10.2,
  l = 4160 mm, D = 200 mm, A_{st} =523 mm²/m (p_t = 0.316), d = 165 mm, f_{ck} = 25 MPa, f_y =500 MPa, w_{DL} = 6.0 kN/m², w_{LL} = 4.0 kN/m², E_c = 25000 MPa, $\tilde{M}_{cr}$ = 16.33 kNm/m., $I_{cr} = 0.8488 \times 10^8$ mm⁴, $I_{gr} = 6.667 \times 10^8$ mm⁴, M_{D+L} = 21.63 kNm/m, $I_{eff,\,D+L} = 1.3315 \times 10^8$ mm⁴, Δ_{D+L} = 11.71 mm, M_D = 12.98 kNm/m, $I_{eff,\,D} = I_{gr}$, Δ_D = 1.40 mm, Δ_L = 10.31 mm

Long-term deflection due to shrinkage: Δ_{sh}

- $\Delta_{sh} = k_3 k_4 \varepsilon_{cs} (l^2/D)$ [refer Eq. 10.22]
  where k_3 = 0.125 for simply supported end conditions,

  $k_4 = 0.72\sqrt{p_t} = 0.72\sqrt{0.316} = 0.405$ (< 1.0) [refer Eq. 10.19, p_c = 0]

  ε_{cs} = 0.0004 (given)

  $\Rightarrow$ $\Delta_{sh} = (0.125)(0.405)(0.0004)(4160)^2/(200) =$ **1.75 mm**

Long-term deflection due to creep: Δ_{cp}

- $E_{ce} = E_c/(1+\theta)$
  $= 25000/(1 + 1.6) = 9615.4$ MPa

  $\Rightarrow$ $m = E_s/E_{ce} = 2 \times 10^5/9615.4 = 20.8$

  $\Rightarrow$ $\rho m = (0.316 \times 10^{-2}) \times 20.8 = 0.0657$

  $\Rightarrow$ $k = \sqrt{2(\rho m) + (\rho m)^2} - \rho m = 0.3027$

  $\Rightarrow$ $kd = 0.3027 \times 165 = 49.95$ mm

  $\Rightarrow$ $I_{cr} = 1000 \times (49.95)^3/3 + (20.8 \times 523) \times (165 - 49.95)^2$
  $= 1.8553 \times 10^8 \text{ mm}^4 < I_{gr} = 6.667 \times 10^8 \text{ mm}^4$

  $\Rightarrow$ $\eta = j(1-k)(b_w/b) = (1 - 0.3027/3)(1 - 0.3027)1.0 = 0.627$

  $$\Rightarrow \quad I_{eff} = \frac{I_{cr}}{1.2 - (\tilde{M}_{cr}/M_{D+L})\eta} = \frac{1.8553 \times 10^8}{1.2 - (16.33/21.63)(0.627)}$$

  $$= 2.5533 \times 10^8 \text{ mm}^4 < I_{gr}$$

- $\Delta_{i+cp} = \dfrac{5}{48}\dfrac{M_D l^2}{E_{ce} I_{eff,D+L}} = \dfrac{5}{48} \times \dfrac{12.98 \times 10^6 \times (4160)^2}{9615.4 \times (2.5533 \times 10^8)} = 9.53$ mm

- $\Delta_i = \dfrac{w_{DL}}{w_{DL} + w_{LL}} \Delta_{D+L} = \dfrac{6}{10} \times 11.71 = 7.03$ mm

$\therefore \quad \Delta_{cp}{}^{\dagger} = \Delta_{i+cp} - \Delta_i = 9.53 - 7.03 =$ **2.50 mm**

Checks on total deflection

1. $\Delta_{D+L} + \Delta_{sh} + \Delta_{cp} = 11.71 + 1.75 + 2.50 =$ **15.96 mm**
   Allowable limit = $l/250 = 4160/250 = 16.64$ mm > 15.96 — OK.
2. $\Delta_L + \Delta_{sh} + \Delta_{cp} = 10.31 + 1.75 + 2.50 =$ **14.56 mm**
   Allowable limit = $l/350 = 11.88$ mm (which is less than 20 mm)
   < **14.56** mm, indicating a marginal excess

Example 10.6

In continuation with Example 10.3, determine the maximum long-term deflections due to shrinkage and creep, and hence apply the checks on the total deflection. Assume an ultimate shrinkage strain $\varepsilon_{cs} = 0.0004$ and an ultimate creep coefficient $\theta = 1.6$.

Solution

- From Example 10.3,
  $l = 6000$ mm, $b = 250$ mm, $D = 400$ mm, $d = 349.5$ mm, $d' = 48$ mm, $A_{st} = 1473$ mm^2 ($p_t = 1.686$), $A_{sc} = 942.5$ mm^2 ($p_c = 1.0787$), $f_{ck} = 25$ MPa, $f_y = 500$ MPa, $w_{DL} = 7.5$ kN/m, plus $W_{DL} = 30$ kN, at midspan, $w_{LL} = 10.0$ kN/m [refer Figure 10.7], $E_c = 25000$ MPa, $\tilde{M}_{cr} = 16.33$ kNm, $I_{cr} = 7.95113 \times 10^8$ mm^4, $I_{gr} = 13.3333 \times 10^8$ mm^4, $M_D = M_1 + M_2 = 33.75 + 45.0 = 78.75$ kNm, $M_{D+L} = 123.8$ kNm; $I_{eff,D} = I_{eff,D+L} = I_{cr} = 7.95113 \times 10^8$ mm^4, $\Delta_{D+L} = 21.65$ mm, $\Delta_D = 13.16$ mm, $\Delta_L = 8.49$ mm.

Long-term deflection due to shrinkage: Δ_{sh}

- $\Delta_{sh} = k_3 k_4 \varepsilon_{cs} (l^2/D)$
  where $k_3 = 0.125$ for simply supported end conditions,
  $p_t - p_c = 1.686 - 1.0787 = 0.6073 > 0.25$ and < 1.0
  $\Rightarrow \quad k_4 = 0.72(p_t - p_c)/\sqrt{p_t} = 0.72(0.6073)/\sqrt{1.686} = 0.337$ (< 1.0) [Eq. 10.19]
  $\varepsilon_{cs} = 0.0004$ (given)
  $\Rightarrow \quad \Delta_{sh} = (0.125)(0.337)(0.0004)(6000)^2/(400) =$ **1.517 mm**

Long-term deflection due to creep: Δ_{cp}

- $E_{ce} = Ec/(1 + \theta) = 25000/(1 + 1.6) = 9615.4$ MPa
  $\Rightarrow \quad m = E_s/E_{ce} = 2 \times 10^5/9804 = 20.8$
  Taking moments of areas of the cracked-transformed section about the NA [Figure 10.7(b)],
  $250(kd)^2/2 + (20.8 - 1)(942.5)(kd - 48) = (20.8 \times 1473)(349.5 - kd)$
  $\Rightarrow \quad 125(kd)^2 + 49299.9(kd) - 11603873 = 0$

† Alternatively, applying the ACI method, $k_r = 0.85$ for $p_c = 0$ [Eq. 10.24] $\Rightarrow \Delta_{cp} = k_r\,\theta\,\Delta_i = 0.85 \times 1.6 \times 7.03 = 9.56$ mm, which is much greater than $\Delta_{cp} = 2.50$ mm obtained as per IS Code procedure.

- Solving, $kd = 165.73$ mm

$\Rightarrow \quad I_{cr} = 250(165.73)^3/3 + (20.8 \times 1473)(349.5 - 165.73)^2 + (19.8 \times 942.5)(165.73 - 48)^2$
$= 16.727 \times 10^8 \text{ mm}^4$

but cannot exceed $I_{gr} = 13.3333 \times 10^8 \text{ mm}^4$

$\Rightarrow \quad I_{eff} = I_{gr} = 13.3333 \times 10^8 \text{ mm}^4$

$$\Rightarrow \quad \Delta_{i+cp} = \frac{5}{48}\frac{l^2}{E_{ce}I_{eff}} \times [M_{1D} + 0.8\, M_{2D}]$$

$$= \frac{5 \times (6000)^2 \times \{33.75 + (0.8 \times 45.0)\} \times 10^6}{48 \times 9615.4 \times (13.3333 \times 10^8)} = 20.4 \text{ mm}$$

$\Delta_i = \Delta_D$ (as $I_{eff,\,D} = I_{eff,\,D+L}$ – refer Example 10.3)

$= 13.16$ mm

$\Rightarrow \quad \therefore \Delta_{cp}{}^{\dagger} = \Delta_{i+cp} - \Delta_i = 20.4 - 13.16 =$ **7.24 mm**

Checks on total deflection

1. $\Delta_{D+L} + \Delta_{sh} + \Delta_{cp} = 21.65 + 1.517 + 7.24 =$ **30.41 mm**
   Allowable limit = $l/250 = 6000/250 = 24.0$ mm < 30.41 mm. Hence, there is an excess of 6.41 mm beyond the permissible limit – which can be overcome by providing a camber of at least 7 mm at the midspan location. [Compensation by camber is usually limited to the dead load deflection. Here, $\Delta_D = 13.16$ mm; hence OK. The camber can be as much as 10 mm.]
2. $\Delta_L + \Delta_{sh} + \Delta_{cp} = 8.49 + 1.517 + 7.24 =$ **17.24 mm**
   Allowable limit = $l/350 = 17.14$ mm (which is less than 20 mm)
   < 17.24 mm
   which represents only a negligible excess of 0.10 mm.

10.5 Serviceability Limit State: Cracking

In regions of tensile stresses, some cracking in concrete is inevitable. The attempt in crack control is to restrict them to a large number of well-distributed minute hairline cracks, as opposed to a few wide cracks, and to limit the maximum crack width to acceptable limits.

10.5.1 Cracking in Reinforced Concrete Members

Cracking of concrete will occur whenever the tensile strength (or the ultimate tensile strain) of concrete is exceeded. As concrete has relatively low tensile strength as well as low failure strain in tension, cracking is usually inevitable in normal reinforced concrete members (other than those in direct compression). However, the degree of cracking (in terms of width and spacing of cracks) can be controlled through proper design. Cracking is considered undesirable, not only for obvious aesthetic reasons, but also because it adversely affects durability (in aggressive environments) and leads to corrosion of the embedded steel. Also, in some cases, such as liquid-retaining structures and pressure vessels, it can adversely affect the basic functional requirements (such as water-tightness in a water tank). Hence, it is important for the designer to have an understanding of the various causes of cracking, the allowable limits on crack-widths under different situations as well as the methods to achieve crack control. It may also be stated that there is presently widespread lack of awareness of these aspects related to the serviceability

† Alternatively, using the ACI formulation, $k_r = 0.85/(1 + 0.5 \times 1.0787) = 0.552$ [Eq. 10.24] $\Rightarrow \Delta_{cp} = k_r\,\theta\Delta_i = 0.552 \times 1.6 \times 13.16 = 11.62$ mm, which is greater than $\Delta_{cp} = 7.24$ mm obtained by the IS Code procedure.

limit state of cracking. In the modern trend of adopting limit states design concepts, the emphasis has been on the limit state of collapse, and often the limit state of serviceability with respect to cracking of concrete gets compromised, as is the case with deflection.

Cracking in reinforced concrete members is attributable to various causes [Ref. 10.18], particularly:

1. flexural tensile stress due to bending under applied loads [Figure 10.14];
2. diagonal tension due to shear and/or torsion;
3. direct tensile stress under applied loads (for example, hoop tension in a circular water tank);
4. lateral tensile strains accompanying high compressive stress/strain due to Poisson effect (as in a compression test, anchorage zones in PSC, etc.) or due to heavy concentrated loads as in a split cylinder test;
5. restraint against volume changes due to shrinkage and temperature [Figure 10.15], as well as due to creep and chemical effects;
6. additional curvatures due to continuity effects, settlement of supports, etc.;
7. discontinuity effects (including stress-concentration), such as with change of section, re-entrant corners, termination/bending of bars, sudden changes in concrete properties, etc.; and
8. impact/dynamic loading and heavy vibrations.

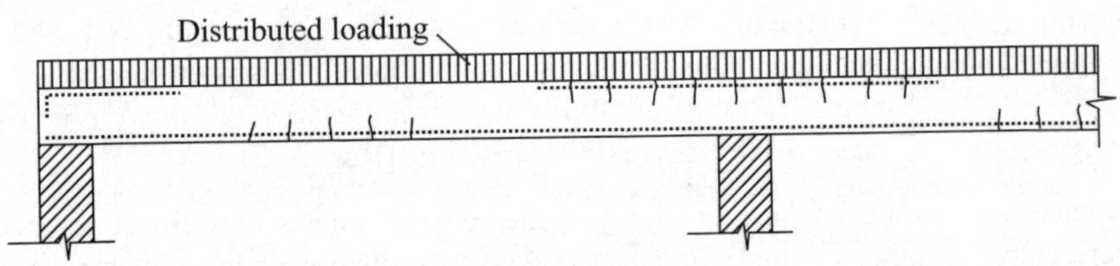

Fig. 10.14 Typical flexural cracks in a continuous one-way slab due to gravity loading.

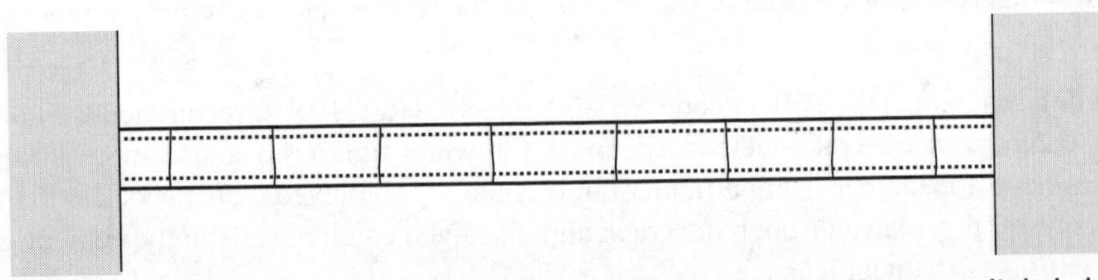

Fig. 10.15 Cracking due to restrained shrinkage and temperature effects in a lightly loaded slab.

Structural cracking in concrete occurs in tension, flexure or a combination of the two effects (eccentric tension). When this happens, splitting of the concrete occurs at the surface, penetrating inwards. Under direct tension, the crack generally runs through the thickness of the member (wall or slab), whereas under flexure, the crack is limited to the flexural tension zone. In all cases, the spacing of cracks as well as width of individual cracks depends not only on the magnitude of tensile force acting, but also on the reinforcement detailing, properties of concrete and thickness of section. It is observed that wide crack spacing is associated with relatively wide crack-widths, which is undesirable. Such cracking is often associated with low reinforcement percentages, wide spacing of bars and the use of high strength reinforcing steels, such as Fe 415 and Fe 500 (because the associated tensile strains at service load levels will be relatively high).

Although cracking of concrete is inevitable, it is desirable to aim for a large number of well-distributed fine hairline cracks, rather than a few but wide cracks. This is the objective of limit state design for the serviceability limit state of cracking.

It should be noted that although through proper design (for example, providing increased thickness), it is possible to contain the tensile stress in concrete within acceptable limits, the occurrence of cracking due to restrained shrinkage and thermal effects and induced tensile strains cannot be altogether eliminated[†].

The discussion in this chapter is primarily limited to the estimation of crack-widths due to applied bending moments and direct tensile forces. The problems associated with the prediction of crack-widths due to restrained deformation are also briefly discussed.

Cracking of concrete cannot be predicted with accuracy, because of inherent randomness in the nature of cracking. The width (and spacing) of cracks is subject to wide scatter, and methods of crack-width calculation only attempt to predict the most probable[‡] maximum crack-width as observed in laboratory tests. The primary objective of calculating crack width is to avoid gross errors in design, which might result in concentration and excessive width of cracks.

10.5.2 Limits on Cracking

Acceptable crack-width depends on the exposure of the structure/member to, and the nature of, the environment, and the function of the structure itself.

The acceptable limits of cracking vary with the type of structure and its environment. The Code (Cl. 35.3.2) recommends a maximum limit of 0.3 mm on the assessed surface width of cracks for concrete structures subject to 'mild' exposure. This limit of 0.3 mm is based essentially on aesthetic considerations, but this limit is also considered to be adequate for the purpose of durability *when the member is completely protected against weather or aggressive conditions* [Ref. 10.2].

However, in the case of 'members where cracking in the tensile zone is harmful either because they are exposed to the effects of weather or continuously exposed to moisture or in contact with soil or ground water' ('moderate' exposure category), the crack-width limit specified by the Code is 0.2 mm. Under more aggressive environments (exposure categories: 'severe', 'very severe' and 'extreme'), a more stringent limit of 0.1 mm is recommended.

For water-retaining structures, the British code BS 8007 (1987) [Ref. 10.19] recommends a limiting surface crack-width of 0.2 mm in general (deemed adequate for water-tightness) and a more stringent limit of 0.1 mm when aesthetic appearance is of particular importance. It is believed that cracks less than 0.2 mm heal autogenously, as water percolates through the crack and dissolved calcium salts in the cement gets deposited on drying, preventing subsequent leakage.

10.5.3 Factors Influencing Crack-widths

Crack-widths in RC members subject to flexure, direct tension or eccentric tension, are influenced by a large number of factors, many of which are inter-related. These include:

- tensile stress in the steel bars;
- thickness of concrete cover;
- diameter and spacing of bars;
- depth of member and location of neutral axis; and
- bond strength and tensile strength of concrete.

† For this reason, even in liquid retaining structures, where proportioning is sometimes done so as to keep tensile stresses in concrete at levels below its tensile strength, some minimum reinforcement is specified by Codes. Also, the designer is required to design the reinforcement to resist fully the applied tension, ignoring the tension-resisting capacity of concrete.

‡ Statistically, with 90 per cent confidence limit, in general.

When a beam is subject to a uniform bending moment [Figure 10.2] and when the limiting tensile strain of concrete is exceeded (at the weakest location), a flexural crack will form, and the concrete in the regions adjoining the crack will no longer be subject to tensile force. Due to the variability in tensile strength and ultimate tensile strain along the length of the beam, discrete cracks will develop at different stages of loading (within ±10 per cent of the 'cracking moment') [Ref. 10.18]. Experimental studies indicate that these initial cracks (sometimes referred to as 'primary' cracks) are roughly uniformly spaced. As discussed earlier (with reference to Figure 10.2), the concrete in-between the cracks resist some tension, and the tensile strain is maximum midway between the cracks. With increase in loading, additional cracks (called 'secondary cracks') will form somewhere midway between these cracks, when the limiting tensile strain capacity is exceeded. Both primary and secondary cracks will widen with increase in loading, and additional cracks may form (as the loading approaches the ultimate load), provided the bond between concrete and steel is capable of sustaining the development of significant tensile strain in the concrete (which can exceed the limiting strain capacity). A similar mechanism of development of primary and secondary cracks is found to occur in RC members subject to direct or eccentric tension [Ref. 10.18]. In all cases of applied loading, the width of the crack is found to be maximum at the surface of the member, reducing (tapering) to a near-zero value at the surface of the reinforcement†. Internal cracks (not visible from outside) are also likely to develop in the tension zone, with the width increasing at distances remote from the reinforcing bar.

Studies have shown that the **width of the crack** at a point depends primarily on the following three key factors:

1. the mean tensile strain (ε_{sm}) in the neighbouring reinforcement;
2. the distance (a_{cr}) to the nearest longitudinal bar that runs perpendicular to the crack; and
3. the distance to the neutral axis location (in the case of flexural cracks).

From the point of view of crack-width control, it is the surface crack-width that is of concern. The most obvious ways of minimising surface crack-widths at service loads are by (1) limiting the tensile stress in the steel (cracked section analysis), (2) minimising the spacing of reinforcing bars, and (3) providing bars as close as possible to the concrete surface in the tension zone (including side face reinforcement in relatively deep beams).

It may be noted that increased cover results in increased crack-widths at the surface. On the other hand, increased cover is highly desirable from the point of view of durability and protection against corrosion of reinforcement. These two aspects appear to be contradictory [Ref. 10.2], but it is always desirable to provide the requisite concrete cover for durability, and to control the crack-width by adopting other measures such as increasing the depth of the flexural member, reducing the bar diameter and spacing, and maintaining low stress levels in the tension steel. The use of low-grade steel (mild steel) as tension reinforcement is particularly desirable in flexural members (such as bridge girders) where both control of crack-width and prevention of reinforcement corrosion are of extreme importance.

In the earlier version of the Code, no explicit recommendations were given regarding procedures to calculate crack-widths. However, in the last revision (2000) of the Code, a procedure is given in Annex F for the estimation of flexural crack-widths (in beams and one-way slabs). Unfortunately, the Code does not emphasise sufficiently on the need to estimate crack-widths, especially where relatively large cover is used. Instead, the

† If, however, the member is very lightly reinforced, the crack-width may be significant at the surface of the reinforcement, and the bar may even yield at the crack location. This condition is, of course, highly undesirable under normal service loads, and can be avoided by providing appropriate minimum reinforcement.

Code has retained a rather outdated clause from the old Code (which was perhaps valid in earlier times when admissible minimum clear covers were 15 mm in slabs and 25 mm in beams). According to this clause (Cl. 43.1), explicit calculations of crack-widths are required only if the spacing of reinforcement exceeds the nominal requirements specified for beams and slabs [refer Section 5.2], regardless of the cover provided. To make matters worse, the clause in the earlier code, limiting the maximum clear cover in any construction to 75 mm has, for some reason, been eliminated. Of course, the highest figure given in Table 16 of the Code for the nominal cover is 75 mm, however, since this is the *minimum* required cover and there is no upper limit specified, a designer may be tempted to give a larger cover. However, as highlighted in a recent study [Ref. 10.21], increased cover implies increased crack-widths, particularly in flexural members. [Code Cl. 21.3.1 recommends, amongst other things, 'sacrificial steel' in tensile zone if the cover exceeds 40 mm for beams and 35 mm for slabs, however this is related to providing fire resistance and to give protection against spalling.]

In flexural members, increased cover leads to increased crack-width. It would appear desirable to specify an upper limit for cover in flexural members – no such limit exists in the current Code IS 456: 2000.

There is little use in providing increased cover to reinforcement (with the desired objective of providing increased durability against chemical attack and corrosion) if that cover is cracked. Such cracking (due to large covers) can be considerable, unless proper precautions are taken during design. Precautionary steps, under such circumstances, include the reduction of the tensile stress in the steel (by providing more reinforcement) and use of more closely spaced bars.

10.5.4 Estimation of Flexural Crack-width

The estimation of the probable maximum width of surface cracks in a flexural member is a fairly complex problem, and despite a fair amount of research in this field over the past four decades, the different equations evolved over the years predict values of crack-widths that are, in some cases, widely different. Different methods (with semi-empirical formulations) have been adopted by different international codes, and these too have undergone revisions over the years.

As with deflection, crack-width calculations are also approximate and subject to wide scatter, due to the uncertainties and variations in the factors involved.

Experiments have shown that the average spacing s_{av} of surface cracks is directly proportional to the distance a_{cr} from the surface of the main reinforcing bar. Cracks are most likely to form on the surface in the tensile zone mid-way between two adjacent bars, as shown in Figure 10.16. The value of a_{cr}, in terms of the bar spacing s, bar diameter d_b and effective cover d_c is given by:

$$a_{cr} = \sqrt{(s/2)^2 + d_c^2} - d_b/2 \qquad (10.30)$$

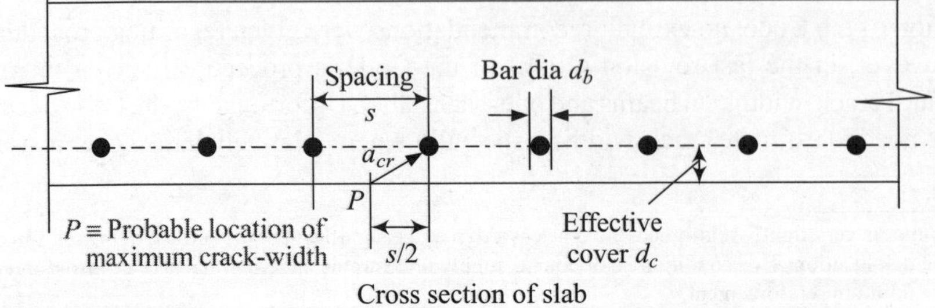

Fig. 10.16 Geometrical parameters of relevance in determining flexural crack-width in a slab.

In the case of a typical rectangular beam, the locations for determining maximum surface crack-widths are mainly at the soffit of the beam (when subject to sagging curvature), at distances where the value of a_{cr} is likely to be maximum [points P_1 and P_2 in Figure 10.17]. Also, points on the side of the beam section, mid-way between the neutral axis and the centreline of reinforcement, should be investigated [point P_3 in Figure 10.17]. The width of flexural crack, w_{cr}, may be expressed as:

$$w_{cr} = \text{constant} \times a_{cr} \times \varepsilon_m \tag{10.31}$$

where ε_m is the mean strain at the level considered and the constant has a value of 3.33 for deformed bars and 4.0 for plain round bars, and the cracks are likely to occur at a mean spacing of $1.67a_{cr}$.

It is seen from Eq. 10.31 that the flexural crack-width at a beam surface is directly proportional to (i) the distance to the nearest longitudinal bar (or the neutral axis for location such as P_3) and (ii) the mean strain in the concrete at the level under consideration.

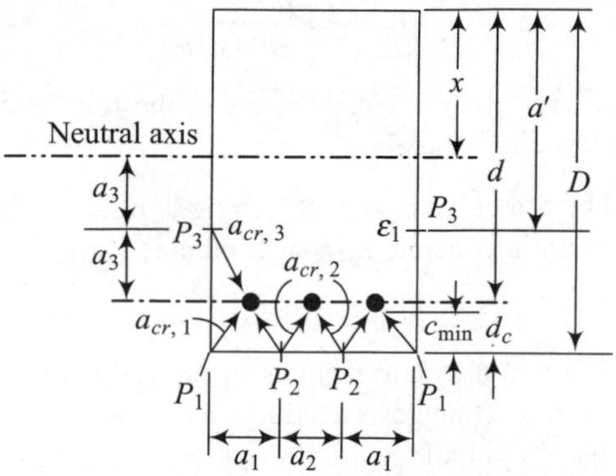

Fig. 10.17 Critical locations for determining flexural crack-width in a typical beam section.

IS 456 Formulation

The IS code in Annex F describes a procedure† for predicting flexural crack-widths, which is apparently borrowed from the British Code [Ref. 10.12]. The expression for w_{cr} takes the form shown in Eq. 10.31:

$$w_{cr} = \frac{3a_{cr}\varepsilon_m}{1 + 2(a_{cr} - C_{\min})/(D - x)} \tag{10.32}$$

where a_{cr} and ε_m are as defined earlier (Eq. 10.31), D is the overall depth of the member, $C_{\min}$ the minimum cover to the main longitudinal bar, and x the neutral axis depth [refer Figure 10.17]. The calculations of ε_m and x are crucial, and must account for the effect of 'tension stiffening'. Accordingly, the British Code BS 8110, on which Eq. 10.31 is based, recommends that they be based on the procedure described in Section 10.3.6 (which involves iterative calculations). It may be noted that the calculations should also accommodate the long-term effects of creep. This is done by taking the value of the allowable tensile stress in concrete at the level of the steel, f_{cts}, to be equal to 0.55 MPa [compared to the value 1.0 MPa for short-term effects, refer Figure 10.4(b)], and by including considerations of creep in the modular ratio. It is also important to note that it is implicitly assumed that the strains in the steel are well within the elastic limit. The Code, accordingly, does not permit the application of Eq. 10.32 to situations where the tensile stress in the steel (at the crack location) exceeds $0.8f_y$. After calculating x and f_{sm}, the average tensile stress in the reinforcement, the value of ε_{m} at any point is easily obtained as:

$$\varepsilon_m = \frac{f_{sm}}{E_s}\,\frac{a' - x}{d - x} \tag{10.33}$$

† However, the manner in which this formulation has been presented in Annex F of the Code lacks clarity, because it is incomplete and the background information regarding the exact procedure to estimate the neutral axis depth, x is not given. Also, it may be noted that while the British Code adopts the same formulation (for the calculation of x) for computations of both crack-widths and deflections (based on 'effective curvature'), the IS Code adopts a different formulation for deflection calculations (based on 'effective second moment of area'), which is borrowed from a much older version of the British Code.

where a' refers to the distance from the extreme compression fibre to the point (such as P_1, P_2, P_3, etc.) at which the surface crack-width is being calculated [refer Figure 10.17].

The calculations, involving an iterative procedure to determine x and f_{sm}, as described above, can be tedious, as shown in Example 10.7. The Code IS 456:2000 allows for an approximation for computing ε_m which involves only the conventional 'cracked' section analysis using the modular ratio concept, whereby x and the 'apparent' strain ε_1 at the location of interest are first calculated (assuming concrete to resist no tension), with

$$\varepsilon_1 = \frac{f_{st}}{E_s}\frac{a' - x}{d - x} \tag{10.34}$$

where f_{st} is the tensile stress in the reinforcement (in MPa units) and E_s (= 2×10^5 MPa) the modulus of elasticity of steel.

The effect of tension stiffening is now accounted for through a term ε_2, such that the desired mean tensile strain in concrete ε_m is now obtained simply as:

$$\varepsilon_m = \varepsilon_1 - \varepsilon_2 \tag{10.35}$$

The strain ε_2 corresponds to the reduction due to tension stiffening effect. For computing this, the Code (Annex F) suggests a reduction in tensile force in reinforcement, equal to the force generated by the triangular distribution of tensile stresses in concrete given in Figure 10.4(b). The tensile stress in concrete at steel level f_{cts} is to be taken as 1.0 MPa (for short-term calculations) and 0.55 N/mm^2 (for inclusion of long-term effects) [refer Annex F of Code]. Accordingly, ε_2 works out to:

$$\varepsilon_2 = f_{cts} \times b(D - x)(a' - x)/\{2E_s A_{st}(d - x)\} \tag{10.35a}$$

The following empirical expression for ε_2 is given in the Code†:

$$\varepsilon_2 = \frac{b(D - x)(a' - x)}{3E_s A_{st}(d - x)} \tag{10.36}$$

where b is the width of the section at the centroid of the tension steel, A_{st} is the area of the tension steel, and $E_s = 2 \times 10^5$ MPa. If the value of ε_2, calculated by Eq. 10.36, exceeds ε_1 (i.e., $\varepsilon_m < 0$), then it should be construed that the section is uncracked.

Considering the crack-width at the surface remote from the compression face [refer Figure 10.17],

$$a' = D$$

whereby Eq. 10.35 simplifies to

$$\varepsilon_m = \frac{1}{E_s}\frac{D - x}{d - x}\left[f_{st} - \frac{b(D - x)}{3A_{st}}\right] \tag{10.37}$$

where f_{st} is the stress at the centroid of the tension steel (cracked section), expressed in MPa units.

Gergely Lutz Formula

The practice in North America [Ref. 10.13, 10.14] is based on a formula due to Gergely and Lutz [Ref. 10.23]. In several European countries, the CEB–FIP procedure [Ref. 10.10] is favoured. Some recent studies

† Note that in the empirical Eq. 10.36, the multiplication factor 1/3 has the unit of stress (N/mm^2).

[Ref. 10.24, and 10.25], which compare the predictions of the prevailing international Code methods with a very large number of experimental test results reported by Clark, Hognestad, Base and others, conclude that the best results are predicted by the Gergely and Lutz formula.

The formula for the maximum probable crack-width, in this case, is given by†:

$$w_{cr} = (11 \times 10^{-6}) \sqrt[3]{d_c (A_e/n)} \left(\frac{D - x}{d - x} \right) f_{st} \tag{10.38}$$

where

$d_c \equiv$ thickness of concrete cover measured from the extreme tension fibre to the centre of the nearest bar;

$A_e \equiv$ effective area of concrete in tension surrounding the main tension reinforcement, having the same centroid as the tension steel [$A_e = 2(D - d)b_w$ in Figure 10.18(a)].

$n \equiv$ number of bars in tension; in case different diameters are used, n shall be taken as the total steel area divided by the area of the largest diameter bar; and

$f_{st} \equiv$ stress (in MPa) at the centroid of the tension steel.

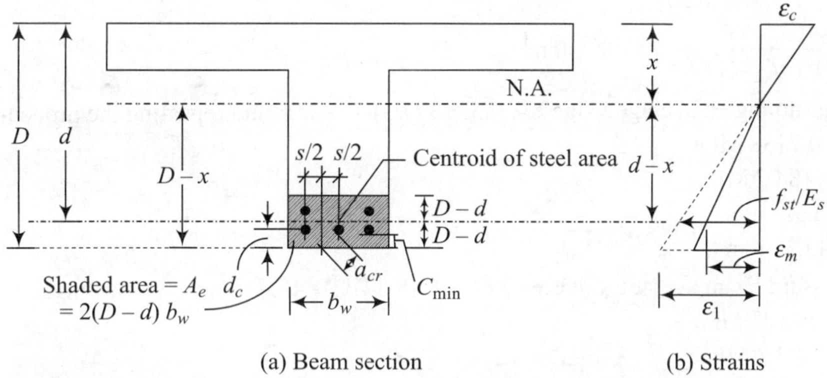

Fig. 10.18 Parameters for crack-width calculation (Gergely-Lutz formula).

Example 10.7

Determine the maximum probable crack-width for the one-way slab designed in Example 5.2 (and analysed for deflection in Example 10.1).

Solution

- From Examples 5.2 and 10.1,

  $D = 200$ mm, $d = 165$ mm, $C_{min} = 30$ mm, $d_b = 10$ mm $d_c = 35$ mm,

  $s = 150$ mm, $A_{st} = 523$ mm²/m (10ϕ @ 150 mm c/c), $p_t = 0.316$,

  $f_y = 500$ MPa, $f_{ck} = 25$ MPa, $f_{cts} = 0.55$ MPa,

  M (at midspan, under service loads) = 21.63 kNm/m.

† Note that for dimensional homogeneity in the empirical Eq. 10.38, the constant 11×10^{-6}, which is obtained from statistical analysis of the experimental data, evidently has the inverse unit of stress.

(a) Based on detailed procedure for calculating x and ε_m

The procedure for calculating the neutral axis depth x is identical to the one described in Example 10.1, except that allowable tensile stress in steel f_{cts} needs to be altered, in order to account for the long-term effects due to creep.

$f_{cts} = 0.55$ MPa [refer Figure 10.4(b)].

Also, the modular ratio† m may be taken as:

$m = 280/(3\sigma_{cbc}) = 280/(3 \times 8.5) = 11.0$

Trial 1: Assume $x \approx d/3 = 165/3 = 55$ mm

$$\Rightarrow \quad f_{ct} = \left(\frac{200 - x}{165 - x}\right) \times 0.55 = 0.725 \text{ MPa}$$

$$\Rightarrow \quad f_{sm} = \left(21.63 \times 10^6 - \frac{1000 \times 200 \times f_{ct} \times (200 - x)}{3}\right) \Big/ 523 \times \left(165 - \frac{x}{3}\right)$$

$= 190.6$ MPa

$$\Rightarrow \quad f_c = \frac{f_{sm} A_{st} + 0.5b(D - x) f_{ct}}{0.5bx} = 5.536 \text{ MPa}$$

$$\Rightarrow \quad x = \frac{165}{1 + f_{sm}/(11 f_c)} = 39.95 \text{ mm}$$

Trial 2: Assuming an average value $x \approx (55 + 39.95)/2 = 47.5$ and repeating the procedure,

$\Rightarrow \quad f_{ct} = 0.7138$ MPa

$\Rightarrow \quad f_{sm} = 184.2$ MPa

$\Rightarrow \quad f_c = 6.35$ MPa

$\Rightarrow \quad x = 45.37$ mm

Trial 3: Assuming an average value $x \approx (47.5 + 45.37)/2 = 46.4$ mm, and repeating the procedure,

$\Rightarrow \quad f_{ct} = 0.7123$ MPa

$\Rightarrow \quad f_{sm} = 183.3$ MPa

$\Rightarrow \quad f_c = 6.49$ MPa

$\Rightarrow \quad$ **$x = 46.2$ mm**, which indicates convergence.

- $w_{cr} = (3a_{cr}\varepsilon_m)/[1 + 2(a_{cr} - C_{min})/(D - x)]$

$$a_{cr} = \sqrt{(s/2)^2 + d_c^{\,2}} - d_b/2 = \sqrt{(150/2)^2 + (35)^2} - 5 = 77.8 \text{ mm}$$

$$\varepsilon_m = \frac{f_{sm}}{E_s} \times \frac{D - x}{d - x} = \frac{183.3}{2 \times 10^5} \times \frac{200 - 46.2}{165 - 46.2} = 0.001187$$

$w_{cr} = (3 \times 77.8 \times 0.001187)/[1 + 2(77.8 - 30)/(200 - 46.2)]$

$= \mathbf{0.171\ mm}$

(b) Based on 'Approximate' procedure of IS 456 (Annex F)

This calls for the conventional cracked section analysis, with the modular ratio m taken as:

$m = 280/(3\sigma_{cbc}) = 280/(3 \times 8.5) = 11.0$

† According to BS 8110, the value of m should be based on E_s/E_{ce}, considering E_{ce} as half the short-term elastic modulus of concrete.

$$k = \sqrt{2(\rho m) + (\rho m)^2} - (\rho m) \text{ where } \rho = p_t/100 = 0.316 \times 10^{-2}$$

$$\Rightarrow \quad k = 0.2312 \Rightarrow x = kd = 0.2312 \times 165 = 38.1 \text{ mm}$$

$$\Rightarrow \quad I_{cr} = (1000)(38.1)^3/3 + (11.0 \times 523)(165 - 38.1)^2 = 1.1108 \times 10^8 \text{ mm}^4$$

$$\Rightarrow \quad f_{st} = \frac{11.0 \times (21.63 \times 10^6) \times (165 - 38.1)}{1.1108 \times 10^8} = 271.8 \text{ MPa}$$

(which is within **275** MPa, the allowable stress for Fe 500 steel, as per working stress design)

$$\varepsilon_1 = \frac{f_{st}}{E_s} \times \frac{D - x}{d - x} = \frac{271.8}{2 \times 10^5} \times \frac{200 - 38.1}{165 - 38.1} = 0.00173$$

$$\varepsilon_2 = \frac{b(D - x)(a' - x)}{3E_s A_{st}(d - x)} = \frac{1000(200 - 38.1)^2}{3(2 \times 10^5)(523)(165 - 38.1)} = 0.000658$$

$$\Rightarrow \quad \varepsilon_m = \varepsilon_1 - \varepsilon_2 = 0.001072 > 0$$

$$\Rightarrow \quad w_{cr} = (3a_{cr}\varepsilon_m)/[1 + 2(a_{cr} - C_{\min})/(D - x)]$$

$$= (3 \times 77.8 \times 0.001072)/[1 + 2(77.8 - 30)/(200 - 38.1)]$$

$$= \mathbf{0.157 \text{ mm}}$$

(which compares reasonably with the value of 0.171 mm obtained by the 'exact' procedure).

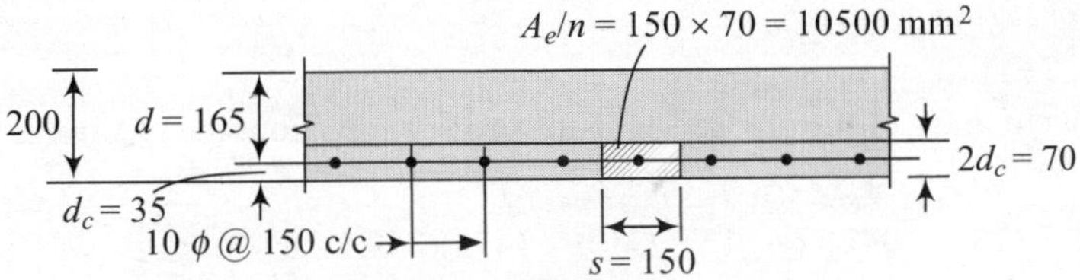

Fig. 10.19 Example 10.7.

Crack-width calculation using Gergely & Lutz formula

- $w_{cr} = (11 \times 10^{-6}) \sqrt[3]{d_c(A_e/n)} \dfrac{D - x}{d - x} f_{st}$ [Eq. 10.38]

where

$d_c = 30 + 10/2 = 35$ mm [refer Figure 10.19]

A_e/n = effective concrete area in tension per bar

$= s(2d_c) = 150 \times 70 = 10500$ mm^2

$$\Rightarrow \quad w_{cr} = (11 \times 10^{-6}) \sqrt[3]{35 \times 10500} \frac{200 - 38.1}{165 - 38.1} \times (271.8)$$

$$= \mathbf{0.273 \text{ mm}}$$

(which is larger than the value of 0.157 mm obtained by the IS Code formula).

Note: It is clear that the maximum probable crack-width is less than 0.3 mm, and hence is acceptable.

Example 10.8

Determine the maximum probable crack-width for the doubly reinforced beam designed in Example 5.4.

Solution

- From Example 5.4,
  D = 400 mm, b = 250 mm, d = 349.5 mm, C_{min} = 30 mm, d' = 48 mm, A_{st} = 1473 mm^2, (3–25ϕ), A_{sc} = 942 mm^2 (3–20ϕ), M_{D+L} (at midspan, under service loads) = 124 kNm, f_{ck} = 25 MPa, f_y = 500 MPa.
  The cross-sectional details are shown in Figure 10.20.

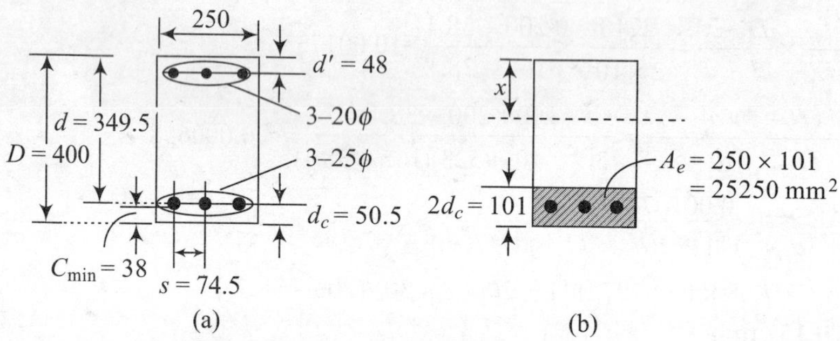

Fig. 10.20 Example 10.8.

- *Depth of neutral axis: x = kd*
  $m = 280/(3 \times 8.5) = 11$
  Taking moments of areas of the cracked-transformed section about the NA [refer Section 4.6.5],
  $b(x)^2/2 + (1.5m - 1)\,A_{sc}(x - d') = mA_{st}(d - x)$
  $\Rightarrow \quad 250(x)^2/2 + (15.5 \times 942)(x - 48) = (11.0 \times 1473)(349.5 - x)$
  $\Rightarrow \quad 125(x)^2 + 30804(x) - 6363797 = 0$
  Solving, x = 133.87 mm
- *Tensile stress in steel under service loads: f_{st}*

$$f_{st} = m\frac{M(d-x)}{I_{cr}}$$

where M = 124 kNm.

$$I_{cr} = 250(133.87)^3/3 + (11.0 \times 1473)(349.5 - 133.87)^2 + (15.5 \times 942) \times (133.87 - 48)^2$$
$$= 10.61 \times 10^8 \text{ mm}^4$$

$$\Rightarrow \quad f_{st} = \frac{11 \times (124 \times 10^6) \times (349.5 - 133.87)}{10.61 \times 10^8}$$
$$= 277 \text{ MPa}$$

(which, incidentally, is nearly equal to (marginally over) σ_{st} = 275 MPa allowed as per working stress design).

Crack-width calculation using IS Code formula

The approximate procedure is followed here. The reader may verify that the detailed procedure yields roughly the same results. Crack-widths are calculated at the three critical positions (P_1, P_2 and P_3) indicated in Figure 10.17.

For position P_1 (corner)

$$a_{cr} = \sqrt{\left(\frac{b-2s}{2}\right)^2 + d_c^2} - d_b/2$$

$$= a_{cr} = \sqrt{(50.5)^2 + (50.5)^2} - 12.5 = 58.9 \text{ mm with } a' = D$$

- $\varepsilon_m = \dfrac{1}{E_s}\dfrac{D-x}{d-x}\left[f_{st} - \dfrac{b(D-x)}{3A_{st}}\right]$ [Eq. 10.37]

$$= \frac{1}{2\times10^5}\frac{400-133.87}{349.5-133.87}\left[277.0 - \frac{250(400-133.87)}{3\times1473}\right]$$

$$= 1.616\times10^{-3}$$

- $C_{min} = 38$ mm
- $w_{cr} = (3a_{cr}\varepsilon_m)/[1 + 2(a_{cr} - C_{\min})/(D-x)]$

  $= (3\times58.9\times1.616\times10^{-3})/[1 + 2(58.9- 38)/ (400 - 133.87)]$

  $=$ **0.247 mm**

For position P_2 (soffit of beam)

$$a_{cr} = \sqrt{(s/2)^2 + d_c^2} - d_b/2$$

$$= \sqrt{(74.5/2)^2 + (50.5)^2} - 12.5 = 50.25 \text{ mm and } a' = D$$

- $\varepsilon_m = \dfrac{1}{E_s}\dfrac{D-x}{d-x}\left[f_{st} - \dfrac{b(D-x)}{3A_{st}}\right]$ [Eq. 10.37]

$$= \frac{1}{2\times10^5}\frac{400-133.87}{349.5-133.87}\left[277.0 - \frac{250(400-133.87)}{3\times1473}\right]$$

$$= 1.616\times10^{-3}$$

- $C_{min} = 38$ mm
- $w_{cr} = (3a_{cr}\varepsilon_m)/[1 + 2(a_{cr} - C_{\min})/(D-x)]$

  $= (3\times50.25\times1.616\times10^{-3})/[1 + 2(50.25 - 38)/(400 - 133.87)]$

  $=$ **0.223 mm**

For position P_3 (side of beam)

$C_e = 30 + 8 + 12.5 = 50.5$ mm

$s = (d - x)/2 = 107.82$ mm

- $a_{cr} = \sqrt{\left(\dfrac{d-x}{2}\right)^2 + (d_c)^2} - 12.5 = \sqrt{(107.82)^2 + (50.5)^2} - 12.5 = 106.6$ mm
- a' = distance of point where crack-width is desired from the extreme compression fibre

  $= 107.82 + 133.87 = 241.69$ mm

ε_1 is the strain at the crack location considering a cracked section

$$\varepsilon_1 = \frac{f_{st}}{2E_s} = \frac{277.0}{2\times2\times10^5} = 6.9\times10^{-4}$$

- $\varepsilon_m = \varepsilon_1 - \dfrac{b_t(D-x)(a'-x)}{3E_s A_{st}(d-x)} = 6.9 \times 10^{-4} - \dfrac{250(400-133.87)(241.69-133.87)}{3 \times 2 \times 10^5 \times 1473(349.5-133.87)}$

  $= 6.524 \times 10^{-4}$

- $w_{cr} = (3a_{cr}\varepsilon_m)/[1 + 2(a_{cr} - C_{\min})/(D - kd)]$

  $= (3 \times 106.6 \times 6.524 \times 10^{-4})/[1 + 2(106.6 - 38)/(400 - 133.87)]$

  $=$ **0.138 mm**

Hence, the maximum probable surface crack-width is **0.247 mm**, and this occurs at the bottom corner (position P_1).

Crack-width calculation using Gergely & Lutz formula

- $d_c = 30 + 8 + 25/2 = 50.5$ mm [refer Figure 10.20a]
  $A_e = 250 \times (2 \times 50.5) = 25250 \text{ mm}^2$ [as shown in Figure 10.20(b)]
  $n = 3$

For positions P_1 and P_2

- $w_{cr} = (11 \times 10^{-6})\ \sqrt[3]{d_c(A_e/n)}\ \dfrac{D-x}{d-x} f_{st}$

  $= (11 \times 10^{-6})\ \sqrt[3]{50.5(25250/3)}\ \dfrac{400-133.87}{349.5-133.87} \times 277.0$

  $=$ **0.283 mm**

Note: The maximum probable crack-width is less than 0.3 mm, and hence is acceptable.

10.5.5 Estimation of Crack-width under Direct and Eccentric Tension

In some reinforced concrete members, such as the walls of water tanks, bins and silos, pressure vessels, suspenders and ties in arch, roof and bridge structures, it is axial (or membrane) tension that is the predominant structural action, and not flexure. In many instances in such members, direct or eccentric tension due to applied loading may act in combination with restraint to volume changes caused by temperature and shrinkage [Ref. 10.18]. This can lead to significant cracking, which should be controlled in the interest of serviceability. In this section, the discussion is limited to cracking caused by applied loading; thermal and shrinkage cracking are discussed in the next section.

Cracking due to direct tension is of somewhat more serious concern than flexural cracking, because it causes a clear separation in the concrete, through the entire thickness of the member, as shown in Figure 10.21. Control of such cracking is therefore of particular importance in liquid retaining structures and pressure vessels.

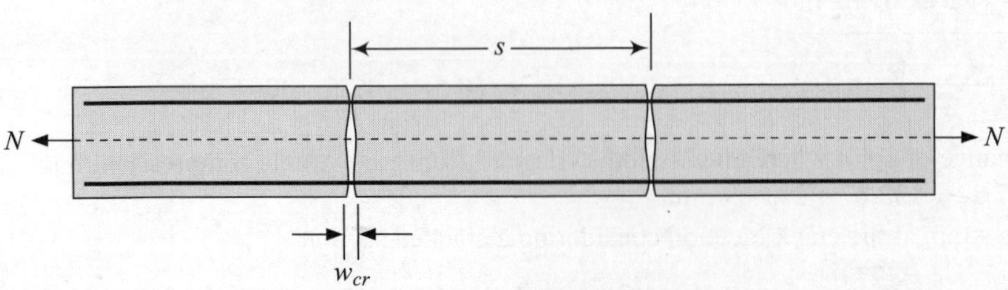

Fig. 10.21 Cracking under direct tension.

At the crack location, the reinforcement is required to resist the entire tension, and the width and spacing of cracks are governed primarily by the reinforcement detailing. If very low percentages of reinforcement are provided, the steel may yield and result in wide crack-widths. However, crack-widths can be significantly controlled by maintaining sufficient reinforcement at close spacing, with relatively low tensile stress and strain in the steel at service loads. As in the case of flexure, the concrete in between the cracks resists some tension ('tension stiffening' effect). The axial stiffness of the member can be greatly reduced by the presence of wide cracks, but this reduction is mitigated by the tension stiffening effect. Recommendations for assessing axial stiffness are given in Ref. 10.18. These may be used in the structural analysis of statically indeterminate reinforced concrete structures involving significant axial tension.

The IS Code does not give any recommendations for estimating crack-widths in members subject to direct or eccentric tension. However, such recommendations are given in the British codes BS 8110 [Ref. 10.12] and BS 8007 [Ref. 10.19], and these are discussed here. BS 8110 permits the extension of the procedure (approximate method) prescribed for crack-width prediction under pure flexure [Eqs 10.34–10.36] to situations of flexure combined with axial tension. When axial tension predominates, the entire section is likely to be under tension with the neutral axis lying outside the section, as shown in Figure 10.22. In such cases, the neutral axis depth x will have a negative value, and this must be taken special note of, while applying Eqs 10.34 and 10.36. In the extreme case of pure tension (i.e., $x \rightarrow -\infty$), it is suggested that it suffices to consider $x = -D$.

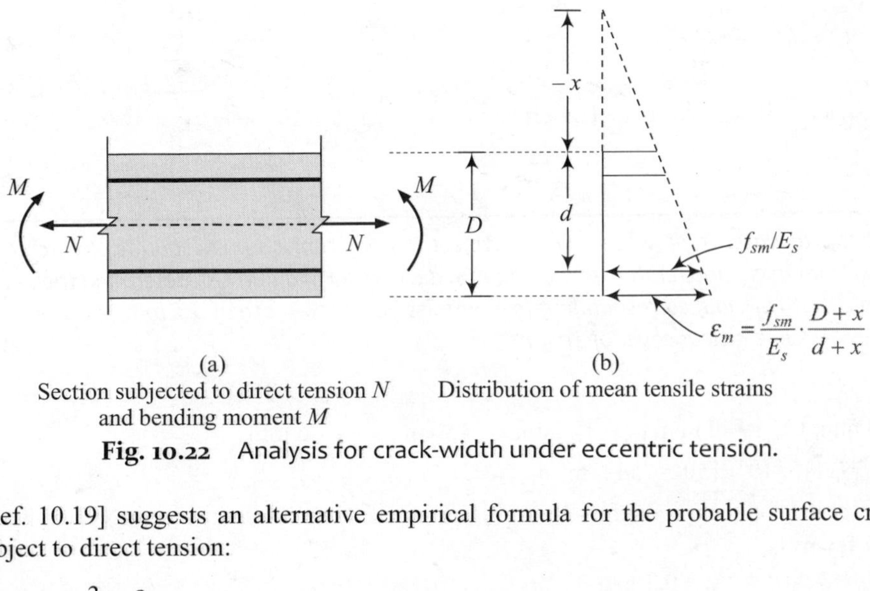

(a)
Section subjected to direct tension N and bending moment M

(b)
Distribution of mean tensile strains

Fig. 10.22 Analysis for crack-width under eccentric tension.

BS 8007 [Ref. 10.19] suggests an alternative empirical formula for the probable surface crack-width in members subject to direct tension:

$$w_{cr} = 3a_{cr}\varepsilon_m \tag{10.39}$$

which has the form given by Eq. 10.31, with the terms a_{cr} and ε_m as defined earlier. The constant, '3' is based on a probability of exceedance of the calculated value of crack-width being equal to about 1 in 100. The expression for the mean tensile strain ε_m is the same as given in Eq. 10.35:

$$\varepsilon_m = \varepsilon_1 - \varepsilon_2$$

where, in the case of flexure, ε_1 is the 'apparent strain' (tensile strain in steel at the crack location) given by Eq. 10.34 and ε_2 is the reduction in strain due to the tension stiffening effect, which is given by:

$$\varepsilon_2 = \frac{f_{ct}A_{gr}}{A_{st}E_s} \tag{10.40}$$

where A_{gr} is the gross area of the cross-section, A_{st} the area of tension steel, and f_{ct} is the allowable tensile stress in concrete. While the above formulas can be used to compute the crack width for an applied tensile force, conversely it can also be used to compute the admissible f_{st} (and hence the tension admissible) for a permissible crack width. For such calculations, the allowable value of f_{ct} is specified as 1.0 MPa if the permissible crack-width is 0.1 mm, and 0.67 MPa if the permissible crack-width is 0.2 mm. For other crack-widths, values of f_{ct} have not been specified by BS 8007 (which is the British code for design of water retaining structures), and linear interpolation or extrapolation are not permitted.

Unlike the British codes (BS 8110 and BS 8007), the ACI codes (ACI 318 for general RC design and ACI 350 for liquid retaining structures) do not specifically recommend any procedure for the estimation of crack-widths under direct or eccentric tension. However, reference is made to the formula given in the ACI 224 Committee Report [Ref. 10.26], which is based on a formula by Broms and Lutz (similar to the one by Gergely and Lutz for flexure). In SI units, this equation takes the following form

$$w_{cr} = 0.02 f_{st} t_e \times 10^{-3} \tag{10.41}$$

where w_{cr} is the maximum probable surface crack-width (in mm), f_{st} is the tensile stress (in MPa) in the steel at the crack, and t_e is the 'effective concrete cover', which may be taken as:

$$t_e = d_c \sqrt{1 + \left(\frac{s}{4d_c}\right)^2} \tag{10.42}$$

where s is the spacing of bars, located at an effective cover d_c.

Example 10.9

Consider a cylindrical water tank, whose wall is subject to hoop tension on account of hydrostatic pressure. If the wall is 250 mm thick, and reinforced with 12 mm dia bars @ 150 mm c/c, determine the allowable hoop tension (per unit width of wall) corresponding to a permissible crack-width of 0.2 mm. Assume M 30 concrete and Fe 500 steel. Assume a clear cover of 40 mm.

Solution

- $D = 250$ mm, $C_{min} = 40$ mm, $d_b = 12$ mm, $s = 150$ mm, $d_c = 46$ mm

  $A_{st} = (113\times10^3)/150 = 754$ mm²/m

  The allowable hoop tension is given by $N = f_{st}A_{st}$, where the allowable value of f_{st} is to be determined.

  BS 8007 formula

  $w_{cr} = 3a_{cr}(\varepsilon_1 - \varepsilon_2) = 0.2$ mm

  where $a_{cr} = \sqrt{(s/2)^2 + d_c^{\,2}} - d_b/2 = \sqrt{(150/2)^2 + (46)^2} - 6 = 82.0$ mm

  $$\varepsilon_2 = \frac{f_{ct}A_{gr}}{E_s A_{st}} = \frac{(0.67)(1000 \times 250)}{(2\times10^5)(754)} = 0.00111; \quad (\text{taking } f_{ct} = 0.67 \text{ MPa})$$

  $$\Rightarrow \quad \varepsilon_1 = \frac{w_{cr}}{3a_{cr}} + \varepsilon_2 = \frac{0.2}{3(82.0)} + 0.00111 = 0.001923$$

$\Rightarrow \quad f_{st} = E_s \varepsilon_1 = (2 \times 10^5)(0.001923) = 384.6$ MPa

(which incidentally is higher than 275 MPa assumed in usual working stress design, but is well within the yield strength).

$\Rightarrow \quad N = f_{st}A_{st} = (384.6 \text{ N/mm}^2)(754 \text{ mm}^2\text{/m}) = 289988.4 \text{ N} = \mathbf{290.0\ kN}$

BS 8100 procedure

$$w_{cr} = \frac{3a_{cr}\varepsilon_m}{1 + 2(a_{cr} - C_{\min})/(D - x)} = 0.2 \text{ mm}$$

$$\Rightarrow \quad \varepsilon_m = 0.2\{1 + 2(a_{cr} - C_{\min})/(D - x)\}/3a_{cr}$$

where, $x = -D = -250$ mm for pure tension [refer Section 10.5.5]

$d = 250 - 40 - 6 = 204$ mm

$$\Rightarrow \quad \varepsilon_m = 0.2\{1 + 2(82 - 40)/(250 + 250)\}/(3 \times 82) = 0.0009496$$

$$\varepsilon_m = \varepsilon_1 - \varepsilon_2$$

$$\varepsilon_2 = \frac{b(D - x)(a' - x)}{3E_s A_{st}(d - x)} = \frac{1000(250 + 250)^2}{3(2 \times 10^5)(754)(204 + 250)} = 0.001217$$

$$\varepsilon_1 = \varepsilon_m + \varepsilon_2 = 0.002167$$

$$\varepsilon_1 = \frac{f_{st}}{E_s}\frac{D - x}{d - x}$$

$\Rightarrow \quad f_{st} = (2 \times 10^5)(0.002167)(204 + 250)/(500) = 393.5$ MPa

$N = f_{st}A_{st} = (393.5 \text{ N/mm}^2)(754 \text{ mm}^2\text{/m}) = 296699 \text{ N} = \mathbf{296.7\ kN}$

(which compares very well with the solution obtained by the BS 8007 formula).

ACI Committee 224 procedure

The effective concrete cover is given by

$$t_e = d_c\sqrt{1 + \left(\frac{s}{4d_c}\right)^2} = 46\sqrt{1 + \left(\frac{150}{4 \times 46}\right)^2} = 59.35 \text{ mm} \qquad \text{[Eq. 10.42]}$$

$\Rightarrow \quad w_{cr} = 0.02 f_{st}\, t_e \times 10^{-3} = 0.2$ mm [Eq. 10.41]

$\Rightarrow \quad f_{st} = 168.5$ MPa

$\Rightarrow \quad N = f_{st}A_{st} = (168.5 \text{ N/mm}^2)(754 \text{ mm}^2\text{/m}) = 127049 \text{ N} = \mathbf{127.0\ kN}$

(which is a conservative estimate in comparison to the BS codes).

10.5.6 Thermal and Shrinkage Cracking

Early Thermal Shrinkage

During mixing of concrete, heat of hydration is generated, causing the temperature of concrete to rise. The temperature at casting may be significantly higher than the ambient temperature, but the peak hydration temperature (which may occur within three days or so after casting) can be considerably higher than the ambient temperature. This difference in temperature (between the peak and ambient temperatures) may vary from 10 to 50°C, depending on various factors, such as the volume of concrete cast, the volume of cement content, the type of cement used, type of formwork, ambient temperature, etc†. The temperature in the middle

† Temperatures increase with the use of rapid-hardening cement or higher-grade cement (with greater fineness), with increased cement content, larger volumes cast (with larger thickness of section) and use of timber formwork (instead of steel).

region is often higher than at the surface (with a gradient of up to 20°C in very thick members). The concrete cools and attains the ambient temperature within seven days or so. This results in shortening of the hardened concrete, and such shortening is sometimes referred to as 'early thermal shrinkage'. The concrete at the surface is subject to tension (and the concrete in the middle region to compression) owing to the temperature gradient across the thickness. Additionally, the overall shortening is frequently restrained by the adjoining concrete, resulting in further development of tensile strains throughout the section. If the overall tensile strain (maximum at the surface regions) exceeds the ultimate tensile strain capacity of the hardening concrete, cracking is likely to occur. Such 'early thermal cracking' can be prevented by controlling the factors affecting the heat of hydration (using a low cement content, using pozzalanic admixtures, using ice to control temperature during mixing, etc.) and by measures to dissipate the heat generated (such as embedded pipes with circulating cold water, often resorted to in mass concreting for concrete dams). Studies have also established that delaying the process of cooling, such as by delaying the formwork removal and insulating the concrete, are also advantageous [Ref. 10.27].

> In the design of liquid storage tanks, where crack-free performance is crucial to prevent leakage of liquid, IS 3370 (Part 2): 2009 calls for provision of adequate minimum reinforcement to control cracking due to early thermal shrinkage (as well as due to seasonal thermal variations); this is discussed in detail in Chapter 18.

Drying Shrinkage

Accompanying the early thermal movement associated with the hardening of concrete, another factor which contributes to the shortening of concrete is *drying shrinkage* [refer Section 2.12.1]. However, unlike early thermal movements, drying shrinkage is a long-term phenomenon. It is best controlled by adopting as low a water-cement ratio as practicable, thereby keeping to a minimum the volume of moisture in the concrete that can evaporate. Cracking due to drying shrinkage occurs due to restraints that cause tensile stresses and strains in the concrete. The external restraints are due to fixity with adjoining members or friction against any surface in contact (such as the earth, in the case of footings supporting walls). There is also internal restraint caused by the embedded steel resisting the free shrinkage of concrete. (It may be noted that such internal restraint does not occur in the case of thermal shrinkage, because the coefficient of thermal expansion for concrete and steel are approximately the same.) If the external restraints are absent, then drying shrinkage can generate a system of self-equilibrating forces, with the concrete in tension and the embedded steel in compression (with longitudinal bond forces at the interface). If the percentage of steel provided is relatively low, cracking of concrete is likely to occur, and the likelihood of such cracking is enhanced in the presence of external restraints.

Other Thermal Effects

There are two other factors that can contribute to thermal cracking. The first is due to seasonal variations in temperature, resulting in volume changes in the hardened concrete. When the season changes from summer to winter, thermal shrinkage occurs, and in the presence of restraints, this can result in cracking. The second factor is due to the differential temperature gradient caused by the action of the sun on the external surface of a slab or a wall, with the other surface relatively insulated ('solar radiation' effect). The presence of restraints restricts the free expansion of the external surface and induces flexural tension on the inner surface, causing possible cracking. The incidence of such cracking particularly needs to be controlled in structural elements such as walls of overhead water-tanks (whose liquid face is prone to cracking).

> Cracking can occur in large unreinforced exposed faces of concrete due to shrinkage and temperature variations. To control such cracks, Code (Cl. 26.5.1.3) requires minimum *side face reinforcements* (refer Section 5.2.2).

Methods of Crack Control and Crack-width Estimation

Cracking due to thermal and shrinkage effects can be effectively controlled by provision of (i) adequate reinforcement and (ii) appropriate 'movement joints', such as contraction and expansion joints [Figure 10.23]. The designer may choose to adopt closely spaced movement joints with low percentage of reinforcement, or widely spaced joints with a relatively high percentage of reinforcement. The choice is governed by factors such as the size of the structure, method of construction and economics [Ref. 10.20].

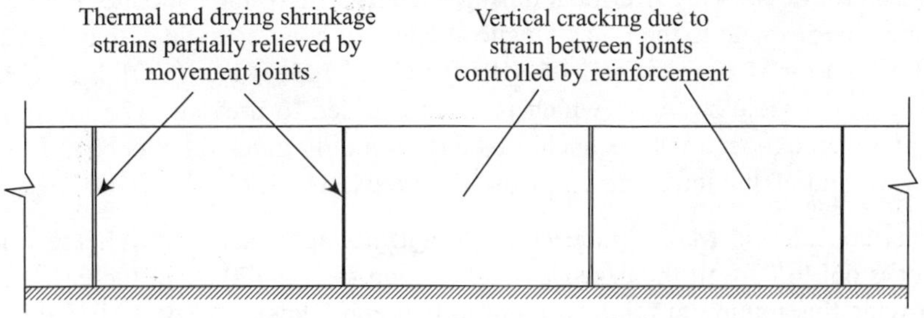

Fig. 10.23 Crack control in a base-restrained wall.

The methods of estimating crack-widths under flexure, direct tension and eccentric tension described earlier can be applied here, provided the magnitude of internal forces are known. Unfortunately, methods to estimate crack-width and spacing due to thermal and drying shrinkage are fraught with various uncertainties. These pertain, not only to uncertainties associated with temperature and shrinkage parameters as well as degree of restraint, but more important, to uncertainties associated with the tensile forces induced in the structure. These are 'deformation-induced forces', which get partially relieved on account of cracking. It would be very conservative to estimate these forces by the usual elastic structural analysis (including finite element analysis), considering all sections to be uncracked, as the tensile forces generated are likely to be high. It would indeed be appropriate to assign appropriate 'effective' stiffnesses (axial and flexural), taking into account the effect of tension stiffening, while performing the structural analysis. However, this is a nonlinear problem, as the amount of tension stiffening depends on the magnitude of internal forces, and these may vary from location to location. The designer must exercise good engineering judgement and caution in estimating the design forces for a maximum permissible crack-width. If the reinforcement provided is inadequate and movement joints are altogether absent, the consequences of thermal and shrinkage cracking can be alarming [Figure 10.24].

Fig. 10.24 Typical thermal and shrinkage cracks in a large reservoir structure. *Photo by Devdas Menon.*

In the case of structures such as water tanks, where crack-width control is of special importance, design codes attempt to achieve such control through guidelines relating to provision of movement joints and minimum reinforcement requirements [Ref. 10.20]. The absolute minimum reinforcement area $(A_{st})_{min}$ is usually governed by the consideration that the steel should not yield when cracking occurs (due to the ultimate tensile strength of concrete being exceeded). Accordingly, considering force equilibrium,

$$(A_{st})_{\min} f_y = A_g f_{ct}$$

$$\Rightarrow \quad (p_t)_{cr} \equiv 100\frac{(A_{st})_{\min}}{A_g} = 100\frac{f_{ct}}{f_y} \qquad (10.43)$$

where $(p_t)_{cr}$ is called the 'critical percentage reinforcement', f_{ct} and f_y denote the limiting tensile strength of concrete and yield strength of steel respectively, and A_g denotes the gross area of the cross-section under consideration. As control of cracking is critical during the early life of the concrete, it is recommended that the value of f_{ct} should correspond to the 3-day tensile strength of concrete, which may be taken as 1.15 MPa for M 25 grade, 1.3 MPa for M 30 grade and 1.6 MPa for M 35 grade [Ref. 10.20]. Eq. 10.43 assumes stress in reinforcement reaching yield strength, which is to be avoided to prevent opening up of cracks due to yielding of steel at the crack locations. As such, this equation only gives the theoretical lower limit for the grade of concrete, without taking into account loads and safety factors.

Thus, for example, considering M 25 grade concrete and a safety factor of 1.5, the critical percentage reinforcement works out to 0.42 in the case of Fe 415 grade steel and 0.69 in the case of Fe 250 steel. It is desirable to provide this minimum reinforcement in two equal layers (in each direction) with minimum cover (from durability point-of-view), and if the member (wall or slab) is very thick (thicker than 600 mm), the calculations may be based on a maximum thickness of 600 mm (i.e., considering only 300 mm on either surface). However, additional reinforcement is called for if movement joints are not provided in large structures, or if high crack-width control is desired. A minimum value of 0.65% is suggested in Ref. 10.28 (referred to in ACI 350), based on considerations of drying shrinkage alone. For large continuous constructions, without expansion joints, this value may be as high as 1.0%, to include the effect of other temperature effects, in the absence of more rigorous analysis.

Finally, it may be mentioned that recent trends in concrete technology suggest that 'high performance concrete' with new materials such as high-volume fly ash (HVFA) have the advantage of well-bonded micro-structure with relatively low potential for shrinkage and thermal cracking [Ref. 10.29]. Such materials, which are also 'sustainable' (low cement consumption), are likely to be used widely in the decades to come.

REVIEW QUESTIONS

10.1 Explain the importance of serviceability limit states in the structural design of reinforced concrete flexural members.

10.2 Is it necessary to limit deflections in reinforced concrete flexural members? Give your reasons.

10.3 Discuss why is it difficult to make an accurate prediction of (a) the total deflection, (b) the maximum crack-width in a reinforced concrete flexural member.

10.4 Distinguish between *short-term* deflection and *long-term* deflection.

10.5 What is meant by the *tension stiffening effect* in reinforced concrete members subject to flexure? Explain with suitable sketches.

10.6 How is the short-term deflection due to live loads alone estimated? What is its relevance?

10.7 Explain the difficulty in estimating the short-term deflection as per IS Code procedure when the applied moment at service loads is marginally less than the cracking moment (calculated using the modulus of rupture of concrete).

10.8 Explain briefly the BS Code procedure of estimating short-term deflections using the concept of 'effective curvature'.

10.9 Discuss how does shrinkage of concrete lead to deflections in reinforced concrete flexural members.

10.10 Does the magnitude of compression reinforcement affect deflections due to (a) shrinkage (b) creep? How?

10.11 Explain the Code procedure for calculating deflection due to creep.

10.12 Explain how temperature effects lead to deflections in reinforced concrete flexural members.

10.13 What are the different options available to a designer with regard to control of cracking in flexural members?

10.14 Explain the major factors which influence crack-widths in flexural members.

10.15 The Code does not call for explicit checks on the serviceability limit states of deflection provided certain requirements are complied with in the design. What are these requirements?

10.16 Are the nominal detailing requirements of the Code adequate for ensuring crack-width control? Comment.

10.17 Discuss the issues involved in designing for achieving control over thermal and shrinkage cracking in large RC structures.

PROBLEMS

10.1 The section of a cantilever beam, designed for a span of 4.0 m is shown in Figure 10.25. The beam has been designed for a bending moment of 200 kNm (at the support) under service loads, of which 60 per cent is due to permanent (dead) loads. The loading is uniformly distributed on the span. Assume M 25 concrete and Fe 500 steel.

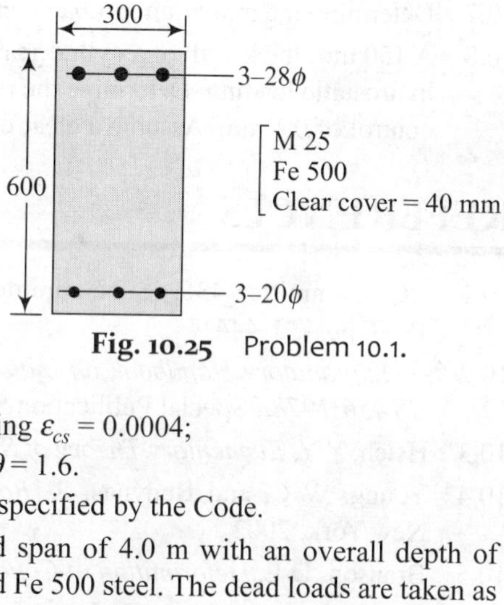

Fig. 10.25 Problem 10.1.

(a) Calculate
   (i) the maximum short-term elastic deflection;
   (ii) the short-term deflection due to live loads alone;
   (iii) the maximum deflection due to shrinkage, assuming $\varepsilon_{cs} = 0.0004$;
   (iv) the maximum deflection due to creep, assuming $\theta = 1.6$.

(b) Check whether the beam satisfies the deflection limits specified by the Code.

10.2 A one-way slab has been designed for a simply supported span of 4.0 m with an overall depth of 170 mm and clear cover of 20 mm, using M 25 concrete and Fe 500 steel. The dead loads are taken as 5.0 kN/m^2 and the live loads as 2.0 kN/m^2. The longitudinal bars are designed as 10 mm ϕ @ 150 c/c. Verify the adequacy of the thickness provided,
   (i) applying the limiting span/effective depth ratio;
   (ii) actual calculation of total deflections.

10.3 For the T-beam designed in Example 5.5, calculate the following:
   (i) short-term deflection due to service loads;
   (ii) incremental short-term deflection due to live loads;
   (iii) long-term deflection due to shrinkage;
   (iv) long-term deflection due to creep.

Hence, verify whether the design satisfies the Code limits on deflection.

10.4 Repeat Problem 10.3 for the continuous T-beam designed in Example 5.6. Assume that 60 per cent of the loading is due to dead (permanent) loads. Also assume that the moments at the two supports are equal to the midspan moment of 533.3 kNm (under service loads) and that the reinforcement provided at the support section is as shown in Figure 10.26.

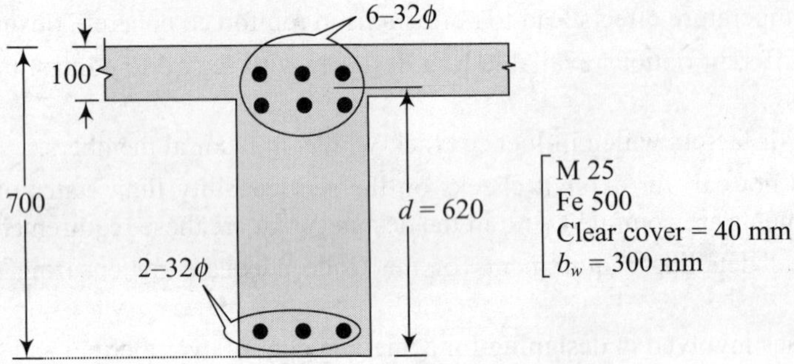

Fig. 10.26 Problem 10.4 – support section.

10.5 Determine the maximum probable crack-width for the cantilever beam of Problem 10.1

10.6 Determine the maximum probable crack-width for the one-way slab of Problem 10.2.

10.7 Determine the maximum probable crack-width for the T-beam of Problem 10.3.

10.8 A 150 mm thick wall of a cylindrical water tank is subject to a direct tensile force of 270 kN/m due to hydrostatic loading. Determine the required spacing of 12 mm dia bars in order to achieve crack-width control of 0.1 mm. Assume a clear cover of 40 mm, M 30 concrete and Fe 500 steel.

REFERENCES

10.1 ACI Committee 435, (Subcommittee 1), *Allowable Deflections*, Journal ACI, Vol. 65, No. 6, June 1968, pp 433–444

10.2 — *Explanatory Handbook on Indian Standard Code of Practice for Plain and Reinforced Concrete (IS 456:1978)*, Special Publication SP:24, Bureau of Indian Standards, New Delhi, 1983

10.3 Hsieh, Y Y, *Elementary Theory of Structures*, Prentice Hall, Inc., New Jersey, 1970

10.4 Young, W C, and Budynas, R, *Roark's Formulas for Stress and Strain*, McGraw-Hill Book Co., New York, 2002

10.5 Branson, D E, *Deformation of Concrete Structures*, McGraw-Hill Inc., New York, 1977

10.6 Yu, W W, and Winter, G, *Instantaneous and Long-time Deflections of Reinforced Concrete Beams under Working Loads*, Journal ACI, Vol. 57, No. 1, July 1960, pp 29–50

10.7 ACI Committee 435, *Deflections of Reinforced Concrete Flexural Members*, Journal ACI, Vol. 63, No. 6, June 1966, pp 637–674

10.8 Beeby, A W, and Miles, J R, *Proposals for the Control of Deflection in the New Unified Code*, Concrete, Vol. 3, March 1969, pp 101–110

10.9 Rao, P S and Subrahmanyam, B V, *Trisegmental Moment-Curvature Relations for Reinforced Concrete Members*, Journal ACI, May 1973, No. 70–39, pp 346–352

10.10 CEB–FIP, *International Recommandations for the Design and Construction of Concrete Structures*, Comité Européen du Béton–Fédération Internationale de la Précontrainte, Paris, 1970

10.11 Prakhya, G K V, and Morely, C T, *Tension Stiffening and Moment-Curvature Relations of Reinforced Concrete Elements*, Journal ACI, Vol. 87, Sept.–Oct. 1990, pp 597–602

10.12 — *Structural Use of Concrete: Part 2: Code of Practice for Special Circumstances*, BS 8110: Part 2: 1985, British Standards Institution, 1985

10.13 — *Commentary on Building Code Requirements for Reinforced Concrete* ACI 318R–05, American Concrete Institute, Detroit, 2005

10.14 CSA Standard A23.3 –04 — *Design of Concrete Structures*, Canadian Standards Association, Mississauga, Ontario, 2004

10.15 ACI Committee 435, *Deflections of Continuous Concrete Beams*, Journal ACI, Vol. 70, No. 12, Dec. 1973, pp 781–787

10.16 ACI Committee 209, *Prediction of Creep, Shrinkage and Temperature Effects in Concrete Structures*, SP–27, Am. Conc. Inst., Detroit, Michigan, USA, 1971, pp 51–93

10.17 ACI Committee 435, *Proposed Revisions by Committee* 435 to ACI *Building Code and Commentary Provisions on Deflections*, Journal of ACI, Vol. 75, No. 6, June 1978, pp 229–238

10.18 ACI Committee 224, *Control of Cracking in Concrete Structures*, Journal ACI, Vol. 69, No. 12, Dec. 1972, pp 717–753

10.19 BS 8007 : 1987 — *Design of Concrete Structures for Retaining Aqueous Liquids*, British Standards Institution, London, 1987

10.20 Anchor, R D, *Design of Liquid Retaining Concrete Structures*, Second edition, Edward Arnold Publishers, London, 1992

10.21 Gouthaman, A and Menon, D, *Increased Cover Specifications in IS 456 (2000) – Crack-width Implications in RC Slabs*, Indian Concrete Journal, Sept. 2001, pp 581–586

10.22 Mosley, W H, Bungey, J.H. and Hulse, R., *Reinforced Concrete Design*, Fifth edition, Macmillan Press Ltd, London, 1999

10.23 Gergely, P and Lutz, L A, *Maximum Crack Width in Reinforced Concrete Flexural Members*, Causes, Mechanism, and Control of Cracking in Concrete, (SP–20), American Concrete Institute, Detroit, 1968, pp 87–117

10.24 Ganesan, N and Shivananda, K P, *Comparison of International Codes for the Prediction of Maximum Width of Cracks in Reinforced Concrete Flexural Members*, Indian Concrete Journal, November 1996, pp 635– 641

10.25 Srinivas, N and Menon, D, *Design Criteria for Crack Control in RC Liquid Retaining Structures – Need for a Revision of IS 3370 (Part II) 1965*, Indian Concrete Journal, Aug. 2001, pp 451–458.

10.26 ACI Committee 224, *Cracking of Concrete Members in Direct Tension*, Journal ACI, Vol. 83, No. 1, Jan-Feb. 1986, pp 3–13

10.27 Fitzgibbon, M E, *Continuous Casting of Concrete,* in "*New Concrete Technologies and Building Design*", ed. Neville, A.M., The Construction Press, 1979

10.28 Vetter, C P, *Stresses in Reinforced Concrete Due to Volume Changes*, Transactions, ASCE, Vol. 98, 1933, pp 1039–1053.

10.29 Mehta, P K, *Concrete Durability: Critical Issues for the Future*, Concrete International, Vol. 19, No. 7, 1997, pp. 27–33

CHAPTER 11

Design of Two-Way Slab Systems

LEARNING OBJECTIVES

After studying this chapter, you will be able to:

- *Describe the structural behaviour of wall-supported, beam-supported and column-supported two-way slabs*
- *Use different methods to compute design moments in two-way slab systems*
- *Interpret the Code provisions for all types of two-way slabs*
- *Design column-supported slabs for shear, and provide for structural integrity*
- *Undertake limit analysis of continuous beams and yield line analysis of slabs*

11.1 Introduction

Slab panels that deform with significant curvatures in two orthogonal directions must be designed as *two-way slabs*, with the principal reinforcement placed in the two directions.

This chapter deals with the design of rectangular two-way slab systems [refer Section 1.6.1], and includes:

- slabs supported on walls (or rigid beams);
- slabs supported on flexible beams; and
- slabs supported directly on columns ('flat plates' and 'flat slabs').

'One-way' slabs are slabs bending with significant curvature, and hence primary moment, only in one direction (ideally, deforming into a cylindrical surface). They are designed for primary moment, considering a typical one-metre-wide strip as a beam. Reinforcements are provided for secondary moments in the transverse direction.

11.1.1 One-Way and Two-Way Actions of Slabs

The design of *one-way* slabs (simply supported/continuous/cantilevered) has already been described in Chapter 5. It was pointed out that 'one-way' action may be assumed when the predominant mode of flexure is in *one* direction alone. Rectangular slabs which are supported only on two opposite sides by unyielding (wall) supports and are uniformly loaded (uniform along the direction parallel to the supports) provide examples of ideal one-way action [Figure 11.1(a)]. The initially plane surface of the slab deforms into a cylindrical surface†, in which curvatures (and hence, primary bending moments) develop only in one direction. For the purpose of analysis and design, the slab may be divided into a parallel series of identical one-way beam-strips, with the *primary* reinforcement placed (with uniform spacing) along each strip [refer Section 4.8]. Some nominal *secondary* reinforcement should also be placed in the perpendicular direction (normal to the beam-strip span) – to take care of tensile stresses that arise due to the secondary bending moments in this direction caused by the Poisson effect [Ref. 11.1], any non-uniform (or concentrated) loading, and temperature and shrinkage effects.

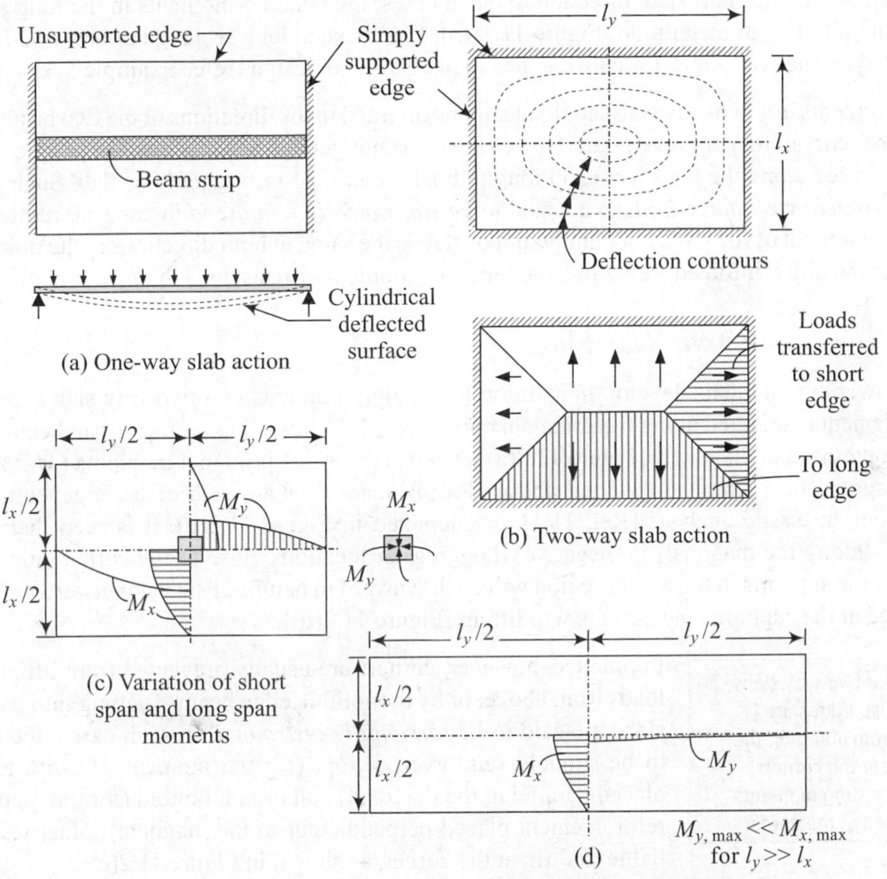

Fig. 11.1 One-way and two-way slab actions.

This primary one-way action [Figure 11.1(a)] ceases to exist if either the support conditions or the loading conditions are altered. For example, if the uniformly loaded rectangular slab of Figure 11.1(a) is supported on all four edges, then the deformed surface of the slab will be *doubly curved*, with the load effects transferred to all the four supporting edges [Figure 11.1(b)].

> **'Two-way' slabs are those with significant curvature, and hence bending moments, in two orthogonal directions.**

† Within the elastic phase, when a plate bends into a *cylindrical* surface, although the curvature in the direction parallel to the axis of the cylinder is zero, the bending moment in this direction is not zero, but is equal to υ times the moment in the direction of the curvature, where υ is the Poisson's ratio of the material of the plate (see also Section 4.8).

Such action is called a *two-way* action, involving significant curvatures along the two principal orthogonal directions. The typical variations of longitudinal and transverse bending moments are depicted in Figure 11.1(c). For the simply supported boundary conditions shown, the bending moments are maximum at the middle of the slab in both directions. Of the two principal moments (M_x, M_y) at the middle point, the one (M_x) along the short span (l_x) is invariably greater, on account of the larger curvature[†].

As the 'aspect ratio' l_y/l_x (i.e., long span/short span) increases, the curvatures and moments along the long span progressively reduce, and more and more of the slab load is transferred to the two long supporting edges by bending in the short span direction. In such cases, the bending moments in the long span direction (M_y) are generally low in magnitude [Figure 11.1(d)]. Hence, such long rectangular slabs ($l_y/l_x > 2$) may be approximated as one-way slabs, for convenience in analysis and design [refer Example 5.3].

The reinforcements in a two-way slab should ideally be oriented in the directions of the two principal moments (i.e., principal curvatures) at every point. However, this is not generally convenient in practice, and the bars are usually placed along the transverse and longitudinal directions[‡] throughout the slab. Such slabs are said to be *orthotropically reinforced.* Slabs are said to be *isotropically reinforced* in case the reinforcements are such that the moment of resistance per unit width of slab is the same in both directions at the point considered. Indeed, isotropically reinforced slab will have the same moment of resistance in *any* direction.

11.1.2 Torsion in Two-Way Slabs

In general, twisting moments develop in addition to bending moments in a two-way slab element – except when the element is oriented along the principal curvatures. These twisting moments can become significant at points along the slab diagonals [Figure 11.2(a)]. The variations of principal moments (M_1, M_2) along and across a diagonal of a simply supported and uniformly loaded square slab of homogeneous material, as obtained from an elastic analysis [Ref. 11.1], are depicted in Figure 11.2(b). It is seen that the principal moment M_1 (along the diagonal) is 'negative' (hogging) at locations close to the corner, and the reactions developed at the supports in the corner region will be downward in nature. If such downward reactions cannot be developed at the supports, the corners will lift up [Figure 11.2(d)].

> **In rectangular two-way slabs, where the slab edges are prevented from lifting off the supports (near the corners) significant twisting moments are developed at the corners.**

In practice, however, corners are usually prevented from lifting up (by wall loads from above, or by monolithic edge beams framing into columns); such slabs are said to be *torsionally restrained.* In such cases, the corners have to be suitably reinforced at top, (for the moment M_1 with reinforcement placed parallel to the diagonal) and also at bottom (for the moment M_2 with reinforcement placed perpendicular to the diagonal); otherwise, cracks are liable to form at the corner, as shown in Figure 11.2(c).

11.1.3 Difference between Wall-Supported Slabs and Beam/Column Supported Slabs

The distributed load w on a typical two-way slab is transmitted partly (w_x) along the short span to the long edge supports, and partly (w_y) along the long span to the short edge supports. In *wall-supported* panels, these portions (w_x, w_y) of the load are transmitted by the respective wall supports directly to their foundations

[†] Assuming linear elastic behaviour, the bending moment along any principal direction is given by the product of the *plate rigidity* (which is similar to *flexural rigidity* in a beam, but also includes a Poisson's ratio contribution) and the curvature along that direction, according to plate theory [Ref. 11.1].

[‡] It may be noted that an orthogonally placed set of reinforcing bars in a slab is capable of generating flexural strength in any direction.

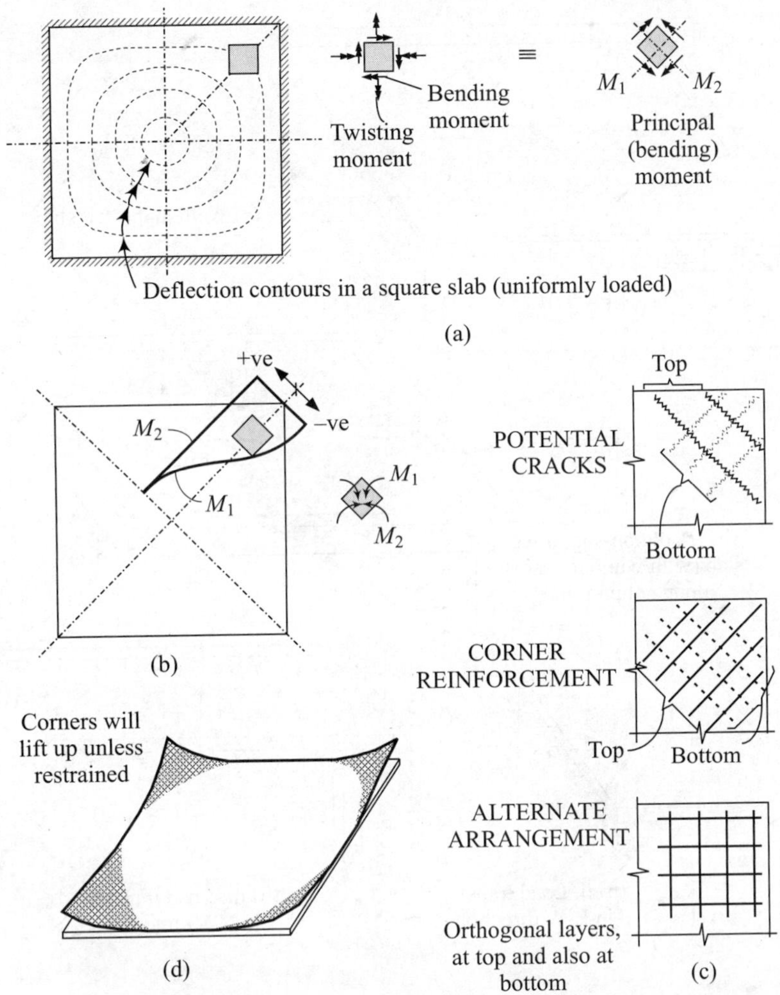

Fig. 11.2 Torsion effects in a two-way slab.

(or other supports) vertically below, as shown in Figure 11.3(a). On the contrary, when the edge supports comprise beams spanning between columns, the portion of the load transmitted by the slab in any one direction is in turn transmitted by the beam in the perpendicular direction to the two supporting columns, as shown in Figure 11.3(b) i.

In general, in *column-supported* slabs, with or without beams along the column lines, 100 per cent of the slab load has to be transmitted by the floor system in *both directions* (transverse and longitudinal) towards the columns (Figure 11.3(b) ii & iii). In such cases, the entire floor system and the columns act integrally in two-way frame action. The analysis of such systems is described in Section 11.4.

> In column-supported slabs, the floor system (slab together with beams, if any) has to transfer the full floor load in both longitudinal and transverse directions.

It may be noted, however, that if beams are provided along the column lines, and if these beams are sufficiently rigid, then the analysis and design of the slab part can be considered separately and treated in same manner as wall-supported slabs.

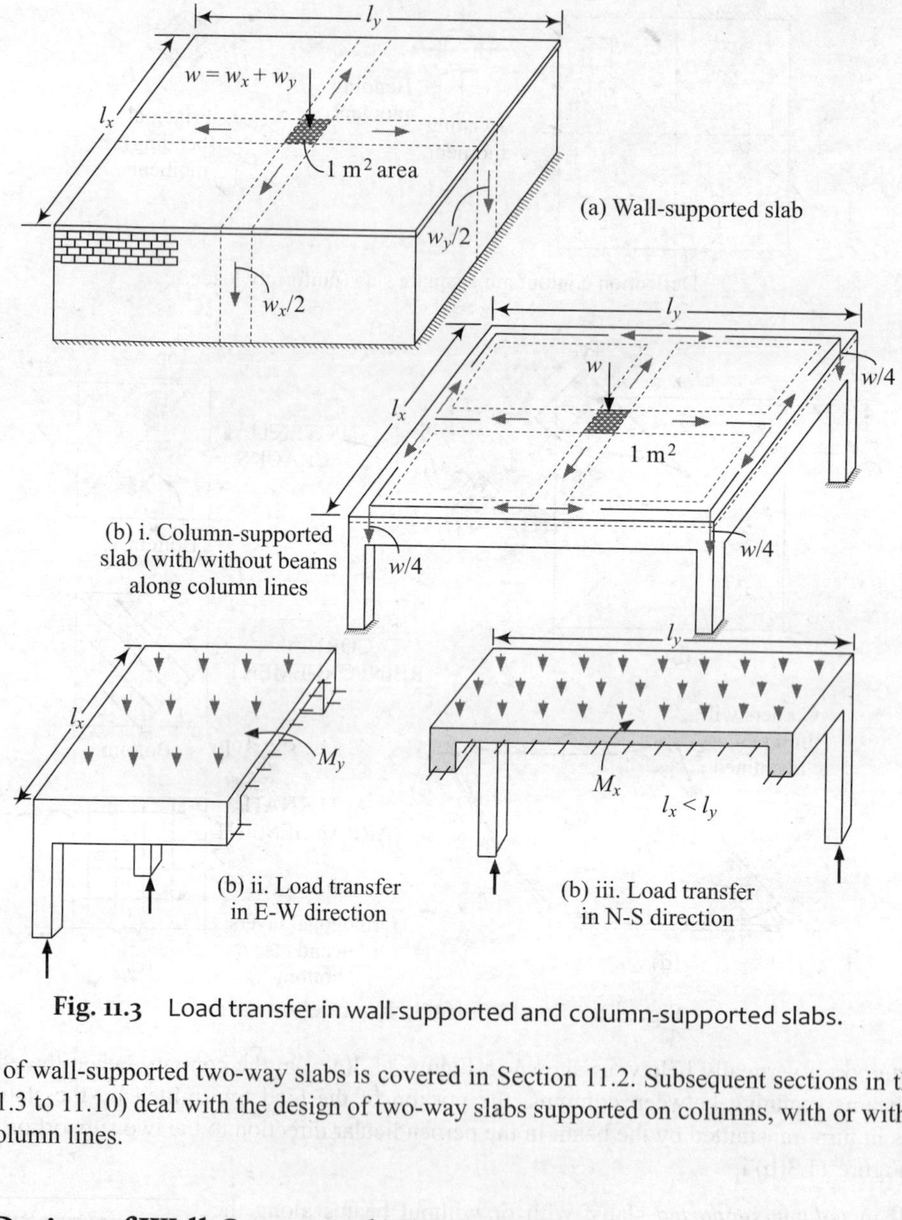

Fig. 11.3 Load transfer in wall-supported and column-supported slabs.

The design of wall-supported two-way slabs is covered in Section 11.2. Subsequent sections in this chapter (Sections 11.3 to 11.10) deal with the design of two-way slabs supported on columns, with or without beams along the column lines.

11.2 Design of Wall-Supported Two-Way Slabs

The design considerations of wall-supported two-way slabs are similar to those pertaining to one-way slabs [refer Chapter 5]. The thickness of the slab is generally based on deflection control criteria, and the reinforcements in the two orthogonal directions are designed to resist the calculated maximum bending moments in the respective directions at the critical sections. [Additional reinforcement may be required at the corners of two-way slabs in some cases, as explained later]. The slab thickness should be sufficient against shear, although shear is usually not a problem in two-way slabs subjected to uniformly distributed loads.

11.2.1 Slab Thickness Based on Deflection Control Criterion

In two-way slabs, the slab depth is generally dictated by deflection control requirements, rather than the flexural strength requirements.

The initial proportioning of the slab thickness may be done by adopting the same guidelines regarding span/effective depth ratios, as applicable in the case of one-way slabs [refer Chapter 5]. The effective span in the *short span* direction should be considered for this purpose. However, the percentage tension reinforcement requirement in the short span direction for a two-way slab is likely to be less than that required for a one-way slab with the same effective span. Hence, the modification factor k_t to be considered for two-way slabs may be taken to be higher than that recommended for one-way slabs [refer Section 5.4.2]. A value of $k_t \approx 1.5$ may be considered for preliminary design. The adequacy of the effective depth provided should be verified subsequently, based on the actual p_t provided.

For the special case of two-way slabs with spans up to 3.5 m and live loads not exceeding 3.0 kN/m^2, the Code(Cl. 24.1, Note 2) permits the slab thickness (overall depth D) to be calculated directly as follows, without the need for subsequent checks on deflection control:

(i) using mild steel (Fe 250 grade),

$$D \geq \begin{cases} l_x/35 & \text{for simply supported slabs} \\ l_x/40 & \text{for continuous slabs} \end{cases} \tag{11.1a}$$

(ii) using Fe 415 grade steel,

$$D \geq \begin{cases} l_x/28 & \text{for simply supported slabs} \\ l_x/32 & \text{for continuous slabs} \end{cases} \tag{11.1b}$$

11.2.2 Methods of Analysis

Over the years, several methods have been developed (Navier and Levy, Westergaard, Rankine-Grashoff, etc.,) and adopted by different codes, most of them simplified to the readily usable format of moment coefficients.

Two-way slabs are highly statically indeterminate†. They may be visualised as being composed of intersecting, closely-spaced grid beam-strips which are subject to flexure, torsion and shear. Owing to the high static indeterminacy, rigorous ('exact') solutions are not generally available. The available solutions, based on the classical theory of plates [Ref. 11.1], for such standard problems as simply supported and uniformly loaded two-way slabs (due to Navier and Levy), need modification to accommodate the differences observed experimentally on account of the non-homogeneous and nonlinear behaviour of concrete. Such solutions have been proposed by Westergaard [Ref. 11.2, 11.3] and others [Ref. 11.4] in the form of convenient moment coefficients, which have been widely used by codes all over the world. Another approximate method, very elementary in approach, is the so-called Rankine-Grashoff method. The main feature of this method is that it simplifies a highly indeterminate problem to an equivalent simple determinate one. This method, as well as its modified version due to Marcus [Ref. 11.5, 11.6] have also been widely in use during the past five decades. Modern computer-based methods include the *finite difference method* [Ref. 11.5] and the *finite element method* [Ref. 11.7]. Other methods, which are particularly suited for limit state design, and are relatively simple, are *inelastic* methods based on *yield line analysis* [Ref. 11.8–11.10], discussed in Section 11.10.

† It should be noted that on account of the multiple load paths possible, two-way slabs are capable of considerable stress redistribution. Hence, the reinforcements in such slabs can be designed in many different ways.

The Code permits '*any acceptable theory*' for the determination of design moments in two-way slabs. Further, for slabs with unyielding supports and carrying uniformly distributed load, the Code gives moment coefficients for rectangular slabs with various support/boundary conditions (refer Sections 11.2.3 and 11.2.4).

According to the Code (Cl. 24.4), two-way slabs may be designed *by any acceptable theory*. In the case of uniformly loaded two-way rectangular slabs, the Code suggests design procedures for

- simply supported slabs whose corners are not restrained from lifting up [Cl. D–2 of the Code].; and
- 'torsionally restrained' slabs, whose corners are restrained from lifting up and whose edges may be continuous or discontinuous [Cl. D–1 of the Code].

Even if relatively stiff beams are provided in rectangular column-supported slabs with beams between the columns, the assumption that the behaviour is akin to wall-supported slabs begins to be questionable when the slab aspect ratio is about 2.0 or more. The use of moment coefficients of the Code is likely to result in under-estimation of the slab moments in the long span direction.

Consider for example a slab aspect ratio exceeding 2.0 (say, 2.5 or 3.0). Such a slab would be normally designed as a one-way slab, and if so, only minimal 'distribution steel' is likely to be provided in the long span direction. However, a more accurate analysis of the beam-slab floor – such as by finite element method or equivalent frame method – will reveal that the long span moment at the slab centre can be quite significant and comparable to the short span moment. [This can also be deduced from the equilibrium conditions of the two one-half segments of the column-supported beam-slab floor shown in Figures 11.3(b)ii and (b)iii. With the aspect ratio l_y/l_x in excess of 2, the *total* moment to be resisted by the *beam and slab* together in the long span direction, M_y {Figure 11.3(b)ii}, is far greater than that in the short direction, M_x {Figure 11.3(b)iii}; while the width of the beam-slab section to resist M_y is lesser ($l_x < l_y$). Roughly, $(M_y/M_x) \alpha (l_y/l_x)^2$]. There is the real possibility of flexural cracks developing under service loads near the slab centre along the short span direction on account of inadequate reinforcement placed in the long span direction. The cracking is likely to be more severe if the supporting edge beams are inverted (as in some cases in practice), on account of the presence of longitudinal (flexural) tension due to flanged beam action. At ultimate loads, plastic hinges may form at the middle of the long span beams, leading to increased deflections and curvatures and, eventually, a yield line formation in the slab as well. With the beams forming plastic hinges and the slab developing yield lines, ultimate failure may result with the formation of a combined beam-slab collapse mechanism (one-way bending in the long span direction). This is different from the typical failure mode of a one-way slab on wall supports, which is also expected with stiff-beam supports. However, if the beams have excessive flexural strength relative to the slab, the slab may fail in the yield line failure mode typical for wall-supported slabs. Nonlinear analysis, such as yield line analysis, is discussed in Section 11.10.

In general, caution needs to be applied while applying moment coefficients (developed for *wall-supported* slabs) to *column-supported slabs* (even with relatively stiff beams between columns), particularly for slabs with high aspect ratios. It would be prudent to carry out a more accurate linear elastic analysis at service loads using Finite Element Analysis (Section 11.2.3) or the Equivalent Frame concept (Section 11.2.4), and Yield Line Analysis (or Nonlinear Finite Element Analysis) at ultimate loads (Section 11.2.6). This will ensure compliance with both serviceability and strength limit states requirements, and can provide for a rational and economical design.

11.2.3 Uniformly Loaded and Simply Supported Rectangular Slabs

The moment coefficients prescribed in the Code (Cl. D–2) to estimate the maximum moments (per unit width) in the short span and long span directions are based on the Rankine-Grashoff theory. According to this theory, the slab can be divided into a series of orthogonal crossing unit (beam) strips, and the load can be apportioned to the short span and long span strips such that the deflections δ of the two strips along the two centre-lines is the same at their intersection [Figure 11.4].

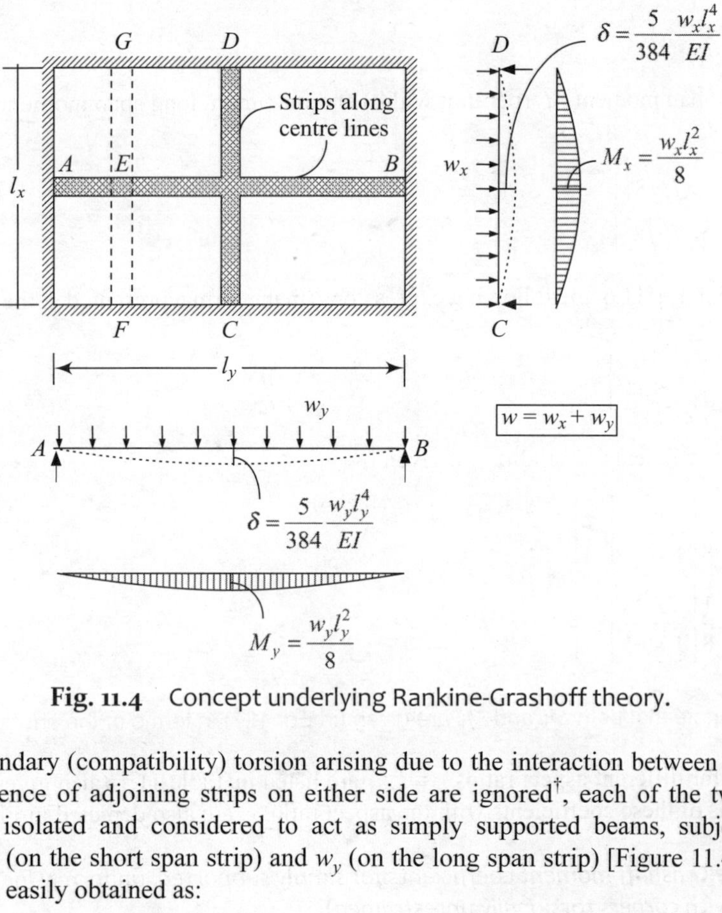

Fig. 11.4 Concept underlying Rankine-Grashoff theory.

If the effect of secondary (compatibility) torsion arising due to the interaction between the interconnecting strips and the influence of adjoining strips on either side are ignored†, each of the two strips along the centrelines can be isolated and considered to act as simply supported beams, subjected to uniformly distributed loads w_x (on the short span strip) and w_y (on the long span strip) [Figure 11.4]. Hence, the mid-point deflection δ is easily obtained as:

$$\delta = \frac{5}{384}\frac{w_x l_x^4}{EI} = \frac{5}{384}\frac{w_y l_y^4}{EI} \tag{11.2}$$

where it is assumed that the second moment of area, I, is the same for both strips. A simple relation between w_x and w_y is obtainable from Eq. 11.2:

$$w_x = w_y (l_y / l_x)^4 \tag{11.3}$$

† It should be noted that these assumptions lead to a high degree of approximation.

Also, in order to satisfy force equilibrium,

$$w_x + w_y = w \tag{11.4}$$

$$\Rightarrow \left.\begin{aligned} w_x &= w\left[\frac{r^4}{1+r^4}\right] \\ w_y &= w\left[\frac{1}{1+r^4}\right] \end{aligned}\right\} \tag{11.5}$$

where $r \equiv l_y/l_x$

The maximum short span moment M_x (per unit width) and maximum long span moment M_y (per unit width) are easily obtained as:

$$\left.\begin{aligned} M_x &= w_x l_x^2/8 \\ M_y &= w_y l_y^2/8 \end{aligned}\right\} \tag{11.6}$$

Substituting Eq. 11.5 in Eq. 11.6, the following expressions (in the format presented in the Code) are obtained:

$$\left.\begin{aligned} M_x &= \alpha_x \; w l_x^2 \\ M_y &= \alpha_y \; w l_x^2 \end{aligned}\right\} \tag{11.7}$$

where the 'moment coefficients' α_x and α_y are given by

$$\left.\begin{aligned} \alpha_x &= \frac{1}{8}\left[\frac{r^4}{1+r^4}\right] \\ \alpha_y &= \frac{1}{8}\left[\frac{r^2}{1+r^4}\right] \end{aligned}\right\} \tag{11.8}$$

It is important to note that both M_x and M_y are given (in Eq. 11.7) in terms of the short span l_x.

Values of α_x and α_y for different aspect ratios $r \equiv l_y/l_x$ are listed in Table 11.1 (also given in Table 27 of the Code). The variations of these coefficients with the aspect ratio, r, are also depicted in Figure 11.5.

Table 11.1 *Rankine-Grashoff moment coefficients for simply supported, uniformly loaded rectangular slabs (with corners torsionally unrestrained)*

l_y/l_x	1.0	1.1	1.2	1.3	1.4
α_x	0.0625	0.0743	0.0843	0.0926	0.0992
α_y	0.0625	0.0614	0.0586	0.0548	0.0506
l_y/l_x	1.5	1.75	2.0	2.5	3.0
α_x	0.1044	0.1130	0.1176	0.1219	0.1235
α_y	0.0464	0.0369	0.0294	0.0195	0.0137

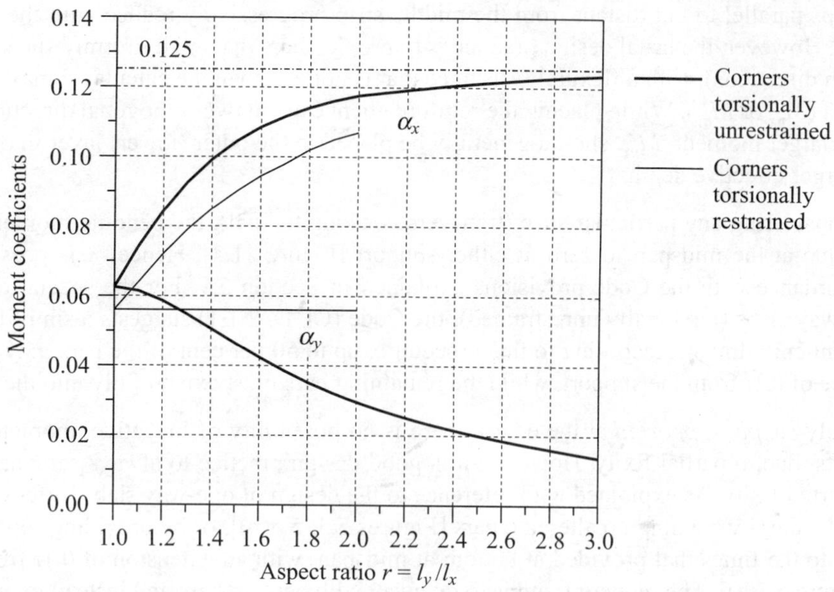

Fig. 11.5 Variation of IS Code moment coefficients α_x, α_y with l_y/l_x for simply supported and uniformly loaded rectangular slabs.

As expected, the short span moment coefficient progressively increases and the long span moment coefficient α_y progressively decreases as the aspect ratio r increases. In the case of a square slab ($l_y/l_x = 1$), $w_x = w_y = w/2$, and $M_x = M_y = \frac{1}{2}(wl_x^2/8) = 0.0625\, wl_x^2$. For high values of l_y/l_x, α_x approaches the 'one-way' value of 1/8 = 0.125 and α_y becomes negligible.

Also shown in Figure 11.5, by means of thinner lines, are the variations of α_x and α_y with r for the case of a rectangular slab with corners torsionally restrained (using Code moment coefficients). This is discussed in Section 11.2.4. It is evident that the corner restraints lead to a reduction in moment coefficients. With regard to the long span moment coefficient, the Code recommends a constant value of $\alpha_y \equiv 0.056$ for all aspect ratios [refer Figure 11.5].

It should be noted that the moments predicted by the Rankine-Grashoff theory are somewhat conservative because the effect of the restraint along the sides of the strips offered by the rest of the slab through torsion, transverse shear and moment are ignored. For example, the slope θ in the elastic curve of the longitudinal strip *AB* at *E* (Figure 11.4) is also the angle of twist at *E* of the transverse strip *GF*. Owing to the torsional stiffness of the strip *GF*, a twisting moment will develop at *E* in the transverse strip *GF* ('secondary torsion' – as explained in Chapter 7). The twisting moments thus developed in the various transverse strips (such as *GF, CD*) at the middle, due to the integral action with the longitudinal middle strip *AB*, effectively reduce the flexure in *AB*. Conversely, the bending in the transverse middle strip *CD* is reduced by torsion in the interconnecting longitudinal strips (parallel to *AB*). Thus, the treatment of strips such as *AB* and *CD* as *discrete strips* free of interaction from the rest of the slab results in conservative estimates of the design bending moments.

Detailing of Reinforcement

The flexural reinforcements in the two directions are provided to resist the maximum bending moments $M_{ux} = \alpha_x w_u l_x^2$ (in the short span) and $M_{uy} = \alpha_y w_u l_x^2$ (in the long span). The steel requirements at the midspan locations in strips parallel to but distant from the middle strip progressively reduce with the distance from the middle strip. However, the usual design practice is to provide bars that are uniformly spaced† throughout the span (in both directions), with a flexural resistance that is not less than the calculated maximum ultimate bending moment (M_{ux} or M_{uy}). While placing the reinforcement cage in two orthogonal directions, the rebars required for the larger moment, M_{ux}, should generally be placed in the outer (lower) layer in order to get the benefit of the larger effective depth.

Furthermore, considering any particular strip (transverse or longitudinal), the bending moment varies from a maximum value at the midspan to zero at either support [Figure 11.4]. Hence, it is possible to curtail the bars in accordance with the Code provisions explained in Section 5.9. For the special case of simply supported two-way slabs (torsionally unrestrained), the Code (Cl. D–2.1.1) suggests a simplified procedure for reinforcement curtailment. According to this procedure, up to 50 per cent of the bars may be terminated within a distance of $0.1l$ from the support, while the remaining bars must extend fully into the supports.

If the slab is truly *simply supported* at the edges, there is no possibility of 'negative' moments developing near the supports, due to partial fixity. However, it is good design practice to always safeguard against the possibility of partial fixity. As explained with reference to the design of one-way slabs [refer Chapter 5] this can be achieved either by bending up alternate bars [Figures 5.3, 5.5(b)], or by providing separate top steel, with area equal to 0.5 times that provided at bottom at midspan, with an extension of $0.1l$ from the face of the support [Figure 5.5(a)]. The modern trend is to do away with bent up bars and instead to opt for separate layers at top and bottom. This type of detailing is illustrated in Example 11.1 [Figure 11.14].

11.2.4 Uniformly Loaded 'Restrained' Rectangular Slabs

The Code (Cl. D–1) uses the term *restrained slabs* to refer to slabs whose corners are prevented from lifting and contain suitable reinforcement to resist torsion [Ref. 11.11]. All the four edges of the rectangular 'restrained' slab are assumed to be supported (tied down) rigidly against vertical translation, and the edges may be either continuous/fixed or discontinuous (simply supported). Accordingly, nine different configurations of restrained rectangular slab panels are possible (as shown in Figure 11.6), depending on the number of discontinuous edges (zero, one, two, three or four) and also depending on whether the discontinuous edge is 'short' or 'long'.

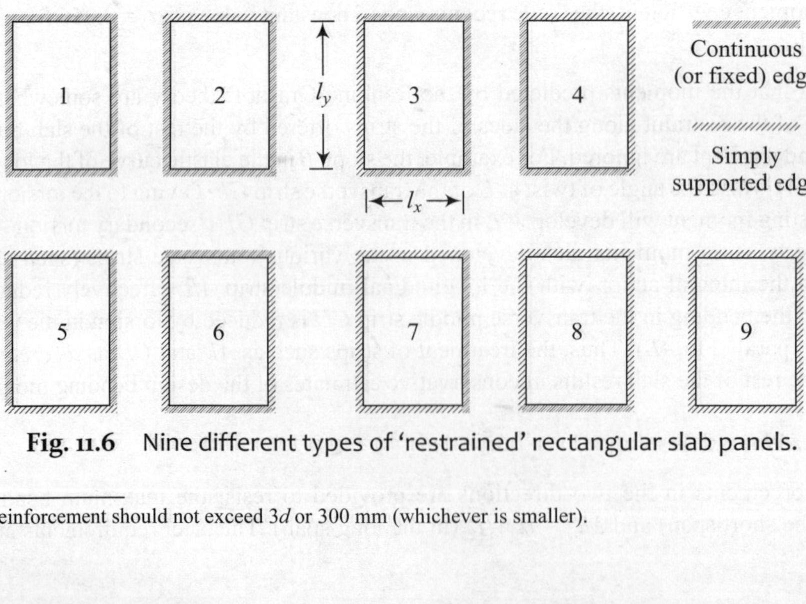

Fig. 11.6 Nine different types of 'restrained' rectangular slab panels.

† The spacing of reinforcement should not exceed $3d$ or 300 mm (whichever is smaller).

Panel type '1' corresponds to the slab with all four edges continuous/fixed, and panel type '9' corresponds to the slab with all four edges simply supported [Figure 11.6]. [Incidentally, there will be several more cases if combinations involving *free* (unsupported) edges are also considered].

The torsional restraint at the corner calls for the provision of special corner reinforcement, as explained earlier [refer Figure 11.2(c)]. The corner restraints have the beneficial effect of reducing the deflections and curvatures in the middle of the slab. Expressions for design moment coefficients for uniformly loaded two-way 'restrained' rectangular slabs with fixed or simply supported edge conditions, based on the classical theory of plates, are available [Ref. 11.1, 11.5, 11.6]. Approximate solutions based on the Rankine-Grashoff theory are also available. Modifications to these solutions were proposed by Marcus ('Marcus correction'), whereby the moment coefficients are reduced to account for the effects of torsional restraint at the corners, as well as torsional resistance of the transverse and longitudinal unit strips [Ref. 11.5]. For example, the 'Marcus correction' in the case of simply supported slabs, results in a reduction in the design moment M_x by about 42 per cent for $l_y/l_x = 1.0$ (square slab) and 9 per cent for $l_y/l_x = 3.0$, when compared to the slab with corners free to lift up [Table 11.1]; these results compare favourably with the rigorous solutions from elastic theory [Ref. 11.5].

However, the moment coefficients recommended in the Code (Cl. D–1) are based on *inelastic analysis* (yield line analysis is discussed in Section 11.10 at the end of this chapter), rather than elastic theory. This analysis is based on the following assumptions:

- the bottom steel in either direction is uniformly distributed over the 'middle strip' which spreads over 75 per cent of the span;
- the 'edge strip' lies on either side of the middle strip, and has a width equal to $l_x/8$ or $l_y/8$ [Figure 11.7];
- top steel is provided in the edge strip adjoining a continuous edge (and at right angles to the edge) such that the corresponding flexural strength (ultimate 'negative' moment capacity) is 4/3 times the corresponding ultimate 'positive' moment capacity due to the bottom steel provided in the middle strip in the direction under consideration;
- the corner reinforcement provided is sufficient to prevent the formation of 'corner levers', i.e., forking of diagonal yield lines near the corners.

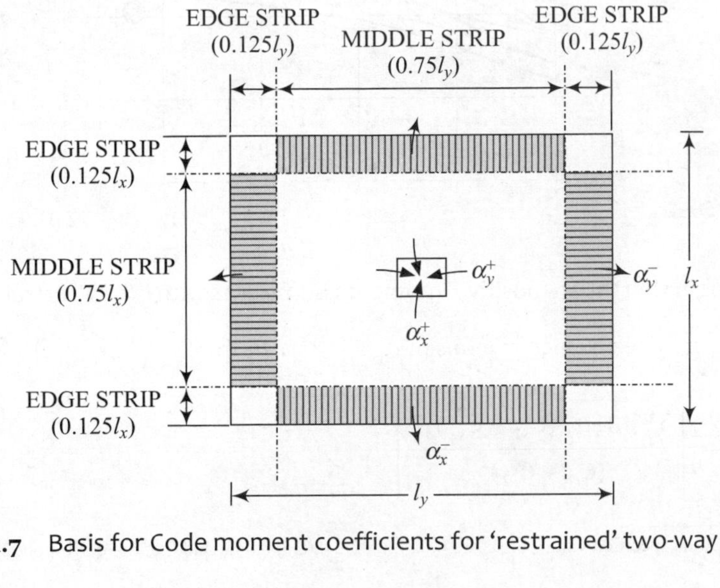

Fig. 11.7 Basis for Code moment coefficients for 'restrained' two-way slabs.

The resulting moment coefficients α_x^+, α_y^+ for 'positive' moments at midspans in the short span and long span directions respectively, and the coefficients α_x^-, α_y^- for 'negative' moments at the continuous edge(s) in the two directions, for the nine different sets of boundary conditions [Figurey-11.6] are listed in Table 26 of the Code. The design factored moment is obtained as

$$M_u = \alpha w_u l_x^2 \tag{11.9}$$

where w_u is the uniformly distributed factored load and l_x the effective short span and α is the appropriate moment coefficient.

'Positive' Moment Coefficients α_x^+, α_y^+

The variations of the short span 'positive' moment coefficient α_x^+, with l_y/l_x is plotted for the nine types of two-way slabs in Figure 11.8. In all cases, there is a marked increase in α_x^+ as l_y/l_x increases from 1.0 to 2.0. The Code recommends a constant value of α_y^+ for all values of l_y/l_x. The value of α_y^+ is obtainable from the following formula [Ref. 11.13]:

$$\alpha_y^+ = (24 + 2n_d + 1.5n_d^2)/1000 \tag{11.10}$$

where n_d denotes the number of discontinuous edges. Corresponding to $n_d = 0, 1, 2, 3$ and 4, the values of α_y^+ are obtained as 0.0240, 0.0275, 0.0340, 0.0435 and 0.0560 respectively†.

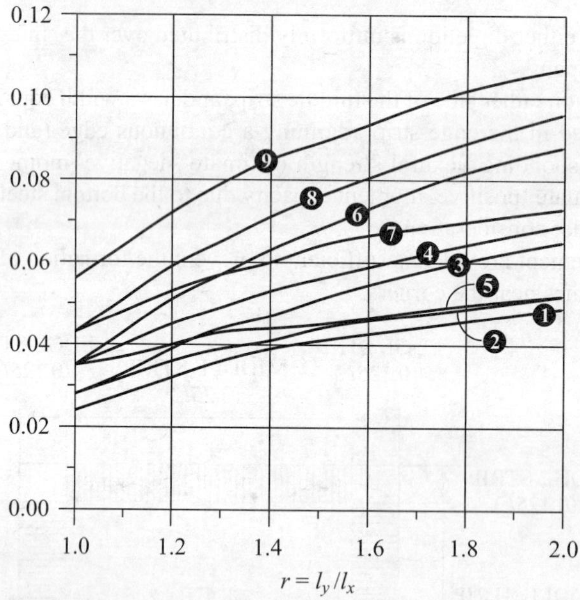

Fig. 11.8 Variations in short span 'positive' moment coefficients with l_y/l_x in 'restrained' two-way slabs.

An expression for α_x^+ may be obtained in terms of α_y^+ and $r \equiv l_y/l_x$ from yield line analysis [Ref. 11.12, 11.13] as follows:

$$\alpha_x^+ = \frac{2}{9}\left[\frac{3 - \sqrt{18\alpha_y^+ (C_{s1} + C_{s2})/r}}{(C_{l1} + C_{l2})^2}\right] \tag{11.11}$$

† In Table 26 of the Code, the specified values of α_y are 0.024, 0.028, 0.035, 0.043, and 0.056 – corresponding to $n_d = 0, 1, 2, 3$ and 4 respectively.

where

$$C = \begin{cases} 1 & \text{for a discontinuous edge} \\ \sqrt{7/3} & \text{for continuous edge} \end{cases} \tag{11.12}$$

and the subscripts s and l denote 'short edge' and 'long edge' respectively, while the additional subscripts '1' and '2' represent the two edges in either direction. Thus, for example, for the slab panel of type '4' ("two adjacent edges discontinuous"), $C_{s1} + C_{s2} = Cl_1 + Cl_2 = 1 + \sqrt{7/3} = 2.5275$. For such a case, $n_d = 2$; hence, applying Eq. 11.10, $\alpha_y^+ = 0.0340$. Further, applying Eq. 11.11,

$$\alpha_x^+ = \frac{2}{9}\left[\frac{3 - \sqrt{18 \times 0.034(2.5275)/r}}{(2.5275)^2}\right] = \frac{2}{9}\left[\frac{3 - 1.9773/r}{6.3884}\right]$$

This results in values of α_x^+ varying from 0.0356 (for $r = 1.0$) to 0.0700 (for $r = 2.0$); the corresponding values given in Table 26 of Code are 0.035 (for $r = 1.0$) and 0.069 (for $r = 2.0$).

Similarly, values of α_x^+ and α_y^+ can be easily obtained for any value of $r \equiv l_y/l_x$ in the range [1.0, 2.0] and given set of boundary conditions. If the value of l_y/l_x exceeds 2.0, the Code (Cl. D–1.11) recommends that the slab should be treated as *one-way* [refer Chapter 5]; the provision of the *secondary reinforcement* in the long span direction is expected to take care of the nominal bending moments that may arise in this direction.

'Negative' Moment Coefficients α_x^-, α_y^-

As explained earlier, the Code moment coefficients have been derived (using yield line analysis) with the basic assumption that the ultimate moment of resistance (for 'negative' moment) at a continuous support is 4/3 times the 'positive' moment capacity in the midspan region. Of course, at a discontinuous support, the 'negative' moment developed is zero[†]. Accordingly,

$$\alpha^- = \begin{cases} 0 & \text{at a discontinuous support} \\ \frac{4}{3}\alpha^+ & \text{at a continuous support} \end{cases} \tag{11.13}$$

Detailing of Flexural Reinforcement

- The bottom steel for the design moments (per unit width) $M_{ux}^+ = \alpha_x^+ w_u l_x^2$ and $M_{uy}^+ = \alpha_y^+ w_u l_x^2$ should be uniformly distributed across the 'middle strips' in the short span and long span directions respectively. The Code (Cl. D–1.4) recommends that these bars should extend to within $0.25l$ of a continuous edge or $0.15l$ of a discontinuous edge. It is recommended [Ref. 11.14] that alternate bars (bottom steel) should extend fully into the support, as shown in Figure 11.9.
- The top steel calculated for the design moments $M_{ux}^- = \alpha_x^- w_u l_x^2$ and $M_{uy}^- = \alpha_y^- w_u l_x^2$ at continuous supports should be uniformly distributed across the 'edge strips' in the long span and short span directions respectively. The Code (Cl. D–1.5) recommends that at least 50 per cent of these bars should extend to a distance of $0.3l$ from the face of the continuous support, on either side. The remaining bars may be curtailed at a distance of $0.15l$ from the face of the continuous support, as shown in Figure 11.9[‡].

---

† However, as explained earlier, the possibility of partial restraint must be considered at the time of detailing.

‡ In Figure 11.9, the top bars and bottom bars are shown as being separate. Alternatively, the bottom bars can be bent up to form the top steel, as shown in Figure 5.5.

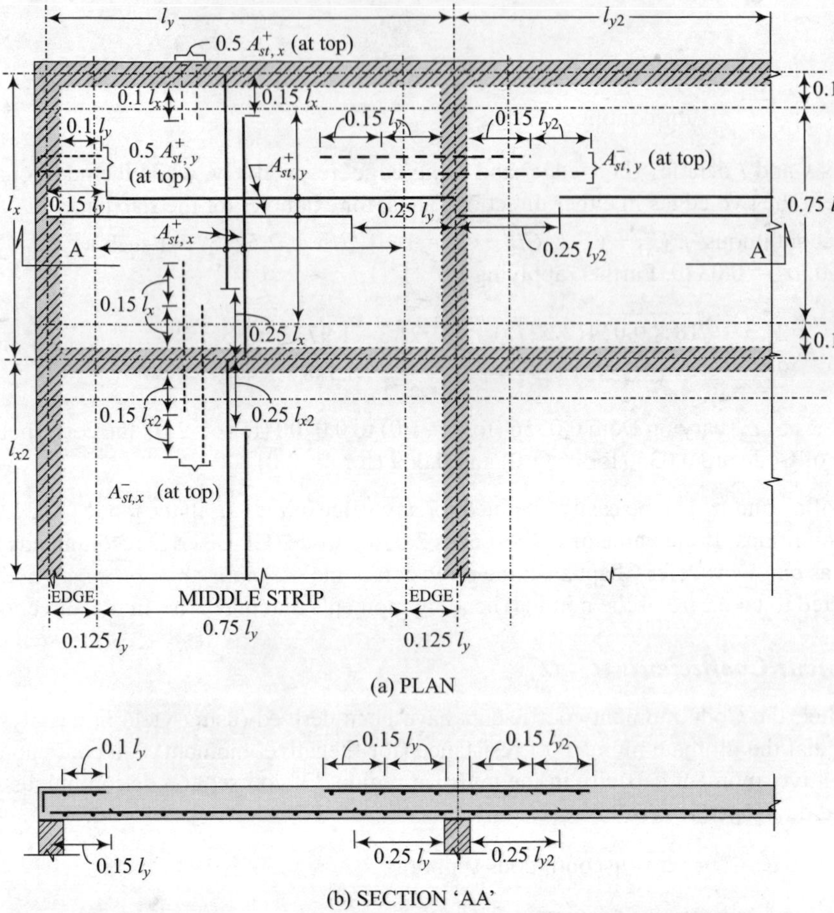

Fig. 11.9 Detailing of flexural reinforcement in two-way 'restrained' rectangular slabs† (excluding corner reinforcement).

- To safeguard against possible 'negative' moments at a discontinuous edge due to partial fixity, the Code (Cl. D–1.6) recommends that top steel with area equal to 50 per cent of that of the bottom steel at mid-span (in the same direction) should be provided, extending over a length of $0.1l$, as shown in Figure 11.9.
- In the edge strip, distribution bars parallel to that edge (conforming to the minimum requirements specified in Section 5.2) should be provided – at top and bottom – to tie up with the main bars [Figure 11.9].

Detailing of Torsional Reinforcement at Corners

Corners of rectangular slabs with discontinuous edge(s) need torsional reinforcement.

Torsional reinforcement is required at the corners of rectangular slab panels whose edges are discontinuous. This can conveniently be provided in the form of a mesh (or grid pattern) at top and bottom. The bars can be made

† For convenience in estimating lengths of bars and locations of bar cut-off points, l_x and l_y may be taken as the spans, measured centre-to-centre of supports.

U-shaped (wherever convenient) and provided in the two orthogonal directions as shown in Figure 11.10 [Ref. 11.14]. The Code (Cl. D–1.8) recommends that the mesh should extend beyond the edge† over a distance not less than one-fifth of the shorter span (l_x). The total area of steel to be provided in *each* of the four layers should be not less than:

- 0.75 $A^{+}_{st,x}$ if both edges meeting at the corner are discontinuous;
- 0.375 $A^{+}_{st,x}$ if one edge is continuous and the other discontinuous.

Here, $A^{+}_{st,x}$ is the area of steel required for the maximum midspan moment in the slab.

It may be noted that if both edges meeting at a corner are continuous, torsional reinforcement is not called for at the corner [refer Cl. D–1.10]. This is indicated in Figure 11.10. [However, this area will have some reinforcement provided anyway, because of the 'negative' moment reinforcements over supports in the edge strips and the distributor reinforcements in the edge strips.]

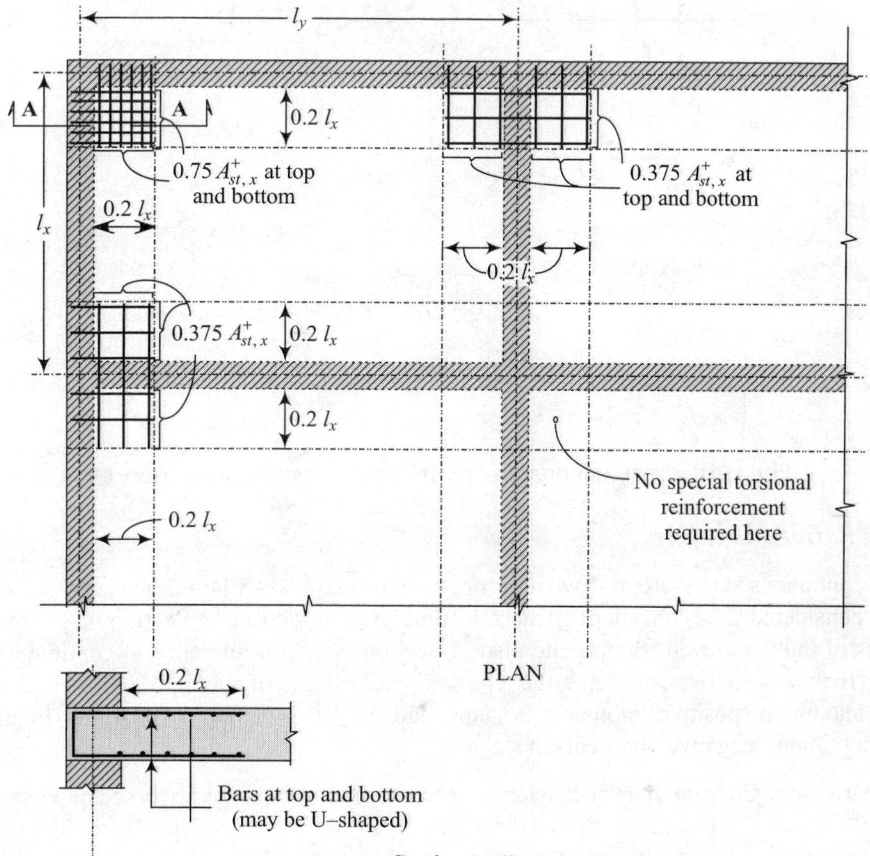

Fig. 11.10 Detailing of torsional reinforcement at corners.

† Here, the term 'edge' refers to the face of the support.

Design 'Negative' Moments at Continuous Supports

In a wall-supported continuous slab system, each rectangular slab panel is analysed separately (for design moments) using the Code moment coefficients. The 'negative' moments (M_1, M_2) calculated for two panels sharing a common continuous edge may not be equal [Figure 11.11] due to one or more of the following reasons:

- the two adjacent spans are unequal;
- the boundary conditions in the two adjoining panels are different; or
- the loading on one panel is different from that in the other panel.

Since the Code moment coefficients are based on *inelastic* analysis, with a fixed ratio (4/3) of 'negative' to 'positive' moment capacities, no redistribution of moments is permissible†. Hence, it is logical to take the *larger* factored moment (M_1 in Figure 11.11) as the design 'negative' moment at the continuous edge.

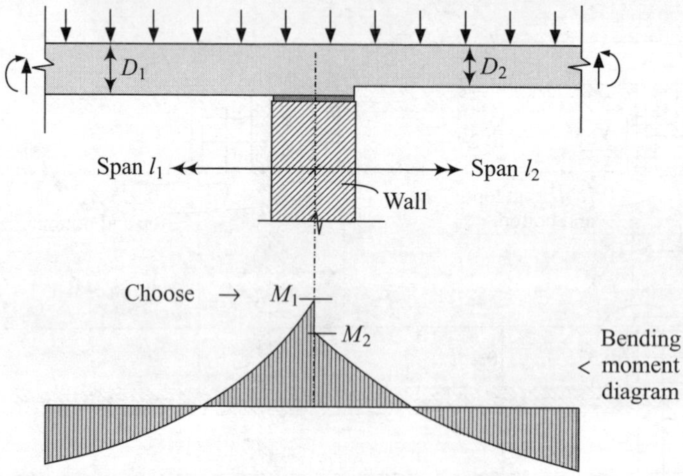

Fig. 11.11 Design 'negative' moment at a continuous support.

Influence of Pattern Loading

In the case of continuous slab systems – whether one-way or two-way – the influence of variability in live loads must be considered. The concept of 'pattern loading' was introduced in Section 9.7, with reference to elastic analysis of multi-storeyed frames, and also in Section 5.6, with reference to continuous beams and one-way slabs. In the case of two-way slabs, the 'checkerboard pattern' of loading [Figure 11.12(a)] generally results in the maximum 'positive' moments in slabs, and the 'strip pattern' of loading [Figure 11.12(b)] results in the maximum 'negative' moments in slabs.

As explained earlier, the Code moment coefficients for 'restrained' slab panels are based on inelastic analysis, and not elastic analysis. Each panel is analysed separately for its worst ('collapse') loading, and hence the concept of pattern loading is not relevant here.

---

† It may be noted that the Code recommends the use of the same moment coefficients for design by the *working stress method*. In a WSM context (i.e., under service loads), it may be argued that the design moments should be obtained through some kind of moment distribution procedure [Ref. 11.5]. However, this is not meaningful in design by LSM. Moreover, the basis of the Code moment coefficients is *inelastic* analysis, and not elastic analysis.

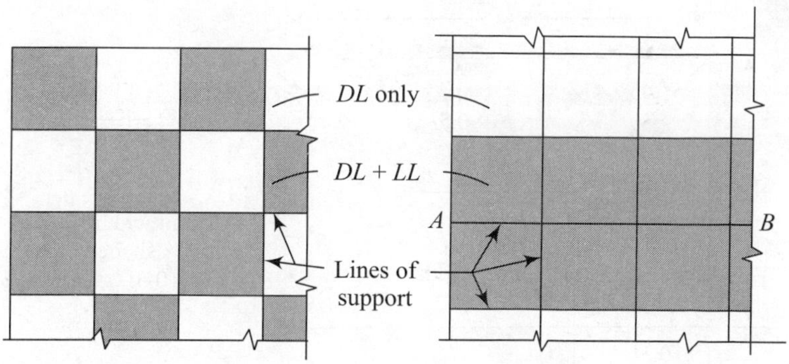

(a) 'checkerboard loading' pattern for maximum 'positive' moments (in panels with LL)

(b) 'strip loading' pattern for maximum 'negative' moments along panel edges/support lines (along AB)

Fig. 11.12 Pattern loadings for maximum slab moments.

Redistribution of Moments

Bending moments in continuous systems, based on elastic analysis, can be redistributed, as explained in Chapter 9, for more economical distribution of reinforcement. However, when the Code moment coefficients for 'restrained' slabs are used, moment redistribution is prohibited [refer Cl. D–1.3], as the coefficients are based on inelastic analysis.

11.2.5 Shear Forces in Uniformly Loaded Two-Way Slabs

Shear is generally not a governing design consideration in wall-supported reinforced concrete slabs subject to uniformly distributed loads. This was explained earlier [refer Example 6.2] with reference to one-way slabs. With two-way action, the shear stresses are likely to be lesser in magnitude, compared to one-way action.

The distribution of shear forces at the various edges of a two-way slab is complicated in general. However, the Code (Cl. 24.5) recommends a simple distribution of loads on the supporting edges (as explained earlier in Section 9.4), according to which, the distribution of load on the short edge is triangular, and the distribution of load on the long edge is trapezoidal, with the lines demarcating the contributing areas at 45 degrees to the boundaries [Figure 11.13]. The critical section for shear† is to be considered d away from the face of the support.

As shown in Figure 11.13, the maximum factored shear force per unit length, V_u, is obtained as:

$$V_u = w_u (0.5 l_{xn} - d) \tag{11.14}$$

where l_{xn} is the *clear span* in the short span direction.

The corresponding nominal shear stress $\tau_v = V_u/bd$ (with b = 1000 mm) should be less than the design shear strength of concrete for slabs, $k\tau_c$ [refer Section 6.6.2]. An average effective depth $d = (d_x + d_y)/2$ may be considered in the calculations.

For a more accurate estimation of load distribution in slabs with different boundary conditions, reference may be made to Ref. 11.16.

† This type of shear is called 'one-way shear' or 'beam shear', which is distinct from 'two-way shear' ('punching shear') applicable for slabs supported on columns [see Section 11.8].

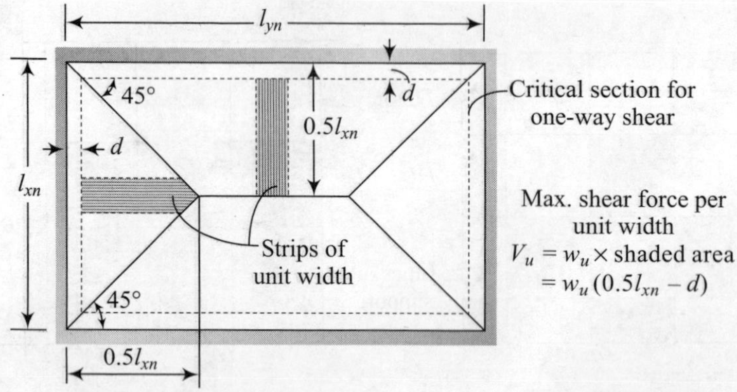

Fig. 11.13 Assumed distribution of loads on the edges of a rectangular slab, uniformly loaded.

Example 11.1

Design a simply supported slab to cover a room with internal dimensions 4.0 m × 5.0 m and 230 mm thick brick walls all around. Assume a live load of 3 kN/m² and a finish load of 1 kN/m². Use M 25 concrete and Fe 500 steel. Assume that the slab corners are free to lift up. Assume mild exposure conditions.

Solution

- Effective short span ≈ 4150 mm

  Assume an effective depth $d \approx \dfrac{4150}{20 \times 1.5} = 138$ mm

  With a clear cover of 20 mm and say, 8ϕ bars, overall thickness of slab $D \approx 138 + 20 + 4 = 162$ mm.

  $\Rightarrow$ Provide $D = 165$ mm

  $\Rightarrow$ $d_x = 165 - 20 - 4 = 141$ mm

  $d_y = 141 - 8 = 133$ mm

  $$\Rightarrow \text{Effective spans} \begin{cases} l_x = 4000 + 141 = 4141 \text{ mm} \\ l_y = 5000 + 133 = 5133 \text{ mm} \end{cases} \Rightarrow r \equiv \frac{l_y}{l_x} = \frac{5133}{4141} = 1.239$$

  [Note that effective span is taken as (clear span + d), as this is less than centre-to-centre span (between supports)].

  Loads on slab:

  (i) self-weight @ 25 kN/m³ × 0.165 m = 4.13 kN/m²

  (ii) finishes (given) = 1.0 "

  (iii) live loads (given) = 3.0 "

  $w = 8.13$ kN/m²

  $\Rightarrow$ Factored load $w_u = 8.13 \times 1.5 = 12.20$ kN/m²

  Design Moments (for strips at midspan, 1 m wide in each direction)

- As the slab corners are torsionally unrestrained, the Rankine-Grashoff method [Cl. D–2 of Code] may be applied:

  short span: $M_{ux} = \alpha_x w_u l_x^2$

  long span: $M_{uy} = \alpha_y w_u l_x^2$

where

$$\alpha_x = \frac{1}{8}\left[\frac{r^4}{1+r^4}\right] = \frac{1}{8}\left[\frac{1.239^4}{1+1.239^4}\right] = 0.0878$$

and $$\alpha_y = \frac{1}{8}\left[\frac{r^2}{1+r^4}\right] = \frac{1}{8}\left[\frac{1.239^2}{1+1.239^4}\right] = 0.0571$$

$\Rightarrow$ $M_{ux} = 0.0878 \times 12.20 \times 4.141^2 = 18.37$ kNm/m

$M_{uy} = 0.0571 \times 12.20 \times 4.141^2 = 11.95$ kNm/m

Design of Reinforcement

- $R_x \equiv \dfrac{M_{ux}}{bd_x^2} = \dfrac{18.37 \times 10^6}{10^3 \times 141^2} = 0.924$ MPa
- $R_y \equiv \dfrac{M_{uy}}{bd_y^2} = \dfrac{11.95 \times 10^6}{10^3 \times 133^2} = 0.6756$ MPa

$$\frac{(p_t)_{\text{reqd}}}{100} \equiv \frac{(A_{st})_{\text{reqd}}}{bd} = \frac{f_{ck}}{2f_y}\left[1-\sqrt{1-4.589R/f_{ck}}\right]$$

$$\Rightarrow \quad \frac{(p_t)_{x,\text{reqd}}}{100} = \frac{25}{2 \times 500}\left[1-\sqrt{1-(4.598 \times 0.924)/25}\right] = 0.222 \times 10^{-2}$$

$\Rightarrow$ $(A_{st})_{x,\text{ reqd}} = (0.222 \times 10^{-2}) \times 1000 \times 141 = 313$ mm²/m

$\Rightarrow$ required spacing of 8ϕ bars $= \dfrac{1000 \times 50.265}{313} = 160$ mm

- Similarly, $\dfrac{(p_t)_{y,\text{reqd}}}{100} = \dfrac{25}{2 \times 500}\left[1-\sqrt{1-(4.598 \times 0.6756)/25}\right] = 0.161 \times 10^{-2}$

$\Rightarrow$ $(A_{st})_{y,\text{ reqd}} = (0.161 \times 10^{-2}) \times 1000 \times 133 = 214.13$ mm²/m

$\Rightarrow$ required spacing of 8ϕ bars $= \dfrac{1000 \times 50.265}{214.13} = 234.7$ mm

Maximum spacing for primary reinforcement = $3d$ or 300 mm

$$= \begin{cases} 3 \times 141 = 423 \text{ mm (short span)} \\ 3 \times 133 = 399 \text{ mm (long span)} \end{cases}$$

- Provide $\begin{cases} 8\phi \text{ @ } 155 \text{ c/c} \quad \text{(short span)} \quad \Rightarrow \quad A_{st,x} = 324.3 \text{ mm}^2/\text{m} \\ 8\phi \text{ @ } 230 \text{ c/c} \quad \text{(long span)} \quad \Rightarrow \quad A_{st,y} = 218.5 \text{ mm}^2/\text{m} \end{cases}$

The detailing is shown in Figure 11.14.

Check for deflection control

- $p_{t,x} = \dfrac{324.3}{10^3 \times 140} \times 100 = 0.230$
- $f_s = 0.58 \times 500 \times 313/324.3 = 280$ MPa

$\Rightarrow$ modification factor $k_t = 1.4$ (from Table 5.2 or Figure 3 of Code)

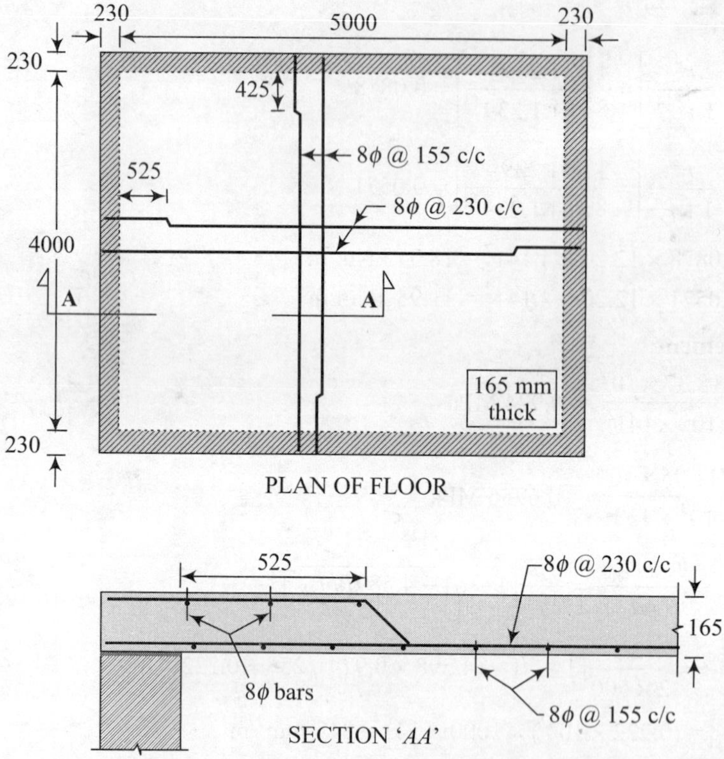

Fig. 11.14 Example 11.1.

$\Rightarrow \quad (l/d)_{max} = 20 \times 1.4 = 28$

$$(l/d)_{provided} = \frac{4141}{141} = 29.36 > 28$$

[This marginal exceedance can be resolved by providing a small pre-camber at the slab centre during construction. Alternatively, more detailed deflection calculations can be carried out, as described in Chapter 10.]

Check for shear†

- average effective depth, $d = (141 + 133)/2 = 137$ mm

$$V_u = w_u(0.5l_{xn} - d) = 12.20(0.5 \times 4.0 - 0.137) = 22.73 \text{ kN/m}$$

$\Rightarrow \quad \tau_v = 22.73 \times 10^3/(1000 \times 137) = 0.166$ MPa

- $p_t = 0.23 \Rightarrow \tau_c = 0.346$ MPa $\Rightarrow k\tau_c > \tau_v$ – Hence, OK.

Example 11.2

Repeat Example 11.1, assuming that the slab corners are prevented from lifting up.

† As explained earlier, a check on shear is not really called for in uniformly loaded, wall-supported two-way slabs. This is evident from the results of this example.

Solution

- [Refer Example 11.1]: Assume $D = 160$ mm (which is 5 mm less than the previous case)
  Assuming 8ϕ bars $\Rightarrow d_x = 160 - 20 - 4 = 136$ mm, $d_y = 136 - 8 = 128$ mm

$$\Rightarrow \begin{cases} l_x = 4000 + 136 = 4136 \text{ mm} \\ l_y = 5000 + 128 = 5128 \text{ mm} \end{cases} \Rightarrow \frac{l_y}{l_x} = 1.240$$

Loads on slab: (same as in Example 11.1, ignoring the slight reduction due to the reduced slab thickness)

- Factored load $w_u = 12.20$ kN/m^2

Design Moments (for middle strips, 1 m wide in each direction).

As the slab corners are to be designed as torsionally restrained, the moment coefficients given in Table 26 of the Code (Cl. D–1) may be applied† for $l_y/l_x = 1.240$:

- *Short span*: $\alpha_x = 0.072 + (0.079 - 0.072) \times \dfrac{1.240 - 1.2}{1.3 - 1.2} = 0.0748$

$$\Rightarrow \quad M_{ux} = \alpha_x w_u l_x^2$$
$$= 0.0748 \times 12.20 \times 4.136^2 = 15.61 \text{ kNm/m}$$

(which, incidentally, is about 15 per cent less than the value of 18.36 kNm/m obtained in Example 11.1)

- *Long span*: $\alpha_y = 0.056$

$$\Rightarrow \quad M_{uy} = \alpha_y w_u l_x^2$$
$$= 0.056 \times 12.20 \times 4.136^2 = 11.69 \text{ kNm/m}$$

(which is comparable to the earlier value of 11.94 kNm/m)

Design of reinforcement

- $R_x \equiv \dfrac{M_{ux}}{bd_x^2} = \dfrac{15.61 \times 10^6}{10^3 \times 136^2} = 0.844$ MPa

$$R_y \equiv \frac{M_{uy}}{bd_y^2} = \frac{11.69 \times 10^6}{10^3 \times 128^2} = 0.714 \text{ MPa}$$

$$\Rightarrow \quad \frac{(p_t)_{x,\text{reqd}}}{100} = \frac{25}{2 \times 500}\left[1 - \sqrt{1 - 4.589 \times 0.844/25}\right] = 0.202 \times 10^{-2}$$

$$\Rightarrow \quad (A_{st})_{x,\text{ reqd}} = (0.202 \times 10^{-2}) \times 1000 \times 136 = 274.72 \text{ mm}^2/\text{m}$$

$$\Rightarrow \quad \text{Required spacing of } 8\phi \text{ bars} = \frac{1000 \times 50.3}{274.72} = 183.1 \text{ mm}$$

Maximum spacing permitted = 3 × 136 = 408 mm, but < 300 mm.

$$\Rightarrow \quad \frac{(p_t)_{y,\text{reqd}}}{100} = \frac{25}{2 \times 500}\left[1 - \sqrt{1 - 4.589 \times 0.714/25}\right] = 0.170 \times 10^{-2}$$

$$\Rightarrow \quad (A_{st})_{y,\text{ reqd}} = (0.170 \times 10^{-2}) \times 1000 \times 128 = 217.6 \text{ mm}^2/\text{m}$$

$$\Rightarrow \quad \text{Required spacing of } 8\phi \text{ bars} = \frac{1000 \times 50.3}{217.6} = 231.2 \text{ mm}$$

Maximum spacing permitted = 3 × 128 = 384 mm, but < 300 mm

† Alternatively, Eqs 11.10, 11.11 may be applied.

- Provide $\begin{cases} 8\,\phi\ @\ 180\ \text{c/c}\ \ \text{(short span)} \\ 8\,\phi\ @\ 230\ \text{c/c}\ \ \text{(long span)} \end{cases}$

The detailing is shown in Figure 11.15.

Check for deflection control

- $p_{t,x} = 0.205$
- $f_s = 0.58 \times 500 \times 274.72/279.25 = 285$ MPa
  $\Rightarrow$ modification factor $k_t = 1.42$ (from Table 5.2 or Figure 3 of Code)

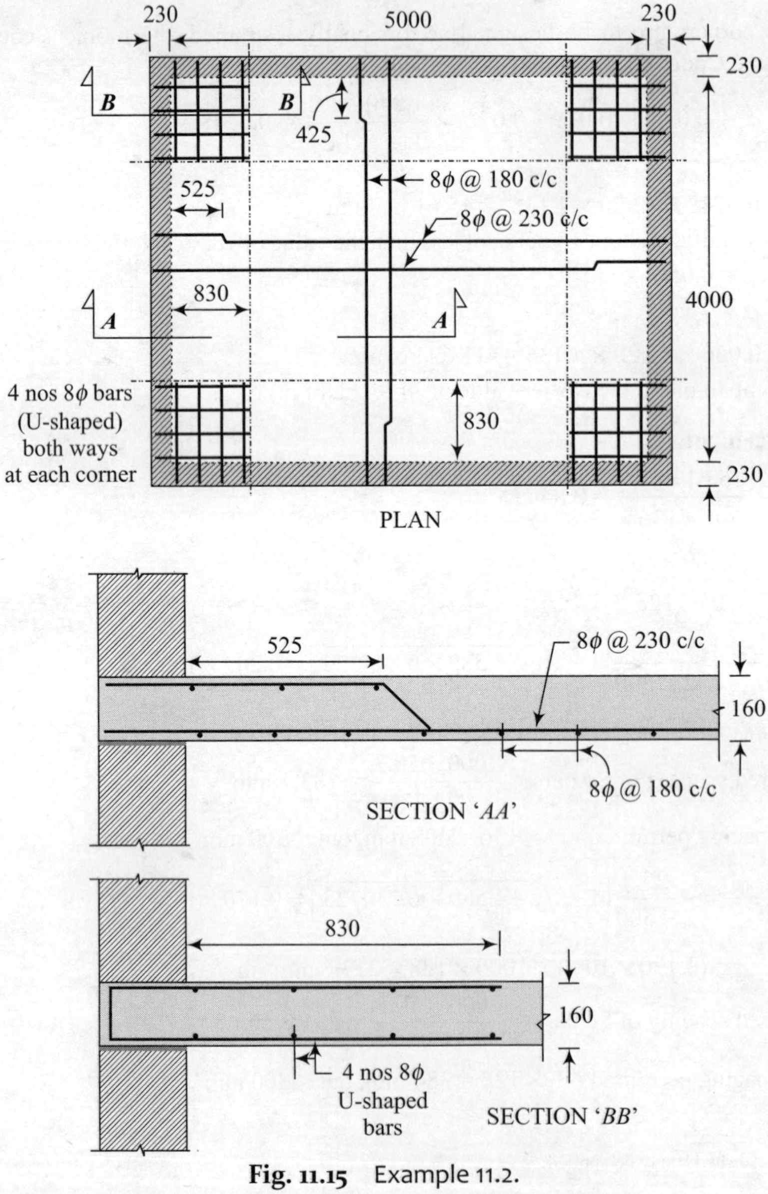

Fig. 11.15 Example 11.2.

- $\Rightarrow \quad (l/d)_{max} = 20 \times 1.42 = 28.4$

$$(l/d)_{provided} = \frac{4136}{136} = 30.4 > 28.4$$

[This marginal exceedance can be resolved by providing a small pre-camber at the slab centre during construction. Alternatively, more detailed deflection calculations can be carried out, as described in Chapter 10.]

Corner Reinforcement

As the slab is designed as 'torsionally restrained' at the corners, corner reinforcement has to be provided [vide Cl. D–1.8 of the Code] over a distance $l_x/5 = 830$ mm in both directions in meshes at top and bottom (four layers), each layer comprising $0.75\ A_{st,\ x}$.

$$\Rightarrow \quad \text{spacing of } 8\phi \text{ bars} = \frac{180}{0.75} = 240 \text{ c/c}$$

Provide 8ϕ @ 240 c/c both ways at top and bottom at each **corner** over an area 830 mm × 830 mm, i.e., 4 bars U-shaped in two directions, as shown in Figure 11.15.

Example 11.3

The floor slab system of a two-storeyed building is shown in Figure 11.16. The slab system is supported on load-bearing masonry walls, 230 mm thick, as shown. Assuming a floor finish load of 1.0 kN/m² and a live load of 4.0 kN/m², design and detail the multi-panel slab system. Use M 25 concrete and Fe 500 steel. Assume mild exposure conditions.

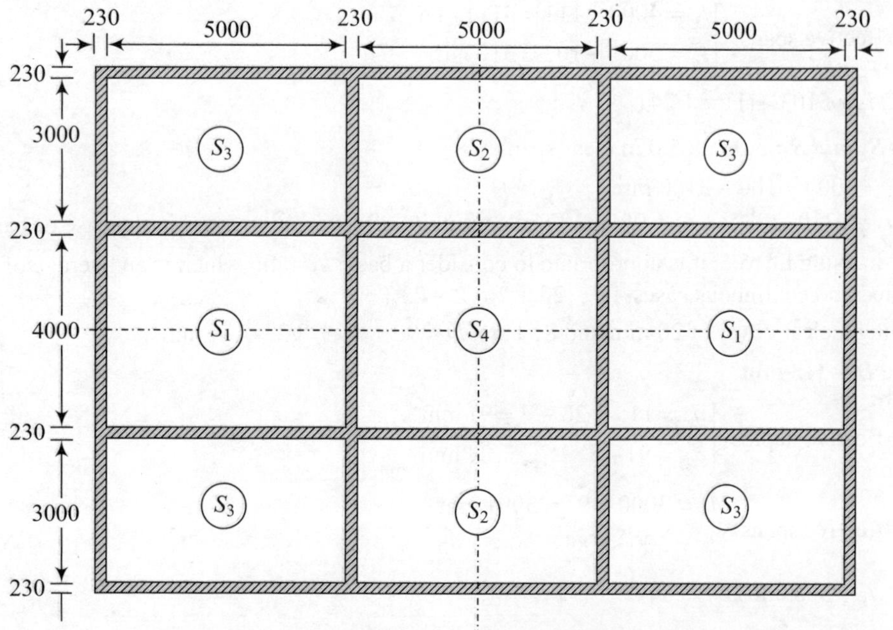

Fig. 11.16 Floor slab system – Example 11.3.

Solution

- The slab system [Figure 11.16] has two axes of symmetry passing through the centre, owing to which the number of different slab panels to be designed is four:

Panel	Clear spans	Boundary conditions	Type [refer Figure 11.16]
S_1	4.0 m × 5.0 m	one short edge discontinuous	2
S_2	3.0 m × 5.0 m	one long edge discontinuous	3
S_3	3.0 m × 5.0m	two adjacent edges discontinuous	4
S_4	4.0 m × 5.0 m	all four edges continuous	1

Slab thicknesses: based on deflection control criteria

- ***Panels S_1 and S_4:*** 4.0 m × 5.0 m clear spans

$l_x \approx 4000 + 150 = 4150$ mm

$$\Rightarrow \quad d_x = \approx \frac{4150}{26 \times 1.5} = 107 \text{ mm}$$

Assuming a clear cover of 20 mm and 8ϕ bars,

$D \approx 107 + 20 + 8/2 = 131$ mm

Provide $\boldsymbol{D}$ **= 135 mm**

$$\Rightarrow \quad \text{Effective depths} \begin{cases} d_x = 135 - 20 - 4 = 111 \text{ mm} \\ d_y = 111 - 8 = 103 \text{ mm} \end{cases}$$

$$\Rightarrow \quad \text{Effective spans}^{\dagger} \begin{cases} l_x = 4000 + 111 = 4111 \text{ mm} \\ l_y = 5000 + 103 = 5103 \text{ mm} \end{cases}$$

$\Rightarrow \quad l_y/l_x = 5103/4111 = 1.241$

- ***Panels S_2 and S_3:*** 3.0 m × 5.0 m clear spans

$\Rightarrow \quad l_x \approx 3000 + 100 = 3100$ mm

$\Rightarrow \quad d_x = \approx 3100/(23 \times 1.5) = 90$ mm [The continuity effect is only partial in the case of panel S_3. Hence, in using Eq. 5.5, it is appropriate to consider a basic *l*/*d* ratio which is an average of the simply supported and continuous cases, i.e., (20 + 26)/2 = 23.]

Assuming a clear cover of 20 mm and 8ϕ bars, $D \approx 90 + 20 + 8/2 = 114$ mm

Provide $\boldsymbol{D}$ **= 115 mm**

$$\Rightarrow \quad \text{Effective depths} \begin{cases} d_x = 115 - 20 - 4 = 91 \text{ mm} \\ d_y = 91 - 8 = 83 \text{ mm} \end{cases}$$

$$\Rightarrow \quad \text{Effective spans} \begin{cases} l_x = 3000 + 91 = 3091 \text{ mm} \\ l_y = 5000 + 83 = 5083 \text{ mm} \end{cases}$$

$\Rightarrow \quad l_y/l_x = 5083/3091 = 1.644$

---

† The width of the continuous support (230 mm) is less than 1/12 of the clear span (4000/12 = 333 mm); hence, the effective span is to be taken as (clear span + *d*) or (centre-to-centre distance between supports), whichever is less [refer Cl. 22.2 of Code].

Loading on slabs

- self-weight of slab $\begin{cases} @\ 25\ \text{kN/m}^3 \times 0.135m = 3.375\ \text{kN/m}^2 & \text{for } S_1, S_4 \\ @\ 25 \quad \times \quad 0.115 \ = 2.875\ \text{kN/m}^2 & \text{for } S_2, S_3 \end{cases}$

  finishes @ 1.0 kN/m^2
  live loads @ 4.0 kN/m^2

- $\Rightarrow$ Factored load $w_u = \begin{cases} 1.5 \times (3.375 + 1.0 + 4.0) = 12.56\ \text{kN/m}^2 & \text{for } S_1, S_2 \\ 1.5 \times (2.875 + 1.0 + 4.0) = 11.81\ \text{kN/m}^2 & \text{for } S_3, S_4 \end{cases}$

Design Moments (using Code moment coefficients for 'restrained' slabs)

- Referring to Table 26 of the Code, or alternatively applying Eqs 11.10–11.12, the following moment coefficients α_x^+, α_y^+ (for 'positive' moments in the middle strip) in the different panels are obtained as:

$$\alpha_x^+, \alpha_y^+ = \begin{cases} 0.037, \ 0.028 & \text{panel } S_1 \\ 0.056, \ 0.028 & \text{"} \quad S_2 \\ 0.060, \ 0.035 & \text{"} \quad S_3 \\ 0.034, \ 0.024 & \text{"} \quad S_4 \end{cases}$$

- The coefficients for the 'negative' moments in the various continuous edge strips are easily obtained as $\alpha^- = (4/3)\alpha^+$
- The corresponding design (factored) moments $M_u = \alpha w_u l_x^2$ in the various panels are accordingly obtained as follows:

Panel		S_1	S_2	S_3	S_4
Load w_u (kN/m^2)		12.56	11.81	11.81	12.56
Span l_x (m)		4.111	3.091	3.091	4.111
Short span moments	M_{ux}^+	7.85	6.32	6.77	7.22
	M_{ux}^-	10.47	8.43	9.03	9.62
Long span moments (kNm/m)	M_{uy}^+	5.94	3.16	3.95	5.09
	M_{uy}^-	7.92	4.21	5.27	6.79

Design 'negative' moments at common supports

- The 'negative' moments at the continuous edges, as obtained from the Code coefficients, are unequal – as shown in Figure 11.17(a). In all such cases, the design 'negative' moment is taken as the *larger* of the two values obtained from either side of the support. The design moments so obtained are shown in Figure 11.17(b).

Flexural reinforcement requirements

- $\dfrac{(p_t)_{\text{reqd}}}{100} \equiv \dfrac{(A_{st})_{\text{reqd}}}{bd} = \dfrac{f_{ck}}{2f_y}\left[1 - \sqrt{1 - 4.598 M_u / (f_{ck} bd^2)}\right]$

  where $f_{ck} = 25$ MPa, $f_y = 500$ MPa, $b = 1000$ mm

Panel S_1: $d_x = 111$ mm, $d_y = 103$ mm

- *short span*: $M_{ux}^+ = 7.85$ kNm/m $\Rightarrow (A_{st})_{\text{reqd}} = 167.65$ mm^2/m

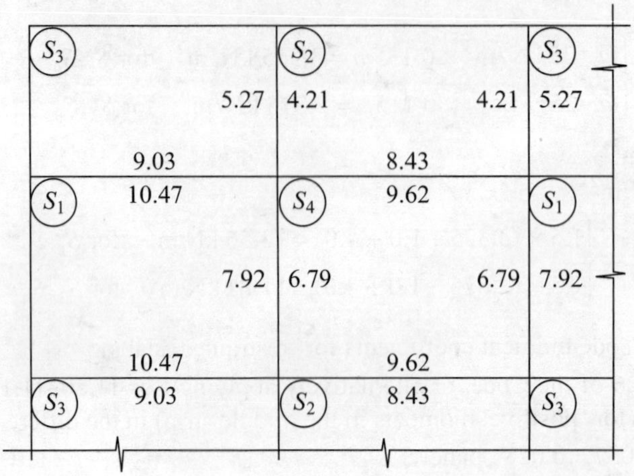

(a) 'negative' moments (kNm/m) at continuous edges for each panel

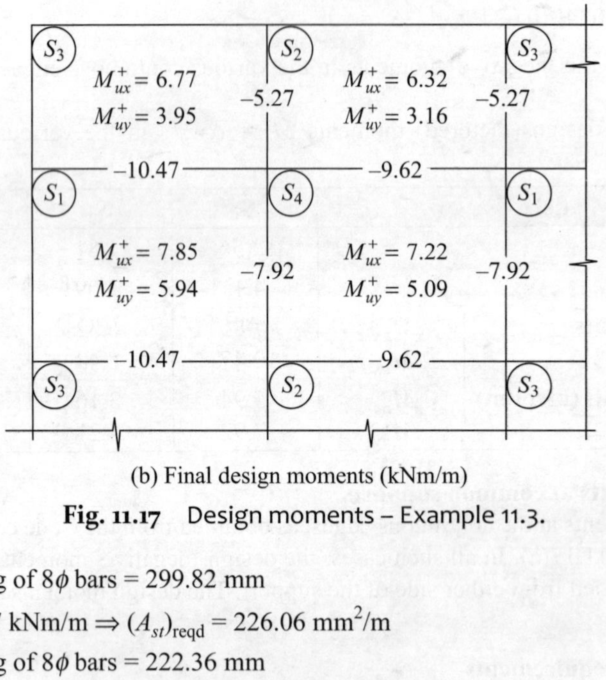

(b) Final design moments (kNm/m)

Fig. 11.17 Design moments – Example 11.3.

$\Rightarrow$ required spacing of 8ϕ bars = 299.82 mm

M^-_{ux} = 10.47 kNm/m $\Rightarrow (A_{st})_{\text{reqd}}$ = 226.06 mm²/m

$\Rightarrow$ required spacing of 8ϕ bars = 222.36 mm

- *long span*: M^+_{uy} = 5.94 kNm/m $\Rightarrow (A_{st})_{\text{reqd}}$ = 136.18 mm²/m

  $\Rightarrow$ required spacing of 8ϕ bars = 369.1 mm – to be limited to 300 mm

  M^-_{uy} = 7.92 kNm/m $\Rightarrow (A_{st})_{\text{reqd}}$ = 183.3 mm²/m

  $\Rightarrow$ required spacing of 8ϕ bars = 274.2 mm

Panel S_2: d_x = 91 mm, d_y = 83 mm

- *short span*: M^+_{ux} = 6.32 kNm/m $\Rightarrow (A_{st})_{\text{reqd}}$ = 165.7 mm²/m

⇒ required spacing of 8ϕ bars = 303 mm – to be limited to $3d_x$ = 273 mm

M_{ux}^{-} = 9.62 kNm/m ⇒ $(A_{st})_{\text{reqd}}$ = 257.62 mm^2/m

⇒ required spacing of 8ϕ bars = 195.11 mm

- *long span*: M_{uy}^{+} = 3.16 kNm/m ⇒ $(A_{st})_{\text{reqd}}$ = 89.46 mm^2/m
  ⇒ required spacing of 8ϕ bars = 561.9 mm – to be limited to $3d_y$ = 249 mm
  M_{uy}^{-} = 5.27 kNm/m ⇒ $(A_{st})_{\text{reqd}}$ = 151.5 mm^2/m
  ⇒ required spacing of 8ϕ bars = 331.78 mm — to be limited to $3d_y$ = 249 mm

Panel S_3: d_x = 91 mm, d_y = 83 mm

- *short span*: M_{ux}^{+} = 6.77 kNm/m ⇒ $(A_{st})_{\text{reqd}}$ = 178 mm^2/m
  ⇒ required spacing of 8ϕ bars = 282.39 mm – to be limited to $3d_x$ = 273 mm
  M_{ux}^{-} = 10.47 kNm/m ⇒ $(A_{st})_{\text{reqd}}$ = 281.99 mm^2/m
  ⇒ required spacing of 8ϕ bars = 178.25 mm
- *long span*: M_{uy}^{+} = 3.95 kNm/m ⇒ $(A_{st})_{\text{reqd}}$ = 112.46 mm^2/m
  ⇒ required spacing of 8ϕ bars = 446.97 mm – to be limited to $3d_y$ = 249 mm
  M_{uy}^{-} = 5.27 kNm/m ⇒ $(A_{st})_{\text{reqd}}$ = 151.5 mm^2/m
  ⇒ required spacing of 8ϕ bars = 331.78 mm – to be limited to $3d_y$ = 249 mm

Panel S_4: d_x = 111 mm, d_y = 103 mm

- *short span*: M_{ux}^{+} = 7.22 kNm/m ⇒ $(A_{st})_{\text{reqd}}$ = 153.8 mm^2/m
  ⇒ required spacing of 8ϕ bars = 326.82 mm – to be limited to 300 mm
  M_{ux}^{-} = 9.62 kNm/m ⇒ $(A_{st})_{\text{reqd}}$ = 206.96 mm^2/m
  ⇒ required spacing of 8ϕ bars = 242.87 mm
- *long span*: M_{uy}^{+} = 5.09 kNm/m ⇒ $(A_{st})_{\text{reqd}}$ = 116.23 mm^2/m
  ⇒ required spacing of 8ϕ bars = 432.45 mm – to be limited to 300 mm
  M_{uy}^{-} = 7.92 kNm/m ⇒ $(A_{st})_{\text{reqd}}$ = 183.3 mm^2/m
  ⇒ required spacing of 8ϕ bars = 274.22 mm

Detailing of Reinforcement

- Based on the requirements of reinforcement calculated above, the detailing of flexural reinforcement in the various middle strips and edge strips is shown in Figure 11.18. For practical convenience, only two different bar spacings (220 mm and 150 mm) are adopted. The detailing is in conformity with the requirements specified in Cl. D–1 of the Code, and satisfies the requirements of minimum spacing.
- Nominal top steel (50 per cent of bottom steel) is provided at the discontinuous edges – against possible 'negative' moments due to partial fixity.

Torsional reinforcement at corners

- As required by the Code, the reinforcement is provided in the form of a mesh, extending over a distance of 0.2*lx* beyond the face of the supporting wall. The bars are provided as U-shaped (i.e., with the mesh extending over top and bottom).
- At the extreme corner of the slab system, required spacing of 8 mm ϕ bars = 4/3 × 220 = 293 mm – over a distance of 0.2 × 3103 = 620 mm.
  ⇒ Provide 3 nos 8 mm ϕ U-shaped bars in both directions at the extreme corner of the slab system – over a distance 620 mm × 620 mm.

- The area of steel required at the other corners, where torsional reinforcement is required, is half the above requirement – however, provide 3 nos 8 mm ϕ at top and bottom. The size of the mesh is 620 mm × 620 mm at the junction of S_2 and S_3, where one edge of the corner is discontinuous.
- The size of the mesh is 0.2 × 4111 ≈ 820 mm at the junction of S_1 and S_3. Provide 3 nos 8 mm ϕ bars at top and bottom.

The detailing is shown in Figure 11.18.

[*Note:* The slab panels satisfy the limiting *l/d* ratios for deflection control; this may be verified.]

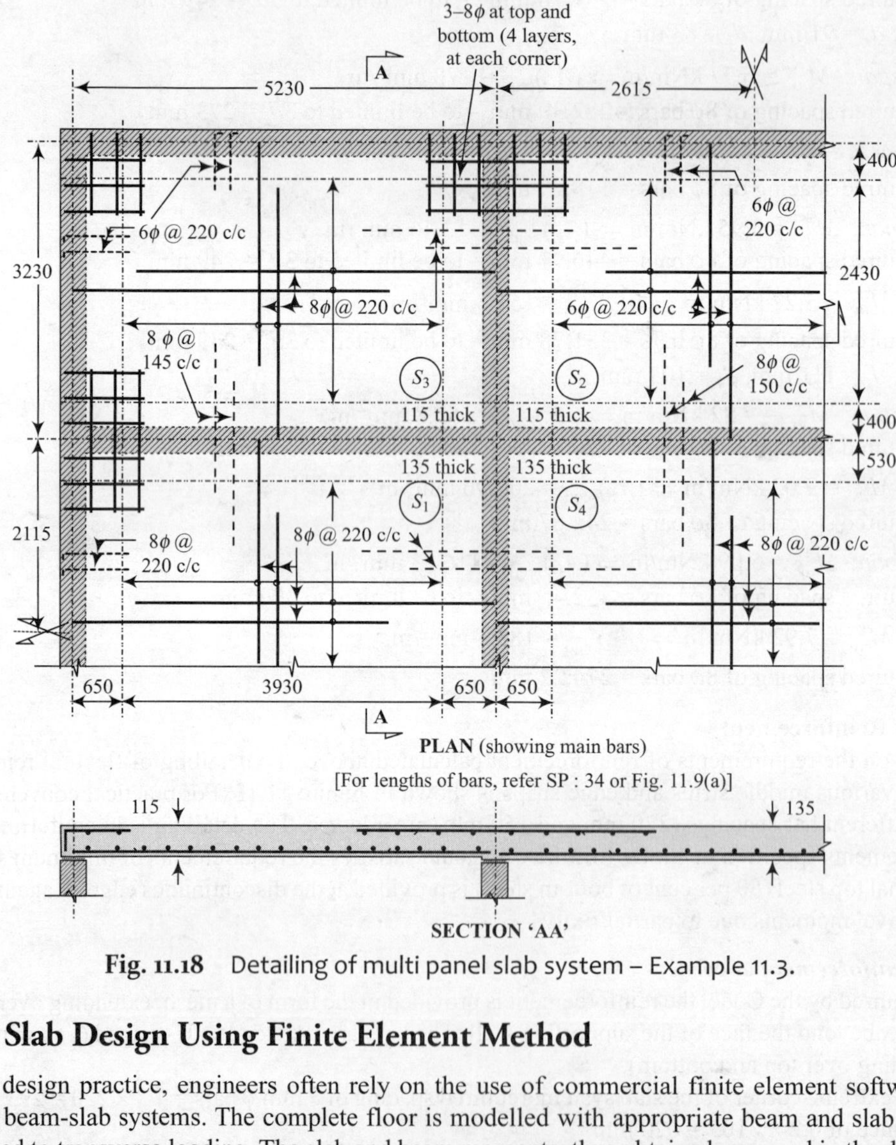

Fig. 11.18 Detailing of multi panel slab system – Example 11.3.

11.2.6 Slab Design Using Finite Element Method

In modern design practice, engineers often rely on the use of commercial finite element software for the analysis of beam-slab systems. The complete floor is modelled with appropriate beam and slab stiffnesses, and subjected to transverse loading. The slab and beam moments, thus obtained, are used in the design. Such a rigorous analysis, which considers the integral behaviour of the beam-slab-column system is essential when the supporting beams along the column lines are shallow (flexible) or absent. Alternatively, the 'equivalent frame method' discussed in Section 11.6 may be used.

In finite element analysis, one of the important criteria is the choice of the structural element used in the analysis. Plate elements, following Kirchhoff-Love's theory, can be used to model thin slabs, whereas Mindlin-Reissner plate theory is used to model thick slabs, where shear deformations can be significant [Ref 11.17]. If the slab element is likely to be subjected to significant in-plane forces, shell elements may be adopted in the finite element model. It may be noted that the results of the finite element analysis are sensitive to the mesh size. It is prudent to carry out a mesh convergence study before finalising the results obtained from a finite element analysis. The additional checks necessary relate to (i) modelling of correct boundary conditions, (ii) size of the element, and (iii) meshing near curved boundaries [Ref 11.18]. In the analysis of the beams under factored loads in the finite element model, the compatibility torsion needs to be properly accounted for, considering the likely torsional cracking, especially under factored loads; a torsion stiffness property modifier of 0.1 is usually adopted in practical design.

> It is seen that results of FEM analysis are significantly affected by the modelling of the beams along the columns and the linkage of the slab elements with beam elements (refer Table 11.2).

It is instructive to study the implications of beam flexibility on the moment field in a column-supported beam-slab system, with reference to the slab in Example 11.2 (with slab depth = 165 mm and load = 12.2 kN/m^2), considering the 230 mm thick masonry wall supports to be replaced by 230 mm wide RC beams. Three different beam depths have been considered in a finite element analysis study – 600 mm (very stiff), 450 mm (stiff) and 300 mm (very flexible) on all four sides, integrally connected to RC columns of size 300 mm × 300 mm of height 4 m (above hinged bases). A 3D rendered view of the beam-slab system with the slabs meshed is shown in Figure 11.19. The results obtained using SAP2000 software are tabulated below. It may be noted that in all these cases, the beam-slab member will be subjected to a net in-plane axial compression, equal to the column base shears in the direction under consideration; however, these are of small magnitudes and can generally be ignored (in this example).

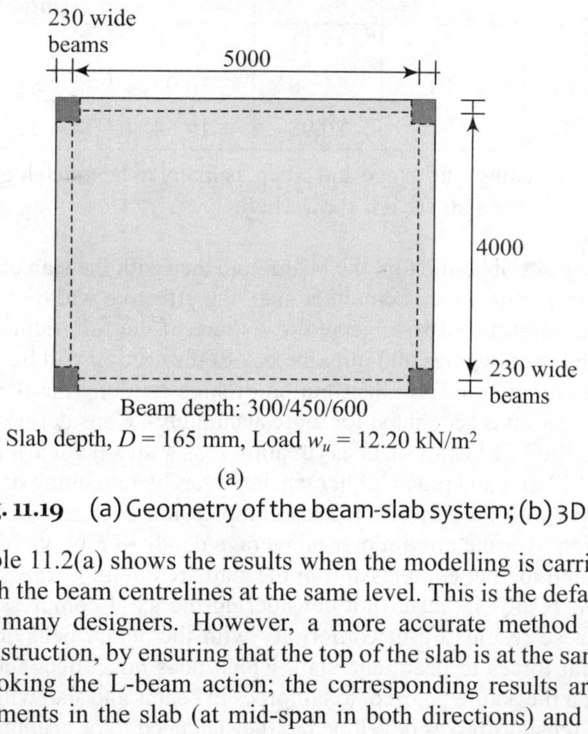

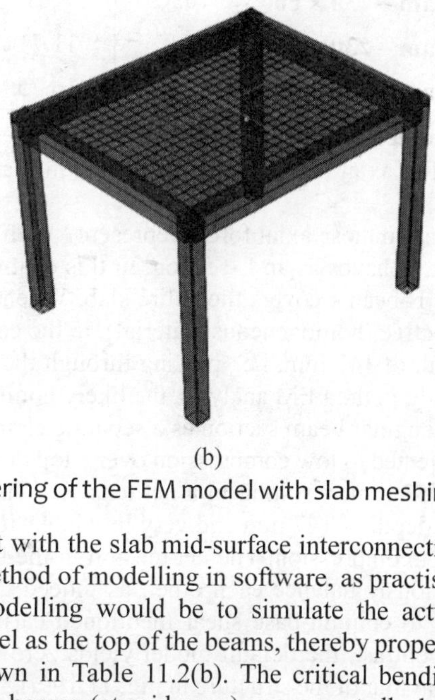

Fig. 11.19 (a) Geometry of the beam-slab system; (b) 3D rendering of the FEM model with slab meshing.

Table 11.2(a) shows the results when the modelling is carried out with the slab mid-surface interconnecting with the beam centrelines at the same level. This is the default method of modelling in software, as practised by many designers. However, a more accurate method of modelling would be to simulate the actual construction, by ensuring that the top of the slab is at the same level as the top of the beams, thereby properly invoking the L-beam action; the corresponding results are shown in Table 11.2(b). The critical bending moments in the slab (at mid-span in both directions) and in the beams (at mid-span) are expectedly less, when the more accurate modelling is done. However, the results show in-plane compressive forces in the slab (primarily in the part close to the beams) and axial tensile forces in the beams (not shown in Table 11.2(b)).

Table 11.2(a) *Results of Finite Element Analysis (by default method, with centrelines of beams coinciding with slab mid-surface)*

Case	Slab – Short span m_x (kNm/m)	Slab – Long span m_y (kNm/m)	Beam – Short span		Beam – Long span		Short-term deflection (service loads)* (mm)
			Mid-span, M_x (kNm)	Support (hogging) I_xM_x (kNm)	Mid-span, M_y (kNm)	Support (hogging) I_yM_y (kNm)	
Beam – 230 × 600	13.49	12.17	38.54	1.39	56.67	3.20	2.72
Beam – 230 × 450	14.07	14.28	30.51	2.84	43.65	5.86	3.47
Beam – 230 × 300	14.87	17.76	16.23	6.83	22.48	14.20	4.68

* The actual total deflection, including the effects of cracking, shrinkage and creep, is likely to be much higher

Table 11.2(b) *Results of Finite Element Analysis (by more accurate method, with top of beams flush with the top of slab)***

Case	Slab – Short span m_x (kNm/m)	Slab – Long span m_y (kNm/m)	Beam – Short span		Beam – Long span		Short-term deflection (service loads)* (mm)
			Mid-span, M_x (kNm)	Support (hogging) I_xM_x (kNm)	Mid-span, M_y (kNm)	Support (hogging) I_yM_y (kNm)	
Beam – 230 × 600	10.82	8.81	22.83	3.32	36.21	6.60	1.92
Beam – 230 × 450	12.07	11.71	20.01	6.18	31.50	10.93	2.81
Beam – 230 × 300	12.67	16.75	14.04	9.34	20.98	15.54	4.52

* The actual total deflection, including the effects of cracking, shrinkage and creep, is likely to be much higher
** The axial forces in the beams and in-plane forces in the slab are not shown here

What do these axial forces represent? With an integral slab at the top, the beam, together with the slab close to it, behaves as an L-section. In this example, considering beams on either side, the effective width of the two L-beams covers the entire slab. When this double-L beam is subjected to flexure, if the full section is effective (homogeneous material), in the case with beam depth = 600 mm, the NA of the section will be at a depth of 147 mm, i.e., passing through the slab (assuming uniform distribution of stresses along the flange width; in the FEM analysis, the likely nonlinear variation is accounted for more accurately). Considering the rectangular beam section as a separate element, as the FEM analysis does (treating it as a line element), it is subjected to low compression over a top depth of 147 mm and much higher tension over the remaining depth of 453 mm, resulting in a net tension. The slab part, on the other hand, has compression over an average top depth of 147 mm and very low intensity tension over the bottom part of average depth 18 mm, yielding a net compression. The net tension in the beams and the net compression in the slab are due to *flexure* and obviously balance each other, as indeed the FEM results indicate (not considering the axial compression due to column-base shear mentioned earlier). These results are in conformity with the actual behaviour. In contrast, the default model yields zero net axial forces in beam and slab, which does not reflect actual behaviour of the structure in Fig. 11.19(a). Note that the nature (sign) of axial forces in beams and slab will be reversed in the case of an upturned beam (and the tensile stresses developed in the slab need to be accounted for in the design, in combination with the bending moments). The significant differences between the values in Tables 11.2(a) and (b) also highlight the need to correctly model and simulate boundary conditions while using Finite Element Method. The need to correctly interpret the results is also critical.

With regard to beam flexibility, a clear trend can be seen in the results. Expectedly, with increasing beam flexibility, the peak moment in the slab mid-span increases in both directions. The increase in short span moment is marginal, whereas the increase in long span moment is significant (exceeding the short span moment when the beam depth is only 300 mm). On the contrary, with increasing beam flexibility, the bending moments at the mid-span of beams are found to decrease significantly in both directions, while the beam end moments (hogging) are found to increase. The wide spectrum in the results obtained for different beam depths point to the importance of carrying out such an analysis to assess the beam-slab behaviour.

It is also instructive to compare the slab moments (based on elastic analysis, considering beam-slab combined action) for the first two cases in the Tables 11.2(a) and (b) with the values obtained in Example 11.2 (based on the Code moment coefficients, derived from yield line analysis, applicable to wall-supported slabs). The third case does not qualify for the application of the moment coefficients, the beams being very flexible. The design moment in the short span direction is 15.61 kNm/m (much higher than the values as per finite element analysis). However, in the long span direction, it is 11.69 kNm/m, which is comparable to the values as per finite element analysis.

In some cases, a finite element analysis is carried out primarily to analyse the beams and columns under various load combinations, without meshing the slabs (i.e., invoking the 'rigid diaphragm' idealisation). The slabs are analysed separately by methods such as the use of moment coefficients. The load transfer from the slab to the beam is assumed to follow the tributary area loading (Figure 9.5). The beams can then be designed either as L- or T-beams, or conservatively as rectangular beams (see Chapter 5). In the finite element analysis given above, the beam bending moment, shear force and axial force obtained are those on the rectangular section line member and accordingly, if the beam is designed for these effects as having a rectangular section, and not flanged section, the axial forces generated in the slab should be accounted for in the slab design. Alternatively, the FEM can be used as an analysis tool to determine the distribution of bending moments, shear forces and axial forces at critical sections of the structure and the various identifiable members/segments such as T-beams, L-beams, slab part (column strip, middle strip, etc., where applicable) designed for their respective shares of bending moment, shear force and axial force. The twisting moments in the slab also need to be accounted for in the design, wherever significant, and Wood-Armer equations can be used for this purpose [Ref 11.19].

It is important to note the limitations of finite element analysis of beam-slab systems carried out assuming linear elastic behaviour. Although sophisticated and computationally intensive, the validity of the results under ultimate loads, by scaling linearly the moments and shear forces using appropriate load factors, is questionable. The linear scaling may be justified when the critical loading conditions for individual sections/ members are different. The analysis properly accounts for the relative stiffnesses of the various elements, but does not account for the relative strengths of these elements (based on the reinforcement provided). Such details are essential while carrying out a nonlinear analysis, which alone can estimate correctly the response at ultimate loads, including the post-yielding response. The ACI 318-19 code cautions the designer to carry out such an inelastic finite element analysis to determine the actual behaviour at ultimate loads. As an alternative, limit analysis, including possible formation of plastic hinges in the beams and yield lines in slabs as discussed in Section 11.10, can be considered for this purpose. Nevertheless, the elastic analysis at service loads is also necessary to ensure adequate serviceability (limiting deflections and crack-widths).

11.2.7 Design of Circular, Triangular and Other Slabs

Non-rectangular slabs, with shapes such as circular, triangular and trapezoidal, are sometimes encountered in structural design practice. Rectangular slabs, supported on three edges or two adjacent edges, are also met with in practice. Classical solutions, based on the elastic theory, are available in the case of rectangular and circular plates, uniformly loaded [Ref. 11.1]. Non-rectangular slabs are sometimes designed by considering the largest circle that can be inscribed within the boundaries of the slabs, and treating these slabs as equivalent circular slabs [Ref. 11.16]. More accurate analyses of stresses in non-rectangular and other slabs are obtainable from the computer-based finite difference method [Ref. 11.6] and finite element method [Ref. 11.7]. Yield line analyses provide simple and useful solutions for slabs of all possible shapes and boundary conditions [Ref. 11.8–11.10]. This is discussed in Section 11.10 at the end of this chapter.

Some of the standard solutions for a few typical cases are given here (without derivation). In all these cases, slabs are assumed to be subjected to uniformly distributed loads w (per unit area).

Circular Slabs, Simply Supported [Figure 11.20]

Elastic theory

- Moment in radial direction $M_r = \frac{w}{16}[(3+\nu)(a^2 - r^2)]$ (11.15a)

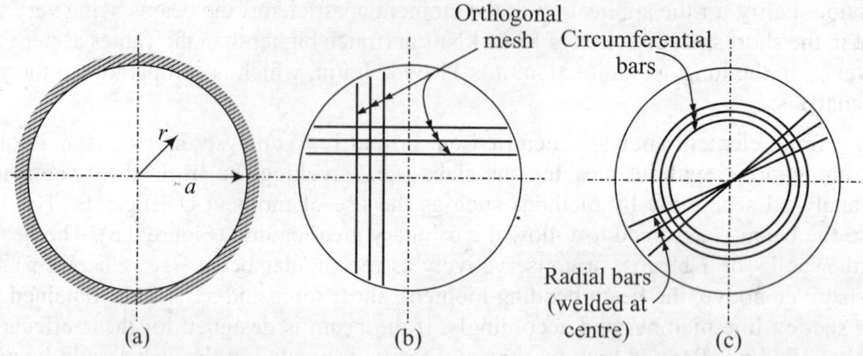

Fig. 11.20 Circular slabs, simply supported and isotropically reinforced.

- Moment in circumferential direction $M_\theta = \frac{w}{16}[a^2(3+\nu) - r^2(1+3\nu)]$ (11.15b)

  where $a \equiv$ radius of the circular slab;
  $r \equiv$ radius where moment is determined ($0 \le r \le a$);
  $\nu \equiv$ Poisson's ratio – may be taken as zero in the case of reinforced concrete.
- Maximum moments (at centre): $M_{r,\max} = M_{\theta,\max} = 3wa^2/16$ (11.15c)
- The two-way reinforcement may be provided by means of an orthogonal mesh with isotropic reinforcement [Figure 11.20(b)]; providing radial plus circumferential reinforcement [Figure 11.20(c)] is also (theoretically) a solution; however, this is not convenient in practice, as the radial bars need to be specially welded at the centre.

Yield line theory (assuming isotropic reinforcement)

- Collapse load $w_u = 6M_{uR}/a^2$

$\Rightarrow$ design moment $M_u = w_u a^2/6$ (11.16)

(which is less than the elastic theory solution: $M_u = w_u a^2/5.333$).

Circular Slabs, Fixed at the Edges

Elastic theory

$$M_r = \frac{w}{16}[a^2(1+\nu) - r^2(3+\nu)] \tag{11.17a}$$

$$M_\theta = \frac{w}{16}[a^2(1+\nu) - r^2(1+3\nu)] \quad (11.17b)$$

where the notations are exactly as mentioned earlier [Figure 11.20]

Design moments(assuming $\upsilon = 0$*):*

$$M^+_{r,\max} = M^+_{\theta,\max} = wa^2/16 \quad \text{('positive' at centre)} \quad (11.17c)$$

$$M^-_{r,\max} = (-)\,wa^2/8;\ M^-_{\theta,\max} = 0 \quad \text{(at edges)} \quad (11.17d)$$

[Top steel is required near the supports, in the radial direction].

Yield line theory (assuming isotropic reinforcement)

- Collapse load $w_u = 6(M^+_{uR} + M^-_{uR})/a^2$

  As the elastic moment at the support is twice that at the centre, it is desirable to provide $M^+_{uR} : M^-_{uR}$ in the ratio 1 : 2

  Accordingly, for design, $M_u^+ = (+)\,wa^2/18$ (11.18a)

  $M_u^- = (-)\,wa^2/9$ (11.18b)

Equilateral Triangular Slabs, Simply Supported [Figure 11.21(a)]

Yield line theory (assuming isotropic reinforcement)

- Collapse load $w_u = 72\ M_{uR}/l^2$

  where l is the length of one side

  $\Rightarrow$ design moment (at midspan) $M_u = w_u l^2/72$ (11.19)

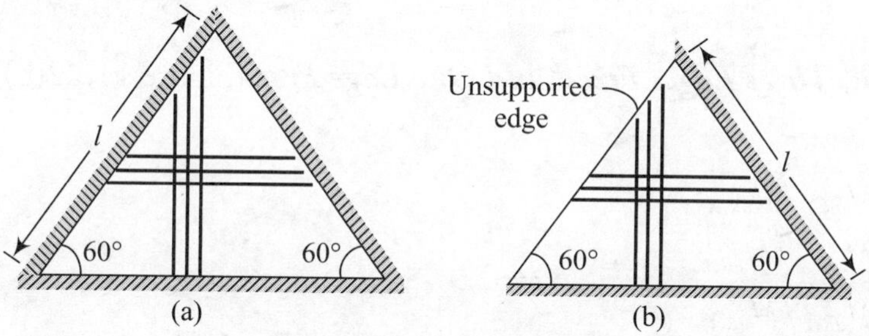

Fig. 11.21 Equilateral triangular slabs, isotropically reinforced.

Equilateral Triangular Slabs, Two Edges Simply Supported and One Edge Free [Figure 11.21(b)]

Yield line theory (assuming isotropic reinforcement)

- Collapse load $w_u = 24M_{uR}/l^2$

  where l is the length of one side

  $\Rightarrow$ design moment (at midspan) $M_u = w_u l^2/24$ (11.20)

Rectangular Slabs, Three Edges Simply Supported and One Edge Free [Figure 11.22(a)]

Yield line theory

Let $\mu \equiv M_{uR,Y}/M_{uR,X}$ and $R \equiv l_Y/l_X$; the X- and Y-directions are as indicated in Figure 11.22(a).

- Design moments:

$$M_{uX} = \begin{cases} \dfrac{w_u R^2 l_X^2}{24\mu}\left\{\sqrt{4+9\mu/R^2}-2\right\} \\ \dfrac{w_u l_X^2}{24}\left\{\sqrt{3+\dfrac{\mu}{4R^2}}-\dfrac{\sqrt{\mu}}{2R}\right\}^2 \end{cases} \text{(whichever is greater)} \tag{11.21}$$

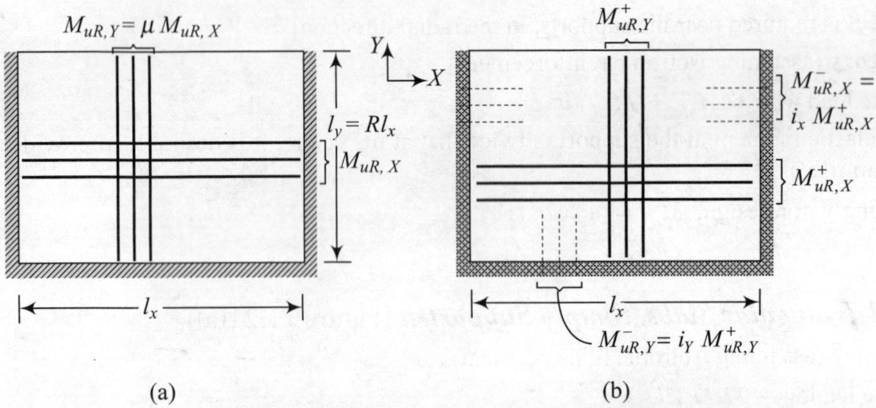

Fig. 11.22 Rectangular slabs, supported on three edges.

- By suitably selecting μ (which can even be taken as unity), design moments M_{uX} and $M_{uY} = \mu M_{uX}$ can be determined.

Rectangular Slabs, Three Edges Fixed and One Edge Free [Figure 11.22(b)]

Yield line theory

Let

$$\mu \equiv M_{uR,Y} / M_{uR,X}$$
$$i_X \equiv M^-_{uR,X} / M^+_{uR,X}$$
$$i_Y \equiv M^-_{uR,Y} / M^+_{uR,Y}$$

- Design moments: $$M^+_{uY} = \begin{cases} \dfrac{w_u l_Y^2 (3-\alpha_1)}{6(i_Y+\alpha_1)} \\ \dfrac{w_u l_Y^2\, \alpha_2^2}{6(1+i_Y)} \end{cases} \text{(whichever is greater)} \tag{11.22}$$

where

$$\alpha_1 \equiv 4\left(\sqrt{4+3K_1}-2\right)/K_1$$

$$K_1 \equiv \frac{\mu(3+i_Y)}{R^2(1+i_X)}$$

$$\alpha_2 \equiv \left(\sqrt{1+3K_2}-1\right)/K_2$$

$$K_2 \equiv \frac{4(1+i_X)}{\mu(1+i_Y)}$$

- By suitably selecting μ, i_X and i_Y, all the design moments can be determined. This is illustrated in Example 11.5.

Rectangular Slabs, Two Adjacent Edges Fixed and the Other Two Free [Figure 11.23]

Yield line theory

- Using the same notations as in the previous case [refer Figure 11.23], design moment:

$$M_{uX}^{+} = \begin{cases} \dfrac{w_u l_X^2}{6} \Big/ \left\{ \dfrac{1+i_X}{\alpha_3^2} + \dfrac{\mu}{R^2} \right\} \\ \dfrac{w_u l_X^2}{6} \Big/ \left\{ i_X + i_Y \mu / R^2 \right\} \end{cases}$$

(whichever is greater) (11.23)

where $\alpha_3 \equiv \left(\sqrt{1+3K_1} - 1\right)/K_1$

- By suitably selecting μ, i_X and i_Y, all the design moments can be determined.

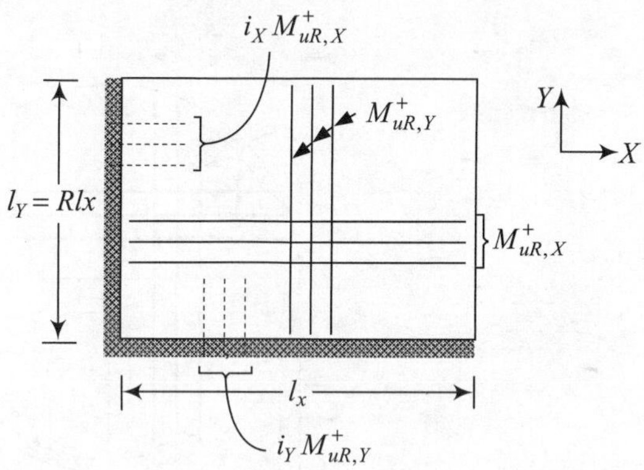

Fig. 11.23 Rectangular slab, two edges fixed and the other two free.

Example 11.4

Design a circular slab of 3.5 m diameter to cover an underground sump. The slab is simply supported at the periphery by a wall 200 mm thick. Assume a finish load of 1.0 kN/m² and live loads of 4.0 kN/m². Use M 25 concrete and Fe 500 steel. Assume mild exposure conditions.

Solution

- Clear span = 3500 – (200 × 2) = 3100 mm

  Assuming a slab thickness of 100 mm, with 20 mm clear cover (*mild* exposure condition) and 8 mm ϕ bars (in an orthogonal mesh), average effective depth d = 100 – 20 – 8 = 72 mm

  ⇒ effective span (diameter) = 3100 + 72 = 3172 mm

  ⇒ effective radius a = 3172/2 = 1586 mm

- *Loads*: (i) self-weight @ 25 kN/m³ × 0.10 m = 2.5 kN/m²

  (ii) finishes = 1.0 ”

  (iii) live loads = 4.0 ”

  w = 7.5 kN/m²

  ⇒ Factored load w_u = 7.5 × 1.5 = 11.25 kN/m²

- *Design moments* (assuming yield line theory with isotopic reinforcement)

$$M_u = w_u a^2/6 = 11.25 \times 1.586^2/6 = 4.72 \text{ kNm/m}$$

$$\Rightarrow \quad R \equiv \frac{M_u}{bd^2} = \frac{4.72 \times 10^6}{10^3 \times 72^2} = 0.910 \text{ MPa}$$

$$\frac{p_t}{100} \equiv \frac{25}{2 \times 500}\left[1 - \sqrt{1 - (4.598 \times 0.910/25)}\right] = 0.219 \times 10^{-2}$$

$$\Rightarrow \quad A_{st,\,\text{reqd}} = (0.219 \times 10^{-2}) \times 10^3 \times 72 = 157.61 \text{ mm}^2/\text{m}$$

$\Rightarrow$ required spacing of 8 mm ϕ bar = $50.3 \times 10^3/157.61$

$= 318.92$ mm

Maximum spacing allowed = $3d = 3 \times 72 = 216$ mm

- Provide **8 mm ϕ 210 c/c both ways** at bottom, as shown in Figure 11.24.

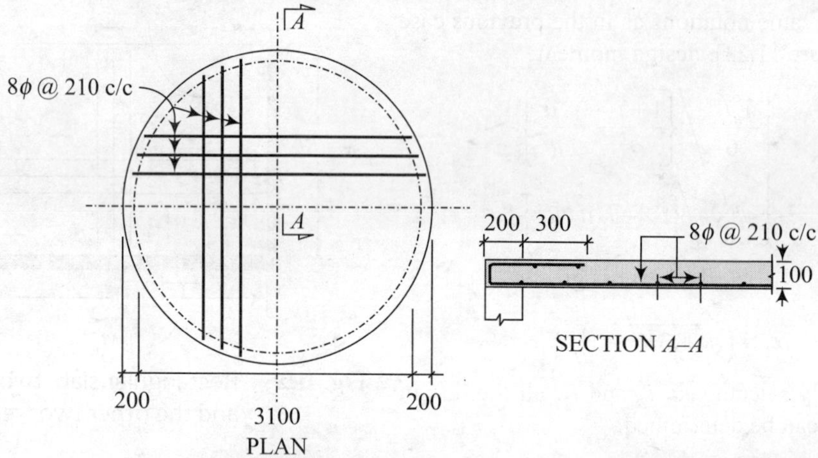

Fig. 11.24 Circular slab – Example 11.4.

Example 11.5

Determine the design moments in a square slab (4 m × 4 m), with three edges continuous and one edge free, subject to a uniformly distributed factored load $w_u = 10.0$ kN/m². Assume the slab to be isotropically reinforced. Also assume that the 'negative' moment capacity at the continuous support to be equal to that at midspan in either direction.

Solution

- Applying the yield line theory solution [Eq. 11.22] with $l_X = l_Y = 4.0$ m, $R = 1$, $\mu = i_X = i_Y = 1$,

$$K_1 = \frac{\mu(3 + i_Y)}{R^2(1 + i_X)} = 2$$

$$K_2 = \frac{4(1 + i_X)}{\mu(1 + i_Y)} = 4$$

$$\Rightarrow \quad \alpha_1 = 4\left(\sqrt{4 + 3K_1} - 2\right)\Big/K_1 = 2.325$$

$$\alpha_2 = \left(\sqrt{1 + 3K_2} - 1\right)\Big/K_2 = 0.651$$

$$\Rightarrow \quad M_{uY}^{+} = \begin{cases} \dfrac{w_u l_Y^2 (3 - \alpha_1)}{6(i_Y + \alpha_1)} = 0.0338\, w_u l_Y^2 \\[2ex] \dfrac{w_u l_Y^2\, \alpha_2^2}{6(1 + i_Y)} = 0.0353\, w_u l_Y^2 \quad \text{(greater)} \end{cases}$$

$$\Rightarrow \quad M_{uY}^{+} = M_{uX}^{+} = M_{uY}^{-} = M_{uX}^{-} = 0.0353 \times 10.0 \times 4.0^2$$

$$= 5.65 \text{ kNm/m}$$

11.2.8 Two-Way Slabs Subjected to Concentrated Loads

Two-way slabs subjected to concentrated loads (such as wheel loads) are frequently encountered in the design of bridge slabs. Analyses by elastic theory have been developed by Westergaard and Pigeaud. However, the theory is mathematically complex, and recourse has to be made to design charts developed for this purpose. The reader may refer to Handbooks such as Ref. 11.16 for such design charts. Yield line analysis (explained in Section 11.10) can also be used.

11.3 Design of Beam-Supported Two-Way Slabs

11.3.1 Behaviour of Beam-Supported Slabs

Slabs supported on beams [refer Figure 1.8] behave differently, when compared to slabs supported on walls, because of the influence of the following three factors:

1. deflections in the supporting beams;
2. torsion in the supporting beams; and
3. displacements (primarily rotations) in the supporting columns.

Deflections in the supporting beams become significant when they have relatively large span/depth ratios and their end connections are relatively flexible. These deflections, caused by relatively low flexural stiffnesses of the beams, get enhanced with time, due to the long-term effects of creep and shrinkage. The support flexibility significantly influences the magnitudes and distributions of bending moments and shear forces in slabs, with the result that the 'moment coefficients' applicable for wall-supported slabs [refer Section 11.2] are not applicable for slabs supported on *flexible* beams.

The monolithic construction of beam and slab results in the twisting of the beam along with the bending of the slab. In statically indeterminate systems, this induces 'secondary torsion' in the beam, whose magnitude depends on the relative torsional stiffness of the beam (which, as discussed in Chapter 7, reduces significantly with the onset of torsional cracking that is likely to occur in torsionally flexible beams). The twisting moment (per unit length) at any location along the length of the beam must be equal to the unbalanced bending moment (if any) per unit length in the slabs on either side at the slab-beam junction. Evidently, the twisting moment will be greater in beams having slabs only on one side. In general, it is observed that, with increase in beam torsional stiffness, there is a consequent decrease in 'positive' moments in interior slab panels, but a significant increase in the 'negative' moment at the discontinuous edge of the exterior panel.

The columns also influence the behaviour of the beam-supported slabs, because they form part of an integral slab-beam-column system which can sway and bend in a variety of ways.

11.3.2 Use of Code Moment Coefficients for Slabs Supported on Stiff Beams

When the supporting beams (and columns) are relatively rigid, the slabs may be *assumed* to be supported on *rigid* (*non-deflecting*) *supports*. The secondary torsion in the beams may also be neglected for convenience. This results in conservative estimates of moments in the slabs, except at the discontinuous edge of the exterior panel (as explained earlier). The latter problem may be resolved by providing suitable top steel at the discontinuous edge of the slab – as required by the detailing requirements of the Code (to account for 'negative' moments due to partial fixity). Furthermore, the minimum stirrup requirements prescribed for beams by the Code provide some measure of torsional strength to the supporting beams. With these assumptions, slabs supported on stiff beams may be designed using the Code moment coefficients of wall-supported slabs [refer Section 11.2].

The Code moment coefficients are based on yield line analysis of *wall-supported* slabs, i.e., slabs with *unyielding* supports. For beam supports to approach this criterion, they have to be unrealistically stiff. Moreover, failure of *beam-supported* slabs can involve combined beam-slab collapse mechanisms (refer Section 11.10.11). For these reasons, it is prudent to be cautious in using Code coefficients for beam-supported slabs.

The Code does not provide any specific recommendations for the procedure for designing beam-supported two-way slabs. Generally, in Indian practice, the design is done by treating continuous beam-supported slabs as identical to continuous wall-supported slabs, for which moment coefficients are readily available in the Code (Table 12 of the Code for one-way slabs, and Table 26 of the Code for two-way slabs). However, this is justifiable only if the supporting beams are adequately stiff.

The Code limitation on beam deflection (Cl. 23.2) does provide some indirect control on the flexural stiffness of the supporting beam. However, the designer must take precautions to ensure that the supporting beams are adequately stiff, in order to justify the application of the Code moment coefficients for the slab design.

Stiff Beams

A simple guideline for selecting the overall depth of a supporting beam D_b (to ensure that it is 'adequately stiff'), is given by the Canadian code [Ref. 11.21]. If D_s is the thickness of the slab, b the width of the beam web and l its clear span, then the ratio, $bD_b^3/(lD_s^3)$, must be not less than 2.0 for the beam to be considered stiff. This implies that the depth of the beam must satisfy the following condition:

$$D_b \geq D_s(2l/b)^{1/3} = 1.26D_s(l/b)^{1/3} \tag{11.24}$$

Considering a square panel with clear spans of 2.8 m and a slab 100 mm thick, the required minimum beam depth, for a beam width of 250 mm, works out to 282 mm. Furthermore, if the panel is rectangular, with clear spans 2.8 m × 5.6 m, and if the slab thickness remains as 100 mm, the required minimum depth of the long span beam (assuming b = 250 mm) is 355 mm, while that of the short span beam is 282 mm.

By treating the beam supports as wall supports, the slab system can be effectively isolated from the integral slab-beam-column system, for design purposes. The reactions due to the gravity loads on the slab are transferred to the supporting stiff beams, as explained in Section 9.4 [refer Figure 9.5]. If the supporting beams are 'secondary' [refer Figure 1.10(c)], then these 'secondary' beams may, in turn, be isolated and assumed to be supported on the 'primary' beams, for design purposes. The primary beams and columns constitute a continuous skeletal framework, which can be separated into plane frames (longitudinal and transverse), and can be designed to resist gravity loads as well as lateral loads [refer Chapter 9].

11.3.3 Slabs Supported on Flexible Beams – Code Limitations

As an alternative to the idealised assumption treating beam-supported slabs as continuous slabs supported on walls, the Code (Cl. 24.3) suggests that slabs monolithically connected with beams may be analysed *as members of a continuous framework with the supports, taking into account the stiffness of such supports*. This suggestion becomes significant in situations where the supporting beams are not adequately stiff.

It may be noted that the ACI Code had made such a treatment mandatory for *all* (flexible) beam-supported two-way slabs, as far back as in 1971, and had altogether dispensed with the use of moment coefficients for such slabs. Another significant change introduced in the 1971 version of the ACI Code was the unification of the design methods for all slabs supported on columns – with and without beams, including flat slabs. This is considered to be an advancement as it ensures that all types of slabs have approximately the same *reliability* (or risk of failure[†]) [Ref. 11.6]. Some other codes, such as the Canadian code [Ref. 11.21], have also incorporated these changes, but retain the moment coefficient method as an alternative for slabs supported on *walls or stiff beams*.

In the IS Code, such a procedure, based on the concept of 'equivalent frame', is prescribed for *flat slabs*. This method [Cl. 31 of the Code] follows closely the extensive research undertaken in this area, since 1956, at the University of Illinois, USA [Ref. 11.11]. However, unlike the ACI and Canadian codes, the IS Code is yet to extend the 'equivalent frame' concept of analysis to beam-supported slabs.

The problem of designing slabs on flexible beams has therefore not yet been satisfactorily addressed by the IS Code. This information is also not generally available in standard Indian books on reinforced concrete design.

A unified procedure for design of column-supported slabs, with and without beams, is presented in the sections below.

In the sections to follow, procedures for analysis and design of beam-supported slabs are described – in line with the by-now-well-established ACI concept of unified procedures for all slabs, supported on columns, with or without beams.

11.3.4 The 'Equivalent Frame' Concept

As mentioned in Section 11.1.3, in the case of beam-supported two-way slabs, 100 per cent of the gravity loads on the slabs are transmitted to the supporting columns, in both longitudinal and transverse directions (see Figure 11.3(b)). The mechanism of load transfer from slab to columns is achieved by flexure, shear and torsion in the various elements. The slab-beam-column system behaves integrally as a three-dimensional system, with the involvement of all the floors of the building, to resist not only gravity loads, but also lateral loads. However, a rigorous three-dimensional analysis of the structure is complex, and not warranted except in very exceptional structures.

The *Equivalent Frame* (or *elastic frame*) method is a simplified procedure for analysis and design of two-way slabs, with or without beams, and supported on columns, treating them as part of a continuous elastic frame, taking into account the stiffness of members.

Conventionally, when stiff beams are provided along column lines, the slab design is separated from the design of beams (and columns), as in the case of wall-supported slabs. The remaining part of the structure, comprising a three-dimensional skeletal framework of beams and columns, is separated for convenience, into (two-dimensional) plane frames in the longitudinal and transverse directions of the building. As the integrally cast slab also contributes to the strength and stiffness of the beams, the beam members are considered as flanged beams (T-beams, L-beams), with *portions of the slab* acting as the flanges of these beams; this concept was explained in Chapter 9. However, when the beams are flexible or absent, it is not appropriate to separate the slab design from the beam design.

In using the concept of a plane frame comprising columns and slab-beam members at various floor levels, fundamentally, the slab-beam member should consist of the *entire floor member* (slab and beam, if any) *tributary* to a line of columns forming the frame. This is illustrated in Figures 11.25(a) and (b), which show how a building structure may be considered as a series of 'equivalent (plane) frames', each consisting of a

[†] It is reported that the application of the 'moment coefficient' procedure to beam-supported slabs results in more conservative designs, with the result that such slabs turn out to be significantly stronger than beamless (flat) slabs, given the same gravity loads and material grades [Ref. 11.6].

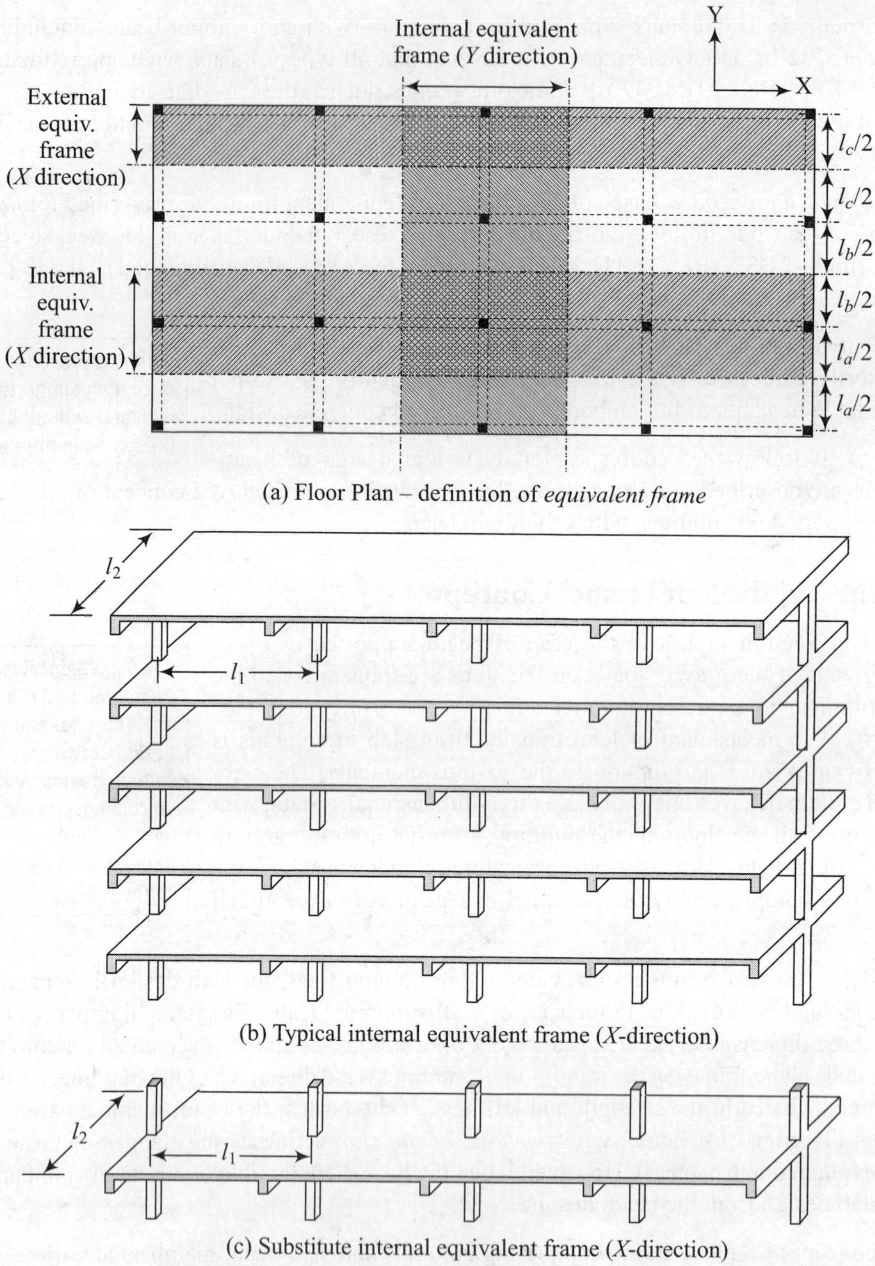

(a) Floor Plan – definition of *equivalent frame*

(b) Typical internal equivalent frame (*X*-direction)

(c) Substitute internal equivalent frame (*X*-direction)

Fig. 11.25 The 'equivalent frame' concept.

row of columns and the portion of the *floor system tributary to it*. The part of the floor bound by the panel centrelines, on either side of the columns, forms the slab-beam member in this plane frame. Such 'equivalent frames' must be considered in both longitudinal and transverse directions; to ensure that load transfer takes place in both directions [Figure 11.25(a)].

The equivalent frames can now be analysed under both gravity loads and lateral loads using the procedures mentioned in Chapter 9. The primary difference between the frame in Figure 9.1(b) and the one in Figure 11.25(b) lies in the width of the slab-beam member and the nature of its connections with the columns. Whereas in the conventional skeletal frame, the full beam is integral with the column, and the rotational restraint offered by the column at the joint is for the entire beam (with both beam and column undergoing the same rotation at the joint), in the 'equivalent frame', the column connection is only over part of the slab-beam member width, and hence the flexural restraint offered by the column to the slab-beam member is only partial. Thus, the rotation of the slab-beam member along a transverse section at the column support will vary, and will be equal to the column rotation only in the immediate vicinity of the column. This, in turn, results in torsion in the portion of the slab transverse to the span and passing through the column (i.e., a cross-beam running over the column).

In the elastic analysis of the plane frame in Figure 9.1(b), it was shown (in Section 9.3) that several approximations can be made, subject to certain limitations. Similar approximations can also be made in the present case.

For example, for the purpose of gravity load analysis, it is possible to simplify the analysis by applying the concept of *substitute frames*. Accordingly, instead of analysing the full 'equivalent frame' [Figure 11.25(b)], it suffices to analyse separate *partial* frames [Figure 11.25(c)], comprising each floor (or roof), along with the columns located immediately above and below. The columns are assumed to be fixed at their far ends [refer Cl. 24.3.1 of the Code]. Such substitute frame analysis is permissible provided the frame geometry (and loading) is relatively symmetrical, so that no significant *sway* occurs in the actual frame under the gravity loading.

Variations of Moments in a Two-Way Slab Panel

Although the horizontal member in the 'equivalent partial frame' in Figure 11.25(c) is modelled as a very wide beam (i.e., slab with or without beam along the column line), it is actually supported on a very limited width. Hence, the outer portions of the member are less stiff than the part along the column line, and the distribution of moment across the width of the member is not uniform – unlike the beam in the conventional plane frame [Figure 9.1(b)]. The probable variations of moments in a typical panel of the 'equivalent frame' are shown in Figure 11.26.

The variation of bending moment in the floor member along the span, under gravity loads is sketched in Figure 11.26(b). Such a variation – with 'negative moments' near the supports and 'positive moments' in the neighbourhood of the midspan – is typical in any beam subject to uniformly distributed loads. In Figure 11.26(b), M_{ab} denotes the total 'negative' moment in the slab-beam member along the support line *AB* (extending over the full width of the panel), and M_{ef} denotes the total 'positive moment' along the middle line *EF* of the panel.

> **The moments in the slab-beam member, obtained from equivalent frame analysis, are distributed laterally between the beam part and the slab part, or between the column strip and the middle strip, as the case may be.**

These moments are distributed across the width of the panel nonuniformly, as sketched in Figure 11.26(c). The actual variation along *AB* or *EF* (marked by the solid line in Figure 11.26(c)) depends on several factors, such as the span ratio l_2/l_1, relative stiffness of beam (if any) along column lines, torsional stiffness of transverse beams at the columns (if any), etc. The actual moment variation is very difficult to predict exactly, and hence suitable approximations need to be made. This is generally achieved by dividing the slab panel into a *column strip* (along the column line) and two *half-middle strips* [Figure 11.26(a)], and by suitably apportioning the total moment (M_{ab} or M_{ef}) to these strips with the assumption that the moment within each strip is uniform. This is indicated by the broken lines in Figure 11.26(c), and is also clearly shown in Figure 11.26(d).

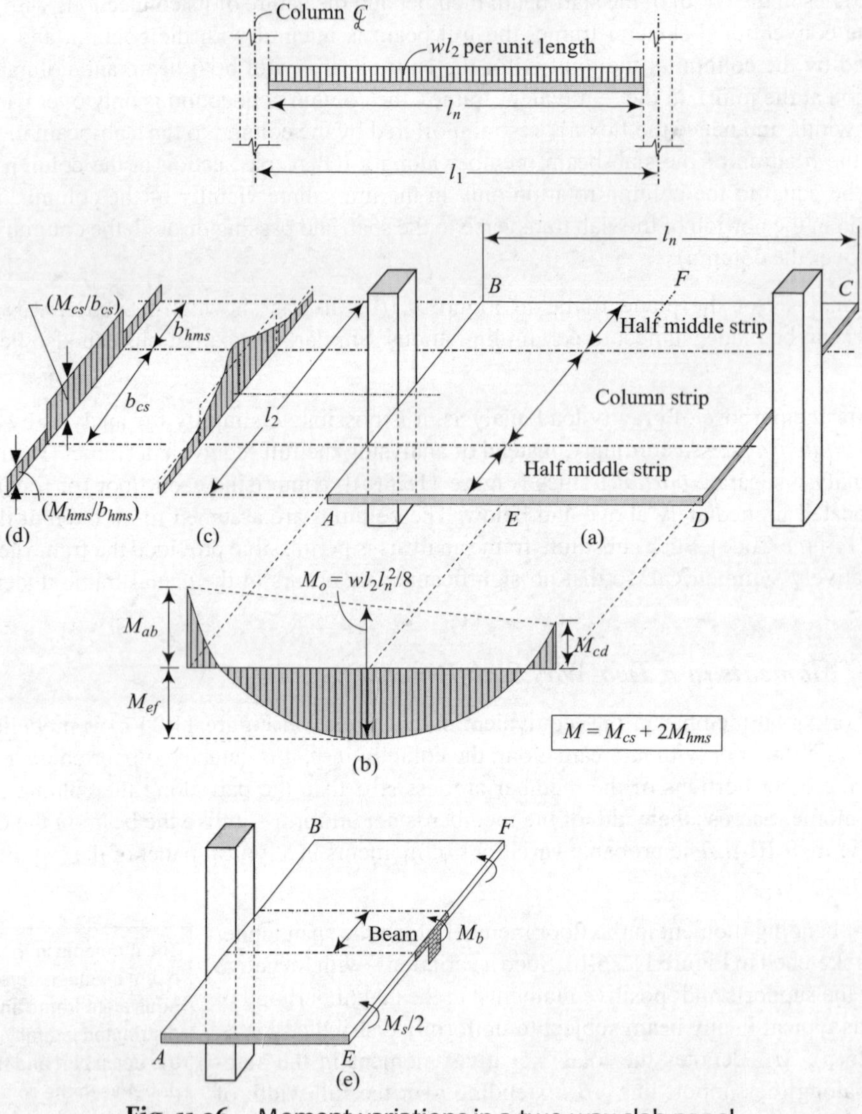

Fig. 11.26 Moment variations in a two-way slab panel

When beams are provided along the column line, the beam portion is relatively stiffer than the slab and resists a major share of the moment at the section. In this case, the moment has to be apportioned between the beam part and the slab part of the slab-beam member as indicated in Figure 11.26(e).

The calculations involved in the design procedure are given in the next section, which follows the unified procedure of design for all types of column-supported slabs – with or without beams (i.e., including flat slabs).

11.4 Design of Column-Supported Slabs (With/Without Beams) Under Gravity Loads

11.4.1 Code Procedures Based on the Equivalent Frame Concept

Two-way slabs supported on columns include *flat plates* [Figure 1.12], *flat slabs* [Figure 1.13], *waffle* (*ribbed*) *slabs* [Figure 1.11], and solid slabs with beams along the column lines [Figure 1.10(b)]. Such slabs may be designed by any procedure which satisfies the basic conditions of equilibrium and geometrical compatibility, and the Code requirements of strength and serviceability. Specific design procedures have been laid out in the Code (Cl. 31) for the design of 'flat slabs', which are defined, according to the Code (Cl. 31.1) as follows:

Equivalent frame concept may be applied to flat plates, flat slabs, ribbed slabs and slabs with beams along column lines.

> The term 'flat slab' means a reinforced concrete slab with or without drops, supported generally without beams, by columns with or without flared column heads. A flat slab may be a solid slab or may have recesses formed on the soffit so that the soffit comprises a series of ribs in two directions.

The above definition is very broad and encompasses the various possible column-supported two-way slabs mentioned earlier, including slabs with beams (note the wording 'generally without beams'). Flat slabs may have an edge beam (indeed they are desirable), which helps in stiffening the discontinuous edge, increasing the shear capacity at the critical exterior column supports and in supporting exterior walls, cladding etc. They also provide restraint at the slab edge, reducing the span moments. Furthermore, they have a favourable effect on the minimum thickness requirement for the slab (see Section 11.4.2). As mentioned earlier, the Code procedure is based on the elastic analysis of 'equivalent frames' [Figure 11.25] under gravity loads, and follows closely the 1977 version of the ACI Code [Ref. 11.11]. However, unlike the unified ACI Code procedure, there is no elaboration in the IS Code (Cl. 31) for the particular case of two-way slabs with beams along column lines as in Figure 1.10(b).

The design procedures described hereinafter† will not only cover the provisions in the prevailing IS Code, but also include provisions in other international codes [Ref. 11.21, 11.22] to cover the case of two-way rectangular slabs supported on flexible beams. These Code procedures are an outcome of detailed analyses of results of extensive tests, comparison with theoretical results based on the theory of plates, and design practices employed successfully in the past. The interested reader may also refer to the background material for the Code procedures presented in Refs. 11.23–11.25. It is assumed that the panels support primarily uniform gravity loading.

The following two methods are recommended by the Code (Cl. 31.3) for determining the bending moments in the slab panel: either method is acceptable (provided the relevant conditions are satisfied):

The DDM is a further simplification, applicable to two-way slab systems meeting certain limitations, and under UD gravity loading.

1. Direct Design Method (DDM)
2. Equivalent Frame Method, also called *Elastic Frame Method* (EFM)

These methods are applicable only to two-way rectangular slabs (not one-way slabs), and, in the case of the Direct Design Method, the recommendations apply to the gravity loading condition alone (and not to the lateral loading condition).

† Other design procedures based on yield line analysis and finite element analysis are also acceptable, provided they satisfy all the requirements mentioned earlier.

Both methods are based on the 'equivalent frame concept' (described in Section 11.3.4). The slab *panel* is defined (Cl. 31.1.1c of the Code) as that part of the slab bounded on each of its four sides by the column centrelines. Each slab panel is divided into *column strips* and *middle strip* [Figure 11.27]. A 'column strip' is defined (Cl. 31.1.1a of the Code) as a design strip having a width equal to the lesser of $0.25l_1$ or $0.25l_2$ on each side of the column centreline, and includes within this width any drop panel or beam (along the column line). Here, l_1 and l_2† are the two spans of the rectangular panel, measured centre-to-centre of the column supports. The 'middle strip' is defined (Cl. 31.1.1b) as a design strip bound on each of its sides by the column strip.

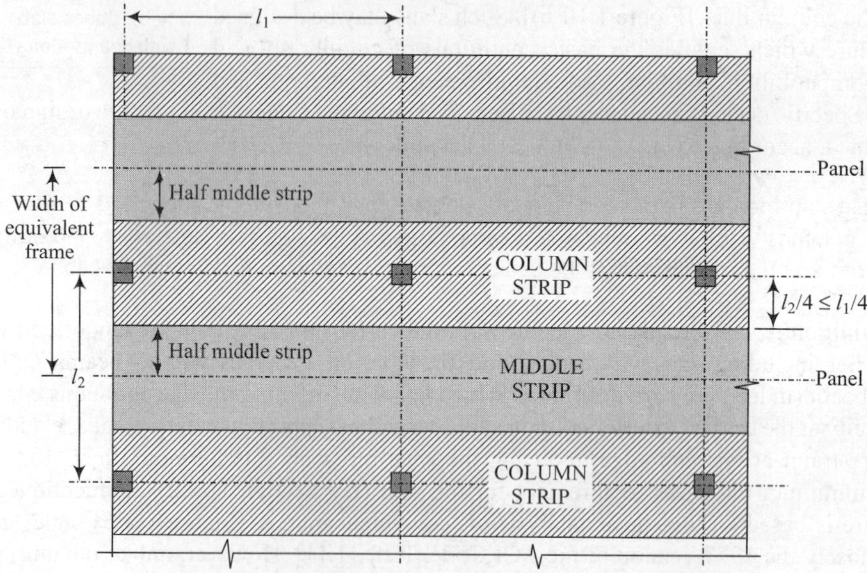

Fig. 11.27 Column strip and middle strip in a slab panel.

While considering an 'equivalent frame' along a column line, the slab width l_2 consists of two half middle strips flanking one column strip, as shown in Figures 11.26(a) and 11.27. When monolithic beams are provided along the column lines, the *effective* (flanged) *beam sections* (which form part of the column strip) are considered to include a portion of the slab on either side of the beam, extending by a distance equal to the projection of the beam above or below the slab (whichever is greater), but not exceeding four times the slab thickness, as shown in Figure 11.28[Ref. 11.21]. In cases where the beam stem is very short, the T-beam may be assumed to have a width equal to that of the column support [Figure 11.28(c)].

The Direct Design Method (described in Section 11.5) and the Equivalent Frame Method (described in Section 11.6) for gravity load analysis differ essentially in the manner of determining the distribution of bending moments along the span in the slab-beam member [Figure 11.26(b)]. The former uses moment coefficients (similar in concept to the simplified Code procedure for continuous beams and one-way slabs – see Sections 5.6.1 and 9.3), whereas the latter requires an elastic partial frame analysis. The procedure for apportioning the factored moments between the middle strip and the column strip (or between the slab and the beam when beams are present along the column line) is identical for both design methods.

† In general, subscript 1 identifies parameters in the direction where moments are being determined, and subscript 2 relates to the perpendicular direction.

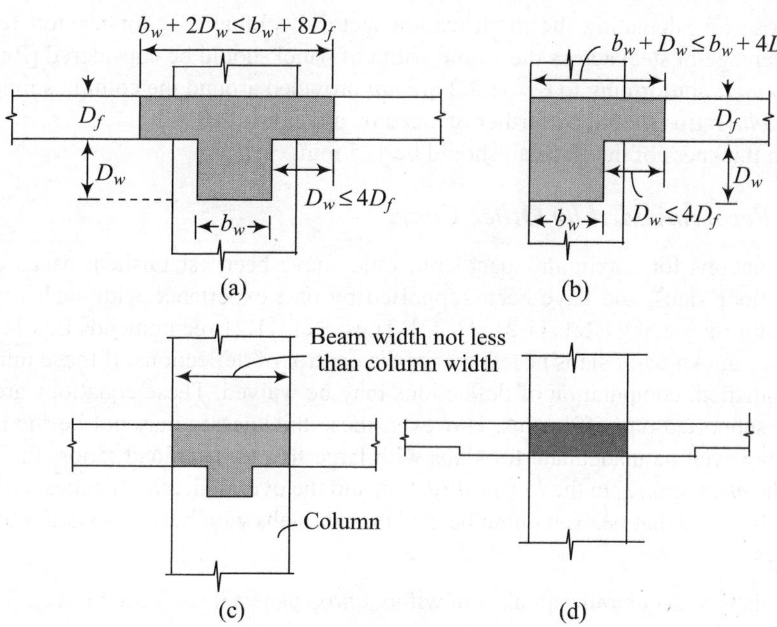

Fig. 11.28 Definition of beam section.

Both methods require the values of several relative stiffness parameters in order to obtain the longitudinal and transverse distribution of factored moments in the design strips. For this purpose, as well as for determining the dead loads on the slab, it is necessary to assume, initially, the gross section dimensions of the floor system (and the columns). These dimensions may need to be modified subsequently, and the analysis and design may therefore need to be suitably revised.

11.4.2 Proportioning of Slab Thickness, Drop Panel and Column Head

Slab Thickness

> **Slab thicknesses are selected, in general, based on *l/d* ratio limits, aimed at controlling deflections. Two-way shear may also be critical.**

The thickness of the slab is generally governed by deflection control criteria. [Shear is also an important design criterion – especially in *flat plates* (slabs without beams and drop panels) and at exterior column supports]. The calculation of deflections of two-way slab systems is quite complex, and recourse is often made to empirical rules which limit maximum span/depth ratios as indirect measures of deflection control. For this purpose, the Code (Cl. 31.2.1) recommends the same *l/d* ratios prescribed (in Cl. 23.2, also refer Section 5.3.2) for flexural members in general, with the following important differences:

- the *longer* span should be considered† (unlike the case of slabs supported on walls or stiff beams, where the *shorter* span is considered);

† These IS Code provisions apply to 'Flat Slabs' as defined in Cl. 31.1. However, it is not clear from the Code whether they apply to slabs with flexible beams between all supports as such slabs are not specifically covered by the Code. Ref. 11.21 does cover such slabs also.

- for the purpose of calculating the modification factor k_t [Table 5.2] for tension reinforcement, an *average* percentage of steel across the whole width of panel should be considered [Ref. 11.11];
- When *drop panels* conforming to Cl. 31.2.2 are *not* provided around the column supports, in flat slabs the calculated *l*/*d* ratios should be further reduced by a factor of 0.9;
- the minimum thickness of the flat slab should be 125 mm.

Slab Thickness Recommended by Other Codes

Other empirical equations for maximum span/depth ratios have been established, based on the results of extensive tests on floor slabs, and have been supported by past experience with such construction under normal values of uniform loading [Ref. 11.21, 11.22]. Thus, Ref. 11.21 recommends Eqs 11.25 to 11.26a for the minimum overall thickness of slabs necessary for the control of deflections. If these minimum thickness requirements are satisfied, computation of deflections may be waived. These equations are also applicable for two-way slabs supported on stiff beams. However, these thicknesses may not be the most economical in all cases, and may even be inadequate for slabs with large live to dead load ratios. In the calculation of span/depth ratio, the *clear span* l_n in the *longer* direction and the overall depth (thickness) of slab *D* are to be considered. It may be noted that 'slabs without beams' include slabs with beams (spandrel beams) *only* along discontinuous edges.

For flat plates and slabs with column capitals, but without drop panels the minimum overall thickness of slab is:

$$D \geq \frac{l_n(0.6 + f_y/1000)}{30} \tag{11.25}$$

However, discontinuous edges shall be provided with an edge beam with stiffness ratio, α_b, of not less than 0.8, failing which the thickness given by Eq. 11.25 shall be increased by 10 per cent in panels with discontinuous edge(s).

For slabs with drop panels, the minimum thickness of slab is:

$$D \geq \frac{l_n(0.6 + f_y/1000)}{30} - \frac{2x_d}{l_n}\Delta_h \tag{11.26}$$

where $(2x_d/l_n)$ is the smaller of the values determined in the two directions, and x_d shall not be taken greater than $l_n/4$, and Δ_h not larger than *D*. Here also, discontinuous edges shall be provided with an edge beam with stiffness ratio, α_b, of not less than 0.8, failing which the thickness given by Eq. 11.25 shall be increased by 10 per cent in panels with discontinuous edge(s).

For slabs with beams between *all* supports, the minimum thickness of slab is:

$$D \geq \frac{l_n(0.6 + f_y/1000)}{30 + 4\beta\alpha_{bm}} \tag{11.26a}$$

where α_{bm} shall not be taken greater than 2.0. This limit is to ensure that with heavy beams all around the panel, the slab thickness does not become too thin. In the above equations,

$x_d \equiv$ dimension from face of column to edge of drop panel, mm;
$f_y \equiv$ characteristic yield strength of steel (in MPa);
$\beta \equiv$ (clear long span)/(clear short span);
$\alpha_{bm} \equiv$ average value of α_b for all beams on edges of slab panel;

$\alpha_b \equiv$ the ratio of the moment of inertia of the beam section to that of a width of slab bounded laterally by the centreline of the adjacent panel (if any) on each side of the beam, equal to I_b/I_s.

$\Delta_h \equiv$ the additional thickness of the drop panel below the soffit of the slab and shall not be taken larger than D

Referring to Figure 11.28,

$$\alpha_b = \frac{I_b}{I_s} \tag{11.27}$$

where I_b is the second moment of area with respect to the centroidal axis of the *gross* flanged section of the beam [shaded area in Figures 11.28(a), (b), (c) and (d)] and $I_s = l_2 D^3/12$. The value of I_b may be taken as:

$$I_b = \frac{bD_b^3}{12}\left(2.5\left(1 - \frac{D}{D_b}\right)\right) \tag{11.27a}$$

where b is the width and D_b the overall depth of the beam.

The minimum thickness for flat slabs obtained from Eq. 11.25 are given in Table 11.3

Table 11.3 *Minimum thicknesses for two-way slabs without beams between interior column supports (Eq. 11.25)*

Steel Grade	Without Drop Panels[1]	
	no edge beam	with edge beam[2]
Fe 250	$l_n/32.1$	$l_n/35.3$
Fe 415	$l_n/26.9$	$l_n/29.6$
Fe 500	$l_n/24.8$	$l_n/27.3$

[1]Thickness to be not less than 125 mm (as per Code).
[2]Edge beam must satisfy $\alpha \geq 0.80$.

Drop Panels

The 'drop panel' is formed by local thickening of the slab in the neighbourhood of the supporting column. Drop panels (or simply, *drops*) are provided mainly for the purpose of reducing shear stresses around the column supports. They also help in reducing the steel requirement for 'negative' moments at the column supports. [Also refer Section 11.7 for calculation of reinforcement at drop panels].

The Code (Cl. 31.2.2) recommends that drops should be rectangular in plan, and have a length in each direction not less than one-third† of the panel length in that direction. For exterior panels, the length, measured perpendicular to the discontinuous edge from the column centreline should be taken as one-half of the corresponding width of drop for the interior panel [Figure 11.29(a)].

The Code does not specify a minimum thickness requirement for the drop panel except that in computation of negative moment reinforcement, the effective depth at the drop panel shall not exceed the thickness of the slab plus one-quarter of the distance between edge of drop and edge of column capital (Cl. 31.7.2). It is, however, recommended [Ref. 11.21, 11.22] that the projection below the slab should not be less than one-fourth the slab thickness, and preferably not less than 100 mm [Figure 11.29(b)].

Column Capital

The 'column capital' (or *column head*), provided at the top of a column, is intended primarily to increase the capacity of the slab to resist *punching shear* [see Section 11.8.2]. The flaring of the column at top is generally done such that the plan geometry at the column head is similar to that of the column.

† This may be interpreted as one-sixth of the centre-to-centre dimension to columns on either side of the centre of the column under consideration, as depicted in Figure 11.29(a).

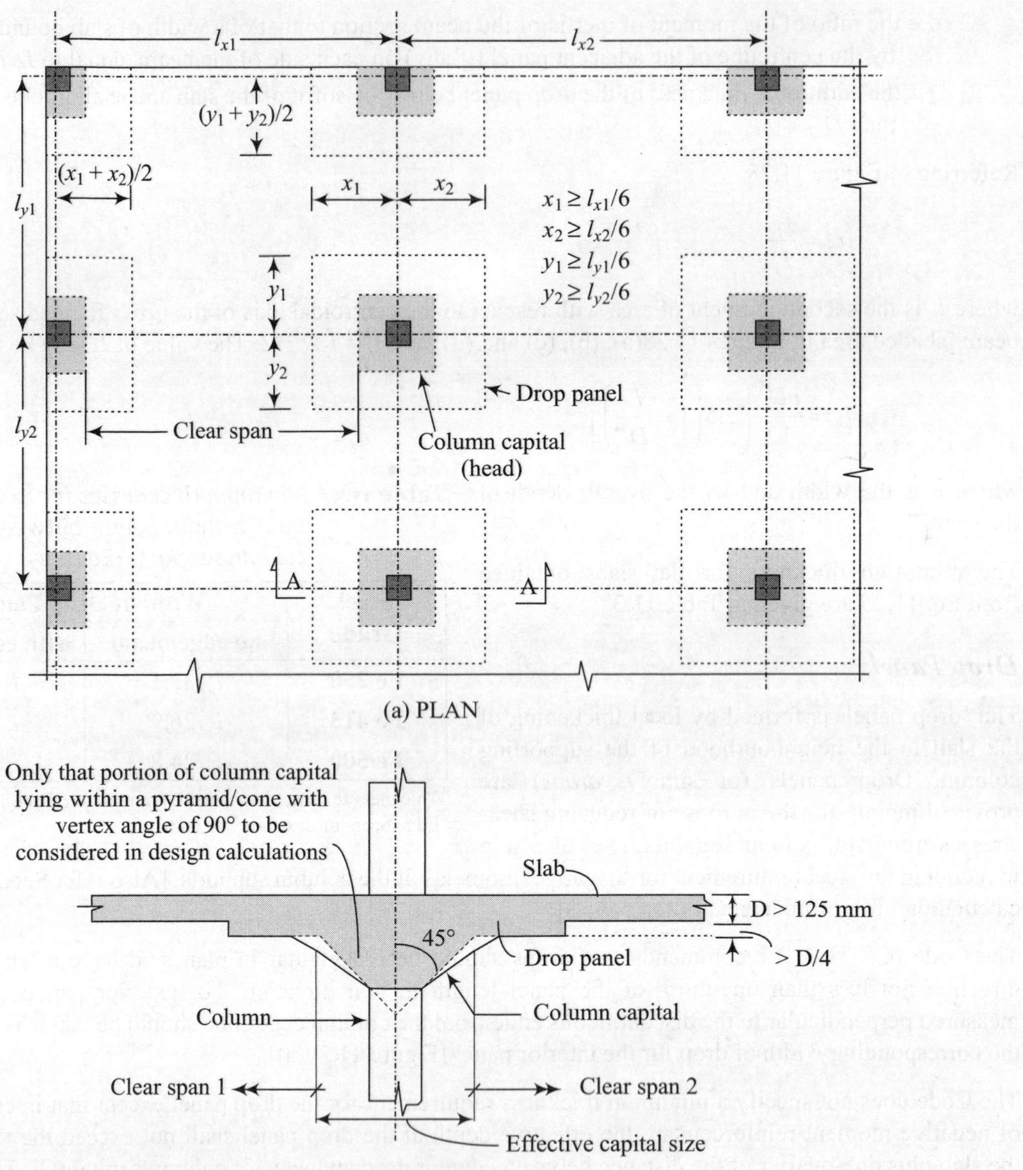

Fig. 11.29 Drop panel and column capital.

The Code (Cl. 31.2.3) restricts the structurally useful portion of the column capital to that portion which lies within the largest (inverted) pyramid or right circular cone which has a vertex angle of 90 degrees, and can be included entirely within the outlines of the column and the column head [Figure 11.29(b)]. This is based on the assumption of a 45° failure plane, outside of which enlargements of the support are considered ineffective in transferring shear to the column [Ref. 11.11].

In the Direct Design Method, the calculation of bending moments is based on a clear span l_n, measured face-to-face of the supports (including column capitals, if any) *but not less than* 0.65 *times the panel span* in the direction under consideration [Cl. 31.4.2.2. of the Code]. When the column (support) width in the direction of span exceeds $0.35l_1$, (to be more precise, $0.175l_1$ on either side of the column centreline), the critical section for calculating the factored 'negative' moment should be taken at a distance not greater than $0.175l_1$ from the centre of the column (Cl.31.5.3).

11.4.3 Transfer of Shear and Moments to Columns in Beamless Two-Way Slabs

Shear forces and bending moments have to be transferred between the floor system and the supporting columns. In slabs without beams along column lines, this needs special considerations.

The design moments in the slabs are computed by frame analysis in the case of the Equivalent Frame Method, and by empirical equations in the case of the Direct Design Method. At any column support, the total unbalanced moment in the slabs must be resisted by the columns above and below in proportion to their relative stiffnesses [Figure 11.30(a)].

In slabs without beams along the column line, the transfer of the unbalanced moment from the slab to the column takes place partly through direct flexural stresses, and partly through development of non-uniform shear stresses around the column head. A part (M_{ub}) of the unbalanced moment M_u can be considered to be transferred by flexure and the balance (M_{uv}) through eccentricity of shear forces, as shown in Figures 11.30(b) and (c). The Code recommendation (Cl. 31.3.3) for the apportioning of M_{ub} and M_{uv} is based on a study described in Ref. 11.26:

$$M_{ub} = \gamma M_u \tag{11.28a}$$

$$M_{uv} = (1-\gamma)M_u \tag{11.28b}$$

where

$$\gamma = \frac{1}{1+\dfrac{2}{3}\sqrt{\dfrac{c_1+d}{c_2+d}}} \tag{11.29}$$

Here, c_1 and c_2 are the dimensions of the equivalent rectangular column, capital or bracket, measured in the direction moments are being determined and in the transverse direction, respectively, and d is the effective depth of the slab at the critical section for shear [refer Section 11.8.2]. For square and round columns, $c_1 = c_2$, and $\gamma = 0.6$.

The width of the slab considered effective in resisting the moment M_{ub} is taken as the width between lines a distance 1.5 times slab/drop thickness on either side of the column or column capital [Figure 11.30(b)], and hence this strip should have adequate reinforcement to resist this moment. The detailing of reinforcement for moment transfer, particularly at the exterior column where the unbalanced moment is usually the largest, is critical for the safety as well as the performance of flat slabs without edge beams.

The critical section considered for moment transfer by eccentricity of shear is at a distance $d/2$ from the periphery of the column or column capital [Figure 11.30(c)]. The shear stresses introduced because of the moment transfer, (assumed to vary linearly about the centroid of the critical section), should be added to the shear stresses due to the vertical support reaction [refer Section 11.8.2].

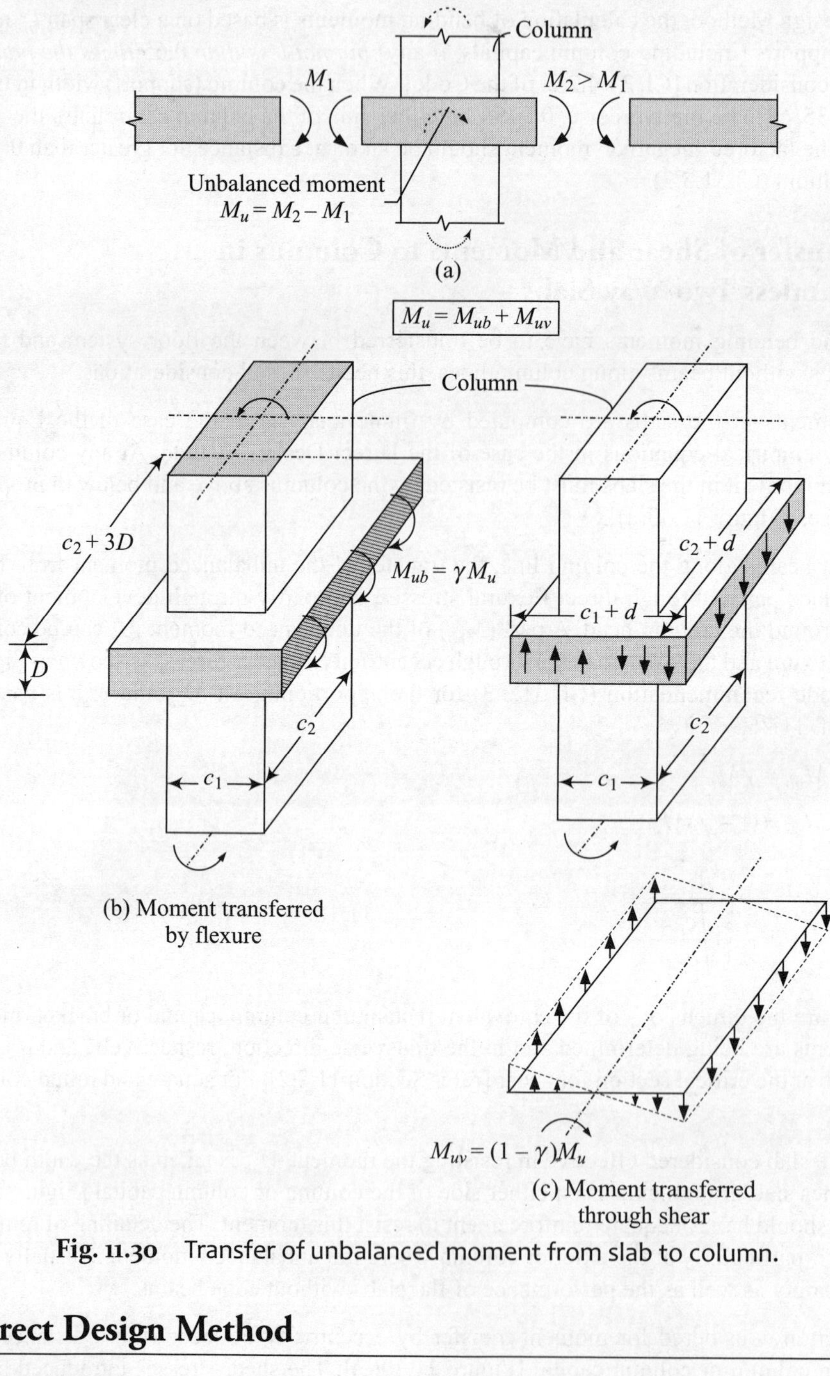

Fig. 11.30 Transfer of unbalanced moment from slab to column.

11.5 Direct Design Method

11.5.1 Limitations

The Direct Design Method (DDM) is a simplified procedure of determining the 'negative' and 'positive' design moments (under gravity loads) at critical sections in the slab (slab-beam member), using empirical moment coefficients. In order to ensure that these design moments are not significantly different from those obtained by an elastic analysis, the Code (Cl. 31.4.1) specifies that the following conditions must be satisfied by the two-way slab systems for the application of DDM.

1. There must be at least three continuous spans in each direction.
2. Each panel must be rectangular, with the long to short span ratio not exceeding 2.0; i.e., there should be significant two-way slab action.
3. The columns must not be offset by more than 10 per cent of the span (in the direction of offset) from either axis between centrelines of successive columns†.
4. The successive span lengths (centre-to-centre of supports), in each direction, must not differ by more than one-third of the longer span.
5. The factored live load must not exceed three times the factored dead load (otherwise, moments produced by pattern loading would be more severe than those calculated by DDM).

There is an additional limitation prescribed by other codes [Ref. 11.21, 11.22], with regard to the application of this method to slab systems with beam between supports. The following condition, relating to the relative effective stiffness of beams in the two perpendicular directions, needs to be satisfied in such cases:

$$0.2 \le \frac{\alpha_{b1} l_2^2}{\alpha_{b2} l_1^2} \le 5.0 \tag{11.30}$$

where α_b is defined by Eq. 11.27, and the subscripts 1 and 2 refer to the direction moments are being determined, and transverse to it, respectively. Ref. 11.21 also limits the live load/dead load ratio to ≤2.0. Furthermore, the loads are assumed to be gravity loads, uniformly distributed over the entire panel.

11.5.2 Total Design Moment for a Span

In any given span, l_1, the *total (factored) design moment* M_o for the span, is expressed as [refer Cl. 31.4.2.2 of the Code]:

$$M_o = w_u l_2 l_n^2 / 8 \tag{11.31}$$

where $w_u \equiv$ factored load per unit area of the slab;

$l_n \equiv$ clear span in the direction of M_o, measured face-to-face of columns‡, capitals, brackets or walls, *but not less than* $0.65 l_1$§;

$l_1 \equiv$ length of span in the direction of M_o; and

$l_2 \equiv$ length of span transverse to l_1.

With reference to Figure 11.26(b), it can be seen that considering statics, the absolute sum of the mid-span 'positive' and average 'negative' design moments in the slab panel must be equal to M_o. The expression for M_o [Eq. 11.31] is obtained as the maximum midspan static moment in an equivalent simply supported span l_n, subjected to a uniformly distributed total load $W = w_u(l_2 l_n)$, where $l_2 l_n$ is the effective panel area on which

† If the column offsets result in variation in spans in the transverse direction, the adjacent transverse spans should be averaged while carrying out the analysis [Cl. 31.4.2.4].

‡ Circular/nonrectangular column supports are to be treated as equivalent square/rectangular supports having the same area (Cl. 31.4.2.3 of the Code).

§ This condition is imposed in order to prevent undue reduction in the design moment when the columns are long and narrow in cross-section or have large brackets or capitals [Ref. 11.11].

w_u acts. When drop panels are used, the contribution of the additional dead load (due to local thickening at drops) should be suitably accounted for; this is illustrated in Example 11.7.

11.5.3 Longitudinal Distribution of Total Design Moment

The typical variation of moments (under gravity loads) in the slab, along the span, has already been introduced in Figure 11.26(b). The Code recommendation (Cl. 31.4.3.3) for the distribution of the calculated 'total design moment', M_o, between critical 'negative' moment sections (at the faces of equivalent rectangular supports) and 'positive' moment sections (at or near midspan) is as depicted in Figure 11.31.

- *Interior span*:
  - 'negative' design moment $M_o^- = 0.65M_o$ (11.32a)
  - 'positive' design moment $M_o^+ = 0.35M_o$ (11.32b)
- *Exterior span*:
  - 'negative' design moment at *exterior* support $M_{o,ext}^- = (0.65/q)M_o$ (11.33a)
  - 'negative' design moment at *interior* support $M_{o,int}^- = (0.75 - 0.10/q)M_o$ (11.33b)
  - 'positive' design moment $M_o^+ = (0.63 - 0.28/q)M_o$ (11.33c)

where $q \equiv 1 + (1/\alpha_c)$ (11.34)

$$\alpha_c \equiv \left(\sum K_c\right)/K_{sb} \tag{11.35}$$

$\sum K_c$ ≡ sum of flexural stiffnesses of columns meeting at the exterior joint; and

K_{sb} ≡ flexural stiffness of the slab (or slab-beam member) in the direction moments are calculated (i.e., along span l_1), at the exterior joint.

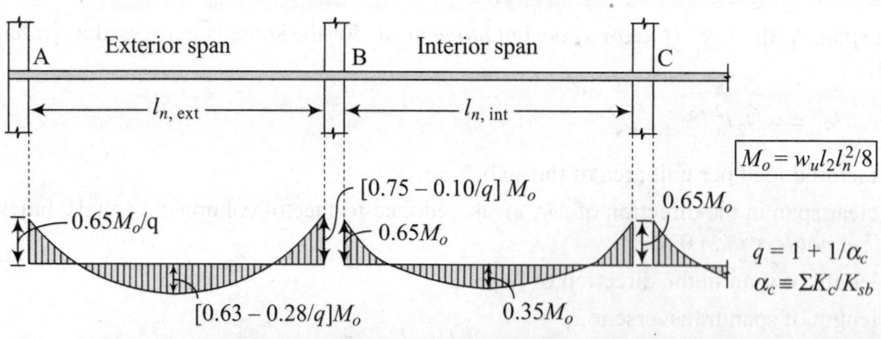

Fig. 11.31 Distribution of M_o into 'negative' and 'positive' design moments (longitudinal).

At interior supports such as B in Figure 11.31, the 'negative' moment sections must be designed to resist the *larger* of the two design 'negative' moments (on either side of the support), unless an analysis is made to distribute the unbalanced moment in accordance with the relative stiffnesses of the elements framing into the support (Cl. 31.4.3.5 of the Code). [However, the moments may be modified as given below.]

The Code (Cl. 31.4.3.4) permits a limited readjustment in the apportioned design moments – but by no more than 10 per cent, because of the approximations and limitations inherent in the Direct Design Method –

provided the total design moment M_o for the panel is not less than the value given by Eq. 11.31. No additional redistribution of moments is permitted.

For the purpose of calculating the flexural stiffness (K_{sb}) of the slab-beam member and that of the column (K_c), it is permitted [Ref. 11.11] to assume that the members are prismatic (i.e., having uniform cross-section throughout their lengths). This is done purely for convenience, and is in keeping with the simplifications underlying DDM. This assumption implies that the contributions of drop panels, column capitals and brackets may be neglected. Furthermore, the increase in the second moment of area of the slab-beam member, between the column centreline and column face, may be neglected. With these simplifications, the flexural stiffness K (of the column or slab-beam member) is simply obtained as:

$$K = 4E_c I/l \tag{11.36}$$

where $E_c \equiv$ short-term modulus of elasticity of concrete (for the grade applicable to the element);
$I \equiv$ second moment of area (considering the *gross* section†); and
$l \equiv$ appropriate centre-to-centre span.

The Code (under Cl. 31) covers only flat slabs, and as such Eq. 11.32 to 11.35 are not specifically meant for use in the case of two-way slabs with flexible beams between column supports. However, other codes [Ref. 11.21] do permit the use of DDM for the latter case mentioned above. For two-way slabs with beams, for interior spans, Eqs 11.32(a), (b) are applicable. For exterior spans, the distribution of M_o for slabs with beams may be made according to the factors given in Table 11.4 – case (2).

Table 11.4 *Moment factors for end span [Ref. 11.21]*

Case	(1) Exterior edge not restrained	(2) Slab with beams between all supports	(3) Slab without beams between interior supports	(4) Exterior edge fully restrained
Interior negative factored moment	0.75	0.70	0.70	0.65
Positive factored moment	0.66	0.59	0.52	0.35
Exterior negative factored moment	0	0.16	0.26	0.65

It may be noted that when the slab is stiffened with beams along the column lines, the calculation of the second moment of area I must logically include the contribution of the portion of the beam projecting below (or above) the slab.

The calculations related to flexural stiffness are required for the purpose of determining the parameter α_c [Eq. 11.35], required for the moment factors in the end span [Eq. 11.33]. An alternative and simpler scheme for end spans (with moment coefficients independent of α_c), suggested in Ref. 11.21, is shown in Table 11.4. [As already indicated above, this Table also covers the case of end spans of two-way slabs with beams between all columns.]

11.5.4 Apportioning of Moments to Middle Strips, Column Strips and Beams

As mentioned earlier [Figures 11.26(c), (d)], the calculated design 'positive' and 'negative' slab moments in the panel in the longitudinal direction have to be apportioned transversely to the design strips of the panel

† In the case of the slab-beam member, the width of the section should be taken as the full panel width, l_2.

(*column strip* (*cs*) and *half middle strips* (*hms*) in flat slabs, and the *beam* part and the *slab* part when there are beams) at all critical sections. This procedure of transverse distribution of moments is common for both Direct Design Method and Equivalent Frame Method.

IS Code Recommendations

The Code recommendations for flat slabs (Cl. 31.5.5) in this regard are based mainly on studies reported in Ref. 11.27:

- *'Negative' moment at exterior support*:
  - *column strip*: $M_{cs,\text{ext}}^{-} = \begin{cases} 1.00 M_{o,\text{ext}}^{-} & \text{if column (or wall) width} < 0.75 l_2 \\ (b_{cs}/l_2) M_{o,\text{ext}}^{-} & \text{otherwise} \end{cases}$ (11.37a)
  - *half middle strip*:

$$M_{hms,\text{ext}}^{-} = \begin{cases} 0 & \text{if col. width} < 0.75 l_2 \\ 0.5(1 - b_{cs}/l_2) M_{o,\text{ext}}^{-} & \text{otherwise} \end{cases} \quad (11.37b)$$

  where b_{cs} is the width of the column strip [Figure 11.26].
- *'Negative' moment at interior support*:
  - *column strip*: $M_{cs,\text{int}}^{-} = 0.75\, M_{o,\text{int}}^{-}$ (11.38a)
  - *half middle strip*: $M_{hms,\text{int}}^{-} = 0.125\, M_{o,\text{int}}^{-}$ (11.38b)
- *'Positive' moment for all spans:*
  - *column strip*: $M_{cs}^{+} = 0.60\, M_o^{+}$ (11.39a)
  - *half middle strip*: $M_{hms}^{+} = 0.20\, M_o^{+}$ (11.39b)

The transverse distribution of moments for a typical exterior slab panel is depicted in Figure 11.32. The moments indicated are assumed to be uniformly distributed across the width of the respective design strips.

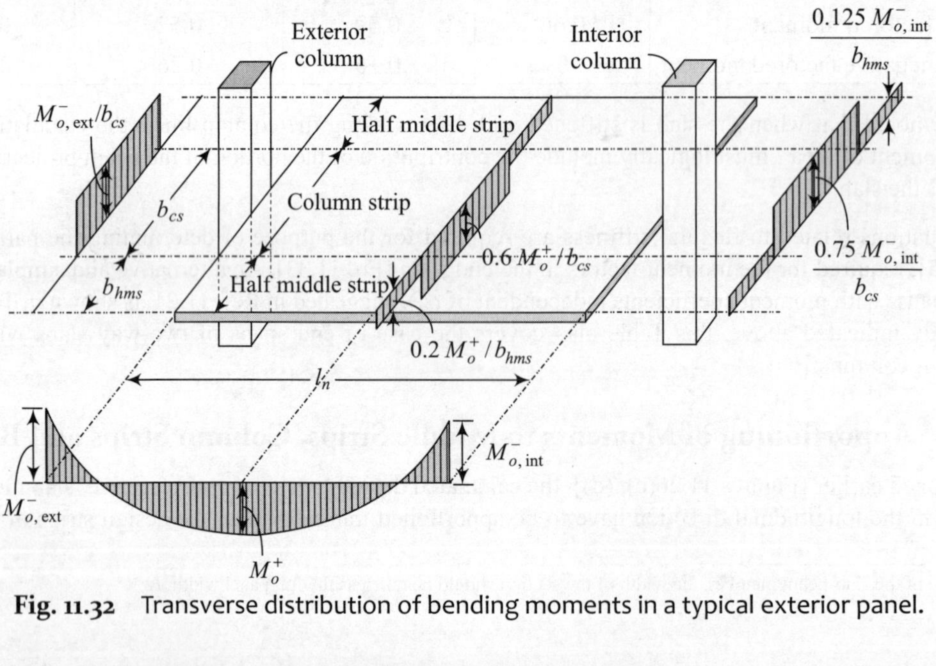

Fig. 11.32 Transverse distribution of bending moments in a typical exterior panel.

In the case of a panel with a discontinuous edge in the direction of M_o (span l_1), such as in the *external* equivalent frame shown in Figure 11.25(a), the design of the half-column strip adjoining and parallel to the discontinuous edge, as well as the middle strip in the panel, depends on whether a marginal beam (with depth > $1.5D_s$) or wall is supporting the slab at the edge. If such a stiffening of the edge exists, the bending moments in the half-column strip should be taken as one-quarter of that for the first interior column strip, and the moments in the middle strip as twice that assigned to the half-middle strip corresponding to the first row of interior columns (Cl. 31.3.2b and 31.5.5.4c of the Code).

Canadian Code Recommendations

A more simplified scheme for transverse distribution of moment, which accounts for the ability of slabs to redistribute moments, is given in the Canadian code [Ref. 11.21]. Slabs are highly statically indeterminate and usually greatly under-reinforced. This leads to the formation of yield lines along sections of peak moment, effecting considerable moment redistribution to sections of lesser moment (see Section 9.7 and Figure 9.12). This inherent ability of the slab gives the designer considerable leeway in adjusting the moment field and designing the reinforcement accordingly, subject to static equilibrium conditions and requirements of strength and serviceability being met. Reflecting this flexibility, for slabs without beams, the Canadian code gives a *range of values* for the column strip share of moment, from which the designer can *choose* an appropriate value; the balance is apportioned to the middle strip. For slabs with beams, the distribution is between the beam part and the slab part, the proportions being dependent on the beam stiffness ratio α_{b1} and the span ratio l_2/l_1. This procedure is applicable to both Direct Design Method and Equivalent Frame Method. These provisions are summarised below, and will be particularly useful for slabs with beams, as IS Code provisions do not cover them:

(a) Slabs without interior beams This includes flat plates and slabs with drop panels and/or column capitals, which may or may not have edge beams along the discontinuous edges (spandrel beams).

(i) Column strip moments: The column strips are designed to resist the total negative or positive moments at the critical sections (given in Figure 11.31 for DDM) multiplied by an appropriate factor within the following ranges:

1. For slabs *without* Drop Panels (with or without spandrel beams):
   (a) Negative moment at interior column 0.70 to 0.90
   (b) Negative moment at exterior column 1.00
   (c) Positive moment in all spans 0.55 to 0.65
2. For slabs *with* Drop Panels (with or without spandrel beams):
   (a) Negative moment at interior column 0.75 to 0.90
   (b) Negative moment at exterior column 1.00
   (c) Positive moment in all spans 0.55 to 0.65

Furthermore, at interior columns, a band of slab with a width extending a distance of $1.5D$ (or $1.5D_D$ for slab with drops) past the sides of the column or the column capital shall be designed to resist at least *one-third* of the total factored negative moment in the entire design strip. Similarly, reinforcement for the total factored negative moment transferred to the *exterior* column shall be placed within such a bandwidth. This is to facilitate the transfer of unbalanced moment to the column by flexure. Further, at the exterior column, the section of slab outside the above band shall be provided with reinforcement not less than that required for temperature and shrinkage effects.

(ii) Middle strip moments: At all critical sections, the portion of the negative and positive moments not resisted by the column strip is assigned proportionately to the two half middle strips on either side of the column strip. A full middle strip in a panel has moments assigned to its two halves from the equivalent frames on either side (Figure 11.33). The middle strip adjacent to and parallel with an edge supported by a wall must be designed for twice the moment assigned to its interior half portion forming part of the equivalent frame along the first row of interior supports (Figure 11.33).

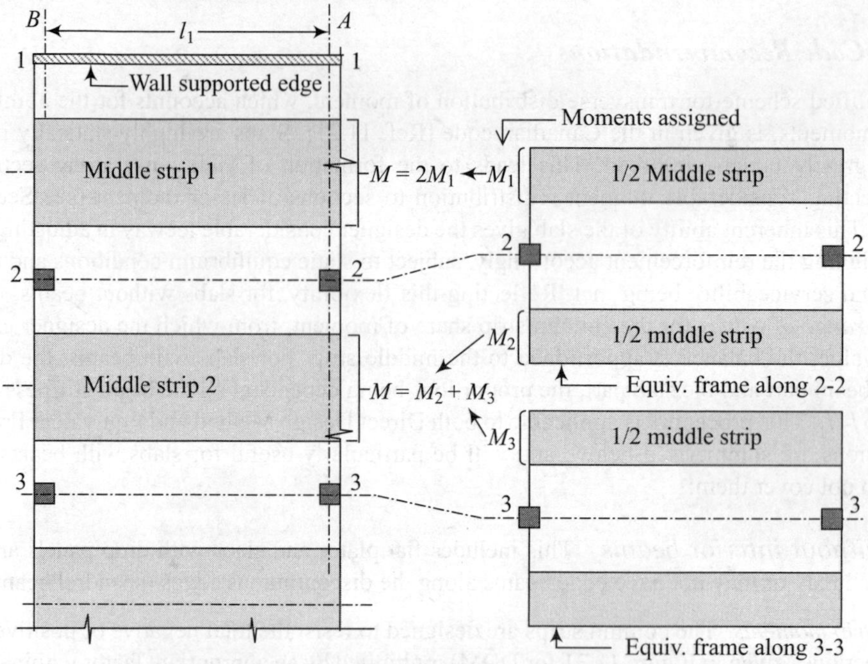

Fig. 11.33 Factored moments in middle strips.

Slab edges must be reinforced with top reinforcement perpendicular to the edge to resist the factored moments caused by edge loads, but not less than the minimum required for temperature and shrinkage. Where the discontinuous edge is not supported by a spandrel beam or wall, or where the slab cantilevers beyond the support, both the top and bottom reinforcement shall be extended to the edge of the slab.

(b) Slabs with beams between all supports In this case, the slab-beam member is divided into the beam part (see Figures 11.26e and 11.28) and the slab part which is the portion of the member outside the beam part.

(i) Moments in beams: The beam shall be designed to resist the following fractions of the total negative and positive moments at the critical sections (given in Figure 11.31 for DDM):

- Negative moment at interior columns and positive moment in all spans – $\dfrac{\alpha_{b1}}{0.3 + \alpha_{b1}}\left(1 - \dfrac{l_2}{3l_1}\right)$ (11.40)
- Negative moment at an exterior column – 100 per cent

The beam must also resist moments due to loads directly applied on it and not considered in slab design such as weight of walls and the beam rib. Here also, the negative moment reinforcement at exterior support must be placed within a band of width b_b extending a distance 1.5D past the sides of the column or the side of the beam web, whichever is larger.

(ii) Moments in slabs: The portion of the negative and positive moments not resisted by the beam is assigned to the slab parts outside the beam. The slab reinforcement for the negative moment at interior supports shall be uniformly distributed over the width of the slab. Positive moment reinforcements may also be distributed uniformly.

(iii) Corner reinforcement: In slabs with beams between supports with a value of α greater than 1.0, top and bottom reinforcement shall be provided at exterior corners of slab for a distance, in each direction, equal to 1/5 of shorter span (see Figures 11.2c and 11.10). This reinforcement shall be adequate to resist a moment per unit width equal to the maximum positive moment per unit width in the slab. As shown in Figure 11.2c, the top reinforcement shall be so placed as to resist moments about axes perpendicular to the diagonal from the corner and the bottom reinforcement to resist moments about axes parallel to the diagonal. Alternatively, the reinforcements may be placed in bands parallel to the sides of the slab.

11.5.5 Loads on the Edge Beam

The IS Code (Cl. 31.3.2) describes a procedure for the design of 'marginal beams' (edge beams) having an overall depth greater than 1.5 times the slab thickness or walls supporting a flat slab. According to this procedure, the slab portion in the 'half-column strip' adjacent to the edge beam (or wall) should be designed to resist one-quarter of the design moment assigned to the 'first interior column strip'. The edge beam or wall should be designed to carry the loads acting directly on it (if any) plus a uniformly distributed load equal to one-quarter of the total load on the slab panel [also refer Section 11.5.8].

11.5.6 Torsion in Edge Beam

Although the IS Code does not offer any specific recommendation for torsion in the transverse beam at the exterior edge, it is evident that some of the 'negative' moment at the exterior edge of the panel ($M^-_{o,\text{ext}}$) will be transferred to the column by torsion in the edge beam [Figure 11.34], and the balance will be transferred to the column through flexure at the column-slab connection.

> **Negative moments developed in the slab at an exterior edge cause a distributed twisting moment on the connected edge beam.**

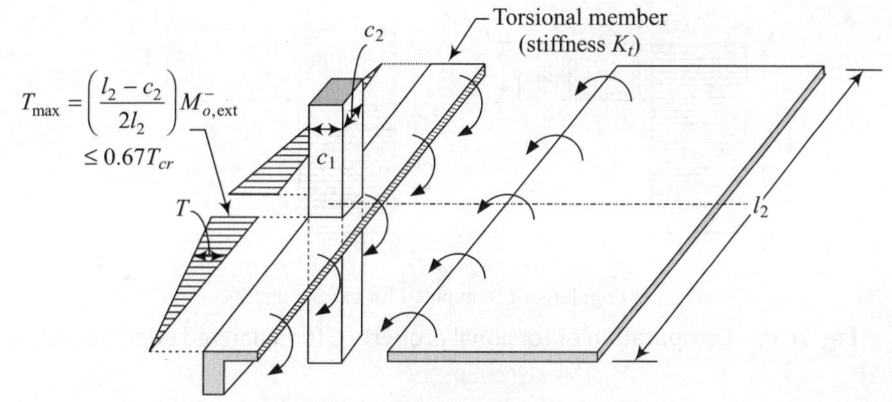

Fig. 11.34 Torsion in edge beam.

The edge beam, therefore, has to be designed as a *spandrel beam* subjected to a torsional moment distributed along its length (in addition to the bending moments and shear force due to the loads indicated in Section 11.5.5). For this purpose, it may be assumed, conservatively, that the entire 'negative' design moment at the exterior support, $M_{o,ext}^{-}$ is uniformly distributed over the width of the design strip, l_2, as shown in Figure 11.33. This results in a linear variation of twisting moment in the edge beam, with a zero value at the mid-span (panel centreline) and a maximum value at the face of the column, as illustrated.

If the maximum torque (T_{max}) exceeds the cracking torque (T_{cr}) of the edge (spandrel) beam, torsional cracking will occur; there will be a reduction in the torsional stiffness and a consequent redistribution of moments[†] [Ref. 11.32] resulting in a relaxation in the induced torque. For this reason, if T_{max} exceeds $0.67T_{cr}$, Ref. 11.21 permits the use of a maximum factored torque of $0.67T_{cr}$, provided a corresponding readjustment is made to the 'positive' moment in the span. If this is done, $M_{o,ext}^{-}$ gets restricted to $2 \times 0.67\ T_{cr} l_2/(l_2 - c_2)$, and the 'positive' moment in the span has to be correspondingly adjusted to maintain the value of M_o [Eq. 11.31].

The design of the edge beam for torsion should conform to the requirements described in Chapter 7.

Some torsion can also be expected to occur in the transverse beams at the interior columns, due to unbalanced moments in the panels on the two sides of these beams. However, such torsion is generally negligible (except in exceptional cases), and hence not considered in design.

Torsional Member and Stiffness

The transverse torsional member (at the edge as in Figure 11.34 or over an interior column) is assumed to have a cross section consisting of the larger of: (i) a portion of the slab having a width equal to that of the column, bracket, or capital measured in the direction l_1 plus that part of the transverse beam (if any) above and below the slab; and (ii) the beam section as defined in Figure 11.28. For the calculation of the torsional stiffness of this member, needed for the Equivalent Frame Method, the torsional property C of the section (refer Section 7.2.3) is needed.

The computation of an exact value of C for a flanged section being very difficult, it suffices to obtain an approximate value for C by subdividing the section into rectangles such that the summation of the C values of the component rectangles results in a maximum value [Figure 11.35]. This is done by subdividing in such a way as to minimise the length of the common boundaries.

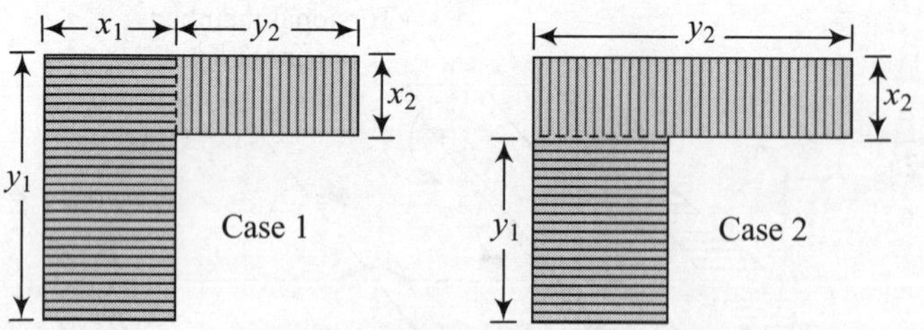

Fig. 11.35 Computation of torsional property C for a flanged edge beam.

† Refer Section 9.7.3 ('torsional plastic hinge').

The expression for C [refer to Section 7.2.3] is accordingly obtained as:

$$C = \sum\left(1 - 0.63\frac{x}{y}\right)\frac{x^3 y}{3} \tag{11.41}$$

where x and y are the short and long dimensions of the rectangular part [Figure 11.35].

11.5.7 Moments in Columns and Pattern Loading

As explained in Section 11.4.3, columns (and walls) built monolithically with the slab must be designed to resist the unbalanced moments transferred from the slab. The total moment transferred to the *exterior* column is the same as the 'negative' design moment ($M^-_{o,\text{ext}}$) at the exterior support, computed by the factors in Figure 11.31 and Table 11.4 for DDM and obtained by frame analysis in EFM. The negative moments at faces of supports computed by these factors for the DDM correspond to the action of full factored live load plus dead load, whereas the maximum unbalanced moment at the *interior* support would occur under pattern loading. Hence, in the case of the *interior* column, the Code (Cl. 31.4.5.2) recommends the use of the following empirical expression[†] for the total unbalanced (factored) moment to be resisted by the column:

$$M_u = \frac{0.08[(w_{u,DL} + 0.5w_{u,LL})l_2 l_n^2 - w'_{u,DL} l'_2 (l'_n)^2]}{1 + 1/\alpha_c} \tag{11.42}$$

where $\alpha_c \equiv (\Sigma K_c / \Sigma K_s)$

$w_{u,DL}$, $w_{u,LL} \equiv$ design (factored) dead and live loads per unit area on the longer span;

$w'_{u,DL} \equiv$ design dead load per unit area on the shorter span;

l_2, $l'_2 \equiv$ lengths transverse to the direction of M_u in the long span and short span respectively;

l_n, $l'_n \equiv$ lengths of clear spans (measured face to face of supports) in the direction of M_u, in the long span and short span respectively;

$\alpha_c \equiv$ relative column stiffness parameter; and

K_c and K_s are flexural stiffnesses of column and slab respectively.

The total unbalanced moment transferred to the column (exterior or interior) should be distributed to the columns above and below the floor under consideration, in direct proportion to their relative stiffnesses.

Furthermore, in the case of beamless slabs, as explained in Section 11.4.3, a fraction, $M_{ub} = \gamma M_u$, of the unbalanced moment is transferred by flexure of a width of slab, and the balance, $M_{uv} = M_u - M_{ub}$, is transferred by shear. The design of the slab should account for the resulting flexural and shear stresses.

Effects of Pattern Loading on Slab Moments

The moments at critical sections in the slab, computed in DDM using the factors in Figure 11.31 also correspond to the application of full factored load (dead load plus live load) on all spans. Due to 'pattern loading' (i.e., occurrence of dead load on all spans and live load only on certain critical spans), it is possible that the 'positive' bending moments could exceed the calculated values for full loading (on all spans), in an extreme case, by as much as 100 per cent [Ref. 11.11]. However, there is no likelihood of a significant increase

[†] This expression for M_u has been derived for the case of two adjacent unequal spans, with full dead load plus half live load on the long span and dead load alone on the short span, thereby (partially) accounting for the effects of pattern loading [Ref. 11.11].

in the calculated 'negative' moment at the support, because the loading pattern for maximum moment for such a case requires full factored loads to be considered on both spans adjoining the support.

If the relative stiffness of the columns, measured by the parameter α_c (defined by Eq. 11.35), is high, such excess of the maximum 'positive' moment under pattern loading (over that calculated with full loading on all spans) is low. The Code (Cl. 31.4.6) prescribes that if α_c is *not* less than a specified value $\alpha_{c,\,min}$, then the possible increase in the design 'positive' moment may be ignored. If, however, the columns lack the desired minimum relative stiffness, i.e., $\alpha_c < \alpha_{c,\,min}$, then the calculated 'positive' design moments should be increased by a factor, δ_s, defined as follows:

$$\delta_s = 1 + \frac{2 - (w_{DL}/w_{LL})}{4 + (w_{DL}/w_{LL})}\left(1 - \frac{\alpha_c}{\alpha_{c,min}}\right) \tag{11.43}$$

where w_{DL} and w_{LL} denote respectively the characteristic (unfactored) dead load and live load per unit area.

The value of $\alpha_{c,\,min}$ depends on the w_{DL}/w_{LL} load ratio, the l_2/l_1 span ratio, as well as the beam stiffness parameter α_b (defined by Eq. 11.27). The values of $\alpha_{c,\,min}$, listed in Table 17 of the Code are for Flat Slabs (i.e., without beams) for which $\alpha_b = 0$; and these are same as the values given as the first set in column 3 of Table 11.5. More comprehensive values for $\alpha_{c,\,min}$, covering values of α_b other than zero, as given in the 1984 revision of the Canadian Code are included in Table 11.5. For intermediate values of w_{DL}/w_{LL}, l_2/l_1 and α_b, linear interpolation may be resorted to. The 2004 revision of the Canadian Code [Ref. 11.21] restricted the use of DDM to cases with $w_{LL}/w_{DL} \leq 2$ and dispensed with the factor δ_s.

Table 11.5 *Values of $\alpha_{c,\,min}$*

w_{DL}/w_{LL}	l_2/l_1	**Beam stiffness parameter α_{b1}**				
		0	**0.5**	**1.0**	**2.0**	**4.0**
2.0	0.5–2.0	0	0	0	0	0
1.0	0.5	0.6	0	0	0	0
	0.8	0.7	0	0	0	0
	1.0	0.7	0.1	0	0	0
	1.25	0.8	0.4	0	0	0
	2.0	1.2	0.5	0.2	0	0
0.5	0.5	1.3	0.3	0	0	0
	0.8	1.5	0.5	0.2	0	0
	1.0	1.6	0.6	0.2	0	0
	1.25	1.9	1.0	0.5	0	0
	2.0	4.9	1.6	0.8	0.3	0
0.33	0.5	1.8	0.5	0.1	0	0
	0.8	2.0	0.9	0.3	0	0
	1.0	2.3	0.9	0.4	0	0
	1.25	2.8	1.5	0.8	0.2	0
	2.0	13.0	2.6	1.2	0.5	0.3

11.5.8 Shears in Two-way Slab Systems with Beams

Two-Way Slab Systems without Beams between Supports

Shear in two-way slabs *without* beams along column lines is discussed in Section 11.8. Here, the slab has to be designed for both one-way shear (beam shear) as for beams, as well as two-way shear.

Two-Way Slab Systems with Flexible Beams between Supports

When there are *stiff* beams, the slab, which transfers the load to the beams, is designed to resist the shear by considering a one-metre-wide strip, in each direction, and designing it as a beam (i.e., beam or one-way shear), as shown in Figure 11.13. In addition, the beam must also be designed to resist the shear due to the loads in the area tributary to it. For this, the Code (Cl. 24.5) suggests that the design shear in *beams supporting solid slabs spanning in two directions at right angles and supporting uniformly distributed loads* may be computed as that caused by loads in tributary areas bounded by 45° lines drawn from the corners of the panels, as explained in Chapter 9 [Figure 9.5]. However, as mentioned earlier, the design of two-way slabs supported on *flexible* beams is not adequately covered in the Code, and hence there are no specific recommendations for determining the design shear forces in such beams.

In two-way slab systems with beams (even *flexible*) between supports, shear design considerations are mostly limited to one-way shear, and Ref. 11.21 recommends a procedure similar to the one discussed in the preceding paragraph. Thus, when the beams have stiffness ratios such that $\alpha_{b1} l_2/l_1 \geq 1.0$, the beam may be considered to be 'adequately stiff' and designed for the shear considering the tributary area as given in Cl. 24.5 (see above and also Figure 9.5). When there are no beams, $\alpha_{b1} l_2/l_1 = 0$, the 'beam' carries no load and the full shear in the panel is transmitted by the slab to the column in two-way action [refer Section 11.8]. Hence, for $0 < \alpha_{b1} l_2/l_1 < 1$, the beam shear may be obtained by linear interpolation assuming that beam carries no load when $\alpha_{b1} = 0$ [Eq. 11.44].

$$V_{\text{flexible beam}} = (\alpha_{b1} l_2/l_1) V_{\text{stiff beam}} \quad \text{for} \quad 0 < \alpha_{b1} l_2/l_1 < 1 \tag{11.44}$$

This means that, in such cases, the beams framing into the column transmit only part of the shear from panels to the column, and the balance shear is transmitted by the slab directly to the columns in two-way shear. In such cases, the total shear strength of the slab-beam-column connection has to be checked to ensure that resistance to the full shear occurring on a panel is provided. This involves the checking of the shear strength of the slab-beam part around the column perimeter as in the case of flat slabs (Section 11.8.2).

It may be noted that, in addition to the shear due to slab loads, beams must also resist shears due to factored loads applied directly on the beams.

The application of the Direct Design Method is illustrated in Example 11.6.

11.6 Equivalent Frame Method

The 'equivalent frame method' (EFM) of design (also called Elastic Frame Method) of two-way beam-supported slabs, flat slabs, flat plates and waffle slabs is a more general (and more rigorous) method than DDM, and is not subject to the limitations of DDM [refer Section 11.5.1]. Furthermore, under lateral loads, recourse has to be taken to design by EFM.

The 'equivalent frame' concept has already been introduced in Section 11.3.4. Such a concept simplifies the analysis of a three-dimensional reinforced concrete building by subdividing it into a series of two-dimensional (plane) frames ('equivalent frames') centred on column lines in longitudinal as well as transverse directions [Figure 11.25]. The 'equivalent frame method' differs from DDM in the determination of the total 'negative' and 'positive' design moments in the slab panels – for the condition of gravity loading. However, the apportioning of the moments to 'column strips' and 'middle strips' (or to beam and slab) across a panel [refer Section 11.5.4] is common to both methods.

11.6.1 Equivalent Frame for Analysis

The bending moments and shear forces in an 'equivalent frame' are obtained in EFM by an elastic analysis†. Such an analysis should generally be performed on the entire plane frame [Cl. 31.5.1(a) of the Code]. However, if the frame is subjected to gravity loading alone, and if the frame geometry and loading are not so unsymmetrical as to cause significant 'sway' (lateral drift) of the frame, each floor may be analysed separately, considering the appropriate 'substitute frame', with the columns attached to the floor assumed fixed at their far ends [Figure 11.25(c)]. A further simplification may be made for the purpose of determining the design moment at a given support or span in the slab-beam member, by assuming the slab-beam member to be fixed at any support two panels distant, provided the slab is continuous beyond this point [refer Cl. 31.5.1(b) of the Code].

The load transfer system in the 'equivalent frame' involves three distinct interconnected elements [Figure 11.36(a)]:

- the slab-beam members (along span l_1);
- the columns (or walls); and
- the torsional members, transverse to the frame (along span l_2) and along the column lines.

In conventional plane frames, the torsional members are absent, and the skeletal frame comprises only beams and columns. However, in the case of the 'equivalent frame', the wide slab-beam member is supported at its support section only over part of its width by the column, and the remaining (and generally substantial) portion is supported by the transverse torsional member, which provides only elastic (flexible) restraint (spring support) – both rotationally (in a twisting mode) and translationally (in a vertical direction). In other words, significantly, the flexural restraint to the slab-beam member (horizontal member) at the support section is less (i.e., the member is more *flexible*), than in the case of a beam-column connection in a conventional plane frame. In effect, it is as though the vertical supporting member (column) has less flexural stiffness than it really has.

The non-uniform translational restraint to the slab-beam member along a transverse line at the column is ignored in frame analysis, its effect being accounted for in the apportioning of the design 'positive' and 'negative' moments over the panel width to column strip and middle strips. However, the increased flexibility of the slab-to-column connection has to be accounted for in some manner in the assessment of the relative stiffnesses of the various members of the 'equivalent frame'. Although the IS Code provisions do not include any specific suggestion as to how this can be done, the ACI Code (on which the EFM procedure of the

† It is now possible to do such analysis of the entire frame by methods such as the *Finite Element Method*. The successive levels of simplifications and approximations given below are for use when such computer-based methods are not resorted to, or are found unnecessary.

IS Code is based) recommends the concept of an 'equivalent column' with stiffness K_{ec} which can be used to replace the actual columns (above and below the floor at any joint) as well as the transverse torsional member at the column under consideration [Figure 11.36(b)].

Thus, for the purpose of gravity load analysis, the *substitute frame* to be analysed by EFM can be modelled as a simple multi-bay, single storeyed portal frame, comprising only horizontal slab-beam members and vertical 'equivalent columns' [Figure 11.36(b)].

The calculation of stiffnesses of the slab-beam members and the equivalent columns are to be based on their respective *gross* concrete sections [Cl. 31.5.1(c) of the Code]. Details of the calculation procedure are discussed in the next section.

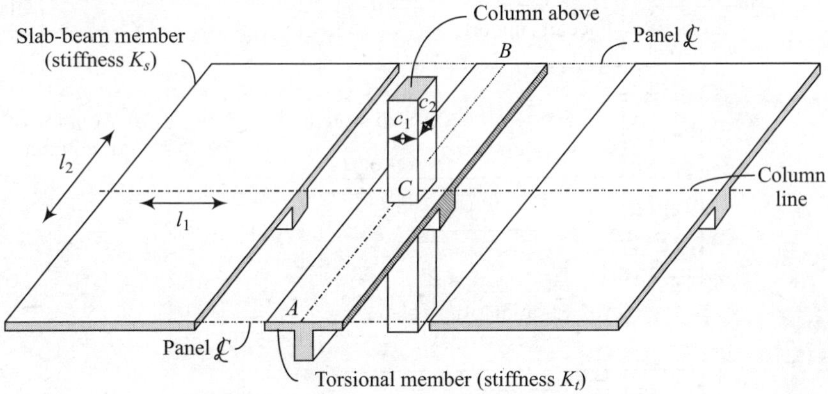

(a) Elements of equivalent frame at a connection

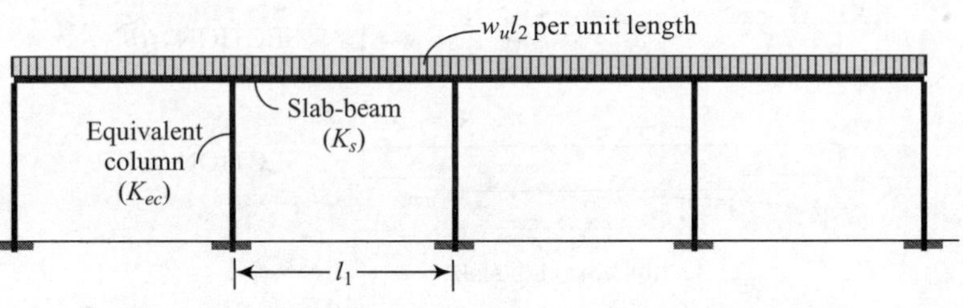

(b) Equivalent frame for analysis

Fig. 11.36 Equivalent frame methods,

11.6.2 Slab-Beam Member

The slab-beam member in an interior frame is bounded laterally by the centreline of the panel on each side of the column line, thus comprising a column strip plus two half-middle strips. For an exterior frame, the slab-beam member extends laterally from the edge to the centreline of the adjacent panel [Figure 11.25(a)]. The slab-beam comprises the slab, drop panel (if provided) and beam(s) (if provided).

The cross-section of the slab-beam member varies along its span, on account of provision of drop panels (if provided) and the increased cross-section within the bounds of the supporting column; the consequent variation of second moment of area along the span must be accounted for in the frame analysis by EFM

[Cl. 31.5.1(d)[†] of the Code]. In order to account for the enhancement in the second moment of area of the slab-beam member in the region between the column face and the column centreline, a magnification factor of $1/(1 - c_2/l_2)^2$ is recommended [Ref. 11.21, 11.22]. The variation of the second moment of area of the slab-beam member in a flat slab (with drop panels) is shown in Figures 11.37(a), (b), (c).

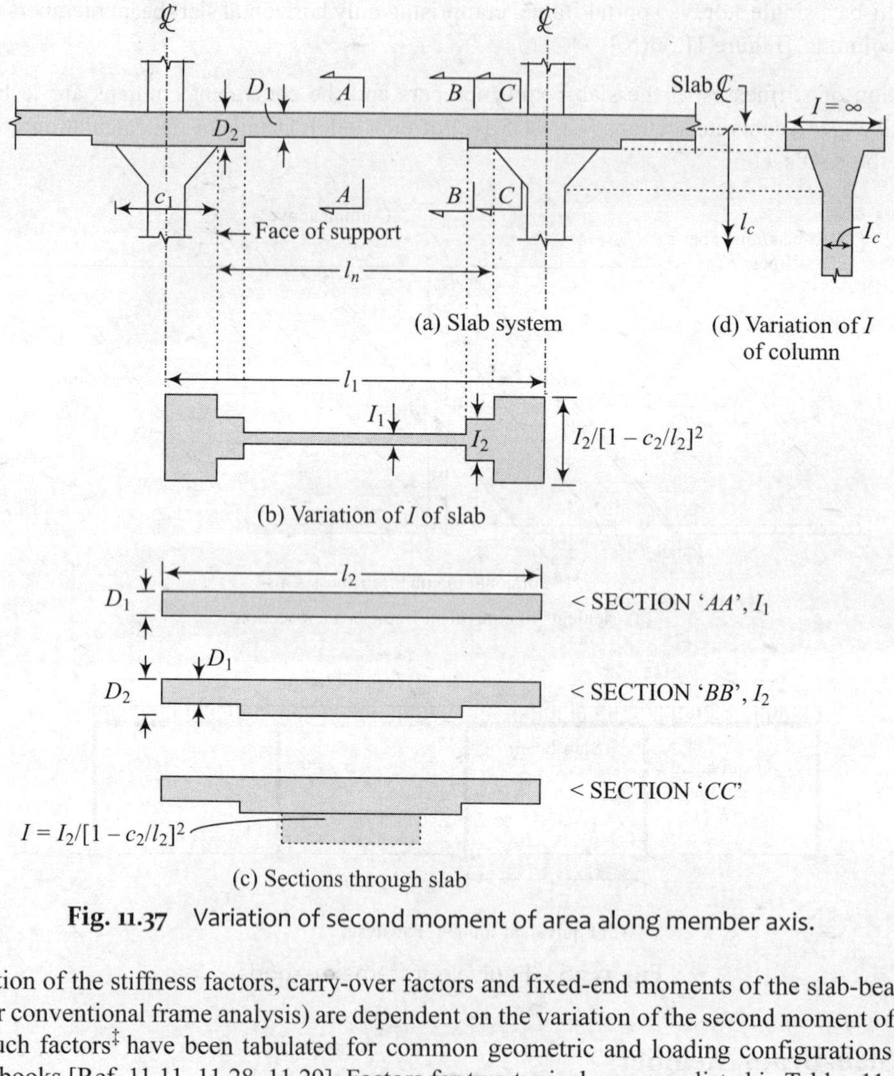

Fig. 11.37 Variation of second moment of area along member axis.

The calculation of the stiffness factors, carry-over factors and fixed-end moments of the slab-beam member (required for conventional frame analysis) are dependent on the variation of the second moment of area along the span. Such factors[‡] have been tabulated for common geometric and loading configurations in various design handbooks [Ref. 11.11, 11.28, 11.29]. Factors for two typical cases are listed in Tables 11.6 and 11.7. The use of such tables is demonstrated in Example 11.7.

[†] With reference to waffle slabs ('recessed' or 'coffered') which are made solid in the region of the columns [Figure 1.11(b)], the Code suggests that the stiffening effect may be ignored provided the solid part of the slab does not extend more than $0.15l_e$ into the span measured from the centreline of the columns.

[‡] However, these factors are not required in modern computer-based analyses using the finite element method; nodes are introduced at the locations where the second moment of area changes.

Table 11.6 *Moment distribution constants for slab-beam elements*

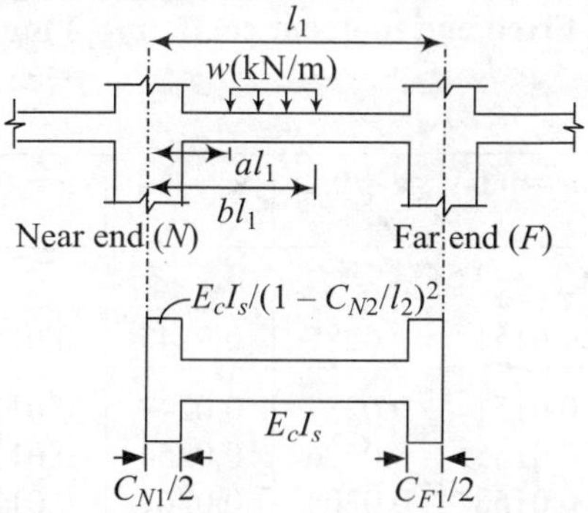

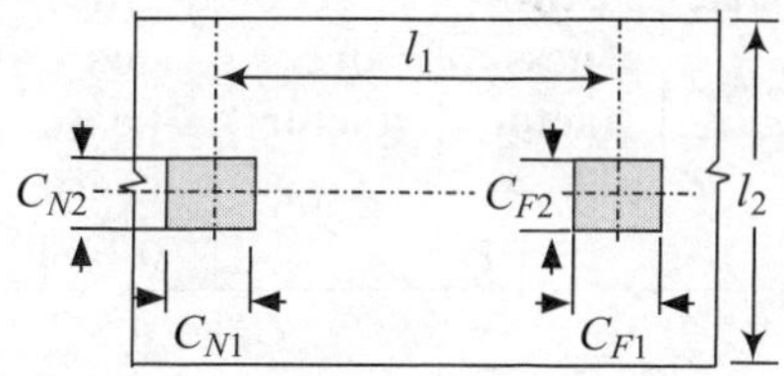

$$FEM_{NF} = \sum_{i=1}^{n} m_{NFi} \, w_i \, l_1^2$$

$$K_{NF} = k_{NF} \, E_c I_s / l_1$$

C_{N1}/l_1	C_{N2}/l_2	Stiffness factor K_{NF}	Carry over factor C_{NF}	Unif. load f.e.m. coeff. (m_{NF})	Fixed end moment coeff. (m_{NF}) for $(b-a)=0.2$				
					$a=0.0$	$a=0.2$	$a=0.4$	$a=0.6$	$a=0.8$
				$C_{F1}=C_{N1}$; $C_{F2}=C_{N2}$					
0.00	–	4.00	0.50	0.0833	0.0151	0.0287	0.0247	0.0127	0.00226
0.10	0.00	4.00	0.50	0.0833	0.0151	0.0287	0.0247	0.0127	0.00226
	0.10	4.18	0.51	0.0847	0.0154	0.0293	0.0251	0.0126	0.00214
	0.20	4.36	0.52	0.0860	0.0158	0.0300	0.0255	0.0126	0.00201
	0.30	4.53	0.54	0.0872	0.0161	0.0301	0.0259	0.0125	0.00188
	0.40	4.70	0.55	0.0882	0.0165	0.0314	0.0262	0.0124	0.00174
0.20	0.00	4.00	0.50	0.0833	0.0151	0.0287	0.0247	0.0127	0.00226
	0.10	4.35	0.52	0.0857	0.0155	0.0299	0.0254	0.0127	0.00213
	0.20	4.72	0.54	0.0880	0.0161	0.0311	0.0262	0.0126	0.00197
	0.30	5.11	0.56	0.0901	0.0166	0.0324	0.0269	0.0125	0.00178
	0.40	5.51	0.58	0.0921	0.0171	0.0366	0.0276	0.0123	0.00156
0.30	0.00	4.00	0.50	0.0833	0.0151	0.0287	0.0247	0.0127	0.00226
	0.10	4.49	0.53	0.0863	0.0155	0.0301	0.0257	0.0128	0.00219
	0.20	5.05	0.56	0.0893	0.0160	0.0317	0.0267	0.0128	0.00207
	0.30	5.69	0.59	0.0923	0.0165	0.0334	0.0278	0.0127	0.00190
	0.40	6.41	0.61	0.0951	0.0171	0.0352	0.0287	0.0124	0.00167
0.40	0.00	4.00	0.50	0.0833	0.0151	0.0287	0.0247	0.0127	0.00226
	0.10	4.61	0.53	0.0866	0.0154	0.0302	0.0259	0.0129	0.00225
	0.20	5.35	0.56	0.0901	0.0158	0.0318	0.0271	0.0131	0.00221
	0.30	6.25	0.60	0.0936	0.0162	0.0337	0.0284	0.0131	0.00211
	0.40	7.37	0.64	0.0971	0.0168	0.0359	0.0297	0.0128	0.00195

Table 11.6 *(contd.)*

C_{N1}/l_1	C_{N2}/l_2	Stiff-ness factor K_{NF}	Carry over factor C_{NF}	Unif. load f.e.m. coeff. (m_{NF})	Fixed end moment coeff. (m_{NF}) for $(b - a) = 0.2$				
					$a = 0.0$	$a = 0.2$	$a = 0.4$	$a = 0.6$	$a = 0.8$
$C_{F1} = 0.5C_{N1}$; $C_{F2} = 0.5C_{N2}$									
0.00	–	4.00	0.50	0.0833	0.0151	0.0287	0.0247	0.0127	0.0023
0.10	0.00	4.00	0.50	0.0833	0.0151	0.0287	0.0247	0.0127	0.0023
	0.10	4.16	0.51	0.0857	0.0155	0.0296	0.0254	0.0130	0.0023
	0.20	4.31	0.52	0.0879	0.0158	0.0304	0.0261	0.0133	0.0023
	0.30	4.45	0.54	0.0900	0.0162	0.0312	0.0267	0.0135	0.0023
	0.40	4.58	0.54	0.0918	0.0165	0.0319	0.0273	0.0138	0.0023
0.20	0.00	4.00	0.50	0.0833	0.0151	0.0287	0.0247	0.0127	0.0023
	0.10	4.30	0.52	0.0872	0.0156	0.0301	0.0259	0.0132	0.0023
	0.20	4.61	0.55	0.0912	0.0161	0.0317	0.0272	0.0138	0.0023
	0.30	4.92	0.57	0.0951	0.0167	0.0332	0.0285	0.0143	0.0024
	0.40	5.23	0.58	0.0989	0.0172	0.0347	0.0298	0.0148	0.0024
0.30	0.00	4.00	0.50	0.0833	0.0151	0.0287	0.0247	0.0127	0.0023
	0.10	4.43	0.53	0.0881	0.0156	0.0305	0.0263	0.0134	0.0023
	0.20	4.89	0.56	0.0932	0.0161	0.0324	0.0281	0.0142	0.0024
	0.30	5.40	0.59	0.0986	0.0167	0.0345	0.0300	0.0150	0.0024
	0.40	5.93	0.62	0.1042	0.0173	0.0367	0.0320	0.0158	0.00235
0.40	0.00	4.00	0.50	0.0833	0.0151	0.0287	0.0247	0.0127	0.0023
	0.10	4.54	0.54	0.0884	0.0155	0.0305	0.0265	0.0135	0.0024
	0.20	5.16	0.57	0.0941	0.0159	0.0326	0.0286	0.0145	0.0025
	0.30	5.87	0.61	0.1005	0.0165	0.0350	0.0310	0.0155	0.0025
	0.40	6.67	0.64	0.1076	0.0170	0.0377	0.0336	0.0166	0.0026
$C_{F1} = 2C_{N1}$; $C_{F2} = 2C_{N2}$									
0.00	–	4.00	0.50	0.0833	0.0151	0.0287	0.0247	0.0127	0.0023
0.10	0.00	4.00	0.50	0.0833	0.0150	0.0287	0.0247	0.0127	0.0023
	0.10	4.27	0.51	0.0517	0.0153	0.0289	0.0241	0.0116	0.0018
	0.20	4.56	0.52	0.0798	0.0156	0.0290	0.0234	0.0103	0.0013
0.20	0.00	4.00	0.50	0.0833	0.0151	0.0287	0.0247	0.0127	0.0023
	0.10	4.49	0.51	0.0819	0.0154	0.0291	0.0240	0.0114	0.0019
	0.20	5.11	0.53	0.0789	0.0158	0.0293	0.0228	0.0096	0.0014

Table 11.7 *Moment distribution constants for slab-beam elements, drop thickness = 0.50D*

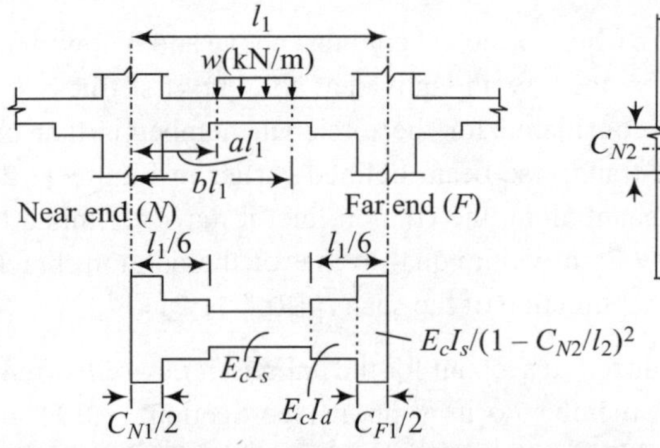

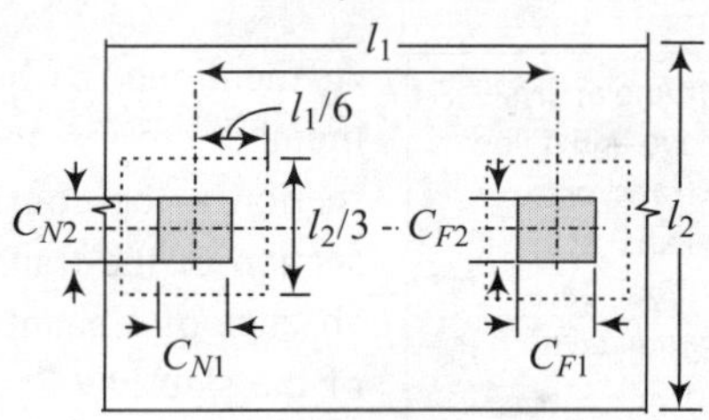

$$FEM_{NF} = \sum_{i=1}^{n} m_{NFi}\, w_i\, l_1^2$$

$$K_{NF} = k_{NF}\, E_c I_s / l_1$$

C_{N1}/l_1	C_{N2}/l_2	Stiff-ness factor K_{NF}	Carry over factor C_{NF}	Unif. load f.e.m. coeff. (m_{NF})	Fixed end Moment coeff. (m_{NF}) for $(b - a) = 0.2$				
					$a = 0.0$	$a = 0.2$	$a = 0.4$	$a = 0.6$	$a = 0.8$
				$C_{F1} = C_{N1}$; $C_{F2} = C_{N2}$					
0.00	–	5.84	0.59	0.0926	0.0164	0.0335	0.0279	0.0128	0.0020
0.10	0.00	5.84	0.59	0.0926	0.0164	0.0335	0.0279	0.0128	0.0020
	0.10	6.04	0.60	0.0936	0.0167	0.0341	0.0282	0.0126	0.0018
	0.20	6.24	0.61	0.0940	0.0170	0.0347	0.0285	0.0125	0.0017
	0.30	6.43	0.61	0.0952	0.0173	0.0353	0.0287	0.0123	0.0016
0.20	0.00	5.84	0.59	0.0926	0.0164	0.0335	0.0279	0.0128	0.0020
	0.10	6.22	0.61	0.0942	0.0168	0.0346	0.0285	0.0126	0.0018
	0.20	6.62	0.62	0.0957	0.0172	0.0356	0.0290	0.0123	0.0016
	0.30	7.01	0.64	0.0971	0.0177	0.0366	0.0294	0.0120	0.0014
0.30	0.00	5.84	0.59	0.0926	0.0164	0.0355	0.0279	0.0128	0.0020
	0.10	6.37	0.61	0.0947	0.0168	0.0348	0.0287	0.0126	0.0018
	0.20	6.95	0.63	0.0967	0.0172	0.0362	0.0294	0.0123	0.0016
	0.30	7.57	0.65	0.0986	0.0177	0.0375	0.0300	0.0119	0.0014
				$C_{F1} = 0.5C_{N1}$; $C_{F2} = 0.5C_{N2}$					
0.00	–	5.84	0.59	0.0926	0.0164	0.0335	0.0279	0.0128	0.0020
0.10	0.00	5.84	0.59	0.0926	0.0164	0.0335	0.0279	0.0128	0.0020
	0.10	6.00	0.60	0.0945	0.0167	0.0343	0.0285	0.0130	0.0020
	0.20	6.16	0.60	0.0962	0.0170	0.0350	0.0291	0.0132	0.0020
0.20	0.00	5.84	0.59	0.0926	0.0164	0.0335	0.0279	0.0128	0.0020
	0.10	6.15	0.60	0.0957	0.0169	0.0348	0.0290	0.0131	0.0020
	0.20	6.47	0.62	0.0987	0.0173	0.0360	0.0300	0.0134	0.0020
				$C_{F1} = 2C_{N1}$; $C_{F2} = 2C_{N2}$					
0.00	–	5.84	0.59	0.0926	0.0164	0.0335	0.0279	0.0128	0.0020
0.10	0.00	5.84	0.59	0.0926	0.0164	0.0335	0.0279	0.0128	0.0020
	0.10	6.17	0.60	0.0907	0.0166	0.0337	0.0273	0.0116	0.0015

Equivalent Columns

For the elastic frame analysis, the columns above and below a joint, and the transverse beams (and/or slabs) acting as torsional members, are replaced by an *equivalent* column.

As mentioned earlier, the actual columns above and below, and the torsional member are replaced by an equivalent column of stiffness K_{ec}. The cross-section to be considered for the torsional member is that of the flanged section of the transverse beam defined earlier in Figure 11.28, and in the absence of a beam along the column line, it may be limited to the portion of the slab having a width equal to that of the column, bracket or capital measured in the direction of the span l_1 [Ref. 11.21].

The concept of an 'equivalent column' is introduced to account for the *increased flexibility* (reduced flexural restraint) of the connection of the slab-beam member to its support (see Section 11.6.1), because of its connection to the column, for most of its width, through a torsional member. This is effected by taking the equivalent (or effective) *flexibility* (inverse of *stiffness*) of the connection as equal to the sum of the flexibilities of the actual columns and the torsional member. The stiffness, K_{ec}, of the equivalent column is thus obtained from:

$$\frac{1}{K_{ec}} = \frac{1}{\sum K_c} + \frac{1}{K_t} \tag{11.45a}$$

$$\Rightarrow \quad K_{ec} = \frac{K_t \sum K_c}{K_t + \sum K_c} \tag{11.45b}$$

Evidently, $K_{ec} \leq \Sigma K_c$; i.e., the effect of the flexibility of the torsional member is to reduce the rotational restraint offered to the slab-beam member at the support section. The condition $K_{ec} = \Sigma K_c$ (implying that the rotation along the entire length AB in Figure 11.36(a) is the same) can be assumed to occur only if the torsional stiffness of the transverse torsional member is infinite or if the column is in fact a wall with a width extending over the full width of the slab-beam member. On the other hand, if $\Sigma K_c = \infty$, $K_{ec} = K_t$, implying that although the column is infinitely stiff, the slab undergoes the same rotation as that of the torsional member along the length AB in Figure 11.36(a) except for the width at the column location.

Another interesting result of $K_{ec} = 0$ is obtained for the hypothetical case of a torsional member with $K_t = 0$, or for the case of a slab simply supported on a masonry wall ($K_c = 0$) throughout the length AB. In the former case, the slab is flexurally unrestrained along the length AB (except for the width c_2 at the column location), and in the latter case, the slab is flexurally unrestrained throughout the entire length AB, and in both cases K_{ec} should naturally be zero.

For the purpose of computing the torsional stiffness of the transverse member, the following approximate expression [Ref. 11.21] is recommended:

$$K_t = \sum \frac{9E_c C}{l_t(1 - c_2/l_t)^3} \tag{11.46}$$

where

$E_c \equiv$ modulus of elasticity of concrete (in the torsional member);

$C \equiv$ torsional property of the cross-section† [refer Eq. 11.41];

$c_2 \equiv$ width of the equivalent rectangular column, capital or bracket, measured transverse to the direction in which moments are being determined; and

$l_t \equiv$ length of attached torsional member, taken as the smaller of l_{2a} or l_{1a} of spans adjacent to the joint; where l_{1a} and l_{2a} are the averages of adjacent spans in l_1 and l_2 directions, respectively.

It should be noted that the concept of the 'equivalent column stiffness', K_{ec}, explained here, is applicable for gravity load analysis, and not for lateral load analysis.

It may be noted that the elastic frame analogy may also be used for the lateral load analysis of this type of unbraced frames, comprising column-supported slab system. However, the Code does not give any guidance on assigning member stiffnesses in such situations. For gravity load analysis, the reduced restraint to the slab-beam member at the column support is accounted for by reducing the effective column stiffness, as explained above. By analogy, for lateral load analysis, the effective stiffness of the slab-beam member has to be reduced. However, it should be realised that, due to the large flexural stiffness of the floor slab in its own plane, the *sway* for all columns in a storey will, in most cases, be very nearly equal. Hence, the columns share the lateral load very nearly in proportion to their stiffnesses; and the column shears determine the column moments at the connection. For this reason, the effective slab-beam member (flexural) stiffness does not usually affect the column moments under lateral load significantly [Ref. 11.32]. However, if the *lateral drift* (sway) is to be computed, a realistic assessment of the effective slab-beam member stiffness is required. Some studies [such as Ref. 11.32] have indicated that calculations with an effective width for the slab-beam member, $b_e = c_2 + 2D$, gives satisfactory drift predictions.

For the calculation of the column stiffness, K_c, the variation of the second moment of area along the height of the actual column should be taken into account. The height of the column l_c, is measured centre-to-centre of floors, and the second moment of area of the column section for the portion integral with the slab-beam member should be taken as infinite [Figure 11.37(d)]. The change in cross-section on account of the column capital and drop panel (wherever provided) should also be considered in computing the stiffness and carry-over factors. To facilitate calculations, these factors have been evaluated for common configurations in various design handbooks [Ref. 11.11, 11.28, 11.29], and are indicated in Table 11.8.

Method of Analysis

The gravity load analysis of the equivalent (substitute) frame, with the appropriate stiffnesses for the slab-beam members and equivalent columns, may be done by any method of structural analysis. For manual calculations, the *moment distribution method* is particularly suitable, as illustrated in Example 11.7.

† For calculation purposes, the torsional member is assumed to have a uniform section throughout its length. In flat slabs, this implies that the provision of drop panels (if any) is ignored.

Table 11.8 *Stiffness and carry-over factors for columns*

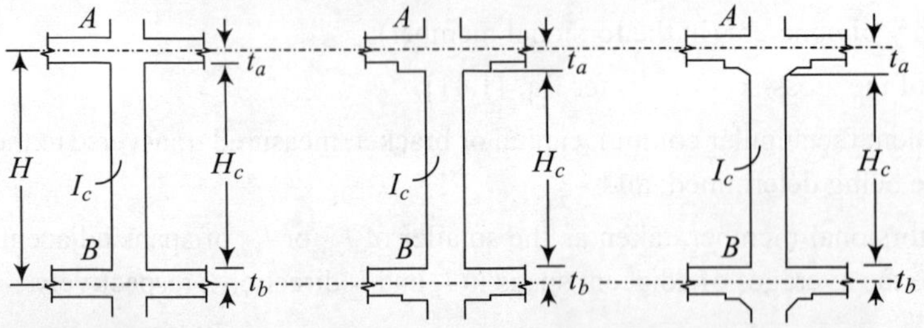

$K_c = k(EI_c)/H$

For values of k_{BA} and C_{BA}, read (t_a/t_b) as (t_b/t_a)

t_a/t_b	H/H_c	1.05	1.10	1.15	1.20	1.25	1.30	1.35	1.40	1.45	1.50
0.0	K_{AB}	4.20	4.40	4.60	4.80	5.00	5.20	5.40	5.60	5.80	6.00
	C_{AB}	0.57	0.65	0.73	0.80	0.87	0.95	1.03	1.10	1.17	1.25
0.2	K_{AB}	4.31	4.62	4.95	5.30	5.65	6.02	6.40	6.79	7.20	7.62
	C_{AB}	0.56	0.62	0.68	0.74	0.80	0.85	0.91	0.96	1.01	1.07
0.4	K_{AB}	4.38	4.79	5.22	5.67	6.15	6.65	7.18	7.74	8.32	8.94
	C_{AB}	0.55	0.60	0.65	0.70	0.74	0.79	0.83	0.87	0.91	0.94
0.6	K_{AB}	4.44	4.91	5.42	5.96	6.54	7.15	7.81	8.50	9.23	10.01
	C_{AB}	0.55	0.59	0.63	0.67	0.70	0.74	0.77	0.80	0.83	0.85
0.8	K_{AB}	4.49	5.01	5.58	6.19	6.85	7.56	8.31	9.12	9.98	10.89
	C_{AB}	0.54	0.58	0.61	0.64	0.67	0.70	0.72	0.75	0.77	0.79
1.0	K_{AB}	4.52	5.09	5.71	6.38	7.11	7.89	8.73	9.63	10.60	11.62
	C_{AB}	0.54	0.57	0.60	0.62	0.65	0.67	0.69	0.71	0.73	0.74
1.2	K_{AB}	4.55	5.16	5.82	6.54	7.32	8.17	9.08	10.07	11.12	12.25
	C_{AB}	0.53	0.56	0.59	0.61	0.63	0.65	0.66	0.68	0.69	0.70
1.4	K_{AB}	4.58	5.21	5.91	6.68	7.51	8.41	9.38	10.43	11.57	12.78
	C_{AB}	0.53	0.55	0.58	0.60	0.61	0.63	0.64	0.65	0.66	0.67
1.6	K_{AB}	4.60	5.26	5.99	6.79	7.66	8.61	9.64	10.75	11.95	13.24
	C_{AB}	0.53	0.55	0.57	0.59	0.60	0.61	0.62	0.63	0.64	0.65
1.8	K_{AB}	4.62	5.30	6.06	6.89	7.80	8.79	9.87	11.03	12.29	13.65
	C_{AB}	0.52	0.55	0.56	0.58	0.59	0.60	0.61	0.61	0.62	0.63
2.0	K_{AB}	4.63	5.34	6.12	6.98	7.92	8.94	10.06	11.27	12.59	14.00
	C_{AB}	0.52	0.54	0.56	0.57	0.58	0.59	0.59	0.60	0.60	0.61
2.2	K_{AB}	4.65	5.37	6.17	7.05	8.02	9.08	10.24	11.49	12.85	14.31
	C_{AB}	0.52	0.54	0.55	0.56	0.57	0.58	0.58	0.59	0.59	0.59
2.4	K_{AB}	4.66	5.40	6.22	7.12	8.11	9.20	10.39	11.68	13.08	14.60
	C_{AB}	0.52	0.53	0.55	0.56	0.56	0.57	0.57	0.58	0.58	0.58
2.6	K_{AB}	4.67	5.42	6.26	7.18	8.20	9.31	10.53	11.86	13.29	14.85
	C_{AB}	0.52	0.53	0.54	0.55	0.56	0.56	0.56	0.57	0.57	0.57
2.8	K_{AB}	4.68	5.44	6.29	7.23	8.27	9.41	10.66	12.01	13.48	15.07
	C_{AB}	0.52	0.53	0.54	0.55	0.55	0.55	0.56	0.56	0.56	0.56
3.0	K_{AB}	4.69	5.46	6.33	7.28	8.34	9.50	10.77	12.15	13.65	15.28
	C_{AB}	0.52	0.53	0.54	0.54	0.55	0.55	0.55	0.55	0.55	0.55

Table 11.8 *(contd.)*

t_a/t_b	H/H_c	1.05	1.10	1.15	1.20	1.25	1.30	1.35	1.40	1.45	1.50
3.2	K_{AB}	4.70	5.48	6.36	7.33	8.40	9.58	10.87	12.28	13.81	15.47
	C_{AB}	0.52	0.53	0.53	0.54	0.54	0.54	0.54	0.54	0.54	0.54
3.4	K_{AB}	4.71	5.50	6.38	7.37	8.46	9.65	10.97	12.40	13.95	15.64
	C_{AB}	0.51	0.52	0.53	0.53	0.54	0.54	0.54	0.53	0.53	0.53
3.6	K_{AB}	4.71	5.51	6.41	7.41	8.51	9.72	11.05	12.51	14.09	15.80
	C_{AB}	0.51	0.52	0.53	0.53	0.53	0.53	0.53	0.53	0.53	0.52
3.8	K_{AB}	4.72	5.53	6.43	7.44	8.56	9.78	11.13	12.60	14.21	15.95
	C_{AB}	0.51	0.52	0.53	0.53	0.53	0.53	0.53	0.52	0.52	0.52
4.0	K_{AB}	4.72	5.54	6.45	7.47	8.60	9.84	11.21	12.70	14.32	16.08
	C_{AB}	0.51	0.52	0.52	0.53	0.53	0.52	0.52	0.52	0.52	0.51
4.2	K_{AB}	4.73	5.55	6.47	7.50	8.64	9.90	11.27	12.78	14.42	16.02
	C_{AB}	0.51	0.52	0.52	0.52	0.52	0.52	0.52	0.51	0.51	0.51
4.4	K_{AB}	4.73	5.56	6.49	7.53	8.68	9.95	11.34	12.86	14.52	16.32
	C_{AB}	0.51	0.52	0.52	0.52	0.52	0.52	0.51	0.51	0.51	0.50
4.6	K_{AB}	4.74	5.57	6.51	7.55	8.71	9.99	11.40	12.93	14.61	16.43
	C_{AB}	0.51	0.52	0.52	0.52	0.52	0.52	0.51	0.51	0.50	0.50
4.8	K_{AB}	4.74	5.58	6.53	7.58	8.75	10.03	11.45	13.00	14.69	16.53
	C_{AB}	0.51	0.52	0.52	0.52	0.52	0.51	0.51	0.50	0.50	0.49
5.0	K_{AB}	4.75	5.59	6.54	7.60	8.78	10.07	11.50	13.07	14.77	16.62
	C_{AB}	0.51	0.51	0.52	0.52	0.51	0.51	0.51	0.50	0.49	0.49
6.0	K_{AB}	4.76	5.63	6.60	7.69	8.90	10.24	11.72	13.33	15.10	17.02
	C_{AB}	0.51	0.51	0.51	0.51	0.50	0.50	0.49	0.49	0.48	0.47
7.0	K_{AB}	4.78	5.66	6.65	7.76	9.00	10.37	11.88	13.54	15.35	17.32
	C_{AB}	0.51	0.51	0.51	0.50	0.50	0.49	0.48	0.48	0.47	0.46
8.0	K_{AB}	4.78	5.68	6.69	7.82	9.07	10.47	12.01	13.70	15.54	17.56
	C_{AB}	0.51	0.51	0.50	0.50	0.49	0.49	0.48	0.47	0.46	0.45
9.0	K_{AB}	4.79	5.69	6.71	7.86	9.13	10.55	12.11	13.83	15.70	17.74
	C_{AB}	0.50	0.50	0.50	0.50	0.49	0.48	0.47	0.46	0.45	0.45
10.0	K_{AB}	4.80	5.71	6.74	7.89	9.18	10.61	12.19	13.93	15.83	17.90
	C_{AB}	0.50	0.50	0.50	0.49	0.48	0.48	0.47	0.46	0.45	0.44

11.6.3 Loading Patterns

When specific gravity load patterns are indicated[†], the equivalent frame should be analysed for those patterns [Cl. 31.5.2.1 of the Code]. When the live load is variable, but does not exceed three-fourths of the dead load, or the nature of the live load is such that all the panels will be loaded simultaneously the Code (Cl. 31.5.2.2) recommends a single loading case of full factored loads (dead plus live) on all spans for analysis for design moments in the slab [Fig. 11.38(a)].

† For example, water tank bases are often two-way slabs (with or without beams) supported on columns. The loading due to water should be expected to act on all the panels (bounded within the tank walls) simultaneously [Ref. 11.11].

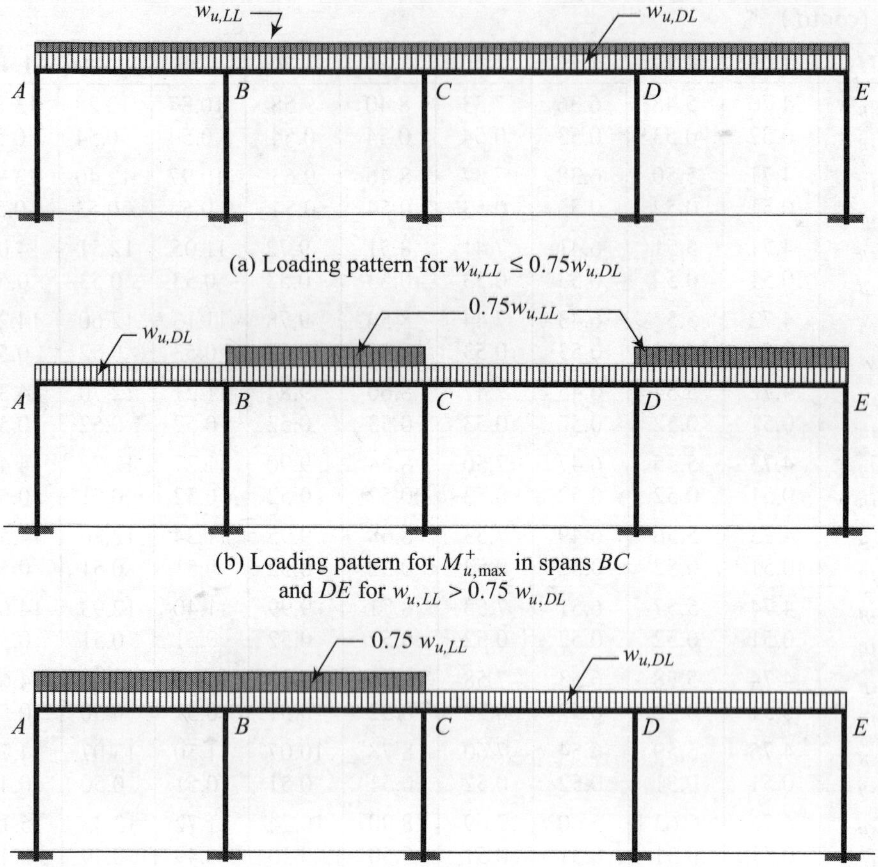

(a) Loading pattern for $w_{u,LL} \leq 0.75 w_{u,DL}$

(b) Loading pattern for $M^{+}_{u,\max}$ in spans *BC* and *DE* for $w_{u,LL} > 0.75\ w_{u,DL}$

(c) Loading pattern for $M^{-}_{u,\max}$ *at* support *B* for $w_{u,LL} > 0.75\ w_{u,DL}$

Fig. 11.38 Gravity loading patterns for equivalent frame analysis.

For larger live load/dead load ratios ($w_{LL}/w_{DL} > 0.75$), it is acceptable to design only for three-fourths of the full live load on alternate spans for maximum 'positive' moments in spans, and on adjacent spans for maximum 'negative' moments at supports, as indicated in Figure 11.38(b) and (c) respectively [Cl. 31.5.2.3 of the Code]. However, in no case must the design moments be taken as less than those occurring with full factored loads (dead plus live) on all spans [Figure 11.38(a)]. The use of only three-fourths of the full design live load for maximum moment loading patterns accounts for possible moment redistribution in the frame [Ref. 11.11].

11.6.4 Design Moments in Slab-Beam Members

The results of the equivalent frame analysis using centreline dimensions gives 'negative' moments at the centreline of the supports, from which the design 'negative' moments at the critical sections have to be deduced, as shown in Figure 11.39. The Code (Cl. 31.5.3.1) recommends that the critical section of the slab-beam member for 'negative' moment at an interior support is to be taken at the face of the support (column, capital or bracket), but in no case at a distance greater than $0.175 l_1$ from the centre of the column.

At an exterior support with a capital or bracket, the critical section is to be taken [Cl. 31.5.3.2 of the Code] at a distance from the face of the column not greater than one-half of the projection of the bracket or capital beyond the face of the column†. These Code specifications are illustrated in Figure 11.39.

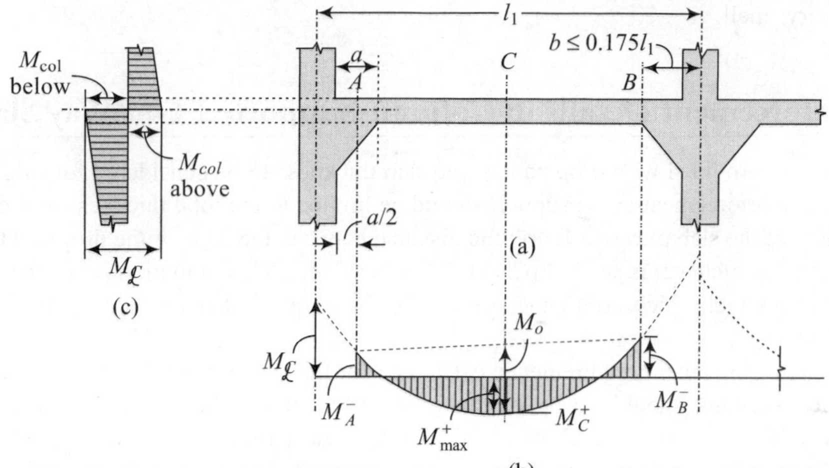

Fig. 11.39 Critical sections for 'negative' design moments in the slab-beam member and column.

The design 'positive' (maximum) moment in the beam-slab member should be obtained from the zero-shear location, which, in general need not correspond to the midspan location [Figure 11.39(b)].

To maintain consistency in design requirements, the Code (Cl. 31.5.4) provides that in a two-way slab system which meets the limitations of DDM (given in Section 11.5.1), but is analysed by EFM, the design moments obtained from equivalent frame analysis, if found excessive, may be reduced in such proportion that the numerical sum of the 'positive' moment at mid-span and the average 'negative' moment used in design need not exceed the value M_o obtained from Eq. 11.31 [Figure 11.39(b)].

The apportioning of the design 'positive' and 'negative' moments in the transverse direction to the column strip and half-middle strips in the case of slabs without beams, and to the beam and slab in the case of slabs with beams between all supports, should be done as explained in Section 11.5.4.

11.6.5 Design Moments in Columns and Torsion in Transverse Beam

The design moments in the 'equivalent columns' are obtained from equivalent frame analysis. The moment (due to gravity loads) is usually significant only at the exterior support. This moment has to be distributed to the actual columns located above and below the floor in proportion to their relative flexural stiffnesses [Figure. 11.39(c)].

At an exterior support, the negative moment in the slab part of the slab-beam member acts as a twisting moment in the torsional member [see Section 11.5.6]. As indicated in Figure 11.34 and conservatively, the twisting moment may be assumed to be uniformly distributed along the length of the torsional member (with

† Circular or regular polygon shaped supports are to be treated as equivalent square supports having the same cross–sectional area [Cl. 31.5.3.3 of the Code].

a maximum value at the face of the column support). The twisting moment will generally be significant only in the presence of an edge beam[†], and the edge beam has to be suitably designed to resist this moment, using the design principles explained in Chapter 7. Transverse beams at interior supports will also be subject to some torsion due to the unbalanced negative moments in the slabs on either side, but the magnitude of this will usually be very small.

11.7 Reinforcement Details in Column-Supported Two-Way Slabs

- When slabs are provided with drop panels, the slab thickness to be considered for calculation of area of 'negative' reinforcement at the support should be limited to the total thickness of the drop panel or the thickness of the slab plus one-fourth the distance between the edge of the drop and the edge of the column capital, whichever is smaller [Cl. 31.7.2 of the Code]. This limitation is intended to discourage the use of excessively thick drop panels solely for the purpose of reducing 'negative' reinforcement area [Ref. 11.11].
- The flexural reinforcement requirements, calculated for the design 'positive' and 'negative' moments at the critical sections, should not be less than the minimum specified for shrinkage and temperature stresses [Cl. 26.5.2.1 and Cl. 26.3.3(b) of the Code]. Furthermore, the Code (Cl. 31.7.1) limits the spacing of bars at critical sections in *flat slabs* to a maximum of twice the slab thickness. This limitation is intended to ensure *slab action*, reduce cracking, and to provide for the distribution of concentrated loads.
- Considerable uncertainties are generally associated with the 'degree of fixity' along the exterior edge of the slab system. The degree of flexural restraint depends on the torsional stiffness of the edge beam (if provided) and interaction with an exterior wall (if provided).
  It is therefore desirable to provide 'negative' moment reinforcement at the discontinuous edge, as required for wall-supported slabs [Cl. D–1.6 of the Code], and to provide proper anchorage for the same. Furthermore, all 'positive' moment reinforcement perpendicular to the discontinuous edge should be extended to the slab edge, and embedded for a length, straight or hooked, of at least 150 mm [Cl. 31.7.4 of the Code].
- For two-way systems supported on relatively stiff beams ($\alpha_{b1} l_2/l_1 > 1.0$), it is necessary to provide the special corner reinforcement at exterior corners, as in the case of wall-supported 'restrained' slabs [refer Cl. D–1 of the Code, and Section 11.2.4].
- The location of bar cut-off or bend points must be based on the moment envelopes (obtainable in the Equivalent Frame Method) and the requirements of development length and bar extensions described in Section 5.9.
- In the case of flat slabs and flat plates, the Code (Cl. 31.7.3) prescribes specific bend point locations and minimum extensions for reinforcement. These recommendations are based on ACI code recommendations and have been incorporated in other international codes [Ref. 11.21, 11.22]. They are depicted in Figure 11.40. Under lateral loads, (combined with gravity loads), the actual lengths of reinforcement should be worked out by equivalent frame analysis, but must not be less than those prescribed in Figure 11.40.

---

† In the absence of a beam, the torsional stiffness K_t will be very low, which means that the slab is nearly unrestrained flexurally at the edges. Hence, the negative moment in the slab part and consequently the twisting moment in the edge portion of the slab (which acts as a torsional member) will be negligible.

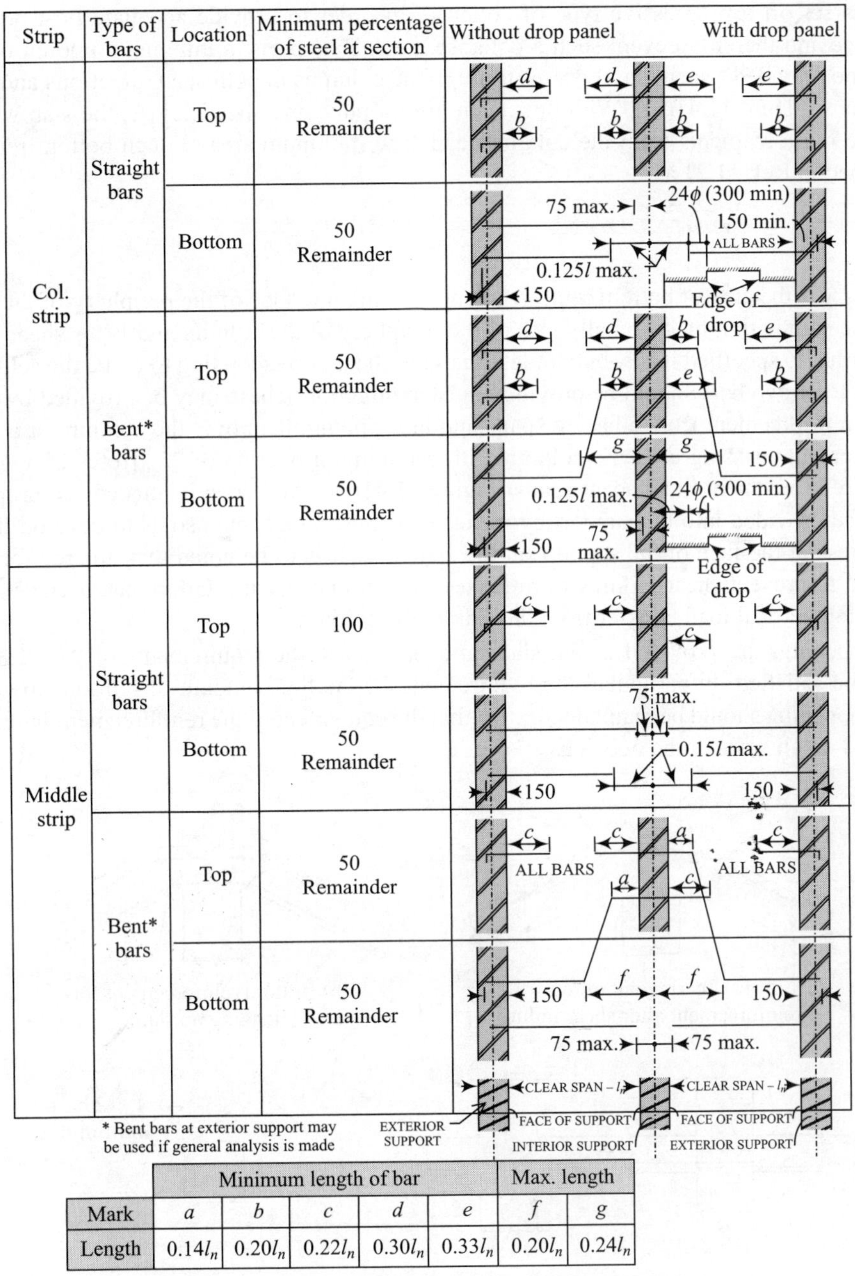

	Minimum length of bar					Max. length	
Mark	a	b	c	d	e	f	g
Length	$0.14l_n$	$0.20l_n$	$0.22l_n$	$0.30l_n$	$0.33l_n$	$0.20l_n$	$0.24l_n$

Fig. 11.40 Minimum lengths of reinforcements in beamless two-way slabs,

- It is seen that punching shear failure (discussed in Section 11.8.2) may lead to the tearing out of the top steel over the support section from the top surface of the slab [Figure 11.41(a)], resulting in a complete 'punch through' at the support. Such a complete failure of one support will result in the slab load in this area getting transferred to the neighbouring support, overloading it, which may, in turn, cause its failure and thus set off a progressive type of collapse. In order to provide adequate post-punching-failure resistance and thereby prevent such a collapse, at slab supports, a minimum amount of *bottom* steel should be provided†, such that it passes through the columns in both span directions and has sufficient anchorage [Figure 11.41(b)]. With this, even after a punching shear failure, the slab will be hanging by these reinforcements from the column head. The minimum area of such bottom reinforcement is prescribed in Ref. 11.21 as:

$$\Sigma A_{sb} = \frac{2V_{se}}{f_y} \geq \frac{2(2w_{DL}l_2l_n)}{f_y} \tag{11.47}$$

where, A_{sb} is the area of bottom reinforcement crossing one face of the periphery of the column, ΣA_{sb} gives the summation of A_{sb} on all faces of the periphery of the column and V_{se} is shear transmitted to column due to specified loads, but not less than the shear corresponding to twice the self-weight of the slab. At least two bars should be provided in each direction. These may be provided by extending the bottom reinforcement from adjacent spans and lap splicing them over the column; or as extra bottom reinforcements passing over the column with a minimum overlap of $2L_d$ [refer Chapter 8] with the bottom reinforcement in adjacent spans [Figure 11.41(d)]. At discontinuous edges, proper anchorage should be provided into the support by means of bends, hooks, etc., so as to develop the full design yield stress at the face of the support on the slab side. It is to be noted that this reinforcement is not intended to prevent shear failures from occurring, but once such a failure has occurred, they help in facilitating vertical load transfer from the slab to the column.

- When openings are provided in flat slabs and flat plates, the requirements of Cl. 31.8 of the Code should be satisfied. In particular, the requirement for the total amount of reinforcement for the slab without opening should be maintained, such that the equivalent of the reinforcement interrupted should be added on all sides of the openings.

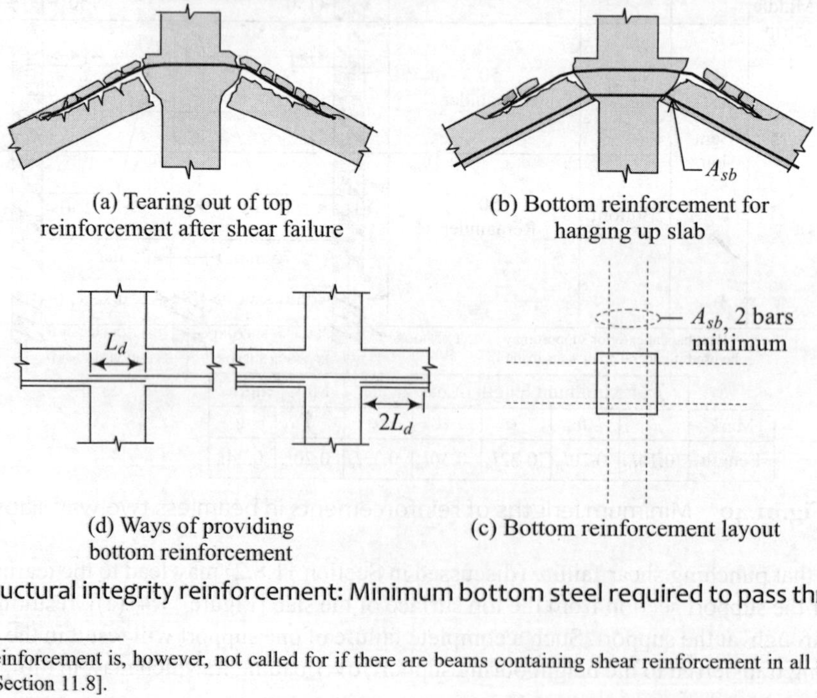

(a) Tearing out of top reinforcement after shear failure

(b) Bottom reinforcement for hanging up slab

(d) Ways of providing bottom reinforcement

(c) Bottom reinforcement layout

Fig. 11.41 Structural integrity reinforcement: Minimum bottom steel required to pass through column.

† Such *integrity* reinforcement is, however, not called for if there are beams containing shear reinforcement in all spans framing into the column [refer Section 11.8].

11.8 Shear in Column-Supported Two-Way Slabs without Beams

Shear in two-way slabs with beams was discussed in Section 11.5.8. There are two types of shear to be considered in the design of two-way slabs supported on columns and without beams:

1. *one-way shear* or *beam shear*, and
2. *two-way shear* or *punching shear*.

As explained in Section 11.5.8, considerations of one-way shear predominate when beams are provided along the column lines; in fact, there is no need to check for two-way shear when the beams provided are relatively stiff. On the other hand, two-way shear considerations predominate in the case of beamless slabs (flat slabs and flat plates). However, both one-way shear and two-way shear need to be checked in two-way slabs supported on flexible beams.†

11.8.1 One-Way Shear or Beam Shear

The slab acts as a wide beam supported on, and spanning between, the columns (and hence, the name *beam shear*, i.e., shear as in the case of beams).The critical section for one-way shear in column-supported slabs is located at a distance d from the face of the concentrated load or reaction area (column, capital or bracket), and extending in a plane across the entire width of the design strip as shown in section 1–1 in Figure 11.42a. The *total* one-way shear at this critical section [Eq. 11.48] shall be distributed between the column strip and the middle strip in proportion to the design negative moments in each strip. The shear stress may be computed taking the full width of the strip (column or middle) considered as a wide beam, or taking a typical segment of slab one metre wide, shown shaded in Figure 11.42a. Assuming the shear to be zero at midspan, the total factored one-way shear force, $V_{u,total}$, at the critical section over its entire length l_2 is given by:

$$V_{u,\text{total}} = w_u l_2 (0.5 l_n - d) \tag{11.48}$$

In the case of a slab with drop panels [Figure 11.42(b)], a second section where one-way shear may be critical is at section 2–2, at a distance d_2 from the edge of the drop panel, where d_2 is the effective depth of the slab outside the drop.

The slab thickness must be adequate to ensure that the shear resistance in one-way action (equal to $\tau_c d$ per unit length) is not less than the factored one-way shear per unit length. However, generally, deflection control criteria are more critical in governing the slab thickness [see Example 11.1], and slabs are mostly safe in one-way shear.

In the vicinity of a corner column, the critical section of the slab for one-way shear is taken along a straight line having a minimum length and located no farther than $d/2$ from the corner column. In case the slab cantilevers beyond the face of the corner column, the critical section may be extended into the cantilevered portion by a length not exceeding d, [Fig. 11.42(c)].

11.8.2 Two-Way Shear or Punching Shear

> For a two-way slab system supported on columns, the critical shear stress consideration is two-way or punching shear

When a large concentrated load is applied on a small slab area‡, there is a possibility of a 'punch through' type of shear failure. A similar situation

† As mentioned earlier, the Code does not adequately cover provisions related to slabs supported on flexible beams. In the general category of flat slabs, the Code (Cl. 31.6) confines its attention to two-way shear alone.

‡ Such a situation is encountered in a footing supporting a column [see Chapter 14].

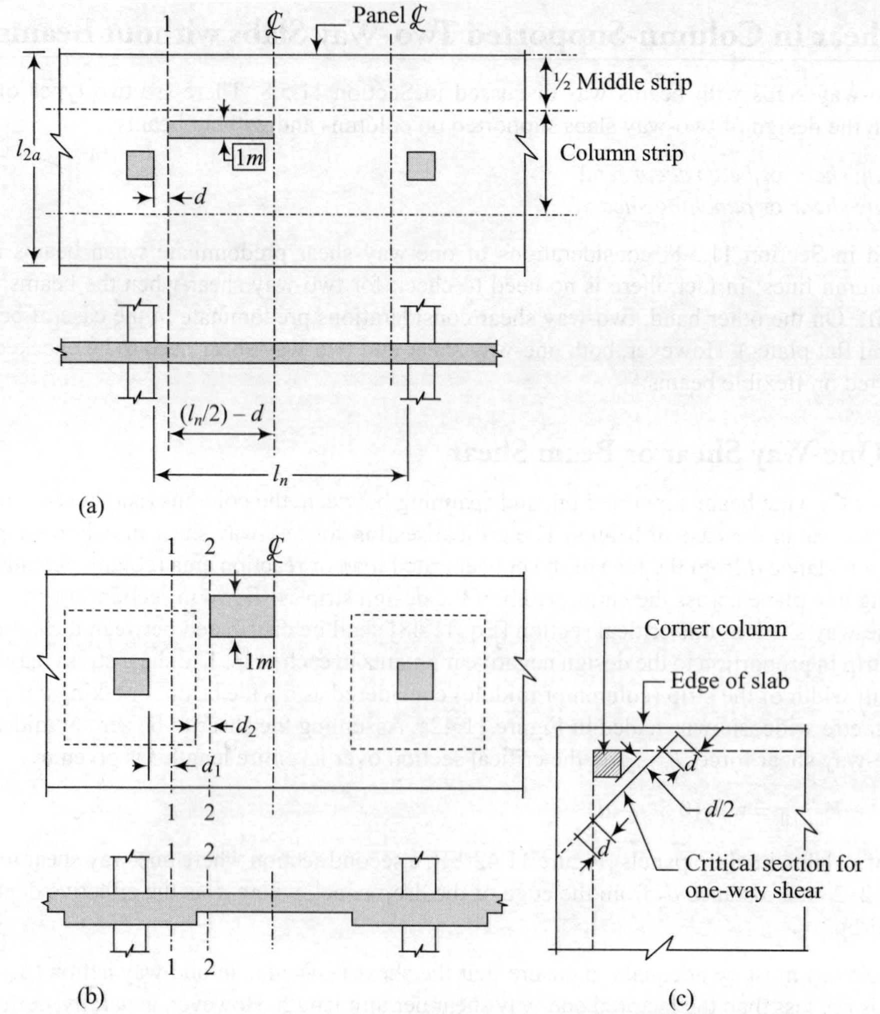

Fig. 11.42 Critical sections for one-way shear.

arises in flat plates and flat slabs supported on columns and subjected to gravity loading and consequent two-way bending. The reaction to the loading on the slab is concentrated on a relatively small area, and if the thickness of the slab is not adequate in this region, shear failure can occur by punching through of the reaction area along a truncated cone or pyramid, with the failure surface sloping outwards in all directions from the perimeter of the loaded (reaction) area, as shown in Figure 11.43(a). The shear associated with this type of failure is termed *two-way shear* or *punching shear* or *perimeter shear*.

Extensive research related to punching shear [Ref. 11.30] indicates that the critical section governing the ultimate shear strength in two-way action of slabs (and footings) is along the perimeter of the loaded area. Furthermore, for square columns and loaded areas, it is found that the ultimate shear stress at this section is a function of two parameters, viz., $\sqrt{f_{ck}}$ and the ratio of the side of the square loaded area to the effective depth of the slab. The shear strength can be made relatively independent of the second parameter by considering a critical section for punching shear at a distance $d/2$ beyond the edge of the loaded area [Figure 11.43(b)].

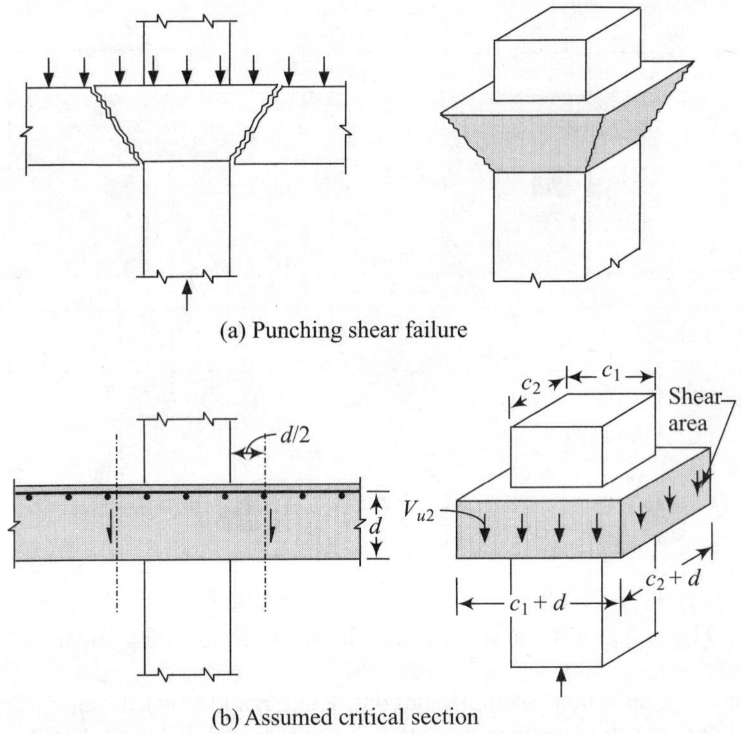

Fig. 11.43 Shear stresses in slabs due to punching shear

An expression for the design shear strength τ_{c2} (in two-way shear), based on Ref. 11.30 and 11.31, is given [Cl. 31.6.3.1 of the Code] as:

$$\tau_{c2} = k_s \left(0.25\sqrt{f_{ck}}\right) \tag{11.49}$$

where $\qquad k_s \equiv 0.5 + \beta_c \leq 1.0 \qquad$ (11.49a)

and β_c† is the ratio of the short side to the long side of the column or capital. The corresponding ultimate shear resistance, V_{c2}, is given by

$$V_{c2} = \tau_{c2} b_o d \tag{11.50}$$

where b_o is the perimeter of the critical section, equal to $2(c_1 + c_2 + 2d)$ for the column, as indicated in Figure 11.43(b).

In general, the factored shear force, V_{u2}, causing punching shear, may be computed as the net upward column reaction minus the downward load within the area of the slab enclosed by the perimeter of the critical section.

In the Equivalent Frame Method, the column reaction can be obtained from frame analysis. In the Direct Design Method, and for preliminary design purposes, V_{u2} may be computed as the total design load acting on the shaded area shown in Figure 11.44.

† Tests have shown that the shear strength reduces with increasing rectangularity of the loaded area [Ref. 11.31].

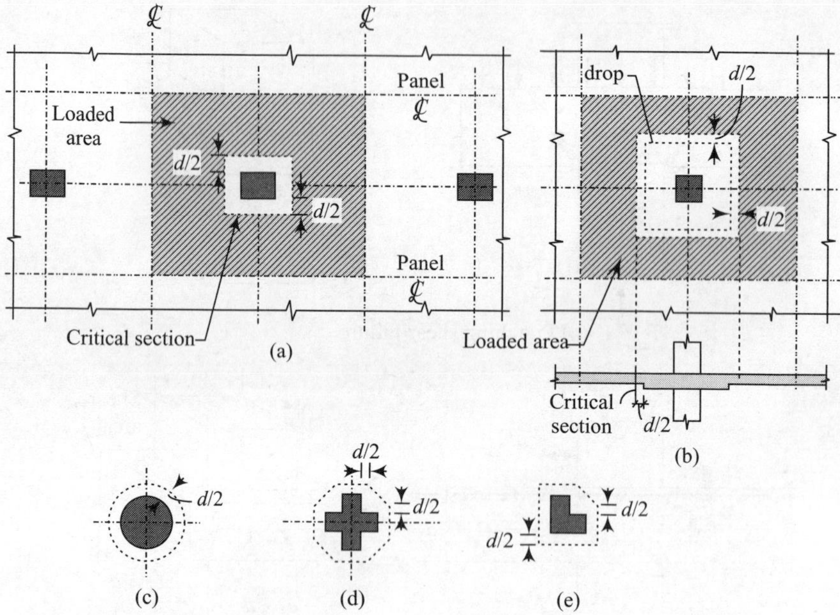

Fig. 11.44 Critical sections and loading for punching shear.

For computing V_{u2} (and V_{c2}), the critical section to be considered should be at a distance $d/2$ from the periphery of the column/capital/drop panel, perpendicular to the plane of the slab [Cl. 31.6.1 of the Code], and having a plan shape geometrically similar to the column section, as shown in Figures 11.44(a), (b), (c). Here, d is to be taken as the effective depth at the section under consideration. For column sections (or loaded areas) with re-entrant corners, a section, no closer than $d/2$ from column face and having the least perimeter, may be taken as the critical section [Figures 11.44(d), (e)].

When openings in the slab are located within a distance of ten times the slab thickness from a concentrated load or reaction area, or within a column strip in a flat slab, the portion of the periphery of the critical section which is enclosed by radial projections of the openings to the centroid of the loaded area must be considered ineffective in computing the shear stress [Cl. 31.6.1.2 of the Code]. Some examples of the effective portions of critical sections for slabs with openings are shown in Figure 11.45.

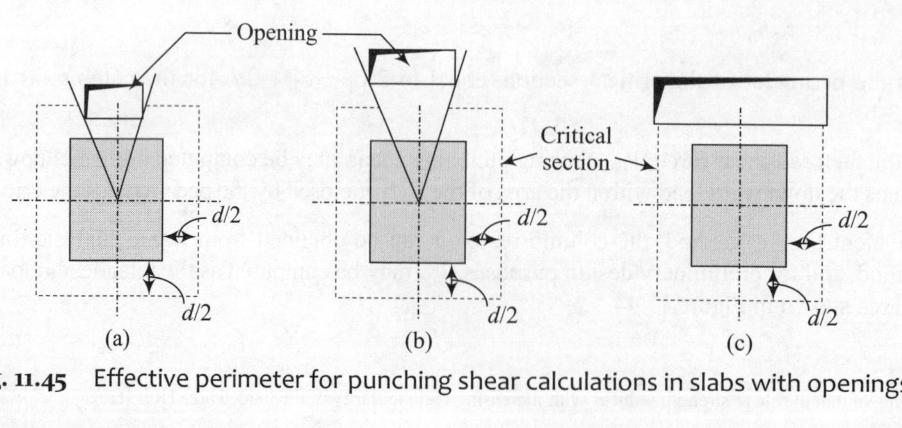

Fig. 11.45 Effective perimeter for punching shear calculations in slabs with openings.

The ultimate shear stress induced by the factored punching shear force V_{u2} at the critical section around a column must be combined with the shear stress due to the transfer of part of the unbalanced slab moment (M_{uv}) to the column through shear [refer Section 11.4.3 and Figure 11.30(c)]. For the purpose of computing shear stresses at the critical section due to M_{uv}, the Code (Cl. 31.6.2.2) recommends that the shear stresses may be assumed to vary linearly about the centroid of the critical section. Accordingly, combining the effects of both V_{u2} and M_{uv}, the shear stress distribution is as shown in Figure 11.46, and the maximum shear stress τ_{v2} (two-way) may be expressed as:

$$\tau_{v2} = \frac{V_{u2}}{b_o d} + \frac{M_{uv}\, c}{J_c} \tag{11.51}$$

where

$b_o \equiv$ perimeter of the critical section;

$J_c \equiv$ property of the critical section analogous to the polar moment of inertia;

$c \equiv$ distance of the point under consideration on the face of critical section to the centroidal axis of the critical section.

Expressions for J_c and c (for maximum shear) are indicated in Figure 11.46 for two typical cases. For other cases, reference may be made to design handbooks such as Ref. 11.28.

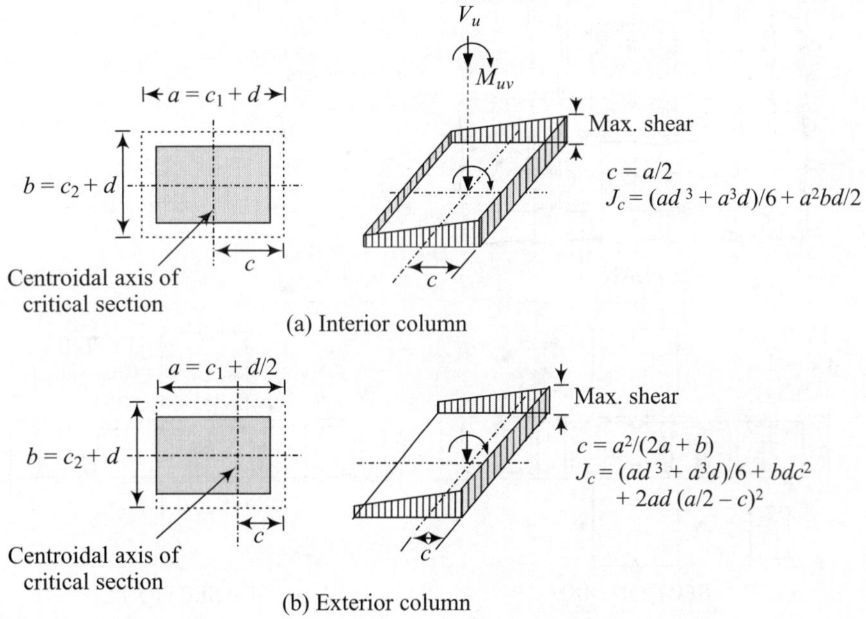

Fig. 11.46 Combined shear due to punching and transfer of unbalanced moment from slab to column.

When there are unbalanced moments about both principal axes, as in the case of a corner column, Eq. 11.51 takes the form:

$$\tau_{v2} = \frac{V_{u2}}{b_o d} + \left[\frac{M_{uv}}{J_c} e\right]_{xx} + \left[\frac{M_{uv}}{J_c} e\right]_{yy} \tag{11.51a}$$

where e is the distance from the respective centroidal axis of the critical section to the extreme point where the stress is being calculated; and the factored shear force and unbalanced moments about the x and y directions are obtained from a consistent loading. Note that, except for a corner column, the maximum values of V_{u2}, $M_{uv\text{-}xx}$ and $M_{uv\text{-}yy}$ occur under different loading conditions.

If the calculated factored shear stress τ_{v2} exceeds the design shear strength τ_{c2} (given by Eq. 11.49), but not $1.5\tau_{c2}$, appropriate shear reinforcement must be provided along the perimeter of the column. The total cross-sectional area A_{sv} of all the stirrup legs in the perimeter is calculated using the following expression [refer Cl. 31.6.3.2 and Ref. 11.11]:

$$A_{sv} = \frac{(\tau_{v2} - 0.5\tau_{c2})b_o d}{0.87 f_y} \tag{11.52}$$

Some typical types of shear reinforcement, recommended in Ref. 11.11 and Ref. 11.14, are shown in Figure 11.47.

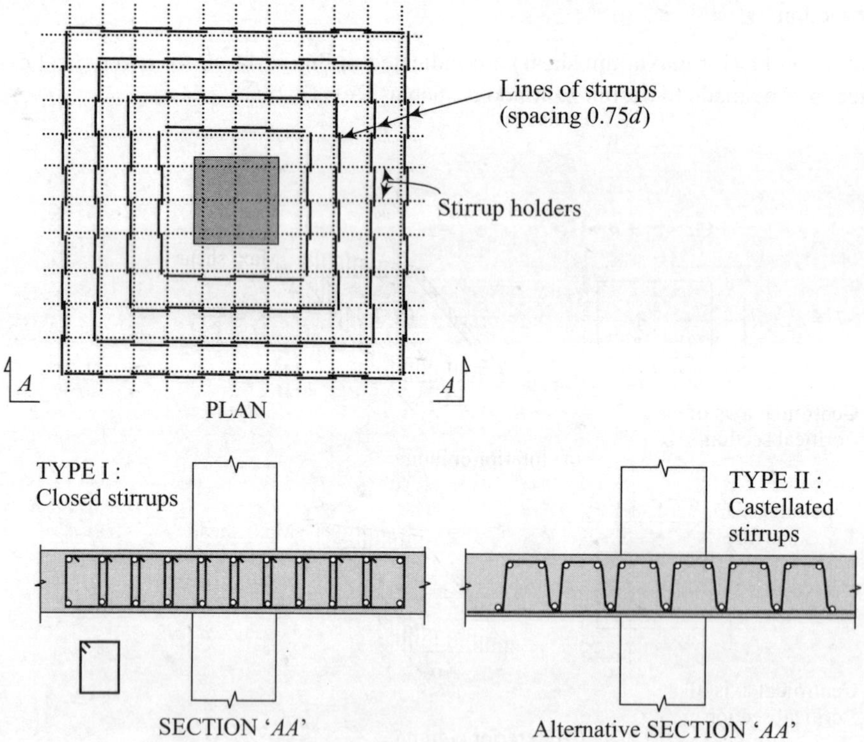

Fig. 11.47 Reinforcement for punching shear.

Stirrups may be *closed* or *castellated* and must pass around one row of tension steel running perpendicular to the stirrups at each face of the relevant section. If the value of τ_{v2} exceeds $1.5\tau_{c2}$, the slab thickness should be suitably increased. Alternatively, reinforcement may be made up of 'shear head reinforcement', consisting of structural steel I-section or channel section embedded within the slab, and designed in accordance with the ACI Code provision [Ref. 11.22]. Generally, when shear reinforcement is provided, the critical section for punching shear gets shifted farther from the column. Hence, the Code (Cl. 31.6.3.2) requires that the shear stresses should be investigated at successive sections (at intervals of $0.75d$, as per Ref. 11.11) more distant from the column, and shear reinforcement should be provided up to a section where the shear stress does not exceed $0.5\tau_{v2}$. It is recommended that the spacing of stirrups should not exceed $0.75d$ and must be continued to a distance d beyond the section at which the shear stress is within allowable limits [Ref. 11.11].

The design of such shear reinforcement is demonstrated in Example 11.7.

11.9 Design Examples of Column-Supported Two-Way Slabs

Two examples are presented here for the design of two-way slabs supported on columns (with or without beams) by the unified approach using the equivalent frame concept. In the first example to follow (Example 11.6), the Direct Design Method is applied, and in the next example (Example 11.7), the Equivalent Frame Method is applied.

Example 11.6: Direct Design Method

The plan of a two-way floor slab system, with beams along the column lines, is shown in Figure 11.48. Based on preliminary estimates, the columns are of size 400 mm × 400 mm and the beams are of size 400 mm × 550 mm. The floor-to-floor height is 3.5 m. Assume a live load of 5.0 kN/m² and a finish load of 1.0 kN/m². Determine the design moments and reinforcement requirements in the various strips in the E–W direction for an edge panel and an interior panel (marked S_1 and S_2 respectively in Figure 11.48), using the Direct Design Method. Assume M 25 concrete and Fe 500 steel.

Solution

The moments in panels S_1 and S_2 in Figure 11.48(a) (in the E-W direction) can be determined by DDM, by considering an 'equivalent frame' along column line 2–2, which is isolated and shown in Figure 11.48(b).

1. Check limitations of DDM

1. There are three continuous spans in each direction.
2. The panels are rectangular with long span/short span ratio = 7.5/6.0
   = 1.25 < 2.0.
3. There are no offset columns.
4. There is no difference in successive span lengths.
5. Assuming the slab to be 200 mm thick, $w_{DL} = 1.0 + (25 \times 0.20) = 6.0$ kN/m²

   $\Rightarrow w_{u,DL} = 6.0 \times 1.5 = 9.00$ kN/m²

   $w_{u,LL} = 5.0 \times 1.5 = 7.50$ "

   $w_u = 16.5$ kN/m²

   $w_{u,LL}/w_{u,DL} = 7.50/9.00 = 0.83 < 3.0$ – OK

   [The more severe condition in Ref. 11.21 is also satisfied as the ratio is < 2.0, and the loads are uniformly distributed gravity loads.]

6. Relative stiffnesses of beams: $\dfrac{\alpha_{b1} l_2^2}{\alpha_{b2} l_1^2}$ where $\alpha_{b1} = I_{b1}/I_{s1}$, $\alpha_{b2} = I_{b2}/I_{s2}$

   As the beam stem dimensions are the same along all edges of the panel, it may be assumed that $I_{b1} \approx I_{b2}$; and $I_{s1} = l_2 D_s^3/12$ and $I_{s2} = l_1 D_s^3/12$;

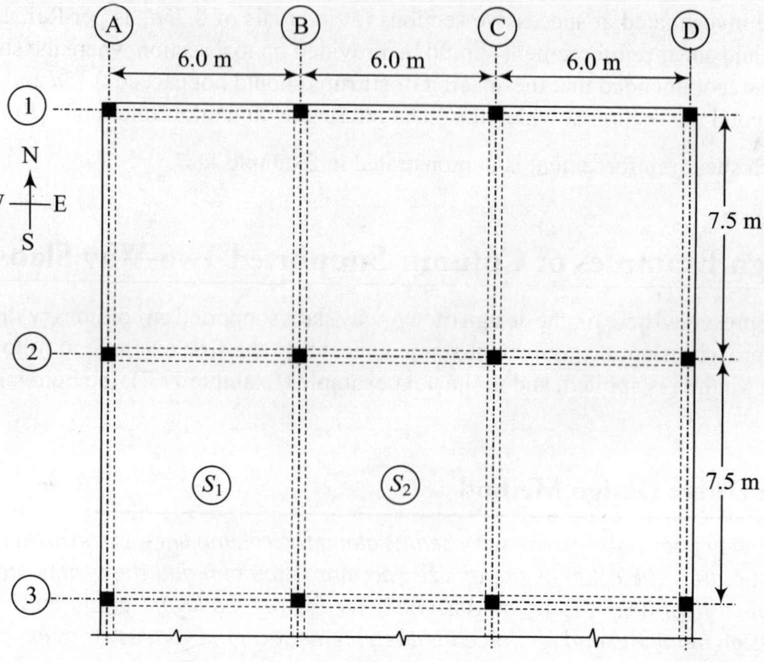

(a) Plan of slab

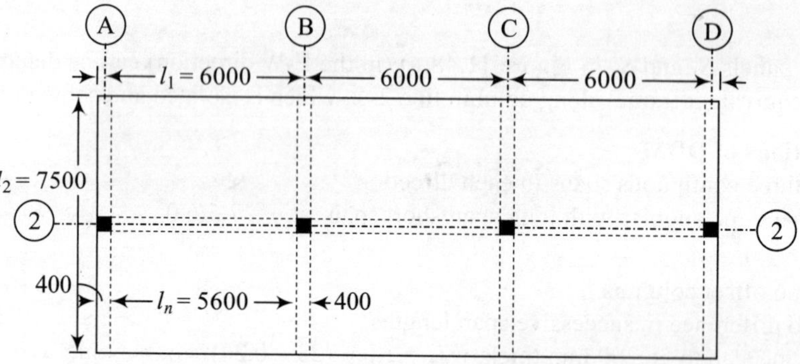

(b) Panel for equivalent frame

Fig. 11.48 Example 11.6.

$$\Rightarrow \quad \frac{\alpha_{b1}}{\alpha_{b2}} \approx \frac{I_{s2}}{I_{s1}} = \frac{l_1}{l_2}$$

$$\Rightarrow \quad \frac{\alpha_{b1} l_2^2}{\alpha_{b2} l_1^2} \approx \frac{l_1}{l_2} \times \frac{l_2^2}{l_1^2} = \frac{l_2}{l_1} = \frac{7.5}{6} = 1.25$$

which lies between 0.2 and 5.0, thereby satisfying Eq. 11.30.

- Hence, all limitations are satisfied, and DDM is applicable.

2. Slab thickness for deflection control

- The critical panel to be considered is the exterior panel $S1$.
- Applying the Canadian Code formula [Eq. 11.26a]:

$$D \geq [l_n(0.6 + f_y/1000)]/\{30 + 4\beta\alpha_{bm}\}$$

where

l_n = 7100 mm (longer clear span)

β = longer clear span/shorter clear span = 7100/5600 = 1.268

f_y = 500 MPa

$\alpha_{bm} \equiv$ average value of α_b for all beams on the edges of panel S_1.

The expression in Eq. 11.27a can be used to compute I_b. However, in this example, the definition for beam sections given in Figure 11.28 will be followed. Accordingly, the beam and slab sections for computing $\alpha_b = I_b/I_s$ along the four edges (along with values of I_b and I_s) are depicted in Figures 11.49(a), (b), (c).

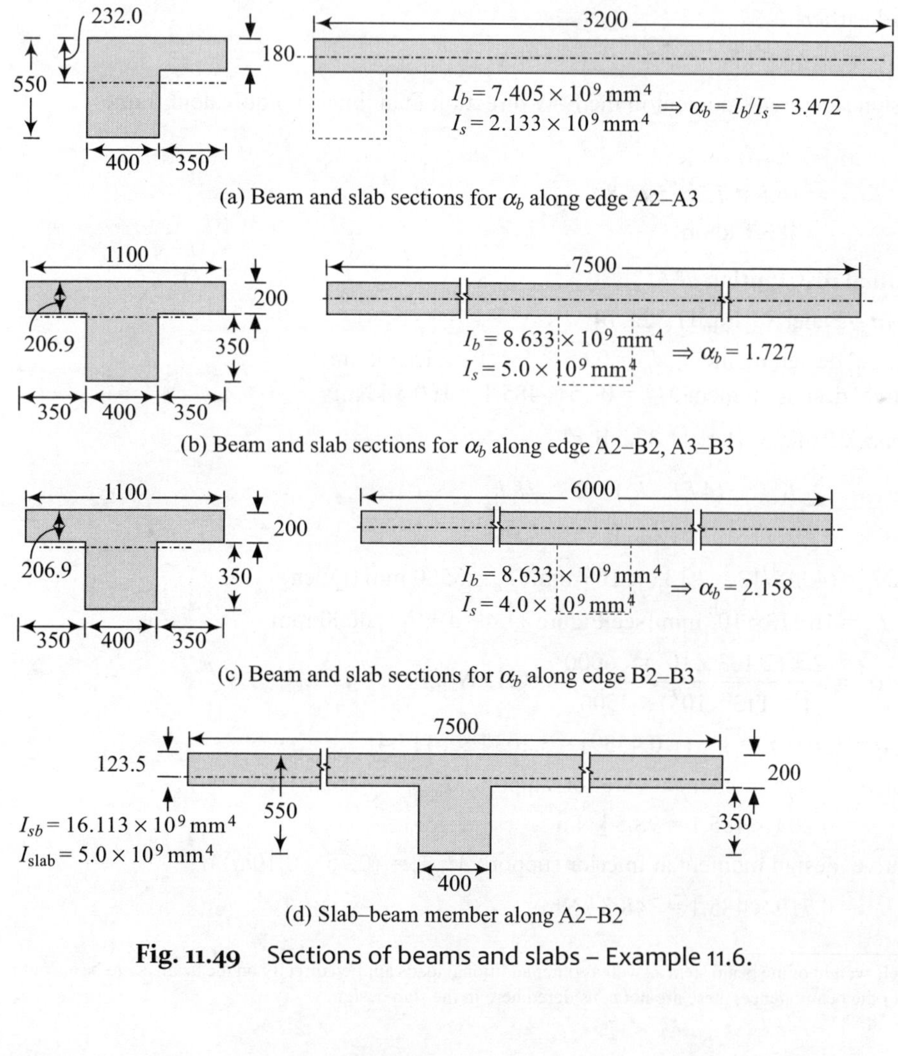

(a) Beam and slab sections for α_b along edge A2–A3

(b) Beam and slab sections for α_b along edge A2–B2, A3–B3

(c) Beam and slab sections for α_b along edge B2–B3

(d) Slab–beam member along A2–B2

Fig. 11.49 Sections of beams and slabs – Example 11.6.

As indicated in Figure 11.49,

$$\alpha_b = \begin{cases} 3.472 & \text{for transverse beams at exterior support} \\ 2.158 & \text{for transverse beams at interior support} \\ 1.727 & \text{for longitudinal beams} \end{cases}$$

$$\Rightarrow \quad \alpha_{bm} = \{3.472 + 2.158 + (1.727 \times 2)\}/4 = 2.271$$

But α_{bm} shall not be greater than 2.0. Using Eq. 11.26a,

$$\Rightarrow \quad D \geq [7100(0.6 + 500/1000)]/\{30 + 4 \times 1.268 \times 2.0\} = 194.5 \text{ mm}$$

[Note that the parameter, $\alpha_{b1}l_2/l_1$, is greater than 1.0 for all the four beams. Hence, the supporting beams can be considered to be 'adequately stiff', whereby the limiting l/d ratios prescribed by the IS Code can be applied, with l taken as the effective *short* span.]

- A slab thickness of 200 mm is therefore adequate.

3. Total (static) design moment

As calculated earlier†,

$$w_u = 16.5 \text{ kN/m}^2$$

⇒ Total design (factored) moment in the E-W direction in an interior equivalent frame:

$$\begin{aligned} M_o &= w_u l_2 l_n^2/8 \\ &= 16.5 \times 7.5 \times 5.6^2/8 \\ &= \mathbf{485.1\ kNm} \end{aligned}$$

4. Longitudinal distribution of M_o

Interior Span – Panel S_2 [Eq. 11.32a, b]

- 'negative' design moment $M_o^- = 0.65 \times 485.1 = 315.3$ kNm
- 'positive' design moment $M_o^+ = 0.35 \times 485.1 = 169.8$ kNm

Exterior Span – Panel S_1 [Eq. 11.33a, b, c]

$$\alpha_c = \frac{\sum K_c}{K_{sb}} = \frac{(4EI_c/h_c) \times 2}{4EI_{sb}/l_1} = \frac{2I_c l_1}{I_{sb}h_c}$$

where $I_c = (400)^4/12 = 2.133 \times 10^9$ mm^4; $h_c = 3500$ mm (given)

$I_{sb} = 16.113 \times 10^9$ mm [see Figure 11.49(d)]; $l_1 = 6000$ mm

$$\Rightarrow \quad \alpha_c = \frac{2 \times (2.133 \times 10^9) \times 6000}{(16.113 \times 10^9) \times 3500} = 0.4539$$

$$\Rightarrow \quad q = 1 + 1/\alpha_c = 1 + (1/0.4539) = 3.203 \text{ [Eq. 11.34]}$$

- 'negative' design moment at exterior support $M_{o,\text{ext}}^- = (0.65/q)M_o$

  $= 0.203 \times 485.1 = 98.5$ kNm

- 'negative' design moment at interior support $M_{o,\text{int}}^- = (0.75 - 0.10/q)M_o$

  $= 0.719 \times 485.1 = 348.8$ kNm

† *Note:* The self-weight of the beam stem as well as other additional loads applied directly on the beam are to be accounted for separately in the design of the beam; hence, these are not considered here in the slab design.

- 'positive' design moment $M_o^+ = (0.63 - 0.28/q)M_o = 0.543 \times 485.1 = 263.4$ kNm
  [Alternatively, following the Canadian code recommendations, the coefficients given in Table 11.4, case (2) may be applied. The corresponding factors there are 0.16, 0.70 and 0.59 respectively, which compare well with the factors above.]
- *Check for effects of pattern loading*:
  Corresponding to $w_{DL}/w_{LL} = 6.0/5.0 = 1.2$, $l_2/l_1 = 7.5/6.0 = 1.25$, and $\alpha_{b1} = 1.727$, referring to Table 11.5, $\alpha_{c,\,\min} = 0$
  Actual $\alpha_c = 0.4539 > 0$; hence, the column stiffness is adequate, and so there is no need to modify the 'positive' design moments to account for the effects of pattern loading.
- The longitudinal distribution of moments (as per IS Code) is shown in Figure 11.50(a). [The 10 per cent modification of bending moments permitted by the Code is not considered here.]

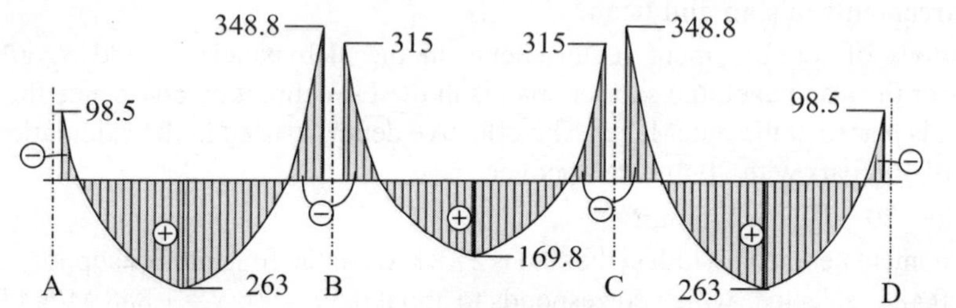

(a) 'positive' and 'negative' design moments

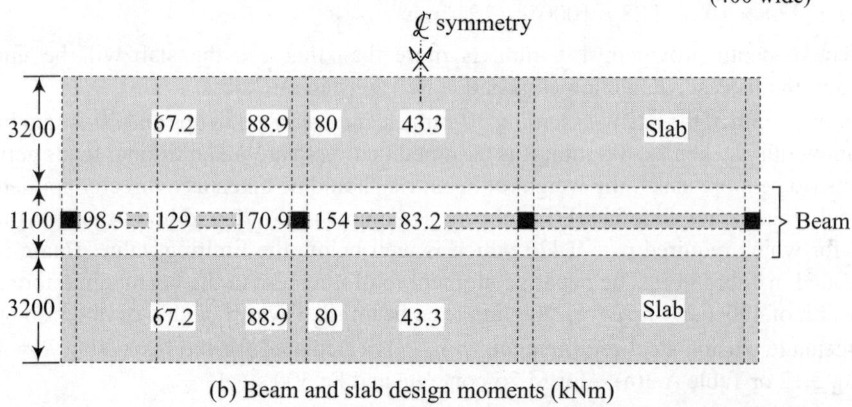

(b) Beam and slab design moments (kNm)

Fig. 11.50 Design moments in various elements in E-W direction – Example 11.6.

5. Transverse distribution of moments in design strips

- At each critical section, part of the design moment is assigned to the beam and the balance to the slab portion. The fraction of the positive moment in all spans and negative moment at interior columns to be resisted by the beam is given by Eq. 11.40, (in this case $\alpha_{b1} = 1.727$), as:

$$\frac{\alpha_{b1}}{0.3 + \alpha_{b1}}\left(1 - \frac{l_2}{3l_1}\right) = \frac{1.727}{0.3 + 1.727}\left(1 - \frac{7.5}{3 \times 6.0}\right) = 0.49 = 49 \text{ per cent.}$$

Hence, the moment share of the slab is 51 per cent.

At the exterior support, the beam must be designed for 100 per cent of the exterior negative moment. Also, the reinforcement for this shall be placed within a band with a width $b_b = 400 + 2 \times 1.5 \times 200 = 1000$ mm.

- These distributed moments in the beam part and the slab part are depicted in Figure 11.50(b). The beam width is 1100 mm [Figure 11.49(c)], and each slab part on either side of beam is 3200 mm wide.
- The factored design moments (in the E-W direction) in the panels S_1 and S_2 of the slab are summarised in Figure 11.51(a). The moments, expressed in kNm per m width of slab, are also indicated in parenthesis in Figure 11.51(a). As the moments on either side of the common continuous support (shared by S_1 and S_2) are unequal, for slab design purposes, it is sufficient and conservative to design for the higher moment – in this case, occurring in panel S_1. [Note that this difference could have been brought down and a more economical design obtained by resorting to the modification of moments by up to 10 per cent as permitted by Code, Cl. 31.4.3.4].

6. Flexural reinforcements in slab and beam

- The calculations of reinforcement requirements in the slab panels S_1 and S_2 are summarised in Table 11.9. For the slab panel, the shorter span is in the E-W direction and hence the reinforcement in this direction is placed at the outer layer. The effective depth, d, used in the calculations is based on the assumption of 10ϕ bars with 20 mm clear cover.

  $\Rightarrow \quad d = 200 - 20 - 10/2 = 175$ mm

  The largest moment per metre width in the slab is 27.8 kNm at the first interior support. If a reinforcement ratio of $p_t = 0.48$ is selected (which corresponds to about 0.5 $p_{t,\,\text{lim}}$), $R = 1.888$ MPa [Table A.2(a)], and the required effective depth is:

  $$d = \sqrt{[27.8 \times 10^6/(1.888 \times 1000)]} = 121 \text{ mm}$$

  The effective depth provided, 155 mm, is more than this and the slab will be under-reinforced throughout. In this case, deflection control dictated the slab thickness.

  The effective depth of the beam, assuming 30-mm clear cover, 8ϕ stirrups and 20ϕ main bars is 502 mm. The beam width is taken as 400 mm. It is assumed that there are no additional loads acting directly on the beams [to be more exact, the weight of beam rib should be taken as a directly applied load, but this being negligible, is not done here]. For the largest moment of 170.9 kNm at the first interior support, $R = 1.7$ for which required $p_t = 0.426$ which is well below the limiting value. Beam reinforcements are indicated in Table 11.9. The negative moment reinforcement in the beam at the top must be spread over a width of $400 + 2 \times 1.5D_s = 1000$ mm (i.e., beam rib + width of slab of 300 mm on either side).
- The percentage tension steel requirement, $(p_t)_{\text{reqd}}$, is calculated for the respective $R \equiv M_u/bd^2$ values, using Eq. 5.12 or Table A.3(a) – for M 25 concrete and Fe 500 steel.
- *Minimum reinforcement*:

  For beam (Cl. 26.5.1.1), $(A_{st})_{\min} = 400 \times 502 \times 0.85/500 = 341 \text{ mm}^2$

  For slab (Cl. 26.5.2.1), $(A_{st})_{\min} = 0.0012\, bD = 0.0012 \times 1000 \times 200 = 240 \text{ mm}^2/\text{m}$

  Maximum spacing of bars: $3d = 3 \times 175 = 525$ mm, to be limited to 300 mm
- Spacing of bars
  - corresponding to $(A_{st})_{\min} = 240 \text{ mm}^2/\text{m}$, using 10$\phi$ bars, spacing required = 1000 × 78.5/240 = 327 mm, minimum 300 mm controls.
  - corresponding to $A_{st} = 381.88 \text{ mm}^2/\text{m}$, at interior support, spacing of 10ϕ bars required = 1000 × 78.5/381.88= 206 mm (at top)

- corresponding to A_{st} = 285.17 mm^2/m, at midspan of panel S_1,
  spacing of 10ϕ bars required = 1000 × 78.5/285.17= 275 mm (at bottom)
- corresponding to A_{st} = 181.1 mm^2/m, at midspan of panel S_2,
  spacing of 10ϕ bars required = 1000 × 78.5/181.1= 434 mm (at bottom)

- There is no negative moment assigned to the slab part at the exterior support. However, the slab at this part has to be provided with the minimum reinforcement. Although the design moment is zero, in order to take care of possible negative moments due to partial fixity, it would be appropriate (Cl. D-1.6) to provide top reinforcement equal to 50 per cent of that provided at mid-span, extending 0.1l into the span (here spacing limitation of 300 mm controls).

Table 11.9 *Slab reinforcement requirements – Example 11.6*

Location	Panel S_1			Panel S_2
	exterior support	**midspan**	**interior support**	**midspan**
1. beam portion				
M_u (kNm)	(–)98.5	(+)129.1	(–)170.9	(+)83.2
$R \equiv \dfrac{M_u}{bd^2}$ (MPa)	0.977	1.281	1.695	0.825
$(p_t)_{reqd}$, (× 10^{-2})	0.236	0.314	0.426	0.198
$(A_{st})_{reqd}$ (mm^2)	473.42	630.88	855.58	396.7
$(A_{st})_{min}$	–	–	–	341
No. of bars	2–20ϕ	2–20ϕ + 1–12ϕ	2–20ϕ + 1–18ϕ	2–18ϕ
2. slab				
M_u (kNm/m)	0.0	(+)21.0	(–)27.8	(+)13.5
R (MPa)	–	0.686	0.908	0.441
$(p_t)_{reqd}$	*	0.163	0.218	0.103
$(A_{st})_{reqd}$ (mm^2/m)	240*	285.17	381.88	181.1
Spacing: required	–	275	206	434
provided	300	200	200	300

* *Note*: $(A_{st})_{min}$ governs.

- Furthermore, all positive moment reinforcement perpendicular to the discontinuous edge should be extended to the slab edge and embedded (Cl. 31.7.4).
- With no moment assigned to the slab at the exterior support, the torsion on the edge beam transmitted by the slab is also zero. In actuality, some torque will be introduced, but this will be low. Therefore, the torsional stresses in the edge beam may be neglected. Similar stresses at interior supports will be even lesser.
- The actual spacings of 10ϕ bars provided in panels S_1 and S_2 are indicated in Table 11.9 and Figure 11.51(b).
- As the supporting beams are 'adequately stiff' ($\alpha_{b1} l_2/l_1$ > 1.0), torsional reinforcement has to be provided at the corners with discontinuous edges in panel S_1 – as in the case of wall-supported slabs (Cl. D-1.9). The area requirement (0.375 A_{st}^{+}) works out to 0.375 × 285.17= 107 mm^2/m, at top and bottom over a square of size 0.2 × 6.0 = 1.2 m. Provide 10ϕ bars at 300 mm spacing.

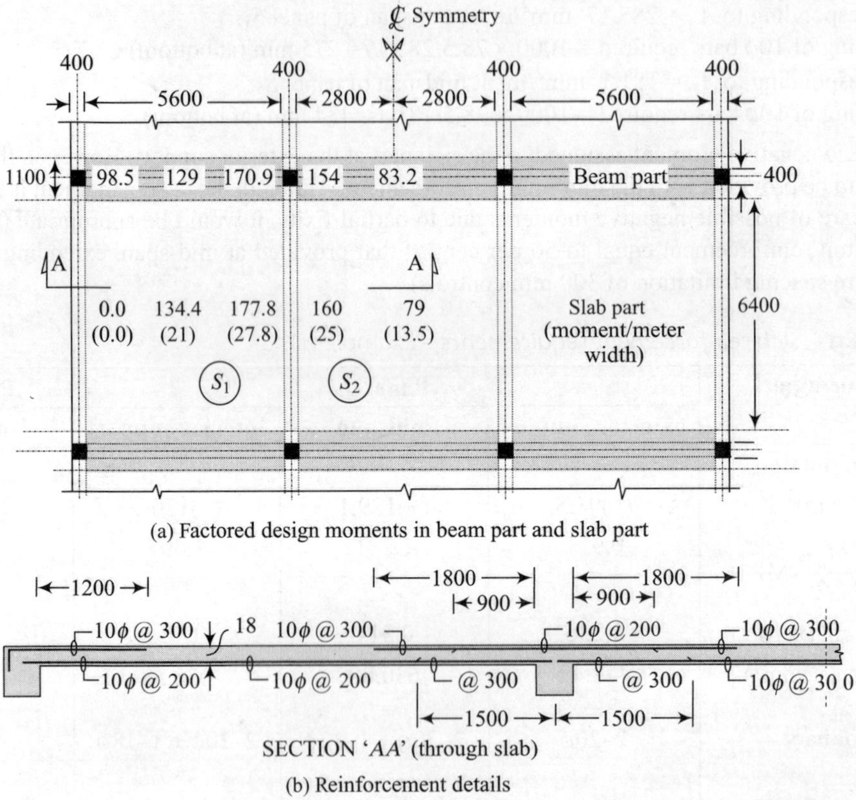

Fig. 11.51 Design moments and reinforcement details in panels S1 and S2 in E-W direction – Example 11.6

7. Transfer of moments to columns

Since beams are provided along column lines, transfer of unbalanced moment to the supporting columns is not critical in this example. The largest unbalanced moment occurs at the exterior support and the beam is designed to resist this in full. The requirement in Cl. 31.3.3 for moment transfer between slab and column through flexure is of primary concern in flat slabs.

8. Shear in slab and beams

Since all beams in this example have the parameter $\alpha_{b1} l_2/l_1$ greater than 1.0, they are adequately stiff. Hence, they are proportioned to resist the full shear from the loads on the respective tributary areas (Figure 11.52) and no part of this need be assigned to the slab to be resisted by two-way action (Section 11.5.8). In beam-supported slabs, the slab shear is essentially that associated with one-way action. For one-way shear in slab, considering a one-metre-wide strip, the distribution of loads as shown in Figure 11.52 may be assumed, with the critical section located d away from the face of the beam. The factored shear force V_u is given by:

$$V_u = w_u\,(0.5 l_n - d)$$

$$= 16.5 \times (0.5 \times 5.6 - 0.175) = 43.32 \text{ kN}$$

$$\Rightarrow \quad \tau_v = 43.32 \times 10^3/(10^3 \times 175) = 0.248 \text{ MPa}$$

shear strength of concrete in one-way shear = $k\tau_c$

where, corresponding to M 25 concrete and $p_t = \dfrac{1000 \times 78.5 \times 100}{200 \times 1000 \times 175} = 0.224$,

$\tau_c = 0.407$ MPa, and $k > 1.0$

$\Rightarrow \quad k\tau_c > \tau_v$ – Hence, OK.

The beam *AB* may be designed for shear due to the load from its tributary area shown shaded in Figure 11.52, as demonstrated in Chapter 6.

Note: As the beams in this example are adequately stiff, the slab system may be alternatively designed by the (much simpler) method of moment coefficients prescribed by the Code for wall-supported slabs.

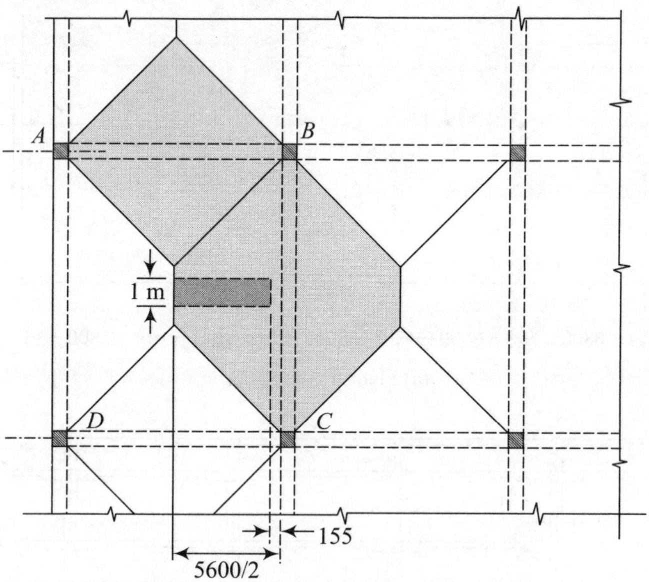

Fig. 11.52 Shear in slab and beams.

Example 11.7: Equivalent Frame Method

The floor plan of a flat slab floor for an office building is shown in Figure 11.53(a). The floor-too-floor height may be taken as 3.3 m. The columns are of size 500 mm × 500 mm. Assume live loads of 2.5 kN/m² and superimposed dead loads of 2.7 kN/m² (comprising finishes: 1.0 kN/m²; partitions: 1.0 kN/m²; false ceiling: 0.2 kN/m², mechanical and electrical fittings: 0.5 kN/m²). Analyse a typical interior bay in the E-W direction, shown shaded in Figure 11.53(a), using the equivalent frame method. Compute the reinforcement requirements in the various design strips of the slab, and check shear stresses. Assume M 25 concrete and Fe 500 steel. Exposure condition is mild.

Solution

1. Slab thickness for deflection control

The same thickness will be provided for the floor slab in all panels. At discontinuous edges, edge beams with a stiffness ratio $\alpha \geq 0.8$ will be provided so that no increase in slab thickness is required for the exterior panels.

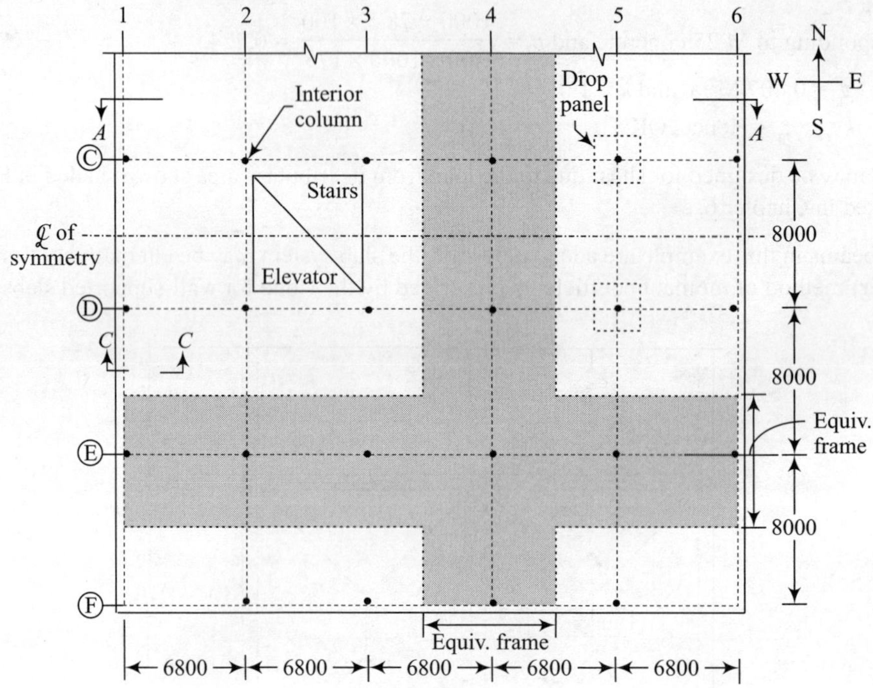

(a) Floor framing plan

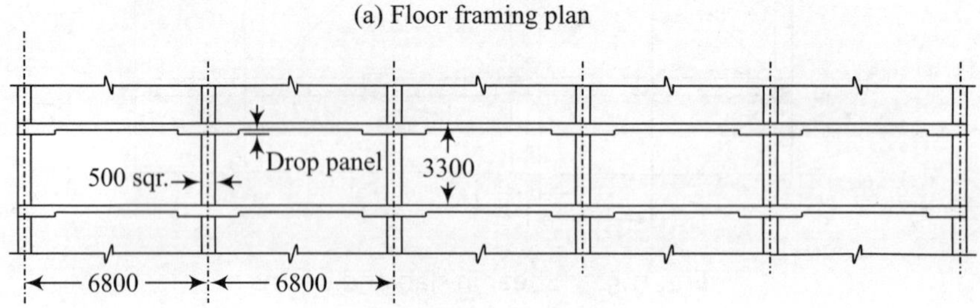

(b) Section *AA* (enlarged)

Fig. 11.53 Example 11.7.

For slabs with drops conforming to the requirements, the Code (Cl. 31.2.1) recommends span to effective depth ratios given in Cl. 23.2, with the longer span considered. For continuous spans, the ratio recommended is 26. For two-way slabs, as already mentioned in Section 11.2.1, the modification factor (Figure 4 of Code) may be taken as 1.5. Considering the larger span, l_n = 7500 mm. With these, the effective depth required is:

$$D \geq 7500/(1.5 \times 26) = 192 \text{ mm}$$

An alternative is to use Eq. 11.26. Assume drop panels extending 1.5 m in each direction from column centre (i.e., 3 m × 3 m panels) and projecting by half the slab thickness below the slab. In Eq. 11.26,

l_n = larger span = 8000-500 =7500 mm

x_d = distance from face of column to edge of drop panel

= 1500 – 250 = 1250 mm < l_n/4, – OK

Of the two directions, the smaller value of $x_d/(l_n/2) = 2 \times 1250/7500 = 1/3$

$$\Delta_h = (D_d - D) = 0.5D, (< D)$$

With these, Eq. 11.26 gives

$$D \geq \frac{7500(0.6 + 500/1000)}{30} - \frac{1}{3} \times 0.5D$$

$$D\,(1 + 1/6) \geq 275; \Rightarrow D \geq (6/7) \times 275 = 235.7 \text{ mm}$$

A slab thickness of 200 mm is selected. This being marginally less than the value calculated above, strictly, a deflection computation is required to check that it is within specified limits.

2. Drop panels

As specified by the Code (Cl. 31.2.2), the minimum extension of the drop panel in each direction from the centre of the column is 1/6 centre-to-centre span, i.e., 6.8/6 = 1.133 m in the E-W direction, and 8.0/6 = 1.333 m in the N-S direction. As assumed earlier, their extension is taken as 1.5 m, resulting in a drop panel size of 3 m × 3 m. The minimum required thickness of the drop panel, projecting below the slab is taken as 100 mm (which is greater than $D/4$). The overall thickness of the drop panel is 300 mm; the entire thickness is effective in calculations of 'negative' moment reinforcement, as this is less than $D + 0.25$ (distance between face of column and edge of drop) = 200 + 0.25(1250) = 512.5 mm [Cl. 31.7.2 of the Code].

3. Edge beam

The edge beam must have a beam stiffness parameter $\alpha_b \geq 0.8$ (to have a favourable effect on the minimum thickness requirement). Assuming a beam of 250 mm width and 450 mm depth [Figures 11.54(a), (b)], the flanged section [Figure 11.54(b)] has a second moment of area which can be shown to be

$$I_b = 2.714 \times 10^9 \text{ mm}^4$$

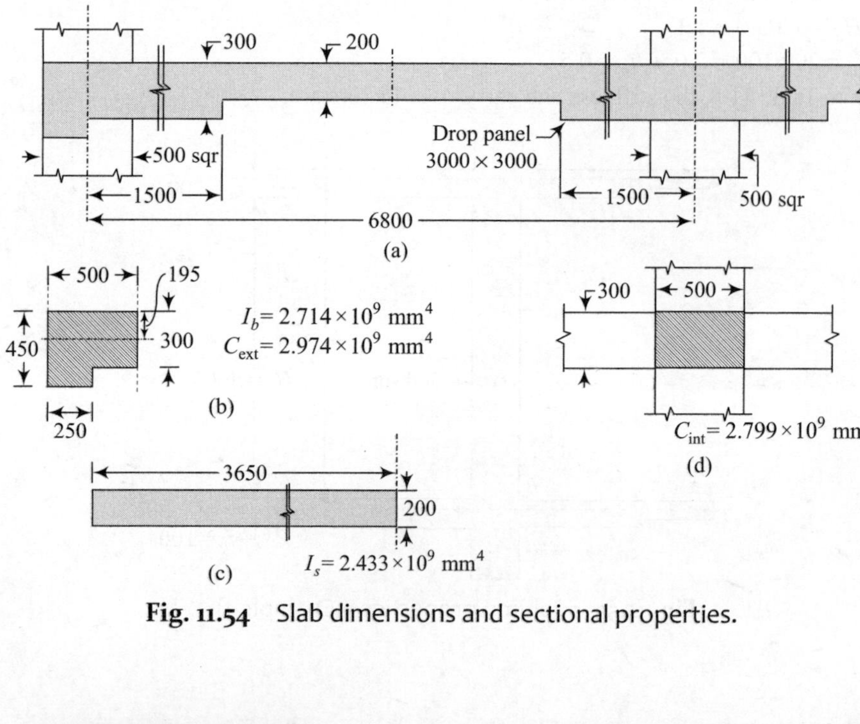

Fig. 11.54 Slab dimensions and sectional properties.

- For the edge beam along the long edge, the associated slab width is 6800/2 + 250 = 3650 mm [Figure 14.54(c)], and the second moment of area of the slab is

$$I_s = 3650 \times 200^3/12 = 2.433 \times 10^9 \text{ mm}^4$$
$$\Rightarrow \quad \alpha_b = I_b/I_s = 2.714/2.433 = 1.115 > 0.8 - \text{OK}$$

- For the edge beam along the short edge, the associated slab width is 8000/2 + 250 = 4250 mm, and

$$I_s = 4250 \times 200^3/12 = 2.833 \times 10^9 \text{ mm}^4$$
$$\Rightarrow \quad \alpha_b = I_b/I_s = 2.714/2.833 = 0.958 > 0.8 - \text{OK}$$

4. Effective depths

- Reinforcement will be placed in the outer layer for the bars in the N-S direction (in order to resist the larger moments in this direction), and in the inner layer for the bars in the E-W direction. Assuming 16ϕ bars with a clear cover of 20 mm, the effective depths are obtained as:

$$d_{N\text{–}S\text{slab}} = 200 - 20 - 16/2 = 172 \text{ mm}$$
$$d_{N\text{–}S\text{drop}} = 300 - 20 - 16/2 = 272 \text{ mm}$$
$$d_{E\text{–}W\text{slab}} = 172 - 16 = 156 \text{ mm}$$
$$d_{E\text{–}W\text{drop}} = 272 - 16 = 256 \text{ mm}$$

5. Factored loads

(i)	self-weight of slab @ 25 × 0.2	= 5.0 kN/m^2
(ii)	superimposed dead load	= 2.7 kN/m^2
(iii)	live load	= 2.5 kN/m^2
		10.2 kN/m^2

$\Rightarrow$ factored load on slab $w_u = 10.2 \times 1.5 = 15.3$ kN/m^2

- additional factored load in drop panel = $(25 \times 0.1) \times 1.5 = 3.75$ kN/m^2

6. Relative stiffness parameters of equivalent frame

a. ***Column stiffness***, K_c [refer Figure 11.55]

$$I_c = (500)^4/12 = 5.208 \times 10^4 \text{ mm}^4$$
$$H/H_c = 3.3/3.0 = 1.1$$
$$t_a/t_b = 200/100 = 2.0, \; t_b/t_a = 0.5$$

Referring to Table 11.8, the stiffness and carry-over factors are:

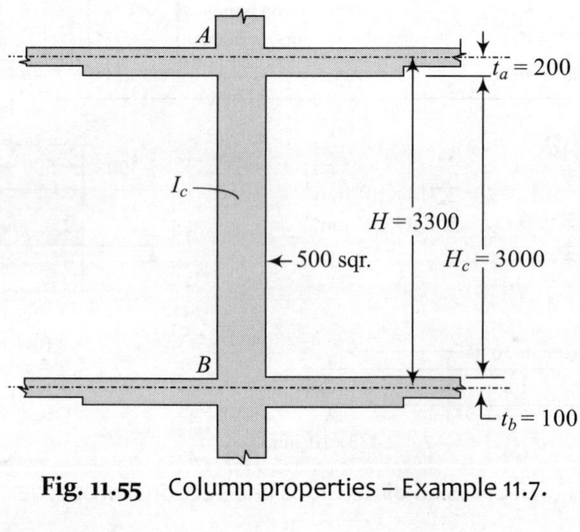

Fig. 11.55 Column properties – Example 11.7.

- for column below, $H/H_c = 1.1$, $t_a/t_b = 2$
  $\Rightarrow \quad K_{AB} = 5.34$, $K_c = KE_cI_c/H = 5.34 \times E_c \times (5.208 \times 10^9)/3300 = (8.427 \times 10^6)E_c$
  $C_{AB} = 0.54$
- for column above, $H/H_c = 1.1$, $t_a/t_b = 0.5$
  $\Rightarrow \quad K_{AB} = 4.85$, $K_c = 4.85 \times E_c \times (5.208 \times 10^9)/3300 = (7.654 \times 10^6)E_c$
  $C_{BA} = 0.595$

b. *Torsional member stiffness*, K_t

- For exterior columns, the long span edge beam [Figure 11.54(b)] acts as the torsional member, having a torsional constant
  $C_{\text{ext}} = (1 - 0.63 \times 150/250) \times (150^3 \times 250)/3 + (1 - 0.63 \times 300/500) \times (300^3 \times 500)/3$
  $= 2.974 \times 10^9 \text{ mm}^4$
  Length of attached torsional member is the smaller of l_{1a} and l_{2a}, = 6800 mm

$$\Rightarrow \quad K_{t,\text{ext}} = \Sigma \frac{9E_cC_{ext}}{l_t(1 - c_2/l_t)^3} \qquad \text{[Eq. 11.46]}$$

$$= \frac{2 \times 9E_c \times (2.974 \times 10^9)}{6800(1 - 500/6800)^3} = (9.899 \times 10^6)E_c$$

- For interior columns, the cross-section of the torsional member is as shown in Figure 11.54(d), having a torsional constant
  $C_{\text{int}} = (1 - 0.63 \times 300/500) \times (300^3 \times 500)/3 = 2.799 \times 10^9 \text{ mm}^4$

$$\Rightarrow \quad K_{t,\text{int}} = \frac{2 \times 9E_c \times (2.799 \times 10^9)}{6800(1 - 500/6800)^3} = (9.317 \times 10^6)E_c$$

c. *Equivalent column stiffnesses*, K_{ec}

$$K_{ec} = \frac{\sum K_c}{1 + \left(\sum K_c/K_t\right)} \qquad \text{[Eq. 11.45(b)]}$$

where $\Sigma K_c = (8.427 + 7.654) \times 10^6 E_c = (16.081 \times 10^6)E_c$

- For external ‘equivalent column’,
  $\Sigma K_c/K_{t,\text{ ext}} = 16.081/9.899 = 1.625$
  $\Rightarrow \quad K_{ec,\text{ext}} = (16.081 \times 10^6)E_c/(1 + 1.625) = (6.126 \times 10^6)E_c$
- For internal ‘equivalent column’,
  $\Sigma K_c/K_{t,\text{ int}} = 16.081/9.317 = 1.726$
  $\Rightarrow \quad K_{ec,\text{int}} = (16.081 \times 10^6)E_c/(1 + 1.726) = (5.899 \times 10^6)E_c$

d. *Slab stiffnesses K_s and fixed-end moment coefficients*

[Although Table 11.7 is strictly applicable for a drop extension of $l_1/6 = 1.13$ m, the same is used in this example for a drop extension of 1.5 m.]

- Referring to Figure 11.54(a) for the slab geometry and Figure 11.56(a) for the loading, and to Table 11.6 for the various stiffness and moment coefficients, with
  $C_{F1} = C_{N1}$; $\quad C_{F2} = C_{N2}$
  $C_{N1}/l_1 = 0.5/6.8 = 0.074$, $C_{N2}/l_2 = 0.5/8.0 = 0.063$

⇒ (interpolating from Table 11.7 for these values),

- stiffness factor $K_{NF} = 5.933$
- carry-over factor $C_{NF} = 0.595$
- FEM coefficient $m_{NF1} = 0.0931$ for uniform load

- For the additional load due to the drop panel, Table 11.7 gives moment coefficients for partial loadings of $0.2l_1$, with $b - a = 0.2$. The drop panel loading, $3.75\ \text{kN/m}^2 \times 3\ \text{m} = 11.25\ \text{kN/m}$ applies over a length of $1.5\ \text{m} = 0.22l_1$ from the column centrelines. An equivalent load acting over a length of $0.2l_1$, equal to $11.25 \times 0.22/0.20 = 12.38\ \text{kN/m}$, may be considered to facilitate the use of Table 11.7 [see Figure 11.56(b)].

  Interpolating from Table 11.7, for $C_{N1}/l_1 = 0.074$ and $C_{N2}/l_2 = 0.063$,
  - for drop panel at near end ($a = 0$), $m_{NF2} = 0.01654$
  - for drop panel at far end ($a = 0.8$), $m_{NF3} = 0.00191$

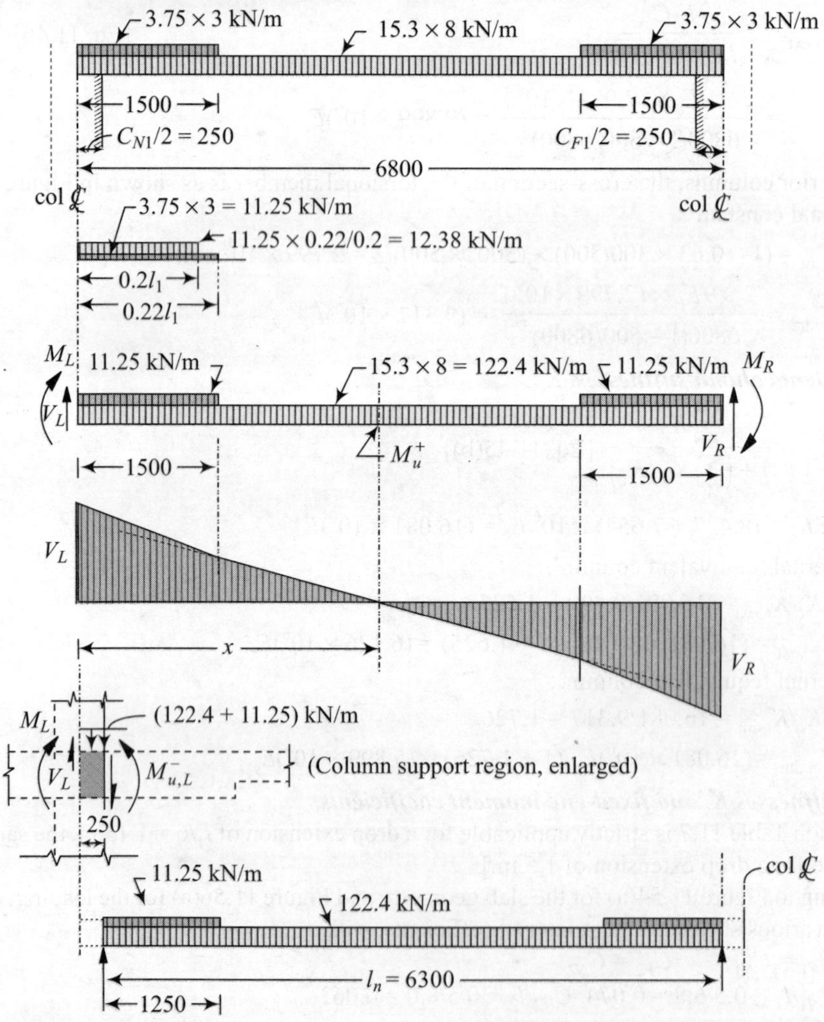

Fig. 11.56 Loading details on slab-beam member – Example 11.7.

- *Slab stiffness* $K_s = K_{NF}E_cI_s/l_1$
  where I_s is the second moment of area of the slab section beyond the drop:
  $$I_s = 8000 \times 200^3/12 = 5.333 \times 10^9 \text{ mm}^4$$
  $$\Rightarrow \quad K_s = 5.933 \times E_c \times (5.333 \times 10^9)/6800 = (4.653 \times 10^6)E_c$$

7. Equivalent Frame Analysis

- The properties of the 'equivalent frame' for analysis by the moment distribution method is indicated in Table 11.10. As the specified live load (2.5 kN/m^2) is less than three-fourths of the dead load (7.7 kN/m^2), it suffices to consider a single loading pattern, comprising full factored dead plus live loads on all spans. The factored loads on each slab-beam member are indicated in Figure 11.56(a).
- The slab fixed-end moments are:
  $$FEM_{NF} = \Sigma m_{NF} w l_1^2$$
  $$= \{(0.0931 \times 15.3 \times 8.0) + (0.01654 + 0.00191) \times 12.38\} \times 6.8^2$$
  $$= 537 \text{ kNm}$$
  The moment distribution factors are calculated based on the relative stiffnesses, and are indicated (for the slab-beam members), along with the carry-over factors in Table 11.10, which also shows the moment distribution procedure.

Table 11.10 *Equivalent frame analysis (moment distribution method) – Example 11.7*

$K_s \times 10^6E_c$ = $K_{ec} \times 10^6E_c$ =	4.653 6.126		4.653 5.899		4.653 5.899					
DF	0.432	0.306	0.306	0.306	0.306	0.306	0.306	0.306	0.306	0.432
COF	0.595		0.595		0.595		0.595		0.595	
FEM	–537	537	–537	537	–537	537	–537	537	–537	537
Bal	232									–232
C.O.		138							–138	
Bal.		–42	–42					42	42	
C.O.	–25			–25			25			25
Bal.	11			8	8	–8	–8			–11
C.O.		6	5		–5	5		–5	–6	
Bal.		–3	–3	2	2	–2	–2	3	3	
C.O.	–2		1	–2	–1	1	2	–1		2
	1	–	–	1	1	–1	–1	–	–	–1
$\Sigma = M_L, M_R$ (kNm)	–320	636	–576	521	–532	532	–521	576	–636	320
V_L, V_R(kN)	387	479	441	425	433	433				
x(m)	3.024		3.465		3.400					
M_u^+ (kNm)	252		171		188					
$M_{u,L}^-$, $M_{u,R}^-$ (kNm)	–227	520	–470	419	–428	428				
$\overline{M}$ (kNm)	617		616		616					
M_o (kNm)	616		616		616					

- With reference to the free-body diagram of a typical slab-beam member shown in Figure 11.56(c), the following expression for maximum shear forces V_L and V_R may be derived, in terms of the moments M_L and M_R, considering static equilibrium:

$$V_L = \frac{122.4 \times 6.8}{2} + (11.25 \times 1.5) - \frac{M_L + M_R}{6.8}$$

$\Rightarrow \quad V_L = [433.0 - (M_L + M_R)/6.8]$ kN

and $\quad V_R = [433.0 + (M_L + M_R)/6.8]$ kN

- The location of maximum 'positive' moment is given by the location of zero shear, marked x from the left support [Figure 11.57(d)]

$$x = \left(\frac{V_L - (11.25 \times 1.5)}{122.4}\right)$$

- The corresponding maximum 'positive' moment is given by:

$$M_u^+ = [M_L + V_L x - (11.25 \times 1.5)(x - 0.75) - 122.4 \times x^2/2] \text{ kNm}$$

- The critical sections for the 'negative' design moments are at the column faces; the moments at the left end ($M_{u,L}^-$) and right end ($M_{u,R}^-$) are, accordingly given by [Figure 11.57(e)].

$$M_{u,L}^- = [M_L + (V_L \times 0.25) - (122.4 + 11.25) \times (0.25)^2/2] \text{ kNm}$$

$$M_{u,R}^- = [M_R - (V_R \times 0.25) + (122.4 + 11.25) \times (0.25)^2/2] \text{ kNm}$$

- The values of V_L, V_R, x, M_u^+, $M_{u,L}^-$ and $M_{u,R}^-$ have been tabulated, using the above formulas for the various spans in Table 11.10†.
- As the slab satisfies the limitations for the Direct Design Method, the sum of the 'positive' moment at midspan and average negative moment, $\overline{M}$, need not exceed M_o, the maximum static moment on the simply supported span $l_n = 6.3$ m [Figure 11.57(f)]:

$$M_o = (122.4 \times 6.3^2/8) + (11.25 \times 1.25^2/2) = 616 \text{ kNm}$$

It is seen that $\overline{M} \approx M_o$ for all the three spans [refer Table 11.10]; hence the proportional reduction in the design moments (for $\overline{M} > M_o$), permitted by the Code, is not applicable here.

8. Transverse distribution of moments

The transverse distribution specified by Code Cl. 31.5.5 is given by Eqs 11.37 to 11.39.

Accordingly:

$\Rightarrow \quad M_{cs,ext}^- = 1.00\ M_{o,ext}^-$ [Eq. 11.37a]

$\Rightarrow \quad M_{hms,ext}^- = 0$

- *'Negative' moment at interior support*

$M_{cs,int}^- = 0.75\ M_{o,int}^-$ [Eq. 11.38a]

$\Rightarrow \quad M_{hms,int}^- = 0.125\ M_{o,int}^-$

- *'Positive' moment*

$M_{cs}^+ = 0.6\ M_o^+$ [Eq. 11.39a]

$\Rightarrow \quad M_{hms}^+ = 0.2 M_o^+$

The distributed moments in the column strips and half-middle strips in the various panels (in the E-W direction) are indicated in Figure 11.57‡.

† These are indicated only for the first three spans, as the six-bay frame is symmetric with respect to its middle.

‡ This distribution is nearly identical to one that will be obtained by following Ref. 11.21 and the median values of the *range* of factors given in Section 11.5.4 (sub-section (a)) for the Canadian Code.

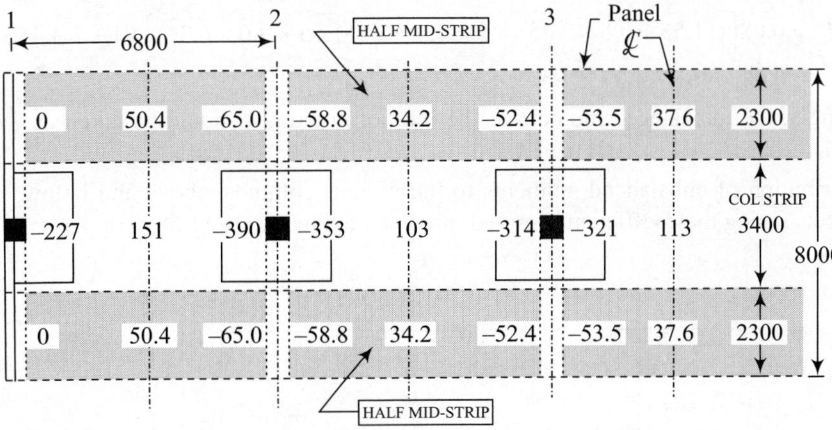

Factored moment	–227	252	–520	–470	171	–419	–428	188	kN/m
Column strip	100	60	75	75	60	75	75	60	Percent
Half mid-strip	0	20	12.5	12.5	20	12.5	12.5	20	Percent

Fig. 11.57 Factored moments in column and middle strips in E-W direction – Example 11.7.

9. Column moments

The total unbalanced slab moments at the various supports are transmitted to the respective columns. At each support, the unbalanced slab moment is shared by the column above and the column below in proportion to their relative stiffnesses.

- Fraction of moment in column above $= \dfrac{7.654}{8.427 + 7.654} = 0.476$

  with a carry-over factor = 0.595 (determined earlier)
- Fraction of moment in column below = 1.0 – 0.476 = 0.524

  with a carry-over factor = 0.54

The unbalanced slab moments are obtainable from Table 11.9:

- at exterior column 1: 320 kNm
- at interior column 2: 636 – 576 = 60 kNm
- at interior column 3: 532 – 521 = 11 kNm

However, at interior column locations, the unbalanced moment should not be less than that given by Eq. 11.42:

$$M_u = 0.08\left[(w_{u,DL} + 0.5w_{u,LL})l_2 l_n^2 - w'_{u,DL} l'_2 (l'_n)^2\right] / (1 + 1/\alpha_c)$$

where $w_{u,DL} = w'_{u,DL} = 7.7 \times 1.5 = 11.55$ kN/m^2 (neglecting drop panel)

$w_{u,LL} = 2.5 \times 1.5 = 3.75$ kN/m^2

$l_2 = l'_2 = 8.0$ m, $l_n = l'_n = 6.3$ m

$$\alpha_c = \sum K_c / k_{sb} = \frac{(8.427 + 7.654) \times 10^6 E_c}{(4.653 \times 10^6) E_c} = 3.456$$

$$\Rightarrow \quad M_u = 0.08\left[(11.55 + 0.5 \times 3.75)(8.0 \times 6.3^2) - (11.55 \times 8.0 \times 6.3^2)\right] \Big/ (1 + 1/3.456)$$

$$= 0.08 \times 461.7 = 37 \text{ kNm}$$

Accordingly, the unbalanced moment at the interior column 3 should be taken as 37 kNm (and not 12 kNm).

The distribution of unbalanced moments to the various columns, above and below, including carry-over effects (using the coefficients derived) are depicted in Figure 11.58.

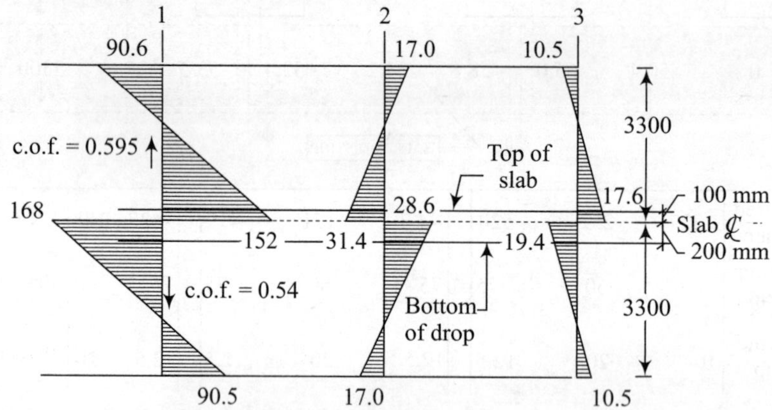

Fig. 11.58 Column moments (kNm) – Example 11.7.

10. Flexural reinforcement

The requirement of flexural (tension) reinforcement at all critical sections is computed in Table 11.11 for the column strip (3400 mm wide for 'positive' moments, and 3000 mm† wide for 'negative' moments), and in Table 11.12 for the middle strip (4600 mm wide for 'positive' moments and 5000 mm wide for 'negative' moments). 16 mm-diameter bars have been used and the Code restrictions of minimum reinforcement and maximum spacing have been adopted.

Table 11.11 *Design of reinforcement in column strip, E-W direction – Example 11.7*

	1			2			3	
Moment in col. strip, M_u (kNm)	227	151	390	353	103	314	321	113
Width of strip, or drop b (mm)	3000	3400	3000	3000	3400	3000	3000	3400
Effective depth d (mm)	256	156	256	256	156	256	256	156
$R \equiv M_u/(bd^2)$ (MPa)	1.155	1.825	1.984	–	1.245	–	1.633	1.366
p [Table A.3(a)]	0.281	0.462	0.508	–	0.305	–	0.409	0.337
$A_{st} = (p/100)bd$ (mm²)	2161	2452	3899	–	1617	–	3140	1786
Number of 16ϕ bars	11	13	20	–	8	–	16	9
Spacing (mm)	272	262	150	–	425	–	187	377

† The effective width of the column strip at supports (for 'negative' moments) is restricted to that of the drop panel, for convenience.

It may be noted that, where the unbalanced slab moment is significant (at the exterior support only, in this Example), adequate reinforcement should be provided over a distance $c_2 + 3D_{drop} = 1400$ mm, centred about the column line, to permit the transfer by flexure from the slab to the column the portion M_{ub} of the unbalanced moment.

$$M_{ub} = 0.6 \times 320 = 192 \text{ kNm} \qquad \text{[Eq. 11.28a]}$$

$$\Rightarrow \quad R \equiv \frac{M_{ub}}{bd^2} = \frac{192 \times 10^6}{1400 \times 256^2} = 2.093 \text{ MPa}$$

$\Rightarrow$ $p_t = 0.539$ [Table A.3(a) or Eq. 5.12, for M 25 and Fe 500]

$\Rightarrow$ $A_{st} = (0.539/100) \times (1400 \times 256) = 1932 \text{ mm}^2$

$\Rightarrow$ No. of 16ϕ bars required = 1932/201 = 10

Thus, at the exterior support, 10 nos of 16ϕ bars must be distributed over a width of 1400 mm centred over the column. The remaining outer portions of the drop panel, with width equal to (3000 – 1400)/2 = 800 mm may be provided with two bars each, to limit the spacing to < $2D$. The column strip 'negative' moment reinforcement at the exterior support, adds up to 10 + (2 × 2) = 14 bars, compared to the 11 bars indicated in Table 11.11.

11. Check on one-way shear stress

There are two critical sections to be considered:

(i) $d = 256$ mm from the face of column; and
(ii) $d = 156$ mm from the edge of drop panel.

Table 11.12 *Design of reinforcement in middle strip, E-W direction – Example 11.7*

		1			2		3	
Moment in col. strip, M_u (kNm)	0	101	130	118	68.4	105	107	75.2
Width of strip 8000 – col. strip b_s (mm)	5000	4600	5000	5000	4600	5000	5000	4600
Effective depth d (mm)	156	156	156	156	156	156	156	156
$R \equiv M_u/(bd^2)$ (MPa)	–	0.902	1.068	–	0.611	–	0.879	0.672
p [Table A.3(a)]	0.002*	0.217	0.259	–	0.145	–	0.211	0.16
$A_{st} = (p/100)bd$ (mm^2)	1200	1556	2021	–	1038	–	1646	1145
Number of 16ϕ bars (No.)	6	8	11	–	6	–	9	6
Spacing (mm)	833†	575†	455†	–	767†	–	556†	767†
Number of 16ϕ bars to limit spacing < $2D$	12	12	13	–	12	–		12

* minimum reinforcement ($A_{st} = 0.0012bD$) governs.
† maximum allowable spacing governs.

From the equivalent frame analysis [Table 11.10], the maximum shear force, equal to 479 kN, is found to be at the exterior face of first interior support. Referring to Figure 11.56(d), with $x = 3.024$ m and $V_R = 479$ kN, and to Figure 11.59,

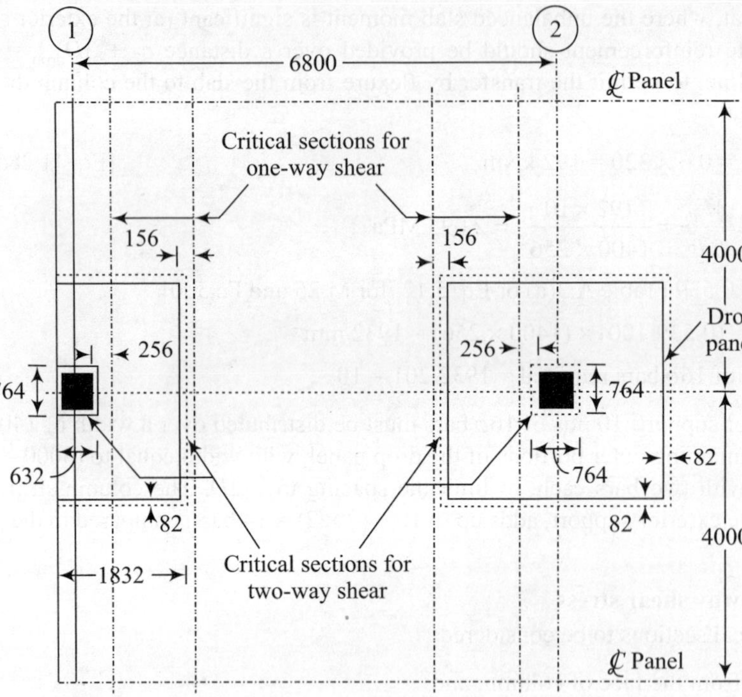

Fig. 11.59 Critical sections for one-way and two-way shear – Example 11.7.

(i) at d = 256 mm from face of column, i.e., 506 mm from centre of column,

$$V_{u1} = 479 - (122.4 + 11.25) \times 0.506 = 411 \text{ kN}$$

Code (Cl. 31.6) regarding shear in flat slabs refers to two-way shear only†. Assuming the shear force to be uniformly distributed over the width of the panel (8.0 *m*), and considering a 1 m strip of the slab outside the drop panel (where d = 156 mm),

$$\tau_{v1} = \frac{(411 \times 10^3)/8.0}{1000 \times 156} = 0.329 \text{ MPa}$$

which is less than $k\tau_c$ given by the Code (Cl. 40.2.1) for $p_t = 0.259$ and M 25 concrete.

(ii) at d = 156 mm from the edge of the drop panel, the shear force and hence the shear stress, will be less than that calculated above.

This will obviously be safe.

12. Check on two-way (punching) shear stress

a. *Interior column*

The maximum column reaction and unbalanced slab moment (in an interior column) occurs at column 2 (or 5). From Table 11.10, the vertical reaction is obtained as the sum of the shears on either side as:

$$R = 479 + 441 = 920 \text{ kN}$$

The effective depth in punching shear calculations may be taken as the average of the effective depths in the E-W and N-S directions. The critical sections are

† Ref. 11.20 specifies that for one-way shear in flat slabs, the total shear across the full width be apportioned between column strip and middle strip in proportion to the factored negative moments in each strip.

(i) $d/2 = (256 + 272)/4 = 132$ mm from the column face all around; and
(ii) $d/2 = (156 + 172)/4 = 82$ mm from the edge of the drop panel,
as indicated in Figure 11.59

(i) For the critical section at $d/2$ from the column face, the punching shear is [Figure 11.56]

$$V_{u2} = 920 - (15.3 + 3.75) \times 0.764^2 = 909 \text{ kN}$$

and the perimeter is

$$b_o = 4 \times 764 = 3056, \text{ with average } d = 264 \text{ mm}$$

The moment transferred by shear is 40 per cent of the unbalanced moment $M_u = 60$ kNm at column 2 [Eq. 11.28b]

$$M_{uv} = 0.4 \times 60 = 24 \text{ kNm}$$

and the parameters c and J_c in Eq. 11.51 [Figure 11.46(a)] are given by:

$$c = (c_1 + d)/2 = 764/2 = 382 \text{ mm}$$

$$J_c = \frac{(c_1+d)d^3}{6} + \frac{(c_1+d)^3 d}{6} + \frac{(c_1+d)^2(c_2+d)d}{2}$$

$$= \frac{764 \times 264^3}{6} + \frac{764^3 \times 264}{6} + \frac{764^3 \times 264}{2}$$

$$= 80.83 \times 10^9 \text{ mm}^4$$

Applying Eq. 11.51,

$$\tau_{v2} = \frac{V_{u2}}{b_o d} + \frac{M_{uv} c}{J_c}$$

$$= \frac{909 \times 10^3}{3056 \times 264} + \frac{(24 \times 10^6) \times 382}{80.83 \times 10^9}$$

$$= 1.127 + 0.113 = 1.240 \text{ MPa}$$

$$\tau_{c2} = k_s\left(0.25\sqrt{f_{ck}}\right) \text{ [Eq. 11.49]}$$

$$= 1.0 \times 0.25\sqrt{25} = 1.25 \text{ MPa}$$

The applied shear stress τ_{v2}, is less than the shear strength τ_{c2}. Hence, shear reinforcement is not required.

(ii) For the critical section $d/2 = 82$ mm from the edge of the drop panel,

$$V_{u2} = 920 - (15.3 \times 3.164^2) - (3.75 \times 3^2) = 733 \text{ kN}$$

$$b_o = 3164 \times 4 = 12656 \text{ mm}, d = 164 \text{ mm}$$

$$\Rightarrow \quad \tau_{v2} = \frac{733 \times 10^3}{12656 \times 164} = 0.354 \text{ MPa}$$

$$<< \tau_{c2} = 1.25 \text{ MPa} - \text{OK}$$

b. *Exterior column*

Owing to the presence of the edge beam, part of the shear will be transmitted by this beam to the column by beam action. However, to simplify calculations, the shear stress is conservatively computed by neglecting the contributions of the edge beam.

The reaction at the exterior column = 387 kN [Table 11.10]

(i) For the critical section, $d/2 = 132$ mm from the column face [Figure 11.59].

$$V_{u2} = 387 - (15.3 + 3.75) \times (0.764 \times 0.632) = 378 \text{ kN}$$

$M_{uv} = 0.4 \times 320 = 128$ kNm

$b_o = (632 \times 2) + 764 = 2028$ mm, $d = 264$ mm

Referring to Figure 11.46(b),

$$c = \frac{(c_1 + d/2)^2}{2c_1 + c_2 + 2d} = \frac{(632)^2}{(2 \times 500) + 500 + (2 \times 264)} = 197 \text{ mm}$$

$$J_c = [(c_1 + d/2)d^3 + (c_1 + d/2)^3 d]/6 + (c_2 + d)dc^2 + 2(c_1 + d/2)(d) \times [(c_1 + d/2)/2 - c]^2$$

$$= [(632)(264)^3 + (632)^3(264)]/6 + (764)(264)(197)^2 + 2(632)(264) \times [632/2 - 197]^2$$

$$= 25.60 \times 10^9 \text{ mm}^4$$

$$\Rightarrow \quad \tau_{v2} = \frac{V_{u2}}{b_o d} + \frac{M_{uv} c}{J_c} = \frac{378 \times 10^3}{2028 \times 264} + \frac{(128 \times 10^6) \times 197}{25.60 \times 10^9}$$

$$= 0.706 + 0.985 = 1.691 \text{ MPa}$$

which is greater than $\tau_{c2} = 1.25$ MPa but less than $1.5\tau_{c2} = 1.875$ MPa.

Hence, shear reinforcement is required, with a total cross sectional area:

$$A_{sv} = \frac{(\tau_{v2} - 0.5\tau_{c2})b_o d}{0.87 f_y} \qquad \text{[Eq. 11.52]}$$

$$= (1.691 - 0.5 \times 1.25)(2028 \times 264)/(0.87 \times 500) = 1312 \text{ mm}^2$$

Using 8 mm ϕ stirrups [Type I arrangement, Fig. 11.47], number of vertical legs required on the three sides (of the rectangle 632mm × 764 mm) = 1312/(50.3) = 26. This can be achieved by providing 8-legged 8 mm ϕ stirrups comprising 4 nos 2-legged closed stirrups [Fig. 11.47] on the two short (764 mm) sides and 10-legged 8 mm ϕ stirrups (comprising 5 nos 2-legged closed stirrups) on the long (764 mm) side. Nominal 10 mm ϕ holder bars may be provided at the stirrup corners if regular top steel and bottom steel are not otherwise available. This arrangement of stirrups should be provided at a spacing of not more than $0.75d = 0.75 \times 264 = 198$ mm ≈ 200 mm and should be continued to a distance $d = 264$ mm beyond the section where the shear stress does not exceed 0.5 τ_{c2}.

- Checking at a section two spacings further removed from the first critical section, and now ignoring the marginal shear stress due to the unbalanced moment,

$$V_{u2} = 387 - (15.3 + 3.75) \times (0.632 + 0.2 \times 2)(0.764 + 0.2 \times 4) = 356 \text{ kN}$$

$$b_o = (632 + 200 \times 2) \times 2 + (764 + 200 \times 4) = 3628 \text{ mm},$$

$$\Rightarrow \quad \tau_{v2} = V_{u2}/(b_o d) = 356 \times 10^3/(3628 \times 264) = 0.373 \text{ MPa}$$

$$< 0.5\ \tau_{c2} = 0.5 \times 1.25 = 0.625\text{MPa} \ - \text{OK.}$$

Thus, it is necessary to provide 2 + 1 = 3 lines of stirrups on all three sides @ 200*mm* c/c – within the drop panel, with the first line of stirrups located $d/2 = 132$ mm away from the column face.

(ii) For the critical section at $d/2 = 82$ mm from the edge of the drop panel [Figure 11.59],

$$V_{u2} = 387 - (15.3 \times 1.832 \times 3.164) - (3.75 \times 3.0 \times 1.75) = 279 \text{ kN}$$

$$b_o = (2 \times 1832) + 3164 = 6828 \text{ mm}, \ d = 164 \text{ mm}$$

$$\Rightarrow \quad \tau_{v2} = \frac{279 \times 10^3}{6828 \times 164} = 0.249 \text{ MPa}$$

$$<< \tau_{c2} = 1.25 \text{ MPa} - \text{OK}$$

11.10 Inelastic Analysis — Yield Line Theory

The methods of analysis of two-way slabs discussed in this chapter so far (except for slabs supported on walls or rigid beams, using moment coefficients or formulas based on yield line theory) are primarily based on *elastic analysis*. It is assumed that under ultimate (factored) loads, the same distribution of bending moments (appropriately factored) may be adopted in design by the limit states method. As discussed in Section 9.7, in statically indeterminate structures, the attainment of the ultimate flexural strength at one section does not necessarily lead to collapse of the structure. Furthermore, after the local yielding and formation of a 'plastic hinge', the further behaviour of the whole structure is inelastic. Greater economy (in terms of less rebars) can generally be achieved by utilising the post-first-yield strength, for which an inelastic analysis is required. This inelastic method is commonly referred to as *limit analysis* in the case of skeletal structures (Section 9.7.1) and *yield line analysis* in the case of slabs (Figure 9.12).

In this Section, the basic concepts underlying the yield line theory are reviewed. This theory [Ref. 11.6, 11.8–11.10] can be applied to all types of slabs (wall-supported/beam-supported/column-supported). It is demonstrated by means of simple examples. Standard formulas, based on this theory, as applied to circular, triangular and rectangular slabs, have already been introduced in Section 11.2.6 and demonstrated in Examples 11.4 and 11.5.

11.10.1 Lower Bound and Upper Bound Methods

The main objective in *inelastic analysis* (or *limit analysis*) of a slab is to determine the *collapse load* of the slab (with prescribed loading and boundary conditions, material properties and reinforcement detailing). According to the basic principles of limit analysis ('uniqueness theorem'), in order to get the correct ('exact') solution, the following three conditions need to be satisfied at the limit state of impending collapse:

1. ***Mechanism condition:*** Sufficient number of plastic hinges should have formed to transform the structure, or part of it, into a hinged (unstable) mechanism which can undergo deformation at constant load;
2. ***Equilibrium condition:*** Equations of static equilibrium should be satisfied at *all* points on the slab;
3. ***Yield (or Safety) condition:*** The ultimate moment capacity of the slab should not be exceeded at any point on the slab.

In general, direct solutions, satisfying all the above three conditions, are not possible in most practical cases. It is, however, possible to get solutions satisfying two of the three conditions (and refine it to meet the third as closely as possible). The resulting collapse load may be a *lower bound* (less than or equal to the true collapse load) or an *upper bound* (greater than or equal to the true collapse load), depending on which two of the three conditions have been explicitly satisfied.

The collapse load, computed on the basis of an assumed distribution of bending moments, satisfying the **equilibrium and yield (safety) conditions**, will be less than or, at best, equal to the true collapse load. This is sometimes referred to as the **lower bound theorem**, and the method of calculation is called the **equilibrium method**. Hillerborg's **strip method**, proposed in 1956, belongs to this category.

The collapse load, computed on the basis of an assumed distribution of plastic hinges (yield lines), satisfying the **mechanism and equilibrium conditions**, will be greater than or, at best, equal to the true collapse load. This is sometimes referred to as the **upper bound theorem**, and the method of calculation is called the **mechanism method**. The **yield line theory**, first proposed in 1923 by Ingerslev, and later developed by Johansen in 1962, belongs to this category.

The equilibrium method and the mechanism methods are demonstrated in Figure 11.60, where, for the sake of simplicity, a fixed-ended beam with uniform ultimate moment capacity, M_{uR}, with a concentrated load P is considered. The bending moment diagram shown at Figure 11.60(a) satisfies equilibrium and by limiting the peak moment at A to M_{uR}, it satisfies the yield condition as well. However, the mechanism condition is not satisfied, since with the yielding at A only, the beam is transformed into a propped cantilever which is stable. Hence this solution, $P = 6.75\ M_{uR}/L$, can only be lower than the true collapse load and hence a *lower bound* one. A second distribution, which also satisfies equilibrium and yield conditions, is shown

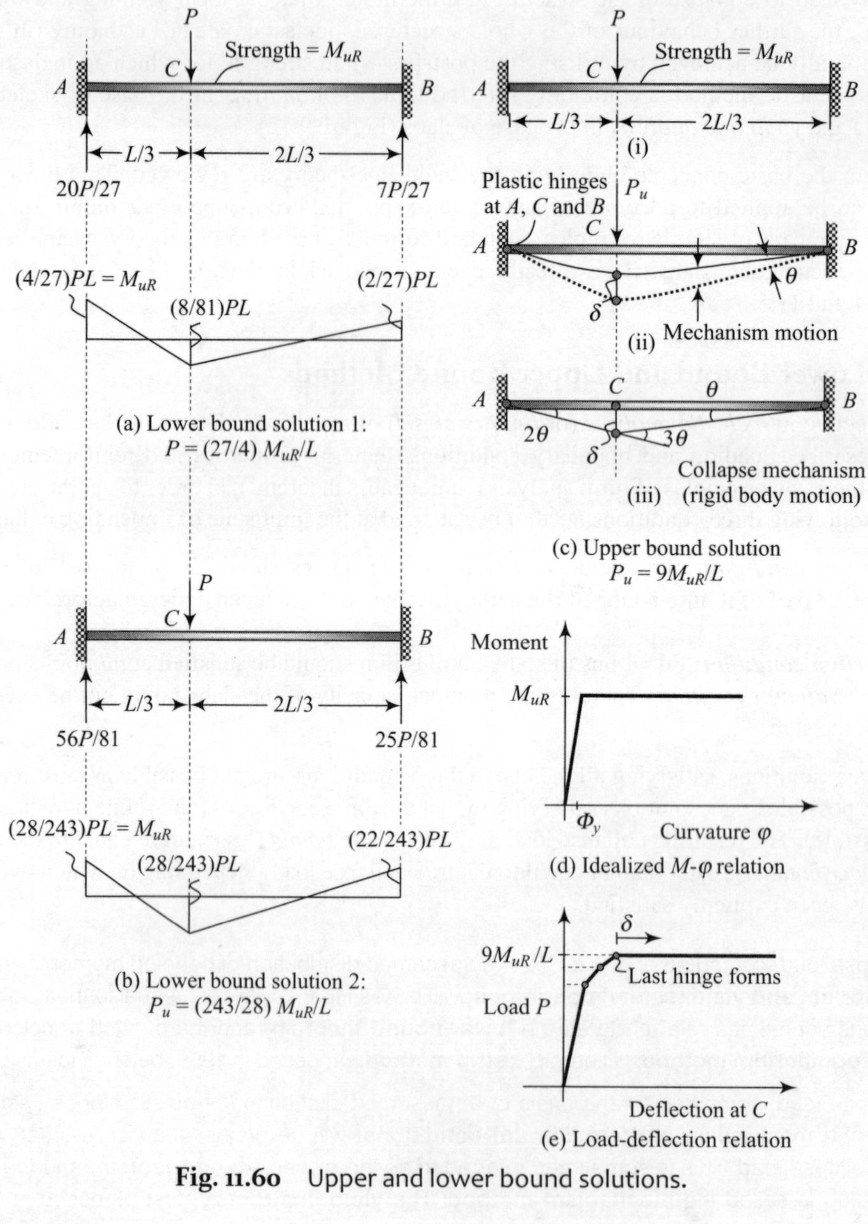

Fig. 11.60 Upper and lower bound solutions.

in Figure 11.60(b)[†], which also is a lower bound solution ($P = 8.68M_{uR}/L$), as no mechanism is formed; however, it is an improved solution, compared to Figure 11.60(a), as it gives a higher load.

The mechanism method is depicted in Figure 11.60(c). Corresponding to an *assumed* collapse mechanism, with plastic hinges forming at *A*, *B* and *C*, the collapse load works out to $P = 9M_{uR}/L$ (see the virtual work method in Section 11.10.5 for detailed calculations). This load is an *upper bound*. However, a check on the bending moment elsewhere, using equilibrium conditions, will show that all moments are less than M_{uR}, and hence the yield condition is also satisfied by the assumed mechanism, and so this is the *correct* solution. It so happens that the correct mechanism was selected in this case. On the other hand, if a solution is selected with any one of the hinge locations changed, the corresponding moment diagram will show that M_{uR} has been exceeded somewhere, whereby the solution is an upper bound, that is, higher than the true collapse load.

An assumed collapse mechanism will also be the correct solution, if it can be shown that the moments in the slab parts between yield lines are within safe limits (*yield condition*).

The mechanism method is simpler and more versatile to apply and is therefore more popular as the method used for inelastic analysis of slabs. However, being an upper bound method, it is likely to over-estimate the true collapse load, and so can be unconservative. The regions of the slab between yield lines are not examined in all but simple cases to ensure that the *yield condition* is satisfied. In order to address this issue (which is a problem with all mechanism methods), it is necessary to investigate as many likely mechanisms (yield line patterns) as possible, and find the minimum collapse load. The associated yield line pattern will be the most probable mode of collapse of the slab.(If *all* possible collapse mechanisms have been considered, admittedly the one giving the lowest load will give the correct solution.) Indeed, the correct solutions for nearly all the common cases are now well established and experimentally validated [Ref. 11.6].

Finally, it may be noted that the inelastic analysis methods, such as yield line theory, estimate the collapse load corresponding to the *flexural collapse* mode only. Other effects, such as due to shear and bond, must be considered separately. In practice, for slabs proportioned and detailed in accordance with Code requirements, these effects are not critical. Shear stresses are generally low and the slab (whose thickness is generally governed by serviceability considerations, rather than strength considerations) is significantly under-reinforced, thereby having adequate 'plastic rotation capacity' required to form all the plastic hinges (yield lines) for a proper collapse mechanism.

11.10.2 Yield Line Patterns

Yield line theory is primarily meant for determining the ultimate (collapse) load of two-way slabs. In general, such slabs are reinforced in two mutually orthogonal directions at bottom and/or at top, with the bars spaced uniformly over various panels. In some cases (such as *skew slabs*), the reinforcement may be non-orthogonal, but uniformly reinforced. Indeed, it is assumed in yield line theory that the flexural strength per unit length of slab is uniform along the yield line. In general, in two-ways slabs, an 'yield line' may cut across bars in the two directions. In one-way slabs of rectangular shape, properly reinforced, the yield line is expected to form in a direction that is perpendicular to the primary reinforcement direction. It is instructive to begin with exploring the simple case of one-way slabs, before considering two-way slabs.

† The reader may work out and see that the solution at (a) is the elastic solution and the one at (b) is the case where the loading is continued after a hinge is formed at *A* until a second hinge is formed at *C* also.

Yield Line Formation in One-way Slabs

Consider a simply supported and uniformly loaded one-way rectangular slab panel, as shown in Figure 11.61(a). Let the effective span be L and the intensity of loading be w (per unit area). The bending moments will vary parabolically along the span, from zero at the supporting edges to a maximum of $wL^2/8$ (per unit width) at mid-span (i.e., along the centre-line), as shown in Figure 11.61(b). As the loading is increased, the bending moments increase until the peak value reaches the ultimate moment capacity. It is convenient to use the notation m_{uR} (in lieu of M_{uR}, used previously) to refer to the ultimate moment capacity per unit width (in kNm/m) in a slab. As the peak moment along the centre-line reaches m_{uR}, in accordance with the idealised M-φ relations assumed [Section 9.7.1 and Figures 9.8, 11.60(d)], localised yielding takes place all along this line, with the curvature increasing at constant moment [Figure 11.61(c)]. In effect, along the centre-line, a 'line hinge' or what is called an '*yield line*'[traditionally shown as a wavy line – Figure 11.61(d)] is formed. This transforms the two halves of the plate into a hinged mechanism (or *collapse mechanism*) with a hinge along the centre-line, which is *unstable* and can collapse with no further increase in load [Figure 11.61(e)]. The maximum load is reached as the collapse mechanism is *just formed* (i.e., the stage of incipient instability) and the corresponding load is the *collapse load*. In this example, at incipient collapse, $m_{uR} = w_uL^2/8$, and the

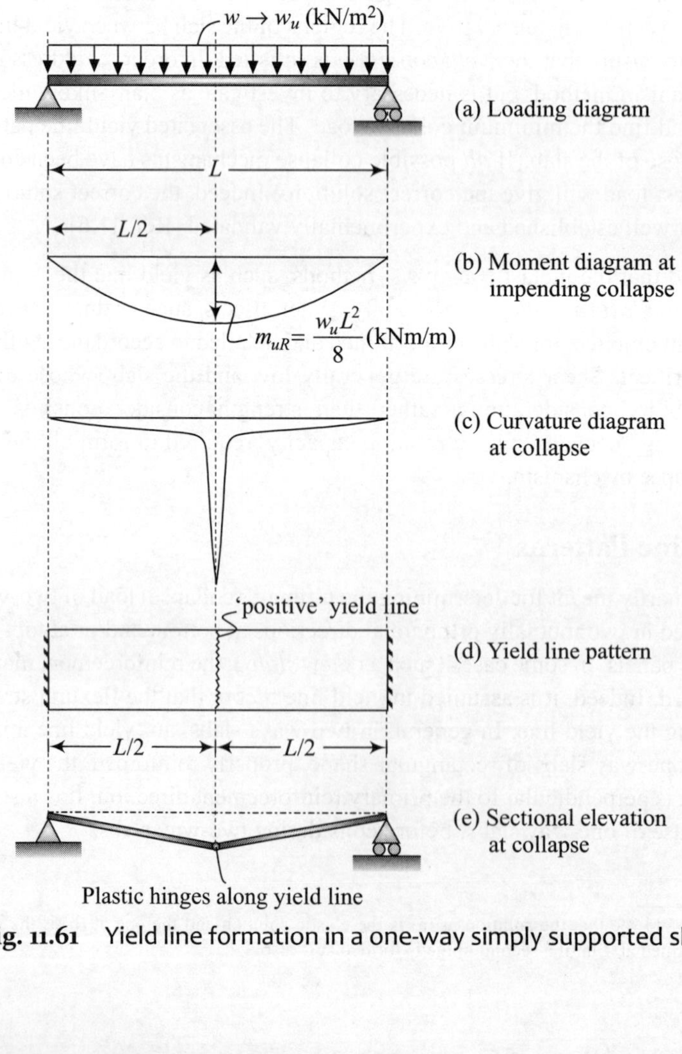

Fig. 11.61 Yield line formation in a one-way simply supported slab.

corresponding load intensity, w_u, is the *collapse load* (in kN/m^2). The *design* ultimate moment of resistance of the slab (including partial safety factors), singly reinforced with uniformly spaced bars (area $A_b = \pi\phi^2/4$, spacing s) is given by (refer Eq. 4.65, considering b = 1000 mm):

$$m_{uR} = 0.87 f_y A_{st}(d - 0.416x_u)$$

$$x_u = \frac{0.87 f_y A_{st}}{0.362 f_{ck}(1000)}; \quad A_{st} = \frac{1000 A_b}{s}$$

$$\Rightarrow \qquad m_{uR} = 0.87 f_y \left(\frac{1000 A_b}{s}\right)\left[d - \frac{f_y}{f_{ck}}\frac{A_b}{s}\right] \tag{11.53}$$

Note that in this example the *moment per unit length of the yield line* is equal to m_{uR}. From a design point-of-view, for an economical design, the factored load is treated as the collapse load, and the primary reinforcement in this one-way slab system is designed to have the design ultimate moment of resistance.

The ***yield line pattern*** in the above case was obvious and the collapse load calculation very simple as the pattern of the bending moment diagram was known. In yield line theory, the convention is to depict yield lines associated with yielding of bottom steel, due to 'positive' (sagging) bending moments with firm lines (shown wavy), and to refer to such lines as ***positive yield lines***. When yield lines are formed due to yielding of top steel, due to 'negative' (hogging) moments, as for example, over the support lines of a continuous slab, *dashed* (broken) lines are used for their depiction, and such yield lines are called ***negative yield lines***.

Just prior to the formation of a mechanism, the various parts of the structure are subjected to bending moments and have associated curvature. As the mechanism is formed, the load and hence the moments and curvature become constant. Any further *mechanism motion* is under constant curvature, i.e., like a *rigid-body rotation* of the already curved parts [see Figure 11.60(c)(ii)]. This means that, for the collapse mechanism motion, *after* the last hinge (or yield line) is *just* formed [see δ in Figure 11.60(e)], at the constant collapse load and constant moment M_{uR} at the hinges/yield lines, the movements are rigid body rotations and displacements are linear as shown in Figure 11.60(c)(iii) [Note that the displacements shown at (iii) are the difference in displacements of the two curves shown at (ii)]. This aspect is convenient in using the 'mechanism method' and the 'virtual work' approach to determine collapse load.

The limit analysis of a uniformly loaded two-span continuous beam (statically indeterminate) was carried out in Chapter 9 (refer Figure 9.9). This analysis is equally applicable for a two-span continuous one-way slab system. Owing to the symmetry in the loading and geometry with respect to the middle support line, the problem can be simplified to that of a single span, simply supported along one edge and 'fixed' along the other edge (propped cantilever), as shown in Figure 11.62(a).

Assume, as in the example in Figure 9.9, that the slab has the same ultimate moment of resistance, m_{uR}, against hogging near the fixed (continuous) edge, as it has against sagging in the span region. In other words, the 'negative' and 'positive' yield lines are assumed to have the same flexural capacity. From the elastic behaviour of a propped cantilever, it is known that the moment distributions will have two peaks, one (–ve) at support, and the other (+ve) in the span and numerically, the former is higher. As the loading on the slab is increased, at some stage of loading (referred to as w_1 in Figure 9.9), the negative yield line will form along the fixed (continuous) edge, and at a later stage ($w_2 = 1.46\ w_1$) the positive yield line will form in the interior of the slab at a distance 0.4142L from the simply supported edge, as analysed earlier [refer Figure 11.62(b)]. The slab is now reduced to an unstable mechanism, and the collapse load has been reached. The resulting yield line pattern is as depicted in Figure 11.62(c). It is assumed that the slab is sufficiently under-reinforced

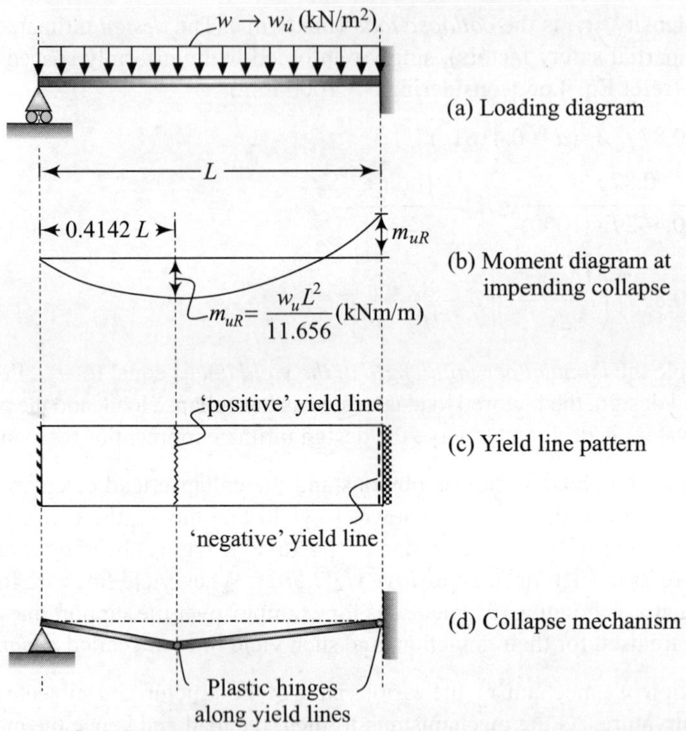

Fig. 11.62 Yield line formation in a one-way propped cantilever slab.

(i.e., the negative yield line has adequate plastic rotation capacity), and thereby capable of attaining the full collapse load, obtained earlier (in Figure 9.9), $w_u = 11.656\ m_{uR}/L^2$. The collapse mechanism is shown in Figure 11.62d.

Yield Line Formation in Two-way Slabs

Consider the ultimate load behaviour of a uniformly loaded rectangular two-way slab panel, simply supported on all four edges, as shown in Figure 11.63(a). Under low loads, before initiation of cracking, the distribution of bending moments will be as predicted by elastic plate theory. Following cracking, there will

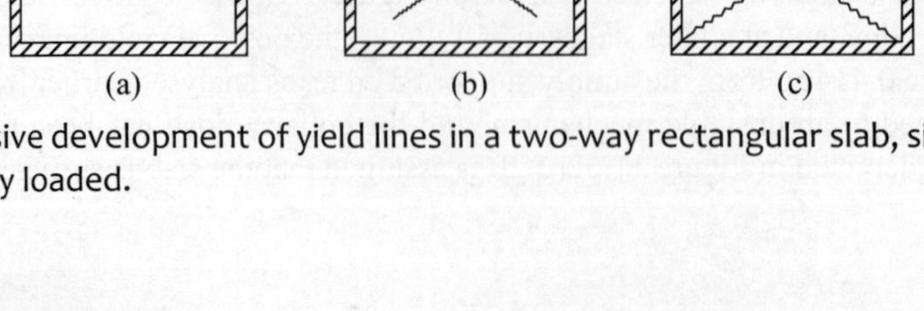

Fig. 11.63 Progressive development of yield lines in a two-way rectangular slab, simply supported and uniformly loaded.

be a reduction in flexural rigidity at the cracked sections, resulting in a redistribution of moments. In this example, it is known that the maximum bending moment (as well as the maximum deflection) will occur at the centre of the slab in the short-span direction. Hence, as the loading intensity is increased, yielding of tension reinforcement is initiated at the centre, and will propagate along the longitudinal centre-line as shown in Figure 11.63(a). This yield line is an idealisation of a band of extensive cracks across which the tension steel has yielded. Considerable redistribution of load effects takes place after yielding, tending generally to enhance the relatively higher moments elsewhere.

Plate theory also indicates development of significant bending moments along the diagonals emanating from the corners of the slab, which are of the same order of magnitude as the moments at mid-span in square slabs, but gradually decrease as the rectangularity increases. In simply supported slabs, whose corners are not held down, the significant moment on the diagonal is such as to develop tension perpendicular to the diagonal at the bottom of the slab. (Indeed, in a square slab, yield lines are initiated from the middle of the slab along these diagonals.) Thus, in the rectangular slab, at some stage, positive yield lines will develop along the diagonals also, as shown in Figure 11.63(b), and the diagonal and central longitudinal yield lines will join up, as shown in Figure 11.63(c). Note that the order in which yield lines are formed is immaterial as long as they have the rotation capacity to undergo further curvature without failure until a mechanism is formed. A system of yield lines forming such a collapse mechanism is called an ***yield line pattern***.

The support condition dictates that a plate segment can rotate only about its support line. Under these conditions, one may expect that at the collapse stage, the slab will break up into segments (that fold up along the likely yield lines) in such a way that their support lines are possible axes of rotation for the supported segment. Thus, for the symmetric conditions in Figure 11.63, with yield lines developing along the longitudinal centre-line and along the four diagonals, and the slab support lines being axes of rotation for the adjoining segments, a likely yield line pattern (with the diagonal yield lines reaching the four corners), leading to collapse is as shown in Figure 11.63(c).

It may so happen that the diagonal yield lines near the corners may not actually converge at the four corners of the slab, and may bifurcate before the corners are reached. In such cases, instead of the yield line pattern shown in Figure 11.63(c), the yield line pattern shown in Figure 11.64(a) may occur, and the latter may give slightly lower collapse loads. For example, as shown in Figure 11.64(a), if the corner A is not held down, it may lift up, the small corner segment (called *corner lever*) rotating about line BC. In Figure 11.64(a), the yield line BC is a negative yield line, which is not likely to form when the corner A is not held down (restrained against uplift) and adequate corner reinforcement is provided (as required, when the corner is held down).

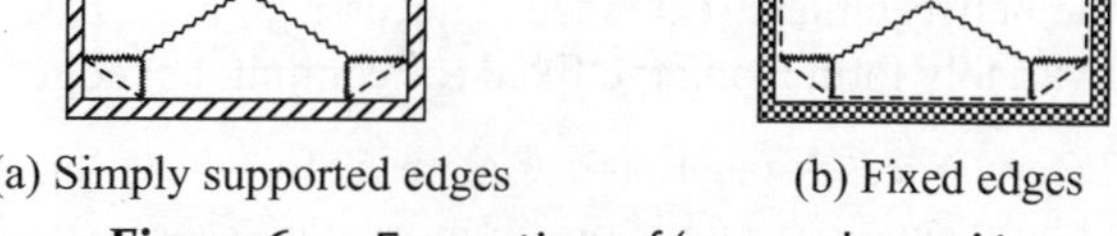

Fig. 11.64 Formation of 'corner levers' in rectangular slabs.

When the slab edges are continuous or fixed, the negative yield lines along the edges form a closed loop, joining up with the negative yield lines at the corners as shown in Figure 11.64(b). Provision of top steel at the corners (so-called 'corner' or 'torsion' reinforcement, as shown in Figure 11.2) tend to diminish the size of the corner levers significantly, and may be conveniently ignored in the calculation of the collapse load. Otherwise, by ignoring the corner levers, the collapse load can be over-estimated up to 10 per cent. This has also been validated by numerous experiments [Ref. 11.8–11.10].

There are two alternative approaches ('virtual work' and 'equilibrium of slab parts') for estimating the collapse load, for any assumed yield line pattern, in a two-way slab. In order to do this, it is necessary to assess the moment capacity of any yield line, which may be inclined to the two orthogonal principal directions. These issues are discussed in Section 11.10.3. However, in order to find the lowest estimate of the collapse load, the appropriate yield line patterns need to be identified in any given situation.

Guidelines for Yield Line Patterns

Based on the previous discussions, the following guidelines can be formed, which help predict yield line patterns.

- Each fractured slab segment rotates about a certain axis, which often corresponds to a line of support, such as a wall or stiff beam or a line passing through a column, or a 'negative' yield line.
- An yield line separating two slab segments will be straight and generally pass through the point of intersection of the two respective axes of rotation of the two segments. When the line of support is curved (for example, at the boundary of a circular slab), it is approximated as a straight line, which implies that the curved arc at the boundary of the fractured slab segment must be small.
- All fractured segments are assumed to be planar.
- 'Positive' yield lines form in the interior regions of the slab and terminate at the slab boundaries.
- 'Negative' yield lines form along the lines of continuous or fixed supports, and sometimes run through or form closed loops within the slab.

Some typical yield line patterns, based on the above guidelines, are depicted in Figure 11.65 for slabs subject to uniform loading. The boundary conditions at the slab edges are shown with hatched lines in the case of simply supported edges, with doubly hatched (criss-crossing hatches) in the case of fixed or continuous edges, and without any hatches (i.e., simple solid lines) in the case of free edges. Columns (or pillars) are marked with small squares.

In all cases, it is interesting to observe the tendency for positive yield lines to occur in the interior regions of the slabs, in between the lines of support. These lines never cross a line of support (including column locations), except at the points of intersection of two lines of support. The directions of the lines of support are not fixed when they pass over columns. However, they must satisfy the rule that when two adjoining lines of support or axis of rotation (extended if necessary, beyond the slab boundaries) intersect, the positive yield line between them (extended if necessary) must pass through the point of intersection. Negative yield lines invariably form along the fixed (or continuous) edges, wherever provided.

Except in cases (such as a square slab) where the locations and directions of the yield lines are known without any uncertainty, one or more dimensional variables (distances or angles of inclination) are identified as unknowns for an assumed yield line pattern. The correct values of these variables are those which yield the minimum collapse load and hence a minimisation (differentiation) procedure will be required. This is demonstrated in the examples to follow. All likely yield patterns have to be analysed this way in order to arrive at the correct yield pattern and the exact collapse load which is the absolute minimum load obtained from amongst all yield patterns.

In the case of slabs subject to concentrated (point) loads, there is a tendency for the positive yield lines to converge at the point load location, as depicted in Figures 11.66(a) and (b). It is not necessary for the positive

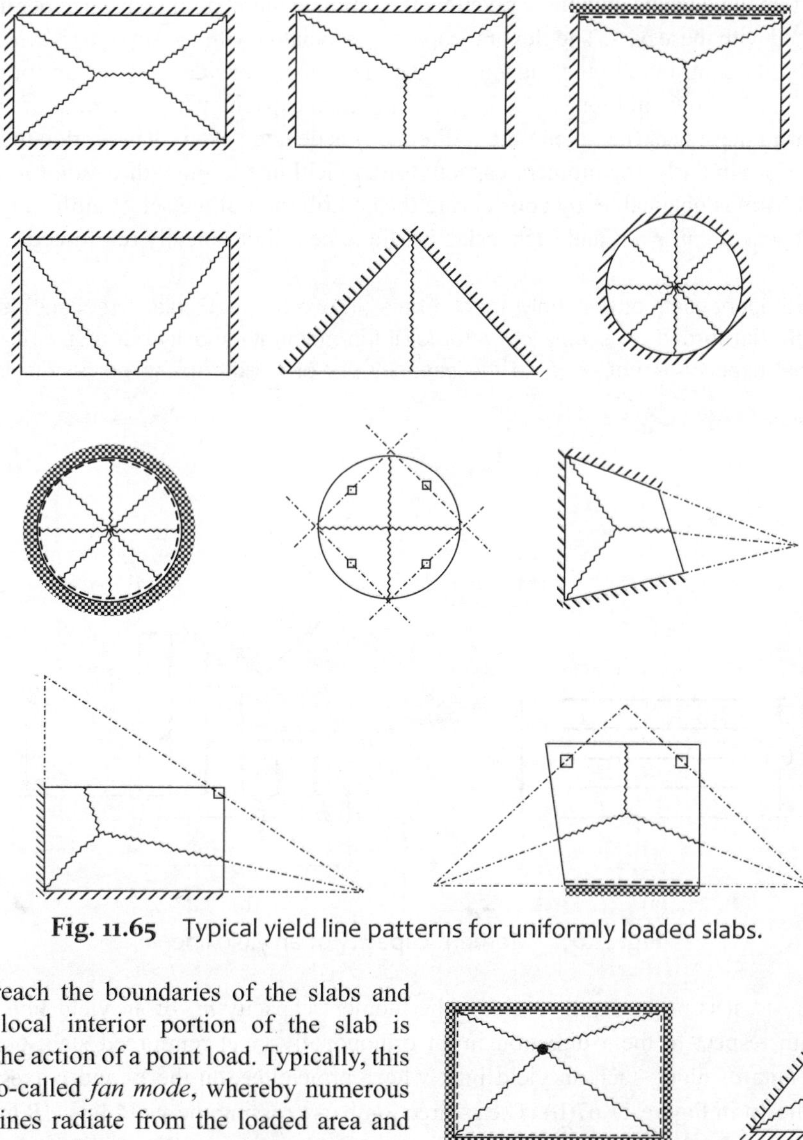

Fig. 11.65 Typical yield line patterns for uniformly loaded slabs.

yield lines to reach the boundaries of the slabs and collapse of a local interior portion of the slab is possible under the action of a point load. Typically, this generates the so-called *fan mode*, whereby numerous positive yield lines radiate from the loaded area and are bounded by a polygon of negative yield lines, which may be approximated as a circle, as shown in Figures 11.66(c) and (d).

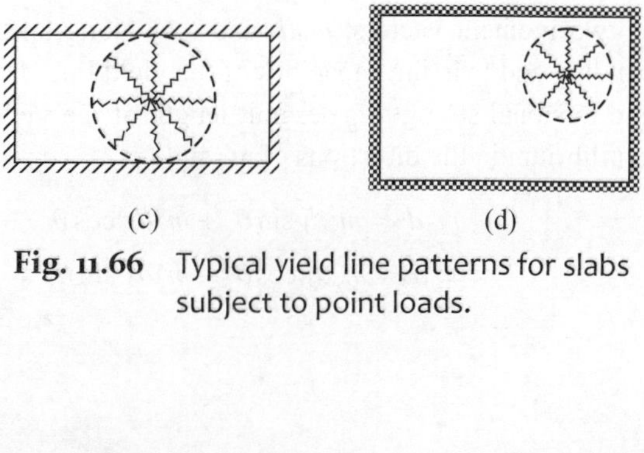

Fig. 11.66 Typical yield line patterns for slabs subject to point loads.

11.10.3 Moment Capacity of an Yield Line

When an yield line forms in a direction that is *perpendicular* to a set of uniformly spaced bars in an orthogonally reinforced slab, then the moment capacity per unit length of that yield line is obviously given by the ultimate moment of resistance per unit width of the slab, m_{uR}, associated with these bars. The flexural capacity associated with the set of bars *parallel* to the yield line will obviously not contribute to the capacity of the yield line. Consider a set of uniformly spaced bars along the x-direction, as shown in Figure 11.67(a). The moment capacity per unit length of an yield line that runs perpendicular to these bars (i.e., along the y-direction) is denoted as m_x, i.e., m_x due to x-direction bars (given by Eq. 11.53). Similarly, the moment capacity of an yield line in the x-direction (m_y per unit length, due to y-direction bars) is obtainable, by considering the contribution of the set of uniformly spaced bars in the y-direction. In general, $m_x \neq m_y$, and such a slab is said to be orthotropically reinforced.

A slab with orthogonal sets of uniformly spaced bars (in two perpendicular directions) is said to be **orthotropically reinforced** (or simply, *orthotropic*) if the moment capacity per unit width of the slab in one principal direction is not equal to the capacity per unit width in the perpendicular direction (i.e., $m_x \neq m_y$).

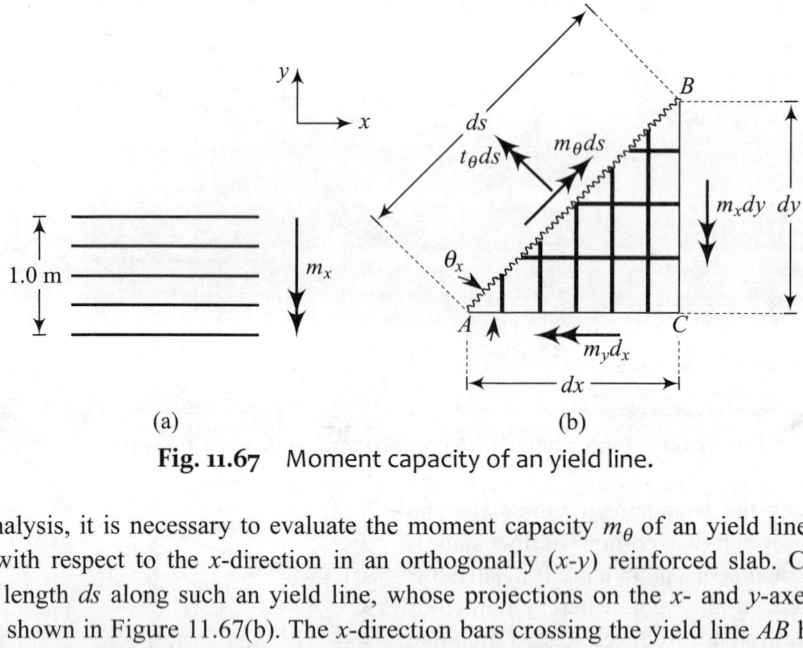

(a) (b)

Fig. 11.67 Moment capacity of an yield line.

In yield line analysis, it is necessary to evaluate the moment capacity m_θ of an yield line that runs at an inclination θ_x with respect to the x-direction in an orthogonally (x-y) reinforced slab. Consider a small element AB of length ds along such an yield line, whose projections on the x- and y-axes are dx and dy respectively, as shown in Figure 11.67(b). The x-direction bars crossing the yield line AB have an ultimate moment capacity of $m_x dy$ whose vector is in the y-direction as shown in the figure. Similarly, the y-direction bars have a moment capacity of $m_y dx$, represented by a horizontal vector. These capacities can be resolved as two moment vectors, $m_\theta ds$ and $t_\theta ds$ along and perpendicular to the yield line, giving respectively the bending and twisting capacities of the yield line AB [Fig. 11.67(b)]. Expressions for the flexural strength m_θ and torsional strength t_θ per unit length of the yield line can now be easily generated considering moment equilibrium in the directions of m_θ and t_θ.

$$m_\theta ds = m_x dy \sin\theta_x + m_y dx \cos\theta_x$$

$$t_\theta ds = m_x dy \cos\theta_x - m_y dx \sin\theta_x$$

Observing that $\frac{dy}{ds} = \sin\theta_x$ and $\frac{dx}{ds} = \cos\theta_x$, the following expressions may be easily derived:

$$m_\theta = m_x \sin^2\theta_x + m_y \cos^2\theta_x \tag{11.54}$$

$$t_\theta = (m_x - m_y)\sin\theta_x \cos\theta_x \tag{11.55}$$

When $m_x = m_y = m$, it follows from the above equations that $m_\theta = m$ and $t_\theta = 0$. In other words, when the flexural capacity per unit width of the slab, provided by the sets of rebars in the two orthogonal directions are exactly equal†, the slab has the same moment capacity in *any* direction. Such a slab is said to be *isotropically reinforced.*

A slab is said to be **isotropically reinforced** (or simply, *isotropic*) if its moment capacity per unit length, *m*, is the same, regardless of its direction. In an orthogonally reinforced slab, this situation occurs when the moment capacities per unit width associated with the two orthogonal sets of reinforcement are equal (i.e., $m_x = m_y = m$). The yield line in such a slab has no torsional strength. Every yield line in an isotropic slab is therefore a line of principal moment.

In an orthotropically reinforced slab, the yield line has a little torsional strength, as indicated by Eq. 11.55. However, in solving problems using yield theory, this usually does not have a role to play, as no relative twisting takes place along the yield lines, as we shall see in the examples to follow.

11.10.4 Yield Line Analysis

Analysis of the collapse load by yield line theory involves the following steps.

1. An appropriate yield line pattern is selected.
2. The moment capacities per unit length of the various yield lines (positive as well as negative) are calculated. (If the slab is isotropically reinforced, all yield lines will have the same capacity, *m*, per unit length).
3. An expression for the collapse load, corresponding to the assumed yield line pattern, is derived, by considering the equilibrium of the slab and its various segments. This may be done by either invoking the concept of virtual work ('Principle of Virtual Displacements') or by the direct use of statics ('Equilibrium of Slab Parts' method).
4. If the yield line pattern involves dimensions that need to be optimised in order to generate the minimum collapse load, this minimisation shall be carried out.
5. Other possible yield line patterns may be investigated, if necessary and steps 1 to 4 repeated, in order to arrive at the smallest value of the collapse load.

11.10.5 Principle of Virtual Displacements

The Principle of Virtual Work is an extremely useful principle in structural analysis to find unknown force/displacement quantities, to set up equilibrium/compatibility relations and to find stiffness/flexibility coefficients [Ref. 11.33]. The principle basically involves equating the total external virtual work, W_E (sum of products of the external forces in the force field and the conjugate displacements in the displacement field) to

† It may be noted that providing bars with the same diameter and same spacing in the two orthogonal directions will, strictly speaking, not provide this condition, because the effective depths are different in the two directions. However, when the bar diameter is very small in relation to the slab thickness, the error in making the assumption of isotropy is not significant.

the total internal virtual work, W_I (sum of products of the internal forces in the force field and the conjugate deformations in the displacement field). This equality, $W_E = W_I$, is valid provided the force field is statically admissible (i.e., in a state of static equilibrium) and the displacement field is kinematically admissible (i.e., satisfying internal compatibility). When the objective is to set up an equilibrium relation in a given (real) force field, as in the present case, a suitable *virtual* (imaginary) displacement field (satisfying compatibility) is visualised, the principle is referred to as the Principle of Virtual Displacements.

In yield line analysis, the virtual displacement field corresponds to the collapse mechanism, with the reference configuration taken as that of the slab at the stage of incipient collapse (with the yield lines fully formed). By imparting a small (virtual) perturbation to the collapse mechanism at this stage, the various slab segments fold up along the yield lines, rotating as rigid bodies (planar elements) about the respective lines of support (axes of rotation). It is thus possible to define the displaced geometry of the slab in this condition, with reference to some reference virtual deflection δ (or rotation θ) at a selected location (usually the maximum deflection or the rotation at a hinge location), satisfying conditions of compatibility, as indicated in the case of the fixed beam in Figure 11.60(c)(ii).

Expression for External Virtual Work

If $\delta(x,y)$ is the virtual deflection at any point (x,y) on the slab (expressed in terms of the reference virtual deflection δ, or rotation θ, as the case may be), and the (real) collapse load intensity at this location is $q_u(x,y)$, then the expression for the external virtual work is given by:

$$W_E = \iint q_u(x,y)\,\delta(x,y)\,dxdy \tag{11.56}$$

If the slab is subject to a uniformly distributed load of intensity, q_o, the above double integral is more easily obtained as a product of q_o and the volume of the space enclosed by the deformed mechanism, expressed in terms of the reference virtual deflection, δ. If the loading is in the form of a line load, instead of a distributed load, the area integral in the above equation will reduce to a line integral. Similarly, if there are concentrated loads acting on the slab, the integration is replaced by summation.

Occasionally, one may encounter a situation (as in an overhang) where the virtual deflection occurs in a direction that is opposite to that of the applied loading; in such a case, the virtual work product corresponding to this load, should be assigned a negative sign. Invariably, however, the total external work, W_E, will have a positive sign. No external work is usually associated with the support reactions, because the deflections at the supports in the collapse mechanism are invariably zero.

Consider the system in Figure 11.60(c)(i) as a one-way slab of span L and width b (in the perpendicular direction), fixed at the two edges A and B, and subject to a line load (such as due to a wall) of intensity P/b per unit width along the line at C. The virtual displacement field is as shown in Figure 11.60(c) (iii), with the yield line along C deflecting uniformly by δ. The total external virtual work is therefore obtained as:

$$W_E = \left(\frac{P_u}{b}\right)(b)(\delta) = P_u\delta$$

Expression for Internal Virtual Work

Considering flexural effects alone, the internal virtual work is obtainable by taking the product of bending moments in the slab (real force field) and the conjugate elemental rotations in the virtual displacement field. However, owing to the mechanism behaviour (rigid body rotations of slab segments), the changes in curvatures in the virtual displacement field are zero, except at the yield line locations, where the rotations can be defined. Thus, for an assumed yield line pattern comprising n yield lines, the internal virtual work is easily obtained as follows:

$$W_I = \sum_{i=1}^{n} (m_i L_i)(\theta_i) \tag{11.57}$$

where θ_i is the rotation (expressed in terms of some reference virtual deflection δ, or virtual rotation θ as the case may be) undergone by the ith yield line, which has a length L_i and a moment capacity per unit length m_i. If the virtual deflections are chosen in the same direction as the deflections at the stage of incipient collapse, the internal work associated with any yield line (whether positive or negative) will invariably be a positive quantity.

For instance, continuing the discussions on the one-way fixed slab AB (span L, width b) subject to a concentrated line load at one-third span location C, the virtual displacement field (deflection δ at the load point C) associated with the collapse mechanism is as shown in Figure 11.60(c)(iii). Compatibility of the virtual displacement field requires that the segment BC should undergo an anti-clockwise rotation†, $\theta = \delta/(2L/3) = 1.5\delta/L$, while the segment AC undergoes a clockwise rotation, $\delta/(L/3) = 2\theta$. If these two segments are considered separately (in sisolation), the exposed end moments in the real force field will act in an anti-clockwise sense at A and C in the free-body AC, while they act in a clockwise sense at C and B in the free-body CB. Assuming the moment capacities of the positive yield line at C, as well as the two negative yield lines at A and B, to be equal to $M_{uR} = mb$, the *external* virtual work product is obtained as $-2(M_{uR})(2\theta)$ for segment AC and $-2(M_{uR})(\theta)$ for segment CB, whereby the total internal virtual work, which is equal to the negative of the external virtual work, is given by $4M_{uR}\theta + 2M_{uR}\theta = 6M_{uR}\theta$. Alternatively, observing that the yield line rotations are given by 2θ, 3θ and θ respectively at A, B and C, as depicted in Figure 11.60(c)(iii), and applying Eq. 11.57,

$$W_I = \left(\frac{M_{uR}}{b}\right)(b)\left[2\theta + 3\theta + \theta\right] = 6M_{uR}\theta$$

Substituting $\theta = 1.5\delta/L$, and invoking the Principle of Virtual Displacements,

$$W_E = W_I \Rightarrow P_u\delta = 6M_{uR}\left(\frac{1.5\delta}{L}\right) \Rightarrow P_u = 9\frac{M_{uR}}{L}$$

In the above example, the yield lines were conveniently aligned in the direction of the axes of rotation (support lines). Moreover, they were horizontal so that the associated rotations were in a vertical plane normal to the yield line, as shown in Figure 11.60(c)(iii).When the yield line forms in an inclined direction to the axes of rotation, as is commonly encountered in two-way slabs, the calculation of the internal virtual work needs to be done carefully. For example, consider a typical case of the yield line AC shown in Figure 11.68(a), separating two triangular segments ADC and ABC, whose respective axes of rotation (supporting edges AD and AB) meet at right angles at A. The yield line AC is inclined in plan to the two orthogonal axes of rotation (making an angle φ_x with the x-axis). In addition, the yield line is also inclined to the horizontal plane. In order to compute the internal work done by the moment along the yield line, it is required to determine the rotation of the two segments at the yield line in a plane perpendicular to it, and this can be complex. However, the procedure can be considerably simplified by resolving the moment and rotation vectors along the two orthogonal directions as shown in Figures 11.68(c),(d) and explained below.

† Assuming small deformations, $\theta = \tan\theta$.

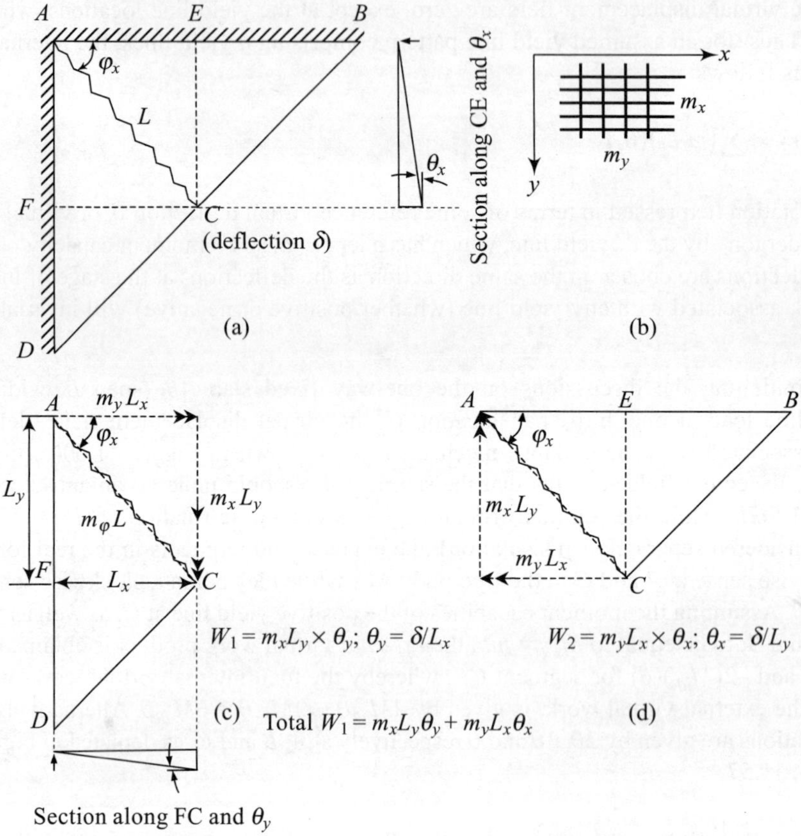

Fig. 11.68 Yield line at an angle to the axis of rotation.

Let the ultimate moment resistance per unit width of slab due to the reinforcements in the x-direction be m_x and due to the reinforcements in the y-direction be m_y respectively, as shown in Figure 11.68(b). The moment resistance per unit length along the yield line, m_φ, can be determined using Eq. 11.54. Now consider the slab segment ACD shown in Figure 11.68(c). The moment along the yield line AC is Lm_φ which can be resolved into moments m_xL_y and m_yL_x about the y- and x-axes respectively (this is the reverse of the process done in Figure 11.57). Here L_x and L_y are the projections of the yield line AC on the x- and y-axes respectively as shown in Figure 11.68(c). The slab segment ACD rotates about the y-axis only ($\theta_y = \delta/L_x$) and hence work is done by the component of moment about y-axis only, that is by m_xL_y. Here θ_y is the rotation of segment ACD about its support line and δ is the virtual displacement at C. Thus the internal work done due to the rotation at the yield line as part of segment ACD is $W_1 = m_xL_y \times \theta_y$. In the same way, the work done by the moment along the yield line as part of segment ABC [Figure 11.68(d)] works out to $W_2 = m_yL_x \times \theta_x$, where $\theta_x = \delta/L_y$. Hence, the total internal work done, W_I, is given by:

$$W_I = (m_xL_y)(\theta_y) + (m_yL_x)(\theta_x) \tag{11.58}$$

Note that the x-direction reinforcement crossing the yield line is over a width of L_y, has a moment capacity of m_xL_y and rotates about y-axis by θ_y giving a work component of $m_xL_y\theta_y$ and this is the first term in Eq. 11.58. Similarly, the y-direction reinforcement crossing the yield line gives the second component. For an isotropically reinforced slab, $m_x = m_y = m$, and Eq. 11.58 reduces to:

$$W_I = (m)(L_y\theta_y + L_x\theta_x) \tag{11.58a}$$

Thus, with inclined yield lines, the fractured segments of the slab may be considered individually and the orthogonal contributions superimposed; in each case, the projected length of the yield line on to the axis of rotation (support line) is considered, along with the moment per unit length equal to that due to reinforcement perpendicular to the axis, and the rotation about the axis.

For example, consider a square slab (side L), simply supported on the four edges, with a symmetrical yield line pattern, as shown in Figure 11.69(a). If the slab is isotropically reinforced, the moment capacity per unit length is $m_x = m_y = m$. Considering a virtual displacement δ at the centre O of the slab, the internal virtual work associated with the yield line for the slab segment AOD (which rotates about line AD as axis) is given by the product of (i) the projected length of yield lines (AO + OD) on the axis of rotation (= L), (ii) moment capacity due to x-direction reinforcement (= m_x = m), and (iii) angle of rotation about axis of rotation ($= \theta_y = 2\delta/L$); giving the result $Lm(2\delta/L) = 2m\delta$ [refer Figure 11.69(b)]. Thus, the total internal work associated with the 4 slab segments, which behave identically, is given by

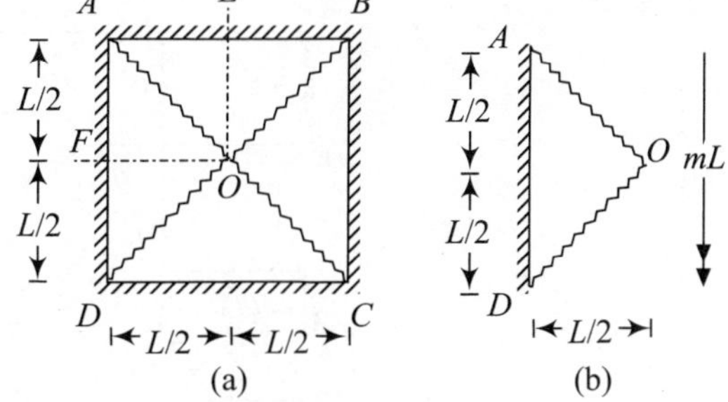

Fig. 11.69 Yield line pattern in a square slab: estimation of internal virtual work.

$$W_I = 4 \times 2m\delta = 8m\delta$$

If the square slab in Figure 11.69(a) is subject to a point load P_u at the centre C, then the external virtual work is easily given by $W_E = P_u\delta$, whereby $W_E = W_I \Rightarrow P_u = 8m$. Similarly, if the slab is subject to a uniformly distributed load of intensity w_u per unit area, $W_E = w_uL^2\delta/3^{\dagger}$, whereby $W_E = W_I \Rightarrow w_u = 24m/L^2$. If the square slab is fixed (or continuous) along the four edges and reinforced at top near these edges such that the negative yield lines forming along these edges have a moment capacity m' per unit length, then each of these 4 yield lines will have an additional internal virtual work contribution, equal to $(m'L)\delta/(L/2) = 2m'\delta$, whereby $W_I = 8(m + m')\delta$. Thus, it can be easily shown that the collapse load, given by the assumed yield line pattern, is $P_u = 8(m + m')$ when the slab is subjected to a point load at the centre, and $w_u = 24(m + m')/L^2$ when the load is uniformly distributed. These are, of course, *upper bound* solutions.

11.10.6 'Equilibrium of Slab Parts' Method

As an alternative to the application of the Principle of Virtual Displacements, the direct application of equations of static equilibrium can be attempted, and in many instances, this method may turn out to be simpler. In this method, the free-bodies of the various fractured slab segments are considered, with appropriate bending moments, twisting moments and shear forces applied at the boundaries (wherever applicable), in addition to the applied external loads.

Consider, for example, the simple case of the one-way fixed slab, subject to a concentrated line load, analysed earlier by the Principle of Virtual Displacements. By considering static equilibrium of the slab at the condition of incipient collapse (assuming the appropriate yield line pattern), the solution for the collapse load can be easily obtained, as shown in Figure 11.70.

† The volume of the deformed pyramid is equal to $L^2(\delta/3)$. Alternatively, we can visualize the total load in each triangular area (of magnitude $wL^2/4$) acting at the centroid of the triangle and undergoing a deflection equal to $\delta/3$, whereby $W_E = 4(wL^2/4)(\delta/3)$ $= wL^2\delta/3$.

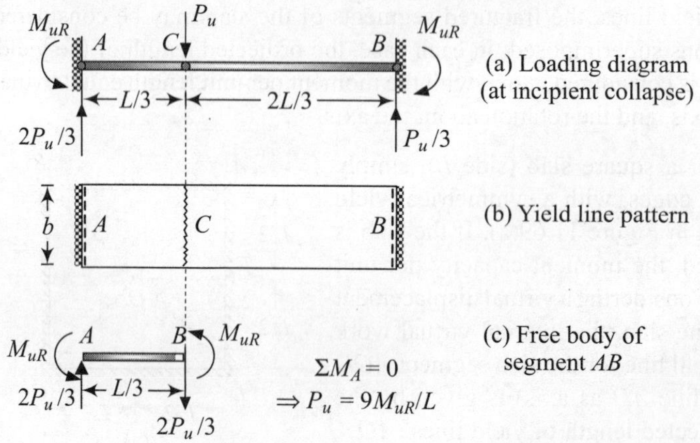

Fig. 11.70 Demonstration of 'Equilibrium of Slab Parts' method.

In two-way slab systems, however, the shear forces along the slab segment boundaries are generally statically indeterminate (in terms of magnitude and distribution). For convenience, they can be resolved into statically equivalent concentrated forces, called *nodal forces*, at the two ends of each yield line on the two-slab segment free-bodies separated by the yield line. When the various segments are joined together, the nodal forces acting at the junctions of yield lines must satisfy force equilibrium. If there is no external load acting at the junction, then the sum of the nodal forces must be equal to zero at the junction. Clearly, when the yield line pattern and loading are symmetrical, the nodal forces at yield line junctions located on any axis of symmetry will all be equal to zero, under distributed loading, as the shear forces along the line of symmetry will be zero. Methods have been proposed by Johansen and later by Wood [Ref. 11.8 and 11.9] to calculate the magnitudes of nodal forces under various conditions. For example, when an yield line intersects a free edge, and the reinforcement mesh comprises rebars that are parallel and perpendicular to the free edge, then it can be shown that the nodal force Q_e is given by:

$$Q_e = \pm m \cot \beta \qquad (11.59)$$

where m is the moment capacity per unit length of the yield line and β is the angle between the yield line and the free edge, as shown in Figure 11.71. In the case of positive yield lines, Q_e will act in the downward direction in the slab segment containing the acute angle ($\beta < 90°$), while it will act upward in the other segment. If the yield line is negative, the directions get reversed, as shown in Figure 11.71. In the special case where the yield line meets the free edge at right angles ($\beta = 90°$), the nodal force is zero.

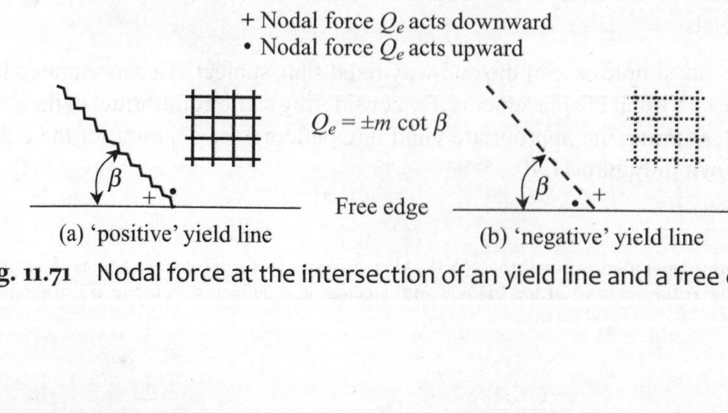

Fig. 11.71 Nodal force at the intersection of an yield line and a free edge.

Another useful finding is that at the junction of three yield lines governed by the same reinforcement mesh, the nodal forces are all zero at the junction, if the yield lines are either all positive moment lines or all negative moment lines.

Consider the square slab in Figure 11.72(a) with a symmetric yield line pattern, subject to a concentrated load P_u at the centre O. The nodal force, acting downward at O, on any of the four triangular slab segments, is obviously equal to $P_u/4$. It is sufficient to consider moment equilibrium of any triangular segment about the supporting edge. The moment $(P_u/4)(L/2)$ must obviously be balanced by the component of the yield line moments, mL, as shown in Figure 11.72(b).

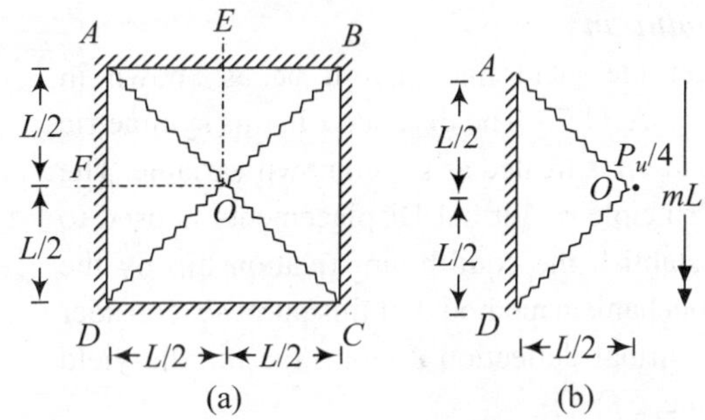

Fig. 11.72 Application of 'Equilibrium of Slab Parts' to a square slab.

$$\sum M_{AD} = 0 \;\Rightarrow\; \left(\frac{P_u}{4}\right)\left(\frac{L}{2}\right) - mL = 0 \;\Rightarrow\; \boxed{P_u = 8m}$$

When the square slab in Figure 11.72(a) is subject to a uniformly distributed load w_u per unit area, the nodal force, acting downward at O, on any of the four triangular slab segments, is obviously equal to zero. The centroid of the loaded triangular area is located at a distance of $(1/3)(L/2)$ from the supporting edge. Accordingly, for this condition, considering equilibrium of the free-body in Figure 11.72(b),

$$\sum M_{AD} = 0 \;\Rightarrow\; \left(w_u \frac{L^2}{4}\right)\left(\frac{1}{3}\frac{L}{2}\right) - mL = 0 \;\Rightarrow\; \boxed{w_u = 24\frac{m}{L^2}}$$

When the four edges of the square slab are fixed or continuous, then the negative yield line moment contributions ($m'L$), which act in the same direction as the positive yield line moment contributions, have to be accounted for. The results obtained will be identical to those obtained earlier by the Principle of Virtual Displacements.

Incidentally, it may be noted that this method accounts for equilibrium of the overall slab segment, defined by an assumed yield line pattern. Hence, it is a *mechanism method*, which yields an *upper bound* solution. The term *equilibrium method* is generally used in connection with an approach that satisfies equilibrium at all points on the beam or slab [as illustrated in Figures 11.60(a) and (b)], and this gives a *lower bound* solution. Hillerborg's strip method (not discussed here) belongs to the latter category. Hence, in order to make this distinction, the method used in yield line theory is called 'Equilibrium of Slab Parts' method.

Various simple applications of this method are demonstrated in the examples to follow.

11.10.7 Examples of Yield Line Analysis

Example 11.8: Rectangular Slab, Isotropically Reinforced

Apply yield line theory to estimate the collapse load of a rectangular slab, simply supported on all four edges, and subject to a uniformly distributed load of intensity w_u per unit area. Assume the slab to have dimensions of a and b along the short span and long span directions. Assume the slab to be isotropically reinforced.

Solution

Let the yield line pattern be as shown in Figure 11.73. The distance x in this symmetric pattern is treated as an unknown variable. The Principle of Virtual Displacements is used to establish the equilibrium relationship by the mechanism method. For this purpose, consider a virtual deflection δ along the middle yield line, EF.

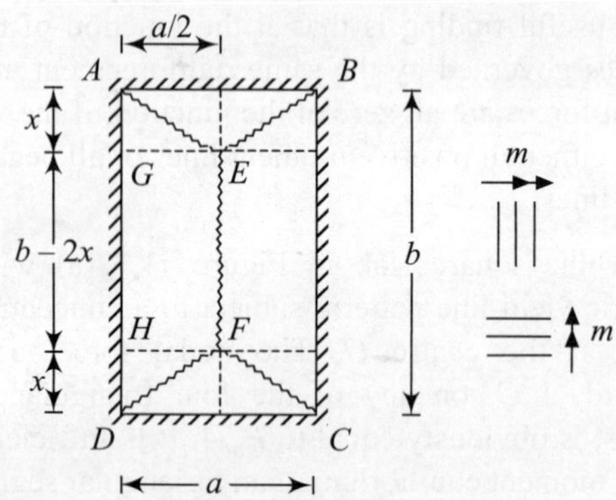

Fig. 11.73 Yield line pattern in a rectangular slab, isotropically reinforced.

Taking advantage of symmetry, the external virtual work can be computed, by considering the contributions of various slab segments, as follows:

$$W_E = (w_u)\left[(\text{area of } \Delta ABE)\left(\frac{\delta}{3}\right) + (\text{area of } \Delta AEG)\left(\frac{\delta}{3}\right)\times 2 + (\text{area of } GEFH)\left(\frac{\delta}{2}\right)\right]\times 2$$

$$\Rightarrow \quad W_E = (w_u)\left[(2ax)\left(\frac{\delta}{3}\right) + a(b-2x)\left(\frac{\delta}{2}\right)\right] = \frac{w_u a\delta}{6}(3b-2x)$$

[Note that the displaced slab is in the form of a hipped roof and the same result can be obtained as the product of load intensity w_u and the volume under the roof]

The internal virtual work can be computed, by considering the contributions of the yield lines EF and four identical inclined yield lines (such as AE). Considering the moment capacity in any direction in this isotropically reinforced slab to be given by m per unit length,

$$W_I = W_{EF} + 4W_{AE}$$

$$W_I = (m)(b-2x)\left(\frac{\delta}{a/2}\times 2\right) + 4(m)\left[(x)\left(\frac{\delta}{a/2}\right) + \left(\frac{a}{2}\right)\left(\frac{\delta}{x}\right)\right]$$

$$= (m)(b)\left(\frac{\delta}{a/2}\times 2\right) + (m)(a\times 2)\left(\frac{\delta}{x}\right) = \frac{2m\delta}{ax}(2bx + a^2)$$

Applying the Principle of Virtual Displacements,

$$W_E = W_I \Rightarrow \frac{w_u a\delta}{6}(3b-2x) = \frac{2m\delta}{ax}(2bx+a^2)$$

$$\Rightarrow \quad \frac{m}{w_u} = \frac{a^2}{12}\times\frac{3bx-2x^2}{2bx+a^2} = \text{constant}\times\frac{u(x)}{v(x)}$$

where $u(x)$ and $v(x)$ represent functions of x. The true solution, for the assumed yield line pattern, corresponds to the maximum value of the ratio m/w_u (i.e., the minimum load). The necessary condition for this is given by equating the derivative of m/w_u to zero.

$$\frac{d(m/w_u)}{dx} = 0 \Rightarrow \text{constant}\times\frac{vu' - uv'}{v^2} = 0$$

$$\Rightarrow \quad vu' - uv' = 0 \Rightarrow (3b - 4x)(2bx + a^2) - (2b)(3bx - 2x^2) = 0$$

Simplifying, $4bx^2 + 4a^2x - 3a^2b = 0 \Rightarrow x = \frac{a}{2}\left[\sqrt{\left(\frac{a}{b}\right)^2 + 3} - \frac{a}{b}\right]$

Substituting this value in the expression for m/w_u, we can derive an expression for the collapse load w (in terms of m, a and b). However, the result is more easily obtained by invoking the 'Equilibrium of Slab Parts' method, and considering equilibrium of the triangular segment ABE alone. Considering moments about the edge AB,

$$\Sigma M_{AB} = 0 \Rightarrow (w_u)\left(\frac{ax}{2}\right)\left(\frac{x}{3}\right) = ma \Rightarrow w_u = \frac{6m}{x^2}$$

$$\Rightarrow \quad w_u = \frac{24m}{a^2}\left[\sqrt{\left(\frac{a}{b}\right)^2 + 3} - \left(\frac{a}{b}\right)\right]^{-2} \qquad (11.60)$$

or alternatively, $m = \frac{w_u a^2}{24}\left[\sqrt{\left(\frac{a}{b}\right)^2 + 3} - \left(\frac{a}{b}\right)\right]^2$

For a square panel, $a = b = L$, the collapse load simplifies to $w_u = 24\frac{m}{L^2}$.

Example 11.9: Rectangular Slab, Orthotropically Reinforced

Repeat Example 11.8, considering the slab to be orthotropically reinforced.

Solution

Let the yield line pattern be as shown in Figure 11.74(a), which is similar to the one in Figure 11.73, and in which the distance x is treated as an unknown variable. Let the bars have an ultimate moment capacity per unit length m in the short span direction, and μm in the long span direction, as shown in Figure 11.74(a). Here, the solution is based on the Equilibrium of Slab Parts method. The free-bodies of slab parts I (triangular) and II (trapezoidal) are shown in Figure 11.74(b). Nodal forces at the junctions of the three yield lines will

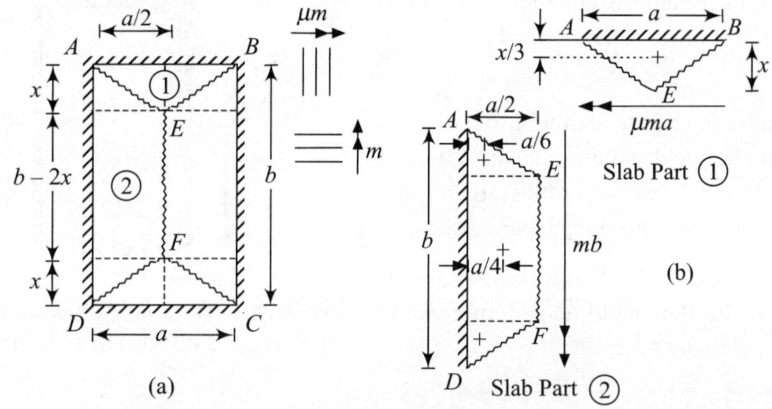

Fig. 11.74 Yield line analysis of a rectangular slab, orthotropically reinforced.

be zero. The resultant moment vectors (associated with the yield lines) in the direction of the supporting slab edges, as well as the locations of the resultant forces (due to the distributed loading) are shown in the two free-bodies.

Equilibrium of Slab Part 1

$$\Sigma M_{AB} = 0 \Rightarrow (w_u)\left(\frac{ax}{2}\right)\left(\frac{x}{3}\right) = \mu m a \Rightarrow \frac{m}{w_u} = \frac{x^2}{6\mu} \quad (1)$$

Equilibrium of Slab Part 2

$$\Sigma M_{AD} = 0 \Rightarrow (w_u)\left[(b-2x)\left(\frac{a}{2}\right)\left(\frac{a}{4}\right) + (x)\left(\frac{a}{2}\right)\left(\frac{1}{3}\times\frac{a}{2}\right)\right] = mb$$

$$\Rightarrow \quad \frac{m}{w_u} = \frac{a^2(3b-4x)}{24b} \quad (2)$$

$$(1) = (2) \Rightarrow \frac{x^2}{6\mu} = \frac{(3a^2b - 4a^2x)}{24b} \Rightarrow (4b)x^2 + (4a^2\mu)x - 3a^2b\mu = 0$$

$$\Rightarrow \quad x = \frac{(-4a^2\mu) + \sqrt{[16a^4\mu^2 + 48a^2b^2\mu]}}{8b}$$

$$\Rightarrow \quad x = \frac{\sqrt{\mu}a}{2}\left[\frac{-a}{b/\sqrt{\mu}} + \sqrt{\left(\frac{a}{b/\sqrt{\mu}}\right)^2 + 3}\right]$$

Substituting Eq. (3) in (1) $\Rightarrow m = \dfrac{w_u a^2}{24}\left[\sqrt{\left(\dfrac{a}{b/\sqrt{\mu}}\right)^2 + 3} - \dfrac{a}{b/\sqrt{\mu}}\right]^2$

$$\Rightarrow \quad w_u = \frac{24m}{a^2}\left[\sqrt{\left(\frac{a}{b/\sqrt{\mu}}\right)^2 + 3} - \frac{a}{b/\sqrt{\mu}}\right]^{-2} \quad (11.61)$$

Substituting $\mu = 1$ in the above equations will yield the same results as obtained in Example 11.8 for the isotropic case.

Similarly, the collapse load for a slab with fixed edges can be derived for the yield pattern shown in Figure 11.75. The negative yield line capacities are im and $i\mu m$ along the short span and long span directions respectively.

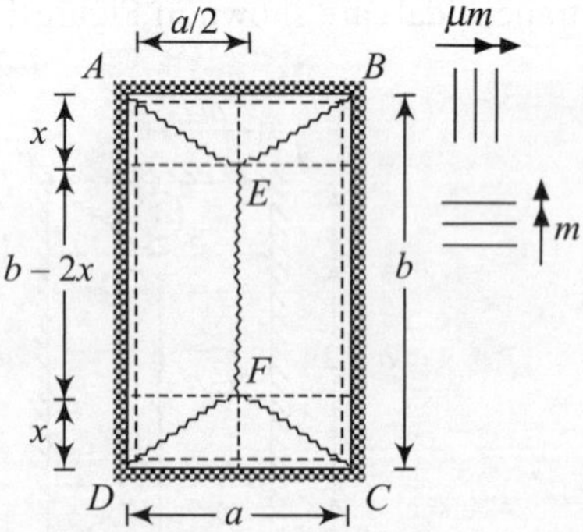

Fig. 11.75 Yield line analysis of a rectangular slab with fixed boundary conditions.

The collapse load w_u for the yield line pattern given in Figure 11.75 can be shown to be:

$$w_u = \frac{24m(1+i)}{a^2}\left[\sqrt{\left(\frac{a}{b/\sqrt{\mu}}\right)^2 + 3} - \frac{a}{b/\sqrt{\mu}}\right]^{-2} \quad (11.62)$$

Example 11.10: Rectangular Slab Supported on Three Edges

Apply yield line theory to estimate the collapse load of a rectangular slab, simply supported on three edges, and subject to a uniformly distributed load of intensity w_u per unit area. Assume the slab to have dimensions of a and b. Assume the slab to be isotropically reinforced.

Solution

There are two yield line patterns that are possible. Intuitively, the one shown in Figure 11.76(a) is more likely to occur when b is much greater than a, while the one in Figure 11.76(b) is likely to occur when a is much greater than b. The distance x in each of these two symmetric yield line patterns is treated as an unknown variable in each analysis. The Principle of Virtual Displacements is used to establish the equilibrium relationship by the mechanism method. For this purpose, consider a virtual deflection δ along the free edge, EF in Figure 11.76(a), and along the middle yield line GH in Figure 11.76(b).

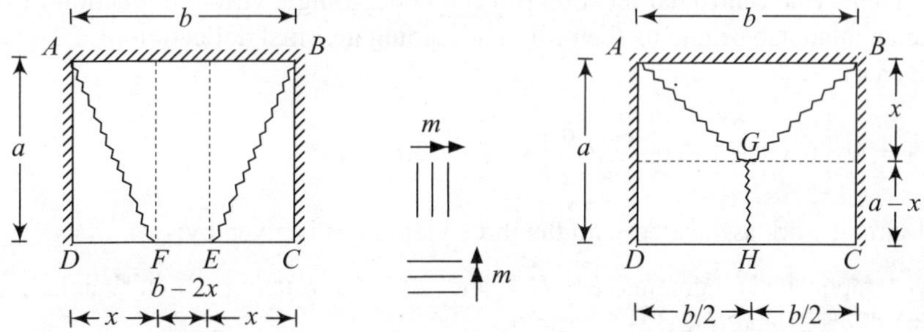

(a) Yield line pattern 1 (b) Yield line pattern 2

Fig. 11.76 Yield line patterns for a rectangular slab supported on 3 edges.

Yield line pattern 1 (Figure 11.76(a)

Considering the action of the uniformly distributed loading on (i) four equal triangular slab segments (the centroidal location undergoing a virtual deflection of $\delta/3$) and (ii) rectangular slab segment bounded between FE and AB (centroid undergoing a virtual deflection of $\delta/2$), the total external virtual work is given by:

$$W_E = w_u\left[2\times(ax)\left(\frac{\delta}{3}\right) + (a)(b-2x)\frac{\delta}{2}\right] = w_u\delta\times a\left(\frac{b}{2}-\frac{x}{3}\right)$$

The total internal virtual work associated with the two identical yield lines is obtainable by summing up the work components in the two orthogonal directions (moment capacity of m per unit length in any direction):

$$W_I = 2\times(m)\left(a\times\frac{\delta}{x} + x\times\frac{\delta}{a}\right) = 2m\delta\left(\frac{x}{a}+\frac{a}{x}\right)$$

$$W_E = W_I \Rightarrow \frac{m}{w_u} = \frac{a\left(\dfrac{b}{2}-\dfrac{x}{3}\right)}{2\left(\dfrac{x}{a}+\dfrac{a}{x}\right)} = \frac{a^2}{12}\times\frac{3bx-2x^2}{x^2+a^2} = \text{constant}\times\frac{f_1(x)}{f_2(x)}$$

For maximum (m/w_u),

$$\frac{\partial(m/w_u)}{\partial x} = 0 \Rightarrow \frac{f_2\times f_1' - f_1\times f_2'}{f_2^2} = 0 \Rightarrow f_2f_1' - f_1f_2' = 0$$

$$\Rightarrow \quad (x^2 + a^2)(3b - 4x) - (3bx - 2x^2)(2x) = 0 \Rightarrow 3bx^2 + 4a^2x - 3a^2b = 0$$

$$\Rightarrow \quad x = \frac{a}{3b}\left[-2a + \sqrt{4a^2 + 9b^2}\right]$$

$$\Rightarrow \quad w_u = \frac{12m}{a^2} \times \frac{x^2 + a^2}{3bx - 2x^2}$$

For example, considering a square panel ($a = b = L$),

$$x = 0.5352L \text{ and } w_u = 14.95\frac{m}{L^2}$$

Yield line pattern 2 (Figure 11.76(b))

Considering the action of the uniformly distributed loading on (i) the rectangular area, bx, comprising three triangular slab segments (the centroidal location of each undergoing a virtual deflection of $\delta/3$) and (ii) the remaining two rectangular slab segments (centroid undergoing a virtual deflection of $\delta/2$), the total external virtual work is given by:

$$W_E = w_u\left[(bx)\left(\frac{\delta}{3}\right) + (a - x)b\frac{\delta}{2}\right] = \frac{w_u b\delta}{6}(3a - x)$$

The total internal virtual work associated with the three yield lines is given by:

(i) for the two trapezoidal segments (*AGHD* and *BGHC*) rotating about *y*-axis, as explained in Fig. 11.67(b), $W_1 = 2\{ma\delta/(b/2)\} = 4ma\Delta\delta/b$.

(ii) for the triangular part *ABG* rotating about *x*-axis, $W_2 = mb\delta/x$.

Thus. the total internal virtual work is:

$$W_I = \frac{4ma\delta}{b} + \frac{mb\delta}{x} = m\delta\frac{4ax + b^2}{bx}$$

$$W_E = W_I \Rightarrow \frac{m}{w_u} = \frac{b^2}{6} \times \frac{3ax - x^2}{4ax + b^2} = \text{constant} \times \frac{f_1(x)}{f_2(x)}$$

For maximum (m/w_u),

$$\frac{\partial(m/w_u)}{\partial x} = 0 \Rightarrow \frac{f_2 \times f_1' - f_1 \times f_2'}{f_2^2} = 0 \Rightarrow f_2 f_1' - f_1 f_2' = 0$$

$$\Rightarrow (4ax + b^2)(3a - 2x) - (3ax - x^2)(4a) = 0$$

Simplifying and solving,

$$\Rightarrow \quad x = \frac{b^2}{4a}\left[\sqrt{1 + 12(a/b)^2} - 1\right]$$

$$\Rightarrow \quad w_u = \frac{6m}{b^2} \times \frac{4ax + b^2}{3ax - x^2}$$

This solution should be compared with the solution obtained earlier for yield line pattern 1, and the lower of the two values should be considered as the collapse load.

For example, considering a square panel ($a = b = L$),

$x = 0.6514L$ and $w_u = 14.14\dfrac{m}{L^2}$, which is less than the value generated by yield line pattern 1 $\left(w_u = 14.95\dfrac{m}{L^2}\right)$.
Hence, for a square panel, the solution is given by $w_u = 14.14\dfrac{m}{L^2}$.

Note: If the three slab edges (other than the free edge) are fixed or continuous, then the contribution of the negative yield lines should be included in the calculation of W_I.

Example 11.11: Circular Slab, Isotropically Reinforced

Apply yield line theory to estimate the collapse load of an isotropically reinforced circular slab of radius R, simply supported on the periphery, and subject to (i) a uniformly distributed load of intensity w_u per unit area and (ii) a concentrated load P_u at the centre. How are these solutions affected if the slab is fixed at the periphery?

Solution

The yield line pattern is likely to have a symmetric 'fan mode' as shown in Figure 11.77(a), with a large number of positive yield lines radiating from the centre to the periphery. When the boundary is fixed, a negative yield line is also likely to form close to the circumference, as shown in Figure 11.77(b). Let m and m' denote the ultimate moment capacities per unit length associated with positive and negative yield lines respectively in this isotropically reinforced slab. Applying a virtual deflection, δ, at the centre of the slab, the deformed shape of the slab (with numerous yield lines) will approach that of a cone. The Principle of Virtual Displacements is used to find the solution.

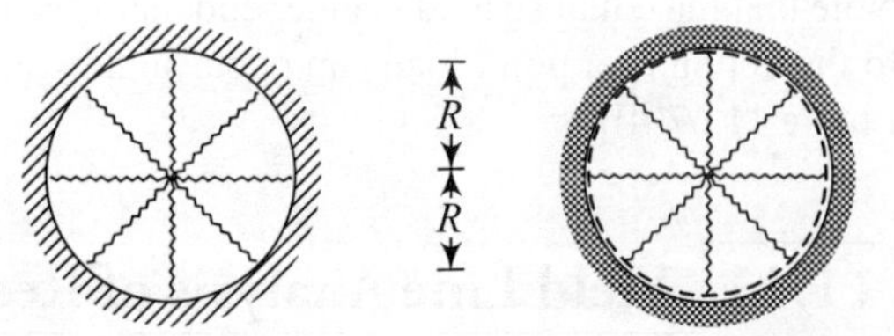

(a) Simply supported (b) Fixed

Fig. 11.77 Yield line patterns for a circular slab.

(i) Uniformly distributed load

Noting that the volume of the cone-shaped deformed shape in the virtual displacement field is given by (πR^2) $(\delta/3)$, the external virtual work is given by

$$W_E = w_u \frac{\pi R^2 \delta}{3}$$

For the purpose of computing the internal virtual work due to the positive yield lines, the projections of the yield lines on the radial and tangential directions can be considered, for convenience. The rotation of each yield line occurs only in the tangential direction. The total projected length of all the positive yield lines in this direction is $2\pi R$, and the tangential rotation at every yield line is given by δ/R. This also holds true for the negative yield line in Figure 11.77(b). Accordingly,

$$W_I = m(2\pi R)\left(\frac{\delta}{R}\right) = 2\pi m\delta \quad \text{[simply supported condition, Figure 11.77(a)]}$$

$$W_I = 2\pi(m + m')\delta \quad \text{[fixed condition, Figure 11.77(b)]}$$

Applying the Principle of Virtual Displacements ($W_E = W_I$),

$$w_u = \frac{6m}{R^2} \text{ when the periphery is simply supported;}$$

$$w_u = \frac{6(m + m')}{R^2} \text{ when the periphery is fixed.}$$

(ii) Concentrated load at centre

The internal virtual work is as calculated above. The external virtual work is given by

$$W_E = P_u \delta$$

Applying the Principle of Virtual Displacements ($W_E = W_I$),

$$P_u = 2\pi m \text{ when the periphery is simply supported;}$$

$$P_u = 2\pi(m + m') \text{ when the periphery is fixed.}$$

Note that the collapse load is independent of the radius of the circle. This implies I 'fan mode' of collapse due to the action of a point load can occur in any slab in a small circle that lies in the interior of the slab [refer Figure 11.67(d)].

11.11 Yield Line Analysis of Rectangular Beam-Supported Slabs

In conventional yield line analysis of slabs discussed above, they are simply supported on or fixed to wall-like non-deflecting level supports along edges, or supported on columns (and sometimes have edges free). In general, after the yield line mechanism is fully formed at the limit state of collapse, the slab segments of the mechanism can rotate about *straight-line axes* through these supports. In the case of beam-supported slabs, it is possible that flexural plastic hinges can form in the beams [Ref. 11.6]. Experimental studies [Ref. 11.34–11.38] have shown the possible occurrence of combined beam-slab failure mechanisms in beam-supported RC slabs, and so these need to be properly accounted for in yield line theory.

Typical yield line patterns that can be expected in the case of rectangular slabs integrally connected to edge beams and supported at the four corners on RC columns are shown in Figure 11.78. If the beams are not integrally connected to RC columns (as in the case of pillar supports), the 'negative' plastic hinges will not form at the beam-pillar interface.

Pattern I (Figure 11.78b) is the failure mechanism typically assumed in conventional analysis of slabs supported on (stiff) beams, having an yield line pattern identical to the one shown earlier in Figure 11.75. In addition to the formation of 'positive' yield lines (associated with moment capacities, m_x and m_y), 'negative' yield lines may also form at the beam-slab interfaces, having moment capacities per unit length, $i_x m_x$ and $i_y m_y$, as shown (limited by the torsional moment capacity of the adjoining beam). However, theoretically, there is a very significant difference between the failure mechanism shown in Figure 11.75 and the one in Figure 11.78(b). While in the former, the negative yield line is straight and level, forming a *straight-line axis* about which the slab segment can rotate (like with a piano-hinge), which is in order; in the latter case, because of the deflection of the beam, the yield line is curved (sagging) and the slab segment has to swing about this *curved axis* (*hinge*), which is kinematically constrained and hence inadmissible. This constraint may tend to inhibit the development of mechanisms with similarly placed yield lines along the beam-slab junction. However, in practical terms, when the beam deflections are negligible, this anomaly could be ignored. [It is pertinent here to note that beam deflection is inversely proportional to its flexural stiffness, and the procedure in Section 11.3.2 does specify *stiff beams* for adopting the Code (Annexure D) moment coefficients (based on Pattern I yield mechanism) for beam supported slab design.]

The beam adjoining a negative yield line such as shown in Figure 11.78(f) is subjected to a uniform twisting moment of im_x per unit length. The maximum torsion on the beam at its ends, $T = im_x \times L_y/2$, has to be limited to the torsional strength of the beam, say T_u. If the value of T calculated as above is more than T_u, torsional yielding will occur at beam ends as T approaches T_u, and the negative yield line will not develop in the slab. With adequate torsion reinforcement and proper detailing, an elastic-plastic torsional response of the beam is possible (See Figure 7.4), in which case two torsional hinges can be assumed to form at beam ends at $T = T_u$. If this happens, the slab segment and attached beam can rotate (twist) together about the torsional hinges to form the mechanism, and the negative yield line will not develop at slab–beam junction (in this case, the 'curved axis of rotation' problem discussed above will not arise as the rotation will be about a straight line joining the two torsional hinges). In general, floor beams are not ordinarily designed and detailed for elastic-plastic torsional response and hence torsional hinges are not often considered in yield line theory. However, the limit on T and hence im_x must be taken in to account.

The solution to the collapse load (uniformly distributed) for this condition is given by Eq. 11.12. Experimental studies have shown that the actual collapse load is likely to be higher on account of tensile membrane action[†] (mobilized under large deflections), which is typically ignored in conventional yield line analysis [Ref. 11.39]. Such a mode of failure, in which the supporting edge beams are assumed to remain intact, while the slab alone collapses, may be referred to as *slab-alone failure*. The conventional procedure (See Section 11.3.2) for design of 'slabs supported on stiff beams' adopts moment coefficients which are based on this pattern of failure. Studies indicate that beams have to be 'very stiff' and strong to result in this pattern of failure. Otherwise, the pattern of failure may be different, as discussed below, making the above conventional design procedure and reinforcing pattern inappropriate (and overly conservative) for the actual failure pattern.

It may be noted that in the conventional procedure, the edge beams are designed to resist the effects of tributary loading transmitted from the slab as well as any distributed (or concentrated) loading acting on it directly. They may be analysed as beams supported on RC columns at the ends (isolated from the slab) and subjected to these loads or, more accurately, by appropriately modelled finite element analysis (of the complete beam-slab system and loading). Either way, the mid-span section of each beam is designed for the corresponding factored bending moment. If the beam is not excessively stiff and strong in relation to the slab (as discussed in the para above), when the maximum beam moment at mid-span reaches its flexural capacity, a plastic hinge develops there. When this happens, as observed experimentally, it will trigger simultaneously an yield line formation in the slab that is kinematically compatible, resulting in a failure mechanism of the entire beam-slab system. This may be referred to as *beam-slab failure*, and can occur typically in three different ways, as depicted in patterns II, III and IV in Figure 11.78.

Pattern II shows the collapse mechanism with slab yield-line midway across the long span joining up with beam hinges, with corresponding negative yield lines close to the short-beam supports, as shown in Figure 11.78c. The entire beam-slab system undergoes a 'one-way' failure in the long span direction. In the failure

[†] Much has been said in technical literature about increase in slab strength due to membrane action. It is debatable whether the strength gain due to the slab becoming a 'hammock' is to be reckoned with.

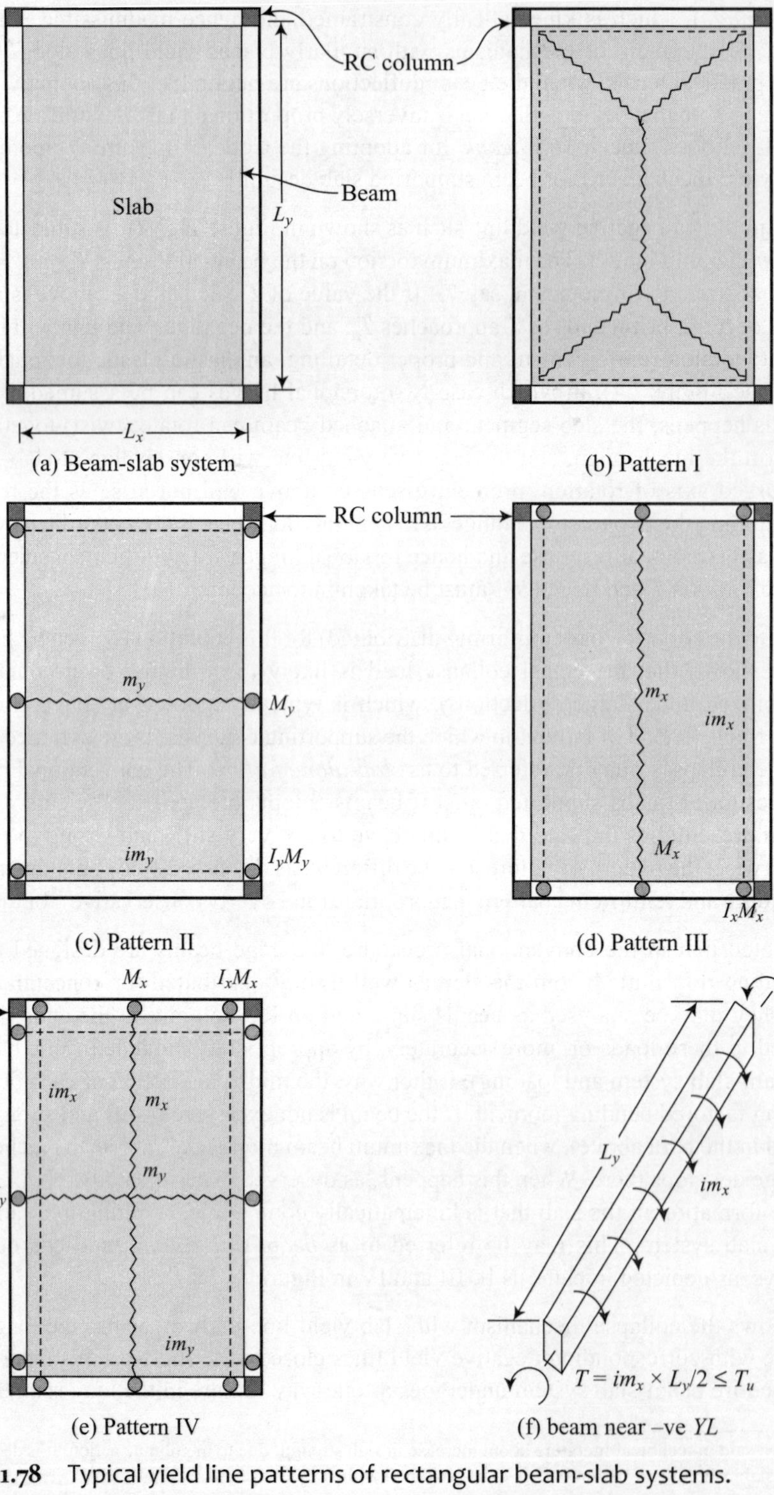

Fig. 11.78 Typical yield line patterns of rectangular beam-slab systems.

mechanism shown in pattern II – found experimentally to be more likely in practice with beams of normal proportions and strength (Ref. 11.34) – the slab steel provided in the short span direction does not yield at collapse, suggesting that it could be reduced, leading to more economical design. Of course, it is necessary to explore all possible failure mechanisms and identify which mechanism is likely to govern (having the lowest collapse load), before such a decision can be made.

With the concept of slab yield lines joining with plastic hinges in beams, as assumed in pattern II, some questions arise which have to be addressed. One of these pertains to the effective beam cross section. With monolithic slab-beam construction, traditionally and rightly, beams are considered to have flanged sections (T, L, etc.). In the beam-slab yield line concept, is the beam section to be taken as rectangular or flanged; and if the latter, what portion of the slab act as flanges and whether this part is to be excluded from the slab yield line? There are studies considering the flanged beam option as well as the rectangular section option. In reality, up until the formation of plastic hinge in the beam, a portion of the slab close to the beam will act as its compression flange, with predominantly compressive stresses in it. As the slab yield line develops and extends towards the beam, with inelastic moment/stress redistribution, the width of this portion will decrease. Since the curvature requirement for formation of slab yield line is usually far greater than that for beam plastic hinge formation, the yield line may join up with the beam hinge only after considerable inelastic rotation takes place at the beam hinge, to match up with the slab's yield curvature. However, even if a short stretch of the slab close to beam does not yield as the ultimate load and collapse mechanism are approached, it appears reasonable to *assume* that the beam consists of only the rectangular section and the slab yield line extends full width, up to the beam face – the slight excess in slab yield line strength reckoned due to inclusion of this short stretch of slab close to beam may be compensated by the under-estimation of beam hinge strength due to ignoring the same stretch acting as beam flange. Test results indicate this assumption to be acceptable.

Another question relates to rotation capacities. The curvature required in the relatively shallow slab to initiate formation of yield-line (i.e. develop m_x or m_y) is far greater than that required for the deeper beam to form a plastic hinge. [The yield curvature, φ_y, can be taken as inversely proportional to the effective depth]. Hence, the beam hinge may have to undergo considerable inelastic rotation without failure (likely far more than required for beam-only mechanisms – Figure 9.9) for the slab yield line to develop fully. While slab yield lines generally have considerable rotation capacity, for beams it is limited. Hence it needs to be ensured that the beam plastic hinges have adequate rotation capacities.

Thus, in the simplified yield line analysis shown here, the total positive yield line flexural strength is taken as the sum of the yield line strength of the slab (m_yL_x) and the plastic hinge moment capacities in the two long-span beams ($2M_y$, M_y being computed for the rectangular beam section). Similarly, the total negative yield line flexural strength is taken as the sum of the yield line strength ($2im_yL_x$) and the negative plastic hinge moment capacities in the two long-span beams ($4I_yM_y$) [Ref 11.36]. As explained earlier, the total strength of a negative yield line along a slab – beam joint is limited to twice the torsional moment capacity of the adjoining beam.

Pattern III, likewise, shows the mechanism with yielding mid-way across the short span, as shown in Figure 11.78d – with a positive yield line running straight down the middle in the long span direction, terminating at the two plastic hinges at the short span beam centres. The total positive yield line flexural strength is obtainable as $m_xL_y + 2M_x$. The total negative yield line flexural strength is obtainable as $2im_xL_y + 4I_xM_x$.

Pattern IV is a combination of patterns II and III, involving the simultaneous development of plastic hinges at the centres and support of all four edge beams and yield lines running down the middle and the beam-slab interface in the two orthogonal directions, as shown in Figure 11.78e. This is the yield line pattern that we can expect in a 'flat plate' without having any edge beams.

Similar yield patterns can be observed in square beam-slab systems as shown in Figure 11.79. Patterns I and III are the biaxially symmetric yield line patterns that can be expected in a perfectly isotropically reinforced square slab. However, in practice, there is likely to be some asymmetry on account of the equally spaced slab reinforcement being provided in two layers (with different effective depths, and hence, slightly different moment capacities), and there is a possibility of yield line pattern II occurring.

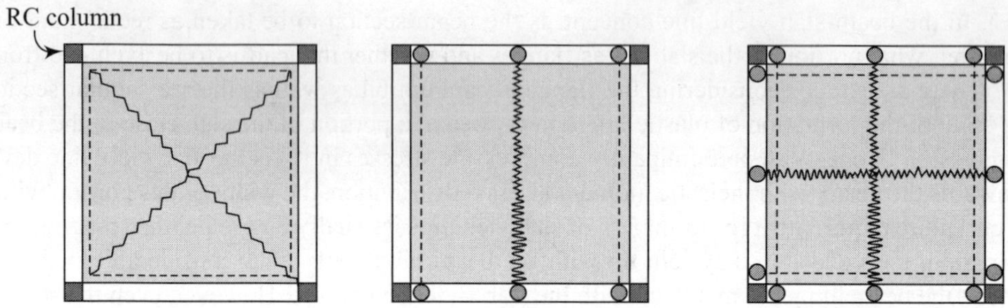

(a) Pattern I (b) Pattern II (c) Pattern III

Fig. 11.79 Typical yield line patterns of a square beam-slab systems.

Finally, it may be noted that while the behaviour of the beam-supported slab is primarily governed by the *relative beam-slab flexural stiffness* in the initial stages of loading (and at service loads), where linear elastic analysis is valid, in the inelastic phase, following the formation of yield lines/plastic hinges, the behaviour is governed primarily by the *relative beam-slab flexural strength and their ductility*. As already discussed in the case of limit analysis of continuous systems (Section 9.6.1), redistribution of moments in the moment field is likely to occur post-yielding. A nonlinear analysis, which accounts for the reinforcement quantities and detailing, is needed to assess the behaviour in this phase. This is, of course, computationally challenging and such fine tuning does not appear to be warranted in the design of regular RC structures. However, an yield line analysis is expected to capture the collapse load and collapse mechanism reasonably well.

In exceptional cases, where the beams have excessive flexural strength, plastic hinge formation in them is unlikely, and a *slab-alone failure* is likely. However, in normal under-reinforced beams, the *combined beam-slab failure* is likely.

11.11.1 Examples of Yield Line Analysis of Beam-Supported Slabs

Example 11.12: Rectangular Beam-Slab System, Orthotropically Reinforced

Apply yield line theory to estimate the collapse load of a rectangular orthotropically reinforced beam-slab, system subjected to a uniformly distributed load of intensity w_u per unit area. Assume the slab to have dimensions of L_x and L_x along the short span and long span directions.

Solution

Pattern I (Fig. 11.78b)

The collapse load formulation given in Example 11.9 (Figure 11.75 and Eq. 11.62) is applicable to beam-slab system with slab-alone failure as given in Figure 11.78(b).

Pattern II

The total collapse load w_u can be found by using the Principle of Virtual Work by applying a virtual displacement δ to the slab centre (Figures 11.78c and 11.80(a)) [Ref. 11.34],

$$W_E = w_u L_x L_y \frac{\delta}{2}$$

$$W_I = (m_y L_x + 2M_y)\frac{2\delta}{L_y/2} + 2(im_y L_x + 2I_y M_y)\frac{\delta}{L_y/2}$$

where m_x and m_y $(= \mu m_x)$ are the moment capacities of slab and M_x and M_y are moment capacities of beam in the short span and long span directions respectively.

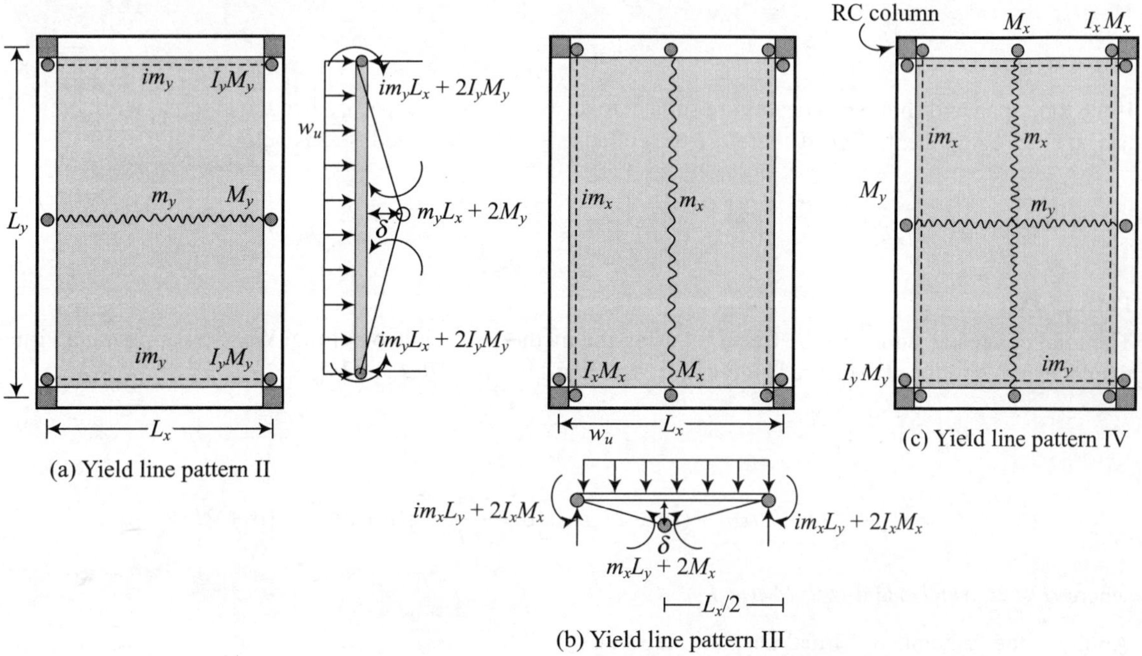

Fig. 11.80 Example 11.12.

Applying the Principle of Virtual Displacements ($W_E = W_I$) and with $L_y/L_x = r$,

$$\Rightarrow \qquad w_u = \frac{8m_x}{r^2 L_x^2}\left[(1+i)\mu + 2(1+I_y)\alpha_y\right]$$

where the $\alpha_y = M_y/(m_x L_x)$

If the long span and short span beams are subject to an additional line load q, then the external work done W_E has an extra component of $qL_y\delta$, therefore the collapse load w_u gets modified as below.

$$w_u = \frac{8m_x}{r^2 L_x^2}\left[(1+i)\mu + 2(1+I_y)\alpha_y\right] - \frac{2q}{L_x} \tag{11.63}$$

Pattern III

Similarly, the total collapse load w_u can be found by using the Principle of Virtual Work by applying a virtual displacement δ to the slab centre [Figures 11.78(d) and 11.80(b)] [Ref. 11.34],

$$W_E = w_u L_x L_y \frac{\delta}{2}$$

$$W_I = (m_x L_y + 2M_x)\frac{2\delta}{L_x/2} + 2(im_x L_y + 2I_x M_x)\frac{\delta}{L_x/2}$$

Applying the Principle of Virtual Displacements ($W_E = W_I$),

$$\Rightarrow \quad w_u = \frac{8m_x}{rL_x^2}\left[(1+i)r + 2(1+I_x)\alpha_x\right]$$

where $\alpha_x = M_x/(m_x L_x)$.

If the long span and short span beams are subject to an additional line load q, then the external work done W_E has an extra component of $qL_x\delta$, therefore the collapse load w_u gets modified as below.

$$w_u = \frac{8m_x}{rL_x^2}\left[(1+i)r + 2(1+I_x)\alpha_x\right] - \frac{2q}{L_y} \tag{11.64}$$

Pattern IV

The total collapse load w_u can be found by using the method Principle of Virtual Work by applying a virtual displacement δ to the slab centre [Figures 11.78(e) and 11.80(c)] [Ref. 11.34],

$$W_E = w_u L_x L_y \frac{\delta}{2}$$

$$W_I = \frac{2m_x L_x}{L_y}\left[(\mu + 2\alpha_y) + (i\mu + 2I_y\alpha_y)\right]\delta + \frac{2m_x L_x}{L_x}\left[(r + 2\alpha_x) + (ir + 2I_x\alpha_x)\right]\delta$$

where $\alpha_x = M_x/(m_x L_x)$ and $\alpha_y = M_y/(m_x L_x)$.

Applying the Principle of Virtual Displacements ($W_E = W_I$),

$$\Rightarrow \quad w_u = \frac{4m_x}{L_x L_y}\left((1+i)\left[\frac{\mu}{r} + r\right] + 2(1+I_y)\frac{\alpha_y}{r} + 2(1+I_x)\alpha_x\right)$$

If the long span and short span beams are subject to an additional line load q, then the external work done W_E has an extra component of $qL_x\delta/2$ and $qL_y\delta/2$, therefore the collapse load w_u gets modified as below.

$$w_u = \frac{4m_x}{L_x L_y}\left((1+i)\left[\frac{\mu}{r} + r\right] + 2(1+I_y)\frac{\alpha_y}{r} + 2(1+I_x)\alpha_x\right) - \frac{q}{L_x} - \frac{q}{L_y} \tag{11.65}$$

This solution should be compared with the solutions obtained earlier for yield line patterns, and the lower of the two values should be considered as the collapse load.

Example 11.13: Collapse Load Estimation of Beam-Slab System (Analysed Using Fem In Section 11.2.6)

Evaluate the collapse load of the rectangular slab supported on beams at the four edges and integrally connected to columns at the four corners, for the three beam sizes, given in Section 11.2.6, using yield line analysis. Assume that the flexural strengths of the slab and beams are exactly equal to values obtained from FEM analysis corresponding to Table 11.2(a) (though in actual reinforcement detailing, the strengths are likely to turn out to be higher). Also, assume that at the slab-beam junctions, top steel is provided, such that it has a hogging moment capacity (im) equal to 50% of the sagging moment (m) in the concerned direction, as per Code requirement. Comment on the results obtained.

Solution

The slab and beam moments obtained from FEM (elastic analysis under factored loads) for the three cases are summarised in Table 11.13 [refer Table 11.12 (a)]. The corresponding input parameters required for yield line analysis are L_x = 4136 mm, L_y = 5128 mm, r = 1.240, ratio of hogging to sagging slab moments i = 0.5, and the other relevant parameters such as orthotropic coefficient (μ), ratio of hogging to sagging beam moments (I_x, I_y) and the constants (α_x, α_y) are given in Table 11.14. The corresponding collapse loads, for all four possible yield line patterns explained in the Example 11.12, calculated using the Eqs 11.62 to 11.65 are given in Table 11.15.

Table 11.13 *Moments obtained from FEM given in Section 11.2.6*

Case	Slab – Short span Moment at centre, m_x (kNm/m)	Slab – Long span Moment at centre, m_y (kNm/m)	Beam – Short span		Beam – Long span	
			Mid-span, M_x (kNm)	Support (hogging) I_xM_x (kNm)	Mid-span, M_y (kNm)	Support (hogging) I_yM_y (kNm)
Beam – 230 × 600	13.49	12.17	38.54	1.39	56.67	3.20
Beam – 230 × 450	14.07	14.28	30.51	2.84	43.65	5.86
Beam – 230 × 300	14.87	17.76	16.23	6.83	22.48	14.20

Table 11.14 *Actual input parameters for collapse load calculation of beam-slab specimens*

Case	$\mu = \frac{m_y}{m_x}$	$I_x = \frac{I_xM_x}{M_x}$	$I_y = \frac{I_yM_y}{M_y}$	$\alpha_x = \frac{M_x}{m_xl_x}$	$\alpha_y = \frac{M_y}{m_xl_x}$	q (kN/m)
Beam – 230 × 600	0.902	0.036	0.056	0.691	1.016	3.450
Beam – 230 × 450	1.015	0.093	0.134	0.524	0.750	2.588
Beam – 230 × 300	1.194	0.421	0.632	0.264	0.366	1.725

Table 11.15 *Estimated collapse loads*

Case	Collapse load (kN/m^2)			
	Pattern I	Pattern II	Pattern III	Pattern IV
Beam – 230 × 600	22.30	12.69	15.40	14.05
Beam – 230 × 450	24.44	12.54	14.94	13.74
Beam – 230 × 300	27.74	12.67	13.97	13.32

From Table 11.15, it is seen that the lowest collapse load corresponds invariably to pattern II, i.e., a combined beam-slab failure along the long span direction. In all cases, the critical collapse load obtained is higher than the factored design load 12.20 kN/m^2 (given in Example 11.2 and Section 11.2.6), thereby assuring Code compliance.

Even when the edge beams are stiff and the results of the elastic FEM analysis suggest predominant bending in the short span direction (Table 11.13), the actual yield line mechanism at collapse (Table 11.15) points to predominant bending in the long span direction.

The collapse load values corresponding to pattern IV are close to the critical values corresponding to pattern II. However, the 'slab alone failure' mechanism, corresponding to pattern I (expected in *wall-supported* slabs), is found to be highly unlikely, predicting collapse load values that are around twice (or more) than the lowest values in all three cases.

Summary: In this Example three beam-supported slabs with different beam stiffnesses were designed, for the slab and beam moments determined using finite element analysis with the simpler (default) modelling. The slab edges were designed for hogging moments equal to 50% of respective mid-span moments.

The yield line analysis, as detailed in this Section, of the beam-supported slabs in this Example, shows that they all have the required ultimate load capacity and will fail in the long span beam-slab failure mode (pattern II). It is also noted that had the design been done by the more accurate finite element analysis, corresponding to Table 11.2(b) (with lower bending moments), and the same analysed by yield line theory as above, the resulting collapse load will fall slightly short of the required strength.

As already stated earlier, elastic theory cannot capture inelastic behaviour, especially in beam-slab systems. For ultimate load evaluations, Codes have been recommending inelastic analyses, such as limit analysis and yield line analysis, under factored loads.

REVIEW QUESTIONS

11.1 Explain clearly the difference in the behaviour of one-way slabs and two-way slabs.

11.2 Explain the need for corner reinforcement in two-way rectangular slabs whose corners are prevented from lifting up.

11.3 Explain the difference in load transfer between wall-supported slabs and beam/column supported slabs.

11.4 Discuss the main considerations that generally govern the thickness of a two-way slab.

11.5 Explain the concept underlying the Rankine-Grashoff theory as applied to uniformly loaded and simply supported rectangular two-way slabs.

11.6 Discuss the assumptions underlying the Code moment coefficients for two-way 'restrained' slabs.

11.7 In the design of a multipanel two-way slab system by the use of the Code moment coefficients, it is found that the design 'negative' moments at continuous supports are often unbalanced. Why does this occur, and how may this problem be resolved?

11.8 Describe how are two-way wall-supported slabs checked for shear.

11.9 How is two-way slab behaviour in a column-supported slab system, with beams along column lines, affected by the stiffnesses of the supporting beams?

11.10 Why is it inappropriate to apply the Code moment coefficients for two-way slabs, if the slabs are supported on flexible beams?

11.11 Explain briefly the 'equivalent frame' concept. Also sketch the variations of moments in a typical two-way slab panel supported on flexible beams.

11.12 Briefly describe the Direct Design Method and compare it with the Equivalent Frame Method.

11.13 What is the function of (i) the *drop panel*, and (ii) the *column capital*, in *flat slab* design?

11.14 Explain how the 'unbalanced' moment is transferred from the slab to the column in flat slabs.

11.15 Discuss briefly how the effects of pattern loading can be included in (i) Direct Design Method (ii) Equivalent Frame Method.

11.16 In flat slabs, what are the parameters, which determine (i) the longitudinal distribution of moments, and (ii) the transverse distribution of moments in a panel?

11.17 In the transverse distribution of moments at critical sections, the column strip is given a larger share than the middle strips. Why?

11.18 Reference 11.8 gives some freedom to the designer in choosing the transverse distribution of moments at critical sections in the slab-beam member in two-way slab systems. How is this justified?

11.19 In flat slab floors, it is desirable to provide an edge beam along the discontinuous edges. Why?

11.20 What are the considerations in the design of edge beams in flat slab floors?

11.21 Explain how shear forces in beams are estimated in two-way slab systems supported on flexible beam.

11.22 Explain the concept of 'equivalent column' in the Equivalent Frame Method.

11.23 What is the difference between one-way shear and two-way shear in column-supported slab systems?

11.24 How is punching shear stress calculated in column-supported slab systems?

11.25 Suggest suitable reinforcement details for resistance against punching shear in flat slabs and flat plates.

11.26 In flat slabs, how can a total punch-through and a progressive collapse prevented?

11.27 Distinguish between *upper bound* and *lower bound* solutions in estimating the collapse load in a slab.

11.28 Describe the steps involved in yield line analysis of slabs. Distinguish between the two alternative methods of formulating the equilibrium condition.

11.29 Show that a concentrated load can result in a local 'fan mode' of collapse in any slab, and show how this load is related to the isotropic flexural strength of the slab.

PROBLEMS

11.1 Design a simply supported slab to cover a hall with internal dimensions 4.0 m × 6.0 m. The slab is supported on masonry walls 230 mm thick. Assume a live load of 3 kN/m^2 and a finish load of 1 kN/m^2. Use M 25 concrete and Fe 500 steel. Assume that the slab corners are free to lift up.

11.2 Repeat Problem 11.1, considering the slab corners to be prevented from lifting up.

11.3 Repeat Problem 11.1, considering the slab to be an internal panel which is part of a multipanel slab system.

11.4 Design the multipanel floor slab system shown in Figure 11.81, assuming a live load of 4.0 kN/m^2 and a floor finish load of 1.0 kN/m^2. The slab is supported on 230 mm thick masonry walls, as shown. Use M 25 concrete and Fe 500 steel.

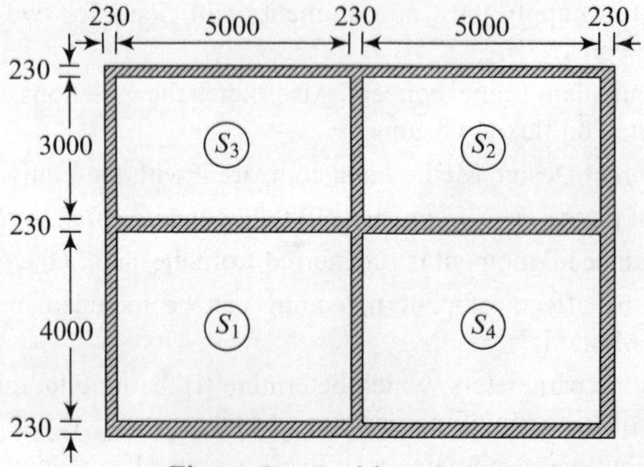

Fig. 11.81 Problem 11.4.

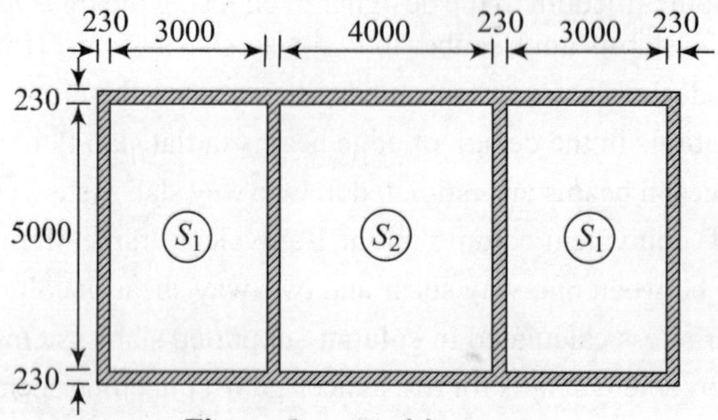

Fig. 11.82 Problem 11.5

11.5 Design the multipanel floor slab system shown in Figure 11.82, assuming a live load of 4.0 kN/m^2 and a floor finish load of 1.0 kN/m^2. The slab is supported on 230 mm thick masonry walls, as shown. Use M 25concrete and Fe 500steel.

11.6 Design the slab panels S_1 and S_2 in the multi-panel floor system of Example 11.6, [Figure 11.48] using the Code moment coefficients, assuming that the supporting beams are adequately stiff. Compare the results with those obtained earlier. (in Example 11.6).

11.7 Design a circular slab of 4.0 m diameter (overall), simply supported at the periphery, by a masonry wall 230 mm thick. Assume a live load of 5.0 kN/m^2 and a finish load of 1.0 kN/m^2. Use M 25concrete and Fe 500steel.

11.8 In continuation with Example 11.6, apply the Direct Design Method to design the corner panel in the slab system [Figure 11.48].

11.9 Repeat Example 11.6, considering the slab system as a *flat slab* system, with suitable beams only along the exterior edges and with suitable drop panels.

11.10 Repeat Example 11.7, applying the Direct Design Method, instead of the Equivalent Frame Method.

11.11 Repeat Example 11.6, applying Equivalent Frame Method instead of the Direct Design Method.

11.12 Redesign the interior equivalent frame in Example 11.7, assuming that beams 300 mm wide and 500 mm deep (overall) are provided along the column lines, and no drop panels are used.

11.13 (a) Sketch the most probable yield line pattern for a uniformly loaded square slab (of side L) supported on columns located at (i) 4 corners, (ii) 3 corners, and (iii) 2 opposite corners.

(b) For case (iii) above, derive an expression for the collapse load w_u (kN/m^2) in terms of the ultimate moment of resistance m (kNm/m) and dimension L (m), assuming the slab to be isotropically reinforced. Hence determine the value of w_u, given L = 3.0 m, effective depth = 100 mm, reinforcement 8 mm ϕ @ 200 mm c/c, M25 concrete and Fe 500 steel.

11.14 A rectangular slab *ABCD* with an aspect ratio of 1.2, is fixed at the edges *AB*, *BC* and *CD*, with the short edge *DA* (length *a*) free. If the slab is isotropically reinforced and subject to a uniformly distributed load, derive, using yield line theory, an expression for the collapse load w_u in terms of the ultimate moment capacities per unit width, m (corresponding to bottom steel) and m' (corresponding to top steel near the supports) and the dimension a.

11.15 Derive an expression for the collapse load w_u (uniformly distributed) of an isotropically reinforced slab panel which is an equilateral triangle (side L), simply supported on two adjacent edges and free along the third edge.

11.16 Derive the expressions for the collapse load w_u (uniformly distributed) of an isotropically reinforced square beam-slab panel (side L), supported at the corners using integrally connected columns as shown in Figure 11.80.

REFERENCES

11.1 Timoshenko, S, and Woinosky-Krieger, S, *Theory of Plates and Shells*, McGraw-Hill Book Co., New York, 1959

11.2 Westergaard, H M and Slater, W A, *Moments and Stresses in Slabs*, Proc. ACI, Vol. 17, 1921, pp 415–538

11.3 Westergaard H M, *Formulas for the Design of Rectangular Floor Slabs and the Supporting Girders*, Proc. ACI, Vol. 22, 1926, pp 26–46

11.4 Di Stasio, J and Van Buren, M P, *Slabs supported on Four Sides*, Proc. ACI Vol. 32, pp 350–364

11.5 Purushothaman, P, *Reinforced Concrete Structural Elements — Behaviour, Analysis and Design,* Tata McGraw Hill Publ. Co. Ltd., New Delhi, 1984

11.6 Park, R and Gamble, W L, *Reinforced Concrete Slabs*, Second Edition, John Wiley & Sons, New York, 2000

11.7 Zienkiewicz, O C, *The Finite Element Method in Engineering Sciences*, Second edition, McGraw-Hill Book Co., London, 1971

11.8 Johansen, K W, *Yield Line Theory*, (translated from the Danish), Cement and Concrete Association, London, 1962

11.9 Jones, L L and Wood, R H, *Yield Line Analysis of Slabs*, Thames and Hudson, Chatto and Windus, London, 1967

11.10 Shukla, S N, *Handbook for Design of Slabs by Yield Line and Strip Methods*, Structural Engineering Research Centre, Roorkee, India, 1973

11.11 — *Explanatory Handbook on Indian Standard Code of Practice for Plain and Reinforced Concrete (IS 456:1978)*, Special Publication SP:24, Bureau of Indian Standards, New Delhi, 1983

11.12 Tayler, R, Hayes, B and Bhai, M, *Coefficients for Design of Slabs by Yield Line Theory*, Concrete, Vol. 13, no. 5, 1969

11.13 —*Structural Use of Concrete: Part 1: Code of Practice for Design and Construction*, BS 8110: Part 1: 1985, British Standards Institution, 1985

11.14 — *Handbook on Concrete Reinforcement and Detailing,* Special Publication SP 34, Bureau of Indian Standards, New Delhi, 1987

11.15 Haan, J, *Structural Analysis of Beams and Slabs*, Sir Isaac Pitman and Sons, London, 1966

11.16 Reynolds, C E and Steedman, J C, *Reinforced Concrete Designer's Handbook*, Rupa & Co., Delhi, 1981

11.17 Krishnamoorthy C S, *Finite Element Analysis: Theory and Programming*, Tata McGraw Hill Education, 1994

11.18 Rombach G A, *Finite Element Design of Concrete Structures*, Thomas Telford Publishing, London, 1994

11.19 Wood, H R, *The Reinforcements of Slabs in Accordance with a Pre-determined Field of Moments*, *Concrete*, Vol. 2, No. 2, 1968, pp 69–76

11.20 Regan, P E and Yu, C W, *Limit State Design for Structural Concrete*, Chatto and Windus, London, 1973

11.21 CSA Standard A23.3–14 — *Design of Concrete Structures*, Canadian Standards Association, Mississauga, Ontario, 2014

11.22 — *Building Code Requirements for Reinforced Concrete*, ACI Standard 318–05, Am. Conc. Inst., Detroit, Michigan, USA, 2005

11.23 Sozen, M A and Siess, C P, *Investigation of Multiple-Panel Reinforced Concrete Floor Slabs: Design Methods — Their Evolution and Comparison*, Journal ACI, Proc. Vol. 60, No. 8, Aug. 1963, pp 999–1028

11.24 Corley, W G, and Jirsa, J O, *Equivalent Frame Analysis for Slab Design*, Journal ACI, Proc. Vol. 67, No. 11, Nov. 1970, pp 875–884

11.25 Gamble, W L, *Moments in Beam Supported Slabs*, Journal ACI, Proc. Vol. 69, No. 3, Mar. 1972, pp 149–157

11.26 Hanson, N W, and Hanson, J M, *Shear and Moment Transfer Between Concrete Slabs and Columns*, Journal, PCA Research and Development Laboratories, Vol. 10, No. 1, Jan. 1968, pp 2–16

11.27 Gamble, W L, Sozen, M A, and Seiss, C P, *Tests on a Two-Way Reinforced Concrete Floor Slab*, Proc. ASCE, Journal of Struct. Div., Vol. 95, No. ST6, June 1969, pp 1073–1096

11.28 *Concrete Design Handbook*, Canadian Portland Cement Association, Ottawa, Canada, 1985

11.29 *Commentary on Building Code Requirements for Reinforced Concrete* (ACI 318–89), American Concrete Institute, Detroit, Michigan, 1989

11.30 ACI–ASCE Committee 326, *Shear and Diagonal Tension*, Journal ACI, Proc. Vol. 59, Nos. 1–3, Jan–March 1962

11.31 ACI–ASCE Committee 426, *The Shear Strength of Reinforced Concrete Members*, Proc. ASCE, Vol. 100, No. ST 8, Aug. 1974, pp 1543–1591

11.32 Pillai, S U, Kirk, W, and Scavuzzo, L, *Shear Reinforcement at Slab-Column Connections in a Reinforced Concrete Flat Plate Structure*, Journal ACI, Proc. Vol. 79, No. 1, Jan.–Feb. 1982, pp 36–42.

11.33 Menon, D, *Structural Analysis*, Narosa Publishing House, Delhi, 2008

11.34 Balakrishnan, B and Menon, D, *Collapse Load Estimation of Rectangular Reinforced Concrete Beam-Slab Systems – New Insights*. ACI Structural Journal, Vol. 115, No. 5, 2018, pp 1279–1294

11.35 Balakrishnan, B and Menon, D, *Yield Line Analysis and Testing of Reinforced Concrete Rectangular Slabs with Primary and Secondary Beams*. ACI Structural Journal, Vol. 116, No. 5, 2019, pp 187–200

11.36 Balakrishnan, B and Menon, D, *Square Beam-Slab Systems: Resolving a Design Controversy Related to Collapse Mechanism*. Journal of The Institution of Engineers (India): Series A, Springer, 2020

11.37 Singh, A, Balakrishnan, B and Menon, D, *Economical and Rational Design of 'One-way' RC Beam-Slab Systems*. Indian Concrete Journal, Vol. 94, No. 3, 2020, pp 12–22

11.38 Singh, A, Balakrishnan, B and Menon, D, *Combined Beam-Slab Collapse Mechanism in Isolated Reinforced Concrete Beam-Slabs — Strength Design and Load Testing*. ACI Structural Journal, Vol. 118, No. 3, May 2021.

11.39 Bailey, C G, *Membrane action of unrestrained lightly reinforced concrete slabs at large displacements*., Engineering Structures, Vol. 23, No. 5, 2001, pp 470–483

CHAPTER 12

Design of Staircases

LEARNING OBJECTIVES

After studying this chapter, you will be able to:

- *Explain the geometrical and structural configurations and general requirements for common types of staircases*
- *Analyse staircase structures for determination of load effects at critical sections, to facilitate design*
- *Design members and detail reinforcements for common types of staircase*

12.1 Introduction

Structurally, a staircase essentially consists of slabs, with or without beams. Design of slabs and beams have already been dealt with. Fresh considerations here relate to evaluation of design moments, shears, etc., in the various elements for the different configurations.

Functionally, the important characteristics defining the user comfort of a staircase are the dimensions of the *tread*, *riser* and *width* of steps, and the number of steps in a *flight*.

The design of staircases is generally included in a first course on reinforced concrete design, and for this reason, this topic is included in this book. It should be noted that, from a structural viewpoint, the staircase merely comprises slab/beam elements, whose basic principles of design have already been dealt with in the previous chapters.

Functionally, the staircase is an important component of a building, and often the only means of access between the various floors in the building. It consists of a *flight* of steps, usually with one or more intermediate *landings* (horizontal slab platforms) provided between the floor levels. The horizontal top portion[†] of a step (where the foot rests) is termed *tread* and the vertical projection of the step (i.e., the vertical distance between two neighbouring steps) is called *riser* [Figure 12.1]. Values of 300 mm and 150 mm are ideally assigned to the tread and riser respectively – particularly in public buildings. However, lower values of tread (up to 250 mm) combined with higher values of riser (up to 190 mm) are resorted to in residential and factory buildings. The *width* of the stair is generally around 1.1–1.6 m, and

[†] The tread is sometimes projected outwards to increase the effective tread width; this projection is termed nosing. Frequently, the nosing is provided in the finish over the concrete tread

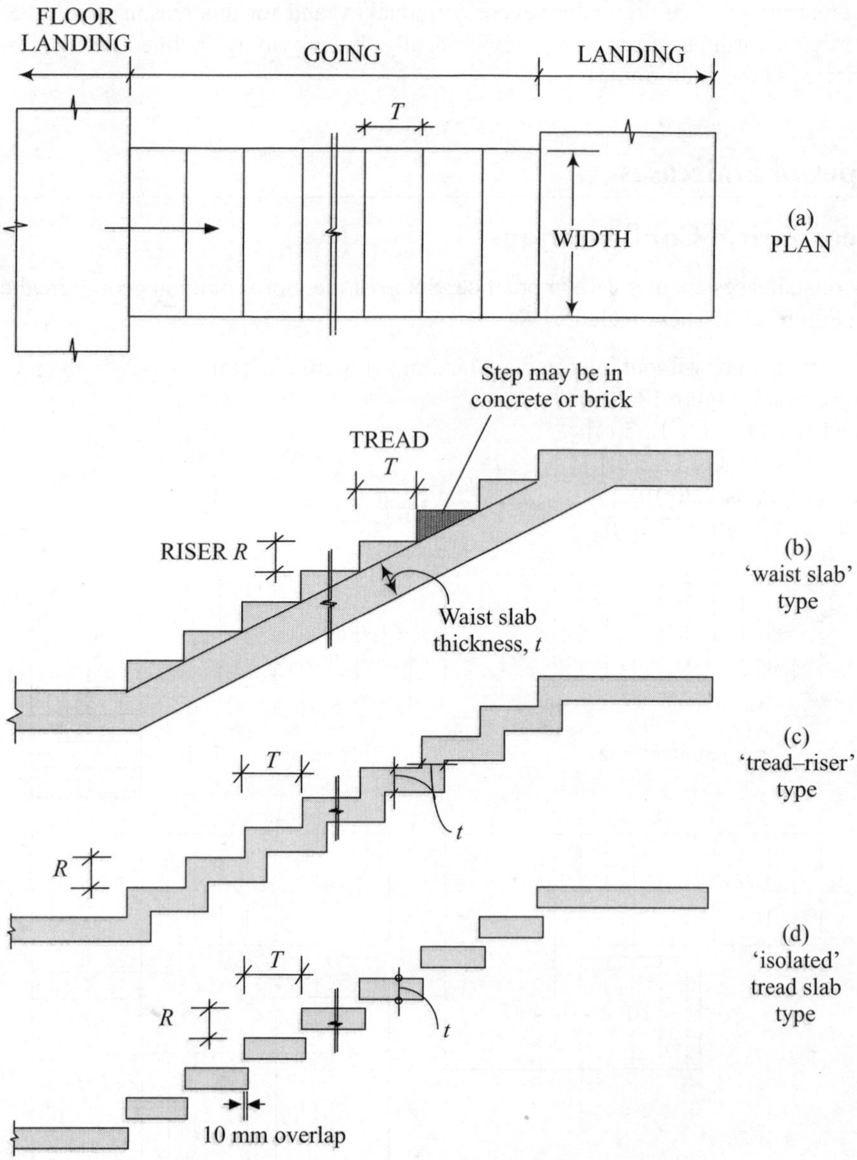

Fig. 12.1 A typical flight in a staircase.

in any case, should normally not be less than 850 mm; large stair widths are encountered in entrances to public buildings. The horizontal projection (plan) of an inclined flight of steps, between the first and last risers, is termed *going*. A typical flight of steps consists of two landings and one going, as depicted in Figure 12.1(a). Generally, risers in a flight should not exceed about 12 in number. The steps in the flight can be designed in a number of ways: with *waist slab*, with *tread-riser* arrangement (without waist slab) or with *isolated tread slabs*, as shown in Figures 12.1(b), (c), (d) respectively.

Staircases are often prone to failure under severe earthquakes, and for this reason should be designed and detailed with care in earthquake-prone regions – ideally, by providing inclined stringer beams that are integrally connected to the main frames.

12.2 Types of Staircases

12.2.1 Geometrical Configurations

A wide variety of staircases are met with in practice. Some of the more common geometrical configurations are depicted in Figure 12.2. These include:

- straight stairs (with or without intermediate landing) [Figure 12.2(a)]
- quarter-turn stairs [Figure 12.2(b)]
- dog-legged stairs [Figure 12.2(c)]
- open well stairs [Figure 12.2(d)]
- spiral stairs [Figure 12.2(e)]
- helicoidal stairs [Figure 12.2(f)]

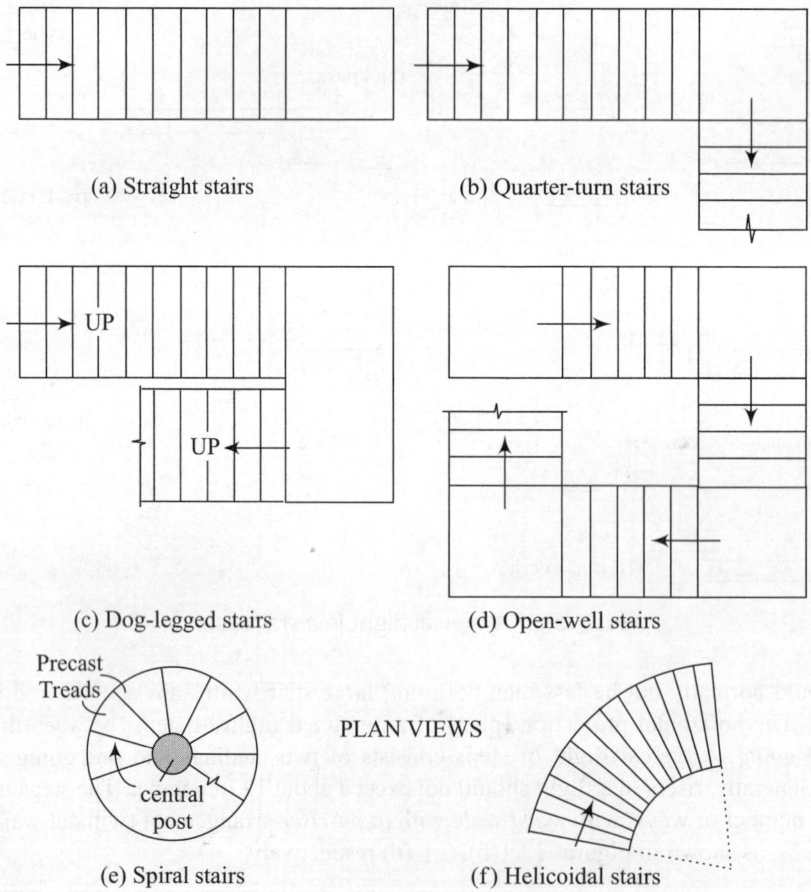

Fig. 12.2 Common geometrical configurations of stairs.

The architectural considerations involved in the selection and location of staircases include accessibility, function, comfort, lighting, ventilation, aesthetics, etc. Structural feasibility also has a major role in deciding the proportioning of the slab thickness (dimension '*t*' in Figure 12.1) which contributes much to the aesthetic appeal of a staircase. Perhaps the most daring of all staircases is the *free-standing staircase* which is supported entirely at the base, and behaves essentially as a cantilever in space [Ref. 12.1, 12.2, 12.7]. The helicoidal staircase (or ramp), with intermediate supports also presents a challenging problem of structural analysis [Ref. 12.3, 12.4, 12.7]. These problems, however, are not discussed in the present chapter, the scope of which is limited to those with simple geometrical configurations.

While some common staircase layouts have been described here, many other elegant and aesthetically appealing layouts have been used in practice, depending on the creative imagination of the architect in charge.

12.2.2 Structural Classification

Structurally, staircases may be classified largely into two categories, depending on the predominant direction in which the slab component of the stair undergoes flexure:

1. stair slab spanning transversely (stair width-wise);
2. stair slab spanning longitudinally (along the incline).

Stair Slab Spanning Transversely

This category generally includes:

1. slab cantilevered from a spandrel beam or wall [Figure 12.3(a)];
2. slab doubly cantilevered from a central spine beam [Figure 12.3(b)]; and
3. slab supported between two stringer beams or walls [Figure 12.3(c)].

The slab component of the stair (whether comprising an isolated tread slab, a tread-riser unit or a waist slab [Figure 12.1]) is supported on its side(s) or cantilevers laterally from a central support [Figure 12.3]. The slab supports gravity loads by bending essentially in a *transverse vertical plane*, with the span along the *width* of the stair.

In the case of the cantilevered slabs [Figures 12.3(a), (b)], it is economical to provide isolated treads[†] (without connected risers), as indicated in Figure 12.1(d). However, the tread-riser type of arrangement [Figure 12.1(c)] and the waist slab type [Figure 12.1(b)] are also sometimes employed in practice, as cantilevers. The spandrel beam is subjected to torsion ('primary torsion'), in addition to flexure and shear.

When the slab is supported at the two sides by means of 'stringer beams' or masonry walls [Figure 12.3(c)], it may be designed as simply supported, but reinforcement at the top should be provided near the supports to resist the 'negative' moments that may arise on account of possible partial fixity.

It may be noted that, although the stair slab spans *transversely*, the supporting spandrel/spine/stringer beams span *longitudinally* along the incline of the stair, framing into supporting columns. The design of the beam is not discussed in this chapter, as all the design principles have already been covered in earlier chapters.

[†] The isolated tread slabs are often *precast*. The treads may form part of a straight flight or a curved flight [Figures 12.2(e), (f)]. For example, in a reinforced concrete chimney or tower, cantilevered tread slabs are fixed to the circular shaft and arranged in a helicoidal pattern.

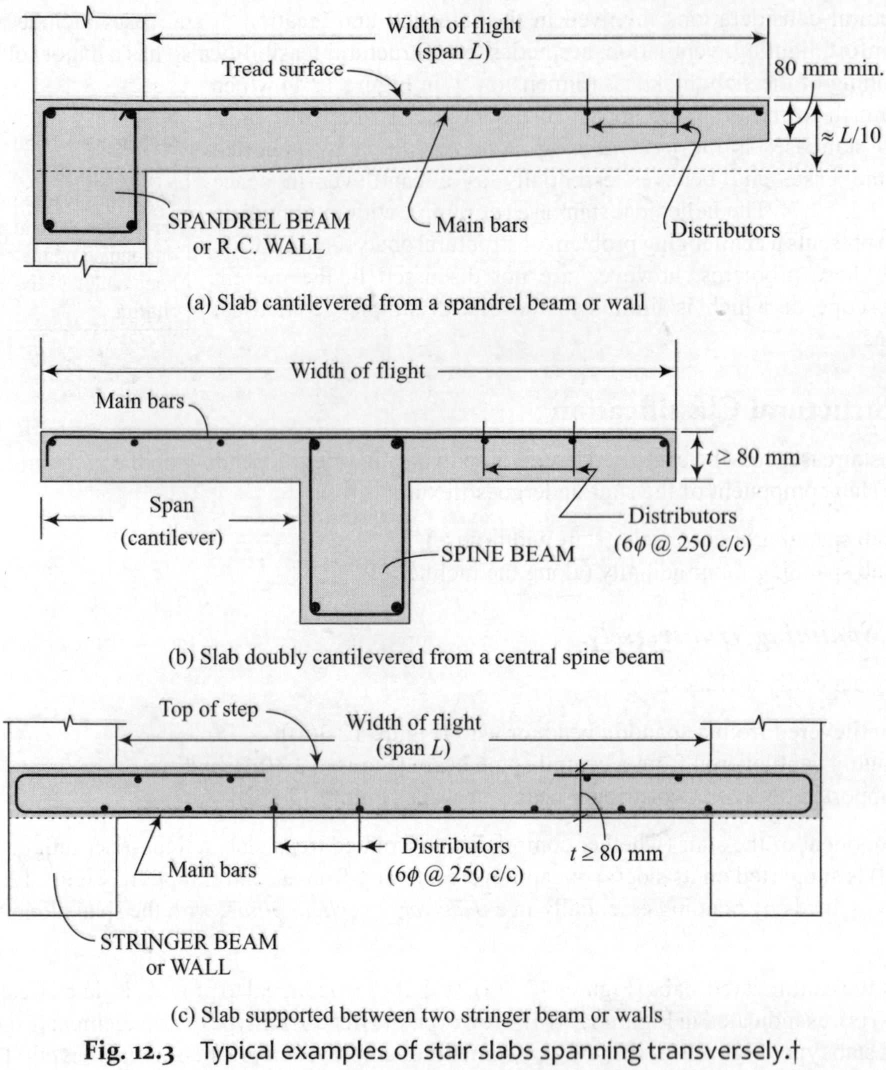

(a) Slab cantilevered from a spandrel beam or wall

(b) Slab doubly cantilevered from a central spine beam

(c) Slab supported between two stringer beam or walls

Fig. 12.3 Typical examples of stair slabs spanning transversely.†

When the slab is doubly cantilevered from a central (spine) beam [Figure 12.3(b)], it is essential to ensure, by proper detailing, that the slab does not separate from the beam when loaded on one side only. This can be done by anchoring the slab reinforcement into the beam, so that the same reinforcement acts as a stirrup in the beam, as shown in Figure 12.3(b). Alternative arrangements are possible; however, it should be ensured that the beam stirrups are 'closed', to provide the desired torsional resistance. When the slab units are precast, suitable mechanical connections have to be provided between the beam and the slab units.

Stair Slab Spanning Longitudinally

In this case, the supports to the stair slab are provided parallel to the riser at two or more locations, causing the slab to bend longitudinally between the supports, as shown in Figure 12.4. It may be noted that longitudinal

† The figures depict transverse sections of the stairs.

bending can occur in configurations other than the straight stair configuration (shown in Figure 12.4), such as quarter-turn stairs, dog-legged stairs, open well stairs and helicoidal stairs [Figure 12.2].

The slab arrangement may either be the conventional 'waist slab' type [Figure 12.1(b)] or the 'tread-riser' type [Figure 12.1(c)]. The slab thickness depends on the 'effective span', which should be taken as the centre-to-centre distance between the beam/wall supports, according to the Code (Cl. 33.1a, c). Figure 12.4(a) shows

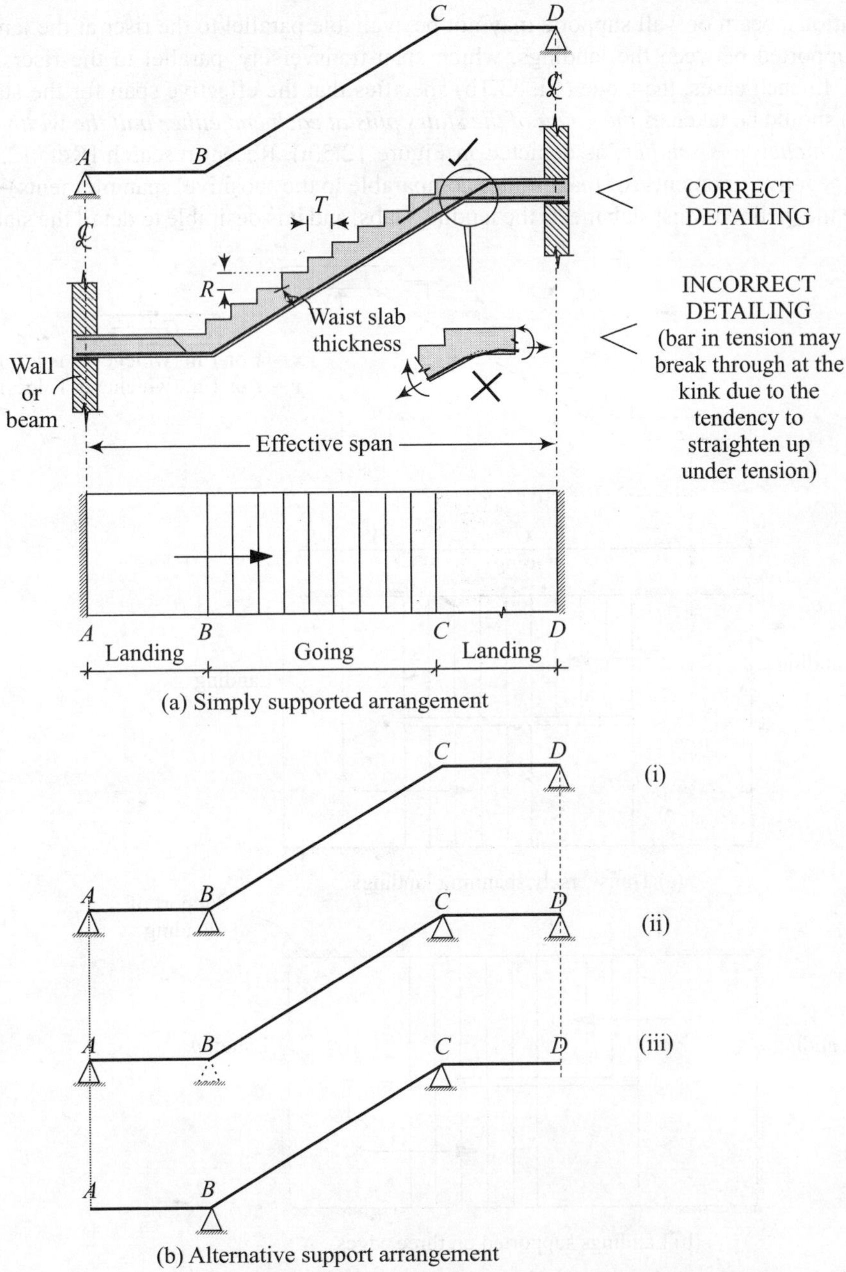

Fig. 12.4 Typical examples of stair slabs spanning longitudinally.

a simple arrangement with simple supports at the far ends of the two landings. However, such an arrangement can result in large slab thicknesses for relatively long spans (4 m or more). In such cases, it is economical to reduce the span, and hence the slab thickness, by providing additional intermediate supports – at locations '*B*' and '*C*', as shown in Figure 12.4(b); this will induce 'negative' moments near the supports, requiring steel at the top in these regions. It is sometimes economical to provide supports at *B* and *C* alone and to treat the landings (*AB*, *CD*) as overhangs – as depicted in the 'balanced cantilever' design shown in Figure 12.4(b)(iii).

In certain situations, beam or wall supports may not be available parallel to the riser at the landing. Instead, the flight is supported between the landings, which span transversely, parallel to the risers, as shown in Figure 12.5(a). In such cases, the Code (Cl. 33.1b) specifies that the effective span for the stairs (spanning longitudinally) should be taken as *the going of the stairs plus at each end either half the width of the landing or one metre, whichever is smaller*, as depicted in Figure 12.5(a). Recent research [Ref. 12.5, 12.6, 12.8] indicates that 'negative' moments (of magnitudes comparable to the 'positive' span moments) develop at the junction where the inclined waist slab meets the landing slabs, and it is desirable to detail the slab accordingly.

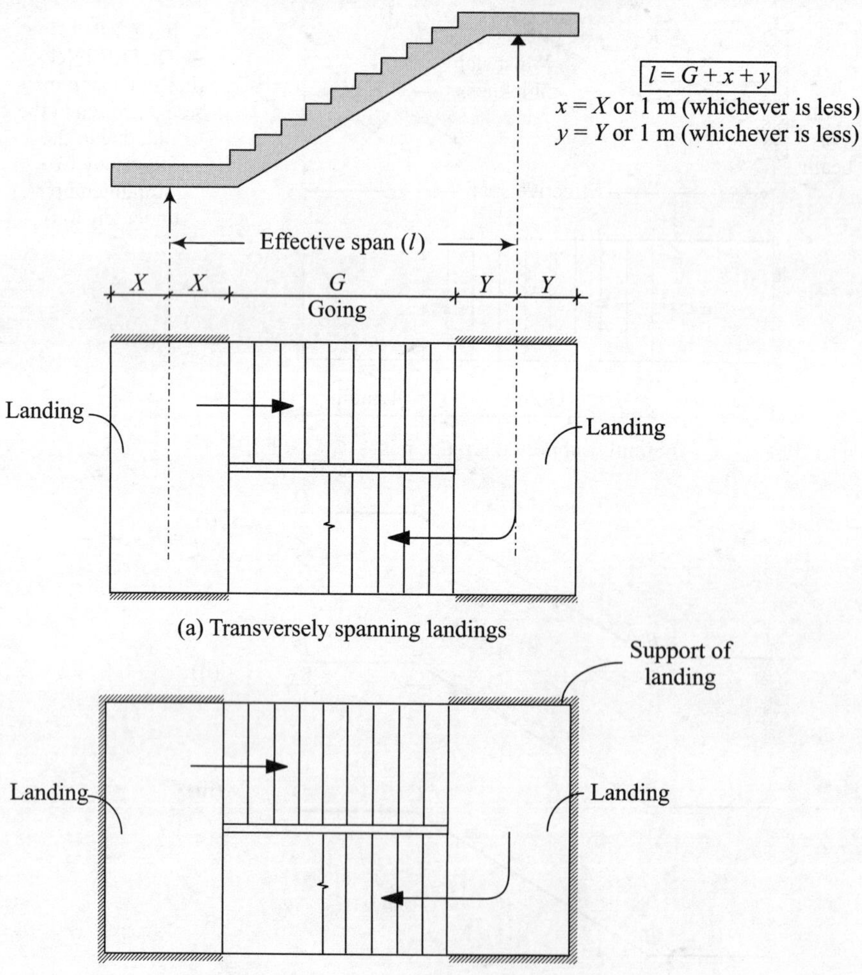

Fig. 12.5 Special support conditions for longitudinally spanning stair slabs.

Another case frequently encountered in residential and office buildings is that of the landings supported on three sides, as shown in Figure 12.5(b). This case has not been explicitly covered by the Code. The ACI Code and BS Code also do not have any special provision as yet for this condition. However, recent studies (based on experiments as well as finite element analysis) reveal that the flight essentially spans between the landing-going junctions, with hogging moments developing at these junctions. It is recommended that an economical and conservative design can be achieved by designing for a 'positive' moment of $wl^2/8$ for the going (at midspan) and a 'negative' moment of $wl^2/8$ at the junction of landing and the going[†]. Here, w is the distributed gravity load acting on the going and l is the length of the going (projected on a horizontal plane) [Ref. 12.5, 12.6, 12.8].

12.3 Loads and Load Effects on Stair Slabs

Stair slabs are usually designed to resist gravity loads[‡], comprising *dead loads* and *live loads*.

12.3.1 Dead Loads

The components of the dead load to be considered comprise:

- self-weight of stair slab (tread/tread-riser slab/waist slab);
- self-weight of step (in case of 'waist slab' type stairs);
- self-weight of tread finish (usually 0.5–1.0 kN/m^2)
- self-weight of hand rails/parapets, if any.

The unit weight of reinforced concrete for the slab and step may be taken as 25 kN/m^3 as specified in the Code (Cl. 19.2.1).

12.3.2 Live Loads

Live loads are generally assumed to act as uniformly distributed loads on the horizontal projection of the flight, i.e., on the 'going'. The Loading Code [IS 875 : 1987 (Part II)] recommends a uniformly distributed load of 5.0 kN/m^2 in general, on the going, as well as the landing. However, in buildings (such as residences) where the specified floor live loads do not exceed 2.0 kN/m^2, and the staircases are not liable to be overcrowded, the Loading Code recommends a lower live load of 3.0 kN/m^2 [Figure 12.6(a)].

Further, in the case of *structurally independent cantilever steps*, the Loading Code requires the tread slab to be capable of safely resisting a concentrated live load of 1.3 kN applied to the free end of each cantilevered tread [Figure 12.6(b)].

It may be noted that the specified live loads are *characteristic* loads; these loads as well as the characteristic dead loads should be multiplied by the appropriate *load factors* in order to provide the *factored loads* required for 'limit state design'.

[†] More detailed expressions for design moments in dog-legged and open-well stairs (with waist slab or with tread-riser) are described in Ref. 12.8.

[‡] In the case of cantilevered tread slabs, the effects of *seismic* loads should also be investigated. The vertical vibrations induced by earthquakes may induce flexural stresses of considerable magnitude. It is desirable to provide bottom steel in the cantilever slabs (near the support locations) to counter the possibility of reversal of stresses.

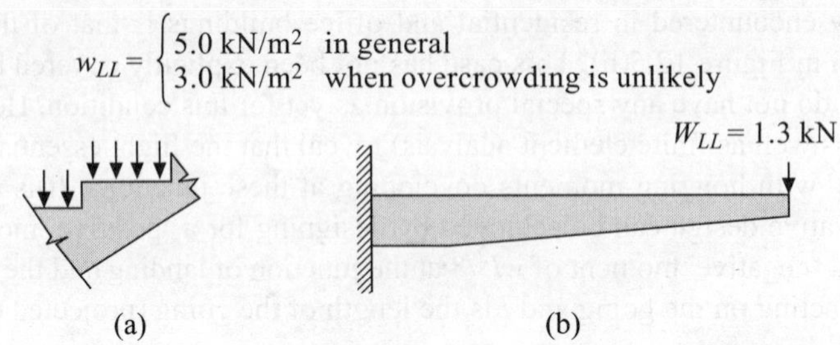

Fig. 12.6 Code specifications for live loads on stair slabs.

12.3.3 Distribution of Gravity Loads in Special Cases

The Code (Cl. 33.2) specifies the following:

- When a staircase takes a right-angled turn [Figures 12.2 b, d], 50 per cent of the gravity loads on the areas (usually landings) common to the two flights (at right angles) may be assumed to act in each direction.
- When a longitudinally spanning flight (or landing) is embedded at least 110 mm into a side wall, then some marginal 'two-way' action can be expected. In such cases, the longitudinally acting component of the gravity load can be assumed to act on a reduced width of flight; a reduction of 150 mm from the face of the side wall is permitted by the Code. Furthermore, the effective width of the section can be increased by 75 mm (into the support) for purposes of design. In other words, if the width of the flight be W (in mm) then the load may be assumed to act over a reduced width (W – 150) mm and the effective width resisting flexure may be taken as (W + 75) mm.

12.3.4 Load Effects in Isolated Tread Slabs

As mentioned earlier, isolated tread slabs [Figure 12.1(d)] are invariably associated with stair slabs spanning transversely. The tread slabs are structurally independent and are designed as simple one-way/cantilever slabs as the case may be.

If the tread slab is simply supported, the thickness required is generally minimal (for stair widths less than 2 m). A slab thickness of 80 mm is usually provided, with minimum reinforcement (comprising at least 3 nos 8 mm ϕ bars). The distribution bars may be of 6 mm ϕ, with a nominal spacing of 250 mm. It suffices to use Fe 250 grade steel in such cases, as the steel requirement is minimal.

In the case of cantilevered tread slabs [Figures 12.3a,b], the slab thickness at support may be taken as at least one-tenth of the effective cantilever span. For large spans, it is economical to taper the slab thickness to a minimum value of 80 mm at the free end, as shown in Figure 12.3(a). The design of a cantilevered tread slab is demonstrated in Example 12.1.

12.3.5 Load Effects in Waist Slabs

In the 'waist slab' type staircase, the longitudinal axis of the flight is inclined to the horizontal and the steps form a series of triangles on top of the waist slab [Figures 12.1(b), 12.7(a)]. The steps[†] are usually treated as non-structural elements and it is the waist slab which is designed to resist the load effects on the stairs.

[†] The steps are sometimes constructed using brickwork.

Some nominal reinforcement is provided in the step (if made in concrete) – mainly to protect the nosing from cracking [Figure 12.7(a)].

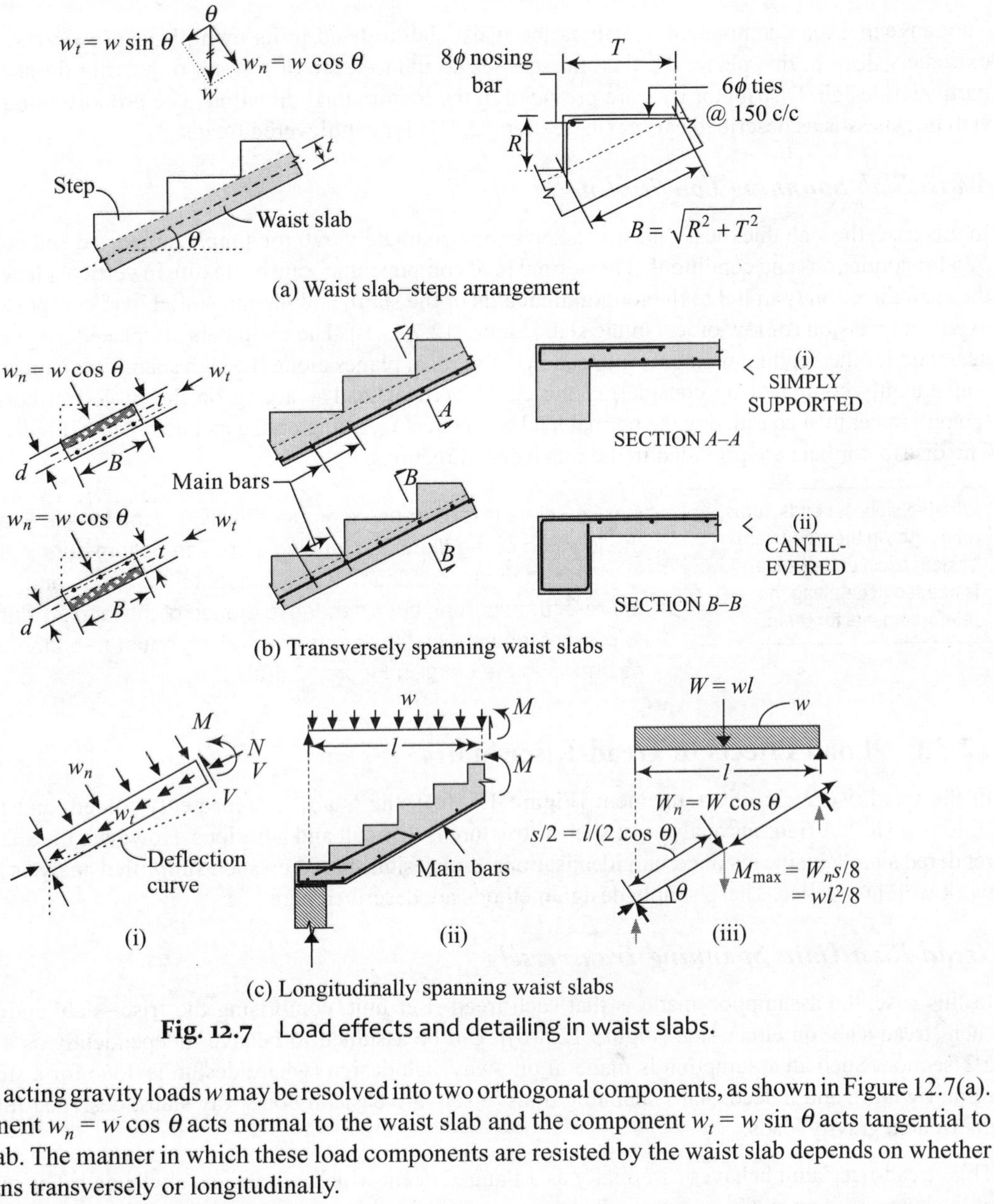

Fig. 12.7 Load effects and detailing in waist slabs.

The vertical acting gravity loads w may be resolved into two orthogonal components, as shown in Figure 12.7(a). The component $w_n = w \cos\theta$ acts normal to the waist slab and the component $w_t = w \sin\theta$ acts tangential to the waist slab. The manner in which these load components are resisted by the waist slab depends on whether the slab spans transversely or longitudinally.

Waist Slab Spanning Transversely

In this case, the normal load component w_n causes the waist slab to bend in transverse planes normal to the sloping surface of the slab. The loading direction, cross-sectional dimensions, neutral axis position, compression zone, main reinforcement and effective depth for a design strip of slab having a width B

corresponding to one tread (one step) are sketched in Figures 12.7(b)(i),(ii) for the simply supported and cantilever cases respectively. As can be seen, the main bars[†] are provided transversely, either at the bottom or top, depending on whether the slab is simply supported or cantilevered.

The tangential load component w_t causes the waist slab to bend in its own plane. However, as the slab is extremely deep in this plane, the flexural stresses so induced are of a small order, and do not call for any particular design. Distributor bars are provided in the longitudinal direction. The proportioning of the waist slab thickness is as described earlier (in Section 12.3.4) for cantilevered treads.

Waist Slab Spanning Longitudinally

In this case, the slab thickness t may be taken as approximately $l/20$ for simply supported end conditions and $l/25$ for continuous end conditions. The normal load component w_n causes flexure in vertical planes containing the span direction (parallel to the longitudinal axis of the slab), and the tangential load component w_t causes axial compression (of low order) in the slab [Figure 12.7(c)(i)]. The main bars are placed longitudinally, and designed for the bending moments induced in the vertical planes along the slab span. These moments may be conveniently computed by considering the entire vertical load w acting on the projected horizontal span (going), rather than considering the normal load component w_n acting on the inclined span s [Figure 12.7(c)(iii)]. The distributor bars are provided in the transverse directions.

With the slopes, bends, turns, joints etc., in the slab/beam of staircases, extreme care is needed in detailing the reinforcements for them.

Care must be taken to ensure proper detailing of the longitudinal bars at the junction of the flight and landing slab. The bottom bars in the waist slab should not be continued to the bottom of the upper landing slab at the re-entrant corner, but extended to the top of the landing slab. This is to prevent the bars (in tension) from breaking out at re-entrant corners, as shown in the detail in Figure 12.4(a).

12.3.6 Load Effects in Tread-Riser Stairs

In the tread-riser type of arrangement [Figure 12.1(c)], the 'slab'[‡] is repeatedly folded, and looks like a 'folded plate'[§]. A rigorous analysis of such a structure is difficult and laborious. However, the analysis can be rendered simple by means of certain idealisations, and designs based on such simplified analysis are found to work well in practice. These simple design methods are described here.

Tread-Riser Units Spanning Transversely

In this case, the assumption made is that each tread-riser unit, comprising the 'riser slab' and one-half of each 'tread slab' on either side [Figure 12.8(b)], can be assumed to behave independently as a beam with a *Z*-section. Such an assumption is made in one-way slab design (where design is done for a standard strip of unit width), and indeed, slabs spanning transversely are basically one-way slabs, designed for uniformly distributed gravity loads.

This 'tread-riser' unit behaves essentially as a flanged beam which is transversely loaded. The overall depth of the beam is given by $(R + t)$, where R is the riser and t the thickness of the 'slab' [Figure 12.8(a)]. Note that

[†] It is desirable to provide a bar in line with every point where the step meets the waist slab, as the effective depth is minimum at this location, if the step is considered to behave integrally with the waist slab. This is shown in Figure 12.7(b).

[‡] Sometimes, this type of stair is referred to as a 'slabless' stair, referring to the absence of a continuous waist slab.

[§] Structurally, it behaves as a 'folded plate' only when spanning transversely.

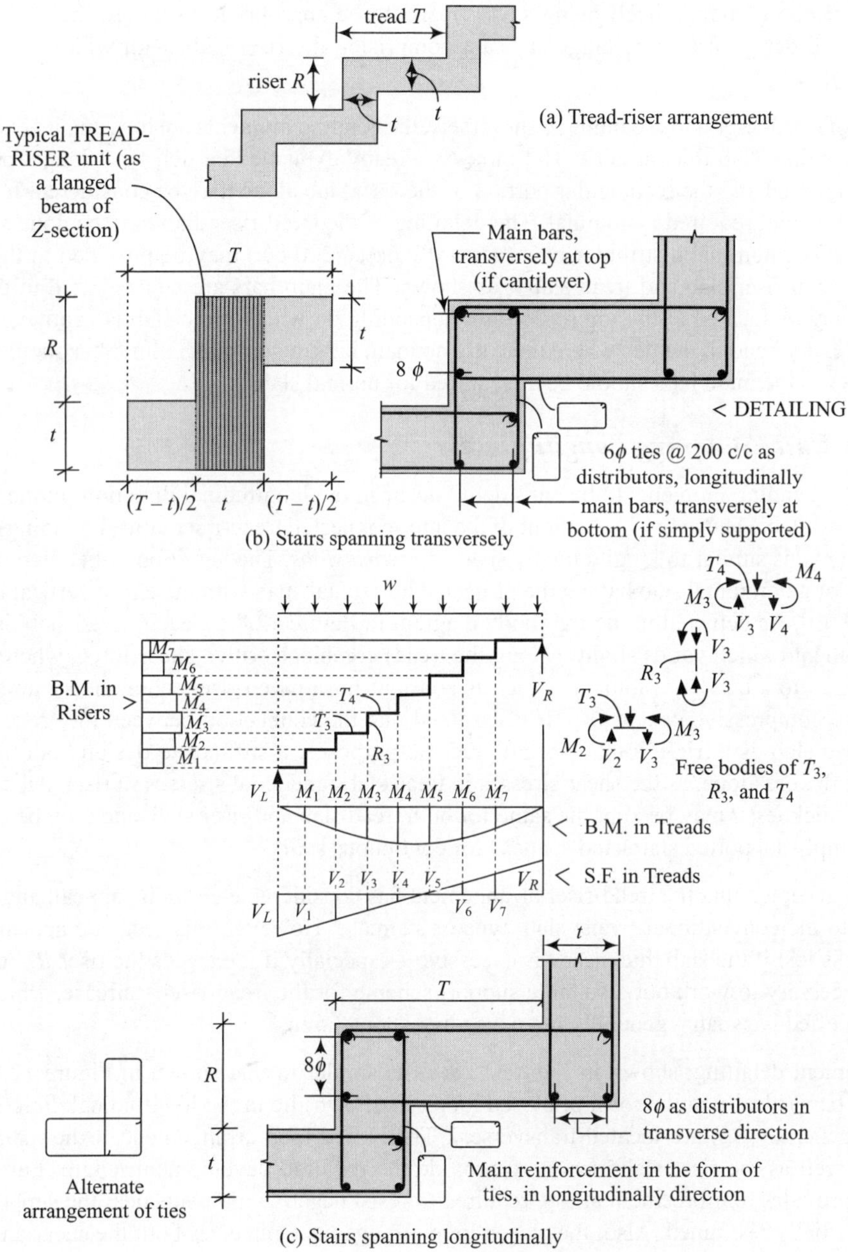

Fig. 12.8 Load effects and detailing in tread-riser units.

with the above assumption, for simply supported stairs, the top flange of this *Z*-section (i.e., half the tread at the top) will be in compression, while the other half of the *same* tread forming the lower flange of the tread-riser unit above will be in tension. Thus, one-half of every tread is in compression and the other in tension. Obviously, the actual behaviour is more complex. The stresses in the flange of the *Z*-section vary from a maximum at the web to zero at their outer edges and hence the full width of flange can not be considered effective. The width of flange itself being small, it would be appropriate to ignore the flange portions of the *Z*-section and design it as a rectangular beam comprising the riser slab, with width t and depth $R + t$ [Figure 12.8(b)].

In most cases of tread-riser units spanning transversely, the bending moments are low, and it generally suffices to provide a nominal slab thickness $t = 100$ mm. As already explained earlier, the 'flange' portions of the beam may be ignored and the rectangular portion of the riser slab alone may be considered. It will be found that the reinforcement required is nominal. The detailing of the tread-riser slab may be done as indicated in Figure 12.8(b). The nominal distributor bars (generally 6ϕ @ 200 c/c) may be provided in the form of ties (stirrups) – in both riser slab and tread slab – as shown. The main bars are concentrated in the 'riser slab' portion, and may be located at the top or bottom, depending on whether the slab is cantilevered or simply supported. At every bend in the ties where there are no main bars, a nominal 8 mm ϕ bar should be provided. The clear cover to the main bars should be as required for normal slabs.

Tread-Riser Units Spanning Longitudinally

In this case, the bending moments to be considered occur in the longitudinal direction, in the 'riser slab' as well as the 'tread slab'. The overall behaviour of the inter-connected tread-riser units, including calculation of bending moments, is similar to longitudinally spanning *waist slabs*. The variation of bending moment along the span is as for a horizontal slab having the projected horizontal span with the entire vertical load acting on it [Figure 12.8(c)]. As depicted in the free-body diagram in Figure 12.8(c), each 'tread slab' is subjected to a bending moment (which varies slightly along the tread) combined with a shear force, whereas each 'riser slab' is subjected to a bending moment (which is constant for a given riser) combined with an axial force (which may be compressive or tensile[†]). It is assumed that the connection between the 'riser slab' and the adjoining 'tread slab' is a 'rigid joint'. For all practical purposes, it suffices to design both tread slabs and riser slabs for flexure alone, as the shear stresses in tread slabs and axial stresses in riser slabs are relatively low. The slab thickness t may be kept the same for both tread slab and riser slab, and may be taken as about span/25 for simply supported stairs and span/30 for continuous stairs.

It is generally accepted that the tread-riser arrangement has considerable aesthetic appeal, and in this sense, it is superior to the conventional 'waist slab' type of staircase. However, this aesthetic appeal of the tread-riser staircase is lost if the slab thickness t is excessive – especially if it exceeds the riser R. For this reason, it becomes necessary to work out a suitable support scheme for the tread-riser staircase, which results in a relatively low effective span – generally not exceeding about 3.5 m.

The reinforcement detailing, shown in Figure 12.8(c), is similar to that shown in Figure 12.8(b) – except that the main bars (ideally in the form of closed loops, as shown) lie in the longitudinal direction, while the distributors (generally 8ϕ) are located transversely. The closed loop arrangement of the main bars (in the tread slab as well as the riser slab) serves to provide the required development length. Furthermore, this arrangement provides reinforcement at top, required to resist negative moments near the supports which are likely to be partially restrained. Also, the closed loop arrangement enhances both the shear and axial force-resisting capacities, as well as ductility of the slabs. The diameter and/or spacing of the main bars in the tread-riser units may be suitably varied along the span (to conform to the bending moment diagram), in order to achieve an economical design.

[†] The axial force is generally tensile in the risers located in the upper half of the flight; this tension is resisted by the closed ties provided as main reinforcement [Figure 12.8(c)].

12.4 Design Examples of Stair Slabs Spanning Transversely

Example 12.1

A straight staircase is made of structurally independent tread slabs, cantilevered from a reinforced concrete wall. Given that the riser is 150 mm, tread is 300 mm, and width of flight is 1.5 m, design a typical tread slab. Apply the live loads specified in the IS Loading Code for stairs liable to be overcrowded. Use M 25 concrete and Fe 250 steel. Assume mild exposure conditions.

Solution

- Given: R = 150 mm, T = 300 mm, W = 1.5 m

  $\Rightarrow$ effective span l = 1.5 m

  It is desirable to make the actual width of the tread slab, B, about 10 mm more than the effective tread, T, so that there is a marginal overlap between adjacent tread slabs [see Figure 12.1(d)]. $\Rightarrow B$ = 310 mm

- Assume a slab thickness at the fixed support, $t \approx \dfrac{l}{10}$ = 150 mm. The slab thickness may be kept constant for a distance of, say, 300 mm, from the support, and tapered to a minimum thickness of 80 mm, as shown in Figure 12.9.

- *Dead Loads:*

  (i) self-weight of tread slab $\approx 25 \text{ kN/m}^3 \times (0.15^{\dagger} \times 0.31) \text{ m}^2$ = 1.162 kN/m

  (ii) finishes $\approx 0.6 \text{kN/m}^2 \times 0.31 \text{ m}$ = 0.186 kN/m

  1.348 kN/m

  $\Rightarrow w_{u,DL} = 1.348 \times 1.5 = 2.022$ kN/m

- *Live Loads:*

  Alternative I: $w_{u,LL} = (5.0 \text{ kN/m}^2 \times 0.3 \text{ m}) \times 1.5 = 2.250$ kN/m

  Alternative II: $W_{u,LL} = 1.3 \text{ kN} \times 1.5 = 1.95$ kN (at free end)

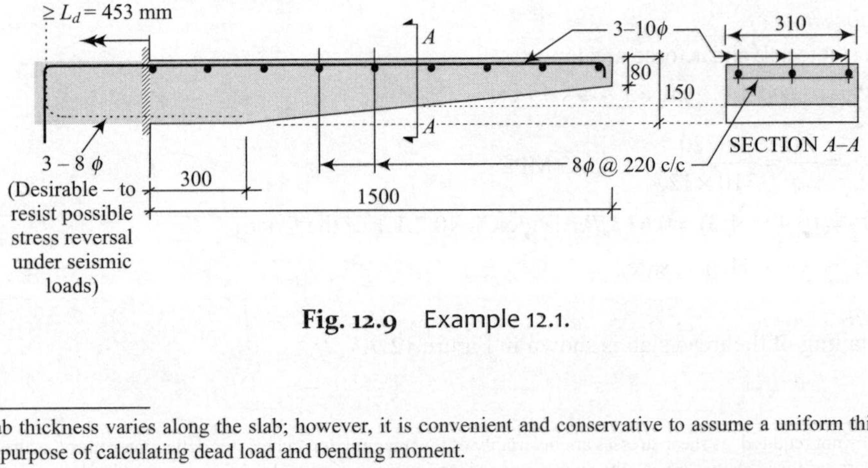

Fig. 12.9 Example 12.1.

[†] The actual slab thickness varies along the slab; however, it is convenient and conservative to assume a uniform thickness equal to 150 mm for the purpose of calculating dead load and bending moment.

- *Design Moment:*

  At fixed end, $M_{u,DL} = 2.022 \times 1.5^2/2 \quad = 2.27 \text{ kNm}$

$$M_{u,LL} = \begin{cases} 2.250 \times 1.5^2/2 & = 2.53 \text{ kNm} \\ 1.95 \times 1.5 & = 2.93 \text{ kNm (more critical)} \end{cases}$$

$$\Rightarrow \quad M_u = 2.27 + 2.93 = 5.20 \text{ kNm}$$

- *Design of Main Bars:*

  Assuming a clear cover of 20 mm (mild exposure) and a bar diameter of 10 mm, effective depth $d = 150 - 20 - 10/2 = 125$ mm.

$$R \equiv \frac{M_u}{bd^2} = \frac{5.20 \times 10^6}{310 \times 125^2} = 1.0735 \text{ MPa}$$

$$\Rightarrow \quad \frac{p_t}{100} \equiv \frac{A_{st}}{bd} = \frac{f_{ck}}{2f_y}\left[1 - \sqrt{1 - 4.598R/f_{ck}}\right]$$

$$= 0.521 \times 10^{-2} \text{ (for } f_{ck} = 25 \text{ MPa and } f_y = 250 \text{ MPa)}$$

  [Alternatively, this is obtainable from design aids Table A.3(a)]

$$\Rightarrow \quad (A_{st})_{\text{reqd}} = (0.521 \times 10^{-2}) \times 310 \times 125 = 202 \text{ mm}^2$$

  Provide 3–10ϕ bars [$A_{st} = 78.5 \times 3 = 235.5 \text{ mm}^2 > 202$]

- Anchorage length required: $L_d = \dfrac{(0.87 \times 250) \times 10}{4 \times 1.2} = 453$ mm [Eq. 8.5]

- *Distributors*

  $(A_{st})_{\min} = 0.0015bt$ (for Fe 250 bars, Cl. 26.5.2.1)

  $= 0.0015 \times 10^3 \times 150 = 225 \text{ mm}^2\text{/m}$ (assuming uniform slab thickness)

  Required Spacing of 8ϕ bars $= \dfrac{50.3 \times 10^3}{225} = 223$ mm

  Provide 8 ϕ distributors @ 220c/c

- *Check for shear†*

  Design (factored) shear force at support:

$$V_u = (2.022 + 2.250) \times 1.5 = 5.72 \text{ kN}$$

$$\Rightarrow \quad \tau_v = \frac{V_u}{bd} = \frac{5720}{310 \times 127} = 0.145 \text{ MPa}$$

$$\tau_c = (0.49 \times 1.3) = 0.63\,MPa \text{ [vide Cl. 40.2.1.1 of the Code]}$$

$$\Rightarrow \quad \tau_v << \tau_c \quad \text{– Hence, safe.}$$

- *Detailing*

  The detailing of the tread slab is shown in Figure 12.9.

† This is generally not required, as shear stresses are invariably of low magnitude. A check for deflection control is also not called for in the case of well-proportioned slabs – especially since the major load component (live load) is a transient load.

Example 12.2

Repeat Example 12.1, considering a tread-riser arrangement spanning transversely.

Solution

- Given (as in previous Example):

  $R = 150$ mm, $T = 300$ mm, $l = 1.5$ m
- Assume a nominal slab thickness $t = 100$ mm.

  Effective depth (assuming 20 mm cover, 10ϕ bars and 8ϕ ties)

  $d = (150 + 100) - 20 - 8 - 10/2 = 217$ mm
- *Load on a typical 'tread-riser' unit* [Figure 12.10(a)]:

  Dead Loads:

  (1) self-weight @ 25 kN/m^3 × (0.3 + 0.15) m × 0.1 m = 1.125 kN/m

  (2) finishes @ 0.6 kN/m^2 × 0.3 m = 0.180 ”

  = 1.305 kN/m

  ⇒ Factored dead load $w_{u,DL} = 1.305 \times 1.5 = 1.958$ kN/m

  Live Loads:

  Alternative I: $w_{u,LL} = 1.5 \times (5.0 \text{ kN/m}^2 \times 0.3 \text{ m}) = 2.250$ kN/m

  Alternative II: $W_{u,LL} = 1.5 \times 1.3 \text{ kN} = 1.95$ kN (at free end)
- *Design Moment*

  Consideration of concentrated live load at the free end [see Example 12.1] will result in a slightly larger design moment of

  $M_u = 1.958 \times 1.5^2/2 + 1.95 \times 1.5 = 5.13$ kNm

  This moment is resisted by the flanged section shown in Figure 12.10(a). Ignoring the contribution of the flanges, and considering a rectangular section with $b = 100$ mm, $d = 217$ mm,

$$R \equiv \frac{M_u}{bd^2} = \frac{5.13 \times 10^6}{100 \times 217^2} = 1.089 \text{ MPa}$$

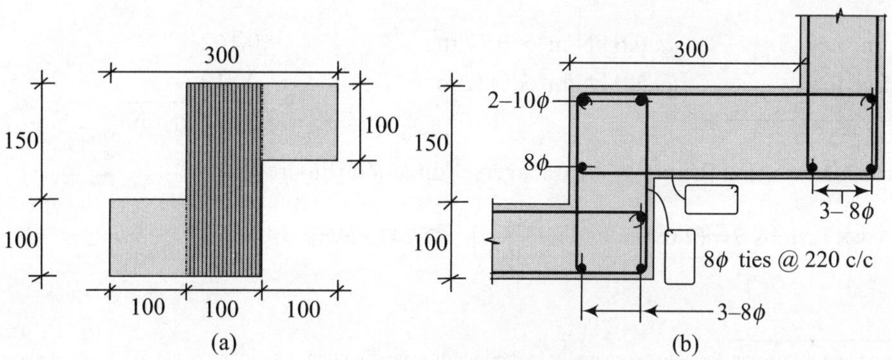

Fig. 12.10 Example 12.2.

- *Design of main bars*

$$\Rightarrow \quad \frac{p_t}{100} \equiv \frac{A_{st}}{bd} = \frac{25}{2\times 250}\left[1-\sqrt{1-4.598\times 1.089/25}\right]$$

$$= 0.529\times 10^{-2}$$

$$(A_{st})_{reqd.} = (0.529\times 10^{-2})\times(100\times 217) = 115\ \text{mm}^2$$

Provide 2–10ϕ bars on top ($A_{st} = 78.5\times 2 = 157\ \text{mm}^2 > 115$)

Anchorage length = 453 mm (as in previous Example)

- *Distributors*

$$(A_{st})_{min} = 0.0015bt \text{ (for Fe 250 bars)}$$
$$= 0.0015\times 1000\times 100 = 225\ \text{mm}^2/\text{m}$$

Provide 8ϕ @ 220c/c distributors (as in Example 12.1). These distributors are provided in the form of closed loops, with a bar (8ϕ minimum) provided transversely at each bend, as shown in Figure 12.10(b).

Example 12.3

Design a 'waist slab' type staircase comprising a straight flight of steps, supported between two stringer beams along the two sides. Assume an effective span of 1.5 m, a riser of 150 mm and a tread of 270 mm. Assume a live load of 3.0 kN/m². Use M 25 concrete and Fe 250 steel. Assume mild exposure conditions.

Solution

- Given R = 150 mm, T = 270 mm, l = 1.5 m

$$\Rightarrow \quad \sqrt{R^2+T^2} = 309\ \text{mm}$$

- Assume a nominal waist slab thickness t = 80 mm [Figure 12.11(a)]. Further, assuming the flexural resistance to be provided entirely by the waist slab, with 20 mm clear cover (mild exposure) and 10ϕ bars, effective depth $d = 80 - 20 - 10/2 = 55$ mm
- *Loads acting vertically over each tread width:*

(1) self-weight of slab @ 25 kN/m³ × (0.080 × 0.309) m² = 0.618 kN/m

(2) self-weight of step @ 25 kN/m³ × $\left(\frac{1}{2}\times 0.15\times 0.27\right)$ m = 0.506 ”

(3) finishes @ 0.6 kN/m² × 0.27 m = 0.162 ”

(4) live loads @ 3.0 kN/m² × 0.27 m = 0.810 ”

w = 2.096 kN/m

Factored load causing flexure in the transverse† direction [Figure 12.11(a)]:

$$(w\times 1.5)\cos\theta = (2.096\times 1.5)\times\left(\frac{270}{309}\right) = 2.747\ \text{kN/m}$$

† The load component $w_t = w \sin\theta$ acting tangentially in the longitudinal direction (i.e., in the plane of the waist slab) results in very low flexural stresses owing to the large depth of the waist slab in its own plane; hence, this is ignored.

⇒ Distributed factored load *per m width* along inclined slab

$$= \frac{2.747}{0.309} = 8.89 \text{ kN/m}^2$$

- *Design of main bars* (spanning transversely). Considering 1-meter-wide strip of the inclined slab spanning between the stringer beams,
Maximum moment at midspan:

$$M_u = \frac{8.89 \times 1.5^2}{8} = 2.50 \text{ kNm/m}$$

$$R \equiv \frac{M_u}{bd^2} = \frac{2.50 \times 10^6}{1000 \times 55^2} = 0.826 \text{ MPa}$$

$$\Rightarrow \quad \frac{p_t}{100} \equiv \frac{A_{st}}{bd} = \frac{f_{ck}}{2f_y}\left[1 - \sqrt{1 - 4.598R/f_{ck}}\right] = 0.395 \times 10^{-2}$$

$$\Rightarrow \quad (A_{st})_{\text{reqd}} = (0.395 \times 10^{-2}) \times 10^3 \times 55 = 218 \text{ mm}^2/\text{m}$$

$$\Rightarrow \text{Required spacing of } 10\phi \text{ bars} = \frac{78.5 \times 10^3}{218} = 360 \text{ mm}$$

$$\text{Required spacing of } 8\phi \text{ bars} = \frac{50.0 \times 10^3}{218} = 229 \text{ mm}$$

(Minimum spacing = $3d = 3 \times 55 = 165$ mm)

Provide 8ϕ bars @ 309/2 = 155 mm c/c, as shown in Figure 12.11(b).

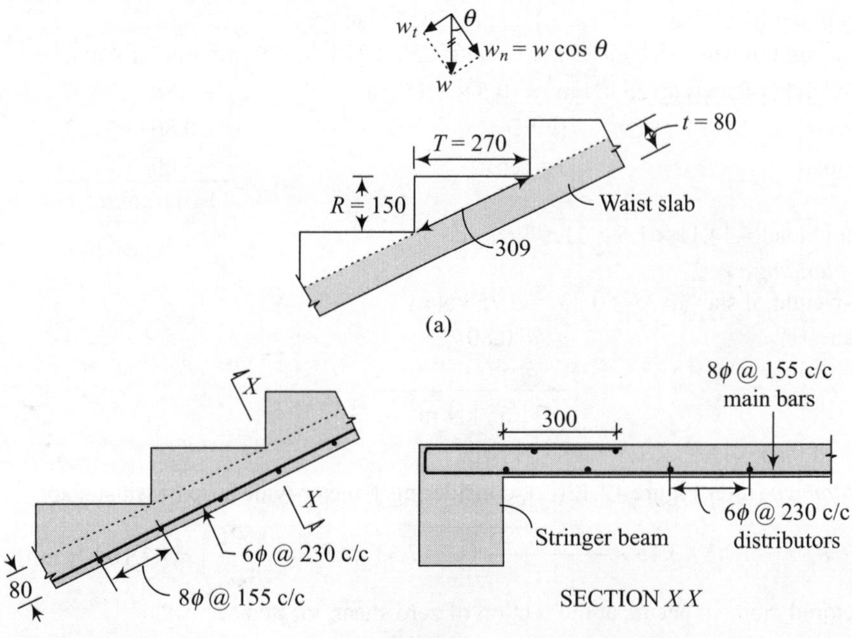

Fig. 12.11 Example 12.3.

- *Distributors* (spanning longitudinally)

$(A_{st})_{min} = 0.0015bt$ (for Fe 250 bars)

$= 0.0015 \times 1000 \times 80 = 120 \text{ mm}^2/\text{m}$

Spacing of 6ϕ bars $= \dfrac{28.3 \times 10^3}{120} = 235$ mm

Provide 6ϕ distributors @ 230 c/c, as shown in Figure 12.11(b)

12.5 Design Examples of Stair Slabs Spanning Longitudinally

Example 12.4

Design the staircase slab, shown in Figure 12.12(a). The stairs are simply supported on beams provided at the first riser and at the edge of the upper landing. Assume a finish load of 0.8 kN/m² and a live load of 5.0 kN/m². Use M 25 concrete and Fe 500 steel. Assume mild exposure conditions.

Solution

- Given: $R = 150$ mm, $T = 300$ mm $\Rightarrow \sqrt{R^2 + T^2} = 335.4$ mm

  Effective span = c/c distance between supports = 4.5 m [Figure 12.12(a)]
- Assume a waist slab thickness $\approx l/20 = 4500/20 = 225$ mm, say 230 mm

  Assuming 20 mm clear cover and 12ϕ main bars,
  effective depth $d = 230 - 20 - 12/2 = 204$ mm.
- *Loads on going* [Ref. Figure 12.12(b)] on projected plan area:

1.	self-weight of waist slab @ 25 kN/m³ × (0.230 × 335.4/300) m		= 6.43 kN/m²
2.	self-weight of steps @ 25 kN/m³ × (0.5 × 0.15) m		= 1.88 ”
3.	finishes	(given)	= 0.80 ”
4.	live load	(given)	= 5.00 ”
			14.11 kN/m²

  $\Rightarrow$ Factored load $= 14.11 \times 1.5 = 21.17 \text{ kN/m}^2$
- *Loads on landing*

1.	self-weight of slab @ 25 × 0.23	= 5.75 kN/m²
2.	finishes	@ 0.80 ”
3.	live loads	@ 5.00 ”
		11.55 kN/m²

  $\Rightarrow$ Factored load $= 11.55 \times 1.5 = 17.33 \text{ kN/m}^2$
- *Design Moment* [refer Figure 12.12(c)], considering 1-meter-wide strip of waist slab:

  $$\text{Reaction } R_1 = \left(21.17 \times 3.45 \times \frac{4.5 - 1.725}{4.5}\right) + \left(17.33 \times 1.05 \times \frac{0.525}{4.5}\right) = 47.16 \text{ kN/m}$$

  Max. factored moment occurs at the section of zero shear, located at

  $x = 47.16/21.17 = 2.228$ m from the left support.

  $$\Rightarrow \quad M_u = (47.16 \times 2.228) - (21.17 \times 2.228^2/2) = 52.53 \text{ kNm/m}$$

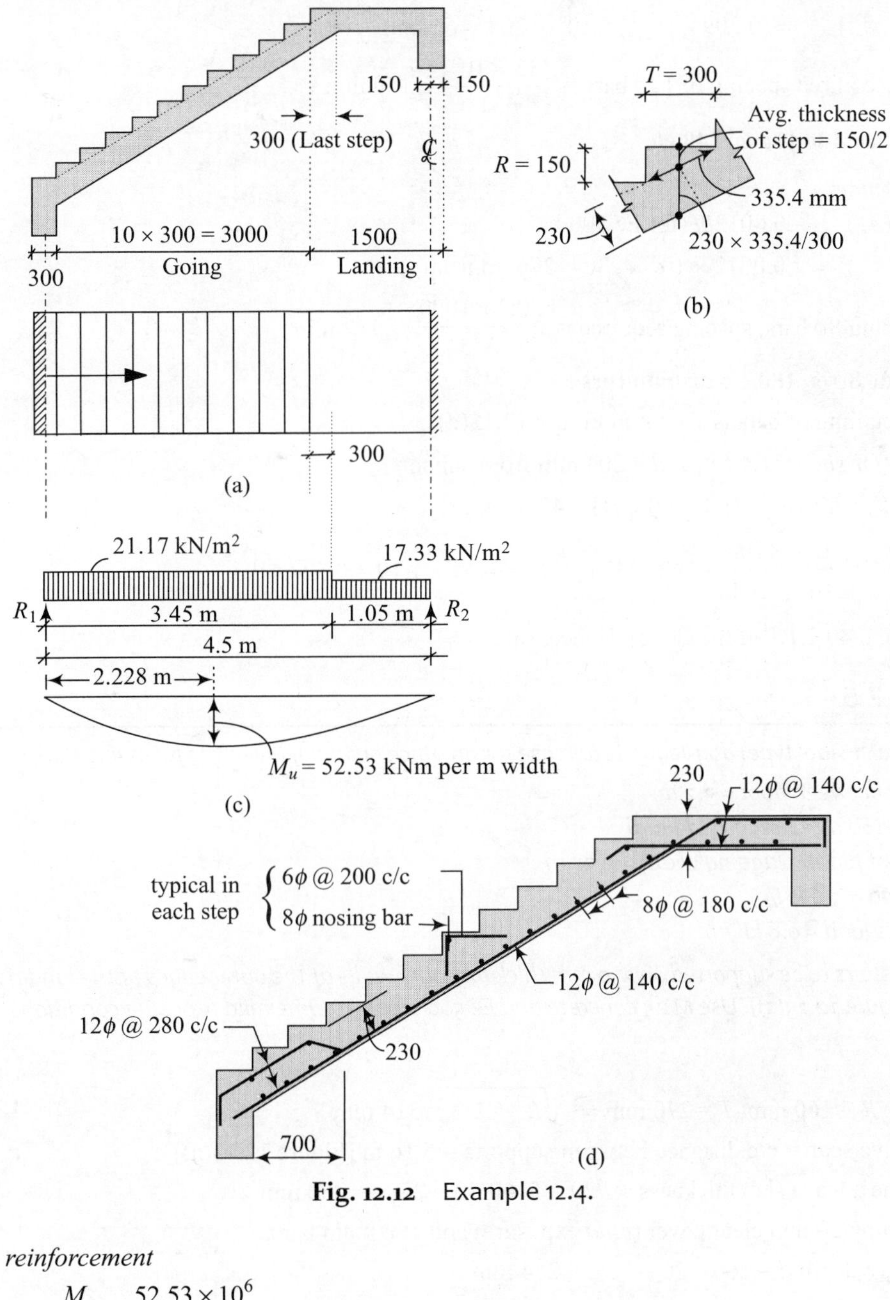

Fig. 12.12 Example 12.4.

- *Main reinforcement*

$$R \equiv \frac{M_u}{bd^2} = \frac{52.53 \times 10^6}{10^3 \times 204^2} = 1.262 \text{ MPa}$$

Assuming f_{ck} = 25 MPa, f_y = 500 MPa,

$$\Rightarrow \quad \frac{p_t}{100} \equiv \frac{A_{st}}{bd} = \frac{f_{ck}}{2f_y}\left[1 - \sqrt{1 - 4.598R/f_{ck}}\right] = 0.309 \times 10^{-2}$$

[This may also be obtained from design aids: Table A.3(a)].

$\Rightarrow \quad (A_{st})_{reqd} = (0.309 \times 10^{-2}) \times 10^3 \times 204 = 631\,\text{mm}^2/\text{m}$

Required spacing of 12ϕ bars $= \dfrac{113 \times 10^3}{631} = 179$ mm

Provide 12ϕ @ 140 c/c

- *Distributors*

  $(A_{st})_{\text{reqd}} = 0.0012bt$ (for Fe 500 bars)

  $= 0.0012 \times 10^3 \times 230 = 276\ \text{mm}^2/\text{m}$

  Assuming 8ϕ bars, spacing required $= \dfrac{50.3 \times 1000}{276} = 182$ mm

  Provide 8ϕ @ 180 c/c distributors

  The detailing of bars is shown in Figure 12.12(d).

- *Check for shear*† (check at $d = 204$ mm from support)

  $V_u = 47.16 - (21.17 \times 0.204) = 42.8$ kN/m

  $\tau_v = \dfrac{42.8 \times 10^3}{10^3 \times 204} = 0.21\ \text{MPa} << \tau_c = 0.44 \times 1.19 = 0.524\ \text{MPa}$

  [refer Cl. 40.2.1.1 of the Code]. Hence, safe.

Example 12.5

Design a ('waist slab' type) dog-legged staircase for an office building, given the following data:

- *height between floor = 3.2 m;*
- *riser = 160 mm, tread = 270 mm;*
- *width of flight = landing width = 1.25 m*
- *live load = 5.0 kN/m²*
- *finishes load = 0.6 kN/m²*

Assume the stairs to be supported on 230 mm thick masonry walls at the outer edges of the landing, parallel to the risers [Figure 12.13(a)]. Use M 25 concrete and Fe 500 steel. Assume mild exposure conditions.

Solution

- Given: $R = 160$ mm, $T = 270$ mm $\Rightarrow \sqrt{R^2 + T^2} = 314$ mm

  Effective span = c/c distance between supports = 5.16 m [Figure 12.13(a)]

- Assume a waist slab thickness $\approx l/20 = 5160/20 = 258 \rightarrow 260$ mm

  Assuming 20 mm clear cover (*mild* exposure) and 12ϕ main bars,

  effective depth $d = 260 - 20 - 12/2 = 234$ mm

  The slab thickness in the landing regions may be taken as 200 mm, as the bending moments are relatively low here.

† As observed earlier in Example 12.1, the slab (if well-proportioned) is invariably safe in shear, and does not require shear reinforcement. Also, as explained earlier, a check for deflection control is not called for here.

- *Loads on going* [Ref. 12.13(b)] on projected plan area:

1.	self-weight of waist slab @ $25 \times 0.26 \times 314/270$		= 7.56 kN/m^2
2.	self-weight of steps @ $25 \times \left(\frac{1}{2} \times 0.16\right)$		= 2.00 ”
3.	finishes	(given)	= 0.60 ”
4.	live load	(given)	= 5.00 ”
			15.16 kN/m^2

$\Rightarrow$ Factored load = $15.16 \times 1.5 = 22.74$ kN/m^2

- *Loads on landing*

1.	self-weight of slab @ 25×0.20	= 5.00 kN/m^2
2.	finishes	@ 0.6 ”
3.	live loads	@ 5.0 ”
		10.60 kN/m^2

$\Rightarrow$ Factored load = $10.60 \times 1.5 = 15.90$ kN/m^2

- *Design Moment* [refer Figure 12.13(b)]

Reaction $R = (15.90 \times 1.365) + (22.74 \times 2.43)/2 = 49.33$ kN/m

Maximum moment at midspan:

$M_u = (49.33 \times 2.58) - (15.90 \times 1.365) \times (2.58 - 1.365/2) - (22.74) \times (2.58 - 1.365)^2/2$
$= 69.30$ kNm/m

- *Main reinforcement*

$$R \equiv \frac{M_u}{bd^2} = \frac{69.30 \times 10^6}{10^3 \times 234^2} = 1.265 \text{ MPa}$$

Assuming $f_{ck} = 25$ MPa, $f_y = 500$ MPa,

$$\frac{p_t}{100} \equiv \frac{A_{st}}{bd} = \frac{25}{2 \times 500}\left[1 - \sqrt{1 - 4.598 \times 1.265/25}\right] = 0.310 \times 10^{-2}$$

[This may also be obtained from design aids Table 3(a)].

$\Rightarrow \quad (A_{st})_{reqd} = (0.310 \times 10^{-2}) \times 10^3 \times 234 = 726 \text{ mm}^2/\text{m}$

Required spacing of 12ϕ bars = $\dfrac{113 \times 10^3}{726}$ = 155 mm

Required spacing of 16ϕ bars = $\dfrac{201 \times 10^3}{726}$ = 276 mm (to be reduced slightly to account for reduced effective depth)

Provide 16ϕ @ 220c/c

- *Distributors*

$(A_{st})_{\text{reqd}} = 0.0012bt$ (for Fe 500 bars)
$= 0.0012 \times 10^3 \times 260 = 312$ mm^2/m

spacing 10ϕ bars = $78.5 \times 10^3/312 = 251$ mm

Provide 10ϕ @ 250 c/c as distributors

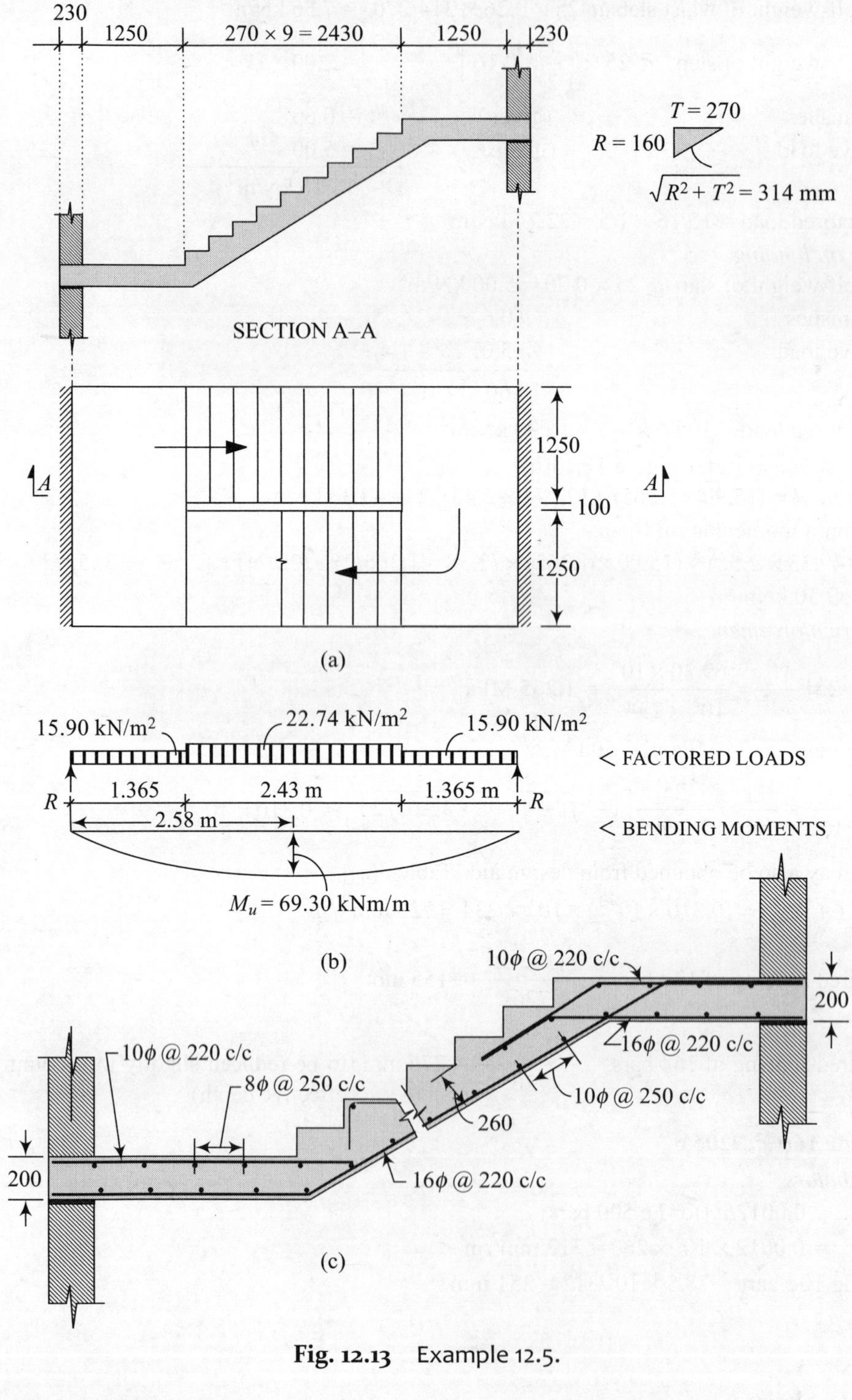

Fig. 12.13 Example 12.5.

The detailing of bars for the first flight is shown in Figure 12.13(c). Some nominal reinforcement (10ϕ @ 220 c/c) is provided in the landing slabs near the support at top to resist possible 'negative' moments on account of partial fixity; 8ϕ @ 250 c/c distributors are also provided.

Example 12.6

Repeat the problem of the dog-legged staircase in Example 12.5, considering the landings to be supported only on two edges perpendicular to the risers [Figure 12.14(a)].

Solution

- The prevailing IS Code recommendations are adopted here for determination of the design moments†.
- Given: $R = 160$ mm, $T = 270$ mm $\Rightarrow \sqrt{R^2 + T^2} = 314$ mm

  As the flight is supported on the landings (whose length is less than 2.0 m), the effective span (as per Code) is given by the c/c distance between landings. $l = 2.43 + 1.25 = 3.68$ m
- Assume a waist slab thickness $\approx 3680/20 = 184 \rightarrow 185$ mm.

  Let thickness of the landing slabs also be 185 mm

  Assuming 20 mm cover and 12ϕ bars, $d = 185 - 20 - 12/2 = 159$ mm
- Loads on going [Ref. 12.14(b)] on projected plan area:

1.	self-weight of waist slab @ $25 \times 0.185 \times 314/270$		$= 5.38$ kN/m^2
2.	self-weight of steps @ $25 \times \left(\frac{1}{2} \times 0.16\right)$		$= 2.00$ "
3.	finishes	(given)	$= 0.60$ "
4.	live load	(given)	$= 5.00$ "
			12.98 kN/m^2

  $\Rightarrow$ Factored load $= 12.98 \times 1.5 = 19.47$ kN/m^2
- *Loads on landing*

1.	self-weight of slab	@ $25 \times 0.185 = 4.63$ kN/m^2
2.	finishes	@ 0.60 "
3.	live loads	@ 5.00 "
		10.23 kN/m^2

  $\Rightarrow$ Factored load $= 10.23 \times 1.5 = 15.35$ kN/m^2

  50% of this load may be assumed to be acting longitudinally,

  i.e., $15.35 \times 1/2 = 7.68$ kN/m^2 [Figure 12.14(b)].

Design of waist slab [refer Figure 12.14(b)]

Reaction on landing $R = (7.68 \times 0.625) + (19.47 \times 2.43/2) = 28.46$ kN/m

- *Design Moment at midspan:*

  $M_u = (28.46 \times 3.68/2) - (7.68 \times 0.625) \times (1.84 - 0.625/2) - 19.47 \times 1.215^2/2 = 30.69$ kN/m

† As explained earlier, this will result in a conservative estimate of sagging moments (and consequently, thicker waist slab) and does not address the development of hogging moments at the going-landing junctions. More rational and economical design procedures are described in Ref. 12.6 and 12.8.

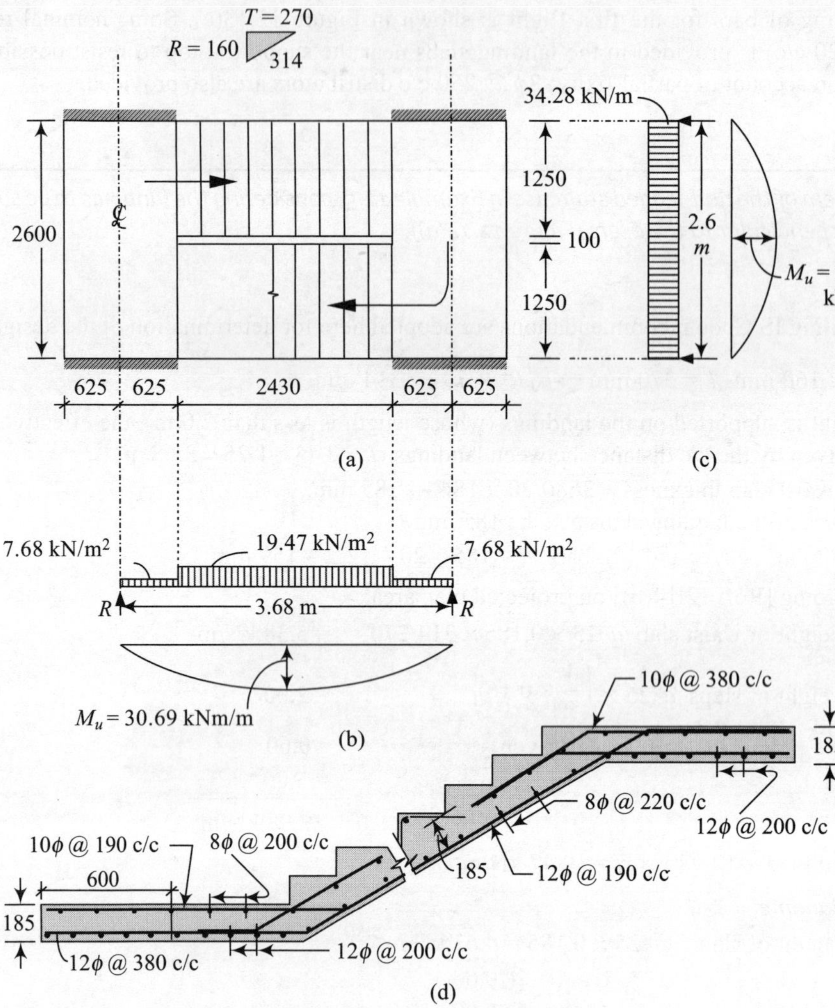

Fig. 12.14 Example 12.6.

- *Main reinforcement*

$$\Rightarrow \quad R \equiv \frac{M_u}{bd^2} = \frac{30.69 \times 10^6}{10^3 \times 159^2} = 1.214 \text{ MPa}$$

Assuming M 25 concrete and Fe 500 steel,

$$\frac{p_t}{100} \equiv \frac{A_{st}}{bd} = \frac{25}{2 \times 500}\left[1 - \sqrt{1 - 4.598 \times 1.214/25}\right] = 0.297 \times 10^{-2}$$

$$\Rightarrow \quad (A_{st})_{\text{reqd}} = (0.297 \times 10^{-2}) \times 10^3 \times 159 = 472 \text{ mm}^2/\text{m}$$

$$\text{Required spacing of } 12\phi \text{ bars} = \frac{113 \times 10^3}{472} = 239 \text{ mm}$$

Provide 12ϕ @ 190 c/c main bars in the waist slab; these bars are continued into the landing slab, as shown in Figure 12.14(d). Nominal top steel 10ϕ @ 190 c/c is also provided at top at the junction of the waist slab with the landing slab to resist possible 'negative' moments.

- *Distributors:*

$$(A_{st})_{min} = 0.0012 \times 1000 \times 185 = 222 \text{ mm}^2/\text{m}$$

Required spacing 8ϕ bars $= \dfrac{50.3 \times 10^3}{222} = 226$ mm

Provide 8ϕ @ 220c/c distributors in the waist slab.

Design of landing slabs [refer Figure 12.14(c)].

The entire loading on the staircase is transmitted to the supporting edges by the bending of the landing slab in a direction parallel to the risers.

- *Loads* (assumed to be uniformly distributed):
(considering the full width of landing of 1.25 m)
(i) directly on landing: 15.35 × 1.25 = 19.19 kN/m
(ii) from going: 19.47 × 2.43/2 = 23.66 "
42.85 kN/m

$\Rightarrow$ Loading on 1 m wide strip = 42.85/1.25 = 34.28 kN/m
Effective span = 2.60 m

- *Design Moment* (at midspan):

$$M_u = 34.28 \times 2.60^2/8 = 29.0 \text{ kNm/m}$$

$$\Rightarrow \quad \frac{M_u}{bd^2} = \frac{29.0 \times 10^6}{10^3 \times 159^2} = 1.147 \text{ MPa}$$

$$\frac{p_t}{100} \equiv \frac{A_{st}}{bd} = \frac{25}{2 \times 500}\left[1 - \sqrt{1 - 4.598 \times 1.147/25}\right] = 0.279 \times 10^{-2}$$

$$\Rightarrow \quad (A_{st})_{reqd} = (0.279 \times 10^{-2}) \times 10^3 \times 159 = 444 \text{ mm}^2/\text{m}$$

Required spacing of 12ϕ bars $= \dfrac{113 \times 10^3}{444} = 254$ mm.

Provide 12ϕ @ 200 c/c at bottom in a direction parallel to the risers.

- The detailing of the staircase (one typical flight) is depicted in Figure 12.14(d). Note that the bars from the waist slab are kept above the main bars of the landing slab so that the desired maximum effective depth is obtained for the main bars in the landing slab. This arrangement is *essential* all the more because the waist slab is supported by the landing, and to facilitate effective load transfer, the waist slab bars must be placed *above* the main bars in the landing. Nominal bars 8ϕ @ 200 c/c are also provided at top in the landing slabs.

Example 12.7

Repeat Example 12.6, considering a 'tread-riser' type of staircase, instead of a 'waist slab' type.

Solution

- Given: (as in Example 12.6) R = 160 mm, T = 270 mm $\Rightarrow \sqrt{R^2 + T^2} = 314$ mm

Effective span of the flight [Figure 12.14(a)]:

$l = 2.43 + 1.25 = 3.68$ m

Assume thickness of tread slab = thickness of riser slab ≈ $l/25 = 147 \rightarrow 145$ mm.

Assuming 20 mm cover and 12ϕ bars, $d = 145 - 20 - 12/2 = 119$ mm

- *Loads on going* [Ref. 12.15(a)] on projected plan area:
  1. self-weight of tread-riser slab @ $25 \times (0.16 + 0.27) \times 0.145/0.27 = 5.77$ kN/m²
  2. finishes = 0.60 "
  3. live load = 5.00 "

  11.37 kN/m²

  ⇒ Factored load = $11.37 \times 1.5 = 17.06$ kN/m²
- *Loads on landing* (assume 175 mm thick)
  1. self-weight of slab @ $25 \times 0.175 = 4.38$ kN/m²
  2. finishes = 0.60 "
  3. live loads = 5.00 "

  9.98 kN/m²

  ⇒ Factored load = $9.98 \times 1.5 = 14.97$ kN/m²

  50% of this load may be assumed to be acting longitudinally, as in Example 12.6; i.e., $14.97 \times 1/2 = 7.49$ kN/m² [refer Figure 12.15(a)]

Design of tread-riser unit

Reaction on landing $R = (7.49 \times 0.625) + (17.06 \times 2.43)/2 = 25.41$ kN/m

- *Design Moment at midspan:*

$$M_u = (25.41 \times 3.68/2) - (7.49 \times 0.625) \times (1.84 - 0.625/2) - 17.06 \times 1.215^2/2$$
$$= 27.01 \text{ kNm/m}$$

$$\Rightarrow \quad R \equiv \frac{M_u}{bd^2} = \frac{27.01 \times 10^6}{10^3 \times 119^2} = 1.907 \text{ MPa}$$

Assuming M 25 concrete and Fe 500 steel,

$$\frac{p_t}{100} \equiv \frac{A_{st}}{bd} = \frac{25}{2 \times 500}\left[1 - \sqrt{1 - 4.598 \times 1.907/25}\right] = 0.486 \times 10^{-2}$$

$$\Rightarrow \quad (A_{st})_{reqd} = (0.486 \times 10^{-2}) \times 10^3 \times 119 = 578 \text{ mm}^2/\text{m}$$

Required spacing of 12ϕ bars = $\dfrac{113 \times 10^3}{578} = 195$ mm.

Provide 12ϕ @ 150 c/c in the form of closed ties [Figure 12.15(b)], as explained earlier in Section 12.3.5 [Figure 12.8(c)].

Distributors: Provide an 8ϕ bar transversely at each bend.

Design of landing slabs

- The entire loading on the staircase is transmitted by flexure of the landing slabs in a direction parallel to the risers.

  Effective span = 2.60 m; effective depth = $175 - 20 - 12/2 = 149$ mm

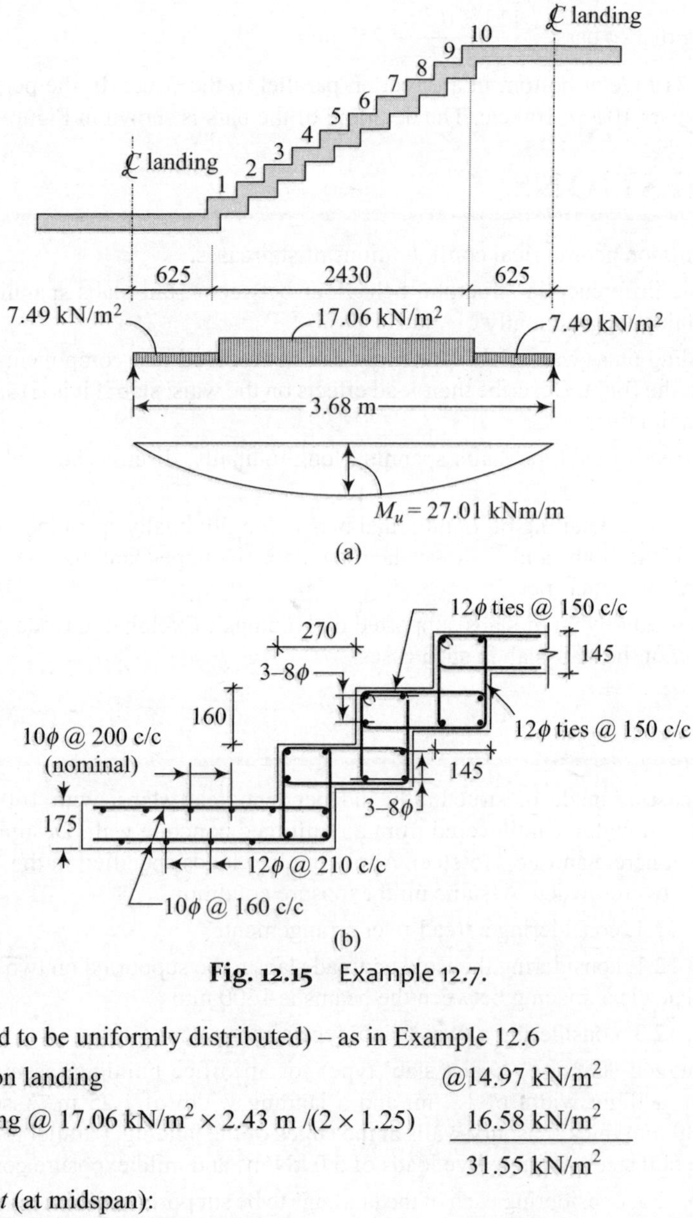

Fig. 12.15 Example 12.7.

- *Loads* (assumed to be uniformly distributed) – as in Example 12.6

(i)	directly on landing	@14.97 kN/m^2
(ii)	from going @ 17.06 kN/m^2 × 2.43 m /(2 × 1.25)	16.58 kN/m^2
		31.55 kN/m^2

- *Design Moment* (at midspan):

$$M_u = 31.55 \times 2.60^2/8 = 26.66 \text{ kN/m}$$

$$\Rightarrow \quad \frac{M_u}{bd^2} = \frac{26.66 \times 10^6}{10^3 \times 149^2} = 1.201 \text{ MPa}$$

$$\Rightarrow \quad \frac{p_t}{100} \equiv \frac{A_{st}}{bd} = \frac{25}{2 \times 500}\left[1 - \sqrt{1 - 4.598 \times 1.201/25}\right] = 0.293 \times 10^{-2}$$

$$\Rightarrow \quad (A_{st})_{\text{reqd}} = (0.293 \times 10^{-2}) \times 10^3 \times 149 = 437 \text{ mm}^2/\text{m}$$

Required spacing of 12ϕ bars = $\dfrac{113\times10^3}{437}$ = 258 mm

Provide 12ϕ @ 210 c/c at bottom in a direction parallel to the risers. In the perpendicular direction, provide nominal bars 10ϕ @ 160 c/c. The detailing of the bars is shown in Figure 12.15(b).

REVIEW QUESTIONS

12.1 Describe the common geometrical configurations of staircases.

12.2 Explain the basic difference in structural behaviour between 'stair slabs spanning transversely' and 'stair slabs spanning longitudinally'.

12.3 The gravity loading on a 'waist slab' type flight can be resolved into components normal to the flight and tangential to the flight. Describe their load effects on the waist slab if it is (i) spanning transversely, (ii) spanning longitudinally.

12.4 In the case of 'tread-riser' type stairs spanning longitudinally, discuss the load effects produced by gravity loading.

12.5 Sketch the appropriate detailing of longitudinal bars in longitudinally spanning 'waist slab' type stairs at the junction of the flight and (i) lower landing slab, (ii) upper landing slab. Is there any special requirement at re-entrant corners?

12.6 Explain what is meant by 'stair slabs supported on landings'. Explain the Code recommendations for the *effective span* of the stair slab in such cases.

PROBLEMS

12.1 A straight staircase is made of structurally independent tread slabs, with 160 mm riser, 280 mm tread, and 1600 mm width, cantilevered from a reinforced concrete wall. Design a typical tread slab, assuming M 20 concrete and Fe 415 steel. Apply the live loads specified in the IS Loading Code for stairs liable to be overcrowded. Assume mild exposure conditions

12.2 Repeat Problem 12.1, considering a tread-riser arrangement.

12.3 Repeat Problem 12.1, considering the isolated tread slabs to be supported on two stringer beams, each 250 mm wide. The clear spacing between the beams is 1600 mm.

12.4 Repeat Problem 12.3, considering a 'waist slab' type arrangement.

12.5 Design a dog-legged staircase ('waist slab' type) for an office building, assuming a floor-to-floor height of 3.0 m, a flight width of 1.2 m, and a landing width of 1.25 m. Assume the stairs to be supported on 230 mm thick masonry walls at the edges of the landing, parallel to the risers. Use M 25 concrete and Fe 500 steel. Assume live loads of 5.0 kN/m^2 and mild exposure conditions.

12.6 Repeat Problem 12.5, considering each of the landings to be supported only on two edges perpendicular to the risers.

12.7 Repeat Problem 12.6, considering a 'tread-riser' type of staircase, instead of a 'waist slab' type.

12.8 Design a single flight straight staircase, with 11 risers, each = 160 mm, and with the tread = 280 mm, and upper and lower landings of 1250 mm width each. The edges of the two landings are simply supported on two masonry walls, 230 mm thick. Design a 'waist slab' type stair, assuming M 25 concrete and Fe 500 steel. Apply the live loads specified in the IS Loading Code for stairs liable to be overcrowded. Assume mild exposure conditions.

12.9 Repeat Problem 12.8, considering a 'tread-riser' type of staircase, instead of a 'waist slab' type.

12.10 Design and detail a typical intermediate flight (shown in section '*AA*') of the 'open-well' staircase, details of which are shown in Figure 12.16. Use M 25 concrete and Fe 500 steel and assume live loads of 5.0 kN/m^2. Assume mild exposure conditions.

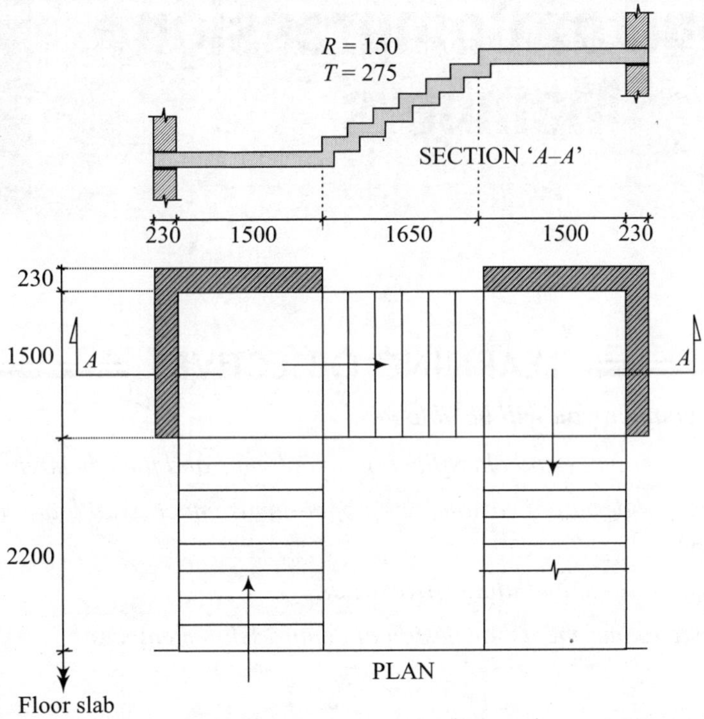

Fig. 12.16 Problem 12.8.

REFERENCES

12.1 Gould, P L, *Analysis and Design of a Cantilever Staircase*, ACI Journal, Vol. 60, July 1963, pp 881–889

12.2 Solanki, H T, *Free Standing Stairs with Slabless Tread-Risers*, Journal ASCE, Structural Div., Vol. 101, August 1975, pp 1733–1738

12.3 Bergman, V R, *Helicoidal Staircases of Reinforced Concrete*, ACI Journal, Vol. 53, October 1956, pp 403–412

12.4 Scordelis, A C, *Internal Forces in Uniformly Distributed Loaded Helicoidal Girders*, ACI Journal, Vol. 56, April 1960, pp 1013–1026

12.5 Ahmed, I, Muqtadir, A and Ahmed, S, *A Design Basis for Stair Slabs Supported at Landing Level*, J. Structural Engg., ASCE, Vol. 121(7), July 1995, pp 1051–1057

12.6 Ahmed, I, Muqtadir A, and Ahmed, S, *Design Provisions for Stair Slabs in the Bangladesh Building Code*, J. Structural Engg., ASCE, Vol. 122(3), March 1996, pp 262–266

12.7 Bangash, M Y H, and Bangash T, *Staircases: Structural Analysis and Design*, A A Balkema, Rotterdam, 1999

12.8 Siva Raman, K V, *R C Stairs Supported on Landing Edges – Elastic Behaviour, Analysis & Design*, M.S. Thesis, Dept. of Civil Engg., Indian Institute of Technology Madras, September 2000

CHAPTER 13

Design of Compression Members

LEARNING OBJECTIVES

After studying this chapter, you will be able to:

- *Explain the different types and classification of columns and their behaviour under loads*
- *Do the analysis and design of various types of columns under axial load and uniaxial/biaxial bending*
- *Describe design of walls, including shear walls*
- *Discuss the Code requirements for design of compression members*

13.1 Introduction

The term 'column', used in this chapter, is representative of all *compression members*, which comprise structural elements subjected predominantly to axial forces.

A 'compression member' is a structural element which is subjected (predominantly) to axial compressive forces. Compression members are most commonly encountered in reinforced concrete buildings as *columns* (and sometimes as reinforced concrete *walls*), forming part of the 'vertical framing system' [refer Section 1.6.2]. Whether the structure is man-made or created by nature, the key element in resisting collapse under gravity load is the column – in buildings and bridges, in trees and plants. Other types of compression members include truss members ('struts'), inclined members and rigid frame members.

The Code defines a 'column' as a compression member having *effective length* greater than three times its least lateral dimension. A shorter vertical compression member is called a *pedestal*.

The 'column' is representative of all types of compression members, and hence, sometimes, the terms 'column' and 'compression member' are used interchangeably. The Code (Cl. 25.1.1) defines the column as a *compression member*, the 'effective length' (see Section 13.2) of which exceeds three times the least lateral dimension. The term 'pedestal' is used to describe a vertical compression member whose 'effective length' is less than three times its least lateral dimension [Cl. 26.5.3.1(h) of the Code]. A member that is subjected simultaneously to axial compression and bending moment is sometimes referred to as a *beam-column*.

13.1.1 Classification of Columns Based on Type of Reinforcement

Reinforced concrete columns may be classified into the following three types based on the type of reinforcement provided:

> **Based on the type of reinforcements, RC columns are classified as *tied columns, spiral columns* and *composite columns.***

1. Tied columns : where the main longitudinal bars are enclosed within closely spaced *lateral ties* [Figure 13.1(a)]
2. Spiral columns (spirally reinforced columns) : where the main longitudinal bars are enclosed within spiral reinforcement [Figure 13.1(b)]
3. Composite columns : where the reinforcement is in the form of structural steel sections or pipes, with or without longitudinal bars [Figure 13.1(c)].

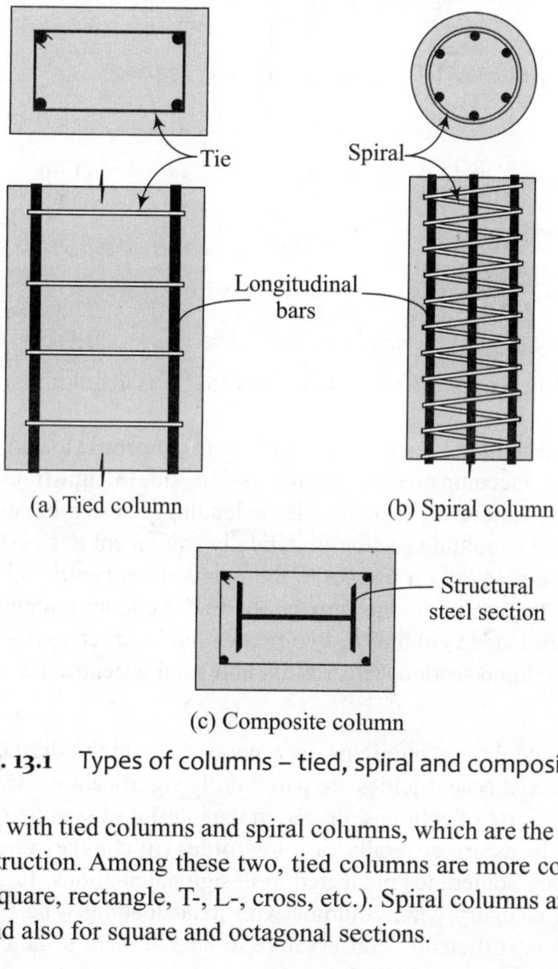

Fig. 13.1 Types of columns – tied, spiral and composite.

This chapter primarily deals with tied columns and spiral columns, which are the most commonly used types in reinforced concrete construction. Among these two, tied columns are more common, being applicable to all cross-sectional shapes (square, rectangle, T-, L-, cross, etc.). Spiral columns are used mainly for columns that are circular in shape, and also for square and octagonal sections.

13.1.2 Classification of Columns Based on Type of Loading

> The loading on a column may be purely axial, eccentric with respect to one axis only, or biaxially eccentric. Columns subjected to significant bending are also referred to as 'beam-columns'.

Columns may be classified into the following three types, based on the nature of loading:

1. Columns with axial loading (applied concentrically) [Figure 13.2(a)]
2. Columns with uniaxial eccentric loading [Figure 13.2(b)]
3. Columns with biaxial eccentric loading [Figure 13.2(c)].

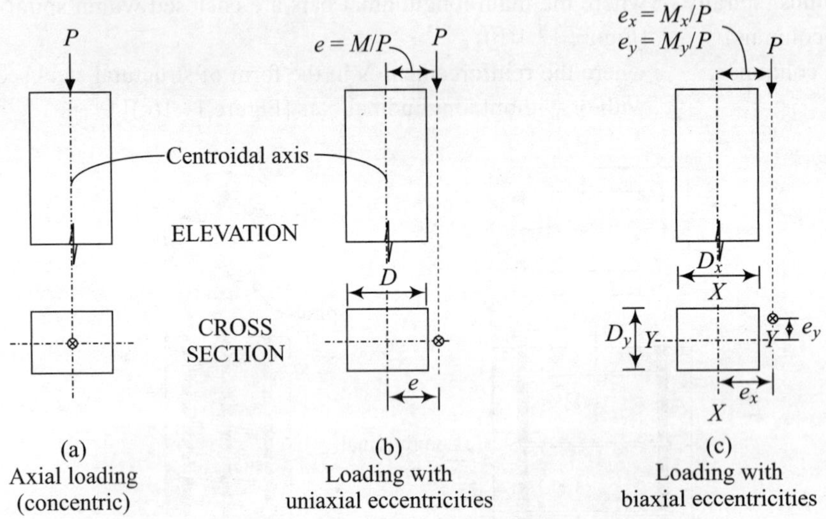

Fig. 13.2 Different loading situations in columns.

The occurrence of 'pure' axial compression in a column (due to concentric loads) is relatively rare. Generally, flexure (and, sometimes, shear[†]) accompanies axial compression – due to 'rigid frame' action, lateral loading and/or actual (or even, unintended/accidental) eccentricities in loading. The combination of axial compression (P) with bending moment (M) at any column section is statically equivalent to a system consisting of the load P applied with an eccentricity $e = M/P$ with respect to the longitudinal centroidal axis of the column section. In a more general loading situation involving *biaxial* bending, bending moments (M_x and M_y) are applied simultaneously on the axially loaded column in two perpendicular directions – about the major axis (XX) and minor axis (YY) of the column section. This results in biaxial eccentricities $e_x = M_x/P$ and $e_y = M_y/P$, as shown in [Figure 13.2(c)].

Columns in reinforced concrete framed buildings, in general, fall into the third category, viz., columns with biaxial eccentricities. The biaxial eccentricities are particularly significant in the case of the columns located in the building corners. In the case of columns located in the interior of symmetrical, simple buildings, these eccentricities under gravity loads are generally of a low order (in comparison with the lateral dimensions of the column), and hence are sometimes neglected in design calculations. In such cases, the columns are assumed to fall in the first category, viz., columns with axial loading. The Code, however, ensures that the design of such columns is sufficiently conservative to enable them to be capable of resisting nominal eccentricities in loading [refer Section 13.3.2].

[†] Considerations of shear in columns are usually neglected because the shear stresses are generally low, and the shear resistance is high on account of the presence of axial compression and the presence of lateral reinforcement.

Frequently, the eccentricity about one axis is negligible, whereas the eccentricity about the other axis is significant. This situation is encountered in the exterior columns of interior frames in a reinforced concrete building, under gravity loads. Under lateral loads (wind or seismic), indeed *all* columns (external as well as internal) in multi-storeyed buildings are subjected to significant uniaxial† bending moments. Such columns fall into the second category, viz., columns with uniaxial eccentricity.

13.1.3 Classification of Columns Based on Slenderness Ratios

Columns (i.e., compression members) may be classified into the following two types, depending on whether *slenderness effects* are considered insignificant or significant:

1. *Short* columns; and
2. *Slender* (or *long*) columns.

'Slenderness' is a geometrical property of a compression member which is related to the ratio of its 'effective length' to its lateral dimension. This ratio, called *slenderness ratio*, also provides a measure of the vulnerability to failure of the column by elastic instability (buckling) – in the plane in which the slenderness ratio is computed. Columns with low slenderness ratios, i.e., relatively short and stocky columns, invariably fail under ultimate loads with the material (concrete, steel) reaching its ultimate strength, and not by buckling. On the other hand, columns with very high slenderness ratios are in danger of buckling (accompanied with large lateral deflection) under relatively low compressive loads, and thereby failing suddenly. Design codes attempt to preclude such failure by specifying 'slenderness limits' to columns [refer Section 13.3.1].

> **IS Code defines the *slenderness ratio* of a column, with respect to buckling about any principal axis of the cross section, as the ratio of the *effective length* to the *depth* of the section associated with the plane of buckling. A more general definition uses the *radius of gyration* instead of the depth of section. Slenderness ratio is a measure of the column's vulnerability to failure by buckling/instability.**

There is another important consequence of slenderness of a column subjected to eccentric compression. When a column is subjected to flexure combined with axial compression, the action of the axial compression in the displaced geometry of the column introduces 'secondary moments' – commonly referred to as the P–Δ effect [refer Section 13.7.1] – which is ignored in the usual 'first-order' structural analysis. These secondary moments become increasingly significant with increasing column slenderness. On the other hand, the secondary moments are negligible in columns with low slenderness ratios; such columns are called *short columns*. Design codes provide guidelines, in terms of slenderness ratios, in drawing the line between 'short columns' (wherein secondary moments can be ignored) and 'slender (or long) columns' (wherein secondary moments must be explicitly considered).

According to the IS Code (Cl. 25.1.2), a compression member may be classified as a 'short column' if its slenderness ratios with respect to the 'major principal axis' (l_{ex}/D_x) as well as the 'minor principal axis' (l_{ey}/D_y) are *both* less than 12‡; otherwise, it should be treated as a 'slender column'. Here l_{ex} and D_x denote the effective length and lateral dimension ('depth') respectively for buckling *in the plane* passing through the longitudinal centroidal axis and normal to the major principal axis; i.e., causing buckling *about the major axis* [refer Figure 13.3]; likewise, l_{ey} and D_y refer to the minor principal axis.

> **A 'short column' is a column whose slenderness ratios, with respect to both principal axes of the cross section, are less than 12.**

† Lateral loads, with their maximum design values, are generally assumed to operate only in one direction *at a time*. The action of lateral loads (especially seismic) in a diagonal direction (inducing biaxial bending in columns) may also have to be investigated in some cases.

‡ In the British Code, this value is specified as 15 for 'braced columns' and 10 for 'unbraced columns' [Ref. 13.2].

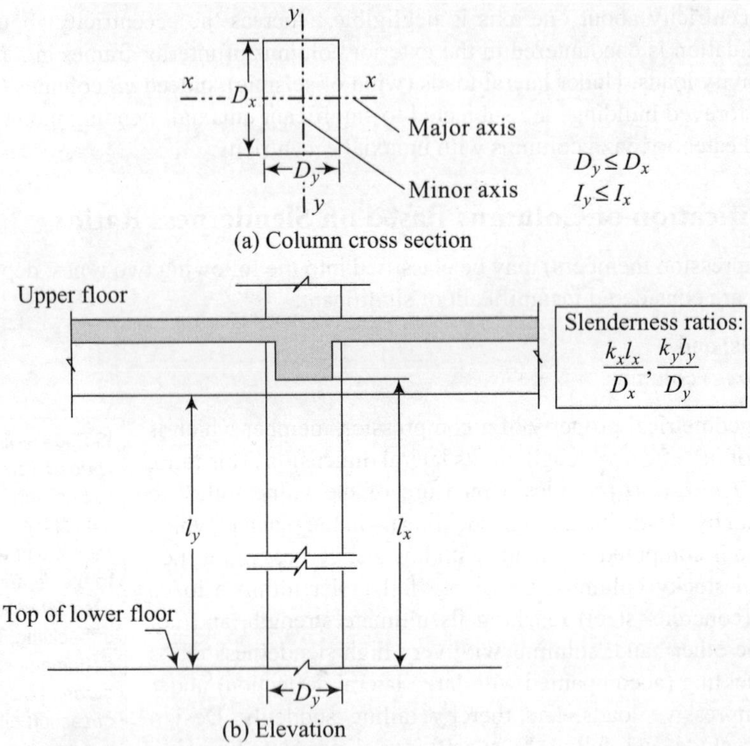

Fig. 13.3 Definitions of unsupported and effective lengths in a rectangular column.

Such a definition is, however, not suitable for non-rectangular and non-circular sections – where the slenderness ratio is better expressed in terms of the *radius of gyration*† r (as in steel columns), rather than the lateral dimension D. In such cases, reference may be made to the ACI Code [Ref. 13.1], which recommends that the dividing line between short columns and slender columns be taken as l_e/r equal to 34 for 'braced columns' and 22 for 'unbraced columns' [refer Section 13.2.3 for definitions of braced/unbraced columns]. Note that, for a square section, the ACI Code limit of 22 works out to an L/D limit of 6.35, compared to the limit of 12 in the IS Code and hence is far more conservative. A more precise definition of this demarcating slenderness ratio, in terms of the magnitudes and directions of the applied primary moments (at the column ends) is given in Section 13.7.1.

The design of slender columns is described in Section 13.7. The design of short columns subject to axial compression, uniaxially eccentric compression and biaxially eccentric compression are described in Sections 13.4, 13.5 and 13.6 respectively. Code requirements relating to slenderness limits, minimum eccentricities and reinforcement are explained in Section 13.3.

The 'effective length' of a column (l_{ex}, l_{ey}) is an important parameter in its design. Methods of estimating the effective length are described in the next section.

† For a solid rectangular section, $r = D/\sqrt{12} \cong 0.3D$; for a circular section, $r = 0.25D$.

13.2 Estimation of Effective Length of a Column

13.2.1 Definition of Effective Length

The *effective length*, l_e, of a column (or other compression member) in a frame (or under any other end conditions) is defined as the length of a hinged-ended column (of the same cross section) whose elastic critical load (Euler formula) is the same as the theoretical critical load of the framed member under consideration. It follows that the effective length of a column for a given plane of bending is the length between the theoretical points of inflection† in the buckled configuration of the column in that plane. The effective length depends on the *unsupported length* l (i.e., distance between lateral connections, or actual length in case of a cantilever) and the boundary conditions at the column ends introduced by connecting beams and other framing members. An expression for l_e may be obtained as

> 'Effective length', l_e, of a column, under any given conditions, is equal to the length of a hinged-ended braced column of the same section and having the same critical load as the given column.

$$l_e = k\,l \tag{13.1}$$

where k is the *effective length ratio* (i.e., the ratio of effective length to the unsupported length – also known as *effective length factor*) whose value depends on the degrees of rotational and/or translational restraints at the column ends.

> 'Effective length ratio/factor', $k = l_e/l$, is the ratio of *effective* length to the *unsupported* length of a column.

Unsupported Length

The Code (Cl. 25.1.3) defines the 'unsupported length' l of a column explicitly for various types of constructions. In conventional framed construction, l is to be taken as *the clear distance between the floor and the shallower beam framing into the columns in each direction at the next higher floor level.* By this, it is implied that when a column is framed in any direction by beams of different depths on either side, then the unsupported length (with respect to buckling about a perpendicular axis) shall be considered, conservatively, with reference to the shallower beam. It may be noted that the unsupported length in one direction may be different from that in the perpendicular direction. For a rectangular column section (width $D_y \times$ depth D_x), we may use the terms, $l_{ex} = k_x l_x$ and $l_{ey} = k_y l_y$ to denote the effective lengths referring to buckling about the major and minor axes respectively, where l_x and l_y denote the corresponding unsupported lengths and k_x and k_y denote the corresponding effective length factors. These concepts are made clear in Figure 13.3, and further illustrated in Examples 13.1 and 13.2.

In the case of 'flat slab construction', the unsupported length l is to be taken as *the clear distance between the floor and the lower extremity of the capital, the drop panel or slab, whichever is the least.*

13.2.2 Effective Length Ratios for Idealised Boundary Conditions

When relative transverse displacement between the upper and lower ends of a column is prevented, the frame is said to be *braced* (against sidesway). In such cases, the effective length ratio k varies between 0.5 and 1.0, as shown in Figure 13.4. The extreme value $k = 0.5$ corresponds to 100 per cent rotational fixity at both the column ends [Figure 13.4(a)] (i.e., when the connecting floor beams have infinite flexural stiffness), and the other extreme value $k = 1.0$ corresponds to zero rotational fixity at both the column ends ('pinned') [Figure 13.4(c)] (i.e., when the beams have zero flexural stiffness). When one end is fully 'fixed' and the other 'pinned', $k = 0.7$ [Figure 13.4(b)].

† When there exists relative translation of the ends of the column member, the points of inflection (zero moment) may not lie within the member. In such cases, they may be located by extending the deflection curve beyond the column end(s) and by applying conditions of symmetry, as shown in Figure 13.4(a), (b).

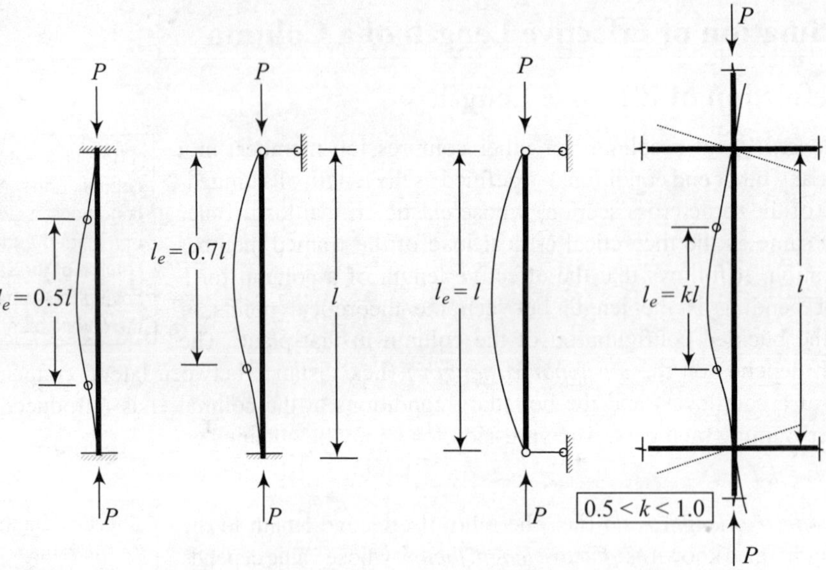

(a) Both ends rotationally fixed

(b) One end rotationally fixed, the other rotationally free

(c) Both ends rotationally free

(d) Both ends partially restrained (rotational)

Fig. 13.4 Effective lengths of columns braced against sidesway.

When relative transverse displacement between the upper and lower ends of a column is not prevented, the frame is said to be *unbraced* (against sidesway). In such cases, the effective length ratio k varies between 1.0 and infinity, as shown in Figure 13.5. The lower limit $k = 1.0$ corresponds to 100 per cent rotational fixity at both the column ends [Figure 13.5(a)], and the upper theoretical $k = \infty$ corresponds to zero rotational fixity at both the column ends, i.e., a column pinned at both ends and permitted to sway (unstable) [Figure 13.5(c)]. When one end is fully 'fixed' and the other 'free', the column acts like a vertical cantilever in the buckled mode, corresponding to which $k = 2$ [Figure 13.5(b)].

Code Recommendations for Idealised Boundary Conditions

> A column is considered *braced against sidesway* if its ends are adequately supported laterally to prevent any lateral relative displacement between the two ends.

Although, in design practice, it is convenient to assume the idealised boundary conditions of either zero or full restraint (rotational and translational) at a column end, the fact is that such idealisations cannot generally be realised in actual structures. For this reason, the Code (Cl. E–1), while permitting these idealisations, recommends the use of 'effective length ratios' $k = l_e/l$ that are generally more conservative than those obtained from theoretical considerations [Figures 13.4, 13.5].

These recommended values of k are as follows:

1. *Columns braced against sidesway*:
   (a) both ends 'fixed' rotationally [Figure 13.4(a)] : 0.65 (instead of 0.5)
   (b) one end 'fixed' and the other 'pinned'[Figure 13.4(b)] : 0.80 (instead of 0.7)
   (c) both ends 'free' rotationally ('pinned') [Figure 13.4(c)] : 1.00

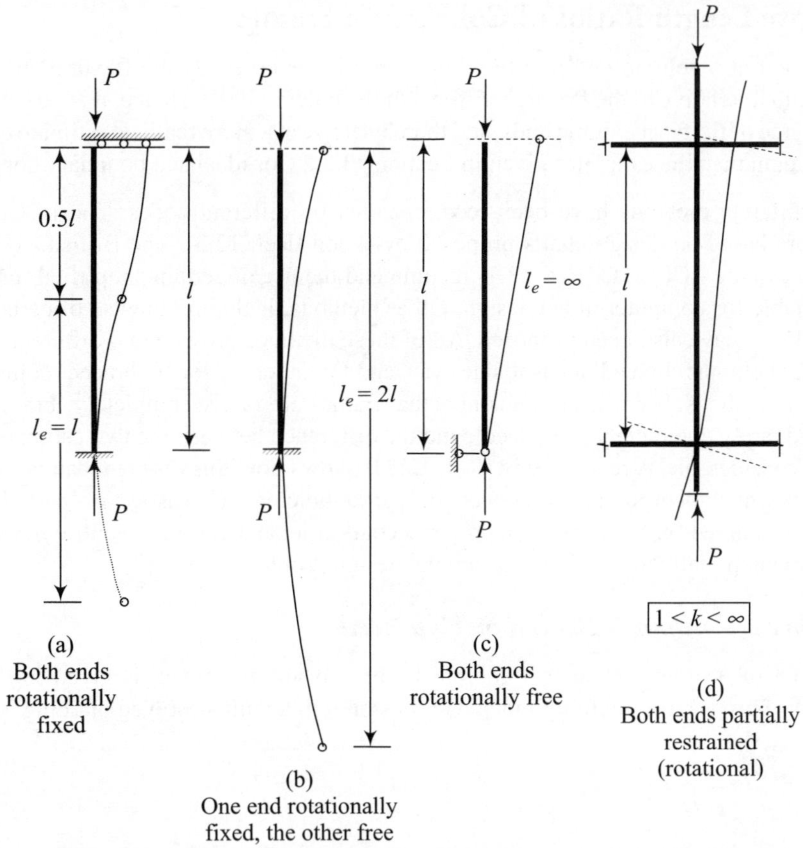

Fig. 13.5 Effective lengths of columns unbraced against sidesway.

2. *Columns unbraced against sidesway*:
   (a) both ends 'fixed' rotationally [Figure 13.5(a)] : 1.20 (instead of 1.0)
   (b) one end 'fixed' and the other 'partially fixed' : 1.50
   (c) one end 'fixed' and the other free [Figure 13.5(b)] : 2.00

The most common case encountered in framed buildings is the one involving partial rotational fixity at both ends of the column. For such a case in a 'braced' frame, $k = 0.85$ may be assumed for preliminary designs – conforming to an average of cases 1(a) and 1(c) indicated above. If the frame cannot be considered to be fully braced†, it is desirable to assume a more conservative estimate – say $k = 1.0$ or more. However, if the frame is clearly 'unbraced', it is necessary to ascertain the effective length ratio more accurately, as described in the next section.

† Generally, the assumption of a fully braced frame can be safely made if there are special bracing elements in a building such as shear walls, shear trusses, etc. [Ref. 13.7] (which are designed to resist practically all the lateral loads on the frame). Even otherwise, if a rigid frame possesses sufficient inherent translational stiffness, and especially if there are in-fill masonry walls, it may be considered to be braced – at least partially, if not fully.

13.2.3 Effective Length Ratios of Columns in Frames

The rotational restraint at a column end in a building frame is governed by the flexural stiffnesses of the members framing into it, relative to the flexural stiffness of the column itself. Hence, it is possible to arrive at measures of the 'degree of fixity' at column ends, and thereby arrive at a more realistic estimate of the effective length ratio of a column than the estimates given in Section 13.2.2 (for idealised boundary conditions).

For this purpose, different methods have been recommended by different codes. The IS Code (Cl. E–1) recommendations are based on design charts proposed by Wood [Ref. 13.3]. The British Code [Ref. 13.2] and the Commentary to the ACI Code [Ref. 13.1] recommend the use of certain simplified formulas, which are particularly suitable for computer-aided design. Other methods, including the use of certain 'alignment charts' [Ref. 13.4, 13.5], have also been proposed. All of these methods provide two different sets of charts/formulas: one set for columns 'braced' against sidesway, and the other set for 'unbraced' columns. This is a shortcoming in these methods, because columns in actual frames are rarely completely 'braced' (prevented from side-sway) and rarely completely 'unbraced', and the difference between the two estimates of effective length ratio can be considerable. A recent study [Ref. 13.22] shows how this problem can be resolved using fuzzy logic concepts, which incorporates the concept of 'partial bracing'. This aspect of 'partial bracing' may be more accurately accounted for by means of a proper second-order analysis of the entire frame [Ref. 13.6]; however, this is computationally too difficult for routine design problems.

Deciding Whether a Column is Braced or Unbraced

An approximate way of deciding whether a column is 'braced' or 'unbraced' is given in the ACI Code commentary. For this purpose, the 'stability index' Q of a storey in a multi-storeyed building is defined as:

$$Q = \frac{\sum P_u}{h_s} \times \frac{\Delta_u}{H_u} \tag{13.2}$$

where $\sum P_u \equiv$ sum of axial loads on all columns in the storey;
$h_s \equiv$ height of the storey;
$\Delta_u \equiv$ elastic first-order lateral deflection of the storey;
$H_u \equiv$ total lateral force acting on the storey.

It can be shown [Ref. 13.8] that, in the absence of bracing elements, the 'lateral flexibility' measure of the storey Δ_u/H_u (storey drift per unit storey shear) may be taken (for a typical intermediate storey) as:

$$\frac{\Delta_u}{H_u} = \frac{h_s^2}{12E_{c,col}\sum(I_c/h_s)} + \frac{h_s^2}{12E_{c,beam}\sum(I_b/l_b)} \tag{13.3}$$

where $\sum(I_c/h_s) \equiv$ sum of ratios of second moment of area to storey height of all columns in the storey in the plane under consideration;
$\sum(I_b/l_b) \equiv$ sum of ratios of second moment of area to span of all floor members in the storey in the plane under consideration;
$E_c \equiv$ modulus of elasticity of concrete.

Equation 13.2 is derived by assuming points of inflection at the mid-heights of all columns and midspan locations of all beams, and by applying the *unit load method* to an isolated storey [Ref. 13.8]. If special bracing elements such as shear walls, shear trusses and infill walls are present, then their effect will be to reduce Δ_u/H_u significantly.

The recommendation given in the ACI Code is that the storey can be considered to be *braced*† only if the stability index $Q < 0.05$.

The application of this concept is demonstrated in Example 13.1.

Use of Code Charts

Charts are given in Figures 26 and 27 of the Code for determining the effective length ratios of braced columns and unbraced columns respectively, in terms of coefficients β_1 and β_2 which represent the degrees of rotational freedom at the top and bottom ends of the column [Ref. 13.7]:

$$\beta = \frac{\sum_{jt} I_c/h_s}{\sum_{jt} I_c/h_s + \sum_{jt} 0.5(I_b/l_b)} \quad \text{for braced columns} \tag{13.4a}$$

$$\beta = \frac{\sum_{jt} I_c/h_s}{\sum_{jt} I_c/h_s + \sum_{jt} 1.5(I_b/l_b)} \quad \text{for unbraced columns} \tag{13.4b}$$

where the notation *jt* denotes that the summation is to be done for the members framing into the top joint (in case of β_1) or the bottom joint (in case of β_2). The increased beam stiffness for unbraced columns [Eq. 13.4b], compared to braced columns [Eq. 13.4a], is attributable to the fact that in the case of the latter (braced), the beams are bent in *single curvature*, whereas in the case of the former, the beams are bent in *double curvature*, in the buckled configuration.

The limiting values $\beta = 0$ and $\beta = 1$ represent 'fully fixed' and 'fully hinged' conditions respectively.

The use of these Code charts (not reproduced in this book) is demonstrated in Examples 13.1 and 13.2.

Use of Formulas

The following formulas, given in BS 8110 [Ref. 13.2] and the Commentary to the ACI Code [Ref. 13.1], provide useful estimates of the effective length ratio k:

$$k = \begin{cases} 0.7 + 0.05\,(\alpha_1 + \alpha_2) \\ 0.85 + 0.05\,\alpha_{\min} \end{cases} \quad \text{whichever is less, for } \textbf{braced} \text{ columns} \tag{13.5a}$$

$$k = \begin{cases} 1.0 + 0.15\,(\alpha_1 + \alpha_2) \\ 2.0 + 0.30\,\alpha_{\min} \end{cases} \quad \text{whichever is less, for } \textbf{unbraced} \text{ columns} \tag{13.5b}$$

$$\text{where } \alpha_1 \equiv \frac{\sum_{jt} I_c/h_s}{\sum_{jt} (I_b/l_b)_{\text{top}}} \text{ and } \alpha_2 \equiv \frac{\sum_{jt} I_c/h_s}{\sum_{jt} (I_b/l_b)_{\text{bottom}}} \tag{13.5c}$$

and $\alpha_{\min}$ is the lesser of the α values determined by Eq. 13.5c.

For a fully fixed condition, $\alpha = 0$ may be considered, and for a 'hinged' condition, $\alpha = 10$ may be considered.

The application of these formulas is demonstrated in Examples 13.1 and 13.2.

† It is found that when $Q < 0.05$, the second-order moments due to the 'lateral drift effect' will be less than 5 per cent of the first-order moments [refer Section 13.7]. It may also be noted that in the earlier versions of ACI 318, the limiting value of Q was specified as 0.04. Code IS 456:2000 (Annex E) gives limiting value for Q as 0.04.

Example 13.1

The framing plan of a multi-storeyed building is shown in Figure 13.6(a). Assume that all the columns have a size 300 mm × 400 mm; the longitudinal beams (global X-direction) have a size 250 mm × 600 mm and the transverse beams (global Y-direction) have a size 250 mm × 400 mm as shown. The storey height h_s = 3.5 m. For a column in a typical lower floor of the building, determine the effective lengths l_{ex} and l_{ey} with respect to the local x- and y- axes (major and minor), as shown in Figure 13.6(b).
For the purpose of estimating the total axial loads on the columns in the storey, assume a total distributed load of 35 kN/m² from all the floors above (combined). Also assume M 25 grade concrete for the columns and M 25 grade concrete for the beams.

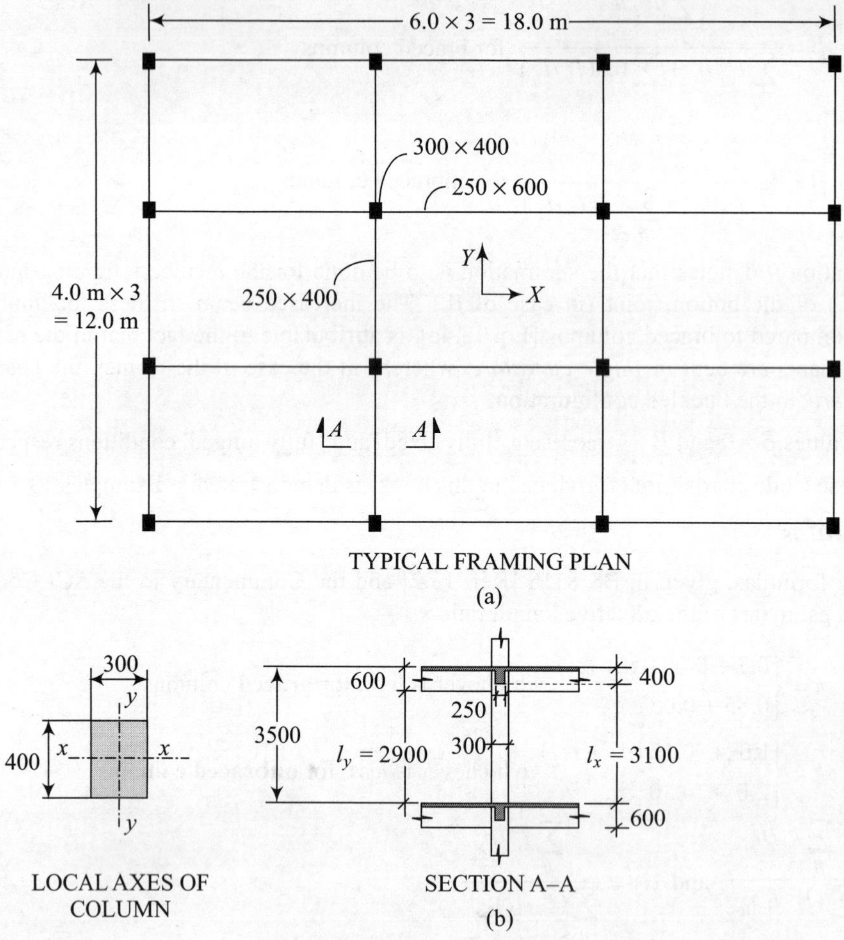

Fig. 13.6 Example 13.1.

Solution

Unsupported lengths of column

l_y = 3500 – 600 = 2900 mm (for buckling about *y*-axis)
l_x = 3500 – 400 = 3100 mm (for buckling about *x*-axis)

Relative stiffness measures of columns and beams

- Columns: 16 nos, 300 mm × 400 mm, $h_s = 3500$ mm

$$\Rightarrow \quad \sum I_c/h_s = 16 \times \frac{400 \times 300^3/12}{3500} = 4114 \times 10^3 \text{ mm}^3 \text{ (for sway in the global } X\text{-direction), and}$$

$$\Rightarrow \quad \sum I_c/h_s = 16 \times \frac{300 \times 400^3/12}{3500} = 7314 \times 10^3 \text{ mm}^3 \text{ (for sway in the global } Y\text{-direction).}$$

- Longitudinal Beams: 12 nos, 250 mm × 600 mm, $l_b = 6000$ mm

$$\Rightarrow \quad \left(\sum I_b/l_b\right)_X = 12 \times \frac{(250) \times (600)^3/12}{6000} = 9000 \times 10^3 \text{ mm}^3$$

- Transverse Beams: 12 nos, 250 mm × 400 mm, $l_b = 4000$ mm

$$\Rightarrow \quad \left(\sum I_b/l_b\right)_Y = 12 \times \frac{(250) \times (400)^3/12}{4000} = 4000 \times 10^3 \text{ mm}^3$$

Columns Braced or Unbraced?

Lateral Flexibility measures of the storey: $(\Delta_u/H_u)_X$ and $(\Delta_u/H_u)_Y$

Ignoring the contribution of in-fill walls [Eq. 13.3]:

- $$\frac{\Delta_u}{H_u} = h_s^2\left[\left\{12E_{c,\text{col}} \times \sum(I_c/h_s)\right\}^{-1} + \left\{12E_{c,\text{beam}} \times \sum(I_b/l_b)\right\}^{-1}\right]$$

  where $E_c = 5000\sqrt{f_{ck}}$ (as per Code Cl. 6.2.3.1)

  For columns, $f_{ck} = 25$ MPa $\Rightarrow E_{c,\text{col}} = 5000\sqrt{25} = 25000$ MPa

  For beams, $f_{ck} = 25$ MPa $\Rightarrow E_{c,\text{beam}} = 5000\sqrt{25} = 25000$ MPa

- Longitudinal direction (global X-direction):

$$\left(\frac{\Delta_u}{H_u}\right)_X = 3500^2\left[(12 \times 25000 \times 4114 \times 10^3)^{-1} + (12 \times 25000 \times 9000 \times 10^3)^{-1}\right]$$

$$= 1.4462 \times 10^{-5} \text{ mm/N}$$

- Transverse direction (global Y-direction):

$$\left(\frac{\Delta_u}{H_u}\right)_Y = 3500^2\left[(12 \times 25000 \times 7314 \times 10^3)^{-1} + (12 \times 25000 \times 4000 \times 10^3)^{-1}\right]$$

$$= 1.5791 \times 10^{-5} \text{ mm/N}$$

Stability Index Q

- Total axial load on all columns ≈ 35 kN/m² × (12.0 m × 18.0 m) = 7560 kN

$$Q = \frac{\Sigma P_u}{h_s} \times \frac{\Delta_u}{H_u} \quad \text{[Eq. 13.2]}$$

Longitudinal direction: $Q_X = \dfrac{7560 \times 10^3}{3500} \times 1.4462 \times 10^{-5} = 0.0312$

Transverse direction: $Q_Y = \dfrac{7560 \times 10^3}{3500} \times 1.5791 \times 10^{-5} = 0.0341$

- As $Q_X = 0.0312 < 0.05$, the storey can be considered 'braced' in the longitudinal direction.
  As $Q_Y = 0.0312 < 0.05$, the storey can be considered 'braced' in the transverse direction.
  Hence, the columns in the storey may be assumed to be 'braced' in both directions. (Note that Q_X and Q_Y are less than the IS Code limit of 0.04 as well)

Effective Lengths by IS Code charts

$$\beta_1 = \beta_2 = \frac{\sum_{jt} I_c/h_s}{\sum_{jt} I_c/h_s + \sum_{jt} 0.5(I_b/l_b)} \quad \text{[Eq. 13.4a]}$$

- *Buckling with respect to minor (local y-) axis:*

$$\sum_{jt}(I_c/h_s) = \frac{400 \times 300^3/12}{3500} \times 2 = 514 \times 10^3 \text{ mm}^3$$

$$\sum_{jt}(I_b/l_b) = \frac{250 \times (600)^3/12}{6000} \times 2 = 1500 \times 10^3 \text{ mm}^3$$

$$\beta_1 = \beta_2 = \frac{514}{514 + 0.5(1500)} = 0.407$$

Referring to Figure 26 of the Code, $k_y = 0.64$

$\Rightarrow \quad l_{ey} = l_y \times k_y = 0.64 \times 2900 = \mathbf{1856\ mm}$

- *Buckling with respect to major (local x-) axis:*

$$\sum_{jt}(I_c/h_s) = \frac{300 \times 400^3/12}{3500} \times 2 = 914 \times 10^3 \text{ mm}^3$$

$$\sum_{jt}(I_b/h_b) = \frac{250 \times (400)^3/12}{4000} \times 2 = 667 \times 10^3 \text{ mm}^3$$

$$\beta_1 = \beta_2 = \frac{914}{914 + 0.5(667)} = 0.733$$

Referring to Figure 26 of the Code, $k_x = 0.82$

$\Rightarrow \quad l_{ex} = l_x \times k_x = 0.82 \times 3100 = = \mathbf{2542\ mm}$

Alternative: Effective Lengths by Formulas [Eq. 13.5a]

$$\alpha_1 = \alpha_2 = \frac{\sum_{jt} I_c/h_s}{\sum_{jt}(I_b/l_b)}$$

- *Buckling with respect to minor (local y-) axis:* $\alpha_1 = \alpha_2 = \dfrac{514}{1500} = 0.3427$

$$\Rightarrow \quad k_y = \begin{cases} 0.7 + 0.05(2 \times 0.3427) = 0.7343 & \text{(lesser)} \\ 0.85 + 0.05(0.3427) = 0.8671 \end{cases}$$

$\Rightarrow \quad l_{ey} = 0.7343 \times 2900 = \mathbf{2129\ mm}$

- *Buckling with respect to major (local x-) axis*: $\alpha_1 = \alpha_2 = \dfrac{914}{667} = 1.3703$

$$\Rightarrow \qquad k_x = \begin{cases} 0.7 + 0.05(2 \times 1.3703) = 0.8370 & \text{(lesser)} \\ 0.85 + 0.05(1.3703) = 0.9185 \end{cases}$$

$$\Rightarrow \qquad l_{ex} = 0.8370 \times 3100 = \mathbf{2595\ mm}$$

- *Note* 1: The use of formulas gives effective lengths that are generally within ± 8 per cent of the corresponding values obtained from the Code charts.
- *Note* 2: Alternatively, the designer may assume idealised boundary conditions – braced columns with partial rotational fixity at top and bottom.

  Assuming a value $k = 0.85$ (as explained in Section 13.2.2)

  $\Rightarrow \qquad l_{ey} = 0.85 \times 2900 = 2465$ mm, and $l_{ex} = 0.85 \times 3100 = 2635$ mm

  This results in a slightly conservative estimate of effective length.
- *Note* 3: A realistic assessment of effective length is called for in the case of *slender* columns. In the present case, as l_{ey}/D_y *and* l_{ex}/D_x are approximately 7, and well below 12, the column is definitely a *short column*, and there is no real need for a rigorous calculation of effective length.

Example 13.2

Repeat the problem in Example 13.1, considering a column size of 250 mm × 250 mm (instead of 300 mm × 400 mm).

Solution

- *Unsupported lengths* of column

  $l_y = 2900$ mm and $l_x = 3100$ mm (as in Example 13.1)
- *Relative stiffness measures* of columns and beams

  Columns: $\sum I_c/h_s = 16 \times (250)^4/(12 \times 3500) = 1488 \times 10^3\ \text{mm}^3$

  Longitudinal Beams: $\left(\sum I_b/l_b\right)_X = 9000 \times 10^3\ \text{mm}^3$ (as in Example 13.1)

  Transverse Beams: $\left(\sum I_b/l_b\right)_Y = 4000 \times 10^3\ \text{mm}^3$ (as in Example 13.1)
- *Lateral Flexibility measures* of the storey:

$$\frac{\Delta_u}{H_u} = h_s^2\left[\left\{12E_{c,\text{col}} \times \sum(I_c/h_s)\right\}^{-1} + \left\{12E_{c,\text{beam}} \times \sum(I_b/l_b)\right\}^{-1}\right]$$

  Substituting $E_{c,\text{col}} = 25000$ MPa, $E_{c,\text{beam}} = 25000$ MPa (as in Example 13.1) and $h_s = 3500$ mm, and values of relative stiffness measures,

  Longitudinal direction (global X-direction): $\left(\dfrac{\Delta_u}{H_u}\right)_X = 3.1979 \times 10^{-5}$ mm/N

  Transverse direction (global Y-direction): $\left(\dfrac{\Delta_u}{H_u}\right)_Y = 3.7650 \times 10^{-5}$ mm/N

  [Comparing these values with those obtained in Example 13.1, it is seen that the reduction in column size results in a drastic increase (more than double) in the lateral flexibility of the storey].

- *Stability Index Q*

$P_u = 7560$ kN (as in Example 13.1)

$$Q_X = \frac{7560 \times 10^3}{3500} \times 3.1979 \times 10^{-5} = 0.0690 > 0.05$$

$$Q_Y = \frac{7560 \times 10^3}{3500} \times 3.7650 \times 10^{-5} = 0.0813 > 0.05$$

Hence, the columns in the storey should be considered as 'unbraced' in both directions.

Effective Lengths by IS Code charts

$$\beta_1 = \beta_2 = \frac{\sum_{jt} I_c/h_s}{\sum_{jt} I_c/h_s + \sum_{jt} 1.5(I_b/l_b)} \qquad \text{[Eq. 13.4b]}$$

- *Buckling with respect to minor (local y-) axis*:

$$\sum_{jt}(I_c/h_s) = \frac{250^4/12}{3500} \times 2 = 186 \times 10^3 \text{ mm}^3 \; ; \; \sum_{jt}(I_b/l_b) = 1500 \times 10^3 \text{ mm}^3$$

(as in Example 13.1)

$$\beta_1 = \beta_2 = \frac{186}{186 + 1.5(1500)} = 0.076$$

Referring to Figure 27 of the Code, $k_y = 1.04$

$\Rightarrow \quad l_{ey} = l_y \times k_y = 1.04 \times 2900 =$ **3016 mm**

- *Buckling with respect to major (local x-) axis*:

$$\sum_{jt}(I_c/h_s) = 186 \times 10^3 \text{ mm}^3; \sum_{jt}(I_b/l_b) = 667 \times 10^3 \text{ mm}^3 \text{ (as in Example 13.1)}$$

$$\beta_1 = \beta_2 = \frac{186}{186 + 1.5(667)} = 0.157$$

Referring to Figure 27 of the Code, $k_x = 1.09$

$\Rightarrow \quad l_{ex} = l_x \times k_x = 1.09 \times 3100 =$ **3379 mm**

Alternative: Effective Lengths by Formulas [Eq. 13.5a]

$$\alpha_1 = \alpha_2 = \frac{\sum_{jt} I_c/h_s}{\sum_{jt}(I_b/l_b)}$$

- *Buckling with respect to minor (local y-) axis*: $\alpha_1 = \alpha_2 = \frac{186}{1500} = 0.124$

$$\Rightarrow \quad k_y = \begin{cases} 1.0 + 0.15(2 \times 0.124) = 1.0372 & \text{(lesser)} \\ 2.0 + 0.30(0.124) = 2.0372 \end{cases}$$

$\Rightarrow \quad l_{ey} = 1.037 \times 2900 =$ **3007 mm**

- *Buckling with respect to major (local x-) axis*: $\alpha_1 = \alpha_2 = \dfrac{186}{667} = 0.2789$

$$\Rightarrow \quad k_x = \begin{cases} 1.0 + 0.15(2 \times 0.2789) = 1.084 & \text{(lesser)} \\ 2.0 + 0.30(0.2789) = 2.084 \end{cases}$$

$$\Rightarrow \quad l_{ex} = 1.084 \times 3100 = \mathbf{3360\ mm}$$

- *Note* 1: The effective lengths predicted by the two different methods are fairly close.
- *Note* 2: Considering the effective lengths given by the Code charts, the slenderness ratios of the column are obtained as follows:

$$l_{ey}/D_y = 3016/250 = 12.1$$
$$l_{ex}/D_x = 3379/250 = 13.5$$

The column should be designed as a 'slender column'.

13.3 Code Requirements on Slenderness Limits, Minimum Eccentricities and Reinforcement

13.3.1 Slenderness Limits

Codes specify limits on slenderness ratios of compression members in order to eliminate buckling/instability failures.

Slenderness effects in columns effectively result in reduced strength, on account of the decrease in critical load with increase in slenderness under axial loading as well as the additional 'secondary' moments introduced [the 'P–Δ moment'; refer Section 13.7]. In the case of very slender columns, failure may occur suddenly under small loads due to instability ('elastic buckling'), rather than due to material failure. The Code attempts to prevent this type of failure (due to instability) by specifying certain 'slenderness limits' in the proportioning of columns.

The Code (Cl. 25.3.1) specifies that the ratio of the unsupported length (l) to the least lateral dimension (d) of a column should not exceed[†] a value of 60:

$$l/d \leq 60 \tag{13.6}$$

Furthermore, in case one end of a column is free (i.e., cantilevered column) in any given plane, the Code (Cl. 25.3.2) specifies that

$$l \leq 100b^2/D \tag{13.7}$$

where D is the depth of the cross-section measured in the plane of the cantilever and b is the width (in the perpendicular direction).

13.3.2 Minimum Eccentricities

As explained in Section 13.1.2, the general case of loading on a compression member is one comprising axial compression combined with biaxial bending. This loading condition is represented by a state of *biaxial eccentric compression*, wherein the axial load P acts eccentric to the longitudinal centroidal axis of the column cross-section, with eccentricities e_x and e_y with respect to the major and minor principal axes [Figure 13.2(c)].

[†] In the case of 'unbraced' columns, it is desirable to adopt a more stringent limit – say, $l/d < 40$.

Very often, eccentricities not explicitly arising out of structural analysis calculations act on the column due to various reasons, such as

In order to account for various uncertainties related to the occurrence of pure axial loading, the Code requires every column to be designed for the applied axial load with a specified minimum eccentricity

- lateral loads not considered in design;
- live load placements not considered in design;
- accidental lateral/eccentric loads;
- errors in construction (such as misalignments); and
- slenderness effects underestimated in design.

For this reason, the Code (Cl. 25.4) requires every column to be designed for a minimum eccentricity e_{min} (in any plane) equal to the unsupported length/500 plus lateral dimension/30, subject to a minimum of 20 mm. For a column with a rectangular section [Figure 13.2], this implies:

$$e_{x,\min} = \begin{cases} l/500 + D_x/30 \\ 20 \text{ mm} \end{cases} \text{(whichever is greater)} \tag{13.8a}$$

$$e_{y,\min} = \begin{cases} l/500 + D_y/30 \\ 20 \text{ mm} \end{cases} \text{(whichever is greater)} \tag{13.8b}$$

For non-rectangular and non-circular cross-sectional shapes, it is recommended [Ref. 13.7] that, for any given plane,

$$e_{\min} = \begin{cases} l_e/300 \\ 20 \text{ mm} \end{cases} \text{(whichever is greater)} \tag{13.8c}$$

where l_e is the *effective length* of the column in the plane considered.

13.3.3 Code Requirements on Reinforcement and Detailing

The Code specifies 0.8 per cent of the gross concrete area (based on the area of concrete required to resist the load) as the minimum longitudinal reinforcement. The maximum is 6 per cent of area of concrete; however, to ease placing and compacting difficulties, a lower percentage is desirable.

Longitudinal Reinforcement (refer Cl. 26.5.3.1 of the Code)

- *Minimum Reinforcement*: The longitudinal bars must, in general, have a cross-sectional area not less than 0.8 per cent of the gross area of the column section. Such a minimum limit is specified by the Code:
  - to ensure nominal flexural resistance under unforeseen eccentricities in loading; and
  - to prevent the yielding of the bars due to creep[†] and shrinkage effects, which result in a transfer of load from the concrete to the steel.

In very large-sized columns (where the large size is dictated, for instance, by architectural considerations, and not strength) under axial compression, the limit of 0.8 per cent of gross area may result in excessive reinforcement. In such cases, the Code allows some concession by permitting the minimum area of steel to be calculated as 0.8 per cent of *the area of concrete required to resist the direct stress, and not the actual (gross) area.*

However, in the case of *pedestals* (i.e., compression members with $l_e/D < 3$) which are designed as plain concrete columns, the minimum requirement of longitudinal bars may be taken as 0.15 per cent of the gross area of cross-section.

[†] Creep effects can be quite pronounced in compression members under sustained service loads [refer Section 13.4.2]. The consequent increase in steel stress (due to creep strain) is found to be relatively high at very low reinforcement percentages: hence, the minimum limit of 0.8 per cent is prescribed [Ref. 13.7].

In the case of reinforced concrete walls, the Code (Cl. 32.5) has introduced detailed provisions regarding minimum reinforcement requirements for vertical (and horizontal) steel. The vertical reinforcement should not be less than 0.15 per cent of the gross area in general. This may be reduced to 0.12 per cent if welded wire fabric or deformed bars (Fe 415/Fe 500 grade steel) is used, provided the bar diameter does not exceed 16 mm. This reinforcement should be placed in two layers if the wall is more than 200 mm thick. In all cases, the bar spacing should not exceed three times the wall thickness or 450 mm, whichever is less.

- *Maximum Reinforcement:* The maximum cross-sectional area of longitudinal bars should not exceed 6 per cent of the gross area of the column section. However, a reduced maximum limit of 4 per cent is recommended in general in the interest of better placement and compaction of concrete – and, in particular, at lapped splice locations.

  In tall buildings, columns located in the lowermost storeys generally carry heavy reinforcement (~4 per cent). The bars are progressively curtailed in stages at higher levels.

- *Minimum diameter/number of bars and their location:* Longitudinal bars in columns (and pedestals) should not be less than 12 mm in diameter and should not be spaced more than 300 mm apart (centre-to-centre) along the periphery of the column [Figure 13.7(a)]. At least 4 bars (one at each corner) should be provided in a column with rectangular cross-section, and at least 6 bars (equally spaced near the periphery) in a circular column. In 'spiral columns' (including noncircular shapes), the

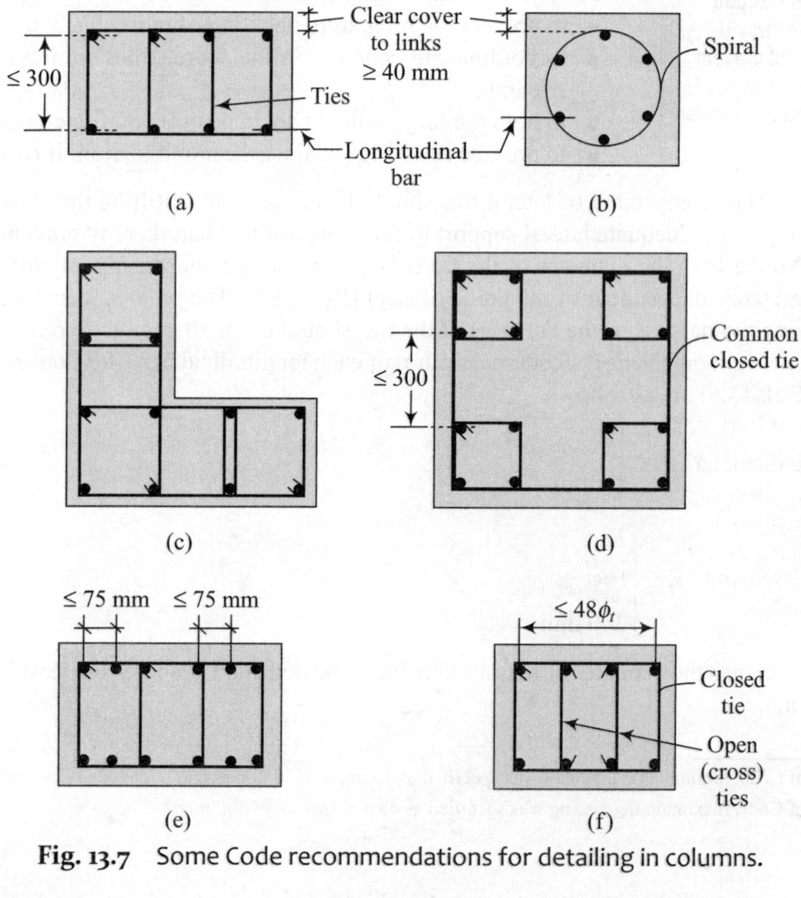

Fig. 13.7 Some Code recommendations for detailing in columns.

longitudinal bars should be placed in contact with the spiral reinforcement, and equidistant around its inner circumference [Figure 13.7(b)]. In columns with T-, L-, or other cross-sectional shapes, at least one bar should be located at each corner or apex [Figure 13.7(c)].

Longitudinal bars are usually located close to the periphery (for better flexural resistance), but may be placed in the interior of the column when eccentricities in loading are minimal. When a large number of bars need to be accommodated, they may be *bundled*, or, alternatively, *grouped*, as shown in [Figure 13.7(d)].

- *Cover to reinforcement*: A minimum clear cover of 40 mm or bar diameter (whichever is greater), to the column ties is recommended by the Code (Cl. 26.4.2.1) for columns in general; a reduced clear cover of 25 mm is permitted in small-sized columns ($D \leq 200$ mm and whose reinforcing bars do not exceed 12 mm) and a minimum clear cover of 15 mm (or bar diameter, whichever is greater) is specified for walls. However, in aggressive environments, it is desirable, in the interest of durability, to provide increased cover [Table 5.1] – but preferably not greater than 75 mm.

Transverse Reinforcement (refer Cl. 26.5.3.2 of the Code)

Transverse reinforcements in columns help to hold longitudinal bars in position during construction, provide lateral support to and prevent buckling of individual bars, confine the concrete, and resist shear and torsion.

- *General:* All longitudinal reinforcement in a compression member must be enclosed within transverse reinforcement, comprising either *lateral ties* (with internal angles not exceeding 135°) or *spirals*. This is required:
  - to prevent the premature buckling of individual bars;
  - to confine the concrete in the 'core', thus improving ductility and strength;
  - to hold the longitudinal bars in position during construction; and
  - to provide resistance against shear and torsion, if required.

- *Lateral Ties:* The arrangement of lateral ties should be effective in fulfilling the above requirements. They should provide adequate lateral support to each longitudinal bar, thereby preventing the outward movement of the bar. The diameter of the tie ϕ_t is governed by requirements of stiffness, rather than strength, and so is independent of the grade of steel [Ref. 13.7]. The *pitch* s_t (centre-to-centre spacing along the longitudinal axis of the column) of the ties should be small enough to reduce adequately the unsupported length (and hence, slenderness ratio) of each longitudinal bar. The Code recommendations (based on Ref. 13.9) are as follows:

$$\text{tie diameter}^{\dagger}\ \phi_t \geq \begin{cases} \phi_{\text{long, max}}/4 \\ 6 \text{ mm} \end{cases} \tag{13.9}$$

$$\text{tie spacing}^{\ddagger}\ s_t \leq \begin{cases} D \\ 16\varphi_{\text{long, min}} \\ 300 \text{ mm} \end{cases} \tag{13.10}$$

where ϕ_{long} denotes the diameter of longitudinal bar to be tied and D denotes the least lateral dimension of the column.

† In earlier version of Code, minimum tie diameter was specified as 5 mm, instead of 6 mm.

‡ In earlier version of Code, maximum tie spacing was specified as $48 \times \phi_t$ instead of 300 mm

Ideally, the tie must turn around (and thereby provide full lateral restraint to) every longitudinal bar that it encloses – particularly the corner bars. When the spacing of longitudinal bars is less than 75 mm, lateral support need only be provided for the corner and alternate bars [Figure 13.7(e)]. The straight portion of a closed tie (between the corner bars) is not really effective if it is large, as it tends to bulge outwards when the concrete core is subjected to compression [Ref. 13.10]. For this reason, supplementary cross ties are required for effective confinement of the concrete. If the longitudinal bars spaced at a distance not exceeding $48\phi_t$ are effectively tied in two directions, then the additional longitudinal bars in between these bars need be tied only in one direction by *open* ties [Figure 13.7(f)].

The ends of every tie (whether closed or open) should be properly anchored. In the case of grouping of longitudinal bars at the corners of a large-sized column [Figure 13.7(d)], each group should be separately tied together, along with a single common closed tie for all groups. The diameter and pitch of this common tie should be computed [Eqs 13.9 and 13.10] by treating each bar group as a single longitudinal bar (of equivalent area); however, the diameter of the common tie need not exceed 20 mm.

Finally, it should be noted that when multiple ties are provided in a column (which is usually the case, except in small-sized columns), the locations of these different ties should preferably be staggered along the longitudinal axis of the column. Extra ties should be provided at lapped splice locations in the longitudinal reinforcement – especially at the bends.

- *Spirals:* Helical reinforcement provides very good confinement to the concrete in the 'core' and enhances significantly the ductility of the column at ultimate loads. The diameter and pitch of the spiral may be computed as in the case of ties [Eqs 13.9, 13.10] — except when the column is designed to carry a 5 per cent overload (as permitted by the Code), in which case

$$\text{pitch } s_t < \begin{cases} 75 \text{ mm} \\ \text{core diameter}/6 \end{cases} \tag{13.11a}$$

$$\text{and } s_t > \begin{cases} 25 \text{ mm} \\ 3\varphi_t \end{cases} \tag{13.11b}$$

The ends of the spiral should be anchored properly by providing one and a half extra turns.

13.4 Design of Short Columns Under Axial Compression

13.4.1 Conditions of Axial Loading

Axial loading on a compression member may be defined as loading that produces a uniform (compressive) *strain* distribution across the cross-section. If the column is symmetrically reinforced, as shown in Figure 13.8(a), the line of action of the load P_o must coincide with the longitudinal centroidal axis of the column section, in order to produce a uniform strain distribution. Equilibrium conditions require the resultant compressive force $C_c + C_s$ in the section to be equal to and act opposite to and through the point of application of the external load P_o [Figure 13.8(a)]. If f_{cc} and f_{sc} denote respectively the stresses in the concrete and the longitudinal steel, corresponding to the uniform compressive strain ε_c, then it follows that

> 'Axial loading' on a RC column is loading that produces a uniform compressive strain across the cross section. For this, in a symmetrically reinforced section, the load should act through the *geometric centroid* of the section. In unsymmetrically reinforced sections, for this condition, the load should act through the *plastic centroid*, which is different from the geometric centroid.

$$\begin{aligned} P_o &= C_c + C_s \\ &= f_{cc}A_c + f_{sc}A_{sc} \end{aligned}$$

$$\Rightarrow \quad P_o = f_{cc}A_g + (f_{sc} - f_{cc})A_{sc} \tag{13.12}$$

where A_g = gross area of cross-section = $A_c + A_{sc}$;

A_{sc} = total area of longitudinal reinforcement = $\sum A_{si}$;

A_c = net area of concrete in the section = $A_g - A_{sc}$

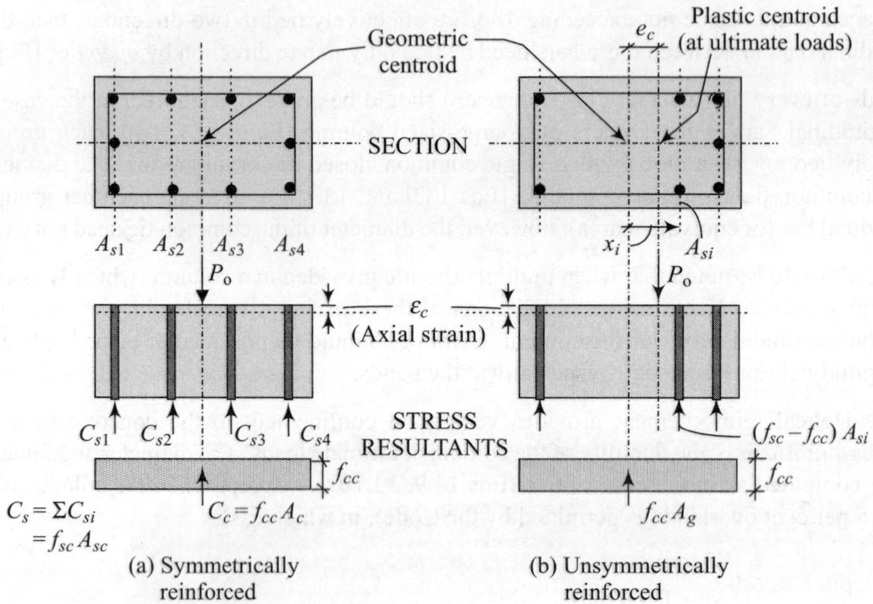

Fig. 13.8 Axial loading on short columns.

When the section is asymmetrically reinforced and subject to axial load conditions [Figure 13.8(b)], Eq. 13.12 remains valid. However, the line of action of the applied load P_o must now be eccentric to the geometric centroidal axis. This eccentricity e_c is easily obtained from moment equilibrium conditions as

$$e_c = \frac{(f_{sc} - f_{cc})\sum A_{si}x_i}{P_o} \tag{13.12a}$$

> The point in a RC cross section, through which only an axial compressive force has to act, in order to produce a uniform compressive strain over the section, is called a 'plastic centroid'.

where x_i = distance measured [+ve as indicated in Figure 13.8(b)] of the ith row of reinforcement of area A_{si} with reference to the geometrical centroid.

At the limit state of collapse, the section would have 'plastified', and for this reason, the axis through which P_o must act for axial load conditions is termed the *plastic centroidal* axis. Under symmetrical reinforcement conditions of axial loading, $e_c = 0$, and the plastic centroid coincides with the geometric centroid.

13.4.2 Behaviour Under Service Loads

Until the early 1950s, reinforced concrete columns were invariably designed using the elastic theory, which involves the concepts of *permissible stresses*, *modular ratio* and *transformed section* [refer Sections 3.2,

4.6]. It was realized subsequently, from extensive experimental investigations, that there can be no fixed ratio of steel stress f_{sc} to concrete stress f_{cc}, even under axial loading conditions [Ref. 13.10]. The ratio of these stresses depended on

1. the amount of creep, which is influenced by the history of sustained loading and numerous factors related to the quality of concrete [refer Section 2.11].
2. the amount of shrinkage, which in turn depended on the age of concrete, method of curing, environmental conditions and several other factors related to the quality of concrete [refer Section 2.12]

In general, the strain in the cross-section ε_c increases with age on account of creep and shrinkage, with a consequent redistribution of stresses in concrete and steel, such that the load shared by the concrete is partially transferred to the steel. Consequently, it becomes difficult to predict the stresses f_{cc} and f_{sc} (in Eq. 13.12) under service loads.

According to conventional working stress method of design, substituting the *permissible stresses* σ_{cc} and σ_{sc} in lieu of f_{sc} and f_{cc} respectively, the design equation is obtained from Eq. 13.12 as

$$P_o = \sigma_{cc} A_g + (\sigma_{sc} - \sigma_{cc}) A_{sc} \tag{13.13}$$

where σ_{sc} is taken approximately as $1.5m\sigma_{cc}$ (as in doubly reinforced beams – refer Section 4.6). However, this assumption renders the steel stress σ_{sc} independent of the grade of steel, and results in unrealistic and uneconomical designs. The Code (B-2.2) in its provision for working stress design, attempts to somewhat remedy this situation by recommending

$$\sigma_{sc} = \begin{cases} 130 \text{ MPa} & \text{for Fe 250 steel} \\ 190 \text{ MPa} & \text{for Fe 415, Fe 500 steels} \end{cases} \tag{13.14a}$$

The allowable stresses in concrete (σ_{cc}) under direct compression are specified as

$$\sigma_{cc} = \begin{cases} 4.0 \text{ MPa} & \text{for M 15} \\ 5.0 \text{ MPa} & \text{for M 20} \\ 6.0 \text{ MPa} & \text{for M 25} \\ 8.0 \text{ MPa} & \text{for M 30} \\ 9.0 \text{ MPa} & \text{for M 35} \end{cases} \tag{13.14b}$$

However, most codes of other countries have dispensed with the *working stress method* (WSM) of design altogether, with the advent of the *ultimate load method* (ULM) of design initially, and the more rational *limit states method* (LSM) of design subsequently (since the 1980s). Indeed, in the revised Indian Code too, priority is given to the LSM design procedure and the WSM is relegated to an Annex.

13.4.3 Behaviour Under Ultimate Loads

Unlike service load conditions, the behaviour of an axially compressed short column is fairly predictable under ultimate load conditions. It is found that the ultimate strength of the column is relatively independent of its age and history of loading. As axial loading is increased, axial shortening of the column increases linearly up to about 80 per cent of the ultimate load P_{uo} (path *OA* in Figure 13.9); this behaviour is found to be independent of the type of transverse reinforcement [Ref. 13.10]. However, beyond the ultimate load (point *B* in Figure 13.9), the behaviour depends on the type and amount of transverse reinforcement.

Tied Columns

Generally, the longitudinal steel would have reached 'yield' conditions at the ultimate load level P_{uo} [point B in Figure 13.9] – regardless of whether transverse reinforcement is provided or not[†]. However, in the absence of transverse reinforcement (or with widely spaced lateral ties), failure will be sudden and brittle, caused by crushing and shearing of the concrete (as in a plain concrete cylinder test – refer Section 2.8) and accompanied by the buckling of longitudinal bars. In the case of tied columns, some marginal ductility [paths BC, BD in Figure 13.9] can be introduced by providing closely spaced lateral ties which undergo yielding in tension prior to collapse of the columns. The descent in the load-axial shortening curve is attributable to 'softening' and micro-cracking in the concrete.

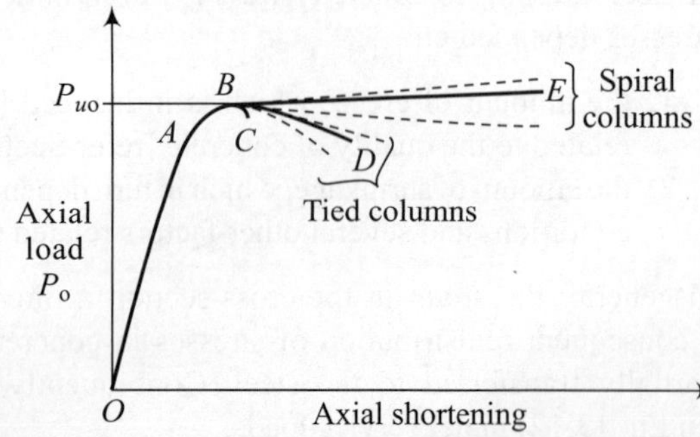

Fig. 13.9 Behaviour of axially loaded tied and spiral columns.

Spiral Columns

> **Spirally reinforced columns fail with considerable ductility. With the specified minimum amount of spiral reinforcement provided, the Code permits a 5 per cent increase in strength for such columns.**

It is with the *spiral column* that substantial ductility is achieved prior to the collapse of the column [path BE in Figure 13.9]. It is found that, approximately at load level P_{uo} [point B in Figure 13.9], the outer shell of the concrete (covering the spiral) spalls off; but the concrete in the 'core', laterally confined by the helical reinforcement, continues to carry load. Collapse ultimately takes place when the spiral reinforcement yields in tension. The load carrying capacity after the spalling can exceed P_{uo} provided the amount of spiral reinforcement is such that the load capacity contributed by it more than makes up for the loss in load capacity due to spalling of the concrete shell. Based on experimental findings [Ref. 13.10], the Code (Cl. 39.4) permits a 5 per cent increase in strength beyond P_{uo}, provided the following requirement is satisfied by the spiral reinforcement:

$$\rho_s \geq 0.36\left(\frac{A_g}{A_{\text{core}}} - 1\right)\frac{f_{ck}}{f_{sy}} \tag{13.15}$$

where $\rho_s \equiv \dfrac{\text{volume of spiral reinforcement}}{\text{volume of core}}$ per unit length of column;

$A_{core} \equiv$ total area of concrete core, measured outer-to-outer of the spirals;

$A_g \equiv$ gross area of cross-section;

$f_{sy} \equiv$ characteristic (yield) strength of spiral, limited to 415 MPa.

However, it may be observed that the 5 per cent increase in strength will be realised only after extensive cracking of concrete and will be accompanied by large deformations. It is stated in the Explanatory Handbook to the Code [Ref. 13.7] that *the permitted increase in design capacity of such columns is because the failure will be gradual and ductile* and not because the Code intends *to make use of increase in capacity beyond the spalling load.*

† It may be noted, however, that, for design purposes, the Code limits the ultimate strain in concrete to 0.002, as a conservative measure. Corresponding to this strain, yield conditions will not be attained in the case of Fe 415 and Fe 500 grades of steel [refer Figures 3.6, 3.7].

In addition to increased ductility and warning prior to collapse, spiral columns exhibit increased toughness (resistance to impact loading) and are particularly effective under dynamic loading conditions (such as seismic loading).

13.4.4 Design Strength of Axially Loaded Short Columns

The maximum compressive strain in concrete under axial loading at the limit state of collapse in compression is specified as $\varepsilon_c = 0.002$ by the Code (Cl. 39.1a). Corresponding to this (somewhat conservative) limiting strain of 0.002†, the design stress in the concrete is $0.67f_{ck}/1.5 = 0.447f_{ck}$ (refer Figure 3.5), and the design stress in steel is $0.87f_y$ in the case of Fe 250 (refer Figure 3.6) and $0.790f_y$ and $0.746f_y$ in the case of Fe 415 and Fe 500 respectively (refer Figure 3.7 and Table 3.2).

Short columns are primarily designed for sectional strength, without any need to consider slenderness effects (additional moments or possible buckling).

Accordingly, under 'pure' axial loading conditions, the design strength of a short column is obtainable from Eq. 13.12 as:

$$P_{uo} = 0.447 f_{ck} A_g + (f_{sc} - 0.447 f_{ck}) A_{sc} \tag{13.16}$$

with

$$f_{sc} = \begin{cases} 0.870 f_y & \text{for Fe 250} \\ 0.790 f_y & \text{for Fe 415} \\ 0.746 f_y & \text{for Fe 500} \end{cases} \tag{13.16a}$$

However, as explained in Section 13.3.2, the Code requires all columns to be designed for 'minimum eccentricities' in loading. Hence, Eq. 13.16 cannot be directly applied. Nevertheless, where the calculated minimum eccentricity (in any plane) does not exceed 0.05 times the lateral dimension (in the plane considered), the Code (Cl. 39.3) permits the use of the following simplified formula, obtained by reducing P_{uo} (from Eq. 13.16) by approximately 10 per cent‡ [Ref. 13.7]:

$$\tilde{P}_{uo} = 0.4 f_{ck} A_g + (0.67 f_y - 0.4 f_{ck}) A_{sc} \tag{13.17}$$

where $\tilde{P}_{uo}$ denotes the design strength in uniaxial compression permitted by the Code (including the effect of minimum eccentricities). It is found that the use of Eq. 13.17 results in a conservative design, compared to the rigorous design involving axial compression and biaxial bending with the minimum eccentricities.

As mentioned earlier, the Code (Cl. 39.4) permits the load capacity be enhanced by 5 per cent when spiral reinforcement is provided, conforming to Eq. 13.15.

Example 13.3

Design the reinforcement in a column of size 450 mm × 600 mm, subject to an axial load of 2400 kN under service dead and live loads. The column has an unsupported length of 3.0 m and is braced against sidesway in both directions. Use M 25 concrete and Fe 500 steel.

† Note that typical stress-strain relations for concrete (see Section 2.8.2 and Figure 2.7) show a decrease in stress after a strain of 0.002 (although the one recommended by the Code [Figure 3.5] does not show this). Thus, beyond a strain $\varepsilon_c = 0.002$, there is strain-softening and in a section under uniform compression, the maximum load carried by *concrete* is at this strain.

‡ The reduction works out as 10 per cent with respect to Fe 415/Fe 500 grades of steel. However, with respect to Fe 250 steel, the reduction in f_{sc} is as high as 30 per cent, while the reduction in f_{cc} is 10 per cent.

Solution

Short Column or Slender Column?

- Given: $l_x = l_y = 3000$ mm, $D_y = 450$ mm, $D_x = 600$ mm

  slenderness ratios $\begin{cases} l_{ex}/D_x = k_x l_x/D_x = k_x \times 3000/600 = 5k_x \\ l_{ey}/D_y = k_y l_y/D_y = k_y \times 3000/450 = 6.67k_y \end{cases}$

  As the column is braced against sidesway in both directions, effective length ratios k_x and k_y are both less than unity, and hence the two slenderness ratios are both less than 12.

- Hence, the column may be designed as a *short column*.

Minimum Eccentricities [Eq. 13.8]

$$e_{x,\min} = \frac{3000}{500} + \frac{600}{30} = 26.0 \text{ mm } (> 20.0 \text{ mm})$$

$$e_{y,\min} = \frac{3000}{500} + \frac{450}{30} = 21.0 \text{ mm } (> 20.0 \text{ mm})$$

- As $0.05D_x = 0.05 \times 600 = 30.0 \text{ mm} > e_{x,\min} = 26.0$ mm
  and $0.05D_y = 0.05 \times 450 = 22.5 \text{ mm} > e_{y,\min} = 21.0$ mm,
  the Code formula for axially loaded short columns can be used.

Factored Load

- P_u = *service load* × *partial load factor*
  $= 2400 \times 1.5 = 3600$ kN

Design of Longitudinal Reinforcement

- $P_u = 0.4 f_{ck} A_g + (0.67 f_y - 0.4 f_{ck}) A_{sc}$ [Eq. 13.17]

  $\Rightarrow \quad 3600 \times 10^3 = 0.4 \times 25 \times (450 \times 600) + (0.67 \times 500 - 0.4 \times 25) A_{sc}$
  $= 2700 \times 10^3 + 325 A_{sc}$

  $\Rightarrow \quad A_{sc} = (3600 - 2700) \times 10^3/325 = 2769 \text{ mm}^2$

- In view of the column dimensions (450 mm, 600 mm), it is necessary to place intermediate bars, in addition to the 4 corner bars:

  Provide **4–25ϕ at corners:** $4 \times 491 = 1964 \text{ mm}^2$
  and **4–20ϕ additional:** $4 \times 314 = 1256 \text{ mm}^2$
  $\Rightarrow \quad A_{sc} = 3220 \text{ mm}^2 > 2769 \text{ mm}^2$

  $\Rightarrow \quad p = (100 \times 3220)/(450 \times 600) = 1.192 > 0.8$ (minimum reinf.) – OK.

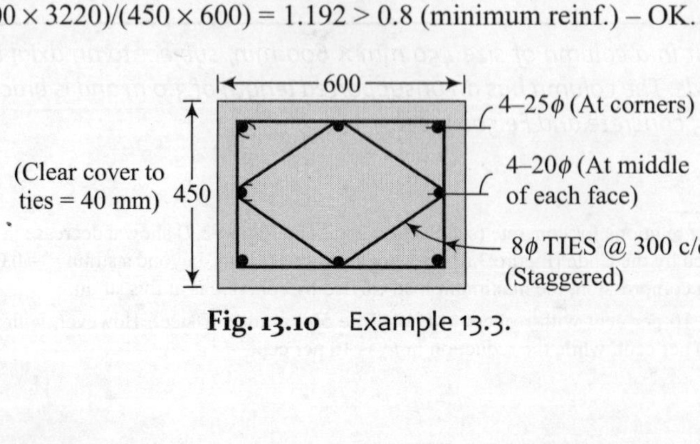

Fig. 13.10 Example 13.3.

Lateral Ties

- Tie diameter $\phi_t > \begin{cases} 25/4 \\ 6 \text{ mm} \end{cases}$: provide 8 mm dia;

  Tie spacing $s_t < \begin{cases} 450 \text{ mm} \\ 16 \times 20 = 320 \text{ mm} \\ 300 \text{ mm} \end{cases}$: provide 300 mm.

  ∴ Provide **8ϕ ties @ 300 c/c**

The detailing of reinforcement is shown in Figure 13.10.

Example 13.4

Design the reinforcement in a spiral column of 400 mm diameter subjected to a factored load of 1500 kN. The column has an unsupported length of 3.4 m and is braced against sidesway. Use M 25 concrete and Fe 500 steel.

Solution

Short Column or Slender Column?

- Given: $l = 3400$ mm, $D = 400$ mm ⇒ slenderness ratio = $l_e/D \leq 3400/400 = 8.5$ (as column is braced).
- As $l_e/D < 12$, the column may be designed as a *short column*.

Minimum Eccentricity

- $e_{\min} = \dfrac{3400}{500} + \dfrac{400}{30} = 20.1$ mm (> 20.0 mm)

  As $0.05D = 20.0$ mm $\approx e_{\min}$, the Code formula for axially compressed short columns may be used.

Factored Load

- $P_u = 1500$ kN (given)
  $= 1.05[0.4f_{ck}A_g + (0.67f_y - 0.4f_{ck})A_{sc}]$
  for spiral columns (appropriately reinforced)

Design of Longitudinal Reinforcement:

- $\dfrac{1500 \times 10^3}{1.05} = 0.4 \times 25 \times \dfrac{\pi \times 400^2}{4} + (0.67 \times 500 - 0.4 \times 25)A_{sc}$

  $\Rightarrow \quad 1428.6 \times 10^3 = 1256.6 \times 10^3 + 325A_{sc}$

  $\Rightarrow \quad A_{sc} = (1428.6 - 1256.6) \times 10^3/325$

  $= 530 \text{ mm}^2$ (equal to 0.42% of gross area)

- $A_{sc,\min}$ at 0.8% of A_g

  $= \dfrac{0.8}{100} \times \dfrac{\pi \times 400^2}{4} = 1005 \text{ mm}^2$

  Provide 6 nos 16ϕ: $A_{sc} = 201 \times 6 = 1206 \text{ mm}^2 > 1005 \text{ mm}^2$.

Design of Spiral Reinforcement:

- Assuming a clear cover of 40 mm over spirals,
  Core diameter = 400 – (40 × 2) = 320 mm

- Assuming a bar diameter of 6 mm and pitch s_t

$$\rho_s \equiv \frac{\text{Volume of spiral reinforcement}}{\text{Volume of core}} \text{ per unit length of column}$$

$$= \frac{(\pi \times 6^2/4) \times \pi \times (320 - 6)/s_t}{\pi \times 320^2/4} = \frac{0.3468}{s_t}$$

- As per the Code requirement (Eq. 13.15, Cl. 39.4.1 of Code)

$$\rho_s \geq 0.36\left(\frac{A_g}{A_{\text{core}}} - 1\right)\left(\frac{f_{ck}}{f_{sy}}\right), \text{ with } f_{sy} \text{ limited to 415 MPa.}$$

Assuming for the spiral reinforcement, $f_{sy} = 415$ MPa

$$\Rightarrow \quad \frac{0.3468}{s_t} \geq 0.36\left(\frac{\pi \times 400^2/4}{\pi \times 320^2/4} - 1\right)\left(\frac{25}{415}\right)$$

$$\Rightarrow \quad s_t \leq 28.4 \text{ mm}$$

- Code restrictions on pitch (Eq. 13.11, Cl. 26.5.3.2d of Code)

$$s_t < \begin{cases} 75 \text{ mm} \\ \text{core dia}/6 = 53.3 \text{ mm} \end{cases}$$

$$s_t > \begin{cases} 25 \text{ mm} \\ 3\phi_t = 18 \text{ mm} \end{cases}$$

Provide 6ϕ spiral @ 28 mm c/c pitch

- The detailing of reinforcement is shown in Figure 13.11.

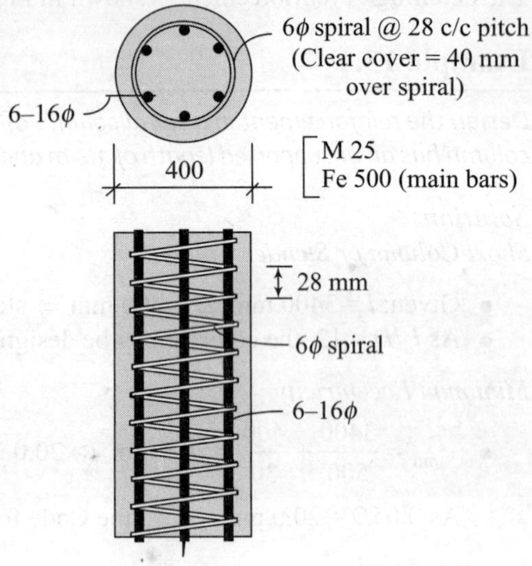

Fig. 13.11 Example 13.4.

13.5 Design of Short Columns Under Compression with Uniaxial Bending

This section deals with the behaviour and design of short compression members subject to axial compression combined with uniaxial bending, i.e., bending with respect to either the major axis or minor axis (but not both). As explained in Section 13.1.2, this loading condition is statically equivalent to a condition of *uniaxial eccentric compression* wherein the factored axial load P_u is applied at an eccentricity $e = M_u/P_u$ with respect to the centroidal axis, M_u being the factored bending moment.

The traditional 'working stress method' of design is not covered in this section, not only because of the fact that it has become obsolete, but also because the Code (Cl. B 4.3) makes it mandatory that designs for eccentric compression by WSM, based on 'cracked section' analysis[†] *should be further checked for their strength under ultimate load conditions to ensure the desired margin of safety*. This condition effectively makes WSM redundant, as it suffices to design in accordance with LSM.

[†] 'Uncracked section' analysis is permitted by the Code (Cl. 46.1) when the eccentricity in loading is so small that the resulting flexural tension, if any, can be borne by the concrete.

13.5.1 Distribution of Strains at Ultimate Limit State

A special limiting case of uniaxial eccentric compression is the condition of zero eccentricity ($e = 0$, i.e., $M_u = 0$) which corresponds to the axial loading condition, discussed in Section 13.4. Corresponding to this condition, the strain across the column section is uniform and limited to $\varepsilon_{cu} = 0.002$ at the *limit state of collapse in compression* (as per the Code).

The other limiting case of uniaxial eccentric compression corresponds to infinite eccentricity ($e = \infty$, i.e., $P_u = 0$), which is equivalent to a condition of 'pure' flexure, discussed in Chapter 4. Corresponding to this condition, the strains are linearly distributed across the section with a 'neutral axis' (NA) located somewhere within the section, and with tensile strains on one side of the NA and compressive strains on the other side. Under ultimate load conditions, i.e., at the *limit state of collapse in flexure*, the strain in the highly compressed edge of the column is specified by the Code as $\varepsilon_{cu} = 0.0035$ [refer Section 4.7].

> **Because of the minimum eccentricity requirement in the Code, all column design involves combined axial load (*P*) and bending moment (*M*). Indeed, pure axial loading and pure bending are the two extreme limits of the general case of combined axial load and bending – one where either *M* = 0, or *P* = 0. The *plane section remaining plane* theory is used throughout. This naturally leads to the *P* – *M* interaction concept.**

In the general case of uniaxial eccentric compression ($M_u \neq 0$, $P_u \neq 0$), it follows that $0 \leq e < \infty$, and for such a condition, the strain profile is non-uniform and assumed to be linearly varying across the section, with the maximum strain in the highly compressed edge, ε_{cu}, having a value between 0.002 and 0.0035 at the ultimate limit state. This is depicted in the Figure 13.12.

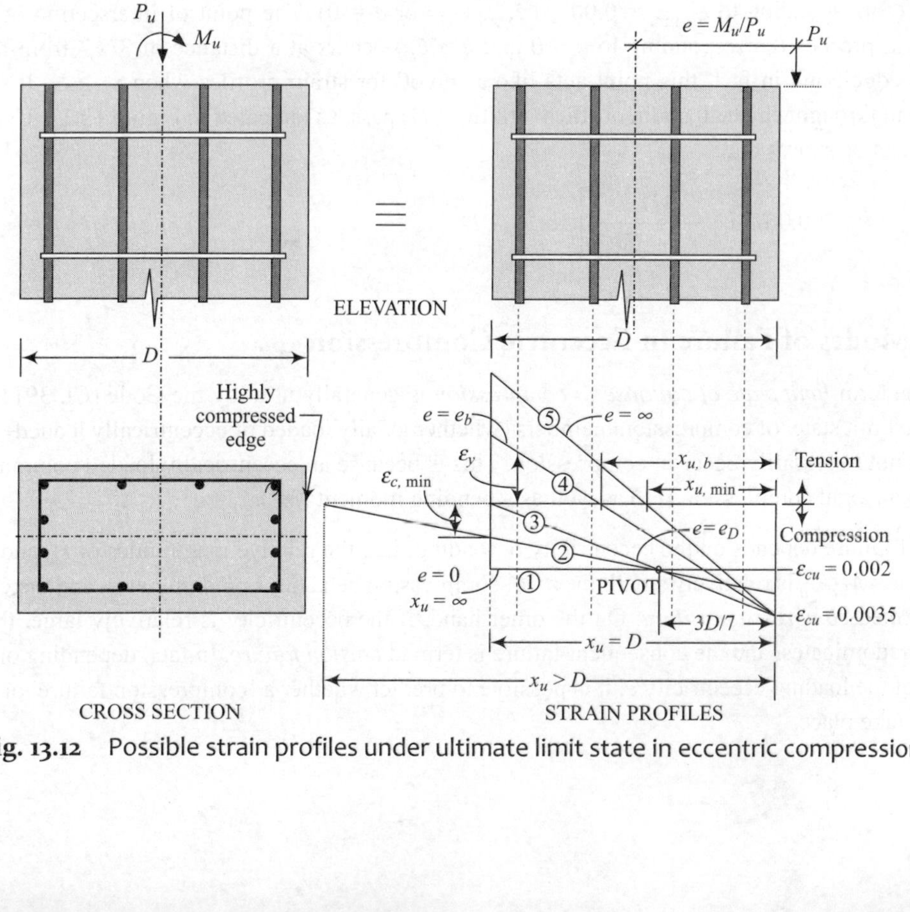

Fig. 13.12 Possible strain profiles under ultimate limit state in eccentric compression.

It may be noted that all the assumptions made in the analysis of the ultimate limit state in flexure [refer Section 4.7] – excluding the one related to the minimum tensile strain ε_{st}^* at the centroid of the tension steel – are also applicable in the case of eccentric compression [refer Cl. 39.1 of the Code]. In fact, the assumption of a linear distribution of strains [Figure 13.12] follows directly from the basic assumption that *plane sections before bending remains plane after bending*; this has been validated experimentally. In the case of eccentric compression, however, the 'depth' of the NA (with reference to the 'highly compressed edge') can vary from a minimum value $x_{u,\min}$ (corresponding to $e = \infty$, i.e., flexure only) to the maximum value $x_u = \infty$ (i.e., no neutral axis(!), corresponding to $e = 0$, i.e., axial compression only).

The Code (Cl. 39.1) permits $\varepsilon_{cu} = 0.0035$ to be considered in cases where the loading eccentricity (i.e., M_u/P_u) is sufficiently high as to induce some tensile strain in the column section, i.e., $x_u \leq D$. The limiting condition for this occurs when the resulting neutral axis coincides with the edge farthest removed from the highly compressed edge, i.e., $x_u = D$, corresponding to which $e = e_{x_u=D} \equiv e_D$, as indicated in Figure 13.12.

When the loading eccentricity is relatively low, such that the entire section is subjected to (non-uniform) compression and the NA lies outside the section ($x_u > D$), the Code (Cl. 39.1b) limits the strain in the highly compressed edge to a value between 0.002 and 0.0035 as follows:

$$\varepsilon_{cu} = 0.0035 - 0.75\,\varepsilon_{c,\min} \text{ for } x_u \geq D \tag{13.18}$$

where $\varepsilon_{c,\min}$ is the strain in the *least compressed edge*, as shown in Figure 13.12. It can be seen that Eq. 13.18 satisfies the limiting strain conditions $\varepsilon_{cu} = 0.0035$ (corresponding to $\varepsilon_{c,\min} = 0$; i.e., $x_u = D$ or $e = e_D$) and $\varepsilon_{cu} = 0.002$ (corresponding to $\varepsilon_{c,\min} = 0.002$; i.e, $x_u = \infty$ or $e = 0$). The point of intersection of these two limiting strain profiles (corresponding to $e = 0$ and $e = e_D$) occurs at a distance of $3D/7$ from the 'highly compressed edge', and in fact, this point acts like a 'pivot' for strain profiles when $x_u \geq D$. It serves as a common point through which all strain profiles (with $x_u \geq D$) pass, as indicated in Figure 13.12. Using similar triangles, it can be shown that:

$$\varepsilon_{cu} = 0.002\left[1 + \frac{3D/7}{x_u - 3D/7}\right] \text{ for } x_u \geq D \tag{13.18a}$$

13.5.2 Modes of Failure in Eccentric Compression

Although the term *limit state of collapse in compression* is generally used by the Code (Cl. 39) to describe the 'ultimate limit state' of compression members (whether axially loaded or eccentrically loaded), the actual failure need not necessarily occur in compression. This is because an eccentrically loaded column section is subjected to an axial compression (P_u) as well as a bending moment (M_u).

The mode of failure depends on the eccentricity of loading; i.e., the relative magnitudes of P_u and M_u. If the eccentricity $e = M_u/P_u$ is relatively small, the axial compression behaviour predominates, and the consequent failure is termed *compression failure*. On the other hand, if the eccentricity is relatively large, the flexural behaviour predominates, and the consequent failure is termed *tension failure*. In fact, depending on the exact magnitude of the loading eccentricity e, it is possible to predict whether a 'compression failure' or a 'tension failure' will take place.

Balanced Failure

In between 'compression failure' and 'tension failure', there exists a critical failure condition, termed 'balanced failure'. This failure condition refers to that ultimate limit state wherein the yielding of the outermost row of longitudinal steel on the tension side and the attainment of the maximum compressive strain in concrete $\varepsilon_{cu} = 0.0035$ at the highly compressed edge of the column occur simultaneously. In other words, both crushing of concrete (in the highly compressed edge) and yielding of steel (in the outermost tension steel) occur simultaneously. In this context, for design purpose, the 'yield strain' ε_y is defined simply as that corresponding to the conventional definition of 'yield point' in the design stress-strain curve for steel [refer Figures 3.6, 3.7].

> The 'balanced condition' for eccentric compression in a column occurs when the yielding of the outermost steel bar on the tension side of the cross section takes place concurrently with the maximum compressive strain in the concrete in the extreme compression fibre reaching $\varepsilon_{cu} = 0.0035$. Note that this is different from balanced condition for pure flexure.

$$\varepsilon_y = \begin{cases} 0.87 f_y/E_s & \text{for Fe 250} \\ 0.87 f_y/E_s + 0.002 & \text{for Fe 415/Fe 500} \end{cases} \tag{13.19}$$

This implies

$$\varepsilon_y = \begin{cases} 0.0010875 & \text{for Fe 250} \\ 0.00380525 & \text{for Fe 415} \\ 0.004175 & \text{for Fe 500} \end{cases} \tag{13.19a}$$

It may be noted that the Code (Cl. 39.7.1.1), in connection with *slender column* design (refer Section 13.7), refers to an axial load, P_b (denoting approximately the *balanced* condition), corresponding to $\varepsilon_y = 0.002$ in the outermost layer of tension steel, for all grades of steel.

The 'balanced strain profile' is depicted, along with other strain profiles in Figure 13.12. The corresponding eccentricity in loading is denoted $e_b \equiv e_{x_u = x_{u,b}}$; i.e., the eccentricity which results in a 'balanced' neutral axis depth $x_u = x_{u,b}$. Evidently, $e_D < e_b < \infty$, where, as explained earlier with reference to Figure 13.12, e_D corresponds to a neutral axis depth $x_u = D$ and $e = \infty$ corresponds to a minimum neutral axis depth $x = x_{u,\min}$ (when $P_u = 0$).

Compression Failure

When the loading eccentricity is less than that corresponding to the 'balanced failure' condition, i.e., when $e < e_b$, 'yielding' of longitudinal steel in tension does not take place, and failure occurs at the ultimate limit state by crushing of concrete at the highly compressed edge. The compression reinforcement may or may not yield, depending on the grade of steel and its proximity to the highly compressed edge.

Tension Failure

When the loading eccentricity is greater than that corresponding to the 'balanced failure' condition, i.e., when $e > e_b$, failure will be initiated by the yielding of the tension steel. The outermost longitudinal bars in the tension side of the neutral axis first undergo yielding and successive inner rows (if provided), on the tension side of the neutral axis, may also yield in tension with increasing strain. Eventually, collapse occurs when the concrete at the highly compressed edge gets crushed.

13.5.3 Design Strength: Axial Load – Moment Interaction

A given column cross section can be subjected to infinite combinations of axial load, P, and moment, M, (= $P \times e$); – i.e., from pure axial load ($e = 0$) to pure moment ($e = \infty$, $P = M/e = 0$). A plot of the ultimate strengths (P_u Vs M_u) covering the full range of e–values is termed an *interaction curve.*

The design strength of an eccentrically loaded short column depends on the eccentricity of loading. For uniaxial eccentricity, e, the design strength (or resistance) has two components: an axial compression component, P_{uR}, and a corresponding uniaxial moment component, $M_{uR} = P_{uR}\, e$.

As seen in Section 13.5.1, there exists a unique strain profile (and neutral axis location) at the ultimate limit state, corresponding to a given eccentricity of loading [Figure 13.12]. Corresponding to this distribution of strains ('strain compatibility'), the stresses in concrete and steel, and hence, their respective resultant forces† C_c and C_s, can be determined. Applying the condition of static equilibrium, it follows that the two design strength components are easily obtainable as

$$P_{uR} = C_c + C_s \tag{13.20}$$

and
$$M_{uR} = M_c + M_s \tag{13.21}$$

where M_c and M_s denote the resultant moments due to C_c and C_s respectively, with respect to the centroidal axis (principal axis under consideration).

From the nature of the equilibrium equations [Eqs 13.20, 13.21], it may be observed that, for a given location of the neutral axis (x_u/D), the design strength values P_{uR} and M_{uR} can be directly determined, and the eccentricity $e = M_{uR}/P_{uR}$ resulting in such a NA location can be deduced. However, given an arbitrary value of e, it is possible to arrive at the design strength (P_{uR} or $M_{uR} = P_{uR}\, e$) using Eq. 13.20, only after first locating the neutral axis – which can be achieved by considering moments of forces C_c and C_s about the eccentric line of action of P_{uR}, and applying static equilibrium. Unfortunately, the expressions for C_c and C_s in terms of x_u (derived in Section 13.5.4) are such that, in general, it will not be possible to obtain a closed-form solution for x_u in terms of e. The relationship is highly nonlinear, requiring a trial-and-error solution.

Interaction Curve

The 'interaction curve' is a complete graphical representation of the design strength of a uniaxially eccentrically loaded column of given proportions. Each point on the curve corresponds to the design strength values of P_{uR} and M_{uR} associated with a specific eccentricity (e) of loading. That is to say, if load P is applied on a short column with an eccentricity e, and if this load is gradually increased till the ultimate limit state (defined by the Code) is reached, and that ultimate load at failure is given by $P_u = P_{uR}$ and the corresponding moment by $M_u = M_{uR} = P_{uR}\, e$, then the coordinates ($M_{uR}$, P_{uR})‡ form a unique point on the interaction diagram (such as point '2' in Figure 13.13). The interaction curve defines the different (M_{uR}, P_{uR}) combinations for all possible eccentricities of loading $0 \le e < \infty$. For design purposes, the calculations of M_{uR} and P_{uR} are based on the *design* stress-strain curves (including the partial safety factors), and the resulting interaction curve is sometimes referred to as the *design interaction curve* (which is different from the *characteristic* interaction curve).

Using the design interaction curve for a given column section, it is possible to make a quick judgement as to whether or not the section is 'safe' under a specified *factored* load effect combination (P_u, M_u). If the point

† Some of the longitudinal steel may be subjected to tension, rather than compression. The term C_s here denotes the net force (assumed positive if compressive) considering all the bars in the section.

‡ It is customary to use the x-axis for M_u values and the y-axis for P_u values.

given by the coordinates (M_u, P_u) falls within the design interaction curve, the column is 'safe'; otherwise, it is not.

In other words, the design interaction curve serves as a *failure envelope*. Of course, it must be appreciated that by the term 'safe', all that is implied is that the risk of failure is deemed by the Code to be acceptably low. It does *not* follow (as some designers are inclined to believe), that if the point (M_u, P_u) falls outside the failure envelope, the column *will* fail!

Salient Points on the Interaction Curve

The salient points, marked 1 to 5 on the interaction curve [Figure 13.13] correspond to the failure strain profiles, marked 1 to 5 in Figure 13.12:

- The point 1 in Figure 13.13 corresponds to the condition of axial loading with $e = 0$. For this case of 'pure' axial compression, $M_{uR} = 0$ and P_{uR} is denoted as P_{uo} (given by Eq. 13.16).

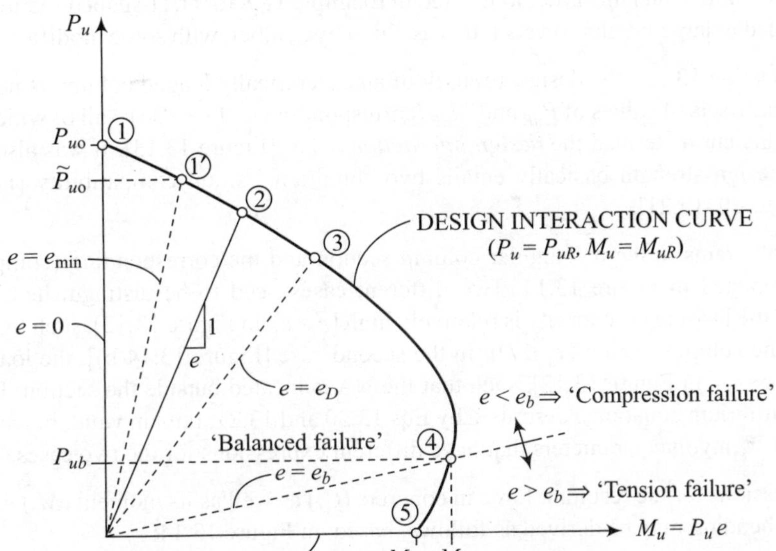

Fig. 13.13 Typical P_u - M_u interaction diagram.

- The point 1′ in Figure 13.13 corresponds to the condition of axial loading with the mandatory minimum eccentricity e_{min} [prescribed by the Code (Cl. 25.4 and 39.3)]. The corresponding ultimate resistance is approximately given by $\tilde{P}_{uo}$ (Eq. 13.17).
- The point 3 in Figure 13.13 corresponds to the condition $x_u = D$ [refer Figure 13.12], i.e., $e = e_D$. For $e < e_D$, the entire section is under compression and the neutral axis is located outside the section ($x_u > D$), with $0.002 < \varepsilon_{cu} < 0.0035$. For $e > e_D$, the NA is located within the section ($x_u < D$) and $\varepsilon_{cu} = 0.0035$ at the 'highly compressed edge' [Figure 13.12]. Point 2 represents a *general* case, with the neutral axis outside the section ($e < e_D$).
- The point 4 in Figure 13.13 corresponds to the *balanced failure* condition, with $e = e_b$ and $x_u = x_{u,b}$ [refer Figure 13.12]. The design strength values for this 'balanced failure' condition are denoted as P_{ub}

and M_{ub}. For $P_{uR} < P_{ub}$ (i.e., $e > e_b$), the mode of failure is called *tension failure*, as explained earlier. It may be noted that M_{ub} is close to the maximum† value of ultimate moment of resistance that the given section is capable of, and this value is higher than the ultimate moment resisting capacity M_{uo} under 'pure' flexure conditions [point 5 in Figure 13.13].

- The point 5 in Figure 13.13 corresponds to a 'pure' bending condition ($e = \infty$, $P_{uR} = 0$); the resulting ultimate moment of resistance is denoted M_{uo} and the corresponding NA depth takes on a minimum value $x_{u,\,min}$.

13.5.4 Analysis for Design Strength

In this section, the detailed calculations for determining the *design strength* of a uniaxially eccentrically loaded column with a rectangular cross-section ($b \times D$) is described in detail. The notation D denotes the 'depth' of the rectangular section in the plane of bending, i.e., either D_x or D_y, depending on whether bending occurs with respect to the major axis or minor axis, and the notation b denotes the 'breadth' (width) of the section (in the perpendicular direction). The basic procedure for other cross-sectional shapes (including circular sections) is similar, and this is demonstrated in Example 13.8 for an H-shaped section. This procedure can also be extended to large tubular towers (such as chimneys), albeit with some modifications [Ref. 13.11].

As explained in Section 13.5.3, the design strength of an eccentrically loaded column is not a unique value, but comprises infinite sets of values of P_{uR} and M_{uR} (corresponding to $0 < e < \infty$) – all of which are describable by means of a single curve, termed the *design interaction curve* [Figure 13.13]. It was also pointed out that the analysis for design strength basically entails two conditions: strain compatibility [Figure 13.12] and equilibrium [Eqs 13.20, 13.21].

The distribution of strains in the rectangular column section and the corresponding (compressive) stresses in concrete are depicted in Figure 13.14. Two different cases need to be distinguished. In the first case [Figure 13.14(a)], the loading eccentricity is relatively high [$e > e_D$ in Figure 13.12], such that the neutral axis is located inside the column section ($x_u \leq D$). In the second case [Figure 13.14(b)], the loading eccentricity is relatively low [$e < e_D$ in Figure 13.12], such that the NA is located outside the section. In both cases, the force/moment equilibrium equations, described by Eqs 13.20 and 13.21, remain valid; however, the formulas for C_c, C_s, M_c and M_s involve parameters that have different expressions for the two cases.

Generalised expressions for the resultant force in concrete (C_c) as well as its moment (M_c) with respect to the centroidal axis of bending may be derived as follows, based on Figure 13.14:

$$C_c = a f_{ck} bD \tag{13.22}$$

$$M_c = C_c(D/2 - \bar{x}) \tag{13.23}$$

where $a \equiv$ stress block area factor

$\bar{x} \equiv$ distance between highly compressed edge and the line of action of C_c (i.e., centroid of stress block area)

† M_{uo} corresponds to the ultimate moment of resistance of an under-reinforced beam section. The presence of some axial compression delays the yielding of the tension steel (and hence, the development of the ultimate limit state), thereby enhancing the moment resisting capacity beyond M_{uo}. However, the presence of axial compression also enhances the compressive stress in concrete, and the gain in M_{uR} due to delayed yielding of tension steel becomes offset by the loss in M_{uR} due to hastening of the compression failure condition, when P_{uR} exceeds P_{ub}.

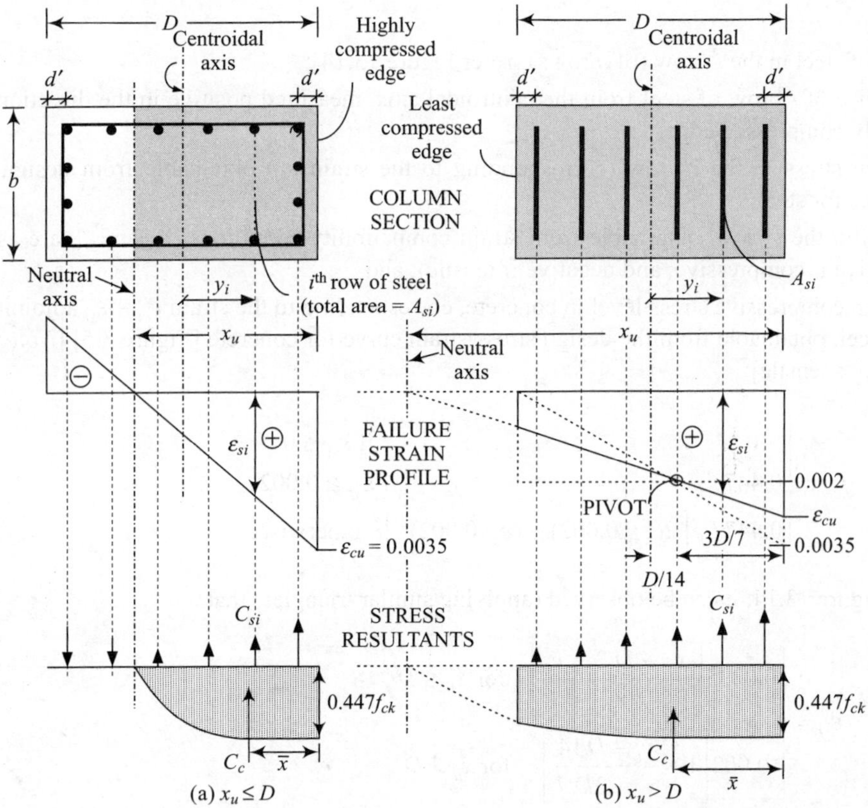

Fig. 13.14 Analysis of design strength of a rectangular section under eccentric compression.

By means of simple integration, it is possible to derive expression for a and $\bar{x}$ for the case (a): $x_u \le D$ [refer Section 4.7] and for the case (b): $x_u > D$ [Ref. 13.12]:

$$a = \begin{cases} 0.362x_u/D & \text{for } x_u \le D \\ 0.447(1 - 4g/21) & \text{for } x_u > D \end{cases} \tag{13.24}$$

$$\bar{x} = \begin{cases} 0.416x_u & \text{for } x_u \le D \\ (0.5 - 8g/49)\{D/(1 - 4g/21)\} & \text{for } x_u > D \end{cases} \tag{13.25}$$

where $$g = 16/(7x_u/D - 3)^2 \tag{13.26}$$

Similarly, the expressions for the resultant force in the steel (C_s) as well as its moment (M_s) with respect to the centroidal axis of bending is easily obtained as

$$C_s = \sum_{i=1}^{n} (f_{si} - f_{ci}) A_{si} \tag{13.27}$$

$$M_s = \sum_{i=1}^{n} (f_{si} - f_{ci}) A_{si} y_i \tag{13.28}$$

where

A_{si} ≡ area of steel in the ith row (of n rows) [refer Figure 13.14];

y_i ≡ distance of ith row of steel from the centroidal axis, measured positive in the direction towards the highly compressed edge;

f_{si} ≡ design stress in the ith row (corresponding to the strain ε_{si}) obtainable from design stress-strain curves for steel;

ε_{si} ≡ strain in the ith row, obtainable from strain compatibility conditions (ε_{si} and f_{si} are assumed to be positive if compressive, and negative if tensile); and

f_{ci} ≡ design compressive stress level in concrete, corresponding to the strain $\varepsilon_{ci} = \varepsilon_{si}$ adjoining the ith row of steel, obtainable from the design stress-strain curve for concrete [Figure 3.5] [*Note:* $f_{ci} = 0$ if the strain is tensile]:

$$f_{ci} = \begin{cases} 0 & \text{if } \varepsilon_{si} \le 0 \\ 0.447 f_{ck} & \text{if } \varepsilon_{si} \ge 0.002 \\ 0.447 f_{ck}\left[2(\varepsilon_{si}/0.002) - (\varepsilon_{si}/0.002)^2\right] & \text{otherwise} \end{cases} \tag{13.29}$$

Also, from Figure 13.14, it can be observed (applying similar triangles) that

$$\varepsilon_{si} = \begin{cases} 0.0035\left[\dfrac{x_u - D/2 + y_i}{x_u}\right] & \text{for } x_u \le D \\ 0.002\left[1 + \dfrac{y_i - D/14}{x_u - 3D/7}\right] & \text{for } x_u > D \end{cases} \tag{13.30}$$

It should be noted that, in the case of *spiral columns*, the Code permits an enhancement in the design strength (both P_{uR} and M_{uR}) by 5 per cent – for short columns only.

Example 13.5

For the column section shown in Figure 13.15(a), determine the design strength components corresponding to the condition of 'balanced failure'. Assume M 25 concrete and Fe 500 steel. Consider loading eccentricity with respect to the major axis alone. Assume 8φ ties and 40 mm clear cover.

Solution

- *Given*: $b = 300$ mm, $D = 500$ mm, $f_{ck} = 25$ MPa, $f_y = 500$ MPa,
  $A_{s1} = A_{s2} = A_{s3} = 2 \times 491 \text{ mm}^2 = 982 \text{ mm}^2$, [as shown in Figure 13.15(b)],
  $y_1 = (-)189.5$ mm, $y_2 = 0$ mm, $y_3 = (+)189.5$ mm with reference to centroidal axis
- ***Neutral axis depth $x_{u,b}$***
  The 'balanced strain' profile is as shown in Figure 13.15(c).

For Fe 500 steel, $\varepsilon_y = \dfrac{0.87 \times 500}{2 \times 10^5} + 0.002 = 0.004175$

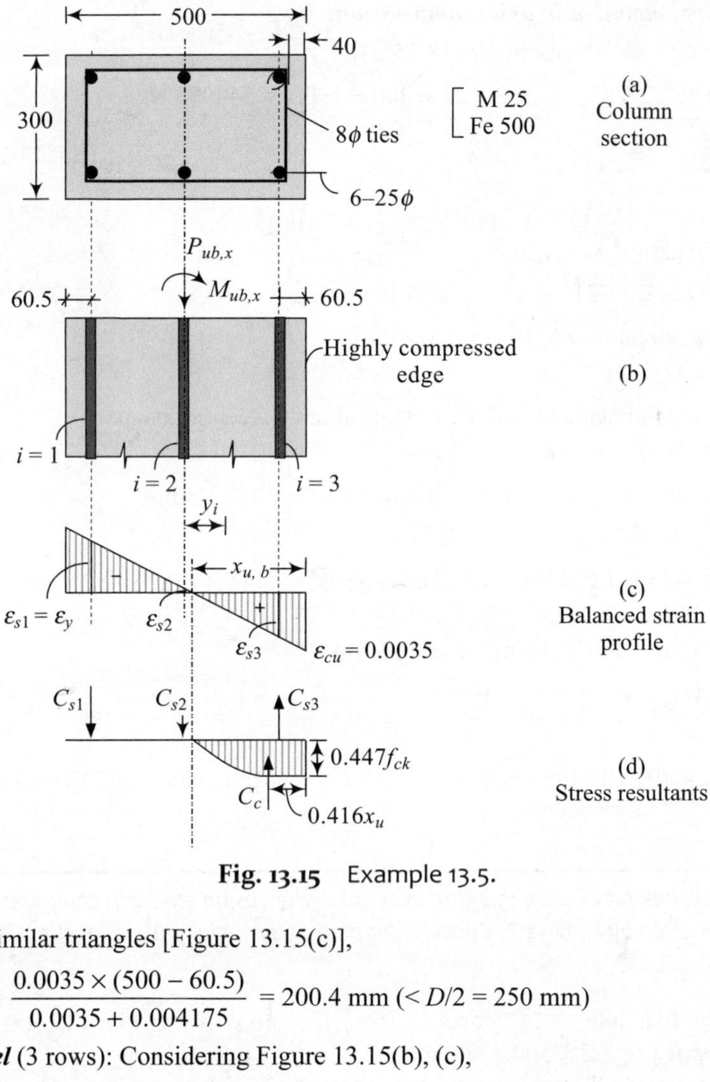

Fig. 13.15 Example 13.5.

Considering similar triangles [Figure 13.15(c)],

$$x_{u,b} = \frac{0.0035 \times (500 - 60.5)}{0.0035 + 0.004175} = 200.4 \text{ mm } (< D/2 = 250 \text{ mm})$$

- ***Strains in steel*** (3 rows): Considering Figure 13.15(b), (c),

$$\varepsilon_{s1} = (-)\varepsilon_y = -0.004175 \text{ (tensile)}$$

$$\varepsilon_{s2} = (-)0.0035 \times \frac{250 - 200.4}{200.4} = -0.000866 \text{ (tensile)}$$

$$\varepsilon_{s3} = (+)0.0035 \times \frac{200.4 - 60.5}{200.4} = +0.002443 \text{ (compression)} > 0.002$$

- ***Design stresses in steel*** (3 rows): Referring to the design stress-strain curve for Fe 500 [Figure 3.7, Table 3.2],

$$f_{s1} = (-)0.87f_y = -435 \text{ MPa}$$

$$f_{s2} = E_s\varepsilon_{s2} = (2 \times 10^5) \times (-)0.000866 = -173.2 \text{ MPa}$$

$$f_{s3} = +[391.3 + \left(\frac{244.3 - 226}{277 - 226}\right) \times (413 - 391.3)] = +399 \text{ MPa}$$

- ***Design strength component in axial compression***: $P_{ub,x}$

$$P_{ub,x} = C_c + C_s \quad \text{[refer Figure 13.15(d)]}$$

$$C_c = 0.362 f_{ck} b x_{u,b} = 0.362 \times 25 \times 300 \times 200.4 = 544086 \text{ N}$$

$$C_s = \sum_{i=1}^{3} C_{si} = \sum (f_{si} - f_{ci}) A_{si} \quad \text{[Eq. 13.27]}$$

$$= [(-435) + (-173.2) + (399 - 0.447 \times 25)] \times 982$$

$$= -216408.3 \text{ N (tensile)}$$

$$\Rightarrow \quad P_{ub,x} = (544.1 - 216.4) \text{ kN} = \mathbf{327.7 \text{ kN}}$$

- ***Design strength component in flexure***: $M_{ub,x}$

$$M_{ub,x} = M_c + M_s$$

where, considering moments of stress resultants about the centroidal axis,

$$M_c = C_c(0.5D - 0.416 x_u)$$

$$= 544086 \times (250 - 0.416 \times 200.4) = 90.66 \times 10^6 \text{ Nmm}$$

$$M_s = \sum C_{si} y_i$$

$$= [(-435)(-189.5) + (-173.2)(0) + (399 - 0.447 \times 25)(189.5)] \times 982$$

$$= 153.1 \times 10^6 \text{ Nmm}$$

$$\Rightarrow \quad M_{ub,x} = (90.66 + 153.1) \text{ kNm} = \mathbf{243.76 \text{ kNm}}$$

[*Note:* $e_{b,x} = \dfrac{M_{ub,x}}{P_{ub,x}} = \dfrac{243.76 \times 10^3}{327.7} = 743.9$ mm $\Rightarrow (e/D)_x = 1.488$ and corresponding $x_{u,b}/D$ $= 200.4/500 = 0.4008$. This implies that *tension failure* occurs only if $(e/D)_x > 1.488$ or $x_u/D < 0.4008$].

Example 13.6

For the column section shown in Figure 13.15(a), determine the design strength components corresponding to a neutral axis location given by $x_u/D = 1.2$. Consider loading eccentricity with respect to the major axis alone.

Solution

- *Given*: Data as in Example 13.5 [Figures 13.15(a), (b)] are shown in Fig. 13.16(a).
- ***Neutral axis depth*** $x_u = 1.2 \times 500 = 600$ mm

  As the NA falls outside the section, the entire section is under compression, and the corresponding failure strain diagram is as shown in Figure 13.14(b).

$$\varepsilon_{cu} = 0.002\left[1 + \frac{3D/7}{x_u - 3D/7}\right] = 0.002\left[1 + \frac{1500/7}{600 - 1500/7}\right] = 0.003111$$

- ***Strains in steel***

  From the distribution of failure strains shown in Figure 13.16(c), by applying similar triangles,

$$\varepsilon_{s1} = (+)0.003111 \times 160.5/600 = +0.000832 \quad < 0.002$$

$$\varepsilon_{s2} = (+)0.003111 \times 350/600 = +0.001815 \quad < 0.002$$

$$\varepsilon_{s3} = (+)0.003111 \times (600 - 60.5)/600 = +0.002797 \quad > 0.002$$

  [Note that these values can alternatively be obtained by applying the generalised formula given by Eq. 13.30]

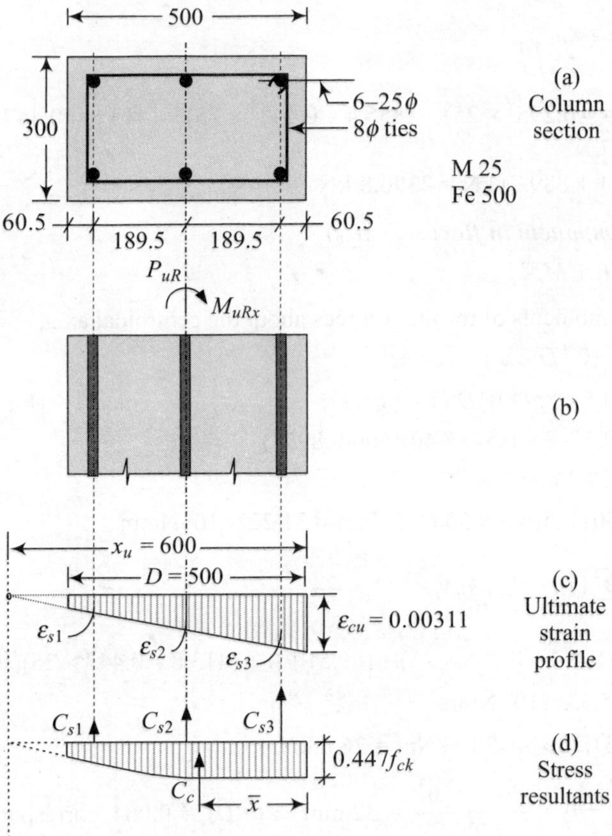

Fig. 13.16 Example 13.6.

- ***Design stresses in steel***

Referring to the design stress-strain curve for Fe 500 [Figure 3.7, Table 3.2],

$$f_{s1} = (2 \times 10^5) \times (+)0.000832 = +166.4 \text{ MPa}$$

$$f_{s2} = +[347.8 + \frac{181.5 - 174}{195 - 174} \times (369.6 - 347.8)] = +355.4 \text{ MPa}$$

$$f_{s3} = +[413 + \frac{279.7 - 277}{312 - 277} \times (423.9 - 413)] = +413.8 \text{ MPa}$$

- ***Design strength component in axial compression: P_{uR}***

$P_{uR} = C_c + C_s$ [refer Figure 13.16(b)]

The properties of the truncated stress block have to be considered [Eqs 13.24–13.26] as $x_u > D$:

$$g = 16/(7x_u/D - 3)^2 \quad \text{[Eq. 13.26]}$$
$$= 16/(7 \times 1.2 - 3)^2 = 0.5487$$
$$a = 0.447 \times (1 - 4g/21) \quad \text{[Eq. 13.24]}$$
$$= 0.447 \times 0.8955 = 0.4003$$

$$\therefore \quad C_c = af_{ck}bD = 0.4003 \times 25 \times 300 \times 500 = 1501125 \text{ N}$$

$$C_s = \sum_{i=1}^{3}(f_{si} - f_{ci})A_{si}$$

$$= [(166.4 - 0.295^{\dagger} \times 25) + (355.4 - 0.443^{\ddagger} \times 25) + (413.8 - 0.447 \times 25)] \times 982$$

$$= 889667 \text{ N}$$

$$\Rightarrow \quad P_{uR} = (1501.1 + 889.7) \text{ kN} = \mathbf{2390.8\ kN}$$

- ***Design strength component in flexure:*** $(M_{uR})_x$

$$(M_{uR})_x = M_c + M_s$$

where, considering moments of resultant forces about the centroidal axis,

$$M_c = C_c(0.5D - \bar{x})$$

$$\bar{x} = (0.5 - 8g/49)\{D/(1 - 4g/21)\} \quad \text{[Eq. 13.25]}$$

$$= (0.5 - 8 \times 0.5487/49)(500/0.8955)$$

$$= 229.2 \text{ mm}$$

$$\Rightarrow \quad M_c = 1501125(0.5 \times 500 - 229.2) = 31.22 \times 10^6 \text{ Nmm}$$

$$M_s = \sum_{i=1}^{3}(f_{si} - f_{ci})A_{si}y_i$$

$$= [(166.4 - 0.295 \times 25)(-189.5) + 0 + (413.8 - 0.447 \times 25)(+189.5)] \times 982$$

$$= 45.33 \times 10^6 \text{ Nmm}$$

$$\Rightarrow \quad (M_{uR})_x = (31.22 + 45.33) \text{ kNm} = \mathbf{76.6\ kNm}$$

[Note that $e_x = \dfrac{(M_{uR})_x}{P_{uR}} = \dfrac{76.6 \times 10^3}{2390.8} = 32$ mm $\Rightarrow (e/D)_x = 0.064$, corresponding to $x_u/D = 1.2$]

Example 13.7

For the column section shown in Figure 13.15(a), determine the design strength components and corresponding eccentricity of loading with respect to the minor axis alone, for the limiting condition of 'no tension' in the section.

Solution

- For bending about the *minor axis*, the column details are as shown in Figure 13.17(a). In this case, $b = 500$ mm, $D = 300$ mm. There are only two rows of steel.

$$A_{s1} = A_{s2} = 3 \times 491 \text{ mm}^2 = 1473 \text{ mm}^2$$

$y_1 = (-)89.5$ mm and $y_2 = (+)89.5$ mm with reference to the centroidal axis.

- ***Neutral axis depth***

$x_u = 300$ mm, as shown in Figure 13.17(c) for the limiting strain profile for 'no tension' (i.e., $x_u = D$)

† Applying Eq. 13.29 with $\varepsilon_{s1} = +0.000832, f_{c1} = 0.447 f_{ck} \times 0.6589 = 0.295 f_{ck}$.

‡ Applying Eq. 13.29 with $\varepsilon_{s2} = +0.001815, f_{c2} = 0.447 f_{ck} \times 0.9914 = 0.443 f_{ck}$.

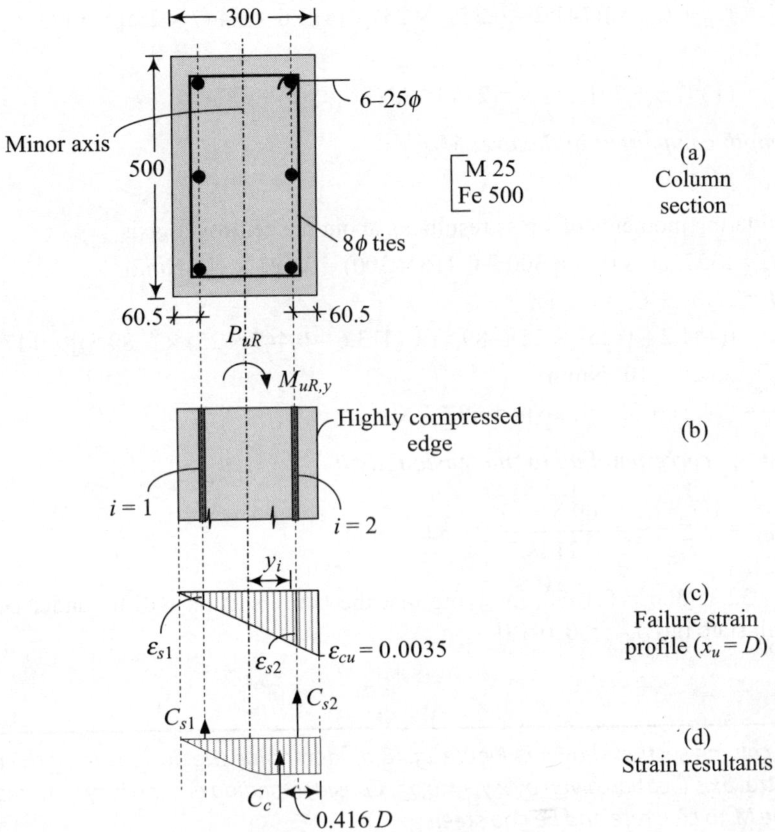

Fig. 13.17 Example 13.6.

- ***Strains in steel*** (2 rows): Considering Figure 13.17(c),

$$\varepsilon_{s1} = (+)0.0035 \times \frac{60.5}{300} = +0.000706 \qquad < 0.002$$

$$\varepsilon_{s2} = (+)0.0035 \times \frac{300 - 60.5}{300} = +0.00279 \qquad > 0.002$$

- ***Design stresses in steel*** (2 rows):
Referring to the design stress-strain curve for Fe 500 [Figure 3.7, Table 3.2],

$$f_{s1} = (2 \times 10^5) \times (+)0.000706 = +141.2 \text{ MPa}$$

$$f_{s2} = +[413 + \frac{279 - 277}{312 - 277} \times (423.9 - 413)] = +413.6 \text{ MPa}$$

- ***Design strength component in axial compression:*** P_{uR}

$$P_{uR} = C_c + C_s \text{ [refer Fig. 13.17(d)]}$$

$$C_c = 0.362 \times 25 \times 500 \times 300 = 1357500 \text{ N}$$

$$C_s = C_{s1} + C_{s2} = [(141.2 - 0.259^{\dagger} \times 25) + (413.6 - 0.447 \times 25)] \times 1473$$
$$= 791222 \text{ N}$$
$$\Rightarrow \quad P_{uR} = (1357.5 + 791.2) \text{ kN} = \mathbf{2148.7 \text{ kN}}$$

- ***Design strength component in flexure:*** $M_{uR,y}$

$$M_{uR,y} = M_c + M_s$$

where, considering moments of stress resultants about the centroidal axis,

$$M_c = 1357500 \times (0.5 \times 300 - 0.416 \times 300) = 34.21 \times 10^6 \text{ Nmm}$$
$$M_s = C_{s1}y_1 + C_{s2}y_2$$
$$= [(141.2 - 0.259 \times 25)(-89.5) + (413.6 - 0.447 \times 25) \times (+89.5)] \times 1473$$
$$= 35.29 \times 10^6 \text{ Nmm}$$
$$\Rightarrow \quad M_{uR,y} = (34.21 + 35.29) \text{ kNm} = \mathbf{69.5 \text{ kNm}}$$

- ***Eccentricity*** $e_{D,y}$ ***corresponding to 'no tension' limit***

$$e_{D,y} = \frac{(M_{uR})_y}{P_{uR}} = \frac{69.5 \times 10^3}{2148.7} = 32.35 \text{ mm}$$

[$\Rightarrow (e/D)_y = 32.35/300 = 0.1078$, implying that the entire section will be under compression at the ultimate limit state if $(e/D)_y < 0.1078$].

Example 13.8

For the H-shaped column section shown in Figure 13.18(a), determine the design strength components corresponding to a neutral axis location given by $x_u/D = 0.75$. Consider loading eccentricity with respect to the major axis alone. Assume M 30 concrete and Fe 500 steel.

Solution

- *Given:* Data as indicated in Figures 13.18(a), (b)

$$A_{s1} = A_{s2} = 314 \times 3 = 942 \text{ mm}^2 \text{ ; } y_1 = -150 \text{ mm}, y_2 = +150 \text{ mm},$$
$$f_{ck} = 30 \text{ MPa}; f_y = 500 \text{ MPa}$$
$$D = 400 \text{ mm} \Rightarrow x_u = 0.75 \times 400 = 300 \text{ mm}$$

- ***Strains in steel*** (2 rows)

Referring to strain profile shown in Figure 13.18(c), $\varepsilon_{cu} = 0.0035$ (as $x_u < D$),

$$\varepsilon_{s1} = (-)0.0035 \times 50/300 = -0.000583 \text{ (tensile)}$$
$$\varepsilon_{s2} = (+)0.0035 \times 250/300 = +0.002917 \text{ (compressive)}$$

- ***Design stresses in steel***

Referring to the design stress-strain curve for Fe 500 [Figure 3.7, Table 3.2],

$$f_{s1} = (2 \times 10^5) \times (-)0.000583 = -116.6 \text{ MPa}$$
$$f_{s2} = +[413 + \frac{291.7 - 277}{312 - 277} \times (423.9 - 413)] = +417.6 \text{ MPa}$$

† Applying Eq. 13.29 with $\varepsilon_{s1} = +0.000706, f_{c1} = 0.447 f_{ck} \times 0.5814 = 0.259 f_{ck}$.

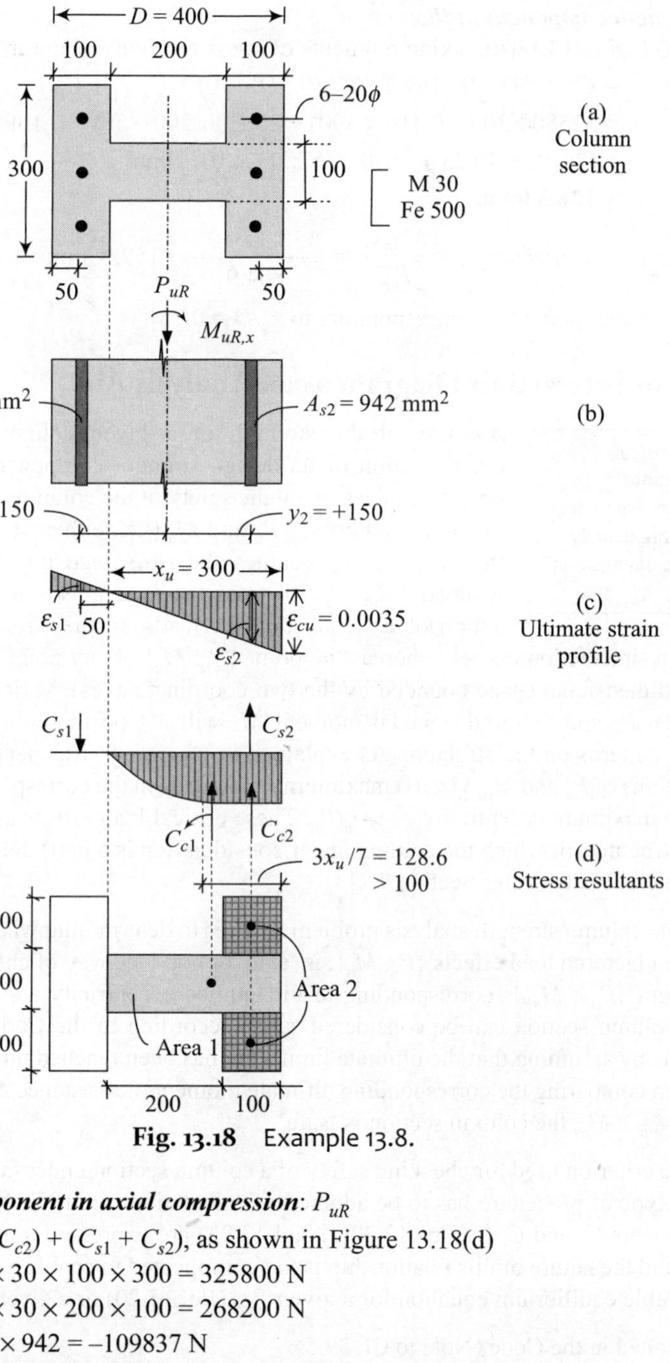

Fig. 13.18 Example 13.8.

- ***Design strength component in axial compression***: P_{uR}

$P_{uR} = (C_{c1} + C_{c2}) + (C_{s1} + C_{s2})$, as shown in Figure 13.18(d)

$C_{c1} = 0.362 \times 30 \times 100 \times 300 = 325800$ N

$C_{c2} = 0.447 \times 30 \times 200 \times 100 = 268200$ N

$C_{s1} = -116.6 \times 942 = -109837$ N

$C_{s2} = +(417.6 - 0.447 \times 30) \times 942 = +380747$ N

$\Rightarrow \quad P_{uR} = (325.80 + 268.20 - 109.84 + 380.75)$ kN = **864.9 kN**

- ***Design strength component in flexure***: $M_{uR,\,x}$

Referring to Figure 13.18(d), taking moments of stress resultants about the centroidal axis of bending,

$$\begin{aligned} M_{uR,\,x} &= C_{c1}(0.5D - 0.416x_u) + C_{c2}(0.5D - 50) + C_{s1}y_1 + C_{s2}y_2 \\ &= 325800(200 - 0.416 \times 300) + 268200(200 - 50) + (-109837)(-150) + (380747)(150) \\ &= (24.50 + 40.23 + 16.48 + 57.11) \times 10^6 \text{ Nmm} \\ &= \mathbf{138.3\ kNm} \end{aligned}$$

- ***Corresponding eccentricity*** $e_x = \dfrac{M_{uR,x}}{P_{uR}} = \dfrac{138.3 \times 10^3}{864.9} = 159.9$ mm

[$\Rightarrow (e/D)_x = 159.9/400 = 0.4$, corresponding to $x_u/D = 0.75$].

13.5.5 Use of Interaction Diagram as an Analysis Aid

> Interaction diagrams can be used as aids to both analysis and design. For wider applicability, they are usually presented in a non-dimensional format.

Analysis of the strength of a given column section basically implies determination of its design strength components P_{uR} and M_{uR} – with the objective of assessing the safety of the column section subjected to specified factored load effects P_u and M_u (i.e., either M_{ux} or M_{uy}). It should be noted that $\{P_{uR}, M_{uR}\}$ denotes the *resistance* inherent in the column section, whereas $\{P_u, M_u\}$ denotes the *load effects* induced in the section by the action of external *factored* loads on the structure. The point $\{P_{uR}, M_{uR}\}$ lies on the design 'interaction curve', whereas the point $\{P_u, M_u\}$ is any point on the 'interaction diagram' (i.e., in the two-dimensional space bounded by the two coordinate axes). Various combinations of factored axial compression P_u and factored uniaxial moment M_u will act on the column section due to different factored loading patterns on the structure. As explained in Chapter 9, it generally suffices to consider two critical combinations of P_u and M_u, viz., (i) maximum P_u along with the corresponding M_u, and (ii) P_u and M_u corresponding to maximum eccentricity $e = M_u/P_u$. These critical load effects are obtainable from structural analyses of the structure (of which the column under consideration is a part) under different loading patterns (gravity loads, lateral loads) [refer Section 9.2].

Thus, in effect, the column strength analysis problem reduces to determining whether a given column section, subjected to given factored load effects $\{P_u, M_u\}$, is 'safe' or not. One way of checking this is by determining the design strength $\{P_{uR}, M_{uR}\}$, corresponding to the applied eccentricity $e = M_u/P_u$, and if $P_{uR} \geq P_u$ and $M_{uR} \geq M_u$, the column section can be considered safe†, according to the Code. An alternative method of checking safety is by assuming that the ultimate limit state has been reached under the factored load P_u, i.e., $P_{uR} = P_u$, and then comparing the corresponding ultimate moment of resistance M_{uR} with the applied factored moment M_u; if $M_{uR} \geq M_u$, the column section is 'safe'.

Regardless of the criterion used for checking safety of a column section under factored load effects $\{P_u, M_u\}$, a trial-and-error type of procedure has to be adopted, if calculations are to be based on first principles. The basic stress resultants C_c and C_s (in Eqs 13.22(c) and 13.23) are expressed in terms of an unknown neutral axis depth (x_u), and the nature of this relationship is too complicated to enable a closed-form solution for x_u – by solving a suitable equilibrium equation for a given P_{uR} (Eq. 13.20) or a given eccentricity‡ e.

Indeed, as mentioned in the Code (Note to Cl. 39.5):

---

† By the term 'safe', it is only implied that the risk of failure (measured in terms of *probability of failure*) is acceptably low [refer Chapter 3].

‡ The problem of determining x_u/D for any given P_{uR} can be more elegantly solved using a suitable numerical procedure [Ref. 13.13]. Thus, a computer program can be written and used to derive the interaction curve coordinates, using increments of P_{uR}, rather than x_u/D.

'The design of a member subject to combined axial load and uniaxial bending will involve lengthy calculation by trial and error. In order to overcome these difficulties, interaction diagrams may be used'.

Although the above statement refers to *design* (discussed in Section 13.5.6), it is equally valid in the case of *analysis*. If an *interaction diagram* [refer Figure 13.13] is readily available (or can be constructed) for the given column section, then the analysis problem simply reduces to determining whether or not the point corresponding to factored load effects $\{P_u, M_u\}$ lies within the envelope of the interaction curve, as explained in Section 13.5.3. Furthermore, the design strength components $\{P_{uR}, M_{uR}\}$ can be easily read off from the interaction curve, corresponding to any given eccentricity e, or given P_u $(= P_{uR})$.

Construction of a Design Interaction Curve

The coordinates of the 'design interaction curve', viz., M_{uR} (on the x-axis) and P_{uR} (on the y-axis), can be determined for any arbitrary neutral axis depth x_u, using Eqs 13.20 and 13.21. The starting value of x_u corresponding to $P_{uR} = 0$, viz., $x_{u,\min}$ [refer Figure 13.12], poses some problem as it is unknown and has to be determined by solving Eq. 13.20 with $P_{uR} = 0$ by trial-and-error. To begin with, a trial value $x_{u,\min} \approx 0.15D$ can be assumed; this, in all probability, will result in a negative value of P_{uR}, which corresponds to a condition of *eccentric tension*. By incrementing x_u/D suitably (in steps of 0.05 or less), the transition between $P_{uR} < 0$ and $P_{uR} > 0$ can be traced. (The 'exact' value of the ultimate moment of resistance M_{uo} corresponding to 'pure bending' ($P_{uR} = 0$), if required, can be obtained by repeated trial-and-error†, using very fine increments of x_u/D).

Having located (approximately) $x_{u,\min}/D$, the coordinates of the design interaction curve can be obtained (using Eqs 13.20, 13.21) and tabulated for incremental values of x_u/D – say, increments of 0.05. The process can be terminated when P_{uR} exceeds the maximum limit $\tilde{P}_{uo}$ permitted by the Code [refer Eq. 13.17], and may be extended to P_{uo} ($e = 0$) [Eq. 13.16]. As the procedure is repetitive, this can be more conveniently done on a computer. The coordinates (M_{uR}, P_{uR}) of the design interaction curve can then be tabulated and/ or plotted. It is useful to include the ratios x_u/D and e/D in the table. The construction and use of a design interaction curve for a typical column section is demonstrated in Examples 13.9 and 13.11.

Example 13.9

For a column section shown in Figure 13.15(a), construct the design interaction curve for axial compression combined with uniaxial bending about the major axis. Hence, investigate the safety of the column section under the following factored load effects:

$P_u = 2275$ kN, $M_{ux} = 46.4$ kNm *(maximum axial compression);*

$P_u = 1105$ kN, $M_{ux} = 125$ kNm *(maximum eccentricity).*

Solution

- *Given*: $b = 300$ mm, $D = 500$ mm, $f_{ck} = 25$ MPa, $f_y = 500$ MPa, $A_{sc} = 2946$ mm^2

  $A_{s1} = A_{s2} = A_{s3} = 2 \times 491$ mm^2 $= 982$ mm^2 [as in Example 13.5]

  $y_1 = -189.5$ mm, $y_2 = 0$ mm, $y_3 = +189.5$ mm

† The problem of determining x_u/D for any given P_{uR} can be more elegantly solved using a suitable numerical procedure [Ref. 13.13]. Thus, a computer program can be written and used to derive the interaction curve coordinates, using increments of P_{uR}, rather than x_u/D.

- *Maximum axial compression resistance*:

$$\tilde{P}_{uo} = 0.4 f_{ck}\, bD + (0.67 f_y - 0.4 f_{ck}) A_{sc} \quad \text{[Eq. 13.17]}$$
$$= (0.4 \times 25 \times 300 \times 500) + (0.67 \times 500 - 0.4 \times 25) \times (2946)$$
$$= (1500\,000 + 957\,450)\ \text{N} = 2457.45\ \text{kN}$$

Interaction Curve Coordinates

The theoretical maximum axial compression (with $e = 0$) is given by Eq. 13.16:

$$P_{uo} = 0.447 f_{ck} bD + (0.746 f_y - 0.447 f_{ck}) A_{sc} \text{ — for Fe 500}$$
$$= (0.447 \times 25 \times 300 \times 500) + (0.746 \times 500 - 0.447 \times 25) \times (2946)$$
$$= (1676250 + 1065936.45)\ \text{N} = 2742\ \text{kN}$$

The coordinates ($M_{uR,x}$, P_{uR}) are derived for $0 \le P_{uR} \le P_{uo}$, considering incremental values of x_u/D, using the equilibrium equations (Eqs 13.20, 13.21). The results, obtained by a computer program, are tabulated in Table 13.1(a). The reader may verify some of the solutions by simple manual calculations. The 'balanced failure' point ($P_{ub,x}$ = 327.7 kN, $M_{ub,x}$ = 243.76 kNm) obtained in Example 13.5 is a salient point on the interaction curve.

An alternative, and perhaps more elegant, computer-based procedure for determining the interaction curve coordinates, is by considering incremental values of P_{uR} (instead of x_u/D). The 'bisection method' was employed here to determine x_u/D (to an accuracy of 10^{-6}) for a given P_{uR}. Thus, it becomes possible to accurately compute $x_{u,\,\min}/D$ and M_{uo}, corresponding to $P_{uR} = 0$; the values are obtained as

$$x_{u,\,\min}/D = 0.312$$
$$M_{uo,\,x} = 230.7\ \text{kNm}$$

The results obtained by this alternative procedure are tabulated in Table 13.1(b). The design interaction curve is plotted in Figure 13.19.

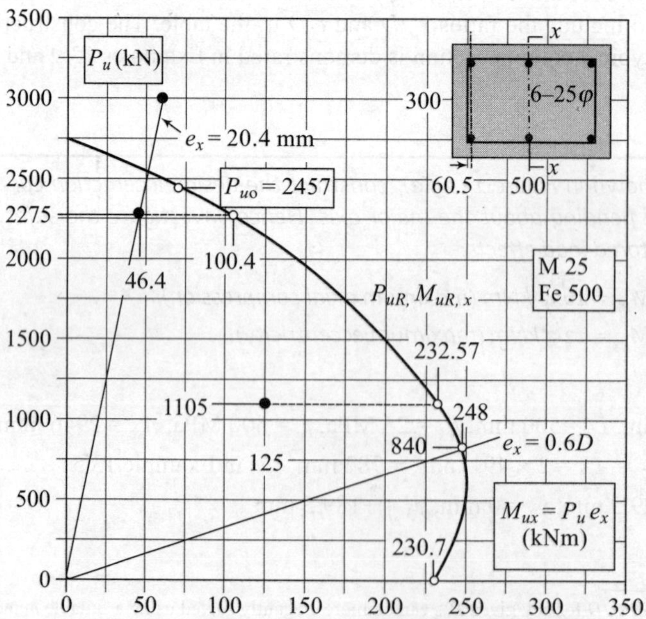

Fig. 13.19 Example 13.9: Interaction diagram.

Table 13.1 *Example 13.9 – Design interaction curve coordinates*

(a)			(b)		
x_u/D	P_{uR} (kN)	$M_{uR,x}$ (kNm)	P_{uR} (kN)	$M_{uR,x}$ (kNm)	x_u/D
0.31	–7.1	230.2	0	230.7	0.312
0.35	139.17	238.2	100	236.7	0.341
0.39	299.40	244.4	200	240.6	0.364
0.43	444.89	248.6	300	244.4	0.390
0.47	579.82	250.9	400	247.5	0.417
0.51	711.56	250.8	500	249.8	0.446
0.55	840.28	248.5	600	251.1	0.476
0.59	975.30	242.7	700	250.9	0.506
0.63	1132.8	230.4	800	249.7	0.537
0.67	1278.0	218.6	900	246.6	0.568
0.71	1412.9	207.2	1000	240.8	0.596
0.75	1539.3	195.8	1100	233.0	0.621
0.79	1658.3	184.4	1200	225.0	0.648
0.83	1771.1	172.8	1300	216.8	0.676
0.87	1878.5	161.0	1400	208.3	0.706
0.91	1981.3	148.8	1500	199.4	0.737
0.95	2079.9	136.1	1600	190.1	0.770
0.99	2175.0	123.1	1700	180.2	0.804
1.03	2243.2	110.9	1800	169.7	0.840
1.07	2296.2	100.9	1900	158.5	0.878
1.11	2341.1	92.4	2000	146.4	0.917
1.15	2379.6	85.1	2100	133.4	0.958
1.19	2412.9	78.8	2200	119.1	1.001
1.23	2441.9	73.3	2300	100.2	1.073
1.27	2466.8	68.3	2400	81.2	1.173
1.31	2488.8	63.9	2500	61.6	1.332
1.35	2508.4	59.9	2600	41.4	1.626
1.39	2525.9	56.4	2700	20.6	2.397
∞	2742.2	0.0	2742	0.0	∞

Safety under given factored load effects

(i) $P_u = 2275$ kN, $M_{ux} = 46.4$ kNm
From Figure 13.19, it can be seen that this point falls within the design interaction curve (failure envelope). Hence, the section is 'safe' under the given load effects.

Alternatively, corresponding to P_{uR} = 2275 kN, $M_{uR,x} \approx 104.41$ kNm (from Figure 13.19). As this ultimate moment of resistance is greater than M_{ux} = 46.4 kNm, the column section is safe.

Alternatively, $e_x = \dfrac{46.4 \times 10^6}{(2275 \times 10^3)}$ = 20.40 mm† (i.e., $(e/D)_x$ = 0.0408). The design strength corresponding to this loading eccentricity can be obtained from Figure 13.19 as the intersection of the design interaction curve with a straight line passing through the origin and the given point. Accordingly,

P_{uR} = 2525 kN > P_u = 2275 kN

M_{uR} = 56.4 kNm > M_u = 46.4 kNm – Hence, safe.

(ii) P_u = 1105 kN, M_{ux} = 125 kNm

This point also falls within the design interaction curve [Figure 13.19]. Hence, the section is 'safe'. Alternatively, corresponding to P_{uR} = 1105 kN (from Figure 13.19),

$M_{uR,x}$ = 232.57 kNm > M_{ux} = 125 kNm – Hence, safe.

Example 13.10

Using the design interaction curve obtained in Example 13.9, determine

(i) the maximum eccentricity e_x with which a factored load P_u = 1400 kN can be safely applied;

(ii) the design strength components corresponding to an eccentricity e_x = 0.6D.

Solution

(i) Considering the design interaction curve in Figure 13.19, or Table 13.1(b) corresponding to $P_{uR} = P_u$ = 1400 kN, the design flexural strength is obtained as

$M_{uR,x}$ = 208.29 kNm

This is the maximum factored moment that can be applied on the column section, in combination with P_u = 1400 kN. The corresponding eccentricity is given by

$$e_x = \frac{M_{ux}}{P_u} = \frac{208.29 \times 10^3}{1400} = \mathbf{148.77\ mm}$$

(ii) $e_x = 0.6D = 0.6 \times 500 = 300$ mm

Draw the radial line with e_x = 0.3, and locate its intersection with the interaction curve. For this, consider a point with coordinates P_u = 1000 kN and M_{ux} = 1000 × 0.30 = 300 kNm. Passing a straight line from the origin to this point on the interaction diagram (extending this line if necessary), to intersect the design interaction curve [see Figure 13.19], the design strength components are obtained as

P_{uR} = **840 kN**

$M_{uR,x}$ = **248 kNm**

Example 13.11

For the column section shown in Figure 13.15(a), construct the design interaction curve for axial compression combined with uniaxial bending about the minor axis. Hence, determine the

(i) maximum eccentricity e_y with which a factored load P_u = 1400 kN can be safely applied; and

(ii) design strength components corresponding to an eccentricity e_y = 180 mm.

† This roughly corresponds to the minimum uniaxial eccentricity (for short columns) specified by the Code.

Solution

- The design interaction curve $P_{uR} - M_{uR,y}$ is constructed in a manner similar to the $P_{uR} - M_{uR,x}$ curve of Example 13.9. In the present case, the depth of the section is taken as 300 mm and the width as 500 mm. There are only two rows of reinforcement to be considered [see Example 13.7]:

$$A_{s1} = A_{s2} = 3 \times 491 = 1473 \text{ mm}^2$$
$$y_1 = -89.5 \text{ mm, and } y_2 = +89.5 \text{ mm}$$

The coordinates of the interaction curve (along with values of x_u/D) are shown in Table 13.2 and plotted in Figure 13.20.

- Some salient points on this interaction curve are

$$\tilde{P}_{uo} = 2457.45 \text{ kN}, P_{uo} = 2742 \text{ kN}$$
(as in Example 13.9)

$$M_{uo,y} = 124.46 \text{ kNm (as against } M_{uo,x} = 230.77 \text{ kNm in Example 13.9)}$$

$$P_{ub,y} = 564.1 \text{ kN}, M_{ub,y} = 159.74 \text{ kNm}$$

(i) Corresponding to $P_{uR} = P_u = 1400$ kN, the design flexural strength is obtained from Table 13.2 or Figure 13.20 as
$M_{uR,y} = 125.2$ kNm (compared to 208.3 kNm in Example 13.10)
This is maximum factored moment M_{uy} that can be applied on the column section, in combination with $P_u = 1400$ kN. The corresponding eccentricity is given by

$$e_y = \frac{M_{uy}}{P_u} = \frac{125.2 \times 10^3}{1400} = \mathbf{89.49 \text{ mm}}$$

(ii) $e_y = 180$ mm
Considering a straight line with slope such that $P_u : M_{uy} = 1000$ kN : 180 kNm, i.e., a slope of 1:e_y, the desired strength components are obtained as the point of intersection of the design curve with this straight line [see Figure 13.20]:

$$P_{uR} = \mathbf{800 \text{ kN}}$$
$$M_{uR,y} = \mathbf{156.87 \text{ kNm}}$$

[In this case, $e_y/D = 180/300 = 0.60$. The results may be compared with $P_{uR} = 800$ kN, $M_{uR,x} = 249.7$ kNm corresponding to $e_x/D = 0.6$, obtained in Example 13.10(ii)].

Table 13.2 *Example 13.11 — Design Interaction Curve Coordinates*

P_{uR} (kN)	$M_{uR,y}$ (kNm)	x_u/D
0	124.5	0.273
100	133.1	0.298
200	141.3	0.327
300	149.2	0.359
400	155.2	0.392
500	159.1	0.431
600	160.1	0.470
700	159.2	0.507
800	156.1	0.537
900	151.4	0.560
1000	146.4	0.585
1100	141.3	0.612
1200	136.1	0.640
1300	130.7	0.669
1400	125.2	0.701
1500	119.5	0.733
1600	113.5	0.768
1700	107.1	0.804
1800	100.3	0.842
1900	93.1	0.882
2000	85.3	0.923
2100	77.0	0.966
2200	67.5	1.015
2300	56.4	1.088
2400	45.3	1.193
2500	34.3	1.354
2600	23.0	1.645
2700	11.6	2.372
2742	0.0	∞

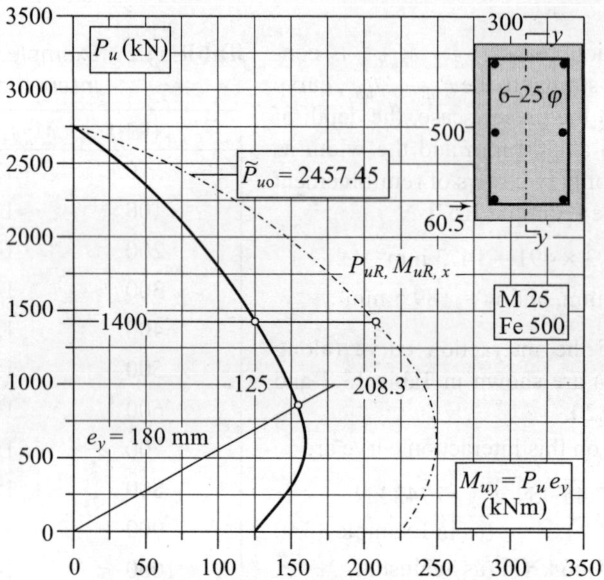

Fig. 13.20 Example 13.11.

13.5.6 Non-dimensional Interaction Diagrams as Design Aids

In a typical *design* situation, the column section has to be designed to resist certain critical combinations of factored axial compression (P_u) and factored bending moment (M_u) – as obtained from structural analyses. Commonly, the overall dimensions of the column are assumed†, and the grades of concrete and steel are specified; of course, these could be changed subsequently – in a redesign. The problem of 'design', therefore, reduces to the provision of longitudinal and transverse reinforcement. Designing of transverse reinforcement is relatively simple, as it is largely a matter of compliance with Code specifications related to bar diameter and spacing [refer Section 13.3.3]. Designing of longitudinal reinforcement can also be made simple by the use of interaction diagrams, as explained in Section 13.5.5. Indeed, as pointed out earlier, in the absence of such analysis/design aids, the problem is difficult to solve as it calls for repeated trial-and-error in order to locate the neutral axis.

The interaction diagrams discussed hitherto [such as Figure 13.19 or Figure 13.20] are applicable only for particular sections, details of which are indicated in the inset of each diagram. The application of the interaction diagram can be rendered more versatile by making coordinates P_u and M_u independent of the cross-sectional dimensions – by defining suitable non-dimensional parameters p_u and m_u:

$$p_u \equiv \frac{P_u}{f_{ck} bD} \tag{13.31}$$

$$m_u \equiv \frac{M_u}{f_{ck} bD^2} \tag{13.32}$$

The $p_u - m_u$ interaction diagram [Figure 13.21] now becomes applicable to all sections geometrically similar to and having the same material (steel) properties as the one shown in the inset of the figure. The design

† Indeed, these dimensions need to be assumed at the stage of structural analysis itself, if the column forms part of a statically indeterminate structure – as is usually the case.

interaction curve has coordinates p_{uR} and m_{uR} (corresponding to P_{uR} and M_{uR}); expressions for p_{uR} and m_{uR} are obtainable from Eqs 13.20–13.30:

$$p_u \equiv \frac{P_u}{f_{ck}bD} = a + \sum_{i=1}^{n}(f_{si} - f_{ci})\frac{k_i p}{100 f_{ck}} \tag{13.33}$$

$$m_u \equiv \frac{M_u}{f_{ck}bD^2} = a\,(0.5 - \bar{x}/D) + \sum_{i=1}^{n}(f_{si} - f_{ci})\frac{k_i p}{100 f_{ck}}\frac{y_i}{D} \tag{13.34}$$

where expressions for the non-dimensional parameters a and $\bar{x}/D$ are obtainable from Eqs 13.24 and 13.25; and k_i is the fraction of the total percentage of reinforcement p located at the ith row, where

$$p \equiv \frac{100 A_s}{bD} \tag{13.35}$$

From the nature of Eqs 13.33 and 13.34, it follows that by selecting p/f_{ck} as a parameter, the interaction diagram (valid for given arrangement of bars), can be rendered independent of the grade of concrete†. A family of non-dimensional design interaction curves ($p_{uR} - m_{uR}$) can thus be generated for a given arrangement of bars. For example, considering the arrangement of six bars in the rectangular column section of Example 13.5 [see Figures 13.15(a), 13.19], with bending about the major axis, a family of interaction curves can be generated, as shown in Figure 13.21 – for some typical values of p/f_{ck} (0.05, 0.10, 0.15, 0.20, 0.25) and specific grade of steel, viz., Fe 500. In this particular arrangement of bars, it is assumed that all the bars are of equal diameter and symmetrically arranged, with one pair of bars located along the major centroidal axis. This is indicated in the inset shown at the top of the figure. The ratio of the effective cover d' to the overall depth D is another parameter of significance. A typical value $d'/D = 0.10$ is assumed in the interaction diagram shown in Figure 13.21. In practice, d'/D usually varies in the range 0.05–0.20, and p/f_{ck} in the range 0.01–0.26. For a fairly exhaustive set of interaction diagrams (including different bar arrangements and grades of steel), reference may be made to the Design Handbook, SP : 16 [Ref. 13.12]

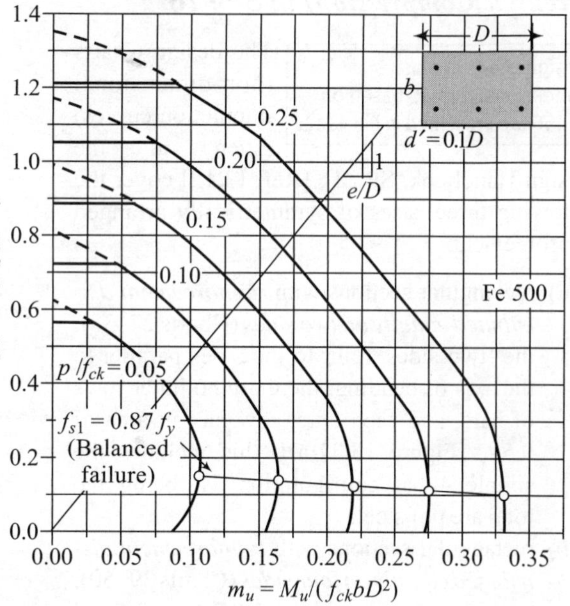

Fig. 13.21 Typical non-dimensional interaction diagram.

It is seen that the different 'balanced failure' condition points on the various design interaction curves of the same 'family' all happen to fall on the same straight line – as indicated in Figure 13.21.

It may also be noted that the non-dimensional design strength components p_{uR} and m_{uR} can be obtained for any given eccentricity e, as the point of intersection of the non-dimensional interaction curve with a straight

---

† Note that the term f_{ci} in Eqs 13.33 and 13.34 is dependent on f_{ck} if $\varepsilon_{si} > 0$ (compressive) [refer Eq. 13.29]. However, it is sufficiently accurate to consider f_{ck} = 20 MPa or 25 MPa for this purpose and thereby make the curves applicable for all grades of concrete [Ref. 13.12].

line passing through the origin and having a slope given by

$$p_u : m_u = 1 : e/D, \text{ as indicated in Figure 13.21.}$$

The non-dimensional interaction curves can be used to handle all types of design and analysis problems. In the design problem, the desired value of percentage reinforcement p can be easily obtained from the family of interaction curves for a given p_u and m_u. This is demonstrated in Examples 13.12–13.14.

Design Charts (for Uniaxial Eccentric Compression) in SP : 16

Design charts in non-dimensional format, based on IS 456 are presented in Ref 13.12.

The design Charts (non-dimensional interaction curves) given in the Design Handbook, SP : 16 [Ref. 13.12] cover the following three cases of symmetrically arranged reinforcement :

(a) rectangular sections with *reinforcement distributed equally on two sides* (Charts 27–38): the 'two sides' refer to the sides parallel to the axis of bending; there are no inner rows of bars, and each outer row has an area of $0.5A_s$ [Figure 13.22(a)], this includes the simple 4–bar configuration; A_s being the total area of steel;

(b) rectangular sections with *reinforcement distributed equally on four sides* (Charts 39–50): two outer rows (with area $0.3A_s$ each) and four inner rows (with area $0.1A_s$ each) have been considered in the calculations†; however, the use of these Charts can be extended, without significant error, to cases of not less than two inner rows (with a minimum area $0.3A_s$ in each outer row), as shown in Figure 13.22(b).

(c) *circular column sections* (Charts 51–62): the Charts are applicable for circular sections with at least six bars (of equal diameter) uniformly spaced circumferentially, as shown in Figure 13.22(c).

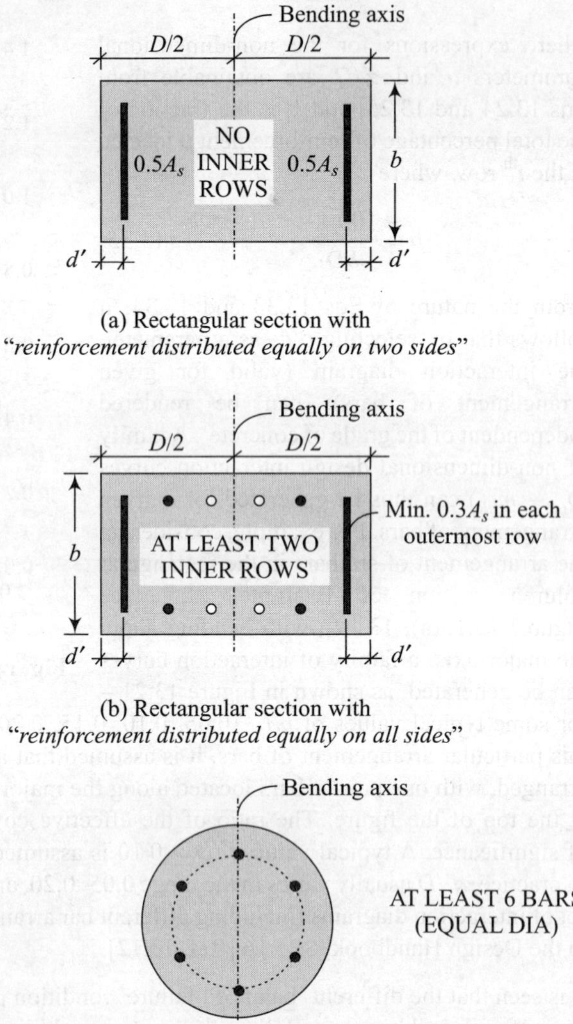

Fig. 13.22 Reinforcement arrangements for which SP : 16 Charts are applicable.

Corresponding to each of the above three cases, there are as many as 12 Charts available – covering

† If bars of equal diameter are used, this is equivalent to using 20 bars. While actually providing reinforcement to conform to A_s computed using these Charts, some adjustments may be called for in practice. Providing a greater proportion of reinforcement (more than $0.3A_s$) on the outermost rows is on the safer side [refer Example 13.13].

the 3 grades of steel (Fe 250, Fe 415, Fe 500), with 4 values of d'/D ratio for each grade (viz., $d'/D = 0.05$, .0.10, 0.15, 0.20). For intermediate values of d'/D, linear interpolation may be done. Each of the 12 Charts of SP : 16 covers a family of non-dimensional design interaction curves with p/f_{ck} values ranging from 0.0 to 0.26.

It may be noted that there are other types of symmetrical reinforcement arrangements such as the 6-bar arrangement of Figure 13.15(a) which are not covered by SP : 16 [Figure 13.22]. In such cases, the designer may make judicious approximations if he still wishes to avail of the SP : 16 Charts. However, a proper course of action would be to construct the proper interaction diagram (as in Examples 13.9 and 13.11) for the section chosen, and thereby to verify the safety of the section; if required, the design should be suitably revised, to make it more economical.

There are other situations, encountered in practice, which are not amenable for the use of SP : 16 Charts. These include cases of

- unsymmetrically arranged reinforcement in rectangular sections;
- non-rectangular and non-circular sections – such as L-shaped, T-shaped, H-shaped, cross shaped sections, etc.

In such cases, it becomes necessary to construct proper interaction diagrams in order to obtain accurate and reliable solutions.

Example 13.12

Using the design aids given in SP : 16, design the longitudinal reinforcement in a rectangular reinforced concrete column of size 300 mm × 600 mm subjected to a factored load of 1400 kN and a factored moment of 280 kNm with respect to the major axis. Assume M 25 concrete and Fe 500 steel.

Solution

- *Given*: $b = 300$ mm, $D = 600$ mm, $f_{ck} = 25$ MPa, $f_y = 500$ MPa, $P_u = 1400$ kN, $M_{ux} = 280$ kNm
- *Arrangement of bars*: As $D = 600$ mm, the spacing between the corner bars will exceed 300 mm; hence inner rows of bars have to be provided to satisfy detailing requirements [refer Section 13.3.3]. Assuming two or more inner rows, the SP : 16 Charts for 'equal reinforcement on four sides' can be made use of [Figure 13.22(b)].
- Assuming an effective cover $d' = 60$ mm,

$$\Rightarrow \quad d'/D = 60/600 = 0.1$$

$$p_u = \frac{P_u}{f_{ck}bD} = \frac{1400 \times 10^3}{25 \times 300 \times 600} = 0.311$$

$$m_u = \frac{M_{ux}}{f_{ck}bD^2} = \frac{280 \times 10^6}{25 \times 300 \times 600^2} = 0.104$$

- Referring to Chart 48 ($d'/D = 0.10$) of SP : 16, it can be observed that, the coordinates $p_u = 0.311$, $m_u = 0.104$ would lie on a design interaction curve with

$$p/f_{ck} \approx 0.06$$

$$\Rightarrow \quad p_{\text{reqd}} = 0.06 \times 25 = 1.5$$

$$\Rightarrow \quad A_{s,\,\text{reqd}} = 1.5 \times 300 \times 600/100 = \mathbf{2700\ mm^2}$$

Detailing of longitudinal reinforcement

- The design chart used refers to the case of 'equal reinforcement on four sides' [Figure 13.22(b)],

Outermost rows

Minimum area required in each outermost row = 0.3 × 2700 = 810 mm^2
Provide 2–25ϕ: area = 491 × 2 = 982 mm^2 > 810 mm^2

Inner rows

Total area required = 2700 – (982 × 2) = 736 mm^2
Provide 4–20ϕ in two inner rows: area = 314 × 4 = 1257 mm^2 > 736 mm^2

- Total area provided = (982 × 2) + 1257 = 3221 mm^2 > 2700 mm^2
(⇒ p = 100 × 3221/(300 × 600) = 1.789)
Assuming 8 mm ties, effective cover = 40 + 8 + (25/2) = 60.5 mm ≈ 60 mm – OK
The detailing is shown in Figure 13.23. Details of transverse reinforcement are also indicated in the figure. (It may be verified that this detailing adequately satisfies the Code requirements).

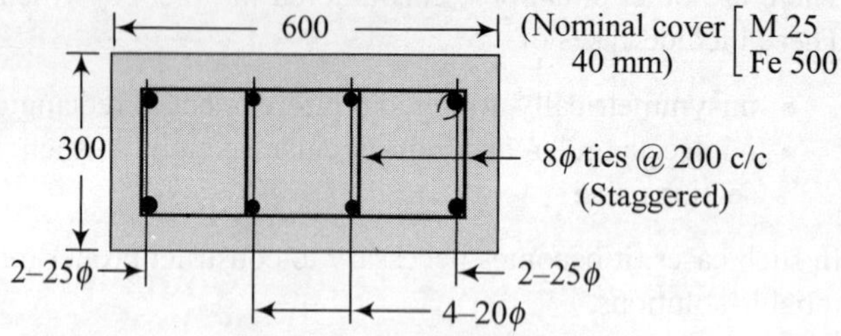

Fig. 13.23 Example 13.12.

Example 13.13

Referring to the column section shown in Figure 13.23, investigate the safety of the column section under uni-axial eccentric compression with respect to the minor axis, considering P_u = 1400 kN and M_{uy} = 200 kNm. If the section is unsafe, suggest suitable modifications to the reinforcement provided.

Solution

- *Given*: b = 600 mm, D = 300 mm, f_{ck} = 25 MPa, f_y = 500 MPa, P_u = 1400 kN, M_{uy} = 200 kNm, A_s = 3221 mm^2, p = 1.789
Effective cover d' = 40 + 8 + 12.5 = 60.5 mm
- The arrangement of bars in this case conforms to 'reinforcement distributed equally on two sides' [Figure 13.23(a)].

$$d'/D = 60.5/300 = 0.202 \approx 0.2$$

$$p/f_{ck} = 1.789/25 = 0.0716 \cong 0.07$$

$$p_u = \frac{P_u}{f_{ck}bD} = \frac{1400 \times 10^3}{25 \times 600 \times 300} = 0.311$$

$$m_u = \frac{M_{ux}}{f_{ck}bD^2} = \frac{200 \times 10^6}{25 \times 600 \times 300^2} = 0.148$$

- Referring to Chart 34 (d'/D = 0.2) of SP: 16, it can be seen that the point p_{uR} = 0.311, m_u = 0.148 lies outside the design interaction curve envelope for p/f_{ck} = 0.07. The value of p/f_{ck} corresponding to p_{uR} = 0.311 and m_{uR} = 0.148 is given by:

$$(p/f_{ck})_{\text{reqd}} = 0.12 > (p/f_{ck})_{\text{provided}} = 0.07.$$

Hence, the given section is **unsafe**.

- ***Revised Design***
Corresponding to $(p/f_{ck})_{\text{reqd}} = 0.12$,

$$p_{\text{reqd}} = 0.12 \times 25 = 3$$

$$\Rightarrow \quad A_{s,\,\text{reqd}} = 3 \times 600 \times 300/100 = 5400 \text{ mm}^2$$

(to be provided equally in two rows)
Provide 4–32ϕ + 4–28ϕ (instead of 4–25ϕ + 4–20ϕ)

$$\Rightarrow \quad A_{s,\,\text{provided}} = (804 + 616) \times 4$$
$$= 5680 \text{ mm}^2 > 5400 \text{ mm}^2 \ (p = 3.156)$$

The detailing for the revised design is shown in Figure 13.24.

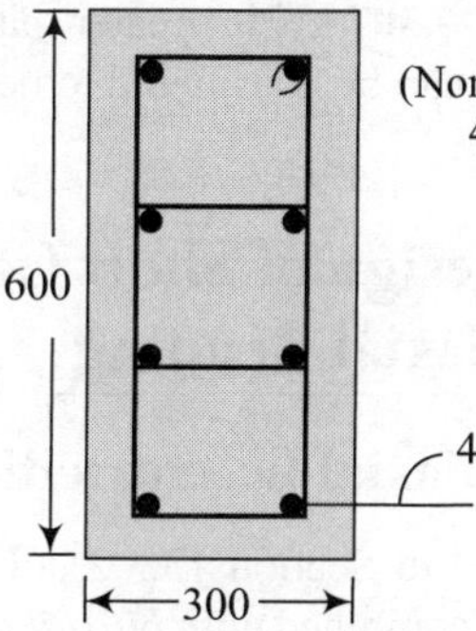

Fig. 13.24 Example 13.13.

Example 13.14

Consider a spiral circular short column, with details as given in Figure 13.11 (Example 13.4). Assess the safety of the column section, when subjected to a factored compressive load of 260 kN and a factored bending moment of 78 kNm. In case the section is found unsafe, redesign the reinforcement.

Solution

- *Given*: diameter D = 400 mm, A_s = 1206 mm^2(6–16ϕ), f_{ck} = 25 MPa, f_y = 500 MPa, P_u = 260 kN, M_u = 78 kNm
- As the spiral reinforcement satisfies the Code requirements (Cl. 39.4.1), as seen in Example 13.4, the design strength (i.e., P_{uR}, M_{uR}) may be enhanced by 5 per cent, as permitted for short columns.
- Effective cover d' = 40 + 6 + 16/2 = 54 mm

$$\Rightarrow \quad d'/D = 54/400 = 0.135 \text{ (which lies between 0.10 and 0.15)}$$

- percentage of reinforcement $p = \dfrac{100A_s}{\pi D^2/4} = \dfrac{100 \times 1206}{\pi \times 400^2/4} = 0.960$

$$\Rightarrow \quad p/f_{ck} = 0.960/25 = 0.0384$$

- ***Eccentricity of loading*** $e = \dfrac{M_u}{P_u} = \dfrac{78 \times 10^3}{260} = 300$ mm

$$\Rightarrow \quad e/D = 300/400 = 0.75$$
$$\Rightarrow \quad p_{uR} : m_{uR} = 1 : 0.75, \text{ or more conveniently, } 0.1 : 0.075$$

Thus, the design strength components p_{uR}, m_{uR} can be obtained as the point of intersection of the design interaction curve with a straight line joining the origin to a point with p_u = 0.1, m_u = 0.075 in the non-dimensional interaction diagram.

- Referring to Chart 60 (d'/D = 0.10) and Chart 61 (d'/D = 0.15) of SP : 16, and interpolating results for d'/D = 0.135 and p/f_{ck} = 0.038, and enhancing the p_{uR}, m_{uR} values by 5 per cent (as permitted by the Code for spiral columns, suitably reinforced),

$$p_{ur} \equiv P_{uR}/(f_{ck}D^2) \approx 0.073 \times 1.05 = 0.0767$$
$$m_{ur} \equiv M_{uR}/(f_{ck}D^3) \approx 0.0565 \times 1.05 = 0.0593$$
$$\Rightarrow \quad P_{uR} = 0.0767 \times 25 \times 400^2 = 306.8 \times 10^3 \text{ N} = \mathbf{307\ kN}$$
$$M_{uR} = 0.0593 \times 25 \times 400^3 = 94.88 \times 10^6 \text{ Nmm} = \mathbf{94.9\ kNm}$$

As P_{uR} = **307** kN is greater than P_u = 260 kN and M_{uR} = **94.9** kNm is greater than M_u = 78 kNm, the section can be considered to be safe, and hence there is no need for a redesign.

13.6 Design of Short Columns Under Axial Compression with Biaxial Bending

13.6.1 Biaxial Eccentricities

As mentioned in Section 13.3.2, all columns are (in a strict sense) to be treated as being subject to axial compression combined with *biaxial* bending, as the design must account for possible eccentricities in loading (e_{min} at least) with respect to both major and minor principal axes of the column section. *Uniaxial loading* is an idealised approximation which can be made when the *e*/*D* ratio with respect to one of the two principal axes can be considered to be negligible. Also, as mentioned in Section 13.4.1, if the *e*/*D* ratios are negligible with respect to both principal axes, conditions of *axial loading* may be assumed, as a further approximation. In the 2000 revision to the Code, it is clarified (Cl. 25.4) that 'where biaxial bending is considered, it is sufficient to ensure that eccentricity exceeds the minimum about one axis at a time'. This implies that if either one or both the factored bending moments M_{ux} and M_{uy} (obtained from analysis) is less than the corresponding value, calculated from minimum eccentricity considerations (Eq. 13.8), it suffices to ensure that at least one of the two minimum eccentricity conditions is satisfied. However, it also becomes necessary to check for the other biaxial bending condition wherein the minimum eccentricity in the other direction is also satisfied. In lieu of the above, of course, it will be sufficient and conservative to ensure that both minimum eccentricities are simultaneously satisfied in a single design check.

The factored moments M_{ux} and M_{uy} acting on a column section (with respect to bending about the major axis and minor axis respectively) can be resolved into a single resultant moment M_u which acts about an axis inclined to the two principal axes [Figure 13.25(a)]:

$$M_u = \sqrt{M_{ux}^2 + M_{uy}^2} \tag{13.36}$$

Alternatively, the resultant eccentricity $e = M_u/P_u$ may be obtained [refer Figure 13.25(b)] as:

$$e = \sqrt{e_x^2 + e_y^2} \tag{13.37}$$

When the column section (including the reinforcement) is axisymmetric (with reference to the longitudinal axis) – as in a circular column – the resultant axis of bending is also a principal axis [Figure 13.25(d)]. In such a situation, the case of biaxial bending simplifies into a case of uniaxial bending. The neutral axis, in this instance, will remain parallel to the resultant axis of bending.

> In columns with non-axisymmetric cross section subjected to biaxial bending, the neutral axis is generally not parallel to the resultant moment vector, and an exact solution is extremely complex. Recourse is made to approximate methods.

However, in the more general case of non-axisymmetric reinforced concrete column sections, the neutral axis is generally not parallel to the resultant axis of bending [Figure 13.25(c)]. In fact, the determination of the exact neutral axis location is a laborious process of trial and error. For a given neutral axis location, however, the failure strain distribution can be drawn (with the same assumptions as in the case of uniaxially eccentric compression) [Figure 13.26].

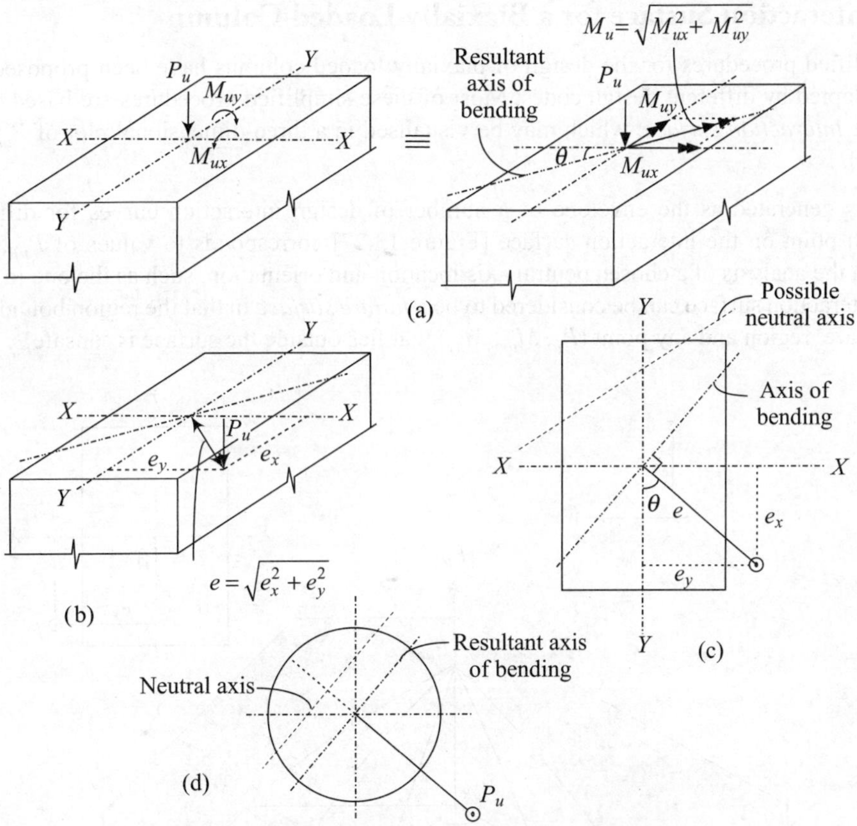

Fig. 13.25 Resultant eccentricity of loading.

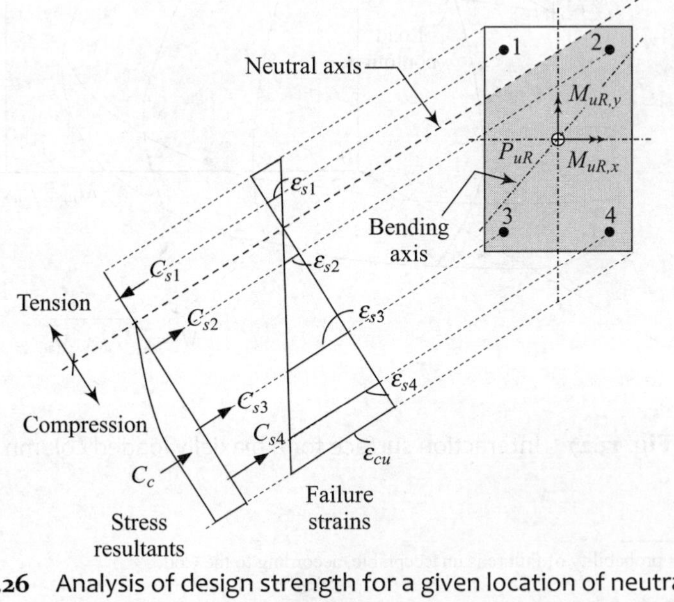

Fig. 13.26 Analysis of design strength for a given location of neutral axis.

13.6.2 Interaction Surface for a Biaxially Loaded Column

Various simplified procedures for the design of biaxially loaded columns have been proposed [Ref. 13.14, 13.15] and adopted by different design codes. Most of these simplified procedures are based on an approximation of the *interaction surface*, which may be visualised in a three-dimensional plot of $P_{uR} - M_{ux} - M_{uy}$ [Figure 13.27].

The surface is generated as the envelope of a number of design interaction curves for different axes of bending. Each point on the interaction surface [Figure 13.27] corresponds to values of P_{uR}, M_{ux} and M_{uy} obtained from the analysis of a chosen neutral axis location and orientation, such as the one in Figure 13.26. The design interaction surface can be considered to be a *failure surface* in that the region bounded within this surface is a 'safe' region and any point (P_u, M_{ux}, M_{uy}) that lies outside the surface is 'unsafe'[†].

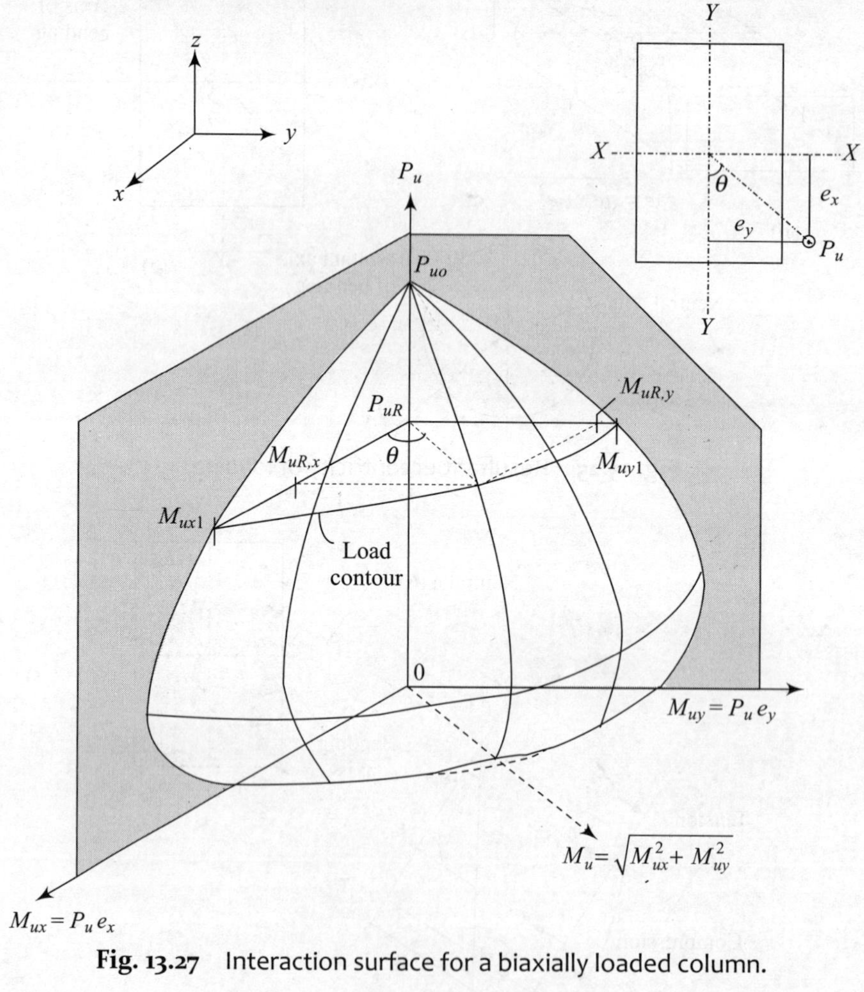

Fig. 13.27 Interaction surface for a biaxially loaded column.

[†] That is, the corresponding probability of failure is unacceptable, according to the Code.

The traces of the interaction surface on the *x-z* and *y-z* (vertical) planes correspond to the design interaction curves for uniaxial eccentricity with respect to the major and minor principal axes respectively. In order to avoid confusion, the notations used for the design flexural strength under uniaxial eccentricity and under biaxial eccentricities, the following notations shall be used in the context of biaxial loading of columns:

$M_{uR,x} \equiv$ design flexural strength with respect to *major* axis under *biaxial* loading, with axial load P_{uR}

$M_{uR,y} \equiv$ design flexural strength with respect to *minor* axis under *biaxial* loading, with axial load P_{uR}

$M_{ux1} \equiv$ design flexural strength with respect to *major* axis under *uniaxial* loading, with axial load P_{uR}, (i.e., $e_y = 0$).

$M_{uy1} \equiv$ design flexural strength with respect to *minor* axis under *uniaxial* loading, with axial load P_{uR}, (i.e., $e_x = 0$).

The notations and their respective meanings are depicted in Figure 13.27, corresponding to an axial compression $P_u = P_{uR}$.

It is interesting to note (in Figure 13.27) that the trace of the interaction surface on a horizontal plane (parallel to the *x-y* plane) at any load level P_u is also an interaction curve – depicting the interaction between the biaxial bending capacities $M_{uR,x}$ and $M_{uR,y}$. Such an interaction curve is sometimes referred to as a *load contour*, as all the points on the curve pertain to a constant axial load level.

13.6.3 Code Procedure for Design of Biaxially Loaded Columns

The simplified method adopted by the Code (Cl. 39.6) is based on Bresler's formulation [Ref. 13.14] for the 'load contour' – whereby an approximate relationship between $M_{uR,x}$ and $M_{uR,y}$ (for a specified $P_u = P_{uR}$) is established. This relationship is conveniently expressed in a non-dimensional form as follows:

$$\left(\frac{M_{ux}}{M_{ux1}}\right)^{\alpha_n} + \left(\frac{M_{uy}}{M_{uy1}}\right)^{\alpha_n} \leq 1 \qquad (13.38)$$

where M_{ux} and M_{uy} denote the factored biaxial moments acting on the column, and (as explained earlier) M_{ux1} and M_{uy1} denote the uniaxial moment capacities with reference to the major and minor axes respectively, all under an accompanying axial load $P_u = P_{uR}$. It may be noted that M_{ux}, M_{uy} (and P_u) are measures of the *load effects* due to *external* loading on the structure, whereas M_{ux1}, M_{uy1} (and P_{uR}) are measures of the inherent *resistance* of the column section.

α_n in Eq. 13.38 is a constant which depends on the factored axial compression P_u and which defines the shape of the 'load contour' [refer Figure 13.28]. For low axial load levels, the load contour (in non-dimensional coordinates) is approximated as a straight line; accordingly, $\alpha_n = 1$. For high axial load levels, the load contour is approximated as the quadrant of a circle; accordingly, $\alpha_n = 2$. For moderate load levels, α_n takes a value between 1 and 2, as shown in Figure 13.28(a). In order to quantitatively relate α_n with P_u, it is convenient to normalise P_u with the maximum axial load capacity of the column (under 'pure compression'). This was denoted as P_{uo} in Section 13.4.3, and defined by Eq. 13.16, with slightly different expressions for different grades of steel. In the context of biaxial loading, the Code (Cl. 39.6) uses the notation P_{uz} (instead of P_{uo}), and suggests the following rounded-off version of Eq. 13.16, applicable for all grades of steel:

$$P_{uz} = 0.45 f_{ck} A_c + 0.75 f_y A_{sc},$$

$$\Rightarrow \quad P_{uz} = 0.45 f_{ck} A_g + (0.75 f_y - 0.45 f_{ck}) A_{sc} \qquad (13.39)$$

where A_g denotes the gross area of the section and A_{sc} the total area of steel in the section.

$\alpha_n = 1$ for $P_u/P_{uz} < 0.2$; $\alpha_n = 2$ for $P_u/P_{uz} > 0.8$; and α_n is assumed to vary linearly for values of P_u/P_{uz} between 0.2 and 0.8 as shown in Figure 13.28(b). Accordingly,

$$\alpha_n = \begin{cases} 1.0 & \text{for } P_u/P_{uz} < 0.2 \\ 2.0 & \text{for } P_u/P_{uz} > 0.8 \\ 0.667 + 1.667\, P_u/P_{uz} & \text{otherwise} \end{cases} \tag{13.40}$$

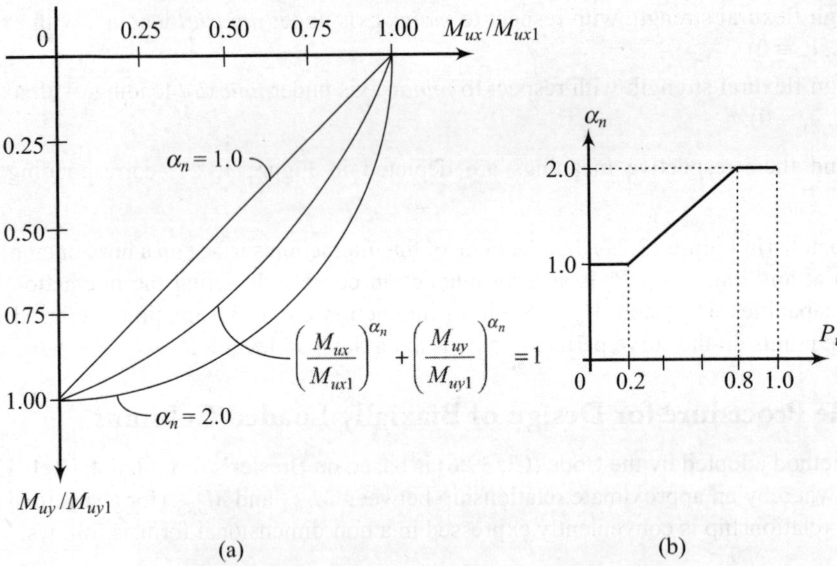

Fig. 13.28 Approximation of load contour.

A recent study [Ref. 13.23], based on rigorous analyses of several rectangular column sections with varying aspect ratios and reinforcement patterns has brought out that the above simplified formulation in the Code turns out to be conservative at very low axial load levels ($0.0 \le P_u/P_{uz} < 0.3$), and a little unconservative at higher axial load levels (levels ($0.5 < P_u/P_{uz} < 0.8$); improved expressions for α_n are proposed.

Rectangular Beam Sections Subject to Biaxial Bending

When there is no axial load on the section, but it is subject to biaxial bending, it behaves as a beam section under biaxial bending. The interaction of ultimate moment capacities, M_{ux} and M_{uy}, in the two orthogonal directions is represented by the load contour corresponding to $P_u/P_{uz} = 0$. For rectangular sections, the Code approximation (as given by Eq. 13.38), with $\alpha_n = 1$, simplifies to:

$$\left(\frac{M_{ux}}{M_{ux1}}\right) + \left(\frac{M_{uy}}{M_{uy1}}\right) \le 1 \tag{13.38a}$$

The use of Eq. 13.38a, assuming a linear interaction, results in conservative designs.

Code Procedure for Columns subject to Biaxial Bending

1. Given P_u, M_{ux}, M_{uy}, verify that the eccentricities $e_x = M_{ux}/P_u$ and $e_y = M_{uy}/P_u$ are not less than the corresponding minimum eccentricities (refer Section 13.6.1).

2. Assume a trial section for the column.
3. Determine M_{ux1} and M_{uy1}, corresponding to the given P_u (using appropriate design aids). Ensure that M_{ux1} and M_{uy1} are significantly greater than M_{ux} and M_{uy} respectively; otherwise, suitably redesign the section†.
4. Determine P_{uz} [Eq. 13.39], and hence α_n [Eq. 13.40].
5. Check the adequacy of the section [Eq. 13.38]; if necessary, redesign the section and check again.

Selection of Trial Section

Generally, in practice, the cross-sectional dimensions of the column are tentatively fixed in advance, and the structural analysis is performed on the basis of these dimensions. Indeed, the biaxial moments obtained from frame analyses (considering various load combinations) are based on the assumed cross-sectional dimensions (required for stiffness calculations). Hence, in the selection of the 'trial section' for the design of biaxially loaded columns, it is only reinforcement details that need to be suitably assumed in practical situations.

One simple way of doing this is by designing the trial section for uniaxial eccentricity, considering a moment of approximately 15 per cent‡ in excess of the resultant moment, i.e.,

$$M_u \cong 1.15\sqrt{M_{ux}^2 + M_{uy}^2} \tag{13.41}$$

This bending moment should be considered to act with respect to the major principal axis if $M_{ux} \geq M_{uy}$; otherwise, it should be with respect to the minor principal axis. The reinforcement may be assumed to be distributed equally on all sides of the section.

Example 13.15

A corner column (400 mm × 400 mm), located in the lowermost storey of a system of braced frames, is subjected to factored loads: P_u = 1300 kN, M_{ux} = 190 kNm and M_{uy} = 110 kNm. The unsupported length of the column is 3.5 m. Design the reinforcement in the column, assuming M 25 concrete and Fe 500 steel.

Solution

- *Given*: $D_x = D_y = 400$ mm, $l = 3500$ mm, $P_u = 1300$ kN, $M_{ux} = 190$ kNm, $M_{uy} = 110$ kNm, $f_{ck} = 25$ MPa, $f_y = 500$ MPa.

Slenderness ratios

- Assuming an effective length ratio of 0.85 for the braced column,

$$l_{ex} = l_{ey} = 0.85 \times 3500 = 2975 \text{ mm}$$

$$\Rightarrow \quad l_{ex}/D_x = l_{ey}/D_y = 2975/400 = 7.44 < 12$$

Hence the column may be designed as a *short column*.

Check minimum eccentricities

- Applied eccentricities: $e_x = 190 \times 10^3/1300 = 146$ mm

$$e_y = 110 \times 10^3/1300 = 84.6 \text{ mm}$$

† This is usually achieved by increasing the percentage of reinforcement and/or improving the grade of concrete; the dimensions may also be increased, if required.

‡ Lower percentages (up to 5 per cent) can be assumed if the axial loading level (P_u/P_{uz}) is relatively high.

Minimum eccentricities as per Code [Eq. 13.8]:

$$e_{x,\,min} = e_{y,\,min} = 3500/500 + 400/30 = 20.3 \text{ mm} > 20 \text{ mm}$$

As the minimum eccentricities are less than the applied eccentricities, no modification to M_{ux}, M_{uy} is called for.

Trial section: Longitudinal reinforcement

- Designing for uniaxial eccentricity with $P_u = 1300$ kN and

$$M_u \approx 1.15\sqrt{M_{ux}^2 + M_{uy}^2}$$
$$= 1.15\sqrt{190^2 + 110^2} = 252 \text{ kNm}$$

- Assuming $d' = 60$ mm,

$$d'/D = 60/400 = 0.15$$
$$\frac{P_u}{f_{ck}bD} = \frac{1300 \times 10^3}{25 \times 400^2} = 0.325$$
$$\frac{M_u}{f_{ck}bD^2} = \frac{252 \times 10^6}{25 \times 400^3} = 0.157$$

- Referring to chart 49 of SP : 16 ('equal reinforcement on all sides'),

$$p/f_{ck} = 0.13$$
$$\Rightarrow \quad p_{reqd} = 0.13 \times 25 = 3.25$$

[*Note:* This relatively high percentage of steel is particularly acceptable for a column located in the lowermost storey of a tall building.]

$$\Rightarrow \quad A_{s,\,reqd} = 3.25 \times 400^2/100 = 5200 \text{ mm}^2$$

- **Provide 12–25ϕ**: $A_s = 491 \times 12 = 5892 \text{ mm}^2 > 5200 \text{ mm}^2$. The arrangement of bars is shown in Figure 13.29.

Uniaxial moment capacities: M_{ux1}, M_{ux2} [Here, due to symmetry, $M_{ux1} = M_{ux2}$]

$$P_u/f_{ck}bD = 0.325 \text{ (as calculated earlier)}$$
$$p_{provided} = 5892 \times 100/400^2 = 3.68$$
$$\Rightarrow \quad p/f_{ck} = 3.68/25 = 0.147$$
$$d' = 40 + 8 + 25/2 = 60.5 \text{ mm (assuming a clear cover of 40 mm and 8 mm ties)}$$
$$\Rightarrow \quad d'/D = 60.5/400 = 0.151 \approx 0.15$$

- Referring to Chart 49 ($d'/D = 0.15$),

$$\frac{M_{ux1}}{f_{ck}bD^2} = 0.18$$
$$\Rightarrow \quad M_{ux1} = M_{uy1} = 0.18 \times 25 \times 400^3 = 288 \times 10^6 \text{ Nmm}$$
$$= 288 \text{ kNm}$$

which is significantly greater than $M_{ux} = 190$ kNm and $M_{uy} = 110$ kNm

Values of P_{uz} and α_n

- $P_{uz} = 0.45f_{ck}A_g + (0.75f_y - 0.45f_{ck})A_{sc}$ [Eq. 13.40]
  $= (0.45 \times 25 \times 400^2) + (0.75 \times 500 - 0.45 \times 25) \times 5892$
  $= (1800 \times 10^3 + 2143.2 \times 10^3)N = 3943$ kN

  $\Rightarrow \quad P_u/P_{uz} = 1300/3943 = 0.330$ (which lies between 0.2 and 0.8)

  $$\Rightarrow \quad \alpha_n = 1.0 + \frac{0.330 - 0.2}{0.8 - 0.2}(2.0 - 1.0) = 1.216$$

  [Alternatively, Eq. 13.40 may be used].

Check safety under biaxial loading

- $$\left(\frac{M_{ux}}{M_{ux1}}\right)^{\alpha_n} + \left(\frac{M_{uy}}{M_{uy1}}\right)^{\alpha_n} = \left(\frac{190}{288}\right)^{1.216} + \left(\frac{110}{288}\right)^{1.216}$$
  $$= 0.603 + 0.31 = 0.913 < 1.0$$

  Hence, the trial section is safe under the applied loading.

Transverse reinforcement

- The minimum diameter ϕ_t and maximum spacing s_t of the lateral ties are specified by the Code [Eq. 13.9, 13.10]:

  $$\phi_t > \begin{cases} 25/4 = 6.25 \text{ mm} \\ 6 \text{ mm} \end{cases}$$

  $\Rightarrow$ Provide 8ϕ ties

  $$s_t < \begin{cases} D = 400 \text{ mm} \\ 16 \times 25 = 400 \text{ mm} \\ 300 \text{ mm} \end{cases}$$

  Provide 8ϕ ties@ 300 c/c as shown in Figure 13.29.

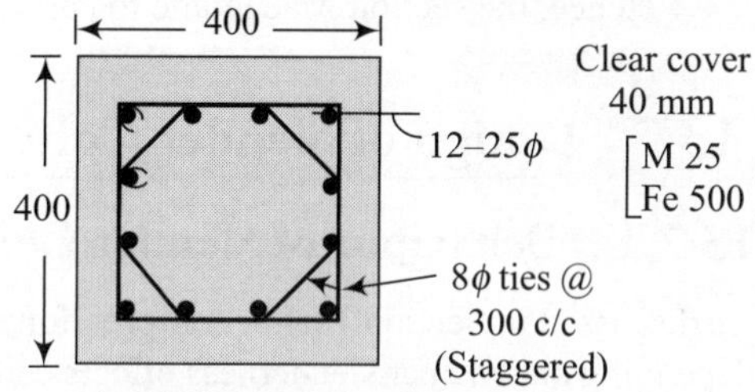

Fig. 13.29 Example 13.15.

Example 13.16

Verify the adequacy of the short column section Figure 13.15(a) under the following load conditions:

$P_u = 1400$ kN, $M_{ux} = 125$ kNm, $M_{uy} = 75$ kNm

The design interaction curves [Figures 13.19, 13.20] derived earlier may be used for this purpose. Assume that the column is a 'short column'.

Solution

- *Given*: $D_x = 500$ mm, $D_y = 300$ mm, $A_s = 2946$ mm^2, $M_{ux} = 125$ kNm, $M_{uy} = 75$ kNm, $f_{ck} = 25$ MPa, $f_y = 500$ MPa [refer Example 13.5].

Applied eccentricities

- $e_x = M_{ux}/P_u = 125 \times 10^3/1400 = 89.3$ mm $\Rightarrow e_x/D_x = 0.179$
  $e_y = M_{uy}/P_u = 75 \times 10^3/1400 = 53.6$ mm $\Rightarrow e_y/D_y = 0.179$
- These eccentricities for the short column are clearly not less than the minimum eccentricities specified by the Code.

Uniaxial moment capacities: M_{ux1}, M_{uy1}

- As determined in Examples 13.10 and 13.11 [also see Figure 13.20], corresponding to P_u = 1400 kN,

$$M_{ux1} = 208.3 \text{ kNm}$$
$$M_{uy1} = 125.3 \text{ kNm}$$

Values of P_{uz} and α_n

- $P_{uz} = 0.45 f_{ck} A_g + (0.75 f_y - 0.45 f_{ck}) A_{sc}$

$$= (0.45 \times 25 \times 300 \times 500) + (0.75 \times 500 - 0.45 \times 25) \times 2946$$
$$= (1687500 + 1071607.5)\ N = 2759 \text{ kN}$$

- $\Rightarrow P_u/P_{uz} = 1400/2759 = 0.507$ (which lies between 0.2 and 0.8)
- $\Rightarrow \alpha_n = 1.0 + \dfrac{0.507 - 0.2}{0.8 - 0.2}(2.0 - 1.0) = 1.513$

Check safety under biaxial bending

- $\left(\dfrac{M_{ux}}{M_{ux1}}\right)^{\alpha_n} + \left(\dfrac{M_{uy}}{M_{uy1}}\right)^{\alpha_n} = \left(\dfrac{125}{208.3}\right)^{1.512} + \left(\dfrac{75}{125.3}\right)^{1.512}$

$$= 0.462 + 0.46$$
$$= 0.922 < 1.0$$

Hence, the section is adequate to carry the given loads.

13.7 Design of Slender Columns

13.7.1 Behaviour of Slender Columns

As discussed in Section 13.1.3, compression members are categorised as being either *short* or *slender* (*long*), depending on whether slenderness effects can be ignored or need special consideration. It was also explained that the *slenderness ratios* (l_{ex}/D_x, l_{ey}/D_y) provide a simple basis for deciding whether a column is short or 'slender'. The behaviour and design of short columns under axial, uniaxial eccentric and biaxial eccentric loading conditions have been extensively described in Sections 13.4, 13.5 and 13.6 respectively.

This section describes the behaviour of slender columns, and shows how this behaviour increasingly deviates from the short column behaviour with increasing slenderness ratios. To begin with, a simple example of a pin-ended column with an eccentrically applied load [Figure 13.30(a)] is considered. The height l between the pinned ends is the 'unsupported length', which, in this case, is also equal to the 'effective length' [refer Figure 13.4(a)]. By considering different heights of the column, with the same cross-section, the effects of different slenderness ratios can be studied. Subjecting the column to a gradually increasing load P, applied at an eccentricity e (with the undeflected longitudinal axis), the behaviour of the column can be observed until failure.

Due to the applied eccentricity e, 'primary moments' $M_{pr} = Pe$ are developed not only at the end sections of the column, but all along the height [Figure 13.30(b)]. The bending of the column causes it to deflect laterally, thereby introducing additional displacement (load) dependent eccentricities. If the lateral deflection of the longitudinal axis is denoted as Δ, then the total eccentricity is $e + \Delta$, and the total moment M at any section is given by

$$M = P(e + \Delta) \quad (13.42a)$$
$$M = M_{pr} + P\Delta \quad (13.42b)$$

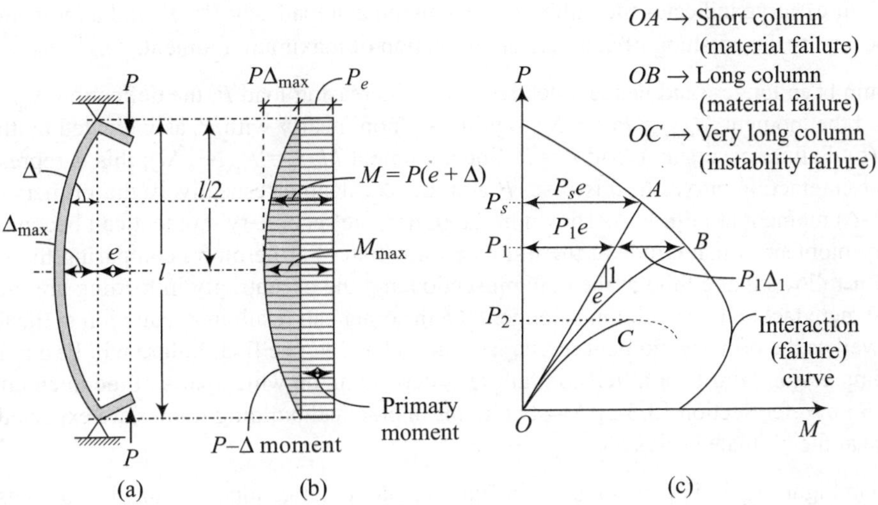

Fig. 13.30 Behaviour of slender columns.

where $P\Delta$ is the 'secondary moment' (also called 'P–Δ moment'), which has a variation along the height of the column that is identical to that of Δ [refer Figures 13.30(a), (b)]. The maximum value of Δ (i.e., Δ_{max}), and hence the maximum value of the total moment $M_{max} = P(e + \Delta_{max})$ occurs at the mid-height section of the column.

> Slender columns have significant lateral deflections (Δ), which increase the effective eccentricity, and the axial load, P, interacting with the lateral deflection causes (additional) 'secondary moments', $= P \times \Delta$, often called 'P-Δ effect'. The increase in moment results in decrease in axial load capacity.

It should be noted that the lateral deflection Δ_{max} is not only due to the curvature produced by the primary moment M_{pr}, but also due to the P–Δ moment. Hence, the variation of M_{max} with P is nonlinear, with M_{max} increasing at a faster rate as P increases. In the case of a very slender column, with increase in lateral deflection, the moment M_{max} may increase so rapidly that a stage may be reached where the section cannot resist any more moment without a decrease in the axial load, resulting in an instability (buckling) failure (see loading path OC in Figure 13.30(c)). On the other hand, in the case of a very short column, the flexural stiffness is so high that the lateral deflection Δ is negligibly small†; consequently, the P–Δ moment is negligible, and the primary moment M_{pr} alone is of significance in such a case.

> Very slender column may fail by buckling (instability) before reaching the cross-sectional strength limit.

Figure 13.30(c) shows the axial load-moment interaction curve (at the ultimate limit state) for the column *section*. This curve, therefore, represents the strength of the column. Also shown in Figure 13.30(c) are three different loading paths OA, OB, OC that are possible (for different slenderness ratios) as the column in Figure 13.30(a) is loaded to failure, with increasing P (and hence, M) and constant eccentricity e. In the case of a very short column, $\Delta_{max} \approx 0$ (as explained earlier) and $M_{max} = Pe$. The resulting P–M path is linear, as indicated by the line OA in Figure 13.30(c). The termination of this line at the point of intersection A with the

† Theoretically, $\Delta_{max} = 0$ only if the effective length $l_e = 0$ or if $e = 0$ (pure axial loading). In practical 'short' columns, some lateral deflection is unavoidable, particularly at high eccentricities of loading. However, it is expected that the P–Δ moment in a short column will not exceed about 5 per cent of the primary moment, and so may be neglected.

interaction (failure) curve indicates the failure of the column at a load, say $P = P_s$ and a moment $M_{max} = P_s e$. The failure occurs by the crushing of concrete at the section of maximum moment.

Had the column been longer (and hence, 'slender'), with increasing load P, the deflection Δ_{max} is no longer negligible, and the moment $M_{max} = P(e + \Delta_{max})$ will vary nonlinearly with P, as indicated by the line OB in Figure 13.30(c). Failure occurs at a load $P = P_1$ and a moment $M_{max} = P_1(e + \Delta_1)$; this is represented by the point B on the interaction curve. In this case, $P_1 e$ and $P_1\Delta_1$, denote respectively the primary moment and secondary (P–Δ) moment at failure. As shown in the figure, the secondary moment can become comparable to the primary moment in magnitude at the ultimate limit state. Furthermore, comparing the loading paths OA with OB, it follows that although the column section and the eccentricity in loading are identical in the two cases, the mere fact that one column is longer than the other can result in a reduction in the load-carrying capacity (as well as the primary moment resistance). In both cases, the final failure will be a material failure – either a 'compression failure' or a 'tension failure' – depending on which parts of the interaction curve the points A and B lie [refer Section 13.5.2]. Most columns in practical building frames are expected to have this type of failure at the ultimate limit state.

If the column in Figure 13.30 is very long, the increase in lateral deflection Δ_{max} may be so excessive that the load-moment path corresponds to OC, with dP/dM reaching zero at the point C. In this case, the column is so slender that it fails by instability (buckling) at a relatively low axial load P_2. This type of failure may occur in very slender columns in unbraced frames.

Braced Slender Columns: Member Stability Effect

As explained in Section 13.2.3, a 'braced column' is one which is not subject to sidesway, i.e., there is no significant relative lateral displacement between the top and bottom ends of the column. The pin-jointed column of Figure 13.30 is a simple example of a braced column. In general, the ends of a braced column (which forms part of a 'braced frame') are partially restrained against rotation (by the connecting beams). The primary moments M_1 and M_2 that are applied at the two ends of the column are determined from a 'first-order' structural analysis; i.e., analysis which assumes linear elastic behaviour, and neglects the influence of change in geometry of the frame due to deflections. The column may be bent in *single curvature* or *double curvature*, depending on the directions of M_1 and M_2 [Figure 13.31]. The notations M_1 and M_2 generally refer to the smaller and larger column end moments, and the ratio M_1/M_2 is considered positive if the column is bent in single curvature, and negative if it is bent in double curvature.

If $M_1/M_2 = +1.0$, the column is bent in symmetrical single curvature, and the slenderness in the column will invariably result in an increased moment as can be seen from Figure 13.30(b). However, in the more general case of unequal end moments ($M_1/M_2 \neq 1.0$), it is not necessary that slenderness will result in a peak moment in the column that is greater than the larger primary end moment M_2 – as indicated by the curves labelled '1' in Figure 13.31. If, however, the column is very slender, and the consequent lateral deflection Δ_2 is sufficiently high (curve '2' in Figure 13.31), the peak in the total moment over the length of the column to be considered in design (i.e., including the additional moment $P\Delta_2$) may exceed the larger end moment M_2. This is less likely in columns bent in double curvature [Figure 13.31(b)]. In fact, the chances of a given slenderness resulting in a peak design moment larger than M_2 fall off significantly as the ratio M_1/M_2 drops below about +0.5 and approaches the limit of –1.0. The possible amplification in bending moment (over the primary moment M_2) on account of lateral displacements (relative to the chord joining the column ends) is termed as *member stability effect*.

'Member stability effect' is the amplification of primary moments in a braced column due to lateral displacement of the column.

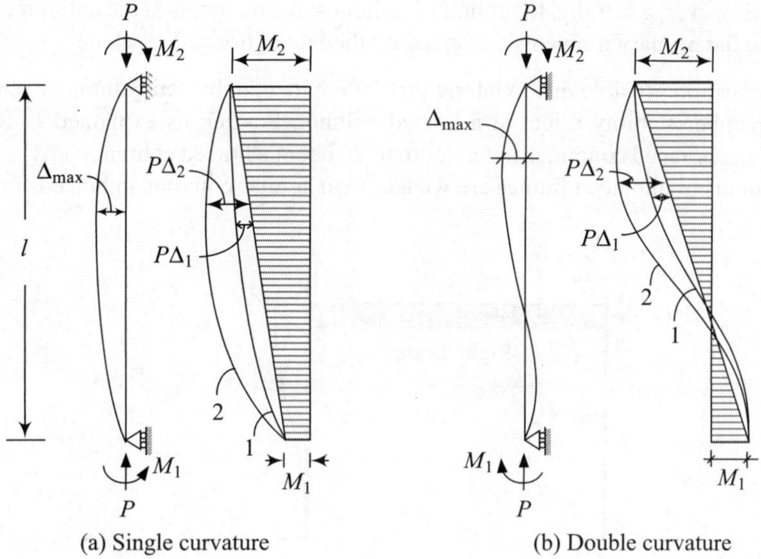

Fig. 13.31 Braced columns: member stability effect.

Thus, the criticality of slenderness effects is also dependent on the ratio M_1/M_2. The ACI Code [Ref. 13.1] recommends that slenderness effects may be ignored (i.e., the column may be designed as a 'short column') if, for a braced column,

$$l_e/r < 34 - 12M_1/M_2 \tag{13.43}$$

where l_e is the effective length and r the radius of gyration. Thus, the slenderness ratio (l_e/r) limit for short columns lies in the range 22–34 in single curvature and 34–46 in double curvature. It is shown [Ref. 13.16] that this slenderness limit [Eq. 13.43] corresponds to effective lengths for which the ultimate axial load capacity, including 'member stability' effect, is at least 95 per cent of the axial compressive strength of the cross-section.

Unbraced Slender Column: Lateral Drift Effect

As explained in Section 13.2.3, an 'unbraced column' is one which is subject to sidesway (or 'lateral drift'), i.e., there is significant lateral displacement between the top and bottom ends of the column. The lateral drift may occur due to the action of lateral loads, or due to gravity loads when the loading or the frame is asymmetric.

> **'Lateral drift effect' is the increase in column end moments due to the vertical load acting on the lateral sway of an unbraced column.**

Considering the simple portal frame of Figure 13.32(a) (in which the beam is assumed to be infinitely rigid, for convenience), the lateral drift (or sidesway) of the column is the relative translational displacement $\Delta\ (= \Delta_A + \Delta_B)$ between the ends of the column. The additional moments at the column ends caused by the action of the vertical load acting on the deflected configuration of the unbraced column is termed the *lateral drift effect*. In unbraced columns, the action of the primary moments (M_1, M_2) generally results in 'double curvature', which is further enhanced by the lateral drift effect. In addition, there is the 'member stability effect' (described earlier) on account of the lateral displacements at points along the length of the column relative to the chord joining the column ends

[Figure 13.32(d)]. However, generally, for unbraced columns, the moments at the column ends are maximum, and these are due to the primary moments enhanced by the lateral drift effect alone.

The moment amplification possible due to lateral drift effect in an unbraced column is generally much more than that due to member stability effect in a braced column. Further, as explained in Section 13.2.3, the effective length of an unbraced column is much more than that of a braced column with the same unsupported length. Hence, columns in unbraced frames are weaker than similar columns in braced frames.

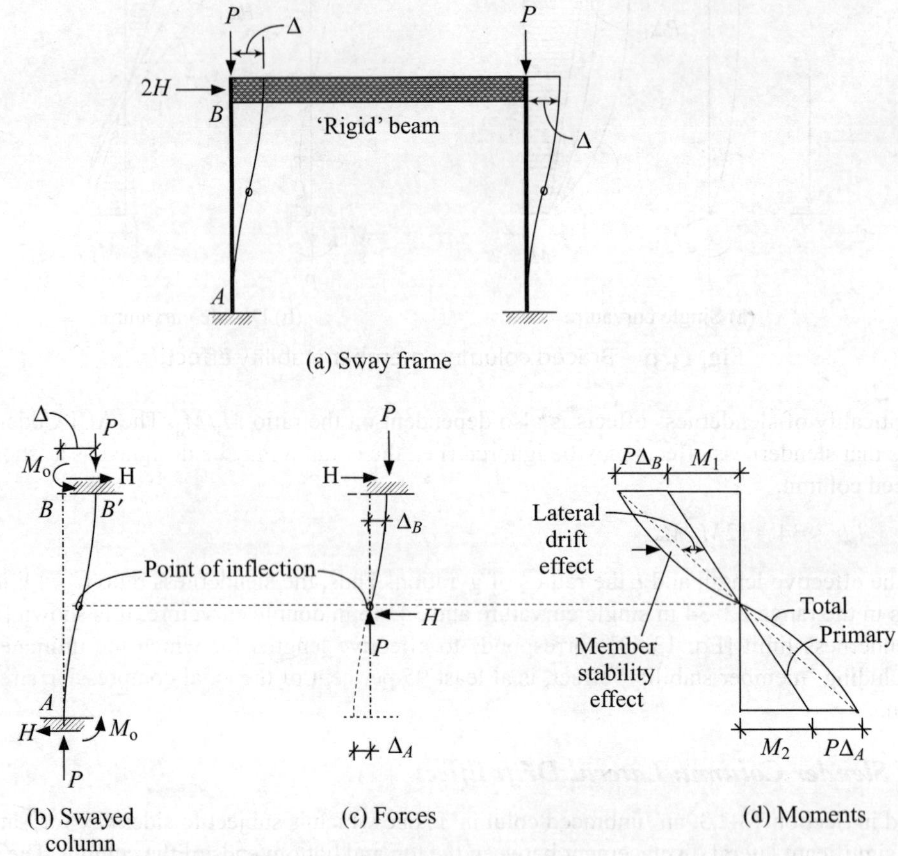

Fig. 13.32 Unbraced columns: lateral drift effect.

13.7.2 Second-Order Structural Analysis of Slender Column Structures

The main problem with slender column design lies in determining the factored moments (including P–Δ effects) to be considered in design. In other words, the problem is essentially one of structural *analysis*, rather than structural *design*. The principles of designing a column section under a given factored axial compression P_u and factored moments M_{ux}, M_{uy} [described in Section 13.6] remain the same for both short columns and slender columns; the only difference is that M_{ux} and M_{uy} must include secondary moment components in slender column design, whereas these secondary moment components (being negligible) are ignored in short column design.

Rigorous Analysis

In general, the Code (Cl. 39.7) broadly recommends that when slender columns are involved in a reinforced concrete structure, a detailed 'second-order' structural analysis should be carried out to determine the bending moments and axial forces for which the slender columns are to be designed. Indeed, such a rigorous analysis is particularly desirable for slender columns in unbraced frames. Such analysis must take into account *all* slenderness effects, viz., the influence of column and frame deflections on moments, effects of axial loads and effects of sustained loads. Realistic moment-curvature relationships should be made use of. The details of procedures for second-order analysis lie outside the scope of this book; these details are presented in Ref. 13.17–13.19.

It should be noted that the *principle of superposition* is not valid in second-order analysis, and for this reason, the load effects due to different load combinations cannot be obtained by an algebraic summing up (with appropriate load factors); each load combination should be investigated separately. This requires substantial computational effort.

13.7.3 Code Procedures for Design of Slender Columns

In routine design practice, only first-order structural analysis (based on the linear elastic theory and undeflected frame geometry) is performed, as second-order analysis is computationally difficult and laborious. In recognition of this, the Code recommends highly simplified procedures for the design of slender columns, which either attempt to predict the increase in moments (over primary moments), or, equivalently, the reduction in strength, due to slenderness effects.

Strength Reduction Coefficient Method

This is a highly simplified procedure, which is given in the Code for the working stress method of design [refer Section 13.4.3]. According to this procedure (B-3.3 of the Code) the *permissible stresses* in concrete and steel [Eqs 13.15, 13.16] are reduced by multiplication with a *strength reduction coefficient* C_r, given by

$$C_r = 1.25 - \frac{l_e}{48d} \tag{13.44a}$$

where d is the least lateral dimension of the column (or diameter of the core in a spiral column). Alternatively, *for more exact calculations,*

$$C_r = 1.25 - \frac{l_e}{160r_{\min}} \tag{13.44b}$$

where $r_{\min}$ is the least radius of gyration of the column. There is some ambiguity in Eqs 13.44(a), (b) regarding the plane in which the effective length l_e is to be estimated. This can be resolved by considering $(l_e/d)_{\max}$ in Eq. 13.44(a) and $(l_e/r)_{\max}$ in Eq. 13.44(b) i.e., considering the maximum effective slenderness ratio of the column.

It is recommended in the Explanatory Handbook to the Code [Ref. 13.7] that instead of applying the strength reduction factor C_r to the 'permissible stresses', this factor may be directly applied to the load-carrying capacity estimated for a corresponding short column. Furthermore, it may be noted that although this method has been prescribed for WSM, it can be extended to the limit state method (LSM) for the case of axial loading (without primary bending moments). This is demonstrated in Example 13.17.

Additional Moment Method

The method prescribed by the Code (Cl. 39.7.1) for slender column design by the limit state method is the 'additional moment method'[†], which is based on Ref. 13.20, 13.21. According to this method, every slender column should be designed for biaxial eccentricities which include the P–Δ moment ('additional moment') components $e_{ax} \equiv M_{ax}/P_u$ and $e_{ay} \equiv M_{ay}/P_u$:

$$\tilde{M}_{ux} = P_u(e_x + e_{ax}) = M_{ux} + M_{ax} \tag{13.45a}$$

$$\tilde{M}_{uy} = P_u(e_y + e_{ay}) = M_{uy} + M_{ay} \tag{13.45b}$$

Here, $\tilde{M}_{ux}$ and $\tilde{M}_{uy}$ denote the total design moments; M_{ux}, M_{uy} denote the *primary* factored moments[‡] (obtained from first-order structural analyses); and M_{ax}, M_{ay} denote the *additional moments* with reference to bending about the major and minor axes respectively.

The essence of this method lies in a simple formulation for the determination of the *additional eccentricities* e_{ax}, e_{ay}. In the basic formulation, the P–Δ effect in a braced slender column with pin-joined ends [Figure 13.30a] is considered. The 'additional eccentricity' e_a is equal to Δ_{max} in Figure 13.30(a), which is a function of the curvatures to which the column is subjected. If the maximum curvature (at mid-height) is denoted as φ_{max}, it can be shown [refer Figure 13.33] that Δ_{max} lies between $\varphi_{max}l^2/12$ and $\varphi_{max}l^2/8$, the former limit corresponding to a linearly varying curvature (with zero at the pin joints and a maximum of φ_{max} at mid height) and the latter corresponding to a constant curvature along the column height [Figures 13.33(b), (c)].

Taking an average value,

$$e_a = \Delta_{max} \approx \varphi_{max}l^2/10 \tag{13.46}$$

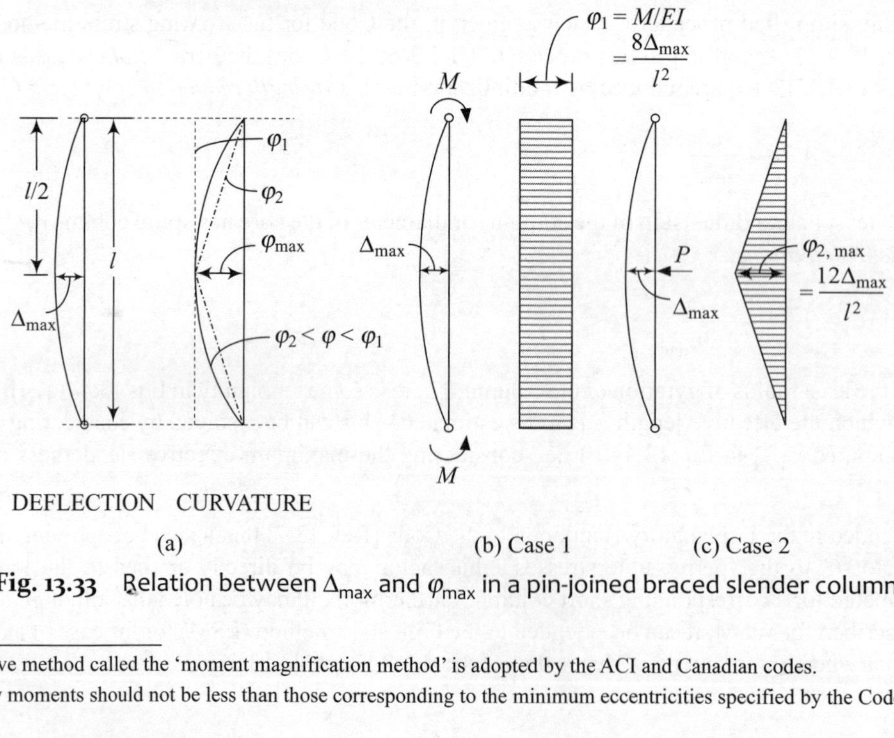

Fig. 13.33 Relation between Δ_{max} and φ_{max} in a pin-joined braced slender column.

† An alternative method called the 'moment magnification method' is adopted by the ACI and Canadian codes.

‡ The primary moments should not be less than those corresponding to the minimum eccentricities specified by the Code.

Failure of the column at the ultimate limit state is expected to occur at the section corresponding to φ_{max}. By making suitable assumptions, φ_{max} can be expressed in terms of the failure strains ε_{cu} and ε_{st} in concrete (at the highly compressed edge) and steel (in the outermost row) respectively, as shown in Figure 13.34. The values of ε_{cu} and ε_{st} evidently depend on the factored axial load P_u (as explained in Section 13.5.1); this determines the location of the point of failure, marked *B* in the interaction curve in Figure 13.30(c).

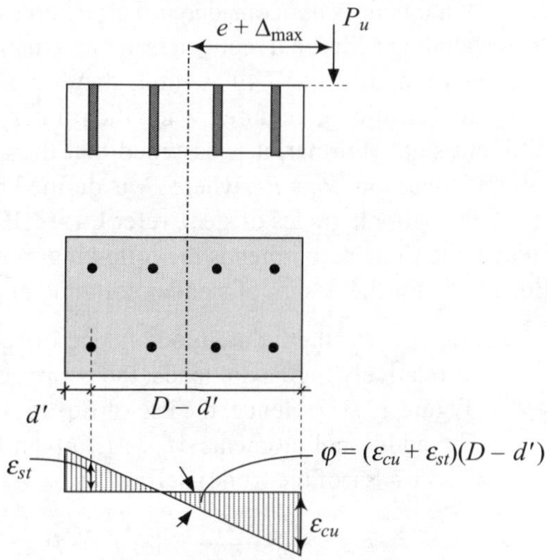

Fig. 13.34 Determination of curvature from failure strain profile.

Assuming that ε_{cu} = 0.0035 and ε_s = 0.002†, $d' \approx 0.1D$ and further assuming (rather conservatively) that the additional moment comprises about 80 per cent of the total moment,

$$\phi_{max} \cong \frac{0.0035 + 0.002}{0.9D} \times 0.8 \approx \frac{1}{200D} \tag{13.47}$$

Combining Eq. 13.47 with Eq. 13.46, the following expression for the additional eccentricity ratio e_a/D is obtained:

$$e_a/D \approx \frac{(l/D)^2}{2000} \tag{13.48}$$

Accordingly, the following expressions for additional moments M_{ax}, M_{ay} [in Eqs 13.45a, b] are obtained, as given in the Code (Cl. 39.7.1):

$$M_{ax} = P_u e_{ax} = \frac{P_u D_x}{2000}(l_{ex}/D_x)^2 \tag{13.49a}$$

$$M_{ay} = P_u e_{ay} = \frac{P_u D_y}{2000}(l_{ey}/D_y)^2 \tag{13.49b}$$

where l_{ex} and l_{ey} denote the *effective lengths*, and D_x and D_y denote the depths of the rectangular column section with respect to bending about the major axis and minor axis respectively. It may be noted that the height l in Eq. 13.48 has been replaced by the effective length l_e in Eq. 13.49 to extend the application of the formulation to the various boundary conditions (other than the pinned-end condition) that occur in practical columns including unbraced columns. It is reported [Ref. 13.7] that the use of Eq. 13.49 has been validated with reference to a large number of experimental tests [Ref. 13.20]. It is seen from Eqs 13.48 and 13.49 that the e_a/D ratio increases with the square of the slenderness ratio l_e/D; e_a/D has a minimum value of 0.072 for l_e/D =12 (transition between 'short column' and 'slender column') and a maximum value of 0.450 for l_e/D = 30 (recommended limit for unbraced columns) and 1.800 for l_e/D = 60 (braced column).

It should be noted that Eq. 13.49 relates to the 'additional moments' to be considered in addition to the maximum factored primary moments M_{ux}, M_{uy} in a column. Under eccentric loading, these primary moments should not be less than those corresponding to the minimum eccentricities specified by the Code. Where a

† This approximately corresponds to the 'balanced failure' condition, whereby $\varepsilon_{st} = \varepsilon_y$ at the cracked section (refer Eq. 13.19). For deflection calculations, the mean steel strain should be considered, including the effect of 'tension stiffening' (refer Chapter 10).

primary moment is not considered, i.e., taken as zero, (as under axial loading), it should be ensured that the corresponding additional moment is not less than that computed from considerations of minimum eccentricity. The derivation of Eq. 13.49 assumes that the column is braced and bent symmetrically in single curvature; some modification is required when the primary moments applied at the column ends are unequal and/or of different signs. Further, it is assumed that the axial load level corresponds approximately to the 'balanced failure' condition, $P_u = P_b$, where P_b is defined by the Code (Cl. 39.7.1.1) as the axial load corresponding to $\varepsilon_y = 0.002$ (for all grades of steel, refer Eq. 13.19). Eq. 13.49 needs to be modified for other axial load levels. Hence, the Code recommends the following modifications to be incorporated with the use of Eq. 13.49 (and Eq. 13.45) for the design of slender columns in general:

- For $P_u > P_b$, the failure mode is one of 'compression failure', and the corresponding e/D ratio is low. At relatively high axial loads, the entire section may be under compression, suggesting low curvatures [Figure 13.35]. Hence, the use of Eq. 13.49 in such situations can result in highly conservative results. The additional moments M_{ax}, M_{ay} given by Eq. 13.49 may be reduced by multiplying factors (refer Cl. 39.7.1.1 of the Code) defined as:

$$k_{ax} = \frac{P_{uz} - P_u}{P_{uz} - P_{b,x}} \quad \text{for } P_u > P_{b,x} \tag{13.50a}$$

$$k_{ay} = \frac{P_{uz} - P_u}{P_{uz} - P_{b,y}} \quad \text{for } P_u > P_{b,y} \tag{13.50b}$$

  where P_{uz} is the maximum 'pure compression' strength of the column and $P_{b,x}$ and $P_{b,y}$ corresponds to the axial strength corresponding to the approximate 'balanced' condition $\varepsilon_{cu} = 0.0035$ and $\varepsilon_y = 0.002$ with respect to bending about the major axis and minor axis respectively. P_{uz} is readily obtainable from Eq. 13.39 and P_b from the interaction curve (refer Figure 13.21) corresponding to a design tensile stress of $f_{yd} = 0.87f_y$ in the outermost layer of steel.

  It can be seen that k varies linearly from zero (for $P_u = P_{uz}$) to unity (for $P_u = P_b$) and is a highly simplified formula. It should also be noted that Eq. 13.50 is not applicable for $P_u < P_b$; i.e., $k_a = 1$ for $P_u < P_b$.

- For *braced columns* subject to unequal primary moments M_1, M_2 at the two ends [Figure 13.31(a)], the value of M_u to be considered in the computation of the total moment $\tilde{M}_u$ in Eq. 13.45 may be taken as

$$M_u = 0.4M_1 + 0.6M_2 \geq 0.4M_2 \tag{13.51}$$

  where M_2 is the higher column end moment. As mentioned earlier, with reference to Figure 13.31, M_1 and M_2 are considered to be of opposite signs if the column is bent in double curvature. In the case of braced columns subject to double curvature, it is possible that the use of Eq. 13.51 in Eq. 13.45 may result in a total moment $\tilde{M}_u$ that is less than M_2; this obviously, cannot be allowed. Hence, a further condition needs to be imposed:

$$\tilde{M}_u \geq M_2 \quad \text{for braced columns} \tag{13.52}$$

- In the case of *unbraced columns*, the lateral drift effect (hitherto not considered) needs to be included [Figure 13.32]. An approximate way of accounting for this is by assuming that the additional moment M_a (given by Eq. 13.49†) acts at the column end where the maximum primary moment M_2 is operational. Hence, for design purposes, the total moment $\tilde{M}_u$ may be taken as

$$\tilde{M}_u = M_2 + M_a \quad \text{for unbraced columns} \tag{13.53}$$

† It is inadvisable to apply the reduction factor k (given by Eq. 13.50) for unbraced columns.

Example 13.17

Determine the maximum factored axial load-carrying capacity of the column in Figure 13.15(a), given that the column is 'braced' against sidesway, and has an unsupported length of 7.0 m. Assume effective length ratios $k_x = k_y = 0.85$.

Solution

- *Given*: (refer Example 13.5): $D_x = 500$ mm, $D_y = 300$ mm, $A_{sc} = 2946$ mm^2, $f_{ck} = 25$ MPa, $f_y = 500$ MPa. Also, $l = 7000$ mm, $k_x = k_y = 0.85$.

Slenderness ratios

- $l_{ex} = 0.85 \times 7000 = 5950 \text{ mm} \Rightarrow l_{ex}/D_x = 5950/500 = 11.90 < 12$
  $l_{ey} = 0.85 \times 7000 = 5950 \text{ mm} \Rightarrow l_{ey}/D_y = 5950/300 = 19.83 > 12$
- Hence, the column has to be treated as a *slender* column.

Strength reduction coefficient method

- Extending the *strength reduction coefficient method* given in the Code (B-3.3) for WSM to LSM,

$$C_r = 1.25 - \frac{(l_e/D)_{\max}}{48}$$
$$= 1.25 - 19.83/48 = 0.837$$

- Considering *short column* behaviour (with dimensions satisfying Cl. 39.3 of the Code),

$$\tilde{P}_{uo} = 0.4 f_{ck} A_g + (0.67 f_y - 0.4 f_{ck}) A_s$$
$$= 2457.45 \text{ kN (as determined earlier in Example 13.9).}$$

- Considering *slender column* behaviour,

$$(P_u)_{\max} = C_r \tilde{P}_{uo}$$
$$= 0.837 \times 2457.45$$
$$= \mathbf{2057\ kN}$$

Note: The safety of the column under this factored load, combined with minimum eccentricities, may now be verified by the *additional moment method* given in the Code for LSM.

Additional moment method

- *Minimum eccentricities*

$$e_{x,\min} = \frac{l}{500} + \frac{D_x}{30} = \frac{7000}{500} + \frac{500}{30} = 30.67 \text{ mm} > 20 \text{ mm}$$

$$e_{y,\min} = \frac{l}{500} + \frac{D_y}{30} = \frac{7000}{500} + \frac{300}{30} = 24.00 \text{ mm} > 20 \text{ mm}$$

- *Primary moments*
  As the column is under axial loading, $M_{ux} = M_{uy} = 0$. However, it must be ensured that the total moments $\tilde{M}_{ux}$, $\tilde{M}_{uy}$ should not be less than those due to corresponding minimum eccentricities.

Additional moments

- Without modification factors:

$$e_{ax} = D_x(l_{ex}/D_x)^2/2000 = 500(11.90)^2/2000 = 35.40 \text{ mm}$$
$$e_{ay} = D_y(l_{ey}/D_y)^2/2000 = 300(19.83)^2/2000 = 58.98 \text{ mm}$$

- Modification factors k_{ax}, k_{ay}

$$k_{ax} = \frac{P_{uz} - P_u}{P_{uz} - P_{b,x}}; \; k_{ay} = \frac{P_{uz} - P_u}{P_{uz} - P_{b,y}}$$

where

$$\begin{aligned} P_{uz} &= 0.45 f_{ck} A_g + (0.75 f_y - 0.45 f_{ck}) A_s \\ &= (0.45 \times 25 \times 300 \times 500) + (0.75 \times 500 - 0.45 \times 25) \times 2946 \\ &= (1687.5 \times 10^3 + 1071.61 \times 10^3)\, N = 2759 \text{ kN} \end{aligned}$$

Referring to Example 13.9 (major axis bending), corresponding to $\frac{x_u}{439.5 - x_u} = \frac{0.0035}{0.002} \Rightarrow \frac{x_u}{D} = \frac{279.7}{500}$ = 0.559, it can be shown, either deriving from first principles, or interpolating from the values in Table 13.1(a), $P_{b,x}$ = 870.2 kN. Similarly, referring to Example 13.11 (minor axis bending), corresponding to $\frac{x_u}{239.5 - x_u} = \frac{0.0035}{0.002} \Rightarrow \frac{x_u}{D} = \frac{152.4}{300} = 0.508$, it can be shown from first principles, or interpolating from the values in Table 13.2, $P_{b,y}$ = 701.8 kN.

$$\begin{aligned} \Rightarrow \quad k_{ax} &= (2759 - 2057)/(2759 - 870.2) = 0.372 \\ k_{ay} &= (2759 - 2057)/(2759 - 701.2) = 0.342 \\ M_{ax} &= P_u(k_{ax} e_{ax}) = 2057 \times (0.372 \times 0.0354) = 27.08 \text{ kNm} \\ M_{ay} &= P_u(k_{ay} e_{ay}) = 2057 \times (0.342 \times 0.05898) = 41.49 \text{ kNm} \end{aligned}$$

- *Total Moments*

$$\begin{aligned} \tilde{M}_{ux} &= M_{ux} + M_{ax} = 0.0 + 27.08 = 27.08 \text{ kNm} \\ &< P_u e_{x,\min} = 2057 \times 0.03067 = \mathbf{63.1\ kNm} \\ \tilde{M}_{uy} &= M_{uy} + M_{ay} = 0.0 + 41.49 = 41.49 \text{ kNm} \\ &< P_u e_{y,\min} = 2057 \times 0.0240 = \mathbf{49.4\ kNm} \end{aligned}$$

Check safety under biaxial loading

- Corresponding to P_u = 2057 kN,

$$\begin{aligned} M_{ux1} &= 139.4 \text{ kNm [refer Table 13.1, Figure 13.19]} > \tilde{M}_{ux} = 63.1 \text{ kNm} \\ M_{uy1} &= 80.79 \text{ kNm [refer Table 13.2, Figure 13.20]} > \tilde{M}_{uy} = 49.4 \text{ kNm} \end{aligned}$$

- P_u/P_{uz} = 2057/2759 = 0.745 (which lies between 0.2 and 0.8)

$$\Rightarrow \quad \alpha_n = 1.0 + \frac{0.745 - 0.2}{0.8 - 0.2}(2.0 - 1.0) = 1.908$$

- $$\begin{aligned} \left(\frac{\tilde{M}_{ux}}{M_{ax1}}\right)^{\alpha_n} + \left(\frac{\tilde{M}_{uy}}{M_{ay1}}\right)^{\alpha_n} &= \left(\frac{63.1}{139.35}\right)^{1.908} + \left(\frac{49.4}{80.79}\right)^{1.908} \\ &= 0.22 + 0.391 \\ &= 0.611 < 1.0 - \text{safe} \end{aligned}$$

- Evidently, P_u = 2057 kN is a slightly conservative estimate of the axial load-carrying capacity of the slender column. This is as expected, owing to the conservatism built into the highly simplified 'strength reduction coefficient' method.

Example 13.18

Design the longitudinal reinforcement for a braced column, 300 mm × 400 mm, subject to a factored axial load of 1500 kN and factored moments of 60 kNm and 40 kNm with respect to the major axis and minor axis respectively at the top end. Assume that the column is bent in double curvature (in both directions) with the moments at the bottom end equal to 50 per cent of the corresponding moments at top. Assume an unsupported length of 7.0 m and an effective length ratio of 0.85 in both directions. Use M 30 concrete and Fe 500 steel.

Solution

- *Given*: $D_x = 400$ mm, $D_y = 300$ mm, $P_u = 1500$ kN; $M_{ux} = 60$ kNm, $M_{uy} = 40$ kNm, at top; $M_{ux} = 30$ kNm, $M_{uy} = 20$ kNm, at bottom; $l = 7000$ mm, $k_x = k_y = 0.85$.

Slenderness ratios

- $l_{ex} = l_{ey} = 0.85 \times 7000 = 5950$ mm

  $\Rightarrow \quad l_{ex}/D_x = 5950/400 = 14.88 > 12$

  $l_{ey}/D_y = 5950/300 = 19.83 > 12$

  Hence, the column should be designed as a *slender column*.

Minimum eccentricities

- $$e_{x,\min} = \frac{l}{500} + \frac{D_x}{30} = \frac{7000}{500} + \frac{400}{30} = 27.33 \text{ mm} > 20 \text{ mm}$$

  $$e_{y,\min} = \frac{l}{500} + \frac{D_y}{30} = \frac{7000}{500} + \frac{300}{30} = 24.00 \text{ mm} > 20 \text{ mm}$$

Primary moments for design

- As the column is braced and bent in double curvature [refer Eq. 13.51],

  $$M_{ux} = (0.6 \times 60 - 0.4 \times 30) = 24 \text{ kNm } (\geq 0.4 \times 60 = 24 \text{ kNm})$$

  $$M_{uy} = (0.6 \times 40 - 0.4 \times 20) = 16 \text{ kNm } (\geq 0.4 \times 40 = 16 \text{ kNm})$$

  $\Rightarrow$ corresponding (primary) eccentricities:

  $$e_x = 24 \times 10^3/1500 = 16 \text{ mm} < e_{x\,\min} = 27.33 \text{ mm}$$

  $$e_y = 16 \times 10^3/1500 = 10.67 \text{ mm} < e_{y\,\min} = 24.00 \text{ mm}$$

  The primary eccentricities should not be less than the minimum eccentricities.

- $\therefore$ Primary moments for design: $M_{ux} = 1500 \times (27.33 \times 10^{-3}) = 41.0$ kNm

  $M_{uy} = 1500 \times (24.00 \times 10^{-3}) = 36.0$ kNm

Additional moments

- Without modification factor, additional eccentricities

  $$e_{ax} = D_x(l_{ex}/D_x)^2/2000$$
  $$= 400(14.88)^2/2000 = 44.28 \text{ mm}$$

  $$e_{ay} = D_y(l_{ey}/D_y)^2/2000$$
  $$= 300(19.83)^2/2000 = 58.98 \text{ mm}$$

- Assuming modification factors $k_{ax} = k_{ay} \approx 0.5$ (to be verified later), additional moments:

$$M_{ax} = P_u(k_{ax}e_{ax}) = 1500(0.5 \times 0.04428)$$
$$= 33.2 \text{ kNm}$$
$$M_{ay} = P_u(k_{ay}e_{ay}) = 1500(0.5 \times 0.05898)$$
$$= 44.2 \text{ kNm}$$

Total factored moments

$$\tilde{M}_{ux} = M_{ux} + M_{ax} = 41.0 + 33.2 = 74.2 \text{ kNm}$$
$$\tilde{M}_{uy} = M_{uy} + M_{ay} = 36.0 + 44.2 = 80.2 \text{ kNm} > \tilde{M}_{ux} = 74.2 \text{ kNm}$$

Trial section

- Designing for a resultant uniaxial moment with respect to the *minor* axis,

$$M_u \approx 1.15\sqrt{74.2^2 + 80.2^2} = 126 \text{ kNm}$$

combined with $P_u = 1500$ kN

$\Rightarrow$ $P_u/f_{ck}bD = (1500 \times 10^3/(30 \times 400 \times 300) = 0.417$

$M_u/f_{ck}bD^2 = 126 \times 10^6/(30 \times 400 \times 300^2) = 0.117$

- Assuming 25ϕ for main bars, 8ϕ ties and 40 mm clear cover, $d' = 60.5$ mm

$\Rightarrow$ $d'/D \approx 60.5/300 = 0.201 \approx 0.20$ with 'equal reinforcement on all sides', and referring to Chart 46 of SP : 16,

$p/f_{ck} = 0.13 \Rightarrow p_{\text{reqd}} = 0.13 \times 30 = 3.9$

$\Rightarrow$ $A_{s,\text{reqd}} = 3.9 \times 300 \times 400/100 = 4680 \text{ mm}^2$

- Provide 8–28ϕ (as shown in Figure 13.35).

$[A_s = 8 \times 616 \text{ mm}^2]$ $4928 > 4680$

$\Rightarrow$ $p_{\text{provided}} = 4928 \times 100/(300 \times 400) = 4.107$

$\Rightarrow$ $p/f_{ck} = 4.107/30 = 0.137$

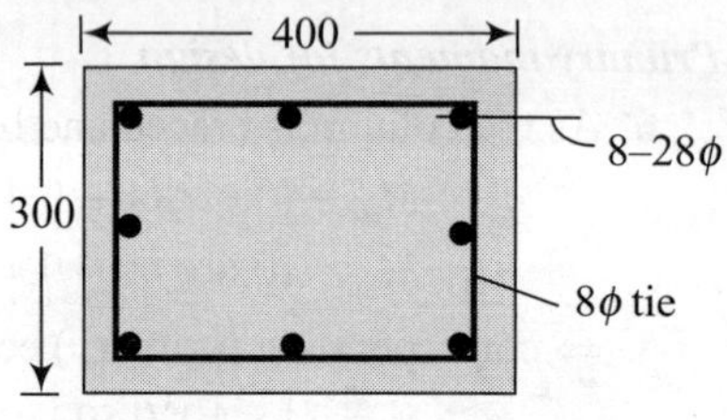

Fig. 13.35 Example 13.18.

Check additional moments

- Assuming a clear cover of 40 mm, $d' = 40 + 8 + 28/2 = 62$ mm

$\Rightarrow$ $d'/D_x = 0.155 \approx 0.15$ and $d'/D_y = 0.207 \approx 0.20$

- Referring to Charts 45 ($d'/D = 0.15$) and 46 ($d'/D = 0.20$) of SP: 16, the ultimate loads $P_{ub,x}$ $P_{ub,y}$ at balanced failure can be determined by considering the stress level $f_{yd} = 0.87f_y$ (marked on the interaction curves).
- Corresponding to $p/f_{ck} = 0.137$,

for $d'/D_x = 0.15$, $P_{ub,x}/f_{ck}bD = 0.03 \Rightarrow P_{ub,x} = 252$ kN

for $d'/D_y = 0.20$, $P_{ub,y}/f_{ck}bD = 0.03 \Rightarrow P_{ub,y} = 108$ kN

- $P_{uz} = 0.45f_{ck}A_g + (0.75f_y - 0.45f_{ck})A_s$

$$= (0.45 \times 30 \times 300 \times 400) + (0.75 \times 500 - 0.45 \times 30) \times 4928$$
$$= (1620 \times 10^3 + 1781.47 \times 10^3) = 3401 \text{ kN}$$

- *Modification factors:*

$$k_{ax} = \frac{P_{uz} - P_u}{P_{uz} - P_{ub,x}} = \frac{3401 - 1500}{3401 - 108} = 0.577$$

$$k_{ay} = \frac{P_{uz} - P_u}{P_{uz} - P_{ub,y}} = \frac{3401 - 1500}{3401 - 0} = 0.559$$

- Hence, the assumed values $k_{ax} = k_{ay} = 0.5$ are fairly accurate. The actual (revised) total moments are obtained as:

$$\tilde{M}_{ux} = 41.0 + 1500(0.577 \times 0.04428) = 79.32 \text{ kNm}$$
$$\tilde{M}_{uy} = 36.0 + 1500(0.559 \times 0.05898) = 85.47 \text{ kNm}$$

Check safety under biaxial bending

- Referring to the design Charts in SP : 16, uniaxial moment capacities corresponding to

$$P_u/f_{ck}bD = 0.417 \quad \text{and} \quad p/f_{ck} = 0.137$$

are obtained as

$$M_{ux1}/f_{ck}bD^2 = 0.15 \text{ (for } d'/D = 0.15)$$
$$M_{uy1}/f_{ck}bD^2 = 0.13 \text{ (for } d'/D = 0.20)$$
$$\Rightarrow \quad M_{ux1} = 0.15 \times 30 \times 300 \times 400^2 = 216 \times 10^6 \text{ Nmm} = 216 \text{ kNm} > \tilde{M}_{ux} = 79.32 \text{ kNm}$$
$$M_{uy1} = 0.13 \times 30 \times 400 \times 300^2 = 140.4 \times 10^6 \text{ Nmm} = 140.4 \text{ kNm} > \tilde{M}_{uy} = 85.47 \text{ kNm}$$

- $P_u/P_{uz} = 1500/3401 = 0.441$ (which lies between 0.2 and 0.8)

$$\Rightarrow \quad \alpha_n = 1.0 + \frac{0.441 - 0.2}{0.8 - 0.2}(2.0 - 1.0) = 1.402$$

- $$\left(\frac{\tilde{M}_{ux}}{M_{ux1}}\right)^{\alpha_n} + \left(\frac{\tilde{M}_{uy}}{M_{uy1}}\right)^{\alpha_n} = \left(\frac{79.318}{216}\right)^{1.402} + \left(\frac{85.47}{140.4}\right)^{1.402}$$
$$= 0.245 + 0.499$$
$$= 0.744 < 1.0 \ \beta. \text{ Hence, safe}$$

13.8 Members with Axial Tension and Bending

13.8.1 Axial Tension with Uniaxial Bending

Occasionally, a concrete member may be subjected to axial tension combined with bending moment (i.e., an eccentric tension). For this case, the axial load-moment interaction diagram may be considered as the extension of the typical ($P_u - M_u$) diagram shown in Figure 13.13 on to the negative P_u side of the axis, as shown in Figure 13.36. In Figure 13.36, the part below $P_u = P_{ub}$ is characterised by tension failure. In the same way, when P_u is negative (i.e., axial force is tensile), tension controls failure. At $M_u = M_{uo}$, (i.e., bending only, axial force $P_u = 0$), the tensile and compressive forces across the cross-section balance ($C_u = T_u$). Evidently, when the net force across the section is tensile, the tensile component T_u will be greater than the compressive part C_u and the neutral axis depth x_u (see Figure 13.14) will be less than the depth for the bending only case. Also, in this case, the peak compressive strain at the extreme compression fibre will be 0.0035 and the maximum tensile strain in the steel farthest from the neutral axis on the tension side greater than ε_y. On the basis of these, the points on the interaction diagram on the tension side (part *ACB* in Figure 13.36) can be determined from the strain distribution and equilibrium considerations. These calculations are demonstrated in Examples 13.19 and 13.20.

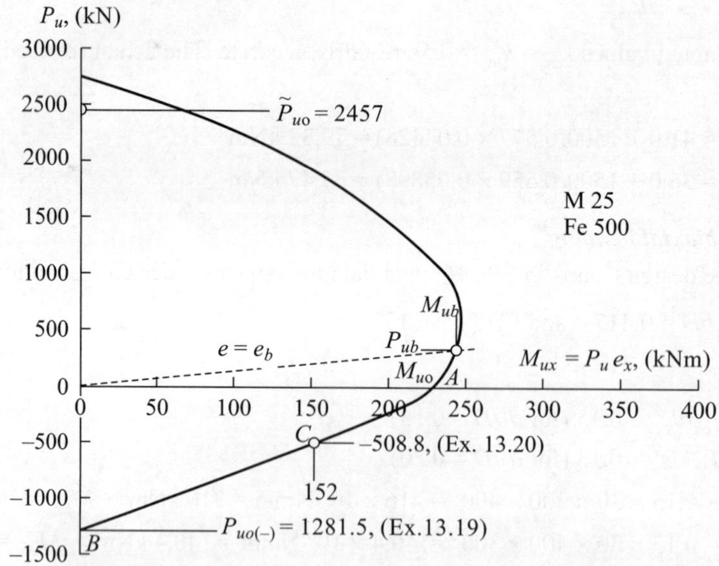

Fig. 13.36 P_u–M_u interaction diagram showing eccentric tension.

The point on the interaction curve corresponding to its intersection with the vertical axis can be obtained by estimating the axial strength in tension of the given section. Since the bending moment applied is zero, the eccentricity is zero and the tensile force is truly axial, passing through the centroidal axis, whereby the strain distribution will be uniform. The concrete will crack well before the steel yields. In any case, in the theory for combined flexure and axial loads, the tensile strength of concrete is ignored. Hence the net axial force is solely due to the tension in the reinforcement, which is easily obtainable as:

$$P_{uo(-)} = 0.87 f_y A_s \qquad (13.54)$$

It is seen that the interaction diagram in the eccentric tension zone is almost linear. Hence, as for a quick approximation, linear interpolation may be carried out, connecting the points joining the 'bending only' point ($P_u = 0$, $M_u = M_{uo}$) to the 'pure axial tension' point ($P_u = P_{uo(-)}$, $M_u = 0$).

13.8.2 Axial Tension and Slenderness Effects

> In columns subjected to axial tension, slenderness is irrelevant and there is no distinction as 'short' or 'long'.

In the case of bending with axial compression, the slenderness of the member is important because of the '$P - \Delta$' effect (see Section 13.7), where the compressive force P interacting with lateral deflection Δ causes increase in the primary moments. In contrast, when the axial force is tensile, its effect will be to straighten the member and any '$P - \Delta$' effect will only *reduce* the primary moment. As such, *slenderness is not a factor* to be considered in the design of members with axial tension and there is no distinction for such a member as 'short' or 'long'.

Example 13.19

For the column section shown in Figure 13.15(a), determine the design tensile strength when no bending moment is acting on the section. Assume M 25 concrete and Fe 500 steel. Assume 8φ ties and 40 mm clear cover.

Solution

- *Given*: $b = 300$ mm, $D = 500$ mm, $f_{ck} = 25$ MPa, $f_y = 500$ MPa, $A_{s1} = A_{s2} = A_{s3} = 2 \times 491$ mm^2 = 982 mm^2 [as shown in Figure 13.15(b)].
- *Axial strength*: $P_{uo(-)} = A_{st} 0.87 f_y = 3 \times 982 \times 0.87 \times 500 \times 10^{-3}$ = **1281.5 kN** (Tensile)
  The corresponding point is shown as *B* in Figure 13.36.

Example 13.20

For the column section shown in Figure 13.15(a), determine the design strength components corresponding to an axial force (tensile) applied at an eccentricity of 300 mm with respect to the major axis. Assume M 25 concrete and Fe 500 steel. Assume 8φ ties and 40 mm clear cover.

Solution

- *Given*: Data as in Example 13.5, $b = 300$ mm, $D = 500$ mm, $f_{ck} = 25$ MPa, $f_y = 500$ MPa, $A_{s1} = A_{s2} = A_{s3} = 2 \times 491$ mm^2 = 982 mm^2, [as shown in Figure 13.15(b)], $y_1 = (-)189.5$ mm, $y_2 = 0$ mm, $y_3 = (+)189.5$ mm with reference to centroidal axis.
- *Neutral axis depth* x_u
  For this section, for the case of bending alone ($P_{u,} = 0$), the neutral axis depth was determined in Example 13.9 [see Table 13.1(b)] as $x_{u,b} = 0.312D = 156$ mm. With the eccentric tensile force [applied as shown in Figure 13.37(b)], the depth of neutral axis, x_u, will be less than 156 mm. This being a tension failure, as ultimate strength is reached, the reinforcement closest to the extreme tension face would have yielded and the maximum compressive strain in concrete would be 0.0035. The corresponding failure strain diagram is as shown on Figure 13.37(c).

For Fe 500 steel, $\varepsilon_y = \dfrac{0.87 \times 500}{2 \times 10^5} + 0.002 = 0.004175$

- *Strains in steel* (3 rows): Considering Figures 13.37(b), (c),

$$\varepsilon_{s1} > (-)\varepsilon_y, \text{ (tensile)}$$

$$\varepsilon_{s2} = (-)0.0035 \times \frac{250 - x_u}{x_u}, \text{ (tensile)}$$

$$\varepsilon_{s3} = (+)0.0035 \times \frac{x_u - 60.5}{x_u}, \text{ (compression)}$$

- *Design stresses in steel* (3 rows): Refer to the design stress-strain curve for Fe 500 [Figure 3.7, Table 3.2],

As $\varepsilon_{s1} > (-)\varepsilon_y, f_{s1} = (-)0.87 f_y = -435$ MPa

As x_u is unknown, the strains in reinforcement groups 2 and 3 are not known yet and the stresses in these will depend on the values of ε_{s2} and ε_{s3}. Hence, particularly with a nonlinear part in the stress-strain relations for Fe 500 steel, a trial-and-error approach has to be adopted. For the first trial, it may

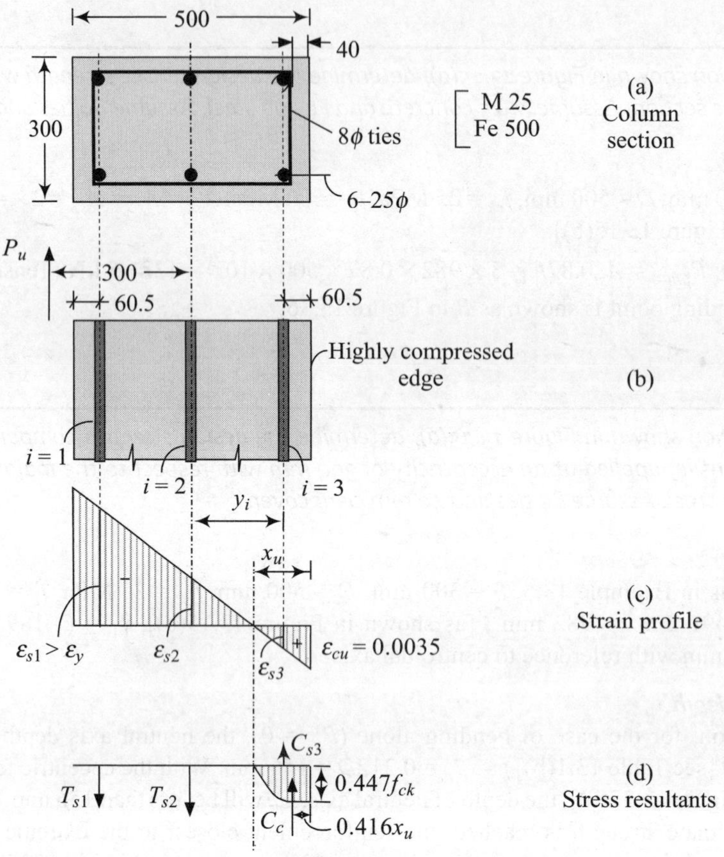

Fig. 13.37 Example 13.20.

be assumed that group 2 steel has also yielded (since $x_u < 156$ mm, this is very likely). As ε_{s3} is less than $0.0035 < \varepsilon_y$, this steel would not have yielded, and it being close to the neutral axis, the stress in it is likely to be relatively low and may be assumed to be in the linear elastic range. Accordingly,

$$f_{s2} = 435 \text{ MPa}$$

$$f_{s3} = +(2 \times 10^5) \times 0.0035 \times \frac{x_u - 60.5}{x_u} \text{ MPa (ignoring the displaced concrete effect).}$$

[Note that it may be simpler to assume a trial value for x_u and refine this through successive trials]

- *Design strength components* [Figure 13.37(d)]

$$C_c = 0.362 f_{ck} b x_u = 0.362 \times 25 \times 300 \times x_u = 2715 x_u \text{ N}$$

$$C_{s3} = A_{s3} f_{s3} = 982 \times (2 \times 10^5) \times 0.0035 \times \frac{x_u - 60.5}{x_u} = 687400 \frac{x_u - 60.5}{x_u}$$

$$T_{s1} = A_{s1} f_{s1} = 982 \times (-)435 = -427170 \text{ N (tensile)}$$

$$T_{s2} = A_{s2} f_{s2} = 982 \times (-)435 = -427170 \text{ N (tensile)}$$

- As these forces are in equilibrium with applied load P_u, taking moments of these about P_u,

$$T_{s1}(300 - 250 + 60.5) + T_{s2}(300) - C_{s3}(300 + 189.5) - C_c(300 + 250 - 0.416 x_u) = 0$$

This gives a 3rd degree equation in x_u. A solution to this equation may be obtained by trial and error . This yields $x_u = 75.9$ mm.

With the above value of x_u, the strains in groups 2 and 3 steels are:

$$\varepsilon_{s2} = (-)0.0035 \times (250 - 75.9)/75.9 = 0.00803 > \varepsilon_y,$$

and hence the assumption that this steel has yielded in tension is valid.

$$\varepsilon_{s3} = (+)0.0035 \times (75.9 - 60.5)/75.9 = 0.000710 \text{ (compression).}$$

Hence the assumption that this steel is in the linear elastic range is also valid. For this strain, the corresponding stress is $f_{s3} = 0.000710 \times 2 \times 10^5 = 142$ MPa.

These values give: $C_{s3} = 139444$ N, $C_c = 206069$ N and a corresponding moment due to these about P_u of 175.1×10^6, which equals the moment of tensile forces, thus satisfying equilibrium condition.

The axial tensile strength is given by:

$$P_{u(-)} = T_{s1} + T_{s2} - C_{s3} - C_c = 2 \times 427170 - 139444 - 206069 = \mathbf{508.8\ kN}$$

The associated moment can be obtained by taking moments of these forces about the centroidal axis:

$$M_u = 427170(189.5 + 0) + 139444 \times 189.5 + 206069(250 - 0.416 \times 75.9)$$
$$= 152.4 \times 10^6 \text{ N} = \mathbf{152\ kNm}$$

As a check, the moment due to eccentric load is:

$$M_u = 508.8 \times 0.300 = 152.6 \text{ kNm} \approx \mathbf{152\ kNm}$$

The corresponding point on the interaction diagram is shown as *C* in Figure 13.36.

13.8.3 Axial Tension with Biaxial Bending

The $P_u - M_u$ interaction diagram on the tension side is very nearly linear as may be seen from the part *ACB* in Figure 13.36. Hence, under biaxial bending with axial tension, the interaction surface may be taken as the linear extension of the trace on the *X-Y* plane of the interaction surface shown in Figure 13.27 (i.e., the curves shown in Figure 13.28a), to the point (B in Figure 13.36) with co-ordinates (0, 0, $-P_{uo(-)}$). Thus, the interaction surface will be conical (inverted), with its apex at B and its base having the shape of the curve in Figure 13.28a. Taking, the linear variation for the trace on the *X-Y* plane as shown in Figure 13.28a ($\alpha_n = 1.0$ for $p_u = 0$, Eq. 13.40), the interaction surface on the tension side will be a plane represented by Eq. 13.55.

$$\left(\frac{P_{u(-)}}{P_{uo(-)}}\right) + \left(\frac{M_{ux}}{M_{uxo}}\right) + \left(\frac{M_{uy}}{M_{uyo}}\right) = 1 \tag{13.55}$$

where $P_{u(-)}$, M_{ux} and M_{uy} denote the factored axial tension and biaxial moments acting on the member, $P_{uo(-)}$ denote the member strength under axial tension only, and M_{uxo} and M_{uyo} denote the uniaxial moment capacities under bending only with reference to the major and minor axes respectively. It may be noted that $P_{u(-)}$, M_{ux}, and M_{uy} are measures of the *load effects* on the member due to *external* loading on the structure, whereas $P_{uo(-)}$, M_{uxo}, and M_{uyo} are measures of the inherent *resistance* of the member section. For safety, the sum of the left-hand side should be ≤ 1.0.

13.8.4 Serviceability Requirements

The procedures given so far in Section 13.8 deal with the estimation of the strength of the section, subject to axial tension and uniaxial or biaxial bending, at the *limit state of collapse*. However, from a design point of view, it is necessary to also ensure that the cracking which occurs in the presence of axial tension meet the serviceability limit state requirements[†]. When axial tension is significant, the crack-width control requirements generally supersede the strength requirements, and hence govern the design. Methods of estimating crack-widths under direct tension and eccentric tension are discussed in Chapter 10.

13.9 Concrete Walls

Walls are vertical elements in which the horizontal length, L_w, is at least six times the thickness, t, and at least one-third the clear height of the element. They may generally be classified as (i) bearing wall, (ii) non-bearing wall, and (iii) shear wall. Earthquake resistant design and detailing of shear walls are not covered here.

> 'Bearing wall' is a wall supporting in-plane vertical loads and bending moments about an in-plane horizontal axis, caused by eccentricity of vertical loads and/or lateral loads

> 'Flexural shear wall' is a shear wall that resists in-plane lateral loads by flexural action.

Bearing wall is a wall that supports factored in-plane vertical loads exceeding about $0.08 f_{ck} A_g$ and moments about a horizontal axis in the plane of the wall (weak axis bending) and associated shear. **Non-bearing wall** is one that supports in-plane vertical loads $\leq 0.08\, f_{ck}\, A_g$ and, in some cases, moment about the weak axis as well. Here A_g is the gross area of a horizontal section of the wall. **Shear wall** is a wall or assembly of interconnected walls forming part of the lateral-load-resisting system of a structure. They support vertical loads, moments about horizontal axes perpendicular to the plane of the wall (strong axis bending) and shear forces acting parallel to the plane of the wall. Weak axis bending may also be present. A shear wall that resists in-plane lateral loads by flexural action is called a **flexural shear wall.** As these walls are governed by flexural action, a more appropriate name would be **slender structural walls**; these usually have a height, H_w, above the section of maximum moment in the wall, that is greater than $2L_w$.

Lateral loads caused by wind and seismic actions tend to generate large lateral forces, deflections, vibrations and over-stressing of members in buildings, if not adequately designed for. **Shear walls** are typically provided in mid-rise and high-rise buildings to enhance their lateral load resisting capacity. Due to the large in-plane stiffness, RC walls provide the much-needed lateral stiffness to the building, thereby reducing the vibrations and keeping the deflections and drifts within permissible limits. It is evident from observations of past earthquake responses that buildings with well-designed shear walls perform better than those which rely completely on rigid frame action [Ref. 11.25].

The shear walls are judiciously placed at specific locations so as to increase the lateral stiffness (in both directions) without introducing torsional irregularities in the building. These walls are usually provided around service cores (lift shafts and stairwells). The shear walls can be constructed in different shapes based on the architectural feasibility. Rectangular walls with and without enlarged boundary elements are commonly provided. Other shapes such as T, C and H shaped flanged walls are also widely adopted [refer Figure 13.38]. It is important to ensure that the shear walls continue from the foundation to the top without any discontinuities. From a functional point of view, openings may sometimes become necessary in the shear walls. In such cases, care must be taken to ensure that the openings are of small size and that they are not staggered along the height of the wall, thereby minimizing the possibility of discontinuity in the vertical reinforcement.

† The Code (Annex B) permits, as an alternative, a 'working stress design' approach to members subject to direct tension. In this method, it is sufficient to ensure that the calculated tensile stress in concrete (based on the *transformed* section) does not exceed the permissible stress specified in Cl. B-2.1.1. The area of steel should be calculated assuming that the concrete does not resist any tension. This procedure usually results in large cross-sections.

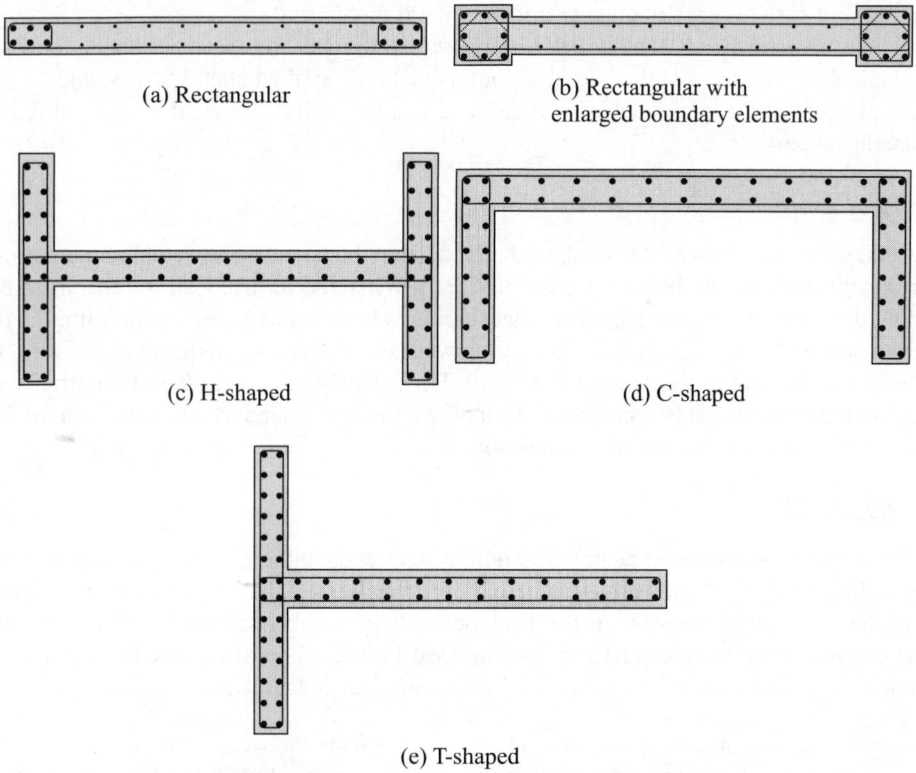

Fig. 13.38 Structural walls – different sectional shapes.

The minimum thickness of bearing walls and shear walls may be taken as not less than the smaller of $L_w/25$ or $H_u/25$, but not less than 150 mm, where H_u is the unsupported vertical height of the wall between horizontal supports [Ref. 13.24]. For non-bearing walls, the minimum thickness may be taken as 1/30 of the unsupported height or length, whichever is shorter, but not less than 100 mm. Without any distinction, IS-456 (Cl. 32.1) specifies a minimum thickness of 100 mm for walls. In addition, the ratio of effective height (H_{we}, see below) to thickness shall not exceed 30.

13.9.1 Braced Walls under In-plane Vertical Loads only

As mentioned above, reinforced concrete walls are subjected to direct compression, with or without flexure and shear. Flexure may result from eccentricity of vertical loads and/or lateral loads. The Code (Cl. 32) permits the design of *braced walls* subjected to *only vertical compression* [Figure 13.39(b)] by an empirical procedure given below. For all other cases, the procedure given in Section 13.9.2 shall be followed.

Braced Walls

A wall may be assumed to be braced if the structure providing lateral support satisfies all the following conditions (Cl. 32.2.1):

(a) Walls or other vertical bracing elements are arranged in two directions so as to provide lateral stability to the structure as a whole;
(b) Lateral forces are resisted by shear in the planes of these walls or by braced elements;

(c) Floor and roof systems are designed to transfer lateral forces; and
(d) Connections between the wall and its lateral supports are designed to resist a horizontal force not less than
  (i) simple static reactions at the lateral supports due to the applied lateral forces; and
  (ii) 2.5 per cent of the total factored vertical load that the wall is designed to carry at the level of the lateral support.

Eccentricity of Load

In braced walls, the eccentricity of the axial vertical load shall be taken as the actual value but not less than $0.05t$, where t is the thickness of the wall (Code Cl. 32.2.2). When the vertical load is transmitted by a floor or roof extending on one side only, the load from that floor is to be taken as acting at one-third the depth of the bearing area measured from the floor-side face of the wall. For floors continuous over the wall, the vertical load may be assumed to act at the centre of the wall. For calculating the *resultant* eccentricity of the *total vertical load* on the wall, all loads transmitted from above the upper support (such as from all floors above this level) may be assumed to have zero eccentricity.

Effective Height, H_{we}

Where the braced wall is restrained against rotation at both ends, either by floors above and below or by intersecting walls on either side, the effective height of the wall, H_{we}, shall be taken as the lesser of $0.75H_w$ and $0.75L_1$ as the case may be, where H_w is the unsupported height of the wall and L_1 is the horizontal distance between the centres of walls giving lateral restraint [see Figure 13.39(a)]. The end condition 'restrained against rotation', required for the k-factor of 0.75 above implies attachment to a member having a flexural

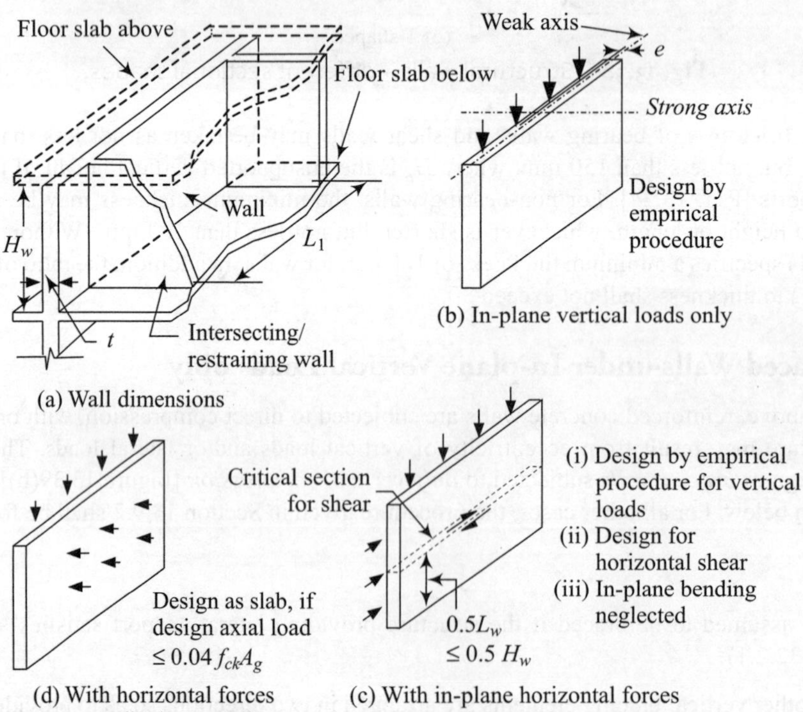

Fig. 13.39 Wall design procedures (weak axis bending).

stiffness, EI/ℓ, at least as large as that of the wall. Where not restrained against rotation at both ends, H_{we} is the lesser of H_w and L_1, which assumes pinned conditions at both ends.

Design Strength

For braced walls subjected to in-plane vertical loads only [Figure 13.39(b)], the design axial strength in compression per unit length of wall, P_{uw}, is given by Eq. 13.56:

$$P_{uw} = 0.3(t - 1.2e - 2e_a)f_{ck} \tag{13.56}$$

where t is the thickness of wall, e is the resultant eccentricity of the total vertical load measured at right angles to the plane of the wall and e_a is the additional eccentricity due to slenderness effect, taken as

$$e_a = \frac{H_{we}^2}{2500t} \tag{13.57}$$

13.9.2 Walls under Combined Vertical and Horizontal Loads

When the horizontal forces are in the plane of the wall [Figure 13.39(c)], Eq. 13.56 may be used for design for vertical forces. In addition, design for horizontal shear may be done as detailed in Section 13.9.3 below. In-plane bending due to the horizontal loads may be neglected if a horizontal section of the wall is under compression considering the vertical compressive stresses due to vertical loads and the flexural stresses under in-plane bending due to horizontal loads.

When the horizontal forces are perpendicular to the wall [Figure 13.39(d)], if the vertical load does not exceed $0.04f_{ck}A_g$, (i.e., the gross average compressive stress is below $0.04f_{ck}$), the wall shall be designed as a transversely loaded slab. Where the axial compressive load is higher, the member has to be designed for the combined effects as a beam-column using the theories of flexure (and axial load) and shear. The axial load eccentricity should not be used to reduce the bending moment caused by the horizontal loads.

13.9.3 Design of Walls for Horizontal Shear

Weak axis bending [Figure 13.39(b)] will cause associated transverse shear (flexural shear), as in the case of a slab, however except where the horizontal forces are perpendicular to the wall [Figure 13.39(d)], resulting shear stresses are very small; design for this kind of shear follows the procedure applicable for slabs. The major consideration for shear in walls pertains to horizontal shear, V_u, resulting from in-plane horizontal forces as shown in Figure 13.39(c). Forces from roof or floor diaphragms, acting parallel to the plane of the wall also induce such shear forces. This is particularly critical in shear walls under seismic loading. Design procedures for in-plane shear forces are different from methods used for flexural shear. The critical section for shear in walls is taken at a distance above base of 0.5 L_w or 0.5 H_w whichever is less.

The nominal shear stress in the wall, τ_{vw}, is given by

$$\tau_{vw} = V_u/(td) = V_u/(t0.8\,L_w) \tag{13.58}$$

where V_u is the (factored) shear force due to design loads and d is taken as $= 0.8 \times L_w$. The Code (Cl. 32.4.2.1) limits the nominal shear stress in walls, τ_{vw}, to a maximum of 0.17 f_{ck}, failing which, the cross-section dimensions have to be increased.

The shear resistance of the wall, V_{rw}, may be taken as

$$V_{rw} = V_{cw} + V_{sw}$$

where V_{cw} is the shear resistance provided by the concrete and V_{sw} is the shear resistance of the reinforcement. The *design shear strength* of concrete in the wall, τ_{cw}, is given by

(a) for $H_w/L_w \leq 1.0$;

$$\tau_{cw} = 0.2\sqrt{f_{ck}}\left(3.0 - \frac{H_w}{L_w}\right) \tag{13.59a}$$

(b) for $H_w/L_w > 1.0$;

$$\tau_{cw} = 0.045\sqrt{f_{ck}}\,\frac{(H_w/L_w + 1)}{(H_w/L_w) - 1)} \tag{13.59b}$$

but not greater than the value given by Eq. 13.59a; however, τ_{cw} shall not be less than 0.15 $\sqrt{f_{ck}}$ in any case. Accordingly, the shear resistance provided by concrete is given by:

$$V_{cw} = \tau_{cw} \times (t0.8\, L_w) \tag{13.60}$$

Design of Shear Reinforcement

The shear resistance to be provided by reinforcement, $V_{sw} = V_u - V_{cw} = V_u - \tau_{cw}\ 0.8\ L_w t$. The part V_{sw} is to be calculated as per Cl. 40.4 of the Code. Reinforcement for shear in walls is provided in the form of horizontal and vertical bars, which correspond to transverse stirrups in beams. The shear resistance of reinforcement in beams in the form of transverse stirrups, as per Cl. 40.4, may be expressed as

$$V_{us} = \frac{0.87 f_y A_{sv} d}{s_v} \tag{13.61a}$$

$$= 0.87 f_y \rho_{sv} db \tag{13.61b}$$

where $\rho_{sv} = A_{sv}/(s_v b)$ is the ratio of transverse shear reinforcement area to the corresponding concrete area. The corresponding expressions for walls, with $d = 0.8\ L_w$ and $b = t$ can be obtained as Eq. 13.62a, b below:

$$V_{sw} = \frac{0.87 f_y A_{vw}(0.8L_w)}{s_{vw}} \tag{13.62a}$$

where A_{vw} is the area of transverse shear reinforcement in the wall and s_{vw} its spacing. Following the format in Eq. 13.61b, and denoting the transverse reinforcement ratio by P_w, $(= A_{vw}/s_{vw}\ t)$, V_{sw} may also be expressed as [Eq. 13.62b]:

$$V_{sw} = 0.87 f_y P_w (0.8 L_w t)$$

$$= (0.87 f_y) A_{av} \tag{13.62b}$$

where, $A_{av} = P_w(0.8\, L_w\, t)$.

The Code (Cl. 32.4.4) uses the latter format and P_w is determined as follows:

(a) for $H_w/L_w \leq 1.0$, P_w = the lesser of the ratios of either the vertical reinforcement area or the horizontal reinforcement area to the cross-sectional area of wall in the respective direction, and
(b) for $H_w/L_w > 1.0$, P_w = the ratio of the horizontal reinforcement area to the cross-sectional area of wall, per vertical metre.

The shear stress τ_v of slender structural walls can be calculated as

$$\tau_v = \frac{V_u}{t_w \times 0.8 \times L_w} \tag{13.63}$$

It may be noted that IS 13920: 2016, which deals with the design of ductile shear walls, limits the maximum shear stress in the wall to 0.25 $\sqrt{f_{ck}}$.

Details of Wall Reinforcement

The Code (Cl. 32.5) requires that the minimum percentage (of gross concrete area) of vertical reinforcement shall be 0.12 for Fe 415 (or higher) grade deformed bars not larger than 16 mm; 0.15 for other type of bars; and 0.12 for welded wire fabric not larger than 16 mm diameter. The corresponding minimum percentages for horizontal reinforcement are 0.20, 0.25 and 0.20 respectively. Note that these minimums may not always be sufficient to resist shrinkage and temperature effects. The vertical reinforcement is provided in each face. For walls thicker than 200 mm, the vertical and horizontal reinforcement shall be provided in two grids, one on each face of the wall. The vertical and horizontal reinforcement in each layer shall not be spaced farther apart than three times the wall thickness or 450 mm, whichever is less. The vertical compression reinforcement need not be enclosed by transverse reinforcement (as per Cl. 26.5.3.2, as for columns) if the area of vertical steel is less than 0.01 times the gross sectional area or where vertical reinforcement is not required for compression. Concentrated vertical reinforcement consisting of not fewer than two 16 mm bars may be provided at each end of all walls.

Example 13.21

The end wall of a 15.2 m × 25.15 m × 7 m high single storey building is shown in Figure 13.40. Reinforced concrete flat roof is provided. Under seismic loading, the horizontal shear transmitted by the roof of the structure to the top of the wall is 1200 kN. Lateral force due to the self-weight of the wall may be taken as 0.8 W. The vertical load on the wall from the roof may be taken as 14 kN/m. The wall is 150 mm thick. Transverse restraint is provided by cross walls at 5 m intervals and the wall may be taken as braced. Design the concrete wall. Use M 25 concrete, Fe 500 steel and IS Code provisions.

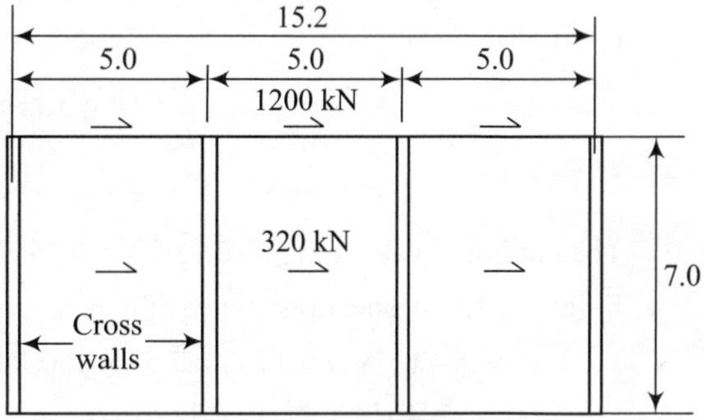

Fig. 13.40 Example 13.21.

Solution

The horizontal forces are in the plane of the wall and hence for vertical forces, the wall may be designed by the empirical method (Cl. 32.3.1).

Design for Vertical Loads

- As the roof slab extends only on one side of the wall, assuming bearing over the full width of wall, the load from the slab (= 14 kN/m) may be taken as acting at one-third the thickness of the wall; i.e., at an eccentricity $e = t/6 = 25$ mm. The self-weight of the wall, assumed to act at the top of the wall at mid-thickness, is $= 1 \times 0.15 \times 7.0 \times 25 = 26.3$ kN. Total vertical load = 14 + 26.3 = 40.3 kN/m.
- Resultant eccentricity of total vertical load is,

$$e = \frac{14 \times 25 + 26.3 \times 0.0}{40.3} = 8.68 \text{ mm}$$

- The wall is restrained against rotation by cross walls spaced at 5 m. Hence the effective height of the wall, H_{we}, is $0.75L_l$ ($< 0.75H_w$) $= 0.75 \times 5 = 3.75$ m.
- Effective height to thickness ratio = 3750/150 = 25 < 30, OK
  Also, the thickness provided is greater than the minimum specified = 100 mm.
  [As per Ref. 13.24, the minimum thickness = $H_u/25 = 7000/25 = 280$ mm]

- The additional eccentricity due to slenderness effect [Eq. 13.57]:

$$= 3.75^2/\{2500(0.15)\} \times 1000 = 37.5 \text{ mm}$$

- *The design axial strength* of the wall per metre length is given by Eq. 13.56:

$$P_{uw} = 0.3(150 - 1.2 \times 8.68 - 2 \times 37.5) \times 25 \times 1000 \text{ N}$$
$$= 484.2 \text{ kN} >> 40.3 \text{ kN} \qquad \text{OK}$$

Design for Horizontal Shear

Shear force from roof at the top of the full wall = 1200 kN. Shear due to seismic effect on self-weight = $0.8W = 0.8 \times 26.3 \times 15.2 = 320$ kN.

Total horizontal shear, $V_u = 1200 + 320 = 1520$ kN

- Check admissible maximum nominal shear stress τ_{vw} (Eq. 13.58):

$$\tau_{vw} = 1520 \times 10^3/(150 \times 0.8 \times 15200) = 0.833 \text{ MPa}$$
$$< 0.17 f_{ck} = 3.4 \text{ MPa} \qquad \text{OK}$$

- *Shear resistance of wall*: Shear resistance provided by concrete is given by Eq. 13.60. The height of wall, $H_w = 7$ m. Ratio $H_w/L_w = 7.0/15.2 = 0.461 < 1.0$, and design shear strength of concrete is given by Eq. 13. 59(a):

$$\tau_{cw} = 0.2\sqrt{f_{ck}}\left(3.0 - \frac{H_w}{L_w}\right) = 0.2\sqrt{25}(3.0 - 0.461)$$
$$= 2.54 \text{ MPa}$$

The minimum value of $\tau_{cw} = 0.15\sqrt{f_{ck}} = 0.15\sqrt{25} = 0.75$ MPa. Hence $\tau_{cw} = 2.54$ MPa.

- From Eq. 13.60, shear resistance of concrete is:

$$V_{cw} = \tau_{cw} \times (t\, 0.8\, L_w) = 2.54 \times 150 \times 0.8 \times 15200 \times 10^{-3}$$
$$= 4633 \text{ kN} > V_u = 1520 \text{ kN}$$

- Since the shear resistance of concrete alone is greater than factored shear force, shear reinforcement is not required for strength and minimum requirements would control.

Reinforcement Detailing

- With Fe 500 grade deformed bars not larger than 16ϕ, the minimum per centages of reinforcement are 0.12 for verticals and 0.20 for horizontals. (These are higher than the minimum requirement for side face reinforcement in Cl. 26.5.1.3). Area of vertical reinforcement per metre length = $0.0012 \times 150 \times 1000 = 180$ mm^2. Required spacing of 10ϕ bars $=1000 \times 78.5/180 = 436$ mm. Similarly, area of horizontal reinforcements = 300 mm^2/m and spacing of 10ϕ bars = 262 mm. Hence provide 10ϕ bars @ 250 mm horizontally and @ 400 mm vertically in a grid pattern. [Note that, where feasible, it is better to give reinforcements in two layers near each face of the wall. In this case, a grid consisting of 10ϕ bars at the maximum spacings of 450 mm vertically and 450 mm horizontally may be provided on each face].
- *Shear resistance of transverse reinforcement*: Although not required for shear strength, for illustration, the resistance V_{sw} of shear reinforcement is computed. Since $H_w/L_w \le 1.0$, P_w is taken as the lesser of the vertical and horizontal reinforcement ratios, which in this case, is the former (considering the single grid arrangement first selected above). With 10ϕ bars @ 400 mm vertically, $P_w = 78.5/(150 \times 400) = 0.00131$. Using Eq. 13.62b:

$$V_{sw} = 0.87 f_y P_w (0.8L_w t)$$

$$= 0.87 \times 500 \times 0.00131 \times 0.8 \times 15200 \times 150 \times 10^{-3}$$

$$= 1039 \text{ kN}$$

Alternatively, Eq. 13.62a gives [with the Code (Cl. 40.4) restriction of f_y to 415 in shear]:

$$V_{sw} = \frac{0.87 f_y A_{vw} (0.8L_w)}{s_{vw}}$$

$$= \frac{0.87 \times 415 \times 78.5 \times 0.8 \times 15.2}{400}$$

$$= 862 \text{ kN}$$

13.9.4 Estimation of Moment Capacity of Slender Structural Walls

The moment of resistance, M_{uv} of the wall section may be calculated as for column sections subjected to combined axial load and moment. Expressions for the moment of resistance (for flexural tension failure and flexural compression failure) of slender rectangular walls with uniformly distributed vertical reinforcement without boundary elements is given in Annex A of IS 13920: 2016 and demonstrated in Example 13.22.

The moment of resistance of walls where flexural tension failure occurs, with $(x_u/L_w) < (x_u^*/L_w)$, can be estimated as:

$$\frac{M_u}{f_{ck} t_w L_w^2} = \varphi \left[\left(1 + \frac{\lambda}{\varphi}\right)\left(\frac{1}{2} - 0.416\frac{x_u}{L_w}\right) - \left(\frac{x_u}{L_w}\right)^2 \left(0.168 + \frac{\beta^2}{3}\right) \right] \qquad (13.64)$$

where, the non-dimensional parameter (x_u/L_w) can be calculated as:

$$\frac{x_u}{L_w} = \left(\frac{\varphi + \lambda}{2\varphi + 0.36}\right) \qquad (13.65)$$

where

$$\varphi = \left(\frac{0.87 f_y \rho}{f_{ck}}\right) \qquad (13.66a)$$

$$\lambda = \left(\frac{P_u}{f_{ck} t_w L_w}\right) \qquad (13.66b)$$

$$\beta = \frac{(0.002 + 0.87 f_y / E_s)}{0.0035} \qquad (13.66c)$$

$$\frac{x_u^*}{L_w} = \frac{0.0035}{0.0035 + (0.002 + 0.87 f_y / E_s)} \qquad (13.67)$$

The moment of resistance of walls where flexural compression failure occurs, with $(x_u^*/L_w) < (x_u/L_w) < 1.0$, can be estimated as:

$$\frac{M_u}{f_{ck} t_w L_w^2} = \alpha_1 \left(\frac{x_u}{L_w}\right) - \alpha_2 \left(\frac{x_u}{L_w}\right)^2 - \alpha_3 - \frac{\lambda}{2} \tag{13.68}$$

where

$$\alpha_1 = \left[0.36 + \varphi\left(1 - \frac{\beta}{2} - \frac{1}{2\beta}\right)\right] \tag{13.69a}$$

$$\alpha_2 = \left[0.15 + \frac{\varphi}{2}\left(1 - \beta + \frac{\beta^2}{3} - \frac{1}{3\beta}\right)\right] \tag{13.69b}$$

$$\alpha_3 = \frac{\varphi}{6\beta}\left(\frac{1}{x_u/L_w} - 3\right) \tag{13.69c}$$

The value of x_u/L_w can be calculated from Eq 13.70:

$$\alpha_1 \left(\frac{x_u}{L_w}\right)^2 + \alpha_4 \left(\frac{x_u}{L_w}\right) - \alpha_5 = 0 \tag{13.70}$$

where $\alpha_4 = \left(\frac{\varphi}{\beta} - \lambda\right)$ and $\alpha_5 = \left(\frac{\varphi}{2\beta}\right)$. A detailed explanation of the derivation can be found in Ref. 13.27.

Boundary elements are portions along the wall edges that are strengthened by longitudinal and transverse reinforcement. The boundary elements may either be enlarged portions called *barbells* [Figure 13.38(b)] or may have the same thickness as that of the wall [Figure 13.38(a)]. It is advantageous to provide the boundary elements as it significantly improves the flexural strength of the wall. The IS 13920: 2016 mandates the requirement of a boundary element in the wall when the extreme fibre compressive stress in the wall due to factored gravity loads plus factored earthquake force exceeds $0.2 f_{ck}$. The boundary elements shall be continued till the location where the compressive stress becomes less than $0.15 f_{ck}$. The percentage of vertical reinforcement in the boundary elements shall not be less than 0.8 per cent, nor greater than 6 per cent.

When boundary elements are present in the wall, the method to estimate the flexural strength of the wall becomes challenging. An exact procedure for developing the *P-M* interaction curve using closed-form equations is available in literature [Ref. 13.26]. Such walls can be designed similar to columns subjected both axial load and bending moment (discussed earlier in this chapter). The boundary elements need to be designed by providing the confining reinforcement as suggested by IS 13920-2016. The area of the confining steel can be calculated as:

$$A_{sh} = \text{Maximum of} \begin{bmatrix} 0.18\, s_v\, h \dfrac{f_{ck}}{f_y}\left(\dfrac{A_g}{A_k} - 1\right) \\ 0.05\, h \dfrac{f_{ck}}{f_y} \end{bmatrix} \tag{13.71}$$

where A_{sh} is the area of the confinement reinforcement, s_v is the vertical spacing between the ties, h is the distance between the bars with cross-ties in plan, A_g is the gross cross-sectional area of the boundary element, A_k is the core cross-sectional area of the boundary element.

Example 13.22

Design a slender shear wall to resist the loads given in the Table. Assume thickness = 300 mm, length = 4500 mm. (Use M 25 concrete & Fe 500 steel)

Load Case	Axial Load kN	Moment kNm	Shear Force kN
Gravity (DL + LL)	2500	75	75
Lateral (WL/EQ)	250	2000	1000

Solution

Factored Axial Load

- Case 1 – (IS 456:2000)

$$P_{max} = 1.2(DL + LL) + 1.2\ EQ/WL$$
$$= 1.2(2500) + 1.2(250) = 3300 \text{ kN}$$

- Case 2 – (IS 13920:2016 Clause 10.4.2.1)

$$P_{min} = 0.8(DL + LL) + 1.2\ EQ/WL$$
$$= 0.8(2500) + 1.2(250) = 2300 \text{ kN}$$

Factored moment (M_u) $= (1.2 \times 75) + (1.2 \times 2000) = 2490$ kNm

Factored shear force (V_u) $= (1.2 \times 75) + (1.2 \times 1000) = 1290$ kNm

Check for Need of Boundary Element

$$I = \frac{t_w L^3}{12} = \frac{300 \times 4500^3}{12} = 2.278 \times 10^{12} \text{ mm}^4,\ A = t_w L = 300 \times 4500 = 135 \times 10^4 \text{ mm}^2$$

$$Z = \frac{I}{y} = \frac{2.278 \times 10^{12}}{2250} = 1.013 \times 10^9 \text{ mm}^3$$

$$f_{c,max} = \frac{P}{A} + \frac{M}{Z} = \frac{3300 \times 10^3}{135 \times 10^4} + \frac{2490 \times 10^6}{1.013 \times 10^9} = 4.90 \text{ MPa}$$

$$f_{c,min} = \frac{P}{A} - \frac{M}{Z} = \frac{3300 \times 10^3}{135 \times 10^4} - \frac{2490 \times 10^6}{1.013 \times 10^9} = -0.01 \text{ MPa}$$

$f_{c,lim} = 0.2 \times f_{ck} = 0.2 \times 25 = 5.0$ MPa (IS 13920 limit, beyond which boundary elements are required)

$f_{c,max} < f_{c,lim}$ Hence, boundary element not needed.

Shear Design

$$\tau_v = \frac{V_u}{t_w \times 0.8 \times L} = \frac{1290 \times 10^3}{300 \times 0.8 \times 4500} = 1.19 \text{ N/mm}^2$$

$$\tau_{v,limit} = 0.25 \times \sqrt{f_{ck}} = 0.25 \times \sqrt{25} = 1.25 \text{ N/mm}^2$$

The limit on τ_v as per IS: 456- Cl. 40.2.3 (Table 20) is not critical (see below)

$\tau_v < \tau_{v,limit}$. But thickness is greater than 200 mm. Hence steel to be provided in 2 layers.

Reinforcement

Providing steel areas of 0.25% of A_g both horizontally and vertically, which cover minimum requirements,

A_{st} required per meter $= 0.0025 \times 1000 \times 300 = 750$ mm^2

A_{st} required per meter in one layer $= 375$ mm^2

Provide 10 ϕ at 200 mm c/c spacing (both vertical and horizontal)

A_{st} provided = 785 mm^2; ρ_t provided = 0.262%.

For ρ_t = 0.25 and M25 concrete, as per IS:456 (Table 20), $\tau_{c,\max}$ = 3.10 MPa > 1.25 MPa (limit above), hence OK.

Shear resisted by concrete, τ_c = 0.36 MPa from Table 19 of the Code.

Shear to be resisted by steel, $V_{us} = (\tau_v - \tau_c)bd = (\tau_v - \tau_c)\, t_w \times 0.8 \times L = (1.19 - 0.36) \times 300 \times 0.8 \times 4500$ = 896400 N = 896 kN.

Required $A_{sv}/s_v = V_{us}/(0.87 f_y \times 0.8 \times L)$ = 896400/(0.87 × 500 × 0.8 × 4500) = 0.572.

For the reinforcement provided, A_{sv}/s_v = 2 × 78.5/200 = 0.785 > 0.572. **Hence safe in shear.**

Moment Capacity of the Wall

Check if $(x_u/L_w) < (x_u{}^*/L_w)$, using Eqs. 13.65 to 13.67,

$$\frac{x_u^*}{L_w} = \frac{0.0035}{0.0035 + (0.002 + 0.87(500/200000))} = 0.456$$

$$\varphi = \left(\frac{0.87 f_y \rho}{f_{ck}}\right) = \left(\frac{0.87 \times 500 \times 2.62 \times 10^{-3}}{25}\right) = 0.0455$$

$$\lambda = \left(\frac{P_u}{f_{ck} t_w L_w}\right) = \left(\frac{3300 \times 10^3}{25 \times 300 \times 2300}\right) = 0.097$$

$$\beta = \frac{(0.002 + 0.87 f_y/E_s)}{0.0035} = \frac{(0.002 + 0.87(500/200000))}{0.0035} = 1.193$$

$$\frac{x_u}{L_w} = \left(\frac{\varphi + \lambda}{2\varphi + 0.36}\right) = \left(\frac{0.045 + 0.097}{2 \times 0.045 + 0.36}\right) = 0.317$$

$(x_u/L_w) = 0.317 < (x_u{}^*/L_w) = 0.453$. From Eq. 13.64,

$$\frac{M_u}{f_{ck} t_w L_w^2} = 0.045\left[\left(1 + \frac{0.097}{0.045}\right)\left(\frac{1}{2} - 0.416 \times 0.317\right) - (0.317)^2\left(0.168 + \frac{1.193^2}{3}\right)\right]$$

$$\frac{M_{uw}}{f_{ck} t_w L_w^2} = 0.0497,\ M_{uw} = 0.0497 \times 25 \times 300 \times 4500^2 \text{ Nm} = 7558.31 \text{ kNm}.$$

Factored moment (M_u) is less than the flexural capacity of the wall. Hence minimum steel provided is adequate. The reinforcement details are given in Fig. 13.41.

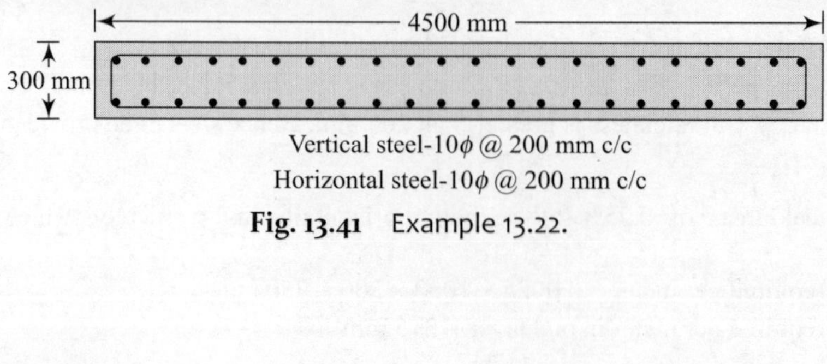

Fig. 13.41 Example 13.22.

REVIEW QUESTIONS

13.1 Discuss *slenderness ratio* of a compression member and its implications

13.2 Distinguish between (i) *unsupported length* and *effective length* of a compression member; (ii) *braced column* and *unbraced column*.

13.3 Explain why does the Code require all columns to be able to resist a *minimum eccentricity* of loading.

13.4 Discuss why the Code specify limits to the minimum and maximum reinforcement in columns.

13.5 A short column, 600 mm × 600 mm in section, is subject to a factored axial load of 1500 kN. Determine the *minimum* area of longitudinal steel to be provided, assuming M 25 concrete and Fe 500 steel.

13.6 Enumerate the functions of the transverse reinforcement in a reinforced concrete column.

13.7 Explain the limitations of the traditional working stress method with regard to the design of axially loaded reinforced concrete column.

13.8 Compare the behaviour of tied columns with spiral columns, subject to axial loading.

13.9 Sketch a typical axial load – moment interaction curve for a column and explain the salient points on it.

13.10 A column is subject to a uniaxially eccentric load which results in a point (on the interaction diagram) that lies (i) marginally outside, or (ii) marginally inside the envelope of the 'design interaction curve'. Comment on the safety of the column for the two situations.

13.11 Explain the reinforcement arrangement details underlying the design interaction curve given in SP : 16 for the condition 'rectangular section with reinforcement distributed equally on four sides'.

13.12 Briefly explain the difficulties in a rigorous analysis for the design strength components of a given rectangular column section under biaxial loading.

13.13 Explain the basis for the simplified Code procedure for analysing the design strength components of a biaxially loaded column with rectangular cross section.

13.14 What is the main difference, in terms of structural behaviour, between a 'short column' and a 'slender column'?

13.15 Distinguish between 'member stability effect' and 'lateral drift effect' in slender column behaviour.

13.16 In frame analysis, the columns are assumed to be fixed at their bases and the foundations have to be designed to resist the base moments as well as axial loads. In the case of slender columns located at the lowermost storey, is it necessary to include 'additional moments' (due to slenderness effect) while designing the foundations? (*Hint:* Does this depend on whether the frame is 'braced' or 'unbraced'?)

13.17 Slenderness effects are not applicable to members under combined bending and axial tension. Explain.

13.18 Explain how rectangular beam sections subject to biaxial bending can be designed using the Code provisions.

13.19 What are the major serviceability considerations in members subjected to combined flexural and axial tension?

13.20 Describe how are reinforced concrete walls classified. Explain the differences in their action.

13.21 Explain where and why shear walls are used. What are the major considerations in their design?

13.22 A column of size 450 mm × 600 mm has unsupported length of 3.0 m. It is braced against sidesway in both directions. As per IS 456: 2000, the minimum eccentricities, in mm, with respect to major and minor axes are:

(A) 20.0 and 20.0 (B) 26.0 and 21.0 (C) 21.0 and 15.0 (D) 26.0 and 20.0

13.23 A tied short column of size 250 mm × 300 mm has four 16 mm dia bars as longitudinal reinforcement. Concrete of M20 and steel of Fe415 grades are used. Neglect eccentricity effect. As per IS 456: 2000, the axial load (compressive) capacity of the column at limit state of collapse (in kN, up to one decimal place), is ________

13.24 A structural member subjected to compression, has one end restrained against both translation and rotation, and the other end restrained against translation only. As per IS 456: 2000, the effective length factor for design is:

(A) 0.50 (B) 0.65 (C) 0.70 (D) 0.80

PROBLEMS

13.1 A seven-storeyed building has a floor-to-floor height of 4*m* and a plan area of 18*m* × 30*m* with columns spaced at 6*m* intervals in the two directions. Assume that all columns have a size 400 mm × 400 mm with M 25 concrete, and all primary beams have a size 250 mm × 600 mm with M 25 concrete.

(a) Determine the *stability indices* of the structure in the transverse and longitudinal directions, considering the second storey. Assume a total distributed load of 50 kN/m^2 from all the floors above combined.

(b) Determine the *effective lengths* of a corner column in the second storey.

13.2 With reference to the short column section shown in Figure 13.42, assuming axial loading conditions, determine the maximum service load that the column can be safely subjected to:

(i) according to the LSM provisions of the Code (assuming a load factor of 1.5)

(ii) according to the WSM provisions of the Code.

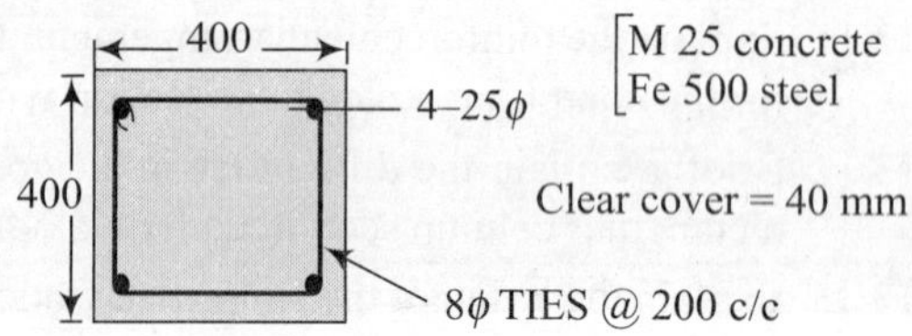

Fig. 13.42 Problem 13.2.

13.3 Repeat Problem 13.2 with reference to the column shown in Figure 13.43. [*Hint*: The 5 per cent increase in strength is allowed subject to certain conditions. Verify].

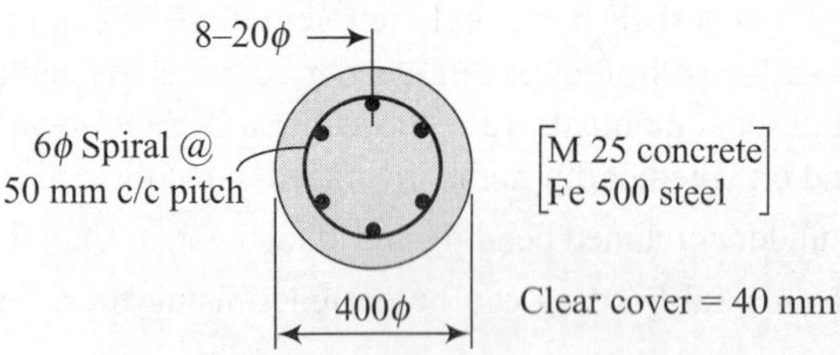

Fig. 13.43 Problem 13.3.

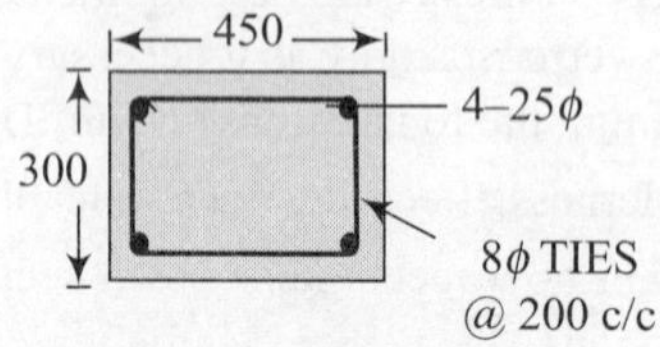

Fig. 13.44 Problem 13.6.

13.4 Design the reinforcement in a column of size 400 mm × 600 mm, subject to a factored axial load of 2500 kN. The column has an unsupported length of 3.0 m and is braced against sidesway in both directions. Use M 25 concrete and Fe 500 steel.

13.5 Repeat Problem 13.4, considering a circular column of 400 mm diameter. Assume (i) lateral ties (ii) spiral reinforcement.

13.6 For the column section shown in Figure 13.42, determine the design strength components corresponding to

(i) the condition of 'balanced failure'
(ii) $x_u/D = 0.55$
(iii) $x_u/D = 1.1$

Assume bending with respect to the major axis.

13.7 Repeat Problem 13.6, considering bending with respect to the minor axis.

13.8 Generate the design interaction curves for the column section in Figure 13.42, considering uniaxial eccentricity with respect to (i) the major axis (ii) the minor axis. [It is convenient to achieve this with the help of a suitable computer program]. Verify with reference to the charts in SP : 16.

13.9 For the L-shaped section shown in Figure 13.45, determine the design strength components corresponding to the neutral axis location shown in the figure.

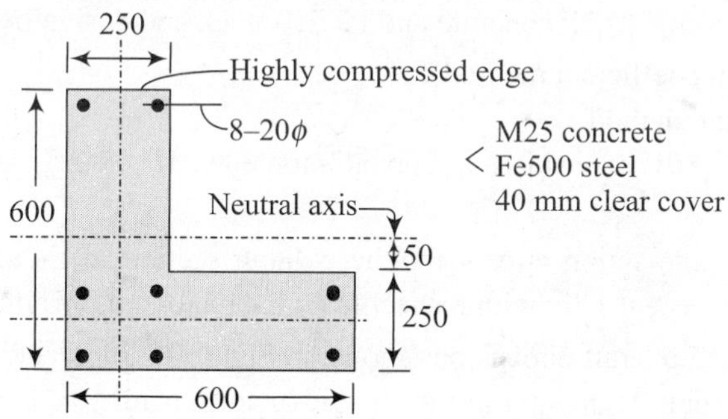

Fig. 13.45 Problem 13.9.

13.10 A short square column 300 mm × 300 mm is reinforced with 4 bars of 25ϕ, placed with a clear cover of 45 mm. Assuming M 25 concrete and Fe 500 steel, determine

(i) the maximum eccentricity with which a factored load of 1250 kN can be safely applied;
(ii) the maximum factored load that can be applied at an eccentricity of 400 mm.

13.11 A short circular tied column 350 mm diameter is reinforced with 6 bars of 20ϕ, placed with a clear cover of 40 mm. It is subject to a factored axial load of 1000 kN, combined with factored bending moments of 50 kNm each applied in two perpendicular directions. The concrete is of grade M 25 and the steel of grade Fe 500. Check the safety of the column. If the column is found to be unsafe, suggest suitable modification to the proposed reinforcement.

13.12 Design a short square column, with effective length 3.0*m*, capable of safely resisting the following factored load effects (under uniaxial eccentricity):

(i) $P_u = 1625$ kN, $M_u = 75$ kNm
(ii) $P_u = 365$ kN, $M_u = 198$ kNm

Assume M 25 concrete and Fe 500 steel.

13.13 Repeat Problem 13.12, considering a suitably proportioned *rectangular* section.

13.14 Repeat Problem 13.12, considering a circular column with spiral reinforcement.

13.15 Design the reinforcement for a column with $l_{ex} = l_{ey} = 3.5m$ and size 300 mm × 500 mm, subject to a factored axial load of 1250 kN with biaxial moments of 180 kNm, and 100 kNm with respect to the major axis and minor axis respectively (i.e., $M_{ux} = 180$ kNm, $M_{uy} = 100$ kNm). Assume M 25 concrete and Fe 500steel.

13.16 Repeat Problem 13.15, considering $P_u = 1500$ kN, $M_{ux} = 100$ kNm, $M_{uy} = 80$ kNm.

13.17 Consider a square column, 400 mm × 400 mm, with 4–25ϕ bars at corners placed with a clear cover of 45 mm, and $l_{ex} = l_{ey} = 12D$, subject to axial loading conditions. Determine the maximum factored axial load P_u that the column can safely carry considering:

(a) short column behaviour under axial loading, assuming $l = 12D$;

(b) short column behaviour under biaxial loading with minimum eccentricities;

(c) slender column behaviour (considering 'additional eccentricities' alone†).

Comment on the results obtained. Assume M 25 concrete and Fe 500 steel.

13.18 Design the reinforcement in a column of size 250 mm × 400 mm, with an unsupported length of 6.0 m, subject to a factored axial load of 1100 kN. Assume the column to be braced, and pinned at both ends in both directions. Assume M 25 concrete and Fe 500 steel, and design by

(i) strength reduction coefficient method;

(ii) additional moment method.

13.19 Repeat Problem 13.18(ii), considering biaxial moments $M_{ux} = M_{uy} = 100$ kNm in addition to $P_u = 1100$ kN.

13.20 Generate the design interaction curves for the column section in Figure 13.42, considering **axial tension** with uniaxial eccentricity with respect to (i) the major axis (ii) the minor axis.

13.21 A concrete wall having overall dimensions shown in Figure 13.39 is 200 mm thick and is reinforced, on each face, with reinforcement forming a grid made up of 10ϕ bars spaced at 400 mm both vertically and horizontally. The vertical loads act with an effective eccentricity of $t/6$ (i.e., at the third point). Compute its design axial strength and horizontal (in-plane) shear strength. Assume Fe 500 reinforcement and M 25 concrete.

REFERENCES

13.1 *Commentary on Building Code Requirements for Reinforced Concrete* ACI 318–95, American Concrete Institute, Detroit, 1995

13.2 *Structural Use of Concrete: Part 1 : Code of Practice for Design and Construction*, BS 8110 : Part 1: 1997, British Standards Institution, London, 1997

13.3 Wood, R H, *Effective Lengths of Columns in Multi-Storey Buildings*, The Structural Engineer, Vol. 57, Nos 7–9 (3 parts), July, August and September 1974

13.4 Kavanagh, T C, *Effective Length of Framed Columns*, Transactions, ASCE, Vol. 127, Part II, 1962, pp 81–101

13.5 Breen J E, MacGregor, J G, and Pfrang, E O, *Determination of Effective Length Factors for Slender Concrete Columns*, Journal ACI, Vol. 69, No. 11, Nov. 1972, pp 669–672

13.6 Timoshenko, S P and Gere, J M, *Theory of Elastic Stability*, Second edition, McGraw Hill International edition, 1963

† That is, assuming zero primary moments.

13.7 *Explanatory Handbook on Indian Standard Code of Practice for Plain and Reinforced Concrete (IS 456:1978)*, Special Publication SP:24, Bureau of Indian Standards, New Delhi, 1983

13.8 Taranath, B S, *Structural Analysis and Design of Tall Buildings*, McGraw-Hill International edition, 1988

13.9 Bresler, B and Gilbert, P H, *The Requirements for Reinforced Concrete Columns*, Journal ACI, Vol. 58, No. 5, November 1961, pp 555–570

13.10 Park, R and Paulay, T, *Reinforced Concrete Structures*, John Wiley & Sons, Inc., New York, 1975

13.11 Rao, P S and Menon, D, *Ultimate Strength of Tubular Reinforced Concrete Tower Sections Under Wind Loading*, Indian Concrete Journal, February 1995, pp 117–123

13.12 *Design Aids (for Reinforced Concrete) to IS 456 : 1978*, Special Publication SP:16, Bureau of Indian Standards, New Delhi, 1980

13.13 Press, W H, Flannery, B P, Teukolsky, S A and Vetterling, W T, *Numerical Recipes in C*, Cambridge University Press, Cambridge, 1988

13.14 Bresler, B, *Design Criteria for Reinforced Concrete Columns Under Axial Load and Biaxial Bending*, Journal ACI, Vol. 57, 1960, pp 481–490

13.15 Gouwens, A J, *Biaxial Bending Simplified, Reinforced Concrete Columns*, ACI Special Publication SP–50, American Concrete Institute, Detroit, 1975, pp 223–261

13.16 MacGregor, J G, Breen, J E, and Pfrang, E O, *Design of Slender Concrete Columns*, Journal ACI, Vol. 67, No. 1, Jan. 1970, pp 6–28

13.17 Wood, B R, Beaulieu, D, and Adams, P F, *Column Design by P–Delta Method*, ASCE Journal of Struct. Div., Vol. 102, Feb. 1976, pp 411–427

13.18 Wood, B R, Beaulieu, D, and Adams, P F, *Further Aspects of Design by P–Delta Method*, ASCE Journal of Struct. Div., Vol. 102, Mar. 1976, pp 487–500

13.19 MacGregor, J G, and Hage, S E, *Stability Analysis and Design of Concrete Columns*, ASCE Journal of Struct. Div., Vol. 10, Oct. 1977, pp 19–53

13.20 Cranston, W B, *Analysis and Design of Reinforced Concrete Columns*, Research Report 20, Cement and Concrete Assn., London, 1972

13.21 CP 110 : 1972 — *The Structural Use of Concrete, Part I*: *Design Materials and Workmanship*, British Standards Institution, London, 1972.

13.22 Menon, D, *Fuzzy Logic Based Estimation of Effective Lengths of Columns in Partially Braced Multi-storey Frames*, Structural Engineering and Mechanics, Vol. 11, No. 3, 2001, pp 287–299.

13.23 Srinivasan, S and Menon, D, *RC Rectangular Column Sections Under Biaxial Eccentric Compression – An Improved Design Recommendation*, Journal of Structural Engg, SERC, Vol. 29, No. 4, Jan-Mar 2003.

13.24 CSA Standard A23.3-04, Design of Concrete Structures, Canadian Standards Association, Mississauga, Canada, 2004

13.25 Fintel, M, *Shear Walls – An Answer for Seismic Resistance?* Concrete International, Vol. 13, No. 7, 1991

13.26 Balakrishnan, B, Geever, I, Jithin, K V, Menon, D, *Generation of P-M Interaction Design Charts for RC Shear Walls*, Indian Concrete Institute, July 2019

13.27 Medhekar, M S and Jain, S K, *Seismic Behaviour, Design and Detailing of RC Shear Walls, Part 1: Behaviour and Strength*, Indian Concrete Journal, Vol. 67, July 1993.

CHAPTER 14

Design of Footings and Retaining Walls

LEARNING OBJECTIVES

After studying this chapter, you will be able to:

- *Explain different types of footings, pile caps and retaining walls, and their structural behaviour*
- *Undertake detailed design of footings, pile caps and retaining walls, including reinforcement detailing*

14.1 Introduction

The function of the foundation is to transmit *safely* to the soil below, all the load effects transferred to it by the superstructure.

In a typical structure built on ground, that part of the structure which is located above ground is generally referred to as the *superstructure*, and the part which lies below ground is referred to as the *substructure* or the 'foundation structure' (or simply, foundation). The purpose of the foundation is to effectively support the superstructure by

1. transmitting the applied load effects (reactions in the form of vertical and horizontal forces and moments) to the soil below, without exceeding the 'safe bearing capacity' of the soil, and
2. ensuring that the *settlement* of the structure is within tolerable limits, and as nearly uniform† as possible.

The primary considerations in footing design are the soil bearing pressure, settlement (overall and differential), instability (overturning, sliding, pullout), and structural strength of the elements in flexure and shear.

Further, the foundation should provide adequate safety against possible *instability* due to *overturning* or *sliding* and/or possible *pullout*. Design against forces inducing overturning and sliding is of special importance in the design of *retaining walls*, whose very purpose is to provide lateral

† Non-uniform (differential) settlement of a structure generally results in significant stresses in the superstructure, which are usually not foreseen in design. In order to avoid this, it is necessary to ensure that the different footings in a building are proportioned in such a way as to result in soil pressures of nearly equal magnitude under their bases (under permanent loads). In those exceptional situations where differential settlements are unavoidable, it is necessary to consider this in the analysis of the structure itself; this will involve a trial-and-adjustment process, as the settlements are not known a priori.

support to earthfill/embankment in order to retain the side of the earthfill in a vertical position. The choice of the type of foundation depends largely on the conditions/parameters of the soil strata on which the structure is to be founded, such as bearing capacity, pressure bulb extent and depth, closeness and nature of the bearing strata, water table level and settlements. This comes under the specialised domain of geotechnical engineering (soil mechanics), and for important structures and/or difficult soil conditions, the type of foundation to be used is based on a soil study by a geotechnical consultant. In the case of retaining walls, the choice of the type of wall is governed by the height of the earth to be retained and other site/soil conditions.

It is not the objective of this book to cover the designs of all the different types of foundations and retaining walls. Nor is it the objective of the Code on Reinforced Concrete Design (IS 456) to do this. The Code recommendations (Cl. 34) are confined to *the design of footings that support isolated columns or walls and rest directly on soil or on a group of piles* [Ref. 14.1]. This chapter is, accordingly, confined to the design of these simple types of footings (including combined footings supporting two columns) as well as retaining walls (*cantilever* and *counterfort* walls). These simple types of footings [Fig. 14.1] are the most widely used types of foundation and are relatively cheap to build. The design of more complex types of foundations (continuous footings, raft foundations, pile foundations, wells and caissons, etc.) is clearly outside the scope of this book, and for this, reference may be made to books on foundation engineering [Ref. 14.2, 14.3] and related IS Codes [IS 2911 (Parts I–III), IS 2950, etc.]. The special codes related to the design of simple footings (discussed in this chapter) are IS 1904:1986 [Ref. 14.4] and IS 1080:1980 [Ref. 14.5].

Sections 14.2–14.6 deal with the types, behaviour and design of footings, while Sections 14.7–14.9 deal with the types, behaviour and design of retaining walls. Design of pile caps is discussed in Section 14.10.

14.2 Types of Footings

'Footings' belong to the category of *shallow foundations* (as opposed to *deep foundations* such as piles and caissons) and are used when soil of sufficient strength is available within a relatively short depth below the ground surface; otherwise, deep foundations are used. When the use of both footings and deep foundations is possible, the deciding factor is usually the cost of construction and, in general, footings are more economical. Shallow foundations comprise not only *footings* (which support columns/walls, and have a limited area/width in plan) but also rafts which support multiple columns on a large plan area). The shallow foundation (footing or raft) has a large plan area in comparison with the cross-sectional area of the column(s) it supports because:

- the loads on the columns (axial thrust, bending moments[†]) are resisted by concrete under compression and reinforcing steel under tension and/or compression, whereas these load effects are transmitted by the footing/raft to a relatively weak supporting soil by *bearing pressures* alone; and
- the 'safe bearing capacity' of the soil is very low (100–400 kPa) in comparison with the *permissible* compressive stresses in concrete (5–15 MPa) and steel (130–190 MPa) in a column under service loads.

14.2.1 Isolated Footings

For ordinary structures located on reasonably firm soil, it usually suffices to provide a separate footing for every column. Such a footing is called an *isolated footing*. It is generally square or rectangular in plan; other

[†] Shear forces are also induced in columns, which may result in significant horizontal forces at column bases, under lateral loads. These are resisted by friction between the underside of the footing and the soil below, and also by passive resistance of the soil adjoining the sides of the footing, and in some cases, by 'keys' cast integrally with the footing.

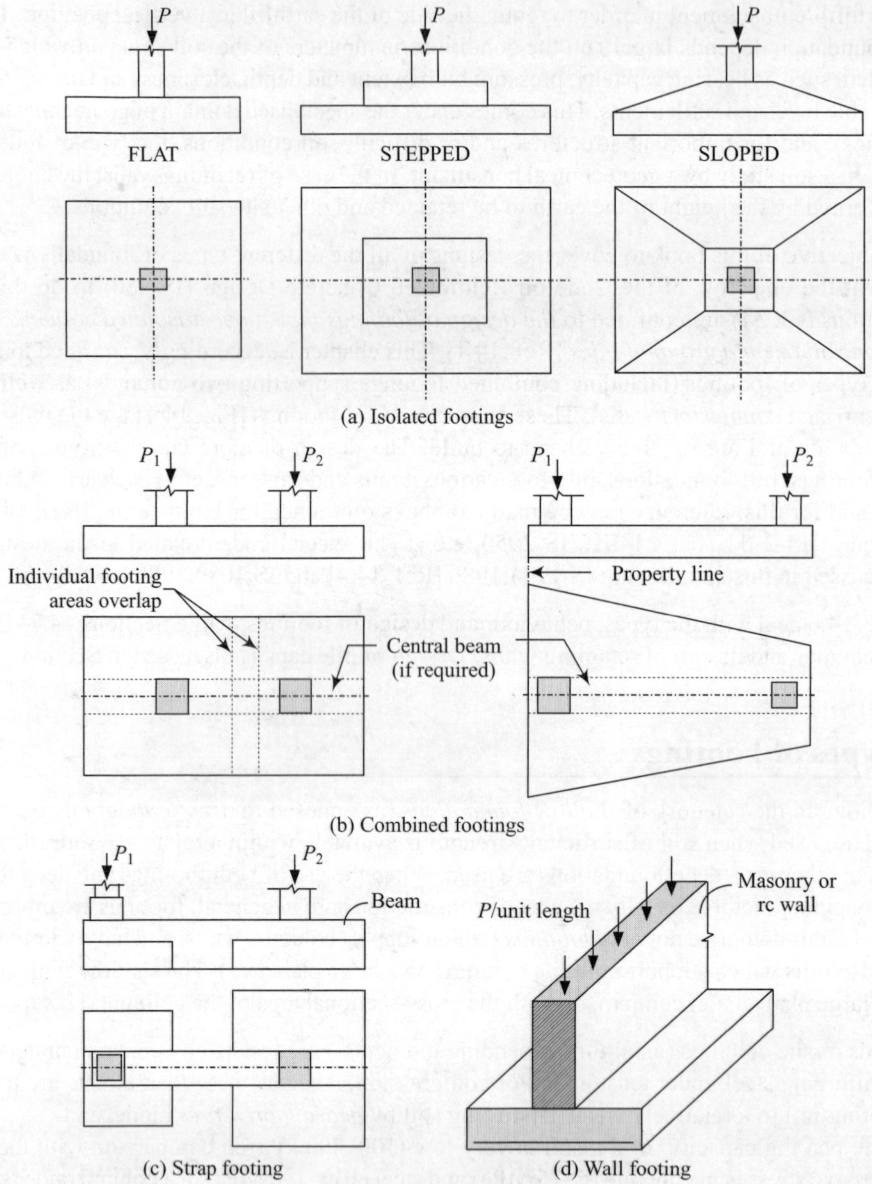

Fig. 14.1 Types of footings.

shapes are resorted to under special circumstances. The footing basically comprises a thick slab which may be flat (of uniform thickness), stepped or sloped (on the upper surface), as shown in Fig. 14.1(a).

The soil bearing pressures from below tend to make the base slab of the footing bend upwards, somewhat into a saucer-like shape (cantilever action), and hence the footing needs to be suitably reinforced by a mesh provided at the bottom of the slab. However, in the exceptional case of very small and relatively thick footings, the structural action is likely to occur, not by bending of the footing slab, but by a lateral dispersion of the compressive stress at the base of the column; in such a case, it suffices to provide a plain concrete *pedestal footing* [refer Section 14.4.7].

The term 'pedestal' is also used to refer to that portion of a column below ground level where the cross-sectional dimensions are enlarged. The provision of a pedestal is optional, but is often resorted to by design engineers, as it results in reduced development length requirements for the column bars, reduced slenderness of the column† (especially when the founding depth is large), increased direct bearing area on the footing base slab, and reduced shear stresses and design moments. Pedestals are also used to support structural steel columns, the load transfer between the steel column and the concrete pedestal being achieved generally through gusseted steel base plates with 'holding down' bolts.

14.2.2 Combined Footings

In some cases, it may be inconvenient to provide separate isolated footings for columns (or walls) on account of inadequate areas available in plan. This may occur when two or more columns (or walls) are located close to each other and/or they are relatively heavily loaded and/or rest on soil with low safe bearing capacity, resulting in an overlap of areas if isolated footings are attempted.

In such cases, it is advantageous to provide a single *combined footing* [Fig. 14.1(b)] for the columns. Often, the term 'combined footing' is used when *two* columns are supported by a common footing, the term 'continuous strip footing' is used if the columns (three or more in number) are aligned in one direction alone, and the term 'raft foundation' ('mat foundation') is used when there is a grid of multiple columns‡. The combining of footings contributes to improved integral behaviour of the structure.

'Combined footings' support two (or more) columns, and are resorted to when isolated footings for these columns tend to overlap, or there is insufficient space for individual footings due to property line limits.

Figure 14.1(b) also shows a two-column combined footing, in which there is a 'property line' limit which restricts the extension of the footing on one side. In this case, the non-availability of space near the exterior column is circumvented by combining the footing with that of an interior column. The width of the footing may be kept uniform or tapered, as shown. The trapezoidal shaped footing (with a larger width near the exterior column) is required when the exterior column is more heavily loaded than the interior column. Another option is a combined footing which is T-shaped. It is sometimes economical to provide a central beam interconnecting the column bases; this causes the base slab to bend transversely, while the beam alone bends longitudinally. Thus, the shape and type of footings to be used is a function of the supported structure and its geometry (column/wall spacing, load intensity, etc.).

An alternative to the conventional combined footing is the *strap footing*, in which the columns are supported essentially on isolated footings, but interconnected with a beam, as shown in Fig. 14.1(c).

14.2.3 Wall Footings

Reinforced concrete footings are required to support reinforced concrete walls, and are also sometimes employed to support load-bearing masonry walls§. *Wall footings* distribute the load from the wall to a wider

† Tie beams are also sometimes provided (for this purpose), interconnecting different columns at the top of pedestal level (about 150 mm below ground level). Plinth beams also serve as tie beams.

‡ The raft foundation consists of a thick slab which may be (i) of uniform thickness (flat plate), (ii) with locally thicker panels near column bases (flat slab), or (iii) with stiffening beams interconnecting the columns.

§ It is more common to have stepped masonry (stone or brick) foundation for masonry walls.

area, and are continuous throughout the length of the wall [Fig. 14.1(d)]. The footing slab bends essentially in the direction transverse to the wall (a 'one-way' slab), and hence is reinforced mainly in the transverse direction, with only distributors in the longitudinal direction.

14.3 Soil Pressures under Isolated Footings

14.3.1 Allowable Soil Pressure

The plan area of a footing base slab is selected so as to limit the maximum soil bearing pressure induced below the footing to within a safe limit. This safe limit to the soil pressure is determined using the principles of soil mechanics [Ref. 14.2, 14.3]. The main considerations in determining the allowable soil pressure, as well as fixing the depth of foundation, are (i) that the soil does not fail under the applied loads, and (ii) that the settlements, both overall and differential, are within the limits permissible for the structure. The safety factor, used in soil mechanics, lies in the range 2–6, and depends on the type of soil, and related uncertainties and approximations.

> **The given allowable safe soil bearing capacity, q_a, usually includes the factor of safety and hence corresponds to service load conditions. If so, the footing area calculations using q_a must be for the service load effects on the footing.**

It should be noted that the value of the *safe soil bearing capacity* ('allowable soil pressure'), q_a, given to the structural designer by the geotechnical consultant[†], is applicable for *service load* conditions, as q_a includes the factor of safety. Hence, the calculation for the required area of a footing must be based on q_a and the *service* load effects[‡]. The 'partial load factors' to be used for different load combinations (*DL, LL, WL/EL*) should, therefore, be those applicable for the *serviceability limit state* and *not* the 'ultimate limit state' [refer Section 3.6.3] when used in association with q_a.

> **'Gross' pressure is the allowable pressure at the foundation base level, *including* the pressure due to the existing overburden; 'net' pressure is the admissible pressure *in excess* of the existing overburded pressure.**

Another point to be noted is that the prescribed allowable soil pressure q_a at a given depth may be expressed in terms of the *gross* pressure, which includes the pressure due to the existing overburden (soil up to the founding depth), or in terms of the *net* pressure (in excess of the existing overburden pressure). Strictly, in traditional geotechnical practise, the latter is recommended [Ref. 14.12].Hence, the total load to be considered in calculating the maximum soil pressure q ($\leq q_a$) should be appropriately taken based on how q_a is specified. If the specified q_a is based on the gross pressure, the calculation of q must include the weight of the footing itself and that of the backfill. Often, in preliminary calculations these weights are accounted for approximately as 10–15 percent of the axial load on the column. However, if the specified q_a is based on the net pressure, the calculation of q may include only the additional weight of the footing arising from the difference in the unit weights of concrete and soil it replaces; this may work out to about 5 per cent of the axial load on the column. However, these assumptions should be verified subsequently.

[†] The soil bearing capacity, according to soil mechanics theory, depends on the size of the footing, and this is to be accounted for (approximately) in the recommendation made in the Soil Report.

[‡] Building codes in some countries (e.g., National Building Code of Canada 2005) have done away with the practice of computing required footing area based on service loads and 'service soil bearing capacity', and have adopted calculations based on factored loads and 'factored soil bearing resistance'.

14.3.2 Distribution of Base Pressure

The distribution of the soil reaction acting at the base of the footing depends on the rigidity of the footing as well as the properties of the soil. The distribution of soil pressure is generally non-uniform. However, for convenience, a linear distribution of soil pressure is assumed in normal design practice.

Concentrically Loaded Footings

Thus, in a symmetrically loaded footing, where the resultant vertical (service) load $P + \Delta P$ (where P is the load from the column and ΔP the weight of footing plus backfill) passes through the centroid of the footing, the soil pressure is assumed to be uniformly distributed [Fig. 14.2], and its magnitude q is given by

$$q = \frac{P + \Delta P}{A} \tag{14.1}$$

where A is the base area of the footing.

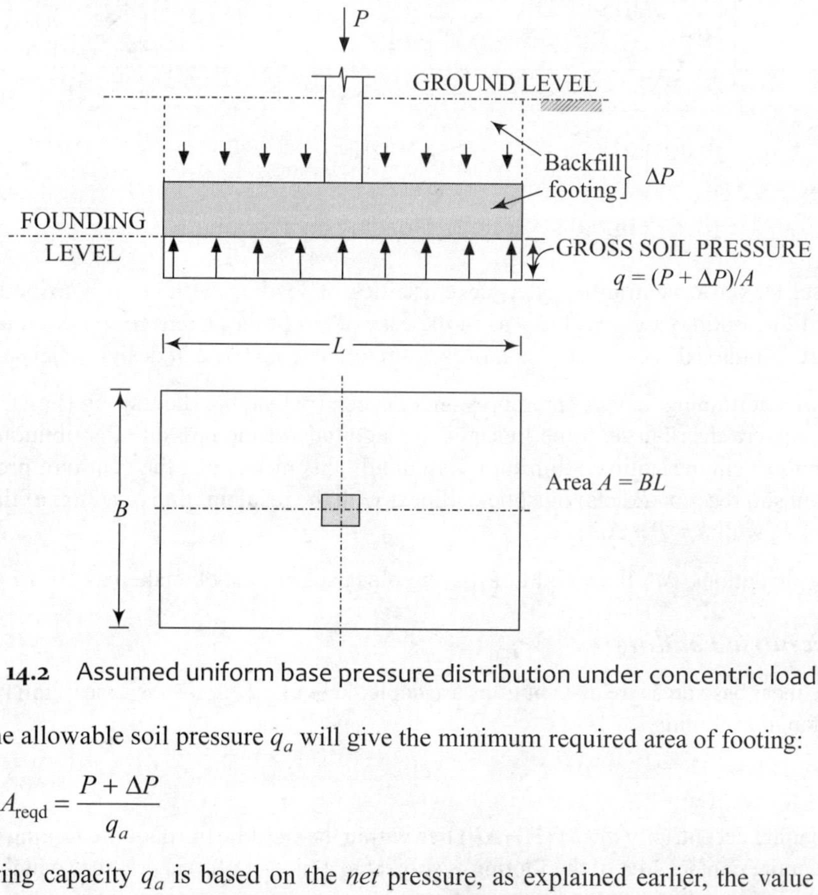

Fig. 14.2 Assumed uniform base pressure distribution under concentric loading.

Limiting q to the allowable soil pressure q_a will give the minimum required area of footing:

$$A_{\text{reqd}} = \frac{P + \Delta P}{q_a} \tag{14.1a}$$

If the safe bearing capacity q_a is based on the *net* pressure, as explained earlier, the value of ΔP may be limited to the product of the volume of the base slab and the difference in the unit weights of concrete and soil; for all practical purposes, this marginal increase may be ignored and $A_{\text{reqd}} = P/q_a$ may be considered.

Eccentrically Loaded Footings

Eccentric loading causes non-uniform stress distribution at the base of footing. Eccentricity may be due to column transmitting a moment, column being eccentric to the footing centroid, or column transmitting a lateral force applied above the foundation level.

The load P acting on a footing may act eccentrically with respect to the centroid of the footing base. This eccentricity e may result from one or more of the following effects:

- the column transmitting a moment M in addition to the vertical load [Fig. 14.3(a)];
- the column carrying a vertical load offset with respect to the centroid of the footing [Fig. 14.3(b)]; and
- the column (or pedestal) transmitting a lateral force located above the foundation level, in addition to the vertical load [Fig. 14.3(c)].

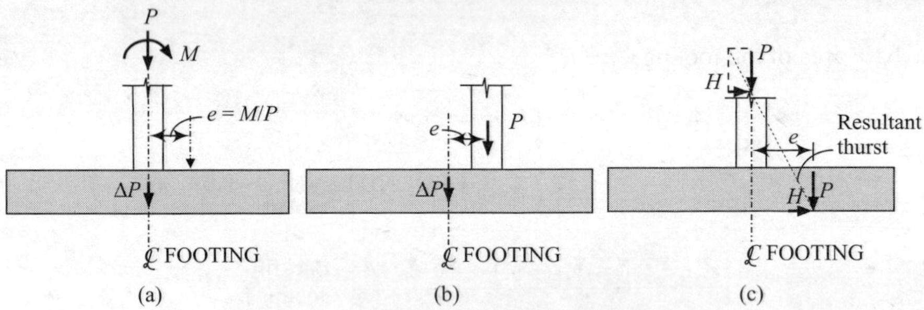

Fig. 14.3 Eccentric loading on a footing.

In a general case, biaxial eccentricities (i.e., eccentricities of loading with respect to both the principal centroidal axes of the footing) are possible – as in the case of a footing for the corner column of a building. However, the case of uniaxial eccentricity† is more commonly encountered in design practise.

For the purpose of determining the base pressures under eccentric loading, the footing is assumed to be rigid and the contact pressure distribution to be linear. The magnitude of the pressure distribution is determined from considerations of simple static equilibrium. Essentially this means that the centre of pressure (through which the resultant soil reaction R acts) must be collinear with the resultant line of action of the eccentrically applied load $P + \Delta P$, with $R = P + \Delta P$ [Fig. 14.4].

For preliminary calculations, ΔP, the weight of footing plus backfill, may be taken as 10–15 percent of P.

Uniaxially Eccentric Loading

Various possible linear base pressure distributions are depicted in Fig. 14.4 for the case of uniaxially eccentric loading on a rectangular footing.

Case 1: $|e| \le L/6$

If the resultant loading eccentricity $e = M/(P + \Delta P)$ lies within the 'middle third' of the footing (i.e., $|e| \le L/6$), it is seen that the entire contact area of the footing is subject to a (non-uniform) pressure which varies linearly

† Eccentricities in loading can be quite significant in footings which support columns that form part of a lateral load resisting frame. However, as the lateral loads are generally assumed to act (with maximum values) in only one direction at a time, the problem is essentially one of uniaxial eccentricity. Eccentricities in both directions should be considered, but usually only one at a time.

from q_{min} to q_{max} [Fig. 14.4(a)]. These pressures are easily obtained by superposing the separate effects due to the direct load $(P + \Delta P)$ and the bending moment $M = (P + \Delta P)\, e$:

$$q_{max,min} = \frac{(P+\Delta P)}{A} \pm \frac{(P+\Delta P)e}{Z} \tag{14.2a}$$

with area $A = BL$ and section modulus $Z = BL^2/6$, where L is the length of the footing in the direction of the eccentricity e, and B the width of the footing. Accordingly,

$$q_{max,min} = \frac{(P+\Delta P)}{A}\left(1 \pm \frac{6e}{L}\right) \quad \text{for } |e| \le L/6 \tag{14.2b}$$

In the limiting case of $|e| = L/6$, $q_{min} = 0$ and $q_{max} = 2(P + \Delta P)/A$, resulting in a triangular pressure distribution. The uniform pressure distribution $q = (P + \Delta P)/A$ [Eq. 14.1] is obtained as special case of Eq. 14.2b, with $e = 0$.

The limiting case of $|e| = L/6$, is valid only for uniaxial bending.

Case 2: $|e| > L/6$

> **Negative pressure (tension) cannot be expected to develop at footing-soil interface; hence when eccentricity *e* exceeds *L*/6, separation or *uplift* is deemed to occur over part of the footing base.**

When the resultant eccentricity e exceeds $L/6$, Eq. 14.2 becomes invalid because it will yield a negative value for q_{min}, implying a tensile force at the interface. However, such tension resisting capacity cannot be practically expected from soil.† Thus, it is seen that the effective length of contact is reduced from L to L', whereby the effective contact area is given by $A' = BL'$. Assuming a triangular pressure distribution (considering the soil under compression alone), and considering equilibrium, the line of action of the resultant soil reaction R must be collinear with the eccentric load $P + \Delta P$, and the magnitude of $R = P + \Delta P$. Thus, R acts at a distance $L'/3 = c = 0.5L - e$ from the location of maximum base pressure [Fig. 14.4(b)].The pressure distribution being triangular, the maximum pressure will be twice the average pressure. Hence:

$$q_{max} = \frac{2(P+\Delta P)}{BL'} \tag{14.3a}$$

$$\left.\begin{aligned} L' &= 3c \\ c &= 0.5L - e \end{aligned}\right\} \tag{14.3b}$$

Thus, it is seen that the effective length of contact is reduced from L to $L' = 3c$, and the maximum soil pressure q_{max} is increased from $(P + \Delta P)/A$(for $e = 0$) to twice the load $(P + \Delta P)$ divided by the effective area BL'. In order to limit q_{max} to the allowable bearing pressure q_a, and also to maximise the effective bearing area ratio L'/L, it may be necessary to design a footing with a large base area. Uplift may be permitted (for the sake of economy) only in the case of extreme incidental loading, and the extent of uplift should typically not exceed 10 percent (i.e., L'/L should not be less than 0.9). Such footings are commonly encountered in industrial buildings where columns are relatively lightly loaded axially, but subject to high bending moments due to lateral wind loads or eccentric gantry crane loads.

---

† In fact, it can be expected that the footing will tend to separate (uplift) from the soil base, thereby developing no pressure whatsoever in the base regions farthest removed from q_{max}.

Highly non-uniform base pressure can lead, over time, to tilting of footing and hence should be avoided.

It may be noted that highly non-uniform base pressures (especially under *sustained* eccentric loads) are undesirable, as this can result in possible tilting of the footing. Hence, proportioning of the footing base should be such as to make the contact pressure as uniform as possible.

In case, footings are likely to be subject to uplift, the possibility of flexural tension developing at top of the footing slab (on account of weight of the footing and soil above in the cantilevering portion) should be accounted for, and nominal top steel provided accordingly.

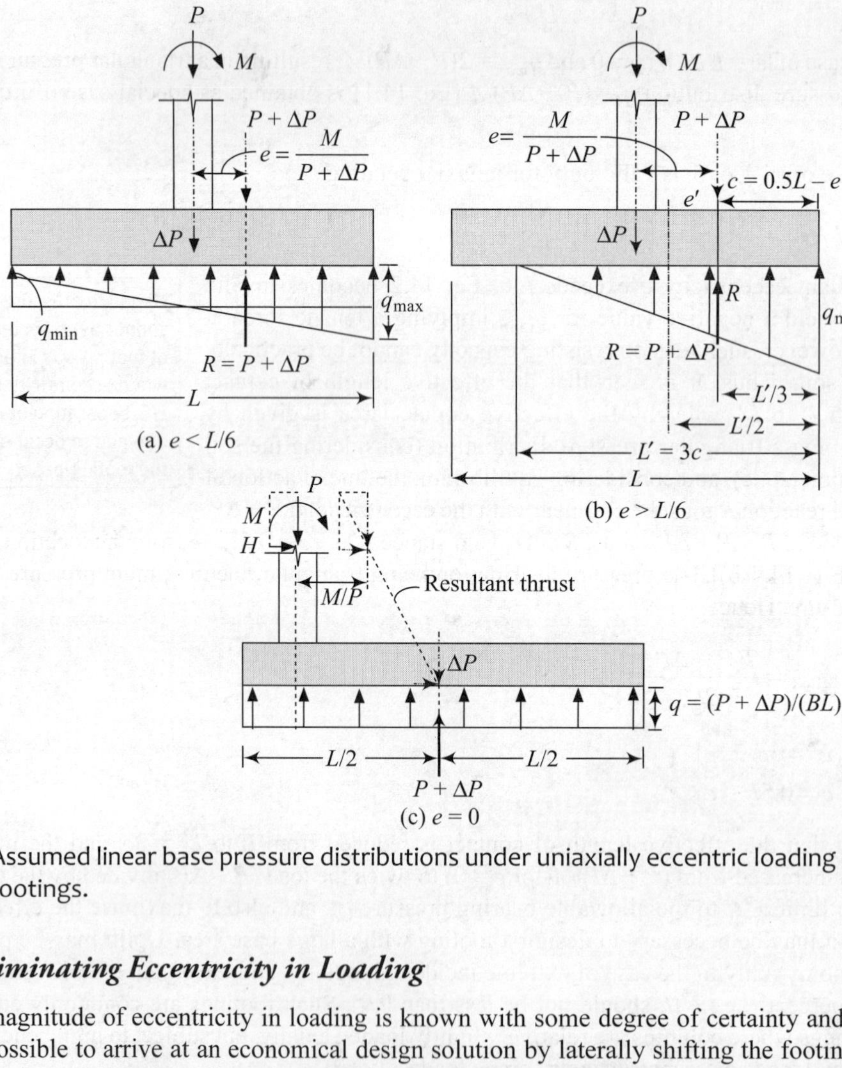

Fig. 14.4 Assumed linear base pressure distributions under uniaxially eccentric loading on rectangular footings.

Case 3: Eliminating Eccentricity in Loading

Where the magnitude of eccentricity in loading is known with some degree of certainty and its direction is fixed, it is possible to arrive at an economical design solution by laterally shifting the footing base, relative to the column, such that the effective eccentricity in loading is reduced considerably, if not eliminated altogether. This is not only desirable from the viewpoint of economy but also desirable from the viewpoint of eliminating possible titling of the footing on account of non-uniform base pressure. The ideal situation of zero effective eccentricity is depicted in Fig. 14.4(c), where it is shown that by suitably offsetting the footing base so that the resultant line of thrust passes through the centroid of the footing, a uniform pressure distribution is obtainable, with $q = (P + \Delta P)/A$. However, some increase in bearing pressure should be considered in practice, to account for possible variations in the estimated M/P ratio.

Indeed, such a design solution becomes impracticable when the M/P ratio is highly uncertain in magnitude, and especially when the bending moment and/or the horizontal force H can be reversible in direction (as under wind loads).

Biaxially Eccentric Loading

In the case of biaxially eccentric loading, the pressure distribution at the bottom of the footing may be assumed to be planar, and the possible planar base pressure distributions are depicted in Fig. 14.5 on a rectangular footing.

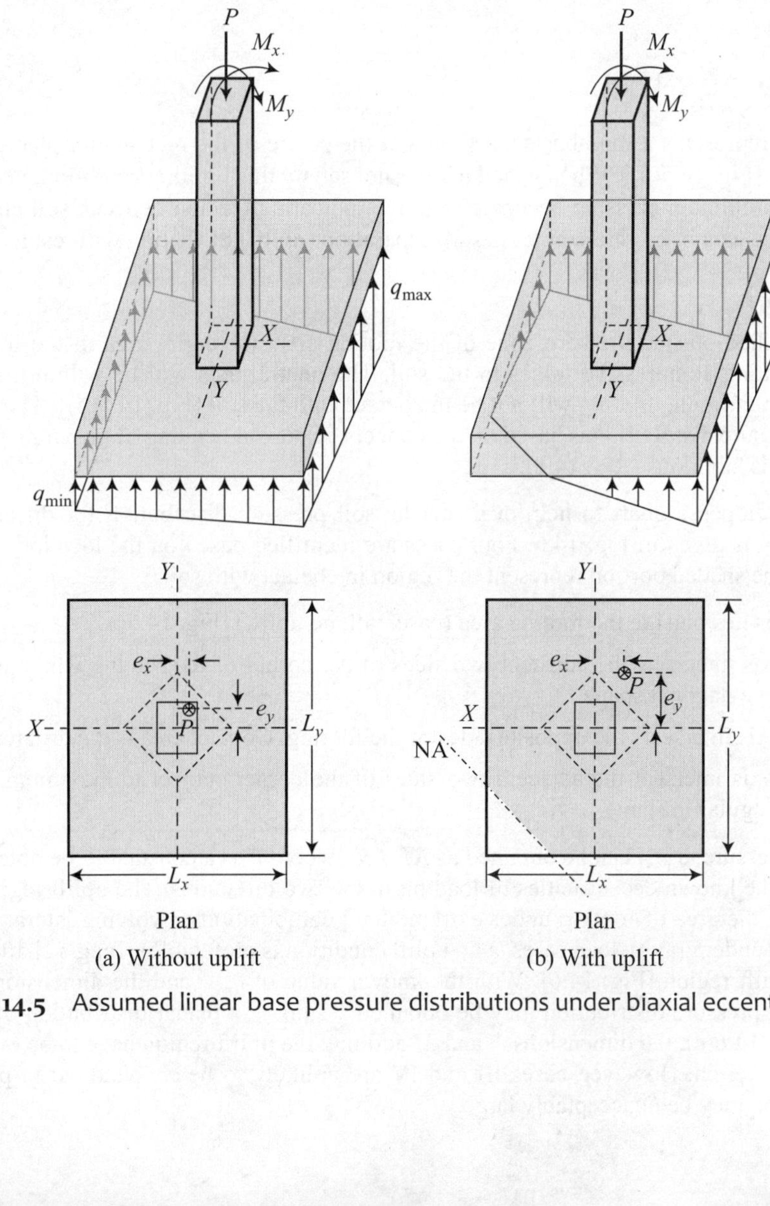

Fig. 14.5 Assumed linear base pressure distributions under biaxial eccentric loading.

Case 1: No Uplift

When the load is applied with eccentricities e_x and e_y along x and y directions respectively, it is seen that the entire contact area of the footing is subject to a (nonuniform) pressure [Fig. 14.5(a)]. The pressure at the four corners may be obtained as

$$q = \frac{P + \Delta P}{A}\left(1 \pm \frac{6e_x}{L_x} \pm \frac{6e_y}{L_y}\right) \tag{14.4a}$$

The limiting case for *no uplift* may be obtained by equating minimum pressure to be greater than or equal to zero to ensure the entire base area to be in compression,

$$q_{\min} = \frac{P + \Delta P}{A}\left(1 - \frac{6e_x}{L_x} - \frac{6e_y}{L_y}\right) \geq 0 \tag{14.4b}$$

Simplifying,

$$\frac{e_x}{L_x/6} + \frac{e_y}{L_y/6} \leq 1 \tag{14.4c}$$

The above condition represents a rhombus shaped area at the centre of the rectangular plan of the footing, referred to as the *kern* [Fig. 14.5(a)]. When e_x and e_y does not satisfy this limiting condition, i.e., the load acts outside the kern, the minimum pressure becomes negative indicating tension between soil and the footing. Since tensile resistance cannot be offered by the soil, separation (uplift) of footing will result.

Case 2: With Uplift

When the load is applied outside the kern zone of the footing area, the entire area of the footing will not contribute in transmitting compressive forces to the soil. The neutral axis will lie within the base area of footing and some portion of the footing will not be in contact with the soil [Fig. 14.5(b)]. The procedure for obtaining the soil pressure distribution is based on the concept of biaxial bending of unsymmetrical sections; however, the method is laborious [Ref. 14.6].

Teng [Ref. 14.7] developed a chart to help evaluate the soil pressure distribution for different values of e_x/L_x and e_y/L_y, which is given in Fig. 14.6. Four cases are identified based on the location of neutral axis [Fig 14.6(c)] where the shaded portion represent the region in contact with soil,

Case I: Neutral axis lies outside the footing area (case with no uplift) [Fig. 14.5(a)]

Case II: Neutral axis intersects the adjacent two sides of the corner of the footing where uplift is likely. Contact area has a pentagonal shape

Case III: Neutral axis intersects the opposite sides of the footing. Contact area is quadrilateral in shape.

Case IV: Neutral axis intersect the adjacent two sides of the corner subject to maximum soil pressure. Contact area is triangular in shape.

The maximum soil pressure, q_{max}, can be obtained as KP/L_xL_y where K is a constant to be obtained from the chart [Fig. 14.6] for the known eccentricities of loading in the two directions. The uplift region should not be more than 10% of the area of footing under extreme load combinations involving lateral loads such as wind and earthquake (under gravity load cases, a no uplift condition is preferable). Teng's chart also provides the dimensions of uplift region [Fig. 14.6]. With the known value of q_{max} and the dimension of the uplift region, the entire soil pressure distribution may be obtained assuming a planar distribution of stresses. For case III shown in Fig. 14.6(c), the dimensions N and M defining the uplift region have to be evaluated using the equations shown therein. However, cases III and IV are unlikely to be encountered in practice as the associated uplift region may be unacceptably large.

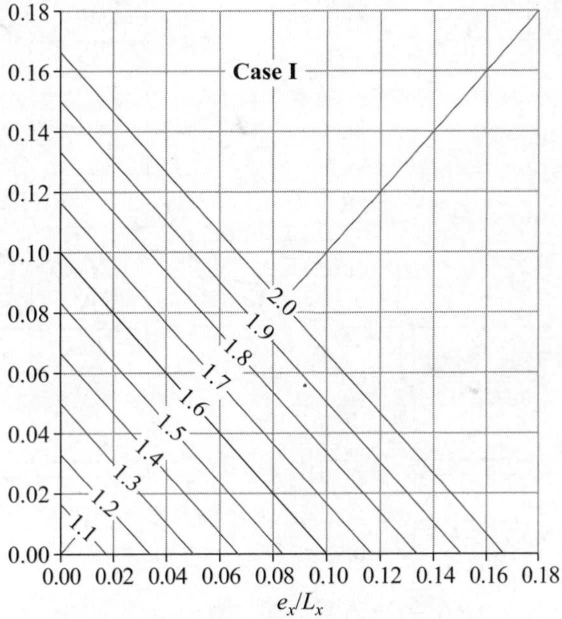

(a) Variation of K for no uplift: Case I

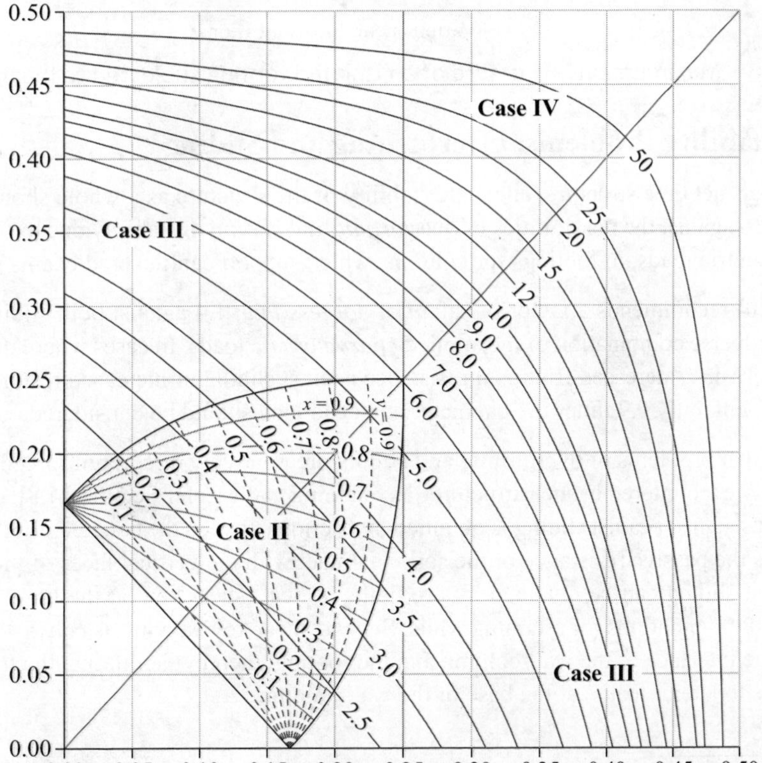

(b) Variation of K for cases with uplift: Case II to IV

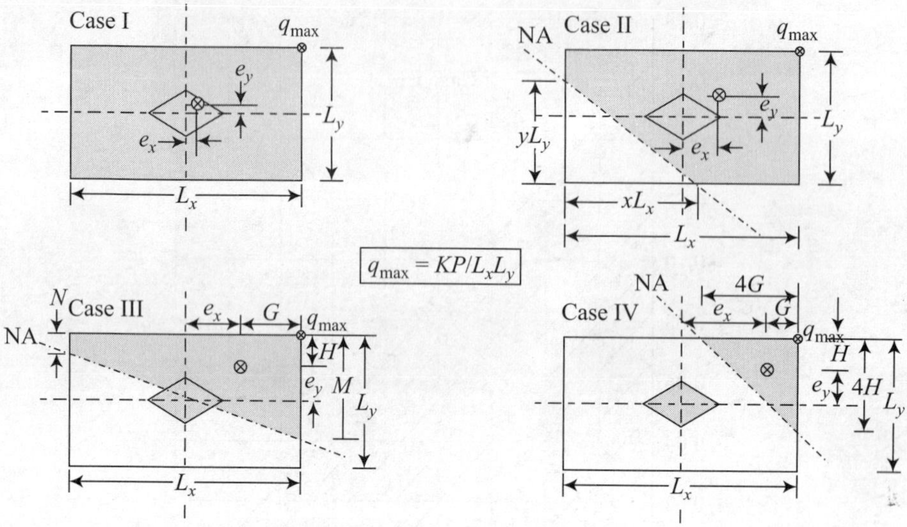

$$G = \frac{L_x[1 + 2(N/M) + 3(N/M)^2]}{4[1 + (N/M) + (N/M)^2]} = 0.5\,L_x - e_x$$

$$H = \frac{M[1 + (N/M) + (N/M)^2 + (N/M)^3]}{4[1 + (N/M) + (N/M)^2]} = 0.5\,L_y - e_y$$

(c) Various neural axes locations

Fig. 14.6 Maximum base pressure of an isolated footing subjected to biaxial moment.

14.3.3 Instability Problems: Overturning and Sliding

When lateral loads act on a structure, adequate stability of the structure as a whole should be ensured at the foundation level – against the possibilities of *overturning* and *sliding*. Instability due to overturning may also occur due to eccentric loads, in footings for columns which support cantilevered beams/slabs.

The Code (Cl. 20) recommends a factor of safety of *not less than* 1.4 against both sliding and overturning† under the most adverse combination of the applied *characteristic* loads. In cases where dead loads contribute to improved safety, i.e., increased frictional resistance against sliding or increased restoring moment against overturning moment, only 0.9 times the characteristic dead load should be considered.

It may be noted that problems of overturning and sliding are relatively rare in reinforced concrete buildings, but are commonly encountered in such structures as retaining walls [refer Section 14.8], chimneys, industrial sheds, etc. The resistance against sliding is obtained by friction between the concrete footing base and the soil below, as well as the passive resistance of the soil in contact with the vertical faces of the footing. Improved resistance against sliding can be obtained by providing a local 'shear key' at the base of the footing, as is sometimes done in foundations for retaining walls. Such a 'shear key' serving as *construction joint*, may also be provided at the interface of the wall/column and the footing, thereby facilitating the transfer of horizontal shear forces (due to lateral loads) at the base of the wall/column.

† Against overturning, the Code (Cl.1 20.1) permits a reduced minimum factor of safety of 1.2 if the overturning moment is entirely due to dead loads. However, it is advisable to apply a uniform minimum factor safety of 1.4 in all cases of loading.

The restoring moment, counterbalancing the overturning moment due to lateral/eccentric loads is generally derived from the weight of the footing plus backfill. In some cases, this may call for footings with large base area [refer Fig. 14.4(b)] and large depths of foundation. However, in cases where the overturning moment (not due to wind or earthquake) is not reversible, the problem can be more economically solved by suitably making the column/wall eccentric to the centre of the footing [refer Fig. 14.4(c)].

Another possibility, relatively rare in practice, is the case of *pullout* of a foundation supporting a tension member. Such a situation is encountered, for example, in an overhead tank (or silo) structure (supported on multiple columns), subjected to a very severe lateral wind load. Under minimal gravity load conditions (tank empty), the windward columns are likely to be under tension, with the result that the forces acting on these column foundations will tend to pull out the column-footing from the soil. The counteracting forces, comprising the self-weight of the footing and the weight of the overburden, should be sufficiently large to prevent such a 'pullout'. If the tensile forces are excessive, it may be necessary to resort to *tension piles* for proper anchorage.

14.4 General Design Considerations and Code Requirements

14.4.1 Factored Soil Pressure at Ultimate Limit State

As mentioned earlier, the area of a footing is fixed on the basis of the allowable bearing pressure q_a and the applied loads and moments under service load conditions (with *partial load factors* applicable for the 'serviceability limit state†'). Once the base area of the footing is determined, the subsequent structural design of the footing is done for the *factored loads*, using the partial load factors applicable for the 'ultimate limit state'. In order to compute the factored moments, shears, etc., acting at critical sections of the footing, a factored soil pressure q_u, corresponding to the factored loads, should be considered.

It may further be noted that the soil pressure which induces moments and shears in the footing base slab are due to the *net pressure* q_{net}, i.e., excluding the pressure induced by the weight ΔP of the footing and the backfill (which are uniformly distributed). This net pressure is due to the concentrated load on the column (from the superstructure) and the moments at the base of the column (or pedestal), if any, as shown in Fig. 14.7. Using *gross pressures* instead of *net pressures* will result in needlessly conservative designs. The 'factored net soil pressure' q_u to be considered in the design of the footing at the limit state is obtainable from the factored loads on the column (P_u, M_u) as shown in Fig. 14.7(b).

14.4.2 General Design Considerations

The major design considerations in the structural design of a footing relate to *flexure*, *shear* (both one-way and two-way action), *bearing* and *bond* (development length). In these aspects, the design procedures are similar to those for beams and two-way slabs supported on columns. Additional considerations involve the transfer of force from the column/pedestal to the footing, and in cases where horizontal forces are involved, safety against sliding and overturning.

† As mentioned in Section 3.6.3, the partial load factor may be taken as unity in general – except for the load combination *DL* + *LL* + *WL*/*EL*, where a partial load factor of 0.8 is applicable for live loads (*LL*) and for wind loads (*WL*)/earthquake loads (*EL*).

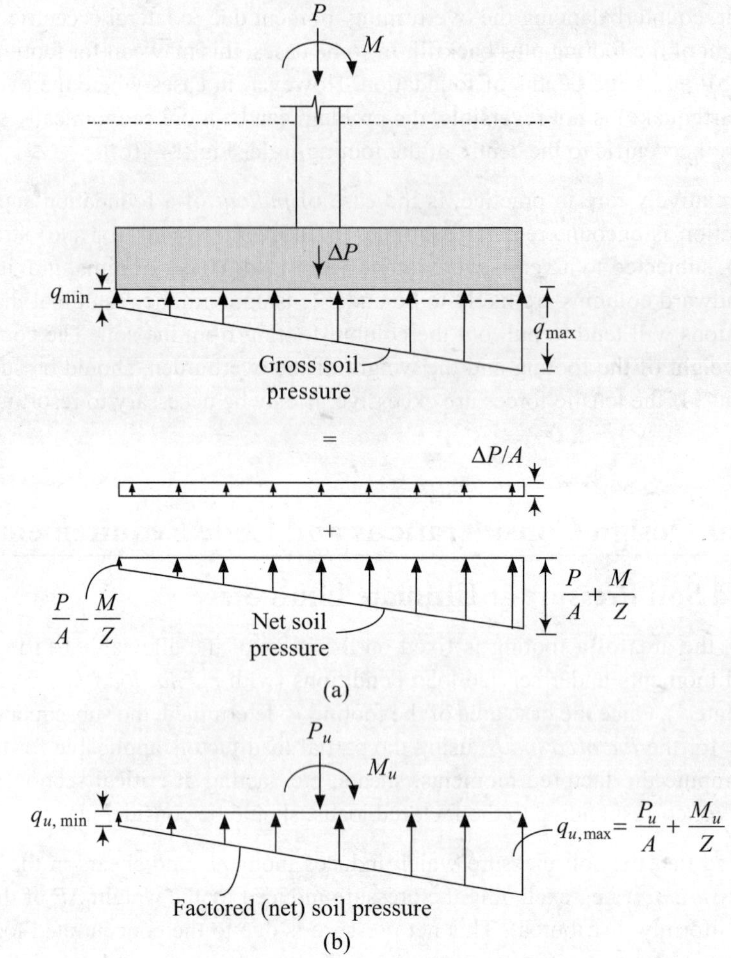

Fig. 14.7 Net soil pressure causing stresses in a footing.

> For footings, deflection control is not a consideration. However, being buried underground, crack control and ensuring protection of reinforcements are important.

Deflection control is not a consideration in the design of footings which are buried underground (and hence not visible). However, control of crack-width and protection of reinforcement by adequate cover are important serviceability considerations, particularly in aggressive environments. It is considered sufficient to limit the crack-width to 0.3 mm in a majority of footings, and for this, the general detailing requirements will serve the purpose (of crack-width control) [Ref. 14.1].

The strut-and-tie model (see Section 17.2 and Example 17.2) may be more appropriate for the design of footings which are relatively deep (clear span to depth ratio < 2.0) and pedestals.

> Although the minimum cover prescribed in the Code (Cl. 26.4.2.2) is 50 mm, it is desirable to provide a clear cover of 75 mm to the flexural reinforcement in all footings.

14.4.3 Thickness of Footing Base Slab

The thickness of a footing base slab is generally based on considerations of shear and flexure, which are critical near the column location. Generally, shear considerations predominate, and the thickness is based on shear criteria. However, in some cases, the minimum thickness may be governed by the development length requirement of the reinforcement from the supported member.

Except in the case of small footings, it is economical to vary the thickness from a minimum at the edge to a maximum near the face of the column, in keeping with the variations in bending moment and shear force. This may be achieved either by sloping the top face of the base slab or by providing a stepped footing.

In any case, the Code (Cl. 34.1.2) restricts the minimum thickness at the edge of the footing to 150 mm for footings in general (and to 300 mm in the case of pile caps). This is done to ensure that the footing has sufficient rigidity to provide the calculated bearing pressures. A 'levelling course' of lean concrete (about 100 mm thick) is usually provided below the footing base.

14.4.4 Design for Shear

It is common practice to design footings without shear reinforcement. Therefore, the minimum thickness (depth) of the footing base slab is most often dictated by the need to check shear stress, and for this reason, the design for shear usually precedes the design for flexure.

Both one-way shear and two-way shear ('punching shear') need to be considered in general [refer Cl. 34.2.4.1 of the Code]. However, in wall footings [Fig. 14.1(d)] and combined footings provided with a central beam [Fig. 14.1(b)], the base slab is subjected to one-way bending, and for this reason, need to be designed for one-way shear alone. The critical section for one-way shear is taken, as for beams, at a distance *d* (effective depth) from the face of the column/pedestal [Fig. 14.8(a)] or wall/beam [Fig. 14.8(d)]. The effective area resisting one-way shear may be rectangular or polygonal, depending on whether the footing is flat [Fig. 14.8(a)] or sloped [Fig. 14.8(c)].

The behaviour of footings in two-way (punching) shear is identical to that of a two-way flat slab supported on columns, discussed in Chapter 11. The critical section for two-way shear is taken at a distance $d/2$ from the periphery of the column, as shown in Fig. 14.8(b), (c).

The design procedures for one-way and two-way shear are identical to those discussed in Chapters 6 and 11, respectively. However, shear reinforcement is generally avoided in footing slabs, and the factored shear force V_u is kept below the factored shear resistance of the concrete V_{uc}[†] by providing the necessary depth. Where, for some reason, there is a restriction on the depth of the footing base slab on account of which $V_u > V_{uc}$, appropriate shear reinforcement should be designed and provided, to resist the excess shear $V_u - V_{uc}$.

Finally, it may be noted that in the case of a column/pedestal with a circular or octagonal cross-section, the Code (Cl. 34.2.2) recommends that an equivalent square section should be considered, for the purpose of locating the critical sections for shear (and moment). The equivalent squares should be inscribed *within* the perimeter of the round or octagonal column or pedestal.

† For the purpose of calculating the design shear strength τ_c of concrete, a nominal percentage of flexural tensile reinforcement ($p_t = 0.25$) may be assumed (in preliminary calculations).

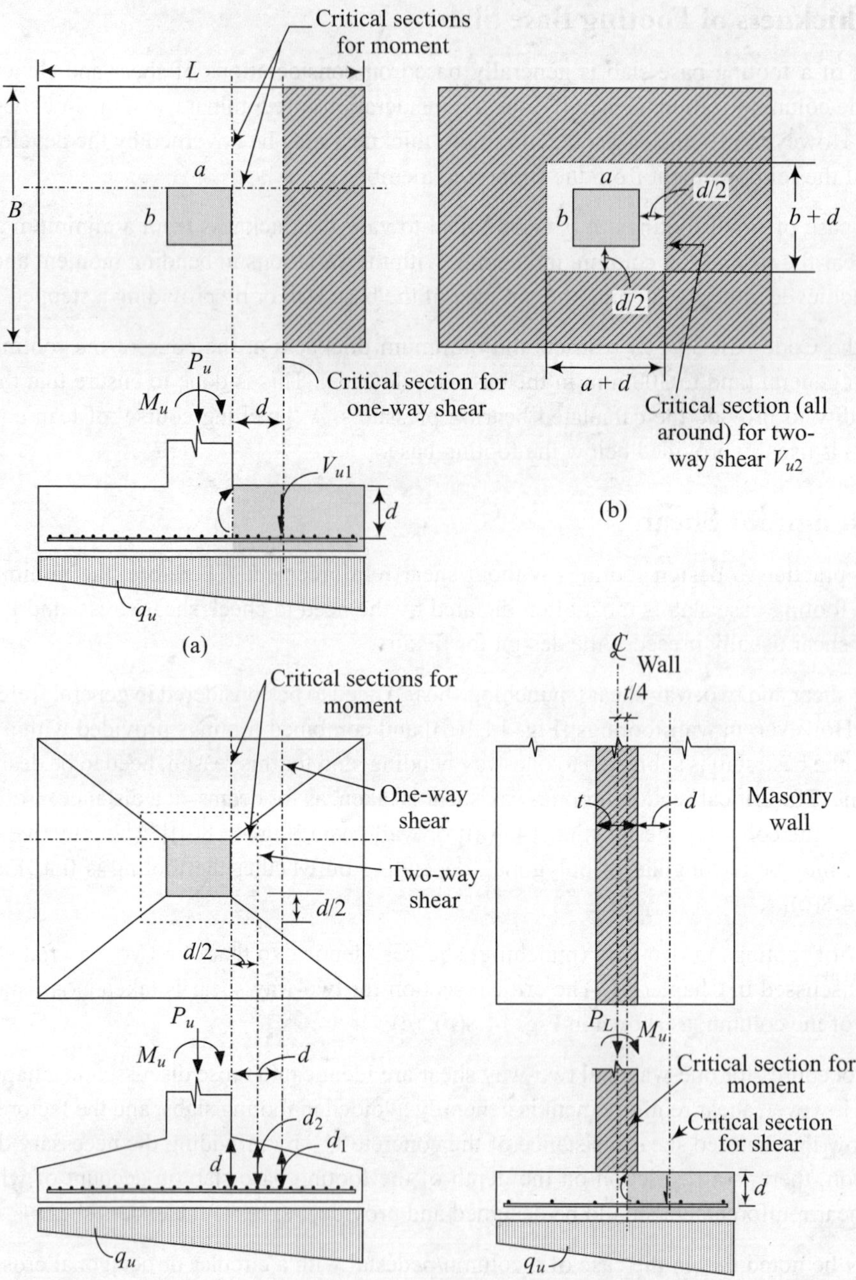

Fig. 14.8 Critical sections for shear and moment.

14.4.5 Design for Flexure

As mentioned earlier, the footing base slab bends upward into a saucer-like shape on account of the net soil pressure q_u from below [Fig. 14.8(a)]. Based on extensive tests, it has been determined that the footing base slab may be designed against flexure by considering the bending moment at a critical section defined as a straight section passing through

- the face of a column, pedestal or wall for a footing supporting a concrete column, pedestal or wall [Fig. 14.8(a)];and
- halfway between the face and centreline of the wall for a footing supporting masonry wall [Fig. 14.8(d)].

In one-way reinforced footings (such as wall footings), the flexural reinforcement (calculated for the moment at the critical section) is placed perpendicular to the wall at a uniform spacing. In the perpendicular direction (along the length of the wall), nominal *distributor* reinforcement should be provided – mainly to account for secondary moments due to Poisson effect and possible differential settlement, and also to take care of shrinkage and temperature effects.

In two-way reinforced square footings also, flexural reinforcement may be placed at a uniform spacing in both directions. In two-way reinforced rectangular footings, the reinforcement in the long direction is uniformly spaced across the full width of the footing, but in the short direction, the Code (Cl. 34.3.1c) requires a larger concentration of reinforcement, as given by Eq. 14.5, to be provided within a central band of width equal to the width B of the footing, or equal to the length of the supported column or wall, whichever is greater:

$$\text{Reinforcement in central band width} = A_{st,\text{short}} \times \frac{2}{\beta + 1} \tag{14.5}$$

where

$A_{st,\text{short}} \equiv$ total flexural reinforcement required in the short direction

and $\beta \equiv$ ratio of the long side (L) to the short side (B) of the footing.

This reinforcement is to be uniformly distributed within the central band width (equal to width B), and the remainder of the reinforcement distributed uniformly in the outer portions of the footing, as shown in Fig. 14.9. This is done to account (approximately) for the observed variation of the transverse bending moment along the length of the footing. However, to expedite fieldwork and minimize the possibility of errors, it is desirable to space the bars in the short direction also *uniformly throughout* by increasing the amount of reinforcement in the two outer portions (i.e., provide the spacing worked out for the central band in the outer portions also; the increase will only be marginal in most cases).

These special detailing requirements are strictly intended for footings with uniform slab thickness. In the case of sloped footings, it usually suffices to provide uniformly distributed reinforcement in the short direction also, as the reduced bending moment in the outer portions is coupled with reduced effective depths in these regions. In the long direction also, the common practice is to provide uniformly spaced reinforcement throughout the width of the footing, despite the variations in depth.

In general, the percentage flexural reinforcement requirement in footing base slabs is low, owing to the relatively large thickness provided on shear considerations. At any rate, the reinforcement should not be less than the minimum prescribed for slabs [refer Chapter 5], unless the footing is designed as a plain concrete (pedestal) footing. Furthermore, the percentage reinforcement provided should be adequate to mobilise the required one-way shear strength in concrete.

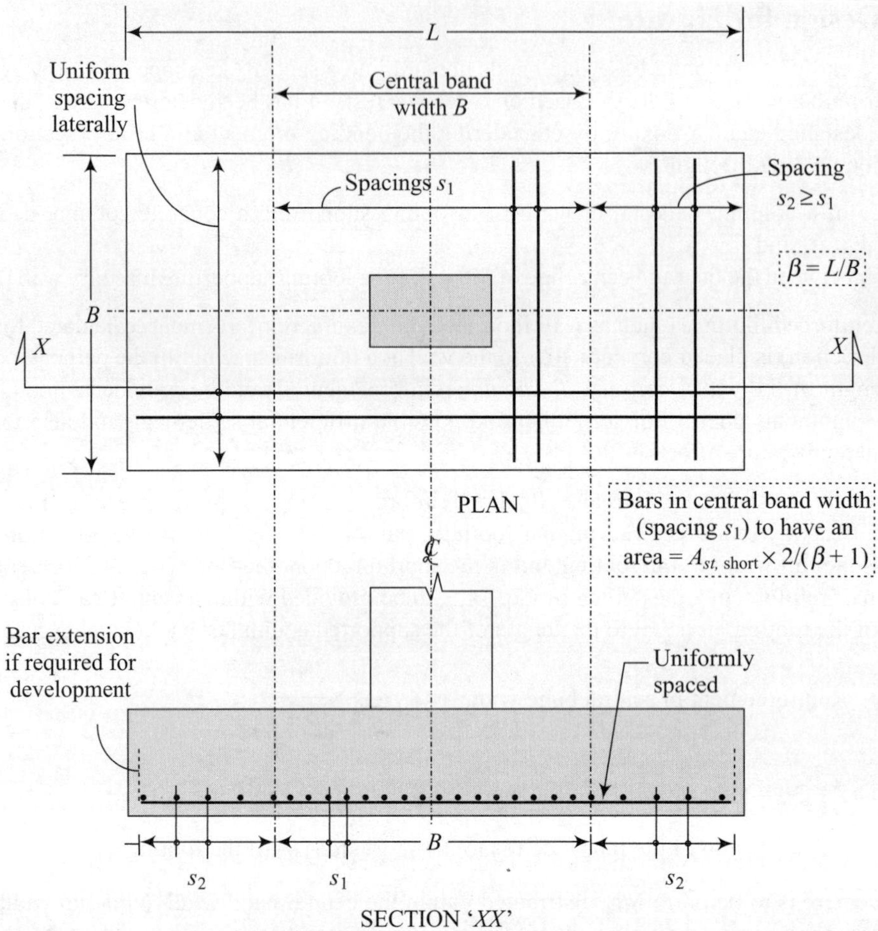

Fig. 14.9 Detailing of flexural reinforcement in a rectangular footing with uniform thickness.

It is advisable to select small bar diameters with small spacings, in order to reduce crack widths and development length requirements.

Development length requirements for flexural reinforcement in a footing should be satisfied at the sections of maximum moment, and also at other sections where the depth is altered. Shortfall in required development length can be made up by bending up the bars near the edges of the footings. This may be required in footings with small plan dimensions.

Furthermore, the longitudinal reinforcement in the column/pedestal must also have the required development length, measured from the interface between the column/pedestal and the footing. When the column is subjected to compression alone (without the bars being subject to tension), it is possible to achieve a full transfer of forces from the column/pedestal to the footing by *bearing*, as discussed in the next section (Section 14.4.6). Where this is not possible, and the transfer of force is accomplished by reinforcement, such reinforcement must also have adequate development length on each side.

14.4.6 Transfer of Forces at Column Base

All forces (axial force, moment) acting at the base of the column[†] (or pedestal) must be transferred to the footing either by compression in concrete or by tension/compression in reinforcing steel. The force transfer achieved through compression in concrete at the interface is limited by the *bearing* resistance of concrete for *either* surface (i.e., supported surface or supporting surface). Under factored loads, the maximum bearing stress $f_{br,\max}$ is limited by the Code (Cl. 34.4) to

$$f_{br,\max} = 0.45 f_{ck} \sqrt{A_1 / A_2} \tag{14.6}$$

where A_2 is the loaded area at the column base, and A_1 the maximum area of the portion of the *supporting* surface that is geometrically similar to and concentric with the loaded area. In the case of stepped or sloping footings, the area A_1 is to be taken as that of the lower base of the largest frustum of a pyramid (or cone) contained wholly within the footing (with area A_2 on top) with a side slope of 1 in 2, as shown in Fig. 14.10(a). The factor $\sqrt{A_1/A_2}$ in Eq. 14.6 allows for the increase in concrete strength in the bearing area in the footing due to confinement offered by the surrounding concrete. This factor $\sqrt{A_1/A_2}$ is limited to 2.0. A limitation on the bearing stress is imposed because very high axial compressive stresses give rise to transverse tensile strains which may lead to spalling, lateral splitting or bursting of concrete. This possibility, however, can be countered by providing suitable transverse and confinement reinforcement.

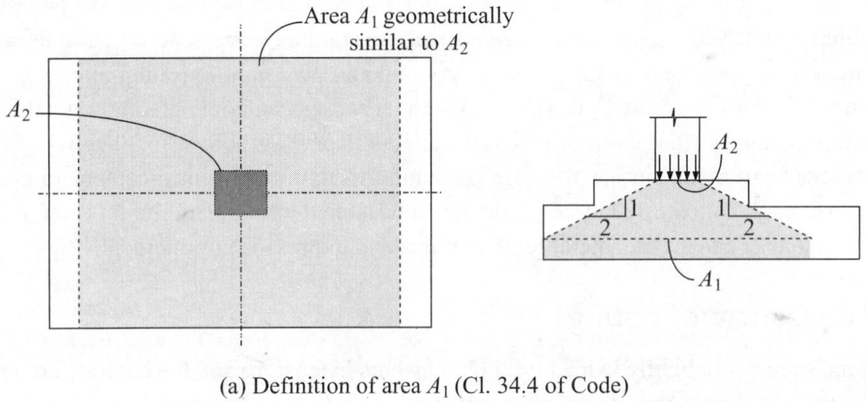

(a) Definition of area A_1 (Cl. 34.4 of Code)

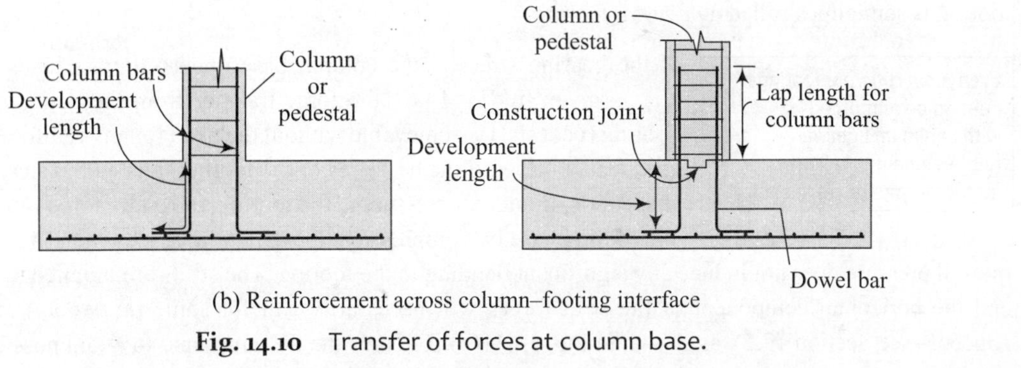

(b) Reinforcement across column–footing interface

Fig. 14.10 Transfer of forces at column base.

[†] This is equally applicable in the case of force transfer from the column base to the pedestal (if provided) and from the pedestal base to the footing.

It should be noted that $f_{br,max}$ may be governed by the bearing resistance of the concrete in the column at the interface (for which $\sqrt{A_1/A_2}$ is obviously unity), rather than that of the concrete in the footing (for which $1 < \sqrt{A_1/A_2} \leq 2$). If the actual compressive stress exceeds $f_{br,max}$, then the excess force is transferred by reinforcement, dowels or mechanical connectors. For transferring a moment at the column base (involving *tension* in the reinforcement), it may be necessary to provide the same amount of reinforcement in the footing as in the column, although some relief in the compression reinforcement is obtainable on account of transfer through bearing. This may be achieved by either continuing the column/pedestal bars into the footing or by providing separate *dowel bars* across the interface as depicted in Fig. 14.10(b). The diameter of dowels should not exceed the diameter of the column bars by 3 mm. Furthermore, the reinforcement provided across the interface must comprise at least four bars, with a total area not less than 0.5 percent of the cross-sectional area of the supported column or pedestal [refer Cl. 34.4.3 of the Code].

Finally, it should be ensured that all reinforcement provided across the interface (whether by extension of column bars or dowels) must have the necessary development length in compression or tension, (as applicable) on both sides of the interface.

Pedestals are used when the bearing stratum is deep below the finished ground floor level and the column is not extended to the top of the footing. These are very short compression members and may be designed as columns while checking bearing and the minimum reinforcement. Lateral support for the pedestal is usually provided by plinth beams/slab at ground level and the surrounding soil. Where pedestals are provided, and full force transfer is possible at the interface of column and pedestal, no reinforcement is theoretically required in the pedestal. However, the Code (Cl. 26.5.3.1h) specifies that nominal longitudinal reinforcement (i.e., in a direction parallel to the column load) of not less than 0.15 percent of the cross-sectional area should be provided, for reasons similar to those pertaining to minimum reinforcement in columns [refer Section 13.3.3]. Although not required by the code, it is advisable to provide minimum (nominal) transverse reinforcement also to take care of the lateral tensile strains and to provide confinement.

14.4.7 Plain Concrete Footings

When the column is relatively lightly loaded (without any bars in tension) and the base area requirement of a footing is relatively low, it may be economical to provide a simple plain concrete block as a footing. Such a footing is sometimes called a *pedestal footing*.

> Even *plain concrete* footings need to be reinforced with minimum nominal reinforcement to take care of tie-forces and for crack control.

If the bearing stress at the column base under ultimate loads is less than $f_{br,max}$ (given by Eq. 14.6), the force transfer from the column base to the footing (pedestal) is achievable without the need for any reinforcement at the interface. Further, if the base area of the footing falls within a certain zone of dispersion of internal pressure in the footing, the entire force is transmitted to the footing base by compression† (*strut action*, as shown in Fig. 14.11a), and the soil pressure does not induce any significant bending in the footing. The struts are inclined to the vertical, and the horizontal component of the strut forces will necessarily call for some *tie action* ('strut and tie' concept– see Section 17.2), as shown in Fig. 14.11(b). To carry the tie forces and to avoid possible cracking

† This is only a convenient idealisation; the actual state of stress is difficult to assess.

of concrete due to the resulting tensile forces, it is necessary to provide some minimum reinforcement to serve as effective ties [Fig. 14.11(b)]. An example of the design of a footing by the strut-and-tie method is presented in Chapter 17 (Example 17.2).

Although, the Code does not specify the need for any reinforcement, a minimum reinforcement is necessary, not only for tie action, but also to provide resistance against temperature and shrinkage effects.

For the purpose of defining this zone of dispersion of internal pressure in the footing, thereby enabling the determination of the required thickness of the footing block, the Code (Cl. 34.1.3) defines an angle α between the plane through the bottom edge of the footing and the corresponding edge of the column at the interface [Fig. 14.9], such that

$$\tan\alpha \geq 0.9\sqrt{100q_{max}/f_{ck}+1} \quad (14.7)$$

where q_{max} is the maximum soil pressure under service loads, as defined earlier [Eq. 14.2a, Fig. 14.4a].

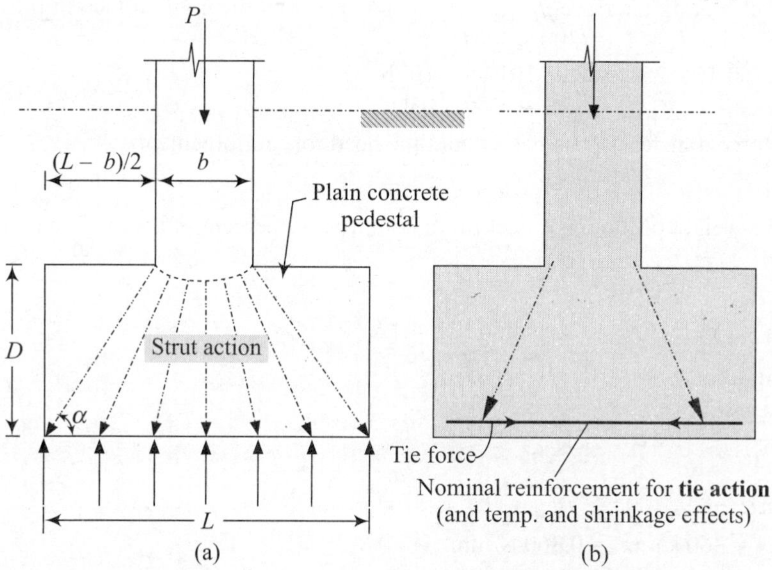

Fig. 14.11 Plain concrete (pedestal) footing.

An expression for the thickness D of the footing block is obtainable [Fig. 14.11] as:

$$D = (L-b)(\tan\alpha)/2$$

$$\Rightarrow \quad D \geq 0.9\sqrt{100q_{max}/f_{ck}+1}\,(L-b)/2 \quad (14.8)$$

where b is the width of the column and the expression for $\tan\alpha$ in Eq. 14.7 governs the minimum thickness of the footing.

The design of a plain concrete footing is demonstrated in Example 14.1.

14.5 Design Examples of Isolated and Wall Footings

Example 14.1 *Design of a plain concrete footing*

Design a plain concrete footing for a column, 300 mm × 300 mm, carrying an axial load of 330 kN (under service loads, due to dead and live loads). Assume an allowable soil bearing pressure of 360 kN/m² at a depth of 1.0 m below ground. Assume M25 concrete and Fe 500 steel.

Solution

Transfer of axial force at base of column

- In order to provide a plain concrete block footing, full force transfer must be possible at the column base, without the need for reinforcement at the interface. That is, the factored axial load P_u must be less than the limiting bearing resistance F_{br}.
- Assuming a load factor of 1.5, $P_u = 330 \times 1.5 = 495$ kN

  Limiting bearing stress $f_{br,\,max} = 0.45 f_{ck}\sqrt{A_1/A_2}$

  At the column-footing interface, $f_{br,\,max}$ will be governed by the column face in this case (and not the footing face), with $A_1 = A_2 = (300 \times 300)$ mm²

  $$\Rightarrow \quad F_{br} = 0.45 \times 25 \times 300^2 = 1012.5 \times 10^3 \text{ N}$$
  $$> P_u = 495 \text{ kN}$$

  Hence, full force transfer is possible without the need for reinforcement.

Size of footing

- Assuming the weight of footing + backfill to comprise 10 percent of the axial load, base area required

  $$= \frac{330 \times 1.1}{360} = 1.01 \text{ m}^2$$

  Provide 1 m × 1 m footing, as shown in Fig. 4.12.

Thickness of footing

- $$D = \left(\frac{1000 - 300}{2}\right) \tan\alpha$$

  where $\tan\alpha \geq 0.9\sqrt{100 q_{max}/f_{ck} + 1}$

  $q_{max} = 360 \text{ kN/m}^2 = 0.360 \text{ N/mm}^2$

  $f_{ck} = 25 \text{ N/mm}^2$

  $$\Rightarrow \quad D \geq 350 \times 0.9\sqrt{100 \times 0.36/25 + 1}$$
  $$= 492 \text{ mm}$$

  Provide 500 mm.

  Hence, provide a concrete block 1000 × 1000 × 500 mm.
- Further, it is necessary to provide minimum reinforcement to provide for 'tie action', and to account for temperature and shrinkage effects:

  $$A_{st,min} = 0.0012BD = 0.0012 \times 1000 \times 500 = 600 \text{ mm}^2$$

  Provide 6–12 mm ϕ bars ($A_{st} = 678$ mm²) both ways with a clear cover of 75 mm, as shown in Fig. 4.12. The spacing is within limits (< 5d or 450 mm).

Check gross base pressure

- Assuming unit weight of concrete and soil as 24 kN/m^3 and 18 kN/m^3 respectively,

$$\text{actual gross soil pressure } q_{max} = \frac{330}{1.0 \times 1.0} + (24 \times 0.50) + (18 \times 0.50)$$
$$= 330.0 + 12.0 + 9.0$$
$$= 351.0 \text{ kN/m}^2$$
$$< q_a = 360 \text{ kN/m}^2 \text{ — Hence, safe.}$$

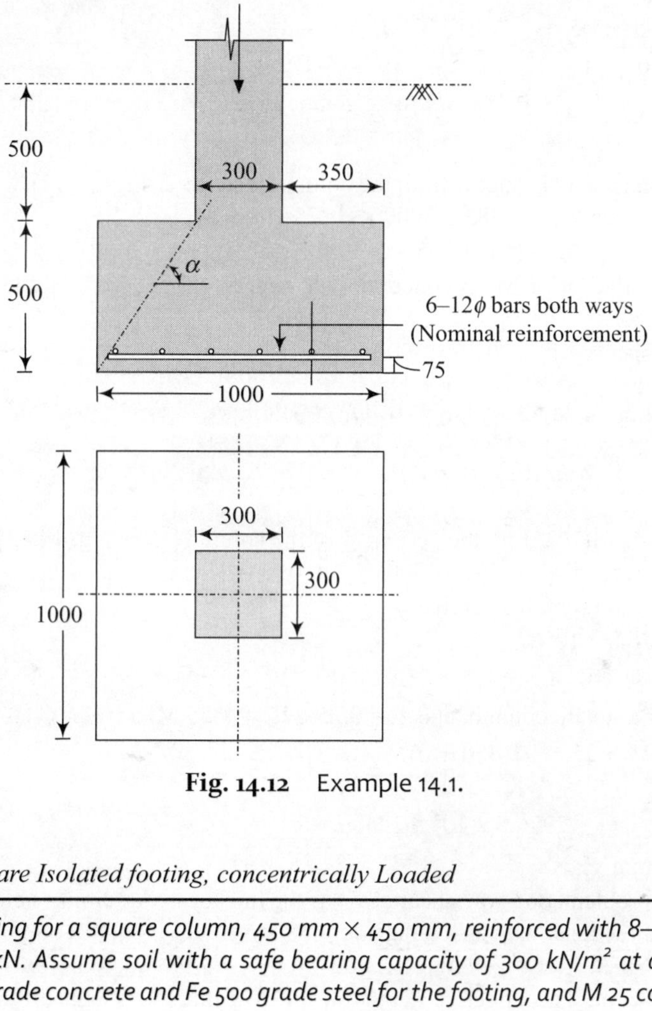

Fig. 14.12 Example 14.1.

Example 14.2 *Square Isolated footing, concentrically Loaded*

Design an isolated footing for a square column, 450 mm × 450 mm, reinforced with 8–25 ϕ bars, and carrying a service load of 2300 kN. Assume soil with a safe bearing capacity of 300 kN/m^2 at a depth of 1.5 m below ground. Assume M 25 grade concrete and Fe 500 grade steel for the footing, and M 25 concrete and Fe500 steel for the column.

Solution

Size of footing

- *Given*: $P = 2300$ kN, $q_a = 300$ kN/m^2 at $h = 1.5$ m

Assuming the weight of the footing + backfill to be 10%[†] of the load $P = 2300$ kN,

base area required $= \dfrac{2300 \times 1.1}{300} = 8.43 \text{ m}^2$

$\Rightarrow$ Minimum size of square footing $= \sqrt{8.43} = 2.904$ m

Assume a 3 m × 3 m footing base

Thickness of footing slab based on shear

- Net soil pressure at ultimate loads (assuming a load factor of 1.5)

$$q_u = \frac{2300 \times 1.5}{3.0 \times 3.0} = 383 \text{ kN/m}^2$$
$$= 0.383 \text{ N/mm}^2$$

(a) One-way shear

- The critical section is at a distance d from the column face [refer Fig. 14.13].

$\Rightarrow$ Factored shear force $V_{u1} = 0.383 \times 3000 \times (1275 - d)$

$= (1464{,}975 - 1149d)$ N

Assuming $\tau_c = 0.36$ MPa(for M 25 concrete with, say, $p_t = 0.25$) [refer Table 6.1 or Table 13 of the Code],

One-way shear resistance $V_{c1} = 0.36 \times 3000 \times d$

$= (1080d)$ N

$$V_{u1} \le V_{c1} \Rightarrow 1464975 - 1149d \le 1080d$$
$$\Rightarrow \quad d \ge 658 \text{ mm}$$

(b) Two-way shear

- The critical section is at $d/2$ from the periphery of the column [refer Fig. 14.13]

$\Rightarrow$ Factored shear force $V_{u2} = 0.383 \times [3000^2 - (450 + d)^2]$

Assuming $d = 658$ mm (obtained earlier[‡])

$$V_{u2} = 2976.8 \times 10^3 N$$

Two-way shear resistance $V_{c2} = k_s \tau_c \times [4 \times (450 + d)d]$

where $k_s = 1.0$ for a square column, and $\tau_c = 0.25\sqrt{25} = 1.25$ MPa (refer Cl. 31.6.3.1 of the Code)

$$\Rightarrow \quad V_{c2} = 1.0 \times 1.25 \times 4d\,(450 + d)$$
$$= (2250d + 5d^2) \text{ N}$$
$$V_{u2} \le V_{c2} \quad \Rightarrow \quad 2976.8 \times 10^3 \le 2250d + 5d^2$$

Solving, $d \ge 579$ mm

- Evidently, in this problem, one-way shear governs the thickness. Assuming a clear cover of 75 mm and 16ϕ bars in both directions, with an average $d = 658$ mm,

thickness $D \ge 658 + 75 + 16 = 749$ mm

Provide $\boldsymbol{D}$ **= 750 mm**. The effective depths in the two directions will differ by one bar diameter, which is not significant in relatively deep square footings. For the purpose of flexural reinforcement calculations, an average value of d may be assumed:

$$\Rightarrow \quad d = 750 - 75 - 16 = \mathbf{659 \text{ mm}}$$

[†] This assumption is verified subsequently.

[‡] Actual effective depth provided cannot be less than this value; hence, the use of this value in this context can only be on a slightly conservative side; such an assumption simplifies calculations.

- Assuming unit weights of concrete and soil as 24 kN/m^3 and 18 kN/m^3 respectively, actual gross pressure at footing base (under service loads)

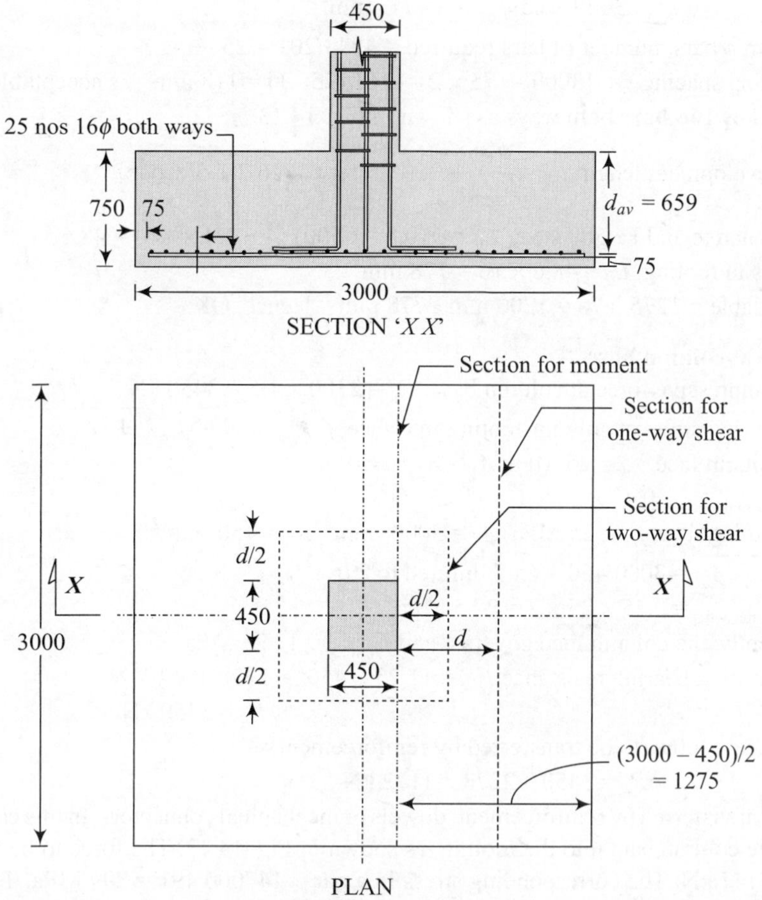

Fig. 14.13 Example 14.2.

$$q = 2300/(3.0 \times 3.0) + (24 \times 0.75) + (18 \times 0.75) = 287 \text{ kN/m}^2 < 300 \text{ kN/m}^2 \text{ – OK.}$$

Design of flexural reinforcement

- Factored moment at column face (in either direction):

$$M_u = 0.383 \times 3000 \times 1275^2/2 = 933.9 \times 10^6 \text{ Nmm}$$

$$\Rightarrow \quad R \equiv \frac{M_u}{Bd^2} = \frac{933.9 \times 10^6}{3000 \times 659^2} = 0.717 \text{ MPa}$$

$$\Rightarrow \quad \frac{(p_t)_{\text{reqd}}}{100} = \frac{25}{2 \times 500}\left[1 - \sqrt{1 - 4.598 \times 0.717/25}\right] = 0.171 \times 10^{-2}$$

$$A_{st,\min} = 0.0012BD = 0.0012 \times 3000 \times 750 = 2700 \text{ mm}^2$$

$$\Rightarrow \quad p_{t,\min} = 100 \times 2700/(3000 \times 659) = 0.137 < 0.171$$

- However, this reinforcement is less than assumed for one-way shear design[†], ($\tau_c = 0.36$ MPa).

  for which $p_t = 0.25$ (for M25 concrete)

  $\Rightarrow \quad A_{st,reqd} = 0.25 \times 3000 \times 659/100 = 4943 \text{ mm}^2$

  Using 16 mm ϕ bars, number of bars required = 4943/201 = 25

  [corresponding spacing $s = \{3000 - (75 \times 2) - 16\}/(25 - 1) = 118$ mm – is acceptable.]

  Provide 25 nos 16ϕ bars both ways as shown in Fig. 14.13

  Required development length $L_d = \dfrac{\phi(0.87 f_y)}{4\tau_{bd}}$ [refer Cl. 26.2.1 of Code]

  For M 25 concrete and Fe 500 steel, $L_d = \phi\,(0.87 \times 500)/(4 \times 1.4 \times 1.6) = 48.6\phi$

  For 16ϕ bars in footing, $L_d = 48.6 \times 16 = 778$ mm

  Length available = 1275 – 75 = 1200 mm >778 mm – Hence, OK.

Transfer of force at column base

- Factored compressive force at column base: $P_u = 2300 \times 1.5 = 3450$ kN

  Limiting bearing stress at column-footing interface, $f_{br,\max} = 0.45 f_{ck}\sqrt{A_1/A_2}$.

  (i) for column face, $f_{ck} = 25$ MPa, $A_1 = A_2 = 450^2 \text{ mm}^2$

  $\Rightarrow f_{br,\max-col} = 0.45 \times 25 \times 1 = 11.25$ MPa

  (ii) for footing face, $f_{ck} = 25$ MPa, $A_1 = 3000^2 \text{ mm}^2$, $A_2 = 450^2 \text{ mm}^2$

  $\Rightarrow \sqrt{A_1/A_2} = 3000/450 = 6.67$, limited to 2.0

  $\Rightarrow f_{br,\max\text{-}ftg} = 0.45 \times 25 \times 2 = 22.5$ MPa

  Evidently, the column face governs, and $f_{br,\max} = 11.25$ MPa

  $\Rightarrow$ Limiting bearing resistance $F_{br} = 11.25 \times 450^2 = 2278.1 \times 10^3$ N

  $< P_u = 3450$ kN

  $\Rightarrow$ Excess force (to be transferred by reinforcement):

  $$\Delta P_u = 3450 - 2278 = 1172 \text{ kN}$$

  This may be transferred by reinforcement, dowels or mechanical connectors. In this case, it is convenient to extend the column bars into the footing, as shown in Fig. 14.13. The force to be transferred per bar = 1172/8 = 147 kN. The corresponding stress in a bar = 147000/491 = 299 MPa. This force has to be developed in the bar through adequate embedment.

  For fully stressed bars in compression (M25, Fe500):

  $$L_d = \frac{\phi(0.87 \times 500)}{4(1.4 \times 1.6 \times 1.25)} = 38.8\phi$$

  $$\Rightarrow \quad \tilde{L}_d = L_d \times (f_s/0.87 f_y)$$
  $$= 38.8 \times 25 \times (299/(0.87 \times 500))$$
  $$= 667 \text{ mm}$$

  Available vertical embedment length in footing (d = 659 mm) < 667mm. As the length available is insufficient, provide two additional 25ϕ bars as dowels, with which the required embedment length becomes 667 × 8/10 = 534 mm < 659 mm available. The bars are bent (with 90° standard bend) into the footing, and may rest directly on the top of the reinforcement layer in the footing, as shown in Fig. 14.13.

[†] Unless the footing dimensions are revised (to result in less shear stress), the reinforcement requirement here will be governed by shear strength requirements, and not flexural strength requirements. In a practical design, this should be investigated.

Alternative Design

- Providing a uniform thickness of 750 mm for the footing slab is rather uneconomical, as such a high thickness is required essentially near the face of the column (due to shear considerations); the effective depth requirement falls off with increasing distance from the critical section for one-way shear; theoretically, only a minimum thickness (150 mm, specified by the Code) need be provided at the edge of the footing.
- However, the slope provided at the top of the footing should preferably not exceed about 1 in 1.5 (i.e., 1 vertical : 1.5 horizontal), as a steeper slope will require the use of additional formwork on top (to prevent the concrete from sliding down).
- As the thickness of the footing near the column base is governed by shear (one-way shear, in this example) and the effective area available at the critical section is a truncated rectangle, the effective depth required is slightly larger than that for a flat footing.
- Assuming a thickness D = 750 mm up to a distance of 660 mm (> d = 659 mm) from the periphery of the column; and providing a slope of 1 in 1.5 over the remaining distance of 1275 – 660 = 615 mm on all four sides [Fig. 14.14], the edge thickness is obtained as 750 – 615/1.5 = 340 mm

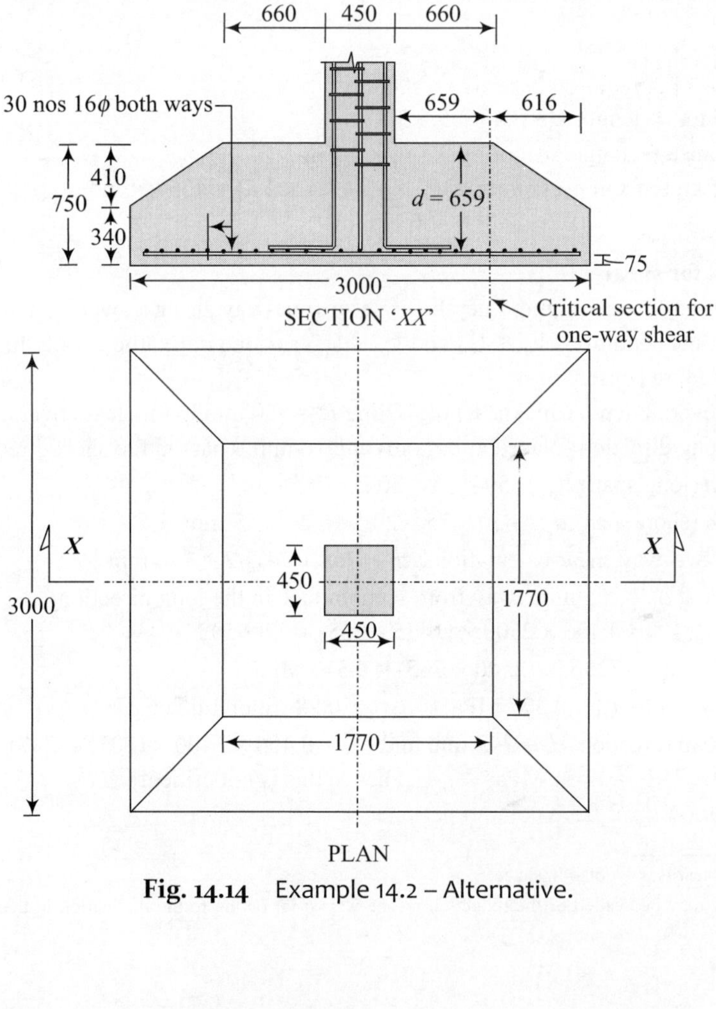

Fig. 14.14 Example 14.2 – Alternative.

⇒ $V_{u1} = 0.383 \times (1275 - 659) \times 3000 = 707784$ N

⇒ $\tau_{v1} = 707784/(3000 \times 659 - 616 \times 410)^{\dagger} = 0.410$ MPa

Providing $p_t = 0.35 \Rightarrow \tau_c = 0.421$ MPa (for M25 concrete) [refer Table 6.1]

$\tau_c > \tau_v$ – Hence, OK.

⇒ $(A_{st})_{reqd} = (0.35/100) \times (3000 \times 659 - 615 \times 410) = 6036$ mm^2

⇒ No. of 16ϕ bars required = 6036/201 = 30 (as shown in Fig. 14.14).

Other alternative designs are possible. These include (i) providing a proper sloped footing with a thickness varying linearly from a minimum at the edge to a maximum‡ at the *face* of the column, and (ii) providing a stepped footing. In the latter case, the section at the step location becomes a critical section at which one-way shear, flexural reinforcement and development length requirements need to be verified.

Example 14.3 *Rectangular Isolated footing, concentrically Loaded*

Redesign the footing for the column in Example 14.2, including a spatial restriction of 2.5 m on one of the plan dimensions of the footing.

Solution

Size of footing

- As in Example 14.2, required base area = 8.43 m^2
  Width B = 2.5 m, ⇒ length L = 8.43/2.5 = 3.37 m
  ⇒ Provide a rectangular footing 3.4 m × 2.5 m.
  ⇒ Net factored soil pressure = 2300 × 1.5/(3.4 × 2.5) = 406 kN/m^2
  = 0.406 N/mm^2

Thickness required for shear

- An exact solution for the required depth for shear (one-way shear as well as two-way shear) may be obtained using the conditions $V_{u1} \le V_{c1}$ and $V_{u2} \le V_{c2}$, as done in Example 14.2. In this example, a trial-and-error procedure is used.
  Assuming an overall depth (thickness) of footing D = 850 mm, with clear cover of 75 mm and 20 mm ϕ bars in the long direction (placed at bottom) and 16 mm ϕ bars in the short direction,
  effective depth (long span) $d_x = 850 - 75 - 20/2 = 765$ mm
  effective depth (short span) $d_y = 850 - 75 - 20 - 16/2 = 747$ mm
  Average d for two-way shear calculations: $d = (765 + 747)/2 = 756$ mm
- One-way shear at d_x = 765 mm away from column face in the long direction:
  $V_{u1} = 0.406 \times 2500 \times (1475 - 765) = 720650$ N
  ⇒ $\tau_{v1} = 720650/(2500 \times 765) = 0.377$ MPa
  For $\tau_c = \tau_{v1} = 0.377$ MPa, $(p_t)_{reqd} = 0.28$ [refer Table 6.1].
  [In the short span direction, d_y = 747 mm and $V_{u1} = 0.406 \times 3400 \times (1025 - 747) = 383751$ N ⇒ τ_{v1} = 383751/(3400 × 747) = 0.151 MPa $\ll \tau_{c,min}$; hence this is not critical].
- Two-way shear (at $d_{av}/2$ from column periphery):

† The area resisting the shear is polygonal in shape.

‡ In this case, advantage may be availed of the reduction in one-way shear owing to the inclination in the compressive force [refer Section 6.4.2].

$$V_{u2} = 0.406 \times [3400 \times 2500 - (450 + 756)^2] = 2860 \times 10^3 \text{ N}$$

$$\Rightarrow \quad \tau_v = 2860 \times 10^3/\{(450 + 756) \times 4 \times 756\} = 0.784 \text{ MPa}$$

$$< k_s\tau_c = 1.0 \times 0.25\sqrt{25} = 1.25 \text{ MPa (refer Cl. 31.6.3.1 of Code). – Hence, OK.}$$

Design of flexural reinforcement

(a) *long direction* (section XX in Fig. 14.15)

- $M_{ux} = 0.406 \times 2500 \times 1475^2/2 = 1104.1 \times 10^6$ Nmm

$$\Rightarrow \quad R \equiv \frac{M_u}{Bd_x^{\,2}} = \frac{1104.1 \times 10^6}{2500 \times 765^2} = 0.755 \text{ MPa}$$

$$\Rightarrow \quad \frac{(p_t)_{\text{reqd}}}{100} = \frac{25}{2 \times 500}\left[1 - \sqrt{1 - 4.598 \times 0.755/25}\right] = 0.18 \times 10^{-2}$$

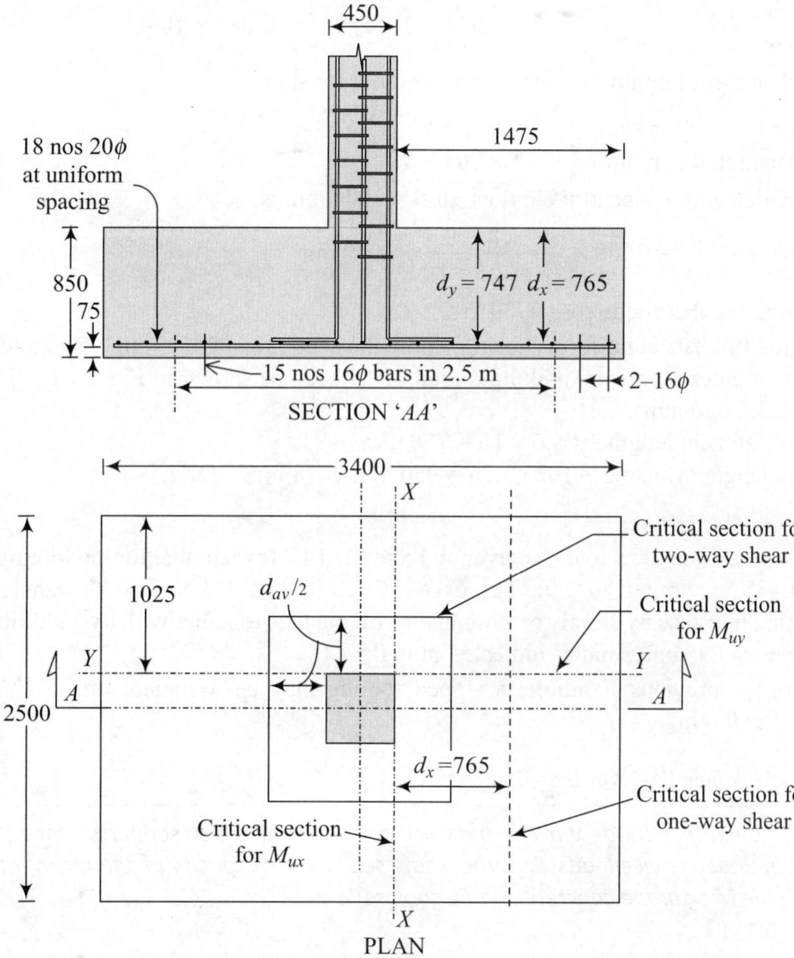

Fig. 14.15 Example 14.3.

- This is less than $p_t = 0.28$ required for one-way shear.

  $\Rightarrow \qquad (A_{st,x})_{reqd} = 0.28 \times 2500 \times 765/100 = 5355 \text{ mm}^2$

  Using 20ϕ bars, number required = 5355/314 = 18

  $\Rightarrow$ Corresponding spacing $s = \{2500 - (75 \times 2) - 20\}/17 = 137$ mm – OK.

  Provide **18 nos 20ϕ** bars at uniform spacing in the long direction.

- Development length required: $L_d = 48.6\phi$ (for M25 concrete, Fe500 steel, as in previous Example)

  $= 48.6 \times 20 = 972$ mm

  Development length available = 1475 – 75 = 1400 mm >972 mm — OK.

(b) *short direction* (section YY in Fig. 14.15)

- $M_{uy} = 0.406 \times 3400 \times 1025^2/2 = 725.1 \times 10^6$ Nmm

  $$\Rightarrow \qquad R \equiv \frac{M_u}{Bd_y^{\,2}} = \frac{725.1 \times 10^6}{3400 \times 747^2} = 0.382 \text{ MPa}$$

  $$\Rightarrow \qquad \frac{(p_t)_{reqd}}{100} = \frac{25}{2 \times 500}\left[1 - \sqrt{1 - 4.598 \times 0.382/25}\right] = 0.089 \times 10^{-2}$$

- This is less than the minimum reinforcement required for slabs:

  $$(A_{st})_{\min} = 0.0012\, bD = 0.0012 \times 3400 \times 850 = 3468 \text{ mm}^2$$

  Using 16ϕ bars, number required = 3468/201 = 18

- A_{st} to be provided within a central band width $B = 2500$ mm is:

  $$3468 \times \frac{2}{\beta + 1} = 3468 \times \frac{2}{(3.4/2.5 + 1)} = 2939 \text{ mm}^2$$

  Using 16ϕ bars, number required = 2939/201 = 15

- Provide **15 nos 16ϕ** bars at uniform spacing within the central band of width 2.5 m, and **2 nos 16ϕ** bars each in the two outer segments; making a total of 19 bars, as shown in Fig. 14.13. The spacings are within limits (3*d*, 300 mm).
- Required development length = $48.6 \times 16 = 778$ mm

  Development length available = 1025 – 75 = 950 mm >778 mm – OK.

Transfer of force at column base

The calculations are identical to those given in Example 14.2 (except that for the footing face, $\sqrt{A_1/A_2}$ = 2500/450 = 5.56, limited to 2.0). The excess force of 1171.9 kN may be transferred across the column-footing interface by simply extending the column bars together with two additional dowel bars, as in the previous Example, and as indicated in Fig. 14.15.

Alternative: As in the previous Example, a sloped footing may be designed; this is likely to be more economical than a flat footing.

Example 14.4 *Masonry Wall footing*

Design a reinforced concrete footing for a 230 mm thick masonry wall which supports a load (inclusive of self-weight) of 200 kN/m under service loads. Assume a safe soil bearing capacity of 150 kN/m² at a depth of 1 m below ground. Assume M 25 grade concrete and Fe 500 grade steel.

Solution

Size of footing

- *Given:* $P = 200$ kN/m, $q_a = 150$ kN/m^2 at a depth of 1 m.

- Assuming the weight of the footing + backfill to constitute 10 percent of the applied load P, and considering a 1 m length of footing along the wall, required width of footing = $\frac{200 \times 1.1}{150}$ = 1.47 m. Provide 1.5 m wide footing.

Thickness of footing based on shear considerations

- Factored net soil pressure (assuming a load factor of 1.5) is:

$$q_u = \frac{200 \times 1.5}{1.5 \times 1.0} = 200 \text{ kN/m}^2 = 0.200 \text{ N/mm}^2$$

- The critical section for (one-way) shear is located at a distance d away from the face of the wall

$$\Rightarrow \quad V_u = 0.200 \times 1000[(1500 - 230)/2 - d]$$
$$= (127000 - 200d) \text{ N}$$

- Assuming nominal flexural reinforcement (p_t = 0.25), τ_c = 0.36 MPa for M25 concrete, the shear resistance of concrete is:

$$V_{uc} = 0.36 \times 1000 \times d = (360d) \text{ N}$$

- $V_u \leq V_{uc} \Rightarrow 127000 - 200d \leq 360d$

$$\Rightarrow \quad d \geq 227 \text{ mm}$$

- Assuming a clear cover of 75 mm and 16ϕ bars,
thickness $D \geq 227 + 75 + 16/2 = 310$ mm
Provide $\boldsymbol{D}$ **= 310 mm** upto a distance of 250 mm from the face of the wall. At the edge of the footing, a minimum thickness of 150 mm may be provided, and the thickness linearly tapered upto 310 mm, as shown in Fig. 14.16.

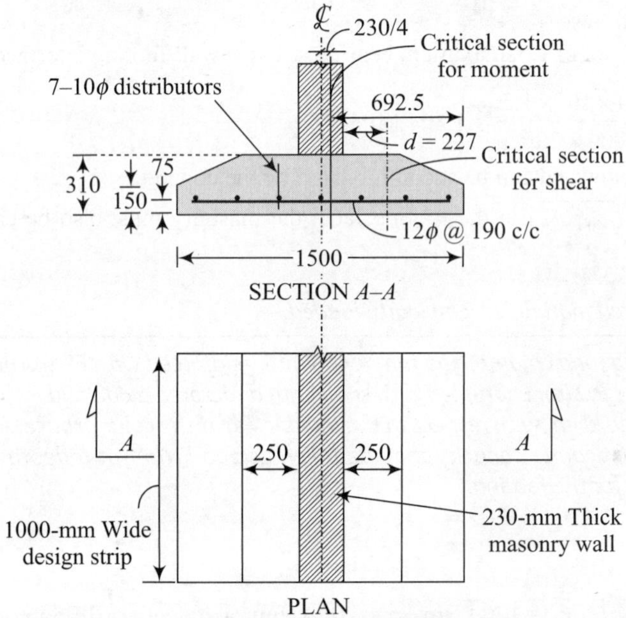

Fig. 14.16 Example 14.4.

Design of flexural reinforcement

- The critical section for maximum moment is located halfway between the centreline and edge of the wall, i.e., at a distance 1500/2 – 230/4 = 692.5 mm from the edge of the footing [refer Fig. 14.6]. Considering a 1 m long footing strip with d = 227 mm,

- $\Rightarrow \quad M_u = 0.200 \times 1000 \times 692.5^2/2 = 48.0$ kNm

$$\Rightarrow \quad R \equiv \frac{M_u}{bd^2} = \frac{48.0 \times 10^6}{1000 \times 227^2} = 0.932 \text{ MPa}$$

$$\Rightarrow \quad \frac{(p_t)}{100} = \frac{25}{2 \times 500}\left[1 - \sqrt{1 - 4.598 \times 0.932/25}\right] = 0.224 \times 10^{-2}$$

which is lesser than the nominal value ($p_t = 0.25$) assumed for τ_c

- $(A_{st})_{reqd} = 0.25 \times 10^{-2} \times 1000 \times 227 = 568$ mm^2 per m length of footing.

$$\Rightarrow \quad \text{Spacing of } 16\phi \text{ bars} = \frac{1000 \times 201}{568} = 353 \text{ mm}$$

$$\text{Spacing of } 12\phi \text{ bars} = \frac{1000 \times 113}{568} = 198 \text{ mm } (< 3d \text{ or } 300 \text{ mm})$$

Provide 12ϕ @ 190 c/c, as shown in Fig. 14.16.

- Development length required = 48.6ϕ (for M 25 concrete, Fe500 steel)
  = 48.6 × 12 = 583 mm†

  Length available = 692.5 – 75 = 617.5 mm >583 mm – OK.

Distributors

Some nominal bars may be provided, to account for possible secondary stresses due to differential settlement.

Provide 10ϕ distributors @ about 200 c/c (7 nos will be adequate) [Fig. 14.16].

Transfer of force at wall base

Assuming a load factor of 1.5, maximum bearing stress at wall/footing interface (loaded area is 230 mm wide)

$$f_{br} = \frac{200 \times 10^3 \times 1.5}{1000 \times 230} = 1.304 \text{ MPa}$$

which is relatively low and can be accommodated by the concrete

[$f_{br,\,max} = 0.45 f_{ck} \sqrt{A_1/A_2}$] in the footing face; the masonry must also be capable of providing this bearing resistance.

Example 14.5 *Isolated footing, eccentrically loaded*

Design an isolated footing for a column, 300 mm × 500 mm, reinforced with 6–25ϕ bars with Fe500 steel and M 25 concrete [refer Fig. 13.14(a), Example 13.5], subject to a factored axial load P_u = 1000 kN and a factored uniaxial moment M_{ux} = 120 kNm (with respect to the major axis) at the column base. Assume that the moment is reversible. The safe soil bearing capacity may be taken as 200 kN/m² at a depth of 1.25 m. Assume M25 concrete and Fe500 steel for the footing.

Solution

Size of footing

- *Given:* P_u = 1000 kN, M_{ux} = 120 kNm, q_a = 200 kN/m^2 at a depth of 1.25 m.
- As the moment is reversible, the footing should be symmetric with respect to the column. Assuming

† This is required with reference to the section of maximum moment. Strictly, development length should also be checked at sections where the thickness is reduced. However, in this case, it can be seen that in the region of tapered thickness, the drop in bending moment (due to cantilever action) is steeper than the drop in effective depth, and hence there is no cause for concern.

the weight of the footing plus backfill to constitute about 15 per cent of P_u, resultant eccentricity of loading at footing base,

$$e = \frac{120 \times 10^3}{1000 \times 1.15}$$

$$= 104 \text{ mm}$$

- Assuming $e < L/6$ (i.e., $L > 6 \times 104 = 624$ mm)

$$\frac{1000 \times 1.15}{BL} + \frac{120}{BL^2/6} \leq (200 \times 1.5^{\dagger}) \text{ kN/m}^2$$

$$\Rightarrow \quad 300BL^2 - 1150L - 720 \leq 0$$

various combinations of width B and length L can satisfy the above equation.

Assuming $B = 1.0 \text{ m} \Rightarrow L \geq 4.381 \text{ m}$

$B = 1.5 \text{ m} \Rightarrow L \geq 3.075 \text{ m}$

$B = 2.0 \text{ m} \Rightarrow L \geq 2.414 \text{ m}$

- An economical proportion of the base slab is generally one in which the projection beyond the face of column (or pedestal) is approximately equal in both directions (for effective two-way behaviour, i.e., $(L - a)/2 \approx (B - b)/2$ [refer Fig. 14.6(a)].
- Provide B = 2000 mm and L = 2450 mm; this gives projection of 850 mm (in the short direction) and 975 mm (in the long direction), as shown in Fig. 14.17.

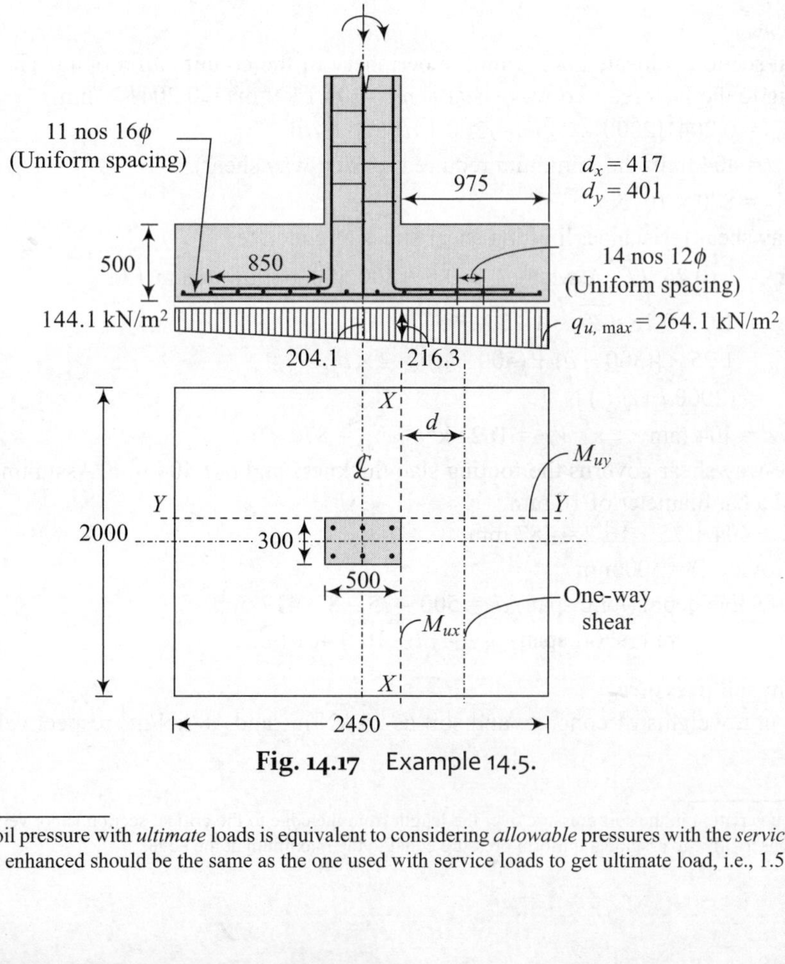

Fig. 14.17 Example 14.5.

---

† Using a *factored* soil pressure with *ultimate* loads is equivalent to considering *allowable* pressures with the *service* loads. However, the factor by which q_a is enhanced should be the same as the one used with service loads to get ultimate load, i.e., 1.5 in this case.

Thickness of footing based on shear

- Factored (net) soil pressure $q_{u,\max} = \dfrac{1000}{2.0 \times 2.45} + \dfrac{120 \times 6}{2.0 \times 2.45^2} = 204.1 + 60.0$
$= 264.1 \text{ kN/m}^2$
- $q_{u,\min} = 204.1 - 60.0 = 144.1 \text{ kN/m}^2$

(*a*) *One-way shear*

- The critical section is located d away from the column face, as shown in Fig. 14.17. The average pressure contributing to the factored one-way shear is[†]

$$q_u = 264.1 - 60.0 \times \{(975 - d)/2\}/1225$$
$$= (240.2 + 0.02449d) \text{ kN/m}^2$$
$$\approx 255 \text{ kN/m}^2 \text{ (assuming } d = 600 \text{ mm conservatively)}$$
$$= 0.255 \text{ N/mm}^2$$
$$\Rightarrow \quad V_{u1} = 0.255 \times 2000 \times (975 - d)$$
$$= (497250 - 510d) \text{ N}$$

- Assuming $\tau_c = 0.36$ MPa (for M25 concrete with nominal $p_t = 0.25$),

$$V_{uc} = 0.36 \times 2000 \times d = (720d) \text{ N}$$

- $V_{u1} \le V_{uc} \Rightarrow 497250 - 510d \le 720d$

$$\Rightarrow \quad d \ge 404 \text{ mm}$$

(*b*) *Two-way shear*

- The critical section is located $d/2$ from the periphery of the column all around. The average pressure contributing to the factored two-way shear is $q_u = 204.1 \text{ kN/m}^2 = 0.2041 \text{ N/mm}^2$

$$\Rightarrow \quad V_{u2} = 0.2041[2000 \times 2450 - (300 + d)(500 + d)]$$

Assuming $d = 404$ mm (the minimum required for one-way shear),

$$V_{u2} = 870 \times 10^3 \text{ N}$$

- For two-way shear resistance, limiting shear stress of concrete

$$\tau_{cz} = k_s(0.25\sqrt{f_{ck}}), \text{ where } k_s = 0.5 + 300/500, \text{ but limited to } 1.0.$$
$$\Rightarrow \quad \tau_{cz} = 1.0 \times 0.25\sqrt{25} = 1.25 \text{ MPa}$$
$$\Rightarrow \quad V_{uc} = 1.25 \times [(300 + d) + (500 + d)] \times 2 \times d$$
$$= (2000d + 5d^2) \text{ N}$$

With $\quad d = 404 \text{ mm} \Rightarrow V_{uc} = 1624 \text{ kN} > V_{u2} = 870 \text{ kN}$

- Hence, one-way shear governs the footing slab thickness and $d \ge 404$ mm. Assuming a clear cover of 75 mm and a bar diameter of 16 mm,

$$D \ge 404 + 75 + 16/2 = 487 \text{ mm}$$

Provide $D = 500$ mm

$$\Rightarrow \quad \text{effective depth (long span) } d_x = 500 - 75 - 8 = 417 \text{ mm}$$
$$\text{effective depth (short span) } d_y = 417 - 16 = 401 \text{ mm}$$

Check maximum soil pressure

- Assuming unit weights of concrete and soil as 24 kN/m^3 and 18 kN/m^3 respectively, at the factored loads,

[†] In this problem, the variation in the soil pressure over the length from the edge to the critical section is not very large. In such cases, it is sufficient and conservative to assume a uniform pressure equal to the maximum at the edge.

$$q_{\text{max-gross}} = \frac{1000}{2.0 \times 2.45} + \{(24 \times 0.5) + 18 \times (1.25 - 0.5)\} \times 1.5 + \frac{120 \times 6}{2.0 \times 2.45^2}$$
$$= 302 \text{ kN/m}^2 \approx 200 \times 1.5 \text{ kN/m}^2 \text{ – Hence, OK.}$$

Design of flexural reinforcement

- The critical sections for moment are located at the faces of the column in both directions (*XX* and *YY*) as shown in Fig. 14.17.

(a) *long span*

- cantilever projection = 975 mm, width = 2000 mm, d_x = 417 mm, q_u = 0.2163 N/mm^2 at face of column, 0.2641 N/mm^2 at footing edge.
- $M_{ux} = (0.2163 \times 2000 \times 975^2/2) + (0.2641 - 0.2163) \times \frac{1}{2} \times 2000 \times 975^2 \times 2/3$
  $= (205.6 + 30.3) \times 10^6 = 236 \times 10^6$ Nmm

  [Note that assuming a uniform soil pressure distribution at 0.2641 N/mm^2 will give M_{ux} = 251 kNm, which is in error by only 6 per cent on the conservative side.]

$$\Rightarrow \quad R \equiv \frac{M_u}{bd_x^2} = \frac{236 \times 10^6}{2000 \times 417^2} = 0.679 \text{ MPa}$$

$$\Rightarrow \quad \frac{(p_t)}{100} = \frac{25}{2 \times 500}\left[1 - \sqrt{1 - 4.598 \times 0.679/25}\right] = 0.161 \times 10^{-2}$$

p_t assumed for one-way shear = 0.25 > 0.161

$\Rightarrow \quad (A_{st})_{\text{reqd}} = 0.25 \times 2000 \times 417/100 = 2085$ mm^2

- Using 16ϕ bars, number required = 2085/201 = 11
  [corresponding spacing = (2000 – 75 × 2 – 16)/10 = 183 mm]

Provide 11 nos 16ϕ bars at uniform spacing in the long direction, as shown in Fig. 14.15.

- Development length required = 48.6ϕ (for M 25 with Fe500)
  = 48.6 × 16 = 778 mm
  < 900 mm available – OK.

(b) *short span*

- cantilever projection = 850 mm, width = 2450 mm, d_y = 401 mm, q_u varies along the section YY, with an average value of 0.2041 N/mm^2 at the middle. Considering a slightly greater value (mean of values at centre and footing edge), $q_u \approx (0.2041 + 0.2641)/2 = 0.2341$ N/mm^2
- $M_{uy} = 0.2341 \times 2450 \times 850^2/2) = 207.2 \times 10^6$ Nmm

$$\Rightarrow \quad R \equiv \frac{M_u}{bd_y^2} = \frac{207.2 \times 10^6}{2450 \times 401^2} = 0.526 \text{ MPa}$$

$$\Rightarrow \quad \frac{(p_t)}{100} = \frac{25}{2 \times 500}\left[1 - \sqrt{1 - 4.598 \times 0.526/25}\right] = 0.124 \times 10^{-2}$$

$\Rightarrow \quad (A_{st})_{\text{reqd}} = 0.124 \times 10^{-2} \times 2450 \times 401 = 1218$ mm^2

$(A_{st})_{\text{min}} = 0.0012 \times 2450 \times 500 = 1470$ mm^2 > 1218 mm^2

- Number of 12ϕ bars required = 1470/113 = 14
  As the difference in dimensions between the two sides (B = 2000 mm, L = 2450 mm) is not significant, it suffices to provide these bars at a uniform spacing.
- **Provide 14 nos. 12ϕ bars** in the short direction at uniform spacing, as shown in Fig. 14.17.
- Development length required = 48.6 × 12 = 583 mm
  < 775 mm available – Hence, OK.

Transfer of forces at column base

- As some of the bars are in tension, no transfer of the tensile force is possible through bearing at the column-footing interface, and these bars may be extended into the footing.
- Required development length of 25ϕ bars in tension = 48.6 × 25
  = 1215 mm
- Length available (including standard 90° bend on top of upper layer of footing reinforcement) = (500 – 75 – 16 – 12) – 5 × 25 + 8 × 25 = 472 mm. The balance, 1215 – 472 = 743 mm, can be made up by extending these bars into the footing beyond the standard bend. A total extension (including the 4ϕ extension of the bend) of 4 × 25 + 743 = 843 ≈ 850 mm needs to be provided beyond the bend point, as shown in Fig. 14.17. [It may be noted that it is much simpler and straight forward to compute the required total length of the bent leg, i.e., the total projection beyond the straight bar centreline, marked as distance BC in Fig. 8.8(c). The straight length available to the top of footing reinforcement = (500 – 75 – 16 – 12) = 397 mm. The required total projection is = $L_d - L_{straight} + 5.5\phi$ = 1215 – 397 + 5.5 × 25 = 955.5 mm, which gives the same result as can be obtained from above as = 843 + 4.5 × 25 = 955.5]. As the moment on the column is reversible, this embedment should be provided for all the column bars.
- Alternatively, a pedestal (with cross-sectional dimensions of, say, 450 mm × 750 mm) may be provided to the column below ground level (or 150 mm below GL), and the longitudinal bars in the pedestal designed to resist the factored axial load-moment combination; small diameter bars (say 16 mm ϕ) may be selected, with the aim of reducing the development length requirements.

Example 14.6 *Isolated footing eccentrically loaded*

Redesign the footing in Example 14.5 for a uniformly distributed base pressure, considering that the applied moment at the column base is entirely due to dead loads (and hence, irreversible).

Solution

- *Given:* (as in the previous Example) P_u = 1000 kN, M_{ux} = 120 kNm, q_a = 200 kN/m^2 at a depth of 1.25 m, f_{ck} = 25 MPa, f_y = 500 MPa

Size of footing

- Required eccentricity between column centroid and footing centroid = M_u/P_u

$$= \frac{120 \times 10^3}{1000} = 120 \text{ mm}$$

- Assuming the weight of the footing + backfill to constitute 10 per cent of P_u, and assuming a load factor of 1.5,

$$\text{base area required} = \frac{1000 \times 1.1}{200 \times 1.5} = 3.67 \text{ m}^2$$

- For economical proportions, the cantilever projections (for flexural design) should be approximately equal in the two directions.

  ⇒ Provide $L = B$ = 1.95 m (Area = 3.80 m^2 > 3.67 m^2)

  With the column offset by 120 mm, this results in cantilever projections of 845 mm and 825 mm in the two directions, as shown in Fig. 14.18.

Thickness of footing based on shear

- Factored (net) soil pressure $q_u = \frac{1000}{1.95 \times 1.95}$ = 263.0kN/m^2
  = 0.263 N/mm^2

(a) *One-way shear*

- The critical section is located d away from the column face [refer Fig. 14.18]

$$V_{u1} = 0.263 \times 1950 \times (845 - d) = (433358 - 512.8d) \text{ N}$$

- Assuming $\tau_c = 0.36$ MPa (for M25 concrete with nominal $p_t = 0.25$),

$$V_{uc} = 0.36 \times 1950 \times d = (702d) \text{ N}$$

- $V_{u1} \le V_{uc} \Rightarrow 433358 - 512.8d \le 702d$

$\Rightarrow \quad d \ge 356.7$ mm

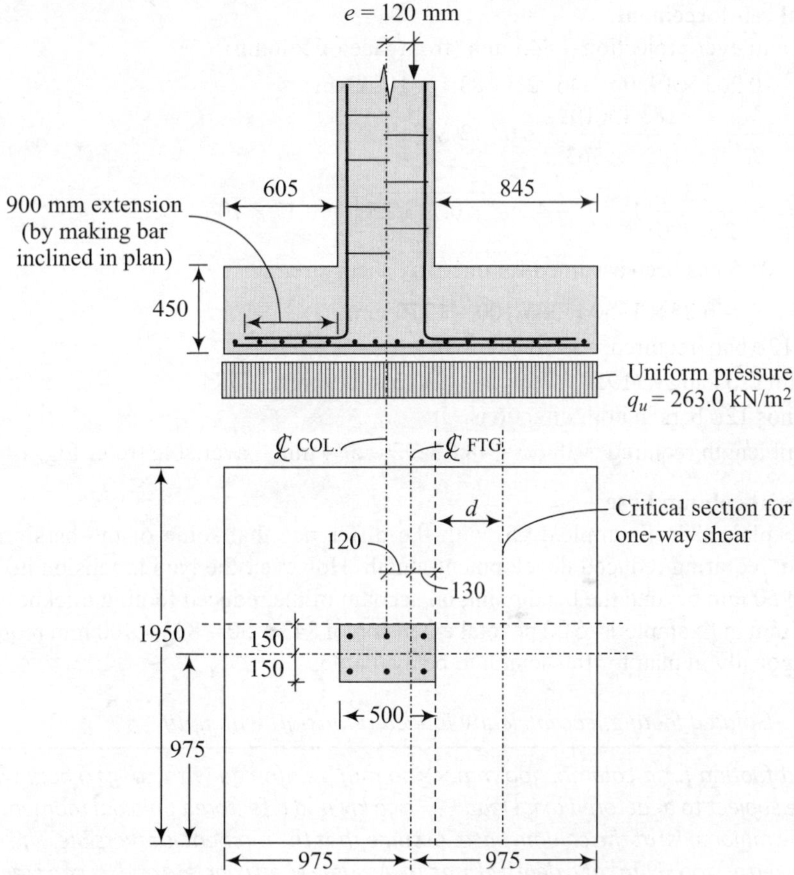

Fig. 14.18 Example 14.6.

(b) *Two-way shear*

- The critical section is located $d/2$ from the column periphery all around.

$$V_{u2} = 0.263 \times [1950^2 - (300 + d)(500 + d)]$$

- Assuming $d \ge 357$ mm, $V_{u2} \le 851976$ N = 852 kN
- Two-way shear resistance (as in Example 14.5)

$$V_{uc} = 1.25 \times [(300 + d) + (500 + d)] \times 2 \times d$$

$$d = 357 \text{ mm} \quad \Rightarrow \quad V_{uc} = 1351.25 \text{ kN} > V_{u2,\max} = 852.0 \text{ kN}$$

Hence, one-way shear governs the thickness. As a square footing is provided and the one-way shear requirement is equally applicable in both directions, the d calculated may be taken as an average depth: $(d_x + d_y)/2$.

Assuming 75 mm clear cover and 12ϕ bars,

$$D \geq 357 + 75 + 12 = 444 \text{ mm}$$

- Provide $D = 450$ mm and consider the average effective depth,

  $d = 450 - 75 - 12 = 363$ mm while designing for flexure.

Design of flexural reinforcement

- Maximum cantilever projection = 845 mm (from face of column)

$$M_u = 0.263 \times 1950 \times 845^2/2 = 183.1 \times 10^6 \text{ kNm}$$

$$\Rightarrow \quad R \equiv \frac{M_u}{Bd^2} = \frac{183.1 \times 10^6}{1950 \times 363^2} = 0.713 \text{ MPa}$$

$$\Rightarrow \quad \frac{p_t}{100} = \frac{25}{2 \times 500}\left[1 - \sqrt{1 - 4.598 \times 0.713/25}\right] = 0.17 \times 10^{-2}$$

$p_t = 0.25$ has been assumed for one-way shear strength

Accordingly, $A_{st} = 0.25 \times 1950 \times 363/100 = 1770 \text{ mm}^2$

Number of 12ϕ bars required = 1770/113 = 16

[corresponding spacing = $(1950 - 75 \times 2 - 12)/15 = 119$ mm – OK].

Provide 16 nos 12ϕ bars in both directions.

Development length required = 48.6ϕ = 48.6 × 12 = 584 mm – available [refer Fig. 14.18].

Transfer of forces at column base

- This is as explained in Example 14.5, with the difference that some of the bars are always under compression, requiring reduced development length. However, the bars in tension need an additional extension of 50 mm beyond the bend point, on account of the reduced footing thickness of 450 mm (as against 500 mm in Example 14.5). The total extension of $843 + 50 = 893 \approx 900$ mm requires reorienting the bars diagonally in plan for this length to be available.

Example 14.7 *Isolated footing, eccentrically loaded (uniaxial) with uplift*

Design an isolated footing for a column, 300 mm × 500 mm, reinforced with 10–32ϕ bars with Fe 500 steel and M 25 concrete subject to a factored axial load P_u = 750 kN and a factored uniaxial moment M_{ux} = 450 kNm (with respect to the major axis) at the column base. Assume that the moment is reversible. The safe soil bearing capacity may be taken as 200 kN/m^2 at a depth of 1.25 m. Assume M 25 concrete and Fe 500 steel for the footing.

Solution

Size of footing

- *Given:* $P_u = 750$ kN, $M_{ux} = 450$ kNm, $q_a = 200$ kN/m^2 at a depth of 1.25 m.
- As the moment is reversible, the footing should be symmetric with respect to the column. Assuming the weight of the footing plus backfill to constitute about 15 per cent of P_u, resultant eccentricity of loading at footing base,

$$e = \frac{450 \times 10^3}{750 \times 1.15}$$

$$= 522 \text{ mm} = 0.522 \text{ m}$$

- Assuming $e > L/6$ and using Eq. 14.3c,

$$q_{max} = \frac{2 \times 750 \times 1.15}{BL'} \leq (200 \times 1.5)\ \text{kN/m}^2$$

$$\Rightarrow \quad BL' \geq 5.75\ \text{m}^2$$

Substituting $L' = 3c$, where $c = 0.5L - e = 0.5L - 0.522$ [see Fig. 14.4(b)]

$$\Rightarrow \quad B(0.5L - 0.522) \geq 1.92$$

$$\Rightarrow \quad 0.5BL - 0.522B \geq 1.92$$

Assuming 5% of footing area to be in uplift;

$$\frac{L - L'}{L} \times 100 \leq 5\text{. Substituting } L - L' = L - 3(0.5L - e) = 3e - 0.5L$$

$$\frac{3e - 0.5L}{L} \times 100 \leq 5$$

$$L \geq 2.85\ \text{m}$$

Assuming $L = 2.85$ m $\Rightarrow$ $B \geq 2.13$ m

- Provide $B = 2250$ mm and $L = 2850$ mm; this gives projection of 975 mm in the short direction and 1175 mm in the long direction, as shown in Fig. 14.19. L' =2709 mm.

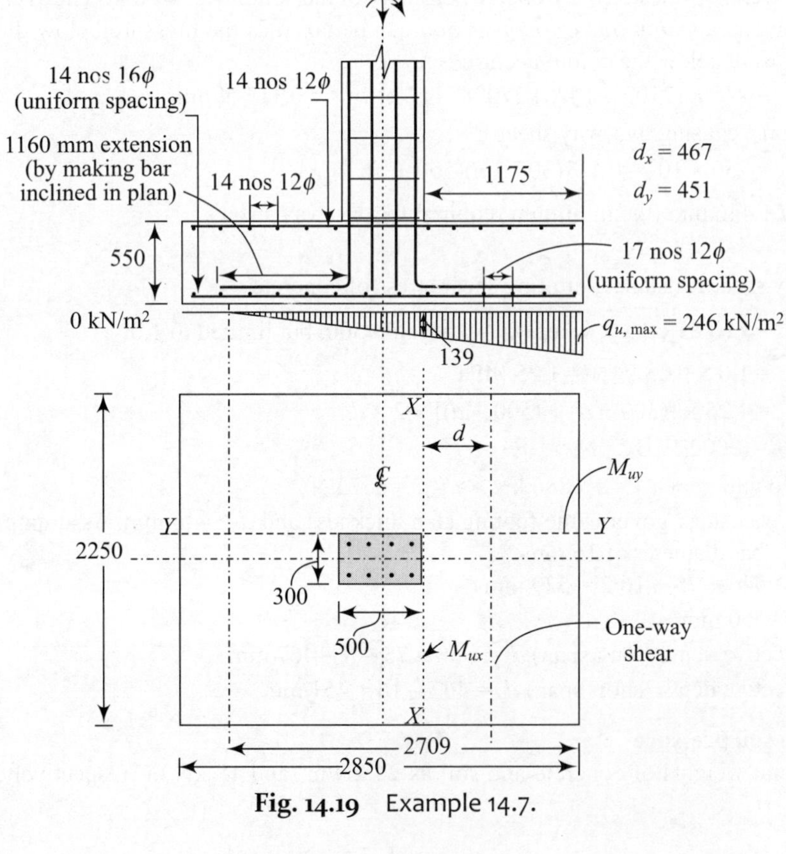

Fig. 14.19 Example 14.7.

Thickness of footing based on shear

Factored (net) soil pressure $q_{u,\max} = \dfrac{2 \times 750}{2.25 \times 2.709} = 246$ kN/m^2 $q_{u,\min} = 0$ kN/m^2

(*a*) *One-way shear*

- The critical section is located d away from the column face, as shown in Fig. 14.19. The pressure at d away from the column face,

$$q_u = \frac{246}{2.709} \times \left(2.709 - \frac{2.85}{2} + \frac{0.5}{2} + d\right)$$
$$= (139.3 + 90.8d) \text{ kN/m}^2$$
$$\approx 194 \text{ kN/m}^2 \text{ (assuming } d = 0.6 \text{ m conservatively)}$$
$$= 0.194 \text{ N/mm}^2$$

$$\Rightarrow \quad V_{u1} = 0.194 \times 2250 \times (1175 - d) + 0.5 \times 2250 \times (0.246 - 0.194) \times (1175 - d)$$
$$= (581625 - 495d) \text{ N}$$

- Assuming $\tau_c = 0.36$ MPa (for M25 concrete with nominal $p_t = 0.25$),

$$V_{uc} = 0.36 \times 2250 \times d = (810d) \text{ N}$$
$$V_{u1} \le V_{uc} \quad \Rightarrow \quad 581625 - 495d \le 810d$$
$$\Rightarrow \quad d \ge 446 \text{ mm}$$

(*b*) *Two-way shear*

- The critical section is located $d/2$ from the periphery of the column all around. The average soil pressure on the footing area *within this critical section* can be taken as the pressure below the column centre. The soil pressure below the column centre is

$$= 246 \times (2709 - 1425)/2709 = 117 \text{ kN/m}^2 = 0.117 \text{ N/mm}^2$$

The shear force causing two-way shear is

$$V_{u2} = 750 \times 10^3 - 0.117(300 + d)(500 + d)$$

Assuming $d = 446$ mm (the minimum required for one-way shear),

$$V_{u2} = 667 \times 10^3 \text{ N}$$

- For two-way shear resistance, limiting shear stress of concrete

$$\tau_{cz} = k_s(0.25\sqrt{f_{ck}}), \text{ where } k_s = 0.5 + 300/500, \text{ but limited to 1.0.}$$
$$\Rightarrow \quad \tau_{cz} = 1.0 \times 0.25\sqrt{25} = 1.25 \text{ MPa}$$
$$\Rightarrow \quad V_{uc} = 1.25 \times [(300 + d) + (500 + d)] \times 2 \times d$$
$$= (2000d + 5d^2) \text{ N}$$

With $d = 446$ mm $\Rightarrow$ $V_{uc} = 1886$ kN >> $V_{u2} = 667$ kN

- Hence, one-way shear governs the footing slab thickness and $d \ge 446$ mm. Assuming a clear cover of 75 mm and a bar diameter of 16 mm,

$$D \ge 446 + 75 + 16/2 = 529 \text{ mm}$$

Provide $D = 550$ mm

$\Rightarrow$ effective depth (long span) $d_x = 550 - 75 - 8 = 467$ mm

effective depth (short span) $d_y = 467 - 16 = 451$ mm

Check maximum soil pressure

- Assuming unit weights of concrete and soil as 24 kN/m^3 and 18 kN/m^3 respectively, at the factored loads,

$$q_{\text{max-gross}} = \frac{2 \times 750}{2.25 \times 2.709} + \{(24 \times 0.550) + 18 \times (1.25 - 0.550)\} \times 1.5$$

$$= 285 \text{ kN/m}^2 \leq 200 \times 1.5 \text{ kN/m}^2 \text{ – Hence, OK.}$$

Design of flexural reinforcement

- The critical sections for moment are located at the faces of the column in both directions (XX and YY) as shown in Fig. 14.19.

(a) *long span*

- Cantilever projection = 1175 mm, width = 2250 mm, d_x = 467 mm, q_u = 0.139 N/mm^2 at face of column, 0.246 N/mm^2 at footing edge.

$$M_{ux} = (0.139 \times 2250 \times 1175^2/2) + (0.246 - 0.139) \times \frac{1}{2} \times 2250 \times 1175 \times \frac{2}{3} \times 1175$$

$$= (215.9 + 110.8) \times 10^6 = 326.7 \times 10^6 \text{ Nmm}$$

$$\Rightarrow \quad R \equiv \frac{M_u}{bd_x^2} = \frac{326.7 \times 10^6}{2250 \times 467^2} = 0.666 \text{ MPa}$$

$$\Rightarrow \quad \frac{(p_t)}{100} = \frac{25}{2 \times 500}\left[1 - \sqrt{1 - 4.598 \times 0.666/25}\right] = 0.158 \times 10^{-2}$$

p_t assumed for one-way shear = 0.25 > 0.158

$\Rightarrow \quad (A_{st})_{\text{reqd}} = 0.25 \times 2250 \times 467/100 = 2627 \text{ mm}^2$

- Using 16ϕ bars, number required = 2627/201 = 14
[corresponding spacing = (2250 – 75 × 2 – 16)/13 = 160 mm]

Provide 14 nos 16ϕ bars at uniform spacing in the long direction, as shown in Fig. 14.19.

- Development length required = 49ϕ (for M 25 with Fe 500)
= 49 × 16 = 784 mm
< 1100 mm available – OK.

(b) *short span*

- cantilever projection = 975 mm, width = 2850 mm, d_y = 451 mm, q_u varies along the section YY, with a value of 0.117 N/mm^2 along the centre line of the column along XX. Considering the mean of values at centre and footing edge, $q_u \approx (0.117 + 0.246)/2 = 0.182$ N/mm^2
- $M_{uy} = 0.182 \times 2850 \times 975^2/2 = 246.5 \times 10^6$Nmm

$$\Rightarrow \quad R \equiv \frac{M_u}{bd_y^2} = \frac{246.5 \times 10^6}{2850 \times 451^2} = 0.425 \text{ MPa}$$

$$\Rightarrow \quad \frac{(p_t)}{100} = \frac{25}{2 \times 500}\left[1 - \sqrt{1 - 4.598 \times 0.425/25}\right] = 0.997 \times 10^{-3}$$

$$\Rightarrow \quad (A_{st})_{\text{reqd}} = 0.997 \times 10^{-3} \times 2850 \times 451 = 1282 \text{ mm}^2$$

$$(A_{st})_{\text{min}} = 0.0012 \times 2850 \times 550 = 1881 \text{ mm}^2 > 1282 \text{ mm}^2$$

Number of 12ϕ bars required = 1881/113 = 17

As the difference in dimensions between the two sides (B = 2250 mm, L = 2850 mm) is not significant, it suffices to provide these bars at a uniform spacing.

Provide 17 nos 12ϕ bars in the short direction at uniform spacing, as shown in Fig. 14.19.

- Development length required = 49 × 12 = 588 mm
  < 900 mm available – Hence, OK.

  As uplift is allowed, minimum top steel is required to resist the small hogging moments generated due to weight of soil including overburden pressure above the uplifted region.

  $(A_{st})_{min} = 0.0012 \times 2250 \times 550 = 1485 \text{ mm}^2$

  Provide 14 nos 12ϕ bars in short and long directions at top.

Transfer of forces at column base

- As some of the bars are in tension, no transfer of the tensile force is possible through bearing at the column-footing interface, and these bars may be extended into the footing.
- Required development length of 32ϕ bars in tension = 49 × 32
  = 1568 mm

  Length available (including standard 90° bend on top of upper layer of footing reinforcement) = (550 – 75 – 16 – 12) – 5 × 32 + 8 × 32 = 543 mm. The balance, 1568 – 543 = 1025 mm, can be made up by extending these bars into the footing beyond the bend. A total extension of 4 × 32 + 1025= 1153 ≈ 1160 mm needs to be provided beyond the bend point, as shown in Fig. 14.19. As the projection in the short span direction is less than 1160 mm, appropriate bent has to be provided to satisfy the development length. As the moment on the column is reversible, this embedment should be provided for all the column bars.

Example 14.8 *Isolated footing, eccentrically loaded (biaxial) with uplift*

Design an isolated footing for a column, 450 mm × 600 mm, reinforced with 10–32ϕ bars with Fe 500 steel and M 25 concrete subject to a factored axial load P_u = 750 kN and factored biaxial moments M_{ux} = 450 kNm (with respect to the major axis) and M_{uy} = 200 kNm (with respect to the minor axis) at the column base. Assume that the moment is reversible. The safe soil bearing capacity may be taken as 200 kN/m² at a depth of 1.25 m. Assume M 25 concrete and Fe 500 steel for the footing.

Solution

Size of footing

- *Given:* $P_u = 750$ kN, $M_{ux} = 450$ kNm, $M_{uy} = 200$ kNm, $q_a = 200$ kN/m² at a depth of 1.25 m.
- As the moment is reversible, the footing should be symmetric with respect to the column. Assuming the weight of the footing plus backfill to constitute about 15 per cent of P_u, resultant eccentricity of loading in two directions at footing base,

$$e_x = \frac{450 \times 10^3}{750 \times 1.15} = 522 \text{ mm} = 0.522 \text{ m}$$

$$e_y = \frac{200 \times 10^3}{750 \times 1.15} = 232 \text{ mm} = 0.232 \text{ m}$$

- Assuming $\dfrac{e_x}{L_x/6} + \dfrac{e_y}{L_y/6} > 1$

  Trial 1: $L_x = 2.85$ m; $L_y = 2.25$ m

  The maximum pressure q_{max} can be obtained from Fig. 14.6

$$\frac{e_x}{L_x} = \frac{0.522}{2.85} = 0.183\,; \quad \frac{e_y}{L_y} = \frac{0.232}{2.25} = 0.103$$

Therefore, the neutral axis location corresponds to Case II; $K \approx 2.9$; $x \approx 0.4$; $y \approx 0.7$

$$q_{\max} = \frac{KP_u}{L_x L_y} = \frac{2.9 \times 750 \times 1.15}{2.85 \times 2.25} = 390.1 > (200 \times 1.5)\ \text{kN/m}^2.$$

Not satisfied; Hence increase the dimensions.

Trial 2: $L_x = 3.1$ m; $L_y = 2.5$ m

The maximum pressure $q_{\max}$ can be obtained from Fig. 14.6

$$\frac{e_x}{L_x} = \frac{0.522}{3.1} = 0.168; \quad \frac{e_y}{L_y} = \frac{0.232}{2.5} = 0.093$$

Corresponding to Case II, $K \approx 2.6$; $x \approx 0.3$; $y \approx 0.5$

$$q_{\max} = \frac{KP_u}{L_x L_y} = \frac{2.6 \times 750 \times 1.15}{3.1 \times 2.5} = 289.4 \le (200 \times 1.5)\ \text{kN/m}^2$$

$$\text{Percentage of area under uplift} = \frac{1}{2}(xy) \times 100 = \frac{1}{2}(0.3 \times 0.5) \times 100 = 7.5\%$$

- Provide $L_x = 3100$ mm and $L_y = 2500$ mm; this gives projection of 1250 mm in the long direction and 1025 mm in the short direction, as shown in Fig. 14.20.

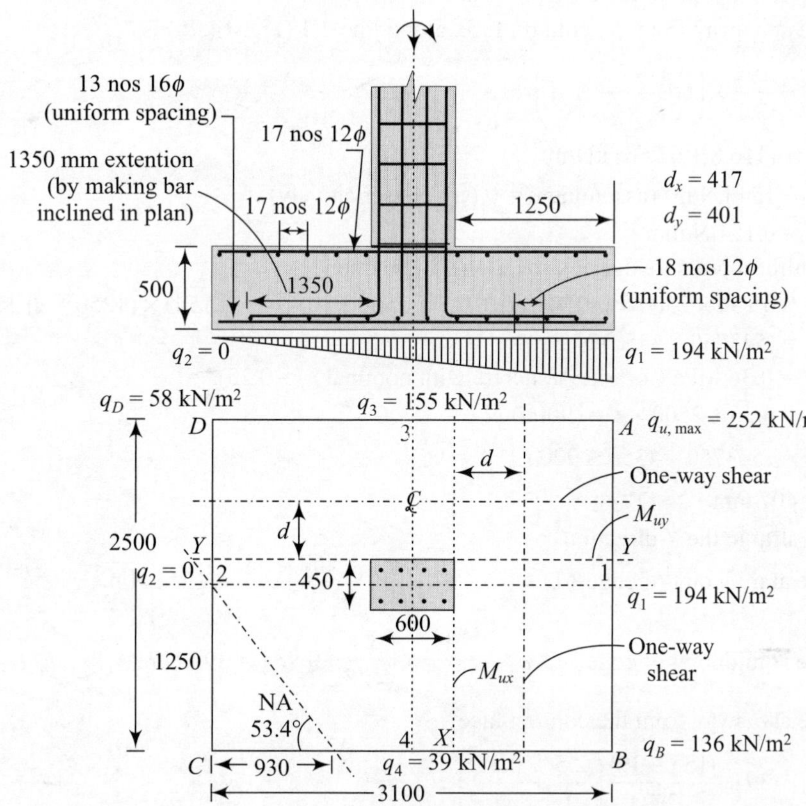

Fig. 14.20 Example 14.8

Thickness of footing based on shear

Factored (net) soil pressure $q_{u,\max} = \dfrac{KP_u}{L_x L_y} = \dfrac{2.6 \times 750}{3.1 \times 2.5} = 252 \text{ kN/m}^2$

The neutral axis in case of biaxial bending is inclined, intersecting sides *BC* at xL_x (= 930 mm) from *C*, and *CD* at yL_y (= 1250 mm) from *C* [Fig. 14.20]. The inclination of neutral axis, θ is obtained as 53.4°. The soil pressure along the neutral axis is zero and the pressure along the axis parallel to the neutral axis is constant. The factored (net) soil pressures q_B and q_D at points *B* and *D*, can be obtained by considering the axis parallel to the neutral axis passing through *B* and *D*, respectively as shown in Fig. 14.20.

By assuming linear distribution of soil pressures,

Factored (net) soil pressure at *B*, $q_B = 136 \text{ kN/m}^2$

Factored (net) soil pressure at *D*, $q_D = 58 \text{ kN/m}^2$

(a) One-way shear

- The critical section is located *d* away from the column face considering strips in X- and Y-directions, as shown in Fig. 14.20.

  Considering strip in the X-direction,

  Soil pressure at midpoint of edge AB, $q_1 = \dfrac{q_{\max} + q_B}{2} = \dfrac{252 + 136}{2} = 194 \text{ kN/m}^2$

  Soil pressure at midpoint of edge CD, $q_2 = 0$

  The pressure at *d* away from the column face, along line 2-1 (Fig. 14.20) is

$$q_a = \frac{194}{3.1} \times \left(\frac{3.1}{2} + \frac{0.6}{2} + d\right)$$
$$= (116.8 + 62.6d) \text{ kN/m}^2$$
$$\approx 154 \text{ kN/m}^2 \text{ (assuming } d = 0.6 \text{ m conservatively)}$$
$$= 0.154 \text{ N/mm}^2$$

  Assuming uniform pressure distribution along Y-direction

$$\Rightarrow \quad V_{u1} = 0.154 \times 2500 \times (1250 - d) + 0.5 \times 2500 \times (0.194 - 0.154) \times (1250 - d)$$
$$= (543750 - 435d) \text{ N}$$

- Assuming $\tau_c = 0.36$ MPa (for M25 concrete with nominal $p_t = 0.25$),

$$V_{uc} = 0.36 \times 2500 \times d = (900d) \text{ N}$$

- $V_{u1} \le V_{uc} \quad \Rightarrow \quad 543750 - 435d \le 900d$

  $\Rightarrow \quad d \ge 407$ mm

  Considering strip in the Y-direction,

  Soil pressure at midpoint of edge AD, $q_3 = \dfrac{q_{\max} + q_D}{2} = \dfrac{252 + 58}{2} = 155 \text{ kN/m}^2$

  Soil pressure at midpoint of edge BC, $q_4 = \dfrac{136}{2.17} \times \left(\dfrac{3.1}{2} - 0.93\right) = 39 \text{ kN/m}^2$

  The pressure at *d* away from the column face,

$$q_a = 39 + \frac{(155 - 39)}{2.5}\left(\frac{2.5}{2} + \frac{0.45}{2} + d\right)$$
$$= (107.4 + 46.4d) \text{ kN/m}^2$$

≈ 135 kN/m^2 (assuming $d = 0.6$ m conservatively)

$= 0.135$ N/mm^2

Assuming uniform pressure distribution along X-direction

$$\Rightarrow \quad V_{u1} = 0.135 \times 3100 \times (1025 - d) + 0.5 \times 3100 \times (0.155 - 0.135) \times (1025 - d)$$
$$= (460737.5 - 449.5d) \text{ N}$$

- Assuming $\tau_c = 0.29$ MPa (for M25 concrete with nominal $p_t = 0.15$),

$$V_{uc} = 0.29 \times 3100 \times d = (899d) \text{ N}$$

- $V_{u1} \leq V_{uc} \quad \Rightarrow \quad 460737.5 - 449.5d \leq 899d$

$$\Rightarrow \quad d \geq 342 \text{ mm}$$

(*b*) *Two-way shear*

- The critical section is located $d/2$ from the periphery of the column all around. Upward soil pressure below column at its centre (middle of line 3-4) in Fig. 14.20 is:

$$= (155 + 39)/2 = 97 \text{ kN/m}^2 = 0.097 \text{ N/mm}^2$$
$$V_{u2} = 750 \times 10^3 - 0.097(600 + d)(450 + d)$$

Assuming $d = 407$ mm (the minimum required for one-way shear),

$$V_{u2} = 666 \times 10^3 \text{ N}$$

- For two-way shear resistance, limiting shear stress of concrete

$$= k_s(0.25\sqrt{f_{ck}}), \text{ where } k_s = 0.5 + 300/500, \text{ but limited to 1.0.}$$

$$\Rightarrow \quad \tau_{cz} = 1.0 \times 0.25\sqrt{25} = 1.25 \text{ MPa}$$
$$\Rightarrow \quad V_{uc} = 1.25 \times [(300 + d) + (500 + d)] \times 2 \times d$$
$$= (2000d + 5d^2) \text{ N}$$

With $\quad d = 407$ mm $\Rightarrow \quad V_{uc} = 1642$ kN $>> V_{u2} = 666$ kN

- Hence, one-way shear governs the footing slab thickness and $d \geq 407$ mm. Assuming a clear cover of 75 mm and a bar diameter of 16 mm,

$$D \geq 407 + 75 + 16/2 = 490 \text{ mm}$$

Provide $D = 500$ mm

$\Rightarrow$ effective depth (long span) $d_x = 500 - 75 - 8 = 417$ mm

effective depth (short span) $d_y = 417 - 16 = 401$ mm

Design of flexural reinforcement

- The critical sections for moment are located at the faces of the column in both directions (XX and YY) as shown in Fig. 14.20.

(a) *long span*

- cantilever projection = 1250 mm, width = 2500 mm, $d_x = 417$ mm,

Assuming a uniform pressure of $q_1 = 0.194$ N/mm^2 along the centre line of the column, the moment at the face of the column may be calculated conservatively as,

$$M_{ux} = 0.194 \times 2500 \times 1250^2/2 = 378.9 \times 10^6 \text{ Nmm}$$

$$\Rightarrow \quad R \equiv \frac{M_u}{bd_x^2} = \frac{378.9 \times 10^6}{2500 \times 417^2} = 0.872 \text{ MPa}$$

$$\Rightarrow \quad \frac{(p_t)}{100} = \frac{25}{2 \times 500}\left[1 - \sqrt{1 - 4.598 \times 0.872/25}\right] = 0.209 \times 10^{-2}$$

p_t assumed for one-way shear = 0.25 > 0.209

$\Rightarrow \quad (A_{st})_{reqd} = 0.25 \times 2500 \times 417/100 = 2606 \text{ mm}^2$

Using 16ϕ bars, number required = 2606/201 = 13
[corresponding spacing = (2500 – 75 × 2 – 16)/12 = 194 mm]

Provide 13 nos 16ϕ bars at uniform spacing in the long direction, as shown in Fig. 14.20.

- Development length required = 49ϕ (for M 25 with Fe 500)
  = 49 × 16 = 784 mm
  < 1250 mm available – OK.

(b) *short span*

- cantilever projection = 1025 mm, width = 3100 mm, d_y = 401 mm,
  Assuming a uniform pressure of $q_2 = 0.155$ N/mm^2 along the centre line of the column, the moment at the face of the column may be calculated as,

$$M_{uy} = 0.155 \times 3100 \times 1025^2/2 = 252.4 \times 10^6 \text{ Nmm}$$

$$\Rightarrow \quad R \equiv \frac{M_u}{bd_y^{\,2}} = \frac{252.4 \times 10^6}{3100 \times 401^2} = 0.506 \text{ MPa}$$

$$\Rightarrow \quad \frac{(p_t)}{100} = \frac{25}{2 \times 500}\left[1 - \sqrt{1 - 4.598 \times 0.506/25}\right] = 0.119 \times 10^{-2}$$

p_t assumed for one-way shear = 0.15 > 0.119

$\Rightarrow \quad (A_{st})_{reqd} = 0.15 \times 3100 \times 417/100 = 1939 \text{ mm}^2$

Using 12ϕ bars, number required = 1939/113 = 18
[corresponding spacing = (3100 – 75 × 2 – 12)/17 = 173 mm]

Provide 18 nos 12ϕ bars at uniform spacing in the short direction, as shown in Fig. 14.20.

- Development length required = 49 × 12 = 588 mm
  < 1025 mm available – Hence, OK.

As uplift is allowed, minimum top steel is required to resist the small hogging moments generated due to weight of soil including overburden pressure above the uplifted region.

$$(A_{st})_{min} = 0.0012 \times 3100 \times 500 = 1860 \text{ mm}^2$$

Provide 17 nos 12ϕ bars in short and long directions at top.

Transfer of forces at column base

- As some of the bars are in tension, no transfer of the tensile force is possible through bearing at the column-footing interface, and these bars may be extended into the footing.
- Required development length of 32ϕ bars in tension = 49 × 32
  = 1568 mm
- Straight length available to top of upper layer of footing reinforcement) = (500 – 75 – 16 – 12) = 397 mm. With 90° bend and extension beyond, total length required beyond the straight portion [Fig. 8.8(c)] is = $L_d - L_{straight} + 5.5\phi$ = 1568 – 397 + 5.5 × 32 = 1347 ≈ 1350 mm. The lengths available in the footing in the long and short directions are 1250 mm and 1025 mm respectively, however in a diagonal direction, up to 1616 mm is available. Hence the column bars may be bent at an angle (in plan) providing the required plan length (total projection beyond the vertical bar) of 1350 mm as shown in Fig. 14.20.

In the short span, the projection is only 1025 mm and hence a second standard 90° bend shall be provided near the outer end. As the moment on the column is reversible, this embedment should be provided for all the column bars.

14.6 Design of Combined Footings

14.6.1 General

As mentioned in Section 14.2.2, a footing supporting more than a single column or wall is called a *combined footing*, and when many columns (more than two) are involved, terms such as *continuous strip footing* (if columns are aligned in one direction only) and *raft foundation* or *mat foundation* are used. Multiple column foundations become necessary in soils having very low bearing capacities. However, even in soils having moderate or high 'safe bearing capacity' adequate for the use of individual footings, combined footings become necessary sometimes — as when

- columns are so closely spaced that isolated footings cannot be conveniently provided, as the estimated base areas tend to overlap; and
- an exterior column located along the periphery of the building is so close to the property line that an isolated footing cannot be symmetrically placed without extending beyond the property line.

14.6.2 Distribution of Soil Pressure

As mentioned earlier (in Section 14.3.2), the prediction of the exact distribution of base pressure under a footing is difficult, as it depends on the rigidity of the footing as well as the properties of the soil. If this is difficult for an isolated footing, indeed, it is more so for a combined footing.

For a very rigid footing supported on an elastic soil base, a straight-line pressure distribution is appropriate. Such an assumption is found to lead to satisfactory designs in the case of relatively rigid footings. However, for relatively flexible footings, such an assumption is not realistic; the problem is rather complex and involves consideration of *soil-structure interaction*.

In this section, only two-column combined footings are considered. The footing is assumed to be rigid and the soil response elastic, and hence a straight-line distribution of soil pressure is assumed.

14.6.3 Geometry of Two-Column Combined Footings

Examples of two-column combined footings are shown in Fig. 14.21. The geometry of the footing base should preferably be so selected as to ensure that the centroid of the footing area coincides with the resultant of the column loads (including consideration of moments if any, at the column bases). This will result in a uniform distribution of soil pressure, which is desirable in order to avoid possible tilting of the footing (as mentioned earlier in Section 14.3.2).

> Usually in the design of two-column combined footings, the plan dimensions are so selected as to have the centroid of footing area coincide with the resultant of the column loads. This results in uniform soil pressure.

The footing may be rectangular or trapezoidal in shape [Fig. 14.21], depending on the relative magnitudes of loads on the two columns which the footing supports. When the exterior column (which has the space limitation for an independent footing) carries the lighter load ($\overline{x} > s/2$), a rectangular footing [Fig. 14.21(b)] or a trapezoidal footing (with a reduced width under the exterior column) as shown in Fig. 14.21(c) may be provided. On the other hand, when the exterior column carries the heavier load [$\bar{x} < s/2$ in Fig. 14.21(e)], the wider end of the trapezoidal footing should be located under the exterior column.

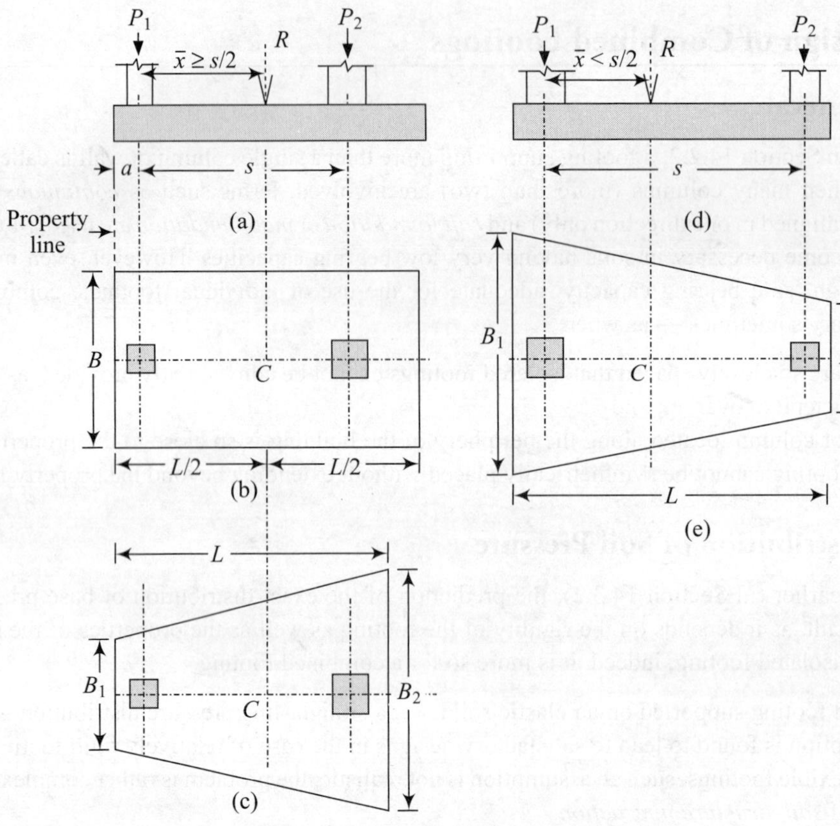

Fig. 14.21 Geometry of two-column combined footings.

14.6.4 Design Considerations in Two-Columns Footings

Fixing Plan Dimensions

As discussed earlier with reference to Fig. 14.21, the plan dimensions of the two-column combined footing may be selected to satisfy the following two requirements:

1. Base area of footing, A = Total (service) load†/q_a.
2. The line of action of the resultant of the column loads must pass through the centroid of the footing.

In the case of a rectangular footing [Fig. 14.21(b)], the second requirement results in a length L of the footing equal to $2(\bar{x} + a)$. The edge distance a may be fixed with reference to a property line (as shown in Fig. 14.21); otherwise, it may be suitably assumed. Having fixed L, the footing width B is obtained as A/L. In the case of a trapezoidal footing [Fig. 14.21(c), (e)], usually the length L is selected first, and the dimensions B_1, B_2 adjusted to satisfy the two requirements cited above.

† Including the weight of the footing plus backfill.

Load Transfer Mechanism

As in the case of isolated footings, the factored net soil pressure q_u is computed as the resultant factored load divided by the base area provided, and the pressure may be assumed to be uniformly distributed† [refer Fig. 14.22].

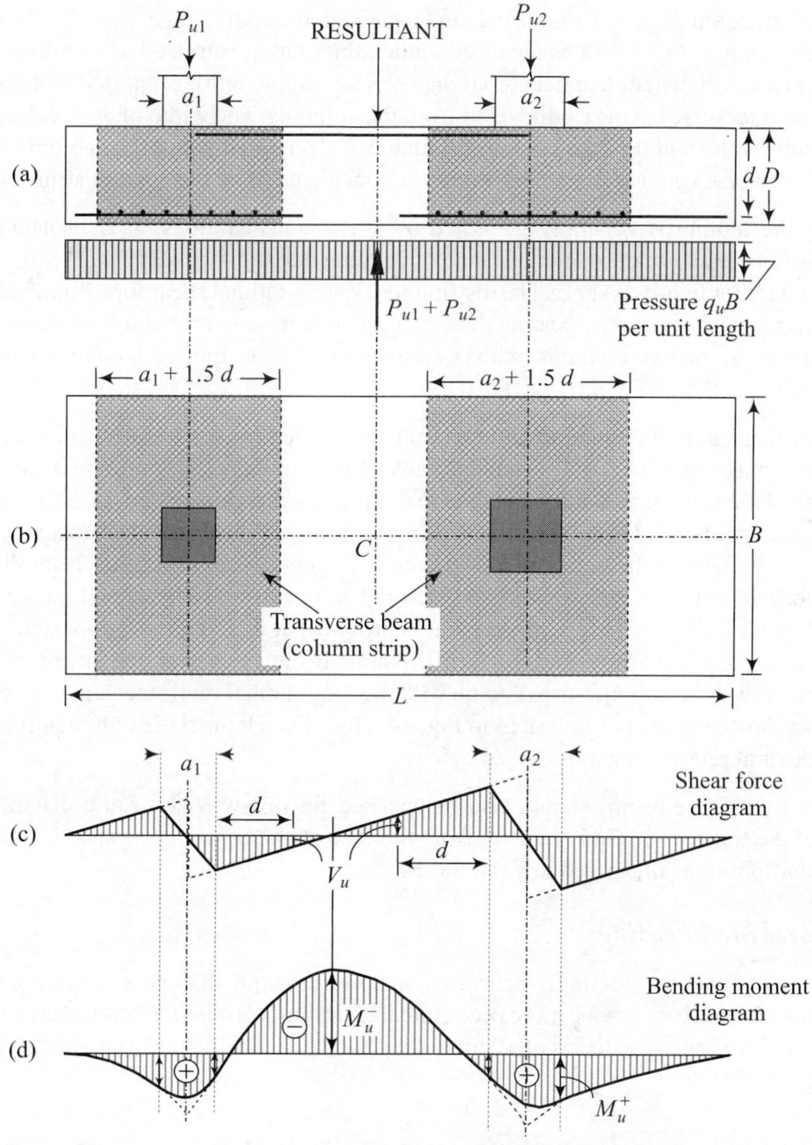

Fig. 14.22 Assumed load transfer in two-column combined footing.

† In cases where the ratio of the column loads $P_1 : P_2$ is subject to uncertainty, or when these loads are accompanied by moments which may be reversible, the line of action of the resultant load will not always match with the centroid of the footing, and the pressure distribution will be nonuniform. However, it is conservative to assume uniform distribution with maximum q_u.

The base slab of the combined footing is subject to two-way bending, and one-way as well as two-way shear (as in the case of isolated footing). In general, the width of the footing (B) is much less than the length (L), with the result that the flexural behaviour is predominantly one-way (i.e., in the longitudinal direction), and the two-way action (i.e., including transverse bending) is limited to the neighbourhood of the column locations.

For the purpose of structural design, a simplified (and usually conservative) load transfer mechanism may be assumed – as shown in Fig. 14.22. In this idealised model, the footing is treated as a uniformly loaded wide longitudinal beam (width B, length L and factored load $q_u B$ per unit length), supported on two column strips, which in turn act as transverse beams cantilevered from the columns. The width of each column strip may be taken approximately as the width of the column (a) plus $0.75d$ on either side of the column [Fig. 14.22(b)]. In designing for transverse bending, the effective part is considered to be the column strips only.

The thickness of the footing is generally governed by shear considerations, as in isolated footings. The critical sections for one-way shear are at a distance d from the column face [Fig. 14.22(c)], and at $d/2$ from each column periphery for two-way shear. The distribution of longitudinal shear forces and bending moments may be easily determined from statics, treating the footing slab as a beam of width B and loading $q_u B$ per unit length, simply supported† on two columns, with overhangs (if any) beyond each column support, as shown in Fig. 14.22(c), (d).

The flexural reinforcement in the longitudinal direction is designed for the 'positive' moment at the face of the column and the maximum 'negative' moment between the columns; the reinforcement is placed at the bottom in the case of the former, and at top in the case of latter, as depicted in Fig. 14.22(a), (d). The flexural reinforcement in the transverse direction (in the column strip) is designed for the 'positive' moment at the section in line with the face of the column, considering the column strip as a beam centrally supported on the column and loaded with uniformly distributed factored soil pressure (whose total magnitude is equal to the factored load on the column). This reinforcement is provided at the bottom, and located in a layer above the longitudinal reinforcement [refer Fig. 14.22(a)]. Nominal transverse reinforcement may be provided elsewhere (i.e., other than the column strips), to tie with the longitudinal reinforcement (wherever provided); these nominal bars, however, are not indicated in Fig. 14.22(a). Development length requirements should be satisfied by the flexural reinforcement provided.

The column strip (transverse beam) should also be checked for one-way shear at a distance, equal to the effective depth of the transverse reinforcement, from the face of the column/pedestal. The design of a two-column rectangular footing is illustrated in Example 14.9.

Beam-Slab Combined Footings

In the case of relatively large footings, providing a uniform large thickness for the entire footing is uneconomical. In such a case, it may be more economical to design a *beam-slab* footing, in which the footing consists of a base slab stiffened by means of a central longitudinal beam (of sufficient depth), interconnecting the columns [Fig. 14.23].

† Although the load transfer mechanism assumes a transverse beam of width $a + 1.5d$ (critical for transverse bending), the *longitudinal* bending moment and shear force diagrams in Fig. 14.22(c), (d) are drawn taking the width of support equal to the column width, as the critical section for positive moment in the longitudinal direction is at the face of the column, and for shear at distances d (one-way) and $d/2$ (two-way) from column face. As the design section for both shear and moment are outside the column section, it suffices to assume the supports to be concentrated at the column centrelines; the corresponding shear force and bending moment distributions are shown by dashed lines in Fig. 14.22(c), (d).

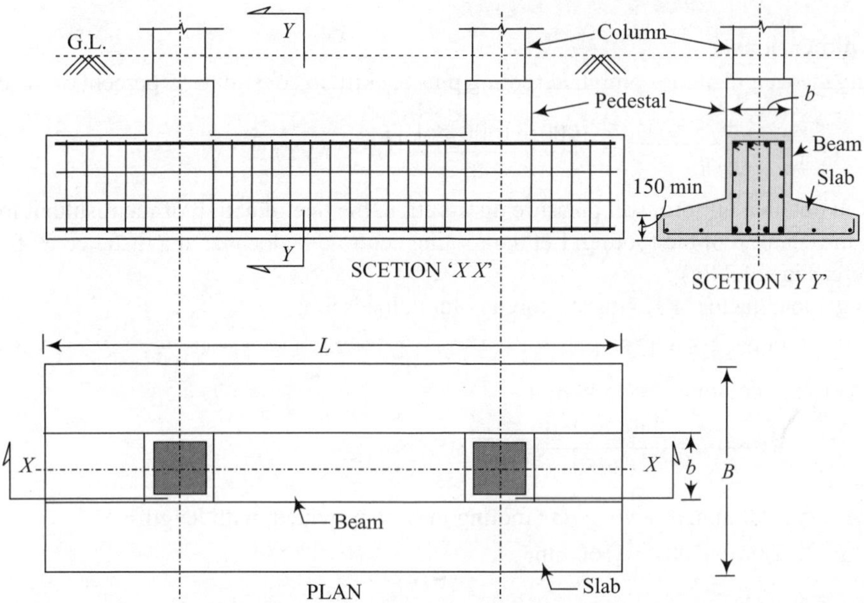

Fig. 14.23 Beam-slab combined footing.

The base slab behaves like a one-way slab, supported by the beam, and bends transversely under the uniform soil pressure acting from below. The loads transferred from the slab are resisted by the longitudinal beam. The size of the beam is generally governed by (one-way) shear at d from the face of the column/pedestal. For effective load transfer, the width of the footing beam should be made equal to the column/pedestal width, and it is advantageous to provide a pedestal to the column. The high shear in the beam will usually call for heavy shear reinforcement, usually provided in the form of multi-legged stirrups [Fig. 14.23].

The base slab may be tapered (if the span $(B - b)/2$ is large), for economy. The thickness of the slab should be checked for one-way shear at d (of slab) from the face of the beam. The flexural reinforcement in the slab is designed for the cantilever moment at the face of the beam, and provided at the bottom, as shown in Fig. 14.23. Two-way shear is not a design consideration in beam-slab footings. The top and bottom reinforcement in the beam should conform to the longitudinal bending moment diagram, and development length requirements should be satisfied.

Example 14.9

Design a combined footing for two columns C_1 (400 mm × 400 mm with 4–25ϕ bars) and C_2 (500 mm × 500 mm with 4–28ϕ bars) supporting axial loads P_1 = 900 kN and P_2 = 1600 kN respectively (under service dead and live loads). The column C_1 is an exterior column whose exterior face is flush with the property line. The centre-to-centre distance between C_1 and C_2 is 4.5 m. The allowable soil pressure at the base of the footing, 1.5 m below ground level, is 240 kN/m^2. Assume steel of grade Fe500 in columns as well as footing, and concrete of M 30 grade in columns and M25 grade in footing.

Solution

Footing base dimensions

- Assuming the weight of the combined footing plus backfill to constitute 15 percent of the column loads,

$$A_{\text{reqd}} = \frac{P_1 + P_2 + \Delta P}{q_a} = \frac{(900+1600)\times 1.15}{240} = 11.98 \text{ m}^2$$

- In order to obtain a uniform soil pressure distribution, the line of action of the resultant load must pass through the centroid of the footing. Let the footing centroid be located at a distance $\overline{x}$ from the centre of C_1 [refer Fig. 14.24(a)]:
- Assuming a load factor of 1.5, the factored column loads are:

$$P_{u1} = 900 \times 1.5 = 1350 \text{ kN}; P_{u2} = 1600 \times 1.5 = 2400 \text{ kN} \quad \Rightarrow \quad P_{u1} + P_{u2} = 3750 \text{ kN}$$

- spacing between columns $s = 4500$ mm

$$\Rightarrow \qquad \overline{x} = \frac{P_{u2}\, s}{P_{u1} + P_{u2}} = \frac{2400 \times 4500}{3750} = 2880 \text{ mm}$$

- As $\overline{x} > s/2 = 2250$ mm, a *rectangular* footing may be provided, with length

  $L = 2(2880 + 200) = 6160$ mm

  Provide $L = 6.16$ m

  $\Rightarrow$ width required $B \geq A/L = 11.98/6.16 = 1.95$ m

  Provide $B = 2.00$ m

Stress resultants in longitudinal direction

- Treating the footing as a wide beam (B = 2000 mm) in the longitudinal direction, the uniformly distributed load (acting upward) is given by

  $q_u B = (P_{u1} + P_{u2})/L = 3750/6.16 = 608.8$ kN/m [as shown in Fig. 14.24(b)].

- The distribution of shear force is shown in Fig. 14.24(c). The critical section for one-way shear is located at a distance d from the (inside) face of C_2, and has a value

  $V_{u1} = 2400 - 608.8(1460 + 250 + d) \times 10^{-3} = (1359 - 0.6088d)$ kN

- The distribution of bending moment is shown in Fig. 14.24(d). The maximum 'positive' moment at the face of column C_2 is given by

  $M_u^+ = 608.8 \times (1.460 - 0.250)^2/2 = 446$ kNm

- The maximum 'negative' moment occurs at the location of zero shear, which is at a distance x from the edge (near C_1) of the footing [Fig. 14.24(c)]:

  $x = 1350/608.8 = 2.2175$ m

- $\Rightarrow$ $M_u^- = 608.8 \times (2.2175)^2/2 - 1350 \times (2.2175 - 0.2) = (-)1227$ kNm

Thickness of footing based on shear

(a) *One-way shear* (longitudinal): V_{u1}

- Assuming $\tau_c = 0.49$ MPa (for M 25 concrete, assuming $p_t = 0.50$)

  $V_{uc} = 0.49 \times 2000 \times d = (980d)$ N

  $V_{u1} \leq V_{uc} \Rightarrow (1359 - 0.6088d) \times 10^3 \leq 980d$

  $\Rightarrow$ $d \geq 855$ mm

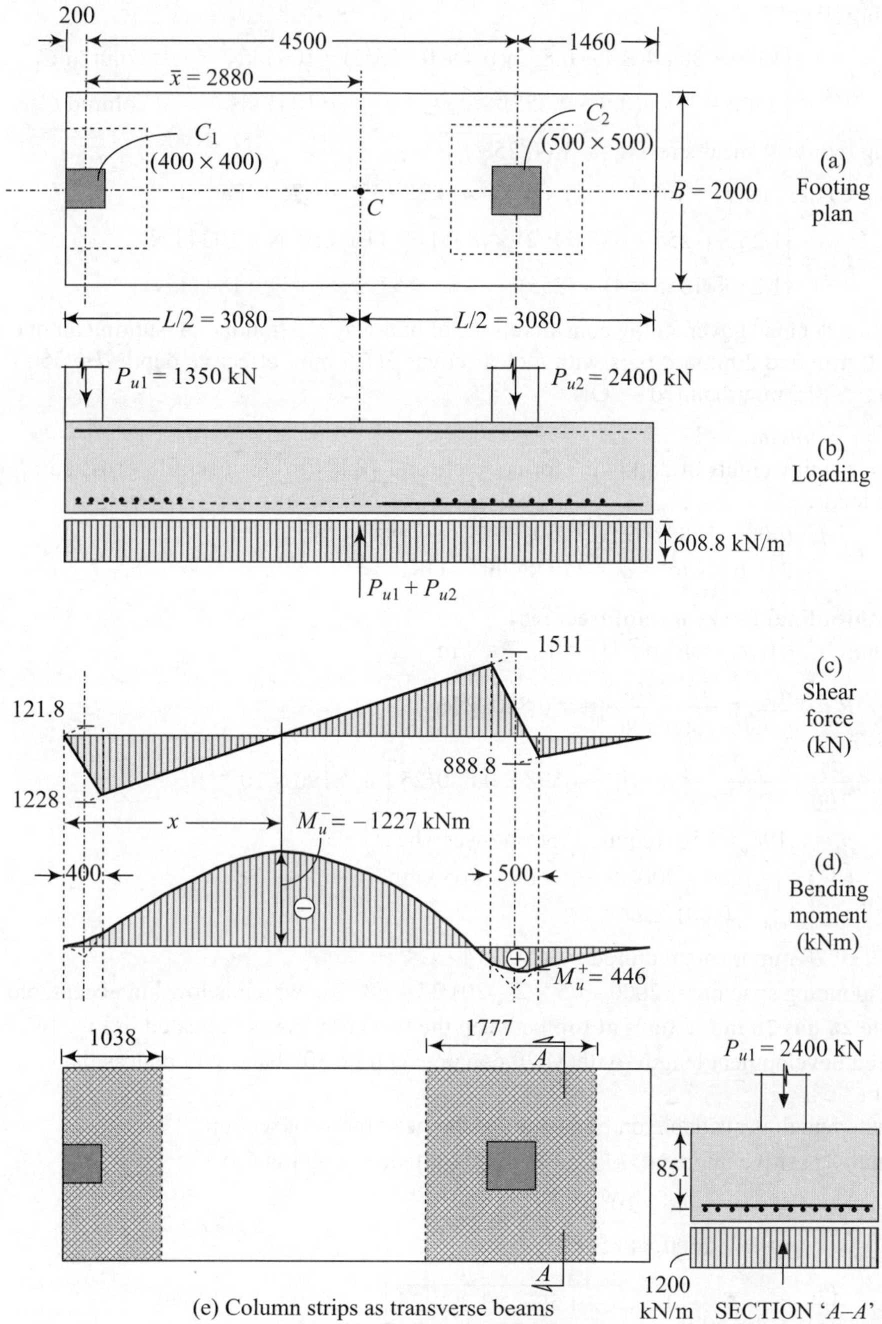

Fig. 14.24 Example 14.9.

(b) *Two-way shear*

- The critical section is located $d/2$ from the periphery of columns C_1 and C_2 [Fig. 14.24(a)], and the factored soil pressure $q_u = (q_u B)/B = 608.8/2.0$
$= 304.4 \text{ kN/m}^2$

Assuming $d = 855$ mm,

$$V_{u2} = \begin{cases} 1350 - 304.4(0.4 + 0.855)(0.4 + 0.855/2) = 1034 \text{ kN} & \text{at column } C_1 \\ 2400 - 304.4(0.5 + 0.855)^2 = 1841 \text{ kN} & \text{at column } C_2 \end{cases}$$

Limiting two-way shear stress $\tau_{c2} = k_s(0.25\sqrt{f_{ck}})$

For square columns, $k_s = 1.0 \;\Rightarrow\; \tau_{c2} = 1.0 \times 0.25\sqrt{25} = 1.25$ MPa

$$\Rightarrow \quad V_{uc} = \begin{cases} 1.25 \times (1255 + 827.5 \times 2) \times (855) = 3110 \times 10^3 \text{ N} > 1034 \text{ kN} \\ 1.25 \times (1355 \times 4) \times (855) = 5793 \times 10^3 \text{ N} > 1841 \text{ kN} \end{cases}$$

Hence, the depth is governed by considerations of one-way shear alone. Assuming an overall thickness **D = 950 mm** and 20 mm ϕ bars with a clear cover of 75 mm, effective depth $d = 950 - 75 - 20/2 = 865$ mm; > 855 mm required — OK.

- *Check base pressure*:
  Assuming unit weights of 24 kN/m^3 for concrete and 18 kN/m^3 for backfill, gross soil pressure under service loads

$$q = (900 + 1600)/(6.16 \times 2.0) + (24 \times 0.95) + (18 \times 0.55)$$
$$= 235.6 \text{ kN/m}^2 < q_a = 240 \text{ kN/m}^2 \text{ – OK.}$$

Design of longitudinal flexural reinforcement

- Maximum 'negative' moment: $M_u^- = 1227$ kN/m

$$\Rightarrow \quad R \equiv \frac{M_u}{Bd^2} = \frac{1227 \times 10^6}{2000 \times 865^2} = 0.820 \text{ MPa}$$

$$\Rightarrow \quad \frac{p_t}{100} = \frac{25}{2 \times 500}\left[1 - \sqrt{1 - 4.598 \times 0.820/25}\right] = 0.196 \times 10^{-2}$$

$$\Rightarrow \quad p_t = 0.196 < 0.50^{\dagger} \text{ required for one-way shear}$$

$$\Rightarrow \quad (A_{st})_{\text{reqd}} = 0.50 \times 2000 \times 865/100 = 8650 \text{ mm}^2$$
$$> (A_{st})_{\min} = 0.0012BD$$

Number of 20 mm ϕ bars required = 8650/314 = 28

[Corresponding spacing = (2000 – 75 × 2 – 20)/27 = 68 mm, which is low but acceptable.]

Provide 28 nos 20 mm ϕ bars at top between the two columns as indicated in Fig. 14.25.

- Required development length (with M 20 concrete and Fe 500 bars) will be less than $L_d = 48.6 \times 20 = 972$ mm
  Adequate length is available on both sides of the peak moment section.
- Maximum 'positive' moment: $M_u^+ = 446$ kNm (at face of column C_2)

$$\Rightarrow \quad R \equiv \frac{M_u}{Bd^2} = \frac{446 \times 10^6}{2000 \times 865^2} = 0.298 \text{ MPa}$$

$$\Rightarrow \quad \frac{p_t}{100} = \frac{25}{2 \times 500}\left[1 - \sqrt{1 - 4.598 \times 0.298/25}\right] = 0.069 \times 10^{-2} \text{ (low)}$$

$$(A_{st})_{\min} = 0.0012\, BD = 0.0012 \times 2000 \times 950 = 2280 \text{ mm}^2$$

† ***Note:*** In general, it is not good practice (and often, not economical) to fix the flexural steel requirement based on shear strength requirements, if the steel requirement is excessive. However, in this situation, $p_t = 0.50$ cannot be considered to be excessive.

- Number of 16 mm ϕ bars required = 2280/201 = 12
  [Corresponding spacing = (2000 – 75 × 2 – 16)/11 = 167 mm – OK.]
  Provide 12 nos 16 mm ϕ barsat bottom as indicated in Fig. 14.25.
- Required development length = 48.6 × 16 = 778 mm, which is available on the side of the column C_2 close to the edge of the footing; by placing the bars symmetrically with respect to column C_2, the required length will be available on both sides of the section of maximum 'positive' moment.

Design of column strips as transverse beams [Fig. 14.24(e)].

(a) *Transverse beam under column* C_1:

- Factored load per unit length of beam = 1350/2.0 = 675 kN/m
  Projection of beam beyond column face = (2000 – 400)/2 = 800 mm
- Maximum moment at column face:

$$M_u = 675 \times 0.80^2/2 = 216 \text{ kNm}$$

- Effective depth for transverse beam (16 mm ϕ bars placed above the 16 mm ϕ longitudinal bars): $d = 950 - 75 - 16 \times 1.5 = 851$ mm
  Width of beam = width of column + 0.75d
  = 400 + 0.75 × 851 = 1038 mm

$$\Rightarrow \quad R \equiv \frac{M_u}{Bd^2} = \frac{216 \times 10^6}{1038 \times 851^2} = 0.287 \text{ MPa (low)}$$

$\Rightarrow$ Provide minimum reinforcement: $A_{st} = 0.0012\, bD$

$\Rightarrow$ $A_{st} = 0.0012 \times 1038 \times 950 = 1183 \text{ mm}^2$

- Number of 16 mm ϕ bars required = 1183/201 = 6
  [Corresponding spacing = (1038 – 75 – 16)/5 = 189 mm]
  Alternatively, no. of 12 mm ϕ bars required = 1183/113 = 11

Provide 11 nos 12 mm ϕ bars

Required development length = 48.6 × 12 = 583 mm < (800 – 75) mm available – OK.

- There is no need to check one-way transverse shear in this case as the critical section (located at $d = 851$ mm from column face) lies outside the footing.

(b) *Transverse beam under column* C_2:

- Factored load per unit length = 2400/2.0 = 1200 kN/m
  Projection beyond column face = (2000 – 500)/2 = 750 mm
  $\Rightarrow$ Moment at column face = $1200 \times 0.75^2/2 = 338$ kNm
- Width of beam = 500 + 1.5 × 851 = 1777 mm

$$\Rightarrow \quad R \equiv \frac{M_u}{Bd^2} = \frac{338 \times 10^6}{1777 \times 851^2} = 0.263 \text{ MPa (low)}$$

$\Rightarrow$ Provide $(A_{st})_{min} = 0.0012 \times 1777 \times 950 = 2026 \text{ mm}^2$

- Number of 12 mm ϕ bars required = 2026/113 = 18

Provide 18 nos 12 mm ϕ bars

- Required development length = 48.6 × 12 = 583 mm is available beyond the column face.
- As in the previous case, check for one-way shear is not called for.

Transfer of force at column base

(a) *Column* C_1:

- Limiting bearing stress at (i) column face $= 0.45 f_{ck} = 0.45 \times 30 = 13.5$ MPa

  (ii) footing face $= 0.45 f_{ck} \sqrt{A_1/A_2}$

  [As the column is located at the edge of the footing, $A_1 = A_2 = 400^2$ mm^2]

  $= 0.45 \times 25 \times 1.0 = 11.25$ MPa, < 13.5 MPa

  $\Rightarrow$ Limiting bearing resistance at column-footing interface

  $F_{br} = 11.25 \times 400^2 = 1800 \times 10^3 \text{ N} > P_{u1} = 1350$ kN – OK.

- Hence, full force transfer can be achieved without the need for reinforcement across the interface. However, it is desirable to provide some nominal dowels (4 nos 20 mm ϕ), as shown in Fig. 14.25.

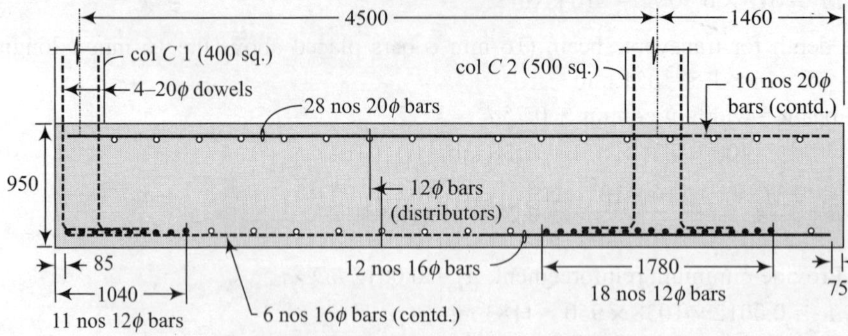

Fig. 14.25 Details of reinforcement, Example 14.9.

(b) *Column* C_2:

- Limiting bearing stress at (i) column face $= 0.45 f_{ck} = 13.5$ MPa (as before)

  (ii) footing face $= 0.45 f_{ck} \sqrt{A_1/A_2}$

  [$A_1 = 2000^2$, $A_2 = 500^2$ mm^2 $\Rightarrow$ $\sqrt{A_1/A_2} = 4.0$, limited to 2.0]

  $= 0.45 \times 25 \times 2.0 = 22.5$ MPa, > 13.5 MPa

  $\Rightarrow$ $F_{br} = 13.5 \times 500^2 = 3375 \times 10^3 \text{ kN} > P_{u2} = 2400$ kN.

- In this case also, full force transfer can be achieved without the need for reinforcement across the interface. However, it is desirable to provide some nominal dowels (4 nos 20 mm ϕ) as shown in Fig. 14.25.

Reinforcement details

- The reinforcement details are indicated in Fig. 14.25. Some of the longitudinal bars at the bottom are shown (arbitrarily) extended across the full length of the footing in order to provide some nominal reinforcement in the large (otherwise unreinforced) area of concrete between the columns and also to tie up with the transverse bars under column C_1. Nominal transverse reinforcement is also indicated at top between the columns, in order to tie up with the main longitudinal bars provided.

14.7 Types of Retaining Walls and their Behaviour

As explained in Section 14.1, retaining walls are used to retain earth (or other material) in a vertical (or nearly vertical) position at locations where an abrupt change in ground level occurs. The wall, therefore, prevents the retained earth from assuming its natural angle of repose. This causes the retained earth to exert a lateral pressure on the wall, thereby tending to bend, overturn and slide the retaining wall structure. The wall, including its supporting footing, must therefore be suitably designed to be *stable* under the effects of the lateral earth pressure, and also to satisfy the usual requirements of strength and serviceability.

Retaining walls are usually of the following types:

1. **Gravity Wall [Fig. 14.26(a)]**

   The 'gravity wall' provides stability by virtue of its own weight, and therefore, is rather massive in size. It is usually built-in stone masonry, and occasionally in plain concrete. The thickness of the wall is also governed by the need to eliminate or limit the resulting tensile stress to its permissible limit (which is very low† in the case of concrete and masonry). Plain concrete gravity walls are not used for heights exceeding about 3 m, for obvious economic reasons.

> 'Gravity walls', usually built in stone masonry, resist the earth pressure and get stability due to their self-weight. Their width is so determined that the resultant line of thrust falls within the middle-third of the cross-section, so that there is no tension developed in the section.

2. **Cantilever Wall [Fig. 14.26(b)]**

   The 'cantilever wall' is the most common type of retaining structure and is generally economical for heights up to about 8 m. The structure consists of a vertical *stem*, and a *base slab*, made up of two distinct regions, viz., a *heel slab* and a *toe slab*. All three components behave as one-way cantilever slabs: the 'stem' acts as a vertical cantilever under the lateral earth pressure; the 'heel slab' acts as a (horizontal) cantilever under the action of the weight of the retained earth (minus soil pressure acting upwards from below); and the 'toe slab' also acts as a cantilever under the action of the resulting soil pressure (acting upward). The detailing of reinforcement (on the flexural tension faces) is accordingly as depicted in Fig. 14.26(b). The stability of the wall is maintained essentially by the weight of the earth on the heel slab plus the self-weight of the structure.

> In these walls, the earth retaining element – the vertical stem – acts as a vertical cantilever.

3. **Counterfort Wall [Fig. 14.26(c)]**

   For large heights, in a cantilever retaining wall, the bending moments developed in the *stem*, *heel slab* and *toe slab* become very large and require large thicknesses. The bending moments (and hence stem/slab thicknesses) can be considerably reduced by introducing transverse supports, called *counterforts*, spaced at regular intervals of about one-third to one-half of the wall height), interconnecting the *stem*‡ with the *heel slab*. The counterforts are concealed within the retained earth (on the rear side of the wall). Such a retaining wall structure is called the *counterfort wall*, and is economical for heights above (approx.) 7 m. The counterforts subdivide the vertical slab (stem) into rectangular panels and support them on two sides (suspender-style), and themselves behave essentially as vertical

> In these structures, the counterforts act as stiff vertical cantilevered beams, and tie up with (support) the vertical slab, which spans horizontally between the counterforts and retains the earth.

† To eliminate tensile stresses, the 'middle third rule' is generally applied, wherein the wall thickness is made sufficiently large, to ensure that the resultant thrust at any cross-section falls within the 'middle third' region of the section.

‡ The toe slab is also frequently interconnected with the stem (in the front side of the wall) by means of a 'front counterfort', whose height is limited by the ground level on the toe side, so that it is concealed and provides free usable space in front of the wall.

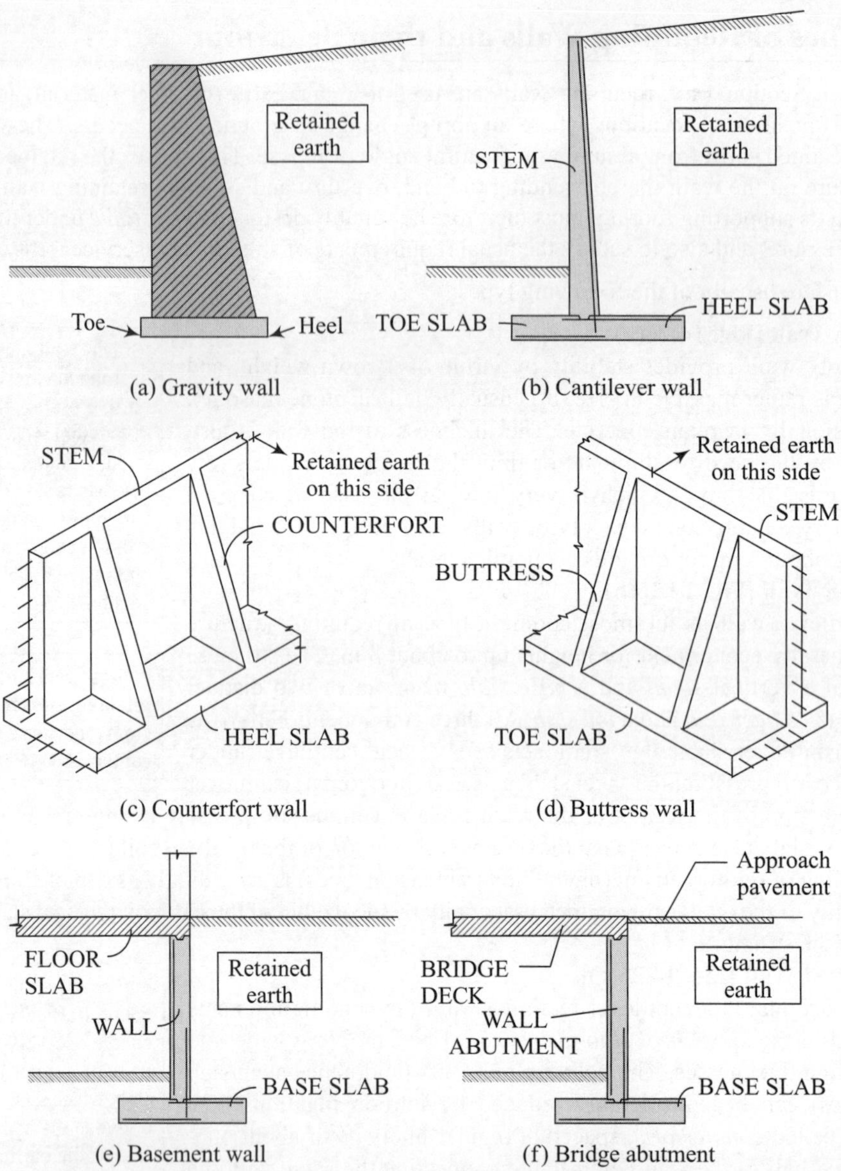

Fig. 14.26 Types of retaining wall structures.

> 'Buttress walls' are very similar to counterfort walls except that while in the latter, the vertical cantilevered beams are on the soil side of the vertical slab, in the former, these beams – called buttresses – are on the front side

cantilever beams of T-section and varying depth. The *stem* and *heel slab* panels between the counterforts are now effectively 'fixed' on three sides (free at one edge), and for the stem the predominant direction of bending (and flexural reinforcement) is now horizontal (spanning between counterforts), rather than vertical (as in the cantilever wall).

4. **Buttress Wall [Fig. 14.26(d)]**

The 'buttress wall' is similar to the 'counterfort wall', except that the transverse stem supports, called *buttresses*, are located in the front side, interconnecting the *stem* with the *toe slab* (and not with the *heel slab*, as with counterforts). Although buttresses are structurally more efficient (and more economical) than counterforts, the counterfort wall is generally preferred to the buttress wall as it provides free usable space (and better aesthetics) in front of the wall.

5. **Other Types of Walls**
   Retaining walls often form part of a bigger structure, in which case their structural behaviour depends on their interaction with the rest of the structure. For example, the exterior walls in the *basement* of a building [Fig. 14.26(e)] and wall-type *bridge abutments* [Fig. 14.26(f)] act as retaining walls which also carry substantial axial loads. In both these situations, the vertical stem is provided an additional horizontal restraint at the top, due to the slab[†] at the ground floor level (in the case of the basement wall) and due to the bridge deck (in the case of bridge abutment). The stem is accordingly designed as a beam-column, fixed at the base and simply supported or partially restrained at the top. The side walls of *box culverts* also act as retaining walls. In this case, the box culvert (with single/multiple cells) acts as a closed rigid frame, resisting the combined effects of lateral earth pressures, dead loads (due to self-weight and earth above), as well as live loads due to highway traffic.

   In the sections to follow, only the cantilever and counterfort retaining walls are discussed – with particular emphasis on the cantilever wall, which is the most common type of retaining wall structure.

14.8 Earth Pressures and Stability Requirements

14.8.1 Lateral Earth Pressures

The lateral force due to earth pressure constitutes the main force acting on the retaining wall, tending to make it bend, slide and overturn. The determination of the magnitude and direction of the earth pressure is based on the principles of soil mechanics, and the reader may refer to standard texts in this specialised area (such as Ref. 14.2, 14.3, 14.8) for a detailed study.

In general, the behaviour of lateral earth pressure is analogous to that of a fluid, with the magnitude of the pressure p increasing nearly linearly with increasing depth z for moderate depths below the surface:

$$p = C\gamma_e z \tag{14.9}$$

where γ_e is the unit weight of the earth and C is a coefficient that depends on its physical properties, and also on whether the pressure is *active* or *passive*. 'Active pressure' (p_a) is that which the retained earth exerts on the wall as the earth moves in the same direction as the wall deflects. On the other hand, 'passive pressure' (p_p) is that which is developed as a resistance when the wall moves and presses against the earth (as on the toe side of the wall). The coefficient to be used in Eq. 14.9 is the *active pressure coefficient*, C_a, in the case of active pressure, and the *passive pressure coefficient*, C_p, in the case of passive pressure; the latter (C_p) is generally much higher than the former (C_a) for the same type of soil.

> 'Active earth pressure' on a retaining wall is the pressure exerted by the retained earth when the earth tends to move in the same direction as the deflection of the wall. 'Passive pressure' is the pressure developed when the wall tends to push against the earth.

In the absence of more detailed information, the following expressions for C_a and C_p, based on Rankine's theory [Ref. 14.2, 14.3], may be used for cohesionless soils and level backfills:

[†] The slab is integrally connected to numerous frames formed by the columns and beams, and the lateral restraint offered by it is due to the high *storey stiffness* at the lowermost storey.

$$C_a = \frac{1 - \sin\phi}{1 + \sin\phi} \tag{14.10a}$$

$$C_p = \frac{1 + \sin\phi}{1 - \sin\phi} \tag{14.10b}$$

where ϕ is the *angle of shearing resistance* (or *angle of repose*). For a typical granular soil (such as sand), $\phi \approx 30°$, corresponding to which, $C_a = 1/3$ and $C_p = 3.0$.

When the backfill is sloped[†], as shown in Fig. 14.27, the expression [Eq. 14.10a] for C_a should be modified as follows:

$$C_a = \left[\frac{\cos\theta - \sqrt{\cos^2\theta - \cos^2\phi}}{\cos\theta + \sqrt{\cos^2\theta - \cos^2\phi}}\right]\cos\theta \tag{14.11}$$

where θ is the angle of inclination of the backfill, i.e., the angle of its surface with respect to the horizontal [Fig. 14.27].

The direction of the active pressure, p_a [given by Eq. 14.9], is parallel to the surface of the backfill. The pressure has a maximum value at the heel, and is equal to $C_a \gamma_e h'$, where h' is the height of the backfill, measured vertically above the heel [Fig. 14.27]. For the case of a level backfill, $\theta = 0$ and $h' = h$, and the direction of the lateral pressure is horizontal and normal to the vertical stem.

The force, P_a, exerted by the active earth pressure, due to a backfill of height h' above the heel, on unit length of wall is accordingly obtained from the triangular pressure distribution [Fig. 14.27] as

$$P_a = C_a \gamma_e (h')^2/2 \tag{14.12}$$

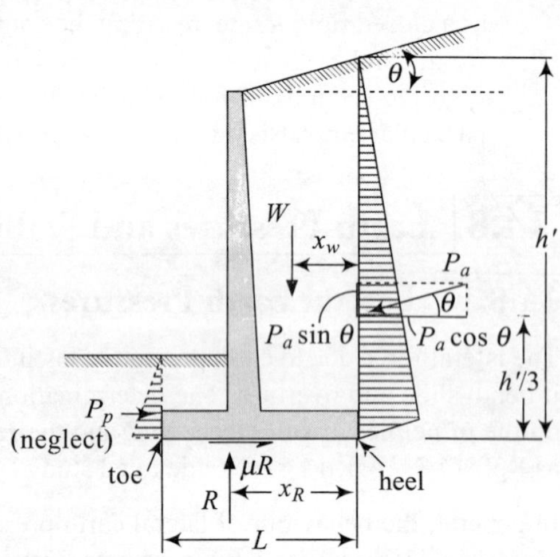

Fig. 14.27 Forces acting on a cantilever retaining wall.

This force has units of kN per m length of the wall, and acts at a height $h'/3$ above the heel at an inclination θ with the horizontal.

The force, P_p, developed by passive pressure on the toe side of the retaining wall is generally small (due to the small height of earth[‡]) and usually not included in the design calculations, as this is conservative.

14.8.2 Effect of Surcharge on a Level Backfill

Frequently, gravity loads act on a level backfill due to the construction of buildings and the movement of vehicles near the top of the retaining wall. These additional loads can be assumed to be static[§] and uniformly distributed on top of the backfill, for calculation purposes. This distributed load w_s (kN/m^2) can be treated as

[†] Sometimes, the term 'inclined surcharge' is used to refer to a sloping backfill; the term 'surcharge' implies the additional height of the backfill (or loading) above the level of the top of the wall [refer Section 14.8.2].

[‡] Strictly, for the full development of passive earth pressure, it is necessary that during the construction of the wall, there should be no disturbance to the soil against which the concrete in the toe slab is placed.

[§] In the case of vehicular traffic and other live loads, the equivalent loading should include a magnification factor for dynamic effects.

statically equivalent to an additional (fictitious) height, $h_s = w_s/\gamma_e$, of soil backfill with unit weight γ_e. This additional height of backfill is called *surcharge*, and is expressed either in terms of height h_s, or in terms of the distributed load w_s [Fig. 14.28].

The presence of the surcharge not only adds to the gravity loading acting on the heel slab, but also increases the lateral pressure on the wall by $C_a\gamma_e h_s = C_a w_s$. The resulting trapezoidal earth pressure distribution is made up of a rectangular pressure distribution (of intensity $C_a w_s$), superimposed on the triangular pressure distribution due to the actual backfill, as shown in Fig. 14.28. The total force due to active pressure acting on the wall is accordingly given by

$$P_a = P_{a1} + P_{a2} \tag{14.13}$$

where,

$$P_{a1} = C_a w_s h = C_a \gamma_e h_s h \tag{14.13a}$$

$$P_{a2} = C_a \gamma_e h^2/2 \tag{14.13b}$$

with the lines of action of P_{a1} and P_{a2} at $h/2$ and $h/3$ above the heel.

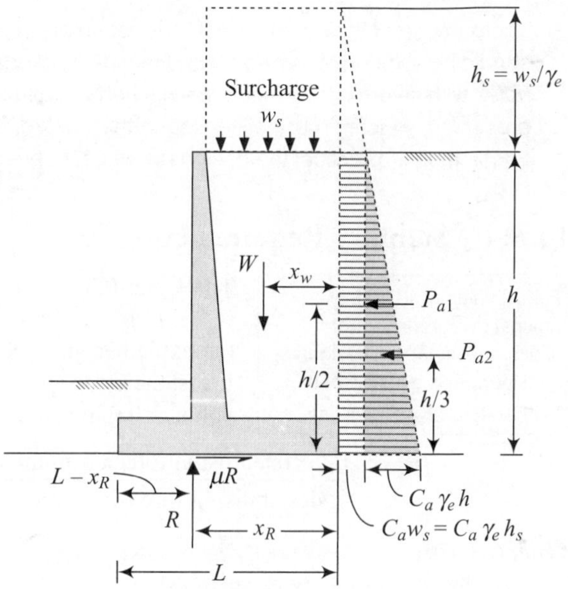

Fig. 14.28 Effect of surcharge on a level backfill.

14.8.3 Effect of Water in the Backfill

When water accumulates in the backfill, it can raise the lateral pressure on the wall to very high levels. If the water in the backfill does not have an escape route, it will build up a hydrostatic pressure on the wall, causing it to behave like a dam. The resulting pressure† distributions are depicted in Fig. 14.29.

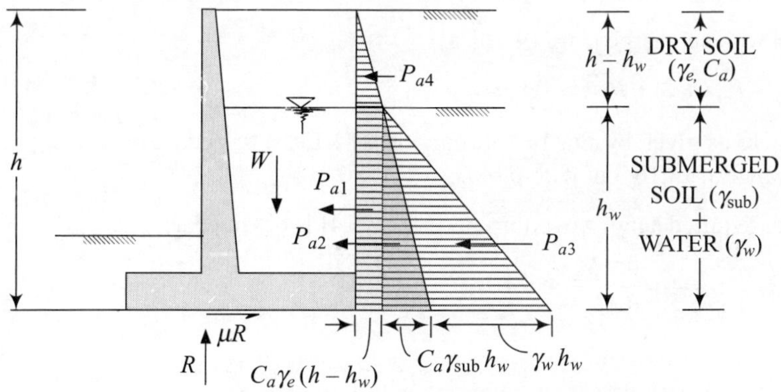

Fig. 14.29 Effect of water in the backfill.

† The presence of water does not significantly alter the shearing resistance of granular soils; hence the coefficient, C_a is practically the same for both dry and submerged conditions.

The purpose of the retaining wall is to retain earth, and not water. Hence, submerged earth conditions should be avoided by providing and maintaining proper drainage facilities (including provision of *weep holes* with inverted filter medium at its head). Failure to do so can result in the building up of enormous pressures, which, if not anticipated in the design, can result in serious failures. Such failures are not uncommon in practice; the designer must accept some responsibility for this.

14.8.4 Stability Requirements

For retaining walls, safety against overturning and sliding are important design considerations because of their vulnerability to such failures.

The Code (Cl. 20) specifies that the factors of safety against overturning (Cl. 20.1) and sliding (Cl. 20.2) should not be less than 1.4. Furthermore (as explained in Section 14.3.3), as the stabilising forces are due to dead loads, the Code specifies that these stabilising forces should be factored by a value of 0.9 in calculating the factor of safety, *FS*. Accordingly,

$$FS = \frac{0.9 \times (\text{stabilising force or moment})}{\text{destabilising force or moment}} \geq 1.4 \tag{14.14}$$

Overturning

If the retaining wall structure were to overturn, it would do so with the toe acting as the centre of rotation. In an overturning context, there is no upward reaction R acting over the base width L. The expressions for the overturning moment M_o and the stabilising (restoring) moment M_r depend on the lateral earth pressure and the geometry of the retaining wall.

For the case of a sloping backfill [Fig. 14.27],

$$M_o = (P_a \cos\theta)(h'/3) = [C_a \gamma_e (h')^3/6]\cos\theta \tag{14.15}$$

$$M_r = W(L - x_w) + (P_a \sin\theta)L \tag{14.16}$$

where W denotes the total weight of the wall structure plus the retained earth resting on the footing[†] (heel slab), and x_w is the distance of its line of action from the heel Fig. 14.27.

For a level backfill with surcharge [Fig. 14.28],

$$M_o = P_{a1}(h/2) + P_{a2}(h/3) \tag{14.17}$$

where P_{a1} and P_{a2} are as given by Eq. 14.13(a) and Eq. 14.13(b) respectively. The expression for M_r is the same as that given by Eq. 14.16, but with $\theta = 0$.

The factor of safety required against overturning [Eq. 14.14] is obtained as

$$(FS)_{overturning} = \frac{0.9\, M_r}{M_o} \geq 1.4 \tag{14.18}$$

Sliding

The resistance against sliding is essentially provided by the friction between the base slab and the supporting soil, given by

$$F = \mu R \tag{14.19}$$

[†] The weight of the earthfill above the toe slab is usually (conservatively) ignored. Similarly, the passive earth pressure P_p [Fig. 14.27] is also usually ignored.

where $R = W$ is the resultant soil pressure acting on the footing base and μ is the coefficient of static friction between concrete and soil. [In a sloping backfill, R will also include the vertical component of earth pressure, $P_a \sin\theta$ (see Fig. 14.27)]. The value of μ varies between about 0.35 (for silt) to about 0.60 (for rough rock) [Ref. 14.2].

The factor of safety against sliding [Eq. 14.14] is obtained as

$$(FS)_{\text{sliding}} = \frac{0.9F}{P_a \cos\theta}, \text{ which should be} \geq 1.4 \tag{14.19a}$$

When active pressures are relatively high (as when surcharge is involved), it maybe difficult to obtain the required factor of safety against sliding, through frictional resistance below the footing alone. In such cases, it is advantageous to use a *shear key* projecting below the footing base, extending throughout the length of the wall [Fig. 14.30]. When the concrete in the 'shear key' is placed in an unformed excavation (against undisturbed soil), it can be expected to develop considerable passive resistance. The shear key (usually square in section, $a \times a$) is best positioned at a distance X_{sk} from the toe in such a way that the flexural reinforcement from the stem can be extended straight into the shear key near its face on the toe side; although in practice they have been positioned at different locations from the toe end to the heel end depending on several other factors.

A 'shear key' is a projection of rectangular section, of adequate depth (a 'key'), provided below the base slab of a retaining wall, throughout its length, to help resist sliding of the wall.

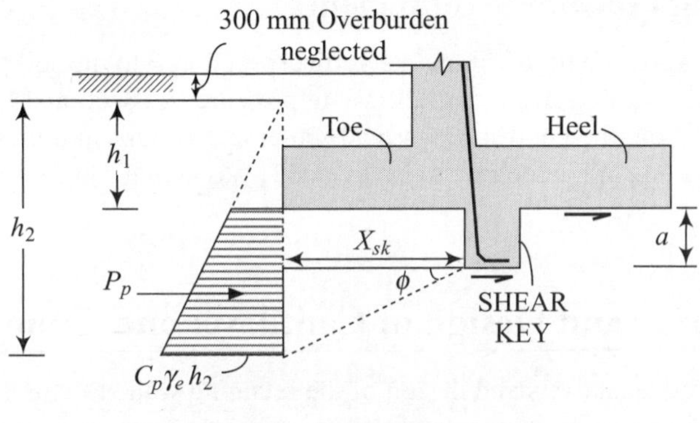

(a) High P_p, no friction below toe

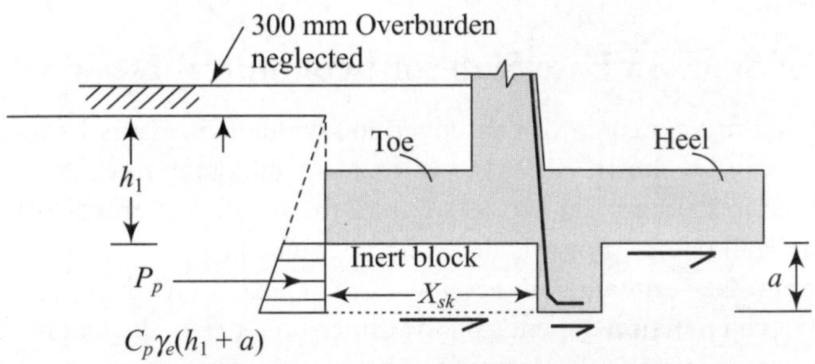

(b) Low P_p, with friction below toe

Fig. 14.30 Sliding resistance due to shear key - two different approaches.

Different procedures have been proposed to estimate this passive resistance P_p, and associated frictional resistance. In one approach [Ref. 14.8], considered relatively conservative, the frictional resistance under the toe region is ignored and the passive pressure is considered over a depth, $h_2 - h_1$, below the toe as shown in Fig. 14.30(a). The overburden due to the top 0.3 m of earth below ground level is usually ignored in the calculation. The resulting value of the sliding resistance is given by:

$$F = C_p\gamma_e\left(h_2^2 - h_1^2\right)/2 + \mu R_{\text{heel}} \tag{14.20a}$$

where R_{heel} is the resultant upward thrust below the heel region including the shear key. Note that if the soil below the base is in submerged condition, γ_e should be replaced with γ_{sub} (see Fig. 14.29).

In another approach, generally found to result in more economical designs [Ref. 14.9], the passive pressure contribution of the soil below the bottom level of shear key is ignored, while the rectangular soil region below the toe is assumed to behave like an 'inert block' as shown in Fig. 14.30(b). The soil-to-soil frictional resistance below the inert block is included in the estimate of sliding resistance. The resulting expression for sliding resistance is given by:

$$F = C_p\gamma_e\left((h_1 + a)^2 - h_1^2\right)/2 + \mu_s R_{toe} + \mu R_{heel} \tag{14.20b}$$

where $\mu_s = \tan\phi$ is the soil-to-soil frictional resistance and ϕ is the angle of repose of soil. This approach is demonstrated in Examples 14.8 and 14.9.

14.8.5 Soil Bearing Pressure Requirements

The base width L must be adequate to distribute the vertical reaction R to the soil without causing excessive settlement or rotation. The required depth and allowable pressure q_a (Section 14.2) are usually prescribed on the basis of a soil study and the control on vertical settlement is built into these recommendations. The designer must ensure that tilting of the footing is also avoided by avoiding a highly non-uniform base pressure in weak soils.

14.9 Proportioning and Design of Cantilever and Counterfort Walls

Prior to carrying out a detailed analysis and design of the retaining wall structure, it is necessary to assume preliminary dimensions of the various elements of the structure using certain approximations. Subsequently, these dimensions may be suitably revised, if so required by design considerations.

14.9.1 Position of Stem on Base Slab for Economical Design

An important consideration in the design of cantilever and counterfort walls is the position of the vertical stem on the base slab. It can be shown [Ref. 14.10] that an economical design of the retaining wall can be obtained by proportioning the base slab so as to align the resultant vertical soil reaction R at the base with the front face of the wall (stem). For this derivation, let us consider the typical case of a level backfill [Fig. 14.31]. The location of the resultant soil reaction, R, is dependent on the magnitude and location of the resultant vertical load, W, which in turn depends on the dimension X (i.e., the length of heel slab, inclusive of the stem thickness). For convenience in the derivation, X may be expressed as a fraction, α_x, of the full width L of the base slab ($X = \alpha_x L$). Assuming an average unit weight γ_e for all material (earth plus concrete) behind the front face of the stem (rectangle *abcd*), and neglecting entirely the weight of concrete in the toe slab,

$$R = W = \gamma_e hX = \gamma_e h\,(\alpha_x L)$$

For a given location of R corresponding to a *chosen value of X*, the toe projection of the base slab (and hence its total width, L) can be so selected by the designer as to give any desired distribution of base soil pressure. Thus, representing the distance, L_R, from the heel to R as a fraction α_R of base width L, [Fig. 14.31], the base pressure will be uniform if L is so selected as to make $\alpha_R = 0.5$. Similarly, for $\alpha_R = 2/3$, the base pressure distribution will be triangular. Thus, for any selected distribution of base pressure, α_R is a constant and the required base width $L = L_R/\alpha_R$.

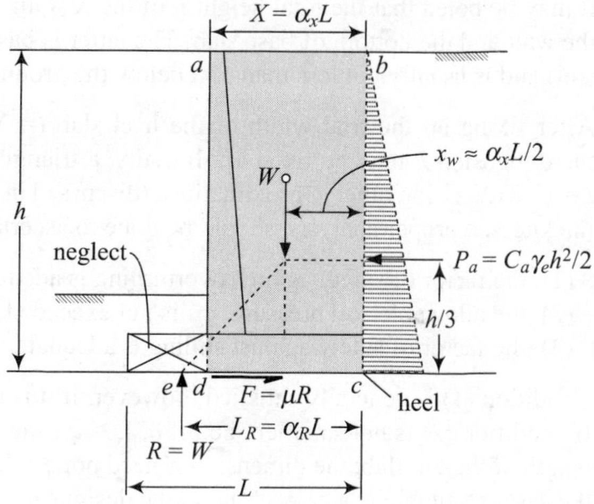

Fig. 14.31 Proportioning of retaining wall.

Considering static equilibrium and taking moments about reaction point e, and assuming $X_w \approx \alpha_X L/2$,

$$W(\alpha_R L - \alpha_X L/2) = P_a h/3$$

$$\Rightarrow \quad \gamma_e h L^2 (\alpha_R \alpha_X - \alpha_X^2/2) = C_a \gamma_e h^3/6$$

$$\Rightarrow \quad \frac{L}{h} = \sqrt{\frac{C_a/3}{2\alpha_R\alpha_X - \alpha_X^2}} \tag{14.21}$$

For economical proportioning for a given height of wall (h), the length of the base (L) must be minimum, i.e., L/h should be minimum. From Eq. 14.21, this implies that $(2\alpha_R\alpha_X - \alpha_X^2)$ should be maximum. α_R being constant for any selected distribution of base pressure, the location of R, and hence the base width is dependent on the variable X, i.e., α_x. For maximising $(2\alpha_R\alpha_x - \alpha_x^2)$,

$$\alpha_X = \alpha_R$$

$$\Rightarrow \quad \alpha_R L = \alpha_X L = X$$

Hence, for an economical design, the soil pressure resultant should line up with the front face of the wall.

Width of Base

Applying the above principle, ($\alpha_X = \alpha_R$), an approximate expression for the minimum length of base slab for a given height of wall is obtained from Eq. 14.21 as:

$$\left(\frac{L}{h}\right)_{\min} \approx \frac{1}{\alpha_R}\sqrt{\frac{C_a}{3}}$$

$$\Rightarrow \quad L_{\min} \approx (h/\alpha_R)\sqrt{C_a/3} \tag{14.22}$$

Alternatively, the minimum width of heel slab is given by

$$X_{\min} = \alpha_X L_{\min} = \alpha_R L_{\min} = h\sqrt{C_a/3} \tag{14.23}$$

The effect of surcharge or sloping backfill may be taken into account, approximately, by replacing h with $h + h_s$, or h', respectively.

Alternatively, and perhaps more conveniently, using the above principle, the heel slab width (X in Fig. 14.31) may be obtained by equating moments of W and P_a about the point d. The required L can then be worked out based on the base pressure distribution desired.

It may be noted that the total height h of the retaining wall is the difference in elevation between the top of the wall and the bottom of base slab. The latter is based on geotechnical considerations (availability of firm soil) and is usually not less than 1 m below the ground level on the toe side of the wall.

After fixing up the trial width of the heel slab (= X) for a given height of wall and backfill conditions, the dimension L may be fixed up. Initially, a triangular pressure distribution may be assumed, resulting in $L = (3/2) X$. Using other approximations (discussed in the next section) related to stem thickness and base slab thickness, a proper analysis[†] should be done to ascertain that

(1) the factor of safety against overturning is adequate;
(2) the allowable soil pressure, q_a, is not exceeded; and
(3) the factor of safety against sliding is adequate.

Condition (1) is generally satisfied; however, if it is not, the dimensions L and X may be suitably increased. If condition (2) is not satisfied, i.e., if $q_{max} > q_a$, the length L should be increased by suitably extending the length of the toe slab; the dimension X need not be changed. If condition (3) is not satisfied, which is usually the case, a suitable 'shear key' should be designed.

14.9.2 Proportioning and Design of Elements of Cantilever Walls

Initial Thickness of Base Slab and Stem

For preliminary calculations, the thickness of the base slab may be taken as about 8 percent of the height of the wall plus surcharge (if any); it should not be less than 300 mm. The base thickness of the vertical stem may be taken as slightly more than that of the base slab. For economy, the thickness may be tapered linearly to a minimum value (but not less than 150 mm) at the top of the wall; the front face of the stem is maintained vertical[‡]. If the length of the heel slab and/or toe slab is excessive, it will be economical to provide a tapered slab.

With the above preliminary proportions, the stability check and determination of soil pressure (at the base) may be performed, and dimensions L and X of the base slab [Fig. 14.31] finalised. It may be noted that changes in thicknesses of base slab and stem, if required at the design stage, will be marginal and will not affect significantly either the stability analysis or the calculated (gross) soil pressures below the base slab.

Design of Stem, Toe Slab and Heel Slab

The three elements of the retaining wall, viz., *stem*, *toe slab* and *heel slab* have to be designed as cantilever slabs to resist the factored moments and shear forces. For this a load factor of 1.5 is to be used.

In the case of the toe slab, the net pressure is obtained by deducting the weight[§] of the concrete in the toe slab from the upward acting gross soil pressure. The net loading acts upward (as in the case of usual footings) and the flexural reinforcement has to be provided at the bottom of the toe slab. The critical section for moment is at the front face of the stem, while the critical section for shear is at a distance d from the face of the stem. A clear cover of 75 mm may be provided in base slabs.

---

† In such an analysis, it will be seen that the actual vertical reaction R below the footing base will be close to, although rarely coincident with, the front face of the stem (as assumed initially).

‡ It is recommended that a batter of 1 : 50 be provided to the front face of the stem during construction, to offset the deflection of the stem or possible forward tilting of the structure [Ref. 14.10].

§ The weight of the earthfill in this region is (conservatively) ignored.

In the case of the heel slab, the pressures acting downward, due to the weight of the retained earth (plus surcharge, if any), as well as the concrete in the heel slab, exceed the gross soil pressures acting upward. Hence, the net loading acts downward, and the flexural reinforcement has to be provided at the top of the heel slab. The critical section for moment is at the rear face of the stem base.

The critical section for shear in the heel slab should be taken at the face of the support and not *d* away from it, because there is no compression introduced by the support reaction, and the probable inclined crack may extend ahead of the rear face of the stem [also refer Fig. 6.6(c)].

In the case of the stem (vertical cantilever), the critical section for shear may be taken *d* from the face of the support (top of base slab), while the critical section for moment should be taken at the face of the support. For the main bars in the stem, a clear cover of 50 mm may be provided. Usually, shear is not a critical design consideration in the stem (unlike the base slab). The flexural reinforcement is provided near the rear face of the stem, and may be curtailed in stages for economy [refer Example 14.9].

Temperature and shrinkage reinforcement ($A_{st,\min}$ = 0.12 percent of gross area) should be provided transverse to the main reinforcement. Nominal vertical and horizontal reinforcement should also be provided near the front face which is exposed.

14.9.3 Proportioning and Design of Elements of a Counterfort Wall

Initial Thicknesses of Various Elements

In a counterfort wall, counterforts are usually provided at a spacing of about one-third to one-half of the height of the wall. The triangular shaped counterforts are provided in the rear side of the wall, interconnecting the stem with the heel slab. Sometimes, small buttresses are provided in the front side below the ground level, interconnecting the toe slab with the lower portion of the stem.

The presence of counterforts enables the use of stem and base slab thicknesses that are much smaller than those normally required for a cantilever wall. For preliminary calculations, the stem thickness and heel slab thickness may be taken as about 5 percent of the height of the wall, but not less than 300 mm. If the front buttress is provided, the thickness of the toe slab may also be taken as $0.05h$; otherwise, it may be taken as in the case of the cantilever wall ($0.08h$). The thickness of the counterforts may be taken as about 6 percent of the height of the wall at the base, but not less than 300 mm. The thickness may be reduced along the height of the wall.

With the above preliminary proportions, the stability check and determination of soil pressures (at the base) may be performed, and dimensions L and X of the base finalised, as in the case of the cantilever wall.

Design of Stem, Toe Slab and Heel Slab

Each panel of the stem and heel slab, between two adjacent counterforts, may be designed as two-way slabs fixed on three sides, and free on the fourth side (free edge). These boundary conditions are also applicable to the toe slab, if buttresses are provided; otherwise, the toe slab behaves as a horizontal cantilever, as in the case of the cantilever wall.

The loads acting on these elements are identical to those acting on the cantilever wall discussed earlier. For the stem, bending in the horizontal direction between counterforts[†] is generally more predominant than

[†] An approximate and conservative estimate of this bending moment can be obtained by treating the slab as one-way continuous slab spanning the counterforts.

bending in the vertical direction. Near the counterforts, the main reinforcement will be located close to the rear face of the stem, whereas midway between counterforts, the reinforcement will be close to the outside face; the latter is indicated in Fig. 14.26(c). These two-ways slabs, subject to triangular/trapezoidal pressure distributions may be designed by the use of moment and shear coefficients (based on plate theory), available in various handbooks, and also in the IS Code for the design of liquid storage structures, viz., IS 3370 (Part 4) [Ref. 14.11]. Alternatively, the slabs may be designed by the yield line theory. An alternative simplified method of analysis is demonstrated in Example 14.12.

Design of Counterforts

The main counterforts should be firmly secured (by vertical and horizontal ties, respectively) to the heel slab, as well as to the vertical stem, as the loading applied on these two elements tend to separate them from the counterforts. The counterfort should be designed to resist the lateral (horizontal) force transmitted by the stem tributary to it. It is designed as a vertical cantilever, fixed at its base. As the stem acts integrally with the counterfort, the effective section resisting the cantilever moment is a flanged section, with the flange under compression. Hence, the counterforts may be designed as T-beams [refer Chapter 5] with the depth of section varying (linearly) from the top (free edge) to the bottom (fixed edge), and with the main reinforcement provided close to the sloping face. Since these bars are inclined (not parallel to the compression face), allowance has to be made for this in computing the area of steel required.

Example 14.10

Determine suitable dimensions of a cantilever retaining wall, which is required to support a 4.0 m high bank of earth above the ground level on the toe side of the wall. Consider the backfill surface to be inclined at an angle of 15° with the horizontal. Assume good soil for foundation at a depth of 1.25 m below the ground level with a safe bearing capacity of 160 kN/m². Further assume the backfill to comprise granular soil with a unit weight of 16 kN/m³ and an angle of shearing resistance of 30°. Assume the coefficient of friction between soil and concrete to be 0.5.

Solution

1. Data given: $h = 4.0 + 1.25 = 5.25$ m; $\mu = 0.5$

$\theta = 15°$ $\qquad \gamma_e = 16$ kN/m³

$\phi = 30°$ $\qquad q_a = 160$ kN/m²

- Earth pressure coefficients: $$C_a = \left[\frac{\cos\theta - \sqrt{\cos^2\theta - \cos^2\phi}}{\cos\theta + \sqrt{\cos^2\theta - \cos^2\phi}}\right]\cos\theta = 0.373$$

$$C_p = \frac{1+\sin\theta}{1-\sin\theta} = 3.0$$

2. Preliminary proportions

- Thickness of footing base slab $\approx 0.08h = 0.08 \times 5.25 = 0.42$ m
  Assume a thickness of 420 mm.
- Assume a stem thickness of 450 mm at the base of the stem, tapering to a value of 150 mm at the top of the wall.
- For an economical proportioning of the length L of the base slab, it will be assumed that the vertical reaction R at the footing base is in line with the front face of the stem. For such a condition, (assuming

the height above top of wall to be about 0.4 m), the length of the heel slab (inclusive of stem thickness) [Eq. 14.23]:

$$X \approx \left(\sqrt{C_a/3}\right)\ h' = \sqrt{0.373/3}\ (5.25 + 0.4) \approx 2.0 \text{ m}$$

- Assuming a triangular base pressure distribution,

$$L = 1.5X = 3.0 \text{ m}$$

- The preliminary proportions are shown in Fig. 14.32(a).

3. Stability against overturning

- Force due to active pressure: $P_a = C_a \gamma_e h'^2/2$

  where $h' = h + (X - 150) \tan\theta$ [Fig. 14.32(a)]

  $= 5250 + 1850 \tan 15° = 5746$ mm

  $P_a = (0.373)(16)(5.746)^2/2 = 98.52$ kN (per m length of wall)

  $\Rightarrow P_a \cos\theta = 98.52 \cos 15° = 95.16$ kN

  $P_a \sin\theta = 98.52 \sin 15° = 25.5$ kN

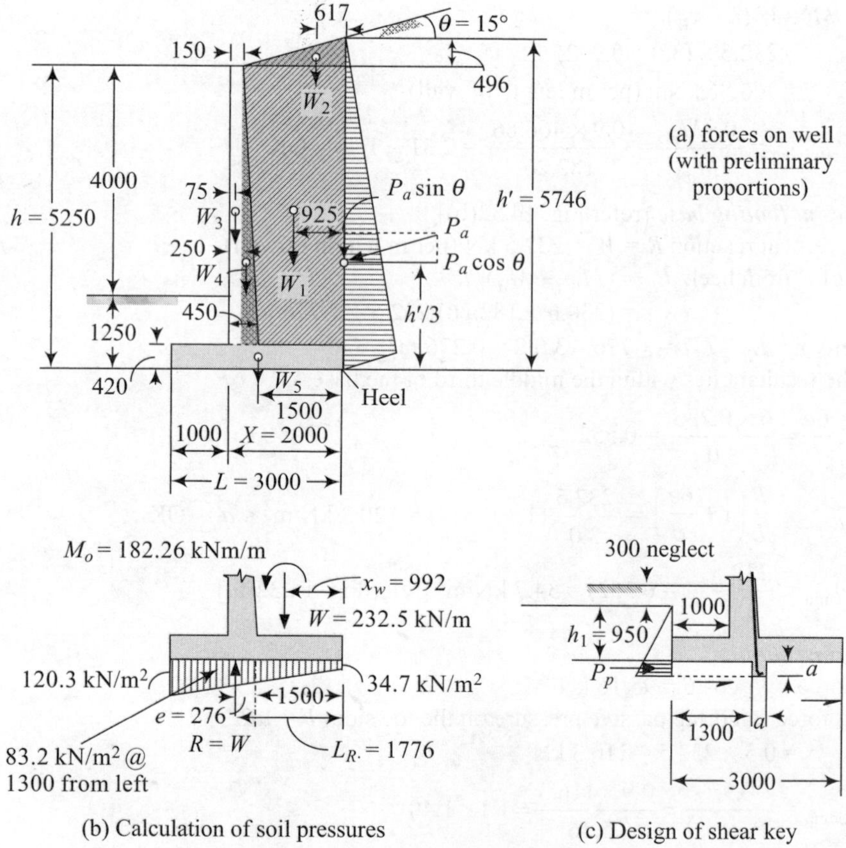

Fig. 14.32 Example 14.10.

- Overturning moment $M_o = (P_a \cos\theta)h'/3 = (95.16)(5.746/3) = 182.26$ kNm
- Line of action of resultant of vertical forces [Fig. 14.32(a)] with respect to the heel can be located by applying statics, considering 1 m length of the wall:

Force (kN)		Distance from heel (m)	Moment (kNm)
$W_1 = (16)(1.85)(5.25 - 0.42)$	= 143.0	0.925	132.3
$W_2 = (16)(1.85)(0.5 \times 0.536)$	= 7.9	0.617	4.9
$W_3 = (25)(0.15)(5.25 - 0.42)$	= 18.1	1.925	34.8
$W_4 = (25 - 16)(4.83)(0.5 \times 0.30)$	= 6.5	1.750	11.4
$W_5 = (25)(3.0)(0.42)$	= 31.5	1.500	47.2
$P_a \sin\theta$	= 25.5	0.000	0.0
	$W = 232.5$		$M_W = 230.6$ kNm

⇒ Distance of resultant vertical force from heel

$$x_W = M_W/W = 230.6/232.5 = 0.992 \text{ m}$$

- Stabilising moment (about toe):

$$M_r = W(L - x_W)$$
$$= 232.5 \times (3.0 - 0.992)$$
$$= 466.86 \text{ kNm (per m length of wall)}$$

$$\Rightarrow (FS)_{\text{overturning}} = \frac{0.9M_r}{M_o} = \frac{0.9 \times 466.86}{182.26} = 2.31 > 1.40 - \text{OK}$$

4. *Soil pressures at footing base* [refer Fig. 14.32(b)]

- resultant vertical reaction $R = W = 232.5$ kN (per m length of wall)
- distance of R from heel: $L_R = (M_W + M_o)/R$
  $= (230.6 + 182.26)/232.5 = 1.776$ m[†]
- eccentricity $e = L_R - L/2 = 1.776 - 3.0/2 = 0.276$ m, $< L/6 = 0.5$
- Hence, the resultant lies within the middle third of the base.

$$\frac{6e}{L} = \frac{6 \times 0.276}{3.0} = 0.552$$

$$\Rightarrow \quad q_{\max} = \frac{R}{L}\left(1 + \frac{6e}{L}\right) = \frac{232.5}{3.0}(1 + 0.552) = 120.3 \text{ kN/m}^2 < q_a - \text{OK}$$

and $$q_{\min} = \frac{232.5}{3.0}(1 - 0.552) = 34.7 \text{ kN/m}^2 \text{ [refer Fig. 14.32(b)]}$$

5. *Stability against sliding*

- Sliding force $= P_a \cos\theta = 95.16$ kN
- Resisting force (ignoring passive pressure on the toe side) $F = \mu R$
  $= 0.5 \times 232.5 = 116.3$ kN

$$\Rightarrow (FS)_{\text{sliding}} = \frac{0.9F}{P_a \cos\theta} = \frac{0.9 \times 116.3}{95.16} = 1.1 < 1.40$$

[†] Note that this value of L_R is different from, although close to, the value of $X = 2.0$ m assumed in the initial proportioning.

- Hence, a *shear key* may be provided to mobilise the balance force through passive resistance.
- Assume a shear key of size $a \times a$, at 1300 mm from toe [Fig. 14.32(c)].

$$F = C_p \gamma_e \left((h_1 + a)^2 - h_1^2\right)/2 + \mu_s R_{\text{toe}} + \mu R_{\text{heel}}$$

$$= 3 \times 16 \times \left((0.95+a)^2 - 0.95^2\right) \Big/ 2 + \tan 30 \times \frac{120.3+83.2}{2} \times 1.3 + 0.5 \times \frac{(83.2+34.7)}{2} \times 1.7$$

$$= 24a^2 + 45.6a + 126.48$$

$$(F.S)_{\text{sliding}} = \frac{0.9(24a^2 + 45.6a + 126.48)}{95.16} > 1.4$$

$\Rightarrow a > 0.39m$. Hence provide a shear key of size 400 mm × 400 mm.

Example 14.11

Repeat the problem in Example 14.10, considering the backfill to be level, but subject to a surcharge pressure of 40 kN/m² (due to the construction of a building). Design the retaining wall structure, assuming M 25 concrete and Fe 500 steel.

Solution

1. *Data given*: (as in Example 14.10)

$h = 4.0 + 1.25 = 5.25$ m $\quad \gamma_e = 16$ kN/m³ $\quad \phi = 30°$ $\quad q_a = 160$ kN/m² $\quad \mu = 0.5$ $\quad w_s = 40$ kN/m²

$\Rightarrow$ Equivalent height of earth as surcharge, $h_s = \dfrac{w_s}{\gamma_e} = \dfrac{40}{16} = 2.5$ m

$\Rightarrow$ $h + h_s = 5.25 + 2.5 = 7.75$ m

- Earth pressure coefficients: $C_a = \dfrac{1 - \sin\phi}{1 + \sin\phi} = 1/3$; $C_p = 1/C_a = 3.0$

2. Preliminary proportions

- Thickness of footing base slab $\approx 0.08(h + h_s) = 0.08 \times 7.75 = 0.620$. Assume a thickness of 620 mm.
- Assume a stem thickness of 650 mm at the base of the stem, tapering to a value of 200 mm at the top of the wall.
- For an economical proportioning of the length L of the base slab, it will be assumed that the vertical reaction R at the footing base is in line with the front face of the stem. For such a condition, the length of the heel slab (inclusive of stem thickness)

$$X \approx \sqrt{C_a/3}(h + h_s) = \sqrt{(1/3)/3}(7.75) = 2.58 \text{ m}$$

Let $X = 2.6$ m.

- Assuming a triangular soil pressure distribution below the base,

$$L = 1.5X = 1.5 \times 2.6 = 3.9 \text{ m}$$

- The preliminary proportions are shown in Fig. 14.33(a)

3. Stability against overturning

- Forces due to active pressure (per m length of wall) [Fig. 14.33(a)]:

$$P_{a1} = C_a w_s h = (1/3)(40)(5.25) = 70.0 \text{ kN}$$

$$P_{a2} = C_a \gamma_e h^2/2 = (1/3)(16)(5.25)^2/2 = 73.5 \text{ kN}$$

$\Rightarrow$ $P_a = 70.0 + 73.5 = 143.5$ kN

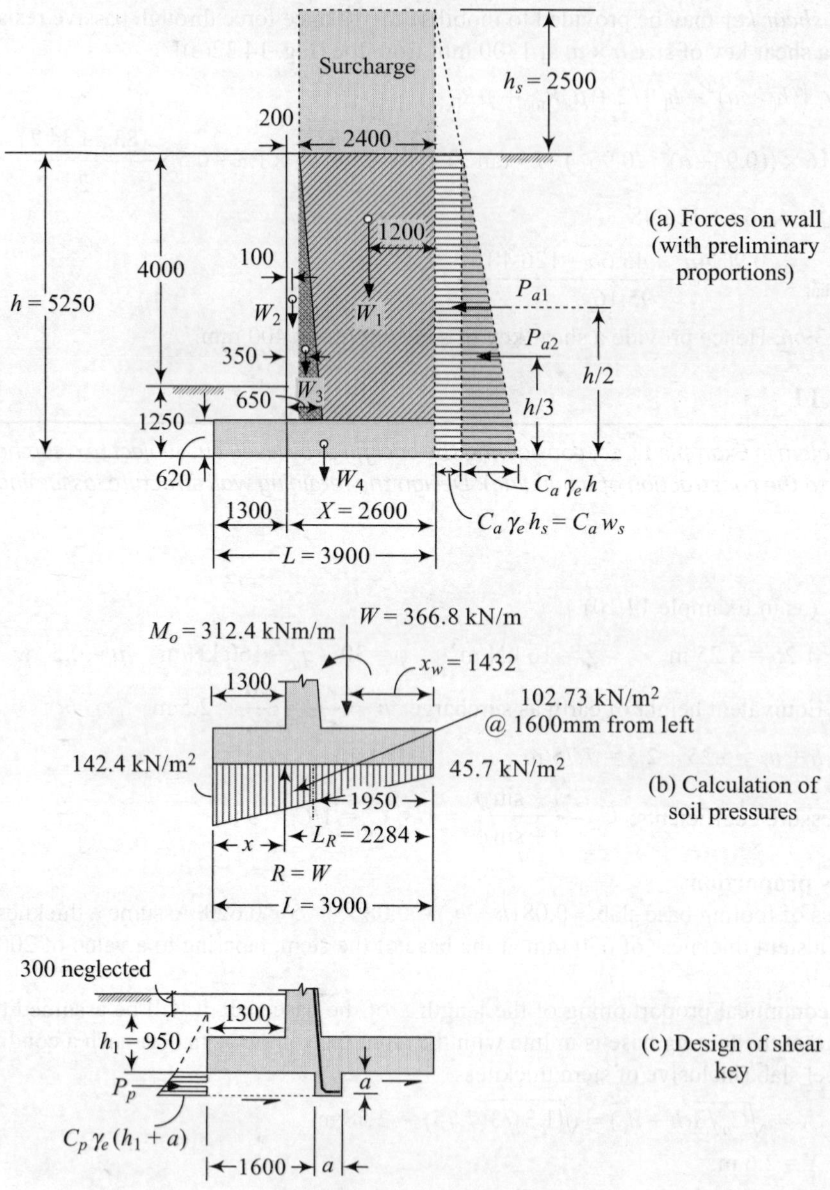

Fig. 14.33 Example 14.11.

- Overturning moment $M_o = P_{a1}h/2 + P_{a2}h/3$

$\Rightarrow \quad M_o = (70.0)(5.25/2) + (73.5)(5.25/3)$

$= 312.4$ kNm (per m length of wall)

- Line of action of resultant of vertical forces [Fig. 14.33(a)] with respect to the heel can be located by applying statics, considering 1 m length of the wall:

Force (kN)		Distance from heel (m)	Moment (kNm)
$W_1 = (16)(2.40)(7.75 - 0.62)$	$= 273.8$	1.20	328.6
$W_2 = (25)(0.20)(4.63)$	$= 23.2$	2.50	58.0
$W_3 = (25 - 16)(0.5 \times 0.45)(4.63)$	$= 9.4$	2.25	21.1
$W_4 = (25)(3.90)(0.62)$	$= 60.4$	1.95	117.8
	$W = 366.8$		$M_W = 525.5$ kNm

$\Rightarrow$ distance of resultant vertical force from heel

$$x_W = M_W/W = 525.5/366.8 = 1.432 \text{ m}$$

Referring to Fig. 14.33(b),

- Stabilising moment (about toe):

$$\begin{aligned} M_r &= W(L - x_W) \\ &= 366.8 \times (3.9 - 1.432) \\ &= 905.3 \text{ kNm (per m length of wall)} \end{aligned}$$

$$\Rightarrow (FS)_{\text{overturning}} = \frac{0.9M_r}{M_o} = \frac{0.9 \times 905.3}{312.4} = 2.61 > 1.40 - \text{OK}$$

4. Soil pressures at footing base [refer Fig. 14.33(b)]

- resultant vertical reaction $R = W = 366.8$ kN (per m length of wall)
- distance of R from heel: $L_R = (M_W + M_o)/R$
  $= (525.5 + 312.4)/366.8 = 2.284$ m[†]
- eccentricity $e = L_R - L/2 = 2.284 - 3.9/2 = 0.334$ m ($< L/6 = 0.65$) indicating that the resultant lies well inside the middle third of the base.

$$\Rightarrow \quad \frac{6e}{L} = \frac{6 \times 0.334}{3.9} = 0.514$$

$$\Rightarrow \quad q_{max} = \frac{R}{L}\left(1 + \frac{6e}{L}\right) = \frac{366.8}{3.9}(1 + 0.514)$$

$$= 142.4 \text{ kN/m}^2 < q_a = 150 \text{ kN/m}^2 - \text{OK.}$$

$$\Rightarrow \quad q_{min} = \frac{R}{L}\left(1 - \frac{6e}{L}\right) = \frac{366.8}{3.9}(1 - 0.514) = 45.7 \text{ kN/m}^2\text{, see Fig. 14.33(b)}$$

5. Stability against sliding

- Sliding force $= P_a = 143.5$ kN (per m length of wall)
- Resisting force (ignoring passive pressure) $F = \mu R$
  $= 0.5 \times 366.8 = 183.4 \text{ kN} > P_a$
- $(F.S)_{\text{sliding}} = \dfrac{0.9F}{P_a} = \dfrac{0.9 \times 183.4}{143.5} = 1.15 < 1.4$
- Hence, a *shear key* needs to be provided to generate the balance force through passive resistance. Providing a shear key of size $a \times a$ mm at 1.6 m from toe [Fig. 14.33(c)],

$$F = C_p \gamma_e \left((h_1 + a)^2 - h_1^2\right)/2 + \mu_s R_{\text{toe}} + \mu R_{\text{heel}}$$

[†] Note that this value of L_R is close to, but not equal to, the value of $X = 2.6$ m assumed in the initial proportioning.

$$= 3 \times 16 \times \left((0.95 + a)^2 - 0.95^2\right)\Big/2 + \tan 30 \times \frac{(142.4 + 102.73)}{2} \times 1.6 + 0.5 \times \frac{(102.73 + 45.7)}{2} \times 2.3$$

$$= 24a^2 + 45.6a + 198.57$$

$$(F.S)_{\text{sliding}} = \frac{0.9(24a^2 + 45.6a + 198.57)}{143.5} > 1.4$$

$\Rightarrow a > 0.44$ m. Hence provide a shear key of size 450 mm × 450 mm.

6. Design of toe slab

- The loads considered for the design of the toe slab are as shown in Fig. 14.34(a). The net pressures, acting upward, are obtained by reducing the uniformly distributed self-weight of the toe slab from the gross pressures at the base.
  Self-weight loading = 25 × 0.62 = 15.5 kN/m^2
- The net upward pressure varies from 126.9 kN/m^2 to 94.7 kN/m^2, as shown in Fig. 14.34(b). The pressure at distance d from face of stem is 108 kN/m^2.
- Assuming a clear cover of 75 mm and 16ϕ bars, $d = 620 - 75 - 8 = 537$ mm
- Applying a load factor of 1.5, the design shear force (at d = 537 mm from the front face of the stem) and the design moment at the face of the stem are given by:

$$V_u = 1.5(126.9 + 108)/2 \times (1.3 - 0.537) = 134.4 \text{ kN/m}$$

$$M_u = 1.5 \times [(94.7 \times 1.3^2/2) + (126.9 - 94.7) \times 0.5 \times 1.3^2 \times 2/3] = 147.2 \text{ kNm/m}$$

- Nominal shear stress $\tau_v = \frac{V_u}{bd} = \frac{134.4 \times 10^3}{10^3 \times 537} = 0.250$ MPa

  From Table 6.1, $\tau_c = 0.325$ MPa, for $p_t = 0.20$ with M25 concrete; alternatively, for a $\tau_c = 0.250$ MPa, the required $p_t = 0.11$ [refer Eq. 6.10].

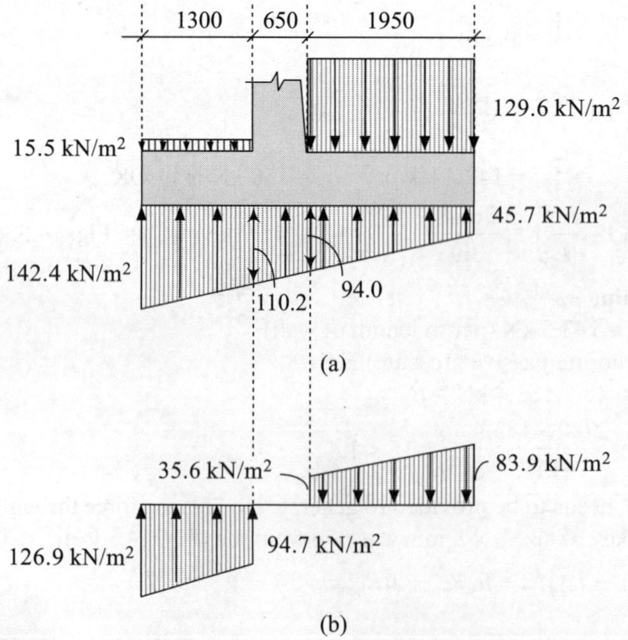

Fig. 14.34 Net soil pressures acting on base slab.

- $R \equiv \dfrac{M_u}{bd^2} = \dfrac{147.2\times10^6}{10^3\times537^2} = 0.510$ MPa

$\Rightarrow \quad \dfrac{(p_t)_{reqd}}{100} = \dfrac{25}{2\times500}\left[1-\sqrt{1-4.598\times0.510/25}\right] = 0.12 \times 10^{-2}$,

which is adequate for shear also

$\Rightarrow \quad (A_{st})_{reqd} = (0.12\times10^{-2})\times10^3\times537 = 645 \text{ mm}^2/\text{m}$

- Using 16ϕ bars, spacing required = 201 × 103/645 = 311 mm
Provide 16ϕ bars @ 300 c/c at the bottom of the toe slab. The bars should extend by at least a distance L_d = 48.6 × 16 = 778 mm beyond the front face of the stem, on both sides. As the toe slab length is only 1.3 m overall, no curtailment of bars is resorted to here.

7. Design of heel slab

- The loads considered for the design of the heel slab are as shown in Fig. 14.34(a). The distributed loading acting downward on the heel slab is given by
  (i) overburden + surcharge @ 16 × (7.75 – 0.62) = 114.1 kN/m²
  (ii) heel slab @ 25 × 0.62 = 15.5 kN/m²
  $\Rightarrow$ w = 129.6 kN/m²
- The net pressure acts downwards, varying between 35.6 kN/m² and 83.9 kN/m² as shown in Fig. 14.34(b).
- Applying a load factor of 1.5, the design shear force and bending moment at the (rear) face of the stem are given by

$$V_u = 1.5(35.6 + 83.9)/2 \times 1.95 = 174.8 \text{ kN/m}$$
$$M_u = 1.5 \times [(35.6 \times 1.95^2/2) + (83.9 - 35.6) \times 0.5 \times 1.95^2 \times 2/3] = 193.4 \text{ kNm/m}$$

- Assuming a clear cover of 75 mm and 16ϕ bars, d = 620 – 75 – 8 = 537 mm
- Nominal shear stress $\tau_v = \dfrac{V_u}{bd} = \dfrac{174.8\times10^3}{10^3\times537}$
$= 0.326$ MPa

Corresponding $\tau_c = 0.325$, with M 25 concrete [refer Table 6.1],
$(p_t)_{reqd} = 0.20$

- $R \equiv \dfrac{M_u}{bd^2} = \dfrac{193.4\times10^6}{10^3\times537^2}$
$= 0.670$ MPa

$\Rightarrow \quad \dfrac{(p_t)_{reqd}}{100} = \dfrac{25}{2\times500}\left[1-\sqrt{1-4.598\times0.670/25}\right]$
$= 0.159\times10^{-2}$
$< 0.20\times10^{-2}$ required for shear

$\Rightarrow \quad (A_{st})_{reqd} = (0.20\times10^{-2})\times10^3\times537$
$= 1074 \text{ mm}^2/\text{m}$

- Using 16ϕ bars, spacing required = 201 × 10³/1074 = 187 mm
Provide 16ϕ bars @ 180 c/c at the top of the heel slab. The bars should extend by at least a distance L_d = 48.6 × 16 = 778 mm beyond the rear face of the stem, on both sides. The bars may be curtailed part way to the heel; however, since the length is relatively short, this is not resorted to in this example.

8. Design of vertical stem

- Height of cantilever above base $h = 5.250 - 0.62 = 4.63$ m
- Assuming a clear cover of 50 mm and 20ϕ bars,
  d (at the base) = 650 – 50 – 10 = 590 mm
- Assuming a load factor of 1.5, maximum design moment

$$M_u = 1.5[C_a w_s h^2/2 + C_a \gamma_e h^3/6]$$
$$= 1.5 \times (1/3)[40 \times 4.63^2/2 + 16 \times 4.63^3/6]$$
$$= 346.7 \text{ kNm/m}$$

$$\Rightarrow R \equiv \frac{M_u}{bd^2} = \frac{346.7 \times 10^6}{10^3 \times 590^2} = 1.00 \text{ MPa}$$

$$\Rightarrow \frac{(p_t)_{\text{reqd}}}{100} = \frac{25}{2 \times 500}\left[1 - \sqrt{1 - 4.598 \times 1.00/25}\right] = 0.242 \times 10^{-2}$$

$$\Rightarrow \quad (A_{st})_{\text{reqd}} = (0.242 \times 10^{-2}) \times 10^3 \times 590 = 1428 \text{ mm}^2/\text{m}$$

- Using 16ϕ bars, spacing required $= \dfrac{201 \times 10^3}{1428} = 140$ mm

  Provide 16ϕ @ 140 c/c, bars extending into the 'shear key'. [This anchorage will be more than the minimum required: $L_d = 48.6 \times 16 = 778$ mm]
- *Check for shear at base*:
  Critical section is at $d = 0.59$ m above base, i.e., at $z_s = 4.63 - 0.59 = 4.04$ m below top edge. Shear force at critical section $= 1.5[C_a w_s z_s + C_a \gamma_s z_s^2/2]$

$$= 1.5 \times (1/3)[40 \times 4.04 + 16 \times 4.04^2/2]$$
$$= 146 \text{ kN/m}$$

$$\tau_v = \frac{146 \times 10^3}{10^3 \times 590} = 0.248 \text{ MPa} < \tau_c \text{ for } p_t = 0.242 - \text{OK}$$

  Note that since the shear stress is low and flexural reinforcement ratio also is low, the thickness of stem at base could be reduced for a more economical design.
- *Curtailment of bars*:
  In general, the curtailment of the bars may be done in two stages (at one-third and two-third heights of the stem above the base) as shown in Fig. 14.35. However, in this example, curtailment is done only at one-third height in order to limit bar spacing. It can be verified that the curtailment satisfies the Code requirements.
- *Temperature and shrinkage reinforcement*
  Provide two-thirds of the (horizontal) bars near the front face (which is exposed to weather and the remaining one-third near the rear face. For the lowermost one-third height of the stem above base,

$$A_{st} = (0.0012 \times 10^3 \times 650) \times 2/3$$
$$= 520 \text{ mm}^2/\text{m}$$

- Using 8ϕ bars, spacing required = 50.3 × 103/520 = 97 mm ≈ 100 mm. Provide 8ϕ @ 100 c/c near front face and 8ϕ @ 200 c/c near rear face in the lowermost one-third height of the wall; 8ϕ @ 200 c/c near front face and 8ϕ @ 400 c/c in the middle one-third height; and 8ϕ @ 300 c/c near front face and 8ϕ @ 500 c/c near the rear face in the top one-third height of the wall.
- Also provide nominal bars 10ϕ bars @ 300 c/c vertically near the front face.
- The detailing is shown in Fig. 14.35.

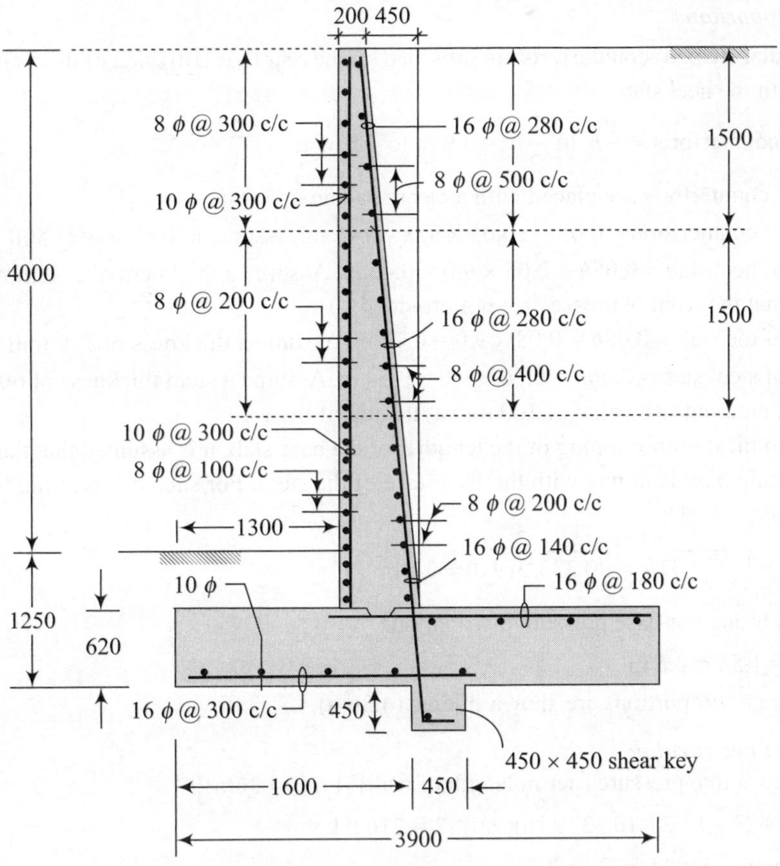

Fig. 14.35 Detailing of cantilever wall — Example 14.11.

Example 14.12

Design a suitable **counterfort** *retaining wall to support a level backfill, 7.5 m high above the ground level on the toe side. Assume good soil for foundation at a depth of 1.5 m below the ground level with a safe bearing capacity of 170 kN/m². Further assume the backfill to comprise granular soil with a unit weight of 16 kN/m³ and an angle of shearing resistance of 30°. Assume the coefficient of friction between soil and concrete to be 0.5. Use M 25 concrete and Fe500 steel.*

Solution

1. *Data given*: $h = 7.5 + 1.5 = 9.0$ m; $\mu = 0.5$

$\theta = 0°$ $\quad \gamma_e = 16$ kN/m^3

$\phi = 30°$ $\quad q_a = 170$ kN/m^2

- Earth pressure coefficients: $C_a = \dfrac{1 - \sin\theta}{1 + \sin\theta} = 0.333$

$$C_p = \frac{1 + \sin\theta}{1 - \sin\theta} = 3.0$$

2. *Preliminary proportions*

- The (triangular shaped) counterforts are provided on the rear (backfill) side of the wall, interconnecting the stem with the heel slab.

  Spacing of counterforts $\approx \frac{1}{3}h$ to $\frac{1}{2}h$ = 3.0 m to 4.5 m

  Assume the counterforts are placed with a clear spacing of 3.0 m.

  Thickness of counterforts $\approx 0.05h = 0.05 \times 9.0 = 0.45$ m. Assume a thickness of 500 mm.
- Thickness of heel slab $\approx 0.05h = 0.05 \times 9.0 = 0.45$ m. Assume a thickness of 500 mm
- Assuming that the front buttresses are not provided,

  Thickness of toe slab $\approx 0.08h = 0.08 \times 9.0 = 0.72$ m. Assume a thickness of 720 mm
- Thickness of stem slab $\approx 0.06h = 0.06 \times 9.0 = 0.54$ m. Assume a stem thickness of 600 mm at the base of the stem, tapering to a value of 300 mm at the top of the wall.
- For an economical proportioning of the length L of the base slab, it is assumed that the vertical reaction R at the footing base is in line with the front face of the stem. For such a condition, (inclusive of stem thickness) [Eq. 14.23]:

$$X \approx \left(\sqrt{C_a/3}\right)h = \sqrt{0.333/3}(9.0) = 3.0 \text{ m}$$

- Assuming a triangular base pressure distribution,

$$L = 1.5X = 4.5 \text{ m}$$

- The preliminary proportions are shown in Fig. 14.36(a).

3. *Stability against overturning*

- Forces due to active pressure (per m length of wall) [Fig. 14.36(a)]:

$$P_a = C_a \gamma_e h^2/2 = (0.333)(16)(9.0)^2/2 = 216.0 \text{ kN}$$

- Overturning moment $M_o = P_a \times h/3$

$$\Rightarrow \quad M_o = 216.0 \times (9.0/3)$$
$$= 648.0 \text{ kNm (per m length of wall)}$$

- Line of action of resultant of vertical forces [Fig. 14.36(b)] with respect to the heel can be located by applying statics, considering 1 m length of the wall (the marginal additional weight due to counterfort is ignored).

Force (kN)		Distance from heel (m)	Moment (kNm)
$W_1 = (16)(2.7)(9.0 - 0.5)$	= 367.20	1.35	495.72
$W_2 = (25)(0.3)(9.0 - 0.5)$	= 63.75	2.85	181.70
$W_3 = (25 - 16)(0.5)(0.3)(9.0 - 0.5)$	= 11.48	2.60	29.85
$W_4 = (25)(3.0)(0.5)$	= 37.50	1.50	56.30
$W_5 = (25)(1.5)(0.72)$	= 27.00	3.75	101.25
	$W = 506.9$		$M_W = 864.8$

$\Rightarrow$ distance of resultant vertical force from heel

$$x_W = M_W/W = 864.8/506.9 = 1.706 \text{ m}$$

Referring to Fig. 14.36(b),

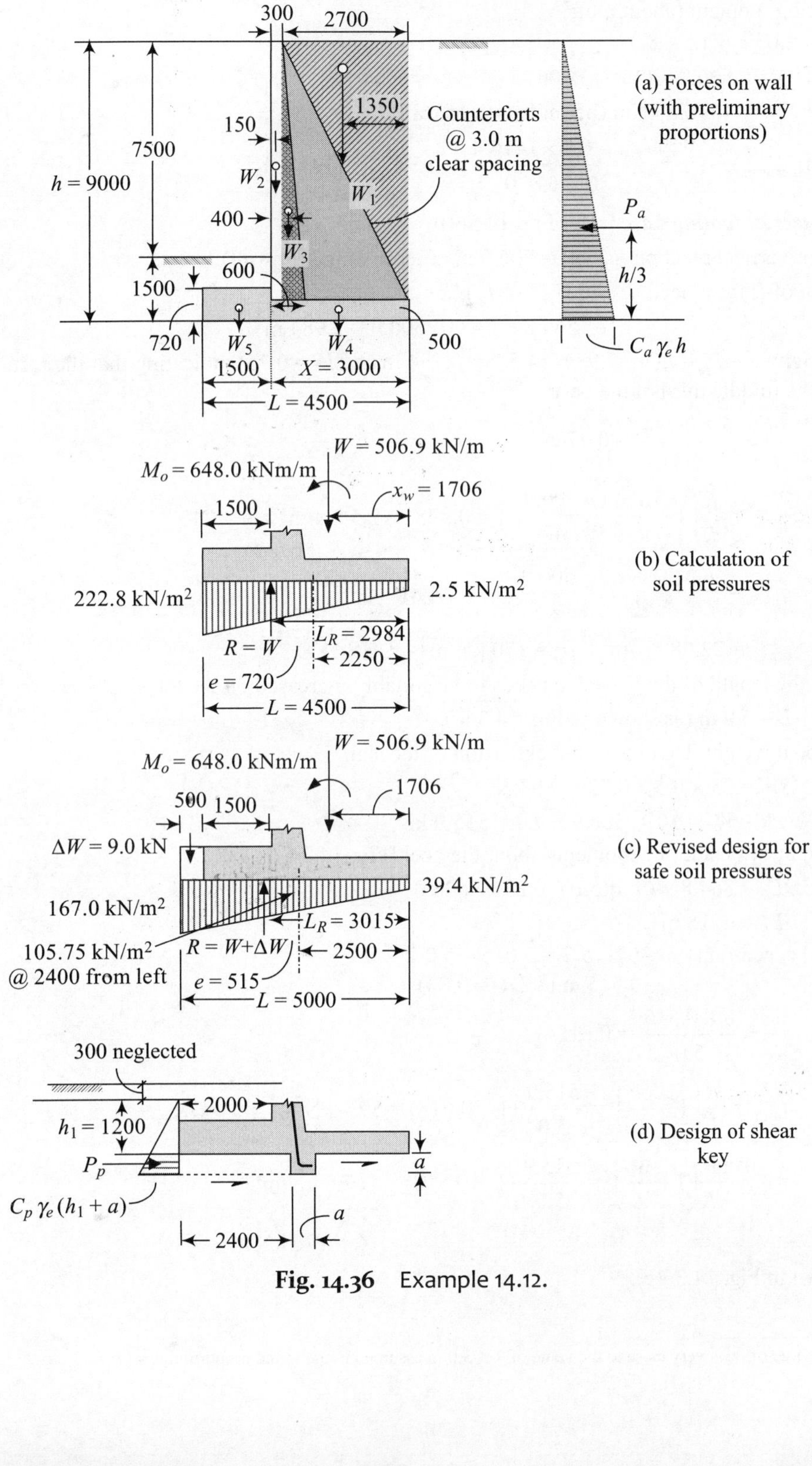

Fig. 14.36 Example 14.12.

- Stabilising moment (about toe):

$$M_r = W(L - x_W)$$
$$= 506.9 \times (4.5 - 1.706)$$
$$= 1416.4 \text{ kNm (per m length of wall)}$$

$$\Rightarrow (FS)_{\text{overturning}} = \frac{0.9M_r}{M_o} = \frac{0.9 \times 1416.4}{648.0} = 1.967 > 1.40 - \text{OK}$$

4. ***Soil pressures at footing base*** [refer Fig. 14.36(b)]

- resultant vertical reaction $R = W = 506.9$ kN (per m length of wall)
- distance of R from heel: $L_R = (M_W + M_o)/R$

$$= (864.8 + 648.0)/506.9 = 2.984 \text{ m}^{\dagger}$$

- eccentricity $e = L_R - L/2 = 2.984 - 4.5/2 = 0.734$ m ($< L/6 = 0.75$) indicating that the resultant lies just inside the middle third of the base.

$$\Rightarrow \quad \frac{6e}{L} = \frac{6 \times 0.734}{4.5} = 0.978$$

$$\Rightarrow \quad q_{\min} = \frac{R}{L}\left(1 - \frac{6e}{L}\right) = \frac{506.9}{4.5}(1 - 0.978) = 2.5 \text{ kN/m}^2 > 0 - \text{OK}$$

$$\Rightarrow \quad q_{\max} = \frac{R}{L}\left(1 + \frac{6e}{L}\right) = \frac{506.9}{4.5}(1 + 0.978)$$

$$= 222.8 \text{ kN/m}^2 > q_a = 170 \text{ kN/m}^2 - \textbf{UNSAFE}.$$

Hence, the length of the base slab needs to be suitably increased on the toe side – say, by 500 mm.

Let $\quad L = 5.0$ m (as shown in Fig. 14.36c).

Additional weight due to 500 mm extension of toe slab

$$\Delta W = 25 \times 0.5 \times 0.72 = 9.0 \text{ kN}$$

$$\Rightarrow \quad R = W + \Delta W = 506.9 + 9.0 = 515.9 \text{ kN}$$

Revised L_R: Considering moments about the heel [Fig. 14.36(c)]

$$515.9L_R = 864.8 + (9.0)(5.0 - 0.25) + 648.0$$

$$\Rightarrow \quad L_R = 3.015 \text{ m}$$

- Revised eccentricity $e = L_R - L/2 = 3.015 - 5.0/2$

$$= 0.515 \text{ m } (< L/6 = 0.83)$$

$$\Rightarrow \quad \frac{6e}{L} = \frac{6 \times 0.515}{5.0} = 0.618$$

$$\Rightarrow \quad q_{\min} = \frac{R}{L}\left(1 - \frac{6e}{L}\right) = \frac{515.9}{5.0}(1 - 0.618) = 39.4 \text{ kN/m}^2 > 0 - \text{OK}$$

$$\Rightarrow \quad q_{\max} = \frac{R}{L}\left(1 + \frac{6e}{L}\right) = \frac{515.9}{5.0}(1 + 0.618) = 167.0 \text{ kN/m}^2$$

$$< q_a = 170 \text{ kN/m}^2 - \text{OK}.$$

as shown in Fig. 14.36(c).

---

† Note that this value of L_R is very close to the value of $X = 3.0$ m assumed in the initial proportioning.

5. *Stability against sliding*

- Sliding force = P_a = 216.0 kN (per m length of wall)
- Resisting force (ignoring passive pressure) $F = \mu R$

$$= 0.5 \times 515.9 = 257.9 \text{ kN} > P_a$$

- $(F.S)_{\text{sliding}} = \dfrac{0.9F}{P_a} = \dfrac{0.9 \times 257.9}{216.0} = 1.075 < 1.4$ – **UNSAFE.**
- Hence, a *shear key* may be provided to mobilise the balance force through passive resistance. Assume a shear key of size $a \times a$, at a distance of 2400 mm from toe as shown in Fig. 14.36(d).

$$F = C_p\gamma_e\left((h_1 + a)^2 - h_1^2\right)/2 + \mu_s R_{\text{toe}} + \mu R_{\text{heel}}$$

$$= 3 \times 16 \times \left((1.2 + a)^2 - 1.2^2\right)\Big/2 + \tan 30 \times \frac{167.0 + 105.75}{2} \times 2.4 + 0.5 \times \frac{(105.75 + 39.4)}{2} \times 2.6$$

$$= 24a^2 + 57.6a + 283.31$$

$$(F.S)_{\text{sliding}} = \frac{0.9(24a^2 + 57.6a + 283.31)}{216} > 1.4$$

- $\Rightarrow a > 0.706$ m. Hence provide a shear key of size 710 mm × 710 mm.

6. *Design of toe slab*

- The loads considered for the design of the toe slab are as shown in Fig. 14.37(a). The net pressures, acting upward, are obtained by reducing the uniformly distributed self-weight of the toe slab from the soil pressures at the base.
  Self-weight loading = 25 × 0.72 = 18.0 kN/m^2

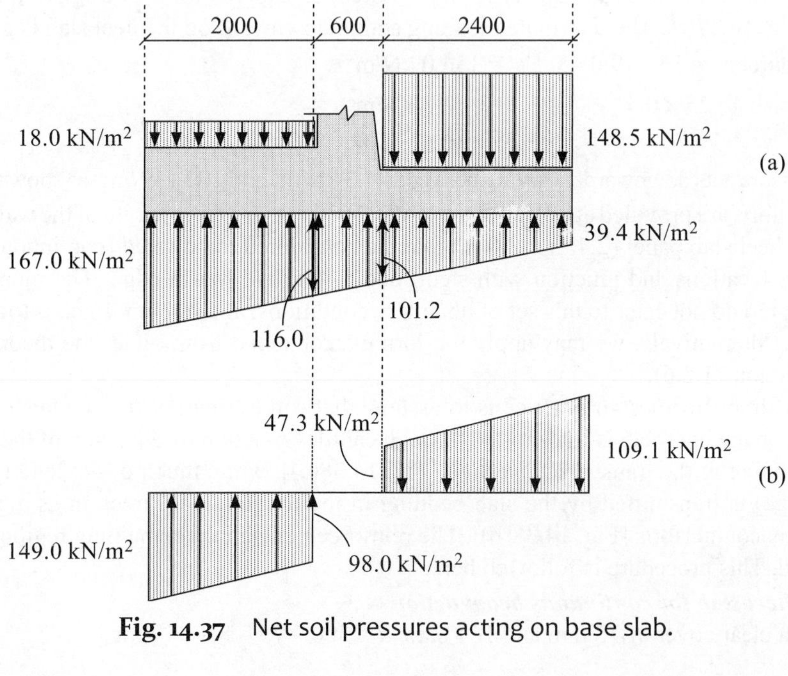

Fig. 14.37 Net soil pressures acting on base slab.

- The net upward pressure varies from 149.0 kN/m^2 to 98.0 kN/m^2, as shown in Fig. 14.37(b).
- Assuming a clear cover of 75 mm and 16ϕ bars, $d = 720 - 75 - 8 = 637$ mm
- Applying a load factor of 1.5, the design shear force (at $d = 637$ mm from the front face of the stem) and the design moment at the face of the stem are given by:

$$V_u \approx 1.5 \times (149.0 + 98.0)/2 \times (2.0 - 0.637) = 252.4 \text{ kN/m}$$

$$M_u = 1.5 \times [(98.0 \times 2.0^2/2) + (149.0 - 98.0) \times 0.5 \times 2.0^2 \times 2/3] = 395.9 \text{ kNm/m}$$

- Nominal shear stress $\tau_v = \dfrac{V_u}{bd} = \dfrac{252.4 \times 10^3}{10^3 \times 637} = 0.396$ MPa

  For a $\tau_c = 0.396$ MPa, the required $p_t = 0.32$ with M 25 concrete [refer Table 6.1]
- $R \equiv \dfrac{M_u}{bd^2} = \dfrac{395.9 \times 10^6}{10^3 \times 637^2} = 0.976$ MPa

$$\Rightarrow \quad \frac{(p_t)_{\text{reqd}}}{100} = \frac{25}{2 \times 500}\left[1 - \sqrt{1 - 4.598 \times 0.976/25}\right] = 0.236 \times 10^{-2}$$

$$< 0.32 \times 10^{-2} \text{ required for shear}$$

$$\Rightarrow \quad (A_{st})_{\text{reqd}} = (0.32 \times 10^{-2}) \times 10^3 \times 637 = 2039 \text{ mm}^2\text{/m}$$

- Using 16ϕ bars, spacing required = 201 × 103/2039 = 98.6 mm
- Using 20ϕ bars, spacing required = 314 × 103/2039 = 154 mm

  Provide 20ϕ bars @ 150 c/c at the bottom of the toe slab. The bars should extend by at least a distance $L_d = 48.6 \times 20 = 972$ mm beyond the front face of the stem, on both sides.

  Distribution steel:

  Provide **10ϕ bars @ 200 c/c** for the transverse reinforcement.

7. ***Design of heel slab***

- The loads (downward loads and upward soil pressures) considered for the design of the heel slab are as shown in Fig. 14.37(a). The distributed loading acting downward on the heel slab is given by

  (i) overburden @ 16 × (9.0 – 0.5) = 136.0 kN/m^2

  (ii) heel slab @ 25 × 0.5 = 12.5 kN/m^2

  ⇒ $w = 148.5$ kN/m^2

  The net pressure acts downwards, varying between 47.3 kN/m^2 and 109.1 kN/m^2 as shown in Fig. 14.37(b).
- The counterforts are provided at a clear spacing of 3.0 m throughout the length of the wall [Fig. 14.36(a)]. Thus, each heel slab panel (2.4 m × 3.0 m) may be considered to be fixed (continuous) at three edges (counterfort locations and junction with stem) and free at the fourth edge. The moment coefficients given in IS 456 do not cater to this set of boundary conditions, and reference needs to be made to other handbooks. Alternatively, we may apply the formulas obtained from yield line theory (such as those given in Section 11.2.6).

  A common simplified design practice is to assume that some tributary (triangular) portion of the net load acting on the heel slab is transmitted through cantilever action by a portion of the slab close to the stem by bending in the transverse direction [Fig. 14.38(a)], while much of the load (particularly near the free edge) is transmitted by the slab bending in the longitudinal direction as a continuous beam supported by counterforts [Fig. 14.38(b)]. The reinforcements in the remaining regions are judiciously apportioned. This procedure is followed here.
- ***Design of heel slab for continuous beam action***

  Assuming a clear cover of 75 mm and 16ϕ bars, $d = 500 - 75 - 8 = 417$ mm

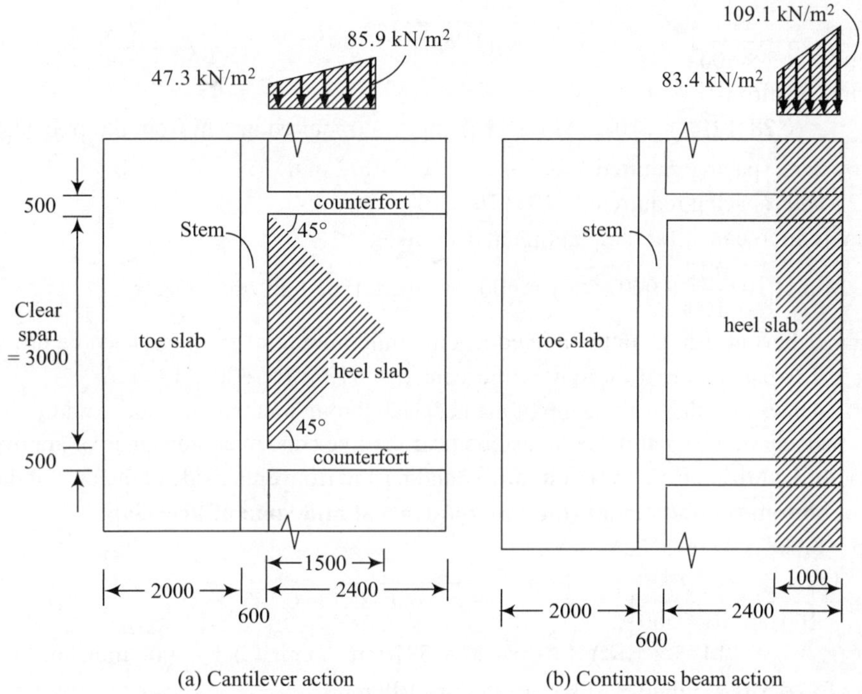

Fig. 14.38 Loading considerations for simplified analysis of heel slab.

Consider a 1 m wide strip near the free edge of the heel (Fig.14.38b). The intensity of pressure at a distance of 1 m from the free edge is 83.4 kN/m^2. Hence, the average loading on the strip may be taken as (83.4 + 109.1)/2 = 96.25 kN/m^2. Applying a load factor of 1.5, $w_u = 1.5 \times 96.25 = 144.4$ kN/m^2. The effective span is given by $l = 3.0 + 0.417 = 3.417$ m

Max. negative moment occurring in the heel slab at the counterfort location is given by†

$$M_{u,-\text{ve}} = w_u l^2/12 = 144.4 \times 3.417^2/12 = 140.5 \text{ kNm/m}$$

Max. mid-span moment may be taken as

$$M_{u,+\text{ve}} = w_u l^2/16 \approx 0.75 \times M_{u,-\text{ve}} = 105.4 \text{ kNm/m}$$

Design shear force

$$V_u = w_u \times (\text{clear span}/2 - d) = 144.4 \times (3.0/2 - 0.417) = 156.4 \text{ kN/m}$$

Design of top reinforcement (for –ve moments) at the counterforts

- Nominal shear stress $\tau_v = \dfrac{V_u}{bd} = \dfrac{156.4 \times 10^3}{10^3 \times 417} = 0.375$ MPa

For a $\tau_c = 0.375$ MPa with M 25 concrete [refer Table 6.1], the required $p_t = 0.28$.

- $R \equiv \dfrac{M_u}{bd^2} = \dfrac{140.5 \times 10^6}{10^3 \times 417^2} = 0.808$ MPa

† In this retaining wall, as in most cases, the design loads are due to earth pressures and self-weight only, which can be classified in the *dead load* category. The moment coefficients for continuous beams given in Cl. 22.5 of the Code, for dead loads, are 1/12 and 1/16 for negative and positive moments respectively, for interior spans. In the retaining wall here, the relatively stiff counterforts give full fixity for the heel slab at its ends and as such, the moment coefficients for the end span may be taken the same as for interior spans.

$$\Rightarrow \frac{(p_t)_{\text{reqd}}}{100} = \frac{25}{2 \times 500}\left[1 - \sqrt{1 - 4.598 \times 0.808/25}\right] = 0.193 \times 10^{-2} < p_t = 0.28$$ required for shear (in the absence of stirrups).

$\Rightarrow (A_{st})_{\text{reqd}} = (0.28 \times 10^{-2}) \times 10^3 \times 417 = 1168$ mm^2/m (required in 1 m from the free edge)

Using 16ϕ bars, spacing required = 201 × 10^3/1168 = 172 mm

Using 12ϕ bars, spacing required = 113 × 10^3/1168 = 96 mm

Minimum reinforcement for temperature and shrinkage:

$$\text{Min. } A_{st} = \frac{0.12}{100}(1000)(500) = 600 \text{ mm}^2/\text{m} < 1168 \text{ mm}^2/\text{m} \text{ – OK.}$$

At a distance beyond 1 m from the free edge, only minimum reinforcement need be provided:

Spacing of 12ϕ bars required for min. reinforcement = 113 × 10^3/600 = 188 mm

Provide **12ϕ bars @ 180 c/c** at the top of the heel slab throughout, and introduce additional 12ϕ bars in between two adjacent bars at the counterforts near the free edge over a distance of approx. 1 m;

i.e., **Provide 5 additional 12ϕ bars on top,** extending 1 m from either side of the face of the counterfort.

Design of bottom reinforcement (for +ve moment) at mid-span of heel slab

- $R \approx 0.75 \times 0.808 = 0.606$ MPa

$$\Rightarrow \frac{(p_t)_{\text{reqd}}}{100} = \frac{25}{2 \times 500}\left[1 - \sqrt{1 - 4.598 \times 0.606/25}\right] = 0.143 \times 10^{-2}$$

$$\Rightarrow (A_{st})_{\text{reqd}} = (0.143 \times 10^{-2}) \times 10^3 \times 417 = 597 \text{ mm}^2/\text{m} < (A_{st})_{\min} = 600 \text{ mm}^2/\text{m}$$

Spacing of 12ϕ bars required = 113 × 10^3 / 600 = 188 mm

Provide **12ϕ bars @ 180 c/c** at the bottom of the heel slab throughout.

Distribution steel:

Provide **10ϕ bars @ 200 c/c** for the transverse reinforcement.

- ***Design of heel slab for cantilever action***

Consider the triangular loading on the heel slab [Fig. 14.38(a)] to be carried by cantilever action with fixity at the face of the stem.

The intensity of load at the face of the stem = 47.3 kN/m^2.

The intensity of load at a distance of 1.5 m from the face of the stem is 85.9 kN/m^2.

Total B.M. due to loading on the triangular portion, is approximately given by

$$\approx \left(\frac{1}{2} \times 3.0 \times 1.5\right) \times \left(66.6 \times \frac{1.5}{3}\right) = 74.93 \text{ kNm}$$

This moment is distributed non-uniformly across the width of 3.0 m. For design purposes, the max. moment intensity (in the middle region) may be taken as two times the average value

$$\Rightarrow M_{\max} = 2 \times (74.93/3.0) = 49.95 \text{ kNm/m}$$

$$d = 417 - 12 = 405 \text{ mm}$$

Applying a load factor of 1.5,

$$R \equiv \frac{M_u}{bd^2} = \frac{1.5 \times 49.95 \times 10^6}{1000 \times 405^2} = 0.457 \text{ MPa}$$

$$\Rightarrow \frac{(p_t)_{\text{reqd}}}{100} = \frac{25}{2 \times 500}\left[1 - \sqrt{1 - 4.598 \times 0.457/25}\right] = 0.107 \times 10^{-2}$$

$$\Rightarrow (A_{st})_{\text{reqd}} = (0.107 \times 10^{-2}) \times 10^3 \times 405 = 434 \text{ mm}^2/\text{m} < (A_{st})_{\min} = 600 \text{ mm}^2/\text{m}$$

(for temperature and shrinkage)

Provide **12ϕ bars @ 180 c/c** at the top of the heel slab throughout.

8. ***Design of vertical stem***

The simplified analysis procedure adopted for the heel slab is used here for the vertical stem also. The cantilever action is limited to the bottom region only (triangular portion) with fixity at the junction of the stem with the base slab. Elsewhere, the stem is treated as a continuous beam spanning between the counterforts. The bending moments reduce along the height of the stem, owing to the reduction in the lateral pressures with increasing height.

Height of stem above base $h = 9.0 - 0.5 = 8.5$ m.

Intensity of earth pressure at the base of the stem is

$$p_a = C_a \gamma_e h = (0.333)(16)(8.5)$$
$$= 45.33 \text{ kN/m}^2 \text{ (linearly varying to zero at the top)}$$

Applying a load factor of 1.5, $w_u = 1.5 \times 45.33 = 68.0$ kN/m^2 at base.

Clear spacing between the counterforts = 3.0 m.

- ***Design of stem for continuous beam action***

At base Assuming a clear cover of 50 mm and 20ϕ bars,

$$d = 600 - 50 - 10 = 540 \text{ mm and effective span, } l = 3.0 + 0.54 = 3.54 \text{ m}$$

Max. –ve moment occurring in the stem at the counterfort location is given by

$$M_{u,-ve} = w_u l^2/12 = 68.0 \times 3.54^2/12 = 71.0 \text{ kNm/m}$$

Max. mid-span moment may be taken as

$$M_{u,+ve} = w_u l^2/16 \approx 0.75 \times M_{u,-ve} = 53.3 \text{ kNm/m}$$

Design shear force

$$V_u = w_u \times (\text{clear span}/2 - d) = 68.0 \times (3.0/2 - 0.54) = 65.3 \text{ kN/m}$$

Design of (rear face) reinforcement for –ve moments at the counterforts

$$\Rightarrow \quad R \equiv \frac{M_u}{bd^2} = \frac{71.0 \times 10^6}{10^3 \times 540^2} = 0.244 \text{ MPa}$$

$$\Rightarrow \quad \frac{(p_t)_{reqd}}{100} = \frac{25}{2 \times 500}\left[1 - \sqrt{1 - 4.598 \times 0.244/25}\right] = 0.057 \times 10^{-2}$$

$$\Rightarrow \quad (A_{st})_{reqd} = (0.057 \times 10^{-2}) \times 10^3 \times 540 = 308 \text{ mm}^2\text{/m}$$

$$\text{Min. } A_{st} = \frac{0.12}{100}(1000)(600) = 720 \text{ mm}^2\text{/m} > 308 \text{ mm}^2\text{/m}$$

Check for shear at base

$$\tau_v = \frac{65.3 \times 10^3}{10^3 \times 540} = 0.121 \text{ MPa} < \tau_c = 0.29 \text{ MPa (for minimum } p_t = 0.15) - \text{OK}$$

(Evidently, it is possible to reduce the thickness of the stem, for economy).

Design of (front face) reinforcement for +ve moments in the mid-span of stem

The minimum reinforcement requirement will govern the design on both faces, since $M_{u,+ve} < M_{u,-ve}$.

Using 12ϕ bars, spacing required = 113 × 1000/ 720 = 156 mm

Provide **12ϕ bars (horizontal) @ 150 c/con both faces** of the stem (up to one-third height above base).

At one-third height above base

$$d = 500 - 50 - 6 = 444 \text{ mm and effective span } l = 3.444 \text{ m}$$

$$M_{u,-ve} = w_u l^2/12 = (68.0 \times 2/3) \times (3.444)^2/12 = 44.81 \text{ kNm/m}$$

$$\Rightarrow \quad R \equiv \frac{M_u}{bd^2} = \frac{44.81 \times 10^6}{10^3 \times 444^2} = 0.227 \text{ MPa}$$

$$\Rightarrow \quad \frac{(p_t)_{reqd}}{100} = \frac{25}{2 \times 500}\left[1 - \sqrt{1 - 4.598 \times 0.227/25}\right] = 0.053 \times 10^{-2}$$

$$\Rightarrow \quad (A_{st})_{reqd} = (0.053 \times 10^{-2}) \times 10^3 \times 444 = 236 \text{ mm}^2/\text{m}$$

$$\text{Min. } A_{st} = \frac{0.12}{100}(1000)(500) = 600 \text{ mm}^2/\text{m} > 236 \text{ mm}^2/\text{m}$$

Using 12ϕ bars, spacing required = 113 × 1000/ 600 = 188 mm

Provide **12ϕ bars (horizontal) @ 180 c/c on both faces** of the stem (in the middle one-third height).

At two-thirds height above base

$$\text{Min. } A_{st} = \frac{0.12}{100}(1000)(400) = 480 \text{ mm}^2/\text{m}$$

Using 10ϕ bars, spacing required = 78.5 × 1000/ 480 = 163 mm

Using 12ϕ bars, spacing required = 113 × 1000/ 480 = 235 mm

Provide **12ϕ bars (horizontal) @ 230 c/con both faces** of the stem (in the upper one-third height).

- ***Design of stem for cantilever action***

  Consider the triangular loading on the stem [Fig. 14.39] to be carried by cantilever action about the face of the stem as follows:

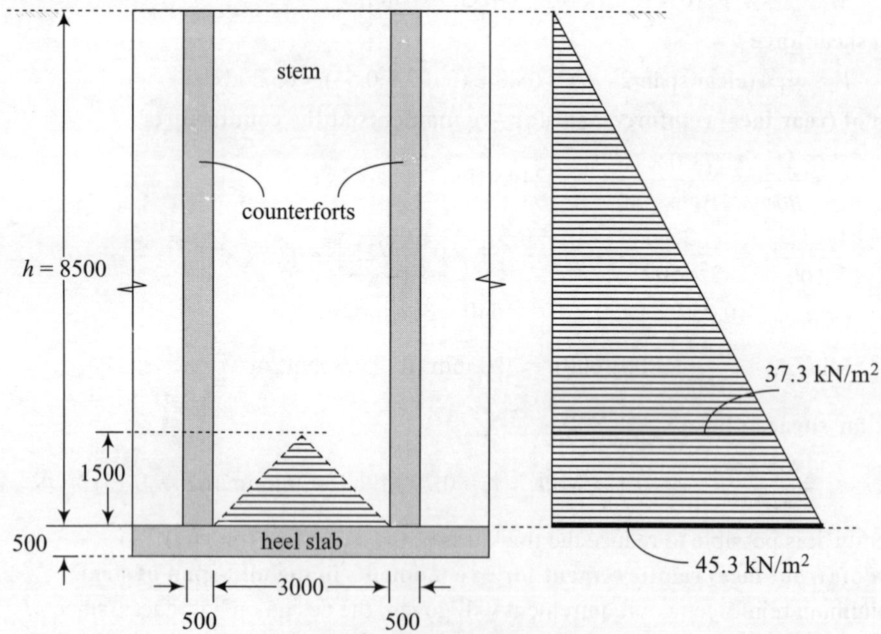

Fig. 14.39 Loading considerations for simplified analysis of stem.

The intensity of horizontal pressure at the base of the stem = 45.3 kN/m^2.

The intensity of horizontal pressure at a distance of 1.5 m from the base of the stem is 37.3 kN/m^2.

Total B.M. due to loading on the triangular portion is approximately given by

$$\approx \left(\frac{1}{2}\times 3.0\times 1.5\right)\times\left[37.3\times\frac{1.5}{3}+(45.3-37.3)\times\frac{1.5}{2\times 3}\right] = 46.5 \text{ kNm}$$

This moment is distributed non-uniformly across the width of 3.0 m. For design purposes, the maximum moment intensity (in the middle region) may be taken as two times the average value

$$\Rightarrow \quad M_{max} = 2\times(46.5/3.0) = 31.0 \text{ kNm/m}$$

effective depth $d = 515 - 12 = 503$ mm. Applying a load factor of 1.5,

$$R \equiv \frac{M_u}{bd^2} = \frac{1.5\times 31.0\times 10^6}{1000\times 503^2} = 0.184 \text{ MPa}$$

$$\Rightarrow \quad \frac{(p_t)_{reqd}}{100} = \frac{25}{2\times 500}\left[1-\sqrt{1-4.598\times 0.184/25}\right] = 0.043\times 10^{-2}$$

(required up to 1.5 m height above base)

$$\Rightarrow \quad (A_{st})_{reqd} = (0.043\times 10^{-2})\times 10^3\times 503 = 217 \text{ mm}^2/\text{m} < (A_{st})_{min} = 720 \text{ mm}^2/\text{m}$$

(for temperature and shrinkage)

The minimum reinforcement requirement will govern the design.
Provide **12ϕ bars (vertical) @ 150 c/c on both faces** of the stem throughout the height of the stem.
The reinforcement details for the stem, toe slab and heel slab are shown in Fig. 14.40

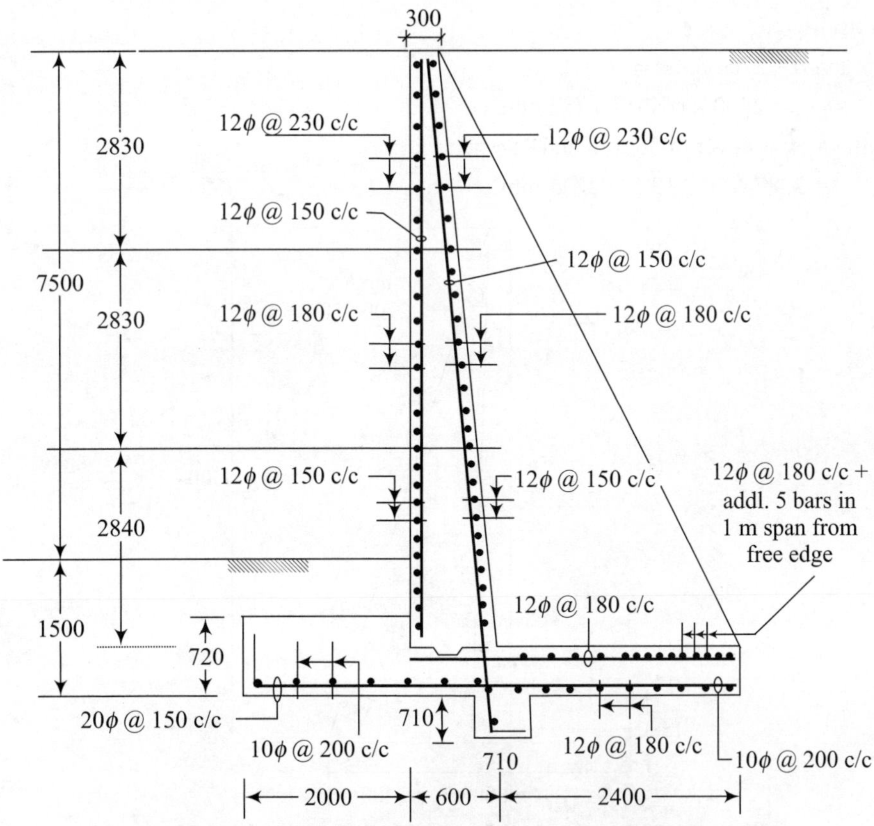

Fig. 14.40 Reinforcement details of stem, toe slab and heel slab.

9. *Design of interior counterfort*

The typical interior counterfort acts as a T-beam of varying section cantilevering out of the base slab. The design should include:

- provision for beam action
- provision of horizontal ties against separation from stem
- provision of vertical ties against separation of base

- ***Design of counterfort for T-beam action***

The thickness of counterforts = 500 mm

Clear spacing of counterforts = 3.0 m

Thus, each counterfort receives earth pressure from a width of

$$l = 3.0 + 0.5 = 3.5 \text{ m}$$

At base The intensity of earth pressure at the base of the stem is

$$p_a = C_a \gamma_e h = (0.333)(16)(8.5) = 45.33 \text{ kN/m}^2$$

Applying a load factor of 1.5,

$$M_u = 1.5 \times \left(\frac{1}{2} \times 45.33 \times 8.5\right) \times 3.5 \times \frac{8.5}{3} = 2866 \text{ kNm}$$

$$V_u = 1.5 \times \left(\frac{1}{2} \times 45.33 \times 8.5\right) \times 3.5 = 1012 \text{ kN}$$

From Fig. 14.41,

$$\tan\theta = 2700/8500 \Rightarrow \theta = 17.6^\circ$$

and $D_{base} = 2400 \times \cos\theta = 2287$ mm

Assuming a clear cover of 50 mm and 25ϕ bars,

$$d = 2287 - 50 - 12.5 = 2224 \text{ mm}$$

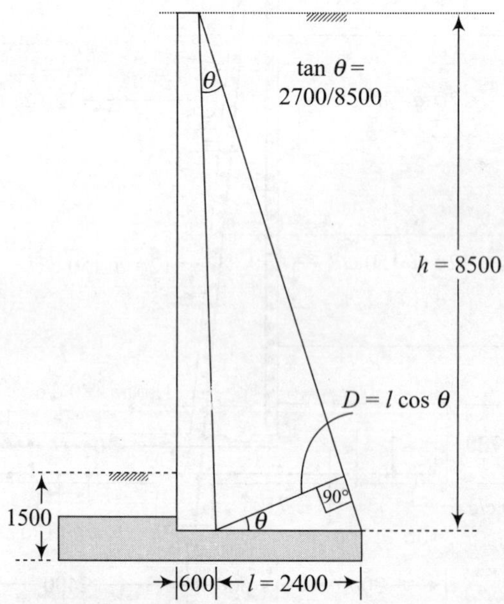

Fig. 14.41 Depth consideration for analysis of counterfort.

- ***Effective flange width*** (Cl 23.1.2 Code):

$$b_f = l_0/6 + b_w + 6D_f \quad \text{[Eq. 4.30]}$$
$$= 8500/6 + 500 + (6 \times 600) = 5517 \text{ mm},$$
$$b_f = b_w + \text{clear span of slab}$$
$$= 500 + 3000 = 3500 \text{ mm}$$

Thus, $b_f = 3500$ mm (least of the above two values)

Approximate requirement of tension steel is given by assuming a lever arm z to be the larger of $0.9d = 2001$ mm and $d - D_f/2 = 1924$ mm, i.e., 2001 mm:

$$(A_{st})_{\text{reqd}} = \frac{M_u}{0.87 f_y z} = \frac{2866 \times 10^6}{0.87(500)(2001)} = 3293 \text{ mm}^2$$

No. of 25ϕ bars required $= \dfrac{3293}{491} = 7$ bars (provide 8 bars in two layers, with 25 ϕ spacer bars)

$\Rightarrow \quad d = 2287 - 50 - 25 - 12.5 = 2199$ mm

Assuming the neutral axis to be located at $x_u = D_f$,

$$M_{uR} = 0.362 \times 25 \times 3500 \times 600 \times (2199 - 0.416 \times 600) = 37048 \times 10^6 \text{ Nmm}$$
$$> M_u = 2866 \times 10^6 \text{ Nmm}$$

This clearly indicates that the neutral axis lies within the flange.

$$R \equiv \frac{M_u}{bd^2} = \frac{2866 \times 10^6}{3500 \times 2199^2} = 0.169 \text{ MPa}$$

$$\Rightarrow \quad \frac{(p_t)_{\text{reqd}}}{100} = \frac{25}{2 \times 500}\left[1 - \sqrt{1 - 4.598 \times 0.169/25}\right] = 0.039 \times 10^{-2}$$

$$\Rightarrow \quad (A_{st})_{\text{reqd}} = (0.039 \times 10^{-2}) \times 3500 \times 2199 = 3002 \text{ mm}^2/\text{m}$$

(which is close to the approximate value of 3293 mm^2 calculated)

Minimum reinforcement in a beam is given by $\dfrac{A_s}{bd} = \dfrac{0.85}{f_y}$

$\Rightarrow \quad A_s = 0.85 \times 500 \times 2199/500 = 1870 \text{ mm}^2 < 3293 \text{ mm}^2$

Provide 8 nos 25ϕ bars in two layers, four bars in each layer with a 25 mm separation.

[*Note:* In the above calculations, the effective depth of section (d) was taken *normal* to the tensile force in reinforcement (say T), and $T = M/(jd)$, where j is the lever arm factor. The same result can be obtained by taking the effective depth along the *horizontal* direction along l at the base of the counterfort, say d_H. The required tensile force component in the *vertical* direction is $T_V = M/(jd_H)$. To provide this vertical component, the tensile force in the inclined reinforcement should be $= T_V/\cos\theta = M/(jd_H \cos\theta) = M/(jd)$ as before, since $d_H \cos\theta = d$.]

Above one-third height from the base

The intensity of earth pressure at h (= 8.5 × 2/3) = 5.67 m from top is

$$p_a = C_a \gamma_e h = 45.33 \times 2/3 = 30.22 \text{ kN/m}^2$$

Applying a load factor of 1.5,

$$M_u = 1.5 \times \left(\frac{1}{2} \times 30.22 \times 5.67\right) \times 3.5 \times \frac{5.67}{3} = 850 \text{ kNm}$$

$$V_u = 1.5 \times \left(\frac{1}{2} \times 30.22 \times 5.67\right) \times 3.5 = 450 \text{ kN}$$

$$D_{h=5.67} = 2287 \times 2/3 = 1525 \text{ mm}$$

Assuming a clear cover of 50 mm and 25ϕ bars,

$$d = 1525 - 50 - 12.5 = 1462 \text{ mm}$$

Approximate requirement of tension steel is given by assuming a lever arm z to be the larger of $0.9d = 1316$ mm and $d - D_f/2 = 1212$ mm, i.e., 1316 mm:

$$(A_{st})_{\text{reqd}} = \frac{M_u}{0.87 f_y z} = \frac{850 \times 10^6}{0.87(500)(1316)} = 1485 \text{ mm}^2$$

$$\text{No. of } 25\phi \text{ bars required} = \frac{1789}{491} \approx 4 \text{ bars}$$

$\Rightarrow$ $d = 1462$ mm

Assuming the neutral axis to be located at $x_u = D_f$,

$$M_{uR} = 0.362 \times 25 \times 3500 \times 500 \times (1462 - 0.416 \times 500) = 19860 \times 10^6 \text{ Nmm}$$

$$> M_u = 850 \times 10^6 \text{ Nmm}$$

This clearly indicates that the neutral axis lies within the flange.

$$R \equiv \frac{M_u}{bd^2} = \frac{850 \times 10^6}{3500 \times 1462^2} = 0.114 \text{ MPa}$$

$$\Rightarrow \quad \frac{(p_t)_{\text{reqd}}}{100} = \frac{25}{2 \times 500}\left[1 - \sqrt{1 - 4.598 \times 0.114/25}\right] = 0.026 \times 10^{-2}$$

$$\Rightarrow \quad (A_{st})_{\text{reqd}} = (0.026 \times 10^{-2}) \times 3500 \times 1462 = 1331 \text{ mm}^2/\text{m}$$

(which is close to the approximate value of 1485 mm^2 calculated)

Minimum reinforcement in a beam is given by $\frac{A_s}{bd} = \frac{0.85}{f_y}$

$$\Rightarrow \quad A_s = 0.85 \times 500 \times 1462/500 = 1243 \text{ mm}^2 < 1331 \text{ mm}^2$$

Curtail 4 nos 25ϕ bars and extend 4 nos 25ϕ bars (rear face).

In order to satisfy the minimum reinforcement criteria, **4 nos 25ϕ bars** may be extended to the top of the counterfort, without any further curtailment.

- **Design of horizontal ties**

  Horizontal tie (closed stirrup) reinforcement in the counterfort serves as shear reinforcement against flexural shear in the counterfort and also as ties resisting the separation of the stem from the counterfort due to the lateral pressure.

At base

Shear reinforcement requirement:

$$V_{u,\text{net}} = V_u - \frac{M_u}{d}\tan\theta$$

$$= 1012 - \frac{2866}{2.199}\tan(17.6) = 598.0 \text{ kN}$$

Nominal shear stress $\tau_v = \dfrac{V_{u,\text{net}}}{bd} = \dfrac{598\times10^3}{500\times2199} = 0.544$ MPa

$$p_t = 100\,A_{st}/b = 100\times(8\times491)/(500\times2199) = 0.357$$

$\Rightarrow$ $\tau_c = 0.416$ MPa

Hence, shear reinforcement is to be provided for a shear force of

$$V_{us} = (\tau_v - \tau_c)bd = (0.544 - 0.416)\,500\times2199$$

$$= 140.8\times10^3 \text{ N}$$

Assuming 10ϕ 2-legged stirrups,

$$A_{sv} = 2\times78.5 = 157 \text{ mm}^2$$

Required spacing $= s_v = \dfrac{0.87 f_y A_{sv} d}{V_{us}} = \dfrac{0.87\times415\times157\times2199}{140.8\times10^3} = 885$ mm

Max. spacing specified by Code $= \begin{cases}0.75d\\300\text{ mm}\end{cases} = 300$ mm (lesser value)

Tie connection requirement:

The tension resisted by the tie reinforcement is given by the lateral pressure on the wall multiplied by the tributary area. At the base ($p_a = 45.33$ kN/m^2), the tensile force intensity is accordingly given by:

$$T = 45.33 \text{ kN/m}^2\times3.5 \text{ m} = 158.7 \text{ kN/m}$$

Applying a load factor of 1.5, the total area of reinforcement required to resist this direct tension = $\dfrac{1.5\times158.7\times10^3}{0.87\times500} = 548$ mm^2/m.

Spacing of 10ϕ 2 legged stirrups required = $2\times78.5\times10^3 / 548 = 286$ mm

This tie reinforcement requirement governs (compared to shear reinforcement requirement).

Provide 10ϕ 2 legged stirrups @ 200 mm c/c in lower one-third region

The tie reinforcement requirement will vary linearly along the height of the stem, as the lateral pressure variation is linear.

At one-third height from the base

$$(A_{st})_{\text{reqd}} = (2/3)\times548 = 366 \text{ mm}^2\text{/m}$$

Spacing of 8ϕ 2 legged stirrups required = $2\times50.3\times10^3/366 = 275$ m

Provide 8ϕ 2 legged stirrups @ 200 mm c/c above one-third height.

These stirrups must enclose two 12ϕ vertical bars placed inside the bends near the outer face of the stem.

- **Design of vertical ties**

  As in the case of the connection between the counterfort and the vertical stem, the connection between the counterfort and the heel slab must be designed to resist the tension arising out of the net downward pressures acting on the heel slab [Fig. 14.38b]. Considering a 1 m strip from the free edge where the pressure is maximum, the average downward pressure is (83.4 + 109.1)/2 = 96.25 kN/m^2, and hence the average tensile force intensity is:

$$T = 96.25 \text{ kN/m}^2 \times 3.5\text{m} = 336.9 \text{ kN/m}$$

Applying a load factor of 1.5, the total area of reinforcement required to resist this direct tension = $\dfrac{1.5 \times 336.9 \times 10^3}{0.87 \times 500} = 1162 \text{ mm}^2\text{/m}$.

Spacing of 10ϕ 2 legged ties required = $2 \times 78.5 \times 10^3/1162 = 135$ mm

Provide **10ϕ 2 legged vertical ties @ 100 mm c/c** up to 1m from the free edge.

The spacing may be increased to 150 mm beyond 1 m, owing to the significant reduction in net pressure.

The counterfort reinforcement details are shown in Fig. 14.42 and Fig. 14.43.

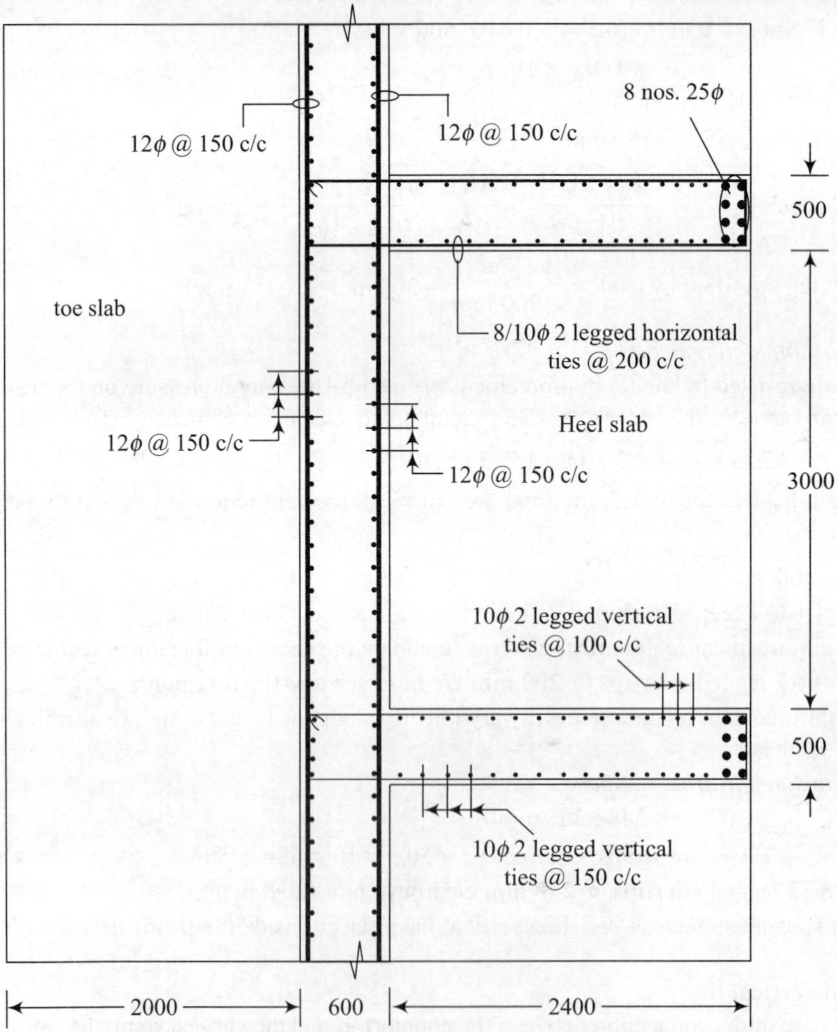

Fig. 14.42 Reinforcement details of stem and counterfort.

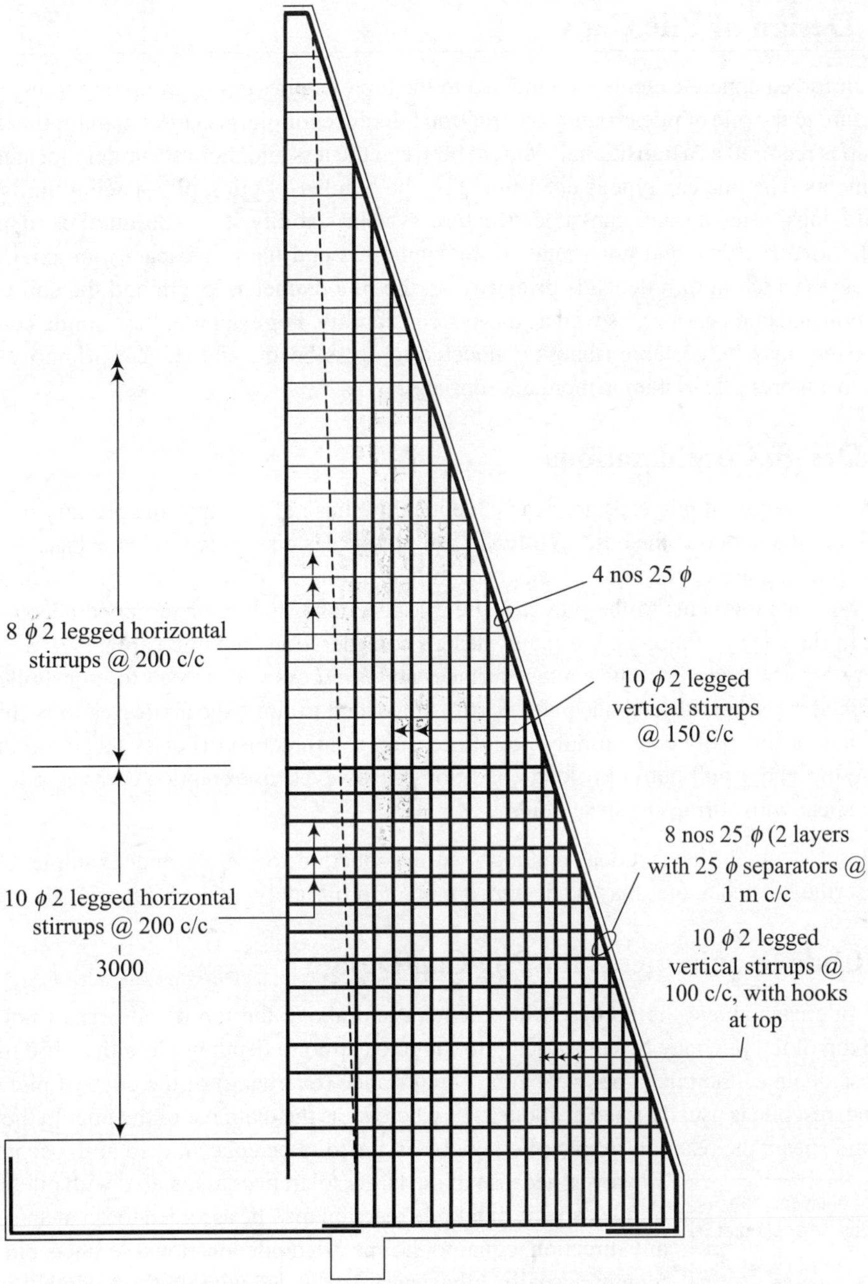

Fig. 14.43 Section through counterfort showing counterfort reinforcement.

14.10 Design of Pile Caps

Pile cap is a reinforced concrete element connected to the top of a pile or pile group that transfers loads from the superstructure to the pile or pile group. Construction tolerance for piles is larger than for the superstructure and the pile cap is required as a transitional element between the less and more accurately located/constructed structural elements. The pile cap type is determined by the number of piles, pile spacing limits, interference with other pile caps, pile-cap and cap-superstructure system stability, etc. The number of piles required depends on the load (vertical and horizontal) to be supported and the pile capacity in axial compression/tension and shear (which in turn depends primarily on the pile diameter, length and the soil characteristics related to friction and end bearing), as well as the system stability. For example, for a single column, a single or two-pile system may be unstable (unless connected to cross beams and subject primarily to only axial load); a three- (or more) pile system is more appropriate.

14.10.1 Design Considerations

The behaviour and design of pile caps are nearly identical to those of footings, the primary difference being in the distribution of reaction at the base. While the soil pressure is distributed over the base of a footing, the reactions on a pile cap are concentrated loads transmitted through the individual piles. Where the column or wall base transmits moments to the pile cap, the pile reactions shall be determined accounting for such moments. As in the case of footings, the major design considerations for pile cap are *flexure*, *shear* (both one-way and two-way), *bearing* at the contact surfaces and *bond*. As with spread footings, pile caps are not usually reinforced for shear, instead adequate depth is provided to limit shear stresses to within admissible limits. Thus, pile caps usually contain only bottom tension reinforcement (unless tension reinforcement is required at the top under pull out/uplift load conditions). However, in exceptional cases, pile caps may be reinforced for shear with stirrups or shear studs.

Deep pile caps, for which the sectional method (see introduction to Ch. 17 and Example 17.6) does not accurately describe the behaviour, may be designed more appropriately by the Strut-and-Tie method.

14.10.2 Code Requirements for Pile Cap Design

The depth of pile caps above the bottom reinforcement and above the top of piles shall not be less than 300 mm. The top of the pile may be embedded into the pile cap for a depth not less than 150 mm. Thus, the minimum gross depth of the pile cap is 450 mm. The distance (overhang) of the edge of pile cap from the centre of the nearest pile is usually fixed at about $2D_p$, where D_p is the diameter of the pile. In the computation of moments and shears the reaction from a pile may be assumed to be concentrated at the centre of the pile. However, because of the larger tolerances associated with piles, in the design of pile cap, the axial pile reaction may be assumed to act at an eccentricity, in any direction, equal to the specified pile location tolerance, but not less than 50 mm. Usually, pile caps are provided with uniform depth throughout. The critical section for moment is the same as in footings, as given in Section 14.4.5 and Fig. 14.6. For one-way shear, for pile caps, the critical section is located at a distance *d* from the face of the column (Cl. 34.2.4.1a), where *d* is the effective depth of the pile cap. For two-way shear, the critical section is located at a distance *d*/2 from the column/pile periphery, as in the case of footings and flat slabs [Fig. 14.6(b)]. For closely spaced piles,

> In the design of pile caps, the pile reaction may be applied at an eccentricity, in any direction, equal to the pile location tolerance, but not less than 50 mm.

the individual critical sections for two-way shear around piles may overlap, in which case a critical section around the pile group may govern.

In computing the external shear on any section, the entire reaction from any pile which is wholly outside the section (i.e., whose centre is located $D_p/2$ or more outside the section) shall be assumed as producing shear (Cl. 34.2.4.2). Similarly, any pile wholly inside the section (i.e., whose centre is located $D_p/2$ or more inside the section) shall be assumed as producing no shear. For intermediate positions of pile centre, linear interpolation between the above limits shall be made. The computation of shear due to a pile reaction at a critical section distant *d* from the column face is depicted in Fig. 14.44. For the case where the critical section passes over a pile, the shear force, V_u, at the critical section due to the pile reaction *R* is given by:

$$V_u = r \times R \tag{14.24}$$

where,

$$r = \frac{c + D_p - d}{D_p} \tag{14.25}$$

Note that the last term in the numerator in Eq. 14.25 is the distance from the column face to the critical section, equal to *d* for one-way shear [shown in Fig. 14.44(b)] and *d*/2 for two-way shear.

For transfer of forces at the base of columns, pile caps and piles, the area of reinforcement across the interface shall not be less than 0.005 times the gross area of the supported member and shall consist of a minimum of four bars (Cl. 34.4.3). When net uplift or moments (resulting in tensile stresses in the reinforcement) are transferred from the column to the pile cap, the reinforcement shall be anchored accordingly.

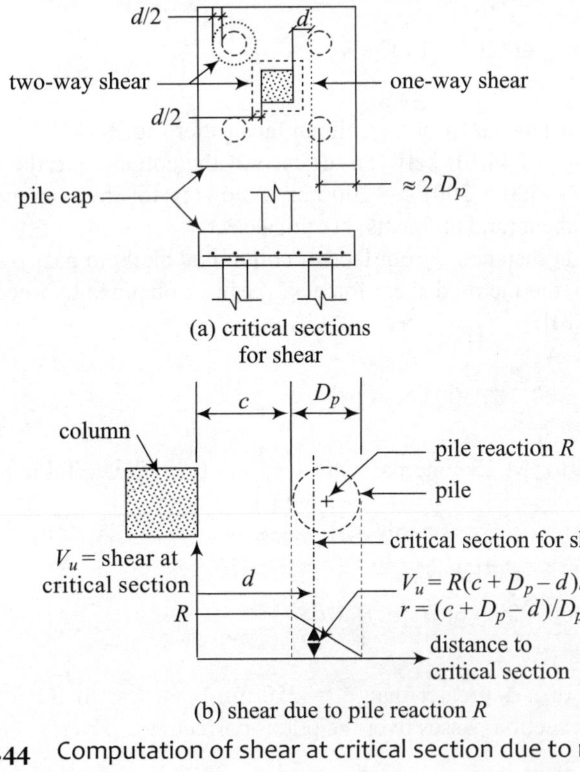

Fig. 14.44 Computation of shear at critical section due to reaction from pile.

Design Procedure

The design procedure is very similar to the design of footings. The required effective depth d is first determined from considerations of one-way shear and two-way shear. For two-way shear, sections distant $d/2$ around the piles are also critical sections. If there is any corner pile enclosed by a pile cap corner that is less than 90° (as with a triangular pile cap for a group of three piles), shear check as for corner columns in flat slab [see Fig. 11.41(c)] also has to be made; however, this may not be critical for deep pile caps. With the largest effective depth determined as above, flexural tension reinforcement is determined as for beams. Finally, the bearing stresses are checked for the columns and the piles.

Example 14.13

Design a suitable **pile cap** *for a reinforced concrete column of size 500 × 500 mm, reinforced with 8–25ϕ bars, carrying a factored axial load of 4000 kN, supported by four symmetrically placed piles, 300 mm diameter, spaced at 1.2 m in both x- and y-directions. The pile location tolerance may be taken as 50 mm. The column and piles are with M 30 concrete and use M 25 concrete for the pile cap. Use Fe 500 steel.*

Solution

Size of Pile cap

- *Given*: Spacing of piles = 1200 mm. The arrangement of piles, pile cap and column is shown in Fig. 14.45(a). Assume a pile cap overhang = $2D_p = 2 \times 300 = 600$ mm. With this, the overall size of the pile cap is 1200 + 2 × 600 = 2400 mm. Assume a 2.4 m × 2.4 m pile cap

Thickness of pile cap based on shear

- The factored pile reaction is = 4000/4 = 1000 kN.

(a) One-way shear

- The critical section is at a distance d from the column face [refer Fig. 14.45].
  The clear distance [c in Fig. 14.44(b)] between the face of the column and the face of the pile at its specified location is (1200 – 500 – 300)/2 = 200 mm. Allowing for the tolerance of 50 mm for pile location, for calculation of shear (and moments) at critical sections, $c = 200 + 50 = 250$ mm. The critical section for one-way shear, at distance d from face of column, is likely to pass over the pile, as shown in Fig. 14.44. Assuming so, the factored shear force, V_{u1}, can be obtained by interpolation as per Code Cl. 34.2.4.2 as [Fig. 14.44(b)]:

$$V_{u1} = 2R(c + D_p - d)/D_p$$
$$= 2000(250 + 300 - d)/300 \text{ kN}$$
$$= (3667 - 6.67\, d) \text{ kN}$$

  Assuming $\tau_c = 0.363$ MPa(for M 25 concrete with, say, $p_t = 0.25$) [refer Table 6.1 or Table 13 of the Code],

  One-way shear resistance $V_{c1} = 0.363 \times 2400 \times d$

$$= (871d) \text{ N}$$

$$V_{u1} \leq V_{c1} \Rightarrow 3667000 - 6670d \leq 871d$$

$$\Rightarrow \quad d \geq 486 \text{ mm}$$

  Since the computed value of d is greater than c (= 250 mm) and less than $c + D_p$ (= 550 mm), the assumption that the critical section passes over the pile is correct.

(b) Two-way shear

Around column

- The critical section is at $d/2$ from the periphery of the column [refer Fig. 14.45]. If the piles are wholly outside this section, 100 percent of pile reactions will contribute to the shear. First assuming that $d/2 < c$ (= 250 mm),

  $\Rightarrow$ Factored shear force $V_{u2} = 4 \times 1000 = 4000$ kN.

  Two-way shear resistance $V_{c2} = k_s \tau_c \times [4 \times (500 + d)d]$

  where $k_s = 1.0$ for a square column, and $\tau_c = 0.25\sqrt{25} = 1.25$ MPa (refer Cl. 31.6.3.1 of the Code)

  $$\Rightarrow \quad V_{c2} = 1.0 \times 1.25 \times 4d(500 + d) = (2500d + 5d^2)\text{ N}$$

  $$V_{u2} \le V_{c2} \quad \Rightarrow \quad 4000 \times 10^3 \le 2500d + 5d^2$$

  Solving, $d \ge 679$ mm

  $d/2 = 340$ mm, is not less than $c = 250$ mm and hence the assumption that the full pile reaction contributes to shear is not valid.

  Hence the critical section passes over the pile and Eq. 14.24 has to be used for computing the shear. In this example, since the pile is along the diagonal, two sides of the critical section for two-way shear will pass over the pile, as shown in Fig. 14.45(b). If the factor r has values r_1 and r_2 in the x- and y-directions, the shear, which is proportional to the partial area beyond the critical section, shown shaded in Fig. 14.45(b) is given by:

  $$V_{u2} = R - R(1 - r_1)(1 - r_2)$$

  and $$r_1 = r_2 = \frac{c + D_p - d/2}{D_p} = \frac{250 + 300 - d/2}{300}$$

  $$V_{u2} = 4 \times 1000\left[1 - \left(1 - \frac{550 - 0.5d}{300}\right)^2\right]$$

  As before, $V_{c2} = (2500d + 5d^2)$ N and

  $$V_{u2} \le V_{c2} \quad \Rightarrow \quad 4000 \times 10^3\left[1 - \left(1 - \frac{550 - 0.5d}{300}\right)^2\right] \le 2500d + 5d^2$$

  Solving, $d = 651$ mm

Around pile

- Factored shear force due to pile reaction = $V_{up} = 1000$ kN

  The critical section is at $d/2$ from the periphery of the pile [refer Fig. 14.44(a)]. Two-way shear resistance $V_{cp} = k_s \tau_c \times [\pi \times (300 + d)d]$ where $\tau_c = 1.25$ MPa

  $$\Rightarrow \quad V_{cp} = 1.0 \times 1.25 \times \pi d(300 + d) = (1179d + 3.93d^2)\text{ N}$$

  $$V_{up} \le V_{cp} \quad \Rightarrow \quad 1000 \times 10^3 \le 1179d + 3.93d^2$$

  Solving, $d \ge 376$ mm

  A more critical section for the pile is along the section ABCD shown in Fig. 14.45. For this section, $V_{cp} = 1.0 \times 1.25 \times d\,\{\pi(300 + d)/4 + 2 \times 600\}$

  $$\Rightarrow \quad V_{cp} = (1795d + 0.982d^2)\text{ N}$$

  $$V_{up} \le V_{cp} \quad \Rightarrow \quad 1000 \times 10^3 \le 1795d + 0.982d^2$$

  Solving, $d \ge 448$ mm

- Evidently, in this problem, two-way shear around the column governs the thickness. Assuming 18ϕ bars in both directions and a minimum embedment of 150 mm of the pile top into the pile cap, with an average d = 651 mm,
  overall thickness $D \geq 651 + 18 + 150 = 819$ mm
  Provide $\boldsymbol{D}$ **= 820 mm**. The effective depths in the two directions will differ by one bar diameter, which is not significant in relatively deep square pile caps. For the purpose of flexural reinforcement calculations, an average value of d may be assumed:
  $\Rightarrow \qquad d = 820 - 150 - 18 = \mathbf{652\ mm}$
- In this example, the pile cap is evenly supported by the piles and no allowance is made for the self-weight of the pile cap in computation of shear forces and bending moments.

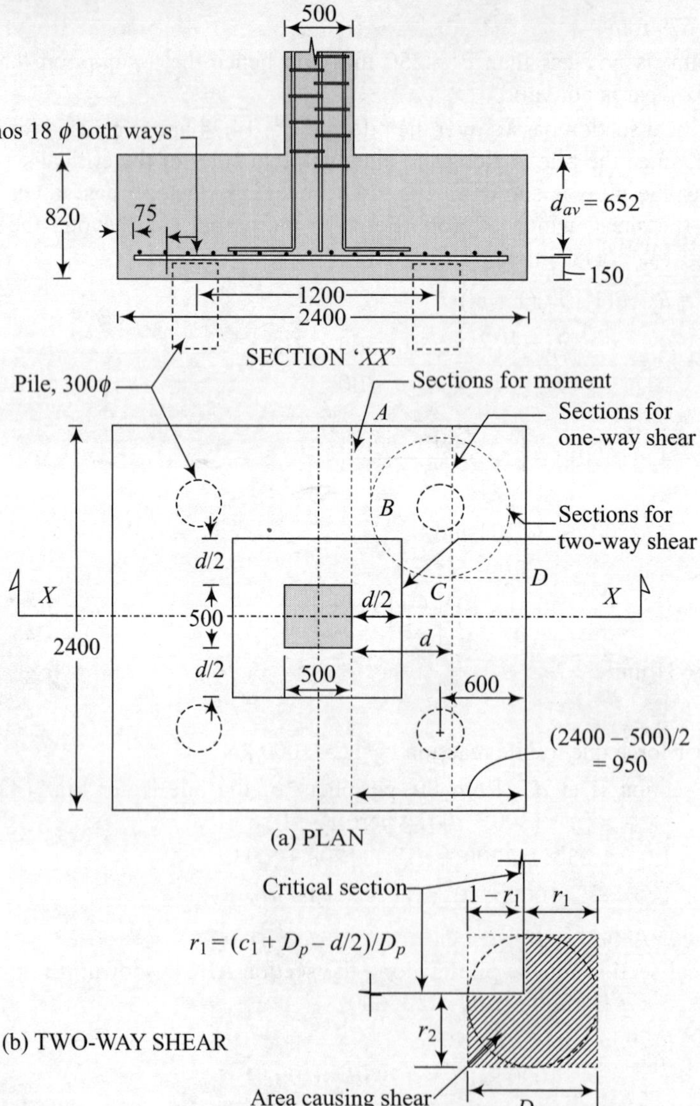

Fig. 14.45 Example 14.13.

Design of flexural reinforcement

- Factored moment at column face (in either direction), including allowance for tolerance:

$$M_u = 2R(c + D_p/2) = 2000 \times 10^3 \times (250 + 150) = 800 \times 10^6 \text{ Nmm}$$

$$\Rightarrow \quad R \equiv \frac{M_u}{Bd^2} = \frac{800 \times 10^6}{2400 \times 652^2} = 0.784 \text{ MPa}$$

$$\Rightarrow \quad \frac{(p_t)_{\text{reqd}}}{100} = \frac{25}{2 \times 500}\left[1 - \sqrt{1 - 4.598 \times 0.784/25}\,\right] = 0.187 \times 10^{-2}$$

$$A_{st,\min} = 0.0012BD = 0.0012 \times 2400 \times 820 = 2362 \text{ mm}^2$$

$$\Rightarrow \quad p_{t,\min} = 100 \times 2362/(2400 \times 652) = 0.151 < 0.187$$

- This reinforcement is less than assumed for one-way shear design, ($p_t = 0.25$, and $\tau_c = 0.363$ MPa). An area of $p_t = 0.25$ may be provided.

$$\Rightarrow \quad A_{st,\text{reqd}} = 0.250 \times 2400 \times 652/100 = 3912 \text{ mm}^2$$

Using 18 mm ϕ bars, number of bars required = 3912/254 = 16

[assuming end cover of 75 mm, corresponding spacing $s = \{2400 - (75 \times 2) - 18\}/(16 - 1) = 149$ mm – is acceptable.]

Provide 16 nos 18ϕ bars both ways as shown in Fig. 14.45

Required development length $L_d = \dfrac{\phi(0.87 f_y)}{4\tau_{bd}}$ [refer Cl. 26.2.1 of Code]

For M 25 concrete and Fe 500 steel, $L_d = \phi(0.87 \times 500)/(4 \times 1.4 \times 1.6) = 48.5\phi$

For 18ϕ bars in footing, $L_d = 48.5 \times 18 = 873$ mm

Length available = 950 – 75 = 875 mm > 873 mm – Hence, OK.

Transfer of force at column base

- Factored compressive force at column base: $P_u = 4000$ kN

Limiting bearing stress at column-pile cap interface, $f_{br,\max} = 0.45 f_{ck}\sqrt{A_1/A_2}$

(i) for column face, $f_{ck} = 30$ MPa, $A_1 = A_2 = 500^2$ mm^2

$$\Rightarrow \quad f_{br,\,max\text{ - }col} = 0.45 \times 30 \times 1 = 13.5 \text{ MPa}$$

(ii) for pile cap face, $f_{ck} = 25$ MPa, $A_1 = 2400^2$ mm^2, $A_2 = 500^2$ mm^2

$$\Rightarrow \quad \sqrt{A_1/A_2} = 2400/500 = 4.8, \text{ limited to } 2.0$$

$$\Rightarrow \quad f_{br,\,\max\text{- ftg}} = 0.45 \times 25 \times 2 = 22.5 \text{ MPa}$$

- Evidently, the column face governs, and $f_{br,\max} = 13.5$ MPa

$\Rightarrow$ Limiting bearing resistance $F_{br} = 13.5 \times 500^2 = 3375 \times 10^3$ N $< P_u = 4000$ kN

$\Rightarrow$ Excess force (to be transferred by reinforcement): $\Delta P_u = 4000 - 3375 = 625$ kN

This may be transferred by reinforcement, dowels or mechanical connectors. In this case, it is convenient to extend the column bars into the pile cap, as shown in Fig. 14.45. The force to be transferred per bar = 625/8 = 78 kN. The corresponding stress in a bar = 78000/491 = 159 MPa. This force has to be developed in the bar through adequate embedment.

For fully stressed bars in compression (M 25, Fe 500):

$$L_d = \frac{\phi(0.87 \times 415)}{4(1.2 \times 1.6 \times 1.25)} = 45.3\phi$$

$\Rightarrow \quad \tilde{L}_d = L_d \times (f_s/0.87 f_y)$
$= 45.3 \times 25 \times (159/(0.87 \times 500))$
$= 414$ mm.

Available vertical embedment length in footing ($d = 652$ mm) > 414 mm. OK.

Minimum required area of reinforcement across the interface
$= 0.005(500 \times 500) = 1250$ mm^2. The area provided is well over this.

Transfer of force at pile-pile cap interface

- Factored reaction from pile: $P_u = 1000$ kN

  Limiting bearing stress at pile-pile cap interface, $f_{br,\max} = 0.45 f_{ck}\sqrt{A_1/A_2}$.
  (i) for pile face, $f_{ck} = 30$ MPa, $A_1 = A_2 = (\pi/4) \times 300^2$ mm^2
  $\Rightarrow \quad f_{br,\max\text{-col}} = 0.45 \times 30 \times 1 = 13.5$ MPa
  (ii) for pile cap face, $f_{ck} = 25$ MPa, $A_1 = (\pi/4) \times 1200^2$ mm^2, $A_2 = (\pi/4) \times 300^2$ mm^2
  $\Rightarrow \quad \sqrt{A_1/A_2} = 1200/300 = 4.0$, limited to 2.0
  $\Rightarrow \quad f_{br,\max\text{-ftg}} = 0.45 \times 25 \times 2 = 22.5$ MPa

- Evidently, the pile face governs, and $f_{br,\max} = 13.5$ MPa

  $\Rightarrow$ Limiting bearing resistance $F_{br} = 13.5 \times \pi \times 300^2/4 = 955 \times 10^3$ N
  $< P_u = 1000$ kN

  The excess force (to be transferred by reinforcement) is only 45 kN. This may be transferred by reinforcement, dowels or mechanical connectors. In this case, it is convenient to extend the pile reinforcement into the pile cap.

REVIEW QUESTIONS

14.1 Describe the main requirements of a foundation system for a structure.

14.2 Discuss why is it necessary to ensure, by proper proportioning of footings, that the bearing pressures underlying all the footings in a building are more-or-less of the same order of magnitude.

14.3 Discuss the situations in which *combined footings* are preferred to *isolated footings*.

14.4 Distinguish among the terms (i) *allowable* soil pressure (ii) *gross* soil pressure (iii) *net* soil pressure, (iv) *factored* soil pressure.

14.5 Describe *eccentric loading* on a footing, and the circumstances under which they occur?

14.6 Why is it desirable to eliminate eccentricity in loading on a footing, wherever possible, by means of proper proportioning?

14.7 From structural analyses, it is found that the following stress resultants develop at a column base under the action of *characteristic* loads:
(i) $P = 475$ kN, $M = 35$ kNm under *dead* loads;
(ii) $P = 380$ kN, $M = 39$ kNm under *live* loads;
(iii) $H = \pm 30$ kN, $P = \pm 12$ kN, $M = \pm 41$ kNm under *wind* loads.
Determine the combined loads to be considered in deciding the area of the footing to be located in a soil with an allowable soil pressure of 200 kN/m^2 at a depth of 1.5 m below ground level.

14.8 Discuss the advantages of providing pedestals to columns.

14.9 Briefly explain the conditions in which transfer of forces at the interface of column (or pedestal) and footing can be achieved without the aid of reinforcement.

14.10 Under what circumstances is a trapezoidal shape preferred to a rectangular shape for a two-column combined footing?

14.11 Describe briefly the load transfer mechanism in a two-column combined footing.

14.12 Explain the purpose of a *retaining wall.* What are the different types of concrete retaining walls?

14.13 Distinguish between *active pressure* and *passive pressure* of earth, in relation to retaining wall structures?

14.14 What is meant by (a) *surcharge* (b) *inclined surcharge*?

14.15 Describe the effect of water in the backfill on the active earth pressure on a retaining wall.

14.16 What is the purpose of a *shear key*? Describe its action.

14.17 Briefly describe the behaviour of the various elements of a *cantilever* retaining wall.

14.18 Briefly describe the behaviour of the various elements of a *counterfort* retaining wall.

14.19 Where are the critical sections for shear located in the case of (a) the *toe slab* (b) the *heel slab* in the design of the base slab of a cantilever retaining wall?

PROBLEMS

14.1 Design a plain concrete footing for a column, 400 mm × 400 mm, carrying an axial (service) load of 400 kN. Assume an allowable soil pressure of 350 kN/m^2 at a depth of 1.0 m below ground. Assume M25 concrete and Fe500 steel.

14.2 Design a square footing for a rectangular column 300 mm × 500 mm, reinforced with 6–25ϕ bars, and carrying a service load of 1250 kN. Assume soil with an allowable pressure of 200 kN/m^2 at a depth of 1.25 m below ground. Assume Fe500 grade steel for both column and footing, and M25 grade concrete for the footing and M30 grade concrete for the column.

14.3 Repeat Problem 14.2, considering a uniaxial moment (with respect to the major axis of the column) of 100 kNm (under service loads – dead plus live) in addition to the axial force of 1250 kN at the column base. Assume a suitable rectangular footing. Also assume that the moment is irreversible.

14.4 Design a square footing for a circular column, 500 mm in diameter, reinforced with 8–25ϕ bars, and carrying an axial load of 2500 kN. Assume soil with a safe bearing capacity of 300 kN/m^2 at a depth of 1.5 m below ground. Assume Fe500 grade steel for both column and footing, and M25 grade concrete for the footing and M30 grade concrete for the column.

14.5 Repeat Problem 14.4, considering a rectangular footing with a spatial restriction of 2.5 m on one of the plan dimensions.

14.6 Determine the base pressure distribution for the rectangular footing of size 5 m × 4 m supporting a column subject to an axial load of 800 kN and biaxial moments of 500 kNm and 400 kNm along major and minor axis respectively.

14.7 Design a square footing for a rectangular column 550 mm × 550 mm, reinforced with 10–25ϕ bars, and carrying an ultimate load of 1000 kN and biaxial moments of 250 kNm along each direction. Assume soil with an allowable pressure of 200 kN/m^2 at a depth of 1.25 m below ground. Assume Fe500 grade steel for both column and footing, and M25 grade concrete for the footing and M 30 grade concrete for the column.

14.8 Design a footing for a 250 mm thick reinforced concrete wall which supports a load (inclusive of self-weight) of 250 kN/m under service loads. Assume a safe soil bearing capacity of 180 kN/m^2 at a depth of 1 m below ground. Assume M25 grade concrete and Fe500 grade steel for both wall and footing. Assume the longitudinal reinforcement of the wall to comprise 0.25 percent of the gross cross-sectional area.

14.9 Repeat Problem 14.8, considering the wall to be made of masonry (instead of reinforced concrete).

14.10 Repeat Problem 14.8, considering a bending moment of 30 kNm/m (reversible) at the base of the wall, in addition to the axial load of 250 kN/m, under service loads.

14.11 Repeat the design of the two-column combined footing of Example 14.9, considering the property line to be located 500 mm away from the centre of column C1.

14.12 Repeat the design of the two-column combined footing of Example 14.9, considering a beam-slab footing, and assuming that the allowable soil pressure is 180 kN/m^2 (instead of 240 kN/m^2).

14.13 Design and detail the stem and base slab of the cantilever retaining wall of Example 14.10.

14.14 Design a cantilever wall to retain earth with a backfill sloped at 20° to the horizontal. The top of the wall is 5.5 m above the ground level, and the foundation depth may be taken as 1.2 m below ground level, with a safe bearing capacity of 120 kN/m^2. Assume that the backfill has a unit weight of 17 kN/m^2 and an angle of shearing resistance of 35°. Further, assume a coefficient of friction between soil and concrete, $\mu = 0.55$. Use M25 concrete and Fe500 steel.

14.15 Repeat Problem 14.14, considering the backfill to be level, with a surcharge, equivalent to an additional 2.52 m of the backfill.

14.16 Suggest suitable proportions for a counterfort retaining wall to support difference in ground elevation of 9 m. The foundation depth may be taken as 1.5 m below ground level, with a safe bearing capacity of 160 kN/m^2. Assume a level backfill with a unit weight of 16 kN/m^3 and an angle of shearing resistance of 30°. Assume a coefficient of friction, $\mu = 0.5$, between soil and concrete. Check the stability of the wall.

14.17 Design and detail the various elements of the counterfort wall structure of Problem 14.16.

REFERENCES

14.1 — *Explanatory Handbook on Indian Standard Code of Practice for Plain and Reinforced Concrete (IS 456:1978)*, Special Publication SP:24, Bureau of Indian Standards, New Delhi, 1983.

14.2 Bowles, J E, *Foundations Analysis and Design*, Third edition., McGraw-Hill Book Co., New York, 1982.

14.3 Peck, R R, Hanson, W E, and Thornburn, T H, *Foundation Engineering*, Second edition, John Wiley & Sons Inc., 1974.

14.4 — *Code of Practice for Structural Safety of Buildings*: *Shallow Foundations*, IS:1904 (third revision), Bureau of Indian Standards, New Delhi, 1986.

14.5 — *Code of Practice for Design and Construction of Simple Spread Foundations*, IS:1080 (First revision), Bureau of Indian Standards, New Delhi, 1980.

14.6 Sarkar, B, *Analysis of isolated footing subjected to axial load and high biaxial moments and numerical approach for its solution,* The Indian Concrete Journal, June 2014, pp 60-80.

14.7 Teng, W C, *Foundation Design*, Prentice Hall of India Private Limited, New Delhi, 1979.

14.8 Huntington, W C, *Earth Pressures and Retaining Walls*, John Wiley, New York, 1968.

14.9 Fisher, G P and Mains, R M, *Sliding Stability of Retaining Walls*, Civil Engineering, July 1952, pp 490.

14.10 Wang, C K and Salmon, C G, *Reinforced Concrete Design*, Fourth edition, Harper & Row, New York, 1985.

14.11 — *Code of Practice for Concrete Structures for Retaining Aqueous Liquids,* Part 4: *Design Tables,* IS: 3370 (Part 4), Bureau of Indian Standards, New Delhi, 2021.

CHAPTER 15

Good Detailing and Construction Practices

LEARNING OBJECTIVES

After studying this chapter, you will be able to:

- *Discuss the importance of detailing in relation to safety, serviceability and structural integrity*
- *Describe with examples, situations requiring special considerations in detailing reinforcements*
- *Explain the importance of quality control and the do's and don'ts in design and construction practices*

15.1 Introduction

The objective of structural design and construction is to build *safe*, *serviceable*, *economical*, *durable*, *aesthetic* and *sustainable* structures. Analysis and design, together, comprise only one of the phases in the process of a building construction. The elaborate computations involved in this phase become worthwhile only if the design is translated into a correspondingly high-quality structure. This necessitates good detailing and construction practices.

In Chapter 3, it was explained that the primary aim of design by the Limit States Method (LSM) is to minimise the probability of failure to an acceptable low value. In this context, *failure* is defined as the attainment of a *limit state*. *Limit states* imply those conditions whereby a structure or any component of it ceases to fulfil the functions for which it has been designed. The limit states include both *ultimate* limit states and *serviceability* limit states. Thus, the term, *failure,* in general, includes both *ultimate failure* – local or overall – (exceeding the load carrying capacity, instability and buckling, overturning, sliding, fatigue and fracture, and progressive type of collapse) under factored loads, and *serviceability failure* (unacceptable deflections and vibrations, excessive cracking, inadequate durability, permanent deformation, leakage, wetting, spalling of concrete, etc.,) under service loads. The structure should also satisfy the fire resistance requirements.

It is comparatively rare that buildings fail in a manner that can be classified as an ultimate limit state failure (collapse). Quite a few of such failures that do occur can be attributed to poor detailing. On the other hand, it is much too common for comfort that buildings (especially those of more recent construction) perform unsatisfactorily in their day-to-day normal service; i.e., fail to meet serviceability criteria.

> **Serviceability failures – routine unsatisfactory performance – are disturbingly common in RC structures.**

In the fifties and sixties, reinforced concrete buildings used to be designed by the working stress method (WSM) with relatively low permissible stresses (for example, 5 MPa for 1:2:4 nominal mix concrete and 140 MPa for mild steel). Moreover, many analysis and design methods used in those days employed approximations which 'erred on the safe side'. Modern structures are designed with higher strength materials, for higher stresses, and by the Limit States Method (allowing for inelasticity and moment redistribution) with 'partial safety factors' lower than the 'factors of safety' inherent in the WSM as practised in the early sixties (see next paragraph). Furthermore, the methods of analysis and design have become more sophisticated and accurate, and the benefit of conservatism in-built in approximate methods is no longer available. As a result, these modern structures are comparatively taller and have longer spans, more slender members, lesser reinforcement and thinner slabs and walls, and are built at a faster pace. They are therefore, more flexible (in terms of deflections) and are more 'crack prone', as compared with the old structures, which used to be low in height, had thicker (stockier) members, were lightly stressed and were built at a slow pace. Thus, *the serviceability criteria assume far greater importance in modern structures*. It is in this context that this chapter is included in this book. It is meant to draw the attention of engineers involved in all the stages of planning, design, detailing, fabrication and construction to these important aspects related to the performance of buildings.

> **Because of several reasons, the real factors of safety inherent in RC structures designed and built over time have come down, while the demands on these structures have increased over the same period. Hence, serviceability checks assume greater importance in modern structures.**

For a comparison of the early 60's design with the current ones, consider the case of the simply supported beam shown in Figure 15.1, which is an example from a 1959 textbook [Ref. 15.1]. With the mild steel reinforcements commonly used then and WSM design (as per IS 456:1953), the admissible service load on this beam, including self-weight, is 15 kN/m. For the same beam today, with LSM design, the common M 25 concrete and Fe 500 steel and load factor of 1.5, the admissible service load works out to 34.5 kN/m, reflecting an increase of 130 per cent!

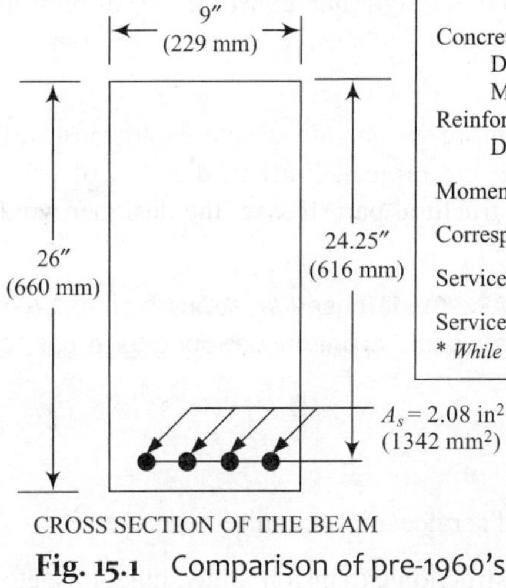

	WSD	LSD
Concrete 1:2:4		
Design stress:	750 psi (5.17 MPa)	25 MPa
Modular ratio:	18	
Reinforcement*		
Design stress:	18000 psi (124 MPa)	500 MPa
Moment capacity:	743,500 in. lbs (84 kNm)	291 kN.m
Corresponding load:	1024 lbs/ft (15 kN/m)	51.7 kN/m
Service load admissible:	15 kN/m	34.5 kN/m

Service load by LSD/service load b yWSD = 2.30

* *While MS was used in 50's, Fe 500 grade steel is used now*

Beam is simply supported
Span, c to c of supports = 22 ft (6.71 m)

CROSS SECTION OF THE BEAM

Fig. 15.1 Comparison of pre-1960's designs with current designs (case 1).

> **Comparisons show that the service load capacity of a typical RC beam, designed using current Code specifications and commonly used grades of concrete and steel, is about *2 to 3 times* that of a beam of identical dimensions and span, designed in the 1950's, using the specifications and grades of materials prevailing then.**

As yet another example, consider the beam in Examples 4.3 and 4.11 in Chapter 4, shown in Figure 15.2. As per IS 456:2000, for this section, the allowable bending moment by WSM is 133 kNm and the ultimate moment (LSM) 348 kNm. By IS 456:1953, the allowable moment works out to 83 kNm. For a 10 m span, the admissible service load by the three methods for a simply supported span, fixed-ended span and fixed-ended span with full redistribution are shown in the table in Figure. 15.2. The admissible service load by the current LSM, even for the simply supported case, is seen to be 2.8 times that by the 1953 code.

For IS 456:2000 calculations, see Examples 4.3 and 4.11

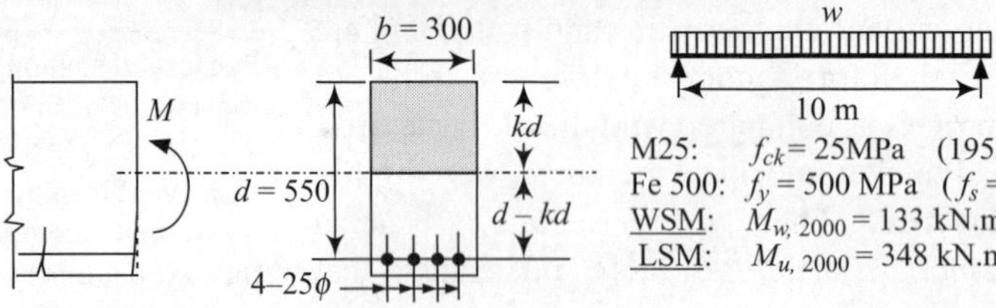

M25: f_{ck} = 25MPa (1953: f_c = 750 psi = 5 MPa)
Fe 500: f_y = 500 MPa (f_s =18,000 psi = 124 MPa)
WSM: $M_{w,\,2000}$ = 133 kN.m; $M_{w,\,1953}$ = 83 kN.m,
LSM: $M_{u,\,2000}$ = 348 kN.m

Admissible service load, *w* in kN/meter, by:

	WSM (1953)	WSM (2000)	LSM (*LF* = 1.5)
S.S. beam *w* =	6.64	10.64	18.56
Fixed ended beam	9.96	15.96	27.84
Fixed ended with redistribution	9.96	18.78	37.12

(*For fixed-ended cases, assume same reinforcements at top at support sections*)

Fig. 15.2 Comparison of pre-1960's designs with current designs (case 2).

Detailing practises, construction practises, quality control in construction, building failures, causes and prevention of cracks/leakage in buildings, etc., are all large enough topics to write separate books and/or publish journals on each of them, as indeed have been done (Ref. 15.2 to 15.9). Nor are all these topics strictly within the scope of this book. As such, an attempt is made here only to draw attention to some of the major and most common causes of failure pertaining to the design (and construction) of reinforced concrete buildings. These are by no means exhaustive. For a more comprehensive coverage, reference may be made to Ref. 15.2–15.12.

In this context it is worthwhile to note that, in most reinforced concrete structures, the cost of the structural part itself forms only a small part of the total cost of the project. Further, the cost of the concrete and reinforcement forms only a fraction of the cost of the structural part. Hence, the designer would do well to remember that:

> aiming for minimum quantities of concrete and reinforcement (based on strength criteria alone) may not lead to significant cost reduction, and may well result in unforeseen long-term cost or failure related to serviceability criteria.

15.1.1 Serviceability Failures

The commonly observed shortcomings in the context of serviceability requirements are:

- leakage from roofs and floors, particularly at construction/expansion joints, junctions, etc.;

- wetting of ceilings, walls (especially around toilet areas), leading to dampness, discoloration, growth of algae and moss on surfaces, growth of vegetation in fissures in walls and around drain pipes, sunshades, ledges, etc.;
- cracking in slabs, beams, columns, walls, etc. (*Structural:* due to direct tension, flexure, shear, fatigue; *Non-structural:* due to creep, shrinkage, temperature, settlement, impact/collision, etc.);
- poor drainage and ponding of water on roof slabs, sunshades, bathrooms, open staircase steps, etc.;
- corrosion of reinforcement and spalling and splitting of concrete, rust staining;
- Flaking, scaling, delamination, pitting, ravelling, pop outs, staining, chloride contamination, efflorescence, carbonation, wear, abrasion, honey combing, freeze–thaw, alkali–silica reactivity (ASR), Ettringite formation, etc.;
- excessive sag/deflections of slabs, beams, etc., permanent deformation, tilt, buckling, settlement, mis-alignment, excessive vibration;
- other issues/causes: temperature changes, chemical attack, moisture absorption, differential foundation movement, design/construction deficiencies, unintended objects in concrete, fire damage, etc.

Many of the above effects are interactive. For example, large deflections of roof slabs can lead to ponding of rain water as well as cracking on the top side in negative moment regions, which in turn can lead to wetting and leakage, and also corrosion of reinforcement.

15.1.2 Reasons for Building Failures

There are many causes that could lead to the failure (*ultimate* and/or *serviceability*) of a structure. Some of these, which must be of concern to the design and construction engineers are listed below:

Failure during construction or soon after	Failure a long time after construction
• Deficiency in design/shift from actual design; • Poor detailing; • Poor quality materials; • Poor quality construction; • Inadequate formwork/scaffolding; • Overloading due to oversight (Ex. Unsymmetrical backfilling of a below ground circular water tank); • Procedural and communication errors, Lack of co-ordination; • Construction mishaps/errors, sabotage; • Unintended objects in concrete (trash, paper, leaves, etc.) – results in voids; • Combinations of the above.	• Failure of a primary load carrying member(s) by accident; • Change in use (change of structural arrangement) or overloading; • Unforeseen disasters like severe earthquake, bomb blast, fire, etc.; • Deterioration arising out of poor-quality materials, design, detailing, construction and/or lack of repair and maintenance; • Exposure to adverse environment, not considered in original design.

A classic example of a 'seemingly harmless' change of structural arrangement leading to catastrophic failure is the 1981 collapse of the suspended walkways across the atrium on the second and fourth floor of Hyatt Regency Hotel in Kansas City, USA. The replacement of continuous suspender rods [Figures 15.3(a), (b)] with two separate rods [Figure 15.3(c)], without corresponding redesign of the joint, resulted in the failure of the upper joint and collapse of both walkways killing 114 persons and injuring over 200; leave alone loss of property, loss of Engineering licenses to many, expensive legal suits and the bankruptcy of several firms. Engineers should be wary of such alterations which may appear innocuous on a cursory glance, but could lead to disastrous results. Incidentally, in this case even the original design failed to meet Code required strength.

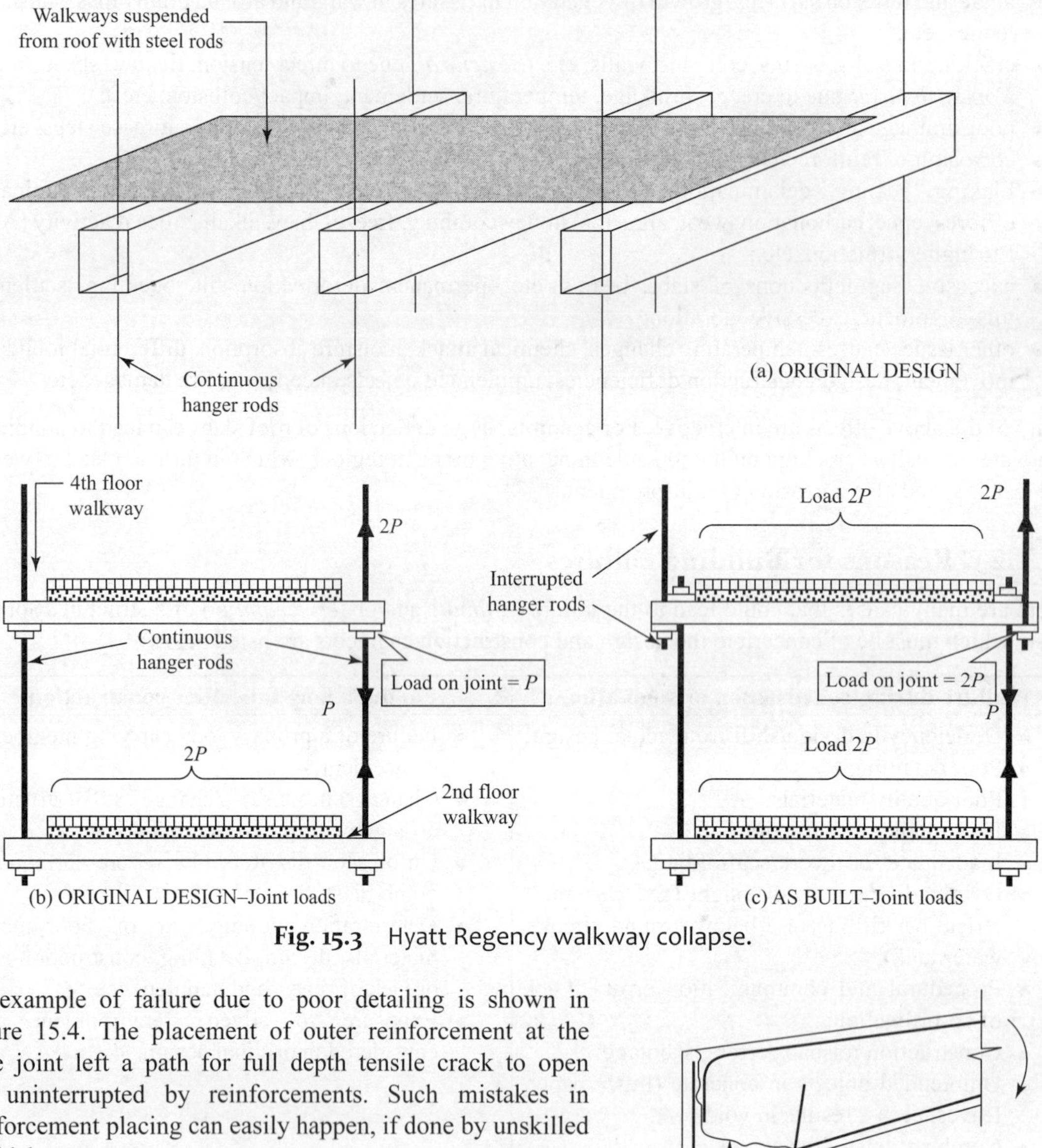

Fig. 15.3 Hyatt Regency walkway collapse.

An example of failure due to poor detailing is shown in Figure 15.4. The placement of outer reinforcement at the knee joint left a path for full depth tensile crack to open up, uninterrupted by reinforcements. Such mistakes in reinforcement placing can easily happen, if done by unskilled field labourers.

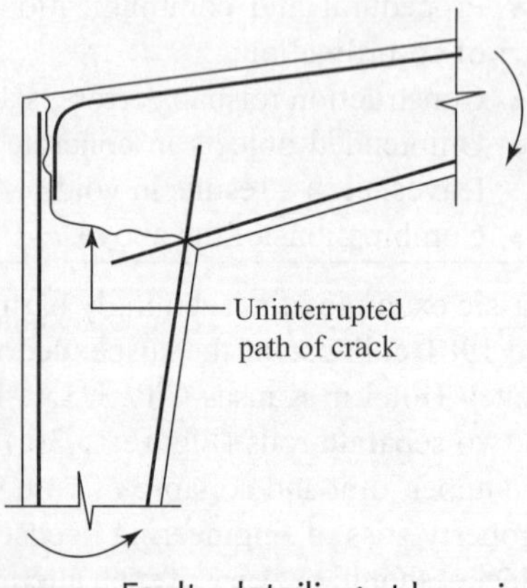

Fig. 15.4 Faulty detailing at knee joint.

15.1.3 Structural Integrity

Some causes for failures long after completion of construction are identified in the above section. Most of these causes such as accidents, overloading and disasters are not directly related to either the design or the construction; usual structures are designed to resist only loads and their effects that may *reasonably be expected.* However, a related design consideration is the need for the structure to have *structural integrity*. A structure is said to have structural integrity if it is able to withstand localised damage or failure of a structural member, caused by any unforeseen or abnormal events (that may *reasonably be expected*) without spread of damage or collapse to a large part of the structure. In other words, the failure of one element should not lead to a *progressive collapse* or *incremental collapse* of the rest of the structure.

'Structural integrity' means the ability of a structure to withstand localised damage/failure without spread of damage/collapse to a large part of the structure.

A typical example of a progressive type of collapse is the failure of a flat plate structure originating from the punching shear failure at one slab-column connection (in the absence of special reinforcement for structural integrity at such connections; refer Section 11.7, Figure 11.40). Punching shear failure at one column can lead to increased shear and moment at adjacent column connections, causing them to fail. Such progressive failure of slab-column joints may lead to the slab falling on to the slab below, causing it to fail as well, and so on vertically down the building. Examples of such progressive collapse are reviewed in Refs. 15.13 and 15.14.

In design, consideration should be given to the integrity of the overall structural system to minimise the likelihood of progressive collapse. This involves a careful selection/review of the structural system, understanding its behaviour under load and possible failure modes and ensuring a robust and stable design with sufficient *redundancy* and *alternative load paths*. Most continuously reinforced cast-in-place concrete structures designed and detailed in accordance with codes will generally possess a satisfactory level of structural integrity. Special provisions for structural integrity may be required for two-way flat slabs at slab-column connections, precast concrete structures, unusual structural systems, and structures exposed to severe loads such as vehicle impact, fire accident or explosion.

Design strategies for structural integrity include (Ref. 15.15):

Control of events causing abnormal loads. An example is protecting columns from vehicle impact by placing energy absorbing devices around the column. However, such measures are, by and large, beyond the scope of structural design.

Design to resist likely abnormal loads. When the loss of a particular member in a structure might lead to a progressive collapse (such as with the failure of one column in a building with less than, say, four columns), then that member should be designed to resist the abnormal event/load. This option is generally less desirable and less economical than the ones given below, but can not be avoided in some cases.

Design for alternate load paths. As mentioned earlier, the basic method of design for structural integrity is to design such that the structure can bridge over the gap left when a structural member is removed. Designers should consider the effect of removal, one at a time, of one span of floor/roof, one column in any one storey or one panel of a load bearing wall in any storey. With the member removed, the structure is checked to ensure that it can support without collapse, the dead load + about one-half of the live load + about one-fifth of the wind load (all at service load levels) plus any debris resulting from the failure. The structure may be permitted to undergo a considerable amount of localized collapse and deformation.

Some of the measures that assist development of alternate load paths are: systematic layout of columns and walls, provision of tying steel at top and bottom of walls to generate beam action in them, minimum reinforcement both ways in slabs to assist development of tensile membrane action while sagging after loss of a support and providing stronger elements where needed to complete an alternate load path. In some cases, provision of lines of weakness may help to limit spread of damage.

Design using local resistance details. This process attempts to provide alternate load paths indirectly, by providing minimum structural resistance with a minimum amount of reinforcement to tie various parts of the structure (Ref. 15.16). Also, strong points are provided in the building to anchor the tie forces. This method is adopted mostly for precast panel buildings. Ties are placed across the joints between floor slabs, across the horizontal joints between the walls above and below a floor and longitudinally and transversely around the periphery of the building.

15.2 Design and Detailing Practices

It is very rare that a building fails as a result of a major design flaw in the design of structural elements. The design codes are fairly conservative, if not up to date, as far as reinforced concrete design is concerned. The engineering curriculum is also reasonably up to date in this regard. Moreover, highly sophisticated and accurate softwares are now available for computer aided analysis, and also for design and drafting. However, in using these softwares, a word of caution is appropriate. The outputs of these programs are only as good as the inputs are! Hence, they should only be used by persons who have a full understanding of what the program does, as well as of the properties of materials, structural behaviour, failure modes, structural system employed, overall deformation patterns, compatibility conditions, load transmission paths to supports, and possible weak links, if any. Furthermore, it is necessary to identify the critical and primary load carrying elements, and to perform an approximate manual check on the stress resultants and design resistance of such members, in order to avoid gross errors. For example, the use of appropriate moment coefficients applied to a simplified substitute frame will yield a rough estimate of moments [refer Chapter 9]. Similarly, an approximate estimation of the ultimate moment of resistance of a beam/slab section can be obtained as $(0.87 f_y A_{st})(0.9d)$.

> While the typical undergraduate curriculum for RC design covers section/member design fairly competently, the coverage of structural integration measures such as joint detailing, reinforcement detailing for appropriate load transfer, considerations of possible failure modes and avoidance measures, construction practices, requirements for formwork. etc., are found wanting.

As mentioned earlier, the analysis of structures for stress resultants and the design of individual elements (critical sections of slabs, beams and columns) for maximum load effects (bending moment, shear and torsion, and axial force) are done, in general, fairly competently. However, the attention given to the combining of these elements together to form the whole structure is generally found wanting both in the engineering curriculum and in many design offices. This includes the attention given to such important details as: termination, extending and bending of bars; anchorage and development; stirrup anchorage; splices; reinforcement placement and construction details at connections (slab-beam, beam-column, rigid frame corners, etc.); detailing reinforcements accounting for load transfer, load paths and stress fields; provision of continuity/discontinuity (as required) at junctions of members; construction sequencing and reinforcement placement to suit; deflection calculations (including long-term deflections) and control; crack control; special cases such as upturned (inverted) beams, edge and spandrel beams, cantilevered members; cover, bar support and reinforcement protection; durability; recognition of and allowance for long-term effects of creep, shrinkage and temperature; providing required camber and slopes; details of control/construction/expansion joints; structures needing special procedures (tanks, chimneys, etc.); special requirements for corrosive environments; sharp discontinuities and stress concentration; design and detailing of formwork; preparation of detailed construction drawings; quality control; and Construction/Project Management..

The practical work in concrete Laboratory Courses in most universities is also found wanting. Experiments and assignments are mostly limited to the standard tests on cement, aggregate and hardened concrete. Applied problems aimed at the understanding of concrete technology (influence of various parameters, and concrete mix design) and fabrication and testing of reinforced concrete elements (design-fabricate-cast-cure-test-analyse type assignments) are seldom included in the laboratory courses.

15.2.1 Reinforcement Layout

Heavy live loads and lack of regularity in framing (widely differing adjoining spans, variation in column sizes and spacings, fluctuations in relative stiffnesses, etc.) can move the point of contra-flexure considerably, thereby affecting the termination, extension and bending of bars considerably. Such lack of regularity could necessitate continuing of top bars over the full length of a short span located between two long ones (common in school buildings, hotels, etc. with narrow central corridors), or may make it impracticable to bend any bar at all, or conversely, may make it possible to bend up considerably more than half the bottom bars in a heavy girder, anchoring and terminating them in a compression zone, or may necessitate provision of stirrups for the full length of a member. Admittedly, considerably improved design skill is required in delineating the reinforcement throughout the length of members than in selecting top and bottom bars for maximum moments. Considering fabrication and placement costs, the reinforcement detail which gives the minimum weight of steel is often not the most economical one.

Concrete being weak in tension, reinforcement is provided to take care of all tensions envisioned by the designer, whether direct/flexural (main reinforcement), diagonal (stirrups), splitting (see Figure 2.11), thermal or due to differential settlements. In flexural members/regions where the assumption that plane sections remain plane is reasonably valid, the magnitude and direction of the tensile stresses can be computed by the theory of flexure. However, in regions of discontinuities (static and/or geometric) where the theory of flexure cannot be applied, the stress trajectories are more complex. For such regions, an appropriate model (see Sections 15.2.3 and 17.2) may be used to conceive the flow of internal stresses/forces.

Suitable reinforcement must be provided across any potential crack in order to inhibit initiation of cracks and to control their widening and propagation once initiated. In particular, attention should be paid to locations at which tensile stresses, not ordinarily calculated, exist – such as due to shrinkage, settlement, temperature and stress concentration effects, and lateral strains due to Poisson effect. Cracking due to thermal and shrinkage movements can be reduced by making provision in the design and construction of structures for unrestrained movement of parts, wherever feasible, by introducing movement joints (expansion joints, control joints and slip joints). Where provision of movement joints is not structurally feasible (as in rigid frames, shell roofs), thermal stresses have to be taken into account at the structural design itself. Even where joints for movement are provided, some amount of restraint to movement due to bond and friction is unavoidable. In cases where the design reinforcement is only in one direction (as in one-way slabs, cantilevered slabs, etc.) cracks could develop across the perpendicular direction due to the induced secondary moment (Poisson effect) and shrinkage in that direction, and it is necessary to provide some reinforcement (variously called as 'distributor reinforcement' or 'temperature reinforcement') in the direction perpendicular to the main reinforcement. In case of members exposed to the sun (sunshades, fins, canopies, balconies, roof slab without adequate insulation cover, etc.), the 'minimum' reinforcement specified by the Code should be increased by 50 to 100 per cent, depending upon the severity of exposure, size of member and local conditions [Ref. 15.5]. Reference may also be made to Section 5.2.2, with regard to the need for *side face reinforcement* to control cracking in large unreinforced exposed faces of concrete members.

15.2.2 Design Drawings

Much time and expense can be saved, and costly mistakes avoided, if simple, clear and complete drawings are prepared. More than serving as a graphic delineation of a structure, a drawing acts as a definite order to workmen to perform certain operations in a specified manner. The drawing also serves as a record of some of the important assumptions made in the design (which, for example, can reveal whether or not future expansion of the structure is possible at a later date). Engineering drawings prepared by the designer should specify grades of concrete and steel, live load, dimensions, reinforcement, lap lengths, concrete cover, and all other information needed for detailing the reinforcement, building the forms, placing the reinforcement and placing the concrete. The designer has full data on the assumptions made, the computations, moment diagrams and the whole philosophy of structural design, and it is his responsibility to define the design requirements by way of anchorages, laps, bends, splices and similar details. Indeed, it is only he who can supply such information to the detailers, fabricators and construction personnel. Hence, design drawings must be complete to the extent that every bit of information regarding the size and arrangement of concrete members, and the size, positioning and detailing of reinforcing bars is completely covered either by a drawing, description, diagram, note, rule, or reference to a standard manual.

Notes and statements should be clear and unambiguous. A note '16 bars 2 ways 2 faces' is highly ambiguous, as it could mean 16 bars each way each face (total 64) or 4 bars each way each face (total 16), or indeed almost anything in between. Instead, the note should have been made explicit, giving the number *each way* in *each face*. Similarly, descriptions are best given in the imperative: 'Do this', 'Bend these bars', rather than 'This may be done', or 'These bars may be bent'. Graphical representations (true-scale elevations, sections, etc.) are preferable to complicated notes and descriptions, to show precisely what is wanted; they are also, to a considerable extent, self-checking.

While, with uniform loads and equal spans, it may be satisfactory to bend bars at the quarter-point and to extend them to the $3/10^{th}$ point as in Figure 5.5 (following standard practices/manuals for such cases), this is not safe as a general practice for all cases. Hence, the drawing should make it clear, by way of a separate section, indicating the departure from standard practice.

15.2.3 Construction Details at Connections and Special Situations

As mentioned before, locations and members needing special detailing considerations are encountered frequently. These include locations of abrupt changes in section size, direction of axis and other sudden discontinuities, edge beams, inverted beams, odd-shaped/sized members, connections, etc. A few such cases are described below. In many such instances, a useful procedure for design and/or detailing is to adopt the *strut-and-tie model* [see Section 17.2].

Offset Columns

When a column in a particular storey is smaller than the one below, some of the vertical bars from below may have to be offset to come within the column above, or dowel splices must be used [Figure 15.5(a)].

The slope of the inclined portion should not exceed 1 in 6. Where column verticals are offset this way, additional ties shall be provided and placed close to the point of bend in the lower column in order to carry the resultant outward transverse force generated due to the change of direction at the bend. When the offset between column faces exceeds 75 mm, the vertical bars in the column below shall be terminated at the floor slab, and splicing of column bars by dowels may be necessary [Figure 15.5(b)]. Dowels may also be necessary when the placing of part of the structure is delayed, and also between various units of structures (such as footings and columns). Dowels should, in general, be of the same size and grade as the bars joined, and should be of sufficient length to splice with the main bars on both sides.

When column bars are spliced, additional ties shall be provided at and near the ends of spliced bars, to provide confinement to the highly stressed concrete in the regions of the bar ends.

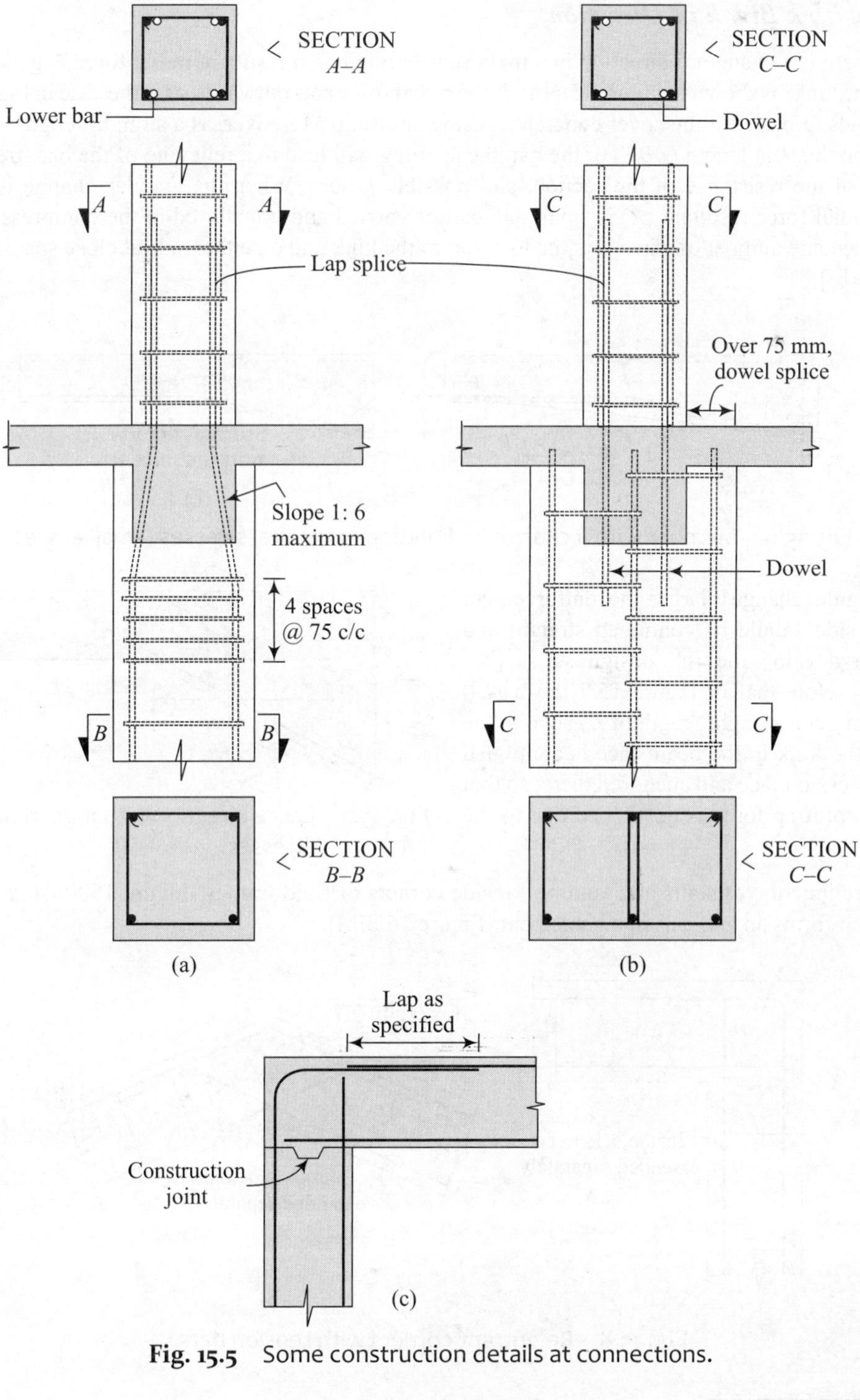

Fig. 15.5 Some construction details at connections.

Members with a Break in Direction

Whenever there is a change of direction in a main reinforcing bar, a resultant radial force is generated at the location of the kink, as shown in Figure 15.6(a). If the radial force acts outwards, as is the case in Figure 15.6(a), this force tends to push out the cover concrete causing splitting. Moreover, as a straight length (such as *AC*) is shorter than the bent length (*ABC*) of the bar, the spalling will lead to a relieving of the bar stress resulting in lowering of the resistance of the section, and possible failure. When the angular change is small (say < 15°) the radial force resultant (*R*) is small and can be carried and transferred to the compression zone by providing adequate number of stirrups at the location of the kink and on either side at close spacing as shown [Figure 15.6(b)].

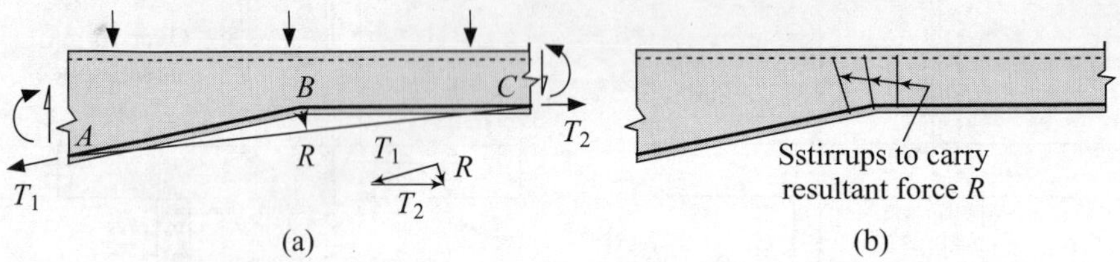

Fig. 15.6 Member with a change in direction in flexural stresses (small angle).

When the angular change is larger, the reinforcement from either side should be continued straight and anchored to develop the full design stress [see Figure 15.7]. Note that in Figure 15.7 the bar *A*, which cannot get a straight length of L_d beyond the location of the kink in the beam face is continued on the compression face and anchored there, so that no outward splitting force is developed due to the bend in this bar.

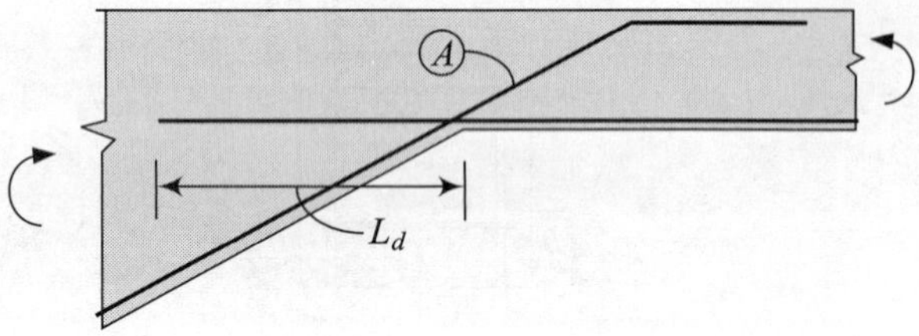

Fig. 15.7 Large directional change in flexural stresses.

Examples are junction of stairs and landing†, inside corners of rigid frames [Figure 15.8(a)] and where the soffit of beam forms an angle as in a gable bent [Figure 15.8(b)].

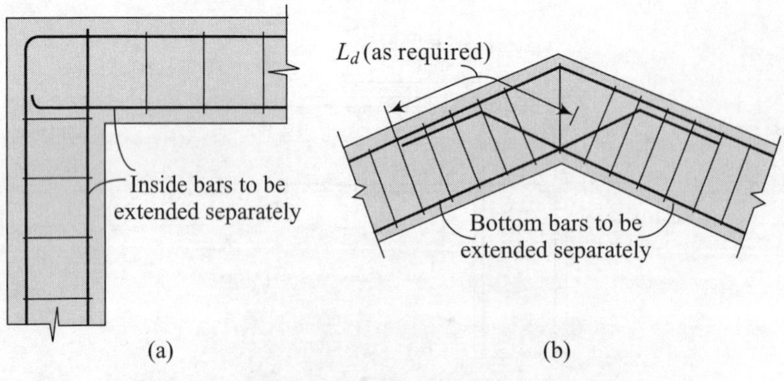

Fig. 15.8 Re-entrant corners with tension bars.

† This detail is indicated in Figure 12.4(a) of Chapter 12.

A similar situation exists when the internal compression force changes direction in such a way that the resultant force acts outward [Figure 15.9(a)]. In the example shown, a breaking away of the flange can be prevented by transverse reinforcement tying the flange to the web of the beam [Figure 15.9(b)].

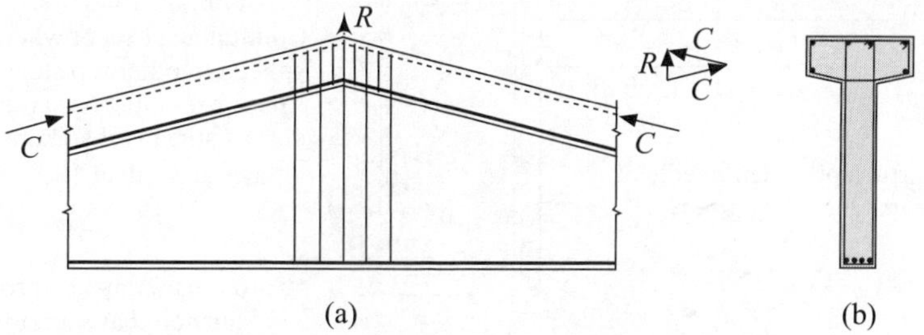

Fig. 15.9 Change in direction of compressive stresses.

Construction and bar placing details of the corner connection of a rigid frame are shown in Figure 15.5(c) – compare Figure 15.4. In detailing such connections, care must be taken particularly in providing full continuity around as large a uniform radius as possible in splicing the top bars from the girder to the outside bars in the column. Rigid corner connections of beams to columns often require closed stirrups or ties around the bend [see also Section 15.2.4 on Rigid Frame Joints]. The designer must provide complete information showing the radius of bend, location and dimensions of the lap splices (or other type of splices) used and stirrup details.

Edge Beams and Slab Edges

In edge and spandrel beams, stirrups must be of the closed type and at least one longitudinal bar should be located at each corner of the beam section. Typical details are shown, for normal and inverted edge/spandrel beams in Figures 15.10(a) and (b) respectively. For easier placing of the longitudinal bars in an inverted beam, two-piece closed stirrups can also be used as shown in Figure 15.10(b). At edges of slabs without edge beam, especially at free edges such as around openings and at edges of cantilevered slabs, it is good practice to provide reinforcement bent around the edges with adequate anchorage lengths as shown in Figure 15.10(c).

Corners of Walls

In concrete walls, horizontal reinforcement may be required to resist moment, shear or temperature and shrinkage effects. All such bars in both faces of wall must be sufficiently extended past a corner or intersection to satisfy development requirements. Typical details are shown in Figure 15.11 for resistance against moment (inward and outward), with the reinforcement from the appropriate faces anchored.

Special Conditions

For special or unusual conditions, adequate details should be shown for proper placing of reinforcement, as the average steel setter cannot be expected to understand engineering principles. Examples are cantilevers and continuous footings, in which the reinforcement is in the opposite side from the one to which the steel setter is accustomed.

There are situations where the embedment length available for end anchorage of bars is insufficient to develop the design stress in the bar through bond. Examples include corbels, deep beams, small size footings, precast beams, etc. In such cases, special devices such as welded cross bars, end plates [Figure 15.12] must be provided.

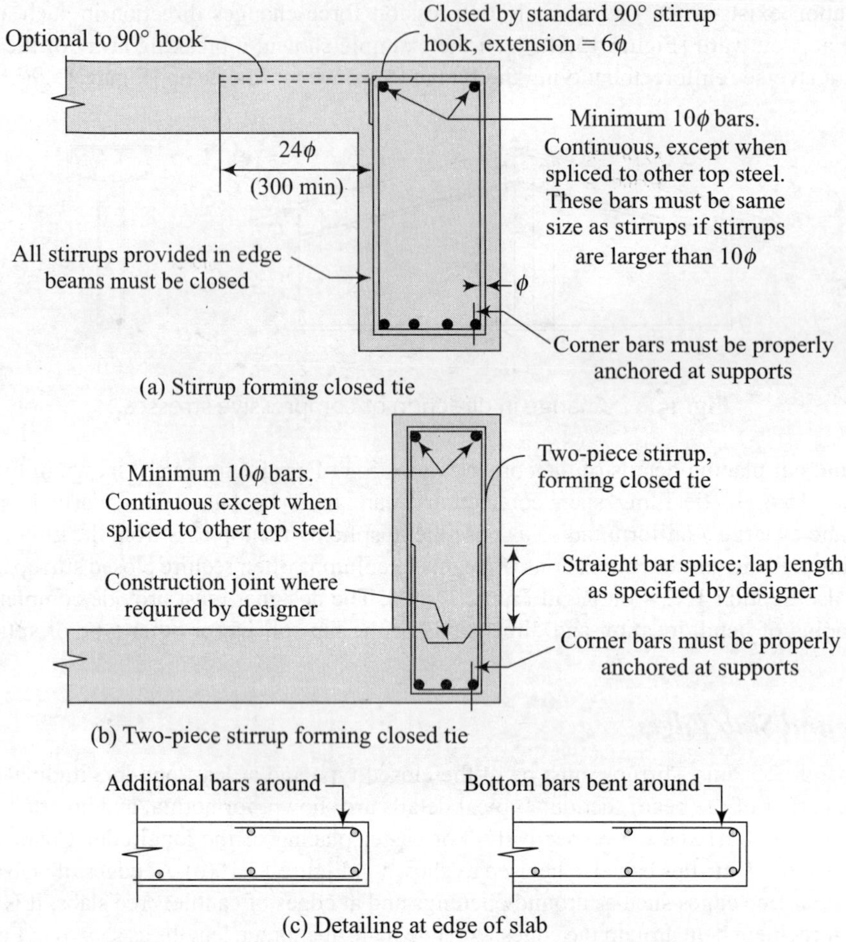

Fig. 15.10 Typical slab edge and spandrel beam details.

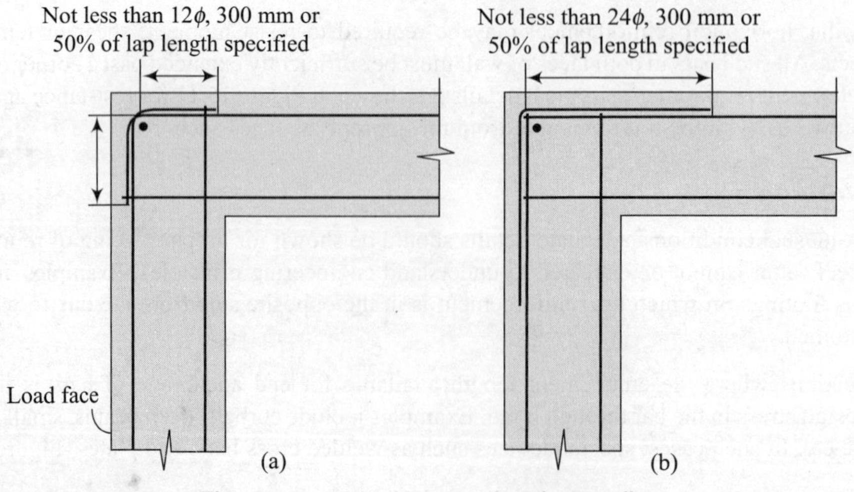

Fig. 15.11 Typical corner details in walls.

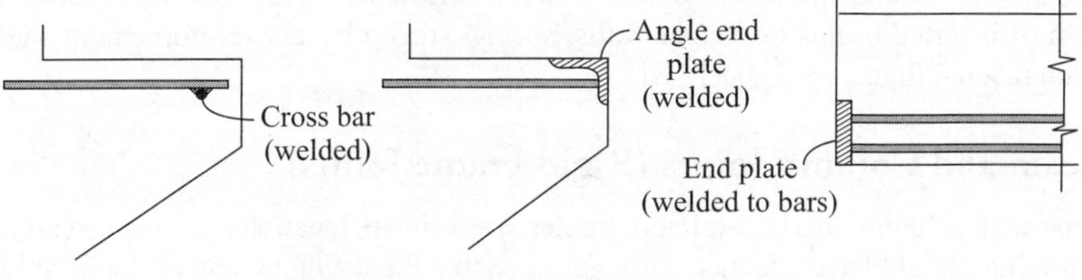

Fig. 15.12 Special anchorage devices.

Intersection of Members

Congestion of steel should be avoided at locations where members intersect, such as intersection of (secondary) beams with girder (primary beam) and girders with column. In the interior beam-column joint, generally there is overcrowding of the negative (top) reinforcement in the beam if they are all placed within the beam width [Figure 15.13(a)]. This usually interferes with proper placing and compaction of the concrete at the joint. The bond developed in these top reinforcements also is relatively inferior. The spreading of the top reinforcement into the adjoining slab, preferably using smaller diameter bars, [Figure 15.13(b)] has been shown to reduce the crack-widths in these beams considerably [Ref. 15.14]. This has the added benefit that the effective depth is slightly increased and the placement and compaction of concrete is facilitated better.

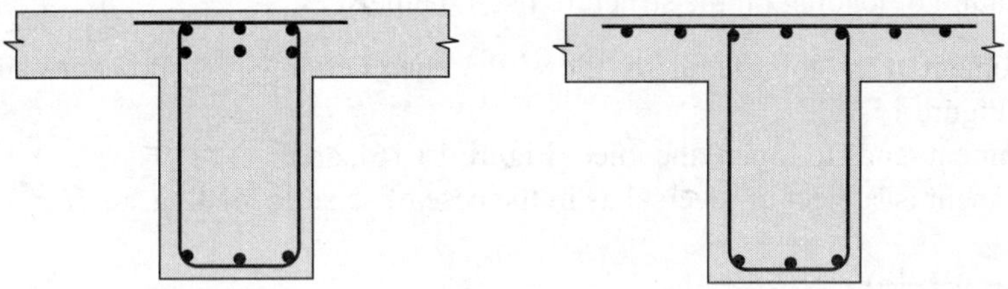

(a) (b)

Fig. 15.13 Negative moment reinforcement at beam-column joint.

At the intersection of a beam and girder, the beam bars should be placed at a different elevation than those in the girder so as to avoid interference. The relative positions of the bars must be in accordance with the load transfer order assumed in design. Thus, the beam reinforcement must come over the girder reinforcement at the intersection [Figure 15.14]. In addition, adequate hanging up bars (suspender stirrups) should be provided in both members in the joint zone as given in Section 6.10. Similarly, at slab-beam junctions, the bottom and

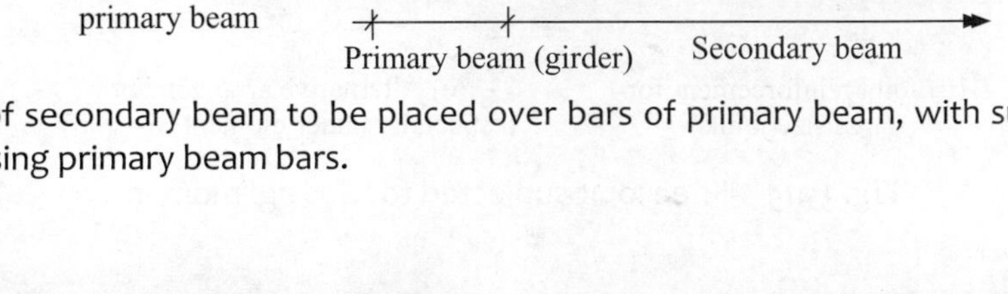

Fig. 15.14 Bars of secondary beam to be placed over bars of primary beam, with suspender stirrups enclosing primary beam bars.

top bars of the slab must be draped over the bottom and top bars in beam respectively. When slabs frame flush with the bottom of inverted beams or hanger walls, special stirrup hanger reinforcement shall be provided [see also Section 6.5 and Figures 6.7 and 15.8].

15.2.4 Beam and Column Joints (Rigid Frame Joints)

Joints of beams and columns in rigid-jointed frames are critical locations requiring careful design and detailing. Such joints should have adequate strength to enable the development, at the joint face, of the full design strengths (and plastic hinges with adequate ductility, if required by design) in the members framing into each joint under the most adverse loading pattern, without distress in the joint itself. This type of rigid connection occurs in rigid jointed multi-storey frames, portal frames, box culverts, at the base of cantilever retaining walls, etc. An example of incorrect detailing of the beam-column joint of a portal frame was shown in Figure 15.4. This allowed a free path for crack propagation, uninterrupted by any reinforcing bar and resulted in the collapse of the structure under dead weight alone [Ref. 15.5].

A simple example of a rigid beam-column joint, for which the design and detailing considerations can be explained with relative ease, is the corner joint of a portal frame, usually called a 'knee joint' [Figure 15.15]. The joint, to be rigid, must have full continuity between the two members. The main flexural reinforcement in the joint zone undergoes a change of direction, and as a result transverse forces are developed, as in the cases considered in Figure 15.15. There can be three types of stress patterns to which the joint zone is subjected to, depending on the nature of loading on the structure itself, namely:

(a) where the moment at the joint tends to 'close' the knee i.e., hogging moment causing tension in the outer fibres [Figure 15.15],
(b) where the moment tends to 'open' the knee [Figure 15.16], and
(c) where the moment is subject to reversal as in the case of seismic loading.

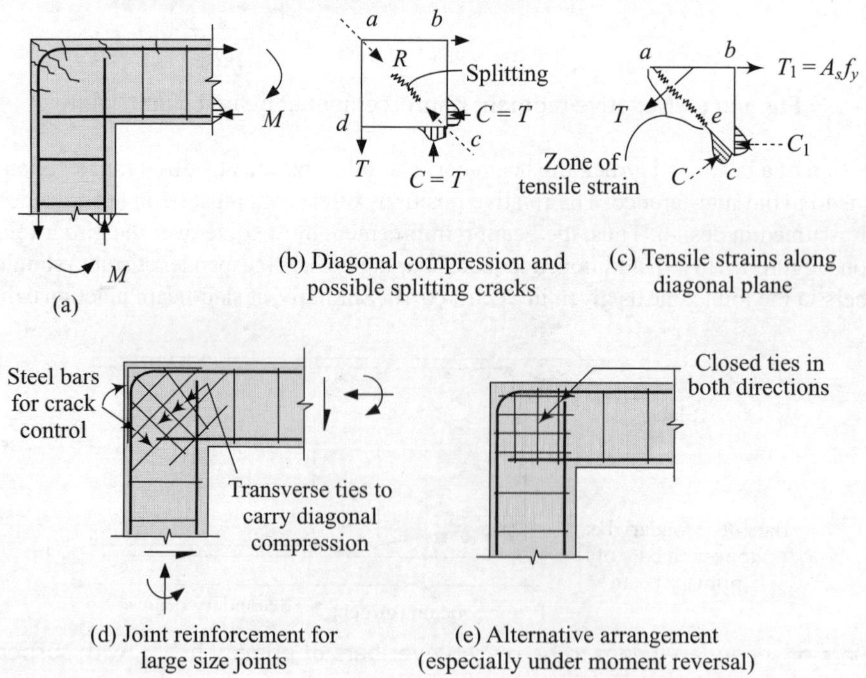

Fig. 15.15 Knee joint subjected to 'closing' moment.

The nature of induced forces in the joint zone in case (a) is shown in Figures 15.15(b) and (c). The diagonal resultant thrust R tends to develop splitting cracks along the diagonal *ac*, analogous to what happens in a split cylinder test. A significant portion (*ae*) of the diagonal *ac* will be under tensile stress and liable to crack, as shown in Figure 15.15(c). It may be noted that the joint is usually subjected to axial forces and shearing forces, in addition to the bending moment. For satisfactory performance in this case, the outer tension bars should be continuous around the corner. The inner bars are in compression; however, the concrete alone may be adequate to carry the compressive forces here. These bars are better continued straight, as shown, rather than being made continuous by bending around near the re-entrant corner. In case these bars are also accounted as contributing part of the required compressive force, they should be continued straight and anchored to develop the design stress at the joint faces along corner *c*. Furthermore, the diagonal compression along *ac* and the possible diagonal cracking along *ae* should be countered. When the members are of small size (as in the case of slab-wall joint or the corner of a small size lightly reinforced and thin-walled box culvert), no special provisions may be needed to carry the diagonal compression and tension along diagonals *ac* and *bd*. However, in large size or heavier reinforced members, the diagonal compression may be resisted, and the diagonal cracking controlled, by secondary reinforcements placed along diagonal directions as shown in Figure 15.15(d). An alternative arrangement is to place these reinforcement orthogonally as in Figure 15.15(e). This arrangement is particularly suited for cases of moment reversals.

The case of a knee joint subjected to 'opening' moment is shown in Figure 15.16. In general, this loading case (moment tending to open the knee joint) is more critical than the case of moment tending to 'close' the knee joint [case (a) discussed in Figure 15.15]. The nature of stresses in the joint and potential crack locations are shown in Figures 15.16(b) and (c). The need to provide reinforcements along diagonal *ac* to carry the resultant tension in this direction and parallel to diagonal *bd* closer to the interior corner *c*, to control flexural cracking are self-evident. The concrete near the corner *a* is stress-free and is likely to spall off, being pushed out by the resultant thrust along *ca*, and nominal reinforcement placed as close to the outer surface as permissible is required to control such cracking. Suggested reinforcing details [Ref. 15.11] for large size joints of type (b) are shown in Figure 15.16(d).

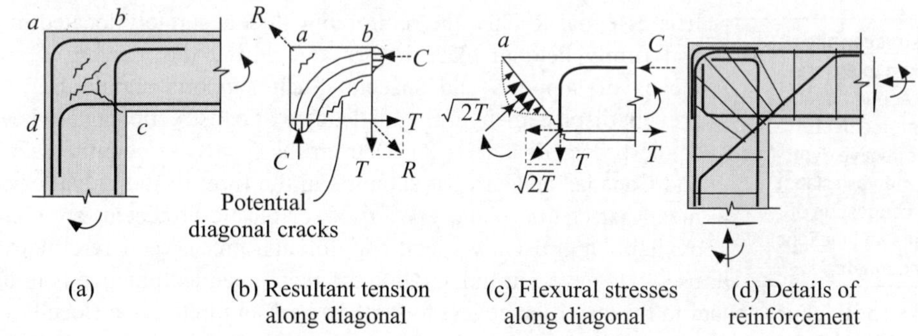

Fig. 15.16 Knee joint subjected to 'opening' moment.

When the moment is subject to reversals, the concrete in the joint zone is likely to crack along both diagonals and significant amounts of secondary reinforcements are required along both diagonals. For this situation it is more convenient to provide an orthogonal mesh of reinforcement (horizontal and vertical) in the joint zone in the form of closed ties. These will resist the horizontal and vertical components of the tensile forces along the diagonal. A model for computing the area of the horizontal and vertical secondary steel (stirrups) required is suggested in Ref. 15.11.

When the joint is subject to high intensity reversed loading for several cycles, the concrete in the joint is likely to be cracked along both principal directions, and it is recommended that the resistance offered by the concrete should not be taken into account.

In multi-storey building frames the joint behaviour is more complex as up to four beams may be framing into a joint with columns above and below at an interior joint. When both beams framing into a joint from opposite directions reach their ultimate capacity and bend in a reverse curvature mode, the diagonal compressive and tensile stresses induced in the joint panel may be very high. Moreover, the beam/column reinforcement may have to develop full anchorage within the joint zone, which may be difficult if the concrete is severely cracked, parallel to both diagonal directions. The joint shear may also be twice as high as that in an exterior joint with beam only on one side. The diagonal compressive stresses and potential diagonal cracking would require an orthogonal mesh of well anchored horizontal and vertical reinforcement ties in the joint region. Furthermore, the concrete in the joint core should be laterally confined. Effective lateral confinement would require cross ties between the legs of the orthogonal ties to prevent the lateral bulging of the concrete in the core.

15.2.5 Construction Joints

It is desirable to indicate at least some of the more obvious construction joints so that all the trades are working along the same line. This also facilitates the designer to indicate shouldered joints [such as in rigid frame bents – see Figure 15.3(c)], reinforced to take moment, shear and thrust. The lapping and splicing of bars should be illustrated clearly, and not just schematically (indicating the amount of steel required at a few points).

Expansion joints are often poorly constructed and leakage through such joints in the roof slab is a common problem. Properly detailed expansion joints for roof slabs, floor slabs and walls are shown in Figure 15.17.

15.2.6 Bar Supports and Cover

> **In many construction sites, measures taken to ensure specified cover and effective depth for reinforcements (particularly effective depth for top reinforcements in slabs) and to avoid congestion of reinforcements (at junctions) are found inadequate.**

It is essential to have the reinforcing steel accurately located in the forms and firmly held in place before and during the placing of concrete by means of supports and spacers. Such supports should be adequate to prevent displacement during the course of construction and to keep the bars at the proper distance (cover) from the forms. In countries such as USA and Canada, standard bar supports in the form of individual or continuous metal bar chairs (plain, galvanised, or plastic protected) are commercially available and usually specified, although precast concrete blocks are also used. However, in India, while the recommended practice is to use precast mortar blocks (of thickness equal to the specified cover) for bottom bars and individual (locally fabricated) metal chairs for top/bent bars, actual site practices vary considerably. It is fairly common to see bottom bars being supported by just slipping in pieces of coarse aggregate between the bar and the formwork (Figure 15.18). Needless to say, these angular aggregate pieces, precariously poised between the formwork and the round steel bars, slip out easily during placing of concrete (if not earlier). The result is that the bar often comes to rest on the formwork with little or no cover. When the formwork is removed, it is a sorry sight to see the bars exposed from underneath slabs and beams at several places! This gets covered up in plaster soon enough to give an appearance that all is well (well, at least for the time being!). However, it is not long before the poorly protected reinforcing bars get corroded, and in this process increase in volume,

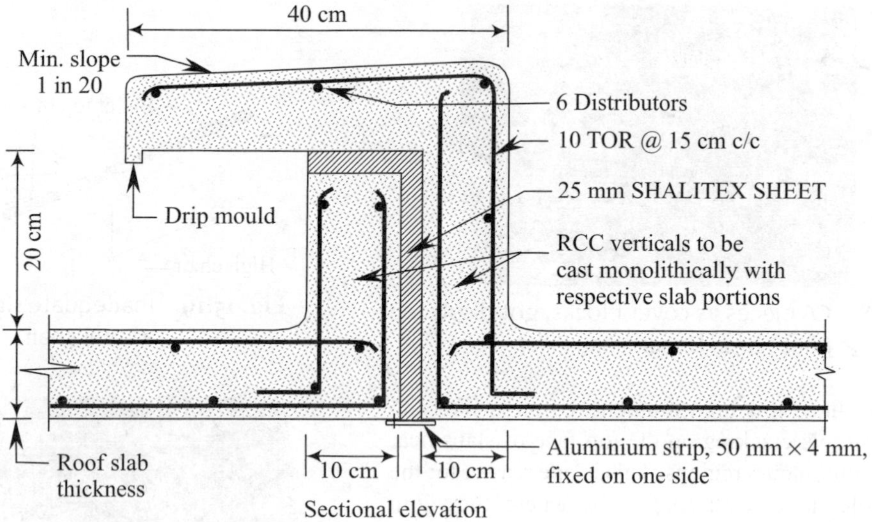

(a) Details of expansion joint in roof slab

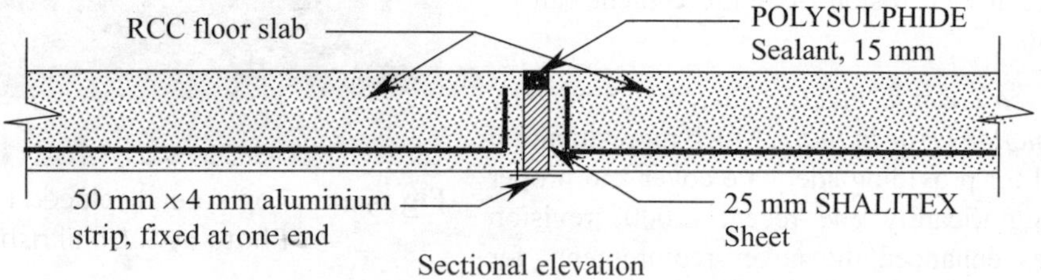

(b) Details of expansion joint in floor slab

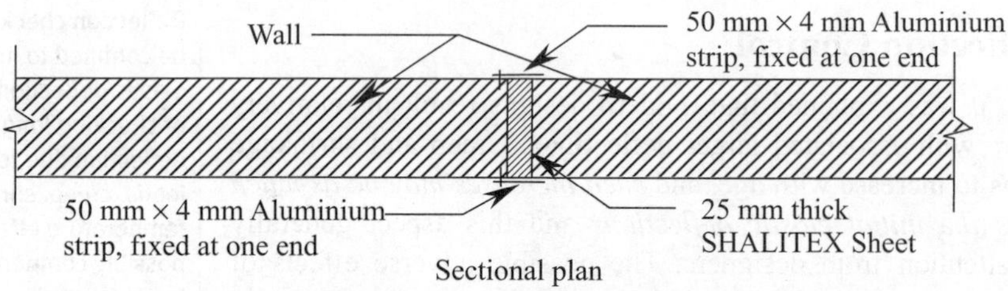

(c) Details of expansion joint in walls

Fig. 15.17 Expansion joint details.

setting up internal bursting stresses in the concrete. In course of time, this causes first cracks in line with the reinforcement, and later spalling of the concrete dislodging the plaster and whatever little concrete cover there is, thereby fully exposing the corroded bars. The seriousness of the resulting damage is obvious to all.

In the case of top bars, locally made individual high chairs are used. However, often these are few and far between, and at times are too flexible [Figure 15.19]. In such cases, with the unskilled workmen frequently stepping on the top bars, the chairs may get bent (sag) or bent bars may get turned sideways, in either case resulting in a reduced effective depth (particularly so in slabs) in the negative moment regions (Figure 15.20).

Fig. 15.18 CA pieces as cover blocks, got displaced. *Photo by S. Unnikrishna Pillai*

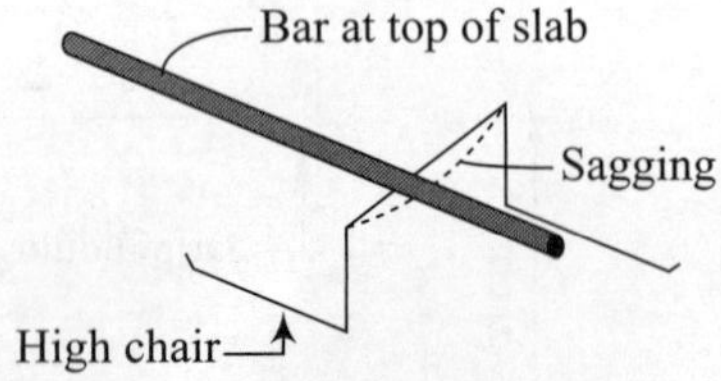

Fig. 15.19 Inadequate rigidity of a steel chair.

A reduced depth in this high moment region is likely to lead to undesirable cracking on the top face of slabs near the support (continuous) regions. This is one reason for the wetting visible underneath roof slabs where they join supporting beams. The multiple and cumulative effects of reduced effective depth at support on deflections, cracking, wetting, leakage, and corrosion of reinforcement can be easily understood.

Inadequate concrete cover for steel bars is a very commonly observed construction error in India. Much more attention needs to be paid for providing adequate cover and proper bar supports. Significantly, the recent (2000) revision of the Code has enhanced the cover requirements for reinforcements, including links.

Fig 15.20 Top steel displaced to bottom. *Photo by S. Unnikrishna Pillai*

15.2.7 Deflection Control

In Section 15.1, it was explained that modern designs result in relatively slender members with associated larger deflections. Creep and shrinkage cause deflections to increase with age, and *such increases may be as much as 2 to 3 times the initial elastic deflections* and this aspect generally receives scant attention from designers. The possible adverse effects of large deflections on a continuous roof slab are schematically shown in Figure 15.21.

Deflection checks appear to be confined to immediate elastic deflection. Importance of checking long-term deflection due to sustained loads, creep, shrinkage and temperature effects, and possibly compensating for it by initial camber, need to be emphasised.

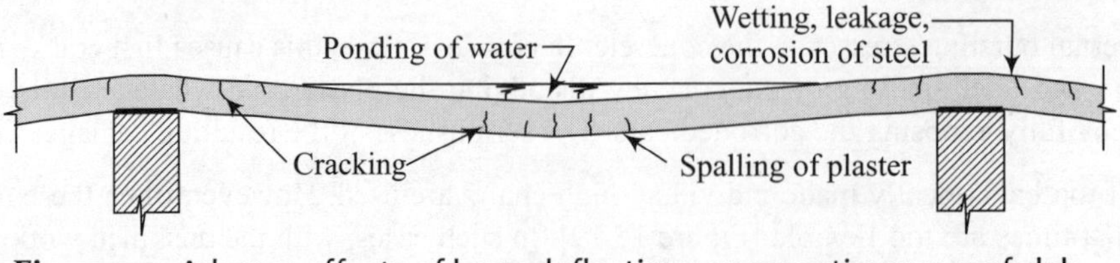

Fig. 15.21 Adverse effects of large deflections on a continuous roof slab.

Beam/slab deflections can also cause cracking in other elements (such as walls) supported by it. These point to the need for deflection calculations and control. While for normal slabs and beams it is enough to control deflections indirectly by limiting span/depth ratios [see Section 5.3], for members which are heavily loaded or exposed to adverse environmental conditions, it is necessary to calculate initial and long-term deflections and to ensure that these are within limits. The limits on span/depth ratios and on deflections specified in the Code (Cl. 23.2) are *not intended to guard against ponding of water on flat roofs*, which is a very common problem with concrete flat roofs in many places. Of late, construction of additional sloping roof on existing flat roofs for protection from rain induced damages is a common sight. For roof slabs, ponding should be checked by calculation of deflections, including added deflection due to ponded water and the long-term effects of all sustained loads, construction tolerances and reliability of provisions for drainage. In medium to large spans where significant deflections can be anticipated, it is desirable to provide initial upward camber in floor slab/beam so as to offset deflection, including long-term effects, especially in roof slabs and cantilevered spans.

15.3 Materials, Quality Control and Construction Practices

Strict adherence to codes and specifications, use of good quality materials, engagement of trained and skilled masons and labour, and good workmanship under strict, honest and competent supervision are prerequisites for avoiding malfunction and failures, and for ensuring high quality structures. Regular materials testing, selection of competent contractors, supervisors, construction engineers and Project Management as well as periodic inspection by regulatory agencies are needed for good quality construction.

Poor quality of construction materials is a real problem in India. Periodic testing of building materials is seldom resorted to in most construction sites. Adulteration of cement has been reported from the sites of even major hydro-electric projects undertaken by large public sector organisations. Reinforcing steel is being supplied by many re-rolling mills in the small-scale sector, which do not have in-house testing and quality control facilities, with the result that there is little guarantee about the strength, ductility, uniformity, and dimensional tolerances of such bars. All these underscores the need for periodic testing and quality control of materials used for construction.

The major reason for poor performance of reinforced concrete structures is the poor quality of construction. This is apparent if one realises that with the same quantity of cement and aggregate, both very poor-quality and very high-quality concrete can be obtained, depending on the water-cement ratio used and degree of control exercised. With reduction in w/c ratio, nearly all the engineering properties of concrete (strength, modulus of elasticity, durability, reduced shrinkage and creep, impermeability, etc.) improve. Reduction in creep and shrinkage also results in reduced long-term curvatures and deflections due to them, and reduced shrinkage cracks in concrete. Yet, most masons routinely use excess water in the mix to save time and labour on compaction and screeding; and this could be a major contributing factor to every one of the serviceability failures listed in Section 15.1. It being *the most important single factor* influencing concrete quality, the quantity of water used in the mix should be the minimum, consistent with requirements of laying and proper compaction. To enable the use of a dry mix (low w/c ratio) and yet get good compaction, *all structural concrete should be compacted using vibrators*. There are other requirements for good quality concrete like grading and cleanliness of aggregates, weight-batching, thorough mixing, adequate curing, etc., and for more details on these and other such requirements, reference may be made to books on *concrete technology* [Ref. 2.1–2.6].

In this context, it is worth noting that *leakage through concrete roof slabs is a very frequent problem in many parts of the country*. Such leakages, if restricted to small areas, can be repaired. However, repair of a poorly built roof slab with extensive leakage spread over large areas is virtually impossible[†]. Therefore, *it is prudent and it pays to do the initial construction meticulously*.

Yet another common mistake seen usually in sites of small projects relates to *too flimsy, poorly detailed* (*with large gaps/holes for example*) *and inadequately supported formwork*. Such forms deflect and vibrate as workmen move about over it. Deflection and vibration during periods of placing, setting and early curing of concrete can result in cracks developing in the concrete. Formwork supports are also frequently seen to be infirm, unstable or yielding (Figure 15.22).

Fig. 15. 22 Failure of formwork during concreting of slab. *Photo by S. Unnikrishna Pillai*

Other common constructions errors include *inadequate curing, improper levels, alignment and slopes, inadequate drainage arrangements, poor bonding between hardened and freshly laid concrete at construction joints, poorly constructed expansion joints, superficial filling of holes cut for plumbing/electrification fixtures, etc.*

Reference has been made here to deterioration arising out of poor-quality materials and construction. Associated with this is the need for timely repair and maintenance. Apart from regular and routine inspection and maintenance, every concrete structure should undergo a special inspection and associated *special repairs* once in 10–15 years. Maintenance engineers should be on the look out for warning signs of impending failures. These include crushed and cracked concrete; severely corroded reinforcement; excessive deflections; damaged columns and beams; unusual vibrations or flexure in stairs, walkways or floors; excessive loading from accumulations or spillage; etc. An annual pre-monsoon inspection and maintenance can eliminate many functional problems likely otherwise. Repairs generally include replacement of spalled concrete, removal and replacement of damaged concrete, guniting, jacketing with fresh RC, sealing of cracks, renewed waterproofing and treatment of corroded reinforcement.

Repairs are expensive and inconvenient and yet they seldom bring the structure to its original (intended) condition. Hence, it pays to be vigilant during design and construction so that such repairs become unnecessary.

15.4 Summary

In this chapter, an attempt has been made to draw attention to some of the essential precautions to be taken and to a few of the very common mistakes with regard to the design, detailing, construction and upkeep of concrete structures. It would be desirable for designers and site engineers to develop a list of 'do's and don'ts' based on codes and specifications, manuals such as Ref. 10.1–10.6, and their own experiences and observations. A partial list of such guidelines is given below:

1. It should be ensured (to the extent possible) that the materials specified can be readily obtained in the size, length and grade required. The quality of materials should be ensured by regular materials testing.
2. Apart from strength and durability considerations, the specification for concrete should also be decided so as to obtain minimum of drying shrinkage and creep.

† *Note:* Various manufactures and proprietary agencies advertise various methods such as tar felting, special plastering with chemical/adhesive cements, etc., for repairing leaky slabs. These may work for small areas and for a short period for larger areas, but do not offer a permanent solution.

3. Concrete mix design should aim at obtaining durable concrete of required strength through proper grading of aggregates, control of w/c ratio, thorough mixing, proper compaction and adequate curing.
4. The quantity of water used in concrete should be the minimum practicable, consistent with requirements for hydration, proper placement and compaction.
5. Consistent with requirements of economy, the integrity of the structure should be improved by building in structural redundancy in the framing system, reinforcement placement, etc.
6. Structural alterations during construction, if essential, shall be made only with the approval of the designer.
7. Flexural members (slabs and beams) should have adequate stiffness so as to limit deflections.
8. In members liable to undergo large deflections, upward camber may be provided to offset the deflections.
9. Reinforcement design and detailing should take care of all tensile stresses in concrete and the control of tensile strains, whether direct, flexural, diagonal, splitting, or due to differential settlements, shrinkage and temperature.
10. Suitable reinforcement should be provided across all potential cracks in concrete, whatever the cause.
11. To minimise shrinkage and temperature stresses, wherever feasible, provision may be made for unrestricted movements of parts, by introducing control/expansion/slip joints.
12. Concrete slabs in exposed situations, such as sunshades, balconies, canopies, open verandas, etc., should be provided with adequate quantities of temperature reinforcement in order to prevent cracks due to shrinkage and contraction.
13. Adequate development length and/or anchorage should be provided so that the computed stress at every section of a reinforcing bar is fully developed on both sides.
14. It should be ensured that hooked and bent bars can be placed conveniently and have adequate concrete protection.
15. Congestion of bars should be avoided at points where members intersect, and it should be ensured that all the reinforcement required can be properly placed.
16. When a member has a break in its direction so that the reinforcement in tension tends to separate from the body of concrete, special anchorage should be provided and properly detailed.
17. When slabs frame flush with bottom of inverted beams or when a load is applied to the side of a member through brackets, ledges or cross beams, special stirrup hanger reinforcement should be provided.
18. Liberal concrete cover for reinforcement should be provided in general, and particularly in humid, wet or aggressive environments. The desired cover should be ensured in actual construction with proper cover blocks/bar supports.
19. Complete and accurate dimensions should be specified in engineering drawings. The notations must be unambiguous and not liable to be misinterpreted.
20. The lengths of laps, points of bend and extension of bars should be specified clearly in drawings.
21. Details of corners, intersection of members, control and construction/expansion joints and similar special locations should be clearly given, with drawings.
22. For special and unusual conditions, adequate details should be shown in drawings so as to ensure proper placing of reinforcement [Examples: cantilevers, continuous footings, hinged base of rigid frames, etc.]
23. Proper bar supports should be provided to ensure that the reinforcing bars are accurately and firmly held in place before and during concreting, and thus the required concrete cover and effective depths are obtained.
24. Concrete should be weigh-batched and mixed with mechanical mixers.
25. Compaction of concrete should be done using vibrators (wherever feasible), enabling the use of low w/c ratio and ensuring better strength and durability.
26. Formwork should be built firmly and with rigid supports and without gaps and holes through which the cement paste can escape resulting in honey-combing.

27. Critical elements such as columns, if found to be defective on removal of formwork, shall be dismantled and rebuilt properly, rather than patched up.
28. Curing of the concrete should be done for durations as recommended by the Code, and should be terminated gradually to prevent quick drying.
29. In case of members which are liable to large deflections (Examples: cantilever beams and slabs), the removal of centering should be delayed as much as possible so that the concrete attains sufficient strength.
30. Adequate slopes for roofs, bathroom floors, etc., should be provided to ensure quick drainage.

REVIEW QUESTIONS

15.1 List the areas in which the basic Reinforced Concrete Design course content in your university is deficient.

15.2 List ten most common construction mistakes in the order of their importance.

15.3 What are the factors in concrete-making that influence creep and shrinkage of the concrete?

15.4 Describe the precautions to be taken (a) at the design stage, (b) at the detailing stage and (c) at the construction stage for ensuring a high-quality structure.

15.5 A multi-storey building frame has been analysed using a commercially available software and the stress resultants obtained. Explain how you would check this to ensure that no gross errors have crept in.

15.6 Explain a few situations where it is desirable to build-in discontinuity in a structure.

15.7 Discuss the types of *serviceability failures* that can occur.

15.8 Describe a 'serviceability failure' that you have observed in a structure you are familiar with, and analyse its causes and effects and suggest remedial/repair measures.

15.9 Explain why serviceability checks assume greater importance in modern concrete structures.

15.10 Explain the concept of 'structural integrity'.

15.11 What are the design strategies to provide structural integrity?

15.12 Give an example of 'progressive collapse'.

15.13 In a three-hour long training programme to be given to masons engaged in construction of concrete structures, list out the important topics that you would include.

15.14 Make a literature survey and write a 'state-of-the-art' report on
(a) Building failure studies;
(b) Deflection calculations and control in concrete structures;
(c) Cracking and control in concrete structures; and
(d) Leakage and control in concrete buildings.

15.15 As a student (group) project, inspect the various structures in the campus and prepare a report on serviceability malfunctions/failures and suggest remedial measures.

REFERENCES

15.1 Jai Krishna and Jain, O P, *Plain & Reinforced Concrete,* Vol. I, Nem Chand & Bros., Roorkee, 1959, pp 260–262

15.2 — *Handbook on Concrete Reinforcement and Detailing*, Special Publication SP 34, Bureau of Indian Standards, New Delhi, 1987

15.3 — *Concrete Materials and Methods of Concrete Construction,* CSA Standards A 23.1–94, Canadian Standards Association, Rexdale (Toronto), Canada, 1994

15.4 — *Structural Failures: Modes, Causes and Responsibilities*, American Society of Civil Engineers, New York, 1973

15.5 Feld, Jacob, *Construction Failures*, John Wiley & Sons, New York, 1968

15.6 — *Handbook on Causes and Prevention of Cracks in Buildings*, Special Publications SP 25, Bureau of Indian Standards, New Delhi, 1984

15.7 — *Formwork Striking Times — Criteria, Prediction and Methods of Assessment*, CIRIA Report, American Society of Civil Engineers, New York, 1996

15.8 Hoover, C A and Greene, M R (editors), *Construction Quality, Education and Seismic Safety*, Earthquake Engineering Research Institute, Oakland, California, 1996

15.9 Grant, E L and Leavenworth, R S, *Statistical Quality Control*, Sixth edition, McGraw-Hill Book Co., New York, 1988

15.10 Levin, R I, Rubin, D S, Stinson, J P and Garden Jr., E S, *Quantitative Approaches to Management*, Eighth edition, McGraw-Hill Book Co., 1992

15.11 Waestlund, G, *Use of High-Strength Steel in Reinforced Concrete*, Journal ACI, Vol. 30, No. 12, June 1959, pp 1237–1250

15.12 Park, R and Paulay, T, *Reinforced Concrete Structures*, John Wiley & Sons, Inc., New York, 1975

15.13 Allen, D E and Shriever, W R, *Progressive Collapse, Abnormal Loads and Building Codes*, in 'Structural Failure: Modes, Causes, Responsibilities', American Society of Civil Engineers, 1973, pp 21–47

15.14 Taylor, D A, *Progressive Collapse*, Canadian Journal of Civil Engineering, Vol. 2, No. 4, Dec. 1975, pp 517–529

15.15 Breen, J E, *Developing Structural Integrity in Bearing Wall Buildings*, Journal of the Prestressed Concrete Institute, Vol. 25, No. 1, Jan.-Feb. 1980, pp 42–73

15.16 Fintel, M, Schultz, D M and Iqbal, M, *Report 2, Philosophy of Structural Response to Normal and Abnormal Loads, Design and Construction of Large-Panel Concrete Structures*, Portland Cement Association, Skokie, Illinois, PCA Publication EB092D, Aug. 1976, p. 133

Special Provisions for Earthquake-Resistant Design

CHAPTER 16

LEARNING OBJECTIVES

After studying this chapter, you will be able to:

- *Explain the importance of ductility in seismic design; and design and detail reinforcement for ductile structural behaviour*
- *Explain the background to seismic design provisions of IS Code and of some related international Codes*

16.1 Introduction

During an earthquake, ground motions occur in a random fashion, both horizontally and vertically, in all directions, radiating from the epicentre. The ground accelerations cause structures to vibrate and induce inertial forces on them. Hence, structures in such locations need to be suitably designed and detailed to ensure stability, strength and serviceability with acceptable levels of safety under seismic effects. The resultant inertial force at any floor level† depends on the mass at the floor level and also the height above the foundation. The inertial forces usually follow a parabolic distribution in regular multi-storey buildings, with maximum values at the top floor levels. In regions of high seismic intensity, it is desirable to minimise the weights at various floor levels, especially the roofs and upper storeys. Also, it is desirable to avoid discontinuities in mass or stiffness in plan or elevation. Torsional effects should particularly be accounted for in buildings with asymmetry in plan‡ or elevation. The codes published by the Bureau of Indian Standards, which specify minimum design requirements for earthquake-resistant design, are listed as Ref. 16.1–16.3. These requirements take into consideration the characteristics and probability of occurrence of earthquakes, the characteristics of the structure and the foundation, and the amount of damage that is considered tolerable. Ref. 16.4–16.7 give details of code provisions in some seismic regions of the world.

† Sufficient number of modes of vibration have to be considered in the 'response spectrum' analysis, as prescribed in IS 1893: 2016, and a suitable mode combination scheme (such as 'SRSS' or 'CQC') has to be employed.

‡ Torsional effects should be considered when the eccentricity between the 'centre of mass' and 'centre of stiffness' at any floor level is significant (more than 5% of the floor plan dimension).

The criteria adopted by codes for fixing the level of the design seismic loading are generally as follows [Ref. 16.7]:

- structures should be able to resist *minor* earthquakes without damage;
- structures should be able to resist *moderate* earthquakes without significant structural damage, but with some non-structural damage; and
- structures should be able to resist *major* earthquakes without collapse, but with some structural and non-structural damage.

The magnitude of the forces induced in a structure due to a given ground acceleration (or given intensity of earthquake) will depend, amongst other things, on the mass of the structure, the material and type of construction, the *damping*, *ductility* and *energy dissipation capacity* of the structure. By enhancing ductility and energy dissipation capacity in the structure, the induced seismic forces can be reduced, and a more economical structure obtained, or alternatively, the probability of collapse reduced. Buildings with lateral load resisting system comprising (i) a *ductile moment-resisting space frame* or (ii) a dual system consisting of ductile moment resisting space frame and ductile flexural (shear) wall, qualify for very low seismic induced forces.

Magnitude of forces induced due to earthquake depends mainly on the mass distribution along the height of the structure, and its damping, ductility and energy dissipation capacity.

Ductility may be broadly defined as the ability of a structure or member to undergo inelastic deformations beyond the initial yield deformation with no decrease in the load resistance.

Since reinforced concrete is relatively less ductile in compression and shear, dissipation of seismic energy is best achieved by *flexural yielding*. A frame of continuous construction, comprising flexural members, columns and their connections, designed and detailed to accommodate reversible lateral displacements after the formation of plastic hinges (without decrease in strength), is known as a *ductile moment-resisting frame*. Similarly, *shear walls* (more appropriately called *flexural walls*), are reinforced concrete structural walls cantilevering vertically from the foundation, and designed and detailed to be ductile and to resist seismic forces and to dissipate energy through flexural yielding at one or more plastic hinges.

A 'ductile moment-resisting frame' is a frame of continuous construction, comprising beams and columns, which will dissipate energy primarily through beam flexural yielding at the plastic hinges.

Modern codes [Ref. 16.1†, 16.4, 16.5] provide for reduction of seismic forces through provision of special ductility requirements. Details for achieving ductility in reinforced concrete structures are given in IS 13920 [Ref. 16.3]. Methods of determining design seismic forces, either in the form of equivalent static lateral loading or through proper dynamic analysis, lie outside the scope of this chapter (for this, see chapter 19); the reader may also refer to the codes, handbooks and other texts [Ref. 16.8–16.10] for this purpose.

This chapter explains the major code provisions, particularly those given in Ref. 16.3, dealing with designing and detailing for ductility in moment-resisting frames and shear walls. Such provisions are mandatory for structures located in relatively high intensity *seismic zones* (zones III, IV and V), specified in IS 1893: 2016 [Ref. 16.1].

† In the recent revision of IS 1893: 2016, the procedure recommended is to first calculate the actual force that may be experienced by the structure during the 'probable maximum earthquake', if it were to remain elastic. Then, the effect of ductile deformation and energy dissipation is accounted for by means of a 'response reduction factor'.

16.2 Importance of Ductility in Seismic Design

16.2.1 Measures of Ductility

As a measure of ductility, the relevant deformation could be chosen as the strain, curvature, rotation or deflection; for plastic hinges in flexural members, the index chosen is usually the rotation.

A general qualitative definition of ductility was given in the preceding section. A quantitative measure of ductility has to be with reference to a load-deformation response. A *ductile* response would be reflected in the deformation increasing at nearly constant load such as was shown in Figure 9.8. Then, the ratio of the ultimate deformation to the deformation at the beginning of the horizontal path (or, at first 'yield') can give a measure of ductility. However, each choice of deformation (*strain, rotation, curvature*, or *deflection*) may give a different value for the ductility measure.

Curvature Ductility

For an under-reinforced beam section in flexure, the moment-curvature (M–φ) relation is typically as shown in Figure 16.1(a). Based on the idealised M–φ behaviour, *curvature ductility*, μ, may be defined as the ratio φ_u/φ_y, where φ_y is the curvature at first yield (idealised), and φ_u the maximum (ultimate) curvature at the section:

$$\mu \equiv \frac{\varphi_u}{\varphi_y} \tag{16.1}$$

Indeed, IS 13920 [Ref. 16.3] defines *curvature ductility* as the ratio of curvature at the ultimate strength to the curvature at first yield of tension steel in the section.

The value of μ is a property of the beam *cross section*, and can be computed easily using the principles described in Chapter 4. It can be shown that 'curvature ductility', μ, of a section *increases* with

- decrease in the percentage tension steel (p_t);
- increase in the percentage compression steel (p_c);
- decrease in the tensile strength of steel;
- increase in the compressive strength of concrete†;
- increase in the compression flange area in flanged beams;
- increase in the transverse (shear) reinforcement, and
- increase in the confinement of concrete and compression reinforcement (by closely spaced hoops, spirals, etc.).

A curvature ductility of at least 5 is considered to be adequate for reinforced concrete [Ref. 16.2].

Different Measures of Ductility

In the case of a beam member [Figure 16.1(b)], it is more difficult to define a unique ductility ratio, as it could be in terms of the curvature (φ) at a particular section, or the rotation (θ) at a joint, or the displacement (Δ) at a selected point. The ductility ratios obtained by the three methods will differ. Furthermore, the rotations and displacements will depend on several factors, such as the span dimensions, shape of the moment diagram, type of support restraints, etc.

† However, very high grades of concrete are undesirable, as they have lower ultimate compressive strains [refer Figure 2.7].

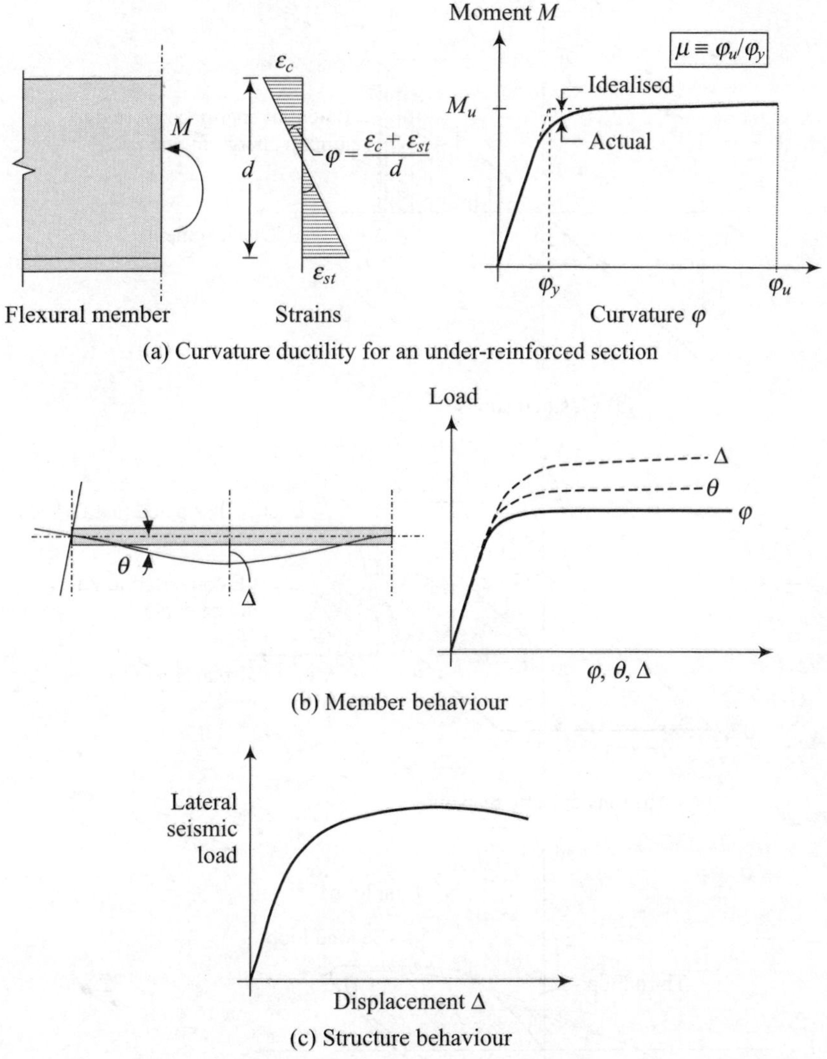

(a) Curvature ductility for an under-reinforced section

(b) Member behaviour

(c) Structure behaviour

Fig. 16.1 Measures of ductility.

The problem becomes more complex when it comes to defining a ductility measure for an entire structure. In general, a reinforced concrete ductile structure will have a load-displacement response as shown schematically in Figure 16.1(c). This ductility is achieved by ensuring ductile member section responses (as indicated by the M–φ relation in Figure 16.1(a)), so that an adequate number of *plastic hinges* [refer Section 9.7] would develop at appropriate locations under extreme lateral seismic forces.

16.2.2 Energy Dissipation by Ductile Behaviour

Under seismic forces, structures are subject to several cycles of reversed cyclic loading. If the structure, modelled (for simplicity) as a single degree-of-freedom system, were to behave in a *linear elastic* manner under reversed cyclic loading, it will exhibit a linear load-displacement behaviour as shown in Figure 16.2(a). The shaded area under the curve denotes the potential energy stored in the structure at the maximum

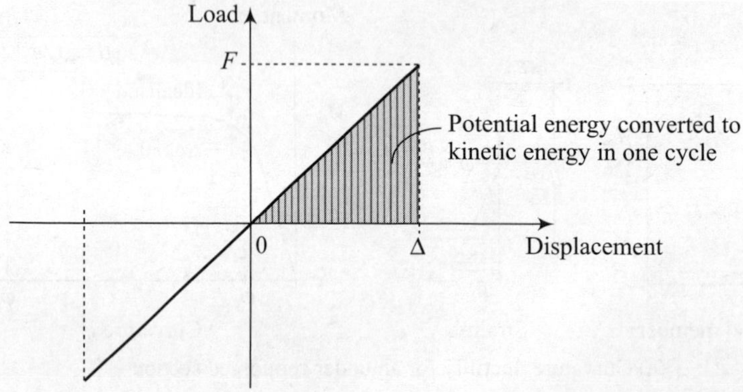

(a) Elastic response

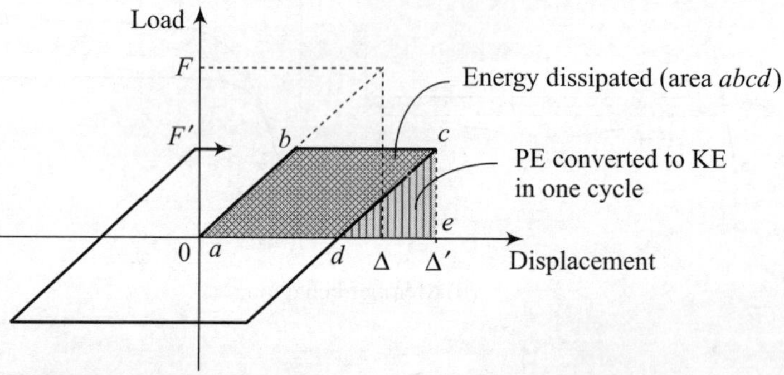

(b) Elastoplastic response

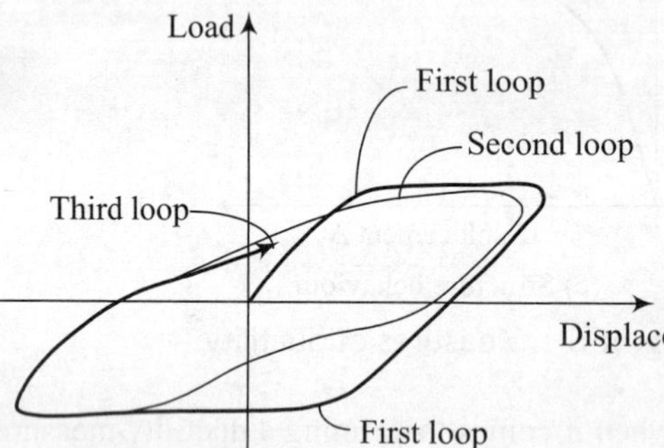

(c) Hysteresis behaviour of reinforced concrete

Fig. 16.2 Load-displacement behaviour under reversed cyclic loading.

displacement position; this gets released and converted to kinetic energy as the structure returns to its zero-load position.

However, if the structure responds in an elastoplastic (ductile) manner, developing fully plastic behaviour at a load level F' (less than F shown in Figure 16.2a), then the load-displacement behaviour is as shown in Figure 16.2(b). In this case, the maximum deflection Δ' is greater than that (Δ) obtained in Figure 16.2(a) for elastic behaviour.

Furthermore, when the structure returns to its zero-load position, the actual energy which gets converted to kinetic energy is limited to the triangular area *cde* in Figure 16.2(b). The remainder of the input energy (given by area *abcd*) gets *dissipated*† by the plastic hinge. In summary, under seismic loadings, for a given energy input, elastoplastic response differs from elastic response in the following ways:

- the energy gets dissipated;
- the induced force is less; and
- the maximum deflection is more.

Thus, while ductility helps in reducing induced forces and in dissipating some of the input energy, it also demands larger deformations to be accommodated by the structure.

It may be noted that the actual behaviour of reinforced concrete is different from the idealised behaviour shown in Figure 16.2(b). As indicated schematically in Figure 16.2(c), the hysteresis behaviour of reinforced concrete is characterised by 'rounding' and 'pinching' of the loops, which is associated with the *Bauschinger effect*‡ in steel, and *stiffness degradation* in concrete (due to repeated opening and closing of cracks and bar slip at anchorage zones) [Ref. 16.11]. This results in the areas within successive loops becoming smaller.

16.2.3 Flexural Yielding in Frames and Walls

As reinforced concrete is relatively less ductile in compression and shear, dissipation of seismic energy is best achieved by flexural yielding. Hence, weakness in compression and shear, in relation to flexure, should be avoided.

In a structure composed of ductile moment-resisting frames and/or shear (flexural) walls, the desired inelastic (ductile) response is developed by the formation of plastic hinges (flexural yielding) in the members, as shown in Figure 16.3.

In the case of ductile frames, plastic hinges may form in the beams or in the columns, as shown in Figure 16.3(a). It is desirable to design the frame such that the plastic hinges form in the beams [Figure 16.3(a)(iii)], and not the columns, because

- plastic hinges in beams have larger rotation capacities than in columns;
- mechanisms involving beam hinges have larger energy-absorptive capacity on account of the larger number of beam hinges (with large rotation capacities) possible;
- eventual collapse of a beam generally results in a localised failure, whereas collapse of a column may lead to a 'global' failure; and
- columns are more difficult to straighten and repair than beams, in the event of residual deformation and damage.

Ductility and strength assessment of an entire structure requires non-linear analysis, considering material and geometric non-linearities. Although ideally, a non-linear dynamic (time history based) analysis is called for, this is computationally very difficult. In practice, a non-linear static analysis, called *pushover analysis*, is now beginning to be used in design offices. Such analysis is facilitated in modern software packages for structural analysis. An introduction to basic concepts of pushover analysis, including details of modelling of plastic hinges in reinforced concrete beam/column elements, is given in Section 16.3.

---

† Gets converted into heat and other forms of nonrecoverable energy.

‡ When reinforcing steel is subjected to reversed cyclic loading, it is found that the yield strength obtained in the reloading or reversed direction is substantially less than the initial yield strength; this is known as the *Bauschinger effect* [refer Figure 2.19].

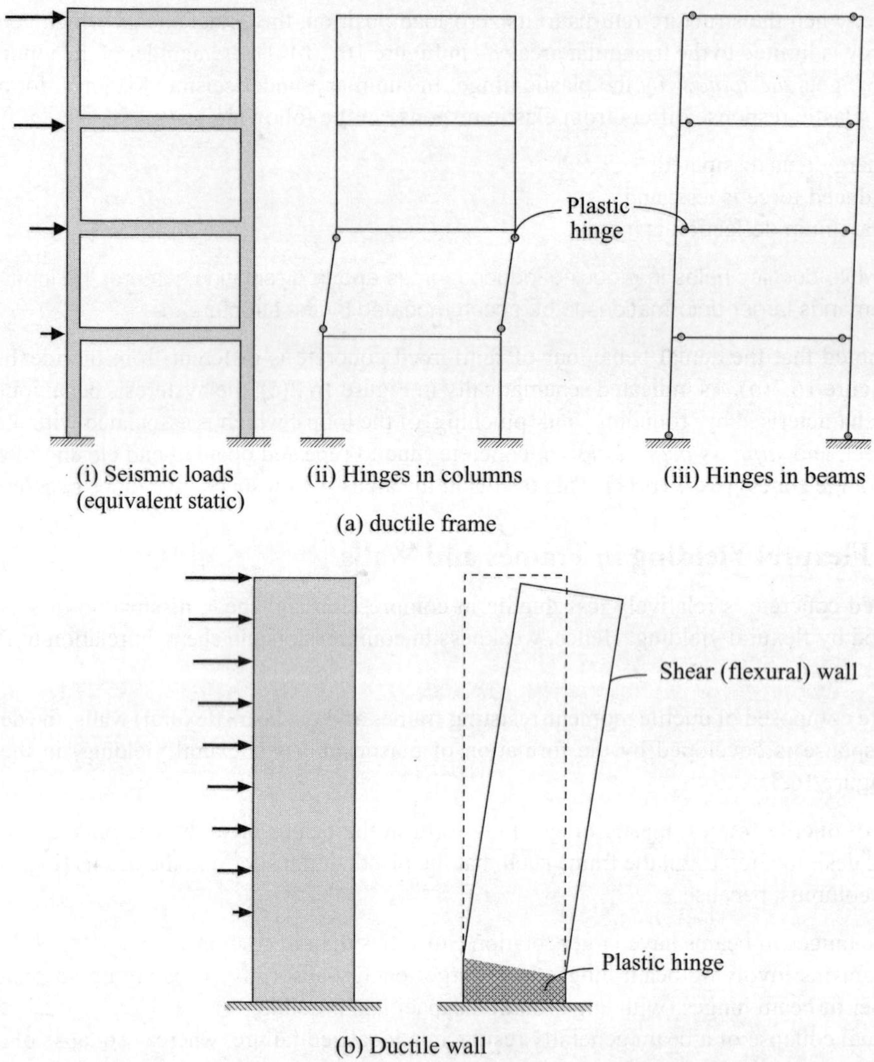

Fig. 16.3 Formation of plastic hinges in a ductile structure.

In pushover analysis, the structure is 'pushed' by applying displacement-controlled lateral loading incrementally on the structure (after applying gravity loading initially) untill global collapse occurs. A force-displacement 'pushover curve' is generated, marked by kinks at various stages, indicating the progressive formation of various flexural and shear plastic hinges.

16.3 Pushover Analysis

16.3.1 Basic Concepts

Pushover analysis is a useful tool for assessing inelastic strength and deformation demands in the structure, and for exposing design weaknesses [Ref. 16.25]. Its foremost advantage is that it facilitates the design engineer to recognize important seismic response quantities and to use engineering judgement to alter suitably the force and deformation demands and capacities that control the seismic response close to failure. For structures that vibrate primarily in the fundamental mode, such an analysis is likely to provide good estimates of global as well as local inelastic deformation demands. It will also expose design weaknesses that may remain hidden in an elastic analysis. Such weaknesses include storey mechanisms, excessive deformations, strength irregularities, and overloads on potentially brittle elements, such as column and connections.

A finite element model of the building (two- or three-dimensional) is subjected to a prescribed lateral load distribution (such as parabolic, triangular or uniform) in the desired horizontal direction. The intensity of the lateral load is slowly increased from zero, under constant gravity loading†, and the sequence of cracks, yielding, plastic hinge formations, and failure of various structural components is recorded. The gravity loading is initially applied incrementally (force-controlled) until the full design load is reached, and subsequently, the lateral loading is applied incrementally under displacement control until the final collapse is reached. A series of iterations is usually required at any stage of displacement-controlled loading to attain force equilibrium.

Local non-linear effects, such as flexural hinges and shear hinges, assumed to occur at the ends of the members, should be appropriately modelled (refer Section 16.3.2). Redistribution of internal forces occurs with progressive plastic hinge formation, and at some hinge locations, local collapse may occur due to the plastic deformation limit being exceeded. The structure is 'pushed' until global collapse, which is triggered when adequate number of plastic hinges form to develop a collapse mechanism or when the system cannot mobilise load paths to sustain force equilibrium (after local hinge break-downs).

The main output of the pushover analysis is in the form of a force-displacement curve, called *pushover curve*. It is a plot of the *base shear* (total lateral load) versus the lateral displacement (drift) at some point at the roof level, including all the stages of lateral load/displacement increments. A typical pushover curve for a plane frame is shown in Figure 16.4. The initial elastic range, as marked in the figure, is followed by onset of

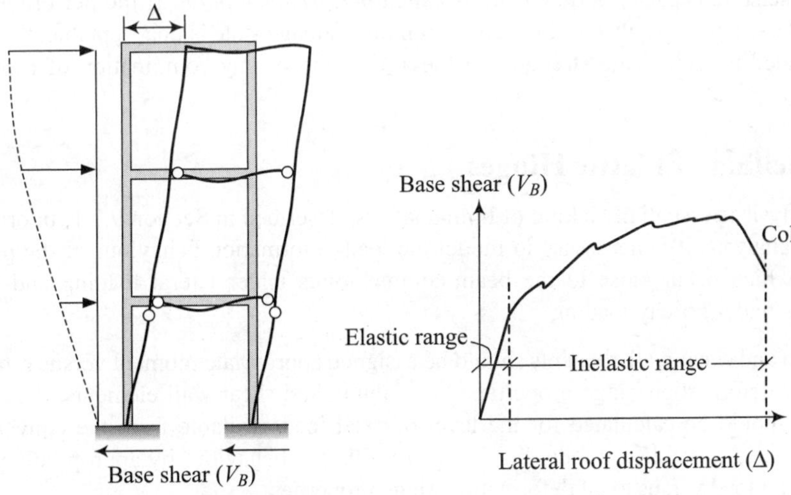

(a) Model of building frame (some plastic hinges shown)

(b) Typical pushover curve

Fig. 16.4 Pushover analysis.

† The criteria recommended by Codes for earthquake load analysis may be used here. As per IS 1893, the gravity load to be considered comprises full dead load plus 25% live load if the live load intensity is less than 3.0 kN/m^2 (otherwise, 50% live load).

yielding of steel at one or more plastic hinges. Full yielding of steel (plastic hinge formation) is generally reflected by a kink in the pushover curve in the inelastic range, as shown. After attaining the peak base shear, further increase in displacement leads to complete collapse.

At any stage of the pushover analysis in the inelastic range, it is possible to note the status of plastic hinge formation in the structure. This knowledge conveys useful information regarding the sequence and locations of plastic hinges, as well as the extent of the plastic deformation at each hinge location. Using this knowledge, it is possible to redesign the various beam/column elements in order to modify and improve the ductile performance of the structure (refer Figure 16.3). This is possible not only with regard to a new building design, but also with regard to retrofit of an existing building [Ref. 16.42].

Recommendations are available [Ref. 16.25, 16.43] to relate the level of damage to a structure to the relative roof displacement (in terms of height of the building) obtained from pushover analysis. The performance may be categorised as 'collapse prevention', 'life safety' or 'immediate occupancy', depending on whether the drift (and hence the damage) level is excessive, moderate or slight. In 'performance-based design', the general objective is to ensure 'life safety' (moderate drift) under the so-called 'design basis earthquake' and 'collapse prevention' (excessive drift) under the 'maximum considered earthquake'. However, in special cases, the performance objectives may be modified. For example, a hospital building (lifeline structure) may be expected to provide for 'life safety' under the maximum considered earthquake and 'immediate occupancy' under the design basis earthquake.

It may be noted that the pushover analysis is approximate and does not account for dynamic characteristics such as hysteresis, higher mode participation, etc. It is known to give good results for regular buildings (without torsional irregularity). In such cases, the pushover curve can be converted to an acceleration versus displacement response spectrum, where it represents the 'seismic capacity' of the structure. It is possible to include in the same plot the 'seismic demand', and to see whether the capacity meets the demand. The meeting point of seismic capacity and demand is called *performance point*. If the performance point does not exist (demand exceeds capacity) or if the corresponding damage state is unacceptable, the system should be suitably upgraded by enhancing strength, stiffness, ductility or any combination of these [Ref. 16.25, 16.42, 16.43].

16.3.2 Modelling of Plastic Hinges

The pushover analysis is essentially a kind of limit analysis, described in Section 9.7.1. In order to carry out such an inelastic analysis, it is necessary to model the load-deformation behaviour of the potential plastic hinge locations, which occur close to the beam-column joints under lateral loading and near mid-span locations in beams under gravity loading.

The beam, column and shear wall elements should be assigned appropriate moment versus rotation and shear force versus shear deformation hinge properties. For column and shear wall elements, the moment versus rotation property should be calculated for the level of axial load available from the conventional gravity load analysis. It is also possible to model bracing and infill wall behaviour by appropriate *equivalent strut modelling* with axial load versus axial deformation hinge properties.

A typical moment versus rotation curve for a beam element is shown in Figure 16.5a. This is idealised into a piecewise linear curve, as shown in Figure 16.5b [Ref. 16.43] defined by the following five points:

1. Point 'A' corresponds to the unloaded condition.
2. Point 'B' corresponds to the onset of yielding.
3. Point 'C' corresponds to the ultimate moment of resistance (M_{uR}).

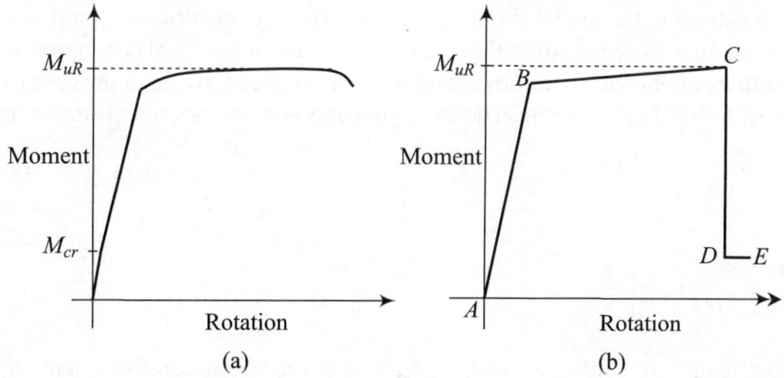

Fig. 16.5 Typical moment-rotation curves for a flexural plastic hinge.

4. Point 'D' corresponds to the drop in strength beyond C. In the absence of the modelling of the descending branch of a load versus deformation curve, the drop is assumed to be vertical. For the computational stability, it is recommended to specify a non-zero residual strength, say 20 per cent of the ultimate strength.
5. Point 'E' corresponds to the maximum deformation capacity with the residual strength. To maintain computational stability, a high value of deformation capacity can be assumed.

In generating the moment-rotation curve, it is necessary to account for the effects of reinforcement detailing. In particular, the beneficial effect of confining stirrups in enhancing the ductility, and to some extent the strength, should be properly accounted for. The stress-strain model for concrete subjected to uniaxial compressive loading and confined by transverse reinforcement shown in Figure 16.6, popularly known as Mander's model [Ref. 16.18, which is an improvement on Ref. 16.15, 16.16 and 16.17] may be used for this purpose. The concrete section may contain any general type of confining steel: either spiral or circular hoops; or rectangular hoops with or without supplementary cross ties.

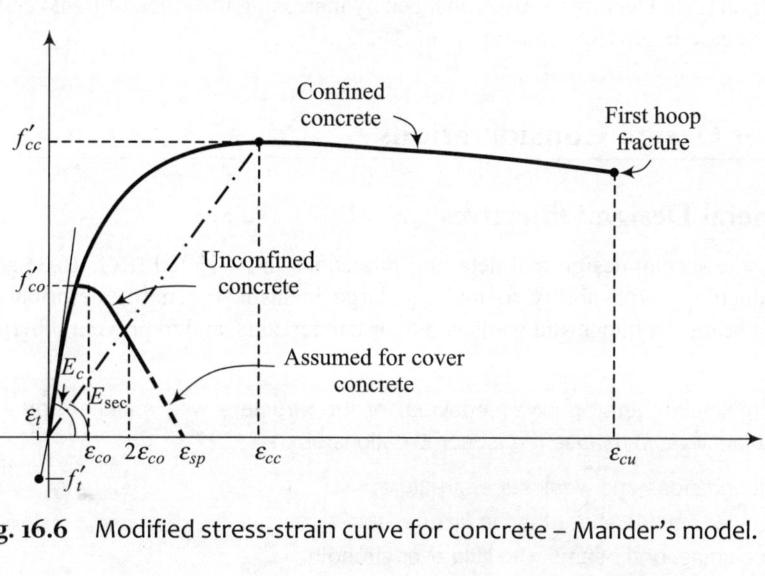

Fig. 16.6 Modified stress-strain curve for concrete – Mander's model.

The salient strain locations in the model (Figure 16.6) are given by the ultimate compressive strain (ε_{cu}), and the strains corresponding to the peak strength, viz., ε_{cc} in the case of confined concrete and ε_{co} (usually 0.002) in the case of unconfined concrete. The corresponding peak strengths are f'_{cc} in the case of confined concrete and f'_{co} in the case of unconfined concrete. The following expressions for critical strains have been proposed:

$$\varepsilon_{cu} = 0.004 + \frac{1.4\rho_s f_{yh}\varepsilon_{sm}}{f'_{cc}} \tag{16.2}$$

$$\varepsilon_{cc} = \varepsilon_{co}\left[1 + 5\left(\frac{f'_{cc}}{f'_{co}} - 1\right)\right] \tag{16.3}$$

where ρ_s = volumetric ratio of confining steel, f_{yh} = grade of the stirrup reinforcement, and ε_{sm} = steel strain at maximum tensile stress.

Improvements to Mander's model have been proposed [Ref 16.19] and validated through experiments. The following expressions for f'_{cc} and ε_{cu} are recommended for use in Mander's model:

$$f'_{cc} = f_{co}\left[1 + 3.7\left(\frac{0.5k_e\rho_s f_{yh}}{f'_{co}}\right)^{0.85}\right] \tag{16.4}$$

$$\varepsilon_{cu} = 0.004 + \frac{0.6\rho_s f_{yh}\varepsilon_{sm}}{f'_{cc}} \tag{16.5}$$

where k_e is a 'confinement effectiveness coefficient' whose value may be taken as 0.75 for rectangular sections.

It has been shown that an increase in the volumetric ratio of confining steel results in not only an increase in ductility (ε_{cu}) but also an increase in compressive strength (f'_{cc}) as well as a marginal increase in the corresponding strain (ε_{cc}). Ductility is also enhanced by increasing the grade of transverse reinforcement, but it reduces with increase in grade of concrete [Ref. 16.22].

16.4 Major Design Considerations

16.4.1 General Design Objectives

The objective of the special design and detailing provisions in IS 13920 [Ref. 16.3] is to ensure adequate toughness and ductility (with ability to undergo large inelastic reversible deformations) for individual members such as beams, columns and walls and their connections, and to prevent other non-ductile types of failure.

In order to maintain overall ductile behaviour of the structure with minimal damage, it becomes necessary to achieve, *in relative terms*, combinations of

- strong foundations and weak superstructure;
- members stronger in shear than in flexure; and
- strong columns, and beams with little over-strength.

Some of the main design considerations in providing ductility include:

- using a low tensile steel ratio (with relatively low-grade steel) and/or using compression steel;
- providing adequate stirrups to ensure that shear failure does not precede flexural failure;
- confining concrete and compression steel by closely spaced hoops or spirals; and
- proper detailing with regard to connections, anchorage, splicing, minimum reinforcement, etc.

Furthermore, continuity in construction and redundancy in structural framing are desirable for the development of more inelastic response, and thereby more moment redistribution and energy dissipation at several plastic hinges. Earthquake is often followed by fire and hence fire resistance should also be a major consideration in building construction in seismic regions.

16.4.2 Requirements of Stability and Stiffness

Under a severe earthquake, it is expected that in a structure designed to resist seismic forces in a ductile manner, large lateral deformations and oscillations will be induced, resulting in the development of reversible plastic hinges at various locations in the ductile frames and walls. The structural system should be so designed as to ensure that the formation of plastic hinges at suitable locations may, at worst, result in the failure of individual elements, but will not lead to instability or progressive collapse. This calls for building-in redundancy into the structural system. Redundancy assists in the development of alternative load paths, thereby helping redistribution of forces, dissipation of energy and avoidance of progressive collapse.

In addition to the requirements of stability and strength to resist seismic forces, the structure must have sufficient *stiffness* to limit the lateral deflection or *drift*. Ref. 16.4 suggests that the anticipated drift due to seismic forces may be taken as three times the lateral deflection obtained from the usual elastic analysis under equivalent factored static loads. [This factor is intended to account for the effects of material and geometric nonlinearities, as well as additional amplification due to dynamic effects]. The inter-storey drift is to be limited to 0.004 times the storey height (under the specified seismic forces) as per IS code [Ref. 16.1]. The effect of drift on the vertical load-carrying capacity of the lateral load resisting system should also be taken into account in the analysis.

16.4.3 Materials

Reinforcing Steel

As mentioned earlier, ductility calls for the use of relatively low grades of steel. Lower grade steel has clearly defined and longer yield plateau, and hence the plastic hinges formed will have larger rotation capacities, leading to greater energy dissipation. Similarly, locations of potential plastic hinges *should not have too much over-strength*, i.e., strength more than the required design strength. Over-strength will result in the section not yielding, as intended, at the expected lateral load levels. This may result in adjoining elements and/or foundations being subjected to loads larger than the design loads, with consequent damage. In other words, the *actual yield strength* of the steel used *should not be markedly higher* than the yield strength specified and used in design computations. Furthermore, yield strength, far in excess of that specified, may lead to excessive shear and bond stresses, as the plastic moment is developed. Another point to note is that, the lower the grade of steel, the higher is the ratio of the *ultimate* tensile strength (f_u) to the *yield* strength (f_y) [refer Section 2.14.2]. A high ratio of f_u/f_y is desirable, as it results in an increased length of plastic hinge (along the member axis), and thereby an increased plastic rotation capacity.

For these reasons, mild steel (Fe 250) is best suited for use as flexural reinforcement in earthquake-resistant design. However, its use will necessitate larger sections of flexural members. Hence, the code [Ref. 16.3] permits the use of the higher-grade Fe 415 (which is most commonly used in practice), but prohibits the use of grades higher than Fe 415. Of late, however, ductile rebars of grade Fe 500, manufactured by special thermo-mechanical treatment (TMT), have become available. The code recommendation is likely to be revised in view of this new technology now available.

Concrete

With regard to the grade of concrete, the code [Ref. 16.3] limits the minimum grade of concrete to M 25 (*for all buildings which are more than* 3 *storeys in height and located in seismic zones III, IV and V*). It may be noted that very high strength concrete is also undesirable because higher compressive strength is associated with lower ultimate compressive strain (ε_{cu}) [refer Section 2.8.2, Figure 2.7] – which adversely affects ductility. Likewise, low density concrete is undesirable because of its relatively poor performance under reversed cyclic loading. The ACI and Canadian codes [Ref. 16.4, 16.6] limit the maximum cylinder strength of low-density concrete for use in earthquake-resistant design to 30 MPa.

16.4.4 Foundations

It is important to ensure that the foundation of a structure does not fail prior to the possible failure of the superstructure. As plastic deformations are permitted to occur at suitable locations in the superstructure under a severe earthquake, the maximum seismic forces transmitted to the foundation will be governed by the lateral loads at which *actual yielding* takes place in the structural elements transferring the lateral loads to the foundation. The ultimate moment, corresponding to 'actual yielding' at a section is obtained as its *characteristic* (nominal) moment capacity†, i.e., without applying partial safety factors (i.e., with $\gamma_c = \gamma_s = 1.0$).

The corresponding moments, shear forces and axial forces transferred from the frames and walls to the foundation system (under conditions of 'actual yielding') should be resisted by the foundation system with the usual margin of safety (i.e., with $\gamma_c = 1.5$ and $\gamma_s = 1.15$) in order to ensure a combination of a relatively stronger foundation and weaker superstructure. Although such a recommendation is yet to be incorporated in the IS codes [Ref. 16.1–16.3], it is in vogue in several international codes (such as Ref. 16.4, 16.7). Such a design concept is necessary to provide for ductile behaviour of the superstructure without serious damage to the foundation.

16.4.5 Flexural Members in Ductile Frames

The code recommendations [Ref. 16.3] for design and detailing of flexural members in earthquake-resistant design are as follows:

- To qualify as 'flexural members', the factored axial stress under earthquake loading should not exceed 0.08 f_{ck}. Further, the overall depth D should not exceed one-fourth of the clear span (to limit shear deformations) and the width b should not be less than 200 mm, with a b/D ratio of more than 0.3 (to avoid lateral instability and provide for improved torsional resistance).
- To ensure significant ductile behaviour even under reversals of displacements in the inelastic range, to avoid congestion of steel, and to limit the shear stresses in beams, the tensile reinforcement ratio ρ_{max} is limited to 0.025 i.e., $p_{t,\,max} = 2.5$.

† Alternatively, this may be taken (conservatively) as 1.4 times the factored moment of resistance (M_{uR}) – as recommended by the code [Ref. 16.3], for estimating plastic moment capacities in the calculation of design shear forces.

- To avoid sudden brittle failure of a beam (when the cracking moment of the section is reached) a minimum reinforcement ratio, $\rho_{min} = 0.24\sqrt{f_{ck}}/f_y$, must be provided at both the top and bottom for the entire length of the member, with at least two bars placed at each face.
- Flexural members of lateral force resisting ductile frames are assumed to yield at the design earthquake. To ensure proper development of reversible plastic hinges near continuous supports (beam-column connections) where they usually develop in such members,
  - The 'positive' moment reinforcement at a joint face must not be less than half the 'negative' moment reinforcement at that joint face;
  - The top and bottom steel at any section along the length of the member should not be less than one-fourth of the 'negative' moment reinforcement at the joint face on either side;
  - Both top and bottom bars must be taken through the column and made continuous wherever possible, in case of an interior joint. In other cases, they must be extended to the far face of the confined column core and provided an anchorage length of $L_d + 10\phi$, where L_d is the development length of the bars (diameter ϕ) in tension [Figure 16.7];
  - Not more than 50 per cent of the bars shall be spliced at one section. Because of the possibility of spalling of the concrete shell (cover) under large reversed strains, lap splices of flexural reinforcement are not permitted in and near possible plastic hinge locations. If welded splices or mechanical connections are used, it must be ensured that not more than 50 per cent of the bars are spliced in the region of potential plastic hinging; and
  - The provisions for redistribution of moments (See Section 9.7.3) shall be used only for vertical load moments and not for lateral load moments.

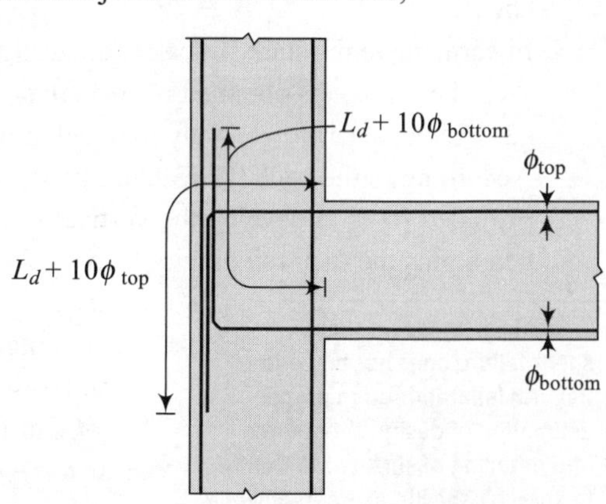

Fig. 16.7 Anchorage of beam bars at an external joint.

- When lap splices are provided (at regions other than plastic hinging regions), transverse reinforcement for confining concrete and to support longitudinal bars, in the form of closed stirrups or 'hoops' (with a 135° hook and $10\phi \geq 75$ mm extension) should be provided over the entire splice length, at a spacing not exceeding 150 mm [Figure 16.8].
- The bar extensions must provide for possible shifts in the inflection points, which may occur under the combined effects of gravity and seismic loadings.

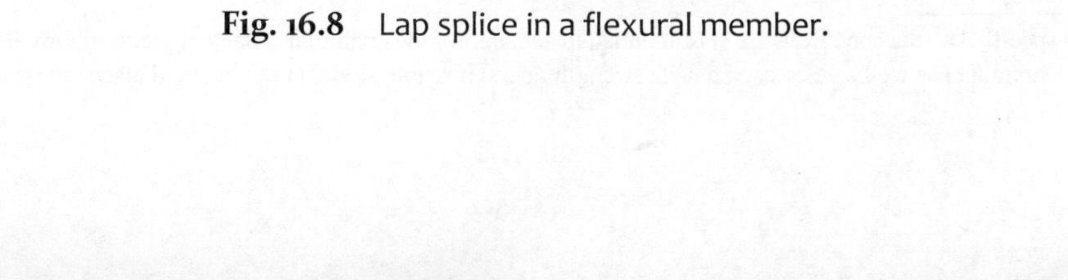

Fig. 16.8 Lap splice in a flexural member.

- During an earthquake, a structure should be capable of undergoing extensive inelastic deformation (through ductile behaviour) without a significant loss in strength. Yielding softens the structure, which effectively increases its time period and reduces the earthquake force. Damping also increases significantly in the inelastic range of response and this further helps to improve the earthquake response. For these desirable effects to take place, it should be ensured that none of the brittle modes of failure (particularly, shear failure) should occur before ductile flexural failure. Hence, the shear design philosophy in an earthquake resistant structure differs significantly from that in an ordinary structure [Ref. 16.34, 16.38]. **Due to extensive cracking in the zones of high shear, it is desirable to completely ignore the shear strength of concrete (τ_c) and to design the stirrups to resist the entire shear.**
- In earthquake resistant structure, the design shear force will be the larger of
  1. Shear force as obtained from analysis for given load combinations, and
  2. Actual shear force likely to develop in a member after flexural failure has taken place.

  According to the code (IS 13920: 2016), the web reinforcement in the form of vertical stirrups shall be provided so as to develop the vertical shear due to formation of the plastic hinges at both ends of the beam plus the factored gravity load on the span.

It is crucial to ensure that shear failure does not precede flexural failure, through proper estimation of design shear force and detailing of stirrups, so that flexural plastic hinges form fully, as anticipated in design, under extreme seismic loading.

- To ensure that a shear failure does not precede the full development of plastic hinges in a beam, the design shear forces in the member should be suitably overestimated, considering plastic moment capacities† of 1.4 M_{uR} at the beam ends, as shown in Figure 16.9(b). The component shear force diagrams, including the effects of factored gravity loads and sway in either direction, are indicated in Figure 16.9(c). The maximum design shear forces (V_u) at the support faces (left or right) are accordingly obtained as:

$$V_{u,\text{left}} = 0.5w_u l_n + 1.4(M^-_{uR,\text{left}} + M^+_{uR,\text{right}})/l_n \tag{16.6a}$$

$$V_{u,\text{right}} = 0.5w_u l_n + 1.4(M^+_{uR,\text{left}} + M^-_{uR,\text{right}})/l_n \tag{16.6b}$$

where l_n is the clear span, and

$$w_u = 1.2(w_{DL} + w_{LL}) \tag{16.6c}$$

assuming that the gravity loads (dead loads w_{DL} and live loads w_{LL}) are uniformly distributed. The ultimate moment capacity M_{uR} for a given section with arbitrary combinations of tension and compression steel (p_t and p_c) may require iterative calculations; alternatively, suitable design aids [Ref. 16.44] can be made use of for this purpose.

- Because of the alternating direction of the shear force due to seismic effects, the direction of the associated diagonal tensile stress also alternates, as shown in Figure 16.10(a). For this reason, *inclined bars* (which are effective only against shear in one direction) are not allowed as effective shear reinforcement.
- Web reinforcement for seismic design must be in the form of closed stirrups, called *hoops*, placed *perpendicular to the longitudinal reinforcement* and must be provided throughout the length of the

† The factor of 1.4 specified by the code [Ref. 16.3] is intended to account for the condition of 'actual yielding' (involving *characteristic* values of material strengths) as well as increased tensile strength due to possible strain hardening, and also some margin of safety.

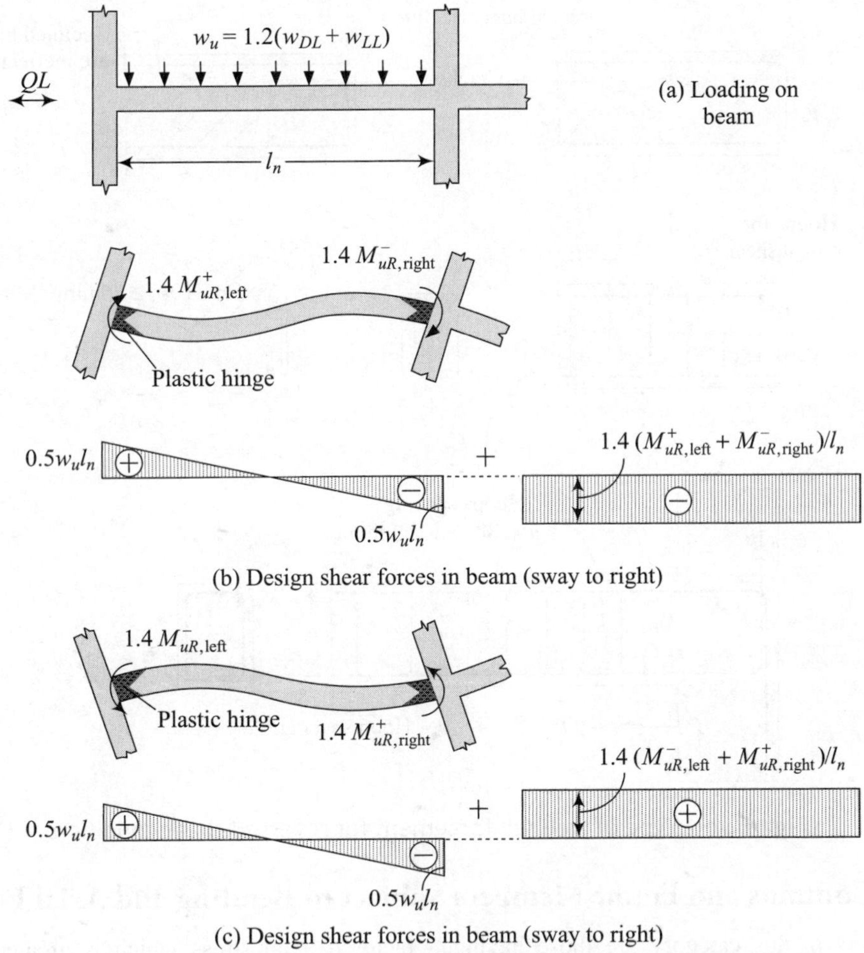

Fig. 16.9 Calculation of design shear forces in beams.

member. These hoops should have a minimum diameter ϕ_s of 8 mm in beams with a clear span exceeding 5 m (6 mm in shorter beams). The free ends of the hoops should be bent at 135° with a minimum bar extension of $10\phi_s$ (but not < 75 mm) [Figure 16.10(b)], so that the ends are adequately anchored in the core of the concrete.

- The hoops serve the additional purposes of confining the concrete and preventing buckling of the longitudinal bars, particularly near the beam-column joints, where reversible plastic hinges are expected to develop and where the concrete cover is liable to spall off after a few cycles of inelastic rotations. The code [Ref. 16.3] specifies a closer spacing of hoops over a length equal to twice the effective depth (i.e., $2d$) from the face of the column. The hoop spacing should not exceed $d/4$ or 8 times the diameter of the smallest longitudinal bar or 100 mm, with the first hoop located at a distance not exceeding 50 mm from the column face. Elsewhere, in the beam, the spacing of hoops should not exceed $d/2$, as shown in Figure 16.10(c).

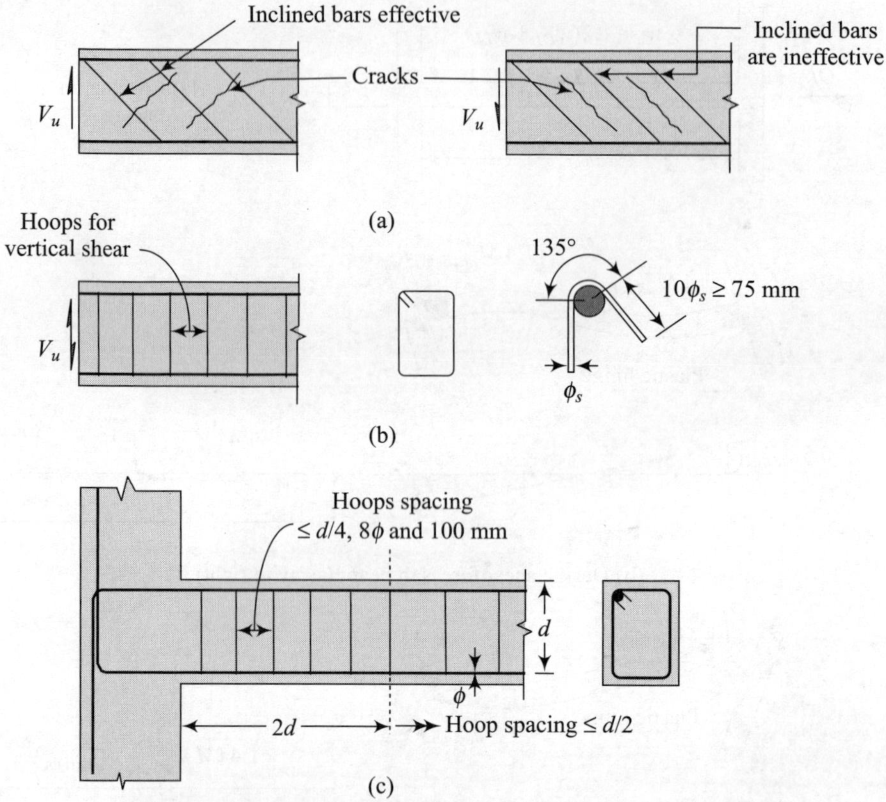

Fig. 16.10 Type of web reinforcement for reversed shear condition.

16.4.6 Columns and Frame Members Subject to Bending and Axial Load

- Members in this category are those having a factored axial stress which is greater than $0.08f_{ck}$ under the effect of seismic forces. Further, the minimum dimension of the member should not be less than 300 mm or 20 times diameter of the largest longitudinal bar, with the ratio of the shortest cross-sectional dimension to the perpendicular dimension preferably not being less than 0.4 [Ref. 16.3].
- To ensure that the combined flexural resistance of the columns is greater than that of the beams at the beam-column joint (so that the plastic hinges form at the beam ends, rather than the column ends), it is necessary to design the column section for a suitably higher moment. The ACI and Canadian codes [Ref. 16.4, 16.7] recommend that the sum of the *factored* moment resistances of the columns framing into the joint be at least 1.1 times the sum of the *characteristic* moment resistances (i.e., $\gamma_c = \gamma_s = 1.0$) of the beams† framing into the joint [Figure 16.11(a)]. The IS 13920: 2016 recommends the relative strength of columns at a joint to be more than 1.4 times the strength of beams in each direction, thus providing a strong column-weak beam design.
- Lap splices are not permitted near the ends of the column where spalling of the concrete shell is likely to occur. Lap splices (suitably designed as tension splices), however, are permitted in the central half of

† The effects of the slab reinforcement within a distance of three times the slab thickness on either side of the beam should be included in calculating the beam moment capacity.

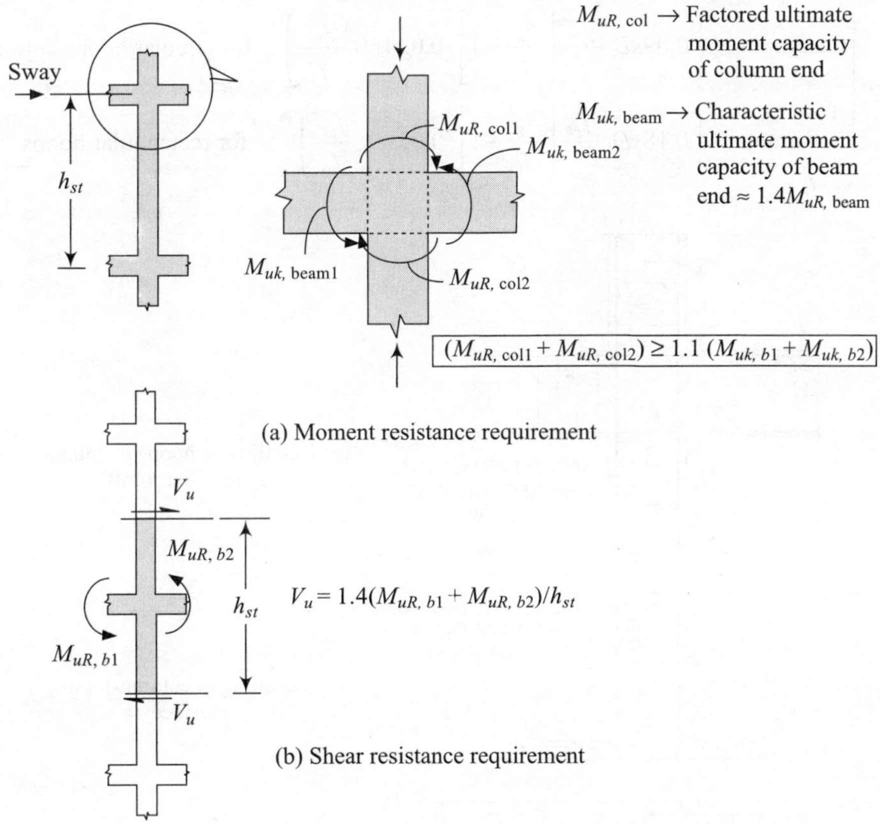

Fig. 16.11 Column resistance requirements.

the member length. Hoops should be provided over the entire splice length at a spacing not exceeding 150 mm (centre-to-centre). Not more than 50 per cent of the bars should be spliced at any section.

- The design shear force in a column should be taken as the larger of (1) the shear force due to the factored loads and (2) the shear force in the column due to the development of the plastic moments (suitably enhanced, as in Eq. 16.6) in the beams framing into the column, given approximately by [Ref. 16.3]:

$$V_u = 1.4(M_{uR,b1} + M_{uR,b2})/h_{st} \tag{16.7}$$

where $M_{uR,b1}$ and $M_{uR,b2}$ are the factored moments of resistance (of opposite sign) of beam ends '1' and '2' framing into the column from opposite faces, and h_{st} is the storey height [refer Figure 16.11(b)].

- Unless a larger amount of transverse reinforcement is required from shear strength considerations, **special confining reinforcement** should be provided as given below. Special confining reinforcement must be provided over a length l_o from each joint face (high moment regions), and on both sides of any section, where flexural yielding may occur under seismic forces [Figure 16.12(a)]. The length l_o should not be less than (a) the larger lateral dimension of the member at the section where yielding may occur, (b) 1/6 of the clear span (height) of the member, and (c) 450 mm. The spacing of hoops used as special confining reinforcement should not exceed 1/4 of the minimum member dimension, but need not be less than 75 mm, or more than 100 mm. The area of cross-section (A_{sh}) of the bar to be used as special confining reinforcement should be taken as

$$A_{sh} \geq \begin{cases} \text{maximum of} \left(0.09sD_k \dfrac{f_{ck}}{f_y}\left[\dfrac{A_g}{A_k} - 1\right], 0.024sD_k \dfrac{f_{ck}}{f_y} \right) & \text{for circular hoops/spiral} \\ \text{maximum of} \left(0.18sD_h \dfrac{f_{ck}}{f_y}\left[\dfrac{A_g}{A_k} - 1\right], 0.05sD_h \dfrac{f_{ck}}{f_y} \right) & \text{for rectangular hoops} \end{cases} \tag{16.8}$$

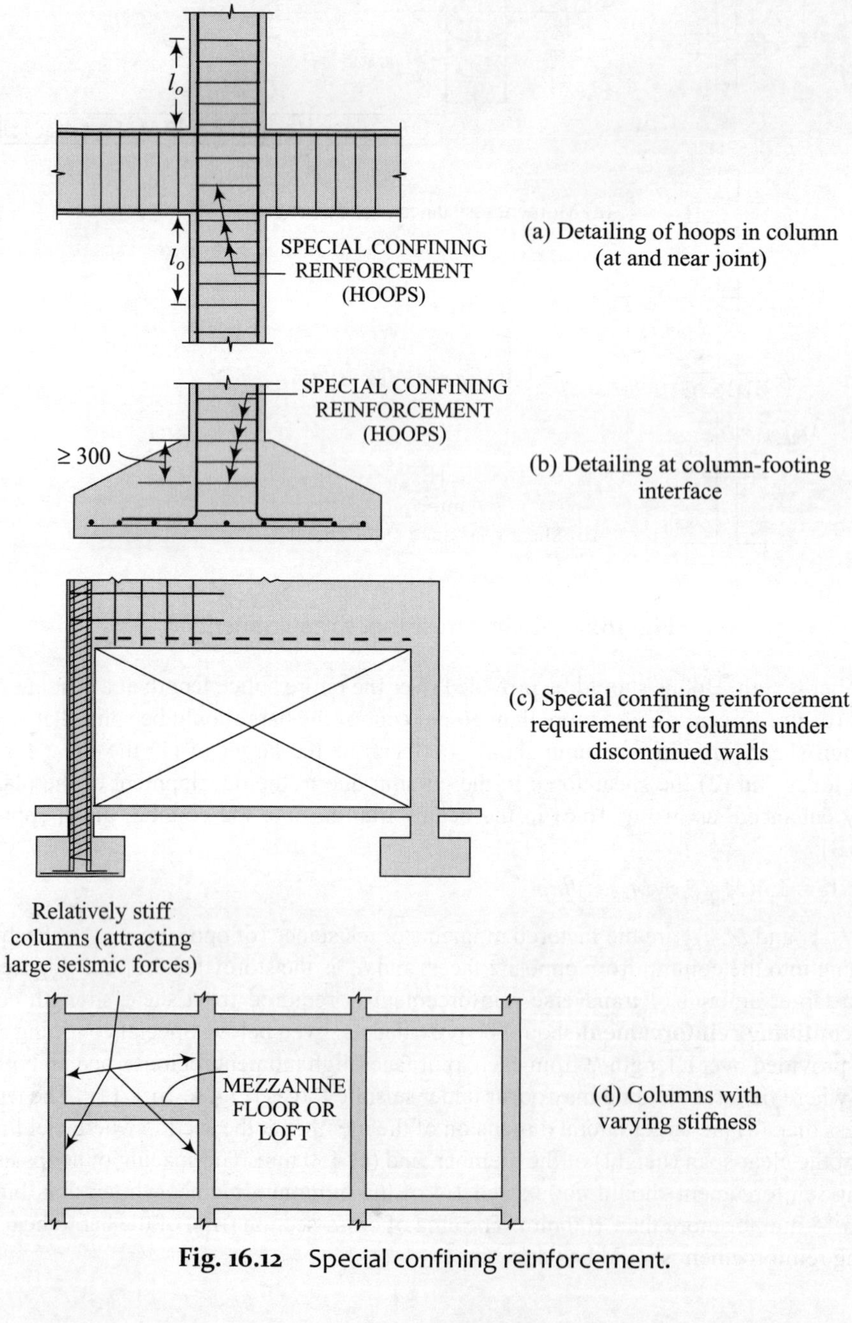

Fig. 16.12 Special confining reinforcement.

where

$s \equiv$ pitch of spiral or spacing of hoops;

$D_k \equiv$ diameter of core, measured to the outside of the spiral or hoop;

$D_h \equiv$ longer dimension of the rectangular hoop, measured to its outer face – not to exceed 300 mm;

$A_g \equiv$ gross area of the column section; and

$A_k \equiv$ area of the concrete core (contained within the outer dimension of the hoop/spiral).

- When a column terminates into a footing or mat, the 'special confining reinforcement' should extend at least 300 mm into the footing or mat, to account for possible development of plastic hinges at the base of a building [Figure 16.12(b)]. Such detailing should also be provided in columns supporting discontinued stiff members (such as walls or trusses) for the full height of the column as shown in Figure 16.12(c). Provision of special confining reinforcement over the full height of the column is also required in cases where there is a significant variation of stiffness along the height of the column – as when mezzanine floors/lofts are provided locally [Figure 16.12(d)] or due to in-filled masonry walls not extending fully over the panel.

16.4.7 Joints in Ductile Frames

- The beam-column joint is a very critical element in reinforced concrete frames, subject to seismic loads. Special attention needs to be paid to (i) minimum column width, (ii) column/beam flexure strength ratio, (iii) joint ductility, (iv) estimation of shear demand and (v) assessment of shear strength, design and detailing of shear reinforcement [Ref. 16.14]. Although IS 13920 is silent on these issues, recommendations are available in other international codes, such as ACI 318-19 [Ref. 16.4] and NZS 3101: 2006 [Ref. 16.45].
- The width of a column framing into a beam-column joint is a vital factor that governs the bond condition of the longitudinal bars in the beam and also contributes to resistance to horizontal shear. Where such reinforcement extends through an interior beam-column joint, straight beam bars may slip within the beam-column joint due to extremely high bond stresses developed during a series of large moment reversals and large inelastic deformations under seismic loading. In order to safeguard against this, ACI 318-19 recommends that the column width should be at least 20 times the beam bar diameter at an interior joint.
- The importance of providing strong column-weak beam design is not often realised in practice. This should be ensured by checking the relative flexural capacities of the columns and beams framing at a joint. ACI 318-19 recommends that the total column flexural strength (above and below the joint) should be at least 20 per cent more than the total beam flexural strength (left top plus right bottom, and also left bottom plus right top).
- Beam-column joints in ductile frames must have adequate shear strength and ductility to facilitate the development of large inelastic reversible rotations, in the event of a severe earthquake. Tests have indicated that the shear strength of joints is dependent primarily on the grade of concrete and detailing of shear reinforcement [Refs 16.4, 16.45]; hence, it is desirable to use high strength concrete in the joint regions, and to achieve good compaction of this concrete [Ref. 16.12].
- The *special confining reinforcement* (hoops) provided near the column ends should be extended through the joint as well [see Figure 16.12(a)]. However, when the joint is 'externally confined', this reinforcement may be reduced to one-half of that required at the end of the column, with the maximum spacing limited to 150 mm (Code Cl. 8.2). A joint is said to be 'externally confined' if beams frame into all the vertical faces of the joint, and if each beam width is at least three-fourths of the column width at the joint [Ref. 16.3 and 16.12].

- Development length requirements of the flexural reinforcement within the joint [refer Figure 16.7] are particularly important. The joint zone is an area of high concentration of beam bars, column bars and hoops. Extreme care is needed in detailing the reinforcement at the beam-column connection in order to provide for proper stress transfer, and to avoid congestion and placing difficulties for both reinforcement and concrete. Many structural failures under seismic loading can be traced to poor detailing of beam-column joints.
- The reinforcements detailed in this chapter pertain to monolithic concrete construction. In *precast* construction, subject to seismic loading, the most critical location is the beam-column connection. However, it has been shown that by careful detailing, ductile beam-column connections (having adequate strength, stiffness, ductility and energy-dissipating capacity) can be made in precast concrete construction as well [Ref. 16.33].

16.4.8 Shear Walls (Flexural Walls)

- Ductile 'shear walls' (more appropriately called *flexural walls*), which form part of the lateral load resisting system, are vertical members cantilevering vertically from the foundation, designed to resist lateral forces in its own plane, and are subjected to bending moment, shear and axial load. Unlike a beam, a wall is relatively thin and deep, and is subjected to substantial axial forces. The wall must be designed as an axially loaded beam, capable of forming reversible plastic hinges (usually at the base†, as shown in Figure 16.3(b)) with sufficient rotation capacity.
- The code [Ref. 16.3] recommends that the thickness of any part of the wall should preferably be not less than 150 mm. Walls that are thin are susceptible to instability (buckling) at regions of high compressive strain. Stability of the compression zones can be improved by local thickening of the wall or by providing flanges or cross walls (which is convenient at such locations as lift cores). Flanged walls also have higher bending resistance and ductility. The code [Ref. 16.3] restricts the effective flange width of flanged walls to (a) half the distance to an adjacent shear wall web, and (b) one-tenth of the total wall height.
- The wall should be reinforced with uniformly distributed reinforcement in vertical direction, with a minimum reinforcement ratio of 0.0025 of the gross section in the web and 0.0080 in the boundary element. In the horizontal direction the minimum reinforcement ratio shall be $0.0025 + 0.5(h_w/L_w - 2)(\rho_v - 0.0025)$. The bar diameter should not exceed one-tenth the wall thickness, and the bar spacing in either direction should not exceed (a) 1/5 of the horizontal length of wall, (b) thrice the wall (web) thickness, and (c) 450 mm. The distributed reinforcement provides the shear resistance, controls the cracking, inhibits local breakdown in the event of severe cracking during an earthquake, and also resists shrinkage and temperature stresses. The vertical reinforcement, comprising both the distributed reinforcement and concentrated reinforcement near wall ends (see below), should be designed for the required flexural and axial load resistance.
- In walls which do not have flanges ('boundary elements'), concentrated vertical reinforcement should be provided towards each end face of the wall, in addition to the uniformly distributed steel. A minimum of 4 nos 12-mm ϕ bars arranged in at least two layers should be provided near each end face of the wall [Ref. 16.3]. The concentrated vertical flexural reinforcement near the ends of the wall must be tied together by transverse ties, as in a column, to provide confinement of the concrete, and to ensure yielding without buckling of the compression bars when a plastic hinge is formed.
- Where the extreme fibre compressive stress in the wall exceeds $0.2\,f_{ck}$, *boundary elements* should be provided along the vertical boundaries of walls. These are portions along the wall edges that are

† Locations of abrupt changes in the strength and stiffness of the lateral load resisting system are also potential zones of flexural yielding in ductile walls.

strengthened by longitudinal and transverse reinforcement, and may have the same or larger thickness as that of the wall web.

- To prevent a premature brittle shear failure of the wall before the development of its full plastic resistance in bending, it is desirable to design the shear resistance of the wall for an overestimated shear force, as in the case of the column. Because of possible severe shear cracking under reversed cyclic loading, the shear carried by concrete in the plastic hinge region is neglected.
- For other details regarding the design of boundary elements, coupled shear walls, walls with openings, etc., reference should be made to Ref. 16.3.

16.4.9 Infill Frames

Generally, in the analysis of multi-storey buildings, the contribution of masonry infill walls is ignored, and the frame analysis is based on the bare RC frame. The mass of the masonry infill is considered, but the stiffness and strength contributions of the masonry infill are neglected. However, the infill frame has some significant effects under lateral loading that merit consideration [Ref. 16.35, 16.36]:

The masonry can be of solid bricks, hollow bricks, concrete blocks etc. Infill walls, confined by beams and columns in the boundary, significantly enhance the lateral strength and stiffness of the building, reducing the lateral drift considerably. The infill walls significantly alter the behaviour of the frames, reducing the moment-resistant *frame action* by incorporating *truss action* (with consequent reduction in bending moments and increase in axial forces in frame members) [Figure 16.13]. The infills are capable of resisting the applied lateral seismic forces through axial compression along the diagonal; there is no tensile resistance capability in the other diagonal, but the cracking induced in the masonry on account of this serves to dissipate energy.

The presence of the infill increases the lateral stiffness and thereby decreases the fundamental time period. Consequently, the seismic demand, in terms of base shear, increases. However, it may be noted that the lateral loading is now resisted not only by the frame but also by the infill walls.

In *regular* multi-storey buildings (with infill frames symmetrically oriented in plan and extending vertically in all the storeys), in general, the neglect of infill frame action results in a conservative estimation of bending moments in columns and beams, as shown in Figure 16.13. Thus, although the bare RC frame of the building considered in design is inconsistent with actual behaviour, the infills in regular framed buildings are expected to significantly reduce the demand on the RC frame members. The resulting design of the frame is thus conservative in such buildings, and this conservatism can prove to be beneficial during extreme seismic events. Numerous cases are cited in the technical literature where brick walls acting together with RC elements have saved buildings from collapse during earthquake.

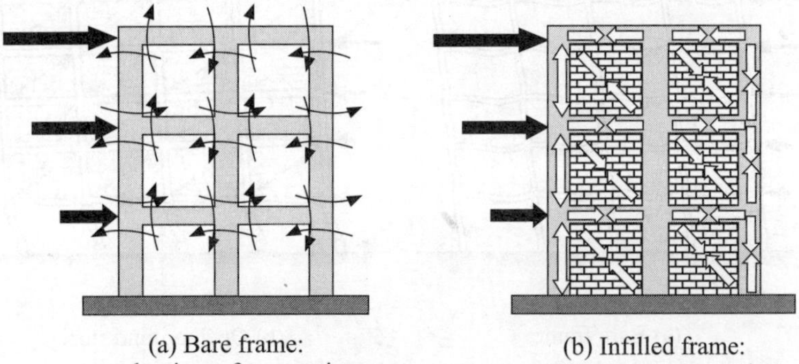

(a) Bare frame: predominant frame action

(b) Infilled frame: predominant truss action

Fig. 16.13 Behaviour of infill frame [Ref. 16.37].

However, when the infill walls are located unevenly in plan and/or elevation in a building, there will be *irregularity* in the framing system, and in such cases, ignoring the infill walls during the analysis can produce unconservative results. Vertical irregularity is typically encountered in 'open ground storey' buildings (discussed in Section 16.4.10), and it has been established that the conventional design of such buildings, based on 'bare frame' analysis, is unsafe [Ref. 16.40]. Similarly, irregularity in plan due to grossly asymmetric infill locations can cause significant eccentricity between the 'centre of rigidity' and 'centre of mass' at various floor levels, resulting in torsional effects that need to be accounted for.

16.4.10 Open Ground Storey Buildings, Soft Storey

Owing to high cost of land and small sizes of plots, parking is often accommodated in the ground storey area of the building itself. In such buildings, the frame bays of the ground storey are not infilled with masonry walls, as in the case of upper stories, and usually, all the panels are left open for parking. Such buildings are called *open ground storey* buildings. The sudden discontinuity in lateral stiffness and mass at the lowermost storey results in a 'soft storey' at the ground floor level.

According to IS 1893: 2016, a *soft storey* is one in which the lateral translational stiffness is less than that in the storey above. As mentioned above, in modern multi-storey construction, such soft stories are commonly encountered in the ground storey. The following effects render open ground storey construction particularly vulnerable to collapse under seismic loading, as evidenced by numerous failures reported in recent earthquakes [Ref. 16.37].

- The deflected shape of the open ground storey frame, under lateral loading, is markedly different from that of the bare frame (or frame with infills in all storeys), as shown in Figure 16.14. The inter-story drift is extremely large in the open ground storey (increasing the *P*-Δ moments), whereas it is relatively very small in the upper storeys [Figure 16.14(b)].
- The behaviour is rendered complex by the abrupt absence of truss action in the ground storey, which has to rely solely on moment-resistant frame action. Furthermore, the presence of infills in the upper floors results in a decrease in the fundamental time period, causing an increase in the base shear, further stressing the ground floor columns.
- Following the initial elastic response, most of the input energy is dissipated by the plastic deformations in the open ground storey columns, and this leads to major overstressing of these elements. The beams at the first-floor level are also affected, but have the beneficial effect of composite action with the infills above. For this reason, plastic hinges are likely to develop in the columns (which is to be avoided – see Section 16.2.3) and not the beams in the open ground storey.

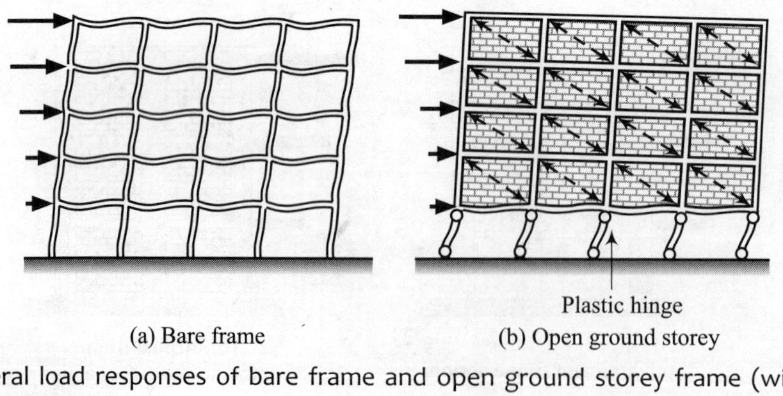

(a) Bare frame (b) Open ground storey

Fig. 16.14 Lateral load responses of bare frame and open ground storey frame (with infills above ground storey).

- If the ground floor columns do not have the desired strength and stiffness, plastic hinges can form easily at the top and bottom of all the columns in this storey, resulting in a *storey mechanism* mode of failure, as shown in Figure 16.14(b). The collapse of the ground storey can be catastrophic, bringing down the entire building, even though the upper storeys may be relatively undamaged. Such a failure is unlikely to occur in the bare frame (or frame with infills in all storeys), where plastic hinges are expected to be more evenly distributed in various storeys (and develop in the beams, rather than the columns).

The design of an open ground storey building should ideally be based on a proper dynamic analysis, including the strength, stiffness and hysteresis effects of infills and inelastic deformations, including effects of member curvature and lateral drift, in all the frame members. However, this is computationally very difficult. The next option is to carry out a linear elastic dynamic analysis (response spectrum) or even an equivalent static analysis, but this should account for appropriate modelling of the infill stiffness appropriately (as discussed in Section 16.4.11). However, in design practice, even this is not usually carried out, due to lack of familiarity with modelling infills.

In lieu of the above rigorous methods of analysis, the earlier version of the code IS 1893 (Part I): 2002, offered a convenient and simple alternative. The designer is permitted to carry out the usual 'bare frame' analysis, ignoring the infill stiffness, but including the mass of the infills at the various floor levels. The frame elements (columns and beams) of the soft storey (in this case, ground storey) are to be designed for 2.5 times the storey shears and moments so calculated under seismic load. This is a rather high penalty†, resulting in heavy reinforcement in the ground storey columns and beams. Recent studies [Ref. 16.46, 16.47] have shown that there is no need to apply this magnification factor to the beams, and that the magnification factor can be much less than 2.5, depending on the infill wall properties (thickness, strength, stiffness, density, spatial distribution, openings) and the building frame geometry (number of bays and storeys, bay widths and storey heights). However, the latest revision of the code IS 1893 (Part I): 2016, regards a building with soft storey as a building having vertical irregularity. RC structural walls or braced frames may be provided in such buildings to minimize the stiffness irregularity but the lateral stiffness in the open storey cannot be less than 80 per cent of the storey above.

16.4.11 Modelling of Infill Walls

Several techniques have been proposed to evaluate the allowable horizontal force of an infilled frame subject to in-plane bending and axial force. The simplest procedure is to model the masonry infill by means of an equivalent compressive diagonal strut [Ref. 16.35]. At the tensile corners of the non-integral infill walls, separation of frame occurs from the infill at early stages. The panels are in contact with the frame only at the compression corners, and this contact is strengthened under increased loading, with high stress concentrations near the corners. The diagonal part of the infill acts as a compressive diagonal strut and is effective in resisting lateral loads. As the tensile corners are subjected to very small stress, the tensile diagonal region is not really effective in resisting lateral loads. Since the infills act as diagonal struts that are active in compression only, an infill wall can be replaced by equivalent struts in the analysis model. Under load reversal, of the two possible diagonal elements in a panel, only the one subject to compression will be active. In structural modelling, either both diagonals (with 'compression-only' stiffness and strength properties) may be modelled, or, more conveniently, to account for both, a single diagonal element active both in compression *and tension* can be used, as indicated in Figure 16.15.

† If this criterion is applied to existing buildings, it will be seen that practically all such buildings will be found to be deficient in terms of compliance with the current code.

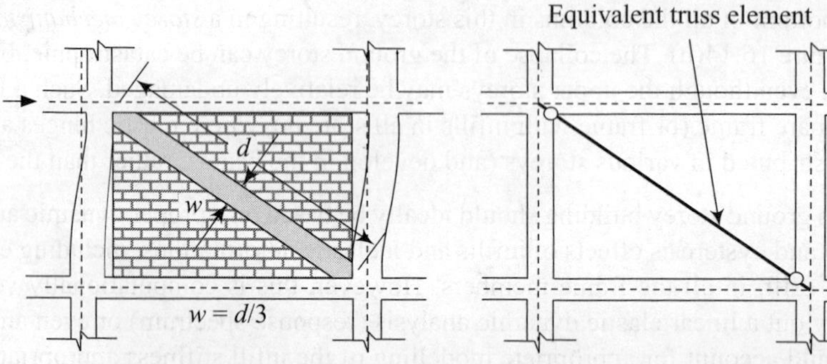

Fig. 16.15 Modelling of an infill wall as equivalent truss element.

Ref. 16.1 suggests the following recommendations for modelling an infill wall using a single equivalent truss element. The depth of the element (w) can be taken as one-third of the diagonal length (d) of the panel, as shown in Figure 16.15(a). The thickness of the element should be taken as the thickness (t) of the infill wall itself. The modulus of elasticity (E) of the truss element can be taken as $550f_m$, where f_m is the compressive strength of the masonry infill.

The latest revision of IS 1893 recommends that the infill masonry walls be modelled as equivalent diagonal struts, having pin-joined connections with the RC frame. For unreinforced masonry walls which do not have openings, the width of the diagonal strut w can be calculated as

$$w = 0.175\alpha_h^{-0.4} L_{ds} \tag{16.9}$$

where

$$\alpha_h = h\left(\sqrt[4]{\frac{Et\sin 2\theta}{4E_f I_c h}}\right)$$

where E_f is the modulus of elasticity of the frame material, I_c is the moment of inertia of the adjoining column, h is the height of the masonry wall, L_{ds} is the length of the diagonal strut and θ is the angle of the diagonal strut with the horizontal.

Openings in the infill walls reduce the infill stiffness. The *opening area ratio* (A_r), defined as the ratio of the area of the opening to the area of the panel, is used as a basis for modifying the stiffness of the equivalent truss element. When this ratio is less than 0.05, the reduction in stiffness can be ignored, and when this ratio exceeds 0.4, the infill stiffness can be completely ignored. For intermediate values of A_r, the stiffness reduction is accounted for by modifying the depth of the truss element, as follows [Ref. 16.41]:

$$w = (0.175\alpha_h^{-0.4} L_{ds})(1 - 2.5A_r) \quad \text{for} \quad 0.05 < A_r < 0.40 \tag{16.10}$$

16.4.12 Modelling of Diaphragms, Chords and Collectors

Diaphragms are horizontal (or nearly horizontal) planar elements that connect with the lateral load resisting (LLR) system, and help to transfer lateral forces to the vertical elements of the LLR system. In typical building structures, floor and roof slabs serve as diaphragms. Indeed, the diaphragms tie the building elements together making the whole structure a three-dimensional system.

Floor diaphragms play an important role in transmitting the inertial forces developed due to the seismic actions to the vertical elements of the lateral load resisting systems (shear walls and columns). In this process, under lateral in-plane inertial forces, the diaphragm itself is subjected to in-plane bending, spanning horizontally between these vertical elements of the lateral load resisting system (Figure 16.16). Although the IS 1893 code is silent on the design aspects pertaining to the diaphragm, a proper design and detailing of the diaphragm is necessary to ensure satisfactory performance of the structure in the event of an earthquake.

Diaphragms can be modelled as *rigid* or *flexible* diaphragms based on their geometry and aspect ratio. Slabs having adequate thickness and regular plan dimensions, with an aspect ratio close to one, may be considered as rigid diaphragms. The rigid diaphragms have infinite in-plane stiffness and hence do not exhibit any membrane deformations. This modelling technique has an advantage of faster computation. However, for slabs having large aspect ratio (rectangular in plan), where in-plane deformations are possible, a flexible diaphragm needs to be adopted. The IS 1893 (Part 1): 2016 recommends that slabs with openings greater than 50 per cent of the total slab area may be assumed to be flexible diaphragms

The diaphragms usually include the slab, *chords* and *collectors* (also known as *distributors*). The in-plane moments in the slab are resisted by the tension and compression *chords* at the ends of the diaphragm, as shown in Figure 16.16. Conventionally, the design of diaphragms is done using the simple beam idealisation. However, a more rational analysis, such as the strut-and-tie method can also be employed to estimate the reinforcement requirements [Ref. 16.49]. A collector element is used to transmit the shear forces from the diaphragms to the vertical elements (walls and columns). These may be locally thickened sections or having the same thickness as that of the slab. The reinforcement provided in the collector elements must be capable to resist the compressive and tensile forces that arise due to the collector action as shown in Figure 16.16. The design procedure for these elements can be found in Ref. 16.49.

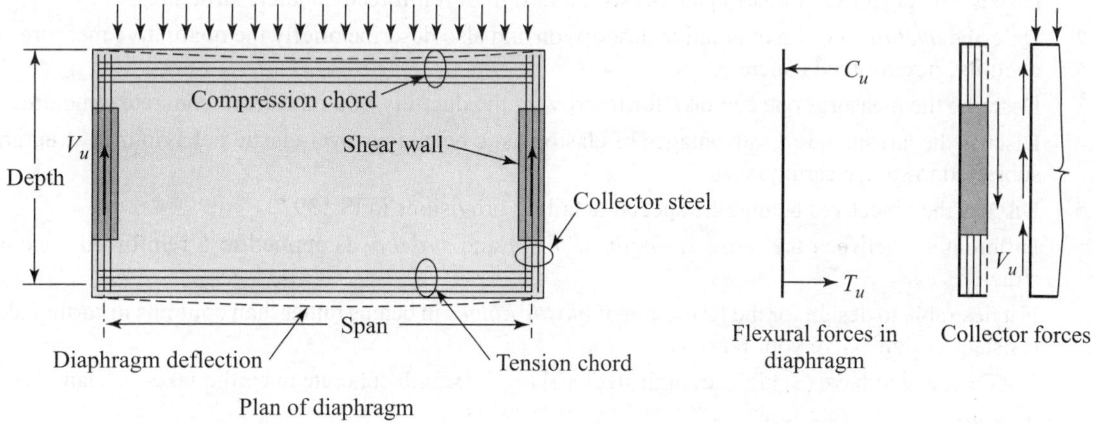

Fig. 16.16 Tension and compression chords in a diaphragm.

16.4.13 Performance Limit States

In several countries, seismic design is in the process of fundamental change. One important reason for the change is that although code-designed buildings performed well (in countries such as USA) in recent earthquakes from a life-safety perspective, the level of damage to structures, economic loss due to non-usage of buildings and costs of repair were unexpectedly high. Conventional methods of seismic design have the objectives to provide for life safety (through strength and ductility) and damage control (through serviceability – drift limits). The design criteria are defined by limits on stresses and member forces calculated from prescribed levels of applied lateral shear force. Performance-based design philosophy involves design criteria that are expressed in terms of achieving stated performance objectives when the structure is subjected to stated levels of seismic hazard [Ref. 16.39]. The performance targets may be a level of stress, a load, a displacement, a limit state or a target damage state not to be exceeded. Required performance criteria for a seismic hazard are 'safety', 'restorability' and 'usability'. Safety refers to protection of human life. Restorability refers to structural integrity. Usability refers to function and habitability.

In earthquake resistant design, the structural displacement is a key parameter which can be used to identify the extent of damage to the structure. Using the displacement based design, a target displacement of the structure can be pre-assigned and the engineer can verify if the structure meets the required performance limits [Ref. 16.48].

16.5 Closure

The purpose of this chapter is to explain the background to the seismic design provisions of the IS code and related international codes. A detailed discussion of seismic analysis and design of reinforced concrete structures is beyond the scope of this book, however, an introduction to the evaluation of seismic forces on buildings is presented in Chapter 19. Rapid advances are being made in this area, and recent publications (for example, Ref. 16.27–16.32) may be consulted for more details.

REVIEW QUESTIONS

16.1 Discuss the objectives of earthquake-resistant design of reinforced concrete structures.

16.2 Describe *ductility*. Give a qualitative description and also describe briefly the qualitative measures of ductility in reinforced concrete.

16.3 Describe the measures one can take for improving the ductility of a reinforced concrete structure.

16.4 Discuss the advantages/disadvantages of elastoplastic behaviour over elastic behaviour in structures subjected to severe earthquakes.

16.5 Discuss the objectives behind the special detailing provisions in IS 13920.

16.6 Differentiate between the terms *strength, stiffness* and *stability* as applied to a reinforced concrete structure.

16.7 Is it desirable to design for the formation of *plastic hinges* in beams rather than columns in earthquake-resistant design? Give your reasons.

16.8 Is it desirable to have (a) high strength steel, (b) high strength concrete in earthquake-resistant design of reinforced concrete structures? Justify your answers.

16.9 Suggest a design procedure for ensuring that the foundation is stronger than the superstructure in earthquake-resistant design.

16.10 Describe the limits placed on tensile reinforcement ratios in beams in earthquake-resistant design. Why are such limits enforced?

16.11 How are the design shear forces estimated in the beams of ductile frames?

16.12 Are inclined stirrups and bent-up bars unsuitable as shear reinforcement in earthquake-resistant design? Discuss.

16.13 Discuss *special confining reinforcement* in columns of ductile frames.

16.14 Explain the design requirements of beam-column joints in earthquake-resistant design.

16.15 Explain the differences between an *ordinary wall* and a *shear wall* in a reinforced concrete tall building, with regard to function, loading and design.

16.16 What are the main design requirements of ductile shear (flexural) walls in earthquake-resistant design?

16.17 Briefly explain the main concepts underlying *pushover analysis*.

16.18 What is the effect of ignoring the contribution of masonry infill in the lateral load analysis of a multi-storey frame?

16.19 In what manner is the behaviour of an 'open ground storey' construction likely to be different from a regular construction in the event of an earthquake?

REFERENCES

16.1 IS 1893 (Part I): 2016 – *Criteria for Earthquake Design of Structures–Part I: General Provisions and Buildings* (Sixth revision), Bureau of Indian Standards, New Delhi, 2005

16.2 IS 4326 : 1993 – *Code of Practice* for *Earthquake Resistant Design and Construction of Buildings*, Bureau of Indian Standards, New Delhi, 1993 (reaffirmed 1998)

16.3 IS 13920 : 2016 – *Ductile Detailing of Reinforced Concrete Structures Subjected to Seismic Forces – Code of Practice*, Bureau of Indian Standards, New Delhi, 1993

16.4 ACI Standard 318-19, *Building Code Requirements for Structural Concrete* and *Commentary* (ACI 318R–19), Am. Conc. Institute, Detroit, Michigan, 2019

16.5 *National Building Code of Canada 2015*, *Part 4*: *Structural Design*, National Research Council of Canada, Ottawa, 2015

16.6 CSA Standard A23.3–14 – *Design of Concrete Structures*, Canadian Standards Association, Rexdale, Ontario, 2014

16.7 *SEAOC, Recommended Lateral Force Requirements and Commentary*, Seismology Committee, Structural Engineer's Association of California, San Francisco, 1980

16.8 *Explanatory Handbook or Codes for Earthquake Engineering,* Special Publication SP 22, Bureau of Indian Standards, New Delhi, 1982

16.9 Newmark, N M and Rosenbleuth, E, *Fundamentals of Earthquake Engineering,* Prentice-Hall, Englewood, Cliffs, N.J., 1971

16.10 Clough, R W and Penzien, J, *Dynamics of Structures*, Second edition, McGraw-Hill International edition, 1993

16.11 Park, R and Paulay, T, *Reinforced Concrete Structures*, John Wiley & Sons, Inc., New York, 1975

16.12 IS 456 (Part I): 2000 – *Plain and Reinforced Concrete-Code of Practice* (Fourth revision), Bureau of Indian Standards, New Delhi, 2000

16.13 *Structural Use of Concrete*: Part 1: *Code of Practice for Design and Construction*, BS 8110: Part 1: 1997, British Standards Institution, London, 1997

16.14 Sarkar, P, Agrawal, R and Menon, D, *Design of Beam-Column Joints Under Seismic Loading – A Review*, Journal of Structural Engineering, SERC, Vol. 33, No. 6, Feb-March 2007, pp 449–458

16.15 Hognestad, E, *A Study of Combined Bending and Axial Load in Reinforced Concrete Members,* Bulletin Series No. 399, 1951, Univ. of Illinois Experimental Station, Urabana, USA

16.16 Kent, D C and Park, R, *Flexural Members with Confined Concrete,* ASCE Journal of the Structural Division, Vol. 97, 1971, pp 1969–1990

16.17 Park, R, Priestley, M J N and Gill, W D, *Ductility of Square-Confined Concrete Columns,* Journal of the Structural Division, ASCE, Vol. 108, 1982, pp 929–950

16.18 Mander, J B, Priestley, M J N and Park, R, *Theoretical Stress–Strain Model for Confined Concrete.* Journal of the Structural Division, ASCE, Vol. 114, 1988, pp 1804–1826

16.19 Panagiotakos, T B and Fardis, M N, *Deformation of Reinforced Concrete Members at Yielding and Ultimate*, ACI Structural Journal, Vol. 98, No. 2, April 2001, pp 135–148

16.20 Saatcioglu, M and Razvi, S, *Strength and Ductility of Confined Concrete.* Journal of the Structural Division, ASCE, Vol. 118, 1992, pp 1590–1607

16.21 Saatcioglu, M and Razvi, S R, *Confinement Model for High-Strength Concrete*, Journal of Structural Engineering, ASCE, Vol. 125, 1999, No. 3, pp 281–289

16.22 Chugh, R, *Studies on RC Beams, Columns and Joints for Earthquake-Resistant Design*, Master of Technology Thesis, Indian Institute of Technology, Madras, India, 2004

16.23 Hakuto, S, Park, R and Tanaka, H, *Effect of Deterioration of Bond of Beam Bars Passing through Interior Beam-Column Joints on Flexural Strength and Ductility*, ACI Structural Journal, Vol. 96, No. 5, 1999, pp 858–864

16.24 SAP 2000NL manual (Version 7.1), *Three Dimensional Static and Dynamic Analysis and Design of Structures*, Computers and Structures, Inc. Berkeley, USA

16.25 ATC-40 (Volume 1): *Seismic Evaluation and Retrofit of Concrete Buildings*, Applied Technology Council, California, 1996

16.26 ACI–ASCE Committee 352, *Recommendations for Design of Beam-Column Joints in Monolithic Reinforced Concrete Structures*, (ACI 352 R–76, Reaffirmed 1981), Am. Conc. Institute, Detroit, 1976

16.27 Arnold, C and Reitherman, R, *Building Configuration and Seismic Design*, John Wiley & Sons, Inc., New York, 1982

16.28 Applied Technology Council, *Tentative Provisions for the Development of Seismic Regulations for Buildings*, ATC 3–06, National Bureau of Standards, Special Publication 510, U.S. Government Printing Office, Washington, D.C., 1978

16.29 Dowrick, D J, *Earthquake Resistant Design*, John Wiley & Sons, Chichester, U.K., 1977

16.30 *Reinforced Concrete Structures in Seismic Zones*, ACI Publication SP–53, Am. Conc. Institute, Detroit, 1977

16.31 *Reinforced Concrete Structures Subjected to Wind and Earthquake Forces*, ACI Publication SP–63, Am. Conc. Institute, Detroit, 1980

16.32 *Earthquake Effects on Reinforced Concrete Structure*, ACI Publication SP–84, Am. Conc. Institute, Detroit, 1985

16.33 Pillai S U, and Kirk, D W, *Ductile Beam-Column Connection in Precast Concrete*, ACI Journal, Vol. 78, Nov–Dec 1981, pp 480–487

16.34 Murty C V R, and Jain S K, *A Review of IS 1893-1984: Provisions on Seismic Design of Buildings,* The Indian Concrete Journal, November 1994, pp 619–629

16.35 Scarlat A S, *Approximate Methods in Structural Seismic Design,* E & FN Spon, London, 1996

16.36 Mallick D V, and Severn R T, *The Behaviour of Infilled Frames,* Proceedings of Institute of Civil Engineers, Vol. 38, Dec 1967, pp 639–656

16.37 *Bhuj, India Earthquake of January 26, 2001: Reconnaissance Report,* Supplement A to Volume 18 Earthquake Spectra, July 2002

16.38 Medhekar M S, Gehad E R, and Jain S K, *Shear Reinforcement for Aseismic Design of Flexural Members,* The Indian Concrete Journal, June 1992, pp 319–324

16.39 Ghobarah A, *Performance Based Design in Earthquake Engineering: State of Development,* Engineering Structures, Vol. 23, 2001, pp 878–884

16.40 Das, S and Nau, J M, *Seismic Design Aspects of Vertically Irregular Reinforced Concrete Buildings*, Earthquake Spectra, Vol. 19, No. 3, 2003, pp 455–477

16.41 Murty C V R, and Jain S K, *Proposed Draft Provisions and Commentary on Indian Seismic Code IS 1893 (Part I): 2002*, IITK-GSDMA project on Building Codes, Indian Institute of Technology, Kanpur, 2005

16.42 Chakrabarti, A, Menon, D and Sengupta, A K (Editors), *Seismic Retrofit of Buildings*, Narosa Publishing House, New Delhi, 2008

16.43 FEMA 273, *NEHRP Guidelines for the Seismic Rehabilitation of Buildings*, Applied Technology Council, USA, 1997

16.44 Chugh, R and Menon, D, *Design Aids for Estimation of Shear in Seismic Design of RC Beams*, Indian Concrete Journal, Vol. 79, March 2005, pp 22–28

16.45 *Concrete Structures Standard, Part I : The Design of Concrete Structures*, New Zealand Standard, New Zealand, 2006.

16.46 Kaushik, H B, *Evaluation of Strengthening Options for Masonry-Infilled RC Frames With Open First-Storey*, PhD. Thesis, Indian Institute of Technology, Kanpur, India, November, 2004

16.47 Davis, R, *Seismic-Resistant Design of Open Ground Storey Buildings*, PhD. Thesis, Indian Institute of Technology, Madras, India, 2008

16.48 Calvi G M, Priestley M J, Kowalsky M J. *Displacement–based Seismic Design of Structures*. Earthquake spectra. 2007; 24(2): 1–24

16.49 Moehle J P, Hooper J D, Kelly D J, Meyer T R, *Seismic Design of Cast-in-place Concrete Diaphragms, Chords and Collectors*. Seismic design technical brief, US Dept. of Commerce, Building and Fire Research Laboratory, National Institute of Standards and Technology. 2010

Selected Special Topics

CHAPTER 17

LEARNING OBJECTIVES

After studying this chapter, you will be able to:

- *Use in design, concepts and procedures such as compression field theory, strut and tie model for design, fire resistance and rating, and green building design*

17.1 Introduction

Typically, beams, columns and walls are analysed and designed by *theory of flexure*, which assumes that 'plane sections remain plane'. Regions of members where this assumption is reasonably valid are termed *flexural regions*. Here, the response of the member is studied section-by-section. The design for flexure discussed in Chapter 5, shear design procedure discussed in Chapter 6 (except Section 6.9) and the modified compression field theory discussed below belong to this category – sometimes referred to as *Sectional Design Methods* – and are applicable for *flexural regions* only. Regions near discontinuities, where the plane section remaining plane assumption is not valid, should be designed by the strut-and-tie method (Section 17.3).

17.2 Design for Shear by Modified Compression Field Theory

17.2.1 Introduction

In flexural regions, the analysis and design for flexure or for the *combined effects* of flexure and concurrent axial force is made in *one step* considering the equilibrium conditions, deformation pattern ('plane section remaining plane'), strain compatibility between concrete and reinforcing bars and the stress-strain relationships of the materials (refer Chapter 13). For shear, in the traditional method given in Chapter 6, the design is done separately and the transverse reinforcement so obtained is placed in addition to the longitudinal reinforcement designed for flexure (and axial load if any). Longitudinal reinforcement requirement for shear is taken care of by detailing provisions (Section 6.6.5). This procedure, widely adopted in practice, does not explicitly account for the interaction among the various stress resultants (shear force, bending moment and axial force). Also, the calculations aim to satisfy equilibrium conditions at the ultimate state only, and do not account for the requirements of deformation compatibility.

There have been attempts to evolve a unified design procedure considering effects of flexure, shear and axial force together. The *Compression Field Theory* [Ref. 17.1–17.4] was an attempt in this direction. However, the mechanics involved are such that an exact solution is complex and intractable. Hence, recourse has been made to several simplifying assumptions, which are perhaps questionable. The theory has undergone many revisions, and in its current format, called *Modified Compression Field Theory* (MCFT), the effects of shear is indeed considered separately and superposed with those of flexure and axial loads; however, several other aspects such as the stress-strain behaviour in compression of cracked reinforced concrete, tensile stresses in the uncracked portion of concrete, compatibility of strains, the variation in the inclination of the diagonal tension cracks (or of the concrete compression struts), contribution of aggregate interlock (interface shear) along cracks, etc are duly accounted for. It may be noted that the current Canadian Code CSA A23.3-14 mandates design for shear and torsion based on the formulations derived from MCFT and its further refinements [Ref. 17.4] and the conventional method has been dispensed with.

> 'Compression field theory' attempts to evolve a unified procedure to design members considering the effects of flexure, shear and axial force together.

The name 'compression field theory' is based on the analogous problem of the post-buckling shear resistance of thin-webbed metal girders (plate girders). Shear initially causes a set of compressive and tensile stresses in orthogonal directions along the diagonals in the web of such girders. However, following the buckling of the thin web due to the diagonal compression, the web cannot resist any more compression and the shear is carried by a 'field of diagonal tension' and the stiffeners [Figure 17.1(a)]. This approach of analysis is known as **tension field theory**. Similarly, in concrete beams, after diagonal cracking, shear would not be resisted by diagonal tension, however a field of diagonal compression and the stirrups would carry shear [Figure 17.1(b)]. This concept is called **compression field theory** [Ref. 17.1].

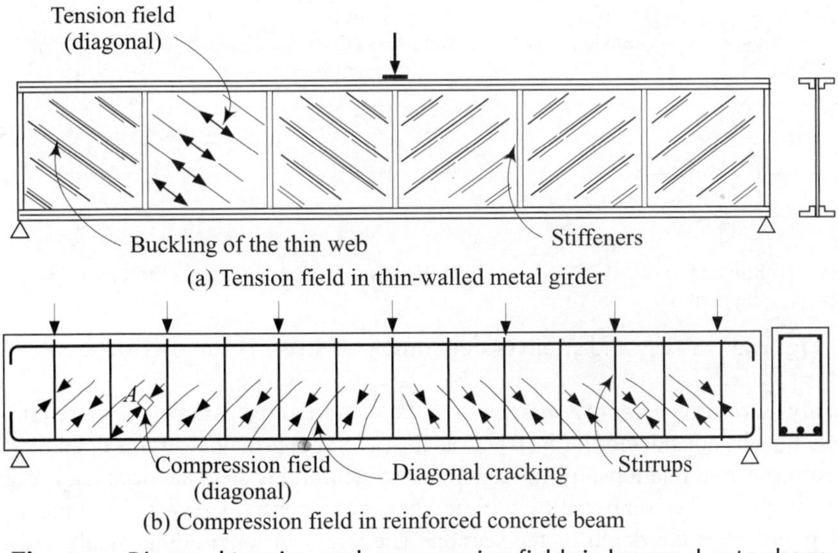

Fig. 17.1 Diagonal tension and compression fields in beams due to shear.

17.2.2 Compression Field Theory – General Concepts

In order to understand the complexity involved in an exact analysis for shear strength, consider the compressive stress trajectories in a beam subjected to a bending moment, M, an axial force, N (considered positive if tensile), and a shear force, V, as shown in Figure 17.2. At any section 1-1, the magnitude and direction of the principal compressive stresses and principal compressive strains will vary over the depth of the section. At the bottom face, the inclination θ will be 90°, and at the top face θ will be 0°. The shear stress will also vary over the depth of section. On a small element such as at A at a depth y, the stresses, strains, and the corresponding Mohr's circles are as shown in Figures 17.2(h)–(l). Concrete is assumed to have no tensile strength. In addition, the directions of principal stresses and principal strains are assumed to coincide.

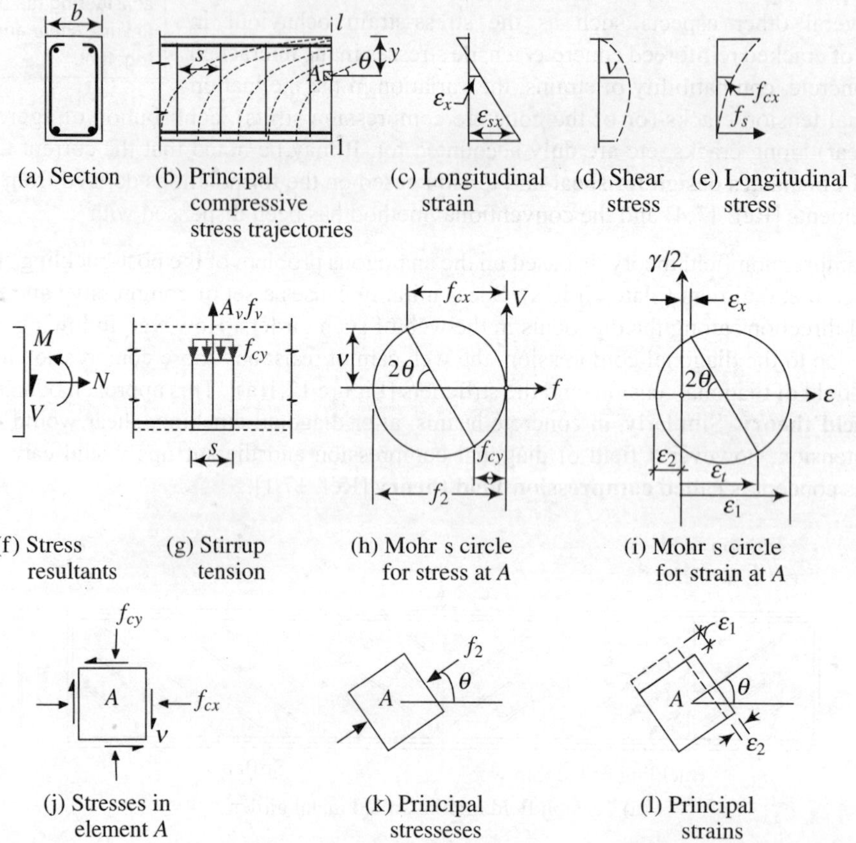

Fig. 17.2 Stress and strain under combined stress resultants M, N, and V.

For a correct analysis, *at each point over the depth* of the section, three parameters are required to be known/computed. These may be considered, for instance, as the (average) principal strains ε_1 and ε_2 and the angle θ. In addition, the stress-strain relationships for concrete and reinforcing steel are necessary. With these known, the principal stress, f_2, can be computed ($f_1 = 0$) and hence the normal stress, f_{cx}, and the tangential (shear) stress, v, at all points over the depth of the section. The stress in longitudinal steel, f_s, can be computed from the steel strain, ε_{sx}, assuming that reinforcing steel carries only axial forces. Thus, the distributions of axial and tangential stresses over the cross section can be obtained as shown schematically in Figures 17.2(e) and (d). [Note that the shapes of the stress and strain diagrams in Figures 17.2(c), (d) and (e) are initially unknown, except that the strain variation may be assumed linear based on 'plane section' theory] By integrating these stresses (multiplied by the width of the cross-section) over the depth of section, the internal stress resultants N, M and V can be obtained [Figure 17.2(f)] which should equal the externally applied axial force, moment and shear at the section (equilibrium condition). The strain in the transverse direction, ε_t, determines the tensile stress, f_v, in the transverse shear reinforcement, and the tension in this reinforcement balances the transverse compressive stress in the concrete, f_{cy}, over the area tributary to it [Figure 17.2(g)] satisfying vertical equilibrium of the element shown.

The strain distribution must also be *compatible* with the geometry of deformation. Thus, assuming that plane sections of the beam remain plane, the distributions of ε_1, ε_2 and θ over the depth must be such that the resulting longitudinal strain, ε_x varies linearly over the depth of the member [Figure 17.2(c)]. Obviously, knowing/assuming, a priori, such distributions of ε_1, ε_2 and θ over the depth at all sections so as to satisfy equilibrium and compatibility conditions is a tall order!

Because of the large number of unknowns involved (i.e., three parameters at every point over the depth), a direct solution to the problem is not possible, and a trial-and-error procedure together with simplifying assumptions has to be used. Two parameters that may be assumed initially are the shear stress distribution and the longitudinal strain distribution (such as a uniform v and a linearly varying ε_x). This gives v and ε_x at all points. Taking trial values of a third parameter also, such as ε_1, and by successive iterations to satisfy equilibrium, compatibility, and stress-strain relations, the appropriate distributions of f_{cx} and v can be found. However, such procedures are lengthy and tedious and seldom resorted to in practice. Hence, several approximations and simplifying assumptions have been introduced in a '*Modified Compression Field Theory*' (MCFT) [Ref. 17.1–17.3]. This is dealt with in Section 17.2.4.

> The 'modified compression field theory' takes into account several aspects such as stress-strain behaviour of cracked and biaxially strained reinforced concrete, tensile stresses in uncracked portion of concrete, compatibility of strains, variation in inclination of diagonal tension cracks, interface shear along cracks, etc.

17.2.3 Stress-Strain Relationship for Diagonally Cracked Concrete

For the evaluation of shear strength, the stress-strain relationship for steel and concrete must be known. The 'compression field' in the web [Figure 17.1(b)] is maintained by *diagonally cracked and biaxially strained* concrete, whose compressive strength will be less than that of uncracked concrete as determined from a cube or cylinder test. The theory of MCFT was developed (and adopted in 1984 in the Canadian Code for design of concrete structures, CSA A23.3-84, and the American bridge design Code, AASHTO-2004) taking concrete strength as the specified 28-day *cylinder strength*, f_c', and the same will be used in this section.

> In the development of MCFT described here, the *cylinder strength* of concrete, f_c', is used as the measure of concrete compressive strength (and not the cube strength, f_{ck}).

The states of stress and strain in element A are shown in Figures 17.2(h) and (j). The maximum (principal) compressive stress in concrete, f_2, is inclined at an angle θ to the axis of the member. The maximum compressive strain along f_2 is ε_2, and the maximum tensile strain, ε_1, is at right angles to the direction of f_2. Because of the low tensile strength of concrete, tensile cracks will develop early along the direction of f_2, and the concrete in between these cracks acts as the parallel compression diagonals. This state of stress, strain and cracking is shown in Figure 17.3(a).

Biaxially strained concrete, as in Figure 17.3(a), with compression in one direction and a concurrent transverse tensile strain is weaker than concrete in uniaxial compression as in a cylinder test [Figure 17.3(b)], where the lateral strain is only due to the Poisson effect. Based on results of tests on concrete panels reinforced with uniform and closely spaced reinforcement along longitudinal and transverse directions and subjected to in-plane shear and normal stresses [Ref. 17.2] the maximum compressive strength, $f_{2,max}$, of concrete in the

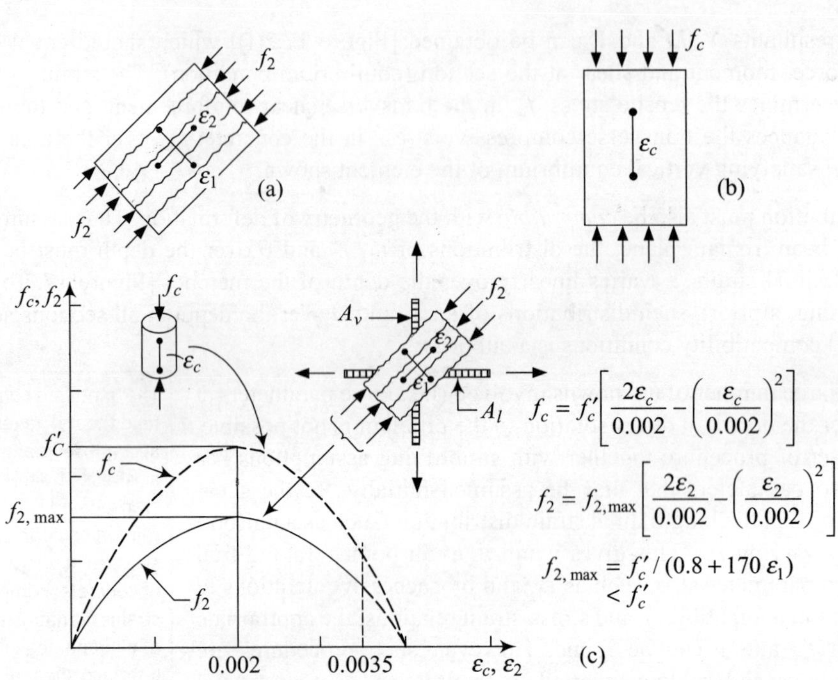

Fig. 17.3 Stress-strain relationship for diagonally cracked concrete.

presence of transverse tensile strain, ε_1, has been obtained as:

$$f_{2,\max} = f_c'/(0.8 + 170\varepsilon_1) \leq f_c' \tag{17.1}$$

where $f_{2,\max}$ = compressive strength of concrete in presence of transverse tensile strain ε_1, (The Code CSA A23.3-14 limits $f_{2,\max} \leq 0.85 f_c'$);

f_c' = specified compressive (cylinder) strength of concrete;

ε_1 = transverse tensile strain;

and the compressive strain in concrete at peak stress is assumed to be 0.002. Note that for cracked concrete, the tensile strain ε_1 represents an *average* value (measured over base lengths including several cracks [Figure 17.3(a)]).

Equation 17.1 gives $f_{2,\max}$, the *maximum strength* of concrete (i.e., at ε_2 = 0.002) under transverse tensile strain ε_1. In general, to compute the stress f_2 corresponding to any principal compressive strain ε_2 (concurrent with transverse tensile strain ε_1), a stress-strain relation for biaxially strained concrete [Figure 17.3(a)] is necessary. For this, it is assumed that the general shape of this stress-strain relation remains the same as for uniaxial compression. One such relationship proposed in Ref. 17.2 is given in Eq. 17.2. Equation 17.2 is also shown in Figure 17.3(c) where it is compared with the parabolic stress-strain diagram for uniaxial compression.

$$f_2 = f_{2,\max}\left[\frac{2\varepsilon_2}{0.002} - \left(\frac{\varepsilon_2}{0.002}\right)^2\right] \tag{17.2}$$

where f_2 is the compressive stress corresponding to compressive strain ε_2 in presence of a transverse tensile strain ε_1, $f_{2,max}$ is given by Eq. 17.1 and the strain corresponding to the peak stress is assumed = 0.002.

For computing $f_{2,max}$, the value of ε_1 used in Eq. 17.1 must be compatible with the associated strain field. The Mohr's circle of strain and the strain directions for the cracked and reinforced concrete element shown in Figure 17.3(c) are as shown in Figures 17.4 (ix, xi). At peak compressive stress, $\varepsilon_2 = -0.002$ and associated ε_x is = strain in longitudinal steel, ε_s. From Mohr's circle of strain [Figure 17.4(ix)]:

$$\varepsilon_x = \varepsilon_s = \frac{\varepsilon_1 - 0.002}{2} - \frac{\varepsilon_1 + 0.002}{2}\cos 2\theta$$

Simplifying, $\varepsilon_1 = \varepsilon_s + (\varepsilon_s + 0.002)\cot^2\theta$ (17.2a)

Similarly, in terms of transverse steel strain ε_t,

$$\varepsilon_1 = \varepsilon_t + (\varepsilon_t + 0.002)\tan^2\theta \tag{17.2b}$$

For longitudinal steel, say, with $f_y = 400$ MPa, as it yields, $\varepsilon_s = 0.002$. With this value for ε_s in Eq. 17.2a, and substituting in Eq. 17.1, the maximum diagonal compressive strength of cracked concrete (for $f_y = 400$ MPa) is obtained as:

$$f_{2,max} = \frac{f_c'}{1.14 + 0.68\cot^2\theta} \le 0.85 f_c' \tag{17.2c}$$

Equation 17.2c gives the admissible peak compressive stress in the compression diagonals corresponding to yielding of longitudinal reinforcement, for $f_y = 400$ MPa.

17.2.4 Analysis Based on Modified Compression Field Theory

(a) Assumptions and Equations – Case of Pure Shear

There are several aspects not considered in the 45° truss analogy. In a beam subjected to M, N and V, the inclination, θ, of the compression diagonals (i.e., of the principal compressive stress, f_2) will not be at 45°; it will vary along the depth of the section and along the span. The concrete between cracks acting as diagonal compression struts will have strength less than that of concrete in uniaxial compression [Figure 17.3 and Eq. 17.2c]. Further, this concrete will develop some tensile stresses f_1 along ε_1 *in-between* the cracks, which will contribute to the shear strength. The shear also necessitates additional longitudinal reinforcement at the flexural steel level. The *modified compression field theory* [Ref. 17.2, 17.3] attempts to take care of all the above aspects more rationally, albeit with several simplifications.

Because of the complexity in considering effects of M, N and V together, the simple case of a symmetrically reinforced beam *under pure shear* is considered first [Figures 17.4(i), (ii)]. Effects of bending moment and axial force are superimposed subsequently. In the development of the theory, flanged sections have generally been used because the variation of shear stress over the depth of the web is nearly uniform and hence the diagonal cracks may be assumed to extend over the full depth at a uniform angle θ.

> **Because of the complexity in arriving at an exact theory, and in order to arrive at a usable format for design, several simplifying assumptions are made in the MCFT.**

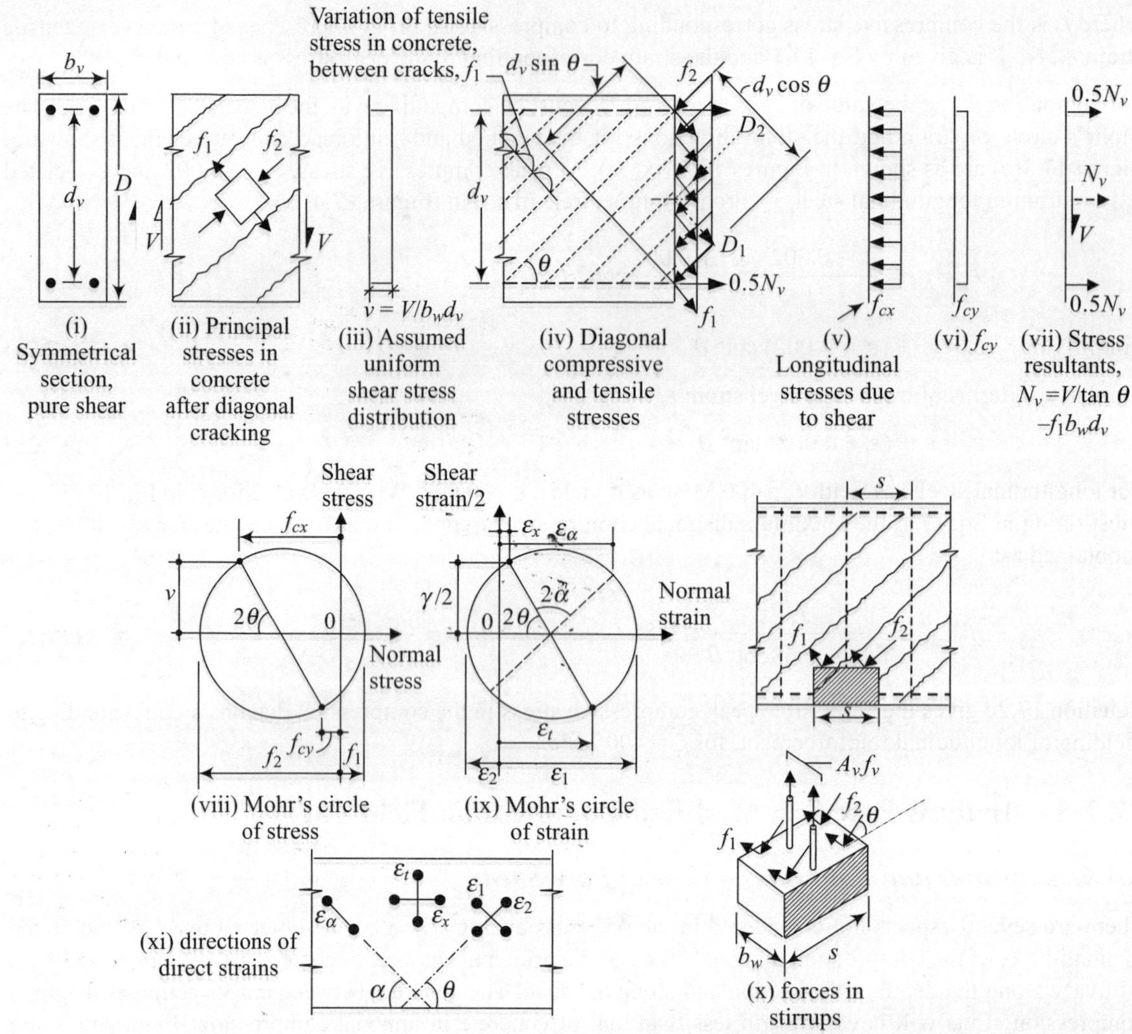

Fig. 17.4 Modified compression field theory – Analysis for shear force V.

Prior to cracking, pure shear causes principal tensile and compressive stresses of equal magnitude along diagonal directions, inclined at 45° to the beam axis. After diagonal tension cracks are formed, the corresponding tensile stress in concrete is reduced to zero at the cracks, while the concrete in-between cracks can still sustain some tensile stresses. Such tensile stresses vary from zero at the cracks to a maximum value in between cracks [Figure 17.4(iv)] and, for deriving equilibrium equations, an *average* value, f_1, is used. This average stress, f_1, is less than the maximum tensile stress reached prior to diagonal cracking. Figure 17.5(c), (d) shows internal forces across section 1-1 mid-way between diagonal cracks and across section 2-2 along a diagonal crack. At the crack, the share of f_1 is taken up by increases in transverse reinforcement stress and/or the interface shear (aggregate interlock), v_{ci}. Furthermore, in deriving these equations, the following simplifying assumptions are made:

(i) The shear stress, v, is uniformly distributed over the web, which has a width b_w and depth d_v (taken as the distance between the resultants of the tensile and compressive forces due to flexure, $\approx 0.9d$), so that,

$$v = \frac{V}{b_w d_v} \tag{17.3}$$

(ii) Under uniform shear stress and with symmetry, the longitudinal strain, ε_x, and the inclination of the principal compressive stress, θ, remain constant over the depth d_v

(iii) Equations 17.1 and 17.2 give the stress-strain relationship in compression for the diagonally cracked concrete.

Shear Strength With these assumptions, the internal forces, stress and strain distributions and the stress resultants at a section subjected to shear only (such as at a point of contraflexure) are as shown in Figure 17.4. The Mohr's circles for (average) stress and strain states at all points on the section are shown in Figures 17.4(viii) and (ix). From the Mohr's circle of stress,

$$v = \frac{f_1 + f_2}{2}\sin 2\theta$$

$$\Rightarrow \qquad f_2 = \frac{v}{\sin\theta\cos\theta} - f_1 \tag{17.4}$$

$$= \frac{V}{b_w d_v \sin\theta\cos\theta} - f_1 \tag{17.5}$$

The force in the transverse reinforcement balances the vertical components of the concrete stresses f_1 and f_2. Considering equilibrium of stirrup forces and vertical components of f_1 and f_2 acting over the concrete area tributary to a stirrup, as shown in Figure 17.4(x),

$$A_v f_v = b_w s(f_2 \sin^2\theta - f_1 \cos^2\theta) \tag{17.6}$$

where f_v is the average stress in the stirrups. Substituting for f_2 from Eq. 17.5,

$$\frac{A_v f_v}{b_w s} = \frac{V}{b_w d_v}\tan\theta - f_1 \tag{17.7}$$

and $$V = \frac{A_v f_v d_v}{s}\cot\theta + f_1 b_w d_v \cot\theta \tag{17.8}$$

$$= V_s + V_c \tag{17.8a}$$

where, $$V_s = \frac{A_v f_v d_v}{s}\cot\theta \tag{17.9}$$

and $$V_c = f_1 b_w d_v \cot\theta \tag{17.10}$$

[*Note:* The diagonal compressive stress in the cracked concrete, f_2, shall be less than the crushing strength of the biaxially strained concrete in compression, represented by Eq. 17.2. This gives an upper limit on V given by Eq. 17.8.]

Equation 17.8 shows that the shear resistance may be considered as consisting of a part, V_s, contributed by the shear reinforcement; and a part, V_c, contributed by the *tensile stresses* in concrete, f_1, (transmitted across cracks via aggregate interlock action – see later, Eq. 17.14). The expression for V_s is the same as that derived earlier in Section 6.7.4 [Eq. 6.18a with $\alpha = 90^o$]. When the transverse reinforcement is placed at an angle α to the beam axis, V_s is given by [compare Eq. 6.18a]:

$$V_s = \frac{A_v f_v d_v}{s}(\cot\theta + \cot\alpha)\sin\alpha \tag{17.9a}$$

The part V_c, given by Eq. 17.10, depends on the average tensile stress, f_1, in the diagonally cracked concrete, and may be expressed as:

$$V_c = \beta\sqrt{f_c'}\, b_w d_v \tag{17.10a}$$

where $\beta = f_1 \cot\theta/\sqrt{f_c'}$ (17.10b)

and β is a factor accounting for the ability of concrete to transmit shear stresses across cracks by aggregate interlock action (see Eq. 17.15a below). In this format, evaluation of shear strength reduces to determination of appropriate values of θ and β and using them in Eqs. 17.9a and 17.10a.

Longitudinal Reinforcement The stresses f_1 and f_2 over a cross section [having resultants D_1 and D_2 – see Figure 17.4(iv)] resulting from shear V has a net axial resultant, N_v, given by:

$$N_v = b_w d_v (f_2 \cos^2\theta - f_1 \sin^2\theta) \tag{17.11}$$

There has to be longitudinal reinforcement to resist this. Thus, shear force necessitates longitudinal reinforcements as well. With longitudinal reinforcement symmetrically placed at top and bottom, the tensile force in each of them will be 0.5 N_v. If A_{sx} is the *total* area of such reinforcement and f_{sx} the tensile stress due to shear, $A_{sx} f_{sx} = N_v$, and substituting for f_2 from Eq. 17.5 into Eq. 17.11,

$$A_{sx} f_{sx} = N_v = V\cot\theta - f_1 b_w d_v \tag{17.12}$$

Both V_c and N_v depend on f_1. There are several considerations in choosing the appropriate value for f_1. In deriving the equations above, *average stresses* and *strains* have been used. In Figure 17.5(c), the *average* tensile stress in concrete, f_1, is assumed to be developed midway between diagonal cracks. As one moves towards the crack, the concrete tensile stress decreases to zero at the crack and the slack is taken up by increases in transverse reinforcement stress and/or the interface shear (through aggregate interlock), v_{ci}. Once the transverse reinforcement yields at a crack (where the stress is maximum), any increase in shear force can be resisted only by increases in shear stresses v_{ci} [Figures 17.5(b) and (d)]. The V_c component due to f_l at section 1-1 and due to v_{ci} at section 2-2 are shown in the vector diagrams in Figures 17.5(c) and (d). Thus, yielding of the transverse reinforcement at a diagonal crack and the limitation on the stress v_{ci} that can be mobilized can limit the magnitude of the effective *average* tension, f_1, that can be transmitted and hence V_c. The magnitude of the shear stress, v_{ci} that can be transmitted between the two sides along the crack interface will depend primarily on the crack width, w, [Figure 17.5(b)]. The crack width, w, in turn depends on the average principal tensile strain, ε_1, and the average spacing, s_θ, of the diagonal cracks. The spacing s_θ itself depends on the type, amount and distribution of the longitudinal and transverse reinforcements. Thus, the value of f_1 depends on a large number of variables. Recommended limiting value of v_{ci} to avoid slipping along cracks is [Ref. 17.1]:

$$v_{ci} = \frac{0.18\sqrt{f_c'}}{0.3 + \dfrac{24w}{a+16}} \tag{17.12a}$$

where, a = the maximum size of aggregate.

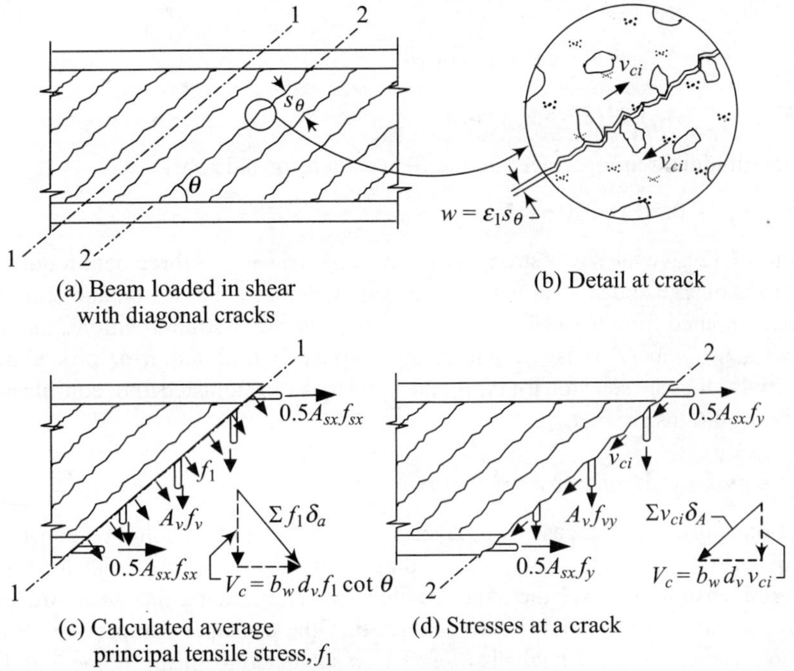

Fig. 17.5 Transmission of forces across diagonal cracks.

The strain in the longitudinal reinforcement also has its peak value at the crack location. Consider the stress patterns given in Figure 17.5. Equating the resultant horizontal force for the *average* stress condition along 1-1 (midway between cracks) shown at (c), and for the conditions at a diagonal crack along 2-2 shown at (d), if yielding of longitudinal bars at the crack is to be avoided,

$$A_{sx}f_y - v_{ci}b_w d_v \cot \theta \geq A_{sx}f_{sx} + b_w d_v f_1 \tag{17.13}$$

where A_{sx} is the *total area* of longitudinal steel (both at top and bottom included). When the transverse reinforcement yields at failure, the shear contribution V_c of the tensile stresses f_1 has to be maintained at the diagonal cracks by the transverse component of the interface shear v_{ci} [Figures 17.5(c) and (d)]. This condition gives:

$$V_c = f_1 b_w d_v \cot \theta = v_{ci} b_w d_v$$

that is, $$f_1 = v_{ci} \tan \theta \tag{17.14}$$

Expressing V_c in terms of β as in Eq. 17.10a, β may be expressed as:

$$V_c = \beta\sqrt{f_c'}\, b_w d_v \tag{17.15}$$

and, $$\beta = v_{ci}/\sqrt{f_c'} \tag{17.15a}$$

Equation 17.12 gives $A_{sx}f_{sx}$. Substituting these values in Eq. 17.13 and simplifying yields:

$$A_{sx}f_y \geq V \cot \theta + f_1 b_w d_v \cot^2 \theta \tag{17.16}$$

Substituting $V_c = f_1 b_w d_v \cot\theta$ from Eq. 17.10

$$A_{sx} f_y \geq V \cot\theta + V_c \cot\theta$$

With $V_c + V_s = V$, $\quad A_{sx} f_y \geq (2V - V_s) \cot\theta$

Considering the longitudinal reinforcement on the flexural tension side only,

$$A_s f_y \geq (V - 0.5V_s) \cot\theta \tag{17.17}$$

Equations 17.8 and 17.12 give the shear strength and the axial tensile reinforcement requirements in the case of pure shear in terms of f_1, θ and steel stress. If three parameters, such as ε_1, ε_2, and θ are known, f_1, f_2, and steel stress can be computed from the respective strains and the stress-strain relations, and the shear strength determined. Stresses f_1, f_2 and f_v must be within their limits. A trial-and-error procedure is presented in Ref. 17.1. In this, trial values are selected for ε_1, θ, and f_v and these are adjusted until equilibrium, compatibility, and limiting stress conditions are met.

(b) Shear with Bending Moment and Axial Force

The previous section considered the case of pure shear where the angle θ could be constant over the depth. In practice, shear occurs in combination with bending moment and, often, axial force as well. Bending moment and/or axial tension increases the axial tensile strain ε_x, reducing the shear strength. With bending moment, the longitudinal strain, ε_x, and the inclination θ of the principal compressive stress vary over the depth of the section. Hence, an exact analysis of a section subjected to shear, moment and axial force, with angle θ and strain ε_x varying over the depth, is very complex and laborious. Therefore, recourse is made to simplifications. One such procedure is to consider the stresses and strains at just one level in the beam depth and to calculate corresponding θ, which is then considered applicable for the entire depth. Again, a trial-and-error process is required for a solution. The strain profile over the depth (linear variation – plane section theory) and the value of θ are adjusted so that the stress limits are not exceeded and the internal stresses are in equilibrium with given bending moment, *M*, and axial force, *N*. Even such a procedure is unsuitable for normal design purposes and further simplifications are needed (see Section 17.2.5).

In Eq. 17.17 giving the longitudinal reinforcement required for shear on each side, including the stresses due to bending moment, *M*, and axial tension, *N*; to avoid yielding of the longitudinal reinforcement on the flexural tension side, we get:

$$A_s f_y \geq \frac{M}{d_v} + 0.5\,\mathrm{N} + (V - 0.5V_s) \cot\theta \tag{17.18}$$

17.2.5 Simplified Design Procedure using Modified Compression Field Theory (MCFT)

One of the simplifying assumptions made is that even under the combined effects of *M*, *V* and *N*, the inclination θ of the diagonal crack is uniform over the depth of the member and may be taken equal to that calculated at the mid-depth of the cross section. The free body diagram of a segment of the beam, separated by such a diagonal crack is idealized and shown in Figure 17.6(a). Considering the forces acting at the section, and taking V_c as the vertical component of the interface shear (see also Figure 17.5(d)), and V_s as the vertical forces in the stirrups crossing the crack, the shear resistance V_r is obtained (using Eqs. 17.9 and 17.10a) as:

$$V_r = V_c + V_s = b_w d_v \beta \sqrt{f_c'} + \frac{A_v d_v f_y}{s} \cot\theta \tag{17.19}$$

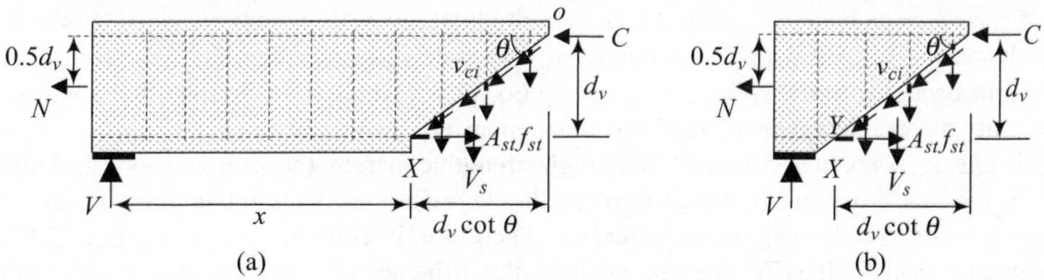

Fig. 17.6 Simplified model for shear resistance.

Factor β The factor β is needed to compute the part V_c. As explained earlier, β and θ depend on several factors. However, in the simplified procedure, all these effects are attempted to be accounted for with two critical parameters, namely the longitudinal strain (ε_x) and the effective (or equivalent) crack spacing (s_{ze}, see below). These two factors are used in the evaluation of, β and θ. [The larger ε_x, the wider the cracks and hence lower the interface shear and its contribution V_c.] It is further assumed that β and θ be based on the value of strain ε_x at mid-depth. Figure 17.7 shows the distribution of longitudinal strains ε_x due to M, V and N. As an approximation, and conservatively, taking the compressive strain close to the top fibre as zero (i.e., in Figure 17.7a, $\varepsilon_c = 0$), ε_x at mid-depth can be taken as one-half the strain at the flexural tensile reinforcement:

$$\varepsilon_x = \frac{M/d_v + 0.5\,V\cot\theta + 0.5N}{2\,A_s E_s} \tag{17.20}$$

$$\approx \frac{M/d_v + V + 0.5\,N}{2\,A_s E_s} \tag{17.21}$$

The simpler Eq. 17.21 is obtained assuming, conservatively, 0.5 cot $\theta \approx 1.0$, thereby making calculation of ε_x independent of θ, to eliminate iterations. If Eq. 17.21 gives a negative value for ε_x, it may be taken as zero. If reinforcement is not fully developed at the critical shear location the term A_s has to be reduced proportionally. Under high axial tension, ε_c may become tensile when either ε_x is calculated as $(\varepsilon_c + \varepsilon_t)/2$, or simply as ε_t.

Using Eq. 17.15(a), β can be determined if the interface shear, v_{ci} is known. However, the latter depends on numerous interacting factors as discussed earlier. Based on detailed analysis by MCFT and experimental results, and assuming an effective crack spacing s_{ze} = 300 mm, an approximate expression for crack width, w, is obtained as given in Eq. 17.22 [Ref. 17.4]. Substituting this w in Eq. 17.12(a) and taking maximum aggregate size as 20 mm, Eq. 17.23 gives the interface shear, v_{ci}.

$$w = 0.2 + 1000\varepsilon_x \tag{17.22}$$

$$v_{ci} = \frac{0.4\sqrt{f_c'}}{1 + 1500\varepsilon_x} \tag{17.23}$$

Introducing a size effect factor for equivalent crack spacing, s_{ze}, other than 300 mm, = 1300/(1000 + s_{ze}), and substituting in Eq. 17.15a, β is given by:

$$\beta = \frac{0.4}{1 + 1500\varepsilon_x}\left(\frac{1300}{1000 + s_{ze}}\right) \tag{17.24}$$

The aggregate interlock (and thereby V_c) depends on the crack width and hence on the crack spacing. The longitudinal spacing at mid-depth between transverse cracks is designated as the *crack spacing parameter*, s_z.

The value of s_z is taken as d_v, or where distributed longitudinal reinforcement is provided, as shown in Figure 17.7(a) whichever is less. Allowing for influence of aggregate size other than 20 mm, [factor $35/(15 + a_g)$] the *effective crack spacing parameter*, s_{ze}, is given by Eq. 17.25, where a_g is the specified nominal maximum size of coarse aggregate. However, s_{ze} shall not be taken as less than $0.85s_z$. For members containing at least minimum stirrups, s_{ze} is taken as 300 mm. With high strength concrete, the stronger paste around aggregates may result in the crack passing (cutting) through the aggregate particles rather than around them. Such smoother crack surfaces reduce aggregate interlock. Therefore, in computing V_c using Eq. 17.19, $\sqrt{f_c'}$ is not to be taken greater than 8 MPa. For the same reason, the influence of aggregate size is not significant with high strength concrete. Hence, it is recommended that in Eq. 17.25, a_g be reduced linearly from the specified size to zero as f_c' increases from 60 to 70 MPa, and taken as zero if f_c' exceeds 70 MPa.

$$s_{ze} = \frac{35s_z}{15 + a_g} \tag{17.25}$$

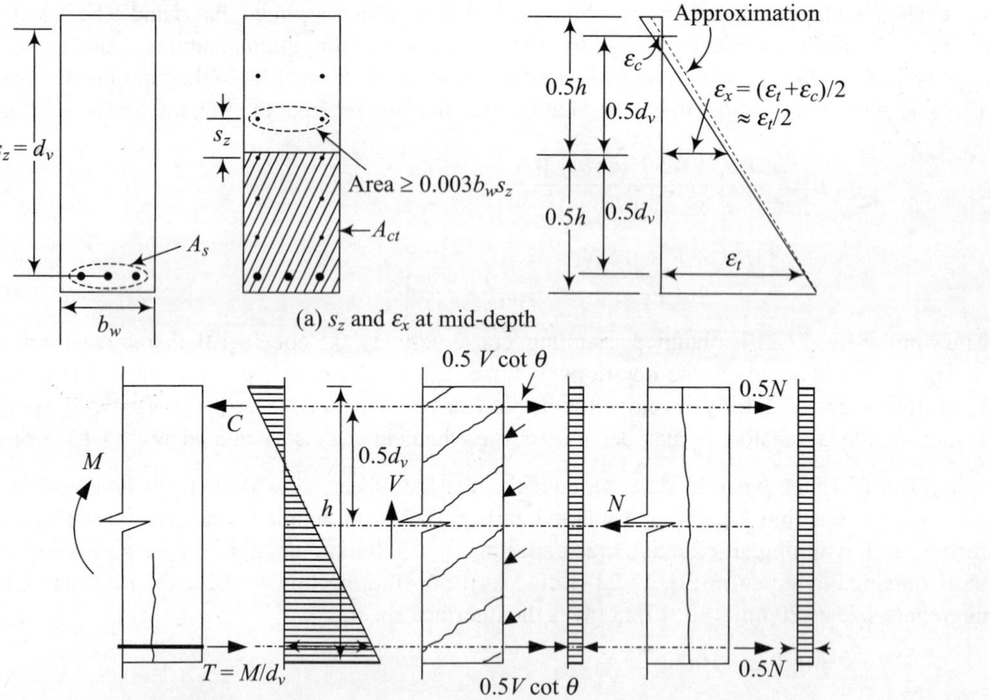

Fig. 17.7 Longitudinal strain at mid-depth.

Angle θ The shear strength component V_s is contributed by a combination of longitudinal and transverse reinforcements in tension and concrete diagonals in compression. In a truss, the diagonal member can be provided at different inclinations to carry a given loading, the change in angle influencing the magnitude of the forces in the members in the bay, mainly in the diagonal and vertical members. In the same way, the reinforced concrete member has the ability to resist shear with different possible inclinations of the compression diagonal. As shown in the next para, to avoid crushing of concrete in diagonal compression, the upper limit of nominal shear stress, $v = V/(b_w d_v)$, is $0.25f_c'$. If θ is too small, concrete crushes in diagonal compression before v reaches its limiting value. If θ is too large, the stirrups do not yield before shear failure. In order to avoid diagonal compression failure of concrete and ensure yielding of stirrups for the condition $v = 0.25f_c'$, the value of θ has been determined as [Ref. 17.4]:

$$\theta = 29° + 7000\varepsilon_x \tag{17.26}$$

Diagonal compression The stress in the compression diagonal, f_2, should be below the compressive strength of the cracked concrete. Equation 17.1 gives the value of $f_{2,max}$ in terms of the principal tensile strain ε_1. An approximate value for $f_{2,max}$ in the normal range of ε_1 is $f_{2,max} = 0.5\,f_c'$. Equation 17.5 gives f_2 in terms of applied shear, V, and the diagonal compressive stress limitation can be expressed as:

$$f_2 = \frac{V}{b_w d_v}(\tan\theta + \cot\theta) - f_1 \le 0.5\,f_c' \tag{17.27}$$

For normal range of θ values, $(\tan\theta + \cot\theta) \approx 2$, and f_1 being very small, this gives:

$$f_2 \approx \frac{2V}{b_w d_v} \le 0.5\,f_c' \tag{17.28}$$

that is,

$$\frac{V}{b_w d_v} \le 0.25\,f_c' \tag{17.29}$$

In deriving Eq. 17.29, an approximate value for $f_{2,max}$ was taken as $0.5f_c'$. A limiting value for $f_{2,max}$ can be obtained in another way. The value of ε_1 at yielding of transverse steel can be obtained by substituting $\varepsilon_t = \varepsilon_y = 0.002$ (assuming $f_y = 400$ MPa) in Eq. 17.2b. With this value for ε_1, Eq. 17.1 gives $f_{2,max}$ as:

$$f_{2,max} = \frac{f_c'}{1.14 + 0.68\tan^2\theta} \le 0.85\,f_c' \tag{17.29a}$$

Value of θ by MCFT is generally $< 45°$. Even (conservatively) with $\theta = 45°$, this gives $f_{2,max} = 0.55f_c'$, which is greater than the $0.5f_c'$ used above; and hence Eq. 17.29 above controls.

[Note that for the same V, members with inclined stirrups have smaller diagonal compressive stresses, f_2, than members with perpendicular stirrups, and hence can withstand higher shears prior to web crushing.]

Longitudinal reinforcement Equation 17.18 (alternatively, taking moments of all forces about point O in Figure 17.6) gives the force, F_{lt}, $(= A_{st}f_{st})$ to be resisted by the longitudinal reinforcement at location X on the flexural tension side:

$$F_{lt} = \frac{M}{d_v} + 0.5\,N + (V - 0.5V_s)\cot\theta \tag{17.30}$$

On the flexural compression side, the net tensile force, F_{lc}, is given by Eq. 17.31. However, usually this gives a negative value as the compression due to flexure exceeds the tension due to shear and axial force.

$$F_{lc} = 0.5\,N + (V - 0.5V_s)\cot\theta - \frac{M}{d_v} \tag{17.31}$$

Anchorage of longitudinal bars at end support At exterior simple supports, although the moment is zero, the longitudinal reinforcement on the flexural tension side has to carry tensile forces due to shear and axial force. Considering Figure 17.6(b) with the point X located at the inside edge of the bearing plate [compare Figure 6.10(b)], or from Eq. 17.30 with $M = 0$, this tensile force is obtained as:

$$F_{lt} = (V - 0.5V_s)\cot\theta + 0.5N \tag{17.31a}$$

Here, V_s is based on the transverse reinforcement provided within the length $d_v \cot\theta$ from the face of support, but need not be taken greater than V. The tension reinforcement should develop this force ($= F_{lt}$) at the point Y [Figure 17.6(b)] where it is intercepted by the potential crack line originating at the inside edge of the bearing area and inclined at angle θ.

Design procedure Shear design involves checking the adequacy of the size of section selected from considerations of flexure and axial loads, and computing the required transverse shear reinforcement and the additional longitudinal reinforcement to carry the applied shear. All the necessary equations for shear design have been developed above. These give *nominal* strengths and to get *factored* values, *resistance factors*, ϕ_c and ϕ_s, have to be applied to steel and concrete strengths. The equations are in terms of two parameters, β and θ. These two can be evaluated from the longitudinal strain ε_x at mid depth and the effective crack spacing parameter s_{ze}. The steps involved are:

(i) Equation 17.29 checks the adequacy of the section in order to limit the diagonal compressive stress in concrete to within limits.

(ii) The nominal shear strength of the section is given by $V = V_c + V_s$, where V_c is the part attributed to concrete and V_s the part contributed by transverse reinforcement. To evaluate these, values of β and θ are needed. For this,

(iii) Compute ε_x and s_{ze} using Eqs. 17.21 and 17.25. With these known,

(iv) Evaluate parameters β and θ with Eqs. 17.24 and 17.26.

(v) Equation 17.15 gives V_c in terms of β; and V_s is given by Eq. 17.9 for vertical stirrups and Eq. 17.9a for inclined stirrups, both in terms of θ.

(vi) Longitudinal steel and their anchorage requirement at support are given by Eqs. 17.30, 17.31 and 17.31a.

17.2.6 CSA Code Provisions for Shear Design

The Canadian Code CSA A23.3-84 first introduced Compression Field Theory for shear design in 1984 as a *General Method*, while retaining the traditional method based on truss model as a *Simplified Method*. Since then, updated versions of the former were included in the Code revisions of 1994, 2004 and 2014 and from 2004 the latter method has been dropped. As one of the first Codes to introduce MCFT, it would be helpful to look at the major provisions in CSA A23.3-14 on shear design by MCFT.

For shear and torsion design of flexural regions, this Code follows the Equations listed in the summary above and developed mostly in Section 17.2.5. The various load and resistance factors are also incorporated. The controlling design equation is:

$$V_r = V_c + V_s \geq V_f \tag{17.32}$$

where, V_r is the factored shear resistance,

V_c is the factored shear resistance attributed to concrete,

V_s is the factored shear resistance provided by the shear reinforcement,

V_f is the factored shear force at the section, and

$$V_c = \lambda\phi_c\beta\sqrt{f_c'}b_w d_v \tag{17.33}$$

For stirrups perpendicular to beam axis:

$$V_s = \frac{A_v\phi_s f_y d_v \cot\theta}{s} \tag{17.34}$$

For transverse reinforcement inclined at an angle a to the longitudinal axis,

$$V_s = \frac{A_v\phi_s f_y d_v(\cot\theta + \cot\alpha)\sin\alpha}{s} \tag{17.35}$$

In the above equations, f_c' is the specified cylinder strength of concrete, ϕ_c (= 0.65) is the material resistance factor for concrete strength in checking for ULS, ϕ_s (= 0.85) is the factor for reinforcing bars and λ is a factor to account for low density concrete.

To limit the diagonal compressive stress to the compressive strength of cracked concrete, V_r is limited to (Eq. 17.29):

$$V_r \le 0.25\phi_c f_c' b_w d_v \tag{17.36}$$

The general requirements for shear reinforcements similar to those given in Chapter 6, such as types, anchorage, minimum required, spacing limitations, etc., are applicable here too (Note that these, in CSA Code are somewhat different from IS Code provisions, and are note detailed fully here). Thus, a minimum area of transverse reinforcement as given by Eq. 17.37 is provided in regions where (a) the factored shear force V_f exceeds V_c, (b) the overall depth of the beam exceeds 750 mm, and (c) the factored torsion T_f exceeds 0.25 T_{cr}, where T_{cr} is the pure torsional cracking resistance given by Eq. 17.38 (Eq. 7.11a with τ taken = $0.38\sqrt{f_c'}$, a lower bound value for concrete stress at cracking).

$$A_{v,\min} = 0.06\sqrt{f_c'}\frac{b_w s}{f_y} \tag{17.37}$$

$$T_{cr} = (A_c^2/p_c)\,0.38\lambda\phi_c\sqrt{f_c'} \tag{17.38}$$

Determination of β and θ For the evaluation of shear strength, the parameters β and θ must be determined. For this, different procedures are presented in the Code. For certain *Special Member Types*, including thin slabs and footings with thickness not greater than 350 mm or beams not thicker than 250 mm, the Code permits β to be taken as 0.21 and θ as 42°. For members meeting certain limitations, a *Simplified Method* (see below) may be used, in lieu of the general method. For members subjected to significant axial tension, β and θ is determined using the *General Method* (see below).

Simplified Method for β and θ This is applicable where the member is not subjected to *significant* axial tension, the specified yield strength of the longitudinal reinforcement does not exceed 400 MPa, and the concrete strength does not exceed 60 MPa. In such cases, θ is taken as 35° and β is determined as given below.

Axial tension is considered 'significant' if it is large enough to crack the flexural compression face of the member, or large enough to cause an increase in stress of over 50 MPa in the flexural tension reinforcement. With 400 MPa grade reinforcement, ε_x at mid-depth is $\approx f_y/(2E_s) \approx 1.0 \times 10^{-3}$ corresponding to flexural tensile failure. A value of 0.85×10^{-3} is recommended for ε_x. With this, Eq. 17.26 gives $\theta = 35°$. Substituting for ε_x in Eq. 17.24 and taking $s_{ze} = d_v$, a simple expression for β is obtained as:

$$\beta = 230/(1000 + d_v) \tag{17.39}$$

Code recommends that β be determined as follows:

(a) If the section contains at least the minimum transverse reinforcement as given by Eq. 17.37, then β may be taken as 0.18;

(b) If the section contains no transverse reinforcement and the specified nominal maximum size of coarse aggregate is not less than 20 mm, then use Eq. 17.39:

(c) Alternatively, value of β for sections containing no transverse reinforcement may be determined for all aggregate sizes by replacing the parameter d_v in Eq. 17.39 by the equivalent crack spacing parameter s_{ze} (Eq. 17.25)

$$s_{ze} = 35s_z/(15 + a_g) \geq 0.85s_z \tag{17.40}$$

where s_z is the crack spacing parameter and a_g is the specified nominal maximum size of coarse aggregate. Parameter s_z is taken as d_v or as the maximum distance between layers of distributed longitudinal reinforcement (Figure 17.7a), whichever is less. Each layer of such reinforcement shall have an area at least equal to $0.003b_w s_z$ (see Figure 17.7).

General Method for β and θ In the general method, the Code specifies that the values of β and θ be determined by Eqs. 17.41 and 17.42 (see Eqs. 17.24 and 17.26 derived above).

$$\beta = \frac{0.40}{(1+1500\varepsilon_x)} \times \frac{1300}{(1000+s_{ze})} \tag{17.41}$$

$$\theta = 29° + 7000\varepsilon_x \tag{17.42}$$

where ε_x is the longitudinal strain at mid-depth of the member (Figure 17.7) due to factored loads, taken positive when tensile and s_{ze} is the equivalent crack spacing parameter. For sections containing at least the minimum transverse reinforcement specified (Eq. 17.37), $s_{ze} = 300$ mm. In other cases, s_{ze} is computed using Eq. 17.40. If f_c' exceeds 70 MPa, a_g in Eq. 17.40 = 0. As f_c' increases from 60 MPa to 70 MPa, a_g reduces linearly to zero.

In lieu of more accurate calculations (Figure 17.7), ε_x may be computed from:

$$\varepsilon_x = \frac{M_f/d_v + V_f + 0.5N_f}{2E_s A_s} \tag{17.43}$$

In Eq. 17.43 (compare Eq. 17.21 above), V_f and M_f are taken as positive, and M_f must be greater than $V_f d_v$. In computing A_s, the area of bars terminated at less than their development length for a given section is reduced in proportion to the shortage in their full development length. If longitudinal bars are terminated in a flexural tension zone, at the cutoff location, ε_x given by Eq. 17.43 must be increased by 50%. If ε_x calculated using Eq. 17.43 is negative, it is taken as zero. Alternatively, ε_x needs to be recalculated with the denominator in Eq. 17.43 taken as $2(E_s A_s + E_c A_{ct})$; however, the resulting ε_x cannot be less than –0.0002. Here A_{ct} is the area of concrete on flexural tension side of the member, as shown in Figure 17.7. The Code also permits the evaluation of β and θ for sections closer than d_v to the face of the support, using values of ε_x calculated at d_v from the face of the support. Where the axial tension is large enough to cause cracking at the compression face of the section, the corresponding increase in ε_x must be taken into account. As an approximation, the Code recommends that in such cases ε_x calculated using Eq. 17.43 be doubled. In Eqs. 17.41 and 17.42, it is permissible to use a value of ε_x greater than that given by Eq. 17.43, provided that ε_x is not greater than 0.003.

Longitudinal reinforcement At every section, longitudinal reinforcement is to be designed for the combined effects of flexure, axial load and shear (see Eq. 17.30). Accordingly, at all sections on the flexural tension side, the factored resistance of the reinforcement (= $\phi_s A_{lt} f_s$) taking account of the stress (= f_s) that can be developed in this reinforcement, shall be greater than F_{lt} given by:

$$\phi_s A_{lt} f_s \geq F_{lt} = M_f / d_v + 0.5N_f + (V_f - 0.5V_s) \cot \theta \tag{17.44}$$

where M_f and V_f are taken as positive, and N_f positive if in tension and negative if in compression. In Eq. 17.44, V_s shall not be taken greater than V_f and d_v may be taken as the flexural lever arm corresponding to the factored moment resistance.

If in Eq. 17.44 the term M_f/d_v is less than the sum of the terms accounting for shear and axial force, longitudinal reinforcement is required on the flexural compression side as well. The factored tensile resistance of this reinforcement, with the stress that can be developed in it, must be greater than F_{lc} given by Eq. 17.45 (see also Eq. 17.31). In Eq. 17.45 also, V_s shall not be taken greater than V_f.

$$\phi_s A_{lc} f_s \geq F_{lc} = 0.5N_f + (V_f - 0.5V_s) \cot \theta - M_f / d_v \tag{17.45}$$

In Eqs. 17.44 and 17.45,

A_{lc} = area of longitudinal reinforcement on flexural compression side
A_{lt} = area of longitudinal reinforcement on flexural tension side
d_v = effective shear depth, taken as the greater of $0.9d$ or $0.72h$ in shear design; but in Eqs 17.44 and 17.45, may be taken as the flexural lever arm corresponding to the factored moment resistance M_r
F_{lc} = required tension force in longitudinal reinforcement in flexural compression side
F_{lt} = required tension force in longitudinal reinforcement in flexural tension side
M_f = factored bending moment
N_f = factored axial load, taken as positive for tension
V_f = factored shear force
V_s = shear resistance provided by shear reinforcement factored by ϕ_s

In the case of members *not* subjected to significant axial tension or significant torsion, Eqs. 17.44 and 17.45 may be satisfied by extending the flexural tension reinforcement by $d_v \cot \theta$ beyond the location needed for flexure alone [compare with Figure 6.10(a)]. Also, as shown by Eq. 17.31a, the bottom longitudinal reinforcement must resist a tensile force T at the inside edge of the bearing area [Figure 17.6(b)] given by:

$$T = (V_f - 0.5V_s) \cot \theta + 0.5N_f \tag{17.46}$$

where V_s is based on the transverse reinforcement provided within a length of $d_v \cot \theta$ from the face of the support, provided that V_s is not greater than V_f.

17.2.7 Combined Shear and Torsion

The shear stress due to torsion and the shear stress due to transverse shear are additive on one side of the cross section and they counteract on the opposite side. The transverse reinforcement is designed considering the side where the stresses are additive. Hence, the transverse reinforcement required may be taken as the sum of that required for the shear and for the coexisting torsion. The equations presented in Section 17.2.5 above are used to compute the area of transverse reinforcement required for shear. Equations based on the *space truss analogy,* with cracks making an angle θ with the longitudinal axis, and assuming that cracked concrete carries no tension, are used for the computation of the transverse reinforcement required for torsion [see Section 7.4.2 and Figure 7.6]. On this basis, the factored torsional resistance of the section, T_r, is given by [see Eq. 7.14a and Figure 7.6]:

$$T_r = 2A_o \frac{\phi_s A_t f_y}{s} \cot\theta \tag{17.47}$$

Here A_t is the area of one leg of *closed* transverse *torsion* reinforcement placed at spacing s. The area enclosed by shear flow path, A_o, may be taken as $0.85A_{oh}$, where A_{oh} is the area enclosed by centerline of exterior closed transverse torsion reinforcement. Angle θ is computed as described in Section 17.2.6. However, when θ and β are determined by the General Method using Eqs. 17.41 to 17.43, to include torsion effects, the value of ε_x should be computed by replacing the term V_f in Eq. 17.43 by the expression:

$$\sqrt{V_f^2 + \left(\frac{0.9 p_h T_f}{2A_0}\right)^2} \tag{17.48}$$

The cross-section dimensions should be adequate to avoid crushing failure of concrete in diagonal compression. This is achieved by restricting the nominal shear stress due to combined shear and torsion. For thin-walled tubular sections, the torsional shear is uniform over the thickness [Chapter 7] and additive with the stress due to transverse shear on one face. Hence, for box type sections, to avoid crushing failure in diagonal compression, the section size shall be such that:

$$\frac{V_f}{b_w d_v} + \frac{T_f p_h}{1.7A_{oh}^2} \le 0.25\phi_c f_c' \tag{17.49}$$

If the wall thickness, t, of the tubular section is less than A_{oh}/p_h, the second term in Eq. 17.49 is replaced with $T_u/(1.7A_{oh}t)$. Note that the nominal shear stress due to pure torsion, based on the *space truss analogy*, is $T_u p_h / A_{oh}{}^2$. However, for pure torsion, the limiting value of diagonal compressive stress is much higher than $0.25\phi_c f_c'$ and is closer to 1.7 times $0.25\phi_c f_c'$ and hence the factor 1.7 in the denominator of the second term of Eq. 17.49 (and Eq. 7.50 below). For other cross-sectional shapes, such as a solid rectangle, torsional shear stress varies over the section from zero to a maximum, with the possibility for considerable redistribution. Allowing for this, a 'root-mean-square' approach is taken, and to avoid crushing failure, the section size shall be such that:

$$\sqrt{\left(\frac{V_f}{b_w d_v}\right)^2 + \left(\frac{T_f p_h}{1.7A_{oh}^2}\right)^2} \le 0.25\phi_c f_c' \tag{17.50}$$

Similarly, to allow for torsion also, the longitudinal reinforcement is proportioned using Eqs. 17.44 and 17.45 with $(V_u - 0.5V_s)$ replaced with the expression in Eq. 17.51.

$$\sqrt{(V_f - 0.5V_s)^2 + \left(\frac{0.45 p_h T_f}{2A_0}\right)^2} \tag{17.51}$$

In calculating stirrup spacing, care must be taken in combining the reinforcement areas required for shear (the A_v/s term in Eq. 17.34) and for torsion (the A_t/s from Eq. 17.47). With closed two-legged stirrups made up of bars having area A_b, the A_v provided (for shear) will be $2A_b$, whereas with the same stirrup for torsion, area A_t provided = A_b. Under combined loading, spacing, s, of closed stirrups must be chosen so that:

$$\frac{A_b}{s} \geq 0.5\frac{A_v}{s} + \frac{A_t}{s} \tag{17.52}$$

17.3 Design Using Strut-and-Tie Model

The regions in reinforced concrete members may be classified as 'B' regions and 'D' regions, where 'B' stands for Beam or Bernoulli and 'D' stands for Discontinuity or Disturbed [Ref. 17.5]. In 'B' regions, the assumption of plane section remaining plane after bending (Bernoulli hypothesis) is considered to be valid, and hence they can be analysed and designed for the resulting stresses with accuracy by traditional sectional methods of design (theory of flexure). In these regions, it is sufficient to consider the effect of the resultant forces (bending moment, shear force, axial force and torsion) acting at any cross-section of the RC beam or column. In contrast, 'D' regions are regions where Bernoulli hypothesis is not valid, and hence traditional methods of design based on flexure theory cannot be strictly used. The 'D' regions occur in RC members due to the presence of concentrated loads (load discontinuity) or sudden changes in cross-sectional dimensions (geometric discontinuity), and cause changes (disturbances) in the stress distribution. For example, in the beam shown in Figure 17.8 (assuming the material to be homogeneous and section to be rectangular), as per elastic theory of flexure, the shear force in the beam cross section at the left support (which is equal to the support reaction) should be *distributed over the depth of the section parabolically*. However, in reality, a force equal to the aggregate shear force over this cross section is applied as a *vertical reaction at the bottom surface*. This replacement, though statically equivalent, will cause changes ('Disturbances') in the stress distribution in the beam locally. Similar is the case at locations of the concentrated load and the support reaction at right or, in general, at other discontinuity (load or geometric) regions. However, as per St. Venant's principle†, such disturbances in the stress field caused by a load or geometric discontinuity ('D' regions) are limited to a distance approximately equal to the member depth, h, from the discontinuity location. Beyond a distance h from the discontinuity, flexure theory would hold good and those portions of the member can be treated as 'B' regions. Thus, Figure 17.8 shows 'B' and 'D' regions of a simply supported beam subjected to

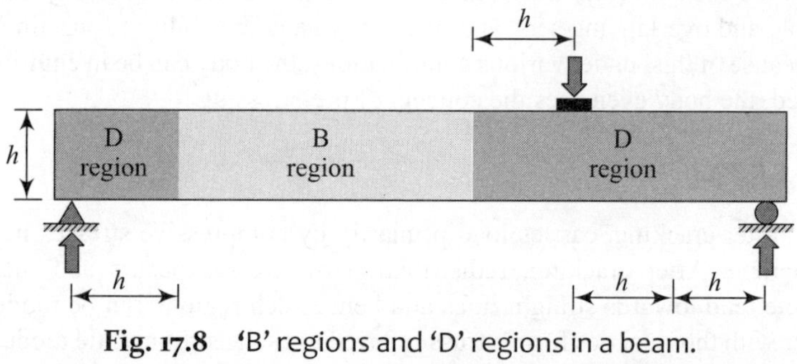

Fig. 17.8 'B' regions and 'D' regions in a beam.

† The *principle of Saint-Venant* states that if the forces acting on a small portion of the surface of an elastic body are replaced by another statically equivalent system of forces acting on the same portion of the surface, this redistribution of loading produces substantial changes in the stresses locally but has a negligible effect on the stresses at distances which are large in comparison with the linear dimensions of the surface on which the forces are changed [Ref. 4.1 – Timoshenko and Goodier: Theory of Elasticity].

a concentrated load. The left shear span (Figure 17.8) includes D-regions, but this region can be conservatively designed using traditional methods of shear and flexure. The right shear span consists of entirely 'D' region where the deep beam action is present. In deep members, the load is primarily transmitted to the supports by strut action along with tie action. Hence it is necessary to study the manner in which the load gets transmitted to the supports. Strut-and-tie is a versatile method to design and detail 'D' regions in RC members.

While D-regions have to be designed by the strut-and-tie method only, the concept and procedure are more universal, and can be used for design in general, including B-regions.

Strut-and-tie method (STM) involves idealising the structural component or part forming the 'D' region as a hypothetical pin-jointed planar or three-dimensional truss (strut-and-tie model) consisting of steel tensile ties and concrete compressive struts, connected at the nodes capable of transferring the loads to the supports or adjacent 'B' regions [Ref. 17.5]. The strut-and-tie method considers the effects of bending moment, shear force, torsion and axial force simultaneously. The strut-and-tie model for a deep beam, subject to two concentrated loads symmetrically located, is shown in Figure 17.9. The method assumes that the regions other than struts, ties and nodes, are ineffective in resisting loads.

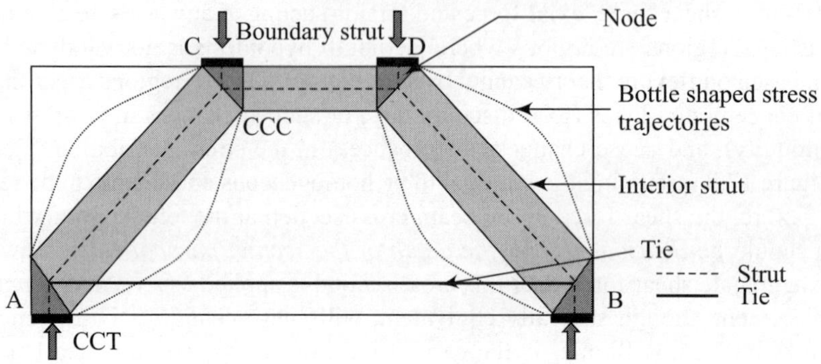

Fig. 17.9 Strut-and-tie model for a deep beam subject to concentrated loads (symmetrically located).

Interestingly, a remarkable example of a strut-and-tie structure is the human body (or for that matter, most vertebrates). In simple terms, it comprises a series of struts in the form of bones interconnected by a series of ties formed by muscular tendons. Without the muscular tendons (the ties), the skeleton would collapse as a set of bones, and without the skeleton (the strut), again we are a heap of flesh! In reality, the tie network is more complex with multiple and overlapping sets, and often they have the ability to sustain compression as well, like a stiff spring. Because of this, under various combinations, the body can be in equilibrium in innumerable configurations. Indeed, the body even uses the concept of pre-stressing†:

17.3.1 Basis of STM

Reinforced concrete, after cracking, carries load primarily by compressive stresses in concrete and tensile stresses in reinforcement. After cracking, redistribution of stresses occurs and the compressive stress trajectories in concrete tend towards straight lines and hence such regions can be modelled as compression struts which, together with the steel ties form a truss referred to as the strut-and-tie model. Based on plasticity theory, which states that any statically admissible stress field that is in equilibrium and in which stress

† For example, when an acrobat pulls himself up holding a cross bar, the muscles crossing the shoulder joints and anchored on either side, contract and introduce a pre-compression on the ball-and-socket type shoulder joints so that the tension applied on the joints due to the weight of body lifted is compensated and there is no danger of pull out at the joint – that is, most of the time!

levels are within the material yield surface, constitutes a lower bound solution [Ref. 17.6], STM provides a lower bound solution. Therefore, the strength obtained from STM is always lower than the member's actual strength, provided the following conditions are satisfied: (a) the chosen truss is in equilibrium, (b) the stresses in concrete and steel are within limits, and (c) plastic material behaviour is ensured. The plasticity theory assumes a rigid-plastic behaviour and this is valid only when the total strains are much higher than the elastic strain [Ref. 17.6]. As concrete is not an elastic-perfectly plastic material, this assumption is valid for beams where yielding of steel occurs before the final failure of the member. This can be ensured by providing sufficient crack control reinforcement thereby preventing the premature diagonal tension failure of the strut. The reinforcement should also be properly detailed to enhance the strain limits of concrete and to prevent local bond or anchorage failure.

17.3.2 Selection of Strut-and-Tie Model

The strut-and-tie model may be chosen by aligning the struts and ties approximately along the elastic compressive and tensile stress fields respectively. Figure 17.10 shows some examples of strut-and-tie models in commonly occurring 'D' regions like beam-column joints, corbel, dapped beam and pile cap. Bridge pier caps are similar to corbels and can be designed using strut-and-tie method [Ref. 17.7, 17.8]. More examples are demonstrated in SP-202 [Ref. 17.9], SP-273 [Ref. 17.10] and *fib* bulletin 61 [Ref. 17.11]. It may be noted that in some cases, more than one model can be conceived.

More than one strut-and-tie configurations are possible for modelling a given problem. Usually, the model with the most direct load path to supports and relatively large angles between strut and tie at nodes will be more efficient.

Selecting the optimum strut and tie model out of the available ones is important. The optimal arrangement would have the members carry the loads with the least forces and deformations possible. From the principle of minimum strain energy for linear elastic behaviour of the struts and ties (after cracking) and assuming the steel ties to be more deformable than concrete struts, the condition in Eq. 17.53 may be used to choose the right strut-and-tie model.

$$\Sigma T_i l_i = \text{Minimum} \tag{17.53}$$

where T_i is the tie force in and l_i the length of the member i. This indicates that a model with the lowest number of ties, tie forces and tie lengths may be adopted. For example, in a deep beam with shear span to depth ratio less than 2, a direct strut model as shown in Figure 17.9 is optimum. However, if shear span to depth ratio is greater than 2, a truss model with vertical ties is preferable. In such situations, a design based on sectional methods based on shear design provision of the code is appropriate. The selection of the model should also consider the anchorage constraints for the reinforcement and constructability of the design [Ref. 17.5]. A statically determinate strut-and-tie model is generally preferred over an indeterminate one because of the ease in evaluation of member forces.

17.3.3 Elements of a Strut-and-Tie Model

The STM is an idealized truss made up of three types of elements (see Figure 17.9), namely (i) *struts* – the compression members made of concrete, (ii) *ties* – the tension members comprising the reinforcing steel, and (iii) *nodes* – the regions where the members of the truss meet, similar to joints in trusses. Distributed loads are idealized as a series of concentrated loads applied at nodes.

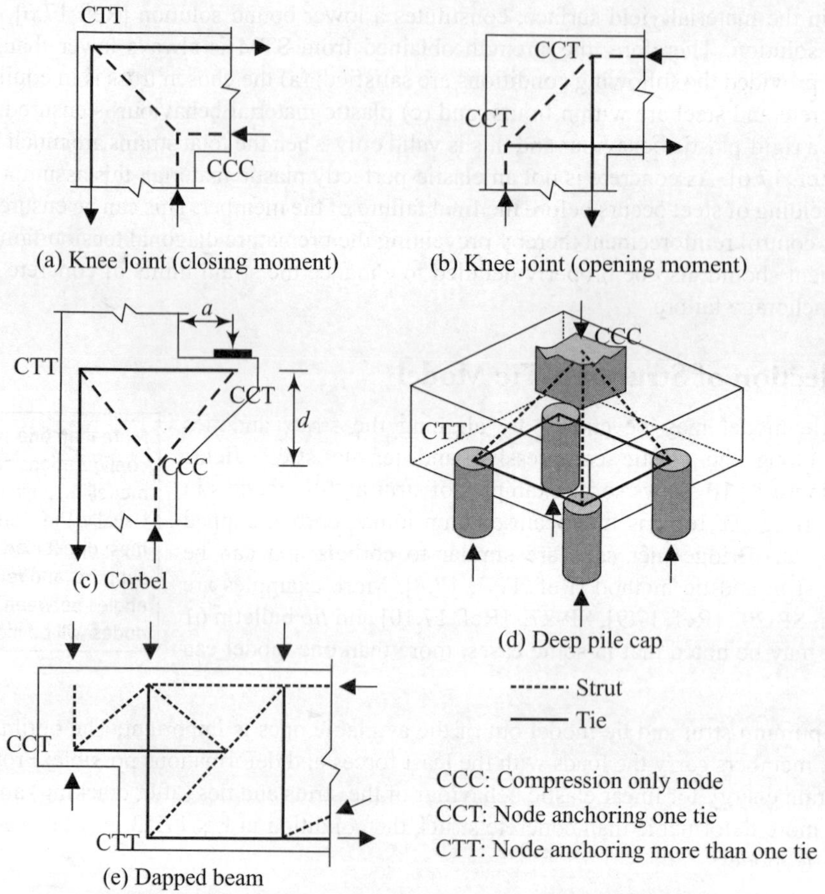

Fig. 17.10 Some examples of strut-and-tie models.

Struts can be classified as 'prismatic', 'fan-shaped' or 'bottle shaped', based on the stress flow within the strut. Struts are usually idealised as prismatic compression members. Boundary struts such as CD in Figure 17.9 may have uniform cross-sections. If the sectional area of a strut differs at the two ends, it is considered as uniformly tapered (strut AC in Figure 17.9). The stress distribution across the cross section of a strut may be assumed to be uniform so that the member force will act along the member centreline. The fan type strut is formed when there is spread of stress flow from a large area to a smaller area as in the diagonal struts in a deep beam subjected to uniformly distributed load or in a wall footing. Bottle shaped struts (interior strut AC in Figure 17.9) occurs when the ends of the struts are bounded usually by bearing plates. Here, the compression stress trajectories tend to spread out transversely from the ends towards the middle and take the shape of a bottle. This bulging of stress trajectories causes transverse tension which can lead to cracking in the direction of the strut. Usually bottle shaped struts are idealised as prismatic struts for convenience and distributed reinforcement is provided to take care of the transverse tension that develops in these struts. For deep beams the crack control reinforcement is provided as an orthogonal mesh. In corbels, as the shear span to depth (a/d) ratios are small (Figure 17.10(c)), horizontal links may be provided as crack control reinforcement. Struts can intersect or overlap only at nodes.

Ties are the tension members in the strut-and-tie model and consist of the reinforcing (or prestressing) steel. These reinforcements may consist of several bars placed in one or more layers, but in the model, they are represented by a single tie having the same total area and centroid. Usually, the surrounding concrete concentric with the axis of the tie is also included in order to delineate the anchorage zone in which tie reinforcements are to be anchored, however the tensile strength of this concrete is ignored. It is important to provide the tie with the required anchorage in or beyond the nodal zones to ensure its yielding, and for the ductility of the structural member. Often nodal regions are small and may not be enough to provide full development length and it may be necessary to increase the dimensions of the member just to provide the required development length. Hooks or mechanical anchorages may also be used. By spreading the tie reinforcement in several layers, the effective area of the nodal zone and hence the anchorage zone can be increased.

Nodal regions are the areas where the truss members meet. As with a pin-jointed truss, all member forces, loads and reactions meeting at a node must form a system of concurrent forces. A node region is bounded by sections of the members meeting at the node and the load or reaction bearing area, if any. Concrete in the nodal zone is subjected to multidirectional compression, with some tensile strains as well in cases where a tie also meet. These regions are generally subject to high stress concentration and a strength check at node faces is warranted to avoid localised failures. The allowable compressive stress in these regions is dependent on the bearing size, degree of confinement and the adverse effects of tensile straining caused by anchoring of tension ties in this region, if any.

In practice, nodes are classified into three major types based on the nature of the forces (Compression or Tension) acting on it: CCC, CCT and CTT nodes. A CCC node anchors three or more struts, with no connecting tie member. If one of the connecting members is a tie, the node is called CCT node. A CTT node anchors at least two ties. The strength of the node depends on the node type. A lower strength is expected for a node where ties are anchored when compared to pure compression node as the strength of concrete is adversely affected by the presence of tension. The types of nodes are shown in Figures 17.9 and 17.10.

It is necessary to dimension the nodal regions for the purpose of checking stresses at node faces and the adjoining struts. The dimensioning of nodes is generally based on the actual stress state considering the stress concentration at the nodes, and also depends on the size of bearing and location and distribution of tie reinforcement (for CCT, CTT nodes), referred to nonhydrostatic proportioning. The node dimensioning of typical CCC, CCT and CTT node are shown in Figure 17.11. The strut width may then be evaluated from geometry (Figure 17.11). Suitable assumptions may be made to obtain the node dimension depending on the problem type. [It may be noted that the effective area of the node region can be increased (and the stresses in the region reduced) by increasing the size of the bearing plates, and by increasing the effective anchorage area of tension ties (wider distribution of tie reinforcement).]

In some cases, it may be necessary to divide a node into two parts to dimension the node (and thereby the struts) correctly. For example, in a simply supported beam subject to a single concentrated load as shown in Figure 17.12, the nodal zone of node A may be divided for dimensioning the node and struts correctly. The single concentrated load is considered as two loads of different magnitudes depending on the fraction of load getting transmitted to each of the two supports. The bearing length share of each part is evaluated by keeping the pressure acting on these two faces same. This way, the strut AC, which carries a higher force gets a proportionately higher width. In some cases, where four or more strut or ties meet at a node, then forces may have to be resolved appropriately based on vector summation for the purpose of dimensioning the node [Ref. 17.5].

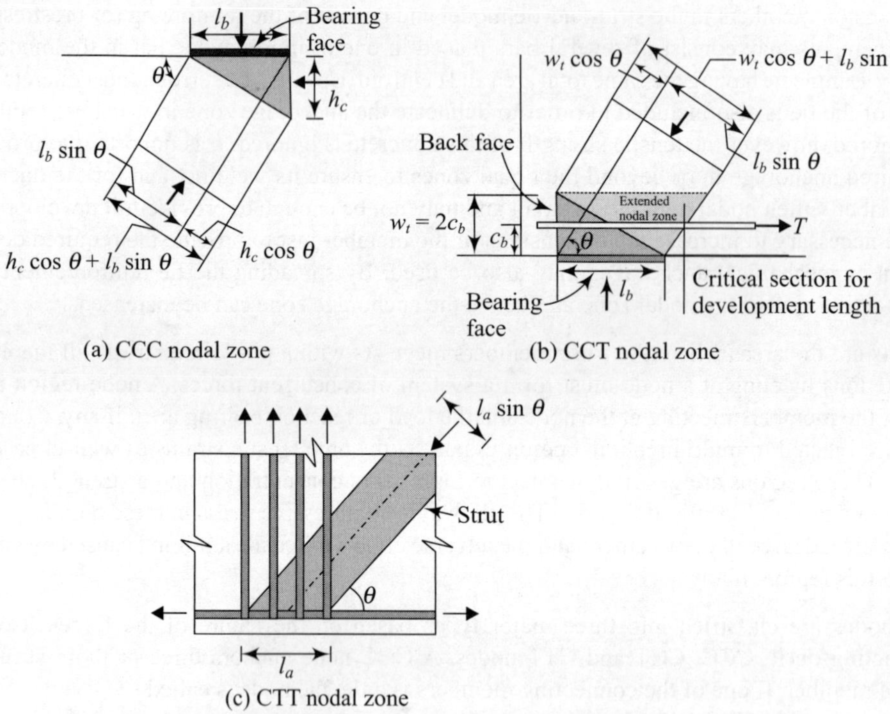

Fig. 17.11 Proportioning of nodes.

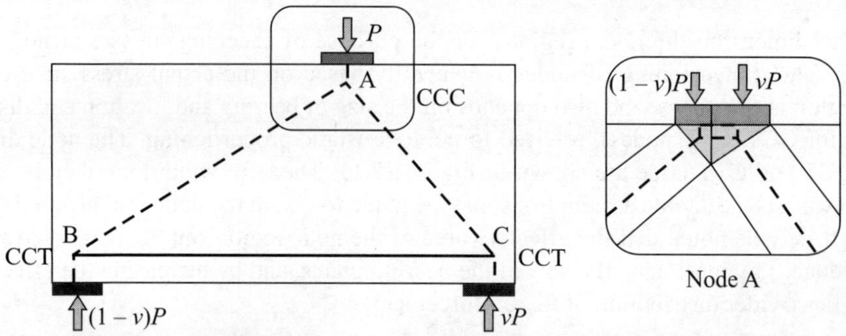

Fig. 17.12 Subdivision of node for proportioning nodal zone.

17.3.4 Members Subject to Unequal and Asymmetric Loads

The ideal strut-and-tie model for a beam with unequal or unsymmetrically applied concentrated loads has the same shape as the bending-moment diagram [Ref. 17.12]. Figure 17.13 shows a simply supported beam subject to two loading conditions: (a) two concentrated loads of magnitudes P and $2P$ symmetrically located and (b) two concentrated loads each with magnitude P located asymmetrically. From the bending moment diagrams, it is evident that the strut-and-tie models will be asymmetric with strut BC inclined as shown in Figure 17.13 for satisfying equilibrium (unless a triangulated truss model is adopted). The strut-and-tie model for these load cases with inclined strut BC could be established experimentally and the failure load is found to depend only on the shear span to depth ratio and the shear force in the failure span [Ref. 17.13, 17.7].

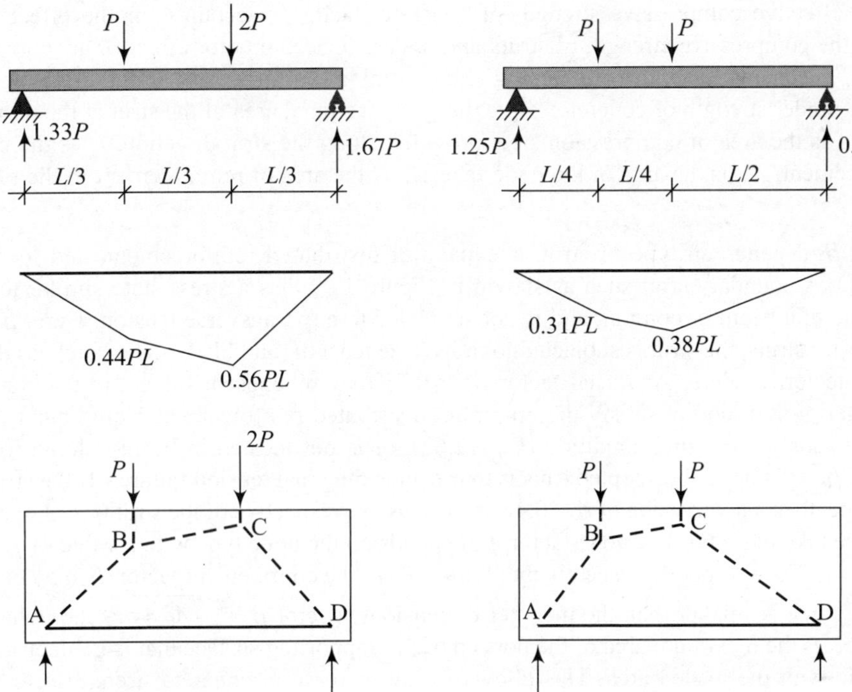

(a) Unequal load case (b) Asymmetric load case

Fig. 17.13 Strut-and-tie models from the shape of the bending moment diagrams.

17.3.5 ACI-318 2019 Provisions

Although IS 456:2000 (Cl. 28) recommends the strut-and-tie model for design of corbels, no guidelines are given for determination of concrete strut and node dimensions and for the allowable stresses. Hence, ACI-318 2019 [Ref. 17.14] strut and tie provisions are discussed here.

ACI-318 requires that the struts, ties and nodal zones have sufficient strength and shall satisfy the conditions in Eq. 17.54.

$$\text{Struts: } \phi F_{ns} \geq F_{us};\ \text{Ties: } \phi F_{nt} \geq F_{ut};\ \text{Nodes: } \phi F_{nn} \geq F_{un} \tag{17.54}$$

where F_{us}, F_{ut} and F_{un} represent the ultimate force in struts, ties and node faces respectively; ϕ is the resistance factor taken as 0.75 for the strut-and-tie method; and F_{ns}, F_{nt} and F_{nn} represent the nominal strength of the struts, ties and node faces respectively, which may be calculated from permissible stresses as follows:

Strut: $$F_{ns} = f_{ce}A_{cs} + A_s'f_s' \tag{17.55}$$

$$f_{ce} = 0.85\beta_s\beta_c f_c' \tag{17.56}$$

Node: $$F_{nn} = f_{ce}A_{nz} \tag{17.57}$$

$$f_{ce} = 0.85\beta_n\beta_c f_c' \tag{17.58}$$

Tie: $$F_{nt} = A_{ts}f_y \tag{17.59}$$

where f_{ce} is the effective compressive strength of concrete; factor β_c accounts for the effect of concrete confinement on the compressive strength of struts and nodes; β_n accounts for effect of anchorage of ties in the nodal zone; β_s accounts for effect of cracking and confining reinforcement on the effective strength of struts; f_c' is the cylinder strength of concrete; A_{cs} is the cross sectional area of the strut at the strut end under consideration; A_s' is the area of compression steel provided along the strut direction, f_s' is the compressive stress in reinforcement, A_{nz} is the area of the node face, A_{ts} is the area of reinforcement in the tie with yield stress f_y.

The strut factor β_s depends on type of strut, adequacy of distributed reinforcement, and location of the strut (Table 17.1). A boundary strut such as shown in Figure 17.9, has a stress state similar to that in the compression zone of a beam or column, and is not subjected to any transverse tension. Here, β_s is taken as 1. In case of interior struts, the strut is subjected to transverse tension (and likely to be cracked) due to bottle shaped stress trajectories. Here, a reduced factor β_s of 0.75 may be chosen, subject to the conditions that follow. If the interior strut do not satisfy the minimum distributed reinforcement requirement (Eqs. 17.60, 17.61) or do not satisfy the sizing condition (Eq. 17.62), or is not located in beam-column joints, then a reduced value of $\beta_s = 0.4$ has to be adopted (this is to preclude diagonal tension failure). If the strut is located in the tension zone, then a lower value of $\beta_s = 0.4$ has to be used irrespective of the strut type. For struts in pile caps, β_s should be taken as 0.60. The node factor, β_n depends on the node type with a value of 1, 0.8 and 0.6 for CCC, CCT and CTT type nodes, respectively (Table 17.1). The confinement factor, β_c may be considered when the bearing area is smaller than the member dimensions. Factor $\beta_c = \sqrt{A_1/A_2} \leq 2.0$, where A_2 is the loaded area and A_1 is the maximum area of the portion of the supporting surface that is geometrically similar to and concentric with the loaded area. This allows for an increase in concrete strength near the bearing zones due to confinement offered by surrounding concrete, and is similar to the factor used for the maximum bearing stress calculation in Section 14.3.6.

The strength of the strut is checked at each end and the lesser value taken. Strut end is usually the node-to-strut interface. Here, the lower of the strength specified for the strut and node has to be considered. The node proportioning as given in Figure 17.11 is used to obtain the width of the strut and node faces.

Table 17.1 *Modification factors β_s and β_n - ACI-318 (2019)*

Strut factor, β_s		Node factor, β_n	
Boundary struts	$\beta_s = 1.0$	CCC node	$\beta_n = 1.0$
Interior struts satisfying the minimum distributed reinforcement (Eq. 17.60, 17.61)	$\beta_s = 0.75$	CCT node	$\beta_n = 0.8$
Interior struts located in regions satisfying the condition in Eq. 17.62	$\beta_s = 0.75$	CTT node	$\beta_n = 0.6$
Interior struts in beam column joints	$\beta_s = 0.75$		
Other interior struts and all struts in tension zones	$\beta_s = 0.40$		
Normal density concrete struts in pile caps (Code Cl. 13.4.6.4)	$\beta_s = 0.60$		

A minimum amount of distributed reinforcement shall be provided in 'D' region across the axes of interior struts primarily to control crack widths at service loads. The reinforcement may be provided as orthogonal grid in horizontal and vertical directions as per Eq. 17.60. The reinforcement can also be provided in one direction, crossing the strut, with the ratio as given in Eq. 17.61.

For distributed reinforcement provided as orthogonal grid (considering the total on both faces plus interior layers, if any, placed in wide members),

$$\frac{A_{sv}}{bs_v} = 0.0025; \quad \frac{A_{sh}}{bs_h} = 0.0025 \tag{17.60}$$

where b is the breadth, A_{sv} is the area of vertical distributed reinforcement provided at spacing s_v and A_{sh} is the area of horizontal distributed reinforcement at spacing s_h.

For distributed reinforcement provided in one direction and crossing the strut at angle α_1, and considering the total on both faces,

$$\frac{A_{svh}}{bs} = \frac{0.0025}{\sin^2 \alpha_1} \tag{17.61}$$

where A_{svh} is the area of distributed reinforcement provided across the strut in one direction at spacing s, and α_1 is the minimum angle between the reinforcement direction and the strut. The spacing of the distributed reinforcement in all the above cases is limited to a maximum of 300 mm, Further, the angle α_1 shall not be less than 40 degrees.

The minimum reinforcement is not required when the strut is laterally restrained. The 'D' region can be considered laterally restrained when (i) the region is continuous perpendicular to the plane of the strut-and-tie model (as in a continuous corbel supporting a slab) or (ii) the concrete restraining the strut extends beyond each side face of the strut a distance more than half the width of the strut or (iii) strut is in a beam-column joint where it is confined by proper detailing.

The member dimensions may be selected using the Eq. 17.62 to prevent premature diagonal tension failure in shear.

$$V_u \leq 0.42\phi \tan\theta \, \lambda_s \sqrt{f_c'}\, bd \tag{17.62}$$

where V_u is the factored shear force at the section in Newtons, f_c' is cylinder strength in MPa, and width b and effective depth d are in mm. Here θ is the angle between the axis of the strut, compression diagonal, or compression field and the tension chord. The size effect modification factor, λ_s , is given by,

$$\lambda_s = \begin{cases} 1 & \text{: if minimum distributed reinforcement is provided} \\ \sqrt{\dfrac{2}{1+0.004d}} \leq 1 & \text{: if minimum distributed reinforcement is not provided} \end{cases} \tag{17.63}$$

where d is the effective depth in mm. As stated earlier and in Table 17.1, with member dimensions satisfying Eq. 17.62, β_s can be taken as 0.75.

The angle between the axes of any strut and any tie meeting at the same node should not be less than 25 degrees. When the angle between the strut and tie decreases, the struts and ties will be aligned almost in the same direction causing incompatibility between the compressive strains in the strut and tensile strains in the tie. This can also result in wide cracks causing reduction in compressive strength of concrete. ACI-318 2019 allows the development length for the ties to be reckoned from the intersection of the extended nodal zone and the tie centroid (Figure 17.11b).

Deep Beam and Corbel: Provisions in ACI-318, 2019

Strut-and-tie method is recommended for design of deep beams and corbels. As per ACI-318, 2019, deep beams are members where clear span does not exceed four times the overall depth or members where concentrated load exists within a distance of two times the depth from the face of the support. The minimum distributed reinforcement of 0.25% in each face has to be provided for these members. This is similar to Eq. 17.60. The spacing of such reinforcement shall not exceed $d/5$ nor 300 mm.

Corbels are short cantilever projection with a/d ratio less than one [Figure 17.10(c)], where a is the distance from the load point to the face of the column and d is the effective depth at column face. Overall depth of corbel at the outside edge of the bearing area should be at least $0.5d$, to avoid premature failure with major diagonal crack propagating to the sloping face.

The depth of the corbel should satisfy Eq. 17.64.

$$V_u \le \left\{ \begin{aligned} &\phi(0.2) f_c' bd \\ &\phi(3.3 + 0.08 f_c') bd \\ &\phi(11) bd \end{aligned} \right\} \tag{17.64}$$

where b is the width of the corbel.

The primary tension reinforcement should be developed at the face of the support and shall be anchored by one of the following: (a) a weld to a transverse bar of at least same diameter as the main reinforcement or (b) bending the primary tension reinforcement back to form a horizontal loop or (c) any other means that develops yield stress at the face of the support. Closed horizontal stirrups shall be provided, spaced such that it is uniformly distributed within $(2/3)d$ measured from the primary tension reinforcement. Corbels with shear span to depth ratios less than 2 shall have a minimum main reinforcement, $A_{sc\text{-min}}$, as given in Eq. 17.65.

$$A_{sc-\min} = 0.04 \left(\frac{f_c'}{f_y} \right) (bd) \tag{17.65}$$

17.3.6 Design Steps using STM

The design steps are as follows:

1. Identify D-region(s) in the member and compute the resultant forces/loads acting on the D-region boundary.
2. Develop an appropriate strut-and-tie model truss suitable to transfer the load across the D-region to the adjacent B region or supports. In this model, the axes of the struts and ties may be chosen to approximately coincide with the axes of the compression and tension fields respectively. A statically determinate truss model is preferable.
3. Compute the forces in the struts and ties of the model truss under the loads acting on D-region boundary.
4. Determine the amount of reinforcement corresponding to the ties and check whether this can be accommodated within the assumed tie region. If not, refine the model by shifting the axis of the tie and repeat the steps.
5. Dimension the nodal regions and check the strengths of struts, ties and nodes as per Code. If the strength of any member or node face is not sufficient, refine the strut-and-tie model (including changes

in the external load/reaction bearing area dimensions, if admissible) and repeat the steps until a suitable configuration is obtained which satisfies the strength check.

6. Detail the main reinforcement with its centroid coinciding with the assumed tie axis location and design the anchorages with full development length being provided beyond the critical section for development.
7. Design and detail the distributed reinforcement.

Example 17.1

The T-beam shown in Figure 17.14(a) is subjected to a specified live load of 28 kN/m and a dead load (including the weight of the beam) of 13 kN/m. A 300 × 500 mm size is selected for the beam and the effective flange width is 3180 mm. Design the required transverse and longitudinal reinforcement for shear and moment using MCFT. Use Fe 415 steel and M 25 concrete. The material resistance factor associated with the cylinder strength, f_c', used in MCFT equations may be taken as $\phi_c = 0.65$.

Solution

MCFT equations are based on the cylinder strength, f_c'. M 25 concrete has $f_{ck} = 25$ MPa. Using Eq. 2.3, for this concrete, f_c' may be taken as $0.8 \times 25 = 20$ MPa.

Shear and moment envelopes

Factored loads are, $w_D = 1.5 \times 13 = 19.5$ kN/m; and $w_L = 1.5 \times 28 = 42$ kN/m

The beam is heavily loaded and the reinforcement may have to be provided in two layers. Assuming a clear cover of 30 mm (moderate exposure), 28ϕ bars in two layers and 10ϕ stirrups, effective depth $d = 500 - (30 + 10 + 28 + 28/2) = 418$ mm

Effective depth for shear (or flexural lever arm) may be taken as:

$$d_v = 0.9\,d = 0.9 \times 418 = 376 \text{ mm}$$

Near the support, where the shear is maximum, assuming that the bars in the top layer have been curtailed, d=446 and $d_v = 401$ mm.

The critical section near the support is at distance d_v from the face of the support, which is at 401 + 120 = 521 mm from the centreline of support.

For the moment envelope, moments are computed at 0.521 m, 0.2L, 0.3L and 0.5L from support centreline, where L is the span. For the shear however, the envelope may be assumed (conservatively) linear between the maximum at support and the maximum at centre of span. The values of M_f and V_f at these sections are tabulated in Table 17.2.

1. Area of reinforcement at mid-span

To choose a trial area of reinforcement at mid-span in order to check assumptions about effective depth calculations above, with assumed lever arm $\approx d_v = 376$ mm,

$$A_s = M_f/(\phi_s f_y d_v)$$
$$= 492 \times 10^6/(0.87 \times 415 \times 376) = 3624 \text{ mm}^2$$

Six 28ϕ bars giving $A_s = 3695$ mm^2, placed in two layers will be adequate and hence the effective depth calculations are OK. This also gives $p_t = 0.0295 < p_{t,\,\text{lim}}$.

2. Check adequacy of the section

Near the support section, where the shear is maximum,

$$b_w = 300 \text{ mm}, d_v = 401 \text{ mm}$$

Admissible maximum V_r is given by Eq. 17.29 or 17.36

$$V_{r,\max} = 0.25\ \phi_c f_c' b_w d_v$$

$$= 0.25 \times 0.65 \times 20 \times 300 \times 401 \times 10^{-3} = 391 \text{ kN}$$

This is greater than the maximum shear at the critical section distant d_v from the face of the support = 219 kN. Hence, the section size is adequate.

3. Design of stirrups

Since stirrups are placed in bands within which the spacing is uniform, the design will be done by calculating the A_v/s requirement at the selected locations along the span and then designing a spacing to meet this.

Section distant d_v from face of support:

The values of parameters θ and β need to be evaluated. As there is no tension in the member, $f_c' < 60$ MPa and $f_y \leq 400$ MPa (this condition is deemed to be satisfied since Fe 415 steel is used), all conditions for use of the *simplified method* are satisfied here; and θ could be taken as 35° and β as 0.18, or β determined using Eqs. 17.39 and 17.40. However, the *general method* will be used here for demonstration. For this, first the value of ε_x at this location is calculated using Eq. 17.43 (note that at all sections, $M_f > V_f d_v$, see below). Assuming three of the six bars are curtailed before this section, $A_s = 1847 \text{ mm}^2$.

At this section, $V_f d_v = 219 \times 0.401 = 87.8 \text{ kNm} < M_f = 120 \text{ kNm}$, – OK

$$\varepsilon_x = \frac{M_f/dv + V_f}{2A_s E_s} = \frac{120 \times 10^6/401 + 219 \times 10^3}{2 \times 200000 \times 1847} = 0.00070$$

The beam will be provided with at least the minimum transverse reinforcement, so that the effective crack spacing parameter, s_{ze}, may be taken as 300 mm. With this, parameter β may be calculated using Eq. 17.41 as:

$$\beta = \frac{0.4}{1 + 1500\varepsilon_x}\left(\frac{1300}{1000 + s_{ze}}\right)\frac{0.4}{1 + 1500 \times 7 \times 10^{-4}} = 0.195$$

From Eq. 17.33, the part V_c of shear resistance is obtained as:

$$V_c = \phi_c b_w d_v \beta \sqrt{f_c'} = 0.65 \times 300 \times 401 \times 0.195\ \sqrt{20} \times 10^{-3}$$

$$= 68.2 \text{ kN}$$

Shear to be carried by transverse reinforcement is $V_s = V_f - V_c = 151$ kN.
Angle θ is computed using Eq. 17. 42 as:

$$\theta = 29° + 7000\varepsilon_x = 29 + 7000 \times 0.0007 = 33.9°$$

Required A_v/s can be calculated using the expression for V_s, (Eq. 17.34)

$$V_s = \frac{\phi_s A_v d_v f_y}{s} \cot\theta$$

or $$\frac{A_v}{s} \geq \frac{V_s}{\phi_s f_y d_v \cot\theta} = \frac{151 \times 10^3}{0.87 \times 415 \times 401 \times \cot 33.9} = 0.701$$

Similar calculations are made for sections at 0.2L, 0.3L and 0.5L and results given in Table 17.2 and plotted in Figure 17.14(e). Note that the minimum shear reinforcement specified by IS-456 gives $A_v/s = 0.4b_w/(0.87f_y) = 0.332$. These requirements are met by 10ϕ two-legged stirrups, placed with the first one along the face of support, followed by six @ 200 mm, four more @ 270 mm and another five more @ 320 mm as shown in Figure 17.14(d). The A_v/s provided are 0.785, 0.581 and 0.490 mm respectively, and are plotted against the requirements in Figure 17.14(e). As all the stirrups crossing a potential inclined crack contribute to V_s, there will not be an abrupt change in shear strength at the location where the stirrup spacing changes. Hence, where the spacing changes, the changeover of A_v/s may be assumed to take effect, linearly, over a length h centred on the location where spacing changes, where h is the overall depth of the member.

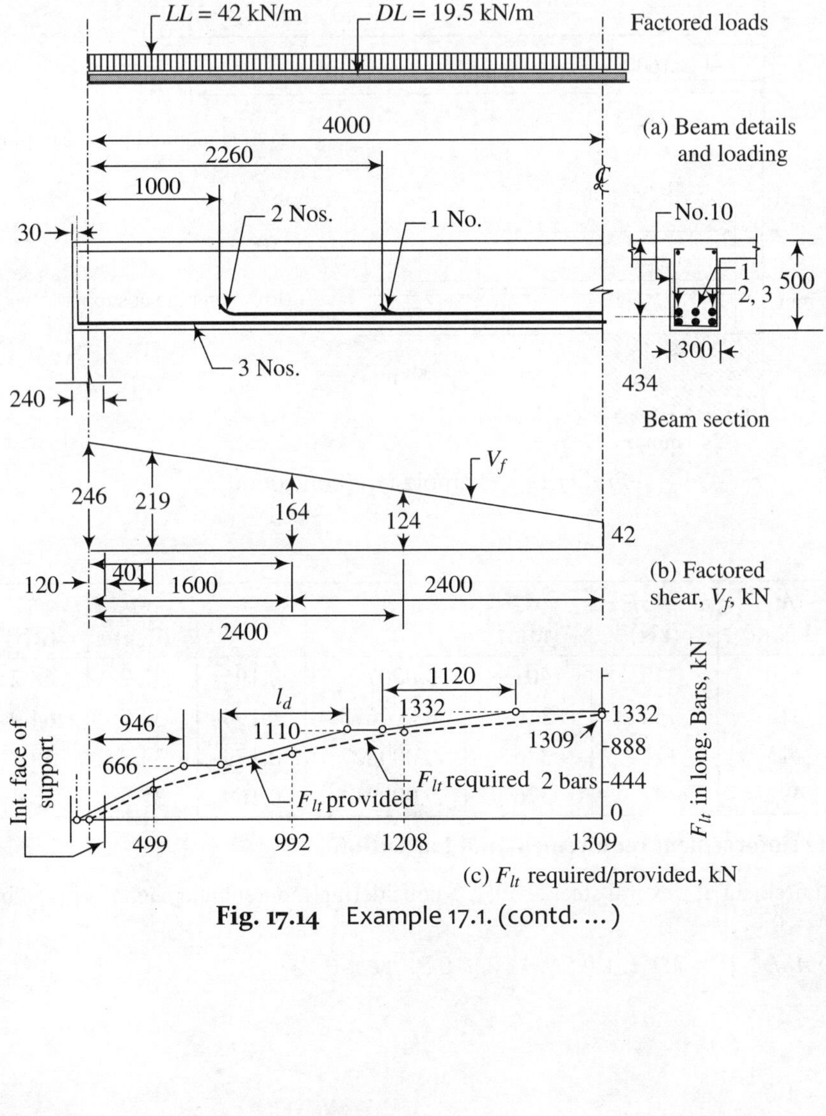

Fig. 17.14 Example 17.1. (contd. ...)

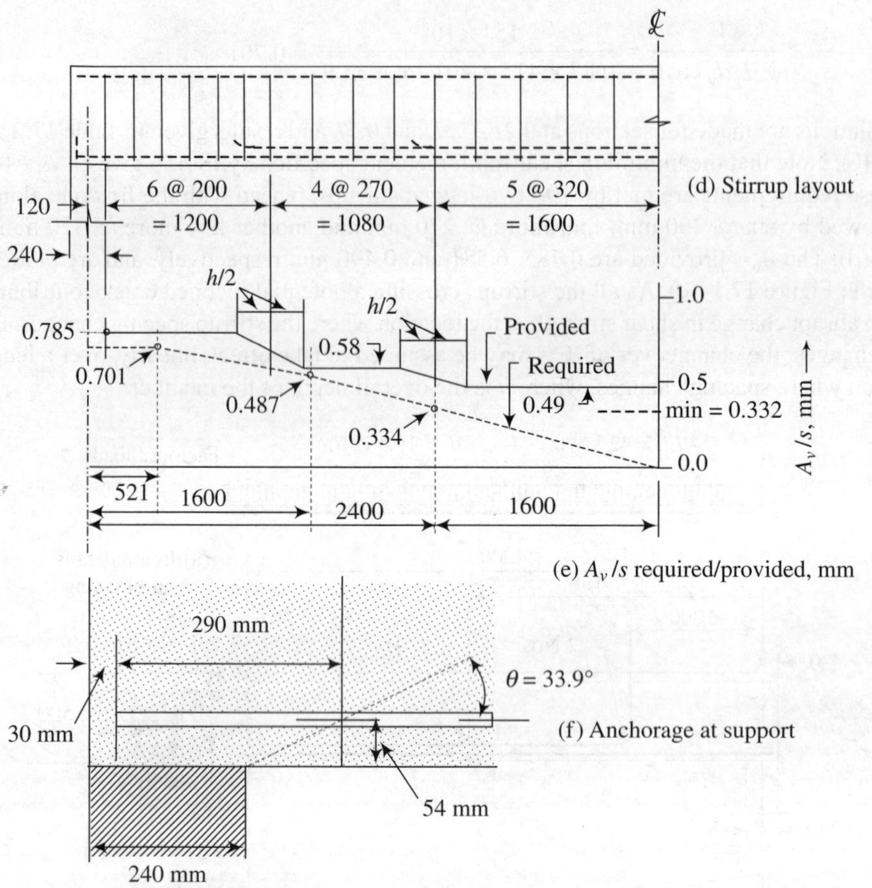

Fig. 17.14 Example 17.1 (concluded).

Table 17.2

Location (m)	M_f (kN.m)	V_f (kN)	d_v (mm)	ε_x	β	Θ (deg)	V_c (kN)	A_v/s (mm)
0.521 m	120	219	401	0.0007	0.195	33.9	68.2	0.701
$0.2L = 1.6$	315	164	376	0.000678	0.198	33.7	64.9	0.487
$0.3L = 2.4$	413	124	376	0.000827	0.179	34.8	58.7	0.334
$0.5L = 4.0$	492	42	376	0.000914	0.169	35.4	55.4	nil

4. Longitudinal reinforcement requirement and bar cut-off

Tensile force requirement at flexural steel level, F_{lt}, considering moment and shear, is given by Eq. 17.30 or Eq. 17.44 with $N = 0$

$$\phi_s A_{lt} f_s \geq F_{lt} = M_f/d_v + 0.5N_f + (V_f - 0.5V_s) \cot \theta$$

At section distant d_v from face of support, V_s corresponds to a stirrup spacing of 200 mm. Substituting the values for this location,

$$F_{lt} = \frac{120 \times 10^6}{401} + \left(219 \times 10^3 - 0.5\frac{0.87 \times 2 \times 78.5 \times 415 \times 401 \times \cot 33.9}{200}\right)\cot 33.9$$

$$= 499 \text{ kN}$$

At $0.2L$, $0.3L$ and $0.5L$, the stirrup spacings are 270 mm, 320 mm and 320 mm respectively and d_v may be taken as 376 mm (at $0.5L$, the required V_s is zero). Results of calculations similar to the above yield values for F_{lt} at $0.2L$, $0.3L$ and $0.5L$ of 992 kN, 1208 kN and 1309 kN respectively. These are plotted in Figure 17.14(c). The bar cut-off should be such that the force developed in longitudinal reinforcement at all sections must exceed the required F_{lt}. The development length for the 28ϕ bars is 40ϕ = 1120 mm. The force per bar when fully developed is 0.87 × 415 × 616 = 222 kN. An arrangement for bar cut-off and the corresponding force developed is also plotted on the 'required F_{lt}' diagram in Figure 17.14(c). The longitudinal reinforcement provided is adequate. Accordingly, the middle bar in the top layer may be cut-off at 2.26 m from center of support and the remaining two bars in this layer at 1 m.

5. Anchorage of longitudinal reinforcement at support

Since sections within a distance d_v from face of support need only be designed for the shear at distance d_v, the values of ε_x and θ computed for the latter section can be used for the support section. The tensile force to be resisted by the longitudinal reinforcement at the point where it is intercepted by a crack originating at the inside edge of the support [Figure 17.14(f)] is given by Eq. 17.31a, where V_s need not be taken greater than V_f:

$$F_{lt} = (V_f - 0.5V_s) \cot \theta + 0.5\, N_f$$

$$= \left(219 \times 10^3 - 0.5\frac{0.87 \times 2 \times 78.5 \times 415 \times 401 \times \cot 33.9}{200}\right)\cot 33.9$$

$$= 200 \text{ kN}$$

The available embedment length at the section (Figure 17.14(f)) is 290 mm. With three bars continued over support, the tensile capacity that can be developed at the critical section is 3 × 222 × 290/1120 = 172 kN which is less than required 200 kN. Hence, the bars may be anchored with standard 90° bends. The anchorage value of a 90° bend = 8ϕ = 224 mm. With this, total effective embedment = 290 – 5ϕ + 8ϕ = 374 mm (see Fig. 8.8) and the tensile capacity = 3 × 222 × 374/1120 = 222.4 kN > 200, hence OK.

The three bars at the support will be fully developed over a distance = 1120 – 84 – 90 = 946 mm from the centre of support. Figure 17.14(c) shows the tensile force developed against the requirements.

Example 17.2

Figure 17.15 shows a continuous beam supporting a monolithically cast cantilever slab. The specified live load on the slab is 2.4 kN/m². In addition, the beam supports a dead load of 12 kN/m, applied directly over the beam width; f_c' = 30 MPa and f_y = 400 MPa. Design the reinforcement for the beam at a critical section near the first interior support.

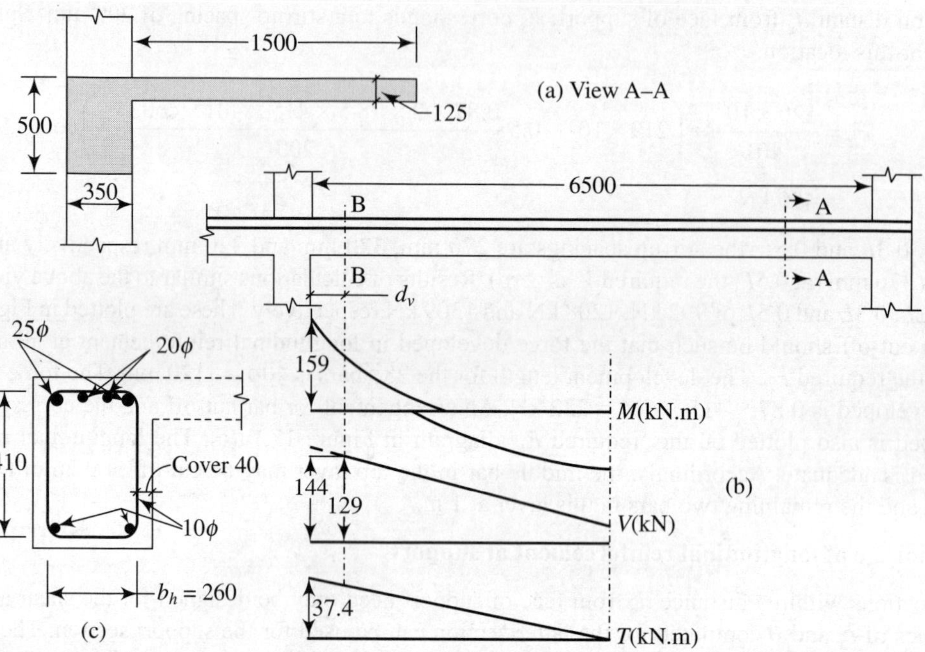

Fig. 17.15 Example 17.2.

Solution

[*Note:* The procedure detailed in Sections 17.2.6 and 17.2.7 are used in this design. Since detailing requirements in CSA Code and IS Code are somewhat different, the design below is limited essentially to checking of section size and determination of longitudinal and transverse reinforcements only]

1. Factored load effects on the beam (Figure 17.15b)
   - Factored Loads from the overhanging portion of the slab per metre length of beam are:
     Dead load: $w_{DL} = 1.50 \times 0.125 \times 1.50 \times 25 = 7.03$ kN/m
     Live load: $w_{LL} = 1.50 \times 1.5 \times 2.4 = 5.40$ kN/m
     Total load from slab: $= 12.43$ kN/m
   - Assuming a beam size of 350 × 500 mm, the torque due to the loads on slab is:
     $T = 12.43(0.175 + 1.5/2) = 11.5$ kN.m/m length
     Factored dead load directly on the beam, including the beam weight, is:
     $1.5(12 + 0.35 \times 0.5 \times 25) = 24.6$ kN/m
     Total dead load on beam = 7.03 + 24.6 = 31.63 kN/m; Total Live load = 5.4 kN/m;
     Total load = 37.0 kN
   - The maximum negative moment in the beam at the face of the first interior column support, using the moment coefficients (Table 9.1) is:
     $$M_f = (w_{u,\mathrm{DL}}/10 + w_{u,LL}/9)l^2 = (31.63/10 + 5.4/9)6.5^2 = 159 \text{ kN.m}$$
   - Maximum shear in the beam at exterior face of first interior support is:
     $$V_{\max} = (0.6w_{u,\mathrm{DL}} + 0.6w_{u,LL})l = 0.6 \times 37.0 \times 6.5 = 144 \text{ kN}$$
   - Maximum torque in beam, at face of support:
     $$T_{\max} = 11.5 \times 6.5/2 = 37.4 \text{ kN.m}$$

The shear and torque vary linearly, with their maxima at the face of the support. Sections located less than a distance d_v from face of the support may be designed for the shear computed at a distance d_v. Assuming 40 mm cover, 10ϕ stirrups and 25ϕ bars,

$$d = 500 - (40 + 10 + 25/2) = 437.5 \text{ mm}$$

Taking d_v as $0.9d = 394$, $\quad d_v = 394$ mm.
At the face of the support, design shear, $V_f = 144 - 37.0 \times 0.394 = 129$ kN and design torque, $T_f = 37.4$ kN.m.

2. Check shear resistance and torsion resistance requirements and adequacy of overall section size
The design condition is that $V_r = V_c + V_s \geq V_f$
To check adequacy of size of section,
$V_{r,\max} = 0.25\phi_c f_c' b_w d_v = 0.25 \times 0.65 \times 30 \times 350 \times 394 \times 10^{-3} = 672$ kN.m >> V_f
(Note that under combined shear and torsion, the requirement in Eq. 17.50 is more critical here, and the check for this is done later below.)
Hence, section size is adequate considering shear alone. To compute factored shear resistance components V_c and V_s, the parameters θ and β are required. Since there is no significant axial tension, $f_y \leq 400$ MPa and $f_c' < 60$ MPa, the *Simplified Method* may be used. Accordingly, $\theta = 35°$ and by providing at least minimum transverse reinforcement, β may be taken as 0.18.
Factored shear resistance provided by concrete, V_c, is (Eq. 17.33),

$$V_c = \lambda\beta\phi_c\sqrt{f_c'}b_w d_v$$

$$= 1.0 \times 0.18 \times 0.65 \times \sqrt{30} \times 350 \times 394 \times 10^{-3} = 88.4 \text{ kN}$$

$V_f = 129$ kN $> V_c = 88.4$ kN, shear reinforcement is required

$$V_s = V_f - V_c = 129 - 88.4 = 40.6 \text{ kN}$$

A minimum area of transverse reinforcement (Eq. 17.37) is required where (a) V_f exceeds V_c and (b) T_f exceeds $0.25\ T_{cr}$.
Pure torsional cracking resistance, T_{cr}, is obtained from (Eq. 17.38) as,

$$T_{cr} = \frac{A_c^2}{p_c} 0.38\lambda\phi_c\sqrt{f_c'}$$

$$A_c = 350 \times 500 = 175 \times 10^3 \text{ mm}^2,\ p_c = 2(350 + 500) = 1700 \text{ mm}$$

$$T_{cr} = \frac{(175 \times 10^3)^2}{1700} \times 0.38 \times 1.0 \times 0.65\sqrt{30} \times 10^{-6} = 24.4 \text{ kN.m}$$

Since $T_f > 0.25\ T_{cr}$, torsion reinforcement is required.
To avoid crushing failure of concrete under diagonal compression, the total nominal shear stress, considering V_f and T_f, must be such that Eq. 17.50 is satisfied, otherwise the section dimensions must be increased. Assuming 40 mm clear cover all around and 10ϕ stirrups, the centreline dimensions of the stirrup cage (Figure 17.14(c)) are 260.0 × 410.0 mm.

$$A_{oh} = 410 \times 260 = 107 \times 10^3 \text{ mm}^2,\ p_h = 2(410 + 260) = 1340 \text{ mm}$$

The right-hand side of Eq. 17.50 is: $0.25\phi_c f_c' = 0.25 \times 0.65 \times 30 = 4.87$ MPa

The left side of Eq. 17.50 is:

$$\sqrt{\left(\frac{129000}{350 \times 394}\right)^2 + \left(\frac{37.4 \times 10^6 \times 1340}{1.7 \times (107 \times 10^3)^2}\right)^2} = 2.74 \text{ MPa} < 4.87 \text{ MPa}$$

Eq. 17.50 is satisfied and the cross-sectional dimensions are adequate.

3. Design of flexural reinforcement

$$R = \frac{M_f}{bd^2} = \frac{159 \times 10^6}{350 \times 437.5^2} = 2.37 \text{ MPa}$$

For this R, from Table A.3(b), for Fe 415 steel and M 35 concrete ($f_c' = 30$ MPa corresponds to $f_{ck} = 37.5$ MPa, hence table for $f_{ck} = 35$ MPa is used here) [alternatively, Eq. 5.12 gives $p_t = 0.00713$]:

$$p_t \approx 0.00717 << p_{t,\max} = 0.0168$$

$$A_{sf} = 0.00717 \times 350 \times 437.5 = 1098 \text{ mm}^2$$

4. Reinforcement for flexural shear: $V_s = V_f - V_c = 129 - 88.4 = 40.6$ kN

Using Eq. 17.34, area of vertical stirrup, A_v, is given by:

$$\frac{A_v}{s} = \frac{V_s \tan\theta}{\phi_s f_y d_v} = \frac{40600 \times 0.700}{0.85 \times 400 \times 394} = 0.212 \text{ mm}^2/\text{mm}$$

Minimum transverse shear reinforcement is given by Eq. 17.37 as:

$$\left(\frac{A_v}{s}\right)_{\min} = \frac{0.06\sqrt{f_c'}b_w}{f_y} = \frac{0.06\sqrt{30}}{400} \times 350 = 0.228 \text{ mm}^2/\text{mm}$$

For satisfying the minimum A_v requirement, Code permits inclusion of transverse torsion reinforcement. Hence, the checking of $A_{v,\min}$ will be done after designing torsion reinforcement (see Para 6 below). Choosing two-legged closed stirrups, area of stirrup required per leg, A_{v1}, is given by:

$$\frac{A_{v1}}{s} = \frac{A_v/s}{2} = \frac{0.212}{2} = 0.106 \text{ mm}^2/\text{mm}$$

5. Torsional reinforcement

Area of stirrup required for torsion, using Eq. 17.47 is, $\dfrac{A_t}{s} = \dfrac{T_f \tan\theta}{2A_o \phi_s f_y}$

$$A_o \approx 0.85\, A_{oh} = 0.85 \times 107 \times 10^3 = 91 \times 10^3 \text{ mm}^2/\text{mm}$$

$$\frac{A_t}{s} = \frac{37.4 \times 10^6 \times 0.700}{2 \times 91 \times 10^3 \times 0.85 \times 400} = 0.423 \text{ mm}^2/\text{mm}$$

The *additional* longitudinal steel required for shear and torsion can be obtained from Eqs. 17.44 and 17.51 as:

$$A_{lt,2} = \frac{1}{\phi_s f_y} \cot\theta \sqrt{(V_f - 0.5V_s)^2 + \left(\frac{0.45 p_h T_f}{2A_0}\right)^2}$$

$$= \frac{1.428}{0.85 \times 400}\sqrt{(129000 - 0.5 \times 40600)^2 + \left(\frac{0.45 \times 1340 \times 37400}{2 \times 91 \times 10^3}\right)^2}$$

$= 457\ \text{mm}^2$ on the flexural tension side.

Total tension reinforcement on the flexural tension side = 1098 + 457 = 1555 mm^2

On the flexural compression side, the longitudinal reinforcement required for moment, shear and torsion is given by Eqs. 17.45 and 17.51. However, the moment term, M_f/d_v (= 404 kN), is greater than the sum of the terms accounting for shear and torsion (= 155 kN) and hence no longitudinal reinforcement is required on the compression side. In other words, the flexural compression is far in excess of the tension due to shear and torsion. However, a minimum of two bars is required at the corners of the closed transverse stirrups as detailed later in Para 7 below.

6. Selection of stirrup and spacing

Total area required for each leg, for resisting shear and torsion, is given by:

$$\left(\frac{A_t}{s}\right)_{\text{total}} = \frac{A_{v1}}{s} + \frac{A_t}{s} = 0.106 + 0.423 = 0.529\ \text{mm}^2/\text{mm}$$

This is more than the minimum requirement of 0.114 mm^2/mm calculated in para 4 above and hence controls.

Using 10ϕ stirrups, $A_v = 78.5$ mm^2, and the required spacing is:

$$s = \frac{A_v}{0.529} = \frac{78.5}{0.529} = 148\ \text{mm}$$

Since T_f exceeds 0.25 T_{cr} as per Code, spacing must not exceed:

$$0.35d_v = 0.35 \times 394 = 138\ \text{mm} < 300\ \text{mm}$$

Select a spacing of 135 mm. The same spacing (135 mm) may be provided for a length of 2 m from supports. Beyond this, the reduced stirrup requirements may be worked out as above.

7. Selection of longitudinal reinforcement

Combined longitudinal reinforcement on the flexural tension side (top face) is:

$$A_l = A_{sf} + A_{lt,2} = 1098 + 457 = 1555\ \text{mm}$$

Provide two 25ϕ bars and 2–20ϕ bars, giving A_s = 1610 mm^2. As explained in Para 5 above, no reinforcement is required on the flexural compression side (bottom face here).

However, inside each corner of the stirrup, at least one longitudinal bar having a diameter not less than $s/16$ (135/16 = 8.44 mm) is a minimum requirement. Hence, provide two 10ϕ bars on the bottom side, as shown in Figure 17.15(c). The longitudinal bars required for torsion must be anchored into the support so as to develop the yield strength at the face of support.

Example 17.3 *Concrete Wall footing*

Design a reinforced concrete footing for a 480-mm thick reinforced concrete wall that supports a load (inclusive of self-weight) of 2100 kN/m under service loads. Assume hard rock with a safe bearing capacity of 1200 kN/m² at a depth of 1 m below ground. Assume M 30 grade concrete and Fe 500 grade steel. Use the strut-and-tie model for the design.

Solution

Size of footing

- Given: $P = 2100$ kN/m, $q_a = 1200$ kN/m at a depth of 1 m.
- Assuming the weight of the footing and backfill to be negligible compared to the wall load, and considering a 1 m length of footing along the wall, required width of footing $= \frac{2100}{1200} = 1.75$ m

  Provide a 1.8 m wide footing.

Thickness of footing based on shear considerations

- Factored net soil pressure (assuming a load factor of 1.5) is

$$q_u = \frac{2100 \times 1.5}{1.8 \times 1.0} = 1750 \text{ kN/m}^2 = 1.75 \text{ N/m}^2$$

- The critical section for (one-way) shear is located at a distance d away from the face of the wall

$$\Rightarrow \quad V_u = 1.75 \times 1000\,[(1800 - 480)/2 - d]$$
$$= (1155000 - 1750d) \text{ N}$$

- Assuming nominal flexural reinforcement ($p_t = 0.25$), $\tau_c = 0.37$ MPa for M30 concrete (see Table 6.1), and the shear resistance of concrete is $V_{cu} = 0.37 \times 1000 \times d = (370d)$ N

$$V_u \le V_{cu} \quad \Rightarrow \quad 1155000 - 1750d \le 370d$$

$$\Rightarrow \quad d \ge 545 \text{ mm}$$

- Assuming a clear cover of 75 mm and 20ϕ bars,
  Thickness $D \ge 545 + 75 + 20/2 = 630$ mm

  Provide a uniform depth $\boldsymbol{D} = \mathbf{640}$ **mm**, as shown in Figure 17.16(a). The entire footing may be classified as 'D' region and strut-and-tie method of design is appropriate.

  Depth to reinforcement, $d = 640 - (75 + 20/2) = 555$ mm

  Lever arm may be assumed as $0.9d = 499.5$ mm

Design of flexural reinforcement by strut-and-tie method

- The assumed strut and tie configuration is shown in Figure 17.16(a). consisting of 10 concrete struts transmitting the wall load to the foundation below. The reinforcement at the bottom provides the tie, connecting all the struts. Each strut transmits the soil reaction from its tributary area, which is 1/10 of the total, to the interface with the wall. Note that several other configurations are also possible.
- The vertical soil reaction on each strut is given by $1750 \times b/10$ or more directly by (the factored wall load)/10 = $2100 \times 1.5/10 = 315$ kN.
  Based on the force distribution in Figure 17.16(a), the compressive forces in the inclined struts and their corresponding tie forces (horizontal component) are worked out in Table 17.3 below. The cumulative tie forces at successive nodes are worked out in Table 17.4. The maximum tie force occurs in members DE and FG.

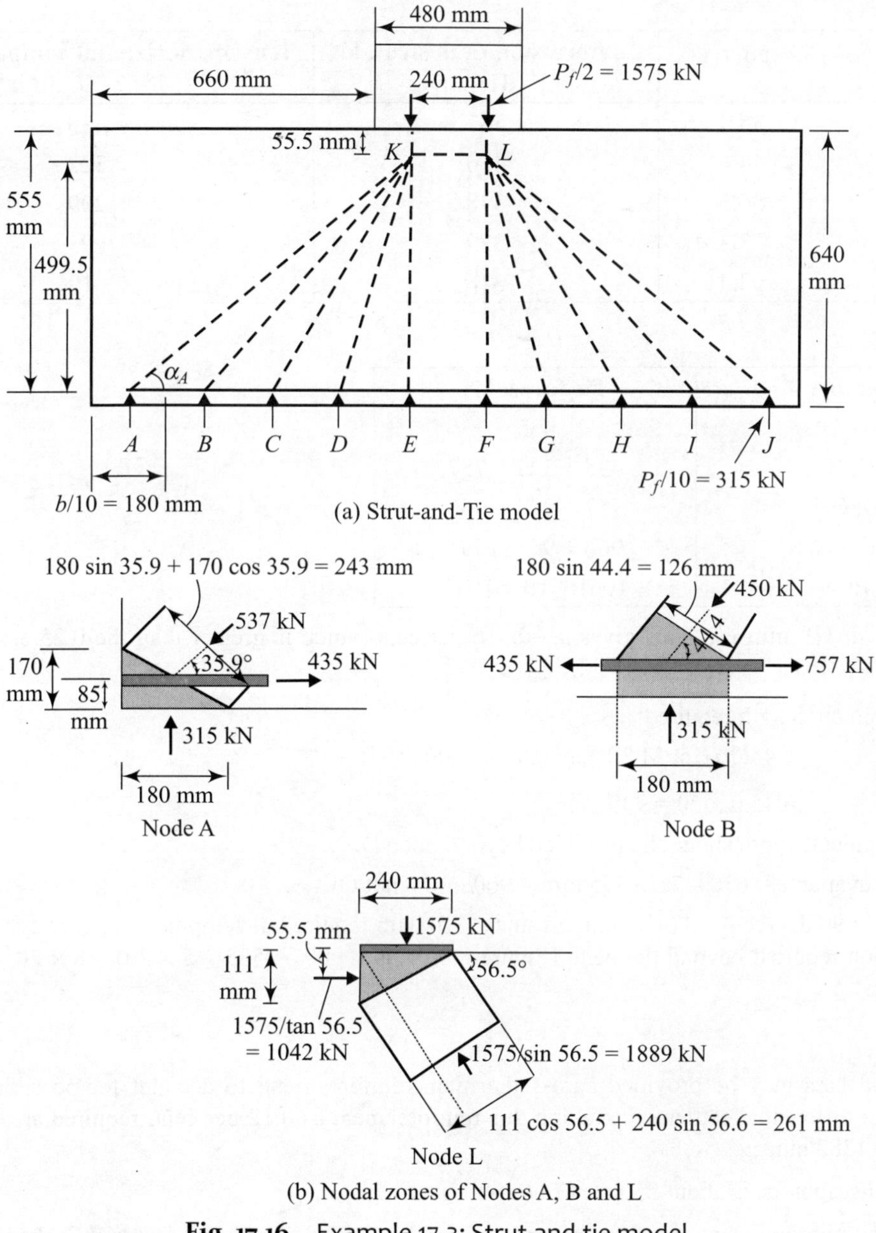

Fig. 17.16 Example 17.3: Strut-and-tie model.

- Required tension reinforcement (for maximum tie force) may be calculated from Eq. below:

$$\phi F_{nt} \geq F_{ut}$$

$$0.75 \times 500 \times A_{st} \geq 1061 \times 10^3$$

$A_{st} \geq 2829$ mm^2 per m length of footing.

$$\Rightarrow \qquad \text{Spacing of } 20\phi \text{ bars} = \frac{1000 \times 314}{2829} = 111 \text{ mm}$$

Table 17.3

Strut	Angle α (°)	Compression C, in strut, kN $C = 315/\sin\alpha$	Tension, horizontal component (kN) $T = 315/\tan\alpha$
AK, JL	35.9	537	435
BK, IL	44.4	450	322
CK, HL	56.5	378	209
DK, GL	73.3	329	95
EK, FL	93.4	316	–19

Table 17.4

Member	Tie force, kN
AB, IJ	435
BC, HI	435 + 322 = 757
CD, GH	757 + 209 = 966
DE, FG	966 + 95 = 1061
EF	1061 – 19 = 1042

Provide 20ϕ @ 110 mm c/c. This gives p_t =0.515 per cent which is greater than the 0.25 assumed while taking τ_c = 0.37 Mpa

- Development length required

  = 45.0ϕ (for M 30 concrete, Fe 500 steel)

  = 45.0 × 20 = 900 mm

  Development length should be provided beyond node D.

  Length available = 630 – 75 = 555 mm < 900 mm – not OK.

  Provide a 90 degree bend (anchorage value = 8ϕ) with required development length beyond the bend. Extension required beyond the bend [Figure 8.8(c)] is = 900 – (555 – 5 × 20) – 8 × 20 = 285 mm ≈ 300 mm.

Distributors

Some nominal bars may be provided across the main reinforcement, to account for possible secondary stresses due to differential settlement. Taking this reinforcement as 0.12 per cent, required area = 0.0012 × 1800 × 640 = 1382 mm^2.

Provide 16ϕ distributors @ about 250 c/c (7 nos will be adequate).

The distributed reinforcement across interior struts is not provided. A reduced factor β_s is therefore chosen for checking of strength of struts.

Check compressive stresses in struts/nodes

The cylinder strength of concrete, f_c' may be taken as $0.8f_{ck}$ = 0.8 × 30 = 24 MPa. Considering an β_s factor of 0.4 for the interior strut (for no minimum distributed reinforcement, Table 17.1) and a confinement factor β_c of 1, the limiting compressive stress, f_{ce} is obtained using Eq. 17.56 as 0.85 × 0.4 × 1 × 24 = 8.16 MPa. Limiting compressive stress for the boundary strut KL and top node face of nodes K and L = 0.85 × 1 × 1 × 24 = 20.4 MPa.

Strut AK

The interior strut AK, has the maximum compressive force of 537 kN. The width of the strut at node *A* may be taken as 180 sin 35.9° + 170 cos 35.9° = 243 mm (Figure 17.16(b))

Strength of the strut = $\phi A_{cs} f_{ce}$ = 0.75 × 1000 × 243 × 8.16 × 10^{-3} = 1487 kN > 537 kN, and hence OK.

Strut BK

The interior strut BK, has a compressive force of 450 kN. The width of the strut at node *A* may be taken as 180 sin 44.4° = 126 mm [Figure 17.16(b)].

Strength of the strut = $\phi A_{cs} f_{ce}$ = 0.75 × 1000 × 126 × 8.16 × 10^{-3} = 771 kN > 450 kN, and hence OK.

Other interior struts may be checked similarly. As the strut forces are smaller than struts AK and BK, this check is not critical.

Node L (and Node K)

The nodal region of node *L* is detailed in Figure 17.16(b).

Five interior struts converge at *L* and the compressive force of the resultant strut is given by C_L = 1575/sin $\alpha_{H'}$ = 1575/sin 56.5 = 1889 kN.

The strut width where it meets the nodal region is 111 cos 56.5 + 240 sin 56.5 = 261 mm [Figure 17.16(b)].

Capacity of this resultant strut = $\phi_{cs} f_{ce}$ = 0.75 × 1000 × 261 × 8.16 × 10^{-3} = 1597 kN > 1575 kN, and hence OK.

Strut KL meeting node L has a compressive force of 1575/tan α_H, = 1575/tan 56.5 = 1042 kN.

The strut width is 2 × 55.5 = 111 mm (Figure 17.15(b)).

Capacity of this boundary strut = $\phi A_{cs} f_{ce}$ = 0.75 × 1000 × 111 × 20.4 × 10^{-3} = 1698 kN > 1042 kN, and hence OK.

Top face of node L has a compressive force of 1575 kN. The bearing width is 240 mm [Figure 17.16(b)].

Capacity of node face = $\phi A_{nz} f_{ce}$ = 0.75 × 1000 × 240 × 20.4 × 10^{-3} = 3672 kN > 1575 kN, and hence OK.

The other nodes are not critical and stress check is not necessary. A separate bearing stress check is not necessary as the top face of node L as it has already been checked above.

Development of wall reinforcement into the footing is not checked in this example. Figure 17.17 shows the detailing of footing.

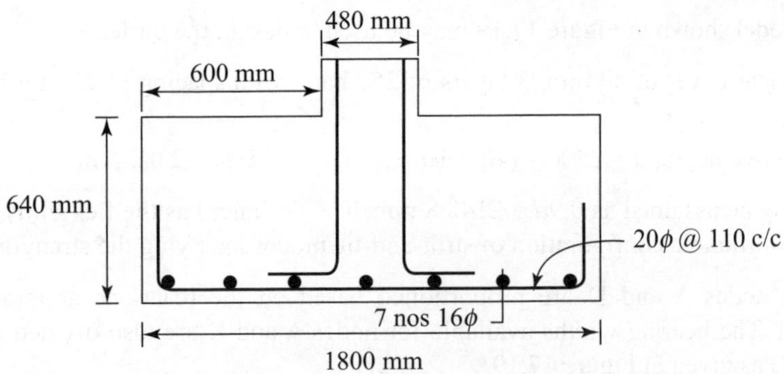

Fig. 17.17 Reinforcement Details, Example 17.3.

Example 17.4 *Deep Beam*

Design a transfer girder supported by two columns of size 450 mm × 450 mm spaced at 6 m (center to center). The girder supports a single column of size 450 mm x 450 mm with a factored axial load of 1800 kN (inclusive of self-weight of girder) located at a distance of 3.5 m from one end. The depth of the girder is restricted to 2.5 m. Use M30 concrete and Fe 500 steel. (Figure 17.18).

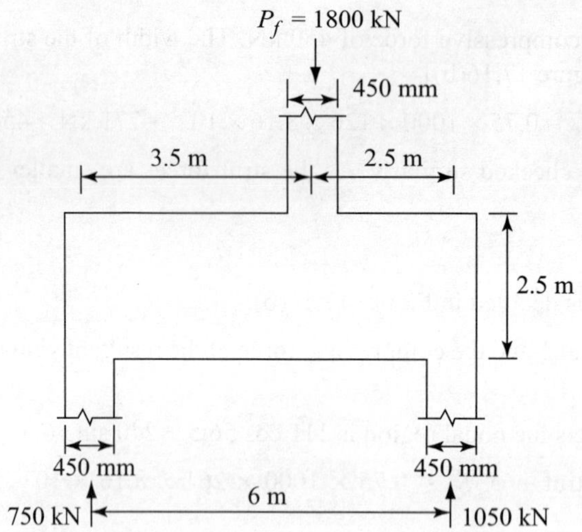

Fig. 17.18 Details of Deep Beam, Example 17.4.

Solution

- The entire girder is classified as 'D' region and strut and tie method of design is appropriate.
- Given: *Factored load,* P_f = 1800 kN

  Provide breadth of the girder, b = 450 mm

  $$\text{Reaction on the right column} = \frac{1800 \times 3.5}{6} = 1050 \text{ kN}$$

  $$\text{Reaction on the left column} = \frac{1800 \times 2.5}{6} = 750 \text{ kN}$$

Strut-and-Tie Model

The strut-and-tie model shown in Figure 17.19 may be used to design the girder.

- Assuming a clear cover of 40 mm, 3 layers of 25ϕ bars (with spacing of 25 mm between layers) and 10ϕ stirrups

  $$\text{Effective depth, } d = 2500 - (40 + 10 + 25 + 25 + 25/2) = 2387.5 \text{ mm}$$

  Lever arm may be assumed as 0.9d = 2148.8 mm. The designer has the flexibility to choose the lever arm to obtain a suitable configuration of strut-and-tie model satisfying the strength check.

  The loads at nodes A and D are proportioned based on the reactions at B and C as shown in Figure 17.19). The bearing widths available for nodes A and K are also divided as per the reactions (Figure 17.12) as given in Figure 17.19.

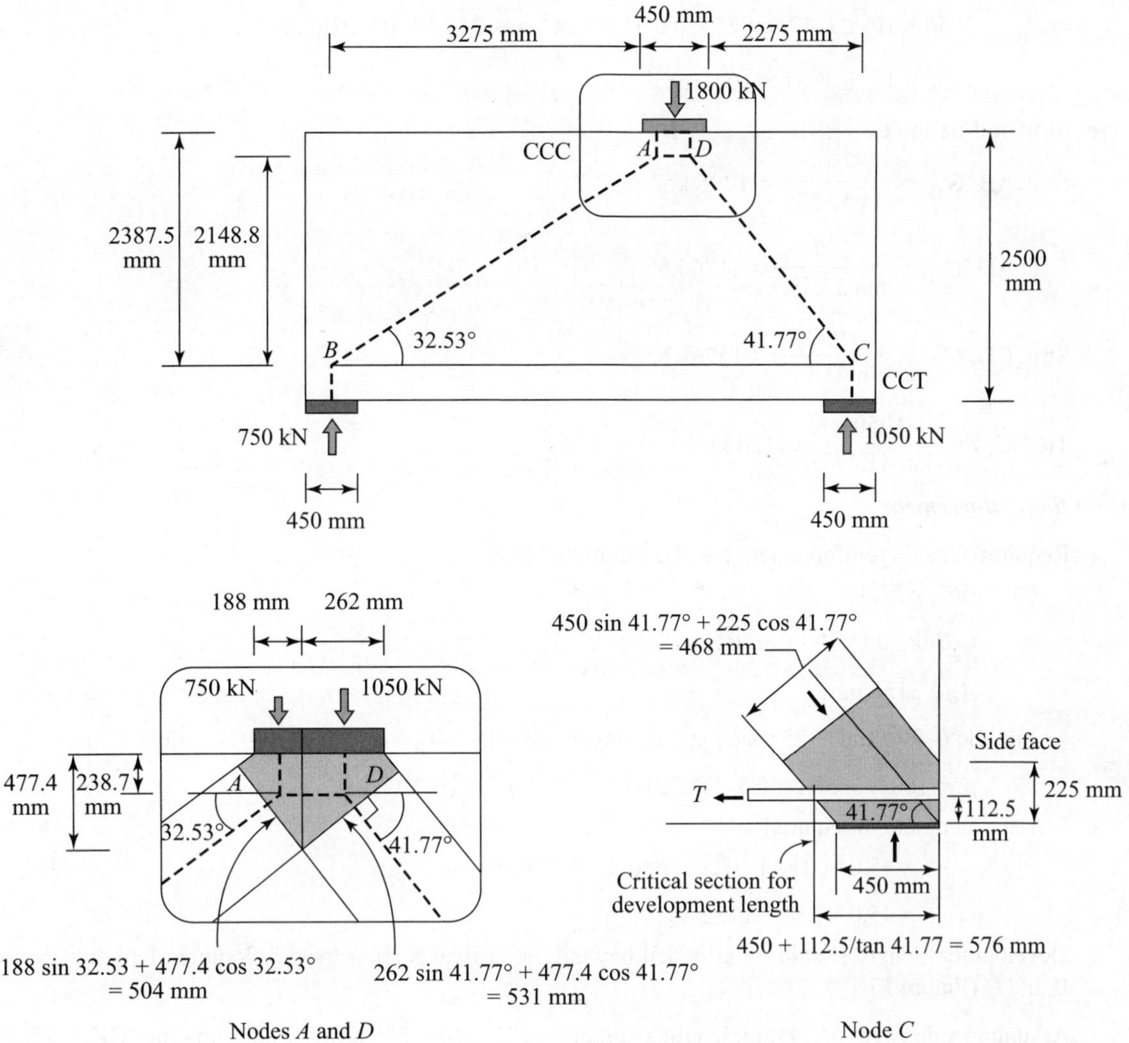

Fig. 17.19 Strut-and-tie model, Example 17.4.

$$\text{Strut angle, } \theta_B = \tan^{-1}\left(\frac{2148.8}{3275 + 188/2}\right) = 32.53°$$

$$\text{Strut angle, } \theta_C = \tan^{-1}\left(\frac{2148.8}{2275 + 262/2}\right) = 41.77°$$

- Depth Check

  Using Eq. 17.52, $V_u \leq 0.42\phi \tan\theta\lambda_s\sqrt{f_c'}\,bd$

  V_u is the maximum factored shear force = 1050 kN, $\lambda_s = 1$ (minimum distributed reinforcement has to be provided for deep beams), f_c' is taken as $0.8f_{ck} = 0.8(30) = 24$ MPa.

$\Rightarrow \quad 1050 \times 10^3 \le 0.42 \times 0.75 \times \tan 41.77° \times 1 \times \sqrt{24} \times 450 \times 2387.5$

$\Rightarrow \quad 1050 \times 10^3 \le 1481 \times 10^3$ Hence OK.

- Strut-and-tie forces

Strut AB, $C_{AB} = \dfrac{750}{\sin 32.53°} = 1395$ kN

Strut AD, $C_{AD} = \dfrac{750}{\tan 32.53°} = 1176$ kN

Strut CD, $C_{CD} = \dfrac{1050}{\sin 41.77°} = 1576$ kN

Tie BC, $T = \dfrac{1050}{\tan 41.77°} = 1176$ kN

Main tie reinforcement

- Required tension reinforcement may be calculated from

$\phi F_{nt} \ge F_{ut}$

$0.75 \times 500 \times A_{st} \ge 1176 \times 10^3$

$A_{st} \ge 3136$ mm^2

$\Rightarrow$ Provide 6–20ϕ and 3–25ϕ bars in three layers for which $A_{st} = 6(314) + 3(491) = 3358 > 3136$.

$p_t = 100 \times 3358/(450 \times 2387.5) = 0.31\,\% > p_{t\text{-min}}\,(= 0.17\%)$

- Development length required

$= 45.0\phi$ (for M 30 concrete, Fe 500 steel)

$= 45.0 \times 25 = 1125$ mm

Development length should be provided beyond the critical section for development length at nodes B and C (Figure 17.19).

Assuming side cover of 30 mm, length available = 576 – 30 = 546 mm < 1125 mm – not OK.

Provide a 90 degree bend (anchorage value = 8ϕ) with required additional length beyond the bend. Extension required beyond the bend = $1125 - (546 - 5 \times 25) - 8 \times 25 = 504$ mm ≈ 510 mm. The 90-degree hook and extension beyond should be confined within the horizontal distributed reinforcements to avoid cracking along the outside of the hooks.

Check compressive stresses in struts/nodes

Limiting compressive stress, f_{ce} for interior struts is obtained using Eq. 17.46, with $\beta_s = 0.75$ and $\beta_c = 1.0$, as $0.85 \times 0.75 \times 1 \times 24 = 15.3$ MPa.

Limiting compressive stress for the boundary strut AD and bearing face of nodes A and D (CCC node) = $0.85 \times 1 \times 1 \times 24 = 20.4$ MPa.

Limiting compressive stress for the nodes B and C (CCT node) = $0.85 \times 0.8 \times 1 \times 24 = 16.32$ MPa.

Node A

Bearing face: Force = 750 kN.

The width of node face = 188 mm (Figure 17.19)

Capacity of the node face = $\phi A_{nz} f_{ce}$ = 0.75 × 188 × 450 × 20.4 × 10^{-3} = 1294 kN > 750 kN, and hence OK.

Boundary strut, *AD*: Force = 1176 kN

The width node face = 477.4 mm (Figure 17.19)

Capacity of the strut = $\phi A_{cs} f_{ce}$ = 0.75 × 477.4 × 450 × 20.4 × 10^{-3} = 3287 kN > 1176 kN, and hence OK.

Interior strut, *AB* connecting Node *A*: Force = 1395 kN

The width of strut-to-node interface = 188 sin 32.53 + 477.4 cos 32.53 = 504 mm (Figure 17.19)

Strength of the strut = $\phi A_{cs} f_{ce}$ = 0.75 × 504 × 450 × 15.3 × 10^{-3} = 2603 kN > 1395 kN, and hence OK.

Node D

Bearing face: Force = 1050 kN.

The width of node face = 262 mm (Figure 17.19)

Strength of the node face = $\phi A_{nz} f_{ce}$ = 0.75 × 262 × 450 × 20.4 × 10^{-3} = 1804 kN > 1050 kN, and hence OK. [Note that at bearing faces of nodes A and D, the loads and bearing widths are taken proportionately and hence it is sufficient to check one only.]

Interior strut, *CD* connecting Node *D*: Force = 1576 kN

The width of strut-to-node interface = 262 sin 41.77 + 477.4 cos 41.77 = 531 mm (Figure 17.19)

Strength of the strut = $\phi A_{cs} f_{ce}$ = 0.75 × 531 × 450 × 15.3 × 10^{-3} = 2742 kN > 1576 kN, and hence OK.

Node B

Bearing face: Force = 750 kN

The width of node face = 450 mm (Figure 17.19)

Capacity of the node face = $\phi A_{nz} f_{ce}$ = 0.75 × 450 × 450 × 16.32 × 10^{-3} = 2479 kN > 750 kN, and hence OK.

Interior strut, *AB* connecting Node *B*: Force = 1395 kN

The width of strut-to-node interface = 450 sin 32.53 +225 cos 32.53= 432 mm (Figure 17.19)

Capacity of the strut = $\phi A_{cs} f_{ce}$ = 0.75 × 432 × 450 × 15.3 × 10^{-3} = 2231 kN > 1395 kN, and hence OK.

Side face (where tie is anchored): Force = 1176 kN

Width of tie = 2(112.5) = 225 mm

Capacity of the strut = $\phi A_{nz} f_{ce}$ = 0.75 × 225 × 450 × 16.32 × 10^{-3} = 1239 kN > 1176 kN

Node C

Bearing face: Force = 1050 kN

The width of node face = 450 mm

Capacity of the node face = $\phi A_{nz} f_{ce}$ = 0.75 × 450 × 450 × 16.32 × 10^{-3} = 2479 kN > 1050 kN, and hence OK.

Interior strut, *CD* connecting Node *C*: Force = 1576 kN

The width of strut-to-node interface = 450 sin 41.77° +225 cos 41.77°= 468 mm (Figure 17.19)

Capacity of the strut = $\phi A_{cs} f_{ce}$ = 0.75 × 468 × 450 × 15.3 × 10^{-3} = 2417 kN > 1576 kN, and hence OK.

Side face (where tie is anchored): Force = 1176 kN

Width of tie = 2(112.5) = 225 mm

Capacity of the strut = $\phi A_c f_{ce} = 0.75 \times 225 \times 450 \times 16.32 \times 10^{-3} = 1239$ kN > 1176 kN

Distributed reinforcement

Minimum distributed reinforcement has to be provided as orthogonal grid in accordance to Eq. 17.50. Assume 2 legged stirrups of 10 mm diameter in horizontal and vertical directions.

$$A_{sv} = A_{sh} = 157 \text{ mm}^2$$

$$\text{Spacing, } s_v = \frac{A_{sv}}{0.0025b} = \frac{157}{0.0025(450)} = 139.6 \text{ mm}$$

Provide 10ϕ two legged stirrups at 130 mm c/c spacing (in vertical and horizontal directions)

Detailing is shown in Figure 17.20.

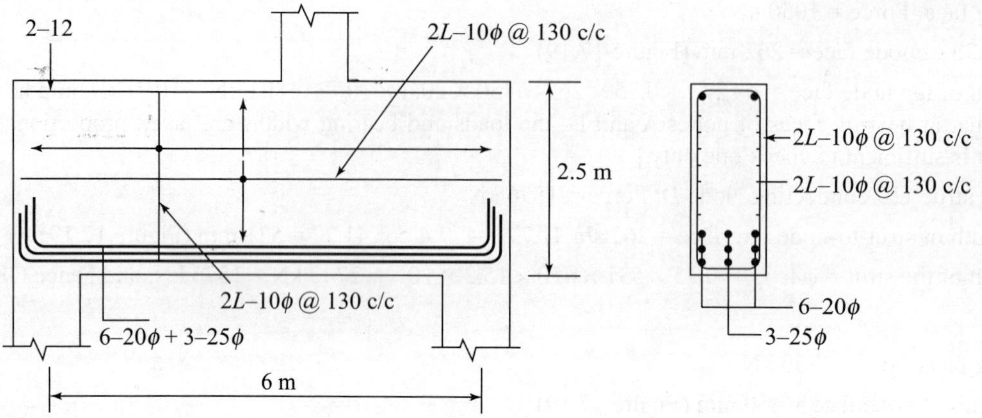

Fig. 17.20 Detailing of Reinforcement, Example 17.4.

Example 17.5 *Corbel*

Design a double corbel projecting from a column of size 350 mm × 350 mm. The corbels support precast beam (on each side) exerting a reaction force of 250 kN (factored) acting at 200 mm from the face of the column. A horizontal tensile force of 60 kN is assumed to develop at the top accounting for creep and shrinkage deformations. Use M 30 concrete and Fe 500 steel.

Solution

- Given: *Factored load,* $V_u = 250$ kN; Axial Tension, $N_u = 60$ kN
  Shear span, $a = 200$ mm

  Cylinder strength of concrete, $f_c' = 0.8 f_{ck} = 0.8(30) = 24$ MPa

Size of the corbel

- Take the width of the corbel, $b = 350$ mm, same as the column depth.
- Provide the corbel with a total overhang of 350 mm from the face of the column.
- Depth may be chosen using Eq. 17.54

$$V_u \le \begin{cases} \phi(0.2) f_c' bd = 0.75(0.2)(24)(350)d = 1260d \\ \phi(3.3 + 0.08 f_c')bd = 0.75(3.3 + 0.08(24))(350)d = 506.5d \\ \phi(11)bd = 0.75(11)(350)d = 2887.5d \end{cases}$$

$\Rightarrow \quad 250 \times 10^3 \le 506.5d$

$d \ge 493.6$ mm

Assuming a clear cover of 30 mm and 16ϕ bars,

Depth of corbel at column face, $D \ge 493.6 + 30 + 16/2 = 531.6$ mm

Provide a depth, $\boldsymbol{D = 540}$ **mm;** Effective depth, $d = 540 - 30 - 16/2 = 502$ mm

Depth at outer edge of bearing should be at least $D/2 = 270$ mm. Provide 270 mm depth at the free end of the corbel as in Figure 17.21.

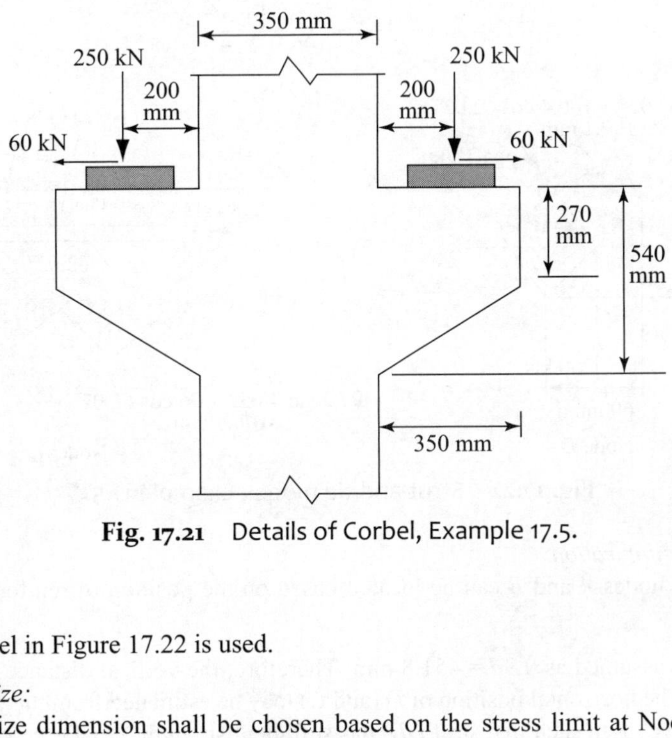

Fig. 17.21 Details of Corbel, Example 17.5.

Strut-and-Tie Model

The strut-and-tie model in Figure 17.22 is used.

- *Bearing plate size:*

  Bearing plate size dimension shall be chosen based on the stress limit at Node A. Vertical force at bearing = 250 kN

  Assume 300 mm × 100 mm bearing plate.

  Stress limit at node A (CCT node), $f_{ce} = 0.85 \times 0.8 \times 1 \times 24 = 16.32$ MPa

  Strength of bearing face = $\phi A_{nz} f_{ce} = 0.75\ (300 \times 100)(16.32) = 367200 > 250 \times 10^3$. Hence assumed bearing plate size is OK.

  Provide 300 mm × 100 mm bearing plate

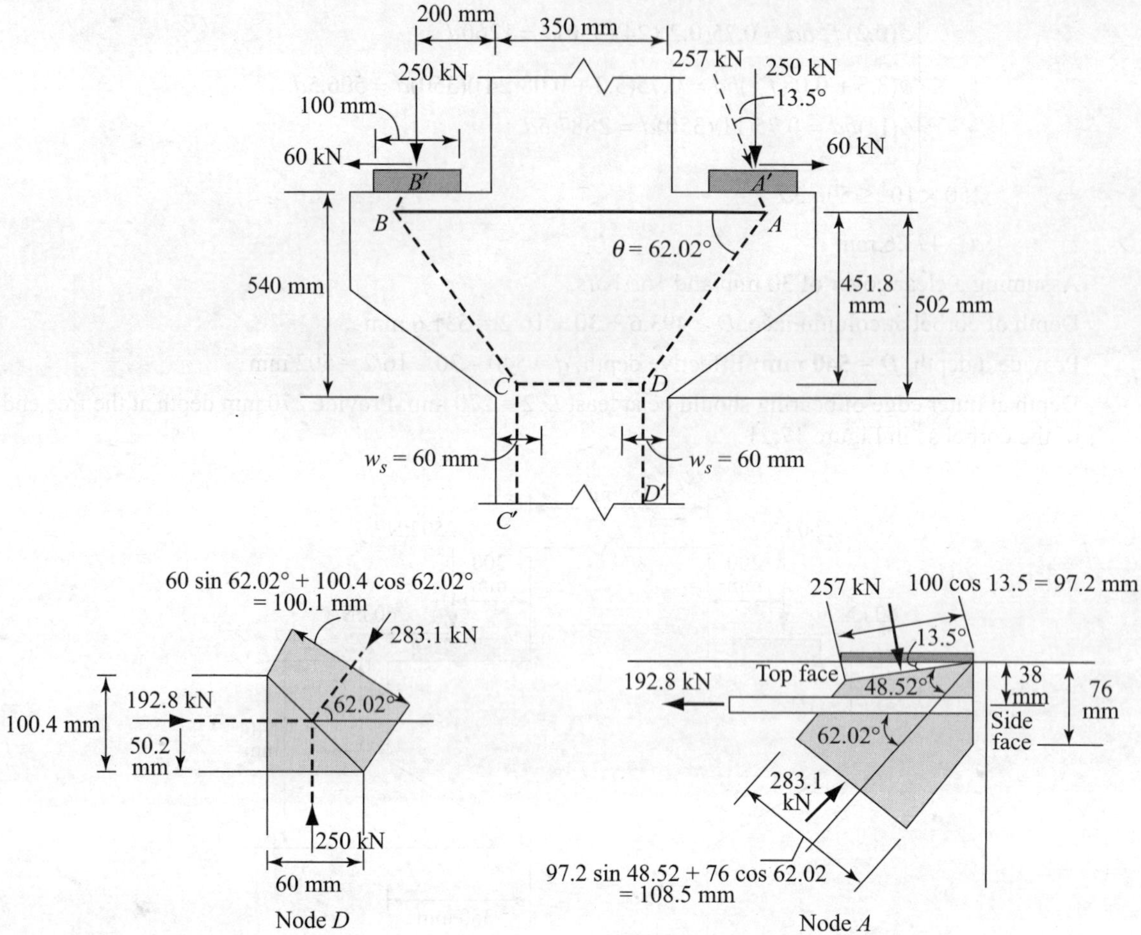

Fig. 17.22 Strut-and-tie model, Example 17.5.

- *Strut-and-Tie Configuration:*

  The positions of nodes A and B can be located based on the position of reinforcement and the shear span.

  The lever arm is assumed as $0.9d = 451.8$ mm. Therefore, the vertical distance between nodes A and $D = 451.8$ mm. The horizontal position of D (and C) may be estimated from the width of strut DD', w_s. Width w_s may be chosen such that strut DD' has sufficient strength, i.e., Force in strut $DD' \leq$ Strength of the strut.

  Force in Strut DD' = 250 kN

  Strength of Strut $DD' = \phi A_{cs} f_{ce}$ where f_{ce} = 20.4 MPa (= $0.85 f_c'$ for boundary strut)

  $$= 0.75(w_s b) f_{ce} = 0.75(350 w_s)(20.4) = 5355 w_s$$

  $\Rightarrow \quad 250 \times 10^3 \leq 5355\, w_s;\ w_s \geq 46.7$ mm

Choose $w_s = 60$ mm. (Fig. 17.22)

Strut angle, $\theta = \tan^{-1}\left(\dfrac{451.8}{200 + 60/2}\right) = 62.02°$

- *Strut-and-Tie Forces:*

Strut AA': The strut force will be resultant of V_u and N_u.

$F_{AA'} = \sqrt{250^2 + 60^2} = 257$ kN at an angle of $\tan^{-1}\left(\dfrac{60}{250}\right) = 13.5°$

Struts DD' & CC': $F_{DD'} = 250$ kN

Struts AD & BC: $F_{AD} = \dfrac{250}{\sin 62.02°} = 283.1$ kN

Strut CD: $F_{CD} = \dfrac{250}{\tan 62.02°} = 132.8$ kN

Tie AB: $F_{AB} = \dfrac{250}{\tan 62.02°} + 60 = 192.8$ kN

Main tie reinforcement

- Required tension reinforcement (corresponding to tie AB) may be calculated from,

$$\phi F_{nt} \geq F_{ut} \quad \Rightarrow \quad \phi f_y A_{st} \geq F_{ut}$$

$$0.75 \times 500 \times A_{st} \geq 192.8 \times 10^3$$

$$A_{st} \geq 514 \text{ mm}^2$$

$\Rightarrow$ **Provide 3–16ϕ** for which $A_{st} = 3(201) = 603 > 514$.

- Minimum reinforcement (Eq. 17.55),

$$A_{sc\text{-}min} = 0.04\left(\frac{f_c'}{f_y}\right)(bd) = 0.04\left(\frac{24}{500}\right)(350)(502) = 337 \text{ mm}^2 < 514 \text{ mm}^2$$

Hence OK.

The main reinforcement is welded at its outer end to a transverse bar of 16ϕ to develop f_y at face of support.

Check for strength of struts/nodes

Nodes need to be proportioned to dimension the node faces and struts connecting the nodes. Node A and Node D dimensions are given in Figure 17.22.

Node A (CCT node)

Force in strut AA' = 257 kN

Bearing width = 100 mm

Strut width of strut AA' = 100 cos 13.5° = 97.2 mm

Stress limit, $f_{ce} = 0.85\beta_n \beta_c f_c'$

Here, $\beta_n = 0.8$ (CCT node). As the bearing plate size is smaller than the size of the member (in the out of plane direction), increase in stress limit due to confinement may be considered. Therefore, confinement factor $\beta_n = \sqrt{A_1/A_2}$, where $A_2 = 300 \times 97.2 = 29160$ mm^2 (area of top face) and $A_1 = 350(97.2 + 50) = 51520$ mm^2 (area of projected area geometrically similar to the top face area). $\beta_n = \sqrt{51520/29160} = 1.33$.

$$f_{ce} = 0.85(0.8)(1.33)(24) = 21.71 \text{ MPa}$$

Strength of the strut = $\phi A_{cs} f_{ce} = 0.75(97.2 \times 300)21.71 \times 10^{-3} = 475.1$ kN > 257 kN, and hence OK.

Side face (where tie is anchored): Force = 192.8 kN

Stress limit, $f_{ce} = 0.85\beta_n\beta_c f_c' = 0.85(0.8)(1)(24) = 16.32$ MPa

Width of tie = 2(38) = 76 mm

Strength of the strut = $\phi A_c f_{ce} = 0.75(76 \times 350)16.32 \times 10^{-3} = 325.6$ kN > 192.8 kN, and hence OK.

Interior strut, *AD* connecting Node *A*: Force = 283.1 kN

Stress limit, $f_{ce} = 0.85\beta_s\beta_c f_c' = 0.85(0.75)(1.33)(24) = 20.20$ MPa

The confinement factor, $\beta_c = 1.33$ may be considered for the strut end *A* connecting with node *A* (the strut end *D* will be checked below). $\beta_s = 0.75$ as minimum distributed reinforcement is to be provided.

The width of strut-to-node interface = 97.2 sin (62.02-13.5) + 76 cos 62.02 = 108.5 mm (Figure 17.22)

Capacity of the strut = $\phi A_{cs} f_{ce} = 0.75(108.5 \times 300) \times 20.20 \times 10^{-3} = 493.1$ kN > 283.1 kN, and hence OK.

Node D (CCC node)

Side face: Force = 192.8 kN

Stress limit, $f_{ce} = 0.85\beta_n\beta_c f_c' = 0.85(1)(1)(24) = 16.32$ MPa

Width of strut *CD* = 2(50.2) = 100.4 mm

Capacity of the strut = $\phi A_{cs} f_{ce} = 0.75(100.4 \times 350)16.32 \times 10^{-3} = 430.1$ kN > 192.8 kN, and hence OK.

Interior strut, *AD* connecting Node *D*: Force = 283.1 kN. For end *D* of strut *AD*, $\beta_c = 1.0$. Stress limit, $f_{ce} = 0.85\beta_s\beta_c f_c' = 0.85(0.75)(1)(24) = 15.3$ MPa

The width of strut-to-node interface = 60 sin 62.02° + 100.4 cos 62.02° = 100.1 mm (Figure 17.22)
Capacity of the strut = $\phi A_{cs} f_{ce} = 0.75(100.1 \times 350) \times 15.3 \times 10^{-3} = 402$ kN > 283.1 kN, and hence OK.

Distributed reinforcement

Minimum distributed reinforcement shall be provided in horizontal direction (Eq. 17.51) within 2/3 *d* distance from the main reinforcement.

Assume 2 legged stirrups of 8 mm diameter.

$$A_{svh} = 157 \text{ mm}^2$$

$$\text{Spacing, } s = \frac{A_{svh}\sin^2\alpha_1}{0.0025b} = \frac{100.5\sin^2 62.02°}{0.0025 \times 350} = 89.6 \text{ mm}$$

Number of strirrups = (2/3)d/s = 3.7.

Provide 4 numbers of 8ϕ two legged stirrups in horizontal direction within a distance of $2/3d \approx 330$ mm from main reinforcement. Detailing is shown in Figure 17.23.

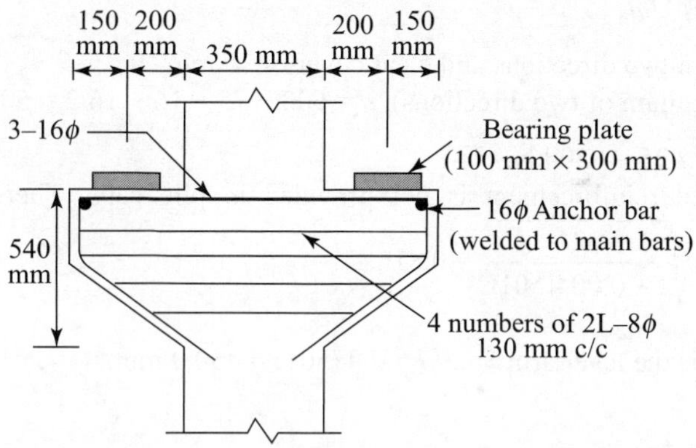

Fig. 17.23 Detailing of Reinforcement, Example 17.5.

Example 17.6 *Pile Cap*

Design a 600 mm deep pile cap of size 2000 mm × 2000 mm for connecting a square column of size 450 mm × 450 mm to four circular piles of diameter 300 mm spaced at a distance of 1.3 m as shown in the plan view in Figure 17.24. The column carries a factored axial load of 1700 kN. Assume M30 concrete and Fe 500 steel.

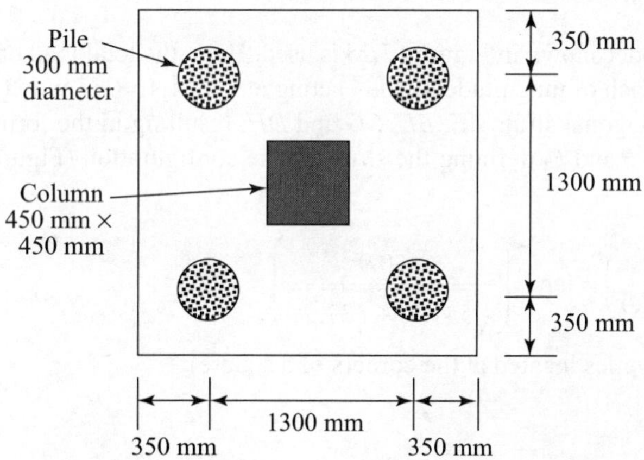

Fig. 17.24 Pile Cap, Example 17.6.

Solution

- Given: P_f = 1800 kN/m
- Assuming the weight of the pile cap small compared the load on the column the reaction on one pile = 1700/4 = 425 kN.

Depth check

- Pile cap is assumed as a deep beam with shear span, a as 1300/2 = 650 mm and width b = 2000 mm. To check for adequacy of depth, using Eq. 17.52.

  $V_u \leq 0.42\phi \tan \theta \lambda_s \sqrt{f_c'}\, bd$

- Assuming 16ϕ bars in two directions and clear cover of 75 mm,
  Effective depth (minimum of two directions), $d = 600 - 75 - 16 - 16/2 = 501$ mm.

- Shear force, $V_u = 2 \times 425 = 850$ kN.
  Minimum distributed reinforcement is not provided in pile caps. Therefore, Size effect factor,

  $$\lambda_s = \sqrt{\frac{2}{1 + 0.004d}} = \sqrt{\frac{2}{1 + 0.004(501)}} = 0.816 \leq 1$$

  $\tan \theta = \dfrac{z}{a}$; where z is the lever arm $\approx 0.9d = 0.9\,(501) = 450.9$ mm.

  $$\tan \theta \approx \frac{450.9}{650} = 0.694$$

  $V_u \leq 0.42\phi \tan \theta \lambda_s \sqrt{f_c'}\, bd$

  $850 \times 10^3 \leq 0.42(0.75)(0.694)(0.816)\sqrt{24}\,(2000)(501)$

  $850 \times 10^3 \leq 875 \times 10^3$ Hence OK.

  Strut-and-Tie Model

  The strut-and-tie model shown in Figure 17.25 is used. Here, the total load on the column is considered as four point loads each of magnitude 425 kN acting at nodes A, B, C and D. The load gets transferred to the piles by the diagonal struts AE, BF, CG and DH, resulting in the formation of ties EF, FG, GH and HE. The angles θ and θ_1 defining the strut-and-tie configuration (Figure 17.25) shall be obtained from geometry.

  $$\text{Angle, } \theta = \tan^{-1}\left(\frac{z}{\text{EO}}\right) = \tan^{-1}\left(\frac{450.9}{\sqrt{537.5^2 + 537.5^2}}\right) = 30.68°$$

  Angle, $\theta_1 = 45°$ (for piles located at the corners of a square)

- *Strut-and-Tie Forces:*

  $$\text{Strut } AE, BF, CG \text{ and } DH\text{: } F_{AE} = \frac{425}{\sin 30.68°} = 832.9 \text{ kN}$$

  $$\text{Struts } AB, BC, CD \text{ and } AD\text{: } F_{AB} = \frac{425}{\tan 30.68°} \cos 45° = 506.5 \text{ kN}$$

  $$\text{Ties } EF, FG, GH \text{ and } EH\text{: } F_{CD} = \frac{425}{\tan 30.68°} \cos 45° = 506.5 \text{ kN}$$

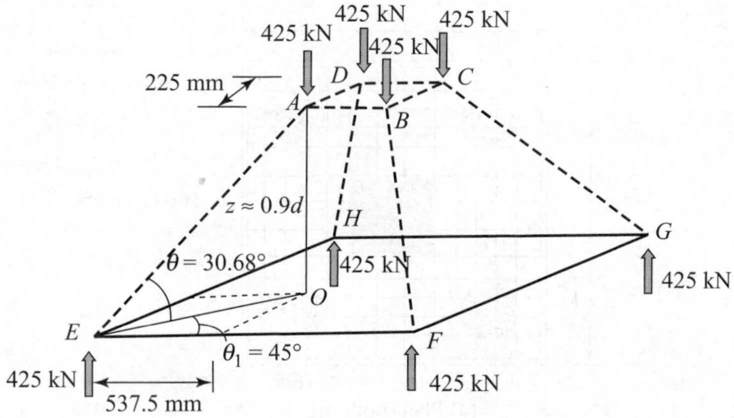

Fig. 17.25 Strut-and-tie model, Example 17.6.

Main tie reinforcement

- Required tension reinforcement (corresponding to each of ties *EF*, *FG*, *GH* and *EH*) may be calculated from,

$$\phi F_{nt} \geq F_{ut} \quad \Rightarrow \quad \phi f_y A_{st} \geq F_{ut}$$

$$0.75 \times 500 \times A_{st} \geq 506.5 \times 10^3$$

$$A_{st} \geq 1351 \text{ mm}^2$$

$\Rightarrow$ **Provide 8–16ϕ** in two layers concentrated over the piles, for which $A_{st} = 8(201) = 1608 > 1351$. [Note that with reinforcement provided in two layers, the lesser effective depth will be 501 – 16 = 485 mm [Figure 17.26(b)]. The average effective depth, considering both directions will be 501 mm, and the depth requirement above (Eq. 17.52) will still be met]

The minimum reinforcement of 0.12% (for slabs) may be provided in region between the piles. This corresponds to 0.0012(1300−300)(600) = 720 mm^2. $\Rightarrow$ **Provide 4–16ϕ** between the piles.

- Development length required
  = 45.0ϕ (for M 30 concrete, Fe 500 steel)

  = 45.0 × 16 = 720 mm

  Development length should be provided beyond the inner face of the piles

  Length available = 350 + 300/2 – 75 = 425 mm – not OK.

  Provide a 90 degree bend with required development length beyond the bend. Extension required beyond the bend may be taken conservatively as = 720 – 425 = 295 mm ≈ 300 mm.

Check for strength of struts/nodes

The shape of nodal zones inside 3D structures like pile cap is complex and this is required to check for the strength of struts/nodes. In a 3-D structure like a pile cap, the concrete in the struts and nodes is highly confined compared to those in a 2-D structure, and hence has significantly enhanced compressive strength.

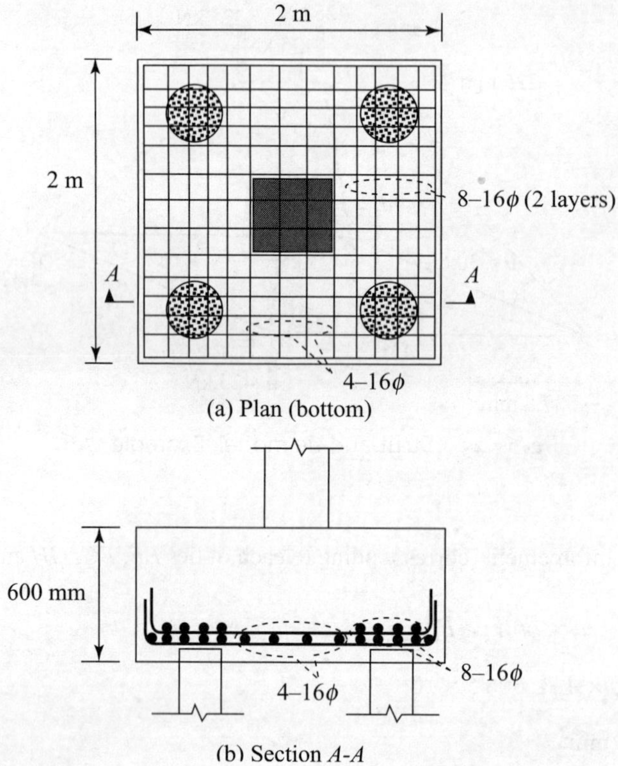

Fig. 17.26 Strut-and-tie model, Example 17.6.

The confinement factor, β_c for the stress limits of nodes and struts (Eqs. 17.46, 17.48) is relatively high as the sizes of the piles and column are much smaller than the size of the pile cap. Therefore, the stress limits for the nodes and struts are larger than for a typical two-dimensional member. Hence, a simplified method (Vide Example 11, SP 273 [Ref. 17.10]) is adopted. In this method, the strength of the nodal zones is assumed to be adequate by limiting the bearing stresses on the piles and the column. It is further assumed that if the strength of nodal zones is adequate, the strength of concrete struts will also be adequate because (i) the available area of struts is larger than that of nodal zones and (ii) the concrete struts in pile caps are well confined all around inside the pile caps.

Bearing stress check on piles:

Compressive force in the piles = 425 kN

Stress limit, $f_{ce} = 0.85\beta_s\beta_c f_c' = 0.85(1)(1)(24) = 20.4$ MPa

Strength = $\phi A_c f_{ce} = 0.75\left(\pi\dfrac{300^2}{4}\right)20.4 \times 10^{-3} = 1081$ kN > 425 kN, and Hence OK.

Bearing stress check on column:

Compressive force in the column = 1700 kN

Stress limit (boundary strut), $f_{ce} = 0.85\beta_s\, \beta_c f_c' = 0.85(1)(1)(24) = 20.4$ MPa

Strength = $\phi A_c f_{ce} = 0.75(450 \times 450)\ 20.4 \times 10^{-3} = 3098$ kN > 1700 kN, and hence OK.

Detailing of the pile cap is given in Figure 17.26.

17.4 Fire Resistance

17.4.1 Introduction

The purpose of this section is to make the reader aware of the need to consider the fire resistance aspect and the related requirements of the applicable building codes, where these can be critical, while designing reinforced concrete structures. It is not the intent here to deal with the behaviour of structures in real fire situations. The objective is only to present some basic information, in order to aid the designer in considering fire hazards and certain fire protection features which could be kept in perspective while doing the structural design and detailing. Indian standard IS 1641 [Ref. 17.15] classifies buildings according to the use or the character of occupancy into 9 groups. Further, the city or area is to be demarcated into distinct Fire Zones (numbered 1–3) based on fire hazard inherent in the buildings and structures in the area, according to occupancy groups. The standard IS 1642 [Ref. 17.16] classifies the types of construction, according to fire resistance ratings, into four categories – Type 1 to Type 4. Restrictions are imposed on admissible Type of construction for new buildings erected in different Fire zones [Ref. 17.15]. The *fire resistance ratings* for structural and non-structural members for various Types of construction are specified in IS 1642 (Table 1, Ref. 17.16). Type 1 construction has the highest fire resistance rating and Type 4 the lowest among the four.

Fire resistance generally refers to the property of a material or assembly to withstand fire or give protection from it. As applied to elements of buildings or a structure, it is characterized by the ability to confine a fire or to continue to perform a given structural function, or both. Resistance to **flame penetration**, **heat transmission** and **failure** are major components. ***Fire resistance rating*** is the *time in hours* or fraction thereof that a material or assembly of materials will withstand the passage of flame and transmission of heat when exposed to fire under specified conditions of test and performance criteria (or as determined by extension or interpretation of information so derived).

The fire resistance rating of building components is determined by standard fire resistance test. In such tests, a building assembly such as a portion of a floor, wall, roof or column is subjected to increasing temperatures that vary with time, approximating the conditions which would prevail during a fire within a moderate size compartment having a relatively small amount of ventilation. Floor and roof specimens are exposed to the fire from below, beams from the bottom and sides, walls from one side and columns from all sides. The end of the test is reached and the fire endurance of the specimen established when (i) specified rise in temperature of unexposed surface, (ii) flame penetration to the unexposed surface through cracks or fissures or (iii) failure to sustain specified load occurs. In general, fire resistance of concrete floor/roof assemblies and walls is governed by heat transmission (i.e., the temperature of the unexposed surface rises by/to a specified value), and columns and beams by failure to sustain the applied load, or beam reinforcement temperature rising to a limiting value. A standard fire resistance test is specified in IS 3809 [Ref. 17.17]. The designer has also the option to use ratings assigned to common assemblies and members in various codes such as Ref. 17.18.

Fire resistance of concrete elements depends upon details such as member size, cover to steel, reinforcement detailing and type of aggregate (normal weight or light weight).

17.4.2 Factors which influence Fire Resistance Ratings of RC Assemblies

Type of Concrete and Aggregates

Concrete is one of the most highly fire resistant structural material used in construction. However, the properties of concrete and reinforcing steel do change significantly at high temperatures caused by fire. For both materials, at high temperatures, the strength and modulus of elasticity are reduced, the coefficient of expansion increases, and creep and stress relaxations are considerably higher.

The compressive strength of concrete during fire exposure mainly depends upon the aggregate it contains. Concrete in which the coarse aggregate is limestone, calcareous gravel, sandstone, blast furnace slag or similar dense material containing not more than 30% quartz performs better during fire exposure, compared with concrete with coarse aggregate such as granite, quartzite, siliceous gravel or other dense materials containing more than 30% quartz. In general, low-density aggregate concretes exhibit better fire performance than natural stone aggregate concretes.

Member Size and Detailing

Other things being equal, the larger the thickness or overall cross-section of an assembly, the greater its fire resistance rating. In slab-like members, such as floors, roofs and walls, the rating can be improved by increasing the thickness. For beams and columns, larger cross sections suffer less average concrete strength loss than smaller ones for a given period of fire exposure, as the larger sections take longer to heat up. Where a plaster finish is used, the plaster thickness can be included in the member thickness for fire resistance requirements. In the case of sections containing cores or voids, an *equivalent thickness* of the slab must be used. For hollow-core concrete slabs and panels having a uniform thickness and cores of constant cross section throughout their length, the equivalent thickness to be used may be obtained by dividing the net cross sectional area of the slab or panel by its width.

Reinforcing Steel and Cover

The loss of strength at high temperatures will be slower for hot rolled reinforcing steel than for cold worked steel and prestressing tendons. Since the load carrying capacity of a member depends largely upon the tensile strength of the reinforcement in it, its fire resistance rating depends upon the type of reinforcing steel and the level of stress in the steel.

The rate at which heat reaches the reinforcement in a member and hence the loss of strength of the reinforcement is inversely proportional to the concrete cover provided. It should be noted that while plaster thickness, where provided, cannot be reckoned as part of cover for meeting the durability requirements (Table 16 of Code), it can be included in the cover thickness for meeting the fire resistance requirements (Table 16A of Code).

Continuity and Restraint (Structural System)

This depends on (1) boundary conditions and (2) type of structural element.

Fire endurance of statically determinate beams and slabs Consider a simply supported reinforced concrete beam, subject to a uniformly distributed load. If the underside of the beam is exposed to fire, this side will expand more than the top, resulting in additional curvature and hence deflection of the beam. If the member is not restrained, no additional stress due to such deformation is likely to be induced (when the temperature gradient across the depth is linear). The compressive strength of concrete and tensile strength of steel will decrease with increase in temperature, and flexural collapse occurs at a 'critical temperature' when the material strength (usually that of steel) lowers to such an extent as to eliminate the margin of safety. The presence of end restraints in such a beam will delay the collapse, as it induces a compressive stress in the steel (and a membrane tension or catenary effect at large deflections); this beneficial effect, however, does not occur in the case of a cantilever or if the top surface of the simply supported member is subject to fire.

Fire endurance of continuous beams and slabs Structures that are continuous or otherwise statically indeterminate undergo changes in stresses when subjected to fire. Such changes in stress result from temperature induced deformations which may be restrained, or changes in strength of materials at high temperatures, or both. The continuous system may fail either by the critical temperature being reached in the reinforcement in the exposed side or by temperature-induced additional stress in the reinforcement in the unexposed side.

Consider a multi-span continuous beam, whose underside is exposed to fire. The bottom of the beam gets hotter than the top and tends to expand more than the top. This differential expansion, under restrained conditions, results in increase in hogging (negative) moments at the interior supports and decrease in sagging (positive) moments in the span regions [Ref. 17.19].

The cover specified by IS 456 for a continuous system for the same endurance rating is less than that for a simply supported system in view of the redundancy in the continuous system. The nominal cover for reinforcement to be provided also depends on the dimensions of the structural element, which govern the rate at which the temperature of steel increases.

Fire Protection Measures

Occasionally, members or assemblies may be provided with fire protection treatments such as plasterboard layers, lightweight aggregate gypsum plaster, fire resistant false ceiling, fire resistant finishes, sprayed fireproofing, etc. When used, contribution of such treatments to the fire resistance must be assessed separately based on test results with such materials.

17.4.3 Code Requirements

In the design of concrete structures, requirements for fire resistance are often overlooked. For example, slab thickness designs adequate from strength and deflection considerations may not provide sufficient fire resistance. As already indicated, the two important design parameters are the member dimensions (especially thickness in the case of slab-like members) and cover to reinforcement. The thickness controls transmission of heat and the cover structural integrity.

The Code (Cl. 21) states that 'a structure or structural element required to have fire resistance should be designed to possess an appropriate degree of resistance to flame penetration; heat transmission and failure'. However, except for giving the minimum requirements of concrete cover and member dimensions for normal-weight aggregate concrete members to have the required fire resistance (Cl. 21.2), the Code does not cover any aspect of design to achieve the required fire resistance ratings. Minimum requirements of member dimensions and concrete cover for normal-weight aggregate concrete members so as to have the required fire resistance are given in Figure 1 and Table 16A of the Code respectively.

It is emphasized that the nominal cover specified in the Code (Cl. 26.4.2) to meet durability requirements may not be sufficient to meet required fire resistance rating. However, too large a cover (in excess of 40 mm for beams and 35 mm for slabs), especially over closely spaced grid type reinforcement layers, may lead to spalling of the cover concrete. In such cases, additional measures should be adopted to give protection against spalling (Code Cl. 21.3.1). Such are the cases falling below the bold line in Table 16A of Code. In column members, when the required cover exceeds 60 mm, wire mesh reinforcement with 1.57 mm diameter wire and 100 mm openings may be incorporated midway in the concrete cover to retain the concrete in position.

Example 17.7

Determine the fire resistance rating of the floor slab designed in Example 5.2. Assume the concrete as normal-weight.

Solution

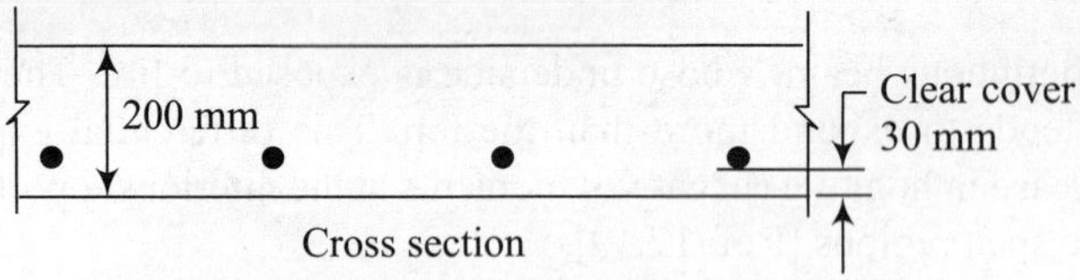

Fig. 17.27 Example 17.7.

The slab cross section is shown in Figure 17.27

- **Rating for transmission of heat**
  From the design, thickness of slab = 200 mm.

  Rating for transfer of heat, as per Fig. 1 of Code (as $D > 170$ mm) is 4 hours (+).
- **Rating for structural integrity**
  Clear concrete cover = 30 mm. The slab is simply supported.

  Referring to Table 16A of Code, the cover is > 25 mm, but less than 35 mm.

  The rating for this cover is 1.5 hours (+).

  Hence, structural integrity governs, and the rating is 1.5 hours.

Example 17.8

Determine the fire resistance rating of the beam and slab floor designed in Example 11.6. Assume the concrete as normal-weight.

Solution

The relevant floor system dimensions are shown in Figure 17.28.

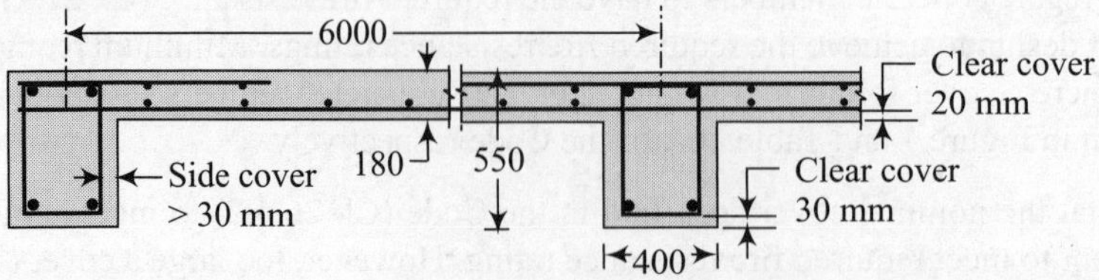

Fig. 17.28 Example 17.8.

- **Fire resistance of the beam section**
  The beam is continuous. For 30 mm cover, from Table 16A of Code, the fire resistance rating is 2 hours. Width of beam is 400 mm. Rating for this, from Figure 1 of Code is in excess of 4 hours. Hence the beam qualifies for a rating of 2 hours
- **Fire resistance of the slab**
  From Figure 1 of Code, for 180 mm thick normal-weight aggregate concrete, rating to resist transfer of heat is in excess of 4 hours.

  From Table 16A, for a clear cover of 20 mm, for continuous slab, the rating is 1.5 hours. Hence, the structural rating controls for the slab and is 1.5 hours.

  Thus, the total floor assembly qualifies for a rating of 1.5 hours.

17.5 Green Building Design

Introduction This Section is primarily meant to increase the awareness of the need for environment-friendly designs, in general. One of the early definitions of Engineering is 'the combination of art and science by which the materials and power of nature are made useful to mankind' [Ref. 17.20]. While service to humanity has always been a major concern in the practice of engineering, the latter's impact on the environment received serious attention only towards the end of the 20th century. We have come to realize that the unmindful exploitation of nature's resources can do irreversible harm to the planet's systems and cycles on which all life depends. Currently, the primary concern in the practice of engineering has shifted towards building a sustainable future through *Sustainable Development*. Sustainable development denotes balancing the need for development and growth for meeting the necessities of the present generation, and the need to protect the natural and built environment for meeting the needs and aspirations of future generations. Buildings need to be routinely designed, constructed and maintained from an environmentally sustainable point of view over its entire life span and hence the effort to 'green' this sector.

Consumption of resources Civil/structural engineering practice involves the use of considerable amounts of natural materials whose progressive depletion and consequent adverse environmental impacts are presently being felt. The unchecked mining of sand (for use as fine aggregate) from and consequent lowering of river beds, leading to quicker run-off, lowered ground water table and dried-up surface wells nearby is a case in point. Products such as cement and steel use considerable energy in their manufacture, which contributes to greenhouse gas emissions. The largest environmental impact attributable to concrete construction, in particular, is the emissions in the cement manufacturing process. The cement industry currently emits 730 to 990 kilograms of CO_2 for every 1000 kg of cement produced, depending on product compositions and process efficiencies which vary from country to country [Ref. 17.21]. Over all, the built environment accounts for a large share of energy use with associated greenhouse gas emissions. *Green building design* envisages increasing the efficiency with which buildings use resources while reducing the building's negative impacts on human health and environment.

Green design The major elements of green buildings include: sustainable sites, water efficiency, energy and atmosphere, materials and resources, indoor environmental quality and innovations in design. Green building practice includes measures that conserve resources, use recycled materials, maximize energy efficiency and otherwise reduce building's impacts on the environment through the complete building life cycle. To evaluate the full environmental impact of a building over its life, a complete life cycle assessment must be carried out addressing all stages including resource extraction, manufacture and transportation of the materials used;

assembly and construction; operation including energy consumption and maintenance; and finally, disposal and reuse of building at end of its life. Planners and designers of reinforced concrete structures have the responsibility to ensure that non-renewable materials are used efficiently and to the minimum, recycled materials are used wherever possible, the initial as well as in-service energy consumption is optimized, renewable sources of energy (solar, wind) are tapped, environment friendly systems (such as rain-water harvesting and ground water recharging) are incorporated and adverse environmental impacts minimized to acceptable levels. Without elaborating, a partial list of steps that can be taken are listed below:

- Recycling concrete products
- Construction waste management
- Use of regional materials
- Structure/Finish combination concrete
- Use of reflective surfaces
- Elevators with regenerative drives
- Green roof
- Building reuse
- Incorporating recycled content material
- Build durable building - longevity
- Conservation via greater efficiency
- Use supplementary cementing materials
- Use of solar power array, water heaters
- Rain-water harvesting
- Wind power
- Resource reuse

Naturally, green building design has to be a cooperative effort involving the entire project team, of which the structural engineer is only a member. As such, a detailed discussion of green building design, which is a rapidly evolving field, is beyond the scope of this book. More information on this topic may be obtained from references 17.21 and 17.22.

17.6 New Materials

17.6.1 Self-Compacted Concrete

Originated in Japan in the late 1980s, *Self-Compacting Concrete* (*SCC*) is a high-performance concrete, designed to *flow* into formwork and consolidate under its own weight, without the aid of mechanical vibration. The fluid consistency and high flowability are achieved through changing the mix proportions (such as increasing cementitious material, increasing paste content, careful selection of aggregate volume and gradation, and lower *w/c* ratio) and by using admixtures such as superplasticizers. The advantages of SCC include rapid placement, reduced labour costs and improved aesthetic appearance of the surface. However, the high flowability may also lead to segregation of course aggregates. The creep and shrinkage of SCC may also be enhanced. More information on this topic may be obtained from Ref. 17.23 and 17.24.

17.6.2 Roller-Compacted Concrete

Use of ***roller-compacted concrete*** originated in Canada in mid-1970s. It is a durable paving material that can carry heavy loads and finds applications as pavements for heavy-duty parking/storage areas and industrial facilities, as base for highway pavements, for gravity dams, etc. While RCC contains the same basic ingredients as conventional concrete – cement, aggregate and water – it is mixed in a drier form (zero slump), placed (usually with asphalt-type paving equipment) and compacted with rollers. Compared with conventional concrete, RCC typically has lower water content, lower paste content, smaller maximum aggregate size and larger fine aggregate content. It must be dry enough to support the weight of the large compaction roller, yet wet enough to facilitate mixing and placement. Use of dense-graded aggregates and low *w/c* ratio gives RCC high-strength properties. Other benefits of RCC are ease and speed of construction and lower cost. More information on this topic may be obtained from Ref. 17.25.

17.6.3 CRS and TMT Rebars

Use of ***corrosion-resistant steel (CRS)*** and ***thermo-mechanically treated (TMT)*** rebars is now being increasingly adopted as a means of enhancing durability of reinforced concrete. In CRS bars, corrosion-resistant elements, such as copper, phosphorus and chromium, are introduced in the manufacturing process. The oxide layer formed on the surface of the rebar, especially due to phosphorus, is found to be relatively dense (with minimal pores) and acts as an inhibitor to corrosion.

Thermo-mechanical treatment (TMT) is an advancement over traditional cold twisting technology in the manufacture of high strength deformed bars. The stage-wise heat treatment process results in a combination of a strong outer layer (of tempered *martensite*) and a ductile inner core (of ferrite-pearlite), giving the bar a combination of strength and ductility.

TMT bars are found to yield very high percentages of elongation (up to 20 per cent) in addition to high strength (500 MPa grade). In conventional cold-twisting of bars, the achievement of high grade was always accompanied by a reduction in ductility, and for this reason the use of Fe 500 bars was discouraged in earthquake-resistant design and detailing. However, in recognition of the changes achieved, the codes are being amended to facilitate the use of Fe 500 ductile bars.

REVIEW QUESTIONS

17.1 Explain *Tension Field Theory*. Where is it applicable?

17.2 Discuss how does the Compression Field Theory differ from the traditional method of design for shear.

17.3 Describe how does the compressive stress-strain relationship of concrete with cracks parallel to the compression differ from that of uncracked concrete. What is the maximum strength of such cracked concrete?

17.4 Enumerate the assumptions used in the Modified Compression Field Theory and critically evaluate them.

17.5 Explain how does an axial tensile force in a beam influence its shear strength.

17.6 Why is the anchorage of flexural tension reinforcement at external support critical?

17.7 Give examples where the Strut-and-Tie Model is most appropriate for design.

17.8 Discuss the design considerations in design using the Strut-and-Tie model.

17.9 In a test for fire resistance of a building component, what are the limiting endurance criteria?

17.10 Describe the factors that influence fire resistance ratings of reinforced concrete assemblies.

17.11 Discuss how can the fire resistance of an already cast floor system improved.

17.12 List out the various measures that can be taken throughout the life cycle of a building by a Building Engineer to promote sustainable development.

PROBLEMS

See Chapters 6 and 7 for problems on shear and torsion design, to be solved using the CFT method.

REFERENCES

17.1 Collins, M P, Mitchell, D, *Prestressed Concrete Structures,* Prentice Hall, Englewood cliffs, NJ, 1991, pp 338–411.

17.2 Vecchio, F J and Collins, M P, *The Modified Compression-Field Theory for Reinforced Concrete Elements Subjected to Shear*, J. ACI, Vol. 83, March-April 1986, pp 219–231

17.3 Collins, M P, Mitchell, D, Adebar, P E, Vecchio, F J, *A General Shear Design Method*, ACI Structural Journal, Vol. 93, No. 1, Jan.–Feb. 1996, pp 36–45

17.4 Bentz, E C and Collins, M P, Development of the 2004 Canadian Standards Association (CSA) A23.3 shear provisions for reinforced concrete, Canadian Journal of Civil Engineering, Vol. 33, 2006, pp. 521–534

17.5 Schlaich, J and Schafer, K, *Design and Detailing of Structural Concrete using Strut-and-tie Models.* The Structural Engineer, Vol. 69, 1991, p 113

17.6 Muttoni, A, Schwartz, J, and Thürlimann, B, *Design of Concrete Structures with Stress Fields,* Birkhäuser Verlag, Switzerland, 1996

17.7 Geevar, I and Menon, D, *Strength of Reinforced Concrete Pier Caps – Experimental Validation of Strut-and-Tie Method,* ACI Structural Journal, 116(1), January 2019

17.8 Geevar, I, Menon, D and Prasad, A M, *Strut-and-Tie-Based Design and Testing of Reinforced Concrete Pier Caps.* ACI Structural Journal, 117(2), March 2020

17.9 SP-208, *Examples for the Design of Structural Concrete with Strut-and-Tie Models*, American Concrete Institute, Michigan, 2002

17.10 SP-273, *Further Examples for the Design of Structural Concrete with Strut-and-Tie Models*, American Concrete Institute, Michigan, 2011

17.11 *fib* bulletin 61, *Design Examples for Strut-and-Tie Models*, International Federation for Structural Concrete, Switzerland, 2011

17.12 Wight, James K and Macgregor, James G, *Reinforced Concrete Mechanics and Design*, Pearson Education Inc., 2012

17.13 Zhang, N, Tan, K H, and Leong, C L, *Single-span Deep Beams Subjected to Unsymmetrical Loads,* Journal of Structural Engineering, 135(3), 2009

17.14 ACI 318, *Building Code Requirements for Structural Concrete and Commentary (ACI 318-19)*, American Concrete Institute, Farmington Hills, USA, 2019.

17.15 — *Fire Safety of Buildings (General): General Principles of Fire Grading and Classification* IS:1641-1988, Bureau of Indian Standards, New Delhi, 1988, 5 pp

17.16 — *Fire Safety of Buildings (General): Details of Construction* IS:1642-1989, Bureau of Indian Standards, New Delhi, 1989, 15 pp

17.17 — *Fire Resistance Test of Structure* IS:3809-1979, Bureau of Indian Standards, New Delhi, 1979.

17.18 — *National Building Code of* Canada *1995: Appendix "D", Fire Performance Ratings*, National Research Council of Canada, Ottawa, 1995

17.19 Gustaferro, A H, *Fire Resistance*, Chapter 7 in *Handbook of Concrete Engineering* edited by Fintel, M., CBS Publishers, 1986, pp 212–226

17.20 Wickenden, W E, A professional Guide to Young Engineers, Engineers' Council for Professional Development New York, 1949, 48 p

17.21 *Guide to Sustainable Design with Concrete* – Version 2.0, Cement Association of Canada, April 2007, 137 p

17.22 *Energy Conservation Building Code – 2007* Manual, Bureau of Energy Efficiency, New Delhi, India

17.23 Okamura, H, *Self-compacting High Performance Concrete*, Concrete International, Vol. 19, No. 7, July 1997, pp. 50–54

17.24 D'Ambrosia, M D and Lange, D A, *Self-Consolidating Concrete*, Structure Magazine, Jan. 2007, pp. 48–50

17.25 Halsted, G, *Production of Roller-Compacted Concrete*, PCA Publication IS332, Portland Cement Association, Skokie, Il. USA, 2006, 8 p

CHAPTER 18

Design of Liquid Storage Tanks

LEARNING OBJECTIVES

After studying this chapter, you will be able to:

- *Describe the structural action and design considerations of common types of liquid storage tanks*
- *Design and detail circular and rectangular water tanks located at or below ground level*
- *Undertake strength and serviceability compliance checks for common types of water tanks*

18.1 Introduction

As mentioned in Chapter 2, reinforced concrete can be advantageously used in the construction of liquid storage structures. Water storage tanks, swimming pools, dams and effluent treatment tanks are a few examples where we commonly encounter the use of reinforced concrete, which has the key advantage of being relatively impermeable (and so, leak-proof), if designed and constructed properly. The components of the RC tank structure (typically walls and slabs) need to be designed to resist hydrostatic (and, in some cases, hydrodynamic) pressures induced by the liquid stored in the tank and external soil pressure in the case of below-ground level tanks. The effects of lateral loads due to wind and earthquake should also be considered, wherever relevant. It is also necessary to consider special loading conditions occurring during construction. Thus, for tanks fully or partially below ground, two loading conditions to be considered are (i) leakage testing stage, prior to backfilling of soil and addition of tank cover/roof and (ii) backfilling prior to adding roof, with tank empty. When liquids other than water (such as chemicals and petroleum products) or hot liquids are stored, specialist literature may have to be referred to, in order to estimate the lateral pressures induced and thermal effects, and to ensure durability of concrete in the presence of possibly aggressive chemical attack. This chapter discusses the design and performance criteria of under-ground, on-ground and over-head tanks, with typical design examples of ground-supported cylindrical and rectangular water storage tanks.

Concrete structures, in general, are required to have adequate strength, serviceability (cracking and deflection control) and durability. The serviceability aspect is especially important in the case of liquid storage tanks, whose main function is to store the liquid, without any leakage or percolation. This can be achieved by means of a strict control on cracking, through proper design and detailing, and proper construction. Hence, serviceability criteria (especially crack-width control) tend to govern the structural design of concrete components and the design and detailing of reinforcement in RC tanks. Requirements of crack-width control and water-tightness are stricter in tanks containing sewage and chemicals.

Crack-width control often governs the design of RC tanks for storage of liquids.

The concrete used in the construction of liquid storage tanks must have low permeability to ensure that there is no leakage. Hence, special attention needs to be paid to the concrete mix used for liquid storage tanks, and also to proper compaction and curing during construction. Further, in case of large tanks, special attention needs to be given to the provision of joints (construction joints, contraction joints, expansion joints, movement joints, etc.).

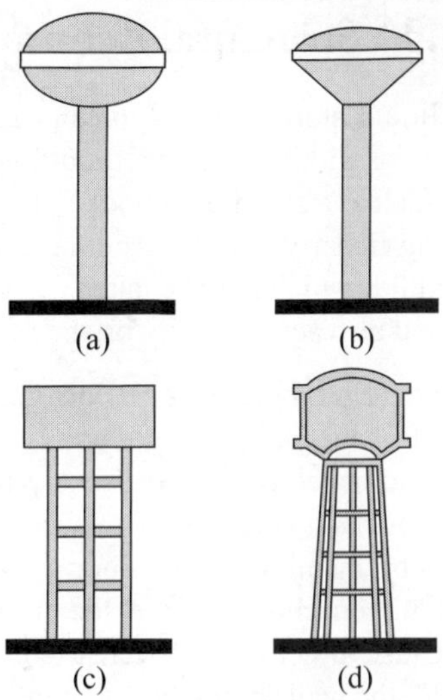

Fig. 18.1 Different types of over-head tanks.

18.2 Types of Tanks

Liquid storage tanks can be broadly classified into three categories: (i) over-head tanks, (ii) under-ground tanks and (iii) on-ground tanks. The most suitable type of the tank, in terms of elevation with respect to ground level, is decided based on the specific application. In some cases, the tank is located partly below ground and partly above ground (see Figure 10.24). Over-head tanks are usually used when there is a need for a pressure head (for distributing stored water to various locations using gravity). Figures 18.1 and 18.2 show different types of over-head tanks (other than the regular tanks kept on the roof-tops of buildings). A variety of other shapes have also been used, primarily based on architectural considerations. Figures 18.1(a) and (b) show schematic sketches of shaft type tanks while Figures 18.1(c) and (d) show schematic sketches of frame-supported tanks. An 'Intze' type tank is shown in Figure 18.1(d); it typically consists of a top spherical dome, top ring beam, cylindrical side wall, bottom ring beam, bottom inverted (frustum of) cone, bottom spherical dome, bottom circular girder, staging and foundation. Intze type tanks are considered to be structurally efficient, involving less material consumption. The main factors affecting the geometry of over-head tanks are storage volume/compartmentalisation, pressure head needed, site/soil conditions, economy, aesthetics and construction expertise. Over-head tanks generally have a capacity ranging from 25 to 500 m^3 (25,000 to 500,000 litres).

Fig. 18.2 Over-head water tanks commonly found in practice. [*Courtesy: D. Menon*]

While there is a wide variety in RC tanks with regard to their shape and location, the discussion in this chapter is largely focused on circular and rectangular tanks located on-ground or underground.

Under-ground tanks are also commonly used to store water. Their size could vary from small tanks to very large tanks. On-ground tanks are usually used in water-treatment and sewage-treatment plants, and in chemical storage facilities. Underground and on-ground tanks are typically circular or rectangular in shape. Rectangular tanks provided below ground, on-ground or on rooftops may comprise single cells or multiple cells (i.e., with partition walls).

18.3 Structural Action

The liquid storage tank typically comprises vertical walls and a horizontal floor (base) slab, forming an enclosure within which the liquid is retained, on top of which a cover slab is often kept (except in an open tank such as a swimming pool). The liquid exerts a hydrostatic pressure, which acts horizontally on the walls, varying linearly with the depth z below the top free surface; it is given by γz, where γ is the unit weight of the liquid (which may be taken as 10 kN/m^3 for water). The maximum pressure is at the base of the tank, and this will also act vertically on the floor slab as a uniformly distributed load (same as the weight of the liquid).

If the tank is on ground or below ground, the water pressure acting downward on the floor slab (plus the self-weight of the slab) will get equilibrated by an equal and opposite soil pressure acting upward on the floor slab, and hence will not cause any flexure in the floor slab. However, if the side wall is rigidly connected to the floor slab (as is usually the case), there will be significant bending moment at the base of the wall, which will get transmitted to the floor slab near the junction (usually, a 'haunch', suitably reinforced, is provided at this junction). Furthermore, the outward pressure on the side walls will generate shear forces at the wall base that cause direct in-plane tension in the floor slab. These moments and direct forces transmitted to the floor slab by the wall should be taken into account in the design of the floor slab. These moments and direct forces can be reduced/eliminated by resorting to sliding joints at the base of the wall, but this is seldom resorted to in practice. In ground supported tanks, the common practice is to thicken the slab locally under the wall (like a cantilever retaining wall base), having a 'toe' projection outward and a 'heel' inside (continuous with the floor slab). The bending moment induced in the ground slab at the inside face of the wall (on the 'heel' side) will be the difference between the design moment at the wall base and the cantilever moment in the toe slab (due to soil pressure acting upwards). It is necessary to ensure that the reinforcement provided in this thickened region of the ground slab adequately accounts for the moment transfer and crack control requirements.

> **There have been different approaches among engineers, in accounting for the wall-base fixity, in the flexural design of wall and floor slab, for tanks supported on ground.**

In reality, as the wall is connected to a relatively thin floor slab, it is unlikely for the wall to develop full fixity at its base; the joint may undergo some rotation, particularly if there is subgrade settlement under the wall base area. The wall-base fixed-moment will get reduced even with slight outward rotation at the base joint. On the other hand, for floors founded on ground, a layer of lean concrete not less than 75 mm thick is placed over the ground and the floor slab is cast over this (with a separating layer of polyethylene sheet). In relatively hard soils, with this layer of concrete base below, and with the upward soil pressure on the toe slab projection on the outside and the downward water pressure on floor slab inside resisting an outward tilt of the base slab, the joint behaviour may be close to fixed-base condition, particularly during the first-time loading. Thus, the actual condition of restraint at the wall base is between fixed and hinged. A conservative design approach therefore would be to design for hoop stresses and 'positive' moments in the wall (tension on the outside face), considering hinged base conditions; and for wall base ('negative') moments considering fixed-base conditions. This will not lead to wasteful design, as minimum reinforcement requirements generally control the design in most cases, as demonstrated in the examples to follow.

For tanks below ground, in the 'tank full' condition, the lateral outward water pressure on the wall may be counteracted by the inward soil pressure from outside the wall and may reduce these moments and direct forces in the wall and floor slab. However, any such relief is suspect, and the Code (IS 3370 - Part 2: Cl. 4.2.6) is specific that *no relief should be given* for such beneficial soil pressure effects on the walls in the 'tank full' condition. In the 'tank empty' condition, under external soil pressure also, the wall and floor slab will be subjected to moments in the opposite direction (to the one mentioned above) and the floor slab to direct compression. Also, for tanks below ground, if the ground water table is located above the level of the tank base, the floor slab will have to be designed to resist the flexural action caused by the ground water pressure acting upwards. Stability of the tank in a 'tank empty' condition also needs to be ensured.

The main structural actions developed in the walls of the tank are (a) direct tension (or compression) and (b) flexural action (involving bending moments and shear forces). In cylindrical tank walls, the predominant structural action is hoop tension (in the circumferential direction) as well as bending (and shear) in the vertical direction, due to hydrostatic pressure. In the case of rectangular tank walls, there is bending (and associated shear) in both vertical and horizontal directions; in addition, there is direct tension in the horizontal direction.

The floor slab and cover slab are typically subject to bending, shear and in-plane forces (tensile or compressive), and often need to be stiffened with intermediate beams (and in some cases, intermediate columns) for an economical design. Further economy can be achieved in large tanks by replacing the flat slabs by dome-shaped shells, in which membrane action (compression) is predominant. In some forms of over-head tanks (as shown in Figure 18.1), the shell shape provided for the tank bottom elements (typically, a truncated cone shape and/or a spherical shell) helps in the development predominantly of hoop tension/compression under the hydrostatic pressure. Adequate steel reinforcement needs to be provided in the design to resist the actions of direct tension and flexural tension, with special attention given to crack control.

In the case of overhead tanks, the supporting staging structure is subject to the effects of gravity load, as well as lateral loads (due to wind and earthquake). If the staging is a framed structure (as discussed in Chapter 1, with reference to Figure 1.7), the columns and beams are subjected to bending moments, shear forces and axial forces. If the staging comprises a shaft (typically cylindrical), it behaves predominantly like a vertical cantilever when subject to lateral loads, while resisting gravity loads through direct compression.

18.4 Design Considerations

18.4.1 Design Code

The Code no longer permits WSM for design of RC tanks for storage of liquids; only LSM is permitted.

The Indian code of practice for 'concrete structures for retaining aqueous liquids' is IS 3370, revised recently in 2021. The standard, first published in 1965, originally had two parts, Part 1 dealing with general requirements and Part 2 with specific design requirements for reinforced concrete tanks. Subsequently, in 1967, Parts 3 and 4 were released: Part 3 relates to prestressed concrete tanks, and Part 4 provides design tables to assist in the analysis of tank walls and slabs in rectangular and cylindrical tanks due to hydrostatic pressure and uniform loading.

Of these four parts of IS 3370, Parts 1 and 2 were revised in 2009, and the changes introduced were intended to bring the code in line with the current code for plain and reinforced concrete, IS 456 (2000). The limit states method of design (for strength and serviceability) was introduced – in line with international codes, but the traditional method of working stress design (given in the 1965 version of the code) was also permitted as an alternative. In the 2021 revision of the code, working stress design has been removed.

With regard to the design of the RC staging for overhead water tanks, the provisions of the code, IS 11682: 1985, titled 'Criteria for design of RCC staging for overhead water tanks' [Ref. 18.8], are applicable.

18.4.2 Concrete

In the revised IS 3370 (Part 1) [Ref 18.1], the exposure condition for the inside of the tank (including the parts enclosing the space above the liquid) has been identified as 'severe', whereby the minimum grade of concrete is specified as M30 for reinforced concrete tanks (with a minimum cement content of 350 kg/m^3 and maximum free water cement ratio of 0.45). However, for small tanks (less than 50 m^3 capacity) located in non-coastal areas, the code permits the use of M25 concrete, in case it is difficult to produce M30 concrete. The code also states that in some cases the exposure condition may be rated as 'very severe' or even 'extreme', and the relevant provisions of IS 456 need to be applied (refer Table 2.1). The nominal cover to reinforcement for 'severe' exposure using M30 concrete is specified in IS 456 as 45 mm (refer Table 5.1), and hence, this is the minimum cover applicable in liquid storage structures, including the roof slab.

Special care needs to be taken to check the cement content in the concrete mixes to minimise the risk of cracking due to thermal-shrinkage effects. The quality of the aggregate also influences the extent of shrinkage which the structure undergoes. Porous aggregates should strictly be avoided [Ref 18.2]. The code [Ref 18.1] restricts the maximum cement content (not including flyash and other mineral additives) to 400 kg/m^3 to reduce the risk of cracking due to drying shrinkage and early thermal cracking.

It is particularly important to minimise permeability of concrete in liquid retaining structures in the interest of leakage prevention and durability; accordingly, the durability provisions discussed in Chapter 2 can be applied to liquid storage structures – to control moisture ingress and corrosion of reinforcement.

18.4.3 Steel Reinforcement

Code specifies minimum 'surface zone' reinforcements as a measure for control of cracking.

Provision of adequate steel reinforcement is important in liquid storage tanks – not only for strength, but more important, to control cracking of concrete. High strength deformed bars are preferred to plain round mild steel bars in liquid storage structures due to increased strength and increased bond resistance [Ref. 18.2]. The minimum reinforcement required to control cracking also depends on the size of the tank and thickness of the member (wall or slab). Crack control is especially needed in the 'surface zones' (on either side of a wall, and at the top and bottom of a slab), and the reinforcement provided in the surface zone is considered effective up to (not more than) a thickness of 250 mm; any additional concrete in the central core (for wall/slab thicknesses exceeding 500 mm) may be ignored for minimum reinforcement calculations.

In ground supported tanks not larger than 14 m (in any horizontal direction), Code IS 3370 (Part 2) [Ref. 18.3] prescribes a minimum reinforcement, in each of two orthogonal directions in each surface zone (not exceeding 250 mm thickness), of 0.24 per cent if high strength deformed bars are used and 0.40 if plain mild steel bars are used. In larger tanks (22 m or larger in any horizontal direction between full movement joints), the minimum reinforcement values are increased to 0.40 and 0.60 per cent, for high strength deformed bars and plain mild steel bars respectively; for lengths between 14 m and 22 m, linear interpolation may be applied. It may be noted that there are additional requirements of minimum reinforcement for temperature and moisture effects (mentioned in Annex A of the code, and explained in Section 18.6.3), which are likely to govern the design. In elevated tanks, the Code prescribes slightly higher minimum reinforcement values of 0.28 and 0.44 percent (for lengths not exceeding 14 m) and 0.42 and 0.66 percent (for lengths exceeding 28 m), for high strength deformed bars and plain mild steel bars respectively.

These minimum reinforcement calculations are to be made with reference to the area of concrete in each of the two 'surface zones', each having a thickness of $D/2$ or 250 mm, whichever is lower (where D is the overall thickness of wall/slab), on either side of vertical walls and top and bottom of slabs. If the thickness of the wall or slab exceeds 500 mm, it suffices to provide the reinforcement in the surface zones (which are vulnerable to cracking), ignoring the additional concrete in the central core. For floor slabs resting on ground, no surface zone need be considered on the bottom side if $D < 300$ mm, and for $D \geq 300$ mm, the thickness of the bottom surface zone may be taken as 100 mm. The bar spacing is limited to 300 mm or the thickness of the member, whichever is less.

The Code permits placement of the entire minimum reinforcement in a single layer (in one face) if the wall thickness is less than 160 mm or slab thickness is less than 180 mm, as it may not be convenient to place the reinforcement in two layers. In the case of ground-supported slabs less than 300 mm thick, the code recommends that the calculated minimum reinforcement be placed in one layer and close to the upper surface (in contact with the liquid), consistent with the nominal cover specified. As noted above, bottom surface zone reinforcement is required to be provided in the ground-supported slab within a surface zone of 100 mm thickness only if the slab thickness exceeds 300 mm [Ref. 18.3].

18.4.4 Loads and Stability Checks

Liquid storage structures are designed for the extreme loading scenarios: 'tank full' and 'tank empty' conditions. For the load combinations specified in the code (given in IS 456), the liquid load is to be treated as 'dead load'. The unit weight of the liquid should be appropriately considered by including the effects of silt or grit, where necessary. For strength design, it is necessary to consider the liquid height up to the full height of the tank, assuming all outlets are blocked. However, for serviceability design, the liquid depth is considered up to the top of the operating level of the tank. In addition to the hydrostatic forces, under-ground tanks are also subjected to earth pressures (and ground water pressures, where applicable). Where a sliding joint is not provided between roof slab and the top of the supporting wall, lateral forces developed due to thermal effects should also be considered.

The effects of lateral loads due to wind and earthquake should also be considered, wherever relevant, particularly in the design of the staging for overhead tanks. In regions with high seismicity, the earthquake induced pressures due to convective and impulsive modes of vibration need to be appropriately accounted for. Additionally, checks on the sloshing wave height need to be carried out to determine the height of free-board [Ref 18.4].

Appropriate stability checks also need to be carried out (typically under the 'tank empty' condition) to ensure adequate safety (as per IS 456) against overturning and sliding. In places where the water-table is high, under-ground tanks need to be checked against the possibility of floatation due to buoyancy and suitably anchored. The base slab must be designed to resist the upward pressure exerted by the ground water, especially in the 'tank empty' condition. The tank walls also need to be designed to resist the soil pressure under saturated/submerged soil condition. In large tanks with internal columns, the base slab must be checked for the effects of upward deflection and cracking.

18.5 Joints in Liquid Storage Tanks

Joints in liquid storage tanks are typically classified under three categories: (1) Movement joints, (2) Construction joints, and (3) Temporary open joints. Procedures for the design, detailing and construction of joints are described at length in IS 3370 (Part 1) [Ref 18.1].

18.5.1 Movement Joints

These joints serve to accommodate relative movements between adjoining parts of the tank, while ensuring water-tightness. Movement joints are further classified under three categories: (a) Contraction joints, (b) Expansion joints and (c) Sliding joints [Ref 18.1].

(a) Contraction joints – A contraction joint accommodates the contraction of concrete. It may be either a *complete contraction joint*, where there is a discontinuity in both concrete and steel [Figure 18.3(a)] or a *partial contraction joint*, where the steel reinforcement runs through continuously, but concrete is discontinuous [Figure 18.3(b)]. In both these joints, there is no initial gap, but discontinuity is introduced during the construction process. A complete contraction joint has a *water bar*, which essentially is a pre-formed strip of impermeable material such as metal or polyvinyl chloride, provided usually in the middle of a wall [as in Figure 18.3(a)] or on the soffit of a floor. On the other hand, in the partial contraction joint the mouth of the joint is filled with a joint sealing compound (such as bitumen or asphalt, with additional fibre or rubber) and strip painted.

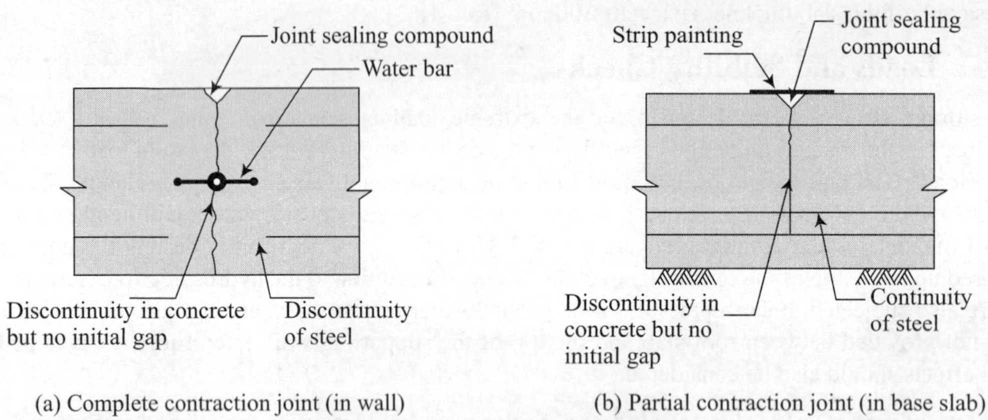

Fig. 18.3 Typical contraction joints.

(b) Expansion joints – An expansion joint accommodates both expansion and contraction of the concrete. It has complete discontinuity in both concrete and steel reinforcement. An expansion type water bar is provided, in the middle of the wall or on the soffit of a floor (as shown in Figure 18.4). The initial gap is filled later with a joint filler (compressible sheet or strip materials used as spacers).

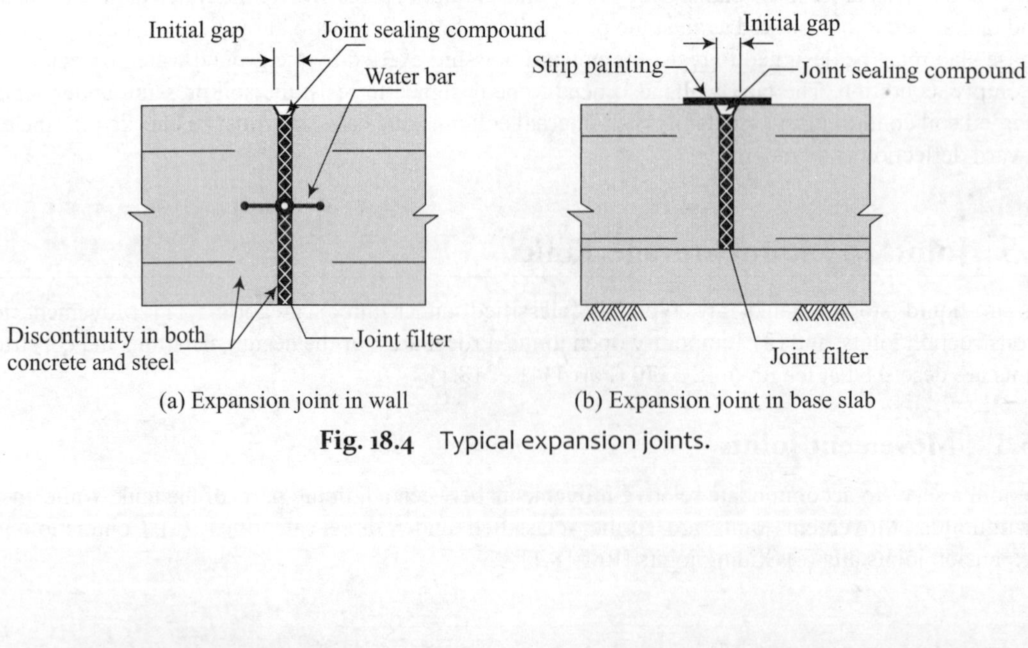

Fig. 18.4 Typical expansion joints.

(c) Sliding joints – A sliding joint is a movement joint that allows minimal restraint to the sliding of one structural member relative to the other. It also has complete discontinuity in both reinforcement steel and concrete. It is typically used in the joint between the wall and floor of cylindrical tanks with flexible joint (as shown in Figure 18.5).

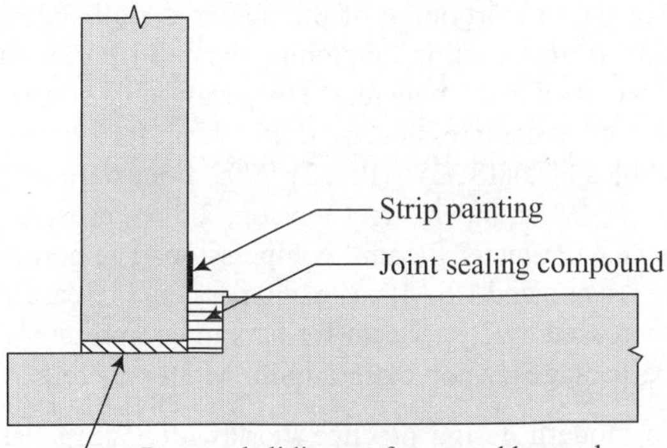

Fig. 18.5 Typical sliding joint.

18.5.2 Construction Joints

A construction joint is provided for ease of construction in a large tank. Special measures need to be taken to ensure that there is no leakage at the construction joint. It is the designer's responsibility to specify the location of the construction joint in a liquid storage tank. The structural continuity assumed in the design has to be realised in practice through proper bonding. Typically, this is achieved by roughening the interface surface of the earlier pour (to provide for aggregate interlock) and applying a surface retarder. The laitance has to be removed (typically using a water jet). At the junction of the tank wall and floor slab, a shear key is sometimes provided (along with a hydrophilic water stop) to ensure effective transmission of shear.

18.5.3 Temporary Open Joints

A temporary open joint is a gap that is temporarily left between the concrete of adjoining parts. The gap is subsequently filled with concrete after the joint surfaces at the interface are suitably prepared. In some cases, jointing materials are provided additionally, to ensure water-tightness, as in the case of contraction joints.

18.6 Design Philosophies

18.6.1 Working Stress Method

Traditionally, liquid storage tanks were designed using the working stress method (WSM) on the theoretical basis of 'no cracking'. This method was retained in the 2009 version of the code as an alternative method of design, in lieu of the limit states method; however, it has now been removed in current (2021) code – in line with international codes [Ref. 18.2, 18.6]. According to WSM based on 'no cracking', it is assumed that if the tank walls and base slabs are made sufficiently thick and adequately reinforced so as to contain the tensile stresses (due to flexure and direct tension) in the concrete within allowable limits, the leakage of the liquid is not expected to occur (assuming the concrete to be impermeable). The whole section of concrete, including the cover to reinforcement, together with the reinforcement, can be taken into account in the calculations for both flexure and direct tension, based on elastic theory, provided the resulting tensile stress in concrete is within specified limits. The limiting of stresses (and thereby, strains) in concrete is for the purpose of ensuring adequate 'resistance to cracking'; the tensile stress in steel, taken as the product of the modular ratio and the tensile stress in the adjoining concrete, is also thus limited for resistance to cracking.

Nevertheless, for 'strength' calculations, in order to safeguard against any possible cracking, the steel reinforcement has to be suitably designed (with reduced allowable tensile stresses), with any capacity of concrete to resist tension completely ignored. According to IS 3370 (Part 2): 2009 (now superseded), the permissible tensile stress under direct tension, bending and shear, was specified as 115 MPa for plain mild steel bars and 130 MPa for high strength deformed bars; for bars in columns subject to direct compression, the corresponding values were specified as 125 MPa and 140 MPa respectively.

For the proportioning of the concrete wall/slab thickness (or beam size), the properties of the 'uncracked transformed section' (including the contribution of reinforcements) can be used to calculate the tensile stress developed in the concrete. The permissible stresses in concrete subject to direct tension and flexural tension, as well as compression, bond and shear, for various grades of concrete, for 'resistance to cracking', are listed in Tables 1-3 of IS 3370 (Part 2): 2009. For example, for M30 concrete, the value of permissible stress is specified as 1.5 MPa under direct tension, 2.0 MPa under flexural tension, 8.0 MPa under direct compression, and 10.0 MPa under flexural compression. The permissible bond stress was specified as 1.0 MPa for plain bars in tension and 1.6 MPa (i.e., 60 per cent increase) for deformed bars in tension (the bond stress values can be increased by 25 per cent for bars in compression). The permissible shear stress value was dependent on the percentage tension steel, and for M 30 concrete, it varied from 0.20 MPa to 0.60 MPa.

In modern design practice worldwide, WSM has been superseded by the Limit States Method, which is found to be more rational, and often, more economical. Nevertheless, WSM is historically relevant, and with this in mind, a simple demonstration of this old method of design is shown in this Chapter with reference to cylindrical water tanks [Example 18.4]. The cracked section and modular ratio concepts of WSM continue to be relevant in the estimation of crack widths (and deflections), as demonstrated in the Examples to follow.

18.6.2 Limit States Method

Although codes of practice for reinforced concrete design had moved on from working stress design to limit states design for general structures in the 1970s, this shift in design philosophy took place only in 2009 in IS codes related to liquid storage tanks, and firmly established in 2021 (eliminating WSM). IS 3370 (Part 2): 2021 recommends the use of the design procedures given in IS 456: 2000 for the limit states of collapse and serviceability, with some additional restrictions related to serviceability.

The design for the limit states of collapse is carried out in a manner similar to that of normal structures, under factored loads, with the specified partial load factors and material safety factors. Typically, this is done by first carrying out the structural analysis of the liquid storage tank under service loads (after assuming proportions for the various members) using elastic theory to determine the critical values of various stress resultants (direct tension or compression, bending moment, shear force, etc.), and then computing their design values, for the limit state considered, by applying the relevant partial load factors. The structural design is then carried out, to check the adequacy of sections selected and to determine the reinforcement requirements.

> Following the introduction of stricter crack control measures in the Code, particularly the requirements of Annex A of IS 3370 (Part 2): 2021 for a limiting crack width of 0.1 mm, it is found that minimum reinforcement requirements often govern the design, unlike in the earlier practice. In such cases, it is sufficient to check the adequacy of the section (with the controlling minimum reinforcement provided) for compliance with the prescribed limit states of collapse and serviceability (crack-width check). Furthermore, no curtailment of reinforcement is normally possible in this case, even if there is a reduction in direct tension or bending moment along the length of the member.

When the tank members are subjected to combined bending and direct tension, as in the case of the wall of a rectangular tank (in the horizontal direction), the interaction must be properly accounted for, as discussed in Section 13.8 of Chapter 13. For a given section (with given reinforcement), it is possible to generate the interaction curve; for a wall (or slab) section, with equal steel provided in two layers, the charts provided in design aids such as SP:16 can be used. Alternatively, it is convenient and conservative to assume a linear interaction between flexural capacity and direct tension capacity, as expressed by the following expression:

$$\frac{N_u}{N_{u0}} + \frac{M_u}{M_{uR}} \leq 1.0 \qquad (18.1)$$

where N_u and M_u are the applied factored direct tension and bending moment values (design strengths) respectively; N_{uo} ($= 0.87f_y A_{st}$) is the capacity in direct tension alone, and M_{uR} is the ultimate moment capacity of the section in flexure alone. The check for crack width under service loads also needs special attention.

The recent (2021) revision to the Code also prescribes a reduction in the estimate of design shear strength of concrete in the presence of direct tension combined with bending. Such a reduction has not been prescribed in IS 456: 2000, although the need for it was pointed out in Chapter 6 of this book (refer Eq. 6.13). The reduction factor, δ, specified in IS 3370 (Part 2): 2021, is as follows:

$$\delta = 1 - 8N_u/(A_g f_{ck}) \qquad (18.1a)$$

where the factored design direct tension, N_u, is expressed in Newtons, the gross sectional area, A_g, is in mm^2 and f_{ck} is in MPa units. Further, the Code states that, in the presence of direct tension, the critical section for shear should be taken at the support face (and not at a distance d away from the face). If shear reinforcement is required, it shall be provided in the form of stirrups, whose spacing should not exceed half the effective depth, *d*, of the member, and also should not be less than 75 mm.

Limiting Crack Width

In liquid storage tanks, the reinforcement requirement is often governed by the serviceability limit state of cracking, and hence, in some cases it is advantageous to carry out this design first, and then check for adequacy of strength at the limit state of collapse under factored loads. A maximum calculated surface crack-width limit of 0.2 mm has been specified in the code. This limit applies to cracks due to *both* (i) direct tension and flexure (Code Annex B) and (ii) restrained temperature and moisture effects (Annex B). This is in line with the recommendation given in other international codes, as cracks less than 0.2 mm wide are believed to heal autogenously, as pointed out earlier [refer Section 10.5.2]. Sometimes, a more stringent requirement of 0.1 mm is also specified in liquid storage tanks [Ref. 18.2]. It may also be noted that IS 456 specifies the surface crack width limit as 0.3 mm for RC structures in general subject to 'mild' exposure, 0.2 mm under 'moderate' exposure and 0.1 mm under 'severe' and more aggressive exposure conditions.

> **The exposure condition for parts of the structure retaining the liquid, or enclosing the space above, being classified as 'severe', it is advised that a crack-width limit of 0.1 mm be aimed at while designing these parts.**

In the recent 2021 Code revision, three categories of "Tightness Class" of particular elements of the tank have been introduced. Tightness Classes 1 and 2 refer to tank elements where the cracks are expected to pass through the full thickness of the section, for which the limiting crack width shall be 0.2 mm. 'Tightness Class 2' is applicable when, in such "through crack" situations, appropriate measures such as liners or water bars are incorporated to prevent leakage of liquid or the limiting crack width is taken as 0.1 mm. 'Tightness Class 3', with limiting crack width of 0.1 mm, is applicable when the cracks do not pass through the full thickness of the section, and a compression zone of at least 50 mm is available. The limiting crack width of 0.1 mm can be exceeded by 0.05 mm in tank elements whose *H*/*t* ratio is 20 or less.

The absence of shear reinforcement can enhance the crack width in the presence of shear in slab; in such cases, the Code recommends checking of crack width for an additional equivalent moment, given by the product of the shear force and one-third of the overall slab thickness.

> In view of the 'severe' exposure condition specified, and in recognition of uncertainties associated with crack-width estimation, it is prudent to aim for a surface crack-width limit of 0.1 mm in liquid storage tanks in design practice, in order to ensure water-tightness, durability and maintenance-free performance.

'Deemed to be Satisfactory' Code Provisions

The crack width on account of direct tension or flexural tension or a combination of the two, needs to be explicitly calculated, in accordance with the procedures given in Annex B of IS 3370 (Part 2): 2021, which are as described in Chapter 10 of this book, and is demonstrated in the Examples to follow. Alternatively, instead of calculating crack widths under the limit state of serviceability, for RC members under direct tension and flexural tension, the code recommends a simple 'deemed to be satisfactory' provision: it is sufficient to ensure that the tensile stress in steel under service conditions does not exceed 115 MPa in the case of plain bars and 130 MPa in the case of high strength deformed bars for a limiting crack width of 0.2 mm. The corresponding values for a limiting crack width of 0.1 mm are 85 MPa for plain bars and 100 MPa for high strength deformed bars – in line with other international codes [Ref 18.2, 18.5]. In the recent code revision, additional "deemed to be satisfactory" criteria have been suggested (in Table 3 of the Code), in terms of maximum bar spacing and maximum tensile stress for bars of high strength deformed bars of various diameters, for a limiting crack width of 0.2 mm in walls and slabs. For example, if the bar diameter is 10 or 12 mm, the maximum permissible spacing is to be limited to 75 mm and the maximum tensile stress to 155 MPa; for the maximum bar diameter of 32 mm, the corresponding limiting spacing is 200 mm and the limiting stress is 135 MPa.

It may be noted that the ultimate tensile stress allowed in steel for strength design under factored loads is $0.87f_y$, which gives values (in MPa) of 435, 361 and 217.5 for Fe500, Fe 415 and Fe 250 grades respectively. If we consider the simplest case of direct tension (as in the case of hoop tension in the wall of a cylindrical tank subject to hydrostatic pressure), and apply the prescribed load factor of 1.5, the corresponding values of limiting stress under service loads (based on strength considerations alone) work out to 290, 241 and 145 MPa for Fe500, Fe 415 and Fe 250 grades steel respectively. These stresses are significantly higher than the limiting 'deemed to be satisfactory' stress values in steel for crack control. A detailed crack-width calculation is likely to reveal that the limiting tensile stress value is likely to lie in between the upper bound of $0.87f_y/1.5$ and the 'deemed to be satisfactory' stress values (which correspond to a lower bound). This is demonstrated in the Examples to follow.

Assessment of Crack Widths in Flexure

According to Annex B-1 of IS 3370 (Part 2): 2021 (and as described earlier in Eq. 10.32), provided the strain in the tension steel does not exceed $0.6f_y/E_s$ and the extreme compressive stress f_c in concrete does not exceed $0.4f_{ck}$, the probable crack width w in flexure at any point on the surface of a wall or slab, with thickness t, can be estimated as:

$$w = \frac{3a_{cr}\varepsilon_m}{1 + \dfrac{2(a_{cr} - C_{\min})}{t - x}} \qquad (18.2)$$

where a_{cr} is the distance from the point under consideration to the surface of the main reinforcing bar (refer Figure 10.16 and Eq. 10.30) and ε_m is the average strain at the level where cracking is being considered, which accounts for the effect of 'tension stiffening'. The code recommends a simplified formulation for ε_m as:

$$\varepsilon_m = \varepsilon_1 - \varepsilon_2 \qquad (18.3)$$

where ε_1 is the 'apparent' strain at the point under consideration at the surface, based on the conventional 'cracked' section analysis using the modular ratio concept (refer Eq. 10.34, with $a' = D = t$), given by:

$$\varepsilon_1 = \frac{f_{st}}{E_s}\frac{t - x}{d - x} \qquad (18.4)$$

The conventional 'cracked' section analysis, using the modular ratio concept, will reveal that the neutral axis depth, x, is typically located close to (and sometimes less than) the effective cover, d', to the 'compression reinforcement', and hence it is sufficient (and appropriate) to perform the analysis considering the wall section to be *singly reinforced*, even if there are two layers of reinforcement. The strain ε_2 in Eq. 18.3 corresponds to the reduction due to tension stiffening effect. The Code (Annex B-3) recommends the following empirical expressions† for ε_2, for concrete in flexure, depending on whether the target crack width is 0.2 mm or 0.1 mm (considering $a' = D = t$):

$$\varepsilon_2 = \frac{1.5b(t-x)^2}{3E_sA_s(d-x)} \quad \text{for } w = 0.1 \text{ mm} \tag{18.5a}$$

$$\varepsilon_2 = \frac{b(t-x)^2}{3E_sA_s(d-x)} \quad \text{for } w = 0.2 \text{ mm} \tag{18.5b}$$

where b is the width of the section at the centroid of the tension steel, x is the depth of neutral axis, d is the effective depth of the section (all dimensions in mm units), E_s (in MPa) is the modulus of elasticity of reinforcing steel and $A_s = \rho bt$ (in mm^2) is the area of the reinforcing steel. For ε_2, the code specifies a reduction factor for special bars, viz. 0.8 for fusion bonded epoxy coated deformed bars, 0.625 for uncoated plain bars and 0.5 for coated plain bars.

The checking for crack width can be done in two ways. The cracked section analysis under service load will give values of f_{st} and x. [Steel stress f_{st} must be less than $0.6f_y$ for flexure and $0.5f_y$ for direct tension]. With these, Eqs 18.4, 18.5, 18.3 and 18.2 will give respectively ε_1, ε_2, ε_m, and w. The computed value of w can be compared with the admissible limit. It is assumed that Eqs 18.5a and 18.5b remain valid for crack-width values in the neighbourhood of $w = 0.1$ mm and 0.2 mm respectively.

Alternatively, by substituting $w = 0.1$ mm or 0.2 mm (as desired) in Eq. 18.2 for a given section with given reinforcement, the corresponding value of ε_m can be determined, which along with the appropriate value of ε_2 from Eq. 18.5, can be substituted in Eq. 18.3, to generate the value of ε_1; if the corresponding value of $\varepsilon_{st} = \varepsilon_1(d-x)/(t-x)$ exceeds $0.6f_y/E_s$ or $0.5f_y/E_s$, the reinforcement has to be suitably increased (typically, by reducing the bar spacing) to ensure compliance with this limit (which ensures that the steel has not yielded). Then, the limiting tensile stress, $(f_{st})_{\text{lim}}$, can be determined using Eq. 18.4. This is the limiting tensile stress in the steel to achieve the desired crack width, and if the calculated stress for the applied moment, M, exceeds this value, the section has to be re-designed suitably. Both procedures are demonstrated in the Examples to follow.

Assessment of Crack Widths in Direct Tension

Cracking due to direct tension penetrates the full depth (or thickness) of the section, unlike a flexural crack, and hence is more likely to allow leakage, unless adequately controlled (refer Figure 10.21). According to Annex B-4 of IS 3370 (Part 2): 2021 (and as described earlier in Eq. 10.39), provided the strain in the tension steel does not exceed $0.5f_y/E_s$, the probable crack width w at any point on the surface (of a wall or slab) in direct tension can be estimated as:

$$w = 3a_{cr}\varepsilon_m \tag{18.6}$$

where a_{cr} and ε_m are as defined earlier (refer Eq. 18.3), and the strain in the steel, $\varepsilon_1 = f_{st}/E_s$, does not exceed $0.5f_y/E_s$. The Code (Annex B-6) recommends the following empirical expressions for ε_2, for concrete in direct tension, depending on whether the target crack width is 0.2 mm or 0.1 mm (with $D = t$):

$$\varepsilon_2 = \frac{bt}{E_sA_s} \quad \text{for } w = 0.1 \text{ mm} \tag{18.7a}$$

$$\varepsilon_2 = \frac{2bt}{3E_sA_s} \quad \text{for } w = 0.2 \text{ mm} \tag{18.7b}$$

† Note that in the empirical Eq. 18.5, the multiplication factor 1/3 has the unit of stress (MPa); likewise, in Eq. 18.7, a multiplying factor of 1.0 MPa is implicit.

By substituting $w = 0.1$ mm or 0.2 mm (as desired) in Eq. 18.6 for a given section with given reinforcement, the corresponding value of ε_m can be determined, which along with the appropriate value of ε_2 from Eq. 18.7, can be substituted in Eq. 18.3, to generate the value of ε_1; if this value of ε_1 exceeds $0.5f_y/E_s$, the reinforcement has to be suitably increased (typically, by reducing the bar spacing) to ensure compliance with this limit. Then, the limiting tensile stress, $(f_{st})_{\lim}$, can be determined as $E_s\varepsilon_1$. This is the limiting tensile stress in the steel to achieve the desired crack width, and if the calculated stress, $f_{st} = N/A_{st}$, under the applied direct tension, N, exceeds this value, the section has to be re-designed suitably. Alternatively, as explained in the case of calculation of crack width due to flexure, the theoretical crack width due to direct tension can also be computed directly and checked with admissible limits. ε_2 needs to be suitably reduced in case of special bars, as mentioned in the flexure case.

Assessment of Crack Widths in Direct Tension Combined with Flexure

When the combined effects of direct tension and flexural tension need to be accounted for (as required in the design of horizontal reinforcement in the walls of rectangular tanks), special attention is required for estimating the crack width, as Annex B of the code does not give any specific recommendations for this. The formulations given below are based on the recommendations given in Ref. 18.9. It is suggested that the crack-width formulation for direct tension (Eq. 18.6) can be used if direct tension, N, predominates (neutral axis lies outside the section, as shown in Figure 10.22). Otherwise, if bending moment, M, predominates (neutral axis lies inside the section; one face of the member is subject to compression), the crack-width formulation for flexure (Eq. 18.2) can be used. In either case, the apparent strain ε_1 has to be properly computed, satisfying force and moment equilibrium using the cracked section and modular ratio concepts of WSM.

It can be shown that the neutral axis will lie outside the section if the following condition (related to eccentricity of loading, M/N) is satisfied (similar to 'middle third rule'):

$$\frac{M}{Nt} < \frac{1}{2}\left(1 - \frac{2d'}{t}\right)^2 \tag{18.8}$$

Case 1: Direct tension predominates

If Eq. 18.8 is satisfied, the entire section will be under eccentric tension (Figure 10.22). If f_{s1} and f_{s2} denote the higher and lower tensile stresses in the two layers of steel, having reinforcement ratios, ρ_1 and ρ_2 respectively (with respect to the gross area, bt), then the expression for the apparent strain ε_1 can be shown to be:

$$\varepsilon_1 = \frac{f_{s1}}{E_s} + \frac{f_{s1} - f_{s2}}{(t - 2d')E_s} \tag{18.9}$$

where d' is the effective cover to the reinforcement, and

$$f_{s1} = \frac{M}{2bt^2\rho_1(0.5 - d'/t)} + \frac{N}{2bt\rho_1} \tag{18.10a}$$

$$f_{s2} = \frac{1}{\rho_2}\left(\frac{N}{bt} - \rho_1 f_{s1}\right) \tag{18.10b}$$

The value of the strain in steel should not exceed $0.5f_y/E_s$, and the maximum calculated tensile stress in the steel under the applied loading (N and M), given by f_{s1}, also should not exceed the limiting tensile stress, $(f_{st})_{\lim}$ (discussed above in relation to direct tension); else, the section has to be re-designed suitably.

Case 2: Flexure predominates

If the neutral axis lies inside the section (i.e., Eq. 18.7 is not satisfied), a small portion of the section will be under flexural compression. As mentioned earlier, it suffices to perform the analysis considering the wall section to be singly reinforced. The equilibrium equations for force and moment can be easily formulated as follows:

$$N = f_{st} A_{st} - \frac{1}{2} f_c bx \tag{18.11}$$

$$M = f_{st} A_{st} \left(\frac{t}{2} - d' \right) + \frac{1}{2} f_c bx \left(\frac{t}{2} - \frac{x}{3} \right) \tag{18.12}$$

where f_c is the maximum compressive stress in the extreme compression face, which is related to the tensile stress in the steel, f_{st}, as follows:

$$f_{st} = m f_c \frac{d - x}{x} \tag{18.13}$$

Clearly, a closed form solution for the neutral axis depth, x, and the stress f_{st} (or f_c) is not possible, and a suitable iterative procedure (say, by assuming an initial trial value of x) has to be employed to arrive at satisfactory convergence. Eq. 18.13 can be substituted in Eq. 18.12 (to obtain f_c using the assumed x) and in Eq. 18.11 (to generate a quadratic equation to solve for an improved value of x) as follows:

$$f_c = \frac{M}{m A_{st} \left(\frac{d - x}{x} \right) \left(\frac{t}{2} - d' \right) + \frac{1}{2} bx \left(\frac{t}{2} - \frac{x}{3} \right)} \tag{18.14}$$

$$\frac{1}{2} f_c bx^2 + (N + A_{st} m f_c) x - A_{st} m f_c d = 0 \tag{18.15}$$

The value of x thus obtained is compared with the trial value of x chosen earlier, and the process repeated, if required, until satisfactory convergence is obtained (ensuring that f_{st} does not exceed $0.6 f_y / E_s$ and f_c does not exceed $0.4 f_{ck}$). If the value of f_{st} thus obtained under the applied loading (M and N) is found to exceed the limiting tensile stress, $(f_{st})_{\lim}$ (discussed above in relation to flexure), the section has to be re-designed suitably. This procedure is demonstrated in the Examples to follow.

Control of Cracking due to Temperature and Moisture Effects

> **Control of cracking due to temperature and moisture effects is important, and generally requires higher amounts of minimum reinforcements, and must necessarily be implemented, irrespective of the design method.**

Cracking of concrete can occur in 'immature concrete' due to restraints to short-term movements: expansion/contraction caused by the heat generated during hydration of the cement paste and the contraction from autogenous shrinkage. In addition, restraints to long-term movements due to drying shrinkage and seasonal variations in temperature can also cause cracking [Ref. 18.2]. In order to achieve crack control due to these temperature and moisture effects, as mentioned above, the Code limits the maximum calculated surface crack width due to these effects as well, to 0.2 mm. Also, in line with international practice, the code gives recommendations for minimum reinforcement and calculations for crack width control in Annex A – for thin and thick sections of relatively long continuous walls or slabs [Ref. 18.3].

It is observed that these important recommendations (relegated to an Annexure in the code and appearing somewhat convoluted in expression) are often overlooked in current design practice in India. Although many designers have switched over from the old working stress method to the limit states design (as this is found to be more economical), considerations of crack width control are generally limited to the provisions of Annex B, while those given in Annex A are typically skipped in practice. The provisions of Annex A call for relatively high values of minimum reinforcement – not encountered in the older version of IS 3370, based on working stress design. The prevailing textbooks in India (on liquid storage tanks) mostly continue with the old working stress method of design, and hence there exists a lack of familiarity with the minimum reinforcement requirements needed to achieve control of cracking due to temperature and moisture effects (as given in Annex A).

Clause 4.5.4 of the code states that "no separate calculation is required for stresses due to moisture or temperature change in concrete", provided the minimum reinforcement requirements (discussed earlier) and a number of precautions are enforced (such as 'avoid cracking of concrete during the construction period and until the tank is put into use'). These measures are difficult to ensure at site. The provisions for crack control (similar to Annex A) are mandated in other international codes for liquid storage tanks, and hence must necessarily be accounted for in the interest of leakage free performance of the tank [Ref. 18.5, 18.6]. Failure to do so can sometimes lead to disastrous consequences; the initial cracking due to early thermal shrinkage effects can widen significantly under hydrostatic pressure, resulting in leakage (see Figure 10.24).

> Cracking due to temperature and moisture effects must necessarily be accounted for in the structural design and detailing of the liquid storage tank – regardless of whether it has been designed by limit states method or working stress method. Indeed, the old saying, 'A structure does not know how it has been designed', is most relevant here.

The provisions of Annex A of the code aim to control cracking due to temperature and moisture effects by (1) recommending a minimum reinforcement ratio 'to be effective in distributing cracking' and (2) requiring the designer to make certain that the reinforcement provided is adequate to ensure that the calculated crack width is acceptably low (i.e., 0.2 mm or 0.1 mm). For practical convenience, the second requirement can also be converted to an equivalent minimum reinforcement ratio or percentage – as demonstrated here.

Minimum Reinforcement to Ensure Distributed Cracking

The first requirement (Annex A-1.2) of minimum reinforcement is intended to negate the potential for the steel to yield once a crack has formed in the immature concrete [Ref. 18.2]. For thin wall or slab sections, the reinforcement ratio provided should be greater than $0.75f_{ct}/f_y$, where f_{ct} is the direct tensile strength of immature concrete having values of 1.15, 1.3, 1.45, 1.6, 1.7, 1.8 and 1.9 MPa for M 25, M 30, M 35, M 40, M 45, M 50 and M 55 concretes respectively and f_y is the characteristic strength of reinforcement. Accordingly, the minimum reinforcement percentages (applicable to each surface zone) can be calculated for various grades of concrete and steel, as summarised in Table 18.1. The minimum reinforcement requirement increases with the grade of concrete but decreases with the grade of steel. For any specified grade of concrete, it is clearly advantageous to use higher grade steel.

Table 18.1 *Minimum reinforcement percentages to ensure distributed cracking due to temperature and moisture in immature concrete, for long continuous wall or floor slabs of thin cross section.*

Grade of concrete	$p_{t,\min}$ for Fe 250	$p_{t,\min}$ for Fe 415	$p_{t,\min}$ for Fe 500
M 25	0.345	0.208	0.173
M 30	0.390	0.235	0.195
M 35	0.435	0.262	0.218
M 40	0.480	0.289	0.240
M 45	0.510	0.307	0.255
M 50	0.540	0.325	0.270
M 55	0.570	0.343	0.285

For ground slabs having a thickness less than 200 mm, the code recommends that the minimum reinforcement may be assessed considering a thickness of 100 mm and placed in a single layer, close to the top surface (with a cover not exceeding 50 mm). For ground slabs from 200 to 500 mm thick, the thickness of the top surface zone may be taken as half the slab thickness (i.e., 100 to 250 mm). Two layers of reinforcement are required (in two surface zones) in the case of ground slabs with thickness exceeding 300 mm (as indicated in Figure 2 of the Code); the reinforcement in the bottom surface zone may be assessed considering a surface zone thickness of 100 mm. In the case of thick ground slabs (more than 500 mm thick), a top surface zone thickness of 250 mm and a bottom surface zone thickness of 100 mm only need to be considered.

Minimum Reinforcement to Achieve Desired Crack Width Control

After ensuring the first requirement of providing minimum reinforcement to ensure *distributed cracking*, the designer is required to further ensure that the reinforcement is adequate to achieve the desired crack width control. To facilitate this, the code (Annex A-1.3 and A-1.4) provides a simple expression to estimate the maximum crack width, w_{max}, as a product of the expected maximum spacing, s_{max}, of the cracks, and the effective strain, ε:

$$w_{max} = s_{max}\varepsilon \tag{18.16}$$

Cracking occurs when the bond force between the reinforcement and concrete exceeds the tensile strength of concrete, whereby it can be shown [Ref. 18.2] that s_{max} can be estimated as:

$$s_{max} = \frac{f_{ct}}{f_b} \times \frac{\phi}{2\rho} \tag{18.17}$$

where f_{ct}/f_b is the ratio of the tensile strength of the concrete to the average bond strength between concrete and steel, ϕ is the size of the reinforcing bar and ρ is the ratio of the area of reinforcement to the gross area of the surface zone. The code suggests that the value of the ratio f_{ct}/f_b can be taken as unity for plain round bars and 2/3 for deformed bars.

The effective contraction strain ε in Eq. 18.16 can be taken as the estimated drying shrinkage strain, ε_{cs}, plus the thermal strain (contraction after peak temperature due to heat of hydration), ε_{te}, minus the average tension strain between the cracks, which is assigned an approximate value of 100 microstrain by the code:

$$\varepsilon = [\varepsilon_{cs} + \varepsilon_{te} - (100 \times 10^{-6})] \tag{18.18}$$

The code (Annex A-1) further suggests that "for walls exposed to normal climatic conditions", the value of ε_{cs} (shrinkage strain in concrete minus creep strain in the immature concrete) can be assigned a value of 100 microstrain ('unless high shrinkage aggregates are used'), whereby Eq. 18.18 reduces to $\varepsilon = \varepsilon_{te}$. Further, ε_{te} can be estimated simply as the product of the coefficient of thermal expansion for immature concrete (which can be taken as half the usual value of the coefficient of thermal expansion for mature concrete, α) and the temperature, T_1, due to cooling from the peak of hydration to ambient temperature. Accordingly, the formula to estimate the maximum crack width due to temperature and shrinkage effects in immature concrete reduces to:

$$w_{max} = s_{max} \times \frac{\alpha}{2} \times T_1 \tag{18.19}$$

In the absence of data for a detailed estimation of the value of T_1 (properly accounting for the temperature of concreting, cement content, thickness of member and material used for shuttering), the code (Annex A-1) recommends a value of 30°C when the concreting is carried out in summer and a value of 20°C when the concreting is carried out in winter.

Using Eq. 18.19 and 18.17, it is possible to work out the minimum reinforcement requirements for any desired target crack width. The results are summarised in Table 18.2 for target crack widths of 0.2 mm and 0.1 mm, considering concreting in summer ($T_1 = 30°C$) and winter ($T_1 = 20°C$), as well as for an intermediate value of $T_1 = 25°C$, which may be used in the absence of more detailed information. While generating this table, the coefficient of thermal expansion of concrete is assumed to be $1.2 \times 10^{-5}/°C$.

In providing for thermal and moisture effects, the minimum reinforcement required for limiting crack width is generally higher than that required for ensuring distributed cracking.

It can be seen from Table 18.2 that the minimum reinforcement percentage required is doubled if the target crack width is 0.1 mm, instead of 0.2 mm. The reinforcement requirement also increases linearly with the temperature T_1 under consideration. For any given combination of target crack width and temperature T_1, it is clearly advantageous to opt for smaller diameter bars (at closer spacing), as this brings down the minimum reinforcement requirement. It should also be noted that the minimum reinforcement value adopted from Table 18.2 cannot be less than the value given in Table 18.1, which shows a dependence on the grades of concrete and steel.

In the case of 'thick' sections (thickness exceeding 500 mm), the above calculations are applicable for the surface zones (not exceeding 250 mm each), according to the code (Annex A-2). While estimating T_1, the average value for the entire thick section should be considered, recognising that the temperature rise due to heat of hydration at the central core region is at least 10°C higher [Ref. 18.3].

Table 18.2 *Minimum reinforcement percentage required to control crack width due to thermal and moisture effects in immature concrete, for long continuous wall or floor slabs of thin cross section.*

		p_t		
T_1		**30°C**	**25°C**	**20°C**
$\phi = 10$ mm	$w = 0.2$ mm	0.30	0.25	0.20
	$w = 0.1$ mm	0.60	0.50	0.40
$\phi = 12$ mm	$w = 0.2$ mm	0.36	0.30	0.24
	$w = 0.1$ mm	0.72	0.60	0.48
$\phi = 16$ mm	$w = 0.2$ mm	0.48	0.40	0.32
	$w = 0.1$ mm	0.96	0.80	0.64
$\phi = 20$ mm	$w = 0.2$ mm	0.60	0.50	0.40
	$w = 0.1$ mm	1.20	1.00	0.80

Additional Reinforcement Required in Large Tanks due to Seasonal Temperature Variation

The code requires consideration of cracking due to another thermal effect arising from a further fall in temperature due to seasonal variation, T_2, in the case of large tanks, where movement joints are not provided at a spacing less than 15 m. This can be accounted for by simply adding T_2 to in Eq. 18.19:

$$w_{max} = s_{max} \times \frac{\alpha}{2} \times (T_1 + T_2) \tag{18.20}$$

However, this is not required for relatively small tanks or where movement joints are suitably provided. The minimum reinforcement values given in Table 18.2 can be suitably extrapolated to include the incremental effect due to T_2.

18.7 Design of Cylindrical Tanks

Cylindrical tanks are economical and commonly used for large tanks. In a cylindrical tank (having a mean radius R and height H), with the circular RC wall free at the top and integrally connected to the floor slab (resting on stable ground), the wall is subjected to hoop (or ring) tension along with bending moment in the vertical direction.

If it is possible to provide an ideal flexible joint at the base of the wall (permitting horizontal translation), as shown in Figure 18.5, then the wall will be free of flexural action, and will resist the hydrostatic pressure entirely through hoop tension. Applying simple static equilibrium (as in the analysis of thin-walled tubes), the value of the hoop tension (per unit height) at any depth z below the top can be shown to be equal to γzR, implying that the hoop tension will vary linearly from zero at the top to a maximum value of γHR at the bottom, as shown in Figure 18.8. The hoop tensile strains induced in the concrete wall will cause the tank wall to move outwards, having a linear lateral deflection profile, with zero deflection at top and maximum deflection at the base, as shown in Figure 18.6. As the tank gets filled and unfilled, the flexible joint at the base is required to respond by moving outward and inward accordingly, retaining water-tightness. This is obviously difficult to achieve and maintain in practice; hence, such a joint is not commonly adopted in practice. It is, however, of academic interest – facilitating easy analysis of the structural action, without the need for complex analytical or numerical solutions. It is pertinent to note here that the linear variation of lateral deflection, increasing with depth, mentioned above and indicated in Figure 18.6 assumes the wall to have uniform 'effective' cross-sectional area from top to bottom. However, in designing the wall, the criterion for both LSM and WSM, is to limit the circumferential (hoop) stress in steel to specified values. Ideally, this implies that the area of circumferential reinforcement (and hence the 'effective' area of the wall section) can be decreased from bottom to top to result in the specified circumferential stress *uniformly* from bottom to top. If this is done, the circumferential stresses, strains and lateral displacements will be *uniform* throughout the depth of the wall (except for the top edge, where theoretically, it will be zero).

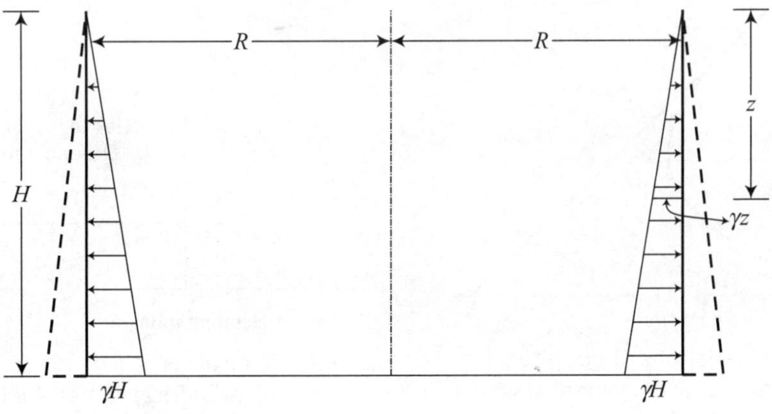

Fig. 18.6 Typical variation of lateral deflection of wall in cylindrical water tank (top free, flexible joint at base).

The common practice is to have the circular wall of the cylindrical tank integrally connected to the base slab, usually with a local thickening of the slab below the wall. Such a connection arrests lateral deflection at the wall base; introducing shear forces horizontally and bending moments along the height of the wall, while reducing the hoop tension (compared to the flexible base condition). The probable lateral deflection profile is as shown in Figure 18.7, and the typical variations of hoop tension and bending moment along the height of the wall are as shown in Figures 18.8 and 18.9 respectively. [It is common practice to extend the floor slab beyond the wall, thereby reducing the soil pressure at the base and providing a place to develop the slab reinforcements.]

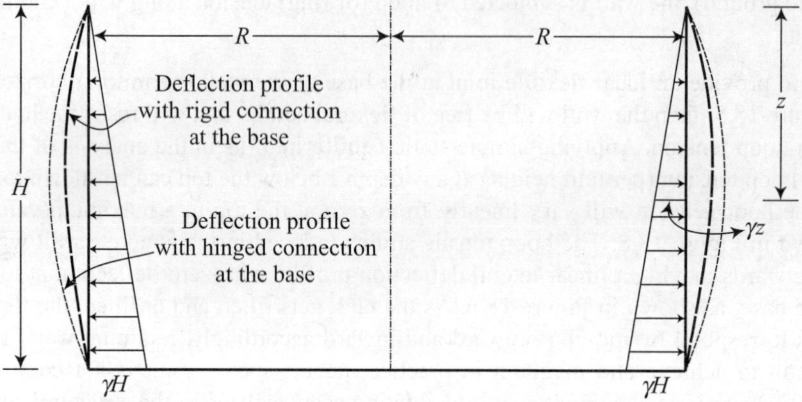

Fig. 18.7 Typical deflection profile of cylindrical wall integrally connected with the base (assuming hinged/rigid connection) and top free.

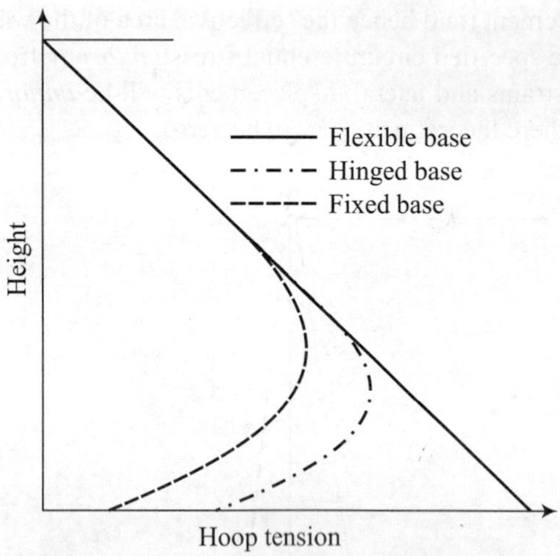

Fig. 18.8 Typical variations of hoop tension in circular wall of cylindrical water tank (top free).

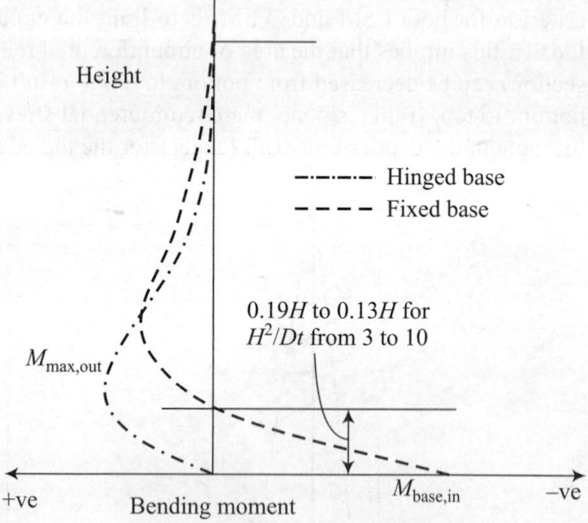

Fig. 18.9 Typical vertical bending moment variation in cylindrical water tank (top free, wall integrally connected to base).

In Figure 18.9, the moments causing flexural tension on the liquid face (having a maximum value $M_{base,in}$ at the base) are designated negative, while the moments causing flexural tension on the outside face (having a maximum value $M_{max,out}$ at a location above the base) are designated positive. The magnitudes of these moments clearly depend on the degree of constraint against rotation at the base.

Although some designers choose to assume full fixity, it should be noted that even a slight rotation at the base (due to subgrade movement) can significantly reduce and even release the assumed $M_{base,in}$ [Ref 18.6], thereby increasing $M_{max,out}$ as well as the maximum hoop tension – as indicated by a hinged base condition. Code IS 3370 Part 4 recommends that it is sufficient to design for the hinged base condition and to provide 'nominal vertical reinforcement in the inside curtain lapped with short dowels across the base joints' to take care of the negative moment at wall base. It is also common practice to provide a haunch thickening (typically of size 150 × 150 mm) at the junction of the wall and the base slab, with nominal haunch reinforcement, as demonstrated in Example 18.5.

18.7.1 Use of Design Tables

It is possible to apply elastic theory and arrive at analytical or numerical solutions for the various stress resultants under different loading and boundary conditions [Ref. 18.7]. IS 3370 Part 4 - Section 3: 2021 and other Handbooks [Ref. 18.12] provide convenient tables and charts for this purpose.

It can be shown that the values of hoop tension and vertical bending moment can be expressed in terms of coefficients that are dependent on the non-dimensional parameter, $H^2/(Dt)$, where t is the thickness of the wall and D the internal diameter. The hoop tension (per unit height) and the vertical moments ($M_{base,in}$ and $M_{max,out}$) (per unit width) are obtained by multiplying the corresponding coefficient with γH^3. The critical design coefficients are summarised in Tables 18.3 and 18.4, corresponding to the fixed base and hinged base conditions respectively. The negative sign for the moment coefficients for $M_{base,in}$ in Table 18.3 indicates flexural tension on the liquid face (at the wall base).

Table 18.3 *Critical design coefficients for cylindrical tanks (internal diameter D, height H, wall thickness t) subject to hydrostatic pressure – with wall free at top and fixed at base*

$H^2/(Dt)$	Hoop tension coefficient ($\times \gamma HD/2$)	Moment $M_{max,out}$ coefficient ($\times \gamma H^3$)	Moment $M_{base,in}$ coefficient ($\times \gamma H^3$)	Shear S_{base} coefficient ($\times \gamma H^2$)
0.4	0.149	0.0021	–0.1205	0.436
0.8	0.263	0.0080	–0.0795	0.374
1.2	0.283	0.0112	–0.0602	0.339
1.6	0.268	0.0121	–0.0505	0.317
2.0	0.285	0.0120	–0.0436	0.299
3.0	0.362	0.0097	–0.0333	0.262
4.0	0.429	0.0077	–0.0268	0.236
5.0	0.477	0.0059	–0.0222	0.213
6.0	0.514	0.0051	–0.0187	0.197
8.0	0.575	0.0038	–0.0146	0.174
10.0	0.608	0.0029	–0.0122	0.158
12.0	0.633	0.0026	–0.0104	0.145
14.0	0.666	0.0023	–0.0090	0.135
16.0	0.687	0.0019	–0.0079	0.127
20.0	0.716	0.0015	–0.0063	0.114
24.0	0.746	0.0012	–0.0053	0.102
32.0	0.782	0.0009	–0.0040	0.089
40.0	0.805	0.0006	–0.0032	0.080
48.0	0.828	0.0006	–0.0026	0.072
56.0	0.838	0.0004	–0.0023	0.067

It can be seen that for shallow tanks with large diameter (having relatively low values of $H^2/(Dt)$, the hoop tension values are relatively low, while the bending action is predominant; the cantilever action is predominant when the walls are assumed to be fixed at the base. On the contrary, for deep tanks with small diameter (having relatively high values of $H^2/(Dt)$, the hoop tension action is predominant, while the bending action is relatively low; one might say, the pipe action is predominant.

Table 18.4 *Critical design coefficients for cylindrical tanks (internal diameter D, height H, wall thickness t) subject to hydrostatic pressure – with wall free at top and hinged at base*

$H^2/(Dt)$	Hoop tension coefficient ($\times \gamma HD/2$)	Moment $M_{max,out}$ coefficient ($\times \gamma H^3$)	Shear S_{base} coefficient ($\times \gamma H^2$)
0.4	0.474	0.0357	0.245
0.8	0.423	0.0329	0.234
1.2	0.362	0.0296	0.220
1.6	0.385	0.0255	0.204
2.0	0.434	0.0219	0.189
3.0	0.519	0.0153	0.158
4.0	0.579	0.0118	0.137
5.0	0.617	0.0094	0.121
6.0	0.643	0.0078	0.110
8.0	0.697	0.0057	0.096
10.0	0.730	0.0045	0.087
12.0	0.750	0.0039	0.079
14.0	0.761	0.0033	0.073
16.0	0.776	0.0029	0.068
20.0	0.817	0.0024	0.062
24.0	0.839	0.0020	0.055
32.0	0.861	0.0014	0.048
40.0	0.880	0.0011	0.043
48.0	0.900	0.0010	0.039
56.0	0.911	0.0008	0.036

Circumferential reinforcement is designed to resist the hoop tension in the tank wall, and vertical reinforcement is designed to resist tension on the outside face of the wall, corresponding to $M_{max,out}$. In walls with fixed base, vertical reinforcement is also designed to resist tension on the inside face of the wall (close to the base), corresponding to $M_{base,in}$. For the fixed-base condition, this negative moment (tension on the inside face) region extends for a height of approximately $0.19H$ to $0.13H$ [for the usual range of $H^2/(Dt)$ varying from 3 to 10] from the bottom end of the wall.

For proportioning the tank wall thickness of a cylindrical tank, the guideline commonly adopted is:

$$t = 0.03H + 50 \tag{18.21}$$

where t and H denote the wall thickness and height of the tank (in mm) respectively. If the tank wall is rigidly connected to the base, vertical bending moments are induced, calling for vertical reinforcements that need to be located close to the inside face (near the bottom) as well as on the outside face. In this case, in order to facilitate placement of two layers of reinforcement (close to the inside face as well as the outside face), with adequate clear cover, the wall thickness must ideally be not be less than 200 mm.

In the vertical direction, the tank wall is also subject to nominal direct compression (due its self-weight and the additional weight of any cover slab on top, if applicable). However, in the design of the vertical reinforcement for flexure, the beneficial effect of this nominal direct compression can be ignored.

18.7.2 Use of Curved Shells for Large Cover Slabs and Floor Slabs

In the case of large tanks, with cylindrical walls, it is structurally efficient (and aesthetic) to provide curved shells (typically dome-shaped) for the roof [Figure 18.10(a)] and also for the base [Figure 18.10(b)]; the alternative solution of providing horizontal slabs (stiffened with intermediate beams) turns out to be relatively more expensive. A dome-shaped roof or floor provides for membrane action in which the concrete in the shell is subject predominantly to direct compression. The dome is supported on a ring beam, in order to carry the outward thrust from the dome efficiently.

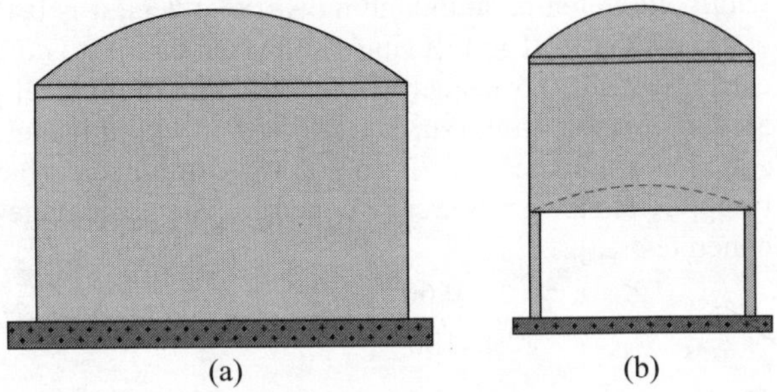

Fig. 18.10 Schematic representation of tanks with dome-shaped roofs and floors.

18.7.3 Design Examples – Cylindrical Tanks

The basic design principles outlined above are demonstrated here with reference to two problems related to cylindrical tanks, open at top – one with a sliding joint between the wall and the base slab (which is more of academic interest, not commonly adopted in practice), and the other with a rigid connection at this interface (commonly adopted in practice). The default method of design is by LSM assuming a limiting crack width of 0.1 mm, using Fe 500 grade steel (along with M 30 grade concrete), as demonstrated by Examples 18.1 and 18.5. Examples 18.3 and 18.6 show how these designs change when the limiting crack width is changed to 0.2 mm. Example 18.2 shows how the design in Example 18.1 is affected by changing the steel grade from Fe 500 to Fe 250, while Example 18.4 shows the implications of changing the design philosophy from LSM to WSM.

Example 18.1

Design a cylindrical water tank of capacity 300 m^3 (300 kL) with a height of 4.0 m, resting on ground, assuming an ideal sliding joint at the base of the wall, and assuming the tank to be open at top. Apply the limit states method of design, considering a limiting crack width of 0.1 mm. Assume M 30 concrete and Fe 500 steel. Also, discuss the implication of using Fe 415 grade steel in lieu of Fe 500.

Solution

Tank Dimensions

- Assuming a free-board of 200 mm
- Total water depth $h = 4.0 - 0.2 = 3.8$ m
- Plan area required $\dfrac{300}{3.8} = 78.95\ \text{m}^2$

- Internal diameter (D) required = $D = \sqrt{\dfrac{4 \times 78.95}{\pi}} = 10.03 \text{ m} \approx 10.1 \text{ m}$ [Radius $R = 5.05$ m]
- Assume thickness of wall $t = 0.03H + 50 = 0.03 \times 4000 + 50 = 170$ mm

Minimum reinforcement

Minimum steel required, as per Cl. 8.1.1 [IS 3370 Part 2] is 0.24%. From Table 18.1, to minimize the crack width due to temperature and moisture effects, it is 0.195%. From Table 18.2, for $T_1 = 25°\text{C}$† and a limiting crack width of 0.1 mm (using 12 mm dia bars), it is 0.6%. Hence, minimum reinforcement calculations are carried out for 0.6% steel. [*Note:* The minimum steel percentage given in Cl. 8.1.1 is to be applied to the area of concrete in the surface zones. For wall thickness, t, up to 500 mm (as in this example), each surface zone has a thickness of $t/2$, so that the combined surface zone thickness will be = t, and the percentage can be applied to the gross area of concrete. The percentages given in Tables 18.1 and 18.2 are based on the gross concrete area].

$$A_{\min} = \frac{0.60}{100} \times 170 \times 1000 = 1020 \text{ mm}^2/\text{m}.$$

Design of horizontal reinforcement in wall for hoop tension

Hoop tension in the wall $N_{\max} = \gamma HD/2$

$$N_{\max} = 10 \times 4.0 \times 10.1/2 = 202.0 \text{ kN/m}$$

The factored hoop tension $N_{u,\max} = 1.5 \times 202.0 = 303.0$ kN/m.

- Area of circumferential steel required using Fe 500 grade steel

$$A_h = \frac{N_{\max}}{0.87 \times f_y} = \frac{303 \times 10^3}{0.87 \times 500} = 697 \text{ mm}^2/\text{m } (p_{t,\text{reqd}} = 0.41\%)$$

$\Rightarrow$ Minimum steel requirement governs the design.

- Providing 12ϕ bars in one layer, required spacing is $\dfrac{\frac{\pi}{4}12^2 \times 1000}{1020} = 110.9$ mm. Hence, provide 12ϕ @ 110 mm c/c ($A_h = 1028 \text{ mm}^2/\text{m}$).

The hydrostatic pressure, and hence the hoop tension, decreases as one moves higher up along the wall, and the reinforcement can be reduced (the spacing of the bars increased); this is demonstrated in Example 18.3 for $w = 0.2$ mm. Here, for $w = 0.1$ mm, the minimum reinforcement requirement of 0.6% governs the design along the full height of the wall.

Crack-width control check under direct tension

- Tensile stress in steel under service loads = $202 \times 10^3/1028 = 196.46$ MPa
- This exceeds the limiting tensile stress in steel of 130 MPa (for high strength deformed bars) as per the 'deemed to satisfy' approach of the code for a crack width of 0.2 mm (and 100 MPa for a crack width of 0.1 mm); hence a rigorous crack-width check is needed (as per Annex B, IS 3370 Part 2).

Considering a crack-width limit of 0.1 mm,

$$w = 3a_{cr}(\varepsilon_1 - \varepsilon_2) = 0.1 \text{ mm}$$

where $a_{cr} = \sqrt{(s/2)^2 + d_c^2} - d_b/2 = \sqrt{(110/2)^2 + (85)^2} - 6 = 95.24$ mm

† In the absence of information on when the concreting is likely to happen, it is prudent to consider an intermediate value of $T_1 = 25°\text{C}$.

$$\varepsilon_2 = \frac{b_t D}{E_s A_h} = \frac{(1000 \times 170)}{(2 \times 10^5)(1028)} = 0.000827$$

$$\Rightarrow \text{ Allowable } \varepsilon_1 = \frac{w_{cr}}{3a_{cr}} + \varepsilon_2 = \frac{0.1}{3(95.24)} + 0.000827 = 0.001177 < \frac{0.5 \times 500}{2 \times 10^5} = 0.00125$$

$\Rightarrow$ Allowable $f_{st} = E_s \varepsilon_1 = (2 \times 10^5)(0.001177) = 235.4$ MPa allowable > 196.4 MPa; hence OK.

[Alternatively, directly calculating the crack width under service loads:

$a_{cr} = 95.24$, $\varepsilon_2 = 0.000827$, $f_{st} = 196.4 < 0.5 \times 500$, and $\varepsilon_1 = f_{st}/E_s = 196.46/(2 \times 10^5) = 0.000982$ and

$w_{cr} = 3a_{cr}(\varepsilon_1 - \varepsilon_2) = 3 \times 95.24 \times (0.000982 - 0.000827) = 0.044$ mm, < 0.1 mm, hence OK]

Design of vertical reinforcement in wall for flexure

Since there is no vertical bending in the wall, minimum reinforcement of 0.6% of the gross cross-sectional area is adequate (to minimize the crack width due to temperature and moisture effects). For wall thickness less than 200 mm, Code Cl. 8.1.1 permits placement of the reinforcement in one layer. [Using 10 mm dia bars, the minimum reinforcement reduces to 0.5% (refer Table 18.2); spacing required is 90 mm, which is rather low, and hence not desirable].

- Provide 12ϕ @ 110 mm c/c at the centre.

The detailing of the tank wall is shown in Figure 18.11.

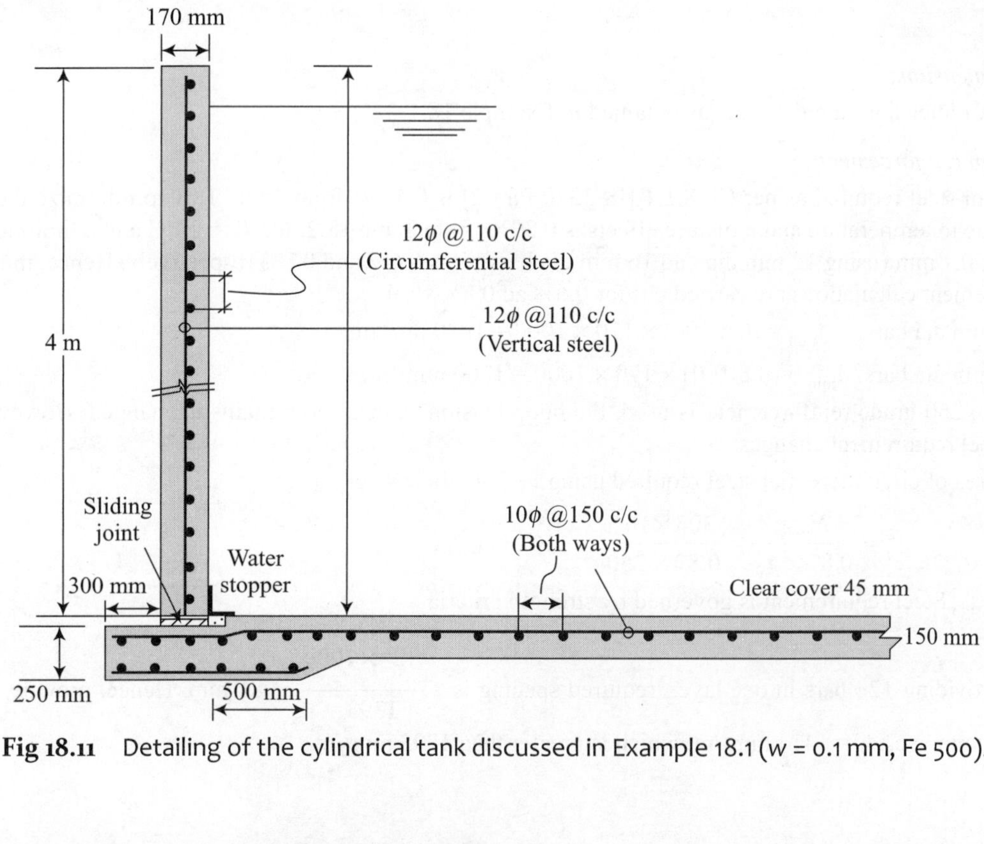

Fig 18.11 Detailing of the cylindrical tank discussed in Example 18.1 (w = 0.1 mm, Fe 500).

Design of tank floor slab

Since the tank is resting on ground, a nominal thickness of 150 mm, with minimum reinforcement, is adequate for the slab. The bar spacing has to be limited to the slab thickness (150 mm); it suffices to use 10 mm diameter bars. Minimum steel requirement (using 10 mm bars) is 0.5% (refer Table 18.2); to be calculated over 100 mm thick surface zone, with steel provided near top – Code Cl. A-1.2).

$$A_{min} = \frac{0.50}{100} A_g = \frac{0.50}{100} \times 100 \times 1000 = 500 \text{ mm}^2/\text{m}$$

- Provide 10ϕ @ 150 mm c/c at the top both ways. Provided steel is 523 mm^2/m > 500 mm^2/m. Hence adequate.

The base slab is thickened locally below the wall and reinforced, as shown in Figure 18.11.

When Fe 415 grade reinforcement is used, the hoop tension calculation in the wall remains unchanged. Although the hoop steel requirement increases due to the reduction in the yield stress of steel (to 839 mm^2/m), the minimum steel requirement of 0.6% governs. Checking the design by providing 12ϕ @ 110 mm c/c (as required by the minimum steel consideration for a crack width of 0.1 mm, using 12ϕ bars), it can be seen that the design satisfies the requirements for both strength and serviceability. This means that there is no advantage in using Fe 500 steel over Fe 415; the reinforcement requirement is identical for both grades in this example.

Example 18.2

Repeat Example 18.1, considering Fe 250 in lieu of Fe 500. Discuss the implications of this change.

Solution

Tank Dimensions

The tank dimensions are the same as obtained in Example 18.1

Minimum reinforcement

Minimum steel required as per Cl. 8.1.1 [IS 3370 Part 2] is 0.40%; from Table 18.1 to minimize the crack width due to temperature and moisture effects is 0.39%; from Table 18.2, for T_1 = 25°C and a limiting crack width of 0.1 mm (using 12 mm dia and 16 mm dia bars), it is 0.6% and 0.8% respectively. Hence, minimum reinforcement calculations are carried out for 0.6% ad 0.8% steel.

For 12 mm dia bars, $A_{min} = (0.6/100) \times 170 \times 1000 = 1020 \text{ mm}^2/\text{m}$.

For 16 mm dia bars, $A_{min} = (0.8/100) \times 170 \times 1000 = 1360 \text{ mm}^2/\text{m}$.

When Fe 250 grade reinforcement is used, the hoop tension calculation remains unchanged. However, the hoop steel requirement changes:

- Area of circumferential steel required using Fe 250 grade steel

$$A_h = \frac{N_{max}}{0.87 \times f_y} = \frac{303 \times 10^3}{0.87 \times 250} = 1393 \text{ mm}^2/\text{m}.$$

$\Rightarrow$ Steel requirement is governed by strength criteria.

- Providing 12ϕ bars in one layer, required spacing is $\dfrac{\frac{\pi}{4}12^2 \times 1000}{1393}$ = 81 mm. Hence, provide 12ϕ @ 80 mm c/c. A_h = 1414 mm^2/m, which is greater than 1393 mm^2/m.

Crack width control check under direct tension

Tensile stress under service loads = 202 × 10³/1414 = 142.9 MPa

This exceeds the limiting tensile stress in steel of 85 MPa (for Fe 250 plain bars) as per the 'deemed to satisfy' approach of the code for a crack width of 0.1 mm; hence a rigorous crack-width check is needed (as per Annex B, IS 3370 Part 2).

Considering a crack-width limit of 0.1 mm,

$$w = 3a_{cr}(\varepsilon_1 - \varepsilon_2) = 0.1 \text{ mm}$$

where $$a_{cr} = \sqrt{(s/2)^2 + d_c^2} - d_b/2 = \sqrt{(80/2)^2 + (85)^2} - 6 = 87.94 \text{ mm}$$

$$\varepsilon_2 = \frac{b_t t}{E_s A_h} = \frac{(1000 \times 170)}{(2 \times 10^5)(1414)} = 0.000601$$

$$\Rightarrow \quad \text{Allowable } \varepsilon_1 = \frac{w_{cr}}{3a_{cr}} + \varepsilon_2 = \frac{0.1}{3(87.94)} + 0.000601 = 0.00098 > \frac{0.5 \times 250}{2 \times 10^5} = 0.000625, \text{ not OK}$$

Increasing the reinforcement to 16ϕ @ 80 mm c/c (A_h = 2513 mm²/m), the tensile stress under service loads works out to: 202 × 10³/2513 = 80.38 MPa, which is less than 85 MPa (limiting tensile stress in steel for a crack width of 0.1 mm). Hence a crack width check is not necessary.

The horizontal reinforcement can be optimized by reducing it to 12ϕ @ 80 mm c/c in the top 2 m of the wall.

Design of vertical reinforcement in wall for flexure

Since there is no vertical bending in the wall, minimum reinforcement of 0.60% of the gross cross-sectional area is adequate.

- Provide 12ϕ @ 110 mm c/c at the centre.

Design of tank floor slab

Since the tank is resting on ground, a nominal thickness of 150 mm for the slab, with minimum reinforcement, is adequate. The bar spacing has to be limited to the slab thickness (150 mm); it suffices to use 10 mm diameter bars. Minimum steel requirement (using 10 mm bars) is 0.5% (refer Table 18.2); to be calculated over 100 mm thick surface zone, with steel provided near top – Code Cl. A-1.2).

$$A_{\min} = \frac{0.50}{100} A_g = \frac{0.50}{100} \times 100 \times 1000 = 500 \text{ mm}^2/\text{m}$$

- Provide 10ϕ @ 150 mm c/c at the top both ways. Provided steel is 523 mm²/m > 500 mm²/m. Hence adequate.

The base slab is thickened locally below the wall and reinforced, as in Example 18.1.

It can be seen that by adopting Fe 250 grade steel (in lieu of Fe 500), the hoop reinforcement requirement substantially increases, due to the lower yield strength of steel. However, the minimum reinforcement requirement governs with respect to vertical steel in the wall and the steel in the base slab, which remains the same as for Fe 500.

Example 18.3

Re-design the tank discussed in Example 18.1, considering a limiting crack width of 0.2 mm in lieu of 0.1 mm. (Use Fe 500 grade steel). Discuss the implications of this change.

Solution

Tank dimensions

The tank dimensions are the same as obtained in Example 18.1

Minimum reinforcement

Minimum steel required as per Cl. 8.1.1 [IS 3370 Part 2] is 0.24%; from Table 18.1 to minimize the crack width due to temperature and moisture effects, it is 0.195% (for Fe 500 steel); from Table 18.2 for $T_1 = 25°C$ and a limiting crack width of 0.2 mm (using 12 mm dia bars), it is 0.30%. Hence, minimum reinforcement calculations are carried out for 0.30% steel. It reduces to 0.25% if 10 mm bars are used.

$$A_{min} = \frac{0.30}{100} \times 170 \times 1000 = 510 \text{ mm}^2/\text{m (using 12 mm dia bars) and } 425 \text{ mm}^2/\text{m (using 10 mm dia bars)}$$

Design of horizontal reinforcement in wall for hoop tension

Area of circumferential steel required using Fe 500 grade steel

$$A_h = \frac{N_{max}}{0.87 \times f_y} = \frac{303 \times 10^3}{0.87 \times 500} = 696.5 \text{mm}^2/\text{m} \; (p_{t,reqd} = 0.41\%)$$

⇒ Steel requirement at the wall base is governed by strength criteria.

- Providing 12ϕ bars in one layer, required spacing is $\dfrac{\frac{\pi}{4}12^2 \times 1000}{696.5} = 162$ mm. Hence, provide 12ϕ @ 160 mm c/c ($A_h = 706.86$ mm^2/m).

Crack width control check under direct tension

- Tensile stress under service loads = $202 \times 10^3/706.86 = 285.77$ MPa
- This exceeds the limiting tensile stress in steel of 130 MPa (for high strength deformed bars) as per the 'deemed to satisfy' approach of the code for a crack width of 0.2 mm; hence a rigorous crack width check is needed (as per Annex B, IS 3370 Part 2).

Considering a crack-width limit of 0.2 mm,

$$w = 3a_{cr}(\varepsilon_1 - \varepsilon_2) = 0.2 \text{ mm}$$

where $a_{cr} = \sqrt{(s/2)^2 + d_c^{\,2}} - d_b/2 = \sqrt{(160/2)^2 + (85)^2} - 6 = 110.7$ mm

$$\varepsilon_2 = \frac{2b_t t}{3E_s A_h} = \frac{2 \times (1000 \times 170)}{3 \times (2 \times 10^5)(706.86)} = 0.000802$$

$$\Rightarrow \text{Allowable } \varepsilon_1 = \frac{w_{cr}}{3a_{cr}} + \varepsilon_2 = \frac{0.2}{3(110.7)} + 0.000802 = 0.001404 > \frac{0.50 \times 500}{2 \times 10^5} = 0.00125$$

This requirement can be met by reducing the bar spacing. It can be shown that providing 12ϕ @ 100 mm c/c satisfies the above condition. The corresponding value of ε_1 works out to 0.001221.

$\Rightarrow$ Allowable $f_{st} = E_s \varepsilon_1 = (2\times10^5)(0.001221) = 244.17$ MPa < 178.6 MPa (as per the revised bar arrangement). Actual f_{st} marginally exceeds the allowable stress. Hence provide 12ϕ @ 150 mm c/c, which satisfies the 0.2 mm crack-width criteria. [$A_h = 1131$ mm^2/m, $f_{st} = 244.17$ MPa, $a_{cr} = 92.61$ mm, $\varepsilon_1 = 0.000893$, $\varepsilon_2 = 0.000501$, $w_{cr} = 0.109$ mm < 0.2 mm]

The hoop tension reduces as we move away from the base of the tank and hence optimisation in steel is possible. It is adequate to provide 10ϕ @ 100 mm c/c in the top 2 m of the wall.

Design of vertical reinforcement in wall for flexure

Since there is no vertical bending in the wall, minimum reinforcement (using 10 mm dia bars) of 0.25% of the gross cross-sectional area is adequate (to minimize the crack width due to temperature and moisture effects).

- Provide 10ϕ @ 170 mm c/c. Provided steel is 461 mm^2/m > 425 mm^2/m. Hence adequate.

Design of tank floor slab

Since the tank is resting on ground, a nominal thickness of 150 mm for the slab, with minimum reinforcement, is adequate. The bar spacing has to be limited to the slab thickness (150 mm); it suffices to use 10 mm diameter bars. Minimum steel requirement (using 10 mm bars) is 0.25% (refer Table 18.2); to be calculated over 100 mm thick surface zone, with steel provided near top – Code Cl. A-1.2).

$$A_{min} = \frac{0.25}{100} A_g = \frac{0.25}{100} \times 100 \times 1000 = 250 \text{ mm}^2/\text{m}$$

- Provide 10ϕ @ 150 mm c/c at top. Provided steel is 523 mm^2/m > 250 mm^2/m. Hence adequate.

The detailing is similar to that shown in Figure 18.11 (with reinforcement diameter/spacing suitably changed).

By changing the limiting crack width to 0.2 mm from 0.1 mm (refer Example 18.1), it can be seen that the minimum reinforcement demand has reduced by half. The circumferential steel design is now governed by the strength criteria, unlike in the case of 0.1 mm limiting crack width, and curtailment of reinforcement over the height of the wall is possible.

Example 18.4

Repeat Example 18.3, using the working stress method of design. Discuss the implications of this change in method of design. Crack-width limit is 0.2 mm. [Note: WSM has been removed in the latest (2021) version of IS 3370 (Part 2); this Example, based on the 2009 version of the code, is shown here, merely for comparison with LSM; such designs based on WSM are now prohibited.]

Solution

Tank dimensions

The tank dimensions are the same as obtained in Example 18.1.

Minimum reinforcement

Although the working stress method does not specify minimum reinforcement based on crack control for thermal and moisture effects, it is prudent to do this using Annex A.

Minimum steel required as per Cl. 8.1.1 [IS 3370 Part 2] is 0.24%; from Table 18.1 to minimize the crack width due to temperature and moisture effects, it is 0.195% (for Fe 500 steel); from Table 18.2 for $T_1 = 25°C$ and a limiting crack width of 0.2 mm (using 16 mm ϕ bars), it is 0.40%. If 12 mm ϕ bars or 10 mm ϕ bars are used the minimum reinforcement percentage changes to 0.30% and 0.25% respectively. Hence, minimum reinforcement calculations are carried out for 0.40%, 0.30% and 0.25% steel.

$$A_{\min} = \frac{0.40}{100} \times 170 \times 1000 = 680 \text{ mm}^2\text{/m. (for 16 mm } \phi \text{ bars)}$$

$$A_{\min} = \frac{0.30}{100} \times 170 \times 1000 = 510 \text{ mm}^2\text{/m. (for 12 mm } \phi \text{ bars)}$$

$$A_{\min} = \frac{0.25}{100} \times 170 \times 1000 = 425 \text{ mm}^2\text{/m. (for 10 mm } \phi \text{ bars)}$$

Design of horizontal reinforcement in wall for hoop tension

Hoop tension $N_{\max}$ calculation remains the same as discussed in Example 18.1. $N_{\max} = 202$ kN/m.

- Area of circumferential steel required
  For strength as per WSM

  $A_h = \frac{N_{\max}}{\sigma_{st}} = \frac{202 \times 10^3}{130} = 1554 \text{ mm}^2\text{/m.}$ ($p_{t,\text{reqd}} = 0.91\%$) [$\sigma_{st}$ for high strength deformed bars is 130 MPa]. This is higher than the minimum requirements $\Rightarrow$ Strength requirement controls.

- Providing 16ϕ bars in one layer, required spacing is $\frac{\frac{\pi}{4}16^2 \times 1000}{1554} = 129$ mm. Hence, provide 16ϕ @ 125 mm c/c for 1 m height above base. Area provided = 1608.5 mm^2.

The concrete stress is limited to σ_{ct} to resist cracking. For M 30 concrete σ_{ct} is taken as 1.5 MPa. Using the provided thickness of the wall, the applied concrete stress can be found.

$$\sigma_{ct} = \frac{\gamma H \frac{D}{2}}{bt + (m-1)A_h} = \frac{10000 \times 4 \times \frac{10.1}{2}}{1000 \times 170 + (9.33 - 1) \times 1608.5} = 1.10 \text{ MPa} < 1.5 \text{ MPa.}$$

Hence provided thickness is adequate and results in an uncracked section.

The hoop tension reduces as we move away from the base of the tank and hence optimisation in steel is possible. The hoop tension and reinforcement required are tabulated below:

H (m)	*N* (kN/m)	A_h (mm^2)	$A_{h,\min}$ (mm^2)	$A_{h,\text{provided}}$
4.0–3.0	202.0	1554	680	16ϕ @ 125 mm c/c
3.0–2.0	151.5	1165	680	16ϕ @ 145 mm c/c
2.0–0.0	101.0	777	510	12ϕ @ 110 mm c/c

Design of vertical reinforcement in wall for flexure

Since there is no vertical bending in the wall, minimum reinforcement of 0.30% of the gross cross-sectional area (since 12 mm ϕ bars are adopted) is adequate.

Provide 12ϕ @ 170 mm c/c, giving an area of 665 mm^2 > 510 mm^2 required.

Design of tank floor slab

Since the tank is resting on ground, a nominal thickness of 150 mm for the slab, with minimum reinforcement of 0.25% (for 10ϕ bars) is adequate, within a surface zone thickness of 100 mm.

Area required = $0.0025 \times 1000 \times 100 = 250$ mm^2.

Provide 10ϕ @ 150 mm c/c (the maximum spacing permissible), giving an area = 524 mm^2 > 250 mm^2 required.

The detailing is similar to that shown in Figure 18.11 (with reinforcement diameter/spacing suitably changed).

It can be seen that although the section thickness has not changed, in comparison with Example 18.3 (based on limit states design), the steel requirement has significantly increased in using the working stress method of design. The design is governed by the strength criteria and exceeds the minimum steel requirements at all sections (for 0.2 mm crack width), and hence curtailment of steel is possible based on the demand at various heights.

If the limiting crack width is restricted to 0.1 mm for a stricter crack-free performance, minimum steel required from Table 18.2 for $T_1 = 25°C$ (using 16 mm ϕ bars) is 0.80%; for hoop tension at wall base, strength requirement still controls.

Example 18.5

Design the tank discussed in Example 18.1, assuming M 30 concrete and Fe 500 steel, considering the tank wall to be integrally connected to the base slab, and free at top. Apply the limit states method of design, limiting the crack width to 0.1 mm.

Solution

Tank dimensions

When the tank wall is integrally connected to the base slab, the lateral loading (hydrostatic pressure) results in bending moments on the two faces of the tank wall, and hence it is prudent to provide two layers of steel. The minimum wall thickness for accommodating two layers of steel is 200 mm; accordingly, a wall thickness of 200 mm is chosen for this design.

The height and diameter are the same as calculated in Example 18.1.

Minimum reinforcement

The determination of minimum reinforcement has already been explained in Example 18.1.

$$p_{t,\min} = 0.6\%$$

$$A_{\min} = \frac{0.60}{100} \times 1000 \times 200 = 1200 \text{ mm}^2/\text{m}$$

Providing 12ϕ bars in two layers, required spacing is $\dfrac{2 \times \frac{\pi}{4} 12^2 \times 1000}{1200} = 188$ mm. Hence, provide 12ϕ @ 185 mm c/c in each of two layers (in both directions), one near the inside face, and the other near the outside face. Area of circumferential steel provided is 1223 mm^2/m; area of vertical steel provided to resist flexure = 1223/2 = 611.5 mm^2/m.

Design values of hoop tension, bending moment (vertical) and shear in the wall

The tank wall needs to be designed for the worst-case scenario. The wall base being monolithically connected to the base slab, which is relatively thin, some rotation at the joint cannot be ruled out, and wall may be considered as only partially fixed at the base. For a conservative design, both fixed- and hinged-base conditions shall be checked, using the coefficients in Tables 18.3 and 18.4 (suitably interpolating). For hoop tension, and vertical bending causing tension on the exterior face of the wall, the hinged-base condition is more critical.

$H^2/Dt = 4000^2/(10100 \times 200) = 7.92$. Coefficients for this may be interpolated from the values given in Tables 18.3 and 18.4 for H^2/Dt ratios of 6.0 and 8.0.

Hoop tension in the wall N_{max} = coefficient × $\gamma HD/2$

coefficient for fixed base = (7.92 – 6.0)/(8.0 – 6.0) × (0.575 – 0.514) + 0.514 = 0.572

coefficient for hinged base = (7.92 – 6.0)/(8.0 – 6.0) × (0.697 – 0.643) + 0.643 = 0.695

As noted above, the governing case for hoop tension occurs in the case of hinged base.

Hoop tension $N_{max} = 0.695 \times 10 \times 4.0 \times 10.1/2 = 140.4$ kN/m

The wall is subjected to flexural tension on the inner face at its base and to tension on the outer face at some distance above the base.

$M_{base,in}$ coefficient for fixed base = (7.92 – 6.0)/(8.0 – 6.0) × (–0.0187 + 0.0146) + 0.0187 = 0.0148

$M_{base,in}$ = coefficient × $\gamma H^3 = 0.0148 \times 10 \times 4.0^3 = 9.472$ kNm/m

$M_{max,out}$ coefficient for hinged base = (7.92 – 6.0)/(8.0 – 6.0) × (0.0057 – 0.0078) + 0.0078 = 0.00578

$M_{max,out}$ = coefficient × $\gamma H^3 = 0.00578 \times 10 \times 4.0^3 = 3.70$ kNm/m

S_{base} coefficient for fixed base = (7.92 – 6.0)/(8.0 – 6.0) × (–0.197 + 0.174) + 0.197 = 0.0148 = 0.175

S_{base} = coefficient × $\gamma H^2 = 0.175 \times 10 \times 4.0^2 = 28.0$ kN/m

The adequacy of the minimum reinforcement provided needs to be checked.

Design of horizontal reinforcement in wall for hoop tension

The factored hoop tension $N_{u,max} = 1.5 \times 140.4 = 210.6$ kN/m.

- Area of circumferential steel required

$$A_h = \frac{N_{u,max}}{0.87 \times f_y} = \frac{210.6 \times 10^3}{0.87 \times 500} = 484 \text{ m}^2/\text{m} < A_{min}$$

  Hence, minimum reinforcement (12ϕ @ 185 mm c/c in two layers, giving A_h = 1223 mm²/m) governs.

Crack width control check under direct tension

- Tensile stress under service loads = $140.4 \times 10^3/1223 = 115$ MPa
- This exceeds the limiting tensile stress in steel of 100 MPa (for high strength deformed bars) as per the 'deemed to satisfy' approach of the code for a crack width of 0.1 mm; hence a rigorous crack-width check is needed (as per Annex B, IS 3370 Part 2).
- Consider a clear cover of 45 mm. Hence, effective cover is 45 + 12/2 = 51 mm

Considering a crack-width limit of 0.1 mm,

$$w = 3a_{cr}(\varepsilon_1 - \varepsilon_2) = 0.1 \text{ mm}$$

where $a_{cr} = \sqrt{(s/2)^2 + d_c^2} - d_b/2 = \sqrt{(185/2)^2 + (51)^2} - 6 = 99.63$ mm

$$\varepsilon_2 = \frac{b_t t}{E_s A_h} = \frac{(1000 \times 200)}{(2 \times 10^5)(1223)} = 0.000818$$

$\Rightarrow$ Allowable $\varepsilon_1 = \dfrac{w_{cr}}{3a_{cr}} + \varepsilon_2 = \dfrac{0.1}{3(99.63)} + 0.000818 = 0.001152 < \dfrac{0.5 \times 500}{2 \times 10^5} = 0.00125,$

$\Rightarrow$ Allowable $f_{st} = E_s \varepsilon_1 = (2 \times 10^5)(0.001152) = 230.5$ MPa, which is higher than the calculated stress of 115 MPa. Hence OK.

Design of vertical reinforcement in wall for flexure

$$M_{\text{base,in}} = 9.472 \text{ kNm/m}; \; M_{\text{max,out}} = 3.7 \text{ kNm/m}$$

It is enough to verify the adequacy of the minimum vertical reinforcement (provided equally near both faces) for strength and crack width, for the higher moment of 9.472 kNm/m.

Max. factored moment at base = $1.5 \times 9.472 = 14.208$ kNm/m

- Area of vertical steel required (on the water face)

$$A_{st} = \frac{30}{2 \times 500}\left[1 - \sqrt{1 - \frac{4.598 \times 14.208 \times 10^6}{30 \times 1000 \times 149^2}}\right] \times 1000 \times 149 = 225 \text{ mm}^2/\text{m} < 611.5 \text{ mm}^2/\text{m provided.}$$

Hence, minimum reinforcement governs.

Flexural crack-width check (using the procedure described in Annex B of IS 3370 Part 2):

The modular ratio m is taken as:

$$m = 280/(3\sigma_{cbc}) = 280/(3 \times 10.0) = 9.33$$

$$k = \sqrt{2(\rho m) + (\rho m)^2} - (\rho m) \text{ where } \rho = (611.5/(1000 \times 149) = 0.410 \times 10^{-2}$$

$$\rho m = 0.410 \times 10^{-2} \times 9.33 = 0.03829$$

$\Rightarrow$ $k = 0.2411 \Rightarrow x = kd = 0.2411 \times 149 = 35.92$ mm

$\Rightarrow$ $I_{cr} = (1000)(35.92)^3/3 + (9.33 \times 611.5)(149 - 35.92)^2 = 0.884 \times 10^8 \text{ mm}^4$

$\Rightarrow$ $f_{st} = \dfrac{9.33 \times (9.472 \times 10^6) \times (149 - 35.92)}{0.884 \times 10^8} = 113.05$ MPa

For a limiting crack width of 0.1 mm,

$$\varepsilon_2 = \frac{1.5b(t-x)^2}{3E_s A_{st}(d-x)} = \frac{1.5 \times 1000(200 - 35.92)^2}{3(2 \times 10^5)(611.5)(149 - 35.92)} = 0.000973$$

$$a_{cr} = \sqrt{(s/2)^2 + d_c^{\ 2}}\ -d_b/2 = \sqrt{(185/2)^2 + (51)^2}\ - 6 = 99.63 \text{ mm}$$

⇒ Allowable ε_1 is given by:

$$\varepsilon_1 = \frac{w\left[1 + \dfrac{2(a_{cr} - C_{\min})}{t - x}\right]}{3a_{cr}} + \varepsilon_2 = \frac{0.1\left[1 + \dfrac{2(99.63 - 51)}{200 - 35.92}\right]}{3 \times 99.63} + 0.000973 = 0.001506$$

Strain at the level of steel $\varepsilon_{st} = 0.001506 \times (149 - 35.92)/(200 - 35.92) = 0.001038 < \dfrac{0.6 \times 500}{2 \times 10^5} = 0.00150$

Allowable stress in steel for 0.1 mm crack width = 0.001038 × (2 × 10^5) = 207.58 MPa > 113.05 MPa (calculated stress for the steel provided). Hence the crack-width limit of 0.1 mm is satisfied.

Shear check at base

Factored shear force = 1.5 × 28 = 42 kN/m

$$\text{Factored shear stress } (\tau_v) = \frac{42 \times 1000}{1000 \times 149} = 0.282 \text{ MPa}$$

For the given grade of concrete (M 30) and p_t provided (0.41%), shear stress capacity of concrete can be found from Table 19 of IS 456:2000.

τ_c = 0.453 MPa. Since $\tau_v < \tau_c$ there is no need of shear reinforcement in the wall. It is good practice to provide a haunch at the base of the wall (running circumferentially, having a nominal dimension of 150 mm × 150 mm.

Design of floor slab

The floor slab (assumed to be 150 mm thick) will be subject to direct tension, and some local bending near the wall, due to the integral connection with the walls. The slab is thickened locally under the wall, with an outward 'toe' projection of 300 mm and a 'heel' projection inside of 500 mm (continuous with the floor slab). The bending moment in the slab at the face of the wall (on the 'heel' side) will be the difference between the design moment at the wall base and the cantilever moment in the toe slab (due to soil pressure acting upwards). Hence, the moment in the floor slab at the joint will be less than the moment in the wall at wall base, and it is adequate to provide the same thickness (200 mm) and reinforcement (12ϕ @ 185 mm c/c) at top (and bottom) in the thickened portion of the base slab.

The shear force at the base of the wall is transferred as direct tension in the floor slab, which is not subject to bending in the interior region. The minimum reinforcement (for 10ϕ) is 0.5% (to be calculated over 100 mm thick surface zone, with steel provided near top)

$$A_{\min} = \frac{0.50}{100} A_g = \frac{0.50}{100} \times 100 \times 1000 = 500 \text{ mm}^2/\text{m}$$

Provide 10ϕ @ 150 mm c/c at top. Provided steel is 523 mm²/m > 500 mm²/m.

Strength check for direct tension:

$N_{u,\text{base}} = 42$ kN/m (horizontal shear force at the wall base, calculated in the earlier step)

$A_{s,\text{reqd}} = 42 \times 1000/(0.87 \times 500) = 96.6$ mm^2/m < 523 mm^2/m provided. Hence adequate.

Hence minimum reinforcement governs the design.

[***Alternative design procedure:*** In the floor slab design above, by providing the same depth and reinforcement as for the wall base, the flexural strength of the floor slab at the joint was ensured. In case a lower depth is provided for the floor slab, the design may be done as demonstrated below (for a depth of 150 mm):

The negative moment in the floor slab at the rigid joint with the wall may be taken, conservatively, as the moment at the wall base = 14.208 kNm/m. With a gross depth of 150 mm for the slab, the effective depth = 99 mm. The required reinforcement area at top of slab for this moment is:

$$A_{st} = \frac{30}{2 \times 500}\left[1 - \sqrt{1 - \frac{4.598 \times 14.208 \times 10^6}{30 \times 1000 \times 99^2}}\right] \times 1000 \times 99 = 351 \text{ mm}^2/\text{m}$$

The shear at wall base = 42 kN, acts as a direct tension in the floor slab. This being relatively very small, a simple procedure of adding the steel area needed for this with the flexural steel is adopted. The area of steel required for this is: $A_s = 42 \times 10^3/(0.87 \times 500) = 96.6$ mm^2/m. Combining this with the flexural steel, the total steel area required = 351 + 96.6 = 448 mm^2.

The minimum reinforcement requirement, at 0.5%, for the top surface zone area (100 mm thick) of floor slab works out to: $0.005 \times 1000 \times 100 = 500$ mm^2/m > 448 mm^2. Hence the minimum requirement controls. Required spacing of 10ϕ bars in one layer at the top is = $(\pi\ 10^2/4) \times 1000/500 = 157$ mm. Hence provide 10ϕ bars @ 150 mm c/c in the top layer in the floor slab in both directions throughout. Check for moment-direct tension interaction may be done as demonstrated in examples to follow.]

Tension crack-width check for floor slab (for a service tension force of 28 kN/m)

Tensile stress = $28 \times 1000/523 = 55$ MPa (in the interior region, where slab thickness is 150 mm)

This is within the limiting stress of 100 MPa (for high strength deformed bars, for a crack width of 0.1 mm) as per the 'deemed to satisfy' approach of the code (Annex B, IS 3370 Part 2); hence a rigorous crack width check is not needed.

The wall bars are bent into the thickened portion of the circular base slab in a radial manner, as shown in Figure 18.12. In the thickened portion the top steel (same steel as provided in the wall 12ϕ @ 185 c/c) is also provided in a radial manner, while the bottom steel in the annular thickened region is provided radially and circumferentially.

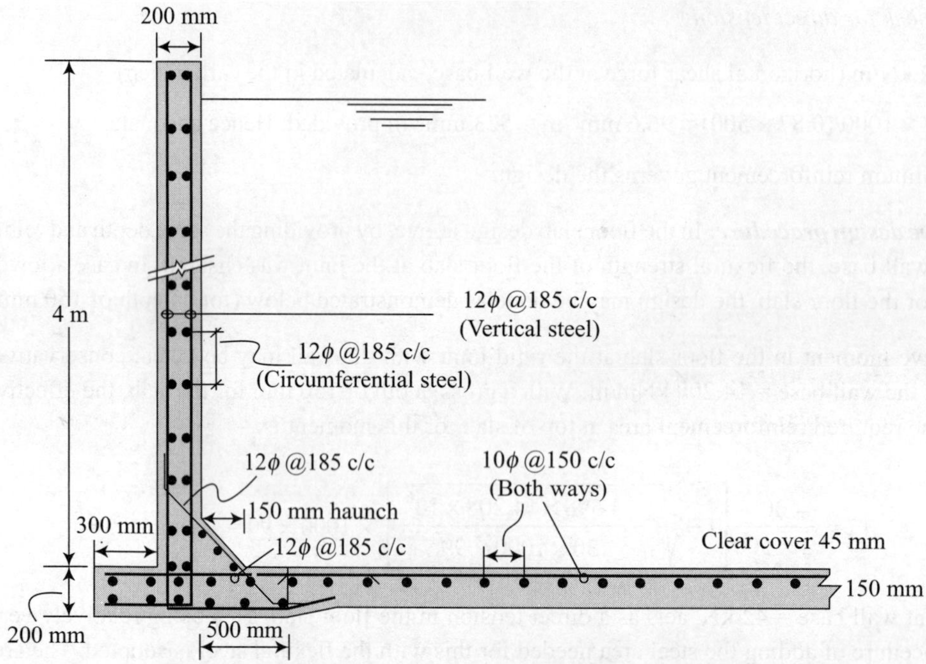

Fig 18.12 Detailing of the cylindrical tank discussed in Example 18.5 (w = 0.1 mm).

Example 18.6

Re-design the tank discussed in Example 18.5, considering a limiting crack width of 0.2 mm in lieu of 0.1 mm. Discuss the implications of this change.

Solution

The dimensions of the tank have already been discussed in Example 18.5.

Minimum steel

The minimum steel percentage are same as that worked out in Example 18.3. $p_{t,\min}$ = 0.30% for 12ϕ bars. It reduces to 0.25% if 10 mm bars are used. However, from Table 18.1 minimum steel needed is 0.195%. Hence it governs for 10 mm bars.

$$A_{\min} = \frac{0.30}{100} \times 200 \times 1000 = 600 \text{ mm}^2\text{/m (using 12 mm dia bars) and } 520 \text{ mm}^2\text{/m (using 10 mm dia bars)}$$

Provide 10ϕ @ 200 mm c/c each in two layers (in both directions), one near the inside face, and the other near the outside face. Area of total circumferential steel provided is 785 mm^2/m; area of vertical steel provided to resist flexure (in each face) = 785/2 = 392.5 mm^2/m

Design values of hoop tension, bending moment (vertical) and shear in the wall

The values are as calculated earlier in Example 18.5.

Hoop tension $N_{\max}$ = 140.4 kN/m, $M_{\text{base,in}}$ = 9.472 kNm/m

$M_{\text{max,out}}$ = 3.70 kNm/m, Shear force at base V = 28 kN/m

It is sufficient to check the adequacy of the minimum steel provided.

- Area of circumferential steel required

$$A_h = \frac{N_{u,\max}}{0.87 \times f_y} = \frac{210.6 \times 10^3}{0.87 \times 500} = 484 \text{ mm}^2/\text{m} < A_{\min} = 785 \text{ mm}^2/\text{m}$$

Hence, minimum reinforcement governs.

- Provide 10ϕ @ 200 mm c/c in two layers. Area of circumferential steel provided is 785 mm^2/m.

Crack-width control check under direct tension

- Tensile stress under service loads = 140.4 × 10^3/785 = 178.9 MPa
- This exceeds the limiting tensile stress in steel of 130 MPa (for high strength deformed bars) as per the 'deemed to satisfy' approach of the code for a crack width of 0.2 mm; hence a rigorous crack-width check is needed (as per Annex B, IS 3370 Part 2).
- Consider a clear cover of 45 mm. Hence, effective cover is 45 + 10/2 = 50 mm, and effective depth = 150 mm,

Considering a crack-width limit of 0.2 mm,

$$w_{cr} = 3a_{cr}(\varepsilon_1 - \varepsilon_2) = 0.2 \text{ mm}$$

where $a_{cr} = \sqrt{(s/2)^2 + d_c^{\,2}} - d_b/2 = \sqrt{(200/2)^2 + (50)^2} - 5 = 106.8$ mm

$$\varepsilon_2 = \frac{2b_t t}{3E_s A_h} = \frac{2 \times (1000 \times 200)}{3 \times (2 \times 10^5)(785)} = 0.000849$$

$$\Rightarrow \quad \text{Allowable } \varepsilon_1 = \frac{w_{cr}}{3a_{cr}} + \varepsilon_2 = \frac{0.2}{3(106.8)} + 0.000849 = 0.001473 > \frac{0.5 \times 500}{2 \times 10^5} = 0.00125,$$

However, by increasing the steel reinforcement to 12ϕ @ 200 mm c/c in two layers, the above criteria can be satisfied, and ε_1 can be worked out to be 0.00122.

$\Rightarrow$ Allowable $f_{st} = E_s \varepsilon_1 = (2 \times 10^5)(0.00122) = 244$ MPa, which is higher than the calculated stress of 124.14 MPa (for revised bar arrangement). Hence OK.

Design of vertical reinforcement in wall for flexure

- It is sufficient to verify the adequacy of the minimum reinforcement (provided equally in two layers) for strength and crack width, for the higher moment of 9.472 kNm/m. Area provided is 10ϕ @ 200 mm c/c in two layers. Area of vertical steel provided near the inside face for negative moment is 785/2 = 392.5 mm^2/m.
- Max. factored moment at base = 1.5 × 9.472 = 14.208 kNm/m
- Area of vertical steel required (on the water face)

$$A_{st} = \frac{30}{2 \times 500}\left[1 - \sqrt{1 - \frac{4.598 \times 14.208 \times 10^6}{30 \times 1000 \times 150^2}}\right] \times 1000 \times 150 = 223.3 \text{ mm}^2/\text{m} < 392.5 \text{ mm}^2/\text{m}$$

Hence, minimum reinforcement governs.

Flexural crack-width check (using the procedure described in Annex B of IS 3370 Part 2):

The modular ratio m is taken as:

$$m = 280/(3\sigma_{cbc}) = 280/(3 \times 10.0) = 9.33$$

$$k = \sqrt{2(\rho m) + (\rho m)^2} - (\rho m) \text{ where } \rho = 392.5/(1000 \times 150) = 0.262 \times 10^{-2}$$

$$pm = 0.262 \times 10^{-2} \times 9.33 = 0.02444$$

$$\Rightarrow \quad k = 0.1980 \Rightarrow x = kd = 0.1980 \times 150 = 29.7 \text{ mm}$$

$$\Rightarrow \quad I_{cr} = (1000)(29.7)^3/3 + (9.33 \times 392.5)(150 - 29.7)^2 = 0.618 \times 10^8 \text{ mm}^4$$

$$\Rightarrow \quad f_{st} = \frac{9.33 \times (9.472 \times 10^6) \times (150 - 29.7)}{0.618 \times 10^8} = 291 \text{ MPa}$$

For a limiting crack width of 0.2 mm,

$$\varepsilon_2 = \frac{b(t-x)^2}{3E_s A_{st}(d-x)} = \frac{1000(200-29.7)^2}{3(2 \times 10^5)(392.5)(150-29.7)} = 0.001023$$

$$a_{cr} = \sqrt{(s/2)^2 + d_c^{\,2}} - d_b/2 = \sqrt{(200/2)^2 + (50)^2} - 5 = 106.8 \text{ mm}$$

$$\Rightarrow \quad \varepsilon_1 = \frac{w\left[1 + \dfrac{2(a_{cr} - C_{\min})}{t-x}\right]}{3a_{cr}} + \varepsilon_2 = \frac{0.2\left[1 + \dfrac{2(106.8-50)}{200-29.7}\right]}{3 \times 106.8} + 0.001023 = 0.002064$$

Strain in level of steel $\varepsilon_{st} = 0.002064 \times (150 - 29.7)/(200 - 29.\ 7) = 0.001458 < \dfrac{0.6 \times 500}{2 \times 10^5} = 0.00150.$

$\Rightarrow$ $f_{st} = E_s \varepsilon_{st} = (2 \times 10^5)(0.001445) = 289$ MPa, which is higher than the induced stress of 173.59 MPa (for the revised steel). Hence OK.

Shear check at base

Factored shear force = 1.5 × 28 = 42 kN/m

Factored shear stress (τ_v) = $\dfrac{42 \times 1000}{1000 \times 149} = 0.282$ MPa

For the given grade of concrete (M 30) and p_t provided (0.24%), shear stress capacity of concrete can be found from Table 19 of IS 456:2000.

$\tau_c = 0.37$ MPa. Since $\tau_v < \tau_c$ there is no need of shear reinforcement in the wall.

Design of floor slab

The design of the floor slab follows the principle explained in Example 18.5, involving a local thickening of the slab below the wall to equal (or exceed) the wall thickness (and providing the same reinforcement as in the wall, in two layers). The base slab (assumed to be 150 mm thick in the interior) can be designed to resist the direct tension and bending that it will be subjected to.

The horizontal shear at the base of the wall is transferred as direct in-plane tension in the floor slab, which is not expected to be subject to bending in the interior region. The bar spacing has to be limited to the slab thickness (150 mm); it suffices to use 10 mm diameter bars. Minimum steel requirement (using 10 mm bars) is 0.25% (refer Table 18.2); to be calculated over 100 mm thick surface zone, with steel provided near top – Code Cl. A-1.2). As per Table 18.1, minimum steel needed is 0.195%.

$$A_{min} = \frac{0.25}{100} A_g = \frac{0.25}{100} \times 100 \times 1000 = 250 \text{ mm}^2/\text{m}$$

- Provide 10ϕ @ 150 mm c/c at top. Provided steel area is 523 mm^2/m > 250 mm^2/m required. Hence adequate.

Due to the change in the limiting crack width to 0.2 mm, the required minimum steel area has reduced significantly, compared to the 0.1 mm crack-width limit; however, the steel provided is more than the minimum due to the limiting spacing requirement of 200 mm.

18.8 Design of Rectangular Tanks

Rectangular tanks are used typically for relatively small tanks, as the cost of shuttering for cylindrical tanks becomes high. Rectangular tanks are uneconomical for large tanks in comparison with cylindrical tanks. The walls of rectangular tanks are typically subject to bending in the vertical and horizontal directions, combined with in-plane tension in the horizontal direction. The stress resultants due to the hydrostatic pressure can be computed either by finite element analysis (increasingly done in design offices) or by applying the moment and shear coefficients available in design handbooks, including IS 3370 (Part 4), assuming various boundary conditions. The procedure is fairly involved, calling for a proper understanding and detailed calculations.

> **Structurally, circular tanks are more efficient than rectangular tanks, although the cost of formwork may be higher.**

The rectangular tank used for storage of water (for domestic supply) typically has a cover or roof slab, which is placed on top of the tank walls, after the tank is constructed and leak tested. Commonly, the vertical bars of the tank wall are extended beyond the wall top and these protruding bars of the finished tank are integrated with the reinforcement of the cover slab before casting it. This provides an effective restraint against horizontal translation of the roof slab, allowing for transmission of horizontal forces between the walls and the slab. The roof slab may exert lateral forces on wall at its top caused by expansion/contraction due to thermal effects. However, this will not occur if sliding joints are provided at the roof slab supports on the walls or if the tank is open (no cover slab).

In the case of the single cell rectangular tank, some portion of the hydrostatic pressure can be considered as causing bending of the walls in the vertical direction (cantilever or propped cantilever action), while the remaining portion can be considered as causing horizontal bending of the walls (box frame action). The maximum shear forces due to vertical bending occurs at the base of the wall, while the maximum shear forces due to horizontal bending occurs at the vertical edges of the wall (due to the restraint provided by the connected cross walls). The latter shear force causes direct in-plane tension in the horizontal direction in the cross wall. Thus, in order to design the tank walls, it is necessary to correctly estimate the distribution and maximum design values of (1) vertical moments and corresponding base shear and (2) horizontal moments and associated shear force, and direct horizontal in-plane tensile forces, in each wall.

> **Walls of rectangular tanks function like two-way slabs under triangular/trapezoidal loading, and are subjected to in-plane direct tension, in addition to flexure in two directions.**

The walls of the tank can be considered to be *hinged* at top in the presence of a cover slab that is dowelled to (or cast integrally with) the vertical walls. At the bottom edges of the walls, there is some degree of rotational restraint due to the integral connection with the base slab. As in the case of cylindrical tanks discussed earlier, it is conservative to design for both boundary conditions at the wall base – *hinged* (which gives a conservative estimate of the maximum moment, $M_{vert,out}$ at a location above the base, causing flexural tension on the outside face) as well as *fixed* (which gives a conservative estimate of the maximum moment, $M_{vert,in}$ at the base, causing flexural tension on the liquid face). This is with regard to bending of the wall in the vertical direction. However, unlike in the cylindrical tank, which is axisymmetric and hence has the same distribution of bending moments at all vertical sections as shown in Figure 18.9), in a rectangular tank, the vertical bending moment profile varies along the length of the wall. The most critical values occur at the middle section (i.e., at $y = 0$ in Figure 18.13) of the wall. If the tank wall is long, the flexural behaviour will approximate that of a propped cantilever, over most of its length away from vertical edges (dominant one-way action). If the rectangular tank is open on top (as in the case of a swimming pool), this behaviour will approximate that of a vertical cantilever, when subject to hydrostatic pressure. As mentioned earlier, the maximum shear forces on account of this vertical bending action develop at the wall base. The tank wall is also subject to direct compression in the vertical direction due to the self-weight of the wall and the load from the cover slab (load from the cover slab area tributary to the wall considered); however, this can be safely ignored in the design of vertical reinforcement in the tank wall.

18.8.1 Use of Design Tables

In order to determine the critical design forces and moments in the walls of a rectangular tank, it is necessary to carry out a structural analysis of this highly indeterminate structure. To facilitate speedy design calculations, IS 3370 (Part 4): Sections 1 and 2: 2021 [Ref. 18.7] provides design tables that can be conveniently used, although the use of computer-aided finite element analysis is also becoming increasingly common in design offices. In the upgraded tables provided in the 2021 version of IS 3370, values of twisting moments M_{xy} have also been introduced, in addition to the orthogonal moments, M_{xx} and M_{yy}. These are typically obtainable from finite element analysis, and the twisting moments, wherever significant, need to be accounted for appropriately in design – typically, by using the Wood-Armer equations. For an orthogonally reinforced wall/slab panels, it is considered conservative to design for equivalent orthogonal moments, $M_{xx} \pm M_{xy}$ and $M_{yy} \pm M_{xy}$. This principle has been invoked in estimating the critical design moment coefficients in the Tables shown below.

The first set of tables given in Section 1 of Ref. 18.7 pertains to individual wall panels with fixed side edges and with (i) top and bottom edges hinged, (ii) top free and bottom hinged, (iii) top free and bottom fixed and (iv) top hinged and bottom fixed. In arriving at the moment and shear coefficients, the walls have been analysed as thin plates subject to hydrostatic pressure. Similar tables are available in other Handbooks, such as Ref. 18.13. All four sets of possible boundary conditions (at top and bottom edges) are depicted in Figure 18.13. As explained earlier, when the walls are rigidly connected to the floor slab, it is appropriate to consider both cases of hinged base and fixed base (as the true condition generally lies in between), and to design for the most critical moments and shears, in order to ensure leakage-free performance.

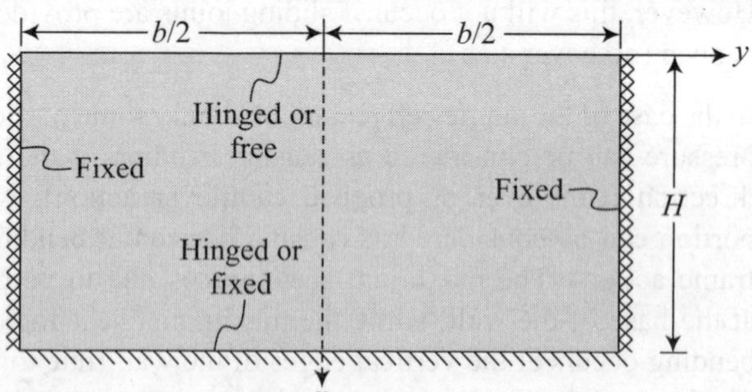

Fig. 18.13 Representation of an individual wall panel with different boundary conditions.

The tables give moment coefficients (horizontal and vertical) at discrete locations along the height of the wall (at close intervals of $x/H = 0.1$ from top to bottom, as shown in Figure 18.13), for six vertical sections

($y/b = 0$, 0.1, 0.2, 0.3, 0.4 and 0.5, where b is the length of the wall). The values are given for width-to-height (b/H) ratios varying from 4.0 to 0.5 at various intervals (typically, intervals of 0.25), and can be interpolated for any intermediate value of b/H. Typical variations of bending moment in the isolated tank wall, in the vertical and horizontal directions, are depicted in Figure 18.14, considering the top edge to be hinged and the bottom edge to be either hinged or fixed. As in the case of cylindrical tanks, the maximum value of the vertical bending moment, causing flexural tension on the liquid face [$M_{vert,in}$, shown negative in Figure 18.14(a)] occurs at the base when the wall base is fixed, while the maximum moment causing flexural tension on the outside face ($M_{vert,out}$, shown positive in Figure 18.14(a)) occurs at a location above the base, and is more critical when the wall base is hinged. With regard to the maximum horizontal moments, it is seen that the maximum values of $M_{hor,in}$ (at the fixed side edge, causing flexural tension on the liquid face) and $M_{hor,out}$ (at the middle of the wall, causing flexural tension on the outside face) are invariably higher when the wall base is hinged (rather than fixed), and generally occur at a level that is around or slightly above one-fourth the height above the base (x/H between ¾ and ½). The maximum values of shear force in the side edges also occur around this height.

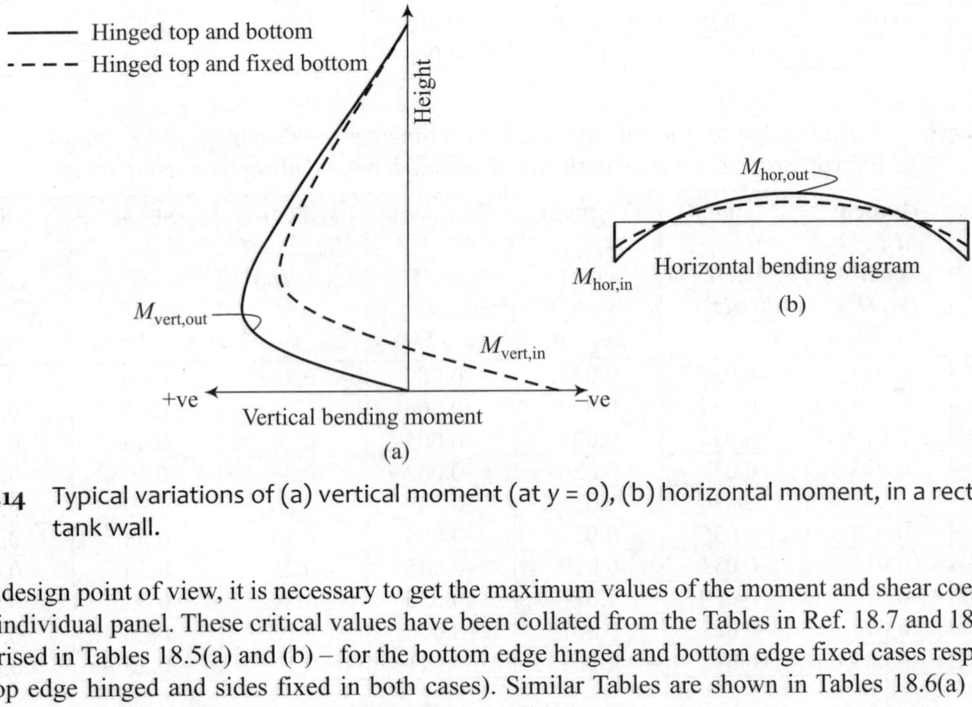

Fig. 18.14 Typical variations of (a) vertical moment (at y = 0), (b) horizontal moment, in a rectangular tank wall.

From a design point of view, it is necessary to get the maximum values of the moment and shear coefficients for the individual panel. These critical values have been collated from the Tables in Ref. 18.7 and 18.13, and summarised in Tables 18.5(a) and (b) – for the bottom edge hinged and bottom edge fixed cases respectively (with top edge hinged and sides fixed in both cases). Similar Tables are shown in Tables 18.6(a) and (b), replacing the hinged condition at top with a top free condition.

The negative sign for the moment coefficients for $M_{hor,in}$ and $M_{vert,in}$ in the Tables indicate flexural tension on the liquid face. These 'negative' moments typically occur at the 'fixity' (restraint) locations – at the sides of the wall or at the base. In practice, a haunch is often provided at these junctions (running vertically at the junction between a wall and a cross wall, and horizontally at the junction of the wall-base and the floor slab); this helps to stiffen the joint and the reinforcement provided at the haunch transversely provide additional moment capacity to resist the 'negative' moments.

Table 18.5(a) *Critical design coefficients for isolated rectangular tank walls (height H, length b) subject to hydrostatic pressure – with two sides fixed, and hinged at top and at base*

b/H	Moment $M_{hor,out}$ coeff ($\times\gamma H^3$)	Moment $M_{hor,in}$ coeff ($\times\gamma H^3$)	Moment $M_{vert,out}$ coeff ($\times\gamma H^3$) ($x = 0$)	Moment $M_{vert,in}$ coeff ($\times\gamma H^3$) ($x = b/2$)	Shear S_{hor} coeff ($\times\gamma H^2$)	Shear $S_{vert,base}$ coeff. ($\times\gamma H^2$)	Shear $S_{vert,top}$ coeff. ($\times\gamma H^2$)
4.00	0.024	–0.064	0.063	–0.013	0.41	0.33	0.17
3.00	0.024	–0.064	0.059	–0.013	0.41	0.33	0.16
2.50	0.024	–0.064	0.054	–0.013	0.41	0.32	0.15
2.00	0.023	–0.064	0.045	–0.012	0.40	0.30	0.13
1.75	0.023	–0.059	0.038	–0.012	0.39	0.28	0.12
1.50	0.021	–0.054	0.032	–0.011	0.38	0.26	0.10
1.25	0.020	–0.047	0.024	–0.009	0.35	0.23	0.07
1.00	0.017	–0.038	0.017	–0.008	0.32	0.20	0.05
0.75	0.012	–0.026	0.011	–0.005	0.26	0.16	0.03
0.50	0.007	–0.014	0.005	–0.003	0.20	0.11	0.01

Table 18.5(b) *Critical design coefficients for isolated rectangular tank walls (height H, length b) subject to hydrostatic pressure – with two sides fixed, hinged at top and fixed at base*

b/H	Moment $M_{hor,out}$ coeff ($\times\gamma H^3$)	Moment $M_{hor,in}$ coeff ($\times\gamma H^3$)	Moment $M_{vert,out}$ coeff ($\times\gamma H^3$) ($x = 0$)	Moment $M_{vert,in}$ coeff ($\times\gamma H^3$) ($x = b/2$)	Shear S_{hor} coeff ($\times\gamma H^2$)	Shear $S_{vert,base}$ coeff. ($\times\gamma H^2$)	Shear $S_{vert,top}$ coeff. ($\times\gamma H^2$)
4.00	0.013	–0.037	0.031	–0.067	0.26	0.40	0.11
3.00	0.013	–0.037	0.029	–0.066	0.26	0.40	0.11
2.50	0.013	–0.037	0.028	–0.065	0.26	0.40	0.11
2.00	0.013	–0.037	0.026	–0.062	0.26	0.39	0.11
1.75	0.013	–0.036	0.024	–0.059	0.26	0.39	0.11
1.50	0.013	–0.036	0.021	–0.053	0.26	0.38	0.11
1.25	0.013	–0.033	0.017	–0.045	0.25	0.36	0.09
1.00	0.012	–0.029	0.017	–0.035	0.24	0.32	0.07
0.75	0.010	–0.022	0.007	–0.023	0.22	0.26	0.05
0.50	0.006	–0.012	0.004	–0.011	0.17	0.20	0.03

The maximum shear associated with vertical bending due to the hydrostatic pressure on the wall occurs at the middle of the wall panel (i.e., $y = 0$), and the maximum values of the shear coefficients at the base ($S_{\text{vert,base}}$) and at the top ($S_{\text{vert,top}}$) are also shown in these tables, along with the maximum shear coefficient associated with horizontal bending (S_{hor}) at the wall side edge. Along the vertical edges, the shear force (S_{hor}) in one wall will cause in-plane tension in the adjoining cross wall in a rectangular tank, and hence these forces are required to be considered while designing the horizontal reinforcement in the wall to resist the combined effects of horizontal bending moment and in-plane tension. Similarly, the values of $S_{\text{vert,base}}$ and $S_{\text{vert,top}}$ can be used to determine the direct tension in the floor slab and roof slab respectively.

Table 18.6(a) *Critical design coefficients for isolated tank walls (height H, length b) subject to hydrostatic pressure – with two sides fixed, free at top and hinged at base*

b/H	Moment $M_{hor,out}$ coefficient ($\times \gamma H^3$)	Moment $M_{hor,in}$ coefficient ($\times \gamma H^3$)	Moment $M_{vert,out}$ coefficient ($\times \gamma H^3$)	Moment $M_{vert,in}$ coefficient ($\times \gamma H^3$)	Shear S_{hor} coefficient ($\times \gamma H^2$)	Shear $S_{vert,base}$ coeff. ($\times \gamma H^2$)
4.00	0.117	–0.317	0.110	–0.063	1.14	0.39
3.00	0.084	–0.205	0.077	–0.041	0.76	0.36
2.50	0.066	–0.150	0.062	–0.030	0.58	0.33
2.00	0.046	–0.098	0.046	–0.020	0.41	0.31
1.75	0.037	–0.077	0.038	–0.015	0.39	0.28
1.50	0.028	–0.063	0.031	–0.013	0.37	0.26
1.25	0.022	–0.050	0.024	–0.010	0.35	0.23
1.00	0.017	–0.038	0.017	–0.008	0.31	0.19
0.75	0.012	–0.026	0.011	–0.005	0.26	0.15
0.50	0.007	–0.014	0.005	–0.003	0.20	0.11

Table 18.6(b) *Critical design coefficients for isolated tank walls (height H, length b) subject to hydrostatic pressure – with two sides fixed, free at top and fixed at base*

b/H	Moment $M_{hor,out}$ coefficient ($\times \gamma H^3$)	Moment $M_{hor,in}$ coefficient ($\times \gamma H^3$)	Moment $M_{vert,out}$ coefficient ($\times \gamma H^3$)	Moment $M_{vert,in}$ coefficient ($\times \gamma H^3$)	Shear S_{hor} coefficient ($\times \gamma H^2$)	Shear $S_{vert,base}$ coefficient ($\times \gamma H^2$)
4.00	0.033	–0.099	0.026	–0.149	0.38	0.50
3.00	0.033	–0.091	0.026	–0.127	0.37	0.50
2.50	0.032	–0.082	0.025	–0.109	0.33	0.48
2.00	0.029	–0.066	0.023	–0.086	0.27	0.45
1.75	0.026	–0.055	0.021	–0.073	0.26	0.43
1.50	0.021	–0.044	0.018	–0.061	0.26	0.40
1.25	0.016	–0.037	0.015	–0.048	0.25	0.36
1.00	0.013	–0.030	0.011	–0.035	0.24	0.32
0.75	0.010	–0.022	0.007	–0.023	0.22	0.26
0.50	0.006	–0.012	0.005	–0.011	0.17	0.19

These coefficients can be considered, without any modification, if the assumed boundary conditions are applicable. In the case of single cell rectangular tanks, the assumption of fixity at the sides of individual wall panels is valid only when the tank is square in plan, as the symmetry of the structure and loading (hydrostatic pressure) will ensure that the corner joints (where adjoining cross walls intersect) do not rotate; the high in-plane stiffness of the walls will also ensure that horizontal translation will not take place. However, in the case of single cell rectangular tanks (not square in plan), the fixed edge moments (in the horizontal direction), obtained using these coefficients, for the two adjoining walls (at the common edge) are usually dissimilar, and the unbalanced moments will cause the edge to rotate. The unbalanced moments need to be suitably distributed so that the final end moments at the common vertical edge is the same in both adjoining walls. This can be done using the moment distribution method. The results of such redistributed moments are available in Ref. 18.7.

The critical values of redistributed horizontal moments for the rectangular tank (with internal plan dimensions of b_1 and b_2, as shown in Figure 18.15), are shown in Tables 18.7(a) and 18.7(b) – for the top edge hinged and top edge free conditions respectively (with bottom edge hinged and sides fixed), and in Tables 18.7(c) and 18.7 (d) – for the top edge hinged and top edge free conditions respectively (with bottom edge fixed and sides fixed). The Tables are in a matrix form, for different combinations of b_1/H and b_2/H. The coefficient values of $M_{\text{hor,out1}}$ and $M_{\text{hor,out2}}$ refer to the longer and shorter walls respectively (Ref. 18.7), while $M_{\text{hor,in}}$ refers to the horizontal moment at the common junction of the two walls. It may be noted that the redistribution in horizontal moments also affects the distribution of vertical moments; however, it is generally conservative to consider the values for the individual walls, without modification. For more accurate results, and to include variations of moments along the height of the wall, the Tables given in Ref. 18.7 may be referred to. Alternatively, a finite element analysis can be carried out to get the results accurately.

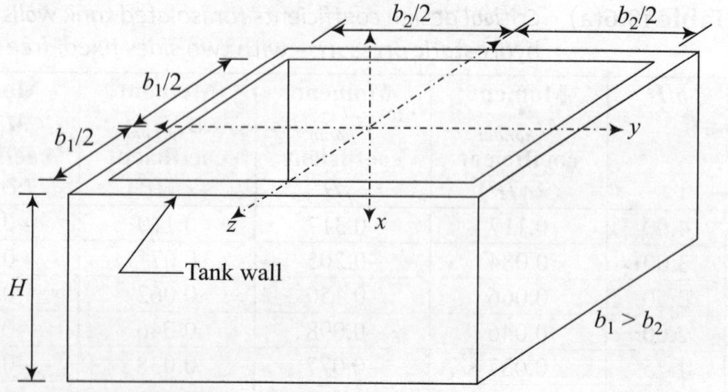

Fig 18.15 Schematic sketch of a rectangular tank showing the sides b_1, b_2 ($b_1 > b_2$) and height H.

Table 18.7(a) *Critical design moment (horizontal) coefficients for rectangular tank walls (height H, long length b_1, short length b_2) subject to hydrostatic pressure – hinged at top and at base*

b_2/H \ b_1/H		4.00	3.00	2.00	1.50	1.00
3.00	$M_{hor,out1}$	0.023				
	$M_{hor,in}$	–0.064				
	$M_{hor,out2}$	0.024				
2.00	$M_{hor,out1}$	0.023	0.024			
	$M_{hor,in}$	–0.062	–0.062			
	$M_{hor,out2}$	0.023	0.023			
1.50	$M_{hor,out1}$	0.024	0.024	0.023		
	$M_{hor,in}$	–0.060	–0.060	–0.058		
	$M_{hor,out2}$	0.021	0.021	0.021		
1.00	$M_{hor,out1}$	0.024	0.024	0.023	0.021	
	$M_{hor,in}$	–0.052	–0.052	–0.051	–0.047	
	$M_{hor,out2}$	0.014	0.015/ –0.024*	0.015/ –0.023*	0.015/ –0.021*	
0.50	$M_{hor,out1}$	0.024	0.025	0.024	0.022	0.018
	$M_{hor,in}$	–0.041	–0.041	–0.041	–0.037	–0.028
	$M_{hor,out2}$	0.014	0.007/ –0.029*	0.007/ –0.027*	0.006/ –0.025*	0.003/ –0.018*

Table 18.7(b) *Critical design moment (horizontal) coefficients for rectangular tank walls (height H, long length b_1, short length b_2) subject to hydrostatic pressure – free at top and hinged at base*

b_2/H \ b_1/H		4.00	3.00	2.00	1.50	1.00
3.00	$M_{hor,out1}$	0.121				
	$M_{hor,in}$	–0.284				
	$M_{hor,out2}$	0.077				
2.00	$M_{hor,out1}$	0.127	0.089			
	$M_{hor,in}$	–0.249	–0.171			
	$M_{hor,out2}$	0.134	0.034/ –0.103*			
1.50	$M_{hor,out1}$	0.129	0.092	0.053		
	$M_{hor,in}$	–0.238	–0.158	–0.086		
	$M_{hor,out2}$	0.031/ –0.160*	0.012/ –0.104*	0.022/ –0.051*		
1.00	$M_{hor,out1}$	0.130	0.094	0.057	0.035	
	$M_{hor,in}$	–0.234	–0.152	–0.078	–0.057	
	$M_{hor,out2}$	0.034/ –0.192*	0.029/ –0.126*	0.005/ –0.061*	0.011/ –0.033*	
0.50	$M_{hor,out1}$	0.128	0.092	0.057	0.037	0.021
	$M_{hor,in}$	–0.253	–0.164	–0.079	–0.049	–0.030
	$M_{hor,out2}$	0.035/ –0.252*	0.024 –0.163*	0.013/ –0.079*	0.024/ –0.042*	0.002/ –0.021*

* Negative values of $M_{hor,out2}$ in the Table indicate that, in a few cases, flexural tension occurs on the inner (liquid) face of the wall; this needs to be accounted for in the design.

Table 18.7(c) *Critical design moment (horizontal) coefficients for rectangular tank walls (height H, long length b1, short length b_2) subject to hydrostatic pressure – hinged at top and fixed at base*

b_2/H \ b_1/H		4.00	3.00	2.00	1.50	1.00
3.00	$M_{hor,out1}$	0.013				
	$M_{hor,in}$	–0.037				
	$M_{hor,out2}$	0.011				
2.00	$M_{hor,out1}$	0.013	0.011			
	$M_{hor,in}$	–0.037	–0.037			
	$M_{hor,out2}$	0.013	0.013			
1.50	$M_{hor,out1}$	0.013	0.011	0.013		
	$M_{hor,in}$	–0.037	–0.036	–0.036		
	$M_{hor,out2}$	0.013	0.013	0.013		
1.00	$M_{hor,out1}$	0.012	0.011	0.012	0.013	
	$M_{hor,in}$	–0.033	–0.033	–0.033	–0.032	
	$M_{hor,out2}$	0.012	0.012	0.012	0.012	
0.50	$M_{hor,out1}$	0.012	0.012	0.013	0.013	0.022
	$M_{hor,in}$	–0.025	–0.025	–0.025	–0.025	–0.021
	$M_{hor,out2}$	0.003/ –0.016*	0.003/ –0.016*	0.003/ –0.016*	0.003/ –0.015*	0.003/ –0.014*

Table 18.7(d) *Critical design moment (horizontal) coefficients for rectangular tank walls (height H, long length b_1, short length b_2) subject to hydrostatic pressure – free at top and fixed at base*

b_2/H \ b_1/H		4.00	3.00	2.00	1.50	1.00
3.00	$M_{hor,out1}$	0.032				
	$M_{hor,in}$	–0.097				
	$M_{hor,out2}$	0.034				
2.00	$M_{hor,out1}$	0.033	0.033			
	$M_{hor,in}$	–0.087	–0.083			
	$M_{hor,out2}$	0.028	0.028			
1.50	$M_{hor,out1}$	0.033	0.033	0.030		
	$M_{hor,in}$	–0.079	–0.074	–0.058		
	$M_{hor,out2}$	0.017	0.017/ –0.038*	0.019/ –0.029*		
1.00	$M_{hor,out1}$	0.034	0.034	0.031	0.024	
	$M_{hor,in}$	–0.069	–0.064	–0.049	–0.041	
	$M_{hor,out2}$	0.007/ –0.050*	0.007/ –0.047*	0.009/ –0.036*	0.010/ –0.024*	
0.50	$M_{hor,out1}$	0.034	0.034	0.032	0.025	0.016
	$M_{hor,in}$	–0.068	–0.064	–0.047	–0.033	–0.024
	$M_{hor,out2}$	0.001/ –0.066*	0.001/ –0.061*	0.001/ –0.047*	0.002/ –0.031*	0.003/ –0.016*

* Negative values of $M_{hor,out2}$ in the Table indicate that, in a few cases, flexural tension occurs on the inner (liquid) face of the wall; this needs to be accounted for in the design.

When the aspect ratio is high (short wall in combination with long wall), the horizontal fixed end moments at the junction become highly dissimilar, and the redistributed negative moment at the junction can be high, causing negative horizontal moments in the middle of the short wall.

18.8.2 Design Examples – Rectangular Tanks

The default method of design adopted here is by LSM, assuming a limiting crack width of 0.1 mm, using Fe 500 grade steel and M 30 grade concrete. Examples 18.7 and 18.8 demonstrate the design of a square tank (b_1/b_2 = 1.0) with and without a cover slab respectively, while Example 18.9 shows the design of a rectangular tank (b_1/b_2 = 2.0) with a cover slab. The implication of changing the limiting crack width to 0.2 mm is also discussed at the end of Example 18.7.

Example 18.7

Design a square water tank of capacity 25 m^3 (25 kL) with a height of 3.0 m, resting on firm ground, considering the tank walls to be integrally connected to the base slab, and having a cover slab at top. Apply the limit states method of design, considering a limiting crack width of 0.1 mm. Assume M 30 concrete and Fe 500 steel.

Solution

Tank Dimensions

- Assuming a free-board of 200 mm
- Total water depth $h = 3.0 - 0.2 = 2.8$ m
- Plan area required $= \dfrac{25}{2.8} = 8.93$ m^2
- Internal dimensions of the tank $= \sqrt{8.93} = 2.99$ m. Hence, consider 3.0 m × 3.0 m square tank.
- Assume thickness of wall $t = 200$ mm (minimum required for two layers of reinforcement)

Minimum reinforcement

Minimum steel required as per Table 5 [IS 3370 Part 2] is 0.24%; from Table 18.1, to minimize the crack width due to temperature and moisture effects, it is 0.195%; from Table 18.2 for $T_1 = 25°$C and a limiting crack width of 0.1 mm (using 12 mm dia bars), it is 0.6%. Hence, minimum reinforcement calculations are carried out for 0.60% steel.

$$A_{min} = \frac{0.60}{100} \times 200 \times 1000 = 1200 \text{ mm}^2/\text{m}$$

Providing 12ϕ bars in two layers, required spacing is 188 mm. Hence, minimum reinforcement requirement in the tank wall in both directions is satisfied by providing 12ϕ @ 185 mm c/c in two layers. Area of steel provided on each face, in each direction, is 1222.6/2 = 611.3 mm^2/m.

Design of wall

For $b/H = 3.0/3.0 = 1.0$ the coefficients of critical moments and shears for the governing cases (whichever is more) can be found in Tables 18.5 (hinged at top, and hinged/fixed at base).

Coefficient for $M_{hor,out} = 0.017$ (hinged at base) $\Rightarrow M_{hor,out} = \text{coeff.} \times \gamma H^3 = 0.017 \times 10 \times 3.0^3 = 4.59$ kNm/m

Coefficient for $M_{hor,in} = 0.038$ (hinged at base) $\Rightarrow M_{hor,in} = \text{coeff.} \times \gamma H^3 = 0.038 \times 10 \times 3.0^3 = 10.26$ kNm/m

Coefficient for $M_{vert,out} = 0.017$ (fixed at base) $\Rightarrow M_{vert,out} = \text{coeff.} \times \gamma H^3 = 0.17 \times 10 \times 3.0^3 = 4.59$ kNm/m

Coefficient for $M_{vert,in} = 0.035$ (fixed at base) $\Rightarrow M_{vert,in} = \text{coeff.} \times \gamma H^3 = 0.035 \times 10 \times 3.0^3 = 9.45$ kNm/m

Coefficient for $S_{hor} = 0.32$ (hinged at base) $\Rightarrow S_{hor} = \text{coeff.} \times \gamma H^2 = 0.32 \times 10 \times 3.0^2 = 28.80$ kN/m

Coefficient for $S_{vert,base} = 0.32$ (fixed at base) $\Rightarrow S_{vert,base} = \text{coeff.} \times \gamma H^2 = 0.32 \times 10 \times 3.0^2 = 28.8$ kN/m

Coefficient for $S_{vert,top} = 0.07$ (hinged at base) $\Rightarrow S_{vert,top} = \text{coeff.} \times \gamma H^2 = 0.07 \times 10 \times 3.0^2 = 6.3$ kN/m

The maximum horizontal moment is higher than the vertical moment in the tank wall; hence, it is prudent to provide the horizontal steel in the outer layer. The shear, S_{hor}, at the side edge of the wall acts as direct tension in the adjoining cross wall ($N = S_{hor}$). Hence, the walls need to be designed to resist combined tension plus bending in the horizontal direction. As the minimum reinforcement of 0.6% provided is substantial, it is sufficient to verify the adequacy of the horizontal and vertical steel provided (and, if required, modified).

Design of horizontal reinforcement in wall for tension + bending

The adequacy of the minimum steel provided, 12ϕ @ 185 mm c/c ($A_s = 611.5$ mm^2/m), on both faces needs to be checked for the critical values of direct tension and bending moment.

Strength check:

$$N_u = 1.5 \times 28.8 = 43.2 \text{ kN/m} \quad \text{and} \quad M_{u,\text{hor}} = 1.5 \times 10.26 = 15.39 \text{ kNm/m}$$

For direct tension plus horizontal bending in the wall, the interaction equation (Eq. 18.1) needs to be satisfied.

$$\frac{N_u}{N_{u0}} + \frac{M_{u,\text{hor}}}{M_{uR}} < 1.0$$

Effective depth $d = t -$ clear cover $- \phi/2 = 200 - 45 - 12/2 = 149$ mm

Effective cover $d' = 45 + 12/2 = 51$ mm.

Reinforcement ratio, $\rho = A_s/bd = 611.3/(1000 \times 149) = 0.004103$

$$\frac{M_{uR}}{bd^2} = 0.87 f_y \rho \left(1 - \frac{f_y}{f_{ck}}\rho\right) = 0.87 \times 500 \times 0.004103 \left(1 - \frac{500}{30} \times 0.004103\right) = 1.663 \text{ MPa}$$

$$M_{uR} = 1.663 \times 1000 \times 149^2 = 36.92 \text{ kNm/m} > 15.39 \text{ kNm/m}$$

Since the steel in provided in two layers, both layers of steel are effective in resisting the tension force. Hence, $A_s = 2 \times 611.5 = 1222.6$ mm²/m.

The tension capacity of the wall (N_{u0}) = 0.87 × 500 × 1222.6 = 531,83 kN/m , substituting in Eq. 18.1,

$$\frac{43.2}{531.83} + \frac{15.39}{36.92} = 0.081 + 0.417 = 0.498 < 1.0. \text{ Hence, the interaction equation is satisfied.}$$

Crack-width check for tension + bending:

Checking if the neutral axis lies within the cross-section or not, using the condition in Eq. 18.7:

$$\frac{M_{\text{hor,out}}}{Nt} = \frac{10.26 \times 1000}{28.8 \times 200} = 1.7812$$

$$0.5\left(1 - \frac{2d'}{t}\right)^2 = 0.5\left(1 - \frac{2 \times 51}{200}\right)^2 = 0.12$$

Since 1.7812 > 0.12, the neutral axis lies well within the section.

The modular ratio m is taken as: $m = 280/(3\sigma_{cbc}) = 280/(3 \times 10.0) = 9.33$

Assuming an x/t value of 0.15 as an initial trial value:

$$x = 0.15 \times 200 = 30 \text{ mm}$$

The value of f_c can be estimated using Eq. 18.13:

$$f_c = \frac{10.26 \times 10^6}{9.33 \times 611.3 \times \left(\frac{149 - 30}{30}\right)\left(\frac{200}{2} - 51\right) + \frac{1}{2} \times 1000 \times 30\left(\frac{200}{2} - \frac{30}{3}\right)}$$

$$= 4.17 \text{ MPa } (< 0.40 f_{ck} = 0.40 \times 30 = 12.0 \text{ MPa})$$

The depth of neutral axis can be calculated by solving the roots of the quadratic equation Eq. 18.14,

$$x_{\text{calc}} = 30.5 \text{ mm}$$

The value of x_{calc} is very close to the assumed value of x, hence satisfactory convergence is achieved.

(It is possible that the convergence may not be achieved in the first iteration and subsequent iterations may be necessary in other problems).

The stress in the steel f_{st} can be calculated using Eq. 18.12,

$$\Rightarrow \quad f_{st} = 9.33 \times 4.17 \times \frac{(149 - 30)}{30} = 154.33 \text{ MPa}$$

For a limiting crack width of 0.1 mm,

$$\varepsilon_2 = \frac{1.5b(t-x)^2}{3E_s A_{st}(d-x)} = \frac{1.5 \times 1000(200-30)^2}{3(2 \times 10^5)(611.3)(149-30)} = 0.000993$$

$$a_{cr} = \sqrt{(s/2)^2 + d_c^{\,2}} - db/2 = \sqrt{(185/2)^2 + (51)^2} - 6 = 99.63 \text{ mm}$$

$$\Rightarrow \quad \varepsilon_1 = \frac{w\left[1 + \dfrac{2(a_{cr} - C_{\min})}{t-x}\right]}{3a_{cr}} + \varepsilon_2 = \frac{0.1\left[1 + \dfrac{2(99.63-51)}{200-30}\right]}{3 \times 99.63} + 0.000993 = 0.001519$$

Strain at the level of steel

$$\varepsilon_{st} = \varepsilon_1 \times (d-x)/(t-x) = 0.001519 \times (149-30)/(200-30) = 0.001063 < \frac{0.6 \times 500}{2 \times 10^5} = 0.00150$$

Allowable stress in steel for 0.1 mm crack width, $(f_{st})_{\lim} = 0.001063 \times (2 \times 10^5) = 212.66 \text{ MPa} > 154.33 \text{ MPa}$ (the calculated actual stress for the steel provided). Hence the 0.1 mm crack width is satisfied.

Design of vertical reinforcement in wall for vertical bending

Maximum vertical bending moment occurs at the wall base. [Note that the same amount of reinforcement is provided horizontally and vertically, and since it is more than adequate for the higher horizontal moment (plus direct tension), as demonstrated above, it should be adequate for the lower vertical moment, despite the slight reduction in effective depth]

$$M_{u,\text{vert}} = 1.5 \times 9.45 = 14.175 \text{ kNm/m}$$

Check adequacy of minimum reinforcement 12ϕ @ 185 mm c/c (611.5 mm^2/m) on both faces

Effective depth $d = t$ – clear cover – ϕ – $\phi/2$ = 200 – 45 – 12– 12/2 = 137 mm

Reinforcement ratio, $\rho = A_s/bd$ = 611.3/(1000 × 137) = 0.004462

$$\frac{M_{uR}}{bd^2} = 0.87 f_y \rho\left(1 - \frac{f_y}{f_{ck}}\rho\right) = 0.87 \times 500 \times 0.004462\left(1 - \frac{500}{30} \times 0.004462\right) = 1.797 \text{ MPa}$$

$$M_{uR} = 1.797 \times 1000 \times 137^2 = 33.73 \text{ kNm/m} > 14.175 \text{ kNm/m}$$

Hence, minimum reinforcement is more than adequate.

Crack-width check for flexure: (for maximum service moment of 9.45 kNm/m)

As the neutral axis is likely to be close to the outer face steel, it suffices to analyse the wall as a singly reinforced section.

The modular ratio m is taken as: $m = 280/(3\sigma_{cbc}) = 280/(3 \times 10.0) = 9.33$

$$\rho = 0.004462 \quad \Rightarrow \quad \rho m = 0.04163$$

$$k = \sqrt{2(\rho m) + (\rho m)^2} - (\rho m) = 0.2499$$

$$\Rightarrow \quad x = kd = 0.2499 \times 137 = 34.24 \text{ mm}$$

$$\Rightarrow \quad I_{cr} = (1000)(34.24)^3/3 + (9.33 \times 611.3)(137 - 34.24)^2 = 0.736 \times 10^8 \text{ mm}^4$$

$$\Rightarrow \quad f_{st} = \frac{9.33 \times (9.45 \times 10^6) \times (137 - 34.24)}{0.736 \times 10^8} = 123.1 \text{ MPa}$$ (exceeding the 'deemed to comply' limit of 100 MPa for a limiting crack width of 0.1 mm).

Hence, a detailed crack-width check is warranted (using the procedure described in Annex B of IS 3370 Part 2).

For a limiting crack width of 0.1 mm,

$$\varepsilon_2 = \frac{1.5b(t-x)^2}{3E_s A_{st}(d-x)} = \frac{1.5 \times 1000(200 - 34.24)^2}{3(2 \times 10^5)(611.3)(137 - 34.24)} = 0.001094$$

$$a_{cr} = \sqrt{(s/2)^2 + d_c^2} - d_b/2 = \sqrt{(185/2)^2 + (63)^2} - 6 = 105.92 \text{ mm}$$

$$\Rightarrow \quad \varepsilon_1 = \frac{w\left[1 + \dfrac{2(a_{cr} - C_{\min})}{t - x}\right]}{3a_{cr}} + \varepsilon_2 = \frac{0.1\left[1 + \dfrac{2(105.92 - 63)}{200 - 34.24}\right]}{3 \times 105.92} + 0.001094 = 0.001572$$

Strain at the level of steel, $\varepsilon_{st} = \varepsilon_1 \times (d - x)/(t - x) = 0.001572 \times (137 - 34.24)/(200 - 34.24) = 0.000975 < \dfrac{0.6 \times 500}{2 \times 10^5} = 0.00150$

Allowable stress in steel for 0.1 mm crack width, $(f_{st})_{\lim} = 0.000975 \times (2 \times 10^5) = 195 \text{ MPa} > 123.1 \text{ MPa}$ (the actual calculated stress for the steel provided). Hence, the 0.1 mm crack-width limit is satisfied.

Shear check

Maximum shear force in the wall occurs at the base and at the vertical edges:

Shear check at junction of wall and base slab

Factored shear force $S_{u,\text{base}} = 1.5 \times 28.8 = 43.2$ kN/m

Factored shear stress $(\tau_v) = \dfrac{43.2 \times 1000}{1000 \times 137} = 0.315$ MPa

For the given grade of concrete (M 30) and p_t provided (0.4462 %), shear stress capacity of concrete can be found from Table 19 of IS 456:2000.

$\tau_c = 0.472$ MPa. Since $\tau_v < \tau_c$ there is no need of shear reinforcement in the wall.

Shear check at junction of walls

Factored shear force $S_{u,hor} = 1.5 \times 28.8 = 43.2$ kN/m

Factored shear stress (τ_v) =(43.2 × 1000)/(1000 × 149) = 0.29 MPa

For the given grade of concrete (M 30) and p_t provided (0.4103 %), shear stress capacity of concrete can be found from Table 19 of IS 456:2000. $\tau_c = 0.453$ MPa. Since the wall is in horizontal tension the design shear strength will decrease as per Eq. 18.1a.

$$\delta = 1 - 8\, N_u / (A_g f_{ck}) = 1 - 8 \times 43.2 \times 1000/(1000 \times 200 \times 30) = 0.9424$$

Design shear strength = $\delta\tau_c = 0.9424 \times 0.453 = 0.427$ MPa > 0.29 MPa

Hence there is no need for shear reinforcement.

It is a good practice to provide haunches at the base and at the vertical edge of the wall. These haunches can have a nominal dimension of 150 mm × 150 mm.

Design of floor slab

The floor slab (assumed to be 150 mm thick) will be subject to direct tension, and some local bending near the junction with the wall, due to the integral connection with the walls. The slab is thickened locally under the wall, with an outward 'toe' projection of 300 mm and a 'heel' inside 500 mm wide (continuous with the floor slab). The bending moment in the floor slab at the face of the wall (on the 'heel' side) will be the difference of the design moment at the wall base and the cantilever moment in the toe slab (due to soil pressure acting upwards). Hence, it is adequate to provide the same thickness (200 mm) and reinforcement (12ϕ @ 185 mm c/c) at top and bottom in the thickened portion of the base slab.

The base shear in the wall is transferred as direct tension to the floor slab, which is not subject to bending in the interior region.

As the tank is resting on ground, a nominal thickness of 150 mm is adequate for the slab. The minimum reinforcement is 0.6% (to be calculated over 100 mm thick surface zone, with steel provided near top)

$$A_{\min} = \frac{0.60}{100} A_g = \frac{0.60}{100} \times 100 \times 1000 = 600 \text{ mm}^2\text{/m}$$

Provide 12ϕ @ 150 mm c/c at top. Provided steel is 753 mm^2/m > 600 mm^2/m.

Strength check for direct tension:

$N_{u,\text{base}} = 43.2$ kN/m (shear force at the wall base, calculated above)

$A_{s,\text{reqd}} = 43.2 \times 1000/(0.87 \times 500) = 99.31$ mm^2/m < 753 mm^2/m provided. Hence adequate.

Hence minimum reinforcement governs the design.

Tension crack-width check for floor slab (for a service tension force of 28.8 kN/m)

Tensile stress = 28.8 × 1000/753 = 38.24 MPa

This is within the limiting stress of 100 MPa (for high strength deformed bars, for a crack width of 0.1 mm) as per the 'deemed to satisfy' approach of the code (Annex B, IS 3370 Part 2); hence a rigorous crack width check is not needed.

Design of Roof Slab

The size of the slab, centre to centre of supports = 3 m + 0.2 m = 3.2 m.

Loading on the slab:

Self-weight of slab = 0.15 × 25 = 3.75 kN/m^2 (assuming 150 mm thick slab)

Finishes = 0.05 × 24 = 1.2 kN/m^2 (assuming a cement mortar finish of 50 mm)

Live load = 1.0 kN/m^2

Total load = 5.95 kN/m^2, Factored load = 1.5 × 5.95 = 8.925 kN/m^2

The bending moment coefficient for an isolated slab whose corners are prevented from lifting up can be found from Table 26 of IS 456:2000, and is 0.056.

$$M_{u,\text{slab}} = 0.056 \times 8.925 \times 3.2^2 = 5.118 \text{ kNm/m}$$

Effective depth of slab = 150 − 45 − 12/2 = 99 mm (clear cover of 45 mm in slab, as slab is enclosing the space above the water, and 12 mm bars used)

Providing a minimum steel area of 0.6% (as per Table 18.2),

$$A_{\text{roof, min}} = \frac{0.60}{100} \times 150 \times 1000 = 900 \text{ mm}^2\text{/m}$$

Provide 12ϕ @ 125 c/c at bottom (A_{roof} = 904.8 mm^2/m), as shown in Figure 18.16.
Reinforcement ratio, $\rho = A_s/bd$ = 904.8/(1000 × 99) = 0.009139

$$\frac{M_{uR}}{bd^2} = 0.87 f_y \rho \left(1 - \frac{f_y}{f_{ck}} \rho\right) = 0.87 \times 500 \times 0.009139 \left(1 - \frac{500}{30} \times 0.009139\right) = 3.370 \text{ MPa}$$

M_{uR} = 3.370 × 1000 × 99^2 = 33.029 kNm/m, which well exceeds the maximum design requirement of 5.118 kNm/m

The tension force acting on the roof slab ($N_{\text{roof}} = S_{\text{top}}$) = 6.3 kN/m

Factored tension force = 1.5 × 6.3 = 9.45 kN/m

The tension capacity of the slab (N_{u0}) = 0.87 × 500 × 904.8 = 393.59 kN/m

Checking the interaction equation

$$\frac{9.45}{393.59} + \frac{5.118}{33.029} = 0.024 + 0.155 = 0.179 < 1.0.$$ Hence, the interaction equation is satisfied.

The minimum reinforcement governs the design. A crack-width check can be carried out to check under the effects of combined bending and tension as explained earlier. The minimum steel provided suffices the 0.1 mm crack-width criteria in this case.

An opening (with a cover) shall be provided appropriately in the roof slab, for access to the inside of the tank for maintenance purposes. Proper detailing of the slab reinforcement is essential around this opening.
The reinforcement detailing is shown in Figure 18.16; the detailing of the vertical haunch along the height of the tank is shown in Figure 18.17.

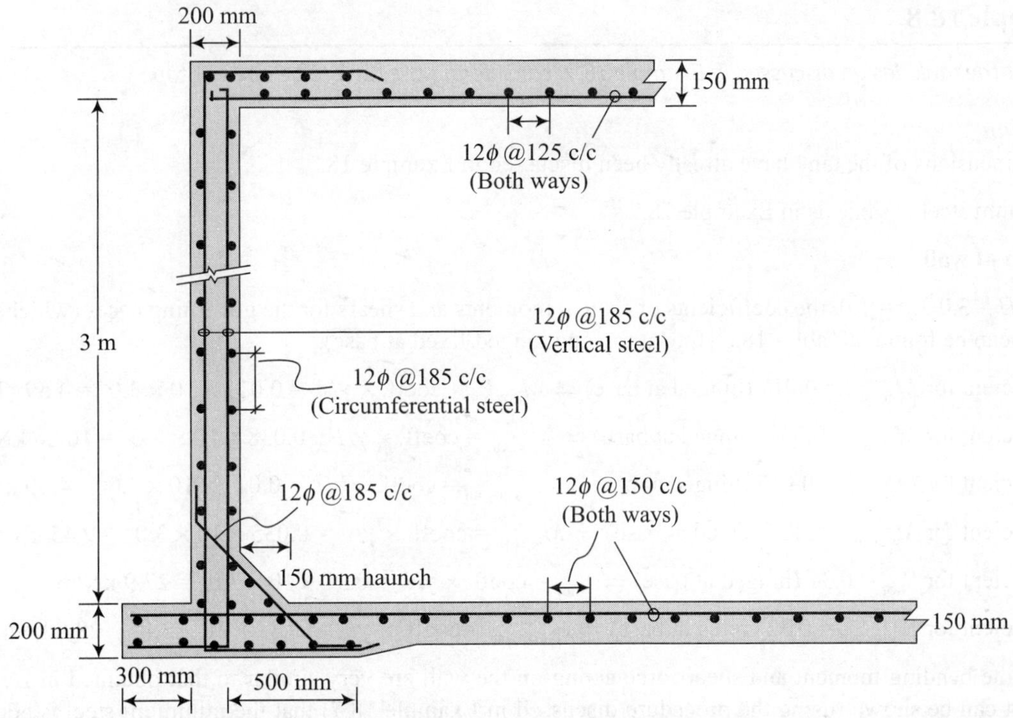

Fig. 18.16 Detailing of the tank designed in Example 18.7.

If the crack width is limited to 0.2 mm instead of 0.1 mm, the minimum steel needed reduces to 0.3%. The design of wall, floor slab and roof slab may be governed by either strength or serviceability criteria and the procedure discussed above can be used to verify this.

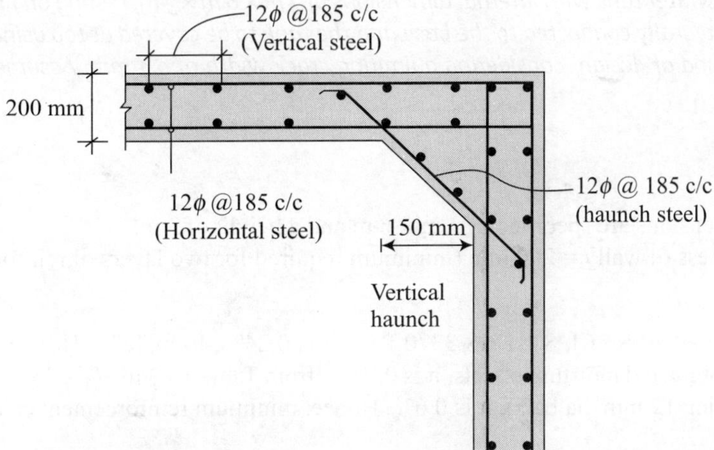

Fig. 18.17 Detailing of corner haunch at the junction of two walls (Example 18.7).

Example 18.8

Repeat the tank design discussed in Example 18.7, considering the tank to be open at top.

Solution

The dimensions of the tank have already been discussed in Example 18.7.

Minimum steel is same as in Example 18.7

Design of wall

For $b/H = 3.0/3.0 = 1.0$, the coefficients of critical moments and shears for the governing cases (whichever is more) can be found in Tables 18.6 (free at top and hinged/fixed at base).

Coefficient for $M_{hor,out} = 0.017$ (hinged at base) $\Rightarrow M_{hor,out} = \text{coeff.} \times \gamma H^3 = 0.017 \times 10 \times 3.0^3 = 4.59$ kNm/m

Coefficient for $M_{hor,in} = 0.038$ (hinged at base) $\Rightarrow M_{hor,in} = \text{coeff.} \times \gamma H^3 = 0.038 \times 10 \times 3.0^3 = 10.26$ kNm/m

Coefficient for $M_{vert,out} = 0.017$ (hinged at base) $\Rightarrow M_{vert,out} = \text{coeff.} \times \gamma H^3 = 0.017 \times 10 \times 3.0^3 = 4.59$ kNm/m

Coefficient for $M_{vert,in} = 0.035$ (fixed at base) $\Rightarrow M_{vert,in} = \text{coeff.} \times \gamma H^3 = 0.035 \times 10 \times 3.0^3 = 9.45$ kNm/m

Coefficient for $S_{hor} = 0.31$ (hinged at base) $\Rightarrow S_{hor} = \text{coeff.} \times \gamma H^2 = 0.31 \times 10 \times 3.0^2 = 27.9$ kN/m

Coefficient for $S_{vert,base} = 0.32$ (fixed at base) $\Rightarrow S_{vert,base} = \text{coeff.} \times \gamma H^2 = 0.32 \times 10 \times 3.0^2 = 28.8$ kN/m

Since the bending moment and shear force acting on the wall are very similar to that obtained in Example 18.7, it can be shown (using the procedure discussed in Example 18.7) that the minimum steel is adequate for both strength and crack-width criteria for the open tank as well. The detailing shown in Figure 18.16 is applicable (without the roof slab).

Example 18.9

Design a rectangular water tank with internal dimensions of 3 m × 6 m × 3 m, resting on firm ground, considering the walls to be integrally connected to the base and the tank to be covered at top using a cover slab. Apply the limit states method of design, considering a limiting crack width of 0.1 mm. Assume M 30 concrete and Fe 500 steel.

Solution

Tank Dimensions

- Tank plan dimensions are specified as 3 m × 6 m and a height of 3 m.
- Assume thickness of wall $t = 200$ mm (minimum required for two layers of reinforcement)

Minimum reinforcement

Minimum steel required as per Cl. 8.1.1 [IS 3370 Part 2] is 0.24%; from Table 18.1, to minimize the crack width due to temperature and moisture effects, it is 0.26%; from Table 18.2 for $T_1 = 25°$C and a limiting crack width of 0.1 mm (using 12 mm dia bars), it is 0.6%. Hence, minimum reinforcement calculations are carried out for 0.60% steel.

$$A_{min} = \frac{0.60}{100} \times 200 \times 1000 = 1200 \text{ mm}^2/\text{m}.$$

Providing 12ϕ bars in two layers, required spacing is 188 mm. Hence, minimum reinforcement requirement in the tank wall in both directions is satisfied by providing 12ϕ @ 185 mm c/c in two layers. Area of steel provided on each face, in each direction, is 1223/2 = 611.5 mm^2/m.

The critical design coefficients can be obtained from Tables 18.7(a) and 18.7(c) (for the horizontal bending $b_1/H = 2.0$ and $b_2/H = 1.0$) and from Tables 18.5(a) and 18.5(b) (for vertical bending and shear). These critical values are tabulated below:

Table 18.8 *Critical design values (Example 18.9)*

	Coefficients		Moment/Shear		Units
	Long wall	Short wall	Long wall	Short wall	
$M_{hor,out}$ (coeff. $\times \gamma H^3$)	0.0230	0.0150	6.21	4.05	kNm/m
$M_{hor,in}$ (coeff. $\times \gamma H^3$)	0.0510	0.0510	13.77	13.77	kNm/m
$M_{vert,out}$ (coeff. $\times \gamma H^3$)	0.0450	0.0170	12.15	4.59	kNm/m
$M_{vert,in}$ (coeff. $\times \gamma H^3$)	0.0620	0.0350	16.74	9.45	kNm/m
S_{hor} (coeff. $\times \gamma H^2$)	0.4000	0.3200	36.00	28.80	kN/m
$S_{vert,base}$ (coeff. $\times \gamma H^2$)	0.3900	0.3200	35.10	28.80	kN/m
$S_{vert,top}$ (coeff. $\times \gamma H^2$)	0.1300	0.0700	11.70	6.30	kN/m

Design of wall

It can be seen from the above table that the vertical moment is higher than the horizontal moment in the long wall. Hence the vertical steel needs to be provided in the outer layer. In the case of short wall, the horizontal moments are higher than the vertical moments, implying that it is beneficial to provide horizontal steel in the outer layer. [If the horizontal steel is provided in the inside layer for the short wall (as in the case of the long wall), it should be checked that this is adequate].

Design of horizontal reinforcement in walls

The adequacy of the minimum steel provided 12ϕ @ 185 mm c/c (A_s = 611.5 mm^2/m) on both faces needs to be checked for the critical combination of direct tension and bending moment. The maximum horizontal moment occurs at the junction of short wall and long wall, and the maximum direct tension occurs in the short wall (obtainable from S_{hor} in the long wall).

For this combination, occurring in the short wall,

$$N_u = 1.5 \times 36.00 = 54.00 \text{ kN/m}; \quad \text{and} \quad M_{u,\text{hor}} = 1.5 \times 13.77 = 20.65 \text{ kNm/m}.$$

Since there is tension and bending in the wall, the interaction equation (Eq. 18.1) needs to be satisfied. As indicated above, in the short wall, the horizontal reinforcement will be placed in the outer layer.

Effective depth, $d = t$ – clear cover – $\phi/2$ = 200 – 45 –12/2 = 149 mm

Effective cover, d' = 45 + 12/2 = 51 mm.

Reinforcement ratio, $\rho = A_s/bd$ = 611.5/(1000 × 149) = 0.004104

$$\frac{M_{uR}}{bd^2} = 0.87 f_y \rho \left(1 - \frac{f_y}{f_{ck}}\rho\right) = 0.87 \times 500 \times 0.004104 \left(1 - \frac{500}{30} \times 0.004104\right) = 1.6631 \text{ MPa}$$

$$M_{uR} = 1.6631 \times 1000 \times 149^2 = 36.92 \text{ kNm/m}$$

which well exceeds the maximum design requirement of 20.65 kNm/m; hence Ok.

Since the steel is provided in two layers, both layers of steel are effective in resisting the direct tension force. Hence $A_s = 2 \times 611.5 = 1223 \text{ mm}^2\text{/m}$.

The tension capacity of the wall (N_{u0}) = 0.87 × 500 × 1223 = 532 kN/m

Checking the interaction equation

$$\frac{54.00}{532} + \frac{20.65}{36.92} = 0.102 + 0.559 = 0.661 < 1.0. \text{ Hence, the interaction equation is satisfied.}$$

The minimum reinforcement governs the design. However, a check is carried out to ensure the crack width is within allowable limits.

Crack-width check for tension + bending

Checking if the neutral axis lies within the cross-section or not, using the condition in Eq. 18.7.

$$\frac{M_{\text{hor,out}}}{Nt} = \frac{13.77 \times 1000}{36.00 \times 200} = 1.913$$

$$0.5\left(1 - \frac{2d'}{t}\right)^2 = 0.5\left(1 - \frac{2 \times 51}{200}\right)^2 = 0.12$$

Since 1.913 > 0.12, the neutral axis lies within the section.

The modular ratio m is taken as: $m = 280/(3\sigma_{cbc}) = 280/(3 \times 10.0) = 9.33$

Assuming an x/t value of 0.154 for the first iteration:

$$x = 0.154 \times 200 = 30.8 \text{ mm}$$

The value of f_c can be estimated using Eq. 18.13,

$$f_c = \frac{13.77 \times 10^6}{9.33 \times 611.5 \times \left(\frac{149 - 30.8}{30.8}\right)\left(\frac{200}{2} - 51\right) + \frac{1}{2} \times 1000 \times 30\left(\frac{200}{2} - 30.8\right)} = 5.61 \text{ MPa}$$

The depth of neutral axis can be calculated by solving the roots of the quadratic equation Eq. 18.14,

$$x_{\text{calc}} = 30.86 \text{ mm}$$

The value of x_{calc} is very close to the assumed value of x, hence convergence is achieved.

The stress in the steel f_{st} can be calculated using Eq. 18.12,

$$\Rightarrow \qquad f_{st} = 9.33 \times 5.61 \times \frac{(149 - 30.8)}{30.8} = 200.92 \text{ MPa}$$

For a limiting crack width of 0.1 mm,

$$\varepsilon_2 = \frac{1.5b(t - x)^2}{3E_s A_{st}(d - x)} = \frac{1.5 \times 1000(200 - 30.8)^2}{3(2 \times 10^5)(611.5)(149 - 30.8)} = 0.000991$$

$$a_{cr} = \sqrt{(s/2)^2 + d_c^{\,2}} - d_b/2 = \sqrt{(185/2)^2 + (51)^2} - 6 = 99.63 \text{ mm}$$

$$\Rightarrow \quad \frac{w\left[1 + \dfrac{2(a_{cr} - C_{\min})}{t - x}\right]}{3a_{cr}} + \varepsilon_2 = \frac{0.1\left[1 + \dfrac{2(99.63 - 51)}{200 - 30.8}\right]}{3 \times 99.63} + 0.000991 = 0.001517$$

Strain at the level of steel $\varepsilon_{st} = \varepsilon_1 \times (d - x)/(t - x) = 0.001517 \times (149 - 30.8)/(200 - 30.8) = 0.001060$ $< \dfrac{0.6 \times 500}{2 \times 10^5} = 0.00150$

Allowable stress in steel for 0.1 mm crack width = $0.001060 \times (2 \times 10^5) = 212.0$ MPa > 200.92 MPa (calculated actual stress for the steel provided). Hence the 0.1 mm crack width is satisfied.

Since $M_{u,\text{hor,out}}$ is lesser than $M_{u,\text{hor,in}}$ a separate design check and crack-width check is not necessary.

Design of vertical reinforcement in wall for vertical bending

The maximum vertical moment occurs at the base of the long wall $M_{\text{vert,in}} = 16.74$ kNm/m. Factored moment $= 1.5 \times 16.74 = 25.11$ kNm/m.

Check adequacy of minimum reinforcement 12ϕ @ 185 mm c/c (611.5 mm^2/m) on both faces.

In the long wall, the vertical reinforcement is placed in the outer layer.

Effective depth $d = t -$ clear cover $- \phi/2 = 200 - 45 - 12/2 = 149$ mm (assuming 12 mm ϕ bars)

Reinforcement ratio, $\rho = A_s/bd = 611.5/(1000 \times 149) = 0.004103$

$$\frac{M_{uR}}{bd^2} = 0.87 f_y \rho\left(1 - \frac{f_y}{f_{ck}}\rho\right) = 0.87 \times 500 \times 0.004103\left(1 - \frac{500}{30} \times 0.004103\right) = 1.663 \text{ MPa}$$

$M_{uR} = 1.663 \times 1000 \times 149^2 = 36.92$ kNm/m, which well exceeds the maximum design requirement of 25.11 kNm/m.

Hence, minimum reinforcement governs.

Flexural crack-width check (for maximum service moment of 16.74 kNm/m)

As the neutral axis is likely to be close to the outer face steel, it suffices to analyse the wall as a singly reinforced section.

The modular ratio m is taken as: $m = 280/(3\sigma_{cbc}) = 280/(3 \times 10.0) = 9.33$

$$\rho = 0.004103 \quad \Rightarrow \quad \rho m = 0.03828$$

$$k = \sqrt{2(\rho m) + (\rho m)^2} - (\rho m) = 0.2411$$

$$\Rightarrow \quad x = kd = 0.2411 \times 149 = 35.92 \text{ mm}$$

$$\Rightarrow \quad I_{cr} = (1000)(35.92)^3/3 + (9.33 \times 611.5)(149 - 35.92)^2 = 0.884 \times 10^8 \text{ mm}^4$$

$$\Rightarrow \quad f_{st} = \frac{9.33 \times (16.74 \times 10^6) \times (149 - 35.92)}{0.884 \times 10^8} = 199.83 \text{ MPa (exceeding the 'deemed to comply' limit of}$$

100 MPa for a limiting crack width of 0.1 mm).

Hence, a detailed crack-width check is warranted (using the procedure described in Annex B of IS 3370 Part 2).

For a limiting crack width of 0.1 mm,

$$\varepsilon_2 = \frac{1.5b(t-x)^2}{3E_s A_{st}(d-x)} = \frac{1.5 \times 1000(200 - 35.92)^2}{3(2 \times 10^5)(611.5)(149 - 35.92)} = 0.000974$$

$$a_{cr} = \sqrt{(s/2)^2 + d_c^2} - d_b/2 = \sqrt{(185/2)^2 + (51)^2} - 6 = 99.63 \text{ mm}$$

$$\Rightarrow \quad \varepsilon_1 = \frac{w\left[1 + \dfrac{2(a_{cr} - C_{\min})}{t - x}\right]}{3a_{cr}} + \varepsilon_2 = \frac{0.1\left[1 + \dfrac{2(99.63 - 51)}{200 - 35.92}\right]}{3 \times 99.63} + 0.000974 = 0.001507$$

Strain at the level of steel $\varepsilon_{st} = \varepsilon_1 \times (d - x)/(t - x) = 0.001507 \times (149 - 35.92)/(200 - 35.92) = 0.001038 < \dfrac{0.6 \times 500}{2 \times 10^5} = 0.00150$

Allowable stress in steel for 0.1 mm crack width = 0.001038 × (2 × 10^5) = 207.6 MPa > 199.83 MPa (actual calculated stress for the steel provided). Hence, the 0.1 mm crack-width limit is satisfied.

Since the check has been done for the maximum vertical bending moment, it is not necessary to carry out checks for other vertical moments as they are lesser and minimum steel is adequate.

Shear check

At base

Factored shear force $S_{u,\text{base}} = 1.5 \times 35.1 = 52.65$ kN/m

Factored shear stress $(\tau_v) = \dfrac{52.65 \times 1000}{1000 \times 149} = 0.353$ MPa

For the given grade of concrete (M 30) and p_t provided (0.41%), shear stress capacity of concrete can be found from Table 19 of IS 456:2000.

$\tau_c = 0.453$ MPa. Since $\tau_v < \tau_c$ there is no need of shear reinforcement in the wall. It is good practise to provide haunches at the base of the wall. These haunches can have a nominal dimension of 150 mm × 150 mm.

The shear force along the vertical edge (for horizontal bending) is less than shear at the wall base, hence a separate check is not necessary.

Shear check at junction of walls

Factored shear force $S_{u,hor} = 1.5 \times 36.0 = 54$ kN/m

Factored shear stress $(\tau_v) = (54 \times 1000)/(1000 \times 137) = 0.394$ MPa

For the given grade of concrete (M 30) and p_t provided (0.41 %), shear stress capacity of concrete can be found from Table 19 of IS 456:2000. $\tau_c = 0.453$ MPa. Since the wall is in horizontal tension the design shear strength will decrease as per Eq. 18.1a.

$$\delta = 1 - 8\,N_u / (A_g f_{ck}) = 1 - 8 \times 43.2 \times 1000/(1000 \times 200 \times 30) = 0.9424 \ (N_u = S_{u,hor} \text{ of short wall})$$

Design shear strength = $\delta\tau_c = 0.9424 \times 0.453 = 0.427 \text{ MPa} > 0.394 \text{ MPa}$

Hence there is no need for shear reinforcement.

It is a good practice to provide haunches at the vertical edge of the wall. These haunches can have a nominal dimension of 150 mm × 150 mm.

The design of floor slab and roof slab are not demonstrated here. These can easily be worked out using the procedures followed in Example 18.7.

The detailing of the wall is similar to that shown in Figures 18.16 and 18.17. However, it should be noted that the placement of horizontal reinforcement in the outer layers is valid in this Example only with respect to the short walls, and not the long walls. In design practice, this difference in detailing (placement of vertical reinforcement in the outer layers) should be made clear in the construction drawing (by means of an additional section cut through the longer wall); the detailing of the haunch in Figure 18.17 will also change accordingly.

REVIEW QUESTIONS

18.1 In what way does the design of liquid storage RC structures call for special attention compared to general RC structures?

18.2 How are liquid storage tanks broadly classified? Give examples.

18.3 Why are cylindrical tanks preferred to rectangular tanks for storage of liquids of large capacity?

18.4 Describe the main structural actions developed in a RC water tank on account of hydrostatic pressure. How is the action different in a rectangular tank, compared to a cylindrical tank?

18.5 Why is it important to examine the implications of the 'tank empty' condition in design?

18.6 Is it advantageous to use high strength deformed bars, compared to mild steel plain bars, in RC water tanks? Discuss.

18.7 What are the different types of movement joints provided in water tanks?

18.8 What are the key assumptions underlying the working stress design of liquid storage tanks?

18.9 What are the 'deemed to be satisfactory' provisions in the Code? What purpose do they serve?

18.10 Discuss the importance of the measures recommended in the Code to control cracking due to temperature and moisture effects.

18.11 Discuss, with the help of sketches, the typical variations of hoop tension and vertical bending moment in a cylindrical tank wall, open at top and rigidly connected to the base below.

18.12 How is the direct tension due to hydrostatic pressure assessed in the walls of a single cell rectangular tank?

18.13 Can the moment coefficients required for the design of a rectangular water tank subject to hydrostatic pressure be taken directly from the corresponding values applicable for an isolated wall panel, fixed at the two sides, with the same boundary conditions at the top and bottom edges? Discuss.

PROBLEMS

18.1 Design a cylindrical water tank of capacity 400 m^3 (400 kL) with a height of 4.0 m, resting on ground, assuming an ideal flexible joint at the base of the wall, and assuming the tank to be open at top. Apply the limit states method of design, considering a limiting crack width of 0.1 mm. Assume M 30 concrete and Fe 500 steel.

18.2 Re-design the tank in Problem 18.1 using Fe 250 steel in lieu of Fe 500. What are the implications of this change?

18.3 Re-design the tank in Problem 18.1, considering a limiting crack width of 0.2 mm in lieu of 0.1 mm. What are the implications of this change?

18.4 Re-design the tank in Problem 18.3 by the working stress method, in lieu of the limit states method. What are the implications of this change?

18.5 Design a cylindrical water tank of capacity 400 m^3 (400 kL) with an internal height of 4.0 m, resting on ground, assuming the wall to be integrally connected to the base slab, and assuming the tank to be open at top. Apply the limit states method of design, considering a limiting crack width of 0.1 mm. Assume M 30 concrete and Fe 500 steel.

18.6 Re-design the tank in Problem 18.5, considering a limiting crack width of 0.2 mm in lieu of 0.1 mm. What are the implications of this change?

18.7 Design a square water tank of capacity 40 m^3 (40 kL) with an internal height of 3.0 m and a cover slab, resting on firm ground, considering the tank walls to be integrally connected to the base slab. Apply the limit states method of design, considering a limiting crack width of 0.1 mm. Assume M 30 concrete and Fe 500 steel.

18.8 Re-design the tank in Problem 18.7, considering a limiting crack width of 0.2 mm in lieu of 0.1 mm. What are the implications of this change?

18.9 Re-design the tank in Problem 18.7, considering the tank to be open at top.

18.10 Design a rectangular water tank with internal dimensions of 4 m (width), 8 m (length) and height of 3.0 m, resting on firm ground, considering the tank walls to be integrally connected to the base slab and with a cover slab on top. Apply the limit states method of design, considering a limiting crack-width of 0.1 mm. Assume M 30 concrete and Fe 500 steel.

REFERENCES

18.1 ___ IS 3370-1 (2021): *Concrete Structures for Retaining Aqueous Liquids – Code of Practice, Part 1 – General Requirements*, Bureau of Indian Standards, New Delhi, 2021

18.2 Forth, J P and Martin A J, *Design of Liquid Retaining Concrete Structures*, Whittles Publishing, 3rd Edition, 2014

18.3 ___ IS 3370-2 (2021): *Concrete Structures for Retaining Aqueous Liquids – Code of Practice, Part 2 – Plain and Reinforced Concrete*, Bureau of Indian Standards, New Delhi, 2021

18.4 ___ IS 1893-2 (2014): *Criteria for Earthquake Resistant Design of Structures, Part 2 – Liquid Retaining Tanks*, Fifth Revision, Bureau of Indian Standards, New Delhi, 2014

18.5 ___ BS 8007 (1987): *Code of Practice for Design of Concrete Structures for Retaining Aqueous Liquids*, British Standards Institution, 1987

18.6 ___ EN 1992-3:2006: Eurocode 2: Design of Concrete Structures – Part 3: Liquid Retaining and Containment Structures, Brussels, 2006

18.7 ___ IS 3370-4 (2021): *Concrete Structures for Retaining Aqueous Liquids, - Code of Practice, Part 4 – Design Tables*, Bureau of Indian Standards, New Delhi, 2021

18.8 ___ IS 11682 (1985): *Criteria for Design of RCC Staging for Overhead Water Tanks*, Bureau of Indian Standards, New Delhi, 1985

18.9 Anchor, R D, *Design of Liquid Retaining Concrete Structures*, Second edition, Edward Arnold Publishers, London, 1991

18.10 A Ghali, *Circular Storage Tanks and Silos*, Second Edition, Taylor and Francis Routledge, 2000

18.11 Reynolds, C E, Steedman, J C and Threlfall, A J, Reynolds's Reinforced Concrete Designer's Handbook, 11th Edition, Taylor and Francis, 2008

18.12 J Munshi, *Rectangular Concrete Tanks*, Revised Fifth Edition, PCA Publication, United States, 1969

18.13 W T Moody, *Moments and Reactions for Rectangular Plates*, Engineering Monograph No. 27, Technical Publication, Department of the Interior, United States, 1963

CHAPTER 19

Estimation of Wind and Seismic Forces on Buildings

LEARNING OBJECTIVES

After studying this chapter, you will be able to:

- *Explain the factors that influence the magnitudes and effects of wind and seismic loads on buildings*
- *Estimate wind and earthquake loads on usual types of buildings*
- *Discuss dynamic analysis options for assessing wind and seismic load effects on buildings*

19.1 Introduction

As discussed in Chapter 1 (Section 1.5), reinforced concrete buildings need to be designed to resist and transmit all the effects of gravity loads (typically, dead loads and live loads) and lateral loads (due to wind and earthquake) to the foundation and ground below. The basic design principles of various RC structural elements, such as beams, slabs, columns, walls (including shear walls), staircases, footings, retaining walls and liquid storage tanks have been discussed (and demonstrated with illustrative examples) in subsequent chapters – primarily for gravity load effects. Gravity load patterns to be considered in framed buildings (continuous systems, in general) have also been discussed in Chapter 9. Basic principles of earthquake-resistant design, including Code provisions for ductile detailing, have been discussed in Chapter 16. The codes of practice to estimate design loads, such as IS 875 (Parts 1-5) and IS 1893 (for earthquake resistant design), have been referred to, but not explained in detail so far in respect of wind and earthquake loadings. This chapter attempts to fill in that gap partly by giving an overview of the procedures to estimate wind and seismic forces on RC buildings – to enable the student to analyse and design typical multi-storeyed RC framed buildings. The focus is on the building as a whole, and not on individual components (such as walls, roofs and projections), which also need special consideration in design.

> Wind and earthquake forces are dynamic and probabilistic in nature. However, for regular low-rise buildings of usual proportions, Codes also present equivalent static forces and methods of analysis.

Loadings due to wind and earthquake are dynamic and probabilistic in nature. Design codes generally permit simplified static analysis for regular buildings to arrive at a reasonably conservative estimate of design forces, although in some cases (typically involving 'irregular' buildings), dynamic analysis is insisted upon. This chapter gives a broad overview of the nature of wind and seismic forces acting on RC buildings and relevant code provisions to estimate them, with a focus on static analysis (including example calculations).

From a design perspective, it is the extreme event (wind or earthquake) that is of significance – something that happens rarely but could happen during the design lifetime of the building. As the simultaneous occurrence of the extreme wind and extreme earthquake is highly unlikely, it suffices to design/check for one of these loads at a time, together with other applicable loads (refer Chapter 3). It is necessary to ensure that the building (including the structural components) has adequate levels of stability, strength and serviceability – under wind/ earthquake, with appropriate combinations of load (and material resistance) factors. In some cases (such as low-rise buildings in low 'seismic zones' and non-cyclone-prone regions), neither wind nor seismic forces may govern the design; in other cases (such as buildings in high seismic zones), the seismic forces are likely to govern, while in some other situations (such as 'super tall'† buildings), wind forces may govern the design. In general, seismic forces tend to govern the design of buildings lower than a critical height (which could vary from five to more than 30 storeys, depending on the building and its location), and could even govern a substantial upper part of taller buildings, while wind forces are likely to govern the design of the lower parts of such buildings [Ref. 19.1].

Essentially, the building behaves like a vertical cantilever (fixed to the ground below), when subject to lateral forces induced by wind or earthquake; the building must therefore have appropriate lateral load resisting mechanisms with adequate strength and stiffness (to limit the lateral drift) and ductility (in earthquake-resistant design). As the height of the building increases, the magnitudes of these forces also increase, resulting in greater 'base shear' and 'base moment' at the base of the building. This is common to both wind and earthquake. However, there are significant differences between the two, with regard to how these forces manifest and how their magnitudes and distribution are affected. There are factors that depend on the geographical location of the building under consideration ('wind zone' or 'seismic zone') and other local site conditions (terrain and topography in the case of wind, and soil conditions in the case of earthquake). There are also factors that depend on the structure itself – notably, its dynamic characteristics (natural vibration frequency and damping); the geometry of the building in plan and elevation (in the case of wind); and distribution of masses at various heights and ductility provisions (in the case of earthquake).

Wind is air in motion relative to the earth's surface, caused primarily by the earth's rotation and differences in terrestrial radiation [Ref. 19.2]. As the wind blows (in the 'atmospheric boundary layer'), it exerts forces on buildings (and other obstructions) that come in the way of its free flow. Wind speed gets translated into wind pressure, which in turn acts as a wind force on the exposed area of the building. As wind speed increases with height above the ground, the wind pressure also increases with height. Furthermore, fluctuations in wind speed and wind gusts (owing to turbulence) result in fluctuations in wind force (in space and time), causing structures to undergo lateral vibrations. However, the mean wind force is high, compared to the fluctuating component, and hence, the lateral deflections are always towards the leeward side of the building, oscillating about a mean deflection profile, as shown in Figure 19.1(a). There is no possibility of reversal of stresses in various members. But the wind direction itself

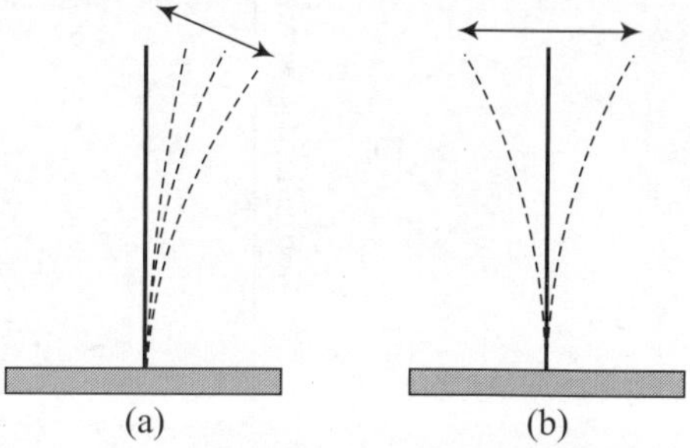

Fig. 19.1 Oscillations induced in a building due to (a) wind, and (b) earthquake.

† IS 16700: 2017 ('Criteria for structural safety of tall concrete buildings') defines a *super tall building* as having a height greater than 250 m, whereas a *tall building* is one that has a height between 50 m and 250 m.

can change and reverse, and this needs to be accounted for in the design. IS 875 (Part-3): 2015 Code† deals with estimation of wind forces on structures [Ref. 19.2].

In the case of earthquake, it is the shaking of the ground under that causes the building to shake (undergo to-and-fro lateral motions with respect to the vertical axis), as depicted in Figure 19.1(b). Consequently, inertial forces are generated by the vibrating masses at various floor levels due to the ground acceleration. [In contrast, weight (due to mass) acts favourably in the case of wind, providing stability to the structure against uplift, overturning and sliding.] The inertial forces thus generated can be considered as 'seismic forces' (lateral forces) acting on the building, which can be analysed (equivalent static analysis), in much the same way as wind forces. The distribution of these seismic forces along the height of the building depends on the mass and height at various floor levels. With increasing height, the seismic force also increases. For this reason, low-rise buildings, with light-weight construction, are typically recommended in high seismic zone regions. The reversed cyclic behaviour shown schematically in Figure 19.1(b) results in reversal of stresses in the various structural elements. IS 1893 (Part 1): 2016 deals with the estimation of seismic forces on structures [Ref. 19.3].

There are additional differences between wind and seismic forces acting on buildings that are noteworthy. Firstly, earthquakes are of much shorter duration than windstorms (with the possible exception of the passage of a tornado) and so can be treated as transient loadings. Secondly, the predominant frequencies of seismic ground motions are typically 10 to 50 times the frequencies of fully developed windstorms, as depicted in Figure 19.2, suggesting that tall and slender buildings are more susceptible to dynamic effects of wind, while seismic forces tend to govern the response of relatively low-rise buildings (with low fundamental time period and correspondingly high natural frequency). Thirdly, the seismic forces generated by earthquake ground motions appear as *fully correlated* equivalent forces acting over the height of a tall building, unlike the *partially correlated* wind forces generated by the eddy structure in windstorms; vortex-shedding forces are also not fully correlated over the height of a slender structure [Ref. 19.4].

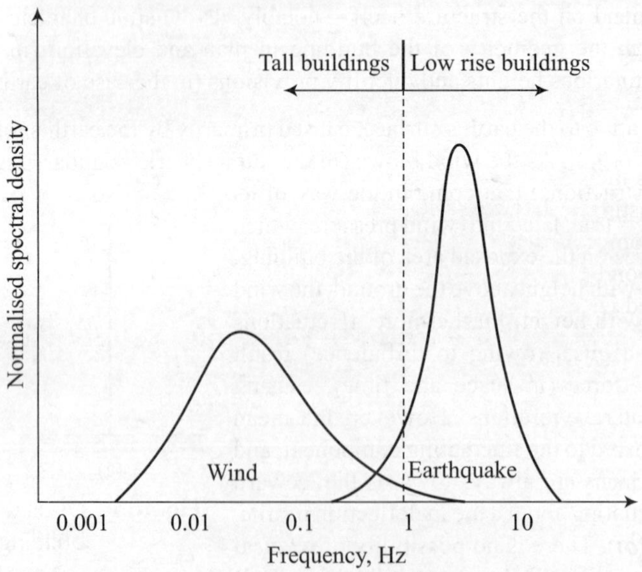

Fig. 19.2 Typical excitation frequencies due to wind and earthquake [Ref. 19.4].

† References to Code 'IS 875 (Part-3)' in this chapter refer to the 2015 (third) revision, and includes amendments to this revision made up to June 2020.

The dynamic response of the building gets amplified when its natural frequency (especially, fundamental frequency) is close to the dominant frequencies encountered in the wind and earthquake 'spectrum' (causing 'resonance'). IS 875 (Part-3) does not require structures with a fundamental natural frequency exceeding 1 Hz to be considered *wind-sensitive*, involving dynamic wind effects to be considered. [The fundamental time period of a typical multi-storeyed building with n storeys is approximately $0.1n$ seconds [Ref. 19.2], whereby the corresponding fundamental natural frequency (in Hz) is obtainable as its reciprocal, $10/n$. Thus, the fundamental natural frequency of a 10 storeyed building is approximately 1 Hz].

19.2 Estimation of Wind Forces

19.2.1 Wind Speed

The flow of wind is relatively uniform above a certain height (called *gradient wind height*), which typically lies between 250 m and 500 m above the ground level, depending on the surface roughness of the terrain. It is this region above the earth's surface that is called the *atmospheric boundary layer* in wind engineering. The wind speed is retarded by the ground surface friction; it increases from a value of zero at the earth's surface to a maximum value, called *gradient speed* (V_g) at the gradient height (Z_g), as shown schematically in Figure 19.3. Above the gradient height, wind speed conditions are independent of the ground surface friction. Below the gradient height, wind speed is turbulent in nature, varying randomly in time and space. At any height, z, above ground, the wind speed, $V_z(t)$, can be conceived as having a mean component, $\bar{V}_z$, plus a fluctuating component (causing 'gustiness'), as indicated in Figure 19.2. [A *Gust* is a positive or negative departure of wind speed from the mean value, lasting for a few seconds but for no more than, say, 2 min over a specified interval of time – the fluctuating component in Figure 19.3]. The magnitudes of both of these components depend not only on height, but also on the approach terrain and topography. However, for the assessment of wind forces on buildings, wind speed is taken as constant up to a height of 10 m, and equal to the value determined for the height of 10 m.

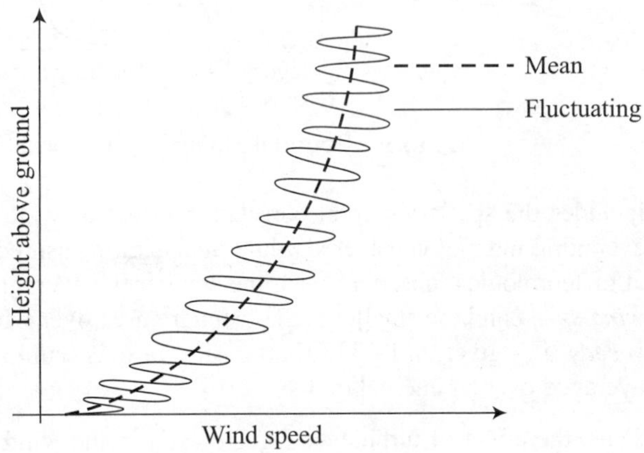

Fig. 19.3 Typical variation of wind speed with height above ground.

For design purpose, the terrains are typically classified into four categories: *category 1* corresponds to 'exposed open', *category 2* corresponds to 'open country', *category 3* corresponds to 'town', and *category 4* corresponds to 'city centre'. With increase in the category number, the surface roughness increases, whereby the gradient height also increases correspondingly, as indicated in Figure 19.4.

Gust Wind Speed (for Static Analysis of 'Rigid' Buildings)

Buildings are located within the gradient height, and hence are subject to buffeting by the turbulent wind. Low-rise and mid-rise buildings (having a height/width ratio less than 5 and a fundamental natural frequency exceeding 1 Hz) are relatively 'rigid', and it suffices to consider an 'equivalent static' wind load, which

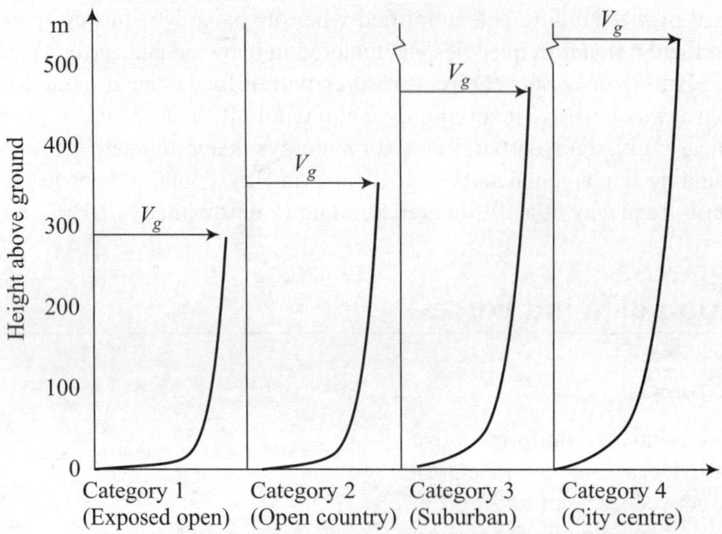

Fig. 19.4 Boundary layer profile for different approach terrains [Ref. 19.2].

includes the spatio-temporal correlation effect of wind gusts. The magnitude of the gust depends on the averaging interval considered while analysing measured wind speed records (using anemometers installed at meteorological observatories): the smaller the averaging interval, the greater is the magnitude of the *gust wind speed* and the smaller is the tributary area over which the gusty winds are correlated. The *basic wind speeds,* V_b, given in IS 875 (Part 3) for various wind zones in India are based on peak gust wind speeds averaged over an interval of 3 s.

Thus, the effect of turbulence ('gustiness') in the wind speed is assumed to be fully accounted for in the specified gust wind speed (basic wind speed), and hence it suffices to simply estimate wind forces on the building, based on these gust wind speeds, and treating these forces as static loads. The wind forces thus estimated are dependent only on the dimensions and geometry, and not on the lateral stiffness (and natural frequency) of the building; in other words, the structure is assumed to be 'rigid' for the purpose of evaluating the wind forces for design.

> Wind loads acting along the height of relatively low-rise 'rigid' buildings are based on *peak gust wind speeds* applicable to the terrain and topography under consideration. They also depend on the exposed area and geometry of the building, and do not involve the dynamic characteristics of the building. In design, these wind forces can be simply treated as *static* loads, as the spatio-temporal correlation effects of wind gusts are already incorporated in the estimation of the basic/design wind speeds.

Hourly Mean Wind Speed and Turbulence Intensity (for Dynamic Analysis of Wind-sensitive Buildings)

However, for a proper dynamic analysis (required for wind-sensitive structures), it is necessary to consider the characteristics of the wind-energy spectrum (refer Figure 19.2) and the natural frequencies of the building. The wind forces induced by the mean wind speed can be considered as statically applied loads, causing a static (mean) response, while the forces induced by the fluctuating component of wind speed cause the vibration in the response [refer Figures 19.1(a) and 19.3]. An 'exact' solution would call for a stochastic dynamic analysis, but this can be greatly simplified and made workable in practice (for the limited purpose of finding the maximum design load effects) by means of the concept of *gust response factor*, *G*, originally proposed by Davenport [Ref. 19.11] and widely adopted by design codes. With this simplification, all that needs to be carried out is an equivalent static analysis, in which the mean wind forces are obtained from the mean wind speeds along the height of the building, and then magnified by the factor *G*.

Such analysis of the building in the direction of the wind flow is called *along-wind analysis*. However, there is another phenomenon that needs to be considered in dynamic analysis of wind-sensitive structures. The building essentially acts like a *bluff* body (in contrast with a *streamlined* body such as an aircraft wing) obstructing the wind flow, causing a 'separation' of the flow at the leading-edge corners; the separated flow on either side tends to form concentrated vortices that are subsequently shed in the 'wake' region on the leeward side of the building, causing the building to vibrate in an 'across-wind' direction (perpendicular to the wind direction) [Ref. 19.4]. Thus, an *across-wind analysis* is also required to be carried out for wind-sensitive buildings. IS 875 (Part 3) recommends a simplified procedure to estimate the wind forces generated in the across-wind direction, and this is also based on the mean wind speed, rather than the gust wind speed.

Buildings that have a height/width ratio more than about 5 or a fundamental natural frequency less than 1 Hz are defined as *wind-sensitive* structures by IS 875 (Part 3): 2015 - Cl. 9. Such flexible slender buildings need to be analysed for dynamic effects of wind in *along-wind* and *across-wind* directions. Associated wind forces depend on the spectral characteristics of the wind and the fundamental natural frequency and damping of the building. The Code recommends a simplified analysis, in which the estimated wind forces can be treated as *equivalent static loads*. These wind forces are estimated, considering the *hourly mean wind speed* and *turbulence intensity* applicable to the location and terrain under consideration.

Flexible slender tall structures, classified as 'wind sensitive', must be analysed for dynamic effects of wind forces.

Meteorological studies have established that a time-averaging interval of one hour is suited for defining the steady mean wind speed. This is called the *hourly mean wind speed, at height z,* $\bar{V}_z$. The variation of hourly mean wind speed with height, *z*, can be represented using a 'log-law model' as given below [Ref. 19.5]:

$$\bar{V}_z = 2.5\, u_* \ln\left(\frac{z}{z_o}\right) \tag{19.1}$$

where u_* is the shear friction speed and z_o is a 'terrain roughness' dimension, which depends on the terrain category. The terrain roughness length value (z_o) is typically specified as 0.002 m for Category 1 (exposed open), 0.02 m for Category 2 (open country), 0.2 m for Category 3 (suburban) and 2.0 m for Category 4 (city centre) [Ref. 19.7].

In order to account for the turbulence in the wind, a non-dimensional factor called *turbulence intensity*, *I(z)*, is defined as the ratio of the standard deviation value of fluctuating wind speed to the mean wind speed. For convenience in design, this standard deviation is assumed to be invariant and equal to the value measured at 10 m above ground level [Ref. 19.6]; hence, with increase in mean wind speed with height, the turbulence intensity, *I*(*z*), decreases with height. The typical values of $I(z = 10\text{ m})$ are 0.11. 0.15, 0.24 and 0.59 for categories 1, 2, 3 and 4 respectively [Ref. 19.7].

The peak gust wind speed, $V(i,t,z)$ of *t* seconds duration, at height *z* in terrain category *i* ($i = 1$ to 4), can be related to the corresponding hourly mean wind speed, $\bar{V}_z(i)$, as given below [Ref. 19.8]:

$$V(i, t, z)/\bar{V}_z(i) = 1 - 0.59\,[I(i, 10)]^{1.13}\,(z/10)^C \ln(t/T) \tag{19.2}$$

where $T = 3600$ s (1 hour) and $C = -I(i, 10\text{ m})$.

Concept of Return Period and Risk Level

From a building design perspective, it suffices to consider the macro-level variation of wind speed with time as being quasi-static. Furthermore, as our interest is in identifying the likely maximum wind forces that act on a building (during its intended lifetime), it is appropriate to analyse measured wind speed data using the concepts of probability and statistics, considering extreme value distributions (refer Figure 3.1 in Chapter 3). Using the annual maximum wind speed data generated by agencies such as the Indian Meteorological Department, it is possible to statistically analyse the data using an appropriate extreme value distribution (such as Gumbel), and this forms the basis of the basic wind speeds described in IS 875 (Part 3).

In a typical extreme value distribution of annual maximum wind speed, the values of wind speed range from zero to infinity. It is necessary to design for some *basic wind speed*, associated with which there is some definite probability, p, of it not being exceeded in any given year.

With reference to the occurrence of extreme events (natural phenomena such as extreme winds, earthquakes and floods), a widely used concept is that of a *return period*, which is the average interval between two successive occurrences of the extreme event (extreme wind speed, in this case). Thus, for example, if a *basic* wind speed is defined as having an annual probability of exceedance p = 0.02 (which is 1 in 50), as shown in Figure 19.5, it implies that the return period is 50 years, i.e., the average interval between two successive occurrences of this wind speed is 50 years.

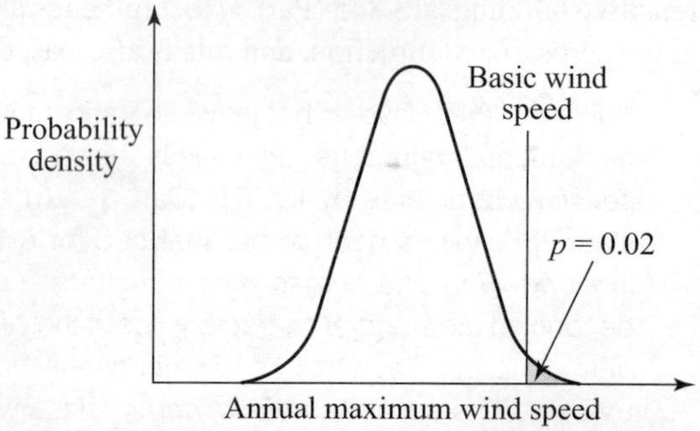

Fig. 19.5 Typical probability distribution of annual maximum wind speed [Ref. 19.5].

A two per cent probability of exceedance may sound reasonably low and acceptable, but it should be noted that this applies to only *one year*, and not to the *entire lifetime* of the building. If we make the assumption that the occurrences of the extreme event are statistically independent, and if the life of the structure is N years, it follows that the probability of the basic wind speed not being exceeded during the life of the building is $(1-p)^N$. If p = 0.02 and N = 50 years, this value works out to 0.364. In other words, the probability that the basic wind speed will be exceeded during the lifetime of the building is as high as 63.6 per cent ('risk level' = 0.636) †. It may also be noted that the wind load acting on the building is proportional to the square of the wind speed. It is possible to work out an appropriate extreme value distribution for the wind load and, conforming to a desired true risk level, arrive at a *characteristic wind speed* to be used in design [Ref. 19.10, 19.11].

For normal buildings, the return period of 50 years, is considered standard. But, for important structures, it may be necessary to reduce the risk by enhancing the design return period. For example, for a nuclear reactor structure, the design return period can be as high as 1000 years or more.

† It may be noted that the current Indian Code specifying design loads, IS 875, does not specify any *characteristic* values for loads. IS 456: 2000 - Cl. 36.2 states that 'since data are not available to express loads in statistical terms, …', the loads given in IS 875 shall be 'assumed' as *characteristic loads*. It can be seen clearly that wind loads based on the *basic wind speed* specified in IS 875 (Part 3) do not, in reality, conform to the IS 456 definition of *characteristic loads*, having a '95 per cent probability of not being exceeded during the life of the structure', as the *basic wind speed* is derived based on the annual maximum wind speed values, instead of all the recorded wind speed values.

Basic Wind Speed (V_b)

For the design of buildings, IS 875 (Part 3): 2015† (Amendment 2 - June 2020) refers to Figure 1 of 'Part 6: Structural design, Section 1- loads, forces and effects, of the National Building Code of India 2016 (NBC-2016)', which presents a 'basic wind speed map' of India showing different wind zones. The country is divided into six wind zones, for which the basic wind speed, V_b, based on a return period of 50 years, is assigned values of 33, 39, 44, 47, 50 and 55 m/s. Annex A to IS 875 (Part 3) also presents, in tabular form, basic wind speed for some important cities and towns in India.

> The basis for all wind load calculations in India is a 'basic wind speed' for the location, determined through statistical analysis of meteorological data and shown in a 'basic wind speed map of India', published in National Building Code of India – 2016.

> *Basic wind speed* is the maximum wind speed (statistically assessed from meteorological data) in a particular wind zone region (described in the Code) having a 50-year return period, at 10 m height above mean ground level in open flat terrain (Category 2), based on peak gust wind speed averaged over 3s.

The basic wind speed values for some important cities (State capitals), zone-wise, are listed in Table 19.1.

Table 19.1 *Basic wind speed for some important cities in India*

Wind Zone	Wind Speed	City
A	33 m/s (118.8 kmph)	Bengaluru
B	39 m/s (140.4 kmph)	Dehradun, Gandhinagar, Kavaratti (Lakshadweep), Panaji, Ranchi, Shimla, Srinagar, Thiruvananthapuram
C	44 m/s (159.4 kmph)	Imphal, Itanagar, Hyderabad, Kohima, Mumbai, Port Blair, Raipur
D	47 m/s (169.2 kmph)	Bhopal, Gangtok, Jaipur, Patna, Tiruchirappalli
E	50 m/s (180 kmph)	Amaravathi, Bhubaneswar, Chandigarh, Chennai, Daman, Dispur, Kolkata, Lucknow, New Delhi, Puducherry, Shillong
F	55 m/s (198 kmph)	Aizawl, Agartala, Leh, Silchar

Design Wind Speed (V_z) *and Hourly Mean Wind Speed* ($\bar{V}_z$)

The *design wind speed* at a height z, V_z, applicable for *rigid* buildings, is obtained by modifying the basic wind speed (V_b) for the location, to include the effects of the risk level assigned to the structure, the terrain roughness (z_o) and height (z), topography of the site, and the vulnerability to cyclonic storms.

> The actual force exerted by wind on a structure or an element of a structure depends on a large number of factors pertaining to the geographical location, terrain/topography, and the use/size/shape/geometry, etc., of the structure/element itself.

Accordingly, the design wind speed V_z, at a height z, is calculated as:

$$V_z = V_b k_1 k_2 k_3 k_4 \tag{19.3}$$

where, V_b is the basic wind speed, k_1 is the *probability factor* (risk coefficient), k_2 is the *terrain roughness and height factor*, k_3 is the *topography factor*, and k_4 is the *importance factor* for cyclonic region.

† IS 875 (Part 3) - 2015 had originally included, as Figure 1, a Basic Wind Speed map of India. However, Amendment No. 2 to this Code dated June 2020 has deleted this Figure 1 from the Code, and in its place, reference is made to 'Figure 1 of Part 6/Section 1 of NBC 2016'.

Similarly, the *design hourly mean wind speed*, $\bar{V}_z$, at height z (required for *wind-sensitive* buildings) is calculated as

$$V_z = V_b k_1 \bar{k}_2 k_3 k_4 \tag{19.4}$$

where $\bar{k}_2$ is the terrain roughness and height factor applicable for hourly mean wind speed (which is different from k_2, applicable for design wind speed V_z (Eq. 19.3).

Probability Factor (Risk Coefficient) (k_1)

The k_1 factor is a statistical parameter which takes into account the degree of reliability required and the life of the structure during which it will be exposed to wind. The basic wind speed is based on a return period of 50 years ($p = 0.02$), whereas the intended design life of a structure may be different, in which case allowance has to be made for the altered wind probability (change in return period) so that the chosen risk level (0.636 for general buildings) remains same. The design life period suggested by Code IS 875 (Part 3) - Cl. 6.3.1 is 50 years for 'all general buildings and structures, and ground based free-standing towers up to 50 m', which correlates with the return period for V_b, and hence this class of structures is assigned the default value of $k_1 = 1.0$.

The Code suggests a higher design life of 100 years for important buildings such as hospitals, communication towers and power plant structures. The corresponding k_1 factor is specified as 1.05 for $V_b = 33$ m/s, 1.06 for $V_b = 39$ m/s, 1.07 for $V_b = 44$ and 47 m/s, and 1.08 for $V_b = 50$ and 55 m/s. For exceptionally important structures, such as nuclear power reactors and satellite communication towers, the corresponding values of k_1 need to be suitably worked out, considering larger return periods ranging from 100 to 1000 years or more, and lower risk levels. The Code gives guidelines to work out these values.

The Code suggests a lower design life of 25 years for buildings presenting a low hazard to life and property, such as farm buildings and isolated towers in wooded areas. The corresponding k_1 factor is specified as 0.94 for $V_b = 33$ m/s, 0.92 for $V_b = 39$ m/s, 0.91 for $V_b = 44$ m/s, 0.90 for $V_b = 47$ and 50 m/s, and 0.89 for $V_b = 55$ m/s.

For temporary sheds, formwork and falsework structures and boundary walls, the Code recommends an even lower design life of 5 years, corresponding to which the k_1 factor is specified as 0.82 for $V_b = 33$ m/s, 0.76 for $V_b = 39$ m/s, 0.73 for $V_b = 44$ m/s, 0.71 for $V_b = 47$ m/s, 0.70 for $V_b = 50$ m/s, and 0.67 for $V_b = 55$ m/s.

Terrain and Height Factor (k_2)

The Code categorises the terrains into the following four types, based on the obstructions which constitute the surface roughness, measurable in terms of the 'terrain roughness' dimension, z_o (refer Eq. 19.1) [the Code terms this as 'the equivalent aerodynamic roughness height']:

- *Category 1* ('exposed open', $z_o = 0.002$ m) refers to exposed open terrain with practically no obstruction to wind flow, where the average height of any object surrounding the building is less than 1.5 m (typically, open sea-coasts and flat plains without trees).
- *Category 2* ('open country', $z_o = 0.02$ m) refers to open terrain with well scattered obstructions whose heights generally range between 1.5 m to 10 m (typically, sparsely built-up outskirts of towns and suburbs); measurement of basic wind speed is based on this criterion.
- *Category 3* ('towns', $z_o = 0.2$ m) refers to terrain with numerous closely spaced obstructions with structures of height up to 10 m and very few isolated tall structures (typically, towns and industrial areas or well-wooded areas).

- *Category 4* ('large city centres', z_o = 2.0 m) refers to terrain with numerous large, high and closely spaced obstructions (typically, well-developed large city centres and well-developed industrial complexes, with structures taller than 25 m).

It is important to note that, with increase in terrain roughness, the design wind speed *reduces*. Hence, when in doubt regarding the terrain category, it is always conservative to consider a lower category. Commonly, the default 'Category 2' ('open country') is considered in design, unless there is clear evidence that the terrain is rougher (Category 3). The code suggests that 'Category 4' 'will not exist in most design situations.'

The Code specifies k_2 factors for the four terrain categories, for heights ranging from 10 m to 500 m. The variation of k_2 with height for the four terrain categories is plotted (in enlarged scale), for heights up to 100 m, in Figure 19.6. [Most buildings encountered in practice lie within 100 m.] It is seen that the basic wind speed (at 10 m height) gets enhanced by 35 per cent at the gradient height (Z_g) in all the four terrain categories. As shown in Figure 19.4, the gradient speed V_g is realised at Z_g = 300 m, 350 m, 450 m and around 550 m for categories 1, 2, 3 and 4 respectively.

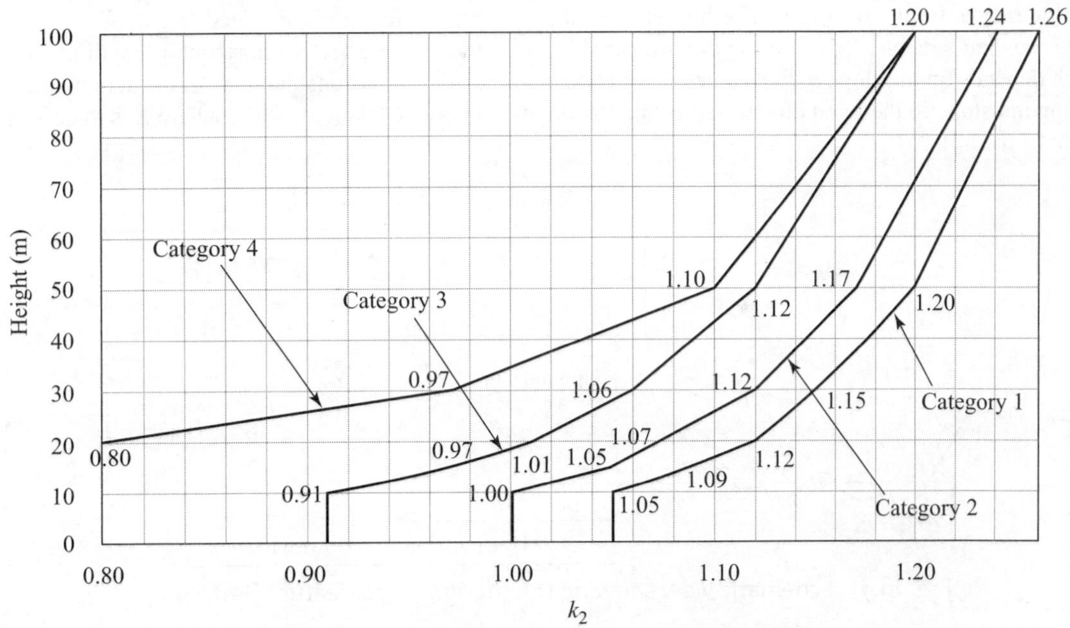

Fig. 19.6 Variation of k_2 with height for different terrain categories.

It may also be noted that the wind speed profile in any specified category develops gradually in height over a horizontal upwind distance, called *fetch*. The Code gives details of the developed height corresponding to fetch distances for the four terrain categories. Thus, for example, for Category 2, for fetch distances of 1, 5, 10 and 50 km, the corresponding developed heights are 45, 100, 140 and 300 m respectively.

For dynamic analysis of wind-sensitive buildings, the terrain roughness and height factor, $\bar{k}_2$, has to be used instead of k_2. (refer Eq. 19.4). It is based on the log-law described earlier (refer Eq. 19.1), and is defined in the Code as follows:

$$\bar{k}_2 = 0.1423\left[\ln\left(\frac{z}{z_{0,i}}\right)\right](z_{0,i})^{0.0706} \tag{19.5}$$

where, as mentioned earlier, $z_{0,i}$ is the aerodynamic roughness height (terrain roughness length) having values (in metres) of 0.002, 0.02, 0.2 and 2.0 m for categories i = 1, 2, 3 and 4 respectively.

Topography Factor (k_3)

The Code prescribes a *topography factor*, k_3, to account for the possible enhancement in wind speed over hills and ridges (i.e., topography where downwind slope exceeds 3°) and cliffs and escarpments (i.e., where downwind side of the crest is relatively flat, less than 3°), when the upwind slope exceeds 3°. The typical topography features and general notations used in IS 875 (Part 3) are shown in Figure 19.7 [Ref. 19.2]. If the upwind slope, θ, is less than about 3°, k_3 may be taken as equal to 1.0; for upwind slopes greater than 3°, the k_3 value ranges from 1.0 to 1.36. The influence of the topographic feature is assumed to extend up to $1.5L_e$ on the upwind side and $2.5L_e$ on the downwind side, where L_e is the effective horizontal length of the hill which depends on the slope θ. For values of θ between 3° and 17°, L_e is considered as L, the actual length of the upwind slope in the wind direction. For higher slopes, L_e may be taken as $Z/0.3$, where Z is the effective height of the hill.

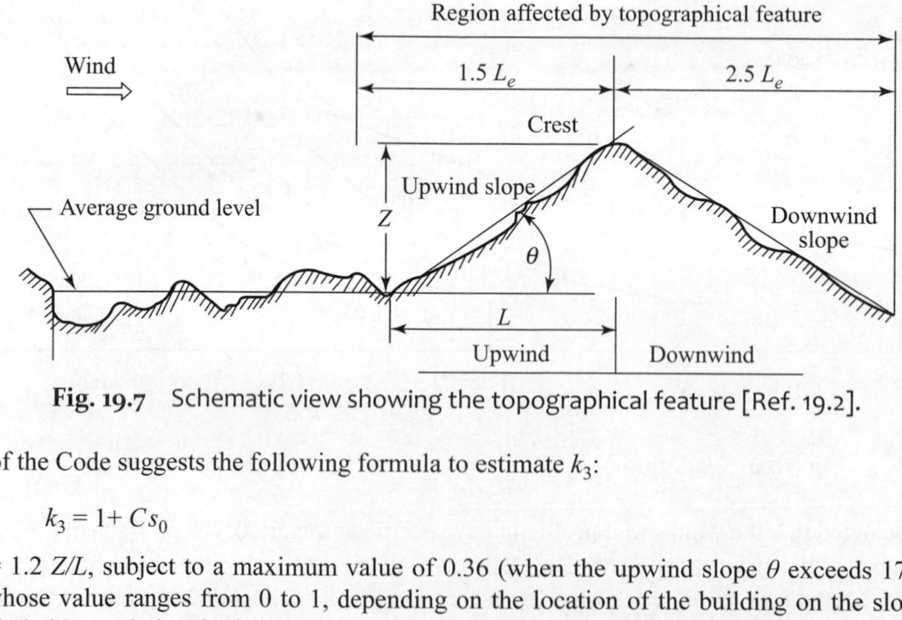

Fig. 19.7 Schematic view showing the topographical feature [Ref. 19.2].

Annex C of the Code suggests the following formula to estimate k_3:

$$k_3 = 1 + Cs_0 \tag{19.6}$$

where C = 1.2 Z/L, subject to a maximum value of 0.36 (when the upwind slope θ exceeds 17°) and s_0 is a factor, whose value ranges from 0 to 1, depending on the location of the building on the slope (upwind or downwind side) and also the height above the ground level under consideration. Annex C of the Code presents separate charts for ridges/hills and cliffs/escarpments to identify the appropriate value of s_0.

For a given upwind slope, the value of s_0 increases gradually from zero at the foot of the hill to a peak value at the crest of the hill, and thereafter decreases on the downwind side; further, it reduces with height above the ground. If the building is located in the close neighbourhood of the crest of the hill (upwind or downwind side), it is conservative to consider the peak conditions at the crest (s_0 = 1), for which Eq. 19.6 reduces to

$$k_3 = 1 + 1.2\ Z/L \tag{19.6a}$$

subject to a maximum value of 1.36.

The variation of k_3 with Z/L is shown in Figure 19.8.

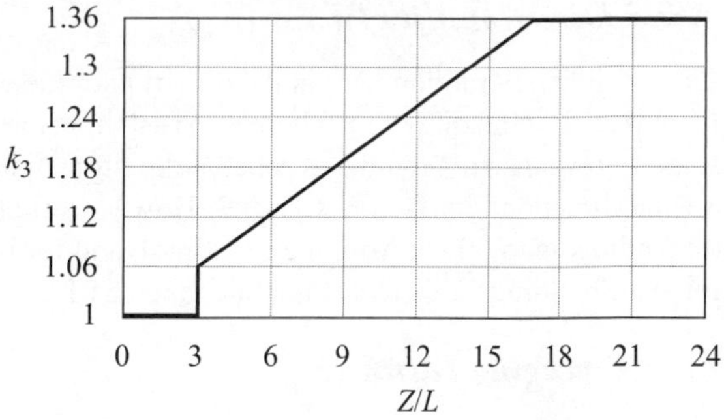

Fig. 19.8 Variation of k_3 with Z/L at the crest of the hill.

Cyclonic Factor (k_4)

The Indian coastline (especially the Coromandel coast) is frequently hit by cyclones, where wind speeds can be dangerously high. In the case of 'super-cyclones', wind speeds over 220 kmph have been recorded in many coastal places. These high-speed winds can cause major destruction to life and property. Recognising this fact, in the recent revision of IS 875 (2015 version), the Code has included the k_4 factor, which accounts for the high wind speeds in a belt of approximately 60 km width along the east coast of India as well as the Gujarat coast. In these regions, the peak wind speeds can exceed by 30% during extreme cyclones, and hence for structures having post-cyclone importance (such as hospitals), the k_4 value is taken as 1.3. For industrial structures, this factor is 1.15 and for all other structures it can be taken as 1.0 [Ref. 19.2].

19.2.2 Design Wind Pressure (p_{dz})

The wind pressure, p_z, at any given height z above the mean ground level is given by:

$$p_z = \frac{1}{2}\rho V_z^2 \tag{19.7}$$

where ρ is the mass density of air (which mainly depends on the atmospheric pressure and air temperature) and V_z is the design wind speed at height z. Taking ρ as equal to 1.20 kg/m^3 (for the average atmospheric conditions in India), the wind pressure, p_z, at height z is obtained as:

$$p_z = 0.6 \times V_z^2 \tag{19.7a}$$

where p_z has units of N/m^2.

[Note that as indicated earlier, the reference velocity used for dynamic analysis is the design hourly mean wind speed, $\bar{V}_{z,d}$ (see Eq. 19.4). The associated design hourly mean wind pressure is designated as $\bar{p}_d$, and obtained as 0.6 $\bar{V}^2_{z,d}$ (N/m^2).]

Allowing for the various influencing factors, the design wind pressure, p_{dz}, to be taken for estimating the wind force on buildings and individual members, can be calculated as

$$p_{dz} = K_d K_a K_c p_z \tag{19.8}$$

where K_d is the *wind directionality factor*, K_a is the *area averaging factor* and K_c is the *combination factor*. The Code specifies that the value of p_{dz} cannot be less than 0.7p_z.

Wind Directionality Factor (K_d)

There is inherent randomness in the direction of the wind flow. Recognising that the wind force is determined for a specific wind direction, whereas in real time, the wind direction is subject to randomness, the Code makes some allowance for 'buildings, open/solid signs, lattice frameworks and trussed towers', and recommends a wind directionality factor, $K_d = 0.9$. However, such reduction is not admissible in areas prone to cyclones (extending up to 60 km from the coastline), and for buildings having circular (or near circular) shape in plan; for such buildings, this factor may be taken as 1.0.

Area Averaging Factor (K_a)

The entire exposed area of the surface of a building or structural element under consideration is unlikely to be subjected to the maximum wind pressure uniformly at any given time. The Code specified pressure coefficients (see below) are based on averaging measured pressure values over *a given (specified)* area. As the exposed area considered (i.e., tributary area) becomes larger, the actual average pressure decreases relative to the above average measured values. This decrease in the actual average pressure, with increase in tributary areas, is accounted for by the 'area averaging factor', K_a. For a tributary area less than 10 m^2, no reduction in wind pressure is recommended, and $K_a = 1.0$. For a tributary area of 25 m^2, K_a is taken as 0.9. For a tributary area greater than or equal to 100 m^2, K_a is taken as 0.8. A linear interpolation of the K_a value is recommended for intermediate values of tributary areas.

Combination Factor (K_c)

The wind force on clad buildings do not have the same pressures on all faces; further, the pressures or suctions-inside and outside are not fully correlated, and their peak values may not occur concurrently. Hence, when taking the combined effect of external and internal pressures on a building frame (discussed below, refer Eq. 19.9), the Code permits a 10 per cent reduction in the design wind pressures ($K_c = 0.9$)†. However, a default value of $K_c = 1.0$ should be considered in Eq. 19.8, when pressure coefficients, C_{pe} and C_{pi}, are not considered.

Wind Pressure Coefficients

For a given wind speed and resulting design wind pressure, the actual wind force exerted on a body/structural element held in the wind stream will depend on several factors, such as its shape, proportions, orientation (to direction of wind), surface roughness/curvature, openings in it (permeability), sharpness of corners, etc. Such influences are accounted for with *pressure coefficients*, C_p, specified for a particular surface or part of the surface of a building. These have been mostly obtained from wind tunnel tests on models. The wind force acting normal to a surface is given by $C_p \times A \times p_d$, where A is the area of the surface.

For the purpose of estimating wind forces on individual members (such as wall or roof or cladding element), the wind force acting normal to the surface is given by:

$$F_z = (C_{pe} - C_{pi}) A_z P_{dz} \tag{19.9}$$

where C_{pe} and C_{pi} are external and internal pressure coefficients respectively, A_z is the surface area of the structural element or cladding at a height of z, and p_{dz} is the design wind pressure at height z.

---

† This positioning of the *Combination factor* K_c in Eq. 19.8 appears to be included prior to defining the *pressure coefficients* in the Code [refer Cl. 7.2 of IS 875 (Part 3)]. For an explanation of K_c, the Code refers to Cl. 7.3.3.13, which points to pressure coefficients applicable to *frames*. It would be therefore appropriate to shift K_c from Eq. 19.8 to Eq. 19.9, as the *combination factor* applicable to *frames* of *clad buildings* (typically, industrial sheds), where 'a reduction factor of $K_c = 0.9$ may be used over the building envelope when roof is subjected to pressure and internal pressure is suction, or vice versa'.

Details of the pressure coefficients, C_{pe} and C_{pi}, for walls or claddings with openings of various sizes (percentage of wall area) and roofs with various slopes (including pitched and hipped) are described in detail in IS:875 (Part 3). The internal pressure coefficient can be positive or negative (indicative of suction).

In this chapter, the focus is on estimation of wind loads on buildings (rather than individual walls and roofs); details of pressure coefficients, C_{pe} and C_{pi}, are not relevant for this purpose.

19.2.3 'Rigid' Building or 'Wind-Sensitive' Building?

The estimation of wind forces on a building depends on whether the building can be categorised as 'rigid' or dynamically 'wind-sensitive'. IS:875 (Part 3), Cl. 9.1 suggests the following guidelines for this classification. A building or structure should be considered to be wind-sensitive (to be examined for dynamic effects of wind) if one of the two criteria given below is satisfied:

(a) the ratio of height to least lateral dimension of the building is more than about 5.0
(b) the natural frequency in the first mode is less than 1.0 Hz.

The fundamental natural frequency (in Hz) is the reciprocal of the fundamental time period, T. In the absence of more precise data, the Code suggests the following approximate formulation to find T (in s):

(a) For moment resistant frames without bracings or shear walls resisting the lateral loads,

$$T = 0.1\,n \tag{19.10}$$

where n is the number of storeys including basement storeys; and

(b) For all other types of buildings

$$T = \frac{0.09H}{\sqrt{d}} \tag{19.11}$$

where H is the total height of the building (in m), and d is the maximum base dimension of the building (in m) in a direction parallel to the applied wind force.

The building can be considered to be 'rigid' if the fundamental natural frequency is greater than (or equal to) 1 Hz *and* the height to least lateral dimension is less than 5.

19.2.4 Wind Forces on 'Rigid' Buildings

The wind force, for 'rigid' buildings (as defined above), at any height z is obtained as:

$$F_z = C_f A_{ez}\, p_{dz} \tag{19.12}$$

where C_f is the *force coefficient* (also called *drag coefficient* as the corresponding force is in the direction of the wind) for the building, A_{ez} is the *effective frontal area* (the projected area normal to the direction of wind) of the building at height z, and p_{dz} is the design wind pressure at height z (refer Eq. 19.8).

The value of the force coefficient is different for the wind acting on different faces of the building. For determining the critical force, the total wind force should be calculated for each wind direction. As the design wind pressure varies with height, the surface area of the building is sub-divided in the vertical direction, and on each such area, the pressure appropriate to it applied. Similarly, in tapered buildings, the force coefficients shall be applied after suitably sub-dividing the area. For all other cases, detailed study needs to be carried out (in the form of wind tunnel tests) or reference made to special publications.

Force coefficients have been derived for various shapes and dimensions based on wind tunnel tests and field studies considering uniform flow. For rectangular clad buildings with flat roofs, the force coefficient values depend on the geometry, depth-to-breadth ratio (a/b in plan) and aspect ratio (h/b in elevation) of the building, and the wind direction. The force coefficients for rectangular clad buildings of uniform section with flat roof are given in Table 19.2, which have been tabulated from graphs given in Figure 4 of IS 875 (Part 3). In Table 19.2, a and b denote the plan dimensions of the building, (b corresponding to the face on which wind is acting), and h the height of the building.

The Code recognises the fact that change in the geometry can affect the response of the building when subjected to wind forces. For buildings that have rounded/chamfered edges, the C_f factor is less than unity in most cases. In such situations, and for other cross-sectional shapes, the values of C_f need to be appropriately selected from the Code [Ref. 19.2] or from special publications/literature.

For buildings with well-rounded surfaces (such as circular or elliptic), the possibility of vortex shedding needs to be examined, and the maximum wind force due to this can occur at a 'critical' wind speed that is much less than the maximum possible at the site under consideration. This needs a special check.

Table 19.2 *Force coefficients (C_f) for rectangular clad building with flat roofs*

a/b	$h/b = 0.25$	$h/b = 0.5$	$h/b = 1.0$	$h/b = 3.0$	$h/b = 5.0$	$h/b = 10$	$h/b = 20$	$h/b = \infty$
0.00	1.200	1.144	1.176	1.250	1.330	1.500	1.750	1.881
0.25	1.200	1.161	1.219	1.301	1.384	1.685	2.026	2.188
0.50	1.200	1.178	1.261	1.352	1.438	1.869	2.301	2.494
0.75	1.200	1.183	1.266	1.362	1.451	1.888	2.397	2.657
1.00	1.200	1.148	1.227	1.307	1.392	1.784	2.188	2.358
1.25	1.200	1.096	1.168	1.248	1.330	1.654	1.975	2.134
1.50	1.164	1.043	1.108	1.188	1.267	1.523	1.761	1.909
1.75	1.129	1.000	1.057	1.143	1.216	1.427	1.622	1.756
2.00	1.094	0.957	1.006	1.097	1.165	1.330	1.483	1.603
2.25	1.071	0.931	0.966	1.066	1.134	1.271	1.392	1.506
2.50	1.047	0.915	0.926	1.034	1.102	1.211	1.301	1.409
2.75	1.024	0.905	0.901	1.000	1.077	1.168	1.262	1.367
3.00	1.000	0.899	0.875	0.966	1.052	1.125	1.222	1.324

19.2.5 Design Examples on 'Rigid' Buildings

In the Examples to follow, the objective is to determine the wind forces on the building at various heights using the formulations prescribed in IS:875 (Part 3). The wind forces at any height are assumed to be uniformly distributed along the breadth of the windward face of the building.

As discussed in Chapter 1 [refer Figure 1.8(b)], the lateral wind loads acting on the exposed surface of the building is effectively resisted by the moment-resisting frames (and shear walls, if any) in the direction of the wind. The whole system acts integrally, with all the frames interconnected at various floor levels by the floor systems, which act as horizontal diaphragms.

In the case of a symmetric building with relatively 'rigid' horizontal diaphragms at the floor levels, the entire building is expected to sway laterally under wind acting on the building. If all the frames are more-or-less equally stiff (including infill walls, if any), they will undergo the same lateral deflection (at any particular floor level), and hence will resist the total wind force (assumed to act at various floor levels) *equally*, regardless of their respective 'tributary areas'.

The 'tributary area' concept is often invoked to estimate the wind forces on any particular frame (based on the spacing of frames in plan), but this could turn out to be unconservative in some cases, such as the end frames, which are typically as stiff as (or stiffer, due to masonry infill walls) the intermediate frames, whereas they have smaller tributary areas.

If the building is unsymmetric, having frames significantly unequal in stiffness, or if the floor diaphragm is relatively flexible (or have openings at some locations), then the deflection may not be equal for all the frames at any floor level, and there is also likelihood of twisting of the building about its vertical axis, involving the simultaneous participation of the frames in the across-wind direction also, while resisting the oncoming wind. A proper three-dimensional analysis of the building frame is warranted in such a case. This is conveniently possible in the design office, by resorting to the software packages commercially available. If shear walls are also present, the analysis must properly account for *shear wall-frame interaction* [refer Figure 1.16(c)].

In the Examples to follow, a symmetric 10-storeyed rectangular building (with moment-resisting frames) is considered, and the total wind force (acting at every floor level) is assessed, in accordance with IS:875 (Part 3). The effects of the various factors (k_1, k_2, k_3 and k_4) are also studied separately, and the results are compared, by locating the same building in different cities, terrains and topographies, and also by changing the function of the building (from office to hospital). The *base shear* (equal to the total force on the building) and the *base moment* (sum of moments of all the floor level forces with respect to the base) provide useful overall measures for comparison (in both the body-fixed axes, *X*- and *Y*-directions).

Furthermore, as the fundamental natural frequency of the building is approximately 1 Hz, it is a borderline case for classification as a 'wind sensitive' building. It is instructive to see how the design wind forces, base shear and base moment values change, when the building is also analysed for dynamic effects of wind, following the Code recommendations. This is taken up later (Example 19.3).

Example 19.1

The framing details for a proposed 10-storey office building in Chennai are shown in Figure 19.9. Compute the lateral wind forces to be used in the design of the building in X- and Y- directions (as shown) at the various floor levels, assuming the 'general' class building, 'Category 2' terrain and level ground.

Solution

Check if the building is 'rigid' or 'dynamically wind sensitive'

The building dimensions are: $l_x = 15$ m, $l_y = 30$ m, $h = 32$ m, whereby $h/l_x = 2.13$, and $h/l_y = 1.06$. The ratios of height to lateral dimensions in both directions are less than 5.0. The fundamental period of the structure (as per Eq. 19.10) is $T = 0.1 \times 10 = 1$ s, whereby the natural frequency ($f = 1/T$) 'does not exceed 1 Hz'. Hence, as per IS:875 (Part 3), the building can be treated as 'rigid' for the purpose of estimation of wind forces.

The values of the various factors for wind force calculation are given in IS 875 (Part 3). The basic wind speed (based on 50-year return period) in Chennai, as per Table 19.1 is: $V_b = 50$ m/s.

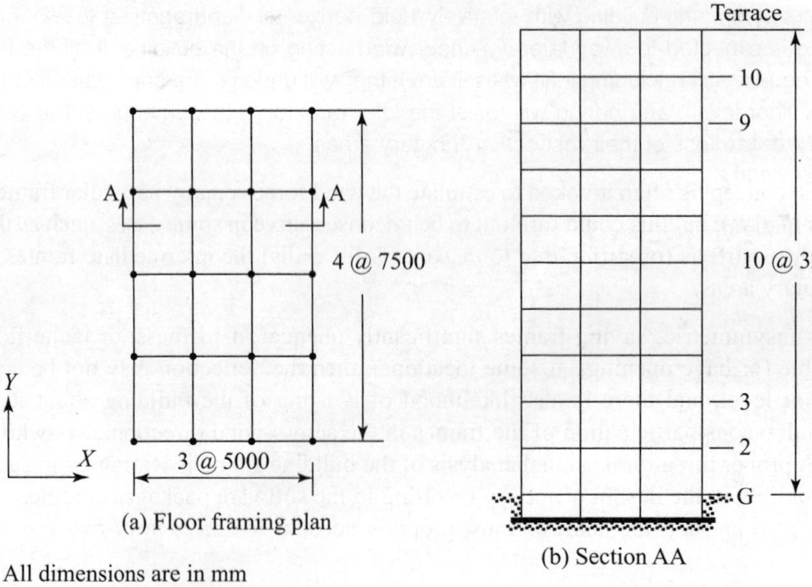

Fig. 19.9 Building configuration used in Example 19.1.

Design wind speed, $V_z = V_b k_1 k_2 k_3 k_4$

where *risk coefficient*, $k_1 = 1.0$ ('general' class of building)

topography factor, $k_3 = 1.0$ (level ground)

cyclonic factor, $k_4 = 1.0$ (office building without any special 'post-cyclonic importance', although located in Chennai, with $V_b = 50$ m/s)

terrain and height factor, k_2 corresponding to 'Category 2' (values of k_2 at various heights (10, 15, 20 and 30 m, can be obtained from Figure 19.6 and interpolated at various floor levels)

With these values,

$$V_z = V_b k_1 k_2 k_3 k_4 = 50 \times 1.0 \times k_2 \times 1.0 \times 1.0 = 50\, k_2 \text{ m/s}$$

The wind pressure at any height z above mean ground level is given by:

$$p_z = 0.6 V_z^2 = 0.6 \times (50 k_2)^2 = 1500 (k_2)^2 \text{ N/m}^2 = 1.5 (k_2)^2 \text{ kN/m}^2$$

Design wind pressure $p_{dz} = K_d K_a K_c p_z$

where *wind directionality factor*, $K_d = 1.0$ (for buildings located in cyclone prone area, Chennai)

area averaging factor in X-direction (for tributary area per floor $= 3.2 \times l_y = 3.2 \times 30 = 96$ m^2, which is less than 100 m^2 but greater than 25 m^2),

$$K_{ax} = 0.8 + 0.1 \times (4/75) = 0.805$$

area averaging factor in Y-direction (for tributary area = $3.2 \times l_x = 3.2 \times 15 = 48$ m^2),

$$K_{ay} = 0.869$$

combination factor, $K_c = 1.0$

[To compute the wind forces at any floor level, the tributary area comprises the area between mid-heights to the floor just below and the one just above.]

X-direction: $p_{dzx} = 1.0 \times 0.805 \times 1.0 \times 1.5(k_2)^2 = 1.208(k_2)^2$ kN/m^2,

not less than $0.7p_z = 0.7 \times 1.5(k_2)^2 = 1.05(k_2)^2$ kN/m^2. Hence, $p_{dzx} = 1.208(k_2)^2$ kN/m^2.

Y-direction: $p_{dzy} = 1.0 \times 0.869 \times 1.0 \times 1.5(k_2)^2 = 1.304(k_2)^2$ kN/m^2,

not less less than $0.7p_z = 0.7 \times 1.5(k_2)^2 = 1.05(k_2)^2$ kN/m^2. Hence, $p_{dzy} = 1.304(k_2)^2$ kN/m^2.

The pressure coefficient C_f (in X and Y directions) depends on the plan aspect ratio (a/b) and height to lateral dimension (h/b). For C_f in X direction: $a = 15$ m, $b = 30$ m, $h = 32$ m. Hence, $a/b = 0.5$ and $h/b = 1.067$. For these ratios, the value of C_{fx} can be found from Table 19.2 as: $C_{fx} = 1.264$ (through interpolation). For C_f in Y direction: $a = 30$ m, $b = 15$ m, $h = 32$ m. Hence, $a/b = 2.0$ and $h/b = 2.13$. For these ratios, the value of C_{fy} can be found from Table 19.2 as: $C_{fy} = 1.057$ (through interpolation).

The wind force, F, acting over an area A is given by: $F_z = C_f \times p_{dz} \times A_z$

Wind force in X direction, $F_{zx} = 1.264 \times 1.208(k_2)^2 \times 96 = 146.52(k_2)^2$ kN

Wind force in Y direction, $F_{zy} = 1.057 \times 1.304(k_2)^2 \times 48 = 66.13(k_2)^2$ kN

For the top floor (roof), the tributary area is half of that calculated for the lower floors. Hence the wind forces in X and Y directions in the top floor are [Note that with these reduced tributary areas, strictly, the applicable area averaging factors will change. However, it is generally satisfactory to ignore this minor difference and use the expressions derived for the floor below, reducing it in proportion with the areas]:

$$F_{zx} = 73.26(k_2)^2 \text{ kN} \quad \text{and} \quad F_{zy} = 33.07(k_2)^2 \text{ kN}$$

Table 19.3 shows the wind force calculation at different heights of the building corresponding to floor levels. The total *base shear* and *base moment* values are also estimated. [For simplicity, the base moment is calculated at the ground level, considering the building to be a vertical cantilever; the actual level of fixity will be below the ground]. The base shear and base moment so determined may be used for assessing wind force effects on the building as a whole, such as overturning, sliding and tension on windward side columns (uplift of foundations).

In design practice, a 3D model of the building as a space frame (with rigid floor diaphragms) is typically used for analysis under gravity and lateral loads to determine the bending moments, shear forces and axial forces in the various frame elements under critical load combinations. The wind forces estimated in Table 19.3 can be used for application at the various floor levels.

In this Example, all the frames in any one direction (X or Y) are likely to sway equally under the action of the lateral loads (assuming rigid floor diaphragm action), and assuming all of them to be equally stiff, will also share the lateral load equally. Hence, it suffices to analyse each frame as a plane frame subjected to the total lateral load divided by the number of resisting frames (5 frames along X direction and 4 frames along Y direction). On this basis, the wind forces acting at the various floor levels can be estimated from Table 19.3; these are shown in Figure 19.10.

Table 19.3 *Calculation of wind forces, Example 19.1*

Floor level	Height, z (m)	k_2 (at nodes)	$F_{zx} = 146.52(k_2)^2$ (kN)	$F_{zy} = 66.13(k_2)^2$ (kN)
Ground/1	0	1.000		
2	3.2	1.000	146.52	66.13
3	6.4	1.000	146.52	66.13
4	9.6	1.000	146.52	66.13
5	12.8	1.028	154.84	69.89
6	16.0	1.054	162.77	73.47
7	19.2	1.0668	166.75	75.27
8	22.4	1.082	171.54	77.43
9	25.6	1.098	176.65	79.73
10	28.8	1.114	181.83	82.07
Terrace	32.0	1.125	92.72*	41.85*
Base shear (kN) = ΣF_z			1,547	698
Base moment (kNm) = $\Sigma F_z \times z$			27,170	12,263

*Estimated using half the tributary area as explained in the solution.

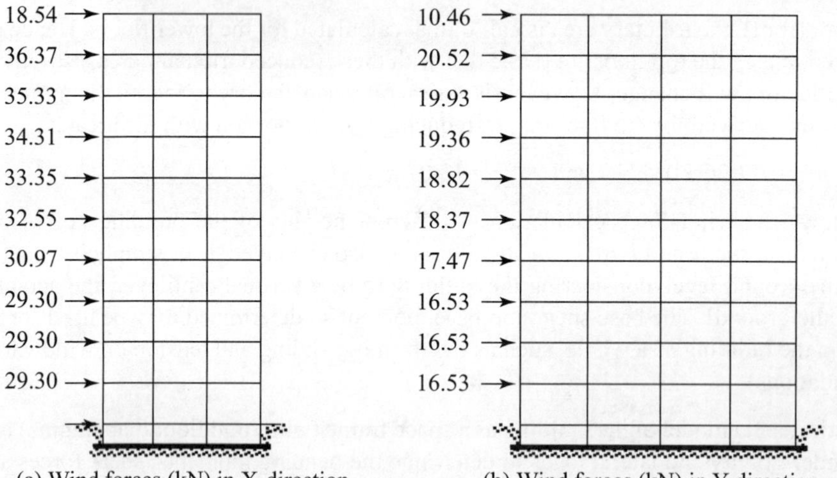

Fig. 19.10 Estimation of wind forces: Example 19.1.

Example 19.2

With reference to the problem in Example 19.1, show how the estimated wind forces change

(a) *if the terrain category of the office building discussed in Example 19.1 changes to 'town' (category 3);*

(b) *if the location of the building is shifted from level ground to the top of a hill (St. Thomas Mount, Chennai). Assume slope to be 9°;*

(c) *if the usage of the building (at Chennai) changes from 'office' to 'hospital';*

(d) *if the location of the office building is changed from Chennai to Bengaluru (level ground).*

Compare and discuss the implications of these changes.

Solution

(a) When the terrain category of the office building (Example 19.1) is changed to 'town':
In this case, all values of the factors, except k_2, remain same as shown in Example 19.1. The factor k_2 changes as shown in Figure 19.6 or Table 2 of the Code. Table 19.4 shows the wind force calculation at different heights of the building.

Table 19.4 *Calculation of wind forces, Example 19.2(a)*

Floor level	Height, z (m)	k_2 (at nodes)	$F_{zx} = 146.52(k_2)^2$ (kN)	$F_{zy} = 66.13(k_2)^2$ (kN)
Ground/1	0	0.91		
2	3.2	0.91	121.34	54.77
3	6.4	0.91	121.34	54.77
4	9.6	0.91	121.34	54.77
5	12.8	0.9436	130.46	58.88
6	16.0	0.978	140.15	63.26
7	19.2	1.0036	147.58	66.61
8	22.4	1.022	153.04	69.08
9	25.6	1.038	157.87	71.26
10	28.8	1.054	162.77	73.47
Terrace	32.0	1.066	83.25*	37.58*
Base shear (kN) = ΣF_z			1,339	605
Base moment (kNm) = $\Sigma F_z \times z$			23,897	10,786

*Estimated using half the tributary area as explained in the solution.

(b) When the building is located on top of a hill with a slope of 9º (Z/L = tan 9º = 0.1584):
In this case, the k_3 value changes to $k_3 = 1 + 1.2\, Z/L = 1.190$ (Eq. 19.6a), all other factors and basic wind speeds remaining the same.
With these values,

$$V_z = V_b k_1 k_2 k_3 k_4 = 50 \times 1.0 \times k_2 \times 1.190 \times 1.0 = 59.5\, k_2 \text{ m/s}$$

The design wind pressure at any height z above mean ground level is given by:

$$p_z = 0.6V_z^2 = 0.6 \times (59.5k_2)^2 = 2124(k_2)^2 \text{ N/m}^2$$

$$p_{dz} = K_d K_a K_c p_z$$

The values of K_d, K_a and K_c are discussed in Example 19.1.

$p_{dzx} = 1.0 \times 0.805 \times 1.0 \times 2.124\ (k_2)^2 = 1.71(k_2)^2$ kN/m^2. However, p_{dz} value cannot be lesser than $0.7p_z = 0.7 \times 2.124(k_2)^2 = 1.487(k_2)^2$ kN/m^2. Hence $p_{dzx} = 1.71(k_2)^2$ kN/m^2.

$p_{dzy} = 1.0 \times 0.869 \times 1.0 \times 2.124(k_2)^2 = 1.846(k_2)^2$ kN/m^2. However, p_{dz} value cannot be lesser than $0.7p_z = 1.487(k_2)^2$ kN/m^2 (calculated above). Hence $p_{dzy} = 1.846(k_2)^2$ kN/m^2.

The values of C_{fx} and C_{fy} are the same as determined in Example 19.1. The wind force, F, acting over an area A is given by:

$$F_z = C_f \times p_{dz} \times A_z$$

Wind force in X direction, $F_{zx} = 1.264 \times 1.710(k_2)^2 \times 96 = 207.49(k_2)^2$ kN

Wind force in Y direction, $F_{zy} = 1.057 \times 1.846(k_2)^2 \times 48 = 93.65(k_2)^2$ kN

For the top floor, the tributary area is half of that calculated for the lower floors. Hence the wind forces in X and Y directions in the top floor are

$$F_{zx} = 103.75(k_2)^2 \text{ kN} \quad \text{and} \quad F_{zy} = 46.83(k_2)^2 \text{ kN}$$

Table 19.5 shows the wind force calculation at different heights of the building.

Table 19.5 *Calculation of wind forces, Example 19.2(b)*

Floor level	Height, z (m)	k_2 (at nodes)	$F_{zx} = 207.49(k_2)^2$ (kN)	$F_{zy} = 93.65(k_2)^2$ (kN)
Ground/1	0	1.000		
2	3.2	1.000	207.49	93.65
3	6.4	1.000	207.49	93.65
4	9.6	1.000	207.49	93.65
5	12.8	1.028	219.27	98.97
6	16.0	1.054	230.51	104.04
7	19.2	1.0668	236.14	106.58
8	22.4	1.082	242.91	109.64
9	25.6	1.098	250.15	112.91
10	28.8	1.114	257.50	116.22
Terrace	32.0	1.125	131.30*	59.26*
Base shear (kN) = ΣF_z			2,190	989
Base moment (kNm) = $\Sigma F_z \times z$			38,475	17,366

*Estimated using half the tributary area as explained in the solution.

(c) When the usage of the building changes to hospital:
In this case, the k_1 value changes to 1.08, and as it is a building having post-cyclone importance, the k_4 value is 1.3, k_3 value remains as 1.0, all other factors and basic wind speeds remaining the same. With these values,

$$V_z = V_b\, k_1 k_2 k_3 k_4 = 50 \times 1.08 \times k_2 \times 1.0 \times 1.3 = 70.2k_2 \text{ m/s}$$

The design wind pressure at any height z above mean ground level is given by:

$$p_z = 0.6V_z^2 = 0.6 \times (70.2k_2)^2 = 2957(k_2)^2 \text{ N/m}^2$$

$$p_{dz} = K_d K_a K_c p_z$$

The values of K_d, K_a and K_c are the same as determined in Example 19.1.

$p_{dzx} = 1.0 \times 0.805 \times 1.0 \times 2.957(k_2)^2 = 2.38(k_2)^2$ kN/m^2. However, p_{dz} value cannot be lesser than $0.7p_z = 0.7 \times 2.957(k_2)^2 = 2.070(k_2)^2$ kN/m^2. Hence $p_{dzx} = 2.38(k_2)^2$ kN/m^2.

$p_{dzy} = 1.0 \times 0.869 \times 1.0 \times 2.957(k_2)^2 = 2.569(k_2)^2$ kN/m^2. This is greater than $0.7p_z$ calculated above. Hence $p_{dzy} = 2.569(k_2)^2$ kN/m^2.

The values of C_{fx} and C_{fy} are the same as in Example 19.1. The wind force, F, acting over an area A is given by:

$$F_z = C_f \times p_{dz} \times A_z$$

Wind force in X direction, $F_{zx} = 1.264 \times 2.38(k_2)^2 \times 96 = 288.83(k_2)^2$ kN

Wind force in Y direction, $F_{zy} = 1.057 \times 2.569(k_2)^2 \times 48 = 130.37(k_2)^2$ kN

For the top floor, the tributary area is half of that calculated for the lower floors. Hence the wind forces in X and Y directions in the top floor are

$$F_{zx} = 144.42(k_2)^2 \text{ kN} \quad \text{and} \quad F_{zy} = 65.19(k_2)^2 \text{ kN}$$

Table 19.6 shows the wind force calculation at different heights of the building.

Table 19.6 *Calculation of wind forces, Example 19.2(c)*

Floor level	Height, z (m)	k_2 (at nodes)	$F_{zx} = 288.83(k_2)^2$ (kN)	$F_{zy} = 130.37(k_2)^2$ (kN)
Ground/1	0	1.000		
2	3.2	1.000	288.83	130.37
3	6.4	1.000	288.83	130.37
4	9.6	1.000	288.83	130.37
5	12.8	1.028	305.23	137.77
6	16.0	1.054	320.86	144.82
7	19.2	1.0668	328.70	148.36
8	22.4	1.082	338.14	152.62
9	25.6	1.098	348.21	157.17
10	28.8	1.114	358.43	161.78
Terrace	32.0	1.125	182.77*	82.50*
Base shear (kN) = ΣF_z			3,049	1,376
Base moment (kNm) = $\Sigma F_z \times z$			53,558	24,174

*Estimated using half the tributary area as explained in the solution.

(d) When the office building (Example 19.1) is shifted to Bengaluru on a level ground:
In this case, the k_1, k_2 and k_4 values are taken as 1.0; however, the basic wind speed changes to 33 m/s (refer Table 19.1).
With these values,

$$V_z = V_b\, k_1 k_2 k_3 k_4 = 33 \times 1.0 \times k_2 \times 1.0 \times 1.0 = 33k_2 \text{ m/s}$$

The design wind pressure at any height z above mean ground level is given by:

$$p_z = 0.6V_z^2 = 0.6 \times (33k_2)^2 = 653.4(k_2)^2 \text{ N/m}^2$$

$$p_{dz} = K_d K_a K_c p_z$$

The value of $K_d = 0.9$ (since it is not a cyclone prone region), K_a and K_c are as determined in Example 19.1.

$p_{dzx} = 0.9 \times 0.805 \times 1.0 \times 0.6534(k_2)^2 = 0.473(k_2)^2$ kN/m^2. However, p_{dz} value cannot be lesser than $0.7p_z = 0.7 \times 0.6534(k_2)^2 = 0.457(k_2)^2$ kN/m^2. Hence $p_{dzx} = 0.473(k_2)^2$ kN/m^2.

$p_{dzy} = 0.9 \times 0.869 \times 1.0 \times 0.6534(k_2)^2 = 0.511(k_2)^2$ kN/m², which is $> 0.7p_z$.
Hence $p_{dzy} = 0.511(k_2)^2$ kN/m².

The values of C_{fx} and C_{fy} are discussed in Example 19.1. The wind force, F, acting over an area A is given by:

$$F_z = C_f \times p_{dz} \times A_z$$

Wind force in X direction, $F_{zx} = 1.264 \times 0.473(k_2)^2 \times 96 = 57.44(k_2)^2$ kN

Wind force in Y direction, $F_{zy} = 1.057 \times 0.511(k_2)^2 \times 48 = 25.93(k_2)^2$ kN

For the top floor, the tributary area is half of that calculated for the lower floors. Hence the wind forces in X and Y directions in the top floor are

$$F_{zx} = 28.72(k_2)^2 \text{ kN} \quad \text{and} \quad F_{zy} = 12.97(k_2)^2 \text{ kN}$$

Table 19.7 shows the wind force calculation at different heights of the building.

Table 19.7 *Calculation of wind forces, Example 19.2(d)*

Floor level	Height, z (m)	k_2 (at nodes)	$F_{zx} = 57.44(k_2)^2$ (kN)	$F_{zy} = 25.93(k_2)^2$ (kN)
Ground/1	0	1.000		
2	3.2	1.000	57.44	25.93
3	6.4	1.000	57.44	25.93
4	9.6	1.000	57.44	25.93
5	12.8	1.028	60.70	27.40
6	16.0	1.054	63.81	28.80
7	19.2	1.0668	65.37	29.51
8	22.4	1.082	67.25	30.35
9	25.6	1.098	69.25	31.26
10	28.8	1.114	71.29	32.18
Terrace	32.0	1.125	36.35*	16.41*
Base shear (kN) = ΣF_z			606	274
Base moment (kNm) = $\Sigma F_z \times z$			10,652	4,808

*Estimated using half the tributary area as explained in the solution.

A comparison of the base shears and base moments of the various cases demonstrated in Examples 19.1 and 19.2 are summarised in Table 19.8.

Table 19.8 *Comparison of base shears and base moments (Examples 19.1 and 19.2)*

Case	Ex 19.1	Ex 19.2(a)	Ex 19.2(b)	Ex 19.2(c)	Ex 19.2(d)
Base shear in X-direction (kN)	1,547	1,339	2,190	3,049	606
Base shear in Y-direction (kN)	698	604	989	1,376	274
Base moment in X-direction (kNm)	27,170	23,897	38,475	53,558	10,652
Base moment in Y-direction (kNm)	12,263	10,786	17,366	24,174	4,808

The following conclusions may be drawn:

- In the case of Example 19.2(a) where the terrain category is changed from 2 ('open country') to 3 ('town'), it can be seen that the base shear and base moment (in both directions) reduce by 13 per cent. This is because the k_2 values are relatively lower in terrain category 3.
- In the case of Example 19.2(b), the building is located on top of a hill where the k_3 value is significantly higher. The base shear and base moments both increase by 42 per cent (in both directions) in comparison with Example 19.1.
- In the case of Example 19.2(c), the function of the building has changed from 'office' to 'hospital), which is an important facility for which a higher risk coefficient k_1 and higher cyclonic factor k_4 (due to its post-cyclonic importance) are applicable. The base shear and base moment are found to nearly double (increase by 97 per cent), in comparison with Example 19.1 (in both directions).
- In the case of Example 19.2(d), the building is shifted to a location (Bengaluru, lowest wind zone), where the basic wind speed is much less (V_b = 33 m/s) compared to Example 19.1 (Chennai, with V_b = 50 m/s). The base shear and base moment reduce by as much as 61 per cent (in both directions). The wind force decreases in proportion to the square of the basic wind speed.

19.2.6 Wind Loads on Dynamically Wind-Sensitive Buildings

In the case of wind sensitive buildings (as defined in Section 19.2.3), dynamic effects of wind need to be considered. Such buildings are to be designed for *along-wind* forces (in the direction of the wind) as well as *across-wind* forces (in the perpendicular direction), for which simplified equivalent static analyses procedures described in the Code may be used, as explained earlier (also refer Figure 19.11). In these analysis procedures, it is important to note that the design wind speed to be used is the one based on the hourly mean wind speed, $\bar{V}_z$, (refer Eq. 19.4), and not the design wind speed V_z (Eq. 19.3) based on peak gust wind speed.

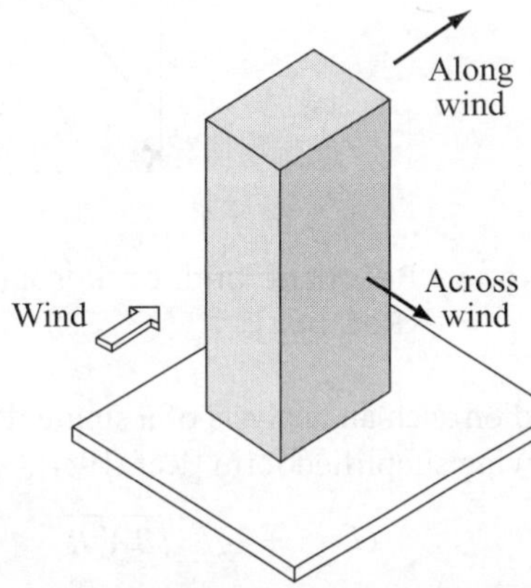

Fig. 19.11 Representation of a building showing along-wind and across-wind directions.

Along-wind Forces

The equivalent static analysis method, based on the concept of *gust factor*, was originally proposed by Davenport [Ref. 19.4, 19.5, 19.10], and has been widely used in design codes and standards worldwide for modelling along-wind loading. The gust factor, G, is defined as the ratio of the expected peak along-wind response to the mean or time-averaged along-wind response over a period of 1 hour. Assuming linear behaviour, it can be applied directly as a dynamic magnification factor on the mean wind force ($C_f A_z \bar{p}_d$) to give the enhanced wind load (including dynamic effects of wind). Thus, introducing the Gust Factor, G, the 'design peak along wind load on the building at any height z', F_z, is given by:

$$F_z = C_{f,z} A_z \bar{p}_d G \tag{19.13}$$

where $C_{f,z}$ is the (drag) force coefficient corresponding to the effective frontal area A_z at any height z (in m^2), and $\bar{p}_d$ is the design hourly mean wind pressure corresponding to the design hourly mean wind speed $\bar{V}_{z,d}$ at height z, obtained as 0.6 $\bar{V}^2_{z,d}$ (N/m^2) [refer Eq. 19.4].

The formula given in the Code to estimate the gust factor G can appear to be formidable, as it involves many factors, which in turn involve many other terms. It is therefore helpful to have a brief overview of the basis of this formulation, which is based on a consideration of the typical 'spectral density' of turbulent wind speed, whose fluctuating wind speed component is modelled as a 'stationary' random process (refer Figures 19.2 and 19.3). The turbulent kinetic wind energy involves a wide band of frequencies ('broad band process'), the along-wind response of a structure (modelled as a single degree of freedom system whose natural frequency is equal to the fundamental natural frequency, f_1, of the structure) is a relatively 'narrow band process'. The response spectral density can be derived from the turbulent wind speed spectral density, assuming linear behaviour, using basic random vibration analysis principles, and takes the form depicted in Figure 19.12. The area under the curve is a measure of the *mean square* fluctuating deflection, and it can be visualised as having a *resonant* part R and a *background* part B, as shown in Figure 19.12. The background part B represents the quasi-static response caused by gusts whose frequencies are less than the natural frequency, f_1, of the structure. [Ref. 19.4].

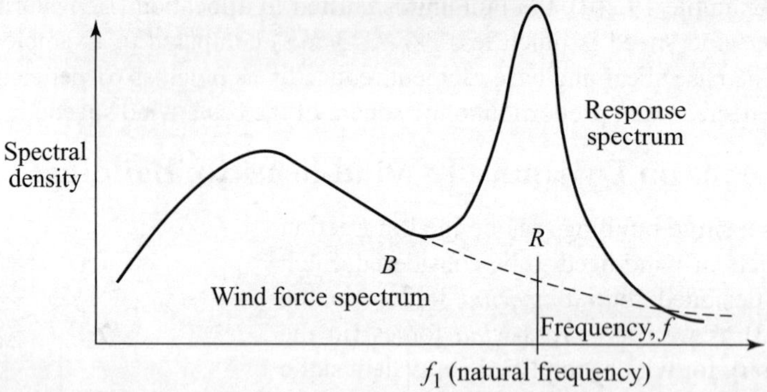

Fig. 19.12 Resonant and background components of fluctuating deflection response spectrum [Ref. 19.4].

Based on such an analysis of a single degree of freedom system, the expression for gust factor, G, takes the following simplified form [Ref. 19.4]:

$$G = 1 + 2gI_z\sqrt{B + R} \tag{19.14}$$

where g is a *peak factor* that depends on the time interval for which the peak response is calculated (typically, one hour) and the frequency range of the response, B and R are the background and resonant response factors (refer Figure 19.12), and I_z is the turbulence intensity at the height z under consideration. Different international standards for wind loading adopt variations of this basic formulation.

The formulation given in IS 875 (Part 3) (Eq. 19.13) is intended to analyse the wind load effects at a level s (above the ground level) on a building of height h (modelled as a vertical cantilever fixed to the base), considering the cumulative effects of the wind forces, F_z, acting above this level ($s < z < h$). Thus, the design peak along wind base bending moment, M_a, can be estimated as follows:

$$M_a = \Sigma F_z z \tag{19.15}$$

The expression for gust factor, G, given in the Code takes the following form:

$$G = 1 + r\sqrt{\left[g_v^2 B_s (1+\phi)^2 + \frac{H_s g_R^2 SE}{\beta}\right]} \tag{19.16}$$

Here, B_s and S address the spatio-temporal correlation between the wind speed fluctuations and wind force fluctuations, which can vary along the height of the building (and are accounted for by the term, s).

The *roughness factor*, r, is taken as twice the longitudinal turbulance intensity $I_{z,i}$, which can be calculated for different terrain categories as:

For terrain category 1: $$I_{z,1} = 0.3507 - 0.0535 \log_{10}\left(\frac{z}{0.002}\right) \quad (19.17a)$$

For terrain category 2: $$I_{z,2} = I_{z,1} + \frac{1}{7}(I_{z,4} - I_{z,1}) \quad (19.17b)$$

For terrain category 3: $$I_{z,3} = I_{z,1} + \frac{3}{7}(I_{z,4} - I_{z,1}) \quad (19.17c)$$

For terrain category 4: $$I_{z,4} = 0.466 - 0.1358 \log_{10}\left(\frac{z}{2}\right) \quad (19.17d)$$

The *peak factor*, g_v, for upwind speed fluctuation is taken as 3.0 for terrain categories 1 and 2, and 4.0 for terrain categories 3 and 4.

The *background factor*, B_s is taken as

$$B_s = \frac{1}{\left[1 + \frac{\sqrt{0.26(h-s)^2 + 0.46b_{sh}^2}}{L_h}\right]} \quad (19.18)$$

where b_{sh} is the average breadth of the structure between heights s and h.

L_h is a measure of *effective turbulence length scale* at the height, h (in m), taken as $85\left(\frac{h}{10}\right)^{0.25}$ for terrain category 1 to 3 and $70\left(\frac{h}{10}\right)^{0.25}$ for terrain category 4.

ϕ is a factor to account for the second order turbulence intensity, to be taken as $\frac{g_v I_{h,i}\sqrt{B_s}}{2}$, where $I_{h,i}$ is the turbulence intensity at height in terrain category i, H_s is the height factor for resonance response calculated as

$$H_s = 1 + \left(\frac{s}{h}\right)^2 \quad (19.19)$$

S is a *size reduction factor* given by

$$S = \frac{1}{\left[1 + \frac{3.5 f_a h}{\bar{V}_{h,d}}\right]\left[1 + \frac{4 f_a b_{0h}}{\bar{V}_{h,d}}\right]} \quad (19.20)$$

where b_{0h} is the average breadth of the structure between 0 and h, f_a is the first mode natural frequency of the building in the along-wind direction (shown as f_1 in Figure 19.12), and $\bar{V}_{h,d}$ is the design hourly mean wind speed at height h (in m/s)

E is the *energy spectrum of turbulence* in the approaching wind stream given by

$$E = \frac{\pi N}{(1 + 70.8N^2)^{5/6}} \tag{19.21}$$

where N is the effective reduced frequency expressed as $\frac{f_a L_h}{\overline{V}_{h,d}}$.

β is the *damping coefficient* of the structure, which may be taken as 0.020 for reinforced concrete structures (and 0.016 for prestressed concrete structures).

g_R is the *peak factor* for resonant response (for a period of 1 hour = 3600 s), given by

$$g_R = \sqrt{[2\ln(3600 f_a)]} \tag{19.22}$$

Across-wind Forces

Conceptually, the dynamic response due to *across-wind* loading is similar to that due to *along-wind* loading. However, there are some significant differences. Firstly, there is a mean along-wind response upon which the fluctuating component is superimposed (refer Figure 19.3), and the maximum wind force is obtained using the gust factor, G (Eq. 19.13). In contrast, the mean across-wind response is typically zero (for symmetrical buildings subjected to symmetric wind flows); the building vibrates in the across-wind direction with respect to the vertical centroidal axis of the building.

Secondly, the across-wind velocity component in the wind flow is small compared to the along-wind velocity. Whereas the spectrum of along-wind force is derived from the corresponding along-wind velocity spectrum, the spectrum of across-wind force is mainly influenced by *vortex shedding* phenomenon in the wake region of the building, with less influence of the fluctuating across-wind velocity in the approach flow. The vortex shedding phenomenon is associated with the non-dimensional 'shedding frequency' of the *Strouhal number*; it is dependent on the geometry/shape of the building in plan and aspect ratio, and there is no generalised analytical approach to evaluate the spectrum of across-wind force, unlike along-wind force.

Hence, the spectrum of across-wind force (in non-dimensional form) is obtained generally from wind tunnel experiments that are specific to the building geometry and aspect ratio. Using these spectra of across-wind force, the dynamic across-wind response is calculated in a manner similar to the along-wind case. Most codes of practice provide equivalent static loading for rectangular buildings with the wind direction normal to either the longer face or shorter face. In such cases, the mean across-wind response will be zero.

The formulation given in IS 875 (Part 3) gives the following expression to estimate the design peak across wind base bending moment, M_c:

$$M_c = 0.5 g_h \overline{p}_h b h^2 (1.06 - 0.06\,k)\sqrt{\left(\frac{\pi C_{fs}}{\beta}\right)} \tag{19.23}$$

where g_h is the peak factor, $= \sqrt{[2\ln(3600 f_c)]}$ in the across-wind direction, $\overline{p}_h$ is the hourly mean wind pressure at height h (in Pa), b is the breadth of the structure normal to the wind (in m), h is the height of the structure (in m), k is the *mode shape power exponent* for representation of the fundamental mode shape as represented by $\psi(z) = \left(\frac{z}{h}\right)^k$, f_c is the first mode natural frequency of the building in the across-wind direction (in Hz). Typical values of k suggested are 0.5 for moment-resisting framed structure, 1.0 for a building with a central core and moment resisting façade, and 1.5 for a uniform cantilever.

The factor C_{fs}, in Eq. 19.22 is the *cross-wind force spectrum coefficient* generalised for a linear mode; it depends on the ratio, $\frac{\bar{V}_{h,d}}{f_c b}$, as well as the height (h): breadth (b): depth (d) ratio of the building, where d is measured parallel to the wind flow. Typical values of C_{fs} are given in IS 875 (Part 3) for square buildings (with $h{:}b{:}d$ = 3:1:1 and 6-9:1:1), and for rectangular buildings (with $h{:}b{:}d$ = 6:1:2 and 6:2:1), considering turbulence intensity values of 0.12 and 0.20 at 0.67h (where the vortex shedding phenomenon is most likely). These are summarised in Tables 19.9(a) and (b), and may be used appropriately, in the absence of more precise data. Interpolation of C_{fs} values may be carried out, wherever possible. When the height to lateral dimension is low (less than 3), suitable values are not provided in the Code. If $\frac{\bar{V}_{h,d}}{f_c b}$ is also small, for such cases, C_f = 0 may be considered (i.e., across-wind loading may be ignored).

Table 19.9 (a) *Values of the cross-wind force spectrum coefficient for buildings square in plan*

$\frac{\bar{V}_{h,d}}{f_c b}$	$I_z = 0.12$ $h{:}b{:}d$ (3:1:1)	$I_z = 0.20$ $h{:}b{:}d$ (3:1:1)	$I_z = 0.12$ $h{:}b{:}d$ (6:1:1)	$I_z = 0.20$ $h{:}b{:}d$ (6:1:1)
2	0.001	0.002	0.001	0.002
4	0.001	0.005	0.001	0.004
6	0.006	0.010	0.007	0.014
8	0.021	0.017	0.031	0.036
10	0.037	0.020	0.074	0.055
12	0.033	0.018	0.072	0.046
14	0.018	0.013	0.033	0.027
16	0.010	0.009	0.012	0.019

Table 19.9 (b) *Values of the cross-wind force spectrum coefficient for buildings rectangular in plan (2:1) and (1:2)*

$\frac{\bar{V}_{h,d}}{f_c b}$	$I_z = 0.12$ $h{:}b{:}d$ (6:2:1)	$I_z = 0.20$ $h{:}b{:}d$ (6:2:1)	$I_z = 0.12$ $h{:}b{:}d$ (6:1:2)	$I_z = 0.20$ $h{:}b{:}d$ (6:1:2)
2	0.001	0.001	0.000	0.001
4	0.001	0.001	0.001	0.002
6	0.001	0.002	0.004	0.005
8	0.011	0.012	0.007	0.010
10	0.045	0.042	0.012	0.017
12	0.005	0.007	0.016	0.023
14	0.002	0.003	0.019	0.028
16	0.001	0.002	0.021	0.032

The across wind load distribution on the building can be obtained from M_c, assuming a linear distribution of loads, as given below:

$$F_{z,c} = \left(\frac{3M_c}{h^2}\right)\left(\frac{z}{h}\right) \tag{19.24}$$

where $F_{z,c}$ is across-wind load per unit height at height z.

Combination of Along-wind and Across-wind Load Effects

The along-wind and across-wind forces, as discussed above, need to be applied simultaneously on the building, to assess their combined effects for design.

Example 19.3

Repeat Example 19.1, treating the building as a dynamically 'wind sensitive' building. Compare the results.

Solution

Since the fundamental period of the structure as per Eq. 19.10 is $T = 0.1 \times 10 = 1$ s, whereby the fundamental natural frequency $f = 1/T = 1$ Hz, this is a borderline case and it is prudent to estimate the wind forces, treating the building as dynamically wind sensitive, even though the height to least lateral dimension is less than 5.

The value of the factor k_1, k_3, k_4 and the basic wind speed V_b are same as discussed in Example 19.1.

The design hourly mean wind speed at height z, $\bar{V}_{z,d} = V_b\, k_1\, \bar{k}_2 k_3 k_4$

The value of the $\bar{k}_2$ factor can be calculated using Eq. 19.5, with $z_{0,i} = 0.02$ (for terrain category 2).

With these values,

$$\bar{V}_{z,d} = V_b\, k_1 \bar{k}_2 k_3 k_4 = 50 \times 1.0 \times \bar{k}_2 \times 1.0 \times 1.0 = 50\bar{k}_2 \text{ m/s}$$

The design hourly mean wind pressure at any height z above mean ground level is given by:

$$\bar{P}_{dz} = 0.6\, \bar{V}_{z,d}^{\,2} = 0.6 \times (50\bar{k}_2)^2 = 1500(\bar{k}_2)^2 \text{ N/m}^2 = 1.5(\bar{k}_2)^2 \text{ kN/m}^2$$

The values of C_{fx} and C_{fy} were evaluated in Example 19.1. The wind force, F_z, acting over an area A_z is given by Eq. 19.13.

Along-wind load calculation

The effective turbulence length scale can be calculated for Terrain category 2 as (refer Section 19.2.6)

$$L_h = 85\left(\frac{32}{10}\right)^{0.25} = 113.69 \text{ m}$$

$$\bar{k}_{2,h} = 0.1423\left[\ln\left(\frac{32}{0.02}\right)\right]0.02^{0.0706} = 0.796$$

$$\bar{V}_{h,d} = 50 \times 1.0 \times 0.796 \times 1.0 \times 1.0 = 39.8 \text{ m/s}$$

$$g_v = 3.0,\ f_a = 1 \text{ Hz},\ b_{oh,x} = 30 \text{ m},\ b_{oh,y} = 15 \text{ m}$$

The *size reduction factor* S in both X- and Y-directions can be calculated using Eq. 19.20.

$$S_x = \frac{1}{\left[1+\dfrac{3.5\times 1\times 32}{39.8}\right]\left[1+\dfrac{4\times 1\times 30}{39.8}\right]} = 0.065$$

$$S_y = \frac{1}{\left[1+\dfrac{3.5\times 1\times 32}{39.8}\right]\left[1+\dfrac{4\times 1\times 15}{39.8}\right]} = 0.105$$

The *roughness factor, r* is twice the *turbulence intensity*, which can be calculated for Category 2, using Eq. 19.17b.

$$I_{h,2} = 0.126 + \frac{1}{7}(0.302 - 0.126) = 0.151$$

$$r = 2\times 0.151 = 0.302$$

As the building is an RC structure, the *damping coefficient* β is taken as 0.02. The effective reduced frequency is calculated as

$$N = \frac{1\times 113.69}{39.8} = 2.855 \text{ Hz}$$

The *energy spectrum of turbulence* is calculated using Eq. 19.21.

$$E = \frac{\pi \times 2.855}{(1+70.8\times 2.855^2)^{5/6}} = 0.045$$

The *peak factor* for resonant response is estimated using Eq. 19.22.

$$g_R = \sqrt{[2\ln(3600\times 1)]} = 4.047$$

Gust factor G: $G = 1 + r\sqrt{\left[g_v^2 B_s (1+\phi)^2 + \dfrac{H_s g_R^2 SE}{\beta}\right]}$

where $\phi = \dfrac{g_v I_{h,i}\sqrt{B_s}}{2}$, and $H_s = 1 + \left(\dfrac{s}{h}\right)^2$ and $B_s = \dfrac{1}{\left[1+\dfrac{\sqrt{0.26(h-s)^2 + 0.46b_{sh}^2}}{L_h}\right]}$

With the various parameters determined as above, Tables 19.10(a) and (b) show the wind force calculations at different heights of the building in X- and Y-directions respectively.

It can be seen that the base shears are higher by 17 and 14 per cent in the X- and Y-directions respectively in comparison with Example 19.1.

Across wind calculation

The h:b:d ratio for the building considered is 2.13:2:1 and the ratio $\dfrac{\overline{V}_{h,d}}{f_c b}$ is less than 2.0. Hence, across wind forces can be considered to be negligible in this case.

Table 19.10(a) Calculation of along wind forces in *X*- direction, Example 19.3

Floor level	Height (m)	$\bar{k}_2$ (Eq. 19.5)	$\bar{p}_d = 0.6\,\bar{V}_{z,d}^2$	H_s (Eq. 19.19)	B_{sx} (Eq. 19.18)	ϕ_x	G_x (Eq. 19.16)	F_x (kN) (Eq. 19.13)
Ground/1	0							
2	3.2	0.548	450.307	1.010	0.819	0.205	2.094	114.44
3	6.4	0.623	581.708	1.040	0.825	0.206	2.101	148.29
4	9.6	0.667	666.361	1.090	0.830	0.206	2.109	170.53
5	12.8	0.698	729.909	1.160	0.834	0.207	2.119	187.65
6	16	0.722	781.194	1.250	0.838	0.207	2.130	201.91
7	19.2	0.741	824.389	1.360	0.842	0.208	2.143	214.34
8	22.4	0.758	861.817	1.490	0.845	0.208	2.157	225.54
9	25.6	0.772	894.909	1.640	0.847	0.208	2.172	235.87
10	28.8	0.785	924.617	1.810	0.848	0.209	2.189	245.54
Terrace	32	0.796	951.602	2.000	0.848	0.209	2.206	127.37
							Base shear (kN)	1,871.5
							Base moment (kNm)	34,938

Table 19.10(b) Calculation of along wind forces in *Y* direction, Example 19.3

Floor level	Height (m)	$\bar{k}_2$ (Eq. 19.5)	$\bar{p}_d = 0.6\,\bar{V}_{z,d}^2$	H_s (Eq. 19.19)	B_{sy} (Eq. 19.18)	ϕ_x	G_y (Eq. 19.16)	F_y (kN) (Eq. 19.13)
Ground/1	0							
2	3.2	0.548	450.307	1.010	0.864	0.211	2.157	49.29
3	6.4	0.623	581.708	1.040	0.873	0.212	2.165	63.91
4	9.6	0.667	666.361	1.090	0.881	0.213	2.176	73.57
5	12.8	0.698	729.909	1.160	0.890	0.214	2.190	81.09
6	16	0.722	781.194	1.250	0.897	0.215	2.205	87.41
7	19.2	0.741	824.389	1.360	0.904	0.215	2.224	93.00
8	22.4	0.758	861.817	1.490	0.910	0.216	2.244	98.11
9	25.6	0.772	894.909	1.640	0.914	0.217	2.266	102.89
10	28.8	0.785	924.617	1.810	0.917	0.217	2.290	107.44
Terrace	32	0.796	951.602	2.000	0.918	0.217	2.316	55.91
							Base shear (kN)	812.6
							Base moment (kNm)	15,210

Only along-wind forces need to be considered. It can be seen that considering the building to be dynamically 'wind-sensitive' results in amplified estimation of the wind forces.

19.2.7 Interference Effect

The procedures for estimating wind forces discussed above are intended for isolated buildings. The presence of another structure in the path of the wind in close vicinity of the building under consideration can affect the wind pressures acting on the building. This is known as *interference effect*, and needs to be accounted for, especially when it causes an enhancement in the wind pressures. The interfering building can also provide a 'shielding effect' that reduces the wind pressures, but this is usually ignored. As discussed in IS 875 (Part 3), 'the actual phenomenon is too complex to justify generalisation of the wind forces/ pressures produced due to interference'. In the case of important structures (tall buildings and towers), where the locations of neighbouring structures are relatively well known, it is desirable to carry out wind tunnel studies or simulation using computational fluid dynamics for a proper understanding of the actual enhancement, due to different directions of the oncoming wind flow.

The term, interference factor (IF), is sometimes used as a multiplying factor to be applied on the design wind forces, to account for the enhancement, with reference to the values applicable for the building considered in isolation. For a preliminary design, specialist literature may be referred to, for appropriate values of IF, depending on the building geometry and location. Some recommendations are also given in IS 875 (Part 3).

19.3 Estimation of Seismic Forces

As discussed in Section 19.1, earthquake loading on a building is essentially a *displacement-induced* loading, unlike wind loading, which is a *force-induced* loading that can be assessed more directly. Although, it would be prudent to perform a *displacement-based design* of structures for earthquake resistance, design codes have traditionally proposed (and continue to propose) a *force-based* design approach for the convenience of structural designers (who are used to treating all loads as forces). In this approach, the inertial forces induced in the building due to the vibrating masses at various floor levels are treated as equivalent *seismic forces*. [The total *base shear* is estimated as a fraction of the weight of the building.] However, unlike the estimation of wind forces (discussed earlier), the estimation of the seismic forces on a building is rather complex and indirect.

> **The forces developed in a building due to an earthquake depend on the resulting peak ground acceleration at the location, the nature of the soil on which the building is founded and the properties of the building structure.**

The seismic force is primarily dependent on the seismology of the region (i.e., the presence of active faults and tectonic plate movements). The motion of the ground during an earthquake is typically expressed in terms of acceleration, velocity or displacement records, measured by seismograms. The value of *peak ground acceleration* (PGA), generally that of the horizontal motion, is used as a measure of the strong motion of any earthquake record, as indicated in Figure 19.13(a). It is used to generate the *response spectrum*, which is a plot of the maximum acceleration of the mass of single degree of freedom (SDOF) systems of different natural periods as a function of the natural periods (of the SDOF systems), under the same earthquake ground motion at their bases. A smoothened average of a number of response spectra (corresponding to various earthquakes) is used to generate a *design response spectrum*, as shown in Figure 19.13(b), that is specified by design codes to facilitate structural design.

The accelerations that occur in the rock layer of the earth's crust during an earthquake get transmitted to the building through the soil over the rock layer. Typically, the rock layer experiences high short period motion; but its response decays rapidly for higher periods. Thus, for buildings located on rock, high intensity ground motion is expected for smaller periods. Conversely soft soils, particularly when they extend to moderate

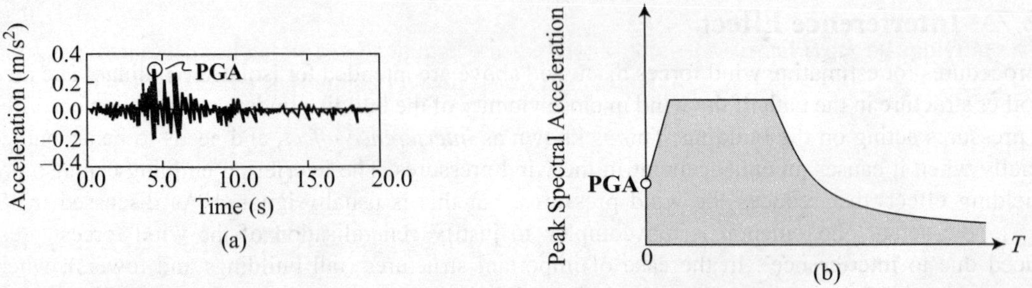

Fig 19.13 Graphical representation of (a) typical ground acceleration record, (b) design response spectrum.

depths (> 50 m), are likely to filter out some of the short period motion and amplify the longer period motion. The nature of the soil layer at a location can be considered to develop a response spectrum for the particular site (*site specific response spectrum*) [Ref. 19.12].

The building's inherent properties, such as *mass*, *damping* and *stiffness*, also affect its vibration response. Structures having higher mass are bound to generate higher inertial forces. Further, stiffer structures also attract higher seismic forces.

Assessment of seismic forces requires an understanding of the structural behaviour under large inelastic and cyclic deformations. Furthermore, some inelastic behaviour (such as *plastic hinge* formation in RC members) and associated damage to the building are generally unavoidable, due to the high magnitude of internal forces generated in the event of an extreme earthquake; it would be economically unviable to design buildings to maintain elastic behaviour. The damage caused in the structural elements (at specific locations) as well as the non-structural elements (such as cracking in the masonry infills) serves to dissipate the energy input caused by the earthquake-induced vibrations.

The Indian Code†, IS 1893, titled *Recommendations for earthquake resistant design of structures*, was first published in 1962, and subsequently revised in 1966, 1970, 1975, 1984, 2002 and 2016. In the 2002 revision, the Code was split into five parts: Part 1 dealing with 'general provisions and buildings', Part 2 with 'liquid retaining tanks', Part 3 with 'bridges and retaining walls', Part 4 with 'industrial structures', and Part 5 with 'dams and embankments'.

19.3.1 Earthquake-resistant Design Philosophy

EQ-resistant design attempts to limit damage to and collapse of the building in a graded manner, depending on the building function and the intensity of the earthquake.

Earthquake-resistant design philosophy is based on the principle that structures should be able to resist: (i) *minor and frequent earthquakes* without any damage, (ii) *moderate earthquakes* without significant structural damage and some non-structural damage, and (iii) *major earthquakes* with some structural and non-structural damage but without collapse and with minimal loss of life [Ref. 19.12]. The term, *Maximum Considered Earthquake* (MCE), is sometimes used to describe the potential 'major earthquake' at the building site under consideration, for which the design at the limit state of collapse has to be carried out, while the term, *Design Basis Earthquake* (DBE), is the earthquake level that forms the general

† References to Code 'IS 1893 (Part 1)' in this Chapter refer to the 2016 (sixth) revision, and includes amendments to this revision made up to November 2020.

basis of earthquake resistant design as per the Code. DBE and MCE correspond respectively to 10% and 2% probability of exceedance in 50 years [Ref. 19.13]. The approximate return periods are 500 years and 2500 years, respectively.

IS 1893 (Part 1) Code deals with seismic force estimation for buildings in India [Ref 19.3]. The Code divides the country into four seismic zones, depending on the severity of the seismic hazard. The representative *peak ground acceleration* (PGA) values in the four zones, as implied by the Code, varies between 0.10*g* (in the lowest seismic Zone II) and 0.36*g* (in the highest seismic Zone V), where *g* is the acceleration due to gravity. The PGA corresponding to DBE is typically taken as 50 per cent of that corresponding to MCE. It may be noted, however, that at some local places (especially near the Himalayan region), the PGA values can well exceed the Code prescribed values. In the 2016 revision of the seismic Code, the usage of the terminology of MCE and DBE have been dispensed with.

Earthquake-resistant design depends heavily on the ductility, redundancy, inelastic behaviour and over-strength built into the structure in order to reduce the induced seismic forces on the building.

The actual elastic forces that develop in structures due to the design earthquake are much larger than the design forces specified in the Code. Factors such as *ductility* obtained through inelastic behaviour and detailing, *redundancy*, reserve strength (*over-strength*) provided, and *post-elastic energy dissipation* in the structure are relied upon to account for this difference between actual elastic and design lateral forces (see *response reduction factor* below). Due to ductility, two things happen – firstly, there is more energy dissipation due to hysteresis; and secondly, the structure becomes 'softer', increasing its natural period, which results in lower induced seismic forces. Redundancy ensures that yielding at one location does not lead to yielding of the structure as a whole, and instead a large number of plastic hinges could form progressively, resulting in significant load redistribution, thereby providing additional safety margin. Over-strength provided, such as for columns relative to the beams at joints, helps avoid collapse and maintain vertical load carrying capacity.

The type of detailing adopted governs the level of damage to the building. By providing appropriate *ductile detailing*, described in IS 13920: 2016 (discussed in Chapter 16), it is possible to ensure the desired performance at MCE, accounting for yielding of structural members at pre-determined locations, thereby ensuring that the collapse of the building is reasonably prevented and the vertical load carrying capacity is not affected even after earthquake. The design and detailing of the structural members should ensure that the building has not only the desired lateral force resistance capacity (*strength*), but also the required large inelastic deformation capacity (*ductility*).

In addition to *strength* and *ductility*, the building should also have adequate lateral *stiffness* for serviceability (to limit the lateral drift under DBE), although the initial stiffness is likely to degrade on account of damage under MCE. Thus, in seismic design the stiffness is governed by the serviceability criteria. Deflection in the structure can lead to distress of non-structural members and may also affect the functionality. The IS 1893 (Part 1) Code imposes a restriction on the lateral deflection to *height*/250 [Ref 19.13].

The *structural configuration* of the building also affects its performance under an earthquake. This is important to bear in mind while planning buildings in high seismic zones. Buildings 'with simple regular geometry and uniformly distributed mass and stiffness in plan and in elevation' are recommended for this purpose [Ref. 19.3, Cl. 7.1]. The Code IS 1893 (Part 1) defines various types of *irregularities in plan*: torsional irregularity, re-entrant corners, floor slabs with excessive cut-outs and out-of-plane offsets, and non-parallel lateral force resisting systems. The Code also defines various types of *irregularities in elevation*: stiffness irregularity (soft storey), mass irregularity, vertical geometric irregularity, in-plane discontinuity in vertical elements resisting lateral force, strength irregularity (weak storey), floating or stub columns, and irregular modes of oscillation in two principal plan directions. Limits on these irregularities have been imposed by IS 1893

(Part 1) for seismic zones III, IV and V, and such buildings need to be analysed and designed with special care.

Four 'main desirable attributes' of an earthquake resistant building, as described in IS 1893 (Part 1): 2016 – Cl.7, are: (1) robust *structural configuration*, (2) a minimum *elastic lateral stiffness*, (3) a *minimum lateral strength* and (4) adequate *ductility*.

These attributes are described in detail in Ref. 19.14 and 19.15.

19.3.2 Code Based Procedure to Estimate Seismic Forces

As mentioned earlier, the current design practice worldwide continues largely to be based on *force-based* earthquake-resistant design of buildings, in which inertial forces acting on the vibrating building are expressed as *equivalent static* lateral forces. In order to simplify and generalise the analysis, the Code provides a *seismic zone map* and a *response spectrum (acceleration)*, based on the PGA values of recorded earthquakes.

The primary quantity involved in such design is the *design seismic base shear*, V_B, which is dependent on the *seismic weight* of the structure, W, and *design horizontal earthquake acceleration coefficient*, A_h. The latter depends on several factors. The seismic hazard at the building site is represented by the seismic zone factor, Z. It is also dependent on the shaking of the building, which is governed by the energy spectrum of the earthquake (at different frequencies), the natural frequencies and damping of the building and the soil types – together represented by a *structural flexibility factor*, S_a/g (also called *design acceleration coefficient*). Another factor, called *response reduction factor*, R, is introduced in order to make the design of normal buildings economically viable by permitting damage, while also ensuring adequate ductility, as discussed earlier. Finally, in order to ensure minimal damage in buildings with special importance (such as hospitals) that are required to survive and function in a post-earthquake scenario, an *importance factor*, I, is also incorporated.

Design Base Shear (V_B)

The *design seismic base shear,* V_B, is the total cumulative (horizontal) lateral force (sum of all the lateral forces acting at various floor levels) that acts at the base of the structure in the considered direction of earthquake shaking – the seismic force the structure is to be designed for. This can be estimated along any principal direction of the building as a fraction of the *seismic weight*, W, of the building:

$$V_B = A_h W \tag{19.25}$$

where A_h is *design horizontal acceleration coefficient*, given by:

$$A_h = \frac{Z}{2}\frac{I}{R}\left(\frac{S_a}{g}\right) \tag{19.26}$$

where the terms *zone factor*, Z, *importance factor*, I, *response reduction factor*, R and *design acceleration coefficient*, S_a/g, are as explained in detail below.

Seismic Weight (W)

The term, *seismic weight*, is used to refer to the gravity load on the building to be considered for the purpose of estimating the design base shear. It must obviously include the full dead load (including partitions), but some allowance in the estimation of live loads is provided for, considering that it would be highly improbable for all the floors of the building to be subject to the full design live load. In the absence of more precise data, the Code recommends that only 50 per cent of the full live load need be considered when the prescribed live load exceeds 3.0 kN/m^2. This is reduced to 25 per cent when the prescribed live load is less than or equal to 3.0 kN/m^2. In regions of severe snow loads (and sandstorms), exceeding 1.5 kN/m^2, 20 per cent of the snow load (or sand load), should be considered while assessing W. While assessing the seismic weight of each floor, the weight of columns and walls (and any other dead weight of significance) should be apportioned appropriately to the floors above and below the storey.

Zone Factor (Z)

The *seismic zone map* given in IS 1893 (Part 1) is broadly based on maximum *intensities*† of recorded earthquakes, also taking into account known *magnitudes* and epicentres, tectonics and lithology. It has been regularly updated over the years, with the increased availability of earthquake records. In the 1970 version of IS 1893, five seismic zones were identified (corresponding to five tectonic units of India, with varying magnitude and frequency of earthquake occurrence); however, Zone I (with the lowest seismic hazard) was upgraded to Zone II in the 2002 version of the Code. Presently, there are four seismic zones in India, denoted as zones II, III, IV and V.

Each seismic zone is assigned a *zone factor*, Z, which is a measure of the PGA (normalised with g), for the level of earthquake for which a structure is to be designed, corresponding approximately to the *maximum considered earthquake* (MCE). The higher the zone, the higher is the value of Z, implying higher seismic forces to be considered in design. Seismic zones II, III, IV and V have been assigned Z values of 0.10, 0.16, 0.24 and 0.36 respectively, according to IS 1893 (Part 1). The seismic zones and zone factors corresponding to some important cities (State capitals) are shown in Table 19.11.

Table 19.11 *Seismic zone factors of important cities in India*

Seismic Zone	Z	Important cities (State capitals)
II	0.10	Bengaluru, Bhopal, Hyderabad, Jaipur, Puducherry, Raipur, Ranchi,
III	0.16	Amaravathi, Bhubaneswar, Chennai, Daman, Gandhinagar, Kavaratti, Kolkata, Lucknow, Mumbai, Panaji, Thiruvananthapuram
IV	0.24	Chandigarh, Dehradun, Gangtok, Gorakhpur, Leh, New Delhi, Patna, Shimla
V	0.36	Aizawl, Agartala, Dispur, Imphal, Itanagar, Kohima, Port Blair, Shillong, Srinagar

Improved analysis is possible by considering seismic *micro-zonation*, based on extensive seismo-tectonic and site specific topographic and geological data. This provides detailed information on earthquake hazard at a resolution that is much finer than the seismic zone maps. The first level micro-zonation maps, in terms of peak ground acceleration (PGA), are presently being developed for selected cities/regions of the country [Ref. 19.14-16].

Importance Factor (I)

The Code recognises the importance of safety of critical facilties and prescribes an enhancement in the lateral forces on the buildings, in terms of the *importance factor*, I (refer Eq. 19.26). The default value of I for normal buildings (with relatively low human occupancy) is 1.0.

† *Magnitude* is a measure of the size of an earthquake, based on the strain energy released along the fault, whereas *intensity* is a measure of the effect of the earthquake (observed damage and human reactions). The Richter scale is commonly used to measure 'magnitude', while the MMI and MSK scales are commonly used to measure 'intensity'.

For critical and lifeline structures, such as hospitals, nuclear facilities, schools, signature buildings, monuments, transit stations, power stations, fire stations and community halls, $I = 1.5$ is prescribed. In order to mitigate loss of life, in buildings with high human occupancy (accommodating more than 200 persons), $I = 1.2$ is typically recommended. In buildings with 'mixed occupancies' (i.e., some portions having less than 200-person occupancy, while others have more), the higher value of I shall be used, considering the analysis of the building as a whole.

The Code also allows for owners and design engineers of buildings to choose higher values of I than those prescribed, with due consideration to 'economy and strategy'.

Design Acceleration Coefficient (S_a/g)

The *response spectrum* is a graphical representation of the maximum response (acceleration, velocity or displacement) of a single-degree-of-freedom (SDOF) linear system for a range of natural vibration periods, with specific damping, subjected to a specific ground motion. It is typically a jagged plot (saw-tooth like), having drastic changes in amplitude for small changes in time period. In order to make this more amenable for practical design, covering an ensemble of earthquake ground motions, a *design acceleration spectrum* (as a smooth average envelope of peak accelerations of SDOF systems) is proposed by design codes. By using such a spectrum, the designer is effectively designing for a range of earthquake ground motions that may be likely at the building site under consideration [Ref. 19.16].

The *design horizontal acceleration coefficient*, A_h, referred to in Eq. 19.25, depends primarily on the value of the maximum acceleration obtained from the design acceleration spectrum prescribed in the Code for a SDOF system for a damping ratio (specified as 5 per cent in the Code) for the expected seismic excitations at the base of the building. The acceleration is normalised with the acceleration due to gravity and called *design acceleration coefficient* (S_a/g), and expressed as a function of the *natural period* (T) of the SDOF system. The typical plot of the design response spectrum is as shown in Figure 19.13 (see also Figure 2 in the Code). The value of S_a/g is typically 1.0 when the time period T is zero, which corresponds to the condition of a fully 'rigid' system (having infinite natural frequency), whereby the structure is expected to have the same acceleration as the ground (PGA) to which it is fixed. The value of S_a/g gets amplified to a peak value of 2.5 for relatively stiff buildings (low-rise buildings) encountered in practice and drops gradually (inversely with respect to T) as the building becomes more flexible (mid-rise and tall buildings) to a minimum value (less than 0.5) for buildings with $T > 4$s.

Multi-storeyed buildings are typically modelled as multi-degree-of-freedom (MDOF) systems (in contrast to SDOF systems), with masses concentrated at the various floor levels located at various heights. The dynamic behaviour is characterised by several natural periods, with corresponding *mode shapes*. In seismic analysis, the response of an MDOF system is evaluated from the response spectrum by considering only the highest period (fundamental natural period) or a few periods and the corresponding ordinates of the spectrum.

As explained earlier, the nature of the soil has a significant influence on the response of flexible buildings; with increase in soil stiffness, the more rapid is the decay in the response with increasing time period. In IS 1893 (Part 1), three different response spectra are prescribed corresponding to three types of soil. *Soil type* I corresponds to 'rock or hard soils', *soil type* II refers to 'medium or stiff soils', while *soil type* III refers to 'soft soil'; detailed descriptions of these three soil types are given in the Code. In terms of the corrected SPT value, N, for the soil, type I is applicable for soils with $N > 30$, type III is applicable for soils with $N < 30$, and type II for values of N in between. The Code also allows the use of *site-specific response spectrum*.

In a departure from earlier versions of the Code, in IS 1893 (Part 1): 2016, the assessment of S_a/g is made dependent on whether the analysis of the response of the structure is carried out by the simplified *equivalent static method* or the more rigorous *response spectrum method* (involving *dynamic analysis*). The only difference in the recommendations for S_a/g is that a constant value of $S_a/g = 2.5$ is now prescribed in the case of equivalent static method for very rigid buildings, with $0 < T < 0.1$s.

However, Cl. 6.4.3 of the Code also specifies an additional constraint, severely limiting the application of the equivalent static method; that it 'may be used for analysis of regular structures with approximate natural period T_a less than 0.4 s'. For such low time periods, the peak value of $S_a/g = 2.5$ is applicable for all soil types. Thus, *in all cases* where equivalent static method can be used, $S_a/g = 2.5$. That being the case, the presentation of Figure 2(a) and the equations in Section 6.4.2 (a) in the Code, giving values of S_a/g for higher values of T (≥ 0.4 s) for 'use in equivalent static method' appears to be rather infructuous; furthermore, these values are identical to those for the *response spectrum method.* However, they may still serve the purpose of facilitating a *preliminary design* of regular multi-storeyed framed buildings (with higher values of T) using the equivalent static method; the final design must be based on dynamic analysis, in compliance with the Code.

The following formulas are recommended by the Code for different soil types, corresponding to 5 per cent damping (for use in the *response spectrum method*). As mentioned above, they can also be used for preliminary design of regular buildings using *equivalent static method*, noting that $S_a/g = 2.5$ for $T < 0.4$s.

For rocky or hard soils
$$\frac{S_a}{g} = \begin{cases} 1+15T & T < 0.10 \text{ s} \\ 2.5 & 0.10 \text{ s} < T < 0.40 \text{ s} \\ \dfrac{1}{T} & 0.40 \text{ s} < T < 4.00 \text{ s} \\ 0.25 & T > 4.00 \text{ s} \end{cases} \qquad (19.27a)$$

For medium stiff soils
$$\frac{S_a}{g} = \begin{cases} 1+15T & T < 0.10 \text{ s} \\ 2.5 & 0.10 \text{ s} < T < 0.55 \text{ s} \\ \dfrac{1.36}{T} & 0.55 \text{ s} < T < 4.00 \text{ s} \\ 0.34 & T > 4.00 \text{ s} \end{cases} \qquad (19.27b)$$

For soft soils
$$\frac{S_a}{g} = \begin{cases} 1+15T & T < 0.10 \text{ s} \\ 2.5 & 0.10 \text{ s} < T < 0.67 \text{ s} \\ \dfrac{1.67}{T} & 0.67 \text{ s} < T < 4.00 \text{ s} \\ 0.42 & T > 4.00 \text{ s} \end{cases} \qquad (19.27c)$$

With regard to *damping ratio*, Cl. 7.2.4 of the Code states that the default value of 5 per cent (of critical damping) assumed in the above formulas (for estimating A_h, and thereby V_B) shall be adopted, considering the high inelastic deformations likely to be experienced by buildings, irrespective of the material of construction (steel, reinforced concrete, masonry, or a combination) and method of analysis (equivalent static or dynamic).

Furthermore, when a number of modes are to be considered in the response spectrum method, the value of the design horizontal seismic coefficient, A_h, as defined by Eq. 19.26, shall be computed for each mode, considering the natural period T corresponding to that mode of oscillation, using Eq. 19.27.

Approximate Fundamental Time Period (T_a)

IS 1893 (Part 1) recommends simplified formulae for estimating the *approximate fundamental natural period* (T_a), in seconds, of buildings with different structural systems for the purpose of estimating the design acceleration coefficient (using Eq. 19.27). For *moment resisting frames* without any infills,

$$T_a = \begin{cases} 0.075h^{0.75} & \text{for RC frame building} \\ 0.080h^{0.75} & \text{for RC-steel composite frame building} \\ 0.085h^{0.75} & \text{for steel frame building} \end{cases} \tag{19.28}$$

where h is the height of the building (in m).

For buildings with *RC structural walls*,

$$T_a = \frac{0.075h^{0.75}}{\sqrt{A_w}} \geq \frac{0.09h}{\sqrt{d}} \tag{19.29a}$$

where A_w is the total effective area (in m^2) of walls in the first storey of the building, given by:

$$A_w = \sum_{i=1}^{N_w}\left[A_{wi}\left\{0.2 + \left(\frac{L_{wi}}{h}\right)^2\right\}\right] \tag{19.29b}$$

where A_{wi} is the effective cross-sectional area of the structural wall i in the first storey (in m^2), L_{wi} is the length of the structural wall i in the first storey in the considered direction of lateral force (in m), d is the base dimension of the building at the plinth level (in m) along the considered direction of earthquake shaking and N_w is the number of walls in the considered direction of earthquake shaking.

For all other buildings,

$$T_a = \frac{0.09h}{\sqrt{d}} \tag{19.30}$$

where h and d are as defined above.

Response Reduction Factor (R)

The calculation of design acceleration coefficient, S_a/g, based on the design response spectrum, assumes linear elastic behaviour of the SDOF system. This will typically result in high seismic force estimates that are usually unviable. It is therefore prudent to allow for limited inelastic yielding, while ensuring that the vertical load carrying capacity of the building is not impaired. Also, by taking advantage of the energy-dissipation capability of the structure, the seismic forces acting on the structure can get significantly reduced. As mentioned in Cl 7.2.6 of the Code, the *response reduction factor, R* attempts to account for the effects of nonlinear behaviour, ductility, redundancy and overstrength normally available in buildings, if designed in compliance with the prescribed standards.

The response reduction factor is essentially a ratio of the seismic base shear for an *elastic* system to the value of base shear for which the structure is to be designed. The quantification of R is rather complex and involves several factors; it is decided based more on engineering judgment than a scientific analysis. In simple terms R can be visualised as a combined effect of reduction (over the elastic response) due to (i) ductility incorporated in the detailing of various elements, R_μ, (ii) redundancy in the system (providing for redistribution of forces following local yielding), R_R, and (iii) inherent overstrength due to the actual strength being more than the required strength demand, R_Ω. This concept is depicted graphically in Figure 19.14, where the base shear, V_B, is plotted against the roof displacement, Δ, of the building [Ref. 19.14].

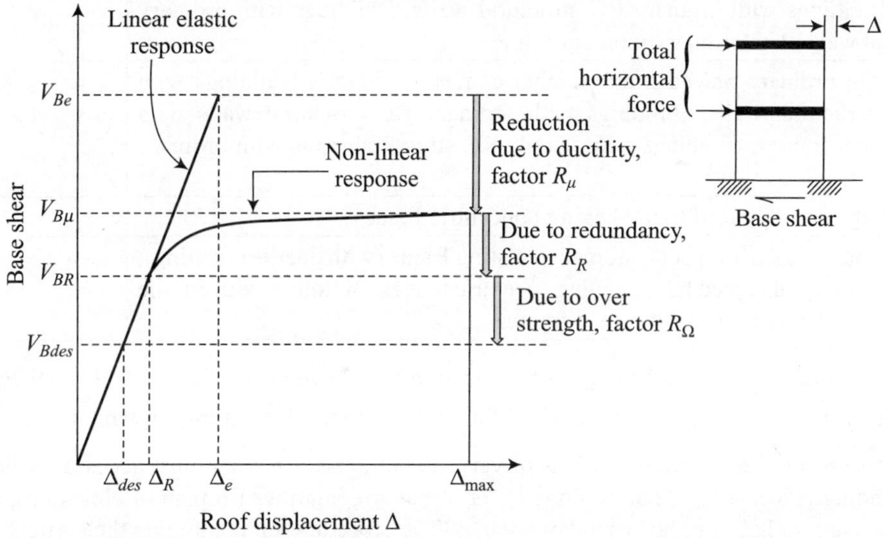

Fig 19.14 Concept of response reduction factor R [Ref. 19.14].

If the design is linear elastic, the corresponding base shear demand V_{Be} will be very high, although the displacement Δ_e will be low. If the actual base shear capacity provided is reduced to $V_{B\mu} = V_{Be}/R_\mu$, to account for the nonlinear response, the corresponding displacement demand is significantly enhanced from Δ_e to Δ_{max} (calling for appropriate ductile detailing). The base shear corresponding to the formation of the first plastic hinge is shown as $V_{BR} = V_{B\mu}/R_R$, and the corresponding displacement is denoted as Δ_R; the increase in displacement demand from Δ_R to Δ_{max} is possible only if there is adequate redistribution of moments in the system and adequate plastic rotation capacities at the yield locations (and no premature failure due to shear, bond, etc.). Taking into account inherent overstrength in the system, the design base shear can now be assessed as $V_{Bdes} = V_{BR}/R_\Omega$, and the overall response reduction factor $R = V_{Be}/V_{Bdes}$ is then given by $R = R_\mu R_R R_\Omega$.

The IS 1893 (Part 1) Code recommends R values for different structural systems. These are tabulated in Table 19.12.

Vertical Acceleration Coefficient (A_v)

Earthquakes also generate vertical ground motions. Since the building usually carries gravity loads, the effect of vertical ground motion on the structure is often ignored in design. However, this can be critical for certain elements such as cantilevers, transfer girders and long-span beams. It is tacitly assumed that the vertical acceleration is two-thirds the peak horizontal acceleration and it has a similar spectral pattern. The expression for the *vertical acceleration coefficient*, A_v, specified by IS 1893 (Part 1) for buildings, is given below:

$$A_v = \frac{2}{3} \times \frac{Z}{2} \times \frac{I}{R} \times 2.5 \tag{19.31}$$

Table 19.12 *Response reduction factors for different structural systems*

Type of structural system	Response reduction factor (R)
RC and steel buildings with ordinary moment resisting frame (without ductile detailing), Buildings with ordinary RC structural walls, Buildings with ordinary RC structural walls with ordinary moment frames	3.0
Buildings with ordinary braced frame having concentric braces, Buildings with ductile RC structural walls, Buildings with ordinary RC structural walls with special moment frames, Buildings with ductile RC structural walls with ordinary moment frames	4.0
Buildings with special braced frame having concentric braces	4.5
RC and steel buildings with special moment resisting frame (with ductile detailing), Buildings with special braced frame having eccentric braces, Buildings with ductile RC structural walls with special moment frames	5.0

Comparing with the expression for the *design horizontal acceleration coefficient* A_h (Eq. 19.26), it follows that the value of A_v is two-thirds the value of A_h, for a relatively rigid structure, for which $S_a/g = 2.5$.

IS 1893 (Part 1) recommends that the effects of vertical earthquake shaking must necessarily be considered when the building is located in Seismic Zone IV or V, has irregularities (in plan or elevation), rests on soft soil, has long spans, or has large horizontal overhangs. The procedure for combining the vertical seismic load effects with the horizontal load effects is discussed in Section 19.3.6.

For determining the induced seismic forces on a building, the Code recommends two main methods, viz., *equivalent static method* and *dynamic analysis method*. However, the former is limited to regular, low-rise, relatively rigid buildings in Zone II.

19.3.3 Types of Seismic Analysis

The IS 1893 (Part 1) Code permits the use of (i) *equivalent static method* and (ii) *dynamic analysis method* to carry out seismic analysis of buildings. However, as mentioned earlier, Cl. 6.4.3 of the Code restricts the equivalent static method to the 'analysis of regular structures with approximate natural period T_a less than 0.4s'. For such low time periods, the peak value of $S_a/g = 2.5$ and is applicable for all soil types (See Figure 2a and Cl. 6.4.2 of Code).

The 2016 revision of IS 1893 (Part 1) restricts the use of the *equivalent static method* of analysis of buildings to 'regular buildings with approximate natural period T_a less than 0.4s' and 'lower than 15 m in Seismic Zone II'. For *all* buildings in higher seismic zones (III, IV and V), and for buildings in Seismic Zone II that are higher than 15 m, or are 'irregular', *linear dynamic analysis* shall be performed – to obtain the design base shear and its distribution to various levels along the height, and to various lateral load resisting elements.

Thus, for the majority of buildings in the country, the *dynamic analysis method* is applicable. It may be done either by the *time history method* (based on an appropriate ground motion, preferably compatible with the design acceleration spectrum in the desired range of natural periods) or the *response spectrum method.* In this chapter, the *equivalent static method* and the *response spectrum method* are discussed and demonstrated. The former method is relatively simple and approximate, while the latter is more rigorous and requires an understanding of structural dynamics. As mentioned earlier, the equivalent static method can be conveniently used for *preliminary design* of regular multi-storeyed framed RC buildings, prior to the use of the more rigorous response spectrum method for final design.

The main difference between the equivalent static method and the response spectrum method lies in the estimation of the base shear and the distribution of lateral forces over the height of the building. In the response spectrum method, the lateral forces account for the properties of the modes of natural vibration of the building, which depend on the distribution of mass and stiffness over the height of the building.

The lateral seismic force at any floor is assumed to act at its *centre of mass* and the total lateral load (equal to the base shear) on the building is effectively resisted by the moment-resisting frames (and shear walls, if any) in the direction under consideration. As in the case of wind loading, the whole system acts integrally, with the floor systems acting as horizontal diaphragms.

> In the case of a 'regular' building with relatively 'rigid' horizontal diaphragms at the floor levels, the entire building is expected to sway laterally in the direction under consideration. With a stiff regular horizontal diaphragm (floor system), if all the frames are more-or-less equally stiff (including infill walls), they will undergo the same lateral deflection (at any particular floor level), and hence will resist *equally* the total seismic load at any given floor level, regardless of the spacing of frames.

However, the effect of in-plane flexibility, if any, of the floor diaphragm must be accounted for, wherever necessary. IS 1893 (Part 1) gives details of the basis for deciding whether a floor diaphragm is flexible or not, depending on the extent of variation in the lateral displacements at the two ends of the building.

19.3.4 Equivalent Static Method

In the equivalent static method, the estimate of seismic forces is based on an approximate estimation of the fundamental period, and the distribution of forces along the height of the building is based on simple formulas appropriate for regular buildings. The base shear, V_B, which is the total horizontal force on the structure, is calculated using Eqs 19.25 and 19.26. The value of the *design acceleration coefficient,* (S_a/g), is required for Eq. 19.26. Although the value of S_a/g, in general, depends on the *approximate fundamental period* (T_a), the equivalent static method is limited to structures with $T_a < 0.4$s, for which $S_a/g = 2.5$ (vide Figure 2a of Code).

The computed value of base shear, V_B, has to be distributed along the height of the building, assuming a somewhat parabolic profile, depending on the magnitude of the seismic weight, W_i, of the ith floor located at a height h_i above the base. The lateral force at floor i, Q_i, is given by:

$$Q_i = \frac{W_i h_i^2}{\sum_{j=1}^{n} W_j h_j^2} V_B \tag{19.32}$$

Example 19.4

Estimate the seismic loads acting in the X- and Y- directions on a three storeyed building having the same plan dimensions as in Example 19.1 (also shown in Figure 19.15), located at Bengaluru and founded on medium type soil. Assume a live load of 3.0 kN/m², a floor finish of 1.5 kN/m², 230 mm thick brick walls at the outer perimeter and 115 mm thick brick walls as internal partitions (between columns). Assume 20% openings in all the walls and a density of 20 kN/m³ (including the cement plaster). Assume that all the ground floor columns are fixed to the base at a depth of 4.5 m, and that the walls of the ground floor are directly supported on separate wall footings (no plinth beams), as shown in Figure 19.15(b). Assume the slabs to be 175 mm thick and the beams to have a width of 300 mm and span/depth ratio of 10. Assume the unit weight of the RC members to be 25 kN/m³. Consider the building to be a special moment resisting frame system, with 400 mm × 400 mm columns.

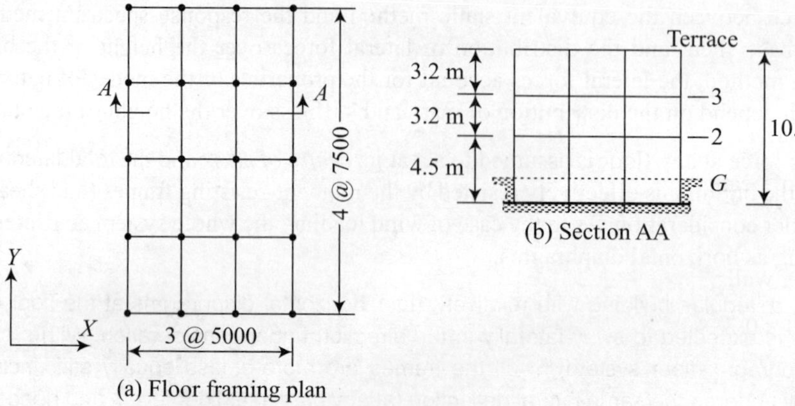

Fig 19.15 Building details for Example 19.4.

Solution

As the building is located in Bengaluru, as per Table 19.11, $Z = 0.10$.

The building is an office building, hence $I = 1.2$

For a special moment resisting frame type structural system, from Table 19.12, $R = 5.0$

Total height of building (from foundation level) = 4.5 + 3.2 + 3.2 = 10.9 m

Lateral dimensions of the building along X (l_x) = 15 m

Lateral dimensions of the building along Y (l_y) = 30 m

Estimation of fundamental period and design acceleration coefficients

As per Eq. 19.30, T_a can be estimated in both X and Y directions.

$$T_{ax} = \frac{0.09 \times 10.9}{\sqrt{15}} = 0.253 \text{ s}$$

$$T_{ay} = \frac{0.09 \times 10.9}{\sqrt{30}} = 0.179 \text{ s}$$

As the approximate time period is less than 0.4 s (in both X and Y directions) and as the building is located in seismic zone II, and has a height less than 15 m, the *equivalent static method* can be used to estimate the seismic forces, as per IS 1893 (Part 1).

The corresponding *design acceleration coefficients*, $S_{ax}/g = S_{ay}/g = 2.5$ (as per Code Figure 2a, for $T_a < 0.4$ s, $Sa/g = 2.5$ for all soil types).

Estimation of seismic weight of the structure

[For estimating the weight, the overall exterior dimensions are taken as 15.4 m × 30.4 m. For ease, in the calculations below, the beam/wall lengths are taken (conservatively) as their full lengths including column overlap.]

$$\text{Slab weight per floor} = 25 \text{ kN/m}^3 \times (15.4 \times 30.4 \times 0.175) \text{ m}^3 = 2048 \text{ kN}$$

Finish load per floor = 1.5 kN/m^2 × (15.4 × 30.4) m^2 = 702 kN

Reduced live load per floor = 0.25 × 3.0 kN/m^2 × (15.4 × 30.4) m^2 = 351 kN

Beams are 300 mm wide and have a span/depth ratio of 10 (i.e., 500 mm and 750 mm deep in X- and Y- directions respectively).

Additional weight of beams per floor = 25 × 0.3 × [{(0.5-0.175) × 15.4 × 5} + {(0.75-0.175) × 30.4 × 4}]

= 712 kN

Self-weight of outer walls (230 mm thick), including 20% openings, per storey

= 20 × 0.23 × 0.8 × [{(3.2 – 0.5) × 15.4 × 2} + {(3.2 – 0.75) × 30.4 × 2}] = 854 kN

Self-weight of partition walls (115 mm thick), including 20% openings, per storey

= 20 × 0.115 × 0.8 × [{(3.2 – 0.5) × 15.4 × 3} + {(3.2 – 0.75) × 30.4 × 2}] = 504 kN

Total weight of walls per storey = 854 + 504 = 1358 kN

Self-weight of all walls in G/1st storey (floor slab at level 4.5 m) = 1358/2 = 679 kN

Self-weight of all walls in 2nd storey (floor slab at level 7.7 m) = 1358 kN

Self-weight of all walls in 3rd storey (roof slab at level 10.9 m) = 1358/2 = 679 kN

Self-weight of all 20 columns in G/1st storey = 25 × 0.4 × 0.4 × (3.2/2 + 4.5/2) × 20 = 308 kN

Self-weight of all 20 columns in 2nd storey = 25 × 0.4 × 0.4 × (3.2/2 + 3.2/2) × 20 = 256 kN

Self-weight of all 20 columns in 3rd storey = 25 × 0.4 × 0.4 × 3.2/2 × 20 = 128 kN

Seismic weight of G/1st floor W_1 (at level 4.5 m) = (2048 + 702 + 351 + 712) + 679 + 308

= 3813 + 667 + 308 = 4788 kN

Seismic weight of 2nd floor W_2 (at level 7.7 m) = 3813 + 1358 + 256 = 5427 kN

Seismic weight of 3rd floor W_3 (at level 10.9 m) = 3813 + 667 + 128 = 4608 kN

Total seismic weight of the building $W = W_1 + W_2 + W_3$ = 4788 + 5427 + 4608 = 14823 kN

Horizontal acceleration coefficient and base shear

In X direction (Eq. 19.26): $A_{hx} = \dfrac{0.10}{2} \times \dfrac{1.2}{5} \times 2.5 = 0.03$

In Y direction: $A_{hy} = \dfrac{0.10}{2} \times \dfrac{1.2}{5} \times 2.5 = 0.03$

Base shear

In X direction (Eq. 19.25): V_{Bx} = 0.03 × 14823 = 445 kN

In Y direction: V_{By} = 0.03 × 14823 = 445 kN

Distribution of lateral forces along the height of the building using Eq. 19.32:

$$Q_1 = \frac{4788 \times 4.5^2}{4788 \times 4.5^2 + 5427 \times 7.7^2 + 4608 \times 10.9^2} \times 445 = 45 \text{ kN}$$

$$Q_2 = \frac{5427 \times 7.7^2}{4788 \times 4.5^2 + 5427 \times 7.7^2 + 4608 \times 10.9^2} \times 445 = 148 \text{ kN}$$

$$Q_3 = \frac{4608 \times 10.9^2}{4788 \times 4.5^2 + 5427 \times 7.7^2 + 4608 \times 10.9^2} \times 445 = 252 \text{ kN}$$

The same force distribution is valid in both X- and Y-directions as the base shear is the same in both directions. Figure 19.16 shows the distribution of forces along the height of the building in X and Y directions.

It may be noted that the storey forces do not change if the soil type changes to hard or soft, as the S_a/g values are the same for all three soil types in both directions.

Although the overall seismic force distribution is the same in both X and Y directions, the actual force per frame will be less along the X direction (as there are 5 frames in this direction), compared to the Y direction (4 frames).

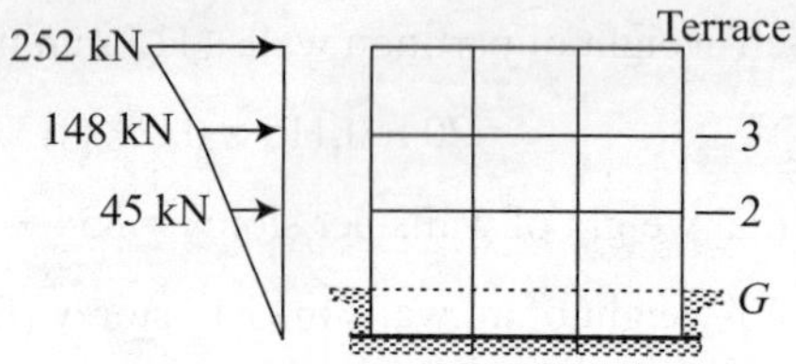

Fig 19.16 Distribution of forces along the height in X and Y directions in Example 19.4.

Example 19.5

Repeat the problem in Example 19.4, assuming the building to be a hospital building.

Solution

If it is a hospital building, then the only change is in the importance factor. $I = 1.5$ for a hospital building.

Hence,

$$A_{hx} = A_{hy} = \frac{0.10}{2} \times \frac{1.5}{5} \times 2.5 = 0.0375$$

$$V_{Bx} = V_{By} = 0.0375 \times 14823 = 556 \text{ kN}$$

Distribution of lateral forces along the height of the building is shown in Figure 19.17.

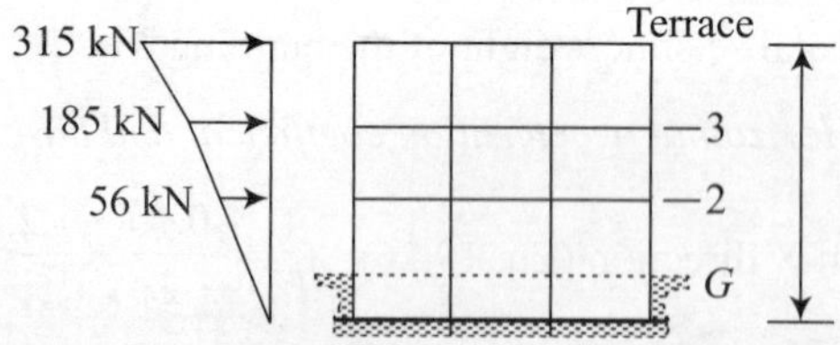

Fig 19.17 Distribution of forces along the height in X and Y directions in Example 19.5.

19.3.5 Response Spectrum Method

The *response spectrum method* of analysis may be applied to estimate the seismic forces on any building using the design acceleration spectrum given in IS 1893 (Part 1) - Figure 2(b) or any site-specific design acceleration spectrum. The Code recommends such an analysis (or alternatively, time history analysis) for all buildings in seismic Zones III, IV and V, and also for buildings higher than 15 m or with $T_a \geq 0.4$ s in Zone II.

This method explicitly accounts for the contributions of higher modes of oscillation (other than the fundamental mode), which in some cases, can significantly affect the response of the structure. In this method, the response of a Multi-Degree-of-Freedom (MDOF) system is expressed as the superposition of various modal responses, each modal response being determined separately from the spectral analysis of single-degree-of-freedom (SDOF) system. The designer is expected to know the details of the mode superposition method of analysis in structural dynamics; this is not covered here as it is beyond the scope of this book. The steps involved are summarised below, and demonstrated with a numerical example. In design practice, this can be conveniently done using standard commercial softwares.

As a first step, the *mass matrix* and the *stiffness matrix* are generated for the lumped mass model (including storey stiffnesses), and the eigen values (natural frequencies) and eigen vectors (mode shapes) of the structure are estimated, considering the undamped free vibration condition. If the analysis is done manually (which is not conveniently possible if the number of storeys exceed 3), the floors can be assumed to be relatively rigid (shear building behaviour), whereby the storey stiffness (in X- or Y-direction) is obtained approximately as a simple summation of the individual column stiffnesses ($12\ EI/L^3$) [Ref. 19.17]. This can be more accurately done in computer-aided analysis (using commercial finite element software), including the flexibility of the floor beams.

The modal mass m_k of the kth mode is calculated as

$$m_k = \frac{\left[\sum_{i=1}^{n} W_i \phi_{ik}\right]^2}{g \sum_{i=1}^{n} W_i (\phi_{ik})^2} \tag{19.33}$$

where g is the acceleration due to gravity, ϕ_{ik} is the mode shape coefficient at floor i in mode k and W_i is the seismic weight of ith storey and n is the number of storeys.

The mode participation factor P_k of the kth mode is calculated as

$$P_k = \frac{\sum_{i=1}^{n} W_i \phi_{ik}}{\sum_{i=1}^{n} W_i (\phi_{ik})^2} \tag{19.34}$$

The design lateral force Q_{ik} at each floor in each mode is calculated as

$$Q_{ik} = A_k \phi_{ik} P_k W_i \tag{19.35}$$

where A_k is the horizontal acceleration coefficient of mode k which is estimated from the time period (T_k) of kth mode.

$$T_k = \frac{2\pi}{\omega_k} \tag{19.36}$$

ω_k is the natural frequency of kth mode, estimated in the first step.

The storey shear in each mode V_{ik} acting in storey i in mode k is calculated as

$$V_{ik} = \sum_{j=i+1}^{n} Q_{ik} \tag{19.37}$$

These individual storey shears can be combined for all modes using the modal combination rules prescribed in the Code. The most common combination rules are the *Square Root of Sum of Squares* (SRSS) method (used when the building does not have closely spaced modes), the *Complete Quadratic Combination* (CQC) method and the *Absolute* (ABS) method (used when the building has a few closely-spaced modes).

The lateral forces in each storey can be obtained (treating the building as a vertical cantilever) as

$$F_{roof} = V_{roof} \tag{19.38a}$$

$$F_i = V_i - V_{i+1} \tag{19.38b}$$

where F_{roof} is the design lateral force at roof level, F_i is the force at floor i. For a building with n storeys, for the first storey, $i = 1$, and $F_n = F_{roof}$.

IS 1893 (Part 1) recommends that, in order to account for the degradation in flexural stiffness due to cracking, for columns 70 per cent of the gross moment of inertia shall be considered, while for beams, only 35 per cent should be considered. This will result in a more correct assessment of the lateral deflections, although it will also imply increased time periods, typically resulting in lower estimates of horizontal acceleration coefficient, S_a/g, and lower base shear. In order to bring in conservatism† in the estimation of seismic forces, the Code recommends that 'the design base shear V_B estimated shall not be less than the design base shear $\bar{V}_B$ calculated using the approximate fundamental time period T_a'.

In case the calculated V_B is less than $\bar{V}_B$, then all the force response quantities shall be scaled up (Code Cl. 7.7.3) by a scale factor, $\bar{V}_B/V_B$. Typically, the scale factor is much greater than unity. Hence, if the objective of the analysis is limited to estimating the seismic forces on the building (and not the lateral displacement), it generally suffices to consider the gross section properties of the various members. Furthermore, on account of the scale factor, the overall base shear (which is equal to the storey shear in the lowest storey) is likely to be the same whether the building is analysed by the simple *equivalent static method* or the more rigorous *response spectrum* method. The only difference will be with respect to the distribution of seismic forces along the height of the building. Typically, the seismic force will be higher at the roof level in the case of the equivalent static method, compared to the response spectrum method, as demonstrated in Example 19.6.

Example 19.6

Repeat the building in Example 19.4, using the response spectrum method of analysis.

Solution

Determination of natural frequencies and mode shapes

Generation of mass matrix:

Using the concept of lumped mass model, the building can be divided into three lumped masses (seismic mass) comprising M_1, M_2, M_3 of the three storeys respectively. From Example 19.4,

$$M_1 = 4788/9.81 = 488 \text{ ton}$$

$$M_2 = 5427/9.81 = 553 \text{ ton}$$

$$M_3 = 4608/9.81 = 470 \text{ ton}$$

† Elements such as masonry infill walls can significantly increase the lateral stiffness of the building; this is often ignored in practice. The increased stiffness will reduce the natural period, and thereby increase the estimated value of S_a/g and base shear.

$$\text{Mass matrix } M = \begin{bmatrix} 488 & 0 & 0 \\ 0 & 553 & 0 \\ 0 & 0 & 470 \end{bmatrix} \text{ton}$$

The total lateral stiffness of each storey is the sum of lateral stiffness of all 20 columns in the given direction. Assuming a shear building behaviour, the storey stiffness can be estimated approximately as

$$k = \frac{12EI}{L^3} \times 20$$

$$E = 5000\sqrt{25} = 25000 \text{ MPa} = 25\times10^6 \text{ kN/m}^2$$

$$I \text{ of each column} = \frac{0.4 \times 0.4^3}{12} = 2.133 \times 10^{-3} \text{ m}^4$$

$$k_1 = 20 \times \frac{12 \times 25 \times 10^6 \times 2.133 \times 10^{-3}}{4.5^3} = 140466.4 \text{ kN/m}$$

$$k_2 = 20 \times \frac{12 \times 25 \times 10^6 \times 2.133 \times 10^{-3}}{3.2^3} = 390625 \text{ kN/m}$$

$$k_3 = k_2 = 390625 \text{ kN/m}$$

As all the columns are assumed to be square, the column stiffness, and hence the storey stiffness is the same in both X and Y directions.

$$\text{Stiffness matrix } K = \begin{bmatrix} k_1 + k_2 & -k_2 & 0 \\ -k_2 & k_2 + k_3 & -k_3 \\ 0 & -k_3 & k_3 \end{bmatrix} = \begin{bmatrix} 531091.4 & -390625 & 0 \\ -390625 & 781250 & -390625 \\ 0 & -390625 & 390625 \end{bmatrix} \text{kN/m}$$

Determining the eigen values (ω) and eigen vectors (ϕ),

$$\omega^2 = \begin{bmatrix} 76.3 & 0 & 0 \\ 0 & 968.5 & 0 \\ 0 & 0 & 2287 \end{bmatrix}$$

$$\phi = \begin{bmatrix} -0.0209 & 0.0336 & -0.0220 \\ -0.0265 & 0.0050 & 0.0329 \\ -0.0291 & -0.0304 & -0.0188 \end{bmatrix}$$

The corresponding mode shapes are shown in Figure 19.18

The natural period can be estimated from Eq. 19.36:

$$T = \begin{bmatrix} 0.72 & 0 & 0 \\ 0 & 0.20 & 0 \\ 0 & 0 & 0.13 \end{bmatrix} \text{s}$$

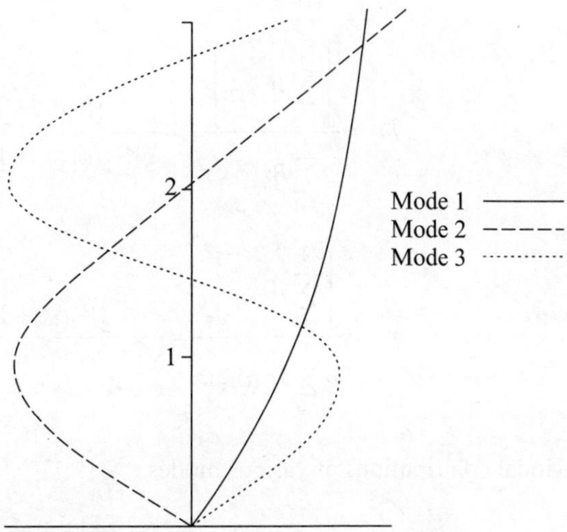

Fig 19.18 Mode shapes obtained in Example 19.6.

[It is noteworthy that the fundamental time period obtained by this analysis, equal to 0.72 s (in both directions), is significantly higher than the approximate T_a values of 0.253 s and 0.179 s along the X- and Y-directions respectively, obtained in Example 19.4].

The modal participation factor P_k of mode k is estimated using Eq. 19.34.

$$P_1 = \frac{\sum_{i=1}^{3} W_i \phi_{i1}}{\sum_{i=1}^{3} W_i (\phi_{i1})^2} = \frac{W_1\phi_{11} + W_2\phi_{21} + W_3\phi_{31}}{W_1(\phi_{11})^2 + W_2(\phi_{21})^2 + W_3(\phi_{31})^2} = -38$$

$$P_2 = \frac{\sum_{i=1}^{3} W_i \phi_{i2}}{\sum_{i=1}^{3} W_i (\phi_{i2})^2} = \frac{W_1\phi_{12} + W_2\phi_{22} + W_3\phi_{32}}{W_1(\phi_{12})^2 + W_2(\phi_{22})^2 + W_3(\phi_{32})^2} = 4.9$$

$$P_3 = \frac{\sum_{i=1}^{3} W_i \phi_{i3}}{\sum_{i=1}^{3} W_i (\phi_{i3})^2} = \frac{W_1\phi_{13} + W_2\phi_{23} + W_3\phi_{33}}{W_1(\phi_{13})^2 + W_2(\phi_{23})^2 + W_3(\phi_{33})^2} = -1.3$$

The modal mass m_k of mode k is estimated using Eq. 19.33.

$$m_1 = \frac{\left[\sum_{i=1}^{3} W_i \phi_{i1}\right]^2}{g\sum_{i=1}^{3} W_i (\phi_{i1})^2} = \frac{[W_1\phi_{11} + W_2\phi_{21} + W_3\phi_{31}]^2}{g[W_1(\phi_{11})^2 + W_2(\phi_{21})^2 + W_3(\phi_{31})^2]} = 1443.5$$

$$m_2 = \frac{\left[\sum_{i=1}^{3} W_i \phi_{i2}\right]^2}{g\sum_{i=1}^{3} W_i (\phi_{i2})^2} = \frac{[W_1\phi_{12} + W_2\phi_{22} + W_3\phi_{32}]^2}{g[W_1(\phi_{12})^2 + W_2(\phi_{22})^2 + W_3(\phi_{32})^2]} = 23.3$$

$$m_3 = \frac{\left[\sum_{i=1}^{3} W_i \phi_{i3}\right]^2}{g\sum_{i=1}^{3} W_i (\phi_{i3})^2} = \frac{[W_1\phi_{13} + W_2\phi_{23} + W_3\phi_{33}]^2}{g[W_1(\phi_{13})^2 + W_2(\phi_{23})^2 + W_3(\phi_{33})^2]} = 1.8$$

Modal contributions of various modes

$$\text{Mode 1, } \frac{m_1}{m_1 + m_2 + m_3} = \frac{1443.5}{1468.6} = 0.98 = 98\%$$

$$\text{Mode 2, } \frac{m_2}{m_1+m_2+m_3} = \frac{23.3}{1468.6} = 0.016 = 1.6\%$$

$$\text{Mode 3, } \frac{m_3}{m_1+m_2+m_3} = \frac{1.8}{1468.6} = 0.0012 = 0.12\%$$

The horizontal acceleration coefficient in each mode A_{hk} can be estimated using Eq. 19.26. Using the periods calculated above, the S_a/g values for the medium soil can be calculated using Eq. 19.27(b), and are obtained as 1.92 for the first mode and 2.5 for the second and third modes.

$$A_{h1} = \frac{Z}{2}\frac{I}{R}\frac{S_{a1}}{g} = \frac{0.1}{2}\frac{1.2}{5}1.92 = 0.023$$

$$A_{h2} = \frac{Z}{2}\frac{I}{R}\frac{S_{a2}}{g} = \frac{0.1}{2}\frac{1.2}{5}2.5 = 0.03$$

$$A_{h3} = \frac{Z}{2}\frac{I}{R}\frac{S_{a3}}{g} = \frac{0.1}{2}\frac{1.2}{5}2.5 = 0.03$$

The lateral force at each floor in each mode can be estimated using Eq. 19.35.

$$\text{In 1}^{\text{st}}\text{ mode: } Q_{i1} = \begin{Bmatrix} A_{h1}P_1\phi_{11}W_1 \\ A_{h1}P_1\phi_{21}W_2 \\ A_{h1}P_1\phi_{31}W_3 \end{Bmatrix} = \begin{Bmatrix} 85.23 \\ 121.96 \\ 114.06 \end{Bmatrix} \text{kN}$$

$$\text{In 2}^{\text{nd}}\text{ mode: } Q_{i2} = \begin{Bmatrix} A_{h2}P_2\phi_{12}W_1 \\ A_{h2}P_2\phi_{22}W_2 \\ A_{h2}P_2\phi_{32}W_3 \end{Bmatrix} = \begin{Bmatrix} 23 \\ 3.9 \\ -20 \end{Bmatrix} \text{kN}$$

$$\text{In 3}^{\text{rd}}\text{ mode: } Q_{i3} = \begin{Bmatrix} A_{h3}P_3\phi_{13}W_1 \\ A_{h3}P_3\phi_{23}W_2 \\ A_{h3}P_3\phi_{33}W_3 \end{Bmatrix} = \begin{Bmatrix} 4.16 \\ -7.05 \\ 3.42 \end{Bmatrix} \text{kN}$$

The storey shears in each mode can be estimated using Eq. 19.37.

$$\text{In 1}^{\text{st}}\text{ mode: } V_{i1} = \sum_{j=i+1}^{n} Q_{i1} = \begin{Bmatrix} Q_{11}+Q_{21}+Q_{31} \\ Q_{21}+Q_{31} \\ Q_{31} \end{Bmatrix} = \begin{Bmatrix} 321.25 \\ 236.02 \\ 114.06 \end{Bmatrix} \text{kN}$$

$$\text{In 2}^{\text{nd}}\text{ mode: } V_{i2} = \sum_{j=i+1}^{n} Q_{i2} = \begin{Bmatrix} Q_{12}+Q_{22}+Q_{32} \\ Q_{22}+Q_{32} \\ Q_{32} \end{Bmatrix} = \begin{Bmatrix} 6.87 \\ -16.13 \\ -20.02 \end{Bmatrix} \text{kN}$$

$$\text{In 3}^{\text{rd}}\text{ mode: } V_{i3} = \sum_{j=i+1}^{n} Q_{i3} = \begin{Bmatrix} Q_{13}+Q_{23}+Q_{33} \\ Q_{23}+Q_{33} \\ Q_{33} \end{Bmatrix} = \begin{Bmatrix} 0.53 \\ -3.64 \\ 3.42 \end{Bmatrix} \text{kN}$$

Using the modal combination rule SRSS, the peak response quantities due to all modes can be calculated as,

$$V_1 = \sqrt{\left[V_{11}^2 + V_{12}^2 + V_{13}^2\right]} = 321 \text{ kN}$$

$$V_2 = \sqrt{\left[V_{21}^2 + V_{22}^2 + V_{23}^2\right]} = 237 \text{ kN}$$

$$V_3 = \sqrt{\left[V_{31}^2 + V_{32}^2 + V_{33}^2\right]} = 116 \text{ kN}$$

The storey forces can be determined using Eq. 19.38.

$$F_{\text{roof}} = F_3 = V_3 = 116 \text{ kN}$$

$$F_{\text{floor 2}} = F_2 = V_2 - V_3 = 237 - 116 = 121 \text{ kN}$$

$$F_{\text{floor1}} = F_1 = V_1 - V_2 = 321 - 237 = 84 \text{ kN}$$

The base shear $V_B = V_1 = 321$ kN. The base shear, $\bar{V}_B$, calculated using the empirical method suggested by the Code, and demonstrated in Example 19.4, is 445 kN. Hence, as discussed in Section 19.3.5, the base shear calculated using the response spectrum method should be scaled up to match the base shear estimated using the empirical method.

The scale factor = 445/321 = 1.386. All the storey forces need to be scaled up accordingly, as shown in Figure 19.19. The forces in X and Y directions remain the same, as the storey stiffness is the same in both directions.

It can be seen that the distribution of forces along the height of the building is significantly different using the equivalent static method and the response spectrum method, although the base shear is the same for both methods (refer Example 19.4).

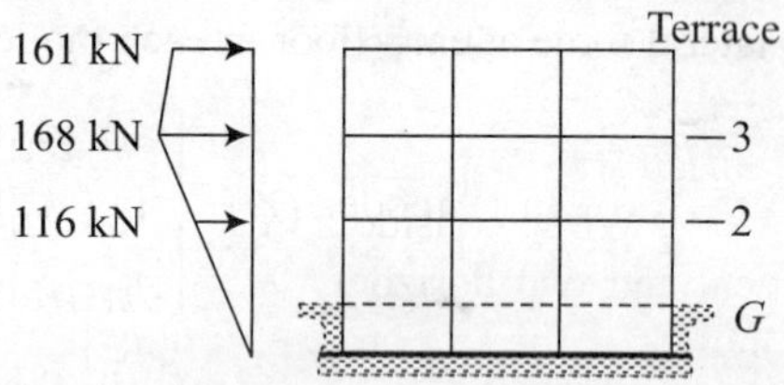

Fig 19.19 Distribution of forces along the height in X and Y directions in Example 19.6.

Example 19.7

Verify the results for the building analysed in Example 19.6 using a commercial software. (a) Analyse the structure using the gross moment of inertia properties and (b) with cracked section modifiers.

Solution

The building is analysed using ETABS commercial software.

The results of the analysis are tabulated below:

Parameter	Gross stiffness properties	Cracked stiffness properties
Time period in X direction	0.93 s	1.25 s
Time period in Y direction	0.83 s	1.07 s
Base shear in X direction	266 kN	193 kN
Base shear in Y direction	301 kN	232 kN

It can be seen that the time period in X and Y directions (in individual fundamental modes) is different from what was obtained in Example 19.6. This is due to the approximation made in the stiffness calculated in Example 19.6. Further, when cracked stiffness properties are applied in the model, the time period increases, leading to a reduction in the base shears. However, it should be noted that the base shears obtained using response spectrum analysis need to be suitably scaled up (Code Cl. 7.7.3), as demonstrated in Example 19.6.

19.3.6 Directional Combination

In the above Examples involving 'regular' rectangular buildings, the columns and frames were conveniently oriented in two mutually orthogonal (*X*- and *Y*-) directions. For such cases, it suffices to design the structure for the seismic forces estimated considering one horizontal direction at a time (and not both directions simultaneously), as in the case of wind loading. Also, as in the case of wind loading, the lateral load resisting system had to account for reversal of direction of loading in both *X*- and *Y*- directions. The appropriate partial load factors discussed in Chapter 3 should be considered, while combining lateral loads with gravity loads.

However, IS 1893 (Part 1) clarifies that when the lateral load resisting elements (walls and columns) are not oriented along mutually orthogonal directions, the building 'shall be designed for the simultaneous effects due to full design earthquake load in one horizontal direction plus 30 per cent of design earthquake load along the other horizontal direction'. This is commonly known as the *100:30 rule*.

Furthermore, in situations where the vertical earthquake load effects also have to be considered (as in irregular buildings, or buildings located in soft soil or in Seismic Zones IV and V), as discussed earlier, the *100:30:30 rule* shall apply, while considering the three directional earthquake ground shaking, according to the Code. While considering 100 per cent of the seismic load effect in any one of the three directions (one vertical and two horizontal), all possible combinations including 30 per cent of the maximum responses computed for the other two directions shall be considered.

As an alternative, the Code also proposes the SRSS method (square root of the sum of the squares of all three components) for the combined effect of the three directional components.

REVIEW QUESTIONS

19.1 What are the major similarities and differences in wind and seismic forces acting on buildings?

19.2 How does wind speed increase with height above ground in different terrains?

19.3 What is the difference between *gust* wind speed and *mean hourly* wind speed, and how are they related?

19.4 How are buildings identified as being dynamically *wind-sensitive*? How is the estimation of wind forces different for such buildings, compared to 'rigid' buildings?

19.5 What is meant by a *return period* for wind speed? How does the Code account for higher return periods (for important structures) in the estimation of design wind speeds?

19.6 How is *basic wind speed* defined in IS: 875 (Part 3): 2015? How is it different from *design wind speed*?

19.7 What are the factors considered in the estimation of *design wind pressure*, as per IS: 875 (Part 3): 2015?

19.8 What is meant by *force coefficient*, and how is it used to estimate wind force on a 'rigid' building?

19.9 Describe briefly the main aspects of earthquake-resistant design philosophy, underlying design codes of practice.

19.10 What are the four 'main desirable attributes' of an earthquake-resistant building, according to IS 1893 (Part 1): 2016?

19.11 What is meant by the terms, *peak ground acceleration* and *spectral acceleration*?

19.12 What is meant by the terms, *zone factor* and *importance factor*, in the estimation of seismic forces?

19.13 How does the *soil type* affect the estimation of seismic forces?

19.14 What is meant by *response reduction factor*? Why are different factors prescribed by IS 1893 for different structural systems?

19.15 What is meant by *equivalent static method* of analysis? What are the restrictions imposed by IS 1893 with respect to use of this method?

19.16 Explain briefly the *response spectrum method* of analysis for estimation of seismic forces.

19.17 What effectively is likely to be the difference in the estimation of seismic forces according to the equivalent static method and the response spectrum method, as per IS 1893?

PROBLEMS

19.1 The framing plan for a proposed 4-storey school building (with square plan) in Bengaluru is shown in Figure 19.20. Compute the lateral wind forces to be used in the design of the building at the various floor levels, assuming the 'general' class building, 'Category 2' terrain and level ground. Consider the floor-to-floor height to be 3.2 m.

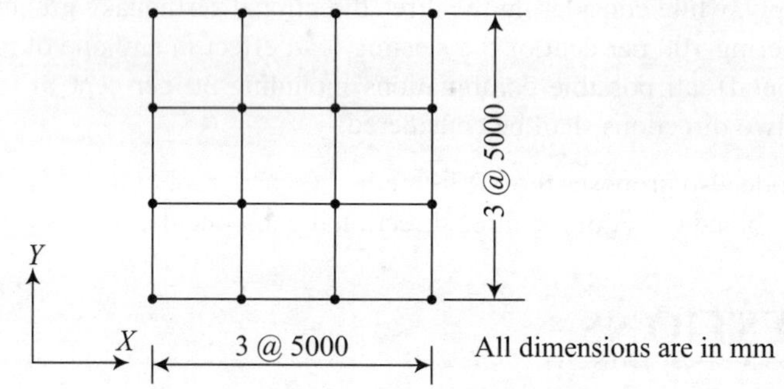

Fig. 19.20 Example 19.1.

19.2 Repeat Problem 19.1, considering the building to be shifted to Chennai and located atop a hill with a slope of 10°.

19.3 Estimate the seismic forces to be considered in design for the building in Problem 19.1, assuming it to be 3-storeyed and founded on hard soil. Assume a live load of 5.0 kN/m^2, a floor finish of 2.0 kN/m^2, and 230 mm thick brick walls at the outer perimeter and 115 mm thick brick walls as internal partitions (between columns). Assume 25% openings in all the walls and a density of 20 kN/m^3 (including the cement plaster). Assume that all the ground floor columns are fixed to the base at a depth of 1.2 m below ground, and that the walls of the ground floor are directly supported on separate wall footings (no plinth beams). Assume the slabs to be 175 mm thick and the beams to have a width of 300 mm and span/depth ratio of 10. Assume the unit weight of the RC members to be 25 kN/m^3. Consider the building to be a special moment resisting frame system, with 400 mm × 400 mm columns. Apply the *equivalent static method.*

19.4 Repeat Problem 19.3 by the *response spectrum method.*

19.5 The framing details for a proposed 7-storey hotel building in Kolkata are shown in Figure 19.21. Compute the lateral wind forces to be used in the design of the building in *X*- and *Y*-directions (as shown) at the various floor levels, assuming the 'general' class building, 'Category 2' terrain and level ground. Consider the floor-to-floor height to be 3.2 m.

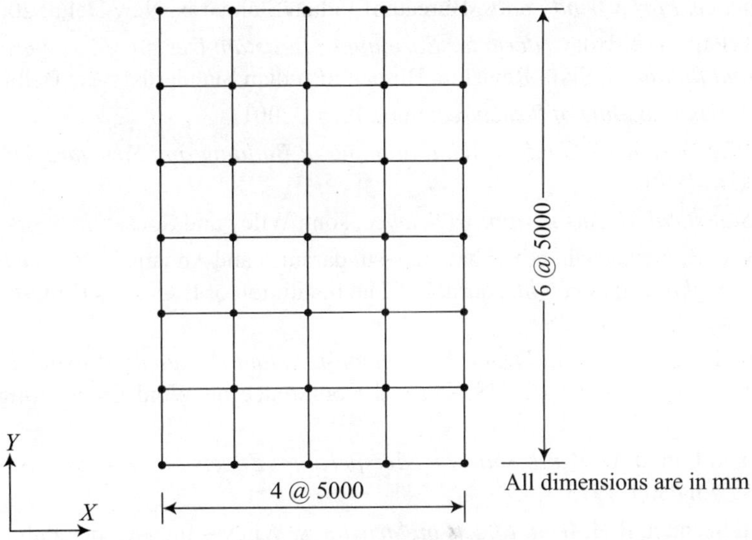

Fig 19.21 Example 19.5.

19.6 Estimate the seismic forces (for preliminary design) acting in the *X*- and *Y*- directions for the building in Figure 19.21, by the *equivalent static method,* assuming it to be founded on medium type soil. Assume a live load of 5.0 kN/m^2, a floor finish of 2.0 kN/m^2, and 230 mm thick brick walls at the outer perimeter and 115 mm thick brick walls as internal partitions (between columns). Assume 25% openings in all the walls and a density of 20 kN/m^3 (including the cement plaster). Assume that all the ground floor columns are fixed to the base at a depth of 1.2 m below ground, and that the walls of the ground floor are directly supported on separate wall footings (no plinth beams). Assume the slabs to be 175 mm thick and the beams to have a width of 300 mm and span/depth ratio of 10. Assume the unit weight of the RC members to be 25 kN/m^3. Consider the building to be a special moment resisting frame system, with 700 mm × 700 mm columns.

19.7 Consider the building in Problem 19.6 to be three-storeyed and located at Bhopal, with 400 mm × 400 mm columns, all other data remaining the same. Estimate the seismic forces by *equivalent static method* and *response spectrum method* and compare the results.

19.8 Consider the 10-storey office building in Chennai in Example 19.1 (Figure 19.9). Using the *equivalent static method,* for a preliminary design, estimate the lateral seismic forces in the *X*- and *Y*-directions at the various floor levels. Assume all other gravity load data (including slab and beam sizes) as given in Example 19.4, except for column sizes, which may be assumed to be 800 mm × 800 mm.

REFERENCES

19.1 Cherry, S, Ward, H S and Dalgliesh, W A, *Earthquake and Wind Loads in Building Design*, The Engineering Journal, Vol. 46, No. 9, September 1963, p. 27–35

19.2 ___ IS 875 (Part 3) (2015): *Design Loads (Other than Earthquake) for Buildings and Structures – Code of Practice, Part 3 Wind Loads*, Bureau of Indian Standards, New Delhi, 2009

19.3 ___ IS 1893 (Part 1) (2016): *Criteria for Earthquake Resistant Design of Structures, Part 1 – General Provisions and Buildings*, Sixth Revision, Bureau of Indian Standards, New Delhi, 2016

19.4 Holmes, J D, *Wind Loading of Structures*, Spon Press, 2001

19.5 Cook, N J, *The Designer's Guide to Wind Loading of Building and Structures, Part 2*, Butterworths Publishers, UK, 1990

19.6 Bury, K V, *Statistical Models in Applied Science*, John Wiley and Sons, New York, 1975

19.7 Venkateswarlu, B, Arunachalam, S, Shanmugasundaram, J and Annamalai, G, *Variation of wind speed with terrain roughness and height*, Journal of The Institution of Engineers (India) – Civil Engineering Division, 69, pp. 228–234, 1989

19.8 Lam, P R and Lam, L C H, *Wind Data for Typhoon-resistant Design of Structures in South China Sea Region*, Proceedings of the Fifth US National Conference on Wind Engineering, Lubbock, Texas, 1985

19.9 Ghoicel, D and Lungu, D, *Wind, Snow and Temperature Effects on Structures Based on Probability*, Abacus Press, England, 1975

19.10 Simiu, E and Scanlan, R H, *Wind Effects on Structures*, Wiley – Interscience Publications, New York, 1996

19.11 Davenport, A G, *Gust Loading Factors*, Journal of Structural Division, ASCE, Vol. 93, No. ST3, 1967, pp 11–33

19.12 Taranath, B S, *Wind and Earthquake Resistant Buildings – Structural Analysis and Design*, Marcel Dekker, New York

19.13 FEMA 356, *Pre-standard and Commentary for the Seismic Rehabilitation of Buildings*, American Society of Civil Engineers, USA, 2000

19.14 Manohar, S and Madhekar S, *Seismic Design of RC Buildings*. Springer India, New Delhi, India; 2015

19.15 Chakrabarti, A, Menon, D, and Sengupta, A K (editors), *Handbook on Seismic Retrofit of Buildings*. Alpha Science International, Limited, 2008

19.16 Agarwal, P and Shrikhande, M, *Earthquake Resistant Design of Structures*, PHI Learning, New Delhi, 2011

19.17 Paz, M and Kim, Y H, *Structural Dynamics*, Springer, 1991

WEB APPENDIX

A

Analysis and Design Aids

Table A.1 ANALYSIS AIDS (WSM) for singly reinforced rectangular beam sections Values of M_{all}/bd^2 (MPa) for given values of p_t

(a) M 20, M 25 concrete grades

(b) M 30, M 35 concrete grades

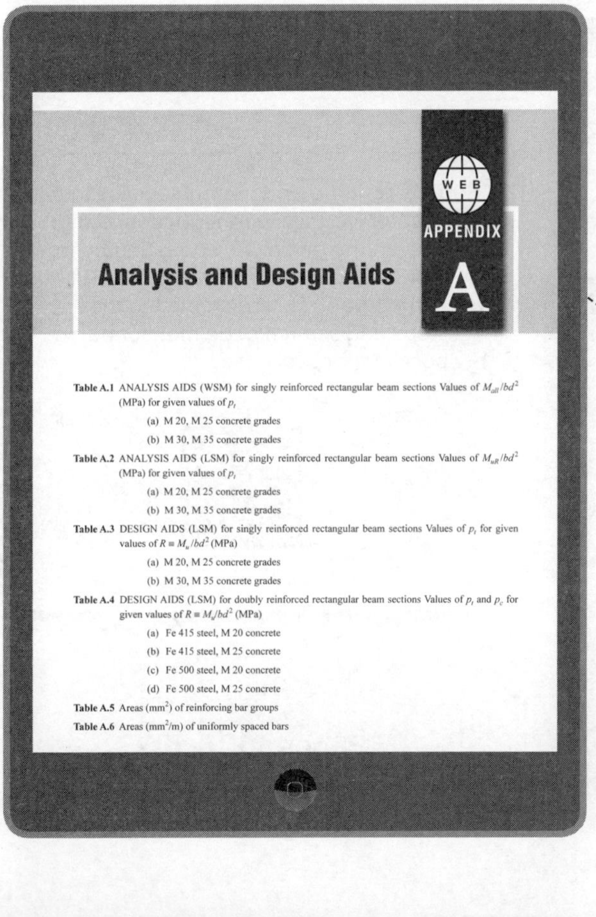

WEB APPENDIX A

Analysis and Design Aids

Table A.1 ANALYSIS AIDS (WSM) for singly reinforced rectangular beam sections Values of M_{all}/bd^2 (MPa) for given values of p_t

(a) M 20, M 25 concrete grades

(b) M 30, M 35 concrete grades

Table A.2 ANALYSIS AIDS (LSM) for singly reinforced rectangular beam sections Values of M_{uR}/bd^2 (MPa) for given values of p_t

(a) M 20, M 25 concrete grades

(b) M 30, M 35 concrete grades

Table A.3 DESIGN AIDS (LSM) for singly reinforced rectangular beam sections Values of p_t for given values of $R \equiv M_u/bd^2$ (MPa)

(a) M 20, M 25 concrete grades

(b) M 30, M 35 concrete grades

Table A.4 DESIGN AIDS (LSM) for doubly reinforced rectangular beam sections Values of p_t and p_c for given values of $R \equiv M_u/bd^2$ (MPa)

(a) Fe 415 steel, M 20 concrete

(b) Fe 415 steel, M 25 concrete

(c) Fe 500 steel, M 20 concrete

(d) Fe 500 steel, M 25 concrete

Table A.5 Areas (mm^2) of reinforcing bar groups

Table A.6 Areas (mm^2/m) of uniformly spaced bars

To read more and get free access to full chapter, visit **www.mheducation.co.in** or scan the given QR Code. Search for ***Reinforced Concrete Design*** or ISBN of the book, and register using the steps and scratch code mentioned on back inner cover.

Pages 973–1020

WEB APPENDIX B

General Data for Dead Loads and Live Loads

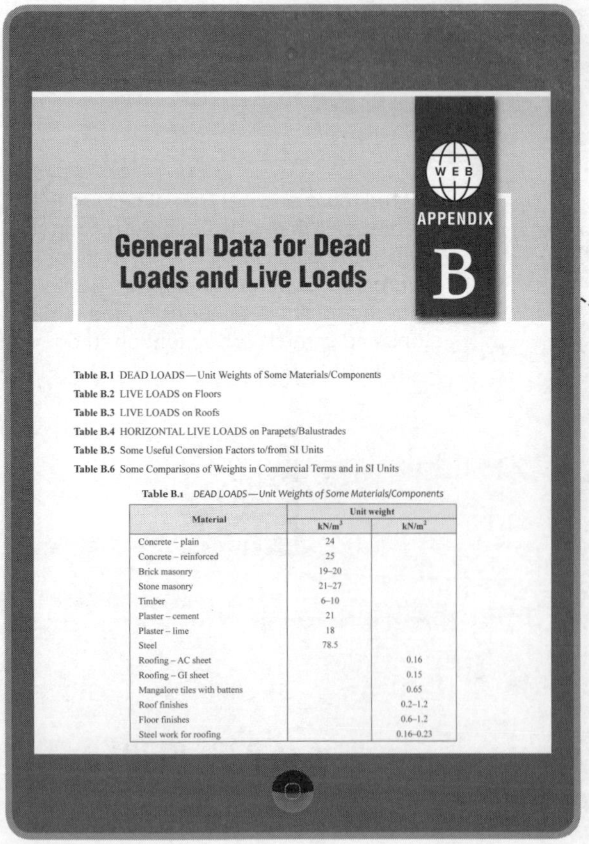

WEB APPENDIX B

General Data for Dead Loads and Live Loads

Table B.1 DEAD LOADS—Unit Weights of Some Materials/Components

Table B.2 LIVE LOADS on Floors

Table B.3 LIVE LOADS on Roofs

Table B.4 HORIZONTAL LIVE LOADS on Parapets/Balustrades

Table B.5 Some Useful Conversion Factors to/from SI Units

Table B.6 Some Comparisons of Weights in Commercial Terms and in SI Units

Table B.1 DEAD LOADS—Unit Weights of Some Materials/Components

Material	Unit weight	
	kN/m^3	kN/m^2
Concrete – plain	24	
Concrete – reinforced	25	
Brick masonry	19–20	
Stone masonry	21–27	
Timber	6–10	
Plaster – cement	21	
Plaster – lime	18	
Steel	78.5	
Roofing – AC sheet		0.16
Roofing – GI sheet		0.15
Mangalore tiles with battens		0.65
Roof finishes		0.2–1.2
Floor finishes		0.6–1.2
Steel work for roofing		0.16–0.23

To read more and get free access to full chapter, visit **www.mheducation.co.in** or scan the given QR Code. Search for ***Reinforced Concrete Design*** or ISBN of the book, and register using the steps and scratch code mentioned on back inner cover.

Pages 1021–1023

Lab Assignments for Students–Design-Build-Test-Analyse Projects

WEB

APPENDIX

C

Notes:

a. These assignments are to be carried out under the guidance of the faculty teaching the subject. Students should discuss the project with the faculty and get additional guidance where required. The guiding faculty member may suitably modify the projects to suit the prevailing local conditions.

b. These practical assignments are intended to supplement the theory dealt with in various chapters and the reference to associated chapters are indicated in parenthesis.

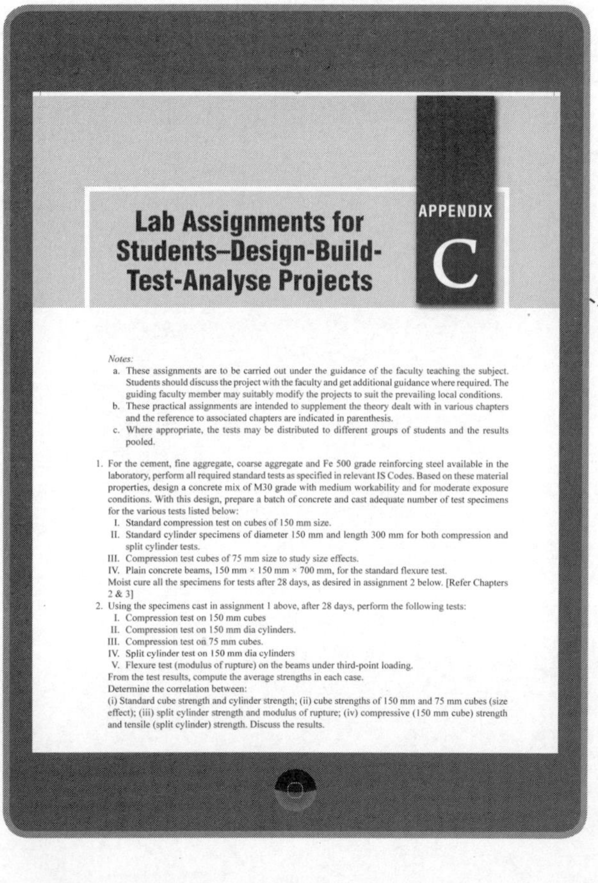

Lab Assignments for Students–Design-Build-Test-Analyse Projects

APPENDIX C

Notes:

a. These assignments are to be carried out under the guidance of the faculty teaching the subject. Students should discuss the project with the faculty and get additional guidance where required. The guiding faculty member may suitably modify the projects to suit the prevailing local conditions.

b. These practical assignments are intended to supplement the theory dealt with in various chapters and the reference to associated chapters are indicated in parenthesis.

c. Where appropriate, the tests may be distributed to different groups of students and the results pooled.

1. For the cement, fine aggregate, coarse aggregate and Fe 500 grade reinforcing steel available in the laboratory, perform all required standard tests as specified in relevant IS Codes. Based on these material properties, design a concrete mix of M30 grade with medium workability and for moderate exposure conditions. With this design, prepare a batch of concrete and cast adequate number of test specimens for the various tests listed below:
   I. Standard compression test on cubes of 150 mm size.
   II. Standard cylinder specimens of diameter 150 mm and length 300 mm for both compression and split cylinder tests.
   III. Compression test cubes of 75 mm size to study size effects.
   IV. Plain concrete beams, 150 mm × 150 mm × 700 mm, for the standard flexure test.

   Moist cure all the specimens for tests after 28 days, as desired in assignment 2 below. [Refer Chapters 2 & 3]
2. Using the specimens cast in assignment 1 above, after 28 days, perform the following tests:
   I. Compression test on 150 mm cubes
   II. Compression test on 150 mm dia cylinders.
   III. Compression test on 75 mm cubes.
   IV. Split cylinder test on 150 mm dia cylinders
   V. Flexure test (modulus of rupture) on the beams under third-point loading.

   From the test results, compute the average strengths in each case.
   Determine the correlation between:
   (i) Standard cube strength and cylinder strength; (ii) cube strengths of 150 mm and 75 mm cubes (size effect); (iii) split cylinder strength and modulus of rupture; (iv) compressive (150 mm cube) strength and tensile (split cylinder) strength. Discuss the results.

To read more and get free access to full chapter, visit **www.mheducation.co.in** or scan the given QR Code. Search for ***Reinforced Concrete Design*** or ISBN of the book, and register using the steps and scratch code mentioned on back inner cover.

Pages 1024–1026

List of Symbols

a — Radius of circular slab; maximum size of aggregate; stress block area factor; shear span

a' — Distance from extreme compression fibre to point of surface crack

a_{cr} — Distance as defined in Fig. 10.36

a_g — Specified nominal maximum size of coarse aggregate

a_v — Distance from face of support ($\leq 2d$) for increase in τ_c

A — Area, mm^2; surface area of a structure or part of a structure for wind loads

A_b — Area of cross section of one bar

A_c — Net area of concrete; area enclosed within perimeter of section under torsion

A_{cs} — Cross sectional area of strut in strut-and-tie model

A_{cv} — Area of concrete section resisting shear in shear-friction

A_{ez} — Effective frontal area for wind force calculation

A_g — Gross area of the section/concrete

A_h — Area of hoop reinforcement in circular tank wall; (seismic) design horizontal acceleration coefficient

A_k — Area of the concrete core, within the outer dimension of hoop/spiral; horizontal acceleration coefficient of mode k

A_l — Total area of longitudinal steel for resisting torsion; area of longitudinal reinforcement

A_{nz} — Area of a face of nodal zone or a section through nodal zone in strut-and-tie model

A_o — Area enclosed by centreline of thin-walled tube; area enclosed by shear flow path

A_{oh} — Area of cross section of bar used as special confining reinforcement

A_r — Opening area ratio in infill wall

A_s — Area of longitudinal bars in flexural tension zone

A'_s — Area of longitudinal bars in flexural compression zone; area of compression reinforcement along a strut in strut-and-tie model

A_{sb} — Area of reinforcement at bottom for hanging up bars

A_{sc} — Area of compression reinforcement

A_{sh} — Area of reinforcement at bottom for hanging up bars; area of horizontal distributed reinforcement

A_{si} — Area of reinforcement in the ith row

A_{st} — Area of tension reinforcement

$A_{st,\text{lim}}$ — Limiting (maximum) area of steel (LSM)

$(A_{st})_{\text{min}}$ — Minimum tension reinforcement

A_{sx} — Total area of longitudinal reinforcement resisting shear

A_{sv} Total cross-sectional area of one stirrup, considering all legs; area of vertical distributed reinforcement

A_{svh} Area of distributed reinforcement across a strut in strut-and-tie model

A_t Cross-sectional area of stirrup bar (each leg)

A_{ts} Area of reinforcement in a tie in strut-and-tie model

A_T Transformed area of reinforced section

A_v Area of shear reinforcement; (seismic) design vertical acceleration coefficient

A_{vf} Area of shear-friction reinforcement

A_w Total effective area of structural walls in the first storey of building (in m^2)

A_{wi} Effective area of wall *i* in the first storey of building (in m^2)

b Width of beam cross section; width of column at beam support; width of the section at centroid of tension steel

b_f Effective width of flange of flanged sections (Tee, Ell, etc.)

b_w Width of web of flanged sections (Tee, Ell, etc.)

b_o Perimeter of critical section for two-way shear

b_1 Width of centreline of thin-walled rectangular tube

b_1, b_2 Longer and shorter plan dimensions of a rectangular tank

B Background factor (to estimate gust factor)

c Shear (stress) resistance due to cohesion in concrete

c_1, c_2 Width of column support along l_1, l_2 directions respectively

C Resultant compressive force in the section; property of the section having the same relationship to the torsional stiffness of a rectangular section as the polar moment of inertia has for a circular section; parameter used to estimate topography factor k_3

C_a Active (soil) pressure coefficient

C_b, C_s, C_{sb} Dimensions as described in Fig. 8.4

C_c Compressive force in concrete

C_f Force (drag) coefficient for wind force

C_{fs} Cross-wind force spectrum coefficient

C_p Passive (soil) pressure coefficient; pressure coefficient for wind

C_{pe} External pressure coefficient for wind load

C_{pi} Internal pressure coefficient for wind load

C_r Strength reduction factor for slender columns - WSM

C_s Compressive force in compression reinforcement; forces in reinforcement in a column section

C_t Creep coefficient

C_u Resultant (ultimate) force in compression (LSD)

C_{uc} Resultant compressive force in concrete

C_{uf} Resultant (ultimate) compressive force in flanges for flanged sections

C_{us} Resultant compressive force in compression reinforcement

C_{uw} Resultant (ultimate) compressive force in web for flanged sections

d Effective depth of beam section; diameter of cylinder; depth of building (in plan); base dimension of the building at the plinth level in the direction of earthquake shaking (in m)

d' Distance between centroid of compression steel and extreme compression fibre in concrete

d_v Effective depth for shear

d_l Depth of centreline of rectangular thin-walled tube

D Overall depth of beam/slab; inside diameter of circular tank

D_b Depth of beam

D_f Thickness of compression flange of flanged sections

D_h Longer dimension of a rectangular hoop, measured to its outer face

D_k Diameter of core, measured to outside of the spiral or hoop
D_p Diameter of pile
DL Dead load
D_s Thickness of slab
D_w Depth of beam of flanged sections (T and L) below flange
D_x, D_y Larger and smaller size of a rectangular column cross section

e Eccentricity
e_a, e_{ax}, e_{ay} Additional eccentricities for slenderness effects in columns/walls
e_c Distance between plastic centroid and geometric centroid of a column cross section
e_x, e_y Eccentricity along X- and Y- directions; eccentricity about X-X/Y-Y axes of a column section
E Young's modulus of elasticity; energy spectrum of wind turbulence
E_c Short term elastic modulus of concrete; static modulus of elasticity
E_{ce} Effective modulus of elasticity of concrete
E_f Modulus of elasticity of frame material in infilled frames
E_s Modulus of elasticity of reinforcing steel

f Flexural stress at any point distant y from neutral axis
f_1, f_2 Principal stresses
f_2 Compressive stress in cracked concrete at strain ε_2, in presence of transverse tensile strain ε_1
$f_{2,max}$ Maximum compressive strength of concrete in presence of transverse tensile strain ε_1
f_a Stress at strain ε_a
f_b Average bond strength between concrete and steel
f_{br} Bearing resistance (stress) of concrete
$f_{br,max}$ Maximum bearing stress
f_c Compressive (maximum) stress in concrete; compressive stress in concrete corresponding to strain ε_c in stress-strain curve
f_{cc} Compressive stress in concrete
f_{ce} Effective compressive strength of concrete in a strut or nodal zone
f_c' Specified cylinder strength of concrete
f_{cc}' Peak compressive strength of confined concrete
f_{ck} Characteristic strength of concrete
f_{cm} Mean compressive strength of concrete
f_{co}' Peak compressive strength of unconfined concrete
f_{ci} Compressive stress in concrete at the level of ith row of reinforcement
f_{cr} Modulus of rupture of concrete
f_{cs} Stress in concrete at tension reinforcement level in transformed section
f_{csc} Stress in concrete at the compression steel level
f_{ct} Splitting tensile strength of concrete; tensile strength of concrete
f_{cts} Allowable tensile stress in concrete at level of tension steel
f_{cx} Normal stress in X-direction
f_{cy} Transverse compressive stress in concrete
f_{max} Maximum stress
f_s Stress in longitudinal steel
f_s' compressive stress in reinforcement along a strut
f_{sc} Mean tensile stress in steel; stress in compression reinforcement
f_{si} Stress in i^{th} row of reinforcement
f_{sm} Stress in tension reinforcement
f_{st}, f_{s1}, f_{s2} Stress in tension reinforcement
f_{sx} Stress in longitudinal reinforcement needed for shear
f_v Tensile stress in transverse shear reinforcement
f_x Flexural stress due to moment M at distance y from NA
f_y Yield strength of reinforcing steel; also stress in the y direction

f_{yh} Yield strength of stirrup reinforcement
f_{yl} Yield strength of longitudinal reinforcement for torsion
F Force in general; frictional resistance
F_i Seismic lateral force at floor i
F_{lc} Net tensile force in flexural compression side including effects of flexure, shear, torsion and axial tension
F_{lt} Force in longitudinal tension reinforcement including effects of flexure, shear, torsion and axial tension
F_{nn} Nominal strength at face of node in strut-and-tie model
F_{ns} Nominal strength of struts in strut-and-tie model
F_{nt} Nominal strength of ties in strut-and-tie model
F_{roof} Seismic design lateral force at roof level
F_{un} Factored compressive force on the face of a node in strut-and-tie model
F_{us} Factored compressive force in a strut in strut-and-tie model
F_{ut} Factored compressive force in a tie in strut-and-tie model
F_z Total wind load on the area
FS Factor of safety

g Acceleration due to gravity; peak factor
G Shear modulus/Modulus of rigidity; gust factor

h Height of column; height of structure above mean ground level; height of building (in m)
h_b Difference in depths of supported and supporting beams (Fig. 6.7)
h_i Height of the ith floor above the base
h_s Height of a storey
h' Height of backfill
H depth of water; height of tank
H_u Total lateral force acting in a storey; unsupported height of wall
H_w Unsupported height of wall
H_{we} Effective height of wall

i, i_x, i_y Ratio of moment capacities per unit length of yield lines in the same direction
I Second moment of area of section about the neutral axis; importance factor (seismic)
I_b Second moment of area of the beam section
I_c Second moment of area of the column section
I_{cr} Second moment of area of the cracked-transformed section
I_{eff} Second moment of area of the effective section
I_{gross} Second moment of area of the gross (uncracked) concrete section
I_s Second moment of area of a width of slab bounded laterally by centrelines of adjacent panel on each side of the beam
I_T Second moment of area of uncracked transformed section about neutral axis
I_x, I_y Ratio of moment capacities of negative and positive plastic hinges in a beam in X-/Y-directions
$I(z)$ Turbulence intensity at height z

j Lever arm factor
j_b Lever arm factor for balanced section
jd Lever arm
J_c Property of critical section analogous to polar moment of inertia

k Neutral axis depth factor; factor for increase in design shear strength of concrete in slabs (Eq. 6.11)
k, k_x, k_y Effective length ratio (factor) for columns; Neutral axis depth factor for balanced section
k_{ax}, k_{ay} Reduction factors for additional moments for slender columns
k_c Modification factor for limiting l/d ratio, dependent on p_c
kd Depth of neutral axis
k_s Factor for design shear strength of concrete in two-way shear

k_t	Modification factor for limiting l/d ratio, dependent on p_t and f_{st}
k_1, k_2, k_3, k_4	Wind speed modification factors
$\bar{k}_2$	Terrain roughness and height factor for hourly mean wind speed
K	St. Venant torsional constant; a constant in general
K_a	Area averaging factor for wind load
K_{ec}	Flexural stiffness of equivalent column
K_c	Flexural stiffness of column; combination factor for wind load
K_d	wind directionality factor
K_{sb}	Flexural stiffness of slab (or slab-beam member) along span l_1
K_t	Torsional stiffness of section; limiting (maximum) moment factor for balanced condition (LSD)
l_o	Distance between points of zero moment in beam; length over which special confining reinforcements are needed (Ch. 16)
l	Unsupported length of column; length of a member or larger horizontal dimension of a building for wind loads
l_e, l_{ex}, l_{ey}	Effective length of column
l_x, l_y	Length of building in X- and Y- directions
l_1, l_2	Spans of rectangular panel, centre to centre of supports, along and transverse to direction of moment calculation, respectively
l_n	Clear span of slab, measured face-to-face of supports in the direction of M_o
L	Length
L_a	Extension of bar beyond theoretical point of cut off
L_o	Anchorage length beyond zero moment location
L_d	Development length
$\tilde{L}_d$	Development length for stress f_s.
L_e	Effective length
L_w	Length (horizontal) of wall
L_x, L_y	Length along X- and Y-directions respectively

LL	Live load
LSM/LSD	Limit states method of design
L_{wi}	Length of structural wall i in the first storey in the direction of earthquake shaking (in m)
m	Modular ratio, $= E_s/E_c$; moment capacity of slab yield line per unit length
m_k	Modal mass of the kth mode
m_x, m_y, m_θ	Moment capacity per unit length in X-/Y-/θ-directions of yield lines in slabs
m_u	Non-dimensional moment in $p_u - m_u$ interaction diagram for columns
M	Bending moment
M_a	Along-wind base bending moment
M_o	Total factored design moment for the span in flat slab panels
M_{all}	Allowable bending moment, WSM
M_b	Moment in the beam part
$M_{base, in}$	Moment in tank wall at base, causing tension on the inside face in vertical bending
M_c	Mass of cement (in kg/m^3); beam moment at centreline of column support; moments in a column section due to compression in concrete; across-wind base bending moment
M_{ca}	Mass of coarse aggregate (in kg/m^3)
M_{cr}	Moment at first crack, cracking moment of section
$\tilde{M}_{cr}$	Limiting value of M_{cr} for deflection calculations
M_{cs}	Moment in the column strip
M_{e1}, M_{e2}	Equivalent bending moment considering torsion
M_f	Factored bending moment
M_{fa}	Mass of fine aggregate (in kg/m^3)
M_{hms}	Moment in half middle strip
$M_{hor, in}$	Moment in rectangular tank wall causing tension on the inside face in horizontal bending
$M_{hor, out}$	Moment in rectangular tank wall causing tension on the outside face in horizontal bending

$M_{\text{hor, out1}}$ Moment in the longer wall of rectangular tank causing tension on the outside face in horizontal bending

$M_{\text{hor, out2}}$ Moment in the shorter wall of rectangular tank causing tension on the outside face in horizontal bending

$M_{\text{max, out}}$ Maximum moment in circular tank wall causing tension on the outside face in vertical bending

M_o Overturning moment

M_r Restoring moment

M_s Moment in a column section due to forces in reinforcement

M_t Effective bending moment due to torsion

M_{wb} Allowable moment for balanced section, WSM

M_u Factored moment due to applied factored loads

M_{uo} Ultimate flexural strength of a short column with no axial load

M_{ub} Part of the unbalanced moment M_u at column supports of flat slabs transferred through flexure; ultimate flexural strength of a short column subjected to axial load and bending, under balanced conditions

M_{uf} Ultimate moment of resistance due to compression in flanges

$M_{u,\text{lim}}$ Limiting moment of resistance, LSD

$M_{u,\text{lim-}DR}$ Limiting moment of resistance of a doubly reinforced section (LSD)

M_{uR} Ultimate moment of resistance (LSD); Ultimate moment resistance of short column under eccentric loading ($= P_{uR}\, e$)

M_{uv} Part of the unbalanced moment M_u at column supports of flat slabs transferred through eccentricity of shear forces

M_{uw} Ultimate moment of resistance due to compression in web

M_{ux} Ultimate moment about Y-axis

$M_{ux,1}$ Uniaxial moment capacity of column section, with axial load P_u, for bending about major axis

M_{uy} Ultimate moment about X-axis

$M_{uy,1}$ Uniaxial moment capacity of column section, with axial load P_u, for bending about minor axis

M_x, M_y Moment about X-X/Y-Y axis of a column cross section; Moment capacities of beam plastic hinges of beams along X-/Y-directions (Section 11.10.8)

$\tilde{M}_{ux}$, $\tilde{M}_{uy}$ Total design moments, including P–Δ moment

$M_{\text{vert, in}}$ Moment in rectangular tank wall causing tension on the inside face in vertical bending

$M_{\text{vert, out}}$ Moment in rectangular tank wall causing tension on the outside face in vertical bending

n Number of reinforcement bars; number of storeys

N Axial force/direct tension; also unfactored permanent compressive force perpendicular to the shear plane

N_f Direct tensile force across shear plane in shear-friction; factored axial load on the section

N_{roof} Factored direct tension in roof slab of a water tank

N_u Factored direct tension due to applied loads

N_{uo} Capacity in direct tension acting alone

N_v Axial tensile force due to shear

N_w Number of structural walls in the direction of earthquake shaking

p Probability of basic wind speed not being exceeded in any given year

p_a Active soil pressure

p_c^* Percentage of compression reinforcement; external perimeter of section under torsion

Percentage of compression reinforcement for balanced section (LSD)

p_d Design wind pressure

$\bar{p}_d$ Hourly mean wind pressure at height h

$p_{d,\,net}$ Total net design wind pressure

p_{dz} Design wind pressure at height z

p_h Perimeter of the centreline of closed transverse torsion reinforcement

p_p Passive pressure of soil

p_t Percentage of tension reinforcement, $= 100A_{st}/bd$

$p_{t,b}$ Percentage tension reinforcement for balanced section, WSM

$p_{t,\lim}$ Limiting (maximum) percentage of tensile steel (LSD)

$(p_t)_{\lim}$ Minimum percentage of tension reinforcement.

p_u Non-dimensional axial load in p_u - m_u interaction diagram for columns

p_z Design wind pressure at height z

P Applied load; axial load on a column

P_o Compressive strength of a short column under axial loading

P_a Force due to active soil pressure

P_f Probability of failure

P_k Mode participation factor of the kth mode

P_p Force due to passive soil pressure

P_u Factored compressive force in the section; Factored axial column load

P_{ub} Ultimate design strength of a short column for balanced conditions under eccentric loading (axial load + bending)

P_{uo} Ultimate design strength of a short column under axial loading

$\tilde{P}_{uo}$ Design strength of a short column in uniaxial compression permitted by Code (for $e_{\min} < 0.05D$)

P_{uR} Ultimate design strength of a short column under eccentric loading (with $M_{uR} = P_{uR}\,e$)

P_{uw} Design axial strength in compression per unit length of wall

P_{uz} Axial load capacity of column used to determine α_n for biaxial bending case

P_w Transverse (horizontal) reinforcement ratio for wall

q Shear flow in thin-walled tube; soil pressure under footings; line load per unit length

q_a Safe bearing capacity of soil at service loads

$q_{\max}$ Maximum soil pressure under footings

$q_{\min}$ Minimum soil pressure

q_{net} Net soil pressure

q_u Factored net soil pressure

Q First moment of area about the NA of portion of section above the layer at distance y from NA; Stability index of a storey

Q_b Moment factor for balanced section (WSM)

Q_i Lateral seismic force at floor i

Q_{ik} Design lateral seismic force at floor i for mode k

QL Wind/Earthquake load

r Aspect ratio, ratio of length of long side to length of short side of a rectangular slab; radius where moment is determined; radius of gyration of section; roughness factor

R Factor $= M_u/(bd^2)$; also, normal reaction across surface of contact; reaction force; riser of step in staircases; inside radius of circular tank; resonant response factor; (seismic) response reduction factor

R_d Design resistance

$R_{\lim}$ Limiting factor $M_{u.\lim}/(bd^2)$

R_n Nominal resistance

R_R Response reduction factor for redundancy

R_μ Response reduction factor for ductile response

R_Ω Response reduction factor for overstrength

s Spacing centre to centre (of beams, reinforcement, stirrups, columns, etc.); pitch of spiral or spacing of hoops; height above ground level

s_h Horizontal clear spacing of bars; spacing of horizontal distributed reinforcement

s_0 parameter used to estimate topography factor k_3

s_{reqd} Required spacing of bars in slab

s_t Pitch of lateral ties

s_v Spacing of stirrups measured along beam axis; spacing of vertical distributed reinforcement

s_z Crack spacing parameter

s_{ze} Effective crack spacing parameter

S Size reduction factor

(S_a/g) (seismic) design acceleration coefficient

S_d Design load effect

S_{hor} Shear force in tank wall related to horizontal bending

S_n Nominal load effect

$S_{vert, base}$ Shear force at base of tank wall related to vertical bending

$S_{vert, top}$, S_{top} Shear force at top of tank wall related to vertical bending

t Time *t*; thickness of concrete wall/slab; tread of steps

t_o Wall thickness of thin-walled tube

T Twisting moment/Torsion; resultant tensile force in the section; tread of steps in staircases; temperature; time in seconds; undamped natural period of oscillation of structure in seconds

T_a Approximate fundamental natural period of building in seconds

T_{cr} Torsional cracking torque in pure torsion

T_i Tie force in member *i* in strut-and-tie model

TL Effects of temperature, creep, shrinkage or support settlement

T_k Time period of the kth mode

T_r Factored torsional resistance of the section

T_u Resultant (ultimate) tensile force in tension reinforcement (LSD); ultimate (factored) torque.

T_{un} Nominal ultimate strength in torsion

T_{uR} Ultimate strength in torsion

u_a Anchorage bond stress

u_{av} Average anchorage bond stress

u_f Flexural bond stress

ULM Ultimate load method of design

v Shear stress

v_{ci} Interface shear stress along crack through aggregate interlock

v_r Factored shear stress resistance = V_r/A_{cv}

V Shear force

V_a Interface shear force

V_b Regional basic wind speed

V_B Design seismic base shear in building frame

$\bar{V}_B$ Design base shear calculated using the approximate fundamental period T_a

V_{Be} Base shear force in building frame under linear elastic response

$V_{B\mu}$ Base shear force in building frame, reduced for ductility effect

V_{BR} Base shear force in building frame at formation of first plastic hinge

V_{Bdes} Design base shear force (for which building designed)

V_{ax} Horizontal component of interface shear V_a.

V_{ay} Vertical component of interface shear V_a.

V_B Design seismic base shear

V_c Shear resistance of concrete

V_{cw} Shear resistance of wall provided by concrete

V_{cz} Shear resistance of uncracked portion of concrete

V_d Dowel force in tension reinforcement

V_e Equivalent shear under combined shear and torsion

V_f Reaction at support, factored shear force

V_g Gradient speed

V_h Resultant horizontal shear force due to torsion, sand heap analogy

V_{ik} The storey shear, acting in storey *i* in mode *k*

V_r Factored shear resistance

V_{rw}	Factored shear resistance of a wall
V_s	Shear resistance of transverse reinforcement
V_{se}	Shear transmitted to column due to specified loads
V_{sw}	Shear resistance due to shear-friction reinforcement in a wall
V_{sn}	Nominal shear resistance due to shear-friction reinforcement
V_u	Factored shear force at a section
$V_{u,\text{net}}$	Net shear force under factored loads
V_{uc}	Ultimate shear resistance of concrete
V_{uR}	Ultimate shear resistance of section
$V_{uR,\text{lim}}$	Limiting (maximum) ultimate shear resistance of section
V_{us}	Ultimate shear resistance of shear reinforcement; Shear resisted by shear reinforcement
V_v	Volume of voids per cubic meter of concrete; resultant vertical shear–sand heap analogy.
V_w	Volume of water per cubic meter of concrete
V_z	Design wind speed at height z
$\bar{V}_z$	Design hourly mean wind speed at height z
w	Uniformly distributed load per unit length; depth of equivalent truss element; width of crack; width of equivalent diagonal strut for infill masonry wall; lesser horizontal dimension of a building or a structural member for wind loads
w_u	Factored uniformly distributed load per unit length
$w_{u,DL}$	Factored uniformly distributed dead load per unit length
$w_{u,LL}$	Factored uniformly distributed live load per unit length
W	Concentrated load; weight; seismic weight
W_i	Seismic weight of the ith floor located at height h_i above the base
W_u	Factored concentrated load
WSM	Working stress method of design
x	Depth of neutral axis of cracked transformed section – elastic theory
x_i	Distance from geometric centroid of column section to the ith row of reinforcement
x_u	Depth of neutral axis at ultimate strength (LSD)
$x_{u,\max}$	Limiting (maximum) depth of neutral axis (LSD)
$x_{u,\max}/d$	Limiting (maximum) neutral axis depth ratio (LSD)
$\bar{x}$	Distance of resultant compression (C_u) from extreme compression fibre = 0.416 x_u; distance to resultant force in general
y	Distance from neutral axis
y_c	Distance from neutral axis to extreme compression fibre
y_f	Depth of equivalent rectangular stress block for flanges (LSM)
y_i	Distance to the ith row of steel from centroidal axis
$y_{\max}$	Maximum value of y, distance to the extreme fibre
y_t	Distance from neutral axis to extreme tension fibre
$\bar{y}$	Depth of neutral axis, working stress design
z	Lever arm; depth below top of liquid; height above ground level
z_o	Terrain roughness dimension/equivalent aerodynamic roughness height
Z	Modulus of section; seismic zone factor; height above ground level
Z_g	Gradient height
α	Angle in general; factor for computing section property for torsional shear calculation for rectangular sections (Eq. 7.4); inclination of diagonal crack due to torsion; constant in Eq. 7.22; inclination of transverse reinforcement to

beam axis; factor representing relative column and beam stiffnesses at a joint, coefficient of thermal expansion of concrete

α_b Ratio I_b/I_s

α_{bm} Average value of α_b

α_c Relative column stiffness parameter, Ratio $\Sigma K_c/K_{sb}$, $\Sigma K_c/\Sigma K_s$

α_f Angle of inclination of shear-friction reinforcement to shear plane

α_n Factor in the interaction equation for biaxially loaded columns

α_x, α_y Factor denoting ratio of beam strength to slab strength (Section 11.10.8)

β Reliability index; inclination of tensile reinforcement to the longitudinal axis of the beam; factor influencing τ_c, (Eq. 6.10a); factor for determining torsional constant K for rectangular sections (Eq. 7.2); ratio of long side to short side of footings; ratio of clear long span to clear short span of rectangular slab panels; coefficient for determining effective length ratios of columns; factor accounting for aggregate interlock action

β_b Ratio of area of bars cut-off to the total area of bars at the section

β_c Ratio of short side to long side of column or column capital; confinement factor for struts and nodes in strut-and-tie model

β_n Factor accounting for effect of tie anchorage in nodal zones in strut-and-tie model

β_s Factor accounting for effects of cracking and confining reinforcement on strength of struts in strut-and-tie model

γ Load factor; fraction of moment at column support in flat slab transferred by flexure; unit weight of liquid/water

γ_c Partial safety factor for concrete strength = 1.5

γ_e Unit weight of earth

γ_Q Partial safety factor for wind or earthquake load

γ_s Partial safety factor for steel strength = 1.15

γ_{sub} Unit weight of submerged soil

δ Multiplying factor for design shear strength of concrete in the presence of axial compression

δ_s Factor for enhancing design positive moment in slabs for $\alpha_c < \alpha_{c,\min}$

Δ Deflection; lateral drift at roof level; lateral deflection/drift of column

Δ_{all} Maximum allowable serviceability limit

Δ_{cp} Deflection due to creep

Δ_{sh} Deflection due to differential shrinkage

Δ_D Deflection due to dead loads

Δ_{D+L} Deflection due to dead + live loads

Δ_i Initial elastic deflection

Δ_{i+cp} Combined initial elastic + creep deflection

Δ_L Deflection due to live loads

Δ_{temp} Deflection due to temperature effects

Δ_u Elastic first-order lateral deflection of a storey

ε Strain

ε_1 Apparent strain at point based on cracked transformed section

ε_1, ε_2 Principal strains at point

ε_2 Reduction in strain due to tension stiffening effect

ε_a Strain at point A

ε_c Compressive strain in concrete at the extreme fibre; compressive strain in concrete

ε_{cc} Strain at peak strength in confined concrete

ε_{cm} Mean strain in extreme compression fibre in concrete

ε_{co} Strain at peak strength in unconfined concrete

ε_{cp} Creep strain

ε_{cs} Ultimate shrinkage strain

ε_{cu} Ultimate compressive strain in concrete

ε_i	Initial elastic strain (instantaneous strain)
ε_m	Average strain at level where cracking is considered
ε_s	Strain in steel reinforcement
ε_{sc}	Strain in compression reinforcement
ε_{sh}	Shrinkage strain at the extreme concrete compression fibre
ε_{si}	Strain in the ith row of steel
ε_{sm}	Mean strain in tension reinforcement; steel strain at maximum tensile stress
ε_{st}	Strain at centroid of tension reinforcement
ε_{st}^*	Code limit (minimum) on strain in tension reinforcement, $= 0.002 + (0.87 f_y/E_s)$
ε_t	Strain in transverse direction
ε_{te}	Thermal strain in concrete
ε_x	Longitudinal (axial) tensile strain
ε_y	Strain at distance y from neutral axis; also yield strain of steel
η	Non-dimensional parameter for computing I_{eff}
θ	Ultimate creep coefficient; also angle θ; inclination of principal stress
λ	Factor to account for low density concrete
λ_s	Size effect factor for shear strength of concrete
μ	Coefficient of friction; Coefficient of orthotropy = ratio of yield line moment capacities in Y- and X-directions = m_y/m_x; curvature ductility
υ	Tangential stress; shear stress; Poisson's ratio
ρ	Reinforcement ration = $A_{st}/(bd)$
ρ_c	Mass density of cement, also of concrete
ρ_{ca}	Mass density of coarse aggregate
ρ_{fa}	Mass density of fine aggregate
ρ_s	Volumetric ratio of spiral reinforcement in columns; volumetric ratio of confining reinforcement at hinging regions
ρ_v	Ratio of shear-friction reinforcement
Σo	Total perimeter of all flexural tension bars at a section
σ	Standard deviation; stress
σ_{cbc}	Permissible compressive stress for concrete in flexure, WSM
σ_{cc}	Permissible stress in compression in concrete, WSM
σ_{sc}	Permissible stress in compression in reinforcement, WSM
$\tilde{\sigma}_{sc}$	Maximum permissible compressive stress in steel (WSM)
σ_{st}	Permissible stress in tension reinforcement, WSM
ϕ	Strength reduction factor/resistance factor; notation for bar diameter, such as 20 ϕ; angle of repose of soil; mode shape
ϕ_c, ϕ_s	Material resistance factor for concrete and steel ($0.65 \approx 1/\gamma_c$ and $0.85 \approx 1/\gamma_s$)
ϕ_{ik}	Mode shape coefficient at floor i in mode k
ϕ_t	Diameter of tie reinforcement
τ	Shear stress
τ_{av}	Average shear stress in a beam section
τ_{bd}	Design bond stress
τ_c	Average design shear strength of concrete
$\tau_{c,\max}$	Upper limit of τ_c.
τ_{cw}	Design shear strength of concrete in wall
$\tau_{t,\max}$	Maximum torsional shear stress
τ_t	Torsional shear stress
τ_v	Nominal shear stress under factored loads
τ_{ve}	Equivalent nominal shear stress under combined shear and torsion
τ_{vw}	Nominal shear stress in walls

φ	Curvature
φ_{cp}	Creep curvature
φ_{cr}	Curvature at cracking moment
φ_{eff}	Effective curvature
φ_i	Initial elastic curvature
φ_{max}	Maximum curvature at mid-height of slender column
φ_{sh}	Curvature due to differential shrinkage
φ_u	Ultimate curvature at section
φ_y	Curvature at yielding of tension reinforcement
ω	frequency

Index